XTRA! QUIZZING

In addition to the open-access chapter-by-chapter quizzes found at the Nelson & Quick Product Support Web site (http://nelson-quick.swlearning.com), Nelson & Quick Xtra! offers you an opportunity to practice for midterms and finals by taking interactive quizzes that span multiple chapters.

TAKE TWO VIDEOS

Take Two Videos are a combination of both workplace and popular film video clips. The Workplace Videos are 8-10 minute clips that focus on workplace situations. Biz Flix are popular Hollywood videos that run from 2-3 minutes in length that bring OB concepts to life through the use of film.

XTRA!

An optional bundle item, if Xtra! is bundled with your NEW textbook, you will receive access to our online study center (access code included in Passport) which includes interactive quizzes, Management videos, and additional activities.

xtra!

Fifth Edition

Organizational Behavior

Foundations, Realities

& Challenges

Debra L. Nelson
Oklahoma State University

James Campbell Quick
University of Texas at Arlington

THOMSON
SOUTH-WESTERN

Australia · Canada · Mexico · Singapore · Spain · United Kingdom · United States

THOMSON

SOUTH-WESTERN

Organizational Behavior: Foundations, Realities & Challenges, 5e

Debra L. Nelson and James Campbell Quick

VP/Editorial Director:
Jack W. Calhoun

VP/Editor-in-Chief:
Dave Shaut

Executive Editor:
John Szilagyi

Developmental Editor:
Leslie Kauffman/LEAP, Inc.

Sr. Production Editor:
Elizabeth A. Shipp

Marketing Manager:
Jacque Carrillo

Sr. Manufacturing Coordinator:
Doug Wilke

Photography Manager:
John Hill

Photography Researchers:
Rose Alcorn
Sam Marshall

Project Management:
LEAP, Inc.

Composition:
GGS Information Services, Inc.

Art Director:
Stacy Jenkins Shirley

Internal Design:
Beckmeyer Design, Inc.

Cover Design:
Beckmeyer Design, Inc.

Cover Image:
Getty Images, Inc.

Printer:
Courier
Kendallville, Indiana

For permission to use material from this text
or product, submit a request online at
http://www.thomsonrights.com. Any
additional questions about permissions
can be submitted by email to
thomsonrights@thomson.com.

For more information
contact South-Western,
5191 Natorp Boulevard,
Mason, Ohio, 45040.
Or you can visit our Internet site at:
http://www.swlearning.com

Brief Contents

Contents

Chapter 11

Power and Political Behavior   354

THINKING AHEAD: CISCO SYSTEMS   355

The Concept of Power   356

Forms and Sources of Power in Organizations   356

Power Analysis: A Broader View   363

Symbols of Power   364

Political Behavior in Organizations   366

Managing Up: Managing The Boss   370

Sharing Power: Empowerment   372

Managerial Implications: Using Power Effectively   376

LOOKING BACK: CISCO SYSTEMS   378

Much has changed in the world since the fourth edition of *Organizational Behavior: Foundations, Realities & Challenges* appeared three years ago, yet little has occurred that refutes much of what we have learned about organizational behavior over the past 100 years. Our knowledge has been refined and advanced in the context of a professional world hungry for positive/authentic leaders who know themselves and act with a spirit of personal integrity. The fifth edition aims to reflect the opportunities and optimism that form a core driving force in the heart of organizational behavior. Opportunity is "a favorable time" or "a chance for progress and advancement." More than responding to change, we encourage students of organizational behavior and leaders in organizations to be the instigators of positive change. Using the knowledge and insights offered in the study of organizational behavior, we can take responsible proaction to create the kinds of organizations in which we not only work and contribute, but ones in which we thrive, grow strong, and experience fulfillment in the spirit of the happy/productive worker. These are favorable times in which to advance the science and practice the art of organizational behavior in such a manner that it is beneficial to all concerned. This includes workers and leaders, men and women, those of all ethnic groups and occupations, and all those of diverse faith traditions.

The distinctiveness of *Organizational Behavior* continues to be reflected in its subtitle: *Foundations, Realities & Challenges.* We chose this subtitle because it represents the solid scholarly foundations on which the science of organizational behavior was built, the realities of contemporary life in organizations, and the challenges that constantly present themselves. "Foundations" refers to the broad and deep research roots of our discipline. Our book is anchored in research tradition and contains not only classic research but also leading-edge scholarship in the field. This research and theory forms the foundations of our knowledge base. "Realities" reflects what is going on in organizations of all types: public and private, large and small, product and service oriented. In our text, these realities take shape as examples from all types of organizations. Some of the examples show successes, while others show failures, of managers applying organizational behavior knowledge in the real world. "Challenges" are the opportunities we have to grow and develop both as individuals and organizations. In the book, they take the form of individual and group activities for proactive learning.

Organizational behavior is the study of individual behavior and group dynamics in organizational settings. It focuses on timeless topics like motivation, leadership, teamwork, and communication. Such issues have captured our attention for decades. Organizational behavior also encompasses contemporary issues in organizations. How do we encourage employees to act ethically, to engage in organizational citizenship behaviors, to go above and beyond the call of duty to exhibit exceptional performance? How do we restructure organizations in the face of increasing competition? What is the new psychological contract between employees and organizations? How have careers changed, and what can we expect in the future? How do you manage employee behavior in virtual organizations or teams? What happens when organizations with strong cultures and a need for constancy face the pressure to become current, competitive, and agile? *Organizational Behavior* thus engages both classic and emerging issues.

Our overarching theme of change has not changed, nor have the four supporting subthemes: globalization, diversity, ethics, and technology. These themes continue to reflect the challenges that managers face. The sequence in which we address these subthemes and the ways in which we elaborate upon them *has* changed, however, as it should. The global marketplace continues to bring with it a world with no boundaries, with no constraints on time and distance. Diversity can be a tremendous asset, with its wealth of skills and knowledge, if managers can build organizational cultures that view differences as assets. While new technologies have vastly improved the efficiency of work, managers must balance high tech with high touch. Managing ethical behavior means doing the right thing in an age of increased white-collar crime and public scrutiny of organizations.

Organizations expect all employees to learn continually. Our book rests on the assumption that learning involves not only acquiring knowledge but also developing skills. The rich theory and research in organizational behavior must be translated into application. Thus, the text presents the opportunity to know concepts, ideas, and theories, and to practice skills, abilities, and behaviors to enhance the management of human behavior at work. Both knowledge and skills are essential for our future managers. We hope the knowledge and skills presented here empower them to succeed in the changing world of work.

SPECIAL FEATURES

Several special features of the book extend the subtitle *Foundations, Realities & Challenges* to specific applications. These features are designed to enhance the application of theory and research in practice, to stimulate student interest and discussion, and to facilitate cognitive as well as skill-based learning. The fifth edition reflects a change in how we refer to some of our special features. You learn in Chapter 1, Figure 1.4, that basic knowledge is concerned with Science, that skill application is concerned with The Real World, and that knowledge and skill development concerns You directly. Therefore, three of the pedagogical features included in each chapter have been retitled Science (Foundations), The Real World (Realities), and You (Challenges).

Foundations

SCIENCE (RENAMED FEATURE) Each chapter includes a Science feature that summarizes a leading-edge research study related to the chapter's topic. This feature exposes students to the way knowledge is advanced in organizational behavior and the scientific nature of the discipline. For example, the Science feature in Chapter 7 shows how political skill may be useful in managing workplace stress and strain.

EXTENSIVE TEXT REFERENCES The book is based on extensive classic and contemporary research literature. At the end of the textbook is a lengthy chapter-by-chapter reference list that students can refer to for in-depth treatments of the chapter topics. In this edition, over 200 new research studies, theory articles, and scholarly books have been reviewed and cited. In addition to this freshening of the content base for the text, chapters have new content and key words that reflect positive changes. For example, two new ideas on motivation—eustress and positive energy/full engagement—appear in Chapter 5, while new focus has been brought to performance management and 360-degree feedback in Chapter 6. Chapter 7 includes new material and emphasis on workaholism, while Chapter 8 brings focus to positive, healthy communication. Diversity and creativity are drawn out in Chapter 9 on teams, while engagement is introduced into Chapter 14 on jobs and the design of work.

Realities

THINKING AHEAD AND LOOKING BACK The opening and closing features for the fifth edition, as in previous editions, frame the chapter with a vignette from one of six focus organizations. The six focus organizations in the fifth edition are all new: Cisco Systems, The Coca-Cola Company, Canine Companions for Independence, Pixar Studios, Virgin Group, Ltd., and Whole Foods Market. As in the past, these organizations represent manufacturing and service, profit and not-for-profit, and large and small organizations. By featuring these six key organizations throughout the book, students can familiarize themselves with the companies in greater depth than a single appearance would allow. The Looking Back feature is a continuation of the Thinking Ahead feature on that particular organization and brings closure to the example.

THE REAL WORLD (RENAMED FEATURE) The purpose of including two new The Real World features in each chapter is to spotlight contemporary organizational life. The realities reflect the themes of globalization, diversity, technology, and ethics. They include not only examples of successes but also examples of failures, which are opportunities for learning. Some are controversial, such as The Real World 1.1 that focuses on the issue of outsourcing jobs from America to lower labor cost economies, such as India or Mexico.

Challenges

YOU (RENAMED FEATURE) What used to be called Challenges in previous editions of our text are now You features in each chapter. These self-assessment exercises provide the student with feedback on an important aspect of the topic. Examples are the learning style inventory (You 1.2) in Chapter 1, in which students discover their own learning preferences, and the tolerance for ambiguity inventory (You 18.1) in Chapter 18, which helps students assess their receptiveness to change. Each You is designed to enhance self-knowledge or to promote skill development in the subject matter. The student is able to use the results of the You for self-discovery and behavioral change.

DISCUSSION AND COMMUNICATION QUESTIONS All students need help in developing their oral and written communication skills. Discussion and communication questions are included at the end of each chapter to give students practice in applying chapter material using some form of communication. The questions challenge students to write memos and brief reports, prepare oral presentations for class, interview experts in the field, and conduct research to gather information on important management topics for discussion in class.

ETHICAL DILEMMAS (NEW FEATURE) Learning to develop moral reasoning and the capacity to resolve ethical dilemmas is hard work. Simple answers to complex questions just do not exist. Therefore, an Ethical Dilemma has been crafted for each chapter that offers students an opportunity to engage in ethical debate and moral reasoning concerning tough decisions and situations. Each chapter feature poses a scenario and then a series of questions for use in probing the ethical dilemma.

EXPERIENTIAL EXERCISES Two group-oriented experiential exercises are included at the end of each chapter. They are designed for students to work in teams to learn more about an important aspect of the chapter's topic. The exercises give students opportunities to develop interpersonal skills and to process their thinking within a teamwork setting. In Experiential Exercise 4.2, for example, students are presented with twelve ethical issues faced in organizations, and meet in groups to discuss all sides of the issue and a proposed resolution. In Chapter 10, Decision Making, Experiential Exercise 10.1 places students in the role of a manager who must make a layoff decision. Students are given summaries of their "employees'" résumés and asked to propose a decision in terms of who should be laid off.

CASES (NEW AND REVISED) A case is included at the end of each chapter. Half of these chapter cases are completely new, and the other half have been extensively updated. Each case is based on a real-world situation that has been modified slightly for learning purposes. Students have an opportunity to discuss and reflect on the content of the case, drawing upon and then applying the content material of the chapter within the framework of the case. All of the Cohesion Cases that appear at the end of the four parts of the book are new and feature an ongoing scenario of the popular high-tech company, Google. Finally, the Biz Flix and Workplace Video Cases are all new, too.

SOME DISTINCTIVE FEATURES STUDENTS LIKE

Organizational Behavior offers a number of distinctive, time-tested, and interesting features for students, as well as new and innovative features. Each chapter begins with a clear statement of learning objectives to provide students with expectations about what is to come. The chapter summaries are designed to bring closure to these learning objectives. Graphics and tables enhance students' ease in grasping the topical material and involve students actively in the learning process. Photos throughout each chapter reinforce, and in many cases supplement, the text.

Interesting and relevant end-of-chapter features such as the list of key terms, review questions, discussion questions, and cases reflect practical and applied aspects of organizational behavior.

Examples from diverse organizations (multinational, regional, not-for-profit, public) and industries (manufacturing, service, defense) are included. These examples are integrated throughout the text. A unique feature of the book is its focus on the six organizations mentioned earlier. These represent many different types of organizations—large and small, for profit and not-for-profit, product and service oriented. The purpose of this approach is to provide a sense of continuity and depth not achieved in single examples.

Study Aids

To help you learn, understand, and apply the material in *Organizational Behavior*, the fifth edition provides many unique and comprehensive study tools.

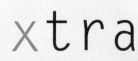

XTRA! WEB SITE Access to a robust set of additional on-line learning tools can be optionally packaged with the text. Found at the Nelson-Quick Xtra! Web site (http://nelsonxtra.swlearning.com), study tools include Author Insights video clips of the authors providing further explanation of complex topics, *Experiencing Organizational Behavior* on-line tutorials, Xtra! quizzes, and various video clips.

STUDY GUIDE (ISBN: 0-324-31826-X) The study guide was prepared by David A. Foote (Middle Tennessee State University). Designed from a student's perspective, the value-laden study guide comes with all the tools necessary to maximize results on exams and in class. Learning objectives and chapter outlines are included, as well as a comprehensive key terms glossary with text page references and numerous self-test questions. Answers with text page references are provided for all self-tests.

INFOTRAC® COLLEGE EDITION With InfoTrac® College Edition, students can receive anytime, anywhere on-line access to a database of full-text articles from hundreds of popular and scholarly periodicals, such as *Newsweek, Fortune, Entrepreneur, Journal of Management,* and *Nation's Business,* among others. Students can use its fast and easy search tools to find relevant news and analytical information among the tens of thousands of articles in the database—updated daily and going back as far as four years—all at a single Web site. InfoTrac® is a great way to expose students to on-line research techniques with the security that the content is academically based and reliable. An InfoTrac® College Edition subscription card is packaged free with new copies of the *Organizational Behavior,* fifth edition text. For more information, visit http://infotrac.thomsonlearning.com.

WEB SITE (HTTP://NELSON-QUICK.SWLEARNING.COM) A rich Web site at http://nelson-quick.swlearning.com complements the text, providing many extras for students. Resources include chapter glossaries, interactive quizzes, and PowerPoint® slides.

EXPERIENCING ORGANIZATIONAL BEHAVIOR An innovative product created by R. Dennis Middlemist of Colorado State University, *Experiencing Organizational Behavior* is a totally on-line collection of Web-based modules that uses the latest Flash technology in its animated scenarios, graphs, and models. Designed to reinforce key management principles in a dynamic learning environment, *Experiencing Organizational Behavior* maintains high motivation through the use of challenging problems. Try it by visiting http://www.experiencingob.com. *Experiencing Organizational Behavior* is available for purchase on-line by each individual module or as a collection of all 13 modules. Access is also available on the Nelson-Quick Xtra! Web site.

SOME DISTINCTIVE FEATURES INSTRUCTORS LIKE

Professors have demanding jobs. They should expect textbook authors and publishers to provide them with the support they need to do an excellent job for students. Among their expectations should be a well-integrated, complete ancillary package. *Organizational Behavior* has this package.

Ancillary Package

A comprehensive set of ancillaries supports the basic text: an instructor's manual with video guide, a test bank, ExamView (computerized testing software), PowerPoint® presentation files, a product support Web site, and a video program. The videos include a variety of short vignettes from real Hollywood films and about real companies with which your students may already be familiar. Using video in the classroom will enhance the text presentation and reinforce its themes, adding continuity and integration to the overall understanding of organizational behavior.

INSTRUCTOR'S MANUAL WITH VIDEO GUIDE (ISBN: 0-324-31827-8) The instructor's manual with video guide for *Organizational Behavior* was prepared by David A. Foote (Middle Tennessee State University), Joseph E. Champoux (University of New Mexico), and B.J. Parker. Each chapter contains the following information:

- Chapter scan—a brief overview of the chapter.
- Suggested learning objectives that are presented in the textbook.
- Key terms—a list of key terms from the chapter.
- The chapter summarized—an extended outline with narratives under each major point to flesh out the discussion and offer alternative examples and issues to bring forward. The extended outlines are several pages long and incorporate many teaching suggestions.
- Answer guidelines for end-of-chapter materials—detailed responses to the review questions, discussion and communication questions, and ethical dilemmas, with suggestions for keeping discussion on track in the classroom.
- Suggested answers for the You features.
- Experiential exercises—a brief description of each exercise as well as a detailed summary of anticipated results. Also included are alternative experiential exercises not found in the text. Discussion questions are provided with selected experiential exercises. Finally, a list of sources for still more may be found under "Extra Experiential Exercises."
- Cases—suggested answers for case discussion questions are provided in a detailed form.
- Integration of Myers-Briggs Type Indicator material (optional)—including full descriptions and exercises in communication, leadership, motivation, decision making, conflict resolution, power, stress and time management, and managing change. For instructors unfamiliar with Myers-Briggs, a general introduction to this instrument is provided at the end of Chapter 3 of the instructor's manual. The introduction includes several good references for additional information about testing.
- Video cases—suggested answers to the Biz Flix and Workplace video cases, including information on how to successfully incorporate the use of video in your lesson plan, are included for all chapters.
- Printouts of the slides from the PowerPoint® Presentation Files.

TEST BANK (ISBN: 0-324-31828-6) The test bank, prepared by Jon G. Kalinowski (Minnesota State University, Mankato), has been thoroughly revised for this edition. The test bank contains more than 1,200 multiple-choice, true/false, matching, and essay questions. Each question has been coded according to Bloom's taxonomy, a widely known testing and measurement device used to classify questions according to level (easy, medium, or hard) and type (application, recall, or comprehension).

EXAMVIEW (ISBN: 0-324-31829-4) This supplement contains all of the questions in the printed test bank. This program is an easy-to-use test creation software compatible with Microsoft Windows and Macintosh. Instructors can add or edit questions, instructions, and answers, and select questions (randomly or numerically) by previewing them on the screen. Instructors can also create and administer quizzes on-line, whether over the Internet, a local area network (LAN), or a wide area network (WAN).

POWERPOINT® PRESENTATION FILES Marilyn Bergmann and Donna Raleigh (University of Wisconsin, Eau Claire) have developed more than 300 PowerPoint® slides for this text. These slides feature figures from the text, lecture outlines, and innovative adaptations to enhance classroom presentation. An enhanced version of the PowerPoint® slides includes clips from the Biz Flix videos featured in the text.

INSTRUCTOR'S RESOURCE CD-ROM (ISBN: 0-324-31830-8) Key instructor ancillaries (instructor's manual, test bank, ExamView, and PowerPoint® slides) are provided on CD-ROM, giving instructors the ultimate tool for customizing lectures and presentations.

WEB SITE (HTTP://NELSON-QUICK.SWLEARNING.COM) *Organizational Behavior* has its own product support Web site at http://nelson-quick.swlearning.com. The full PowerPoint® presentation is available for you to download as lecture support. The instructor's manual is also available for download. A multiple-choice and true/false tutorial to help your students study for exams is also featured.

WEBTUTOR™ ADVANTAGE ON WEBCT™ AND ON BLACKBOARD® WebTutor™ Advantage complements *Organizational Behavior* by providing interactive reinforcement. WebTutor™ Advantage's on-line teaching and learning environment brings together content management, assessment, communication, and collaboration capabilities for enhancing in-class instruction or for delivering distance learning. For more information, including a demo, visit http://webtutor.swlearning.com.

"TAKE 2" VIDEO PROGRAM (ISBN: 0-324-32196-1, 0-324-32195-3) Available in both VHS and DVD formats, an all-new video program has been developed especially for use with *Organizational Behavior*. Video segments have been selected to support the themes of the book and to deepen students' understanding of the organizational behavior concepts presented throughout the text. Biz Flix video cases, developed by Joseph E. Champoux of the University of New Mexico, incorporate clips from popular films such as *8 Mile, Meet the Parents,* and *Reality Bites* into the classroom. Companies profiled in the Workplace video series include CVS Corporation, Buffalo Zoo, and Fannie Mae, among others. Information on using the videos can be found in the Instructor's Manual.

CNN VIDEO: MANAGEMENT AND ORGANIZATIONS (ISBN: 0-324-15179-9) Forty-five minutes of short segments from CNN, the world's first 24-hour all-news network, are available on VHS cassette to use as lecture launchers, discussion starters, topical introductions, or directed inquiries.

ORGANIZATIONAL BEHAVIOR: EXPERIENCES AND CASES (ISBN: 0-324-04850-5) Written by Dorothy Marcic, Joseph Seltzer, and Peter Vaill, *Organizational Behavior: Experiences and Cases* contains experiential exercises and cases that emphasize management skill development and practical application of theory integral to the study of organizational behavior.

OUR REVIEWERS ARE APPRECIATED

We would like to thank our professional peers and colleagues who reviewed the text to evaluate scholarly accuracy, writing style, and pedagogy. The many changes we made are based on their suggestions. We gratefully acknowledge the help of the following individuals:

Robert F. Abbey, Jr., *Troy State University*
Stephen R. Ball, *Cleary University*
Talya Bauer, *Portland State University*
Mark C. Butler, *San Diego State University*
Jacqueline A. Gilbert, *Middle Tennessee State University*
Don Jung, *San Diego State University*
Jalane M. Meloun, *Barry University*
Floyd S. Ormsbee, *Clarkson University*
Linda Beats Putchinski, *University of Central Florida*
Elizabeth C. Ravlin, *University of South Carolina*
Harriet L. Rojas, *Indiana Wesleyan University*
Chris John Sablynski, *California State University, Sacramento*
M. Shane Spiller, *Morehead State University*
William H. Turnley, *Kansas State University*

ACKNOWLEDGMENTS

The fifth edition of *Organizational Behavior* represents a team effort, and we are grateful to each and every team member who made the process run smoothly. Our editor **John Szilagyi** has been a great coach, advocate, friend, and guide who says "yes" more often than "no." **Leslie Kauffman**, our developmental editor, kept us focused on the goal and the yard markers as we all moved down the field on the fifth edition. **Libby Shipp**, our production editor, was a great master of the important elements of production, keeping us all on task and on time. **Malvine Litten** did another excellent job of project management for the textbook, and we are grateful for her eagle eye with the details.

Mark Phillips was an invaluable help in the revision process. His creative touch can be seen throughout the fifth edition. **Bret Simmons**, North Dakota State University, provided many suggestions and insights that shaped this edition.

Faye Cocchiara joined the team at the first planning session and made immense contributions throughout with her great eye for opportunities. In the process, her own research contributions to organizational behavior are reflected in references to her work on diversity, positive stereotypes, and within-group variance. **Marilyn Macik-Frey** added value with her communication expertise, shared with the team.

Joanne H. Gavin switched roles from the fourth to the fifth edition, taking on the mantle of ethicist in the current edition. Her own scholarship on virtue ethics, character, and personal integrity are reflected in the special feature she has pioneered and in the citations to her research. **David J. Gavin** continues to be a positive source of ideas and feedback on many aspects of producing a book from his life as an executive and an editor.

Joseph Champoux of the University of New Mexico was kind enough to lend us materials from his *At the Movies* series of texts for our new Biz Flix video cases, and **B.J. Parker** wrote our all-new Workplace video cases.

Michael McCuddy of Valparaiso University did his customary outstanding job on the cases that appear at the end of each chapter and the cohesion cases that appear at the end of each part. He has a way of making organizational problems fascinating to students. **Jeff McGee** was most helpful with small business and entrepreneurship advice and contacts. **Burley Walker** helped with production operations definitions and content for the design of work. Additionally, **Carol Byrne** and **Ruthie Brock,** business librarians at the University of Texas at Arlington, provided much support in the preparation of this textbook.

Preparation of the ancillary materials to enhance classroom efforts required a host of people. **David A. Foote,** Middle Tennessee State University, **Joseph E. Champoux,** the University of New Mexico, and **B.J. Parker** created a superb Instructor's Manual and Video Guide. **Jon Kalinowski** of Minnesota State University, Mankato, was great in preparing the Test Bank that accompanies the textbook. Many thanks go to **Marilyn Bergmann** and **Donna Raleigh,** University of Wisconsin, Eau Claire, for developing the PowerPoint® Presentation files, and to **David A. Foote,** Middle Tennessee State University, for revising the Study Guide. We are also grateful to **Floyd Ormsbee,** Clarkson University, who wrote the quizzes for the Xtra! Web site.

We are fortunate to have several colleagues who have made helpful contributions and supported our development through all five editions of the textbook: **Mike Hitt** of Texas A & M University; **Lisa Kennedy** of Baylor College of Medicine; **Raj Basu, Ken Eastman, Mark Gavin,** and **Robert Dooley,** all of Oklahoma State University; **David Mack, David Gray, Myrtle Bell, Ken Price, Jim Lavelle,** and **Steve Colburn,** all of the University of Texas at Arlington; **Juliana Lilly** of Sam Houston State University; and **J. Lee Whittington** of University of Dallas.

Our families and friends have encouraged us throughout the development of the book. They have provided us with emotional support and examples for the book and have graciously allowed us the time to do the book justice. We are truly grateful for their support.

This book has been a labor of love for both of us. It has made us better teachers and also better learners. And that is our wish for you!

Debra L. Nelson
James Campbell Quick

Debra L. Nelson

Dr. Debra L. Nelson is The CBA Associates Professor of Business Administration and Professor of Management at Oklahoma State University. She received her Ph.D. from the University of Texas at Arlington, where she was the recipient of the R. D. Irwin Dissertation Fellowship Award. Dr. Nelson is the author of over 80 journal articles focusing on organizational stress management, gender at work, and leadership. Her research has been published in the *Academy of Management Executive, Academy of Management Journal, Academy of Management Review, MIS Quarterly, Organizational Dynamics, Journal of Organizational Behavior*, and other journals. In addition, she is coauthor/coeditor of several books, including *Organizational Behavior: Foundations, Realities, and Challenges* (5th ed., Thomson/South-Western, 2006), *Organizational Leadership* (Thomson/South-Western, 2004), *Gender, Work Stress and Health* (American Psychological Association, 2002), *Advancing Women in Management* (Blackwell, 2002) and *Preventive Stress Management in Organizations* (American Psychological Association, 1997). Dr. Nelson has also served as a consultant to several organizations including AT&T, American Fidelity Assurance, Sonic, State Farm Insurance Companies, and Southwestern Bell. She has presented leadership and preventive stress management seminars in a host of organizations, including Blue Cross/Blue Shield, Conoco, Oklahoma Gas and Electric, Oklahoma Natural Gas, and Preview Network Systems. She was honored with the Greiner Graduate Teaching Award in 2001, the Chandler-Frates and Reitz Graduate Teaching Award in 1997, the Regents' Distinguished Teaching Award in 1994, and the Burlington Northern Faculty Achievement Award at OSU in 1991. Dr. Nelson also serves on the editorial review boards of the *Academy of Management Executive* and *Leadership*.

James Campbell Quick

Dr. James Campbell (Jim) Quick is John and Judy Goolsby Distinguished Professor, Executive Director of the Goolsby Leadership Academy, and Professor of Organizational Behavior in the College of Business Administration at the University of Texas at Arlington. He is former Associate Editor of *The Academy of Management Executive*. He earned an A.B. with Honors from Colgate University, where he was a George Cobb Fellow and Harvard Business School Association intern. He earned an M.B.A. and a Ph.D. at the University of Houston. He completed post-graduate courses in behavioral medicine (Harvard Medical School) and combat stress (University of Texas Health Science Center at San Antonio).

Dr. Quick is a Fellow of the Society for Industrial and Organizational Psychology, the American Psychological Association, the American Psychological Society, and the American Institute of Stress. He was awarded the 2002 Harry and Miriam Levinson Award by the American Psychological Foundation.

Dr. Quick framed preventive stress management with his brother (Jonathan D. Quick, MD, MPH). He has received over $250,000 in funded support for research, scholarship and intellectual contributions from the Society for Human Resource Management, Hospital Corporation of America, the State of Texas, and the American Psychological Association. His articles have been published in leading journals such as the *Academy of Management's Journal, Review*, and *Executive, Journal of Organizational Behavior, Air University Review, Stress Medicine*, and the *Journal of Medical Education*. He received the 1990 Distinguished Professional Publication Award for *Corporate Warfare: Preventing Combat Stress and Battle Fatigue*, coauthored with Debra L. Nelson and his brother for the American Management Association's *Organizational Dynamics*.

He is coauthor of *The Financial Times Guide to Executive Health* (Prentice Hall/Financial Times, 2002) which appears in seven languages, *Preventive Stress Management in Organizations* (American Psychological Association, 1997), originally published in 1984 and released as *Unternehmen ohne Stress* in German, and *Stress and Challenge at the Top: The Paradox of the Successful Executive* (John Wiley & Sons, 1990). He is coeditor of the *Handbook of Occupational Health Psychology* (APA, 2002), *The New Organizational Reality: Downsizing, Restructuring, and Revitalization* (APA, 1998), *Stress and Well-Being at Work* (APA, 1992), and *Work Stress: Health Care Systems in the Workplace* (Praeger Scientific, 1987), for which he has received the 1987 Distinguished Service Award from the UTA College of Business. He is a member of Beta Gamma Sigma and Phi Beta Delta honor societies and the Great Southwest Rotary Club, where he is a past president and a Paul Harris Fellow.

Dr. Quick was the American Psychological Association's stress expert to the National Academy of Sciences on National Health Objectives for the Year 2000. Dr. Quick was a scientific exchange delegate to the People's Republic of China.

Dr. Quick was recognized with the Texas Volunteer Recognition Award (American Heart Association, 1985), a listing in *Who's Who in the World*, 7th Edition (1984–85), *The Maroon Citation* (Colgate University Alumni Corporation, 1993), two Minnie Stevens Piper Professorship Award nominations (1995, 2001), and a *Presidential Citation* from the American Psychological Association (2001).

Colonel Quick, U.S. Air Force (Retired), was the Senior Individual Mobilization Augmentee at the San Antonio Air Logistics Center (AFMC), Kelly AFB, Texas, in his last assignment. He was Distinguished Visiting Professor of Psychology, 59th Medical Wing (1999). His awards and decorations include *The Legion of Merit, Meritorious Service Medal*, and *National Defense Service Medal with Bronze Star*.

Jim is married to the former Sheri Grimes Schember.

To our students, who challenge us to be better than we are, who keep us in touch with reality, and who are the foundation of our careers.

PART 1

Introduction

© Noah Berger/Bloomberg News/Landov

Chapter 1

Organizational Behavior and Opportunity

THINKING AHEAD: CISCO SYSTEMS

Opportunity Calls for Cisco

Cisco Systems got a rude wake-up call in 2001 when its revenues were headed down and its top customers were threatening to revolt and bolt. Cisco's wake-up call came from some of the biggest telecom companies in the world, which included Level 3 Communications and AT&T. The call came in April 2001 when several Cisco executives were summoned to a conference on the Colorado campus of Level 3 Communications, the fiber-optic network operator. In addition to elite engineers from Level 3 Communications were their elite peers from AT&T and a half-dozen other big-time telecom players. These big telecom companies were all major buyers of Cisco networking gear, and their message was very clear—it jarred the Cisco executives. The engineers reported significant technological problems with Cisco routers. The telecom giants gave Cisco a choice: Either fix it or risk losing some of your biggest customers.[1]

The message from the telecom engineers was that the software on the Cisco routers that linked telecom networks stank. The software crashed parts of the networks as often as once a month, sometimes for as long as thirty minutes. Within the telecom industry, the acceptable crash standard was more like "a few minutes" about "once a year." Cisco's software was way off standard and therefore performing at a totally unacceptable level. This confrontation with Cisco by the major telecom companies came during a difficult time in the industry. For Cisco, Spring 2001 was a rather dark time. The Internet and technology bubbles were bursting, taking Cisco off its pinnacle as the most valuable corporation on earth, worth more than half a trillion dollars.

Cisco was able to see opportunity in the wake-up call. Mighty Cisco was a proud young company built on the technological excellence and expertise of its computer science and engineering origins. Cisco saw, as did its rivals, a goldmine in Internet-based networks. In the telecom industry, phone companies had been accumulating multiple networks over several decades. While one of these networks carried traditional phone traffic, another was connecting corporate headquarters with regional offices, while still another was carrying secure transmissions of data, voice, and video information. While the phone companies were operating through traditional networks, Internet protocol (IP) networks were vastly cheaper to build and operate. Cisco, which was founded on the Blue Box router that allowed corporations to connect their various computers, was ideally positioned to take advantage of the phone companies' transition to a new breed of phone company—the Internet service provider.

Human Behavior in Organizations

1. Define *organizational behavior*.

Human behavior in organizations is complex and often difficult to understand. Organizations have been described as clockworks in which human behavior is logical and rational, but they often seem like snake pits to those who work in them.[2] The clockwork metaphor reflects an orderly, idealized view of organizational behavior devoid of conflict or dilemma because all the working parts (the people) mesh smoothly. The snake pit metaphor conveys the daily conflict, distress, and struggle in organizations. Each metaphor reflects reality from a different perspective—the organization's versus the individual's point of view. These metaphors reflect the complexity of human behavior, the dark side of which is seen in cases of air rage and workplace violence. On the positive side, the Gallup Organization's Marcus Buckingham suggests that people's psychological makeup is at the heart of the emotional economy.[3]

This chapter is an introduction to organizational behavior. The first section provides an overview of human behavior in organizations, its interdisciplinary origins, and behavior in times of change. The second section presents an organizational context within which behavior occurs and briefly introduces the six focus companies used selectively in the book. The third section highlights the *opportunities* that exist in times of *change* and *challenge* for people at work.[4] The fourth section addresses the ways people learn about organizational behavior and explains how the text's pedagogical features relate to the various ways of learning. The final section of the chapter presents the plan for the book.

Organizational behavior is individual behavior and group dynamics in organizations. The study of organizational behavior is primarily concerned with the psychosocial, interpersonal, and behavioral dynamics in organizations. However, organizational variables that affect human behavior at work are also relevant to the study of organizational behavior. These organizational variables include jobs, the design of work, communication, performance appraisal, organizational design, and organizational structure. Therefore, although individual behavior and group dynamics are the primary concerns in the study of organizational behavior, organizational variables are also important.

opportunities
Favorable times or chances for progress and advancement.

change
The transformation or modification of an organization and/or its stakeholders.

challenge
The call to competition, contest, or battle.

organizational behavior
The study of individual behavior and group dynamics in organizations.

This section briefly contrasts two perspectives for understanding human behavior, the external and the internal perspectives. The section then discusses six scientific disciplines from which the study of organizational behavior has emerged and concludes with a discussion of behavior in times of change.

Understanding Human Behavior

The vast majority of theories and models of human behavior fall into one of two basic categories. One category has an internal perspective, and the other has an external perspective. The internal perspective considers factors inside the person to understand behavior. This view is psychodynamically oriented. People who subscribe to this view understand human behavior in terms of the thoughts, feelings, past experiences, and needs of the individual. The internal perspective explains people's actions and behavior in terms of their history and personal value systems. The internal processes of thinking, feeling, perceiving, and judging lead people to act in specific ways. The internal perspective has given rise to a wide range of motivational and leadership theories. This perspective implies that people are best understood from the inside and that people's behavior is best interpreted after understanding their thoughts and feelings.

The other category of theories and models of human behavior takes an external perspective. This perspective focuses on factors outside the person to understand behavior. People who subscribe to this view understand human behavior in terms of external events, consequences of behavior, and the environmental forces to which a person is subject. From the external perspective, a person's history, feelings, thoughts, and personal value systems are not very important in interpreting actions and behavior. This perspective has given rise to an alternative set of motivational and leadership theories, which are covered in Chapters 5 and 12 of the text. The external perspective implies that a person's behavior is best understood by examining the surrounding external events and environmental forces.

The internal and external perspectives offer alternative explanations for human behavior. For example, the internal perspective might say Mary is an outstanding employee because she has a high need for achievement, whereas the external perspective might say Mary is an outstanding employee because she is paid extremely well for her work. Kurt Lewin captured both perspectives in saying that behavior is a function of both the person and the environment.[5]

Interdisciplinary Influences

Organizational behavior is a blended discipline that has grown out of contributions from numerous earlier fields of study, only one of which is the psychological discipline from which Kurt Lewin came. These interdisciplinary influences are the roots for what is increasingly recognized as the independent discipline of organizational behavior. The sciences of psychology, sociology, engineering, anthropology, management, and medicine have each contributed to our understanding of human behavior in organizations.

Psychology is the science of human behavior and dates back to the closing decades of the nineteenth century. Psychology traces its own origins to philosophy and the science of physiology. One of the most prominent early psychologists, William James, actually held a degree in medicine (M.D.). Since its origin, psychology has itself become differentiated into a number of specialized fields, such as clinical, experimental, military, organizational, and social psychology. Organizational psychology includes the study of many topics, such as work motivation, which are also covered by organizational behavior.[6] Early psychological research for the American military during World War I had later implications

psychology

The science of human behavior.

sociology
The science of society.

Systems View

engineering
The applied science of energy and matter.

anthropology
The science of the learned behavior of human beings.

management
The study of overseeing activities and supervising people in organizations.

medicine
The applied science of healing or treatment of diseases to enhance an individual's health and well-being.

2. Identify four action steps for responding positively in times of change.

for sophisticated personnel selection methods used by corporations such as Johnson & Johnson, Valero Energy, and Chaparral Steel.[7]

Sociology, the science of society, has made important contributions to knowledge about group and intergroup dynamics in the study of organizational behavior. Because sociology takes society rather than the individual as its point of departure, the sociologist is concerned with the variety of roles within a society or culture, the norms and standards of behavior in groups, and the consequences of compliant and deviant behavior. For example, the concept of *role set,* a key contribution to role theory in 1957 by Robert Merton, was used by a team of Harvard educators to study the school superintendent role in Massachusetts.[8] More recently, the role set concept has been used to study the effects of codes of ethics in organizations.[9]

Engineering is the applied science of energy and matter. Engineering has made important contributions to our understanding of the design of work. By taking basic engineering ideas and applying them to human behavior at work, Frederick Taylor had a profound influence on the early years of the study of organizational behavior.[10] Taylor's engineering background led him to place special emphasis on human productivity and efficiency in work behavior. His notions of performance standards and differential piece-rate systems have had lasting impact. Taylor's original ideas are embedded in organizational goal-setting programs, such as those at Black & Decker, IBM, and Weyerhaeuser.[11]

Anthropology is the science of human learned behavior and is especially important to understanding organizational culture. Cultural anthropology focuses on the origins of culture and the patterns of behavior as culture is communicated symbolically. Research in this tradition has examined the effects of efficient cultures on organization performance[12] and how pathological personalities may lead to dysfunctional organizational cultures.[13] Schwartz used a psychodynamic, anthropological mode of inquiry in exploring corporate decay at General Motors and NASA.[14]

Management, originally called administrative science, is a discipline concerned with the study of overseeing activities and supervising people in organizations. It emphasizes the design, implementation, and management of various administrative and organizational systems. March and Simon take the human organization as their point of departure and concern themselves with the administrative practices that will enhance the effectiveness of the system.[15] Management is the first discipline to take the modern corporation as the unit of analysis, and this viewpoint distinguishes the discipline's contribution to the study of organizational behavior.

Medicine is the applied science of healing or treatment of diseases to enhance an individual's health and well-being. Medicine has long-standing concern for both physical and psychological health, as well as for industrial mental health.[16] More recently, as the war against acute diseases is being won, medical attention has shifted to more chronic diseases, such as hypertension, and to occupational health and well-being.[17] Individual behavior and lifestyle patterns play important roles in treating chronic diseases.[18] These trends have contributed to the growth of corporate wellness programs, such as Johnson & Johnson's "Live for Life Program." The surge in health care costs over the past two decades has contributed to increased organizational concern with medicine and health care in the workplace.[19]

Behavior in Times of Change

Early research with individuals, groups, and organizations in the midst of environmental change found that change is often experienced as a threat which leads to a reliance on well-learned and dominant forms of behavior.[20] That is, in the

The Outsourcing of America

© Sherwin Crasto/Reuters/Landov

Many help desk and tech support hotlines are routed to India. The next time you call up your phone company to question something on your billing statement, there is a high probability that the voice on the other end of the line is in India.

Dramatic advances in the Internet and networking technology enable companies like Procter & Gamble to leverage business process outsourcing (BPO). BPO has its roots in IT outsourcing, which IBM and EDS began doing in the early 1990s. The pace of the dot.com boom years and the pressures surrounding Y2K forced the outsourcing of coding jobs to places like India and Bulgaria. Procter & Gamble was able to take advantage of the rise of BPO, which offered the company hyperflexibility and positive change from the Information Age. Procter & Gamble found that expense reports could be processed in another country, anywhere in the world, when all parties involved in the transactions had access to the same computer network.

The company has saved $1 billion since 1999 by concentrating back-office work in Costa Rica, the Philippines, and Britain. In addition to saving money, BPO can result in better quality work and lower turnover because it attracts top people in new countries. While outsourcing American jobs may sound negative to some, The Conference Board takes a more positive view. The U.S. economy often creates more jobs than it loses annually. For example, the U.S. services sector may lose 10 million jobs in a year while creating 12 million, for a net gain of 2 million jobs. In addition, the outsourcing of America helps to spread wealth from rich nations to poorer ones, which itself may be a net positive for the global economy.

SOURCE: D. Kirkpatrick, "The Net Makes It All Easier–Including Exporting U.S. Jobs," *Fortune* (May 26, 2003): 146, http://www.fortune.com/fortune/subs/columnist/0,15704,450755,00.html.

midst of change, people often become rigid and reactive, rather than open and responsive. This may be useful if the change is neither dramatic nor rapid because we are often effective at coping with incremental change. However, if significant change occurs, then rigid and well-learned behavior may be counterproductive. Outsourcing is a significant change in American industry that is described in The Real World 1.1. Big changes disrupt people's habitual behavior and require learning if they are to be managed successfully. Eric Brown of ProLine International offers some sage words of advice to see the opportunity in change.[21] He recommends adapting to change by seeing it as positive and challenge as good rather than bad. His action steps for doing this are to (1) have a positive attitude, (2) ask questions, (3) listen to the answers, and (4) be committed to success.

However, success is never guaranteed, and change sometimes results in failure. If this happens, do not despair. Some of the world's greatest leaders, such as Winston Churchill, experienced dramatic failure before achieving lasting success. The key to their eventual success was their capacity to learn from the failure and to respond positively to the opportunities presented to them. One venture capitalist with whom the authors have worked likes to ask those seeking to build a business to tell him about their greatest failure. What the venture capitalist is looking for in the answer is how the executive responded to the failure and what he or she learned from the experience. While change carries with it the risk of failure as well as the opportunity for success, it is often how we behave in the midst of change that determines which outcome results.

The Organizational Context

3. Identify the important system components of an organization.

A complete understanding of organizational behavior requires both an understanding of human behavior and an understanding of the organizational context within which human behavior is acted out. The organizational context is the specific setting within which organizational behavior is enacted. This section discusses several aspects of this organizational context and includes specific organizational examples. First, organizations are presented as systems. Second, the formal and informal organizations are discussed. Finally, six focus companies are presented as contemporary examples, which are drawn on throughout the text.

Organizations as Open Systems

Just as two different perspectives offer complementary explanations for human behavior, two other perspectives offer complementary explanations of organizations. Organizations are open systems of interacting components, which are people, tasks, technology, and structure. These internal components also interact with components in the organization's task environment. Organizations as open systems have people, technology, structure, and purpose, which interact with elements in the organization's environment.

What, exactly, is an organization? Today, the corporation is the dominant organizational form for much of the Western world, but other organizational forms have dominated other times and societies. Some societies have been dominated by religious organizations, such as the temple corporations of ancient Mesopotamia and the churches in colonial America.[22] Other societies have been dominated by military organizations, such as the clans of the Scottish Highlands and the regional armies of the People's Republic of China.[23, 24] All of these societies are woven together by family organizations, which themselves may vary from nuclear and extended families to small, collective communities.[25, 26] The purpose and structure of the religious, military, and family organizational forms may vary, but people's behavior in these organizations may be very similar. In fact, early discoveries about power and leadership in work organizations were remarkably similar to findings about power and leadership within families.[27]

Organizations may manufacture products, such as aircraft components or steel, or deliver services, such as managing money or providing insurance protection. To understand how organizations do these things requires an understanding of the open system components of the organization and the components of its task environment.

Katz and Kahn and Leavitt set out open system frameworks for understanding organizations.[28] The four major internal components are task, people, technology, and structure. These four components, along with the organization's inputs, outputs, and key elements in the task environment, are depicted in Figure 1.1. The *task* of the organization is its mission, purpose, or goal for existing. The *people* are the human resources of the organization. The *technology* is the wide range of tools, knowledge, and/or techniques used to transform the inputs into outputs. The *structure* is the systems of communication, systems of authority, and the systems of workflow.

In addition to these major internal components, the organization as a system also has an external task environment. The task environment is composed of different constituents, such as suppliers, customers, and federal regulators.

task
An organization's mission, purpose, or goal for existing.

people
The human resources of the organization.

technology
The tools, knowledge, and/or techniques used to transform inputs into outputs.

structure
The systems of communication, authority and roles, and workflow.

Task environment:
Competitors
Unions
Regulatory agencies
Clients

Inputs:
Material
Capital
Human

Structure

Task

Technology

People
(Actors)

Outputs:
Products
Services

Organizational boundary

SOURCE: Based on Harold Leavitt, "Applied Organizational Change in Industry: Structural, Technological, and Humanistic Approaches," in J. G. March, ed., *Handbook of Organizations* (Chicago: Rand McNally, 1965), p. 1145. Reprinted by permission of James G. March.

Thompson describes the task environment as that element of the environment related to the organization's degree of goal attainment; that is, the task environment is composed of those elements of the environment related to the organization's basic task.[29] For example, when steel was a major component in the production of cars, U.S. Steel was a major supplier for General Motors and Ford Motor Company—U.S. Steel was a major component of their task environments. As less steel and more aluminum was used to make cars, U.S. Steel became a less important supplier for General Motors and Ford—it was no longer a major component in their task environments.

The organization system works by taking inputs, converting them into throughputs, and delivering outputs to its task environment. Inputs consist of the human, informational, material, and financial resources used by the organization. Throughputs are the materials and resources as they are transformed by the organization's technology component. Once the transformation is complete, they become outputs for customers, consumers, and clients. The actions of suppliers, customers, regulators, and other elements of the task environment affect the organization and the behavior of people at work. For example, Onsite Engineering and Management experienced a threat to its survival in the mid-1980s by being totally dependent on one large utility for its outputs. By broadening its client base and improving the quality of its services (that is, its outputs) over the next several years, Onsite became a healthier, more successful small company. Transforming inputs into high-quality outputs is critical to an organization's success.

The Formal and Informal Organization

The open systems view of organization may lead one to view the design of an organization as a clockwork with a neat, precise, interrelated functioning. The

4. Describe the formal and informal elements of an organization.

formal organization
The official, legitimate, and most visible part of the system.

informal organization
The unofficial and less visible part of the system.

Hawthorne studies
Studies conducted during the 1920s and 1930s that discovered the existence of the informal organization.

formal organization is the official, legitimate, and most visible part that enables people to think of organizations in logical and rational ways. The snake pit organizational metaphor mentioned earlier has its roots in the study and examination of the *informal organization*, which is unofficial and less visible. The informal elements were first fully appreciated as a result of the *Hawthorne studies*, conducted during the 1920s and 1930s. It was during the interview study, the third of the four Hawthorne studies, that the researchers began to develop a fuller appreciation for the informal elements of the Hawthorne Works as an organization.[30] The formal and informal elements of the organization are depicted in Figure 1.2.

Potential conflict between the formal and informal organization makes an understanding of both important. Conflicts between these two elements erupted in many organizations during the early years of the twentieth century and were embodied in the union–management strife of that era. The conflicts escalated into violence in a number of cases. For example, during the 1920s supervisors at the Homestead Works of U.S. Steel were issued pistols and boxes of ammunition "just in case" it became necessary to shoot unruly, dangerous steelworkers. Not all organizations are characterized by such potential formal–informal, management–labor conflict. During the same era, Eastman Kodak was very progressive. The company helped with financial backing for employees' neighborhood communities, such as Meadowbrook in Rochester, New York. Kodak's concern for employees and attention to informal issues made unions unnecessary within the company.

1.2 **FIGURE 1.2** Formal and Informal Organization

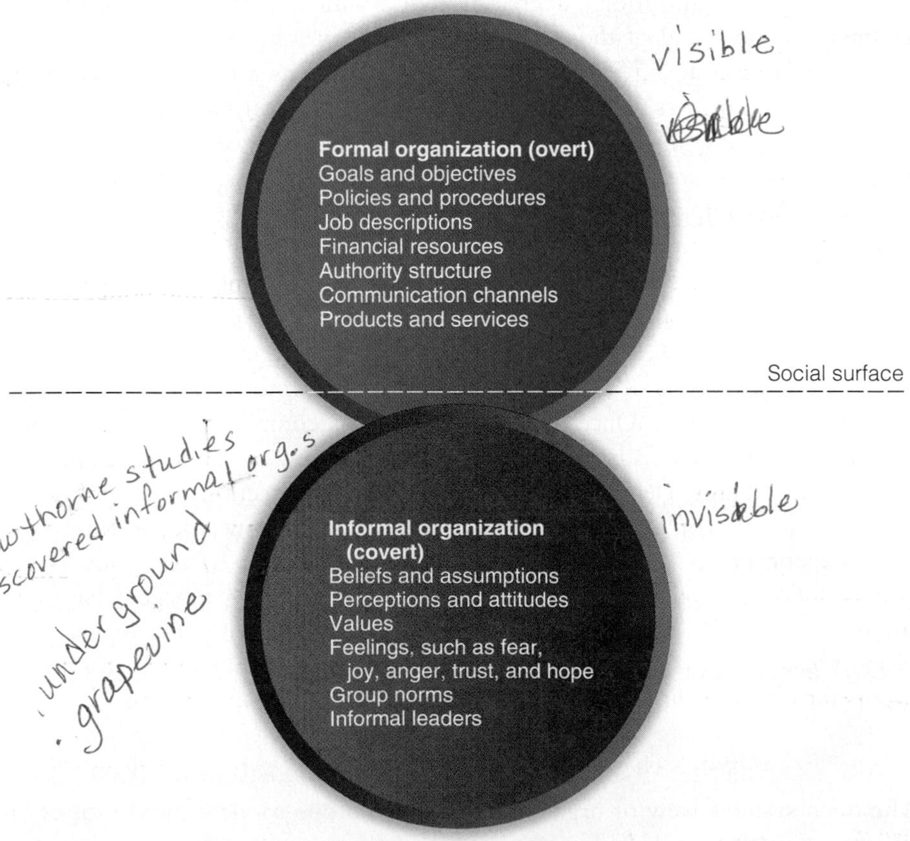

The informal elements of the organization are frequent points of diagnostic and intervention activities in organization development, though the formal elements must always be considered as well because they provide the context for the informal.[31] These informal elements are important because people's feelings, thoughts, and attitudes about their work do make a difference in their behavior and performance. Individual behavior plays out in the context of the formal and informal elements of the system, becoming organizational behavior. The uncovering of the informal elements in an organization was one of the major discoveries of the Hawthorne studies.

Six Focus Organizations

Organizational behavior always occurs in the context of a specific organizational setting. Most attempts at explaining or predicting organizational behavior rely heavily on factors within the organization and give less weight to external environmental considerations.[32] Students can benefit from being sensitive to the industrial context of organizations and from developing an appreciation for each organization as a whole.[33] In this vein, six organizations are each featured in the Thinking Ahead and Looking Back sections of three chapters. Cisco Systems is illustrated in this chapter. We challenge you in each chapter to anticipate what is in the Looking Back feature once you read Thinking Ahead.

The U.S. economy is the largest in the world, with a gross domestic product of more than $10.9 trillion in 2003. Figure 1.3 shows the major sectors of the economy. The largest sectors are service (44 percent) and product manufacture of nondurable goods (21 percent) and durable goods (8 percent). Taken together, the production of products and the delivery of services account for 73 percent of the U.S. economy. Government and fixed investments account for the remaining 27 percent. Large and small organizations operate in each sector of the economy shown in Figure 1.3.

The private sectors are an important part of the economy. The manufacturing sector includes the production of basic materials, such as steel, and the production of finished products, such as automobiles and electronic equipment. The service sector includes transportation, financial services, insurance, and retail sales. The government sectors, which provide essential infrastructure, and nonprofit organizations are also important to our collective well-being because they meet needs not addressed in these economic sectors. We have chosen organizations that can reflect the manufacturing service, retail, and nonprofit sections of business. These six organizations are Cisco Systems, The Coca-Cola Company, Pixar Animation Studios, Virgin Group, Ltd., Whole Foods Market, Inc., and Canine Companions for Independence.

Each of these six organizations makes an important and unique contribution to the manufacturing or service sectors of the national economy and/or to our national well-being. These organizations are not alone, however. Hundreds of other small, medium, and large organizations are making valuable and significant contributions to the economic health and human welfare of the United States. Brief examples from many organizations are used throughout the book. We hope that by better understanding these organizations, you may have a greater appreciation for your own organization and others within the diverse world of private business enterprises and nonprofit organizations.

CISCO SYSTEMS Which is more impressive: Cisco Systems' 2003 sales of $18.9 billion or Cisco's 2003 cash and investments balance of $20.7 billion?[34] While the Internet and technology sector bubbles destroyed many companies

5. Understand the diversity of organizations in the economy, as exemplified by the six focus organizations.

[Handwritten margin notes:]

Sectors of GNP
svc. 44% trans., finac. svcs., retail
product manuf. 21% (basic mat.) auto.
durable goods 8%
—————
73%

Gov. + fixed investments = 27%
non-profits
infrastructure

FIGURE 1.3

U.S. Gross Domestic Product (Approximately $10.9 Trillion for 2003)

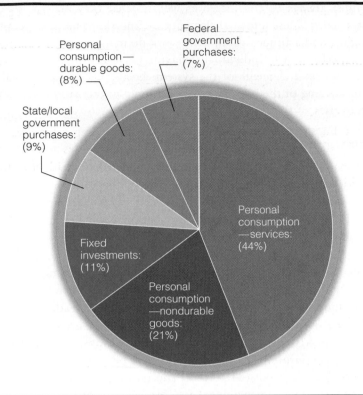

and humbled others, Cisco's bread-and-butter business of selling the routers and switches that power the Internet continues to grow. In addition, Cisco is actively working to expand the worldwide on-line market from its corporate headquarters in San Jose, California. In 150 countries like Afghanistan, 10,000 Cisco academies are training more than 400,000 future network professionals to help their communities enter the Information Age. Networks are at the heart of Cisco's business and are essential for business, education, government, and home communications.

Cisco has had deep roots in technology from its founding in 1984 by a group of computer scientists from Stanford University. Cisco has grown to 36,000 employees worldwide, and its engineers have factored prominently in the development of Internet protocol (IP)-based networking technologies. We take many of these networking technologies for granted today. The firm currently pours 18 percent of annual revenues back into research and development, an investment it hopes will pay dividends in the future. Cisco operates on twin core values of customer focus and corporate citizenship, which are expressed through global involvement in education, community, and philanthropic efforts.

THE COCA-COLA COMPANY Invented by Atlanta pharmacist John Pemberton in 1886, Coca-Cola got its name from two ingredients—coca leaves and kola nuts. Within four years after druggist Asa Chandler purchased The Coca-Cola Company in 1891, the soda fountain drink was available in all states, and in Canada and Mexico by 1898. The firm went public in 1919 and expanded overseas with the slogans, "The Pause that Refreshes" in 1929 and "It's the Real Thing" in 1941. Nearly nine decades later, The Coca-Cola Company (Coke) is "It"—the world's top soft-drink company with its number-one-selling

Coca-Cola Classic and number-three-selling Diet Coke. While it commands about 50 percent of the global soft-drink market, Coca-Cola has moved beyond soda to juice products, bottled water, and other noncarbonated products, but not without fierce competition and a few setbacks. The most well-known of these setbacks was its introduction and swift pullback of New Coke in 1985.

Headquartered in Atlanta, Georgia, Coke now markets products under the Coca-Cola, Barq's, Fruitopia, Minute Maid, POWERade, Sprite, and Dasani brands. The introduction of Vanilla Coke in 2002 was Coke's biggest new product launch since New Coke. In an attempt to boost the younger consumer's interest in its flagship cola, the company launched new marketing and ad campaigns in 2003 by changing the graphics on Coke bottles and cans back to a more traditional look. For fiscal year 2003, Coca-Cola had operating revenues of $21 billion.[35]

PIXAR ANIMATION STUDIOS Combine cutting-edge technology and old-fashioned storytelling and what do you get? In the case of Pixar Studios, you get movies that kids and parents love. With a shelf full of awards and a string of blockbusters including *Monsters, Inc.* and *Finding Nemo* as well as *Cars*, scheduled for a holiday release in 2005, Pixar is the world's leading digital animation studio.

Founded in 1986, Pixar spent more than nine years bringing its first full-length film, *Toy Story*, to the screen. While best known for its high-tech animation tools and flashy CEO Steve Jobs, Pixar's culture is built solidly around great storytelling. At its eclectic California campus, 700 employees revise and refine the stories and characters that eventually become Pixar's movies. The formula has paid off handsomely for Pixar and its former release partner, Walt Disney Pictures; today, the firm has annual revenues of over $262 million (2003 annual report), up from only $14 million just five years earlier.[36] But as the cutting-edge software tools developed at Pixar become more common in the industry, how will it keep its edge? Can it stay competitive by releasing only one movie every eighteen months as it does now, especially if one of those releases is not a blockbuster? And what will happen now that its distribution deal with Disney has ended?

Pixar CEO Steve Jobs, Disney Studios Richard Cook, and producer for the film, John Lasseter pose for photographers during the premiere of the Walt Disney Pictures and Pixar Animation movie *Finding Nemo.*

VIRGIN GROUP, LTD. The Virgin Group may well be one of the most recognizable brands in the world. Founded in 1970 by Richard Branson, then a 17-year-old boarding school dropout, Virgin began as a mail-order record company aptly named "Virgin" because of Branson's lack of experience at the time. More than thirty years later, the Virgin Group can best be described as a conglomerate of consumer products and services selling everything from air and rail travel to soft drinks, though its biggest breadwinners are by far its travel operations led by Virgin Atlantic.

Knighted in 2000, Sir Richard Branson remains the chairman, president, and CEO of the Virgin Group family of companies. Though his holdings are mostly private, Sir Richard's net worth was estimated at $2.6 billion in 2003. Virgin's growth plan can hardly be described as deliberate or strategic. Branson had one simple goal—"to be a disrupter, taking on industries that either charged too much (music), held consumers hostage (cell phone companies), or treated consumers badly and bored them to tears (airlines)." By 2003, Branson had amassed an empire of more than two-hundred entertainment, media, and travel companies worldwide; operations in Africa, Asia, Australia, Europe, and North America; and revenues in excess of $5 billion.[37]

WHOLE FOODS MARKET, INC. The world's number one natural foods chain, Whole Foods Market, operates more than one hundred forty stores in twenty-five states, Washington, D.C., and Canada. Whole Foods has pioneered the supermarket concept in health foods retailing, offering more than 1,200 items in four lines of private label products. Led by John Mackey in 1980 with a $10,000 loan from his father, Whole Foods Market was born as a meager 11,000-square-foot supermarket in Austin, Texas. Capitalizing on the increased health consciousness among consumers coupled with their desire for natural and organic foods, Whole Foods became an instant success and expanded its operations to Houston, Dallas, and Louisiana in the mid- to late-1980s.

By 1992, the chain debuted its first private label products and went public with twelve stores. Soon, every competitor in the fragmented health foods industry became a potential acquisition for Whole Foods. Its biggest acquisition came in 1996 with the purchase of Fresh Fields' twenty-two stores on the East Coast and Chicago. By 2003, Whole Foods had crossed the border into Canada, opening its first foreign store in downtown Toronto. Whole Foods Market has since expanded into related businesses such as nutritional supplements and now sells on-line through a co-branding operation with Gaiam.com. Based in Austin, Texas, the chain has over 24,000 employees and reported revenues for fiscal 2003 of over $3.1 billion.[38]

CANINE COMPANIONS FOR INDEPENDENCE Founded in 1975, Canine Companions for Independence (CCI) was the first organization to expand the concept of guide dogs beyond helping the blind. Based in Oceanside, California, and operating from five regional training centers, CCI places more than one-hundred highly trained service dogs each year (more than two-thousand to date), helping individuals with disabilities achieve greater independence. Service dogs perform tasks such as retrieving dropped objects, opening and closing doors, turning lights on, and signaling deaf individuals when the phone or doorbell rings. While a dog's two-year education program, including medical care, food, and specialized training, costs close to $13,000, the recipient pays only a $100 fee to receive the dog.

CCI's annual income is over $11 million, from sources including individual donations, fundraisers, and gifts from charitable foundations. Its paid staff of one hundred twenty six is supplemented by a network of volunteers who breed and raise puppies especially for CCI, normally paying food and veterinary expenses themselves. CCI has a simple mission: to help disabled people do more for themselves and live more independent lives.[39]

Change Creates Opportunities

6. Recognize the opportunities that change creates for organizational behavior.

Change creates opportunities and risks, as mentioned earlier in the chapter. Global competition is a leading force driving change at work. Competition in the United States and world economies has increased significantly during the past couple of decades, especially in industries such as banking, finance, and air transportation. Corporate competition creates performance and cost pressures, which have a ripple effect on people and their behavior at work. While one risk for employees is the marginalization of part-time professionals, good management practice can ensure the integration of these part-time profession-

Carly Drives Change

Hewlett-Packard (HP) was a time-honored company competing in the high-tech sector, intense environment of Silicon Valley when a burst of publicity made Carly Fiorina a prime candidate for HP's CEO job in 1998. She became the first outsider to lead HP and the highest-profile female CEO in the United States. This combination was rich with opportunity, challenge, excitement, and, yes, risk. The risks overcame her in 2005, when she resigned as CEO. She faced a huge, complicated challenge in successfully orchestrating the HP–Compaq transaction in the face of serious opposition to the deal from within the Hewlett and Packard founding families. Former Time, Inc. Chairman Richard Munro had seen Carly swagger with overwhelming self-confidence early in her career when the two served together as Kellogg outside directors. He hoped that when she ran into the frustrations which all executives eventually experience that it would refine her as a person, not break her. Carly did succeed in putting the HP–Compaq deal together, if only by a razor-thin margin and withstanding a court challenge. She now runs one of the world's largest enterprises with at least $70 billion a year in revenue and the number one position in a half-dozen key markets. Carly drove change at HP, which created both the opportunity and danger for her to reshape HP. Despite her initial success at HP, Carly encountered the kind of frustration about which Mr. Munro was concerned. The question is whether she will grow from the experience.

SOURCE: G. Anders, "The Carly Chronicles," *Fast Company* 67 (February 2003): 66–76, http://www.fastcompany.com/magazine/67/carly.html.

als.[40] The competition may lead to downsizing and restructuring, yet it provides the opportunity for revitalization as well.[41] Further, small companies are not necessarily the losers in this competitive environment. Scientech, a small power and energy company, found it had to enhance its managerial talent and service quality to meet the challenges of growth and big-company competitors. Product and service quality is one tool that can help companies become winners in a competitive environment. Problem-solving skills are another tool used by IBM, Control Data Services, Inc., Northwest Airlines, and Southwest Airlines to help achieve high-quality products and services.

Too much change leads to chaos; too little change leads to stagnation. Former CEO Carly Fiorina created dramatic change at Hewlett-Packard (HP). The Real World 1.2 focuses on her success with the HP–Compaq transaction. What are your perceptions of change? Complete You 1.1 and see how you perceive change.

Four Challenges for Managers Related to Change

Chapter 2 develops four challenges for managers related to change in contemporary organizations: globalization, workforce diversity, ethics and character, and technological innovation. These are four driving forces creating and shaping changes at work. Further, success in global competition requires organizations to be more responsive to ethnic, religious, and gender diversity as well as personal integrity in the workforce, in addition to responding positively to the competition in the international marketplace. Workforce demographic change and diversity are critical challenges in themselves for the study and management of organizational behavior.[42] The theories of motivation, leadership, and group behavior based on research in a workforce of one composition may not be applicable in a workforce of a very different composition.[43] This may be especially

Analyze Your Perceptions of a Change

Everyone perceives change differently. Think of a change situation you are currently experiencing. It can be any business, school-related, or personal experience that requires a significant change in your at- titude or behavior. Rate your feelings about this change using the following scales. For instance, if you feel the change is more of a threat than an opportu- nity, you would circle 0, 2, or 4 on the first scale.

1. Threat	0	2	4	6	8	10	Opportunity
2. Holding on to the past	0	2	4	6	8	10	Reaching for the future
3. Immobilized	0	2	4	6	8	10	Activated
4. Rigid	0	2	4	6	8	10	Versatile
5. A loss	0	2	4	6	8	10	A gain
6. Victim of change	0	2	4	6	8	10	Agent of change
7. Reactive	0	2	4	6	8	10	Proactive
8. Focused on the past	0	2	4	6	8	10	Focused on the future
9. Separate from change	0	2	4	6	8	10	Involved with change
10. Confused	0	2	4	6	8	10	Clear

How positive are your perceptions of this change?

SOURCE: H. Woodward and S. Buchholz, *Aftershock: Helping People through Corporate Change*, p. 15. Copyright (c) 1987 John Wiley & Sons, Inc. Reprinted by permission of John Wiley & Sons, Inc.

problematic if ethnic, gender, and/or religious differences lead to conflict be- tween leaders and followers in organizations. For example, the Russian military establishment has found ethnic and religious conflicts between the officers and enlisted corps a real impediment to unit cohesion and performance at times.

Global Competition in Business

Managers and executives in the United States face radical change in response to increased global competition. According to noted economist Lester Thurow, this competition is characterized by intense rivalry between the United States, Japan, and Europe in core industries.[44] Economic competition places pressure on all cat- egories of employees to be productive and to add value to the firm. The uncer- tainty of unemployment resulting from corporate warfare and competition is an ongoing feature of organizational life for people in companies or industries that pursue cost-cutting strategies to achieve economic success. The global competi- tion in the automotive industry among the Japanese, U.S., and European car com- panies embodies the intensity that can be expected in other industries in the future.

Some people feel that the future must be the focus in coming to grips with this international competition, whereas others believe we can deal with the fu- ture only by studying the past.[45] Global, economic, and organizational changes have dramatic effects on the study and management of organizational behav- ior. How positive were your perceptions of the change you analyzed in You 1.1? Are you an optimist who sees opportunity, or a pessimist who sees threat?

Customer Focused for High Quality

Global competition has challenged organizations to become more customer fo- cused, to meet changing product and service demands, and to exceed customers' expectations of high quality. Quality has the potential for giving organizations in viable industries a competitive edge in meeting international competition.

Quality became a rubric for products and services of high status. Total quality is defined in many ways.[46] Total quality management (TQM) is the total dedication to continuous improvement and to customers so that the customers' needs are met and their expectations exceeded. Quality is a customer-oriented philosophy of management with important implications for virtually all aspects of organizational behavior. Quality cannot be optimized, because customer needs and expectations are always changing. Quality is a cultural value embedded in highly successful organizations. Ford Motor Company's dramatic metamorphosis as an automotive leader is attributable to the decision to "make quality Job One" in all aspects of the design and manufacture of cars.

Quality improvement enhances the probability of organizational success in increasingly competitive industries. One study of one hundred ninety-three general medical hospitals examined seven TQM practices and found them positively related to the financial performance of the hospital.[47] Quality improvement is an enduring feature of an organization's culture and of the economic competition we face today. It leads to competitive advantage through customer responsiveness, results acceleration, and resource effectiveness.[48] The three key questions in evaluating quality-improvement ideas for people at work are these: (1) Does the idea improve customer response? (2) Does the idea accelerate results? (3) Does the idea increase the effectiveness of resources? A "yes" answer means the idea should be implemented to improve quality.

Six Sigma is a philosophy for company-wide quality improvement developed by Motorola and popularized by General Electric. The Six Sigma program is characterized by its customer-driven approach, its emphasis on decision making based on quantitative data, and its priority on saving money.[49] It has evolved into a high-performance system to execute business strategy. Part of its quality program is a 12-step problem-solving method specifically designed to lead a Six Sigma "Black Belt" to significant improvement within a defined process. It tackles problems in four phases: (1) measure, (2) analyze, (3) improve, and (4) control. In addition, it demands that executives be aligned to the right objective and targets, quality improvement teams be mobilized for action, results be accelerated, and sustained improvement be monitored. Six Sigma is set up in a way that it can be applied to a range of problems and areas, from manufacturing settings to service work environments. Table 1.1 contrasts Six Sigma and TQM. One study compared Six Sigma to two other methods for quality improvement (specifically, Taguchi's methods and the Shainin system)

Six Sigma

A high-performance system to execute business strategy that is customer-driven, emphasizes quantitative decision making, and places a priority on saving money.

TABLE 1.1	Contrasting Six Sigma and Total Quality Management
SIX SIGMA	**TOTAL QUALITY MANAGEMENT**
Executive ownership	Self-directed work teams
Business strategy execution system	Quality initiative
Truly cross-functional	Largely within a single function
Focused training with verifiable return on investment	No mass training in statistics and quality Return on investment
Business results oriented	Quality oriented

SOURCE: M. Barney, "Motorola's Second Generation," *Six Sigma Forum Magazine* (May 2002): 13.

and found it to be the most complete strategy of the three, with a strong emphasis on exploiting statistical modeling techniques.[50]

Behavior and Quality at Work

Whereas total quality may draw on reliability engineering or just-in-time management, total quality improvement can be successful only when employees have the skills and authority to respond to customer needs.[51] Total quality has direct and important effects on the behavior of employees at all levels in the organization, not just on employees working directly with customers. Chief executives can advance total quality by engaging in participative management, being willing to change everything, focusing quality efforts on customer service (not cost cutting), including quality as a criterion in reward systems, improving the flow of information regarding quality-improvement successes or failures, and being actively and personally involved in quality efforts. While serving as chairman of Motorola, George Fisher, emphasized the behavioral attributes of leadership, cooperation, communication, and participation as important elements in the company's Six Sigma program.

Quality improvement continues to be important to our competitiveness. The U.S. Department of Commerce's sponsorship of an annual award in the name of Malcolm Baldrige, former secretary of commerce in the Reagan administration, recognizes companies excelling in quality improvement and management. The Malcolm Baldrige National Quality Award examination evaluates an organization in seven categories: leadership, information and analysis, strategic quality planning, human resource utilization, quality assurance of products and services, quality results, and customer satisfaction.

According to George H. W. Bush, "Quality management is not just a strategy. It must be a new style of working, even a new style of thinking. A dedication to quality and excellence is more than good business. It is a way of life, giving something back to society, offering your best to others."

Quality is one watchword for competitive success. Organizations that do not respond to customer needs find their customers choosing alternative product and service suppliers who are willing to exceed customer expectations. With this said, you should not conclude that total quality is a panacea for all organizations or that total quality guarantees unqualified success.

Managing Organizational Behavior in Changing Times

Over and above the challenge of quality improvement to meet international competition, managing organizational behavior during changing times is challenging for at least four reasons: (1) the increasing globalization of organizations' operating territory, (2) the increasing diversity of organizational workforces, (3) the continuing demand for higher levels of moral and ethical behavior at work, and (4) continuing technological innovation with its companion need for skill enhancement. These are the important issues to address in managing people at work.

Each of these four issues is explored in detail in Chapter 2 and highlighted throughout the text because they are intertwined in the contemporary practice of organizational behavior. For example, the issue of women in the workplace concerns workforce diversity and at the same time overlaps the globalization issue. Gender roles are often defined differently in various cultures, and sexual harassment is a frequent ethical problem for organizations in the United States, Europe, Israel, and South Africa. For another example, process and technology innovations require attention to behavioral issues if they are to be successful.

Innovation in a Supportive, Safe Workplace

An environment that fosters teamwork and the freedom to brainstorm new ideas helps nurture process innovations.

© Digital Vision

Innovation has been the industrial religion since the late twentieth century because business sees it as the key to increasing profits and market share. It often focuses on technology and processes. A recent study focused on process innovations, which are deliberate organizational attempts to change production and service processes. Innovations are often driven through total quality management (TQM), lean production, or just-in-time production (JIT). However, implementation of process innovations has often been found to have no effect on performance. These researchers suggest that successful adoption of process innovations requires attention to organizational culture and human behavior. Innovations and technological advances that fail to consider people and behavior may be doomed to fail. Therefore, organizations must support employee initiative while creating psychological safety for employees to take interpersonal risk. This longitudinal study was conducted in forty-seven mid-sized German companies. The authors were interested in seeing the effects of process innovations, in organizationally supportive and psychologically safe workplaces, on firm performance. They found that organizational support and psychological safety were positively related to return on assets and goal achievement. Thus, the study suggests that attention to behavioral factors is important along with technical factors in implementing successful process innovations in organizations.

SOURCE: M. Baer and M. Frese, "Innovation Is Not Enough: Climates for Initiative and Psychological Safety Advantage: The Role of Structural Control and Exploration," *Journal of Organizational Behavior* 24 (2003): 45–68.

The Science feature considers one study of innovation in forty-seven German companies. Therefore, students of organizational behavior appreciate and understand these important issues.

Learning about Organizational Behavior

Organizational behavior is based on scientific knowledge and applied practice. It involves the study of abstract ideas, such as valence and expectancy in motivation, as well as the study of concrete matters, such as observable behaviors and medical symptoms of distress at work. Therefore, learning about organizational behavior includes at least three activities, as shown in Figure 1.4. First, the science of organizational behavior requires the mastery of a certain body of *objective knowledge*. Objective knowledge results from research and scientific activities, as reflected in the Science feature in each chapter. Second, the practice of organizational behavior requires *skill development* based on knowledge and an understanding of yourself in order to master the abilities essential to success. The You features in each chapter challenge you to know yourself and apply what you are learning. Third, both objective knowledge and skill development must be applied in real world settings. The Real World features in each chapter open windows into organizational realities where science and skills are applied.

Learning is challenging and fun because we are all different. Student diversity is best addressed in the learning process through more options for students and

7. Demonstrate the value of objective knowledge and skill development in the study of organizational behavior.

objective knowledge
Knowledge that results from research and scientific activities.

skill development
The mastery of abilities essential to successful functioning in organizations.

FIGURE 1.4   Learning about Organizational Behavior

scientific knowledge + applied practice (abstract ideas + observable behaviors)

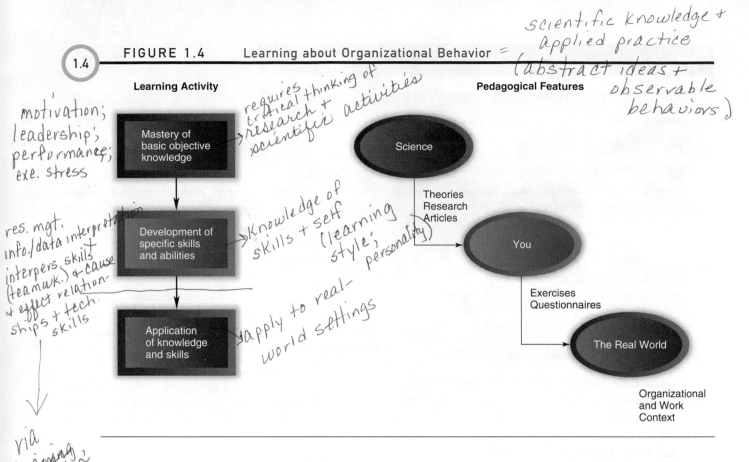

Learning Activity

motivation; leadership; performance; exe. stress

Mastery of basic objective knowledge

requires critical thinking of research + scientific activities

Development of specific skills and abilities

res. mgt. info./data interpretation interpers. skills (teamwk.) + cause + effect relationships + tech. skills

Knowledge of skills + self (learning style; personality)

Application of knowledge and skills

via education, practice + feedback

apply to real-world settings

Pedagogical Features

Science

Theories Research Articles

You

Exercises Questionnaires

The Real World

Organizational and Work Context

greater responsibility on the part of students as coproducers in the effort and fun of learning.[52] For those who are blind or have vision impairments, learning can be a special challenge. And, like these cases, agencies such as Canine Companions for Independence make important contributions. To gain a better understanding of yourself as a learner, so as to maximize your potential and develop strategies in specific learning environments, you need to evaluate the way you prefer to learn and process information. You 1.2 offers a short, quick way of assessing your learning style. If you are a visual learner, then use charts, maps, PowerPoint slides, videos, the Internet, notes, or flash cards, and write things out for visual review. If you are an auditory learner, listen, take notes during lectures, and consider taping them so you can fill in gaps later; review your notes frequently; and recite key concepts out loud. If you are a tactile learner, trace words as you are saying them, write down facts several times, and make study sheets.

Objective Knowledge

Objective knowledge, in any field of study, is developed through basic and applied research. Research in organizational behavior has continued since early research on scientific management. Acquiring objective knowledge requires the cognitive mastery of theories, conceptual models, and research findings. In this book, the objective knowledge in each chapter is reflected in the notes that support the text and in the Science feature included in each chapter. Mastering the concepts and ideas that come from these notes enables you to intelligently discuss topics such as motivation, performance, leadership,[53] and executive stress.[54]

We encourage instructors and students of organizational behavior to think critically about the objective knowledge in organizational behavior. Only by engaging in critical thinking can one question or challenge the results of specific research and responsibly consider how to apply research results in a particular work setting. Rote memorization does not enable the student to appreciate the

Learning Style Inventory

Directions: This twenty-four-item survey is not timed. Answer each question as honestly as you can. Place a check on the appropriate line after each statement.

	OFTEN	SOMETIMES	SELDOM
1. Can remember more about a subject through the lecture method with information, explanations, and discussion.			1 x
2. Prefer information to be written on the chalkboard, with the use of visual aids and assigned readings.	5		
3. Like to write things down or to take notes for visual review.	5		
4. Prefer to use posters, models, or actual practice and some activities in class.	~5		
5. Require explanations of diagrams, graphs, or visual directions.		3 x	
6. Enjoy working with my hands or making things.			1
7. Am skillful with and enjoy developing and making graphs and charts.	5 x		1
8. Can tell if sounds match when presented with pairs of sounds.	5 x		
9. Remember best by writing things down several times.	5		
10. Can understand and follow directions on maps.	5		
11. Do better at academic subjects by listening to lectures and tapes.			1 x
12. Play with coins or keys in pockets.			1
13. Learn to spell better by repeating the word out loud than by writing the word on paper.			1
14. Can better understand a news development by reading about it in the paper than by listening to the radio.	5		
15. Chew gum, smoke, or snack during studies.	5		
16. Feel the best way to remember is to picture it in your head.	5		
17. Learn spelling by "finger spelling" words.	5		
18. Would rather listen to a good lecture or speech than read about the same material in a textbook.	5		1
19. Am good at working and solving jigsaw puzzles and mazes.	5		
20. Grip objects in hands during learning period.		3	
21. Prefer listening to the news on the radio rather than reading about it in the newspaper.		3	
22. Obtain information on an interesting subject by reading relevant materials.		3	
23. Feel very comfortable touching others, hugging, hand-shaking, etc.	5		
24. Follow oral directions better than written ones.		3	

Scoring Procedures

Score 5 points for each OFTEN, 3 points for each SOMETIMES, and 1 point for each SELDOM.

Visual Preference Score 5 Points for questions 2 + 3 + 7 + 10 + 14 + 16 + 19 + 22   = 30 34
Auditory Preference Score 5 Points for questions 1 + 5 + 8 + 11 + 13 + 18 + 21 + 24 = 18
Tactile Preference Score 5 Points for questions 4 + 6 + 9 + 12 + 15 + 17 + 20 + 23 = 20

Learning Styles

SOURCE: Adapted from J. N. Gardner and A. J. Jewler, *Your College Experience: Strategies for Success, Third Concise Edition* (Belmont, Calif.: Wadsworth/ITP, 1998), pp. 62–63; E. Jensen, *Student Success Secrets*, 4th ed. (Hauppauge, N.Y.: Barron's, 1996), pp. 33–36.

complexity of specific theories or the interrelationships among concepts, ideas, and topics. Good critical thinking, in contrast, enables the student to identify inconsistencies and limitations in the current body of objective knowledge.

Critical thinking, based on knowledge and understanding of basic ideas, leads to inquisitive exploration and is a key to accepting the responsibility of coproducer in the learning process. A questioning, probing attitude is at the core of critical thinking. The student of organizational behavior should evolve into a critical consumer of knowledge related to organizational behavior—one who is able to intelligently question the latest research results and distinguish plausible, sound new approaches from fads that lack substance or adequate foundation. Ideally, the student of organizational behavior develops into a scientific professional manager who is knowledgeable in the art and science of organizational behavior.

Skill Development

Learning about organizational behavior requires doing as well as knowing. The development of skills and abilities requires that students be challenged by the instructor and by themselves. Skill development is a very active component of the learning process. The You features in each chapter give you a chance to learn about yourself, challenge yourself, and developmentally apply what you are learning.

The U.S. Department of Labor is concerned that people achieve the necessary skills to be successful in the workplace.[55] The essential skills identified by the Department of Labor are (1) resource management skills, such as time management; (2) information management skills, such as data interpretation; (3) personal interaction skills, such as teamwork; (4) systems behavior and performance skills, such as cause–effect relationships; and (5) technology utilization skills, such as troubleshooting. Many of these skills, such as decision making and information management, are directly related to the study of organizational behavior.[56]

Developing skills is different from acquiring objective knowledge in that it requires structured practice and feedback. A key function of experiential learning is to engage the student in individual or group activities that are systematically reviewed, leading to new skills and understandings. Objective knowledge acquisition and skill development are interrelated. The process for learning from structured or experiential activities is depicted in Figure 1.5. The student engages in an individual or group-structured activity and systematically reviews that activity, which leads to new or modified knowledge and skills.

If skill development and structured learning occur in this way, there should be an inherently self-correcting element to learning because of the modification of the student's knowledge and skills over time.[57] To ensure that skill development does occur and that the learning is self-correcting as it occurs, three basic assumptions that underlie the previous model must be followed.

First, each student must accept responsibility for his or her own behavior, actions, and learning. This is a key to the coproducer role in the learning process. A group cannot learn for its members. Each member must accept responsibility for what he or she does and learns. Denial of responsibility helps no one, least of all the learner.

Second, each student must actively participate in the individual or group-structured learning activity. Structured learning is not passive; it is active. In group activities, everyone suffers if just one person adopts a passive attitude. Hence, all must actively participate.

Third, each student must be open to new information, new skills, new ideas, and experimentation. This does not mean that students should be indiscrimi-

FIGURE 1.5   Learning from Structured Activity

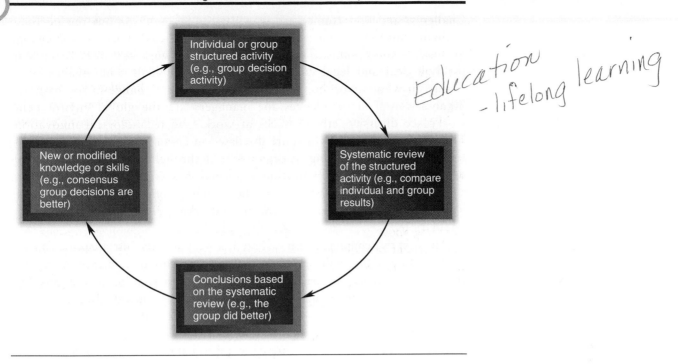

Education – lifelong learning (handwritten annotation)

---

nately open. It does mean that students should have a nondefensive, open attitude so that change is possible through the learning process.

Application of Knowledge and Skills

The Real World features in each chapter give you a window into organizational realities and potentially assess your own knowledge of the real world at work. Understanding organizational behavior includes an appreciation and understanding of working realities, as well as of science and of yourself.

One of the advantages of structured, experiential learning is that a person can explore new behaviors and skills in a comparatively safe environment. Losing your temper in a classroom activity and learning about the potential adverse impact on other people will probably have dramatically different consequences from losing your temper with an important customer in a tense work situation. The ultimate objective of skill application and experiential learning is that one transfers the process employed in learning from structured activities in the classroom to learning from unstructured opportunities in the workplace.

Although organizational behavior is an applied discipline, a student is not "trained" in organizational behavior. Rather, one is "educated" in organizational behavior and is a coproducer in learning. The distinction between these two modes of learning is found in the degree of direct and immediate applicability of either knowledge or skills. As an activity, training more nearly ties direct objective knowledge or skill development to specific applications. By contrast, education enhances a person's residual pool of objective knowledge and skills that may then be selectively applied later—sometimes significantly later—when the opportunity presents itself. Hence, education is highly consistent with the concept of lifelong learning. Especially in a growing area of knowledge such as organizational behavior, the student can think of the first course as the outset of lifelong learning about the topics and subject.

Plan for the Book

Challenge and opportunity are watchwords in organizations during these changing times. Managers and employees alike are challenged to meet change in positive and optimistic ways: change in how work gets done, change in psychological and legal contracts between individuals and organizations, change in who is working in the organization, and change in the basis for organization. Four challenges for managers are the global environment, workplace diversity, ethical issues at work, and technological innovation. These four challenges, which are discussed in detail in Chapter 2, are shaping the changes occurring in organizations throughout the world. For example, the increasing globalization of business has led to intense international competition in core industries, and the changing demographics of the workplace have led to gender, age, racial, and ethnic diversity among working populations.

The first two chapters compose Part 1 of the book, the introduction. Against the backdrop of the challenges discussed here, we develop and explore the specific content subjects in organizational behavior. In addition to the introduction, the text has three major parts. Part 2 addresses individual processes and behavior. Part 3 addresses interpersonal processes and behavior. Part 4 addresses organizational processes and structure.

The five chapters in Part 2 are designed to help the reader understand specific aspects of human behavior. Chapter 3 discusses personality, perception, and attribution. Chapter 4 examines attitudes, values, and ethics. What was your attitude toward change in You 1.1? Chapters 5 and 6 address the broad range of motivational theories, learning, and performance management in organizations. Finally, Chapter 7 considers stress and well-being at work, including healthy aspects of life at work.

Part 3 is composed of six chapters designed to help the reader better understand interpersonal and group dynamics in organizations. Chapter 8 addresses communication in organizations. Chapter 9 focuses on teamwork and groups as an increasingly prominent feature of the workplace. Chapter 10 examines how individuals and groups make decisions. Chapter 11 is about power and politics, one very dynamic aspect of organizational life. Chapter 12 addresses the companion topics of leadership and followership. Finally, Chapter 13 examines conflict at work, not all of which do we consider bad.

The five chapters in Part 4 are designed to help the reader better understand organizational processes and the organizational context of behavior at work. Chapter 14 examines traditional and contemporary approaches to job design. Chapter 15 develops the topics of organizational design and structure, giving special attention to contemporary forces reshaping organizations and to emerging forms of organization. Chapter 16 addresses the culture of the organization. Chapter 17 focuses on the important issue of career management. Finally, Chapter 18 brings closure to the text and the main theme of change by addressing the topic of managing change.

Managerial Implications: Foundations for the Future

Managers must consider personal and environmental factors to understand fully how people behave in organizations and to help them grow to be all they can be. Human behavior is complex and at times confusing. Characteristics of the organizational system and formal–informal dynamics at work are important environmental factors that influence people's behavior. Managers should look for similarities and differences in manufacturing, service-oriented, nonprofit, and governmental organizations.

Change may be seen as a threat or as an opportunity by contemporary managers. In the Looking Back feature, you see how John Chambers took advantage of the opportunity that called on Cisco Systems. Changing customer demands for high-quality outputs challenge companies to beat the global competition. Globalization, workforce diversity, ethics, and technology are four challenges for managers that are developed in Chapter 2. Another aspect of meeting the competition is learning. Managers must continually upgrade their knowledge about all aspects of their businesses, to include especially the human side of the enterprise. They must hone both their technical and interpersonal skills, engaging in a lifelong educational process. This is a fun and somewhat unpredictable process that can at times be frustrating while always challenging and exciting.

Several business trends and ongoing changes are affecting managers across the globe. These include continuing industrial restructuring, a dramatic increase in the amount and availability of information, a need to attract and retain the best employees, a need to understand a wide range of human and cultural differences, and a rapid shortening of response times in all aspects of business activities. Further, the old company towns are largely relics of the past, and managers are being called on to reintegrate their businesses with communities, cultures, and societies at a much broader level than has ever been required before. Trust, predictability, and a sense of security become important issues in this context. Reweaving the fabric of human relationships within, across, and outside the organization is a challenge for managers today.

Knowledge becomes power in tracking these trends and addressing these issues. Facts and information are two elements of knowledge in this context. Theories are a third element of a manager's knowledge base. Good theories are tools that help managers understand human and organizational behavior, help them make good business decisions, and inform them about actions to take or to refrain from taking. Managers always use theories, if not those generated from systematic research, then those evolved from the manager's implicit observation. Theories tell us how organizations, business, and people work—or do not work. Therefore, the student is challenged to master the theories in each topic area, then apply and test the theory in the real world of organizational life. The challenge for the student and the manager is to see what works and what does not work in their specific work context.

LOOKING BACK: CISCO SYSTEMS

Chambers Answers the Phone

John Chambers came to Cisco in 1991 riding a wave of high-powered sales positions at IBM and Wang. He was named CEO in 1995 and aimed to help Cisco cement its control in the Internet gear market. Even though the company enjoyed 70-percent control of the market for routers, switches, and related gear in large corporate computer networks, these markets had seen only single-digit growth for years. While positive, energetic, and optimistic, Chambers had no illusions concerning what the company was up against in Spring 2001. He saw opportunity in telecommunications and with the phone companies. Therefore, the combination of the phone companies' fury and Cisco's internal bickering drove home the message to Chambers that change was needed and a certain amount of damage control was essential.

Cisco's base was as a networking powerhouse that built the most dominant equipment for routing data in corporations. Now the company had to remake that equipment to handle all different kinds of media that can be turned into digital data, especially voice media. The convergence of the computing and telecommunication industries over several decades had now created an exciting opportunity for the convergence of data, voice, and video. Chambers saw this convergence occurring over a single Internet protocol infrastructure, the hottest being IP telephony—Internet phone calls—made possible by voice over Internet protocol (VOIP).[58] VOIP is growing rapidly for long-distance calls. For example, about 37 percent of international calls originating from India use VOIP. The software to manage Internet telephone calls improves daily, and costs are dropping. For instance, no additional charges are applied when using broadband connections.

When Internet-based telephony arrived in 2003, so too did Cisco's opportunity to regain its dominance in the market. The next step beyond VOIP is to combine it with Wi-Fi. Wi-Fi is wireless broadcast technology that allows digital devices within a several-hundred-foot range to connect at broadband speeds to the Internet. The combination of VOIP with Wi-Fi allows for free calling with mobility, a significant advance over the still expensive cell phone networks. In 2003, Cisco shipped its first wireless IP phone for offices with plans for phones for any Wi-Fi access point. In addition, free calling with mobility can be a money-saving feature on cell phones that use conventional cell frequencies when out of Wi-Fi range. By seeing opportunity in the midst of the tech sector downturn and phone company fury, John Chambers and Cisco were able to respond positively to market changes and lead with technological advances.

Chapter Summary

1. Organizational behavior is individual behavior and group dynamics in organizations.

2. Change is an opportunity when one has a positive attitude, asks questions, listens, and is committed to succeed.

3. Organizations are open systems composed of people, structure, and technology committed to a task.

4. Organizations have formal and informal elements within them.

5. Manufacturing organizations, service organizations, privately owned companies, and nonprofit organizations all contribute to our national well-being.

6. The changes and challenges facing managers are driven by international competition and customer demands.

7. Learning about organizational behavior requires a mastery of objective knowledge, specific skill development, and thoughtful application.

Key Terms

anthropology (p. 6)
challenge (p. 4)
change (p. 4)
engineering (p. 6)
formal organization (p. 10)
Hawthorne studies (p. 10)
informal organization (p. 10)

management (p. 6)
medicine (p. 6)
objective knowledge (p. 19)
opportunities (p. 4)
organizational behavior (p. 4)
people (p. 8)
psychology (p. 5)

Six Sigma (p. 17)
skill development (p. 19)
sociology (p. 6)
structure (p. 8)
task (p. 8)
technology (p. 8)

Review Questions

1. Define *organizational behavior*. What is its focus?

2. Identify the four action steps for responding positively to change.

3. What is an organization? What are its four system components? Give an example of each.

4. Briefly describe the elements of the formal and the informal organization. Give examples of each.

5. Discuss the six focus organizations used in the book.

6. Describe how competition and total quality are affecting organizational behavior. Why is managing organizational behavior in changing times challenging?

Discussion and Communication Questions

1. How do the formal aspects of your work environment affect you? What informal aspects of your work environment are important?

2. What is the biggest competitive challenge or change facing the businesses in your industry today? Will that be different in the next five years?

3. Describe the next chief executive of your company and what she or he must do to succeed.

4. Discuss two ways people learn about organizational behavior.

5. Which of the focus companies is your own company most like? Do you work for one of these focus companies? Which company would you most like to work for?

6. *(communication question)* Prepare a memo about an organizational change occurring where you

work or in your college or university. Write a 100-word description of the change and, using Figure 1.1, identify how it is affecting the people, structure, task, and/or technology of the organization.

7. *(communication question)* Develop an oral presentation about the changes and challenges facing your college or university based on an interview with a faculty member or administrator. Be prepared to describe the changes and challenges. Are these good or bad changes? Why?

8. *(communication question)* Prepare a brief description of a service or manufacturing company, entrepreneurial venture, or nonprofit organization of your choice. Go to the library and read about the organization from several sources, then use these multiple sources to write your description.

Ethical Dilemma

The afternoon was as gloomy as Brian's mood. It had not been a very productive day. All Brian could think about was the decision before him. He found the current situation interesting in that he had never before struggled with decisions. In the past, he had always been able to make quick and good decisions. His gut gave him the answer and he trusted his instincts. This time he felt nothing, and he was unsure how to proceed without that guiding force.

Brian Cowell was 62 years old and the CEO of Data Solutions, a company he had run for the last 20 years. Brian had been very successful at the helm of the company. Data Solutions had grown from a small data processing business to one of the largest employers in the area. Brian's good instincts had guided them through the challenging times of the '80s and '90s, and the company was in just the right place to meet the challenges ahead. Or was it? This was the question that plagued Brian.

Changes in technology were providing some interesting possibilities for the future. A part of Brian said that he needed to step up and help Data Solutions move into the global environment. He could lead Data Solutions into the global marketplace and continue the growth he had begun so many years ago. That was a big step and would take Brian down a very challenging road. The other option was to continue on the company's current path. Not a bad one, the company had been the most profitable in its history last year and everyone was very happy. Deep inside, Brian knew the answer. Move the company forward to the next logical step: globalization. But Brian was tired and really wanted to spend his last years at Data Solutions reaping the benefits of his hard work, not gearing up for the biggest challenge of his career. Didn't he deserve the right to enjoy his final years at Data Solutions?

Questions

1. Does Brian have an obligation to lead the company to globalization?

2. What is Brian's responsibility to himself and his family?

3. Consider Brian's decision in light of rule, virtue rights, and justice theories.

Experiential Exercises

1.1 What's Changing at Work?

This exercise provides an opportunity to discuss changes occurring in your workplace and university. These changes may be for the better or the worse. However, rather than evaluating whether they are good or bad changes, begin by simply identifying the changes that are occurring. Later, you can evaluate whether they are good or bad.

Step 1. The class forms into groups of approximately six members each. Each group elects a spokesperson and answers the following questions. The group should spend at least five minutes on each question. Make sure that each member of the group makes a contribution to each question. The spokesperson for each group should be ready to share the group's collective responses to these questions.

    a. *What are the changes occurring in your workplace and university?* Members should focus both on internal changes, such as reorganizations, and on external changes, such as new customers or competitors. Develop a list of the changes discussed in your group.

    b. *What are the forces that are driving the changes?* To answer this question, look for the causes of the changes members of the group are observing. For example, a reorganization may be caused by new business opportunities, by new technologies, or by a combination of factors.

    c. *What signs of resistance to change do you see occurring?* Change is not always easy for people or organizations. Do you see signs of resistance, such as frustration, anger, increased absences, or other forms of discomfort with the changes you observe?

Step 2. Once you have answered the three questions in Step 1, your group needs to spend some time evaluating whether these changes are good or bad. Decide whether each change on the list developed in Step 1a is a good or bad change. In addition, answer the question "Why?" That is, why is this change good? Why is that change bad?

Step 3. Each group shares the results of its answers to the questions in Step 1 and its evaluation of the changes completed in Step 2. Cross-team questions and discussion follow.

Step 4. Your instructor may allow a few minutes at the end of the class period to comment on his or her perceptions of changes occurring within the university, or businesses with which he or she is familiar.

1.2 My Absolute Worst Job

Purpose: To become acquainted with fellow classmates.
Group size: Any number of groups of two.
Exercise schedule:

1. Write answers to the following questions:

    a. What was the worst job you ever had? Describe the following:
       (1) The type of work you did
       (2) Your boss
       (3) Your coworkers
       (4) The organization and its policies
       (5) What made the job so bad

    b. What is your dream job?

2. Find someone you do not know, and share your responses.

3. Get together with another dyad, preferably new people. Partner "a" of one dyad introduces partner "b" to the other dyad, then "b" introduces "a". The same process is followed by the other dyad. The introduction should follow this format: "This is Mary Cullen. Her very worst job was putting appliqués on bibs at a clothing factory, and she disliked it for the following reason. What she would rather do is be a financial analyst for a big corporation."

4. Each group of four meets with another quartet and is introduced, as before.

5. Your instructor asks for a show of hands on the number of people whose worst jobs fit into the following categories:

    a. Factory
    b. Restaurant
    c. Manual labor
    d. Driving or delivery
    e. Professional
    f. Health care
    g. Phone sales or communication
    h. Other

6. Your instructor gathers data on worst jobs from each group and asks the groups to answer these questions:

    a. What are the common characteristics of the worst jobs in your group?
    b. How did your coworkers feel about their jobs?
    c. What happens to morale and productivity when a worker hates the job?
    d. What was the difference between your own morale and productivity in your worst job and in a job you really enjoyed?
    e. Why do organizations continue to allow unpleasant working conditions to exist?

7. Your instructor leads a group discussion on Parts (a) through (e) of Question 6.

SOURCE: D. Marcic, "My Absolute Worst Job: An Icebreaker," *Organizational Behavior: Experiences and Cases* (St. Paul, Minn.: West, 1989), 5–6. Copyright 1988 Dorothy Marcic. All rights reserved. Reprinted by permission.

TAKE 2

Biz Flix | 8 Mile

Jimmy "B-Rabbit" Smith, Jr., (Eminem) wants to succeed as a rapper and to prove that a white man can create moving sounds. His job at the North Detroit Stamping (NDS) plant fills his days while he pursues his music at night—and sometimes on the plant's grounds. The film's title refers to Detroit's northern city boundary, well known to local people. *8 Mile* is a gritty look at Detroit's hip-hop culture in 1995 and Jimmy's desire for acceptance by it. Eminem's original songs, "Lose Yourself" and "8 Mile," received several award nominations. "Lose Yourself" won the 2003 Academy Award for best original song.

The scene has two parts. It is an edited composite of two brief NDS plant sequences that appear in different places in the film. Part I of the scene appears early in the film in the sequence "The Franchise." Part II appears in the last twenty-five minutes of the film in the "Papa Doc Payback" sequence. Jimmy arrives late for work in the first part of the scene, after riding the city bus because his car did not start. The second part occurs after his beating by Papa Doc (Anthony Mackie) and Papa Doc's gang. The film continues to its end with Jimmy's last battle (a rapper competition).

What to Watch for and Ask Yourself:

> What is your perception of the quality of Jimmy's job and his work environment?

> What is the quality of Jimmy's relationship with Manny (Paul Bates), his foreman? Does it change? If it does, why?

> How would you react to this type of work experience?

Workplace Video | CVS Corporation: Foundations of Behavior in Organizations

The CVS Corporation is a drugstore chain of over 4,000 stores that sells prescription drugs and a variety of general merchandise, including over-the-counter drugs, greeting cards, photo finishing services, beauty products, and convenience foods. When CVS recently began a rapid expansion of its retail operations, management decided the company needed to quickly develop new talent for local, district, and regional management positions. To achieve this objective, CVS created a new initiative called Emerging Leaders, a program that provides skills and training for future leadership within the organization.

The program begins by identifying and recruiting employees with traits deemed necessary to become leaders in the company. CVS assigns mentors to these potential leaders and offers continuous learning opportunities so they can develop skills for moving up in the organization. The video case offers an example: Regional Manager Jeff Raymond is assigned to be a mentor for new Emerging Leader Todd Peloquin, a district manager at the company. In turn, Peloquin educates individual subordinate store managers about Emerging Leaders and encourages them to take the opportunity to enter the program as a stepping-stone to career growth. This process motivates CVS employees by providing a clear path to advancement and enables them to gain a broad perspective of the company and its goals that they would not have been able to obtain on their own.

By identifying potential leaders with the right personality traits and equipping them with the essential tools needed to handle any situation, the CVS Corporation's Emerging Leaders program ensures the firm's continued growth and success.

Questions

1. *What key personality traits does CVS management look for when trying to identify a good potential leader?*
2. *What do managers at CVS consider to be a pitfall that prevents employees from pursuing leadership opportunities at the company?*
3. *How does CVS teach complex problem-solving skills to employees in the Emerging Leaders program?*

Johnson & Johnson: Using a Credo for Business Guidance

Johnson & Johnson, founded by Robert Wood Johnson and his brothers James and Mead in 1886, has grown into the world's most comprehensive manufacturer of health care products and related services for the consumer, pharmaceutical, and medical devices and diagnostics markets. Today, Johnson & Johnson consists of more than 200 operating companies, employing approximately 109,100 employees, with more than 50,000 of those in the United States. Johnson & Johnson has operations in 57 nations and sells products in over 175 nations. Johnson & Johnson's product categories include, but are not limited to: allergy, colds, and flu; baby care; cardiology; dental care; diabetes care; first aid; medical devices and diagnostics; oncology; prescription drugs; skin and hair care; and vision care. The company's sales have increased each year for 71 consecutive years, and in 2003, global sales were $41.9 billion and net earnings were $7.2 billion. In 2004, Johnson & Johnson was ranked seventh on *Fortune's* 2004 Most Admired Companies list.

The worldwide success of Johnson & Johnson is widely attributed to an unwavering commitment to a business philosophy that puts customers first and stockholders last. Robert Wood Johnson II first articulated this business philosophy in 1943; it was called the *Johnson & Johnson Credo*. Like his father before him, Robert Wood Johnson II could be dogmatic, autocratic, prone to micromanagement. Yet, he was not as inflexible as many people thought; in fact, he encouraged innovation in every part of the company. There was, however, one thing about which Robert Wood Johnson II was inflexible—adherence to the Johnson & Johnson Credo. Even after the company went from being family-owned to having public ownership and trading of its stock in the early 1960s, the Johnson & Johnson Credo has provided fundamental managerial and operational guidance to which the company has unwaveringly adhered.

The key points of the Johnson & Johnson Credo address the company's four responsibilities. In descending order of emphasis, these responsibilities may be summarized as follows:

- The company's first responsibility is to meet the needs of everyone who uses the company's products by providing quality products that are reasonably priced and by ensuring that suppliers and distributors have the opportunity to make a fair profit.

- The company's second responsibility is to the company's employees throughout the world, treating them fairly and with dignity, seeking to involve them, and providing them with competent and ethical management.

- The company's third responsibility is to the various communities where it operates, seeking to improve those communities and sharing in the burden of such improvements.

- The company's last responsibility is to the stockholders, seeking to make a sound profit to provide a fair return to the owners and to enable the company to innovate and grow so that fair returns are maintained in the future.

The full Credo was in a format that people could understand, and Robert Wood Johnson II demanded that people adhere to it. Very importantly, the company created appropriate organizational mechanisms to bring the Credo to life, and to support and reinforce it. The Johnson & Johnson Credo "may sound a bit corny—and so may J&J's devotion to it: It's posted in every J&J facility around the world and carved in an eight-foot chunk of limestone at company headquarters in New Brunswick, N.J. But Johnson made sure everyone bought into it."

The Credo has served Johnson & Johnson well during normal operating conditions and in times of crisis, such as in 1982 and 1986 when the Tylenol® acetaminophen product was adulterated with cyanide and used as a murder weapon. During the Tylenol® crises, Johnson & Johnson's "managers and employees made countless decisions that were inspired by the philosophy embedded in the Credo." Tylenol® was immediately cleared from store shelves and the company was very proactive and open in addressing each crisis. As a result, Johnson

& Johnson's good reputation was maintained and the Tylenol® business was reinvigorated.

The Johnson & Johnson Credo continues to guide the company's decisions and actions regarding its responsibilities to customers, employees, the community, and stockholders. The Credo guides Johnson & Johnson's operations in Africa, Asia and the Pacific Rim, Eastern and Western Europe, Latin America, the Middle East, and North America. Ralph Larsen, a former chief executive officer of Johnson & Johnson, maintains that the Credo provides a constant source of guidance for the company and that it is the foundation for everything the company does.

Discussion Questions

1. From your perspective, what role(s) should business play in the contemporary world?

2. What implications does the Credo have for Johnson & Johnson's view of the role(s) it should play in the contemporary world?

3. What implications does the Johnson & Johnson Credo have for the attitudes and job behavior of the company's employees?

4. Would you like to work for a company like Johnson & Johnson? Why or why not?

SOURCE: This case was written by Michael K. McCuddy, The Louis S. and Mary L. Morgal Chair of Christian Business Ethics and Professor of Management, College of Business Administration, Valparaiso University. This case was developed from material contained on the Johnson & Johnson Web site at http://www.jnj.com and in the following articles: "Johnson & Johnson," *FSB: Fortune Small Business* (April 2003): 90–93; T. Kinni, "Words to Work By: Crafting Meaningful Corporate Ethics Statements," *Harvard Management Communication Letter* (January 2003): 3–4.

Chapter 2

Challenges for Managers

LEARNING OBJECTIVES

After reading this chapter, you should be able to do the following:

1 Describe the dimensions of cultural differences in societies that affect work-related attitudes.

2 Explain the social and demographic changes that are producing diversity in organizations.

3 Describe actions managers can take to help their employees value diversity.

4 Discuss the assumptions of consequential, rule-based, and character ethical theories.

5 Explain six issues that pose ethical dilemmas for managers.

6 Understand the alternative work arrangements produced by technological advances.

7 Explain the ways managers can help employees adjust to technological change.

THINKING AHEAD: PIXAR ANIMATION STUDIOS

A Dream Challenged from the Start

Ed Catmull is president of Pixar Animation Studios, the outfit behind such cartoon classics as *Toy Story* and *Monsters, Inc.* His ascent to the presidency and the work he leads is in some ways an unlikely story. As with most healthy children, Ed had a dream growing up. His dream was to be a Disney animator. Unfortunately, he was confronted with the reality of his limited drawing abilities. During Ed's childhood, animation was done by gifted artists who drew Mickey Mouse, Donald Duck, Minnie Mouse, and Goofy. These animators were the cornerstones for the whole fantasy and dreamworld that Walt Disney imagined and then created. Fortunately for Ed Catmull, animation did not remain trapped in a time warp, and his own career redirection became a detour that ultimately led him back to the fulfillment of his dream.

Pixar was the heart of the Walt Disney Pictures dreamworld and a household name synonymous with family entertainment at its finest.[1] While Disney had its fingers everywhere—in radio, television, theme parks—Pixar had released only five features since its 1995 debut with *Toy Story*. However, Pixar had come to stand for traditional Disney values before their partnership ended. The promise of *Toy Story*, which was the first computer-animated feature film with extraordinary creativity and intelligence, was further fulfilled with *A Bug's Life* (1998), *Toy Story 2* (1999), and *Monsters, Inc.* (2001). Pixar extends from a solid platform of computer-generated special effects with roots in the 1970s revolution in computer graphics.

While Pixar lives in a fantasy world of dreams first created by Disney, it would be a mistake to think it's all fun and games without substance. For example, Pixar's 2003 release, *Finding Nemo*, has sparkling visual clarity that also comes very close to realism. The witty humor, the adventure, and the dazzling excitement are all there.

These eye-popping features aim to grab kids' attention, while the story line is built on a parable for their parents. Like the darkest of Disney's fairy tales, *Finding Nemo* begins with a barracuda devouring Nemo's mother and hundreds of his would-be siblings. Only Nemo and his father, Marlin, survive. The film is then the story of Nemo growing up, just as the kids in the theater are growing up. In *Finding Nemo*, Pixar delivers a message of substance and positive value for parents while entertaining their children.

Ed Catmull grew up to live out his dream. How did he do it when faced with his limited drawing abilities?

Management Challenges in a New Time

Most U.S. executives continue to believe that U.S. firms are encountering unprecedented global competition.[2] Globalization is being driven on the one hand by the spread of economic logics centered on freeing, opening, deregulating, and privatizing economies to make them more attractive for investment and, on the other hand, by the digitization of technologies that is revolutionizing communication.[3] The challenges for managers in this context are manifest in both opportunities and threats, as were briefly touched upon in Chapter 1. The long, robust economic expansion in the United States during the 1990s led to a bubble that burst and several years of economic difficulty. Managers are challenged to lead people in the good times and the bad times, as Anne Mulcahy has done at Xerox, because business cycles ultimately produce both. Thus, the opportunities and threats for managers are history-dependent.

What major challenges must managers overcome in order to remain competitive? Chief executive officers of U.S. corporations cite four issues that are paramount: (1) globalizing the firm's operations to compete in the global village, (2) leading a diverse workforce, (3) encouraging positive ethics, character, and personal integrity, and (4) advancing and implementing technological innovation in the workplace.[4,5]

Successful organizations and managers respond to these four challenges as opportunities rather than as threats. Our six focus companies—Cisco Systems, The Coca-Cola Company, Pixar Animation Studios, Virgin Group Ltd., Whole Foods Market, and Canine Companions for Independence—and their managers have wrestled with one or more of these four challenges as they pursue success and achievement. We see in the Looking Back feature later in this chapter how Ed Catmull responded positively to the challenge described in the Thinking Ahead feature. You read in Chapter 1 how John Chambers of Cisco Systems, in a similar vein, responded positively when opportunity called. In this chapter, we focus attention on these four challenges that, when well managed, lead to success and healthy organizational outcomes.

Globalization has led to the emergence of the global village in the world economy. The Internet along with rapid political and social changes have broken down old national barriers to competition. What has emerged is a world characterized by an ongoing process of integration and interconnection of states, markets, technologies, and firms. This world as a global macroeconomic village is a boundaryless market in which all firms, large and small, must compete.[6]

2. *Managing a diverse workforce* is something organizations like Alcon Laboratories and Coors Brewing Company do extremely well. Both companies reap success from their efforts. The workforce of today is more diverse than ever before. Managers are challenged to bring together employees of different backgrounds in work teams. This requires attention to more than surface-level diversity; it requires attention to deep-level diversity.[7]

3. *Good character*, *ethical behavior*, and *personal integrity* are what managers in organizations like Johnson & Johnson are known for. The company's credo guides employee behavior and has helped employees do the right thing in some tough situations. Ethical behavior in business has been at the forefront of public consciousness for some time now. Insider trading scandals, influence peddling, and contract frauds are in the news daily. It need not be that way. Many executives lead with a spirit of personal integrity.[8]

4. *Technological innovation* is one of the keys to strategic competitiveness. Imagine yourself as a small business owner of a package delivery firm. You'll be competing with FedEx, the proud owner of the most technologically advanced package tracking and delivery system in the world. Would you be able to compete? Technological change can be complex and risky. The boom and bust of 1999 and 2000 in the New Economy showed the risks for the dot.com companies of dealing with leading-edge technology.

Organizations and managers who see opportunity in these four challenges will remain competitive, more than just survive in today's turbulent environment. Throughout the book, we'll show you how organizational behavior can contribute to managing the challenges with optimism and hope.

The Global Village

Only a few years ago, business conducted across national borders was referred to as "international" activity. The word *international* carries with it a connotation that the individual's or the organization's nationality is held strongly in consciousness.[9] *Globalization*, in contrast, implies that the world is free from national boundaries and that it is really a borderless world.[10] U.S. workers are now competing with workers in other countries. Organizations from other countries are locating subsidiaries in the United States, such as the U.S. manufacturing locations of Honda, Mazda, and Mercedes.

Similarly, what were once referred to as multinational organizations (organizations that did business in several countries) are now referred to as transnational companies. In *transnational organizations*, the global viewpoint supersedes national issues.[11] Transnational organizations operate over large global distances and are multicultural in terms of the people they employ. 3M, Dow Chemical, Coca-Cola, and other transnational organizations operate worldwide with diverse populations of employees.

from multi-national to transnational

transnational organization
An organization in which the global viewpoint supersedes national issues.

Changes in the Global Marketplace

Social and political upheavals have led organizations to change the way they conduct business and to encourage their members to think globally. Toyota is one Japanese company thinking big, thinking globally, and thinking differently, as described in The Real World 2.1. The collapse of Eastern Europe was followed quickly by the demise of the Berlin Wall. East and West Germany were united into a single country. In the Soviet Union, perestroika led to the liberation of the satellite countries and the breaking away of the Soviet Union's member nations. Perestroika also brought about many opportunities for U.S.

Toyota Learns to Speak to Gen Y

Toyota has big ambitions about winning in the global competition described in these first two chapters. The auto company aims to surpass General Motors as the world's biggest automaker. On the way, its goal is to increase its global market share from 10 percent in 2002 to 15 percent in the next decade. To gain new customers, Toyota must go beyond its relationship with baby boomers, the generation that helped nudge its market share to 11.3 percent in 2003. So the company is looking to the boomers' kids: the 60-million-strong Generation Y, or millennials in the United States. To get the attention of Toyota's executive committee members, chief engineer Tetsuya Tada did the unthinkable—skipped the numbers and played a seven-minute music video. The message: If Toyota hoped to win the eight- to twenty-three-year-olds in Gen Y worldwide, it must revamp both its product and its thinking. By 2020, Gen Y will dominate global car sales. The company chose an ad agency that would reach Gen Y, a generation that is a lot more respectful than the generation before it; a generation that wants to see an array of personalities, not just actors or models; and a generation that likes to discover brands on its own. The new rules of engagement for Toyota that emerged were: (1) keep the respect, (2) keep an array of options, and (3) keep it quiet.

SOURCE: F. Warner, "Learning How to Speak to Gen Y," *Fast Company* 72 (July 2003): 36–37, http://www.fastcompany.com/magazine/72/smartcompany.html.

---

businesses, as witnessed by the press releases showing extremely long waiting lines at Moscow's first McDonald's restaurant.

Business ventures in China have become increasingly attractive to U.S. businesses. Coca-Cola has led the way. One challenge U.S. managers have tackled is attempting to understand the Chinese way of doing business. Chinese managers' business practices have been shaped by the Communist Party, socialism, feudalistic values, and *guanxi* (building networks for social exchange). Once *guanxi* is established, individuals can ask favors of each other with the expectation that the favor will be returned. For example, it is common in China to use *guanxi*, or personal connections, to conduct business or to obtain jobs. The term *guanxi* is sometimes a sensitive word, because Communist Party policies oppose the use of such practices to gain influence. In China, the family is regarded as being responsible for a worker's productivity, and in turn, the company is responsible for the worker's family. Because of socialism, Chinese managers have very little experience with rewards and punishments and are reluctant to use them in the workplace. The concept of *guanxi* is not unique to China. There are similar concepts in many other countries, including Russia and Haiti. It is a broad term that can mean anything from strongly loyal relationships to ceremonial gift-giving, sometimes seen as bribery. *Guanxi* is more common in societies with underdeveloped legal support for private businesses.[12]

To work with Chinese managers, Americans can learn to build their own *guanxi*; understand the Chinese chain of command; and negotiate slow, general agreements in order to interact effectively. Using the foreign government as the local franchisee may be effective in China. For example, KFC Corporation's operation in China is a joint venture between KFC (60 percent) and two Chinese government bodies (40 percent).[13]

In 1993, the European Union integrated fifteen nations into a single market by removing trade barriers. At that time, the member nations of the European Union were Belgium, Denmark, France, Germany, Greece, Ireland, Italy, Luxembourg, the Netherlands, Portugal, Spain, Austria, Finland, Sweden, and

---

guanxi

The Chinese practice of building networks for social exchange.

the United Kingdom. As of 2004, Estonia, Hungary, Latvia, Lithuania, Malta, Poland, Slovakia, and Slovenia were also members. The integration of Europe provides many opportunities for U.S. organizations, including 350 million potential customers. Companies like Ford Motor Company and IBM, which entered the market early with wholly owned subsidiaries, will have a head start on these opportunities.[14] Competition within the European Union will increase, however, as will competition from Japan and the former Soviet nations.

The United States, Canada, and Mexico have dramatically reduced trade barriers in accordance with the North American Free Trade Agreement (NAFTA), which took effect in 1994. Organizations have found promising new markets for their products, and many companies have located plants in Mexico to take advantage of low labor costs. DaimlerChrysler, for example, has a massive assembly plant in Saltillo. Prior to NAFTA, Mexico placed heavy tariffs on U.S. exports. The agreement immediately eliminated many of these tariffs and provided that the remaining tariffs be phased out over time.

All of these changes have brought about the need to think globally. Managers can benefit from global thinking by taking a long-term view. Entry into global markets requires long-term strategies.

Understanding Cultural Differences

One of the keys for any company competing in the global marketplace is to understand diverse cultures. Whether managing culturally diverse individuals within a single location or managing individuals at remote locations around the globe, an appreciation of the differences among cultures is crucial. Edgar Schein suggests that to understand an organization's culture, or more broadly any culture, it is important to dig below the surface of visible artifacts and uncover the basic underlying assumptions at the core of the culture.[15] His definition of organizational culture is the pattern of basic assumptions that a given group has invented, discovered, or developed in learning to cope with its problems of external adaptation and internal integration, and that have worked well enough to be considered valid. These basic assumptions are then taught to new members as the correct way to perceive, think, and feel in relation to those problems. We develop Schein's culture model of basic assumptions, values, visible artifacts, and creations more fully in Chapter 16.

Microcultural differences (i.e., differences within cultures) can play an important role in understanding the global work environment.[16] Knowing cultural differences in symbols is extremely important. Computer icons may not translate well in other cultures. The thumbs up sign, for example, means approval in the United States. In Australia, however, it is an obscene gesture. And manila file folders, like the icons used in Windows applications, aren't used in many European countries and therefore aren't recognized.[17]

Do cultural differences translate into differences in work-related attitudes? The pioneering Dutch researcher Geert Hofstede focused on this question.[18] He and his colleagues surveyed 160,000 managers and employees of IBM who were working in sixty different countries.[19] In this way, the researchers were able to study individuals from the same company in the same jobs, but working in different countries. Hofstede's work is important, because his studies showed that national culture explains more differences in work-related attitudes than do age, gender, profession, or position within the organization. Thus, cultural differences do affect individuals' work-related attitudes. Hofstede found five dimensions of cultural differences that formed the basis for work-related attitudes. These dimensions are shown in Figure 2.1 and are described next.

1. Describe the dimensions of cultural differences in societies that affect work-related attitudes.

FIGURE 2.1   Hofstede's Dimensions of Cultural Differences

2.1

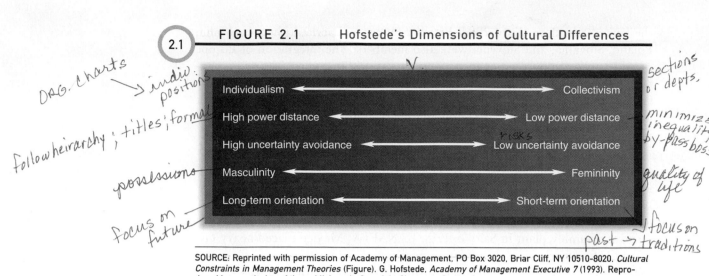

Handwritten annotations:
ORG. charts → indiv positions
follow heirarchy; titles; formal
possessions
focus on future
V
risks
sections or depts.
minimize inequality; by-pass boss
quality of life
✓ focus on past → traditions

SOURCE: Reprinted with permission of Academy of Management, PO Box 3020, Briar Cliff, NY 10510-8020. *Cultural Constraints in Management Theories* (Figure). G. Hofstede, *Academy of Management Executive 7* (1993). Reproduced by permission of the publisher via Copyright Clearance Center, Inc.

individualism

A cultural orientation in which people belong to loose social frameworks, and their primary concern is for themselves and their families.

collectivism

A cultural orientation in which individuals belong to tightly knit social frameworks, and they depend strongly on large extended families or clans.

INDIVIDUALISM VERSUS COLLECTIVISM In cultures where *individualism* predominates, people belong to loose social frameworks, but their primary concern is for themselves and their families. People are responsible for taking care of their own interests. They believe that individuals should make decisions. Cultures characterized by *collectivism* are tightly knit social frameworks in which individual members depend strongly on extended families or clans. Group decisions are valued and accepted.

The North American culture is individualistic in orientation. It is a "can-do" culture that values individual freedom and responsibility. In contrast, collectivist cultures emphasize group welfare and harmony. Israeli kibbutzim and the Japanese culture are examples of societies in which group loyalty and unity are paramount. Organization charts show these orientations. In Canada and the United States, which are individualistic cultures, organization charts show individual positions. In Malaysia, which is a collectivist culture, organization charts show only sections or departments.

This dimension of cultural differences has other workplace implications. Individualistic managers, as found in Great Britain and the Netherlands, emphasize and encourage individual achievement. In contrast, collectivistic managers, such as in Japan and Colombia, seek to fit harmoniously within the group. They also encourage these behaviors among their employees. There are also cultural differences within regions of the world. Arabs are more collectivist than Americans. Within the Arab culture, however, Egyptians are more individualistic than Arabs from the Gulf States (Saudi Arabia, Oman, Bahrain, Kuwait, Quatar, United Arab Emirates). This may be due to the fact that Egyptian businesspeople tend to have longer and more intense exposures to Western culture.[20]

power distance

The degree to which a culture accepts unequal distribution of power.

SW

POWER DISTANCE The second dimension of cultural differences examines the acceptance of unequal distribution of power. In countries with a high *power distance*, bosses are afforded more power simply because they are the bosses. Titles are used, formality is the rule, and authority is seldom bypassed. Power holders are entitled to their privileges, and managers and employees see one another as fundamentally different kinds of people. India is a country with a high power distance, as are Venezuela and Mexico.

In countries with a low power distance, people believe that inequality in society should be minimized. People at various power levels are less threatened by, and more willing to trust, one another. Managers and employees see one another as similar. Managers are given power only if they have expertise. Employees frequently bypass the boss in order to get work done in countries with a low power distance, such as Denmark and Australia.

UNCERTAINTY AVOIDANCE Some cultures are quite comfortable with ambiguity and uncertainty, whereas others do not tolerate these conditions well. Cultures with high *uncertainty avoidance* are concerned with security and tend to avoid conflict. People have a need for consensus. The inherent uncertainty in life is a threat against which people in such cultures constantly struggle.

Cultures with low uncertainty avoidance are more tolerant of ambiguity. People are more willing to take risks and are more tolerant of individual differences. Conflict is seen as constructive, and people accept dissenting viewpoints. Norway and Australia are characterized by low uncertainty avoidance, and this trait is seen in the value placed on job mobility. Japan and Italy are characterized by high uncertainty avoidance, so career stability is emphasized.

MASCULINITY VERSUS FEMININITY In cultures that are characterized by *masculinity*, assertiveness and materialism are valued. Men should be assertive, tough, and decisive, whereas women should be nurturing, modest, and tender.[21] Money and possessions are important, and performance is what counts. Achievement is admired. Cultures that are characterized by *femininity* emphasize relationships and concern for others. Men and women are expected to assume both assertive and nurturing roles. Quality of life is important, and people and the environment are emphasized.

Masculine societies, such as in Austria and Venezuela, define gender roles strictly. Feminine societies, in contrast, tend to blur gender roles. Women may be the providers, and men may stay home with the children. The Scandinavian countries of Norway, Sweden, and Denmark exemplify the feminine orientation.

TIME ORIENTATION Cultures also differ in *time orientation*; that is, whether the culture's values are oriented toward the future (long-term orientation) or toward the past and present (short-term orientation).[22] In China, a culture with a long-term orientation, values such as thrift and persistence, which focus on the future, are emphasized. In Russia, the orientation is short-term. Values such as respect for tradition (past) and meeting social obligations (present) are emphasized.

U.S. CULTURE The position of the United States on these five dimensions is interesting. Hofstede found the United States to be the most individualistic country of any studied. On the power distance dimension, the United States ranked among the countries with weak power distance. Its rank on uncertainty avoidance indicated a tolerance of uncertainty. The United States also ranked as a masculine culture with a short-term orientation. These values have shaped U.S. management theory, so Hofstede's work casts doubt on the universal applicability of U.S. management theories. Because cultures differ so widely on these dimensions, management practices should be adjusted to account for cultural differences. Managers in transnational organizations must learn as much as they can about other cultures in order to lead their culturally diverse organizations effectively.

uncertainty avoidance
The degree to which a culture tolerates ambiguity and uncertainty.

masculinity
The cultural orientation in which assertiveness and materialism are valued.

femininity
The cultural orientation in which relationships and concern for others are valued.

time orientation
Whether a culture's values are oriented toward the future (long-term orientation) or toward the past and present (short-term orientation).

Planning for a Global Career

Think of a country you would like to work in, do business in, or visit. Find out about its culture, using Hofstede's dimensions as guidelines. You can use a variety of sources to accomplish this, particularly your school library, government offices, faculty members, or others who have global experience. You will want to answer the following questions:

1. Is the culture individualistic or collectivist?
2. Is the power distance high or low?
3. Is uncertainty avoidance high or low?
4. Is the country masculine or feminine in its orientation?
5. Is the time orientation short-term or long-term?
6. How did you arrive at your answers to the first five questions?
7. How will these characteristics affect business practices in the country you chose to investigate?

expatriate manager

A manager who works in a country other than his or her home country.

Careers in management have taken on a global dimension. Working in transnational organizations may well give managers the opportunity to work in other countries. *Expatriate managers*, those who work in a country other than their home country, benefit from having as much knowledge as possible about cultural differences. Because managers are increasingly exposed to global work experiences, it is never too early to begin planning for this aspect of your career. You 2.1 asks you to begin gathering information about a country in which you would like to work, including information on its culture.

International executives are executives whose jobs have international scope, whether in an expatriate assignment or in a job dealing with international issues. What kind of competencies should an individual develop in order to prepare for an international career? There seem to be several attributes, all of them centering around core competencies and the ability to learn from experience. Some of the key competencies are integrity, insightfulness, risk taking, courage to take a stand, and ability to bring out the best in people. Learning-oriented attributes of international executives include cultural adventurousness, flexibility, openness to criticism, desire to seek learning opportunities, and sensitivity to cultural differences.[23]

Understanding cultural differences becomes especially important for companies that are considering opening foreign offices, because workplace customs can vary widely from one country to another. Carefully searching out this information in advance can help companies successfully manage foreign operations. Consulate offices and companies operating within the foreign country are excellent sources of information about national customs and legal requirements. Table 2.1 presents a business guide to cultural differences in three countries: Japan, Mexico, and Saudi Arabia.

Another reality that can affect global business practices is the cost of layoffs in other countries. The practice of downsizing is not unique to the United States. Dismissing a forty-five-year-old middle manager with twenty years of service and a $50,000 annual salary can vary in cost from a low of $13,000 in Ireland to a high of $130,000 in Italy.[24] The cost of laying off this manager in the United States would be approximately $19,000. The wide variability in costs stems from the various legal protections that certain countries give workers. In Italy, laid-off employees must receive a "notice period" payment (one year's pay if they have nine years or more of service) plus a severance payment (based on pay and years of service). U.S. companies operating overseas often

TABLE 2.1   Business Guide to Cultural Differences

COUNTRY	APPOINTMENTS	DRESS	GIFTS	NEGOTIATIONS
Japan	Punctuality is necessary when doing business here. It is considered rude to be late.	Conservative for men and women in large to medium companies, though pastel shirts are common. May be expected to remove shoes in temples and homes, as well as in some ryokan (inn) style restaurants. In that case, slip-on shoes should be worn.	Important part of Japanese business protocol. Gifts are typically exchanged among colleagues on July 15 and January 1 to commemorate midyear and the year's end, respectively.	Business cards ("meishi") are an important part of doing business in Japan and key for establishing credentials. One side of your card should be in English and the reverse in Japanese. It is an asset to include information such as membership in professional associations.
Mexico	Punctuality is not always as much of a priority in Mexican business culture. Nonetheless, Mexicans are accustomed to North Americans arriving on time, and most Mexicans in business, if not government, will try to return the favor.	Dark, conservative suits and ties are the norm for most men. Standard office attire for women includes dresses, skirted suits, or skirts and blouses. Femininity is strongly encouraged in women's dress. Women business travelers will want to bring hosiery and high heels.	Not usually a requirement in business dealings though presenting a small gift will generally be appreciated as a gesture of goodwill. If giving a gift, be aware that inquiring about what the receiver would like to receive can be offensive.	Mexicans avoid directly saying "no." A "no" is often disguised in responses such as "maybe" or "We'll see." You should also use this indirect approach in your dealings. Otherwise, your Mexican counterparts may perceive you as being rude and pushy.
Saudi Arabia	Customary to make appointments for times of day rather than precise hours. The importance Saudis attach to courtesy and hospitality can cause delays that prevent keeping to a strict schedule.	Only absolute requirement of dress code in the Kingdom is modesty. For men, this means covering everything from navel to knee. Females are required to cover everything except the face, hands and feet in public; they can wear literally anything they want providing they cover it with an abaya (standard black cloak) and headscarf when they go out.	Should only be given to the most intimate of friends. For a Saudi to receive a present from a lesser acquaintance is so embarrassing that it is considered offensive.	Business cards are common but not essential. If used, the common practice is to have both English and Arabic printed, one on each side so that neither language is perceived as less important by being on the reverse of the same card.

SOURCE: Adapted from information obtained from business culture guides accessed online at http://www.executiveplanet.com.

adopt the European tradition of training and retraining workers to avoid over-staffing and potential layoffs. An appreciation of the customs and rules for doing business in another country is essential if a company wants to go global.

Developing Cross-Cultural Sensitivity

As organizations compete in the global marketplace, employees must learn to deal with individuals from diverse cultural backgrounds. Stereotypes may pervade employees' perceptions of other cultures. In addition, employees may be unaware of others' perceptions of the employees' national culture. A potentially valuable exercise is to ask members of various cultures to describe one another's cultures. This provides a lesson on the misinterpretation of culture.

Intel wants interns and employees to understand the company's culture, but more importantly, it wants to understand the employees' cultures. In an effort to increase diversity, Intel's proportion of ethnic minorities in managerial positions increased from 13 percent in 1993 to 20 percent in 2003, and is still climbing.[25] Many individuals feel their cultural heritage is important and may walk into uncomfortable situations at work. To prevent this, Intel's new workers are paired carefully with mentors, and mentors and protégés learn about each others' cultures.

Cultural sensitivity training is a popular method for helping employees recognize and appreciate cultural differences. Another way of developing sensitivity is to use cross-cultural task forces or teams. The Milwaukee-based GE Medical Systems Group (GEMS) has 19,000 employees working worldwide. GEMS has developed a vehicle for bringing managers from each of its three regions (the Americas, Europe, and Asia) together to work on a variety of business projects. Under the Global Leadership Program, several work groups made up of managers from various regions of the world are formed. The teams work on important projects, such as worldwide employee integration to increase the employees' sense of belonging throughout the GEMS international organization.[26]

The globalization of business affects all parts of the organization, and human resource management is affected in particular. Companies have employees around the world, and human resource managers face the daunting task of effectively supporting a culturally diverse workforce. Human resource managers must adopt a global view of all functions, including human resource planning, recruitment and selection, compensation, and training and development. They must have a working knowledge of the legal systems in various countries, as well as of global economics, culture, and customs. Human resource managers must not only prepare U.S. workers to live outside their native country but also help foreign employees interact with U.S. culture. Global human resource management is a complex endeavor, but it is critical to the success of organizations in the global marketplace.

Globalization is one challenge managers must meet in order to remain competitive in the changing world. Related to globalization is the challenge of managing an increasingly diverse workforce. Cultural differences contribute a great deal to the diversity of the workforce, but there are other forms of diversity as well.

The Diverse Workforce

Workforce diversity is an important issue for organizations. The United States, as a melting pot nation, has always had a mix of individuals in its workforce. We once sought to be all alike, as in the melting pot, but we now recognize

The Positive Value of an Open Mind

Open-minded people in a diverse work climate are found to embrace demographic differences more readily than their close-minded counterparts.

© Ryan McVay/Photodisc

Workforce 2000 and *Opportunity 2000* focus attention on initiatives by organizations to diversify their workforces and the effects of this diversification. Relational demography researchers think that people in work groups and organizations compare their own demographic characteristics, such as sex, race, tenure, and age, with those of other members. Further, they think that perceived similarity or dissimilarity influences work-related outcomes. A study examined the effects of dogmatism (i.e., close-mindedness) on the rela-

tionship of demographic perceptions with self-esteem, trust in coworkers, and attraction to coworkers. The researchers reasoned that the more open-minded people are, the more positively they will respond to demographic differences (for example, race and sex dissimilarity), while the more dogmatic or close-minded they are, the more negatively they will respond to demographic differences. The positive responses would be higher self-esteem, greater trust in coworkers, and greater attraction to coworkers. These ideas were tested in three organizations: a *Fortune 500* computer hardware firm, a manufacturer of printed circuit boards, and a university. The results supported the basic theory, and the researchers concluded that demographic dissimilarity leads to positive outcomes when people are open-minded and to negative outcomes when they are close-minded.

SOURCE: P. Chattopadhyay, "Can Dissimilarity Lead to Positive Outcomes: The Influence of Open versus Closed Minds," *Journal of Organizational Behavior* 24 (2003): 295–312.

and appreciate individual differences. *Diversity* encompasses all forms of differences among individuals, including culture, gender, age, ability, religion, personality, social status, and sexual orientation. Catalyst's Sheila Wellington believes 2003 was the year in which business made the case for diversity and inclusion, and then matched it with action.

Attention to diversity has increased in recent years. This is largely because of the changing demographics of the working population. Managers feel that dealing with diversity successfully is a paramount concern for two reasons. First, managers need to know how to motivate diverse work groups. Second, managers need to know how to communicate effectively with employees who have different values and language skills.

Several demographic trends are affecting organizations. By the year 2020, the workforce will be more culturally diverse, more female, and older than ever. In addition, legislation and new technologies have brought more workers with disabilities into the workforce. Hence, learning to work together is an increasingly important skill. The Science feature examines a study suggesting the importance of also working with an open mind. Alcon Laboratories, the Swiss-owned and Fort Worth-based international company whose mission is to improve and preserve eyesight and hearing, creates an opportunity for learning to work together through diversity training.[27] Valuing diversity in organizations is an important issue.[28]

diversity

All forms of individual differences, including culture, gender, age, ability, religion, personality, social status, and sexual orientation.

Cultural Diversity

Cultural diversity in the workplace is growing because of the globalization of business, as we discussed earlier. People of diverse national origins—Koreans,

2. Explain the social and demographic changes that are producing diversity in organizations.

Bolivians, Pakistanis, Vietnamese, Swedes, Australians, and others—find themselves cooperating in teams to perform the work of the organization. In addition, changing demographics within the United States significantly affect the cultural diversity in organizations. By 2020, minorities will constitute more than one-half of the new entrants to the U.S. workforce. The participation rates of African-Americans and Hispanic Americans in the labor force increased dramatically in recent years. By 2020, white non-Hispanics will constitute 68 percent of the labor force (down from 83 percent in 2002); 14 percent of the workforce will be Hispanic (up from 12 percent); African-Americans' share will remain at 11 percent, and 5 percent will be Asian.[29]

These trends have important implications for organizations. African-Americans and Hispanic Americans are overrepresented in declining occupations, thus limiting their opportunities. Further, African-Americans and Hispanic Americans tend to live in a small number of large cities that are facing severe economic difficulties and high crime rates. Because of these factors, minority workers are likely to be at a disadvantage within organizations. It does not have to be this way. For example, by monitoring its human resource systems, Coco-Cola has made substantial progress on diversity.[30]

The jobs available in the future will require more skill than has been the case in the past. Often, minority workers have not had opportunities to develop leading-edge skills. Minority skill deficits are large, and the proportions of African-Americans and Hispanic Americans who are qualified for higher level jobs are often much lower than the proportions of qualified whites and Asian Americans.[31] Minority workers are less likely to be prepared because they are less likely to have had satisfactory schooling and on-the-job training. Educational systems within the workplace are needed to supply minority workers the skills necessary for success. Companies such as Motorola are already recognizing and meeting this need by focusing on basic skills training.

The globalization of business and changing demographic trends present organizations with a tremendously culturally diverse workforce. This represents both a challenge and a risk. The challenge is to harness the wealth of differences that cultural diversity provides. The risk is that prejudices and stereotypes may prevent managers and employees from developing synergies that can benefit the organization.

Gender Diversity

The feminization of the workforce has increased substantially. The number of women in the labor force increased from 31.5 million in 1970 to 64 million in 2003. This increase accounts for almost 60 percent of the overall expansion of the entire labor force in the United States for this time period. In 2004, women made up over 60 percent of the labor force, and it is predicted that by the year 2010, 70 percent of new entrants into the workforce will be women and/or people of color. Women are better prepared to contribute in organizations than ever before. Women now earn 32 percent of all doctorates, 52 percent of master's degrees, and 50 percent of all undergraduate degrees. Thus, women are better educated, and more are electing to work. In 2004, almost 58 percent of U.S. women were employed.[32] However, women comprised only 13.6 percent of corporate board members in 2003.

Women's participation in the workforce is increasing, but their share of the rewards of participation is not increasing commensurately. Women hold only 15.7 percent of corporate officer positions in the *Fortune 500* companies.[33] In 2003, only eight *Fortune 500* companies had women CEOs.[34] Former HP CEO

Carly Fiorina was the exception, not the rule. Salaries for women persist at a level of 78 percent of their male counterparts' earnings.[35] Furthermore, because benefits are tied to compensation, women also receive lower levels of benefits.

In addition to lower earnings, women face other obstacles at work. The *glass ceiling* is a transparent barrier that keeps women from rising above a certain level in organizations. In the United States, it is rare to find women in positions above middle management in corporations.[36] The ultimate glass ceiling may well be the corporate board room and the professional partnership. One study found no substantive increase in female corporate board members between 1996 and 2002.[37] While women account for 40 percent of the legal professionals, they are not 40 percent of the partners.

There is reason to believe that, on a global basis, the leadership picture for women is improving and will continue to improve. For example, the number of female political leaders around the world increased dramatically in recent decades. In the 1970s there were only five such leaders. In the 1990s, twenty-one female leaders came into power. Countries such as Ireland, Sri Lanka, Iceland, and Norway all had female political leaders in the 1990s. Women around the world are leading major global companies, albeit not in the United States. These global female business leaders do not come predominantly from the West. In addition, a large number of women have founded entrepreneurial businesses. Women now own one-third of all American businesses, and these women-owned businesses employ more people than the entire *Fortune 500* combined.[38]

Removing the glass ceiling and other obstacles to women's success represents a major challenge to organizations. Policies that promote equity in pay and benefits, encourage benefit programs of special interest to women, and provide equal starting salaries for jobs of equal value are needed in organizations. Corporations that shatter the glass ceiling have several practices in common. Upper managers clearly demonstrate support for the advancement of women, often with a statement of commitment issued by the CEO. Women are represented on standing committees that address strategic business issues of importance to the company. Women are targeted for participation in executive education programs, and systems are in place for identifying women with high potential for advancement.[39] Three of the best companies in terms of their advancement and development of women are Motorola, Deloitte & Touche, and the Bank of Montreal.[40]

Although women in our society have adopted the provider role, men have not been as quick to share domestic responsibilities. Managing the home and arranging for child care are still seen as the woman's domain. In addition, working women often find themselves having to care for their elderly parents. Because of their multiple roles, women are more likely than men to experience conflicts between work and home. Organizations can offer incentives such as flexible work schedules, child care, elder care, and work site health promotion programs to assist working women in managing the stress of their lives.[41]

More women in the workforce means that organizations must help them achieve their potential. To do less would be to underutilize the talents of half of the U.S. workforce.

The glass ceiling is not the only gender barrier in organizations. Males may suffer from discrimination when they are employed in traditionally female jobs

© Bryan Haraway/Bloomberg News/Landov

Carly Fiorina, former CEO of Hewlett-Packard

glass ceiling
A transparent barrier that keeps women from rising above a certain level in organizations.

such as nursing, elementary school teaching, and social work. Males may be overlooked as candidates for managerial positions in traditionally female occupations.[42]

Age Diversity

The graying of the U.S. workforce is another source of diversity in organizations. Aging baby boomers (those individuals born from 1946 through 1964) contributed to the rise of the median age in the United States to thirty-six in the year 2000—six years older than at any earlier time in history. This also means that the number of middle-aged Americans is rising dramatically. In the workforce, the number of younger workers is declining, as is the number of older workers (over age sixty-five). The net result will be a gain in workers aged thirty-five to fifty-four. By 2030, there will be seventy million older persons, more than twice their number in 1996. People over age sixty-five will comprise 13 percent of the population in 2010, and 20 percent of the population by 2030.[43]

This change in worker profile has profound implications for organizations. The job crunch among middle-aged workers will become more intense as companies seek flatter organizations and the elimination of middle-management jobs. Older workers are often higher paid, and companies that employ large numbers of aging baby boomers may find these pay scales a handicap to competitiveness.[44] However, a more experienced, stable, reliable, and healthy workforce can pay dividends to companies. The baby boomers are well-trained and educated, and their knowledge can be a definite asset to organizations.

Another effect of the aging workforce is greater intergenerational contact in the workplace.[45] As organizations grow flatter, workers who were traditionally segregated by old corporate hierarchies (with older workers at the top and younger workers at the bottom) are working together. Four generations are co-operating: the silent generation (people born from 1930 through 1945), a small group that includes most organizations' top managers; the baby boomers, whose substantial numbers give them a strong influence; the baby bust generation, popularly known as Generation X (those born from 1965 through 1976); and the subsequent generation, tentatively called Generation Y or the baby boomlet.[46] Although there is certainly diversity within each generation, each generation differs in general ways from other generations.

The differences in attitudes and values among these four generations can be substantial, and managers face the challenge of integrating these individuals into a cohesive group. Currently, as already noted, most positions of leadership are held by members of the silent generation. Baby boomers regard the silent generation as complacent and as having done little to reduce social inequities. Baby boomers strive for moral rights in the workplace and take a more activist position regarding employee rights. The baby busters, newer to the workplace, are impatient, want short-term gratification, and believe that family should come before work. They scorn the achievement orientation and materialism of the baby boomers. Managing such diverse perspectives is a challenge that must be addressed.

One company that is succeeding in accommodating the baby busters is Patagonia, a manufacturer of products for outdoor enthusiasts. Although the company does not actively recruit twenty-year-olds, approximately 20 percent of Patagonia's workers are in this age group because they are attracted to its products. To retain baby busters, the company offers several options, one of which is flextime. Employees can arrive at work as early as 6 A.M., and work as late as 6 P.M., as long as they work the core hours between 9 A.M. and 3 P.M. Workers also have the option of working at the office for five hours a day and at home for three hours.

Personal leaves of absence are also offered, generally unpaid, for as much as four months per year. This allows employees to take an extended summer break and prevents job burnout. Patagonia has taken into consideration the baby busters' desires for more time for personal concerns and has incorporated these desires into the company.[47]

Younger workers may have false impressions of older workers, viewing them as resistant to change, unable to learn new work methods, less physically capable, and less creative than younger employees. Research indicates, however, that older employees are more satisfied with their jobs, are more committed to the organization, and possess more internal work motivation than their younger cohorts.[48] Research also indicates that direct experience with older workers reduces younger workers' negative beliefs.[49] Motivating aging workers and helping them maintain high levels of contribution to the organization is a key task for managers.

Ability Diversity

The workforce is full of individuals with different abilities, presenting another form of diversity. Individuals with disabilities are an underutilized human resource. An estimated 50 million individuals with disabilities live in the United States, and their unemployment rate is estimated to exceed 50 percent.[50] Nevertheless, the representation of individuals with disabilities in the workforce has increased because of the Americans with Disabilities Act, which went into effect in the summer of 1992. Under this law, employers are required to make reasonable accommodations to permit workers with disabilities to perform jobs. The act defines a person with a disability as "anyone possessing a physical or mental impairment that substantially limits one or more major life activities."[51] It protects individuals with temporary, as well as permanent, disabilities. The act's protection encompasses a broad range of illnesses that produce disabilities. Among these are acquired immune deficiency syndrome (AIDS), cancer, hypertension, anxiety disorders, dyslexia, blindness, and cerebral palsy, to name only a few.

Some companies recognized the value of employing workers with disabilities long before the legislation. Pizza Hut employs 3,000 workers with disabilities and plans to hire more. The turnover rate for Pizza Hut workers with disabilities is only one-fifth of the normal turnover rate.[52]

McDonald's created McJOBS, a program that has trained and hired more than 9,000 mentally and physically challenged individuals since 1981.[53] McJOBS is a corporate plan to recruit, train, and retain individuals with disabilities. Its participants include workers with visual, hearing, or orthopedic impairments; learning disabilities; and mental retardation. Through classroom and on-site training, the McJOBS program prepares individuals with disabilities for the work environment. Before McJOBS workers go onsite, sensitivity training sessions are held with store managers and crew members. These sessions help workers without disabilities understand what it means to be a worker with a disabling condition. Most McJOBS workers start part time and advance according to their own abilities and the opportunities available. Some McJOBS workers with visual impairments prefer to work on the back line, whereas others who use wheelchairs can work the drive-thru window.

Companies like Pizza Hut and McDonald's have led the way in hiring individuals with disabilities. One key to the success of these firms is helping able-bodied employees understand how workers with disabilities can contribute to the organization. In this way, ability diversity becomes an asset and helps organizations meet the challenge of unleashing the talents of workers with disabilities.

Differences Are Assets

Diversity involves much more than culture, gender, age, ability, or personality. It also encompasses religion, social status, and sexual orientation. The scope of diversity is broad and inclusive. All these types of diversity lend heterogeneity to the workforce.

The issue of sexual orientation as a form of diversity has received increasing attention from organizations. Approximately 1.5 million households in the United States are identified as homosexual domestic partnerships.[54] Sexual orientation is an emotionally charged issue. Often, heterosexual resistance to accepting gay, lesbian, or bisexual workers is caused by moral beliefs. Although organizations must respect these beliefs, they must also send a message that all people are valued. The threat of job discrimination leads many gay men and lesbians to keep their sexual orientation secret at work. This secrecy has a cost, however. Closeted gay workers report lower job satisfaction and organizational commitment and more role conflict and conflict between work and home life issues than do openly gay workers or heterosexual workers.[55] To counteract these problems, companies like NCR are seeking gay job applicants. Other companies like IBM, Ford Motor Company, J.P. Morgan Chase, and American Airlines are offering benefits, training, support groups, and marketing strategies in support of gay rights. These initiatives help gay employees become more integrated and productive organizational members. Education and training can be supplemented by everyday practices like using inclusive language—for example, using the term "partner" instead of "spouse" in verbal and written communication.

Part of the challenge in managing diversity lies in attempting to combat prejudices and discrimination. Whereas prejudice is an attitude, discrimination is behavior. Both are detrimental to organizations that depend on productivity from every single worker. Often, in studies of ratings of promotion potential, minorities are rated lower than whites, and females are rated lower than males.[56] The disparity between the pay of women and minority-group members relative to white men increases with age.[57] It is to organizations' benefit to make sure that good workers are promoted and compensated fairly, but as the workforce becomes increasingly diverse, the potential for unfair treatment also increases.

Diversity is advantageous to the organization in a multitude of ways. Some organizations have recognized the potential benefits of aggressively working to increase the diversity of their workforces. Yum! Brands' Kentucky Fried Chicken (KFC) has a goal of attracting and retaining female and minority-group executives. A president of KFC's U.S. operations said, "We want to bring in the best people. If there are two equally qualified people, we'd clearly like to have diversity."[58]

In an effort to understand and appreciate diversity, Alcon Laboratories developed a diversity training class called Working Together. The course takes advantage of two key ideas. First, people work best when they are valued and when diversity is taken into account. Second, when people feel valued, they build relationships and work together as a team.[59] Even majority group man-

3. Describe actions managers can take to help their employees value diversity.

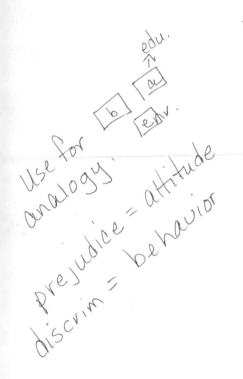

agers may be more supportive of diversity training if they appreciate their own ethnic identity. One evaluation of diversity training found that participants were more favorable if the training was framed with a traditional title and had a broad focus.[60] Further, women react more positively to diversity training than men. Companies can get positive payoffs from diversity training and should, therefore, measure the effect of training.

Managing diversity is one way a company can become more competitive. It is more than simply being a good corporate citizen or complying with affirmative action.[61] It is also more than assimilating women and minorities into a dominant male culture. Managing diversity includes a painful examination of hidden assumptions that employees hold. Biases and prejudices about people's differences must be uncovered and dealt with so that differences can be celebrated and exploited to their full advantage.

Diversity's Benefits and Problems

Diversity can enhance organizational performance. Table 2.2 summarizes the main benefits, as well as problems, with diversity at work. Organizations can reap five main benefits from diversity. First, diversity management can help firms attract and retain the best available human talent. The companies that appear at the top of "Best Places to Work" lists are usually excellent at managing diversity. Second, diversity can enhance marketing efforts. Just as workforces are becoming more diverse, so are markets. Having a diverse workforce can help the company improve its marketing plans by drawing on insights of employees from various cultural backgrounds. Third, diversity promotes creativity and innovation. The most innovative companies, such as HP, deliberately put together diverse teams to foster creativity. Fourth, diversity results in better problem solving. Diverse groups bring more expertise and experience to bear on problems and decisions. They also encourage higher levels of critical thinking. Fifth, diversity enhances organizational flexibility. Inflexible organizations are characterized by narrow thinking, rigidity, and standard definitions of "good" work styles. In contrast, diversity makes an organization challenge old assumptions and become more adaptable. These five benefits can add up to competitive advantage for a company that manages diversity well.

Lest we paint an overly rosy picture of diversity, we must recognize its potential problems. Five problems are particularly important: resistance to change, lack of cohesiveness, communication problems, conflicts, and decision making. People are more highly attracted to, and feel more comfortable with, others like themselves. It stands to reason that diversity efforts may be met with considerable resistance when individuals are forced to interact with others unlike themselves. Managers should be prepared for this resistance rather than naively assuming that everybody supports diversity. (Managing resistance to change is

2.2	TABLE 2.2	Diversity's Benefits and Problems

BENEFITS	PROBLEMS
• Attracts and retains the best human talent	• Resistance to change
• Improves marketing efforts	• Lack of cohesiveness
• Promotes creativity and innovation	• Communication problems
• Results in better problem solving	• Interpersonal conflicts
• Enhances organizational flexibility	• Slowed decision making

presented at length in Chapter 18.) Another potential problem with diversity is the issue of cohesiveness, that invisible "glue" that holds a group together. Cohesive, or tightly knit, groups are preferred by most people. It takes longer for a diverse group of individuals to become cohesive. In addition, cohesive groups have higher morale and better communication. We can reason that it may take longer for diverse groups to develop high morale.

Another obstacle to performance in diverse groups is communication. Culturally diverse groups may encounter special challenges in terms of communication barriers. Misunderstandings can occur that can lower work group effectiveness. Conflicts can also arise, and decision making may take more time.[62]

In summary, diversity has several advantages that can lead to improved productivity and competitive advantage. In diverse groups, however, certain aspects of group functioning can become problematic. The key is to maximize the benefits of diversity and prevent or resolve the potential problems.

Pillsbury is one company that lays out the performance case for managing and valuing differences. Pillsbury's managers argue that the same business rationale for cross-functional teams is relevant to all kinds of diversity. Managing differences includes bringing race and gender, as well as marketing expertise, into a team. To open up a very profitable baked-goods market in a tough-to-crack niche, Pillsbury hired some Spanish-speaking Hispanics. The company lacked the language expertise and cultural access to the Hispanic community. Pillsbury's vice president of human resources conducted his own study of the food industry, asking an independent group to rate the diversity performance of ten companies and correlating it with financial performance over a ten-year period. Along with many other studies, the Pillsbury research suggests that diversity is a strong contributor to financial performance.[63]

Whereas the struggle for equal employment opportunity is a battle against racism and prejudice, managing diversity is a battle to value the differences that individuals bring to the workplace. Organizations that manage diversity effectively can reap the rewards of increased productivity and improved organizational health. Another aspect of a healthy organization is employees of good character, ethical behavior, and personal integrity.

Ethics, Character, and Personal Integrity

4. Discuss the assumptions of consequential, rule-based, and character ethical theories.

In addition to the challenges of globalization and workforce diversity, managers frequently face ethical challenges and dilemmas in organizations. Some organizations display good character, and their executives show personal integrity in addressing ethical dilemmas. Johnson & Johnson employees operate under an organizational credo, presented later in this section. Another organization that manages ethical issues well is Merck & Company. This pharmaceutical company's emphasis on ethical behavior has earned it recognition as one of America's most admired companies in *Fortune*'s polls of CEOs.

Despite the positive way some organizations handle ethical issues, however, unethical conduct does sometimes occur. A few of the ethical problems that managers report as toughest to resolve include employee theft, environmental issues, comparable worth of employees, conflicts of interest, and sexual harassment.[64]

How can people in organizations rationally think through ethical decisions so that they make the "right" choices? Ethical theories help us understand, evaluate, and classify moral arguments; make decisions; and then defend conclusions about what is right and wrong. Ethical theories can be classified as consequential, rule-based, or character.

Consequential theories of ethics emphasize the consequences or results of behavior. John Stuart Mill's utilitarianism, a well-known consequential theory, suggests that right and wrong are determined by the consequences of the action.[65] "Good" is the ultimate moral value, and we should maximize the most good for the greatest number of people. But do good ethics make for good business?[66] Right actions do not always produce good consequences, and good consequences do not always follow from right actions. And how do we determine the greatest good—in short-term or long-term consequences? Using the "greatest number" criterion can imply that minorities (less than 50 percent) might be excluded in evaluating the morality of actions. An issue that may be important for a minority but unimportant for the majority might be ignored. These are but a few of the dilemmas raised by utilitarianism.

In contrast, rule-based theories of ethics emphasize the character of the act itself, not its effects, in arriving at universal moral rights and wrongs.[67] Moral rights, the basis for legal rights, are associated with such theories. In a theological context, the Bible, the Talmud, and the Koran are rule-based guides to ethical behavior. Immanuel Kant worked toward the ultimate moral principle in formulating his categorical imperative, a universal standard of behavior.[68] Kant argued that individuals should be treated with respect and dignity and that they should not be used as a means to an end. He argued that we should put ourselves in the other person's position and ask if we would make the same decision if we were in that person's situation.

Corporations and business enterprises are more prone to subscribe to consequential ethics than rule-based ethics, in part due to the persuasive arguments of the Scottish political economist and moral philosopher Adam Smith.[69] He believed that the self-interest of human beings is God's providence, not the government's. Smith set forth a doctrine of natural liberty, presenting the classical argument for open market competition and free trade. Within this framework, people should be allowed to pursue what is in their economic self-interest, and the natural efficiency of the marketplace would serve the well-being of society. However, an alternative to those theories is offered through virtue-ethics.

Character theories of ethics emphasize the character of the individual and the intent of the actor, in contrast to either the character of the act itself or the consequences of the act. These theories emphasize virtue-ethics and are based on an Aristotelean approach to character. Robert Solomon is the best known advocate of this Aristotelean approach to business ethics.[70] He advocates a business ethics theory that centers on the individual within the corporation, thus emphasizing both corporate roles and personal virtues. The center of Aristotle's vision was on the inner character and virtuousness of the individual, not on the person's behavior or actions. Thus, the "good" person who acted out of virtuous and "right" intentions was one with integrity and ultimately good ethical standards. For Solomon, the six dimensions of virtue-ethics are community, excellence, role identity, integrity, judgment (phronesis), and holism. Further, "the virtues" are a shorthand way of summarizing the ideals that define good character. These include honesty, loyalty, sincerity, courage, reliability, trustworthiness, benevolence, sensitivity, helpfulness, cooperativeness, civility, decency, modesty, openness, and gracefulness, just to name a few.

Cultural relativism contends that there are no universal ethical principles and that people should not impose their own ethical standards on others. Local standards should be the guides for ethical behavior. Cultural relativism encourages individuals to operate under the old adage "When in Rome, do as the Romans do." Unfortunately, strict adherence to cultural relativism can lead

---

consequential theory
An ethical theory that emphasizes the consequences or results of behavior.

rule-based theory
An ethical theory that emphasizes the character of the act itself rather than its effects.

character theory
An ethical theory that emphasizes the character, personal virtues, and integrity of the individual.

individuals to deny accountability for their own decisions and to avoid difficult ethical dilemmas.

5. Explain six issues that pose ethical dilemmas for managers.

People need ethical theories to help them think through confusing, complex, difficult moral choices and ethical decisions. In contemporary organizations, people face ethical and moral dilemmas in many diverse areas. The key areas we address are employee rights, sexual harassment, romantic involvements, organizational justice, whistle-blowing, and social responsibility. We conclude with a discussion of professionalism and codes of ethics.

Employee Rights

Managing the rights of employees at work creates many ethical dilemmas in organizations. Some of these dilemmas are privacy issues related to technology. Computerized monitoring, discussed later in the chapter, constitutes an invasion of privacy in the minds of some individuals. The use of employee data from computerized information systems presents many ethical concerns. Safeguarding the employee's right to privacy and at the same time preserving access to the data for those who need it requires that the manager balance competing interests.

Drug testing, free speech, downsizing and layoffs, and due process are but a few of the issues involving employee rights that managers face. Perhaps no issue generates as much need for managers to balance the interests of employees and the interests of the organization as the reality of AIDS in the workplace. New drugs have shown the promise of extended lives for people with human immunodeficiency virus (HIV), and this means that HIV-infected individuals can remain in the workforce and stay productive. Managers may be caught in the middle of a conflict between the rights of HIV-infected workers and the rights of their coworkers who feel threatened.

Employers are not required to make concessions to coworkers, but employers do have obligations to educate, reassure, and provide emotional support to coworkers. Confidentiality may also be a difficult issue. Some employees with HIV or AIDS do not wish to waive confidentiality and do not want to reveal their condition to their coworkers because of fears of stigmatization or even reprisals. In any case, management should discuss with the affected employee the ramifications of trying to maintain confidentiality and should assure the employee that every effort will be made to prevent negative consequences for him or her in the workplace.[71]

Laws exist that protect HIV-infected workers. As mentioned earlier, the Americans with Disabilities Act requires employees to treat HIV-infected workers as disabled individuals and to make reasonable accommodations for them. The ethical dilemmas involved with this situation, however, go far beyond the legal issues. How does a manager protect the dignity of the person with AIDS and preserve the morale and productivity of the work group when so much prejudice and ignorance surround this disease? Many organizations, such as Wells Fargo, believe the answer is education.[72] Wells Fargo has a written AIDS policy because of the special issues associated with the disease—such as confidentiality, employee socialization, coworker education, and counseling—that must be addressed. The Body Shop's employee education program consists of factual seminars combined with interactive theater workshops. The workshops depict a scenario in which an HIV-positive worker must make decisions, and the audience decides what the worker should do. This helps participants explore the emotional and social issues surrounding HIV.[73] Many fears arise because of a lack of knowledge about AIDS.

How Much Do You Know about Sexual Harassment?

Indicate whether you believe each statement below is true (T) or false (F).

_____ **1.** Sexual harassment is unprofessional behavior.

_____ **2.** Sexual harassment is against the law in all fifty states.

_____ **3.** Sexual advances are a form of sexual harassment.

_____ **4.** A request for sexual activity is a form of sexual harassment.

_____ **5.** Verbal or physical conduct of a sexual nature may be sexual harassment.

_____ **6.** Sexual harassment occurs when submission to sex acts is a condition of employment.

_____ **7.** Sexual harassment occurs when submission to or rejection of sexual acts is a basis for performance evaluation.

_____ **8.** Sexual harassment occurs when such behavior interferes with an employee's performance or creates an intimidating, hostile, and offensive environment.

_____ **9.** Sexual harassment includes physical contact of a sexual nature, such as touching.

_F_ **10.** Sexual harassment requires that a person have the intent to harass, harm, or intimidate.

All of the items are true except item 10, which is false. While somewhat ambiguous, sexual harassment is defined in the eyes of the beholder. Give yourself 1 point for each correct answer. This score reflects how much you know about sexual harassment. Scores can range from 0 (poorly informed about sexual harassment) to 10 (well informed about sexual harassment). If your score was less than 5, you need to learn more about sexual harassment.

SOURCE: See W. O'Donohue, ed., Sexual Harassment (Boston: Allyn and Bacon, 1997) for theory, research and treatment. See http://www.eeoc.gov/stats/harass.html for the latest statistics.

2. Sexual Harassment

According to the Equal Employment Opportunity Commission, sexual harassment is unwelcome sexual attention, whether verbal or physical, that affects an employee's job conditions or creates a hostile working environment.[74] Court rulings, too, have broadened the definition of sexual harassment beyond job-related abuse to include acts that create a hostile work environment. In addition, Supreme Court rulings presume companies are to blame when managers create a sexually hostile working environment. Some organizations are more tolerant of sexual harassment. Complaints are not taken seriously, it is risky to complain, and perpetrators are unlikely to be punished. In these organizations, sexual harassment is more likely to occur. Sexual harassment is also more likely to occur in male-dominated workplaces.[75] Managers can defend themselves by demonstrating that they took action to eliminate workplace harassment and that the complaining employee did not take advantage of company procedures to deal with harassment. Even the best sexual harassment policy, however, will not absolve a company when harassment leads to firing, demotions, or undesirable working assignments.[76] How much do you know about sexual harassment? Complete You 2.2 to get an idea.

There are three types of sexual harassment. *Gender harassment* includes crude comments or sexual jokes and behaviors that disparage someone's gender or convey hostility toward a particular gender. *Unwanted sexual attention* involves unwanted touching or repeated unwanted pressures for dates. *Sexual coercion* consists of implicit or explicit demands for sexual favors by threatening negative job-related consequences or promising job-related rewards.[77] Recent theory has focused attention on the aggressive behavior of sexual harassers.[78]

Sexual harassment costs the typical *Fortune 500* company $6.7 million per year in absenteeism, turnover, and loss of productivity. Valeant Pharmaceuticals International has paid out millions to settle four sexual harassment complaints against former CEO Milan Panic. One U.S. airline reached a $2.6 million settlement with the EEOC in 2001 after the agency found widespread sexual harassment of female employees at the airline's New York JFK International Airport facility. Plaintiffs may now sue not only for back pay but also for compensatory and punitive damages. And these costs do not take into account the negative publicity that firms may encounter from sexual harassment cases, which can cost untold millions. Sexual harassment can have strong negative effects on victims. Victims are less satisfied with their work, supervisors, and coworkers and may psychologically withdraw at work. They may suffer poorer mental health and even exhibit symptoms of post-traumatic stress disorder in conjunction with the harassment experience. Some victims report alcohol abuse, depression, headaches, and nausea.[79]

Several companies have created comprehensive sexual harassment programs that seem to work. Atlantic Richfield (ARCO), owned by British Petroleum and a player in the male-dominated energy industry, has a handbook on preventing sexual harassment that includes phone numbers of state agencies where employees can file complaints. In essence, it gives employees a road map to the courthouse, and the openness seems to work. Lawsuits rarely happen at ARCO. When sexual harassment complaints come in, the company assumes the allegations are true and investigates thoroughly. The process has resulted in the firing of highly placed managers—the captain of an oil tanker was fired for sexually harassing coworkers. Other companies believe in the power of training programs. Some of the best training programs use role-playing, videotapes, and group discussions of real cases to help supervisors recognize unlawful sexual harassment and investigate complaints properly.

Romantic Involvements

Hugging, sexual innuendos, and repeated requests for dates may constitute sexual harassment for some, but they are a prelude to romance for others. This situation carries with it a different set of ethical dilemmas for organizations.

A recent fax poll indicated that three-fourths of the respondents felt it was okay to date a coworker, while three-fourths disapproved of dating a superior or subordinate. In *Meritor vs. Vinson*, the Supreme Court ruled that the agency principle applies to supervisor–subordinate relationships. Employers are liable for acts of their agents (supervisors) and can thus be held liable for sexual harassment. Other employees might claim that the subordinate who is romantically involved with the supervisor gets preferential treatment. Dating between coworkers poses less liability for the company because the agency principle does not apply. Policing coworker dating can also backfire: Wal-Mart lost a lawsuit when it tried to forbid coworkers from dating.

Workplace romances may result, for the participants, in experiences that can be positive or negative, temporary or permanent, exploitative to nonexploitative. The effects of office romances can similarly be positive or negative, or they can simply be mild diversions. Romances can be damaging to organizational effectiveness, or they can occasionally enhance effectiveness through their positive effects on participants. Two particular kinds of romances are hazardous in the workplace. Hierarchical romances, in which one person directly reports to another, can create tremendous conflicts of interest. Utilitarian romances, in which one person satisfies the needs of another in exchange for task-related or career-related favors, are potentially damaging in the workplace. Though most managers realize that workplace romance cannot be eliminated through rules and policies, they believe that intervention is a must when romance constitutes a serious threat to productivity or workplace morale.[80]

quid pro quo

4 Organizational Justice

Another area in which moral and ethical dilemmas may arise for people at work concerns organizational justice, both distributive and procedural. *Distributive justice* concerns the fairness of outcomes individuals receive. For example, the salaries and bonuses of U.S. corporate executives became a central issue with Japanese executives when former President George H.W. Bush and American CEOs in key industries visited Japan in 1992. The Japanese CEOs questioned the distributive justice in keeping the American CEOs' salaries at high levels at a time when so many companies were in difficulty and laying off workers.

distributive justice
The fairness of the outcomes that individuals receive in an organization.

Procedural justice concerns the fairness of the process by which outcomes are allocated. The ethical questions here do not concern the just or unjust distribution of organizational resources. Rather, the ethical questions in procedural justice concern the process. Has the organization used the correct procedures in allocating resources? Have the right considerations, such as competence and skill, been brought to bear in the decision process? And have *or* the wrong considerations, such as race and gender, been excluded from the decision process? Some research has shown cultural differences in the effects of distributive and procedural justice, such as between Hong Kong and the United States.[81]

procedural justice
The fairness of the process by which outcomes are allocated in an organization.

5 Whistle-Blowing

Whistle-blowers are employees who inform authorities of wrongdoings by their companies or coworkers. Whistle-blowers can be perceived as either heroes or "vile wretches" depending on the circumstances of the situation. For a whistle-blower to be considered a public hero, the gravity of the situation that the whistle-blower reports to authorities must be of such magnitude and quality as to be perceived as abhorrent by others.[82] In contrast, the whistle-blower is considered a vile wretch if others see the act of whistle-blowing as more offensive than the situation the whistle-blower reports to authorities.

whistle-blower
An employee who informs authorities of the wrongdoings of his or her company or coworkers.

Whistle-blowing is important in the United States because committed organizational members sometimes engage in unethical behavior in an intense desire to succeed. Many examples of whistle-blowing can be found in corporate America. For example, one former Coke employee made a number of allegations against the company and issued an ultimatum: Coke must pay him almost $45 million or he would go to the media.[83] While a Georgia state court dismissed most of the allegations, Coke still had to defend itself against claims related to wrongful termination. One of the former employee's allegations relating to a falsified marketing test did have the effect of Coke making a public apology and offering to pay Burger King $21 million.

© Paul O'Driscoll/Bloomberg News/Landov

A suit against Coca-Cola for wrongful termination and falsified market testing resulted in an outlay of cash in the millions of dollars.

Organizations can manage whistle-blowing by communicating the conditions that are appropriate for the disclosure of wrongdoing. Clearly delineating wrongful behavior and the appropriate ways to respond are important organizational actions.

Social Responsibility

social responsibility
The obligation of an organization to behave in ethical ways.

Corporate *social responsibility* is the obligation of an organization to behave in ethical ways in the social environment in which it operates. Ethical conduct at the individual level can translate into social responsibility at the organizational level. When Malden Mills, the maker of Polartec, burned down in 1995, the company's president, Aaron Feuerstein, paid workers during the months it took to rebuild the company. Although doing so cost the company a lot of money and was not required by law, Feuerstein said his own values caused him to do the socially responsible thing. Malden Mills recovered financially and continues its success with Polartec.

Socially responsible actions are expected of organizations. Current concerns include protecting the environment, promoting worker safety, supporting social issues, and investing in the community, among others. Some organizations, like IBM, loan executives to inner-city schools to teach science and math. Other organizations like Patagonia demonstrate social responsibility through environmentalism. Firms that are seen as socially responsible have a competitive advantage in attracting applicants.[84]

Codes of Ethics

One of the characteristics of mature professions is the existence of a code of ethics to which the practitioners adhere in their actions and behavior. An example is the Hippocratic oath in medicine. Although some of the individual differences we address in Chapter 4 produce ethical or unethical orientations in specific people, a profession's code of ethics becomes a standard against which members can measure themselves in the absence of internalized standards.

No universal code of ethics or oath exists for business as it does for medicine. However, Paul Harris and four business colleagues, who founded Rotary International in 1905, made an effort to address ethical and moral behavior right from the beginning. They developed the four-way test, shown in Figure 2.2, which is now used in more than 166 nations throughout the world by the 1.2 million Rotarians in more than 30,000 Rotary clubs. Figure 2.2 focuses the questioner on key ethical and moral questions.

Beyond the individual and professional level, corporate culture is another excellent starting point for addressing ethics and morality. In Chapter 16 we

2.2 **FIGURE 2.2** The Four-Way Test

The Four-Way Test
OF WHAT WE THINK, SAY, OR DO

1. Is it the TRUTH?
2. Is it FAIR to all concerned?
3. Will it build GOODWILL and better friendships?
4. Will it be BENEFICIAL to all concerned?

examine how corporate culture and leader behavior trickle down the company, setting a standard for all below. In some cases, the corporate ethics may be captured in a regulation. For example, the Joint Ethics Regulation (DOD 5500.7-R, August 1993) specifies the ethical standards to which all U.S. military personnel are to adhere. In other cases, the corporate ethics may be in the form of a credo. Johnson & Johnson's credo, shown in Figure 2.3, helped hundreds of employees ethically address the criminal tampering with Tylenol products. In its 1986 centennial annual report, J & J attributed its success in this crisis, as well as its long-term business growth (a compound sales rate of 11.6 percent for 100 years), to "our unique form of decentralized management, our adherence to the ethical principles embodied in our credo, and our emphasis on managing the business for the long term."

Individual codes of ethics, professional oaths, and organizational credos all must be anchored in a moral, ethical framework. They are always open to question and continuous improvement using ethical theories as a tool for reexamining the soundness of the current standard. Although a universal right and wrong may exist, it would be hard to argue that there is only one

FIGURE 2.3   The Johnson & Johnson Credo

2.3

We believe our first responsibility is to the doctors, nurses, and patients,
to mothers and all others who use our products and services.
In meeting their needs everything we do must be of high quality.
We must constantly strive to reduce our costs
in order to maintain reasonable prices.
Customers' orders must be serviced promptly and accurately.
Our suppliers and distributors must have an opportunity
to make a fair profit.

We are responsible to our employees,
the men and women who work with us throughout the world.
Everyone must be considered as an individual.
We must respect their dignity and recognize their merit.
They must have a sense of security in their jobs.
Compensation must be fair and adequate,
and working conditions clean, orderly, and safe.
Employees must feel free to make suggestions and complaints.
There must be equal opportunity for employment, development
and advancement for those qualified.
We must provide competent management,
and their actions must be just and ethical.

We are responsible to the communities in which we live and work
and to the world community as well.
We must be good citizens—support good works and charities
and bear our fair share of taxes.
We must encourage civic improvements and better health and education.
We must maintain in good order
the property we are privileged to use,
protecting the environment and natural resources.

Our final responsibility is to our stockholders.
Business must make a sound profit.
We must experiment with new ideas.
Research must be carried on, innovative programs developed
and mistakes paid for.
New equipment must be purchased, new facilities provided,
and new products launched.
Reserves must be created to provide for adverse times.
When we operate according to these principles,
the stockholders should realize a fair return.

code of ethics to which all individuals, professions, and organizations can subscribe.

Technological Innovation

A fourth challenge that managers face is effectively managing technological innovation. *Technology* consists of the intellectual and mechanical processes used by an organization to transform inputs into products or services that meet organizational goals. Managers face the challenge of rapidly changing technology and of putting the technology to optimum use in organizations. The inability of managers to incorporate new technologies successfully into their organizations is a major factor that has limited economic growth in the United States.[85] Although the United States still leads the way in developing new technologies, it lags behind in making productive use of these new technologies in workplace settings.[86] Good-to-great organizations avoid technology fads and bandwagons, yet become pioneers in the application of carefully selected technologies.[87] The Real World 2.2 discusses how Sony effectively translates Japanese technological innovations for U.S. markets.

The Internet has radically changed the way organizations communicate and perform work. By integrating computer, cable, and telecommunications technologies, businesses have learned new ways to compete. For example, Kmart takes advantage of the Internet through BlueLight.com for on-line retailing. In networked organizations, time, distance, and space become irrelevant. A networked organization can do business anytime and anywhere, which is essential in the global marketplace. This allows retailers to drastically cut their investments in inventories. The World Wide Web has created a virtual commercial district. Customers can book air travel, buy compact discs, and "surf the Net" to conduct business around the globe.[88]

The Internet and electronic innovation have made surveillance of employees more widespread. However, companies need to balance the use of spyware, monitoring of employee e-mails and Web sites, and video monitoring systems with respect for employee rights to privacy. Managers with excellent interpersonal skills go a long way in ensuring high productivity, commitment, and appropriate behavior on the part of employees versus the use of intense employee performance monitoring systems using electronic surveillance. Companies with clearly written policies that spell out their approach to monitoring employees may succeed better in walking the fine line between respecting employees' privacy and protecting the interests of the organization.

One fascinating technological change is the development of *expert systems*, computer-based applications that use a representation of human expertise in a specialized field of knowledge to solve problems. Expert systems can be used in many ways, including providing advice to nonexperts, providing assistance to experts, replacing experts, and serving as a training and development tool in organizations.[89] They are used in medical decision making, diagnosis, and medical informatics.[90] Anheuser-Busch has used an expert system to assist managers in ensuring that personnel decisions comply with antidiscrimination laws.[91]

Robots, another technological innovation, were invented in the United States, and advanced research on *robotics* is still conducted here. However, Japan leads the world in the use of robotics in organizations. Organizations in the United States have fewer total robots than were added in 1989 alone in Japan.[92] Robots in Japan are treated like part of the family. They are even

technology
The intellectual and mechanical processes used by an organization to transform inputs into products or services that meet organizational goals.

expert system
A computer-based application that uses a representation of human expertise in a specialized field of knowledge to solve problems.

robotics
The use of robots in organizations.

Sony . . . In English

Most geeks know that Tokyo's Akihabara district is the world's showcase for the newest, coolest, and sometimes weirdest technotoys from Japan. Frequently, Tokyo's technological innovations translate flawlessly into the U.S. market. But sometimes the translation from Japanese technological innovation into English is not so smooth. A marketing team at the American outpost of Sony's Video Audio Integrated Operations (VAIO) division is tasked with the responsibility of figuring out which Sony products fit into which category. This team translates Sony into English. One of their big challenges is a product dubbed the U, which is the smallest laptop computer in the world. Less than seven inches wide with a six-inch diagonal screen, the U makes an ordinary lap-

top look sumo-sized. The U is ideally designed for Japanese culture and the Japanese commuter. The only people in Tokyo who have the luxury of a lap when commuting are the first people on the train. So the U can be gripped at the base with two hands and the thumbs can rest on the keyboard, thus giving its users the experience of what might be called a "standing" computer. While the overwhelming emotional response of Americans to the U is "Wow," the question of its utilization is more challenging. Hence, another opportunity to translate Sony into English.

the U

SOURCE: D. McGray, "Translating Sony into English," *Fast Company* 66 (January 2003): 38, http://www.fastcompany.com/online/66/dispatches.html.

---

named after favorite celebrities, singers, and movie stars. Whereas Japanese workers are happy to let robots take over repetitive or dangerous work, Americans are more suspicious of labor-saving robots because employers often use them to cut jobs.[93] The main reason for the reluctance of U.S. organizations to use robots is their slow payout. Robotics represents a big investment that does not pay off in the short term. Japanese managers are more willing to use a long-term horizon to evaluate the effectiveness of robotics technology. Labor unions may also resist robotics because of the fear that robots will replace employees.

Some U.S. companies that experimented with robotics had bad experiences. Deere & Company originally used robots to paint its tractors, but the company scrapped them because programming the robots for the multitude of types of paint used took too long. Now Deere uses robots to torque cap screws on tractors, a repetitive job that once had a high degree of human error.

It is tempting to view technology from only the positive side; however, a little realism is in order. Some firms that have been disappointed with costly technologies are electing to *de*-engineer. And computer innovations often fail; 42 percent of information technology projects are abandoned before completion, and half of all technology projects fail to meet managers' expectations. Pacific Gas and Electric (part of PG&E Corporation) spent tens of millions of dollars on a new IBM-based system. Deregulation then hit the utility industry, and customers were permitted to choose among utility companies. Keeping up with multiple suppliers and fast-changing prices was too much, and the massive new system couldn't handle the additional burden quickly enough. It was scrapped in favor of a new project using the old first-generation computer system, which is being updated and gradually replaced. Because some innovations fail to live up to expectations, and some simply fail, it is important to effectively manage both revolutionary and evolutionary approaches to technological transitions.[94]

—tech. risk

6. Understand the alternative work arrangements produced by technological advances.

telecommuting

Transmitting work from a home computer to the office using a modem.

Technological advances have been responsible, to a large degree, for the advent of alternative work arrangements, the nontraditional work practices, settings, and locations that are now supplementing traditional workplaces. One alternative work arrangement is *telecommuting,* transmitting work from a home computer to the office using a modem. IBM, for example, was one of the first companies to experiment with the notion of installing computer terminals at employees' homes and having employees work at home. By telecommuting, employees gain flexibility, save the commute to work, and enjoy the comforts of being at home. Telecommuting also has disadvantages, however, including distractions, lack of opportunities to socialize with other workers, lack of interaction with supervisors, and decreased identification with the organization. Despite these disadvantages, telecommuters still feel "plugged in" to the communication system at the office. Studies show that telecommuters often report higher satisfaction with office communication than do workers in traditional office environments.[95]

Estimates are that about 28 million Americans are telecommuting. Why do companies encourage telecommuting? Cost reductions are an obvious motivator. Since 1991, AT&T has gained $550 million in cash flow from eliminating office space and reducing overhead costs. Another reason is to increase productivity. At IBM, a survey of telecommuters indicated that 87 percent believed they were more productive in the alternative work arrangement. Telecommuting also allows companies access to workers with key skills regardless of their locations. Alternative workplaces also give companies an advantage in hiring and keeping talented employees, who find the flexibility of working at home very attractive.

There is a spectrum of other alternative work arrangements. *Hoteling* is a shared-office arrangement wherein employees have mobile file cabinets and lockers for personal storage, and "hotel" work spaces are furnished for them. These spaces must be reserved instead of being permanently assigned. The computer system routes phone calls and e-mail as necessary. Individuals' personal photos and memorabilia are stored electronically and "placed" on occupants' computer desktops upon arrival.

Satellite offices comprise another alternative work arrangement. In such offices, large facilities are broken into a network of smaller workplaces that are located close to employees' homes. Satellites are often located in comparatively inexpensive cities and suburban areas. They usually have simpler and less costly furnishings and fixtures than the more centrally located offices. Satellites can save a company as much as 50 percent in real estate costs and can be quite attractive to employees who do not want to work in a large urban area. This can broaden the pool of potential employees, who can communicate with the home office via various technologies.[96]

All of these alternative work arrangements signal a trend toward *virtual offices,* in which people work anytime, anywhere, and with anyone. The concept involves work being where people are, rather than people moving to where the work is. Information technologies make connectivity, collaboration, and communication easy. Critical voice-mails and messages can be delivered to and from the central office, a client's office, the airport, the car, or home. Wireless Internet access and on-line meeting software such as WebEx make it possible for employees to participate in meetings anywhere at any time.

Emerging Managerial Realities

Technological innovation affects the very nature of the management job. Managers who once had to coax workers back to their desks from coffee breaks now find that they need to encourage workers mesmerized by new technology to take more frequent breaks.[97] Working with a computer can be stressful, both physically and psychologically. Eye strain, neck and back strain, and headaches can result from sitting at a computer terminal too long. In addition, workers can become accustomed to the fast response time of the computer and expect the same from their coworkers. When coworkers do not respond with the speed and accuracy of the computer, they may receive a harsh retort.

Computerized monitoring provides managers with a wealth of information about employee performance, and it holds great potential for misuse as mentioned earlier in this section. The telecommunications, airline, and mail-order merchandise industries make wide use of systems that secretly monitor employees' interactions with customers. Employers praise such systems because they improve customer service. Workers, however, are not so positive; they react with higher levels of depression, anxiety, and exhaustion from working under such secret scrutiny. At Bell Canada, operators were evaluated on a system that tabulated average working time with customers. Operators found the practice highly stressful, and they sabotaged the system by giving callers wrong directory assistance numbers rather than taking the time to look up the correct ones. As a result, Bell Canada now uses average working time scores for entire offices rather than for individuals.[98]

New technologies and rapid innovation place a premium on a manager's technical skills. Early management theories rated technical skills as less important than human and conceptual skill. This is past reality. Managers today must develop technical competence in order to gain workers' respect. Computer-integrated manufacturing systems, for example, have been shown to require managers to use participative management styles, open communication, and greater technical expertise to be effective.[99] In a world of rapid technological innovation, managers must focus more carefully on helping workers manage the stress of their work. They must take advantage of the wealth of information at their disposal to motivate, coach, and counsel workers rather than try to control them more stringently or police them. The management of intellectual property, however, cannot be left to technology managers or corporate lawyers.[100] Roughly 75 percent of *Fortune 100's* total market capitalization is in intangible assets, such as patents, copyrights, and trademarks. Managers and companies with well-conceived strategies and policies for their intellectual property can use it for competitive advantage in the global marketplace.

intellectual property

Technological change occurs so rapidly that turbulence characterizes most organizations. Workers must constantly learn and adapt to changing technology so that organizations can remain competitive. Managers must grapple with the challenge of helping workers adapt and make effective use of new technologies.

Helping Employees Adjust to Technological Change

Most workers are well aware of the benefits of modern technologies. The availability of skilled jobs and improved working conditions have been by-products of innovation in many organizations. Technology is also bringing disadvantaged individuals into the workforce. Microchips have dramatically increased opportunities for workers with visual impairments. Information can be decoded into speech using a speech synthesizer, into braille using a hard-copy printer, or into enlarged print visible on a computer monitor. Workers with visual impairments are no longer dependent on sighted persons to translate printed information for them, and this has opened new doors of opportunity.[101] Engineers at Carnegie Mellon University have developed PizzaBot, a robot that individuals with disabilities can operate using a voice-recognition system. Despite these and other benefits of new technology in the workplace, however, employees may still resist change.

Technological innovations bring about changes in employees' work environments, and change has been described as the ultimate stressor. Many workers react negatively to change that they perceive as threatening to their work situation. Many of their fears center around loss—of freedom, of control, of the things they like about their jobs.[102] Employees may fear deterioration of their quality of work life and increased pressure at work. Further, employees may fear being replaced by technology or being displaced into jobs of lower skill levels.

7. Explain the ways managers can help employees adjust to technological change.

Managers can take several actions to help employees adjust to changing technology. The workers' participation in early phases of the decision-making process regarding technological changes is important. Individuals who participate in planning for the implementation of new technology gain important information about the potential changes in their jobs; therefore, they are less resistant to the change. Workers are the users of the new technology. Their input in early stages can lead to a smoother transition into the new ways of performing work.

Managers should also keep in mind the effects that new technology has on the skill requirements of workers. Many employees support changes that increase the skill requirements of their jobs. Increased skill requirements often lead to increases in job autonomy, more responsibility, and potential pay increases, all of which are received positively by employees. Whenever possible, managers should select technology that increases workers' skill requirements.

Providing effective training about ways to use the new technology also is essential. Training helps employees perceive that they control the technology rather than being controlled by it. The training should be designed to match workers' needs, and it should increase the workers' sense of mastery of the new technology.

Support groups within the organization are another way of helping employees adjust to technological change. Technological change is stressful, and support groups are important emotional outlets for workers. Support groups can also function as information exchanges so that workers can share advice on using the technology. Workers feel less alone with the problem when they know that other workers share their frustration.

reinvention
The creative application of new technology.

A related challenge is to encourage workers to invent new uses for technology already in place. *Reinvention* is the term for creatively applying new technology.[103] Innovators should be rewarded for their efforts. Individuals who explore the boundaries of a new technology can personalize the technology and adapt it to their own job needs, as well as share this information with others in the work group. In one large public utility, service representatives (without their supervisor's knowledge) developed a personal note-passing system that later became the basis of a formal communication system that improved the efficiency of their work group.

Managers face a substantial challenge in leading organizations to adopt new technologies more humanely and effectively. Technological changes are essential for earnings growth and for expanded employment opportunities. The adoption of new technologies is a critical determinant of U.S. competitiveness in the global marketplace.

Managerial Implications: Beating the Challenges

Organizational success depends on managers' ability to address the challenges of globalization, workforce diversity, ethics, and technological innovation. Failure to address the challenges can be costly. Think about Pepsi's losses to Coke in the global cola wars. Coke is winning the battle and capitalizing on the huge opportunities and profits from global markets. A racial discrimination lawsuit against Texaco not only cost the company millions in a settlement but also damaged the company's reputation. Mitsubishi suffered a similar fate in a sexual harassment scandal. Failure to address these challenges can mean costly losses, damage to reputations, and ultimately an organization's demise.

These four challenges are important because the way managers handle them shapes employee behavior. Developing global mindsets among employees expands their worldview and puts competition on a larger scale. Knowing that diversity is valued and differences are assets causes employees to think twice about engaging in behaviors that are discriminatory. Valuing technological change leads employees to experiment with new technologies and develop innovative ways to perform their jobs. Sending a message that unethical behavior is not tolerated lets employees know that doing the right thing pays off.

These four challenges are recurring themes that you will see throughout our book. We show you how companies are tackling these challenges and how organizational behavior can be used to create opportunity in organizations, which is a must if they are to remain competitive.

LOOKING BACK: PIXAR ANIMATION STUDIOS
The Dream Becomes Reality

Rather than moving forward in frustration given the limits of his drawing abilities, Ed Catmull turned in a new direction. He enrolled in the University of Utah's computer science program. His classmates included Jim Clark, John Warnock, and others who became the forefront of a revolution in computer graphics. Clark went on to become founder of Silicon Graphics and Netscape, while Warnock founded Adobe Systems. Catmull was in the midst of this hotbed of change, challenge, and exciting times. He ultimately earned his Ph.D. and ran a research laboratory before landing at Lucasfilm in 1979. That was the time in which *Star Wars* was a recent phenomenon and George Lucas had recognized the value of computer-generated special effects. From Lucasfilm, Catmull truly began coming home to his dream of being an animator. Steve Jobs bought Lucasfilm's computer division for $10 million in 1986, and Catmull became one of the cofounders of a new, stand-alone company christened Pixar. Over the decades, Pixar has forged an innovative culture and distinctive competence.[104]

Embedding a culture of innovation in a fantasy industry can be a challenge in itself. When asked about whether he was concerned that others were stealing his ideas early on, Walt Disney responded by saying that he could create ideas faster than others could steal them. Disney planned to stay ahead of the curve. So, too, with Pixar; it stays ahead of the curve. Pixar recognizes that as soon as you are successful, competitors jump on the bandwagon. And, imitators can do a great job of replicating cutting-edge creations. Therefore, Pixar treats every one of its movie creations as a stepping stone on a positive learning curve in which it learns what works and what does not work. Pixar wants to be a stepping stone for itself, benefiting from its own learning, rather than a stepping stone for others who would aspire to climb over Pixar in their own ascent.

Pixar's distinctive competence lies in its creation of a variety of original software programs and wealth of technical wizardry. It is the only major studio working exclusively in computer-generated animation. Pixar's program can model surface textures, such as metal, cloth, or hair, and create lighting effects, such as bright sunlight or flickering candlelight. The studio's RenderMan program captures all the data and helps artists create the final images. RenderMan won an Academy Award for technical achievement in 2001. More than bells and whistles, Pixar has distinctive competence in the good stories that emerge from its movie scripts; that is the foundation of its business.

Chapter Summary

1. To ensure that their organizations meet the competition, managers must tackle four important challenges: globalization, workforce diversity, ethical behavior, and technological change at work.

2. The five cultural differences that affect work-related attitudes are individualism versus collectivism, power distance, uncertainty avoidance, masculinity versus femininity, and time orientation.

3. Diversity encompasses gender, culture, personality, sexual orientation, religion, ability, social status, and a host of other differences.

4. Managers must take a proactive approach to managing diversity so that differences are valued and capitalized upon.

5. Three types of ethical theories include consequential theories, rule-based theories, and character theories.

6. Ethical dilemmas emerge for people at work in the areas of employee rights, sexual harassment, romantic involvements, organizational justice, whistle-blowing, and social responsibility.

7. Alternative work arrangements, facilitated by technology, are changing the way work is performed.

8. Through supportive relationships and training, managers can help employees adjust to technological change.

Key Terms

character theory (p. 53)

collectivism (p. 40)

consequential theory (p. 53)

distributive justice (p. 57)

diversity (p. 45)

expatriate manager (p. 42)

expert system (p. 60)

femininity (p. 41)

glass ceiling (p. 47)

guanxi (p. 38)

individualism (p. 40)

masculinity (p. 41)

power distance (p. 40)

procedural justice (p. 57)

reinvention (p. 64)

robotics (p. 60)   technology (p. 60)   transnational organization (p. 37)
rule-based theory (p. 53)   telecommuting (p. 62)   uncertainty avoidance (p. 41)
social responsibility (p. 58)   time orientation (p. 41)   whistle-blower (p. 57)

Review Questions

1. What are Hofstede's five dimensions of cultural differences that affect work attitudes? Using these dimensions, describe the United States.

2. What are the primary sources of diversity in the U.S. workforce?

3. What are the potential benefits and problems of diversity?

4. What is the reality of the glass ceiling? What would it take to change this reality?

5. What are some of the ethical challenges encountered in organizations?

6. Describe the difference between distributive and procedural justice.

7. Why do employees fear technological innovations, and how can managers help employees adjust?

Discussion and Communication Questions

1. How can managers be encouraged to develop global thinking? How can managers dispel stereotypes about other cultures?

2. Some people have argued that in designing expert systems, human judgment is made obsolete. What do you think?

3. Why do some companies encourage alternative work arrangements?

4. What effects will the globalization of business have on a company's culture? How can an organization with a strong "made in America" identity compete in the global marketplace?

5. Why is diversity such an important issue? Is the workforce more diverse today than in the past?

6. How does a manager strike a balance between encouraging employees to celebrate their own cultures and forming a single unified culture within the organization?

7. Do you agree with Hofstede's findings about U.S. culture? Other cultures? On what do you base your agreement or disagreement?

8. (*communication question*) Select one of the four challenges (globalization, diversity, ethics, technology) and write a brief position paper arguing for its importance to managers.

9. (*communication question*) Find someone whose culture is different from your own. This might be a classmate, an international student, or a Native American at your university. Interview the person about his or her culture, using Hofstede's dimensions. Also ask what you might need to know about doing business in the person's country (e.g., customs, etiquette). Be prepared to share this information in class.

Ethical Dilemma

Jill Warner, President of Ace Toys, sat looking at the monthly profit and loss statement. For the fifth month in a row, the company had lost money. Labor costs were killing them. Jill had done everything she could think of to reduce costs and still produce a quality product. She was beginning to face the fact that soon she would no longer be able to avoid the idea of out-sourcing. It was a concept that Jill had done everything to avoid, but it was beginning to look inevitable.

Jill felt strongly about making a quality American product using American workers in an American factory. But if things continued the way they were, she was going to have to do something. She owed it to her stockholders and board of directors to keep the company financially healthy. They had entrusted her with the future of the company, and she could not let them down. It was not her money or company to do with as she pleased. Her job was to make sure that Ace Toys flourished.

However, if she chose to outsource the production segment of the company, only management and the sales force would keep their jobs. How could she face the 500 people who would lose their jobs? How would the small community that depended on those 500 jobs survive? She also worried about the customers who had come to depend on Ace Toys to produce a safe product that they could give to their children with confidence. Would that quality suffer if she sent production halfway around the world? How could she ensure that the company she hired to produce their toys would live up to Ace's standards? Would the other company pay a fair wage and not employ children? The questions seemed endless, but Jill needed to decide how to save the company.

Questions

1. Is sending jobs out of the country unethical?

2. Using rule, virtue, right, and justice theories, evaluate Jill's options.

Experiential Exercises

2.1 International Orientations

1. Preparation (preclass)
Read the background on the International Orientation Scale and the case study "Office Supplies International—Marketing Associate," complete the ratings and questions, and fill out the self-assessment inventory.

2. Group Discussions
Groups of four to six people discuss their answers to the case study questions and their own responses to the self-assessment.

3. Class Discussion
Instructor leads a discussion on the International Orientation Scale and the difficulties and challenges of adjusting to a new culture. Why do some people adjust more easily than others? What can you do to adjust to a new culture? What can you regularly do that will help you adjust in the future to almost any new culture?

Office Supplies International—Marketing Associate*
Jonathan Fraser is a marketing associate for a large multinational corporation, Office Supplies International (OSI), in Buffalo, New York. He is being considered for a transfer to the international division of OSI. This position will require that he spend between one and three years working abroad in one of OSI's three foreign subsidiaries: OSI-France, OSI-Japan, or OSI-Australia. This transfer is considered a fast track career move at OSI, and Jonathan feels honored to be in the running for the position.

Jonathan has been working at OSI since he graduated with his bachelor's degree in marketing ten years ago. He is married and has lived and worked in Buffalo all his life. Jonathan's parents are first-generation German Americans. His grandparents, although deceased, spoke only German at home and upheld many of their ethnic traditions. His parents, although quite "Americanized," have retained some of their German traditions. To communicate better with his grandparents, Jonathan took German in high school but never used it because his grandparents had passed away.

In college, Jonathan joined the German Club and was a club officer for two years. His other collegiate extracurricular activity was playing for the varsity baseball team. Jonathan still enjoys playing in a summer softball league with his college friends. Given his athletic interests, he volunteered to be the athletic programming coordinator at OSI, where he organizes the company's softball and volleyball teams. Jonathan has been making steady progress at OSI. Last year, he was named marketing associate of the year.

His wife, Sue, is also a Buffalo native. She teaches English literature at the high school in one of the middle-class suburbs of Buffalo. Sue took five years off from teaching after she had a baby but returned to teaching this year when Janine, their five-year-old daughter, started kindergarten. She is happy to be resuming her career. One or two nights a week, Sue volunteers at the city mission where she works as a career counselor and a basic skills trainer. For fun, she takes both pottery and ethnic cooking classes.

Both Sue and Jonathan are excited about the potential transfer and accompanying pay raise. They are, however, also feeling apprehensive and cautious. Neither Sue nor Jonathan has ever lived away from their families in Buffalo, and Sue is concerned about giving up her newly reestablished career. Their daughter Janine has just started school, and Jonathan and Sue are uncertain whether living abroad is the best thing for her at her age.

Using the following three-point scale, try to rate Jonathan and Sue as potential expatriates. Write a sentence or two on why you gave the ratings you did.

Rating Scale

1. Based on this dimension, this person would adjust well to living abroad.

2. Based on this dimension, this person may or may not adjust well to living abroad.

3. Based on this dimension, this person would not adjust well to living abroad.

Jonathan's International Orientation

rating dimension	rating and reason for rating
International attitudes	
Foreign experiences	
Comfort with differences	
Participation in cultural events	

Sue's International Orientation

rating dimension	rating and reason for rating
International attitudes	
Foreign experiences	
Comfort with differences	
Participation in cultural events	

Discussion Questions: Office Supplies International

1. Imagine that you are the international human resource manager for OSI. Your job is to interview both Jonathan and Sue to determine whether they should be sent abroad. What are some of the questions you would ask? What critical information do you feel is missing? It might be helpful to role-play the three parts and evaluate your classmates' responses as Jonathan and Sue.

2. Suppose France is the country where they would be sent. To what extent would your ratings change? What else would you change about the way you are assessing the couple?

3. Now answer the same questions, except this time they are being sent to Japan. Repeat the exercise for Australia.

4. For those dimensions that you rated Sue and Jonathan either 2 or 3 (indicating that they might have a potential adjustment problem), what would you suggest for training and development? What might be included in a training program?

5. Reflect on your own life for a moment and give yourself a rating on each of the following dimensions. Try to justify why you rated yourself as you did. Do you feel that you would adjust well to living abroad? What might be difficult for you?

rating dimension	rating and reason for rating France, Japan, Australia (or other)
International attitudes	
Foreign experiences	
Comfort with differences	
Participation in cultural events	

6. Generally, what are some of the potential problems a dual-career couple might face? What are some of the solutions to those problems?

7. How would the ages of children affect the expatriate's assignment? At what age should the children's international orientations be assessed along with their parents?

International Orientation Scale

The following sample items are taken from the International Orientation Scale. Answer each question and give yourself a score for each dimension. The highest possible score for any dimension is 20 points.

Dimension 1: International Attitudes

Use the following scale to answer questions Q1 through Q4.

1	*Strongly agree*
2	*Agree somewhat*
3	*Maybe or unsure*
4	*Disagree somewhat*
5	*Strongly disagree*

Q1. Foreign language skills should be taught as early as elementary school. _____

Q2. Traveling the world is a priority in my life. _____

Q3. A year-long overseas assignment (from my company) would be a fantastic opportunity for my family and me. _____

Q4. Other countries fascinate me. _____

Total Dimension 1 _____

Dimension 2: Foreign Experiences

Q1. I have studied a foreign language.

1	Never
2	For less than a year
3	For a year
4	For a few years
5	For several years

Q2. I am fluent in another language.

1	I don't know another language.
2	I am limited to very short and simple phrases.
3	I know basic grammatical structure and speak with a limited vocabulary.
4	I understand conversation on most topics.
5	I am very fluent in another language.

Q3. I have spent time overseas (traveling, studying abroad, etc.).

1	Never
2	About a week
3	A few weeks
4	A few months
5	Several months or years

Q4. I was overseas before the age of 18.

1	Never
2	About a week
3	A few weeks
4	A few months
5	Several months or years

Total Dimension 2 _____

Dimension 3: Comfort with Differences

Use the following scale for questions Q1 through Q4.

1	*Quite similar*
2	*Mostly similar*
3	*Somewhat different*
4	*Quite different*
5	*Extremely different*

Q1. My friends' career goals, interests, and education are . . . _____

Q2. My friends' ethnic backgrounds are . . . _____

Q3. My friends' religious affiliations are . . . _____

Q4. My friends' first languages are . . . _____

Total Dimension 3 _____

Dimension 4: Participation in Cultural Events

Use the following scale to answer questions Q1 through Q4.

1	*Never*
2	*Seldom*
3	*Sometimes*
4	*Frequently*
5	*As often as possible*

Q1. I eat at a variety of ethnic restaurants (e.g., Greek, Polynesian, Thai, German). _____

Q2. I watch the major networks' world news programs. _____

Q3. I attend ethnic festivals. _____

Q4. I visit art galleries and museums. _____

Total Dimension 4 _____

Self-Assessment Discussion Questions:

Do any of these scores suprise you?

Would you like to improve your international orientation?

If so, what could you do to change various aspects of your life?

*"Office Supplies International—Marketing Associate" by Paula Caligiuri. Copyright © 1994 by Paula Caligiuri, Ph.D. Information for The International Orientation Scale can be obtained by contacting Paula Caligiuri, Ph.D. at 732-445-5228 or e-mail: paula@caligiuri.com. Reprinted by permission of the author.

Dorothy Marcic and Sheila Puffer, Management International, West Publishing, 1994. *All rights reserved. May not be reproduced without written permission of the publisher.*

2.2 Ethical Dilemmas

Divide the class into five groups. Each group should choose one of the following scenarios and agree on a course of action.

1. Sam works for you. He is technically capable and a good worker, but he does not get along well with others in the work group. When Sam has an opportunity to transfer, you encourage him to take it. What would you say to Sam's potential supervisor when he asks about Sam?

2. Your boss has told you that you must reduce your work group by 30 percent. Which of the following criteria would you use to lay off workers?

   a. Lay off older, higher paid employees.
   b. Lay off younger, lower paid employees.
   c. Lay off workers based on seniority only.
   d. Lay off workers based on performance only.

3. You are an engineer, but you are not working on your company's Department of Transportation (DOT) project. One day you overhear a conversation in the cafeteria between the program manager and the project engineer that makes you reasonably sure a large contract will soon be given to the ABC Company to develop and manufacture a key DOT subsystem. ABC is a small firm, and its stock is traded over the counter. You feel sure that the stock will rise from its present $2.25 per share as soon as news of the DOT contract gets out. Would you go out and buy ABC's stock?

4. You are the project engineer working on the development of a small liquid rocket engine. You know that if you could achieve a throttling ratio greater than 8 to 1, your system would be considered a success and continue to receive funding support. To date, the best you have achieved is a 4 to 1 ratio. You have an unproven idea that you feel has a 50 percent chance of being successful. Your project is currently being reviewed to determine if it should be continued. You would like to continue it. How optimistically should you present the test results?

5. Imagine that you are the president of a company in a highly competitive industry. You learn that a competitor has made an important scientific discovery that is not patentable and will give that company an advantage that will substantially reduce the profits of your company for about a year. There is some hope of hiring one of the competitor's employees who knows the details of the discovery. Would you try to hire this person?

Each group should present its scenario and chosen course of action to the class. The class should then evaluate the ethics of the course of action, using the following questions to guide discussion:

1. Are you following rules that are understood and accepted?

2. Are you comfortable discussing and defending your action?

3. Would you want someone to do this to you?

4. What if everyone acted this way?

5. Are there alternatives that rest on firmer ethical ground?

Scenarios adapted from R. A. DiBattista, "Providing a Rationale for Ethical Conduct from Alternatives Taken in Ethical Dilemmas." *Journal of General Psychology* 116 (1989): 207–214; discussion questions adapted with the permission of The Free Press, a Division of Simon & Schuster, Inc. from *The Manager as Negotiator: Bargaining for Cooperation and Competitive Gain* by David A. Lax and James K. Sebenius 0-02-918770-2. Copyright © 1986 by David A. Lax and James K. Sebenius.

Biz Flix | Mr. Baseball

The New York Yankees trade aging baseball player Jack Elliot (Tom Selleck) to the Chunichi Dragons, a Japanese team. This lighthearted comedy traces Jack's bungling entry into Japanese culture and exposes his cultural misconceptions, which almost cost him everything—including his new girlfriend Hiroko Uchiyama (Aya Takanashi). Unknown to Jack, Hiroko's father is "The Chief" (Ken Takakura), the Chunichi Dragons' manager. After Jack slowly begins to understand Japanese culture and Japanese baseball, his teammates finally accept him. This film shows many examples of Japanese culture, especially its love for baseball.

The *Mr. Baseball* scene takes place after "The Chief" has removed Jack from a baseball game. It shows Jack dining with Hiroko and her grandmother (Mineko Yorozuya), grandfather (Jun Hamamura), and father. The film continues with a dispute between Jack and Hiroko. Jack also learns from "The Chief" what he must do to succeed on the team.

What to Watch for and Ask Yourself:

> Does Jack Elliot behave as if he had cross-cultural training before arriving in Japan?

> Is he culturally sensitive or insensitive?

> What do you propose that Jack Elliot do for the rest of his time in Japan?

Workplace Video | Merrill Lynch: Telecommuting

Merrill Lynch & Co., Inc., is a holding company that provides investment banking, financing, insurance, financial advice, and related products and services on a global basis. The company serves an array of clients including individual investors, small businesses, corporations, financial institutions, and government agencies.

In the mid-1990s, Merrill Lynch found itself battling low employee morale and high turnover rates. Information-technology workers and other employees at the New York-based investment-services firm were leaving to work for popular businesses such as Cisco and Sun Microsystems. Executives assessed the situation and decided to implement a controversial new solution called telecommuting, a work arrangement that enables employees to work at home and transmit information to the office using a modem. Worker surveys conducted at Merrill Lynch had discovered that employees wanted the option to work from home, and in response, the company set up an Alternative Work Arrangement Department to manage its new telecommuting program. Thousands of employees signed up for the program, and within one year the company saw a 30 percent increase in its worker satisfaction rating. In addition, worker productivity began to rise and the company started reaping enormous savings due to office-space reductions and shrinking overhead costs.

Since the 1990s, telecommuting has evolved into an enormously popular work arrangement for many businesses. The number of telecommuters in the U.S. today is estimated to be about 28 million. Furthermore, analysts expect that the boundaries of the traditional office will continue to expand outward as wireless and broadband technologies create even more possibilities for the telework revolution. For employees at Merrill Lynch and other companies around the world, setting up an office at home or in other remote locations is no longer a wistful dream—it's a reality.

Questions

1. *Why does Janice Miholics of the AWA Department at Merrill Lynch say that that the traditional work environment is about "face time" and that telecommuting is a "leap of faith" for employers?*
2. *List at least five benefits telecommuting offers to employees.*
3. *List at least five benefits telecommuting offers to employers.*

Growth Challenges for Harley-Davidson

In 1903, William Harley and Arthur Davidson produced the first Harley-Davidson motorcycle for sale to the public. Manufactured in a wooden shed, measuring 150 square feet, the first year's production was just three motorcycles. The first Harley-Davidson dealer, C.H. Lang of Chicago, Illinois, sold one of these three motorcycles

From these humble beginnings, Harley-Davidson grew rapidly to become the largest motorcycle manufacturer in the world by the early 1920s. The company's dealer network exploded as well. In 1920, over 2,000 dealers in 67 countries worldwide sold new Harley-Davidson motorcycles. By the 1930s, nearly all of Harley-Davidson's American competition was gone. During World War II, Harley-Davidson suspended nearly all production of civilian motorcycles in order to produce motorcycles for the military. However, once the war ended, the company quickly converted back to production for the civilian market.

In subsequent decades Harley-Davidson continued to grow, both domestically and internationally. This growth was fueled in part through acquisitions. Some of these acquisitions enabled Harley-Davidson to capitalize on new technologies. For instance, in the early 1960s Harley-Davidson acquired a significant position in the Tomahawk Boat Manufacturing Company in recognition of the increasing relevance of fiberglass components in motorcycle manufacturing. In 1969, Harley-Davidson merged with American Machine and Foundry (AMF).

Over the years, other competitors—many from overseas—entered the American marketplace. The early 1970s marked the beginning of a decade of transition in the American motorcycle industry that nearly resulted in the demise of Harley-Davidson. However, in 1981 Harley-Davidson senior executives bought the company from the AMF corporate owners. The new owners proceeded to turn Harley-Davidson around in a dramatic fashion. Product innovations that demonstrated a new commitment to quality were initiated. Production methods were refined and streamlined.

In 1983, two events occurred that played significant roles in Harley-Davidson's future success. One event was the receipt of tariff relief from the International Trade Commission on all imported Japanese motorcycles with engines 700cc or larger. This relief was in response to Japanese motorcycle manufacturers stockpiling unsold motorcycles in the United States. Then in 1987, Harley-Davidson made business and American history by petitioning "the International Trade Commission for early termination of the five-year tariffs on heavyweight motorcycles." Harley-Davidson was confident in its ability to compete effectively in the international marketplace.

The formation of the Harley Owners Group® (H.O.G.) was the second event that played a significant role in Harley-Davidson's success after 1983. This was one of the company's most unique endeavors. H.O.G. organized rallies and other riding activities for its members. These clubs were responsible for transforming motorcycling into a family-oriented social sport. According to the company's 2003 annual report, there were 840,000 proud members and 1,370 H.O.G. chapters worldwide.

Harley-Davidson has a loyal customer base. In 2000, 45 percent of the Harley-Davidson purchasers were previous Harley-Davidson owners. Another 30 percent switched to Harleys from competitive brands, and the remaining 25 percent had not owned a motorcycle in the preceding five years or were new to motorcycling.

While Harley-Davidson has a loyal customer base, the composition of that base has been changing. From the late 1980s to the late 1990s, the number of female Harley customers more than tripled, the median age of purchasers rose by almost 10 years (from 34.7 to 44.4), and the median income almost doubled (from $38,400 to $73,600). In 2002, the average annual income of Harley-Davidson customers was $78,000, and about 9 percent of the customer base consisted of women.

Harley-Davidson's core business is the heavyweight highway motorcycle. It had 48 percent of the United States market share in 2003, up from 12.5 percent in 1983. However, this is not the type of motorcycle that appeals to 25- to 34-year old men. This market segment seems to prefer sleeker, sportier motorcycles—and it is a market segment that Harley-Davidson must consider in terms of future growth. Harley-Davidson's continued success in the future is likely to be influenced by its ability to adapt to changing market preferences.

Since Harley-Davidson's initial public offering of stock in 1986, the company has had record revenues and earnings in each of the following 18 years. In 2003, consolidated revenue was $4.62 billion, a 13 percent increase over the previous year, and net income was $760.9 million, a 31.1 percent increase from 2002. This record-setting trend seems to be continuing. In the first quarter of 2004, for instance, the company's U.S. dealer network reported a historic high first-quarter sales of motorcycles.

According to Harley-Davidson's 2003 annual report, this sustained record performance is attributable to the company's ability to bring new products to market, attract new customers, retain existing customers, and responsibly expand capacity. "Harley-Davidson has established a goal to create and fulfill the demand for 400,000 motorcycles in 2007." To stimulate this demand, the company is developing new motorcycles that have the "classic Harley-Davidson look, sound, and feel." The company is also expanding its manufacturing capacity.

Will Harley-Davidson be able to achieve the goal of creating and fulfilling the demand for 400,000 motorcycles in 2007, given the changing nature of the motorcycle market?

Discussion Questions

1. How can Hofstede's dimensions of cultural differences help Harley-Davidson understand the challenges the company may face in pursuing global growth?
2. How might technology affect Harley-Davidson's competitive position in the global marketplace?
3. How is diversity affecting the growth of Harley-Davidson's business?
4. What ethical challenges do you think Harley-Davidson is likely to encounter as it further develops its presence in the global marketplace?

SOURCE: This case was written by Michael K. McCuddy, The Louis S. and Mary L. Morgal Chair of Christian Business Ethics and Professor of Management, College of Business Administration, Valparaiso University. This case was developed from material contained on the Harley-Davidson, Inc., Web site at http://www.harley-davidson.com and in the following articles: "Harley 1, Wall Street 0," *Dealernews* (May 2004): 52; J. Heylar, "Will Harley-Davidson Hit the Wall?" *Fortune* (August 12, 2002): accessed on http://www.fortune.com; and J. Perry, M. Lavelle, and M. Barnett, "Made in America," *U.S. News & World Report* (May 17, 2004): 50–53.

Google™ (A)

Google Inc., is a privately held and highly profitable company. As one of the most successful startup companies to come out of California's Silicon Valley, Brin and Page decided to take the company public, filing a registration with the U.S. Securities and Exchange Commission on April 29, 2004, for an initial public offering (IPO) of the company's stock.

The company's name is a play on the word *googol*, which is the number 1 followed by 100 zeros. "Google's use of the term reflects the company's mission to organize the immense, seemingly infinite amount of information available on the Web." The driving passion behind Google is to organize the world's information and to make it universally accessible and useful.

The Founding of Google

Sergey Brin and Larry Page founded Google when they were doctoral students in computer science at Stanford University. Brin and Page collaborated on a research project that took "a unique approach to solving one of computing's biggest challenges: retrieving relevant information from a massive set of data." Their research project involved the development of a search engine named *BackRub*, which had a unique approach to analyzing links to a web site. Brin and Page broke away from the common practice of designing a search engine to focus on the frequency with which a given word appeared on a web site. Instead of this approach, they developed a search engine that reflected both the relevance of a web site to a search query and the number of other web pages that are linked to that particular site.

BackRub, in conjunction with the use of many low-end personal computers linked together, provided the foundation for what would eventually become Google Inc. Initially, Brin and Page were not interested in founding a company based on the technology they had developed. Rather, they were looking for partners who had an interest in licensing their technology. Rebuffed by potential partners—including friend and Yahoo! founder David Filo—Brin and Page soon decided to go into business on their own.

They suspended their graduate studies, developed a business plan, and sought investment capital. Andy Bechtolsheim, a founder of Sun Microsystems, was impressed with Brin and Page's product demonstration and immediately wrote a check for $100,000 to Google Inc. Unfortunately, Brin and Page could not cash the check, as they had not yet established Google as a legal entity. The check sat in a desk for a couple of weeks as Page and Brin scrambled to incorporate Google. On September 7, 1998, Google Inc., opened for business in Menlo Park, California.

Google's Rapid Growth

The company grew rapidly, and by February 1999, the search engine was handling more than a half-million queries a day. Google continued its exponential growth as its "features and performance attracted new users at an astounding rate." Google quickly outgrew its Menlo Park location, moved to an office in Palo Alto, and then settled at its present headquarters location—the Googleplex in Mountain View, California. By June 2000, Google averaged 18 million user queries per day, and by the end of 2000, usage had exploded to more than 100 million search queries per day. By the first quarter of 2004, this had grown to a daily rate of more than 200 million searches of 6 billion web pages—this represents 138,000 queries every minute of every day in approximately 90 languages around the globe.

In a few short years, Google has worked itself into the position of providing what is widely recognized as the world's best Internet search engine. As of mid-2004, Google has become one of the five most popular sites on the Internet, being used by millions of people around the world. More than half of Google's user traffic is outside the United States, and there are almost 82 million unique global users per month. Google provides an interface in 97 languages and gives results in 35 languages. Google is the most popular search engine in Australia, France, Germany, Italy, the Netherlands, Spain, Switzerland, and the United Kingdom. Through its partnerships with companies such as America Online and Netscape, Google answers more queries than any other on-line service.

As Google grew, it developed alliances and partnerships with various companies. Chief among these partnerships were financing from venture capitalists, but there were numerous others as well. In June 2000, Google and Yahoo! announced their partnership wherein Google's search technology was licensed to Yahoo! Similar agreements soon followed with major Internet portals in China and Japan. Partnerships were also developed with Universo Online in Latin America and Lycos Korea. At about the same time, Google acquired Deja.com and integrated the Internet's largest Usenet archive into a searchable format.

Generating Revenue

Although Google attracted substantial amounts of investment capital as it grew, the company had yet to establish any substantive way to generate revenues in its first couple of years of operation. Under increasing pressure from the company's board of directors, Brin and Page recruited Eric Schmidt in 2001 to be Google's chief executive officer. Schmidt was charged with providing the organizational and operational expertise and leadership for Google, while Brin and Page provided the engineering, technological, and product development leadership.

A significant aspect of Schmidt's role was to help grow the business by building the necessary corporate infrastructure and ensuring that product quality remained high while product development cycle times were minimized. With Schmidt's help and guidance, Google developed and marketed several revenue generating ventures. These include the following: a web-based advertising program called *Google AdWords for Advertisers*; a service called *Google AdSense* that places relevant advertisements on search result and content pages; a service called *Google Search Services* that enables web site publishers to provide Google web and site search on their own web pages; technology known as *The Google Search Appliance* that enables search across an individual web site or intranet; and the delivery of Google search results on mobile devices through *Google Wireless Services*.

While the Google search engine remains a free service to users, the company's revenue generating ventures have become quite lucrative. In its April 29, 2004, filing with the Securities and Exchange Commission, Google reported net income of $105.6 million on revenue of $961.9 million for calendar year 2003. The unaudited figures for the first quarter of 2004 were $389.6 million in revenue and $64.0 million in net income. These figures compare to revenue of $220,000 and a loss of $6.1 million in calendar year 1998, when Google was founded.

Google's Future

Google seems to be well-positioned for future success. According to Piper Jaffray analyst Safia Rashtchy, Google had about one-fourth of the search industry's $4 billion annual revenue in 2003. Annual industry revenue is expected to triple to $12 billion by 2008. Simply maintaining its market position would enable Google to expand revenues to $3 billion over this time period.

However, AOL, eBay, and Amazon, among others, are expected to compete for some of Google's advertising revenues. Moreover, search engine competition from Yahoo! and Microsoft will likely become quite intense. Yahoo! has been a licensee of Google's search technology but has invested more than $1 billion, including the acquisition of Inktomi and Overture Service, both reputable search engine companies, in a bid to compete directly with Google. Microsoft is developing for release in 2006 a new operating system that contains a richer search engine than Google's current search engine. Microsoft's incursion into search engine technology could have serious implications for Google's popularity and growth in the future.

In 2004, Google reached an important juncture in its development and corporate history. On April 29, 2004, Google filed documents with the Securities and Exchange Commission of the United States for its initial public offering (IPO) of stock. As of the time this case was written, Google announced that its stock would be listed on NASDAQ but had not announced a date for the actual IPO auction of Google shares.

Even though the company is going public, Brin and Page have designed a dual-class voting structure for post-IPO ownership that would leave them in control, thereby enabling them to continue to operate Google as they have since its founding.

Brin, Page, and Schmidt believe that Google will rise to any future challenges it encounters because of two competitive advantages: surprise and innovation.

Discussion Questions

1. What can a potential entrepreneur learn from Sergey Brin and Larry Page?
2. What lessons about leading and managing organizations does Google provide?
3. Which of the organizational challenges—globalization; managing a diverse workforce; technological innovation; and ethics, character, and personal integrity—are likely to have the greatest impact on Google's future operations? Explain your answer.

SOURCE: This case was written by Michael K. McCuddy, The Louis S. and Mary L. Morgal Chair of Christian Business Ethics and Professor of Management, College of Business Administration, Valparaiso University. This case was developed from material contained on the Google Inc., web site at http://www.google.com and in the following articles: *Form S-1 Registration Statement Under The Securities Act of 1933: Google Inc.* (April 29, 2004): accessed at http://sec.gov/Archives/edgar/data/1288776/00011931250407339/ds1.htm; S. Levy, "Next Frontiers: All Eyes on Google," *Newsweek* (March 29, 2004): 48–50, 52, 54–56, 58; and F. Vogelstein, "Can Google Grow Up? Google Is One of the Best Things to Happen to the Net. So Will Its IPO, Expected This Spring, Be a Must-Buy? A Look Inside Reveals a Talented Company Facing Trouble," *Fortune* (December 8, 2003): accessed at http://www.fortune.com.

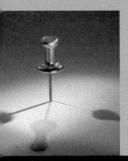

PART 2

Individual Processes and Behavior

© Reuters/CORBIS

Chapter 3

Personality, Perception, and Attribution

THINKING AHEAD: THE COCA-COLA COMPANY

Managing Perceptions from the Beginning

The history of The Coca-Cola Company is a story of perception, misperception, and shaped perception. Coke was devised in 1886 by John Pemberton, a pharmacist, who developed it as a potential headache remedy. His customers perceived it as something good to drink, headache or not. Sadly, Pemberton was unable to recognize Coke's potential, since it did not fit his perspective as a pharmacist. He soon sold the business for less than $3,000.

By the 1890s, Asa Candler became Coke's best salesperson, and by putting the familiar logo everywhere, he quickly grew the drink into a national brand. Unfortunately, Candler's perception of Coke was as a fountain drink, so when he was approached with the idea of putting it in bottles, he showed little interest. In 1899, he sold the rights to bottle Coke to two attorneys for the grand price of $1.

Coke first began managing perceptions of its product around the turn of the twentieth century. As copycat colas glutted the market, Coke moved to ensure its product's distinctiveness. In 1915, it moved from the traditional straight-sided bottle to its distinctive patented "contour" bottle design. Almost a century later, this unique shape is still associated with Coke; around the world, the unique curved bottle is perceived as signifying the original Coca-Cola.

Robert Woodruff led The Coca-Cola Company for almost sixty years, beginning in 1923. Whereas others saw soft drinks as something to be enjoyed occasionally, Woodruff was so intent on making Coke a part of American daily life that he actually sent armies of women door to door, installing Coke-branded bottle openers in American homes so housewives could more easily open the newly developed six-packs. Woodruff was also a visionary in perceiving the entire globe as his potential market, rather than just the United States. In an era when most American firms never looked abroad, Coke became one of the first worldwide brands.

Perhaps Coke's best-known television commercial was released in 1971, as young people from around the world gathered on a hilltop in Italy to sing, "I'd like to buy the world a Coke." By associating itself with the young people of the '60s and '70s, Coke helped create the perception that it was the drink for their generation.

In the Looking Back feature, we'll see how Coke handled an innovation that could have changed the perceptions of its customers for the worse.[1]

Individual Differences and Organizational Behavior

1. Describe individual differences and their importance in understanding behavior.

individual differences
The way in which factors such as skills, abilities, personalities, perceptions, attitudes, values, and ethics differ from one individual to another.

In this chapter and continuing in Chapter 4, we explore the concept of *individual differences*. Individuals are unique in terms of their skills, abilities, personalities, perceptions, attitudes, values, and ethics. These are just a few of the ways individuals may be similar to or different from one another. Individual differences represent the essence of the challenge of management, because no two individuals are completely alike. Managers face the challenge of working with people who possess a multitude of individual characteristics, so the more managers understand individual differences, the better they can work with others. Figure 3.1 illustrates how individual differences affect human behavior.

3.1 FIGURE 3.1   Variables Influencing Individual Behavior

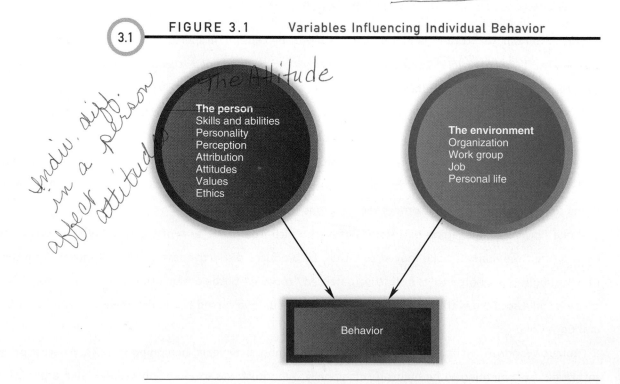

The basis for understanding individual differences stems from Lewin's early contention that behavior is a function of the person and the environment.[2] Lewin expressed this idea in an equation: B = f(P, E), where B = behavior, P = person, and E = environment. This idea has been developed by the *interactional psychology* approach.[3] Basically, this approach says that in order to understand human behavior, we must know something about the person and something about the situation. There are four basic propositions of interactional psychology:

1. Behavior is a function of a continuous, multidirectional interaction between the person and the situation.
2. The person is active in this process and is both changed by situations and changes situations.
3. People vary in many characteristics, including cognitive, affective, motivational, and ability factors.
4. Two interpretations of situations are important: the objective situation and the person's subjective view of the situation.[4]

The interactional psychology approach points out the need to study both persons and situations. We will focus on personal and situational factors throughout the text. The person consists of individual differences such as those we emphasize in this chapter and Chapter 4: personality, perception, attribution, attitudes, values, and ethics. The situation consists of the environment the person operates in, and it can include things like the organization, work group, personal life situation, job characteristics, and many other environmental influences. One important and fascinating individual difference is personality.

Personality

What makes an individual behave in consistent ways in a variety of situations? Personality is an individual difference that lends consistency to a person's behavior. *Personality* is defined as a relatively stable set of characteristics that influence an individual's behavior. Although there is debate about the determinants of personality, we conclude that there are several origins. One determinant is heredity, and some interesting studies have supported this position. Identical twins who are separated at birth and raised apart in very different situations have been found to share personality traits and job preferences. For example, about half of the variation in traits like extraversion, impulsiveness, and flexibility was found to be genetically determined; that is, identical twins who grew up in different environments shared these traits.[5] In addition, the twins held similar jobs.[6] Thus, there does appear to be a genetic influence on personality.

Another determinant of personality is the environment a person is exposed to. Family influences, cultural influences, educational influences, and other environmental forces shape personality. Personality is therefore shaped by both heredity and environment.

Personality Theories

Four major theories of personality are the trait theory, psychodynamic theory, humanistic theory, and the integrative approach. Each theory has influenced the study of personality in organizations.

interactional psychology
The psychological approach that emphasizes that in order to understand human behavior, we must know something about the person and about the situation.

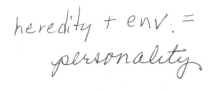

2. Define *personality*.

personality
A relatively stable set of characteristics that influence an individual's behavior.

3. Explain four theories of personality.

trait theory

The personality theory that states that in order to understand individuals, we must break down behavior patterns into a series of observable traits.

TRAIT THEORY Some early personality researchers believed that to understand individuals, we must break down behavior patterns into a series of observable traits. According to *trait theory*, combining these traits into a group forms an individual's personality. Gordon Allport, a leading trait theorist, saw traits as broad, general guides that lend consistency to behavior.[7] Thousands of traits have been identified over the years. Raymond Cattell, another prominent trait theorist, identified sixteen traits that formed the basis for differences in individual behavior. He described traits in bipolar adjective combinations such as self-assured/apprehensive, reserved/outgoing, and submissive/dominant.[8]

More recently, researchers have argued that all traits can be reduced to five basic factors. The "Big Five" traits include extraversion, agreeableness, conscientiousness, emotional stability, and openness to experience.[9] Descriptions of the "Big Five" are shown in Table 3.1. The Big Five are broad, global traits that are associated with behaviors at work.

From preliminary research, we know that introverted and conscientious employees are less likely to be absent from work.[10] In making peer evaluations, individuals with high agreeableness tend to rate others more leniently, while individuals with high conscientiousness tend to be tougher as raters.[11] Extraverts tend to have higher salaries, receive more promotions, and are more satisfied with their careers.[12] Across lots of occupations, people who are conscientious are more motivated and are high performers.[13] When you view more specific occupations, however, different patterns of the Big Five factors are related to high performance. For customer service jobs, individuals high in emotional stability, agreeableness, and openness to experience perform best. For managers, emotional stability and extraversion are traits of top performers.[14] The Big Five framework has also been applied across cultures. It has held up well among Spanish and Mexican populations.[15] It remains to be seen whether or not the Big Five traits will emerge in studies of cultures that are extremely different from Western cultures.[16]

The trait approach has been the subject of considerable criticism. Some theorists argue that simply identifying traits is not enough; instead, personality is dynamic and not completely stable. Further, early trait theorists tended to ignore the influence of situations.[17] Also, the trait theory tends to ignore process—that is, how we get from a trait to a particular outcome.

TABLE 3.1	The "Big Five" Personality Traits
Extraversion	The person is gregarious, assertive, and sociable (as opposed to reserved, timid, and quiet).
Agreeableness	The person is cooperative, warm, and agreeable (rather than cold, disagreeable, and antagonistic).
Conscientiousness	The person is hardworking, organized, and dependable (as opposed to lazy, disorganized, and unreliable).
Emotional stability	The person is calm, self-confident, and cool (as opposed to insecure, anxious, and depressed).
Openness to experience	The person is creative, curious, and cultured (rather than practical with narrow interests).

SOURCES: P. T. Costa and R. R. McCrae, *The NEO-PI Personality Inventory* (Odessa, Fla.: Psychological Assessment Resources, 1992); J. F. Salgado, "The Five Factor Model of Personality and Job Performance in the European Community," *Journal of Applied Psychology* 82 (1997): 30–43.

PSYCHODYNAMIC THEORY Based on the work of Sigmund Freud, *psychodynamic theory* emphasizes the unconscious determinants of behavior.[18] Freud saw personality as the interaction among three elements of personality: the id, ego, and superego. The id is the most primitive element, the source of drives and impulses that operate in an uncensored manner. The superego, similar to what we know as conscience, contains values and the "shoulds and should nots" of the personality. There is an ongoing conflict between the id and the superego. The ego serves to manage the conflict between the id and the superego. In this role, the ego compromises, and the result is the individual's use of defense mechanisms such as denial of reality. The contribution of psychodynamic theory to our understanding of personality is its focus on unconscious influences on behavior.

HUMANISTIC THEORY Carl Rogers believed that all people have a basic drive toward self-actualization, which is the quest to be all you can be.[19] The *humanistic theory* focuses on individual growth and improvement. It is distinctly people centered and also emphasizes the individual's view of the world. The humanistic approach contributes an understanding of the self to personality theory and contends that the self-concept is the most important part of an individual's personality.

INTEGRATIVE APPROACH Recently, researchers have taken a broader, more *integrative approach* to the study of personality.[20] To capture its influence on behavior, personality is described as a composite of the individual's psychological processes. Personality dispositions include emotions, cognitions, attitudes, expectancies, and fantasies.[21] *Dispositions*, in this approach, simply mean the tendencies of individuals to respond to situations in consistent ways. Influenced by both genetics and experiences, dispositions can be modified. The integrative approach focuses on both person (dispositions) and situational variables as combined predictors of behavior.

Personality Characteristics in Organizations

Managers should learn as much as possible about personality in order to understand their employees. Hundreds of personality characteristics have been identified. We have selected five characteristics because of their particular influences on individual behavior in organizations: locus of control, self-efficacy, self-esteem, self-monitoring, and positive/negative affect. Because these characteristics affect performance at work, managers need to have a working knowledge of them.

LOCUS OF CONTROL An individual's generalized belief about internal (self) versus external (situation or others) control is called *locus of control*. People who believe they control what happens to them are said to have an internal locus of control, whereas people who believe that circumstances or other people control their fate have an external locus of control.[22] Research on locus of control has strong implications for organizations. Internals (those with an internal locus of control) have been found to have higher job satisfaction and performance, to be more likely to assume managerial positions, and to prefer participative management styles.[23] You can assess your locus of control in You 3.1.

psychodynamic theory
The personality theory that emphasizes the unconscious determinants of behavior.

humanistic theory
The personality theory that emphasizes individual growth and improvement.

integrative approach
The broad theory that describes personality as a composite of an individual's psychological processes.

4. Identify several personality characteristics and their influences on behavior in organizations.

locus of control
An individual's generalized belief about internal control (self-control) versus external control (control by the situation or by others).

What's Your Locus of Control?

Below is a short scale that can give you an idea of your locus of control. For each of the four items, circle either choice a or choice b.

1. a. Becoming a success is a matter of hard work; luck has little or nothing to do with it.
   b. Getting a good job depends mainly on being in the right place at the right time.
2. a. The average citizen can have an influence in government decisions.
   b. This world is run by the few people in power, and there is not much the little guy can do about it.

3. a. As far as world affairs are concerned, most of us are the victims of forces we can neither understand nor control.
   b. By taking an active part in political and social affairs, people can control world events.
4. a. With enough effort we can wipe out political corruption.
   b. It is difficult for people to have much control over the things politicians do in office.

Scoring Key:

The internal locus of control answers are:
1a, 2a, 3b, 4a
The external locus of control answers are:
1b, 2b, 3a, 4b

Determine which category you circled most frequently using the key to the left. This gives you an approximation of your locus of control.

SOURCES: T. Adeyemi-Bello, "Validating Rotter's Locus of Control Scale with a Sample of Not-for-Profit Leaders," *Management Research News* 24 (2001): 25–35; J. B. Rotter, "Generalized Expectancies for Internal vs. External Locus of Control of Reinforcement," *Psychological Monographs* 80, whole No. 609 (1966).

Internals and externals have similar positive reactions to being promoted, which include high job satisfaction, job involvement, and organizational commitment. The difference between the two is that internals continue to be happy long after the promotion, whereas externals' joy over the promotion is short lived. This might occur because externals do not believe their own performance led to the promotion.[24]

Knowing about locus of control can prove valuable to managers. Because internals believe they control what happens to them, they will want to exercise control in their work environment. Allowing internals considerable voice in how work is performed is important. Internals will not react well to being closely supervised. Externals, in contrast, may prefer a more structured work setting, and they may be more reluctant to participate in decision making.

general self-efficacy

An individual's general belief that he or she is capable of meeting job demands in a wide variety of situations.

- confidence
- overcome obstacles

SELF-EFFICACY *General self-efficacy* is a person's overall view of himself/herself as being able to perform effectively in a wide variety of situations.[25] Employees with high general self-efficacy have more confidence in their job-related abilities and other personal resources (i.e., energy, influence over others, etc.) that help them function effectively on the job. People with low general self-efficacy often feel ineffective at work and may express doubts about performing a new task well. Previous success or performance is one of the most important determinants of self-efficacy. People who have positive beliefs about their efficacy for performance are more likely to attempt difficult tasks, to persist in overcoming obstacles, and to experience less anxiety when faced with adversity.[26] People with high self-efficacy also value the ability to provide input, or "voice," at work. Because they are confident in their capability to provide meaningful input, they value the opportunity to participate.[27]

There is another form of self-efficacy, called task-specific self-efficacy, which we will cover in Chapter 6. Task-specific self-efficacy is a person's belief that he or she can perform a specific task (for example, "I believe I can do this sales presentation today."). In contrast, general self-efficacy is more broad (for example, "I believe I can perform well in just about any part of the job.").

SELF-ESTEEM *Self-esteem* is an individual's general feeling of self-worth. Individuals with high self-esteem have positive feelings about themselves, perceive themselves to have strengths as well as weaknesses, and believe their strengths are more important than their weaknesses.[28] Individuals with low self-esteem view themselves negatively. They are more strongly affected by what other people think of them, and they compliment individuals who give them positive feedback while cutting down people who give them negative feedback.[29]

Evaluations from other people affect our self-esteem. For example, you might be liked for who you are or you might be liked for your achievements. Being liked for who you are is more stable, and people who have this type of self-esteem are less defensive and more honest with themselves. Being liked for your achievement is more unstable; it waxes and wanes depending on how high your achievements are.[30]

A person's self-esteem affects a host of other attitudes and has important implications for behavior in organizations. People with high self-esteem perform better and are more satisfied with their jobs.[31] When they are involved in a job search, they seek out higher status jobs.[32] A work team made up of individuals with high self-esteem is more likely to be successful than a team with low or average self-esteem.[33]

Very high self-esteem may be too much of a good thing. When people with high self-esteem find themselves in stressful situations, they may brag inappropriately.[34] This may be viewed negatively by others, who see spontaneous boasting as egotistical. Very high self-esteem may also lead to overconfidence and to relationship conflicts with others who may not evaluate this behavior favorably.[35] Individuals with high self-esteem may shift their social identities to protect themselves when they do not live up to some standard. Take two students, Denise and Teresa, for example. If Denise outperforms Teresa on a statistics exam, Teresa may convince herself that Denise is not really a good person to compare against because Denise is an engineering major and Teresa is a physical education major. Teresa's high self-esteem is protecting her from this unfavorable comparison.[36]

Self-esteem may be strongly affected by situations. Success tends to raise self-esteem, whereas failure tends to lower it. Given that high self-esteem is generally a positive characteristic, managers should encourage employees to raise their self-esteem by giving them appropriate challenges and opportunities for success.

SELF-MONITORING A characteristic with great potential for affecting behavior in organizations is *self-monitoring*—the extent to which people base their behavior on cues from other people and situations.[37] High self-monitors pay attention to what is appropriate in particular situations and to the behavior of other people, and they behave accordingly. Low self-monitors, in contrast, are not as vigilant to situational cues and act from internal states rather than paying attention to the situation. As a result, the behavior of low self-

self-esteem
An individual's general feeling of self-worth.

self-monitoring
The extent to which people base their behavior on cues from other people and situations.

Are You a High or Low Self-Monitor?

For the following items, circle T (true) if the statement is characteristic of your behavior. Circle F (false) if the statement does not reflect your behavior.

1. I find it hard to imitate the behavior of other people.   T   F

2. At parties and social gatherings, I do not attempt to do or say things that others will like.   T   F

3. I can only argue for ideas that I already believe.   T   F

4. I can make impromptu speeches even on topics about which I have almost no information.   T   F

5. I guess I put on a show to impress or entertain others.   T   F

6. I would probably make a good actor.   T   F

7. In a group of people, I am rarely the center of attention.   T   F

8. In different situations and with different people, I often act like very different persons. T   F

9. I am not particularly good at making other people like me.   T   F

10. I am not always the person I appear to be.   T   F

11. I would not change my opinions (or the way I do things) in order to please others or win
their favor.   T   F

12. I have considered being an entertainer.   T   F

13. I have never been good at games like charades or at improvisational acting.   T   F

14. I have trouble changing my behavior to suit different people and different situations.   T   F

15. At a party, I let others keep the jokes and stories going.   T   F

16. I feel a bit awkward in company and do not show up quite as well as I should.   T   F

17. I can look anyone in the eye and tell a lie with a straight face (if it is for a good cause). T   F

18. I may deceive people by being friendly when I really dislike them.   T   F

Scoring:

To score this questionnaire, give yourself 1 point for each of the following items that you answered T (true): 4, 5, 6, 8, 10, 12, 17, and 18. Now give yourself 1 point for each of the following items that you answered F (false): 1, 2, 3, 7, 9, 11, 13, 14, 15, and 16. Add both subtotals to find your overall score. If you scored 11 or above, you are probably a *high self-monitor*. If you scored 10 or under, you are probably a *low self-monitor*.

SOURCE: From *Public Appearances, Private Realities: The Psychology of Self-Monitoring* by M. Snyder. Copyright © 1987 by W. H. Freeman and Company. Used with permission.

monitors is consistent across situations. High self-monitors, because their behavior varies with the situation, appear to be more unpredictable and less consistent. You can use You 3.2 to assess your own self-monitoring tendencies.

Research is currently focusing on the effects of self-monitoring in organizations. In one study, the authors tracked the careers of 139 MBAs for five years to see whether high self-monitors were more likely to be promoted, change employers, or make a job-related geographic move. The results were "yes" to each question. High self-monitors get promoted because they accomplish tasks through meeting the expectations of others and because they seek out central positions in social networks.[38] They are also more likely to use self-promotion to make others aware of their skills and accomplishments.[39] However, the high self-monitor's flexibility may not be suited for every job, and the tendency to move may not fit every organization.[40] Because high self-monitors base their behavior on cues from others and from the situation, they demonstrate higher levels of managerial self-awareness. This means that, as managers, they assess their own workplace behavior accurately.[41] Managers who are high self-monitors are also good at reading their employees' needs and changing the way they interact with employees depending on those needs.[42]

Although research on self-monitoring in organizations is in its early stages, we can speculate that high self-monitors respond more readily to work group norms, organizational culture, and supervisory feedback than do low self-monitors, who adhere more to internal guidelines for behavior ("I am who I am"). In addition, high self-monitors may be enthusiastic participants in the trend toward work teams because of their ability to assume flexible roles.

5 POSITIVE/NEGATIVE AFFECT Recently, researchers have explored the effects of persistent mood dispositions at work. Individuals who focus on the positive aspects of themselves, other people, and the world in general are said to have *positive affect*.[43] In contrast, those who accentuate the negative in themselves, others, and the world are said to possess *negative affect* (also referred to as negative affectivity).[44] Positive affect is linked with job satisfaction, which we discuss at length in Chapter 4. Individuals with positive affect are more satisfied with their jobs.[45] Employees with positive affect are also absent from work less often.[46] Individuals with negative affect report more work stress.[47] Individual affect also influences the work group. Positive individual affect produces positive team affect, and this leads to more cooperation and less conflict within the team.[48]

Positive affect is a definite asset in work settings. Managers can do several things to promote positive affect, including allowing participative decision making and providing pleasant working conditions. We need to know more about inducing positive affect in the workplace.

The characteristics previously described are but a few of the personality characteristics that affect behavior and performance in organizations. Negative affect, for example, affects work stress as you'll see in Chapter 7. Another personality characteristic related to stress is Type A behavior, also presented in Chapter 7. You'll see other personality characteristics woven in throughout the book. Can managers predict the behavior of their employees by knowing their personalities? Not completely. You may recall that the interactional psychology model (Figure 3.1) requires both person and situation variables to predict behavior. Another idea to remember in predicting behavior is the strength of situational influences. Some situations are *strong situations* in that they overwhelm the effects of individual personalities. These situations are interpreted in the same way by different individuals, evoke agreement on the appropriate behavior in the situation, and provide cues to appropriate behavior. A performance appraisal session is an example of a strong situation. Employees know to listen to their boss and to contribute when asked to do so.

A weak situation, in contrast, is one that is open to many interpretations. It provides few cues to appropriate behavior and no obvious rewards for one behavior over another. Thus, individual personalities have a stronger influence in weak situations than in strong situations. An informal meeting without an agenda can be seen as a weak situation.

Organizations present combinations of strong and weak situations; therefore, personality has a stronger effect on behavior in some situations than in others.[49]

Measuring Personality

Several methods can be used to assess personality. These include projective tests, behavioral measures, and self-report questionnaires.

positive affect
An individual's tendency to accentuate the positive aspects of himself or herself, other people, and the world in general.

negative affect
An individual's tendency to accentuate the negative aspects of himself or herself, other people, and the world in general.

strong situation
A situation that overwhelms the effects of individual personalities by providing strong cues for appropriate behavior.

5. Explain how personality is measured.

projective test

A personality test that elicits an individual's response to abstract stimuli.

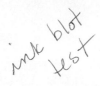

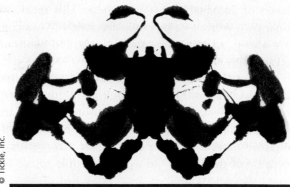

The *projective test* is one method used to measure personality. In these tests, individuals are shown a picture, abstract image, or photo and are asked to describe what they see or to tell a story about what they see. The rationale behind projective tests is that each individual responds to the stimulus in a way that reflects his or her unique personality. The Rorschach ink

The Rorschach ink blot test asks viewers to describe what they see in the abstract images shown to them.

blot test is a projective test commonly used to assess personality.[50] Like other projective tests, however, it has low reliability. The individual being assessed may look at the same picture and see different things at different times. Also, the assessor may apply his or her own biases in interpreting the information about the individual's personality.

behavioral measures

Personality assessments that involve observing an individual's behavior in a controlled situation.

There are *behavioral measures* of personality as well. Measuring behavior involves observing an individual's behavior in a controlled situation. We might assess a person's sociability, for example, by counting the number of times he or she approaches strangers at a party. The behavior is scored in some manner to produce an index of personality. Some potential problems with behavioral measures include the observer's ability to stay focused and the way the observer interprets the behavior. In addition, some people behave differently when they know they are being observed.

self-report questionnaire

A common personality assessment that involves an individual's responses to a series of questions.

The most common method of assessing personality is the *self-report questionnaire*. Individuals respond to a series of questions, usually in an agree/disagree or true/false format. One of the more widely recognized questionnaires is the Minnesota Multiphasic Personality Inventory (MMPI). The MMPI is comprehensive and assesses a variety of traits, as well as various neurotic or psychotic disorders. Used extensively in psychological counseling to identify disorders, the MMPI is a long questionnaire. The Big Five traits we discussed earlier are measured by another self-report questionnaire, the NEO Personality Inventory. Self-report questionnaires also suffer from potential biases. It is difficult to be objective about your own personality. People often answer the questionnaires in terms of how they want to be seen, rather than as they really are.

Another approach to applying personality theory in organizations is the Jungian approach and its measurement tool, the MBTI® instrument. The Myers-Briggs Type Indicator® instrument has been developed to measure Jung's ideas about individual differences. Many organizations use the MBTI instrument, and we will focus on it as an example of how some organizations use personality concepts to help employees appreciate diversity.

Application of Personality Theory in Organizations: The Myers-Briggs Type Indicator® Instrument

One approach to applying personality theory in organizations is the Jungian approach and its measurement tool, the MBTI instrument.

6. Discuss Carl Jung's contribution to our understanding of individual differences, and explain how his theory is used in the Myers-Briggs Type Indicator® instrument.

MBTI, Myers-Briggs, Myers-Briggs Type Indicator, and *Introduction to Type* are registered trademarks or trademarks of the Myers-Briggs Type Indicator Trust in the United States and other countries.

Swiss psychiatrist Carl Jung built his work on the notion that people are fundamentally different, but also fundamentally alike. His classic treatise *Psychological Types* proposed that the population was made up of two basic types—Extraverted types and Introverted types.[51] He went on to identify two types of Perceiving (Sensing and Intuition) and two types of judgment (Thinking and Feeling). Perceiving (how we gather information) and Judging (how we make decisions) represent the basic mental functions that everyone uses.

Jung suggested that human similarities and differences could be understood by combining preferences. We prefer and choose one way of doing things over another. We are not exclusively one way or another; rather, we have a preference for Extraversion or Introversion, just as we have a preference for right-handedness or left-handedness. We may use each hand equally well, but when a ball is thrown at us by surprise, we will reach to catch it with our preferred hand. Jung's type theory argues that no preferences are better than others. Differences are to be understood, celebrated, and appreciated.

During the 1940s, a mother–daughter team became fascinated with individual differences among people and with the work of Carl Jung. Katharine Briggs and her daughter, Isabel Briggs Myers, developed the *Myers-Briggs Type Indicator® instrument* to put Jung's type theory into practical use. The MBTI instrument is used extensively in organizations as a basis for understanding individual differences. More than 3 million people complete the instrument per year in the United States.[52] The MBTI instrument has been used in career counseling, team building, conflict management, and understanding management styles.[53] In Experiential Exercise 3.1 at the end of this chapter, you can assess your own MBTI type. You might find it helpful to do this before reading on.

Myers-Briggs Type Indicator (MBTI)® instrument
An instrument developed to measure Carl Jung's theory of individual differences.

to understand indiv. diff.

The Preferences

There are four scale dichotomies in type theory with two possible choices for each scale. Table 3.2 shows these preferences. The combination of these preferences makes up an individual's psychological type.

EXTRAVERSION/INTROVERSION   The *Extraversion/Introversion* preference represents where you get your energy. The Extraverted type (E) is energized by interaction with other people. The Introverted type (I) is energized by time alone. Extraverted types typically have a wide social network, whereas Introverted types have a more narrow range of relationships. As articulated by

Extraversion
A preference indicating that an individual is energized by interaction with other people.

Introversion
A preference indicating that an individual is energized by time alone.

⑶·² TABLE 3.2   Type Theory Preferences and Descriptions

EXTRAVERSION	INTROVERSION	THINKING	FEELING
Outgoing	Quiet	Analytical	Subjective
Publicly expressive	Reserved	Clarity	Harmony
Interacting	Concentrating	Head	Heart
Speaks, then thinks	Thinks, then speaks	Justice	Mercy
Gregarious	Reflective	Rules	Circumstances
SENSING	**INTUITION**	**JUDGING**	**PERCEIVING**
Practical	General	Structured	Flexible
Specific	Abstract	Time oriented	Open ended
Feet on the ground	Head in the clouds	Decisive	Exploring
Details	Possibilities	Makes lists/uses them	Makes lists/loses them
Concrete	Theoretical	Organized	Spontaneous

Jung, this preference has nothing to do with social skills. Many Introverted types have excellent social skills but prefer the internal world of ideas, thoughts, and concepts. Extraverted types represent approximately 70 percent of the U.S. population.[54] Our culture rewards Extraverted types and nurtures them. Jung contended that the Extraversion/Introversion preference reflects the most important distinction between individuals.

WHAT'S A PET HAVE TO DO TO GET A LITTLE ACTION AROUND HERE, HUH??

INTROVERTED OWNER, EXTRAVERTED PETS

© Rubberball Productions/Getty Images

In work settings, Extraverted types prefer variety, and they do not mind the interruptions of the phone or visits from coworkers. They communicate freely but may say things that they regret later. Introverted types prefer quiet for concentration, and they like to think things through in private. They do not mind working on a project for a long time and are careful with details. Introverted types dislike telephone interruptions, and they may have trouble recalling names and faces. You may be surprised to learn that one of the world's most successful CEOs is an Introverted type. Read about Michael Dell's personality in The Real World 3.1.

Sensing

Gathering information through the five senses.

Intuition

Gathering information through "sixth sense" and focusing on what could be rather than what actually exists.

SENSING/INTUITION The *Sensing/Intuition* preference represents perception or how we prefer to gather information. In essence this preference reflects what we pay attention to. The Sensing type (S) pays attention to information gathered through the five senses and to what actually exists. The Intuitive type (N) pays attention to a "sixth sense" and to what could be rather than to what actually exists.[55] Approximately 70 percent of people in the United States are Sensing types.[56]

At work, Sensing types prefer specific answers to questions and can become frustrated with vague instructions. They like jobs that yield tangible results, and they enjoy using established skills more than learning new ones. Intuitive types like solving new problems and are impatient with routine details. They enjoy learning new skills more than actually using them. Intuitive types tend to think about several things at once, and they may be seen by others as absentminded. They like figuring out how things work just for the fun of it.

Thinking

Making decisions in a logical, objective fashion.

Feeling

Making decisions in a personal, value-oriented way.

THINKING/FEELING The *Thinking/Feeling* preference represents the way we prefer to make decisions. The Thinking type (T) makes decisions in a logical, objective fashion, whereas the Feeling type (F) makes decisions in a personal, value-oriented way. The general U.S. population is divided 50/50 on the Thinking/Feeling type preference, but it is interesting that two-thirds of all males are Thinking types, whereas two-thirds of all females are Feeling types. It is the one preference in type theory that has a strong gender difference. Thinking types tend to analyze decisions, whereas Feeling types sympathize. Thinking types try to be impersonal, whereas Feeling types base their decisions on how the outcome will affect the people involved.

In work settings, Thinking types tend to show less emotion, and they may become uncomfortable with people who do. They are likely to respond more

Michael Dell: Square and Vanilla?

© Bryan Haraway/Bloomberg News/Landov

Michael Dell doesn't let his extreme Introversion hinder him from running his highly successful corporation.

Think all top executives are outgoing like Jack Welch or flashy like Ted Turner? Think again. One of the world's top-performing CEOs is a raging Introverted type with an egoless demeanor. Once, when he heard about the exploits of another, more flamboyant CEO, he held up a piece of paper and remarked, "See this? It's vanilla and square, and so am I."

Interviews with Dell, Inc., employees showed that they viewed Michael Dell as impersonal and aloof. This forced him to admit that he is hugely shy, and

personality tests confirmed it. He shows a clear preference for Introversion. He also is responsible for Dell's rise from anonymity to what some feel is the best-run company in technology. Michael Dell is a stickler for cost-cutting and a driver for continuous improvement. He entered the industry selling PCs from his University of Texas dorm room, and despite his journey to success, he still sees Dell, Inc., as a challenger rather than a market leader.

Part of the company's success is due to Michael Dell's understanding of his personality traits and his willingness to co-lead the firm—self-sacrifices that employees are expected to emulate. Dell and Kevin Rollins, president, have offices separated by a glass wall and work in tandem to lead the company. While Dell is more entrepreneurial, Rollins is more rigid, which makes for a good balance. Yet, Dell still finds time for introverted activities. He reserves an hour in the morning and each afternoon for nothing but reading and responding to e-mail.

Knowing his personality, along with his strengths and weaknesses, has proved to be a formula for success. Michael Dell is one of the longest-tenured company founders who remain CEOs.

SOURCE: A. Park and P. Burrows, "What You Don't Know About Dell," *Business Week* (November 3, 2003): 74–84.

---

readily to other people's thoughts. They tend to be firm minded and like putting things into a logical framework. Feeling types, in contrast, tend to be more comfortable with emotion in the workplace. They enjoy pleasing people and may enjoy frequent praise and encouragement.

JUDGING/PERCEIVING The *Judging-Perceiving* dichotomy reflects one's orientation to the outer world. The Judging type (J) loves closure. Judging types prefer to lead a planned, organized life and like making decisions. A person with a preference for Perceiving (P), in contrast, prefers a more flexible and spontaneous life and wants to keep options open. Imagine two people, one with a preference for Judging and the other for Perceiving, going out for dinner. The J asks the P to choose a restaurant, and the P suggests ten alternatives. The J just wants to decide and get on with it, whereas the P wants to explore all the options.

For Judging types in all arenas of life, and especially at work, they love getting things accomplished and delight in marking off the completed items on their calendars. Perceiving types tend to adopt a wait-and-see attitude and to collect new information rather than draw conclusions. Perceiving types are curious and welcome new information. They may start too many projects and not finish them.

Judging Preference

Preferring closure and completion in making decisions.

Perceiving Preference

Preferring to explore many alternatives and flexibility.

3.3

TABLE 3.3 Characteristics Frequently Associated with Each Type

Introverted Types	SENSING TYPES		INTUITIVE TYPES	
	ISTJ Quiet, serious, earn success by thoroughness and dependability. Practical, matter-of-fact, realistic, and responsible. Decide logically what should be done and work toward it steadily, regardless of distractions. Take pleasure in making everything orderly and organized—their work, their home, their life. Value traditions and loyalty.	**ISFJ** Quiet, friendly, responsible, and conscientious. Committed and steady in meeting their obligations. Thorough, painstaking, and accurate. Loyal, considerate, notice and remember specifics about people who are important to them, concerned with how others feel. Strive to create an orderly and harmonious environment at work and at home.	**INFJ** Seek meaning and connection in ideas, relationships, and material possessions. Want to understand what motivates people and are insightful about others. Conscientious and committed to their firm values. Develop a clear vision about how best to serve the common good. Organized and decisive in implementing their vision.	**INTJ** Have original minds and great drive for implementing their ideas and achieving their goals. Quickly see patterns in external events and develop long-range explanatory perspectives. When committed, organize a job and carry it through. Skeptical and independent, have high standards of competence and performance for themselves and others.
	ISTP Tolerant and flexible, quiet observers until a problem appears, then act quickly to find workable solutions. Analyze what makes things work and readily get through large amounts of data to isolate the core of practical problems. Interested in cause and effect, organize facts using logical principles, value efficiency.	**ISFP** Quiet, friendly, sensitive, and kind. Enjoy the present moment, what's going on around them. Like to have their own space and to work within their own time frame. Loyal and committed to their values and to people who are important to them. Dislike disagreements and conflicts, do not force their opinions or values on others.	**INFP** Idealistic, loyal to their values and to people who are important to them. Want an external life that is congruent with their values. Curious, quick to see possibilities, can be catalysts for implementing ideas. Seek to understand people and to help them fulfill their potential. Adaptable, flexible, and accepting unless a value is threatened.	**INTP** Seek to develop logical explanations for everything that interests them. Theoretical and abstract, interested more in ideas than in social interaction. Quiet, contained, flexible, and adaptable. Have unusual ability to focus in depth to solve problems in their area of interest. Skeptical, sometimes critical, always analytical.

(continued)

The Sixteen Types

The preferences combine to form sixteen distinct types, as shown in Table 3.3. For example, let's examine ESTJ. This type has Extraversion, Sensing, Thinking, and Judging preferences. ESTJs see the world as it is (S); make decisions objectively (T); and like structure, schedules, and order (J). Combining these qualities with their preference for interacting with others makes them natural managers. ESTJs are seen by others as dependable, practical, and able to get any job done. They are conscious of the chain of command and see work as a series of goals to be reached by following rules and regulations. They may have little tolerance for disorganization and have a high need for control. Research results from the *MBTI Atlas* show that most of the 7,463 managers studied were ESTJs.[57]

There are no good and bad types, and each type has its own strengths and weaknesses. There is a growing volume of research on type theory. The MBTI instrument has been found to have good reliability and validity as a measure-

SENSING TYPES		INTUITIVE TYPES	
ESTP Flexible and tolerant, they take a pragmatic approach focused on immediate results. Theories and conceptual explanations bore them—they want to act energetically to solve the problem. Focus on the here-and-now, spontaneous, enjoy each moment that they can be active with others. Enjoy material comforts and style. Learn best through doing.	**ESFP** Outgoing, friendly, and accepting. Exuberant lovers of life, people, and material comforts. Enjoy working with others to make things happen. Bring common sense and a realistic approach to their work and make work fun. Flexible and spontaneous, adapt readily to new people and environments. Learn best by trying a new skill with other people.	**ENFP** Warmly enthusiastic and imaginative. See life as full of possibilities. Make connections between events and information very quickly, and confidently proceed based on the patterns they see. Want a lot of affirmation from others, and readily give appreciation and support. Spontaneous and flexible, often rely on their ability to improvise and their verbal fluency.	**ENTP** Quick, ingenious, stimulating alert, and outspoken. Resourceful in solving new and challenging problems. Adept at generating conceptual possibilities and then analyzing them strategically. Good at reading other people. Bored by routine, will seldom do the same thing the same way, apt to turn to one new interest after another.
ESTJ Practical, realistic, matter-of-fact. Decisive, quickly move to implement decisions. Organize projects and people to get things done, focus on getting results in the most efficient way possible. Take care of routine details. Have a clear set of logical standards, systematically follow them and want others to also. Forceful in implementing their plans.	**ESFJ** Warmhearted, conscientious, and cooperative. Want harmony in their environment, work with determination to establish it. Like to work with others to complete tasks accurately and on time. Loyal, follow through even in small matters. Notice what others need in their day-by-day lives and try to provide it. Want to be appreciated for who they are and for what they contribute.	**ENFJ** Warm, empathetic, responsive, and responsible. Highly attuned to the emotions, needs, and motivations of others. Find potential in everyone, want to help others fulfill their potential. May act as catalysts for individual and group growth. Loyal, responsive to praise and criticism. Sociable, facilitate others in a group, and provide inspiring leadership.	**ENTJ** Frank, decisive, assume leadership readily. Quickly see logical and inefficient procedures and policies, develop and implement comprehensive systems to solve organizational problems. Enjoy long-term planning and goal setting. Usually well informed, well read, enjoy expanding their knowledge and passing it on to others. Forceful in presenting their ideas.

Extraverted Types

NOTE: I = Introversion; E = Extraversion; S = Sensing; N = Intuition; T = Thinking; F = Feeling; J = Judging; and P = Perceiving.

ment instrument for identifying type.[58, 59] Type has been found to be related to learning style, teaching style, and choice of occupation. For example, the MBTI types of engineering students at Georgia Tech were studied in order to see who was attracted to engineering and who was likely to leave the major. STs and NTs were more attracted to engineering. Es and Fs were more likely to withdraw from engineering courses.[60] Type has also been used to determine an individual's decision-making style and management style.

Recent studies have begun to focus on the relationship between type and specific managerial behaviors. The Introverted type (I) and the Feeling type (F), for example, have been shown to be more effective at participative management than their counterparts, the Extraverted type and the Thinking type.[61] Companies like AT&T, ExxonMobil, and Honeywell use the MBTI instrument in their management development programs to help employees understand the different viewpoints of others in the organization. The MBTI instrument can also be used for team building. Hewlett-Packard and Armstrong World Industries use the MBTI instrument to help teams realize that diversity and differences lead to successful performance.

Type theory is valued by managers for its simplicity and accuracy in depicting personalities. It is a useful tool for helping managers develop interpersonal skills. Managers also use type theory to build teams that capitalize on individuals' strengths and to help individual team members appreciate differences.

It should be recognized that there is the potential for individuals to misuse the information from the MBTI instrument in organizational settings.[62] Some inappropriate uses include labeling one another, providing a convenient excuse that they simply can't work with someone else, and avoiding responsibility for their own personal development with respect to working with others and becoming more flexible. One's type is not an excuse for inappropriate behavior.

We turn now to another psychological process that forms the basis for individual differences. Perception shapes the way we view the world, and it varies greatly among individuals.

Social Perception

7. Define *social perception* and explain how characteristics of the perceiver, the target, and the situation affect it.

social perception

The process of interpreting information about another person.

Perception involves the way we view the world around us. It adds meaning to information gathered via the five senses of touch, smell, hearing, vision, and taste. Perception is the primary vehicle through which we come to understand ourselves and our surroundings. As you saw in the Thinking Ahead feature, companies like Coca-Cola rely heavily on consumers' perceptions of their marketing efforts. In this chapter, we focus specifically on one particular type of perception—social perception. *Social perception* is the process of interpreting information about another person. Virtually all management activities rely on perception. In appraising performance, managers use their perceptions of an employee's behavior as a basis for the evaluation.

One work situation that highlights the importance of perception is the selection interview. The consequences of a bad match between an individual and the organization are devastating for both parties, so it is essential that the data gathered be accurate. Typical first interviews are brief, and the candidate is usually one of many seen by an interviewer during a day. How long does it take for the interviewer to reach a decision about a candidate? In the first four to five minutes, the interviewer often makes an accept or reject decision based on his or her perception of the candidate.[63]

Perception is also culturally determined. Based on our cultural backgrounds, we tend to perceive things in certain ways. Read the following sentence:

Finished files are the result of years of scientific study combined with the experience of years.

Now quickly count the number of *F*s in the sentence. Individuals for whom English is their second language see all six *F*s. Most native English speakers report that there are three *F*s. Because of cultural conditioning, *of* is not an important word and is ignored.[64] Culture affects our interpretation of the data we gather, as well as the way we add meaning to it.

Valuing diversity, including cultural diversity, has been recognized as a key to international competitiveness.[65] This challenge and others make social perception skills essential to managerial success.

Three major categories of factors influence our perception of another person: characteristics of ourselves, as perceivers; characteristics of the target per-

FIGURE 3.2   A Model for Social Perception

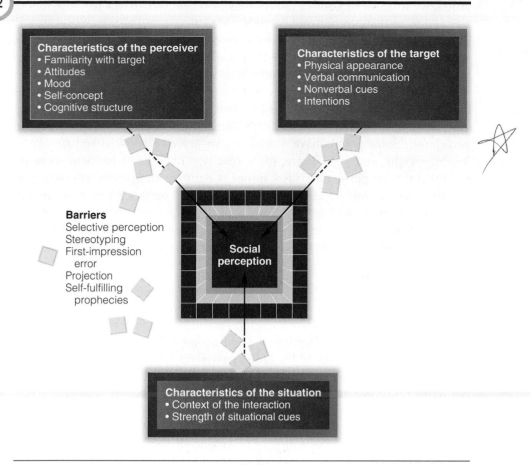

Characteristics of the perceiver
- Familiarity with target
- Attitudes
- Mood
- Self-concept
- Cognitive structure

Characteristics of the target
- Physical appearance
- Verbal communication
- Nonverbal cues
- Intentions

Barriers
Selective perception
Stereotyping
First-impression
  error
Projection
Self-fulfilling
  prophecies

**Social
perception**

Characteristics of the situation
- Context of the interaction
- Strength of situational cues

son we are perceiving; and characteristics of the situation in which the interaction takes place. Figure 3.2 shows a model of social perception.

Characteristics of the Perceiver

Several characteristics of the perceiver can affect social perception. One such characteristic is *familiarity* with the target (the person being perceived). When we are familiar with a person, we have multiple observations on which to base our impression of him or her. If the information we have gathered during these observations is accurate, we may have an accurate perception of the other person. Familiarity does not always mean accuracy, however. Sometimes, when we know a person well, we tend to screen out information that is inconsistent with what we believe the person is like. This is a particular danger in performance appraisals where the rater is familiar with the person being rated.

The perceiver's *attitudes* also affect social perception. Suppose you are interviewing candidates for a very important position in your organization—a position that requires negotiating contracts with suppliers, most of whom are male. You may feel that women are not capable of holding their own in tough negotiations. This attitude will doubtless affect your perceptions of the female candidates you interview.

Mood can have a strong influence on the way we perceive someone.[66] We think differently when we are happy than we do when we are depressed. In addition, we remember information that is consistent with our mood state better than information that is inconsistent with our mood state. When in a positive mood, we form more positive impressions of others. When in a negative mood, we tend to evaluate others unfavorably.

Another factor that can affect social perception is the perceiver's *self-concept*. An individual with a positive self-concept tends to notice positive attributes in another person. In contrast, a negative self-concept can lead a perceiver to pick out negative traits in another person. Greater understanding of self allows us to have more accurate perceptions of others.

Cognitive structure, an individual's pattern of thinking, also affects social perception. Some people have a tendency to perceive physical traits, such as height, weight, and appearance, more readily. Others tend to focus more on central traits, or personality dispositions. Cognitive complexity allows a person to perceive multiple characteristics of another person rather than attending to just a few traits.

Recent research has identified a rare new ability called *synesthesia* that affects an individual's perceptual skills. See whether you are a synesthete in The Real World 3.2.

Characteristics of the Target

Characteristics of the target, who is the person being perceived, influence social perception. *Physical appearance* plays a big role in our perception of others. The perceiver will notice the target's physical features like height, weight, estimated age, race, and gender. Clothing says a great deal about a person. Blue pin-striped suits, for example, are decoded to mean banking or Wall Street. Perceivers tend to notice physical appearance characteristics that contrast with the norm, that are intense, or that are new or unusual.[67] A loud person, one who dresses outlandishly, a very tall person, or a hyperactive child will be noticed because he or she provides a contrast to what is commonly encountered. In addition, people who are novel can attract attention. Newcomers or minorities in the organization are examples of novel individuals.

Physical attractiveness often colors our entire impression of another person. Interviewers rate attractive candidates more favorably, and attractive candidates are awarded higher starting salaries.[68, 69] People who are perceived as physically attractive face stereotypes as well. We will discuss these and other stereotypes later in this chapter.

Verbal communication from targets also affects our perception of them. We listen to the topics they speak about, their voice tone, and their accent and make judgments based on this input.

Nonverbal communication conveys a great deal of information about the target. Eye contact, facial expressions, body movements, and posture all are deciphered by the perceiver in an attempt to form an impression of the target. It is interesting that some nonverbal signals mean very different things in different cultures. The "okay" sign in the United States (forming a circle with the thumb and forefinger) is an insult in South America. Facial expressions, however, seem to have universal meanings. Individuals from different cultures are able to recognize and decipher expressions the same way.[70]

The *intentions* of the target are inferred by the perceiver, who observes the target's behavior. We may see our boss appear in our office doorway and think, "Oh no! She's going to give me more work to do." Or we may perceive that her intention is to congratulate us on a recent success. In any case, the perceiver's interpretation of the target's intentions affects the way the perceiver views the target.

PART 2 [INDIVIDUAL PROCESSES AND BEHAVIOR

Synesthesia: Unusual Perception

Quick, find all the 2s in the box on the top. If you're like most people, the only way for you to pick out the 2s is to methodically examine each number in the box. But for a small group of people called "synesthetes," this task is both instantaneous and effortless. Why? Because when they look at the same box of numbers, they see a unique color code, making the 2s stand out in sharp contrast to the 5s (like the box on the bottom).

Synesthesia, from the Greek words for "perception" and "together," is a rare condition in which the perception of one sensory input creates an additional perception. So for some synesthetes, sights have sounds and sounds have tastes. For others, music evokes brilliant colors, with the shade depending on the instrument being played. One researcher, who himself has synesthesia, recalls attending a concert as a child and being convinced that the lights were dimmed so the audience could see the colors better. In his mind's eye, violins produce bright shades of burgundy, piano music is purple, and cellos produce sounds that are a rich shade of gold.

While people have described the perception of synesthesia for centuries, scientists have often written it off as a figment of imagination, an artifact of childhood memories, or even a side effect of illicit drug use. While synesthetes have known all along that these experiences were real, not until recently have scientists become convinced. A 2002 study using the box of 2s and 5s shown here provided the definitive evidence that synesthesia is a neurological phenomenon rather than the result of an overactive imagination.

What can synesthesia teach us about organizational behavior? First, people see the world differently. Successful managers often surround themselves with advisors and team members who see the world from a slightly different perspective. Second, what seems impossible to one person may be child's play to another. Not surprisingly, a large number of synesthetes enjoy creative endeavors such as composing or painting. Sometimes, the solution to a seemingly impossible task is simply to ask for help.

SOURCES: T. J. Palmeri, R. Blake, R. Marois, M. A. Flanery, and W. Whetsell, Jr., "The Perceptual Reality of Synesthetic Colors," *Proceedings of the National Academy of Sciences of the United States of America* 99 (2003): 4127–4131; V. S. Ramachandran and E. M. Hubbard, "Hearing Colors, Tasting Shapes: Color-Coded World," *Scientific American* (April 14, 2003), http://www.sciam.com/article.cfm?articleID=000AB1B4-A5D0-1E8F-8EA5809EC588 0000; V. S. Ramachandran, and E. M. Hubbard, "Neural Cross Wiring and Synesthesia [Abstract]," *Journal of Vision* 1(3) (2001): 67a; and A. Underwood, "Real Rhapsody in Blue," *Newsweek* (November 25, 2003), http://msnbc.msn.com/id/3540645/.

Characteristics of the Situation

The situation in which the interaction between the perceiver and the target takes place also influences the perceiver's impression of the target. The *social context* of the interaction is a major influence. Meeting a professor in his or her office affects your impression in a certain way that may contrast with the impression you would form had you met the professor in a local restaurant. In Japan, social context is very important. Business conversations after working hours or at lunch are taboo. If you try to talk business during these times, you may be perceived as rude.[71]

discounting principle

The assumption that an individual's behavior is accounted for by the situation.

The *strength of situational cues* also affects social perception. As we discussed earlier in the chapter, some situations provide strong cues as to appropriate behavior. In these situations, we assume that the individual's behavior can be accounted for by the situation, and that it may not reflect the individual's disposition. This is the *discounting principle* in social perception.[72] For example, you may encounter an automobile salesperson who has a warm and personable manner, asks about your work and hobbies, and seems genuinely interested in your taste in cars. Can you assume that this behavior reflects the salesperson's personality? You probably cannot, because of the influence of the situation. This person is trying to sell you a car, and in this particular situation he or she probably treats all customers in this manner.

You can see that characteristics of the perceiver, the target, and the situation all affect social perception. It would be wonderful if all of us had accurate social perception skills. Unfortunately, barriers often prevent us from perceiving another person accurately.

Barriers to Social Perception

8. Identify five common barriers to social perception.

Several factors lead us to form inaccurate impressions of others. Five of these barriers to social perception are selective perception, stereotyping, first-impression error, projection, and self-fulfilling prophecies.

selective perception

The process of selecting information that supports our individual viewpoints while discounting information that threatens our viewpoints.

We receive a vast amount of information. *Selective perception* is our tendency to choose information that supports our viewpoints. Individuals often ignore information that makes them feel uncomfortable or threatens their viewpoints. Suppose, for example, that a sales manager is evaluating the performance of his employees. One employee does not get along well with colleagues and rarely completes sales reports on time. This employee, however, generates the most new sales contracts in the office. The sales manager may ignore the negative information, choosing to evaluate the salesperson only on contracts generated. The manager is exercising selective perception.

stereotype

A generalization about a group of people.

A *stereotype* is a generalization about a group of people. Stereotypes reduce information about other people to a workable level, and they are efficient for compiling and using information. Stereotypes become even stronger when they are shared with and validated by others.[73] Stereotypes can be accurate; when they are accurate, they can be useful perceptual guidelines. Some of the time, however, stereotypes are inaccurate. They harm individuals when inaccurate impressions of them are inferred and are never tested or changed.[74] The Science feature shows how stereotypes about names may lead to discrimination in the hiring process.

In multicultural work teams, members often stereotype foreign coworkers rather than getting to know them before forming an impression. Team members from less developed countries are often assumed to have less knowledge simply because their homeland is economically or technologically less developed.[75] Stereotypes like these can deflate the productivity of the work team, as well as create low morale.

Attractiveness is a powerful stereotype. We assume that attractive individuals are also warm, kind, sensitive, poised, sociable, outgoing, independent, and strong. Are attractive people really like this? Certainly, all of them are not. A study of romantic relationships showed that most attractive individuals do not fit the stereotype, except for possessing good social skills and being popular.[76]

Some individuals may seem to us to fit the stereotype of attractiveness because our behavior elicits from them behavior that confirms the stereotype. Consider, for example, a situation in which you meet an attractive fellow student. Chances are that you respond positively to this person, because you as-

What's in a Name?

What's in a name? When it comes to hiring, maybe more than you think. Widely reported studies have shown, unfortunately, that stereotypes based on names and negative attributions are still present in the hiring process.

Researchers at MIT and the University of Chicago mailed 5,000 résumés in response to job ads posted in the *Boston Globe* and the *Chicago Tribune*. Four résumés were sent for each job advertised; two represented excellent qualifications, one each with a "black" and a "white" sounding name. Two less-qualified résumés were also sent, again one with a black and one with a white sounding name. The names were chosen after a study of birth certificates. White names included Greg, Neil, Emily, and Jill, among others. Black names included Kareem, Tamika, Rasheed, and Aisha.

Researchers found that the callback rates on identical résumés were substantially higher for white-sounding names than for black-sounding names. There was as much discrimination in less skilled jobs (cashier, mailroom worker) as was found in more highly skilled jobs like manager and assistant to the president.

Another study showed that the attributions employers make about names may explain their behavior in hiring. The more black-sounding a person's name, the more employers may believe that the candidate's parents have a lower socioeconomic status, and thus the candidate is from a poorer, less educated family.

Taken together, the studies demonstrate that among some employers, stereotypes and false attributions can lead to discrimination in hiring.

SOURCES: M. Bertrand and S. Mullainathan, "Are Emily and Greg More Employable than Lakisha and Jamal? A Field Experiment on Labor Market Discrimination," *American Economic Review*, 94 (2004): 991–1013.

sume he or she is warm, sociable, and so on. Even though the person may not possess these traits, your positive response may bring out these behaviors in the person. The interaction between the two of you may be channeled such that the stereotype confirms itself.[77]

Stereotyping pervades work life. When there is a contrast against a stereotype, the member of the stereotyped group is treated more positively (given more favorable comments or pats on the back). For example, a female softball player may be given more applause for a home run hit than a male teammate. This occurs because some people may stereotype women as less athletic than men, or because they hold female players to a lower standard. Either way, the contrast is still part of stereotyping.[78]

First impressions are lasting impressions, so the saying goes. Individuals place a good deal of importance on first impressions, and for good reason. We tend to remember what we perceive first about a person, and sometimes we are quite reluctant to change our initial impressions.[79] *First-impression error* occurs when we observe a very brief bit of a person's behavior in our first encounter and infer that this behavior reflects what the person is really like. Primacy effects can be particularly dangerous in interviews, given that we form first impressions quickly and that these impressions may be the basis for long-term employment relationships.

What factors do interviewers rely on when forming first impressions? Perceptions of the candidate, such as whether they like the person, whether they trust the person, and whether or not the person seems credible, all influence the interviewer's decision. Something seemingly as unimportant as the pitch of your voice can leave a lasting impression. Speakers with higher vocal pitch are believed to be more competent, more dominant, and more assertive than those with lower voices. This belief can be carried too far; men whose voices are high

first-impression error *3.*
The tendency to form lasting opinions about an individual based on initial perceptions.

projection 4

Overestimating the number of people who share our own beliefs, values, and behaviors.

self-fulfilling prophecy 5

The situation in which our expectations about people affect our interaction with them in such a way that our expectations are fulfilled.

impression management

The process by which individuals try to control the impressions others have of them.

enough that they sound feminine are judged the least favorably of all by interviewers. This finding is ironic, given that research has found that students with higher vocal pitch tend to earn better grades.[80]

Projection, also known as the false-consensus effect, is a cause of inaccurate perceptions of others. It is the misperception of the commonness of our own beliefs, values, and behaviors such that we overestimate the number of others who share these things. We assume that others are similar to us, and that our own values and beliefs are appropriate. People who are different are viewed as unusual and even deviant. Projection occurs most often when you surround yourself with others similar to you. You may overlook important information about others when you assume we are all alike and in agreement.[81]

Self-fulfilling prophecies are also barriers to social perception. Sometimes our expectations affect the way we interact with others such that we get what we wish for. Self-fulfilling prophecy is also known as the Pygmalion effect, named for the sculptor in Greek mythology who prayed that a statue of a woman he had carved would come to life, a wish that was granted by the gods.

Early studies of self-fulfilling prophecy were conducted in elementary school classrooms. Teachers were given bogus information that some of their pupils had high intellectual potential. These pupils were chosen randomly; there were really no differences among the students. Eight months later, the "gifted" pupils scored significantly higher on an IQ test. The teachers' expectations had elicited growth from these students, and the teachers had given them tougher assignments and more feedback on their performance.[82] Self-fulfilling prophecy has been studied in many settings, including at sea. The Israeli Defense Forces told one group of naval cadets that they probably wouldn't experience seasickness, and even if they did, it wouldn't affect their performance. The self-fulfilling prophecy worked! These cadets were rated better performers than other groups, and they also had less seasickness. The information improved the cadets' self-efficacy—they believed they could perform well even if they became seasick.[83]

The Pygmalion effect has been observed in work organizations as well.[84] A manager's expectations of an individual affect both the manager's behavior toward the individual and the individual's response. For example, suppose your initial impression is that an employee has the potential to move up within the organization. Chances are you will spend a great deal of time coaching and counseling the employee, providing challenging assignments, and grooming the individual for success.

Managers can harness the power of the Pygmalion effect to improve productivity in the organization. It appears that high expectations of individuals come true. Can a manager extend these high expectations to an entire group and have similar positive results? The answer is yes. When a manager expects positive things from a group, the group delivers.[85]

Impression Management

Most people want to make favorable impressions on others. This is particularly true in organizations, where individuals compete for jobs, favorable performance evaluations, and salary increases. The process by which individuals try to control the impressions others have of them is called *impression management*. Individuals use several techniques to control others' impressions of them.[86]

Some impression management techniques are self-enhancing. These techniques focus on enhancing others' impressions of the person using the technique. Name-dropping, which involves mentioning an association with important people in the hopes of improving one's image, is often used. Managing one's appearance is another technique for impression management. Individuals dress carefully for interviews because they want to "look the part" in order to get the job. Self-descriptions, or statements about one's characteristics, are used to manage impressions as well.

Another group of impression management techniques are *other-enhancing*. The aim of these techniques is to focus on the individual whom one is trying to make an impression rather than on one's self. Flattery is a common other-enhancing technique whereby compliments are given to an individual in order to win his or her approval. Favors are also used to gain the approval of others. Agreement with someone's opinion is a technique often used to gain a positive impression. People with disabilities, for example, often use other-enhancing techniques. They may feel that they must take it upon themselves to make others comfortable interacting with them. Impression management techniques are used by individuals with disabilities as a way of dealing with potential avoidance by others.[87]

Are impression management techniques effective? Most research on this topic has focused on employment interviews; the results indicate that candidates who engage in impression management by self-promoting performed better in interviews, were more likely to obtain site visits with potential employers, and were more likely to get hired.[88, 89] In addition, employees who engage in impression management are rated more favorably in performance appraisals than those who do not.[90]

Impression management seems to have an impact on others' impressions. As long as the impressions conveyed are accurate, this process can be beneficial to organizations. If the impressions are found to be false, however, a strongly negative overall impression may result. Furthermore, excessive impression management can lead to the perception that the user is manipulative or insincere.[91] We have discussed the influences on social perception, the potential barriers to perceiving another person, and impression management. Another psychological process that managers should understand is attribution.

Attribution in Organizations

As human beings, we are innately curious. We are not content merely to observe the behavior of others; rather, we want to know *why* they behave the way they do. We also seek to understand and explain our own behavior. *Attribution theory* explains how we pinpoint the causes of our own behavior and that of other people.[92]

The attributions, or inferred causes, we provide for behavior have important implications in organizations. In explaining the causes of our performance, good or bad, we are asked to explain the behavior that was the basis for the performance.

Internal and External Attributions

Attributions can be made to an internal source of responsibility (something within the individual's control) or an external source (something outside the individual's control). Suppose you perform well on an exam in this course. You might say you aced the test because you are smart or because you studied hard. If you attribute your success to ability or effort, you are making an internal attribution.

Alternatively, you might make an external attribution for your performance. You might say it was an easy test (you would attribute your success to degree of task difficulty) or that you had good luck. In this case, you are attributing your performance to sources beyond your control, or external sources. You can

what can we attribute our beh. to? & others' beh.

attribution theory
A theory that explains how individuals pinpoint the causes of their own behavior and that of others.

9. Explain the attribution process and how attributions affect managerial behavior.

see that internal attributions include such causes as ability and effort, whereas external attributions include causes like task difficulty or luck.

Attribution patterns differ among individuals.[93] Achievement-oriented individuals attribute their success to ability and their failures to lack of effort, both internal causes. Failure-oriented individuals attribute their failures to lack of ability, and they may develop feelings of incompetence as a result of their attributional pattern. Evidence indicates that this attributional pattern also leads to depression.[94] Women managers, in contrast to men managers, are less likely to attribute their success to their own ability. This may be because they are adhering to social norms that compel women to be more modest about their accomplishments or because they believe that success has less to do with ability than with hard work.[95]

Attribution theory has many applications in the workplace. The way you explain your own behavior affects your motivation. For example, suppose you must give an important presentation to your executive management group. You believe you have performed well, and your boss tells you that you've done a good job. To what do you attribute your success? If you believe careful preparation and rehearsal led to your success, you're likely to take credit for the performance and to have a sense of self-efficacy about future presentations. If, however, you believe that you were just lucky, you may not be motivated to repeat the performance because you believe you had little influence on the outcome.

One situation in which a lot of attributions are made is the employment interview. Candidates are often asked to explain the causes of previous performance (Why did you perform poorly in math classes?) to interviewers. In addition, candidates often feel they should justify why they should be hired (I work well with people, so I'm looking for a managerial job). Research shows that successful and unsuccessful candidates differ in the way they make attributions for negative outcomes. Successful candidates are less defensive and make internal attributions for negative events. Unsuccessful candidates attribute negative outcomes to things beyond their control (external attributions), which gives interviewers the impression that the candidate failed to learn from the event. In addition, interviewers fear that the individuals would be likely to blame others when something goes wrong in the workplace.[96]

Attributional Biases

The attribution process may be affected by two very common errors: the fundamental attribution error and the self-serving bias. The tendency to make attributions to internal causes when focusing on someone else's behavior is known as the *fundamental attribution error*.[97] The other error, *self-serving bias*, occurs when focusing on one's own behavior. Individuals tend to make internal attributions for their own successes and external attributions for their own failures.[98] In other words, when we succeed, we take credit for it; when we fail, we blame the situation on other people.

Both of these biases were illustrated in a study of health care managers who were asked to cite the causes of their employees' poor performance.[99] The managers claimed that internal causes (their employees' lack of effort or lack of ability) were the basis for their employees' poor performance. This is an example of the fundamental attribution error. When the employees were asked to pinpoint the cause of their own performance problems, they blamed a lack of support from the managers (an external cause), which illustrates self-serving bias.

fundamental attribution error
The tendency to make attributions to internal causes when focusing on someone else's behavior.

self-serving bias
The tendency to attribute one's own successes to internal causes and one's failures to external causes.

There are cultural differences in these two attribution errors. As described previously, these biases apply to people from the United States. In more fatalistic cultures, such as India's, people tend to believe that fate is responsible for much that happens. People in such cultures tend to emphasize external causes of behavior.[100]

In China, people are taught that hard work is the route to accomplishment. When faced with either a success or a failure, Chinese individuals first introspect about whether they tried hard enough or whether their attitude was correct. In a study of attributions for performance in sports, Chinese athletes attributed both their successes and failures to internal causes. Even when the cause of poor athletic performance was clearly external, such as bad weather, the Chinese participants made internal attributions. In terms of the Chinese culture, this attributional pattern is a reflection of moral values that are used to evaluate behavior. The socialistic value of selfless morality dictates that individual striving must serve collective interests. Mao Ze-dong stressed that external causes function only through internal causes; therefore, the main cause of results lies within oneself. Chinese are taught this from childhood and form a corresponding attributional tendency. In analyzing a cause, they first look to their own effort.[101]

The way individuals interpret the events around them has a strong influence on their behavior. People try to understand the causes of behavior in order to gain predictability and control over future behavior. Managers use attributions in all aspects of their jobs. In evaluating performance and rewarding employees, managers must determine the causes of behavior and a perceived source of responsibility. One tough call managers often make is whether allegations of sexual harassment actually resulted from sexual conduct, and if harassment did occur, what should be done about it. To make such tough calls, managers use attributions.

Attribution theory can explain how performance evaluation judgments can lead to differential rewards. A supervisor attributing an employee's good performance to internal causes, such as effort or ability, may give a larger raise than a supervisor attributing the good performance to external causes, such as help from others or good training. Managers are often called on to explain their own actions as well, and in doing so they make attributions about the causes of their own behavior. We continue our discussion of attributions in Chapter 6 in terms of how attributions are used in managing employee performance by presenting Kelley's attribution theory.

Managerial Implications: Using Personality, Perception, and Attribution at Work

Managers need to know as much as possible about individual differences in order to understand themselves and those with whom they work. An understanding of personality characteristics can help a manager appreciate differences in employees. With the increased diversity of the workforce, tools like the MBTI can be used to help employees see someone else's point of view. These tools can also help make communication among diverse employees more effective.

Managers use social perception constantly on the job. Knowledge of the forces that affect perception and the barriers to accuracy can help the manager form more accurate impressions of others.

Determining the causes of job performance is a major task for the manager, and attribution theory can be used to explain how managers go about determining causality. In addition, knowledge of the fundamental attribution error and self-serving bias can help a manager guard against these biases in the processes of looking for causes of behavior on the job.

In this chapter, we have explored the psychological processes of personality, perception, and attribution as individual differences. In the next chapter, we will continue our discussion of individual differences in terms of attitudes, values, and ethics.

LOOKING BACK: THE COCA-COLA COMPANY

The New Coke: A Fiasco or Success?

In 1985, The Coca-Cola Company did the unthinkable and changed the taste of Coca-Cola, the world's most popular soft drink, for the first time in ninety-nine years. While drinkers loved the new taste in lab tests, they perceived that Coke (the original Coke) was part of their American heritage, even though a surprising number could not perceive the difference in blind taste tests. Protests followed, and consumers hoarded the "old" Coke. The Coca-Cola Company received over 1,500 calls a day on its consumer hotline. In response to this outcry, the original formula for Coke finally returned. Following the return of the original Coke, the company received 31,600 calls of appreciation on the hotline.

Ironically, Coke's Web site now portrays this episode as a positive event that both demonstrated people's devotion to the product and marked the beginning of Coke's return to cola dominance. The company hails the decision to try new Coke as one of taking intelligent risks. Coke has managed to perceive (or spin), at least publicly, this huge failure as a success!

Ironically, from 1886 to 1960, Coca-Cola sold exactly one product: Coca-Cola. But from 1961 to today, the company's perception of itself has changed from a maker of one soft drink to a producer of beverages for every taste in 200 different countries. Coke, today, has more than 300 different products, including juices, teas, and athletic drinks.[102]

We'll explore more of Coca-Cola's global challenges in Chapter 18.

Chapter Summary

1. Individual differences are factors that make individuals unique. They include personalities, perceptions, skills and abilities, attitudes, values, and ethics.

2. The trait theory, psychodynamic theory, humanistic theory, and integrative approach are all personality theories.

3. Managers should understand personality because of its effect on behavior. Several characteristics affect behavior in organizations, including locus of control, self-esteem, self-monitoring, and positive/negative affect.

4. Personality has a stronger influence in weak situations, where there are few cues to guide behavior.

5. One useful framework for understanding individual differences is type theory, developed by Carl Jung and measured by the Myers-Briggs Type Indicator (MBTI).

6. Social perception is the process of interpreting information about another person. It is influenced by characteristics of the perceiver, the target, and the situation.

7. Barriers to social perception include selective perception, stereotyping, first-impression error, projection, and self-fulfilling prophecies.

8. Impression management techniques such as name-dropping, managing one's appearance, self-descriptions, flattery, favors, and agreement are used by individuals to control others' impressions of them.

9. Attribution is the process of determining the cause of behavior. It is used extensively by managers, especially in evaluating performance.

Key Terms

attribution theory (p. 103)

behavioral measures (p. 90)

discounting principle (p. 100)

extraversion (p. 91)

feeling (p. 92)

first-impression error (p. 101)

fundamental attribution error (p. 104)

general self-efficacy (p. 86)

humanistic theory (p. 85)

impression management (p. 102)

individual differences (p. 82)

integrative approach (p. 85)

interactional psychology (p. 83)

introversion (p. 91)

intuiting (p. 92)

Judging Preference (p. 92)

locus of control (p. 85)

Myers-Briggs Type Indicator (MBTI) (p. 91)

negative affect (p. 89)

Perceiving Preference (p. 92)

personality (p. 83)

positive affect (p. 89)

projection (p. 102)

projective test (p. 90)

psychodynamic theory (p. 85)

selective perception (p. 100)

self-esteem (p. 87)

self-fulfilling prophecy (p. 102)

self-monitoring (p. 87)

self-report questionnaire (p. 90)

self-serving bias (p. 104)

sensing (p. 92)

social perception (p. 96)

stereotype (p. 100)

strong situation (p. 89)

thinking (p. 92)

trait theory (p. 84)

Review Questions

1. What are individual differences, and why should managers understand them?

2. Define *personality*, and describe its origins.

3. Describe four theories of personality and explain what each contributes to our knowledge of personality.

4. Describe the eight preferences of the Myers-Briggs Type Indicator. How does this instrument measure Carl Jung's ideas?

5. What factors influence social perception? What are the barriers to social perception?

6. Describe the errors that affect the attribution process.

Discussion and Communication Questions

1. What contributions can high self-monitors make in organizations? Low self-monitors?

2. How can managers improve their perceptual skills?

3. Which has the stronger impact on personality: heredity or environment?

4. How can managers make more accurate attributions?

5. How can managers encourage self-efficacy in employees?

6. How can self-serving bias and the fundamental attribution error be avoided?

7. *(communication question)* You have been asked to develop a training program for interviewers. An integral part of this training program focuses on helping interviewers develop better social per-

ception skills. Write an outline for this section of the training program. Be sure to address barriers to social perception and ways to avoid these barriers.

8. *(communication question)* Form groups of four to six, then split each group in half. Debate the origins of personality, with one half taking the position that personality is inherited, and the other half taking the position that personality is formed by the environment. Each half should also discuss the implications of its position for managers.

Ethical Dilemma

Alice loves to hire new people. As manager of the Medicare Reimbursement department of a large hospital, she sees it as a great responsibility to aggressively pursue and hire the best people. She has already experienced the challenges of hiring the wrong person. She knows a bad personality match could undermine the culture she has worked so hard to build. Alice plans to do everything in her power to never repeat the mistake of a bad hire again.

This latest hire, however, is proving to be a bigger challenge than she had expected. The problem is that the position requires a good deal of specialized knowledge. Alice needs someone who knows the current Medicare regulations and who would be able to decipher new ones. The pool of candidates with this knowledge is extremely small. Truthfully, she has interviewed only one person with the skills and knowledge that she needs.

Jana had interviewed two weeks ago. She knew the regulations better than anyone Alice has ever met. Every question Alice asked, Jana answered. What an asset Jana would be to the department. The dilemma is that Jana seems to be extremely extroverted, needing and wanting a lot of social involvement. This job would not offer that opportunity. Even worse, Mike, the main person with whom Jana would be working, is an extreme introvert. He rarely speaks to anyone and prefers that people speak to him as little as possible. Alice can see nothing but problems between these two employees.

Alice does not know what to do. She values Mike a great deal and does not want to do anything to make him unhappy in his job. But she desperately needs someone in this vacant position. She has been depending on everyone to pitch in and cover the workload for weeks now. She knows that has to stop. Yet, is it fair to bring in someone she feels sure would be unhappy in the job and would ultimately quit? She may even end up losing both Jana and Mike. She has no idea what is the right thing to do.

Questions

1. Who are the stakeholders affected by Alice's decisions?

2. How much importance should Alice place on Mike's needs and wants?

3. Using rule, virtue, right, and justice theories, evaluate Alice's decision alternatives.

Experiential Exercises

3.1 MBTI Types and Management Styles

Part I. This questionnaire will help you determine your preferences. For each item, circle either a or b. If you feel both a and b are true, decide which one is more like you, even if it is only slightly more true.

1. I would rather
   a. Solve a new and complicated problem.
   b. Work on something I have done before.

2. I like to
   a. Work alone in a quiet place.
   b. Be where the action is.

3. I want a boss who
   a. Establishes and applies criteria in decisions.
   b. Considers individual needs and makes exceptions.

4. When I work on a project, I
   a. Like to finish it and get some closure.
   b. Often leave it open for possible changes.

5. When making a decision, the most important considerations are
   a. Rational thoughts, ideas, and data.
   b. People's feelings and values.

6. On a project, I tend to
   a. Think it over and over before deciding how to proceed.
   b. Start working on it right away, thinking about it as I go along.

7. When working on a project, I prefer to
   a. Maintain as much control as possible.
   b. Explore various options.

8. In my work, I prefer to
   a. Work on several projects at a time and learn as much as possible about each one.
   b. Have one project that is challenging and keeps me busy.

9. I often
   a. Make lists and plans whenever I start something and may hate to seriously alter my plans.
   b. Avoid plans and just let things progress as I work on them.

10. When discussing a problem with colleagues, it is easy for me to
    a. See "the big picture."
    b. Grasp the specifics of the situation.

11. When the phone rings in my office or at home, I usually
    a. Consider it an interruption.
    b. Do not mind answering it.

12. Which word describes you better?
    a. Analytical.
    b. Empathetic.

13. When I am working on an assignment, I tend to
    a. Work steadily and consistently.
    b. Work in bursts of energy with "down time" in between.

14. When I listen to someone talk on a subject, I usually try to
    a. Relate it to my own experience and see if it fits.
    b. Assess and analyze the message.

15. When I come up with new ideas, I generally
    a. "Go for it."
    b. Like to contemplate the ideas some more.

16. When working on a project, I prefer to
    a. Narrow the scope so it is clearly defined.
    b. Broaden the scope to include related aspects.

17. When I read something, I usually
    a. Confine my thoughts to what is written there.
    b. Read between the lines and relate the words to other ideas.

18. When I have to make a decision in a hurry, I often
    a. Feel uncomfortable and wish I had more information.
    b. Am able to do so with available data.

19. In a meeting, I tend to
    a. Continue formulating my ideas as I talk about them.
    b. Only speak out after I have carefully thought the issue through.

20. In work, I prefer spending a great deal of time on issues of
    a. Ideas.
    b. People.

21. In meetings, I am most often annoyed with people who
    a. Come up with many sketchy ideas.
    b. Lengthen meetings with many practical details.

22. I am a
    a. Morning person.
    b. Night owl.

23. What is your style in preparing for a meeting?
    a. I am willing to go in and be responsive.
    b. I like to be fully prepared and usually sketch an outline of the meeting.

24. In a meeting, I would prefer for people to
    a. Display a fuller range of emotions.
    b. Be more task oriented.

25. I would rather work for an organization where
    a. My job is intellectually stimulating.
    b. I am committed to its goals and mission.

26. On weekends, I tend to
    a. Plan what I will do.
    b. Just see what happens and decide as I go along.

27. I am more
    a. Outgoing.
    b. Contemplative.

28. I would rather work for a boss who is
    a. Full of new ideas.
    b. Practical.

In the following, choose the word in each pair that appeals to you more:

29. a. Social.
    b. Theoretical.

30. a. Ingenuity.
    b. Practicality.

31. a. Organized.
    b. Adaptable.

32. a. Active.
    b. Concentration.

SCORING KEY

Count one point for each item listed below that you have circled in the inventory.

Score for I	Score for E	Score for S	Score for N
(2a)	2b	(1b)	1a
(6a)	6b	(10b)	10a
(11a)	11b	(13a)	13b
(15b)	15a	(16a)	16b
(19b)	19a	(17a)	17b
(22a)	22b	(21a)	21b
(27b)	27a	(28b)	28a
(32b)	32a	(30b)	30a

Total
Circle the one with more points—I or E.
Circle the one with more points—S or N.

Score for T	Score for F	Score for J	Score for P
3a	(3b)	(4a)	4b
5a	(5b)	(7a)	7b
12a	(12b)	(8b)	8a
14b	(14a)	(9a)	9b
20a	(20b)	18b	(18a)
(24b)	24a	(23b)	23a
25a	(25b)	(26a)	26b
29b	(29a)	(31a)	31b

Total
Circle the one with more points—T or F.
Circle the one with more points—J or P.

Your score is
I or E 6
S or N 8
T or F 7
J or P 7

Part II. The purpose of this part of the exercise is to give you experience in understanding some of the individual differences that were proposed by Carl Jung and are measured by the MBTI.

Step 1. Your instructor will assign you to a group.

Step 2. Your group is a team of individuals who want to start a business. You are to develop a mission statement and a name for your business.

Step 3. After you have completed Step 2, analyze the decision process that occurred within the group. How did you decide on your company's name and mission?

Step 4. Your instructor will have each group report to the class the name and mission of the company, and then the decision process used. Your instructor will also give you some additional information about the exercise and provide some interesting insights about your management style.

SOURCE: "MBTI Types and Management Styles" from D. Marcic and P. Nutt, "Personality Inventory," in D. Marcic, ed., *Organizational Behavior: Experiences and Cases* (St. Paul: West, 1989), 9–16. Reprinted by permission.

3.2 Stereotypes in Employment Interviews

Step 1. Your instructor will give you a transcript that records an applicant's interview for a job as a laborer. Your task is to memorize as much of the interview as possible.

Step 2. Write down everything you can remember about the job candidate.

Step 3. Your instructor will lead you in a discussion.

SOURCE: Adapted from D. A. Sachau and M. Hussang, "How Interviewers' Stereotypes Influence Memory: An Exercise," *Journal of Management Education* 16 (1992): 391–396. Copyright © 1992 by Sage Publications. Reprinted with permission of Sage Publications, Inc.

Biz Flix | The Breakfast Club

John Hughes's careful look at teenage culture in a suburban Chicago high school focuses on a group of teenagers from the school's different subcultures. They start their Saturday detention with nothing in common, but over the course of a day, they learn each other's innermost secrets. The highly memorable characters—the Jock, the Princess, the Criminal, the Kook, and the Brain—leave lasting impressions. If you have seen the film, try to recall which actor or actress played each character.

The scene from *The Breakfast Club* is an edited version of the "Lunchtime" sequence that appears in the first third of the film. Carefully study each character's behavior to answer the following questions. The rest of the film shows the growing relationships among the detainees as they try to understand each other's personality.

What to Watch for and Ask Yourself:

> Which Big Five personality dimensions describe each character in this scene?

> Which characters show positive affect? Which show negative affect?

> Refer to the Myers-Briggs Type Indicator (MBTI) section in this chapter. Which of the sixteen types shown in Table 3.3 best describes each character? Why?

Workplace Video | Le Meridien: Managing the New Workplace

Le Meridien is a chain of over 130 luxury hotels in 56 countries. The hotel is famous for offering a unique European experience to its more than 100,000 visitors each year.

Le Meridien is part of the new workplace, using a management paradigm that stresses employee empowerment, teamwork, and collaboration. Managers at Le Meridien are responsible for managing various functional teams and overseeing a multinational staff. The climate of diversity at Le Meridien requires that managers recognize how different personality characteristics affect behavior within the organization.

Bob van den Oord, assistant general manager at Le Meridien, is famous for his "management by walkabout" style—a daily routine of monitoring all the major hotel operations and staff by literally walking through the entire hotel. Van den Oord also holds daily and weekly meetings at which managers may discuss their schedule of events and duties while receiving important feedback.

On any given day, Bob van den Oord and his employees may welcome honeymooners, international tourists, business travelers, convention groups, and holiday revelers. Since providing customer service is the backbone of the hotel industry, management's effectiveness in dealing with all kinds of people is crucial to Le Meridien's success.

Questions

1. *Choose one of the managers or team leaders spotlighted in the video and identify traits that make that person an effective employee for Le Meridien.*
2. *Why is it important for today's managers to know as much as possible about individual differences?*
3. *What attitudes and behaviors can cause managers to be ineffective in working with diverse groups of people?*

Sir Richard Branson: The Development of an Entrepreneur

Virgin is one of the most respected brands in Great Britain and is rapidly becoming an important global brand as well. The Virgin brand was started in the 1970s with a small mail order record company that grew out of a student magazine. Since then Richard Branson has developed the Virgin brand into a veritable entrepreneurial empire.

Branson: The Background of a Developing Entrepreneur

In the first chapter of his autobiography, Richard Branson reminisces about some of his childhood experiences—ones that would have a profound effect on his development as an adult and an entrepreneur. Branson writes that his parents, especially his mother, continually set challenges for him and his sisters, Vanessa and Lindi, in order to make them independent. These challenges were physical in nature rather than academic. According to Branson, he and his sisters were soon setting physical challenges for themselves.

A loving family played an important role in Branson's development. "We were a family that would have killed for each other—and we still are," says Branson. Teamwork was also a hallmark of the family. Branson's parents treated him and his two sisters as equals. They valued their children's opinions and only provided advice when the children asked for it. Branson's mother was very entrepreneurial, as was his Aunt Clare. Each developed several different ways of making money.

Despite his enormous entrepreneurial success, Branson still lacks a high school diploma. In school, he was a pitiful student but a superb athlete. Though he was dyslexic and had vision problems, his inability to read, write, and spell, and his poor performance on tests were blamed on stupidity or laziness. In commenting on Branson's academic miseries as a child in relation to his athletic and future entrepreneurial successes, one observer noted:

In the end, it was the tests that failed. They totally missed his ability and passion for sports. They had no means to identify ambition, the fire inside that drives people to find a path to success that zigzags around the maze of standard doors that won't open. They never identified the most important talent of all. It's the ability to connect with people, mind to mind, and soul to soul. It's that rare power to energize the ambitions of others so that they, too, rise to the level of their dreams.

A passion for sports, adventure, family, and entrepreneurship define Sir Richard's life. Branson has broken several air and land speed and distance records while racing boats and hot air balloons in his pursuit of adventure. He structures his work schedule so that he has ample time to spend with his family and friends. Indeed, Branson's efforts to synthesize work, play, and life seem to be the hallmark of his business model and business success.

Branson: The Entrepreneur

Branson began building his entrepreneurial empire in his teenage years. At the age of 17, being frustrated with the rules and regulations of schools and brimming with activism, Branson and a friend, Jonny Gems, started a magazine called *Student*. The magazine tied many schools together and focused on the students themselves rather than the schools. After publishing the first issue of *Student*, Branson received a note from the headmaster of the school that he and Gems attended. The headmaster wrote: "Congratulations, Branson. I predict that you will either go to prison or become a millionaire."

Branson dropped out of school and continued to pursue his entrepreneurial interests. His next venture was a discount music business called Virgin Records. Then entrepreneurial venture after entrepreneurial venture developed, and as the saying goes: "The rest is history!" Sir Richard—knighted by the Queen of England in 2000—has mostly majority stakes in over 200 companies that constitute his $7.9 billion entrepreneurial empire. The companies cut across a diverse array of business lines, including Virgin Atlantic

Airlines, Virgin Books, Virgin Limousines, Virgin Megastores, Virgin Vacations, Necker Island, Radio Free Virgin, Virgin Cola, and V2 Music, among numerous others.

Branson is not a conventional businessperson—and he never intended to be one. In fact, Sir Richard is about as far removed from the stereotypic CEO as one can possibly imagine. "He continues to be a corporate iconoclast, defying conventional wisdom, pushing the envelope, poking fun at the big guys, saying exactly what he thinks and doing exactly what he wants." Branson has irreverence for authority that he claims to have inherited from both of his parents.

Branson relishes becoming involved in "industries that charge too much (music) or hold consumers hostage (cellular) or treat them badly and bore them to tears (airlines)." His aim is to upset the status quo in these types of industries.

Branson also relishes teamwork and brings it into play in his entrepreneurial ventures. He has an "advisory team, whose job is to capture his entrepreneurial ideas and wrestle them into some kind of corporate structure that is both attractive to investors and palatable to him." Branson also gives others opportunities to develop their ideas into business ventures that he backs.

Sir Richard's entrepreneurial ventures and work pique his intellectual curiosity and provides the education he was never able to get in school. "What really sets him apart from other CEOs is that he

doesn't mind surprises. He thrives on them. Start-up problems don't bother him at all. Neither do unforeseen battles."

Discussion Questions

1. Using the various personality characteristics discussed in this chapter, how would you describe Sir Richard Branson's personality?

2. What perceptions have you formed of Richard Branson? How do you think your perceptions are affected by characteristics of you as the perceiver and Branson as the perceptual target? To what extent have the barriers to social perception influenced your view of Branson?

3. How do attributions factor into understanding the background of Branson's entrepreneurial development?

SOURCE: This case was written by Michael K. McCuddy, The Louis S. and Mary L. Morgal Chair of Christian Business Ethics and Professor of Management, College of Business Administration, Valparaiso University. This case was developed from material contained on the Virgin Group Web site at http://www.virgin.com and in the following articles: J. Hopkins, "Entrepreneurs Are Born, But Can They Be Taught?" *USA Today* (April 7, 2004): accessed from http://search.epnet.com/direct.asp?an=JOE398148936304$db=f5h; B. Morris, "Richard Branson: What a Life. 'I don't think of work as work and play as play. It's all living.'" *Fortune* (October 6, 2003): accessed at http://www.fortune.com; and J. Shepler, "Richard Branson's Virgin Success: The Incredible Triumph of an Enigmatic Entrepreneur," accessed at http://www.johnshepler.com.

Chapter 4

Attitudes, Values, and Ethics

After reading this chapter, you should be able to do the following:

1 Explain the ABC model of an attitude.

2 Describe how attitudes are formed.

3 Define *job satisfaction* and *organizational commitment* and discuss the importance of these two work attitudes.

4 Identify the characteristics of the source, target, and message that affect persuasion.

5 Distinguish between instrumental and terminal values.

6 Explain how managers can deal with the diverse value systems that characterize the global environment.

7 Describe a model of individual and organizational influences on ethical behavior.

8 Discuss how value systems, locus of control, Machiavellianism, and cognitive moral development affect ethical behavior.

THINKING AHEAD: WHOLE FOODS MARKET

Values Driven

Whole Foods Market, the world's largest natural and organic foods market, was founded in Austin, Texas, in 1980. For six consecutive years, Whole Foods has earned the distinction of being one of *Fortune*'s Top 100 Companies to Work For. Its motto, "Whole Foods, Whole People, Whole Planet™," reflects the company's commitment to customer satisfaction and wellness and employee excellence and happiness. The company was the first grocer in the United States to have its retail operations certified organic. Its customers are focused on healthy living and eating well. By 2004, Whole Foods had 150 stores and $3 billion in sales.

The company extends its philosophy to working closely with local farmers, in many cases displaying a minibiography of the farmer near the produce sold in its markets. In addition to foods, the Whole Body department offers herbal teas, essential oils, books, vitamins and supplements, and yoga products. Whole Foods replaced 10 percent of its electricity with clean wind energy, making it one of the largest private purchasers of wind energy in the nation. It maintains strict environmental policies and gives a minimum of 5 percent of profits each year to community and nonprofit groups.

But even Whole Foods experiences controversy. Two animal rights groups, Vegetarians International Voice for Animals (VivaUSA) and People for the Ethical Treatment of Animals (PETA), attacked the company for doing business with farms that abuse ducks. PETA members stormed the podium at Whole Foods' annual shareholder meeting, and company executives walked out. This conflict presented a dilemma: given its values and image, what would Whole Foods do? We'll continue the story in the Looking Back feature at the end of the chapter.[1, 2]

In this chapter, we continue the discussion of individual differences we began in Chapter 3 with personality, perception, and attribution. Persons and situations jointly influence behavior, and individual differences help us to better understand the influence of the person. Our focus now is on three other individual difference factors: attitudes, values, and ethics.

Attitudes

attitude

A psychological tendency expressed by evaluating an entity with some degree of favor or disfavor.

An *attitude* is a psychological tendency that is expressed by evaluating a particular entity with some degree of favor or disfavor.[3] We respond favorably or unfavorably toward many things: animals, coworkers, our own appearance, politics.

Attitudes are important because of their links to behavior. Attitudes are also an integral part of the world of work. Managers speak of workers who have "bad attitudes" and conduct "attitude adjustment" talks with employees. Often, poor performance attributed to bad attitudes really stems from lack of motivation, minimal feedback, lack of trust in management, or other problems. These are areas that managers must explore. Despair, Inc., has created a business based on a humorous look at attitudes. The Real World 4.1 shares its story.

It is important for managers to understand the antecedents to attitudes as well as their consequences. Managers also need to understand the different components of attitudes, how attitudes are formed, the major attitudes that affect work behavior, and how to use persuasion to change attitudes.

The ABC Model

1. Explain the ABC model of an attitude.

Attitudes develop on the basis of evaluative responding. An individual does not have an attitude until he or she responds to an entity (person, object, situation, or issue) on an affective, cognitive, or behavioral basis. To understand the complexity of an attitude, we can break it down into three components, as depicted in Table 4.1.

affect

The emotional component of an attitude.

These components—affect, behavioral intentions, and cognition—compose what we call the ABC model of an attitude.[4] *Affect* is the emotional component of an attitude. It refers to an individual's feeling about something or someone. Statements such as "I like this" or "I prefer that" reflect the affective component of an attitude. Affect is measured by physiological indicators such as galvanic skin response (changes in electrical resistance of skin that indicate emotional arousal) and blood pressure. These indicators show changes in emo-

TABLE 4.1   The ABC Model of an Attitude

	COMPONENT	MEASURED BY	EXAMPLE
A	Affect	Physiological indicators	
		Verbal statements about feelings	I don't like my boss.
B	Behavioral intentions	Observed behavior	
		Verbal statements about intentions	I want to transfer to another department.
C	Cognition	Attitude scales	
		Verbal statements about beliefs	I believe my boss plays favorites at work.

SOURCE: Adapted from M. J. Rosenberg and C. I. Hovland, "Cognitive, Affective, and Behavioral Components of Attitude," in M. J. Rosenberg, C. I. Hovland, W. J. McGuire, R. P. Abelson, and J. H. Brehm, *Attitude Organization and Change* (New Haven, Conn.: Yale University Press, 1960). Copyright 1960 Yale University Press. Used with permission.

A New Twist on Attitudes at Despair, Inc.

Despair, Inc.'s, seemingly de-motivating slogans are, in fact, motivators in that they generate humor.

© 2004 Despair, Inc.

You've seen the sweet-sounding motivational posters and feel-good slogans on coffee mugs. Stores in shopping malls specialize in motivational products like "Do Your Best" posters that display soaring eagles. Despair, Inc., offers an alternative, reminding us that "Eagles may soar, but buzzards don't get sucked into jet engines." The company offers a complete line of "demotivators" that are guaranteed to give a laugh. One poster, for example, describes idiocy: "Never underestimate the power of stupid people in large groups." On burnout: "Attitudes are contagious. Mine might kill you."

Is Despair, Inc., really promoting bad attitudes with its demotivators? Hardly. Studies have shown that humor at work is important, and that in fact it is related to individual and work-unit performance. Humor relieves tension, reduces hostility, and improves morale. By encouraging laughter at work, Despair products, in a bizarre way, might be motivating people.

In its brochure, Despair, Inc., even refers to motivation in the "positively negative way." Despair's thoughts on motivation: "If a pretty poster and a cute saying are all it takes to motivate you, you probably have a very easy job—the kind robots will be doing soon."

SOURCE: F. Sala, "Laughing All the Way to the Bank," *Harvard Business Review* 81 (2003): 16–17.

---

tions by measuring physiological arousal. An individual's attempt to hide his or her feelings might be shown by a change in arousal.

The second component is the intention to behave in a certain way toward an object or person. Our attitudes toward women in management, for example, may be inferred from observing the way we behave toward a female supervisor. We may be supportive, passive, or hostile, depending on our attitude. The behavioral component of an attitude is measured by observing behavior or by asking a person about behavior or intentions. The statement "If I were asked to speak at commencement, I'd be willing to try to do so, even though I'd be nervous" reflects a behavioral intention.

The third component of an attitude, cognition (thought), reflects a person's perceptions or beliefs. Cognitive elements are evaluative beliefs and are measured by attitude scales or by asking about thoughts. The statement "I believe Japanese workers are industrious" reflects the cognitive component of an attitude.

The ABC model shows that to thoroughly understand an attitude, we must assess all three components. Suppose, for example, you want to evaluate your employees' attitudes toward flextime (flexible work scheduling). You would want to determine how they feel about flextime (affect), whether they would use flextime (behavioral intention), and what they think about the policy (cognition). The most common method of attitude measurement, the attitude scale, measures only the cognitive component.

As rational beings, individuals try to be consistent in everything they believe in and do. They prefer consistency (consonance) between their attitudes and behavior. Anything that disrupts this consistency causes tension (dissonance), which motivates individuals to change either their attitudes or their behavior to return to a state of consistency. The tension produced when there is a conflict between attitudes and behavior is *cognitive dissonance.*[5]

cognitive dissonance

A state of tension that is produced when an individual experiences conflict between attitudes and behavior.

Suppose, for example, a salesperson is required to sell damaged televisions for the full retail price, without revealing the damage to customers. She believes, however, that doing so constitutes unethical behavior. This creates a conflict between her attitude (concealing information from customers is unethical) and her behavior (selling defective TVs without informing customers about the damage).

The salesperson, experiencing the discomfort from dissonance, will try to resolve the conflict. She might change her behavior by refusing to sell the defective TV sets. Alternatively, she might rationalize that the defects are minor and that the customers will not be harmed by not knowing about them. These are attempts by the salesperson to restore equilibrium between her attitudes and behavior, thereby eliminating the tension from cognitive dissonance.

Managers need to understand cognitive dissonance because employees often find themselves in situations in which their attitudes conflict with their behavior. They manage the tension by changing their attitudes or behavior. Employees who display sudden shifts in behavior may be attempting to reduce dissonance. Some employees find the conflicts between strongly held attitudes and required work behavior so uncomfortable that they leave the organization to escape the dissonance.

Attitude Formation

2. Describe how attitudes are formed.

Attitudes are learned. Our responses to people and issues evolve over time. Two major influences on attitudes are direct experience and social learning.

Direct experience with an object or person is a powerful influence on attitudes. How do you know that you like biology or dislike math? You have probably formed these attitudes from experience in studying the subjects. Research has shown that attitudes that are derived from direct experience are stronger, held more confidently, and more resistant to change than attitudes formed through indirect experience.[6] One reason attitudes derived from direct experience are so powerful is their availability. This means that the attitudes are easily accessed and are active in our cognitive processes.[7] When attitudes are available, we can call them quickly into consciousness. Attitudes that are not learned from direct experience are not as available, so we do not recall them as easily.

social learning
The process of deriving attitudes from family, peer groups, religious organizations, and culture.

In *social learning*, the family, peer groups, religious organizations, and culture shape an individual's attitudes in an indirect manner.[8] Children learn to adopt certain attitudes by the reinforcement they are given by their parents when they display behaviors that reflect an appropriate attitude. This is evident when very young children express political preferences similar to their parents'. Peer pressure molds attitudes through group acceptance of individuals who express popular attitudes and through sanctions, such as exclusion from the group, placed on individuals who espouse unpopular attitudes.

Substantial social learning occurs through *modeling*, in which individuals acquire attitudes by merely observing others. After overhearing other individuals expressing an opinion or watching them engaging in a behavior that reflects an attitude, the observer adopts the attitude.

For an individual to learn from observing a model, four processes must take place:

1. The learner must focus attention on the model.

2. The learner must retain what was observed from the model. Retention is accomplished in two basic ways. In one, the learner "stamps in" what

was observed by forming a verbal code for it. The other way is through symbolic rehearsal, by which the learner forms a mental image of himself or herself behaving like the model.

3. Behavioral reproduction must occur; that is, the learner must practice the behavior.

4. The learner must be motivated to learn from the model.

SW Airlines

Culture also plays a definitive role in attitude development. Consider, for example, the contrast in the North American and European attitudes toward vacation and leisure. The typical vacation in the United States is two weeks, and some workers do not use all of their vacation time. In Europe, the norm is longer vacations; and in some countries, *holiday* means everyone taking a month off. The European attitude is that an investment in longer vacations is important to health and performance.

Attitudes and Behavior

If you have a favorable attitude toward participative management, will your management style be participative? As managers, if we know an employee's attitude, to what extent can we predict the person's behavior? These questions illustrate the fundamental issue of attitude–behavior correspondence, that is, the degree to which an attitude predicts behavior.

This correspondence has concerned organizational behaviorists and social psychologists for quite some time. Can attitudes predict behaviors like being absent from work or quitting your job? Some studies suggested that attitudes and behavior are closely linked, while others found no relationship at all or a weak relationship at best. Attention then became focused on when attitudes predict behavior and when they do not. Attitude–behavior correspondence depends on five things: attitude specificity, attitude relevance, timing of measurement, personality factors, and social constraints.

Individuals possess both general and specific attitudes. You may favor women's right to reproductive freedom (a general attitude) and prefer pro-choice political candidates (a specific attitude) but not attend pro-choice rallies or send money to Planned Parenthood. That you don't perform these behaviors may make the link between your attitude and behavior on this issue seem rather weak. However, given a choice between a pro-choice and an anti-abortion political candidate, you will probably vote for the pro-choice candidate. In this case, your attitude seems quite predictive of your behavior. The point is that the greater the attitude specificity, the stronger its link to behavior.[9]

Another factor that affects the attitude–behavior link is relevance.[10] Attitudes that address an issue in which we have some self-interest are more relevant for us, and our subsequent behavior is consistent with our expressed attitude. Suppose there is a proposal to raise income taxes for those who earn $150,000 or more. If you are a student, you may not find the issue of great personal relevance. Individuals in that income bracket, however, might find it highly relevant; their attitude toward the issue would be strongly predictive of whether they would vote for the tax increase.

The timing of the measurement also affects attitude–behavior correspondence. The shorter the time between the attitude measurement and the observed behavior, the stronger the relationship. For example, voter preference polls taken close to an election are more accurate than earlier polls.

Personality factors also influence the attitude–behavior link. One personality disposition that affects the consistency between attitudes and behavior is self-monitoring. Recall from Chapter 3 that low self-monitors rely on their internal states when making decisions about behavior, while high self-monitors are more responsive to situational cues. Low self-monitors therefore display greater correspondence between their attitudes and behaviors.[11] High self-monitors may display little correspondence between their attitudes and behavior because they behave according to signals from others and from the environment.

Finally, social constraints affect the relationship between attitudes and behavior.[12] The social context provides information about acceptable attitudes and behaviors.[13, 14] New employees in an organization, for example, are exposed to the attitudes of their work group. Suppose a newcomer from Afghanistan holds a negative attitude toward women in management because in his country the prevailing attitude is that women should not be in positions of power. He sees, however, that his work group members respond positively to their female supervisor. His own behavior may therefore be compliant because of social constraints. This behavior is inconsistent with his attitude and cultural belief system.

Work Attitudes

Attitudes at work are important because, directly or indirectly, they affect work behavior. Chief among the things that negatively affect employees' work attitudes are jobs that are very demanding, combined with a lack of control on the part of the employee.[15] A positive psychological climate at work, on the other hand, can lead to positive attitudes and good performance.[16] A study found that when hotel employees offered helpful, concerned service, hotel customers developed a warmer, more positive attitude toward the hotel itself. This attitude resulted in greater customer loyalty, greater likelihood that the customers would stay at the hotel, and even a willingness to pay more for the same service. Customer attitudes were strongly influenced by employee gestures, facial expressions, and words. In this study, customer attitudes were crucial to the success of the firm, and employee behaviors were crucial in forming customer attitudes, meaning firms can "train" their employees to "train" customers to have better attitudes![17]

Although many work attitudes are important, two attitudes in particular have been emphasized. Job satisfaction and organizational commitment are key attitudes of interest to managers and researchers.

3. Define *job satisfaction* and *organizational commitment* and discuss the importance of these two work attitudes.

job satisfaction

A pleasurable or positive emotional state resulting from the appraisal of one's job or job experiences.

JOB SATISFACTION Most of us believe that work should be a positive experience. *Job satisfaction* is a pleasurable or positive emotional state resulting from the appraisal of one's job or job experiences.[18] It has been treated both as a general attitude and as satisfaction with five specific dimensions of the job: pay, the work itself, promotion opportunities, supervision, and coworkers.[19] You can assess your own job satisfaction by completing You 4.1.

An individual may hold different attitudes toward various aspects of the job. For example, an employee may like her job responsibilities but be dissatisfied with the opportunities for promotion. Characteristics of individuals also affect job satisfaction.[20] Those with high negative affectivity are more likely to be dissatisfied with their jobs. Challenging work, valued rewards, opportunities for advancement, competent supervision, and supportive coworkers are dimensions of the job that can lead to satisfaction.

Assess Your Job Satisfaction

Think of the job you have now or a job you've had in the past. Indicate how satisfied you are with each aspect of your job below, using the following scale:

1 = Extremely dissatisfied
2 = Dissatisfied
3 = Slightly dissatisfied
4 = Neutral
5 = Slightly satisfied
6 = Satisfied
7 = Extremely satisfied

1. The amount of job security I have.
2. The amount of pay and fringe benefits I receive.
3. The amount of personal growth and development I get in doing my job.
4. The people I talk to and work with on my job.
5. The degree of respect and fair treatment I receive from my boss.
6. The feeling of worthwhile accomplishment I get from doing my job.
7. The chance to get to know other people while on the job.
8. The amount of support and guidance I receive from my supervisor.
9. The degree to which I am fairly paid for what I contribute to this organization.
10. The amount of independent thought and action I can exercise in my job.
11. How secure things look for me in the future in this organization.
12. The chance to help other people while at work.
13. The amount of challenge in my job.
14. The overall quality of the supervision I receive on my work.

Now, compute your scores for the facets of job satisfaction.

Pay satisfaction:

Q2 + Q9   = Divided by 2:

Security satisfaction:

Q1 + Q11   = Divided by 2:

Social satisfaction:

Q4 + Q7 + Q12   = Divided by 3:

Supervisory satisfaction:

Q5 + Q8 + Q14   = Divided by 3:

Growth satisfaction:

Q3 + Q6 + Q10 + Q13 = Divided by 4:

Scores on the facets range from 1 to 7. (Scores lower than 4 suggest there is room for change.)

This questionnaire is an abbreviated version of the Job Diagnostic Survey, a widely used tool for assessing individual's attitudes about their jobs. Compare your scores on each facet to the following norms for a large sample of managers.

Pay satisfaction:	4.6
Security satisfaction:	5.2
Social satisfaction:	5.6
Supervisory satisfaction:	5.2
Growth satisfaction:	5.3

How do your scores compare? Are there actions you can take to improve your job satisfaction?

SOURCE: *Work Redesign* by Hackman/Oldham, © 1980. Reprinted by permission of Pearson Education, Inc., Upper Saddle River, N.J.

There are several measures of job satisfaction. One of the most widely used measures comes from the Job Descriptive Index (JDI). This index measures the specific facets of satisfaction by asking employees to respond yes, no, or cannot decide to a series of statements describing their jobs. Another popular measure is the Minnesota Satisfaction Questionnaire (MSQ).[21] This survey also asks employees to respond to statements about their jobs, using a five-point scale that ranges from very dissatisfied to very satisfied. Figure 4.1 presents some sample items from each questionnaire.

FIGURE 4.1   Sample Items from Satisfaction Questionnaires

4.1

Job Descriptive Index

Think of the work you do at present. How well does each of the following words or phrases describe your work? In the blank beside each word given below, write

__Y__   for "Yes" if it describes your work
__N__   for "No" if it does NOT describe it
__?__   if you cannot decide

WORK ON YOUR PRESENT JOB:

_____ Routine
_____ Satisfying
_____ Good

Think of the majority of the people that you work with now or the people you meet in connection with your work. How well does each of the following words or phrases describe these people? In the blank beside each word, write

__Y__   for "Yes" if it describes the people you work with
__N__   for "No" if it does NOT describe them
__?__   if you cannot decide

COWORKERS (PEOPLE):

_____ Boring
_____ Responsible
_____ Intelligent

Minnesota Satisfaction Questionnaire

1 = Very dissatisfied
2 = Dissatisfied
3 = I can't decide whether I am satisfied or not
4 = Satisfied
5 = Very satisfied

On my present job, this is how I feel about:

_____ The chance to work alone on the job (independence)
_____ My chances for advancement on this job (advancement)
_____ The chance to tell people what to do (authority)
_____ The praise I get for a good job (recognition)
_____ My pay and the amount of work I do (compensation)

SOURCES: The Job Descriptive Index is copyrighted by Bowling Green State University. The complete forms, scoring key, instructions, and norms can be obtained from Dr. Patricia C. Smith, Department of Psychology, Bowling Green State University, Bowling Green, OH 43403. Minnesota Satisfaction Questionnaire from D. J. Weiss, R. V. Davis, G. W. England, and L. H. Lofquist, *Manual for the Minnesota Satisfaction Questionnaire* (University of Minnesota Vocational Psychology Research, 1967).

Managers and employees hold a common belief that happy or "satisfied" employees are more productive at work. Most of us feel more satisfied than usual when we believe that we are performing better than usual.[22] Interestingly, the relationship between job satisfaction and performance is quite a bit more complex than that. Are satisfied workers more productive? Or, are more productive workers more satisfied? The link between satisfaction and performance has been widely explored. One view holds that satisfaction causes good performance. If this were true, then the manager's job would simply be to keep workers happy. Although this may be the case for certain individuals, job satisfaction for most people is one of several causes of good performance.

Another view holds that good performance causes satisfaction. If this were true, managers would need to help employees perform well, and satisfaction would follow. However, some employees who are high performers are not satisfied with their jobs.

The research shows modest support for both views, but no simple, direct relationship between satisfaction and performance has been found.[23] One reason for these results may be the difficulty of demonstrating the attitude–behavior links we described earlier in this chapter. Future studies using specific, relevant attitudes and measuring personality variables and behavioral intentions may be able to demonstrate a link between job satisfaction and performance.

Another reason for the lack of a clear relationship between satisfaction and performance is the intervening role of rewards. Employees who receive valued rewards are more satisfied. In addition, employees who receive rewards that are contingent on performance (the higher the performance, the larger the reward) tend to perform better. Rewards thus influence both satisfaction and performance. The key to influencing both satisfaction and performance through rewards is that the rewards are valued by employees and are tied directly to performance.

rewards infl' job sat

Job satisfaction has been shown to be related to many other important personal and organizational outcomes. Job satisfaction is related to *organizational citizenship behavior*—behavior that is above and beyond the call of duty. Satisfied employees are more likely to help their coworkers, make positive comments about the company, and refrain from complaining when things at work do not go well.[24] Going beyond the call of duty is especially important to organizations using teams to get work done. Employees depend on extra help from each other to get things accomplished. When massive wildfires swept through California in 2003, most businesses in the San Diego area closed for one or more days as choking black smoke filled the air and thousands of homes were threatened. Aplus.net, an Internet presence provider, chose to remain open; however, due to the danger involved, the company did not require its employees to report to work. Yet, in spite of thick smoke, most of the firm's employees came to work anyway, even though some were unsure if their homes would be waiting for them when they left work that evening.[25] Because of their willingness to go the extra mile, Aplus.net and its customers remained up and running throughout the fires. The firm reported in November that the massive fires had no negative impact on its financial results for the quarter.

Satisfied workers are more likely to want to give something back to the organization because they want to reciprocate their positive experiences.[26] Often, employees may feel that citizenship behaviors are not recognized because they occur outside the confines of normal job responsibilities. Organizational citizenship behaviors (OCBs) do, however, influence performance evaluations. Employees who exhibit behaviors such as helping others, making suggestions for innovations, and developing their skills receive higher performance ratings.[27]

Individuals who identify strongly with the organization are more likely to perform OCBs.[28] High self-monitors, who base their behavior on cues from the situation, are also more likely to perform OCBs.[29] Good deeds, in the form of OCBs, can be contagious. One study found that when a person's close coworkers chose to perform OCBs, that person was more likely to reciprocate. When the norm among other team members was to engage in OCBs, the individual worker was more likely to offer OCBs. The impact of one worker's OCBs can spread throughout an entire department.[30]

Although researchers have had a tough time demonstrating the link between job satisfaction and individual performance, this has not been the case for the link between job satisfaction and organizational performance. Companies with satisfied workers have better performance than companies with dissatisfied workers.[31] This may be due to the more intangible elements of performance,

organizational citizenship behavior
Behavior that is above and beyond the call of duty.

like organizational citizenship behavior, that contribute to organizational effectiveness but aren't necessarily captured by just measuring individual job performance.

Job satisfaction is related to some other important outcomes. People who are dissatisfied with their jobs are absent more frequently. The type of dissatisfaction that most often leads employees to miss work is dissatisfaction with the work itself. In addition, dissatisfied workers are more likely to quit their jobs, and turnover at work can be very costly to organizations. Dissatisfied workers also report more psychological and medical problems than do satisfied employees.[32]

Like all attitudes, job satisfaction is influenced by culture. American workers tend to hold to the "Protestant work ethic," which values work for its own sake and makes it a central part of their lives. Consistent with this basic view, American managers place a high value on outcomes such as autonomy, independence, and achievement. Koreans, in contrast to Americans, generally grow up in a more authoritarian system, which places greater value on family and less value on work for its own sake. Americans place greater value on and find greater job satisfaction through intrinsic job factors, whereas Koreans prefer extrinsic factors.[33]

This finding was echoed in a study comparing job satisfaction across 49 countries. Job characteristics and job satisfaction were more tightly linked in richer countries, more individualistic countries, and smaller power-distance countries. These findings suggest that cultural differences have strong influences on job satisfaction and the factors that produce job satisfaction.[34]

Because organizations face the challenge of operating in the global environment, managers must understand that job satisfaction is significantly affected by culture. Employees from different cultures may have differing expectations of their jobs; thus, there may be no single prescription for increasing the job satisfaction of a multicultural workforce.

ORGANIZATIONAL COMMITMENT The strength of an individual's identification with an organization is known as *organizational commitment*. There are three kinds of organizational commitment: affective, continuance, and normative. *Affective commitment* is an employee's intention to remain in an organization because of a strong desire to do so. It consists of three factors:

> A belief in the goals and values of the organization

> A willingness to put forth effort on behalf of the organization

> A desire to remain a member of the organization.[35]

Affective commitment encompasses loyalty, but it is also a deep concern for the organization's welfare.

Continuance commitment is an employee's tendency to remain in an organization because the person cannot afford to leave.[36] Sometimes, employees believe that if they leave, they will lose a great deal of their investments in time, effort, and benefits and that they cannot replace these investments.

Normative commitment is a perceived obligation to remain with the organization. Individuals who experience normative commitment stay with the organization because they feel that they should.[37]

Certain organizational conditions encourage commitment. Participation in decision making and job security are two such conditions. Certain job characteristics also positively affect commitment. These include autonomy, responsibility, and interesting work.[38]

organizational commitment

The strength of an individual's identification with an organization.

affective commitment

The type of organizational commitment that is based on an individual's desire to remain in an organization.

continuance commitment

The type of organizational commitment that is based on the fact that an individual cannot afford to leave.

normative commitment

The type of organizational commitment that is based on an individual's perceived obligation to remain with an organization.

Affective and normative commitments are related to lower rates of absenteeism, higher quality of work, increased productivity, and several different types of performance.[39] Managers should encourage affective commitment because committed individuals expend more task-related effort and are less likely than others to leave the organization.[40]

Managers can increase affective commitment by communicating that they value employees' contributions, and that they care about employees' well-being.[41] Affective commitment also increases when the organization and employees share the same values, and when the organization emphasizes values like moral integrity, fairness, creativity, and openness.[42] Negative experiences at work can undoubtedly diminish affective commitment. One such experience is discrimination. Perceived age discrimination, whether for being too old or too young, can dampen affective commitment.[43]

Several researchers have examined organizational commitment in different countries. One study revealed that American workers displayed higher affective commitment than did Korean and Japanese workers.[44] Another study showed that Chinese workers place high value on social relationships at work and that those with stronger interpersonal relationships are more committed to their organizations.[45] The authors suggest that Chinese firms improve employee commitment and retention by organizing activities to help cultivate relationships among employees. This means that expatriate managers should be sensitive to the quality of relationships among their Chinese employees if they want to improve organizational commitment.

Job satisfaction and organizational commitment are two important work attitudes that managers can strive to improve among their employees. And these two attitudes are strongly related. Both affective and normative commitment are related to job satisfaction. Increasing job satisfaction is likely to increase commitment as well. To begin with, managers can use attitude surveys to reveal employees' satisfaction or dissatisfaction with specific facets of their jobs. Then they can take action to make the deficient aspects of the job more satisfying. Work attitudes are also important because they influence business outcomes. Job satisfaction and organizational citizenship behavior are linked to customer satisfaction and company profitability.[46]

Persuasion and Attitude Change

To understand how attitudes can change, it is necessary to understand the process of persuasion. The days of command-and-control management, in which executives simply told employees what do to, are long gone. Modern managers must be skilled in the art of persuasion.[47] Through persuasion, one individual (the source) tries to change the attitude of another person (the target). Certain characteristics of the source, target, and message affect the persuasion process. There are also two cognitive routes to persuasion.

4. Identify the characteristics of the source, target, and message that affect persuasion.

SOURCE CHARACTERISTICS Three major characteristics of the source affect persuasion: expertise, trustworthiness, and attractiveness.[48] A source who is perceived as an expert is particularly persuasive. Trustworthiness is also important. John Mack, head of Credit Suisse First Boston (CSFB), understands the importance of trust. When he came to CSFB, the investment bank was a huge mess, but in a short time Mack achieved amazing results by persuading his employees to trust him. First, he told CSFB's bankers that their pay packages were excessive and the firm could not afford them. The bankers gave back more than $400 million in cash bonuses. Next, he asked CSFB's executives to give up some of the richest pay packages in the business. Mack was able to convince them to give up amounts that sometimes exceeded $20 million, all so that younger executives could receive bonuses and remain with the firm. And when lawyers discovered an e-mail suggesting a top CSFB employee had covered up wrongdoing from federal regulators, Mack immediately contacted federal regulators to blow the whistle. John Mack's employees trust him because he doesn't just talk about teamwork, integrity, and trust; he demonstrates them in his own career. This trustworthiness allowed him to persuade his employees to help him save the firm.[49] Finally, attractiveness and likability play a role in persuasion. Attractive communicators have long been used in advertising to persuade consumers to buy certain products. As a source of persuasion, managers who are perceived as being experts, who are trustworthy, or who are attractive or likable will have an edge in changing employee attitudes.

TARGET CHARACTERISTICS Some people are more easily persuaded than others. Individuals with low self-esteem are more likely to change their attitudes in response to persuasion than are individuals with high self-esteem. Individuals who hold very extreme attitudes are more resistant to persuasion, and people who are in a good mood are easier to persuade.[50] Undoubtedly, individuals differ widely in their susceptibility to persuasion. Managers must recognize these differences and realize that their attempts to change attitudes may not receive universal acceptance.

MESSAGE CHARACTERISTICS Suppose you must implement an unpopular policy at work. You want to persuade your employees that the policy is a positive change. Should you present one side of the issue or both sides? Given that your employees are already negatively inclined toward the policy, you will have more success in changing their attitudes if you present both sides. This shows support for one side of the issue while acknowledging that another side does exist. Moreover, refuting the other side makes it more difficult for the targets to hang on to their negative attitudes.

Messages that are obviously designed to change the target's attitude may be met with considerable negative reaction. In fact, undisguised deliberate attempts at changing attitudes may cause attitude change in the opposite direction! This is most likely to occur when the target of the persuasive communication feels her or his freedom is threatened.[51] Less threatening approaches are less likely to elicit negative reactions. The emotional tone of the message is also important. Persuasion is more successful when messages are framed with the same emotion as that felt by the receiver.[52]

COGNITIVE ROUTES TO PERSUASION When are message characteristics more important, and when are other characteristics more important in persuasion? The elaboration likelihood model of persuasion, presented in Figure 4.2, proposes that persuasion occurs over two routes: the central route and the peripheral route.[53] The routes are differentiated by the amount of elaboration, or scrutiny, the target is motivated to give the message.

The *central route* to persuasion involves direct cognitive processing of the message's content. When an issue is personally relevant, the individual is motivated to think carefully about it. The listener may nod his/her head when the argument is strong and shake his/her head if the argument is weak.[54] In the central route, the content of the message is very important. If the arguments presented are logical and convincing, attitude change will follow.

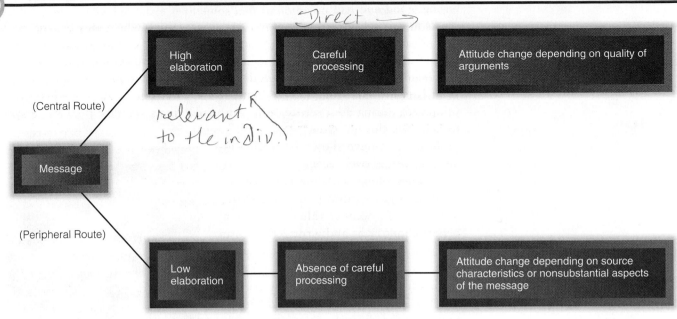

SOURCE: Adapted from R. E. Petty and J. T. Cacioppo, "The Elaboration Likelihood Model of Persuasion," in L. Berkowitz, ed., *Advances in Experimental Social Psychology*, vol. 19 (New York: Academic Press, 1986), 123–205.

In the *peripheral route* to persuasion, the individual is not motivated to pay much attention to the message's content. This is because the message may not be perceived as personally relevant, or the individual may be distracted. Instead, the individual is persuaded by characteristics of the persuader—for example, expertise, trustworthiness, and attractiveness. In addition, the individual may be persuaded by statistics, the number of arguments presented, or the method of presentation—all of which are nonsubstantial aspects of the message.

The elaboration likelihood model shows that the target's level of involvement with the issue is important. That involvement also determines which route to persuasion will be more effective. In some cases, attitude change comes about through both the central and the peripheral routes. To cover all of the bases, managers should structure the content of their messages carefully, develop their own attributes that will help them be more persuasive, and choose a method of presentation that will be attractive to the audience.[55]

We have seen that the process of persuading individuals to change their attitudes is affected by the source, the target, the message, and the route. When all is said and done, however, managers are important catalysts for encouraging attitude change. This is a difficult process. Recently, researchers have proposed that people hold attitudes at two different levels.

Values

Another source of individual differences is values. Values exist at a deeper level than attitudes and are more general and basic in nature. We use them to evaluate our own behavior and that of others. As such, they vary widely among individuals. *Values* are enduring beliefs that a specific mode of conduct or end state of existence is personally or socially preferable to an opposite or converse mode of conduct or end state of existence.[56] This definition was proposed by

values

Enduring beliefs that a specific mode of conduct or end state of existence is personally or socially preferable to an opposite or converse mode of conduct or end state of existence.

Rokeach, an early scholar of human values. Values give us a sense of right and wrong, good and bad.

As individuals grow and mature, they learn values, which may change over the life span as an individual develops a sense of self. Cultures, societies, and organizations shape values. Parents and others who are respected by the individual play crucial roles in value development by providing guidance about what is right and wrong. Values come to the forefront of an individual's development during adolescence, and many individuals stabilize their value systems during this life stage.

Businesses have shown increasing interest in values over recent years. This interest goes along with the emphasis on ethics in organizations that we described in Chapter 2. Because values are general beliefs about right and wrong, they form the basis for ethical behavior. Some companies value personal growth and freedom. More than a quarter century ago (1979), Intel began offering sabbaticals to workers at all levels. Today, every full-time Intel employee qualifies for eight weeks of time off with full pay and benefits every seven years. Intel says sabbaticals help employees recharge and return to work ready for new challenges. Employees have used their sabbaticals to pursue hobbies, take classes, and even climb the Himalayas. Other companies that offer sabbaticals include Hallmark,

Sabbaticals, whether used for scaling mountains or just recharging, can enable employees to return to work with renewed vigor.

Apple Computers, and Ralston Purina Company. Unfortunately, certain values can lead to an organization's downfall. The Real World 4.2 describes the combination of values that led to HealthSouth's meltdown. We will focus on the importance of shared values in the organization in Chapter 16. Our emphasis in this chapter is on values as sources of variation among individuals.

Instrumental and Terminal Values

5. Distinguish between instrumental and terminal values.

instrumental values

Values that represent the acceptable behaviors to be used in achieving some end state.

terminal values

Values that represent the goals to be achieved or the end states of existence.

Rokeach distinguished between two types of values: instrumental and terminal. *Instrumental values* reflect the means to achieving goals; that is, they represent the acceptable behaviors to be used in achieving some end state. Instrumental values identified by Rokeach include ambition, honesty, self-sufficiency, and courage. *Terminal values*, in contrast, represent the goals to be achieved or the end states of existence. Rokeach identified happiness, love, pleasure, self-respect, and freedom among the terminal values. A complete list of instrumental and terminal values is presented in Table 4.2. Terminal and instrumental values work in concert to provide individuals with goals to strive for and acceptable ways to achieve the goals.

Americans' rankings of instrumental and terminal values have shown remarkable stability over time.[57] Rokeach studied their rankings in four national samples from 1968, 1971, 1974, and 1981. There was considerable stability in the rankings across the studies, which spanned a thirteen-year period. Most of the values shifted only one position in the rankings over this time span. The

A Simple Recipe for Corporate Meltdown

What do Enron, WorldCom, Tyco, and HealthSouth have in common? First, they were all run by their founders, who were hard-striving entrepreneurs. In fact, not one of these companies lasted longer than its founder's managerial span. Second, each company possessed a set of values that proved to be disastrous.

HealthSouth was the nation's largest provider of rehabilitative health care and outpatient surgery services. An SEC investigation of accounting fraud at the company led to the firing of HealthSouth's chairman, and the company's stock was delisted by the New York Stock Exchange. History repeated itself at HealthSouth because, like the other companies mentioned above, it fit the pattern of three specific elements mixed together:

1. *A baby company's culture in a giant company's body.* The company never grew from one person's idea into an institution with an identity of its own. No value ranked higher than blind obedience to the founding CEO.

2. *A sense of entitlement, which leads to greed.* The founders and employees believed that they deserved everything because they had created success.

3. *Slavery to Wall Street's expectations.* Executives at HealthSouth were expected to make their numbers and satisfy Wall Street; if they didn't, their huge stock holdings and options would fall, threatening their personal wealth.

The combination of these three value-laden elements led HealthSouth, like its predecessors, into scandal and eventual meltdown.

SOURCE: J. Colvin, "History Repeats Itself at HealthSouth," *Fortune* (May 12, 2003): 40, http://www.fortune.com/fortune/valuedriven/0,15704,448251,00.html.

---

highest ranked instrumental values were honesty, ambition, responsibility, forgiving nature, open-mindedness, and courage. The highest ranked terminal values were world peace, family security, freedom, happiness, self-respect, and wisdom.

Although the values of Americans as a group have been stable, individuals vary widely in their value systems. For example, social respect is one terminal value that people differ on. Some people desire respect from others and work diligently to achieve it, and other people place little importance on what others

TABLE 4.2 Instrumental and Terminal Values

INSTRUMENTAL VALUES

Honesty	Ambition	Responsibility
Forgiving nature	Open-mindedness	Courage
Helpfulness	Cleanliness	Competence
Self-control	Affection/love	Cheerfulness
Independence	Politeness	Intelligence
Obedience	Rationality	Imagination

TERMINAL VALUES

World peace	Family security	Freedom
Happiness	Self-respect	Wisdom
Equality	Salvation	Prosperity
Achievement	Friendship	National security
Inner peace	Mature love	Social respect
Beauty in art and nature	Pleasure	Exciting, active life

SOURCE: Table adapted with the permission of The Free Press, a Division of Simon & Schuster, Inc., from *The Nature of Human Values* by Milton Rokeach. Copyright © 1973 by The Free Press.

think of them. Individuals may agree that achievement is an important terminal value but may disagree on how to attain that goal.

Age also affects values. Baby boomers' values contrast with those of the baby busters, who are beginning to enter the workforce. The baby busters value family life and time off from work and prefer a balance between work and home life. This contrasts with the more driven, work-oriented value system of the boomers. The United States is not the only nation affected by age differences in values. Many European nations have found that values of young workers differ from those of older generations. Younger generations place more emphasis on personal development at work and on good pay as compared with previous generations.

Work Values

Work values are important because they affect how individuals behave on their jobs in terms of what is right and wrong.[58] Four work values relevant to individuals are achievement, concern for others, honesty, and fairness.[59] Achievement is a concern for the advancement of one's career. This is shown in such behaviors as working hard and seeking opportunities to develop new skills. Concern for others is shown in caring, compassionate behaviors such as encouraging other employees or helping others work on difficult tasks. These behaviors constitute organizational citizenship, as we discussed earlier. Honesty is providing accurate information and refusing to mislead others for personal gain. Fairness emphasizes impartiality and recognizes different points of view. Individuals can rank-order these values in terms of their importance in their work lives.[60] You 4.2 gives you a chance to see what your work values are and whether they match those of an organization.

Although individuals' value systems differ, sharing similar values at work produces positive results. Employees who share their supervisor's values are more satisfied with their jobs and more committed to the organization.[61] Values also have profound effects on the choice of jobs. Traditionally, pay and advancement potential have been the strongest influences on job choice decisions. One study, however, found that three other work values—achievement, concern for others, and fairness—exerted more influence on job choice decisions than did pay and promotion opportunities.[62]

This means that organizations recruiting job candidates should pay careful attention to individuals' values and to the messages that organizations send about company values. A new "name and shame" report published in Australia by RepuTex is designed to embarrass companies that behave unethically. Nineteen groups graded each of Australia's top companies on corporate governance policies, environmental friendliness, and workplace practices. The 500-page report named Westpac, a major bank, as the most ethical firm in Australia. Westpac was the only company in the country's top 100 to receive the AAA rating.[63]

Cultural Differences in Values

As organizations face the challenges of an increasingly diverse workforce and a global marketplace, it becomes more important than ever for them to understand the influence of culture on values. Doing business in a global marketplace often means that managers encounter a clash of values among different cultures. Take the value of loyalty, for example. In Japan, loyalty means "compassionate overtime." Even though you have no work to do, you should stay late to give moral support to your peers who are working late.[64] In contrast, Koreans value loyalty to the person for whom one works.[65] In the United States,

What Do You Value at Work?

The fifty-four items listed below cover the full range of personal and institutional values you'd be likely to encounter at any company. Divide it into two groups: the twenty-seven that would be the most evident in your ideal workplace and the twenty-seven that would be the least. Keep halving the groups until you have a rank-ordering, then fill in the numbers of your top and bottom ten choices. Test your fit at a firm by seeing whether the company's values match your top and bottom ten.

TOP TEN CHOICES

BOTTOM TEN CHOICES

THE CHOICE MENU
YOU ARE: 1. Flexible. **2.** Adaptable. **3.** Innovative. **4.** Able to seize opportunities. **5.** Willing to experiment. **6.** Risk-taking. **7.** Careful. **8.** Autonomy-seeking. **9.** Comfortable with rules. **10.** Analytical. **11.** Attentive to detail. **12.** Precise. **13.** Team-oriented. **14.** Ready to share information. **15.** People-oriented. **16.** Easygoing. **17.** Calm. **18.** Supportive. **19.** Aggressive. **20.** Decisive. **21.** Action-oriented. **22.** Eager to take initiative. **23.** Reflective. **24.** Achievement-oriented. **25.** Demanding. **26.** Comfortable with individual responsibility. **27.** Comfortable with conflict. **28.** Competitive. **29.** Highly organized. **30.** Results-oriented. **31.** Interested in making friends at work. **32.** Collaborative. **33.** Eager to fit with colleagues. **34.** Enthusiastic about the job.
YOUR COMPANY OFFERS: 35. Stability. **36.** Predictability. **37.** High expectations of performance. **38.** Opportunities for professional growth. **39.** High pay for good performance. **40.** Job security. **41.** Praise for good performance. **42.** A clear guiding philosophy. **43.** A low level of conflict. **44.** An emphasis on quality. **45.** A good reputation. **46.** Respect for the individual's rights. **47.** Tolerance. **48.** Informality. **49.** Fairness. **50.** A unitary culture throughout the organization. **51.** A sense of social responsibility. **52.** Long hours. **53.** Relative freedom from rules. **54.** The opportunity to be distinctive or different from others.

SOURCE: M. Siegel, "The Perils of Culture Conflict." Reprinted from the November 9, 1998, issue of *Fortune* by special permission; copyright © 1998, Time Inc. All rights reserved.

family and other personal loyalties are more highly valued than is loyalty to the company or one's supervisor.

Cultures differ in what they value in terms of an individual's contributions to work. Collectivist cultures such as China and Mexico value a person's contributions to relationships in the work team. In contrast, individualist cultures (the United States, the Netherlands) value a person's contribution to task accomplishment. Both collectivist and individualist cultures value rewards based on individual performance.[66] Iran also represents a collectivist culture. Iranian managers' values, which include little tolerance for ambiguity, high need for structure, and willingness to sacrifice for the good of society, are greatly influenced by Islam. Belonging, harmony, humility, and simplicity are all values promoted by Islam.[67]

Values also affect individuals' views of what constitutes authority. French managers value authority as a right of office and rank. Their behavior reflects this value, as they tend to use power based on their position in the organization. In contrast, managers from the Netherlands and Scandinavia value group inputs to decisions and expect their decisions to be challenged and discussed by employees.[68]

Value differences between cultures must be acknowledged in today's global economy. We may be prone to judging the value systems of others, but we should resist the temptation to do so. Tolerating diversity in values can help us understand other cultures. Value systems of other nations are not necessarily right or wrong—they are merely different. The following suggestions can help managers understand and work with the diverse values that characterize the global environment:[69]

6. Explain how managers can deal with the diverse value systems that characterize the global environment.

1. Learn more about and recognize the values of other peoples. They view their values and customs as moral, traditional, and practical.

2. Avoid prejudging the business customs of others as immoral or corrupt. Assume they are legitimate unless proved otherwise.

3. Find legitimate ways to operate within others' ethical points of view—do not demand that they operate within your value system.

4. Avoid rationalizing "borderline" actions with excuses such as the following:
   > "This isn't really illegal or immoral."
   > "This is in the organization's best interest."
   > "No one will find out about this."
   > "The organization will back me up on this."

5. Refuse to do business when stakeholder actions violate or compromise laws or fundamental organizational values.

6. Conduct relationships as openly and aboveboard as possible.

As business becomes more global, questions involving values become even more complex. For instance, in many foreign countries, "facilitating payments" are often paid to government officials to secure basic services, such as the installation of a telephone. U.S. firms doing business in these countries are often expected to offer such payments, even though U.S. law would classify these payments as illegal bribery. In response to billions of dollars in bribes and facilitating payments paid out by U.S. firms, Congress passed the 1988 Foreign Corrupt Practices Act, which prohibits such payments. However, in order to prevent U.S. firms from operating at a disadvantage overseas, the act specifically allows payments that are made to facilitate "routine government action," such as installing a phone or unloading cargo. In such situations, U.S. firms may pay bribes and avoid prosecution under the statute.[70]

Values are important because they provide guidance for behavior. They are intertwined with the concept of ethics, the next dimension of individual differences to be examined.

Ethical Behavior

ethical behavior

Acting in ways consistent with one's personal values and the commonly held values of the organization and society.

Ethics is the study of moral values and moral behavior. *Ethical behavior* is acting in ways consistent with one's personal values and the commonly held values of the organization and society.[71] As we saw in Chapter 2, ethical issues are a major concern in organizations. With all the corporate ethical scandals, many CEOs are on trial for unethical behavior. Will linking CEO pay to firm performance help firms perform better? What happens when the firm is in a

Pigs in Pinstriped Suits

Martha Stewart, Sotheby's Alfred Taubman, Enron's Kenneth Lay, and Tyco's Dennis Koslowski are all subjects of recent CEO trials. Big-spending, insider-trading CEOs are front-page news, giving the impression that CEO greed is rampant worldwide. Executive salaries and perks are massive, and some executives continue to earn big bucks when the firms they lead are failing. One suggested remedy is to link the CEO's pay with firm performance. That way, when the firm performs poorly, the CEO's earnings also suffer.

While stock options (which gain value as the firms' share prices rise) are often cited as a sure way to tie executives' pay to firm performance, boards of di-

rectors don't always enforce the rules. In some cases, when share prices fall and the executives' stock options become worthless, boards actually reprice the options, in effect removing any penalty for poor firm performance. While this action is often taken to ensure that the poorly performing CEO doesn't jump ship, a five-year study found that executives who received this amazingly lucrative deal were no more likely to remain with the firm than those who didn't. In the end, the only apparent effect was to slap them on the wrist and get the money presses rolling again.

SOURCE: M. C. Carter and L. J. Lynch, "The Effect of Stock Option Repricing on Employee *Turnover*," *Journal of Accounting and Economics*," 37 (2004): 91–112.

downslide, and CEO pay falls, too—will the CEO leave the firm? Find out by reading the Science feature.

There is evidence that paying attention to ethical issues pays off for companies. In the early 1990s, James Burke, then the CEO of Johnson & Johnson, put together a list of companies that devoted a great deal of attention to ethics. The group included Johnson & Johnson, Coca-Cola, Gerber, Kodak, 3M, and Pitney Bowes. Over a forty-year period, the market value of these organizations grew at an annual rate of 11.3 percent, as compared to 6.2 percent for the Dow Jones industrials as a whole.[72] Doing the right thing can have a positive effect on an organization's performance.[73]

Ethical behavior in firms can also lead to practical benefits, particularly in attracting new talent. Firms with better reputations are able to attract more applicants, creating a larger pool from which to hire, and evidence suggests that respected firms are able to choose higher-quality applicants.[74]

Failure to handle situations in an ethical manner can cost companies. Employees who are laid off or terminated are very concerned about the quality of treatment they receive. Honestly explaining the reasons for the dismissal and preserving the dignity of the employee will reduce the likelihood that the employee will initiate a claim against the company. One study showed that less than 1 percent of employees who felt the company was being honest filed a claim; more than 17 percent of those who felt the company was being less than honest filed claims.[75]

Unethical behavior by employees can affect individuals, work teams, and even the organization. Organizations thus depend on individuals to act ethically. For this reason, more and more firms are starting to monitor their employees' Internet usage. "LittleBrother" and "SurfControl Web Filter" are just two of several software packages that allow system administrators to easily monitor employee Web usage, flagging visits to specific Web sites by using neural network technology to classify URL content and block Web traffic.

Although some employees have complained that this type of monitoring violates their privacy, the courts have generally disagreed, arguing that employees are using company hardware and software, hence the company is entitled to monitor what employees do with it. In one such case, Michael Smyth was fired from his job with Pillsbury Co. after company employees read inflammatory comments he made in several e-mails to his supervisor. Smyth sued for wrongful termination, claiming that his right to privacy was violated because the firm had told employees their e-mail would remain confidential. Despite these promises, the court ruled that Smyth had no reasonable expectation of privacy while using the firm's equipment; further, it said, Smyth's right to privacy was outweighed by the firm's need to conduct business in a professional manner. Only future court cases will clarify where a firm's effort to monitor potentially unethical behavior actually crosses its own ethical line.[76]

Today's high-intensity business environment makes it more important than ever to have a strong ethics program in place. In a survey of more than 4,000 employees conducted by the Washington, D.C.–based Ethics Resource Center, one-third of the employees said that they had witnessed ethical misconduct in the past year. If that many employees actually saw unethical acts, imagine how many unethical behaviors occurred behind closed doors! The most common unethical deeds witnessed were lying to supervisors (56 percent), lying on reports or falsifying records (41 percent), stealing or theft (35 percent), sexual harassment (35 percent), drug or alcohol abuse (31 percent), and conflicts of interest (31 percent).[77]

One of the toughest challenges managers face is aligning the ideal of ethical behavior with the reality of everyday business practices. Violations of the public's trust are costly. Since Jack in the Box restaurants' *E. coli* crisis, the company has faced image and financial problems. And Firestone Inc., after spending more than a third of a billion dollars replacing allegedly defective tires on Ford sport utility vehicles in 2000, still faces an uncertain future including billions of dollars in lawsuits. Studies show that firms experience lower ac-

TABLE 4.3 — Ethical Issues from One Week in *The Wall Street Journal*

1. **Stealing:** Taking things that don't belong to you.
2. **Lying:** Saying things you know aren't true.
3. **Fraud and deceit:** Creating or perpetuating false impressions.
4. **Conflict of interest and influence buying:** Bribes, payoffs, and kickbacks.
5. **Hiding versus divulging information:** Concealing information that another party has a right to know or failing to protect personal or proprietary information.
6. **Cheating:** Taking unfair advantage of a situation.
7. **Personal decadence:** Aiming below excellence in terms of work performance (e.g., careless or sloppy work).
8. **Interpersonal abuse:** Behaviors that are abusive of others (e.g., sexism, racism, emotional abuse).
9. **Organizational abuse:** Organizational practices that abuse members (e.g., inequitable compensation, misuses of power).
10. **Rule violations:** Breaking organizational rules.
11. **Accessory to unethical acts:** Knowing about unethical behavior and failing to report it.
12. **Ethical dilemmas:** Choosing between two equally desirable or undesirable options.

SOURCE: Kluwer Academic Publishers, by J. O. Cherrington and D. J. Cherrington. "A Menu of Moral Issues: One Week in the Life of *The Wall Street Journal*." *Journal of Business Ethics* 11 (1992): 255–265. Reprinted with kind permission of Springer Science and Business Media.

counting returns and slow sales growth for as long as five years after being convicted of a corporate illegality.[78]

The ethical issues that individuals face at work are complex. A review of articles appearing in *The Wall Street Journal* during just one week revealed more than sixty articles dealing with ethical issues in business.[79] As Table 4.3 shows, the themes appearing throughout the articles were distilled into twelve major ethical issues. You can see that few of these issues are clear-cut. All of them depend on the specifics of the situation, and their interpretation depends on the characteristics of the individuals examining them. For example, look at issue 2: lying. We all know that "white lies" are told in business. Is this acceptable? The answer to this question varies from person to person. Thus, the perception of what constitutes ethical versus unethical behavior in organizations varies among individuals.

Ethical behavior is influenced by two major categories of factors: individual characteristics and organizational factors.[80] Our purpose in this section is to look at the individual influences on ethical behavior. We examine organizational influences throughout the remainder of the book—particularly in Chapter 16, where we focus on creating an organizational culture that reinforces ethical behavior.

The model that guides our discussion of individual influences on ethical behavior is presented in Figure 4.3. It shows both individual and organizational influences.

Making ethical decisions is part of each manager's job. It has been suggested that ethical decision making requires three qualities of individuals:[81]

7. Describe a model of individual and organizational influences on ethical behavior.

1. The competence to identify ethical issues and evaluate the consequences of alternative courses of action

2. The self-confidence to seek out different opinions about the issue and decide what is right in terms of a particular situation

3. Toughmindedness—the willingness to make decisions when all that needs to be known cannot be known and when the ethical issue has no established, unambiguous solution.

FIGURE 4.3   **Individual/Organizational Model of Ethical Behavior**

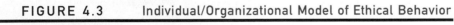

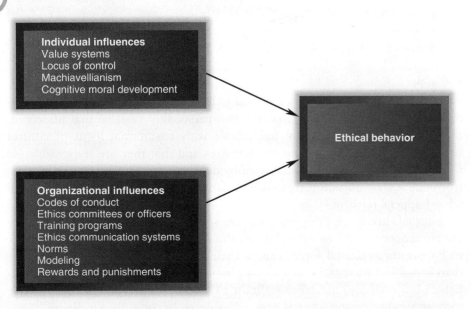

What are the individual characteristics that lead to these qualities? Our model presents four major individual differences that affect ethical behavior: value systems, locus of control, Machiavellianism, and cognitive moral development.

Value Systems

8. Discuss how value systems, locus of control, Machiavellianism, and cognitive moral development affect ethical behavior.

Values are systems of beliefs that affect what the individual defines as right, good, and fair. Ethics reflects the way the values are acted out. Ethical behavior, as noted earlier, is acting in ways consistent with one's personal values and the commonly held values of the organization and society.

Employees are exposed to multiple value systems: their own, their supervisor's, the company's, the customers', and others'. In most cases, the individual's greatest allegiance will be to personal values. When the value system conflicts with the behavior the person feels must be exhibited, the person experiences a value conflict. Suppose, for example, that an individual believes honesty is important in all endeavors. Yet this individual sees that those who get ahead in business fudge their numbers and deceive other people. Why should the individual be honest if honesty doesn't pay? It is the individual's values, a basic sense of what is right and wrong, that override the temptation to be dishonest.[82]

Some companies promote volunteering and being involved in community activities as a way to instill values.

Pharmaceutical maker Eli Lilly believes it has a responsibility to strengthen the communities in which it operates and does business. Consequently, Lilly encourages its employees to be involved in volunteer and community service activities. A Lilly Web site spells out the details of its "Employee Volunteerism Policy," which states that employees who take work time to be involved in company-sponsored service activities are allowed to count their service hours as "company business" rather than unpaid time off.[83]

Locus of Control

Another individual influence on ethical behavior is locus of control. In Chapter 3, we introduced locus of control as a personality variable that affects individual behavior. Recall that individuals with an internal locus of control believe that they control events in their lives and that they are responsible for what happens to them. In contrast, individuals with an external locus of control believe that outside forces such as fate, chance, or other people control what happens to them.[84]

Internals are more likely than externals to take personal responsibility for the consequences of their ethical or unethical behavior. Externals are more apt to believe that external forces caused their ethical or unethical behavior. Research has shown that internals make more ethical decisions than do externals.[85] Internals also are more resistant to social pressure and are less willing to hurt another person, even if ordered to do so by an authority figure.[86]

Machiavellianism

Another individual difference that affects ethical behavior is Machiavellianism. Niccolò Machiavelli was a sixteenth-century Italian statesman. He wrote *The Prince*, a guide for acquiring and using power.[87] The primary method for achieving power that he suggested was manipulation of others. *Machiavellianism*, then, is a personality characteristic indicating one's willingness to do whatever it takes to get one's own way.

A high-Mach individual behaves in accordance with Machiavelli's ideas, which include the notion that it is better to be feared than loved. High-Machs tend to use deceit in relationships, have a cynical view of human nature, and have little concern for conventional notions of right and wrong.[88] They are skilled manipulators of other people, relying on their persuasive abilities. Low-Machs, in contrast, value loyalty and relationships. They are less willing to manipulate others for personal gain and are concerned with others' opinions.

High-Machs believe that the desired ends justify any means. They believe that manipulation of others is fine if it helps achieve a goal. Thus, high-Machs are likely to justify their manipulative behavior as ethical.[89] They are emotionally detached from other people and are oriented toward objective aspects of situations. And high-Machs are likelier than low-Machs to engage in behavior that is ethically questionable.[90] Employees can counter Machiavellian individuals by focusing on teamwork instead of on one-on-one relationships where high-Machs have the upper hand. It is also beneficial to make interpersonal agreements public and thus less susceptible to manipulation by high-Machs.

Machiavellianism
A personality characteristic indicating one's willingness to do whatever it takes to get one's own way.

Cognitive Moral Development

An individual's level of *cognitive moral development* also affects ethical behavior. Psychologist Lawrence Kohlberg proposed that as individuals mature, they move through a series of six stages of moral development.[91] With each successive stage, they become less dependent on other people's opinions of right and wrong and less self-centered (acting in one's own interest). At higher levels of moral development, individuals are concerned with broad principles of justice and with their self-chosen ethical principles. Kohlberg's model focuses on the decision-making process and on how individuals justify ethical decisions. His model is a cognitive developmental theory about how people think about what is right and wrong and how the decision-making process changes through interaction with peers and the environment.

Cognitive moral development occurs at three levels, and each level consists of two stages. In Level I, called the premoral level, the person's ethical decisions are based on rewards, punishments, and self-interest. In Stage 1, the individual obeys rules to avoid punishment. In Stage 2, the individual follows the rules only if it is in his or her immediate interest to do so.

In Level II, the conventional level, the focus is on the expectations of others (parents, peers) or society. In Stage 3, individuals try to live up to the expectations of people close to them. In Stage 4, they broaden their perspective to include the laws of the larger society. They fulfill duties and obligations and want to contribute to society.

In Level III, the principled level, what is "right" is determined by universal values. The individual sees beyond laws, rules, and the expectations of other people. In Stage 5, individuals are aware that people have diverse value systems. They uphold their own values despite what others think. For a person to be classified as being in Stage 5, decisions must be based on principles of justice and rights. For example, a person who decides to picket an abortion clinic

cognitive moral development
The process of moving through stages of maturity in terms of making ethical decisions.

just because his religion says abortion is wrong is not a Stage 5 individual. A person who arrives at the same decision through a complex decision process based on justice and rights may be a Stage 5 individual. The key is the process rather than the decision itself. In Stage 6, the individual follows self-selected ethical principles. If there is a conflict between a law and a self-selected ethical principle, the individual acts according to the principle.

As individuals mature, their moral development passes through these stages in an irreversible sequence. Research suggests that most adults are in Stage 3 or 4. Most adults thus never reach the principled level of development (Stages 5 and 6).

Since it was proposed, more than thirty years ago, Kohlberg's model of cognitive moral development has received a great deal of research support. Individuals at higher stages of development are less likely to cheat,[92] more likely to engage in whistle-blowing,[93] and more likely to make ethical business decisions.[94, 95]

Kohlberg's model has also been criticized. Gilligan, for example, has argued that the model does not take gender differences into account. Kohlberg's model was developed from a twenty-year study of eighty-four boys.[96] Gilligan contends that women's moral development follows a different pattern—one that is based not on individual rights and rules but on responsibility and relationships. Women and men face the same moral dilemmas but approach them from different perspectives—men from the perspective of equal respect and women from the perspective of compassion and care. Researchers who reviewed the research on these gender differences concluded that the differences may not be as strong as originally stated by Gilligan. Some men use care reasoning, and some women may use justice reasoning when making moral judgments.[97]

There is evidence to support the idea that men and women view ethics differently. A large-scale review of sixty-six studies found that women were more likely than men to perceive certain business practices as unethical. Young women were more likely to see breaking the rules and acting on insider information as unethical. Both sexes agreed that collusion, conflicts of interest, and stealing are unethical. It takes about twenty-one years for the gender gap to disappear. Men seem to become more ethical with more work experience; the longer they are in the workforce, the more their attitudes become similar to those held by women. There is an age/experience effect for both sexes: Experienced workers are more likely to think lying, bribing, stealing, and colluding are unethical.[98]

Individual differences in values, locus of control, Machiavellianism, and cognitive moral development are important influences on ethical behavior in organizations. Given that these influences vary widely from person to person, how can organizations use this knowledge to increase ethical behavior? One action would be to hire individuals who share the organization's values. Another would be to hire only internals, low-Machs, and individuals at higher stages of cognitive moral development. This strategy obviously presents practical and legal problems.

There is evidence that cognitive moral development can be increased through training.[99] Organizations could help individuals move to higher stages of moral development by providing educational seminars. However, values, locus of control, Machiavellianism, and cognitive moral development are fairly stable in adults.

The best way to use the knowledge of individual differences may be to recognize that they help explain why ethical behavior differs among individuals and to focus managerial efforts on creating a work situation that supports ethical behavior.

Most adults are susceptible to external influences; they do not act as independent ethical agents. Instead, they look to others and to the organization for guidance. Managers can offer such guidance by encouraging ethical behavior through codes of conduct, ethics committees, ethics communication systems, training, norms, modeling, and rewards and punishments, as shown in Figure 4.3. We discuss these areas further in Chapter 16.

Managerial Implications: Attitudes, Values, and Ethics at Work

Managers must understand attitudes because of their effects on work behavior. By understanding how attitudes are formed and how they can be changed, managers can shape employee attitudes. Attitudes are learned through observation of other employees and by the way they are reinforced. Job satisfaction and organizational commitment are important attitudes to encourage among employees, and participative management is an excellent tool for doing so.

Values affect work behavior because they affect employees' views of what constitutes right and wrong. The diversity of the workforce makes it imperative that managers understand differences in value systems. Shared values within an organization can provide the foundation for cooperative efforts toward achieving organizational goals.

Ethical behavior at work is affected by individual and organizational influences. A knowledge of individual differences in value systems, locus of control, Machiavellianism, and cognitive moral development helps managers understand why individuals have diverse views about what constitutes ethical behavior.

This chapter concludes our discussion of individual differences that affect behavior in organizations. Attitudes, values, and ethics combine with personality, perception, and attribution to make individuals unique. Individual uniqueness is a major managerial challenge, and it is one reason there is no single best way to manage people.

LOOKING BACK: WHOLE FOODS MARKET

Walking the Talk

CEO John Mackey and his leadership team had a problem. Whole Foods was facing a major campaign by PETA and VivaUSA against the grocer for buying ducks from farmers who engaged in inhumane practices. Pressures were mounting.

Mackey wrote to Lauren Ornelas, VivaUSA's director, and began discussions with her. Following these interactions, Whole Foods pledged to uphold humane standards for animals whose meat will be sold in its stores. It refused to do business with farms that abuse ducks.

Was the decision motivated by profit or political correctness, or was it a value-driven decision in line with Whole Foods' mission? Mackey himself claimed that

Whole Foods did not respond to coercion; he reexamined the activists' claims and decided they were right. In fact, the incident caused Mackey himself to change from being a conventional vegetarian to a vegan (abstaining from all foods with animal by-products). Mackey said he could not oppose the argument that eating animals causes pain and suffering to the animals.[100, 101]

Chapter Summary

1. The ABC model of an attitude contends that an attitude has three components: affect, behavioral intentions, and cognition. Cognitive dissonance is the tension produced by a conflict between attitudes and behavior.

2. Attitudes are formed through direct experience and social learning. Direct experience creates strong attitudes because the attitudes are easily accessed and active in cognitive processes.

3. Attitude–behavior correspondence depends on attitude specificity, attitude relevance, timing of measurement, personality factors, and social constraints.

4. Two important work attitudes are job satisfaction and organizational commitment. There are cultural differences in these attitudes, and both attitudes can be improved by providing employees with opportunities for participation in decision making.

5. A manager's ability to persuade employees to change their attitudes depends on characteristics of the manager (expertise, trustworthiness, and attractiveness), the employees (self-esteem, original attitude, and mood), the message (one-sided versus two-sided), and the route (central versus peripheral).

6. Values are enduring beliefs and are strongly influenced by cultures, societies, and organizations.

7. Instrumental values reflect the means to achieving goals; terminal values represent the goals to be achieved.

8. Ethical behavior is influenced by the individual's value system, locus of control, Machiavellianism, and cognitive moral development.

Key Terms

affect (p. 116)
affective commitment (p. 124)
attitude (p. 116)
cognitive dissonance (p. 117)
cognitive moral development (p. 137)

continuance commitment (p. 124)
ethical behavior (p. 132)
instrumental values (p. 128)
job satisfaction (p. 120)
Machiavellianism (p. 137)
normative commitment (p. 124)

organizational citizenship behavior (p. 123)
organizational commitment (p. 124)
social learning (p. 118)
terminal values (p. 128)
values (p. 127)

Review Questions

1. Describe the ABC model of an attitude. How should each component be measured?

2. How are attitudes formed? Which source is stronger?

3. Discuss cultural differences in job satisfaction and organizational commitment.

4. What are the major influences on attitude–behavior correspondence? Why do some individuals seem to exhibit behavior that is inconsistent with their attitudes?

5. What should managers know about the persuasion process?

6. Define *values*. Distinguish between instrumental values and terminal values. Are these values generally stable, or do they change over time?

7. What is the relationship between values and ethics?

8. How does locus of control affect ethical behavior?

9. What is Machiavellianism, and how does it relate to ethical behavior?

10. Describe the stages of cognitive moral development. How does this concept affect ethical behavior in organizations?

Discussion and Communication Questions

1. What jobs do you consider to be most satisfying? Why?

2. How can managers increase their employees' job satisfaction?

3. Suppose you have an employee whose lack of commitment is affecting others in the work group. How would you go about persuading the person to change this attitude?

4. In Rokeach's studies on values, the most recent data are from 1981. Do you think values have changed since then? If so, how?

5. What are the most important influences on an individual's perceptions of ethical behavior? Can organizations change these perceptions? If so, how?

6. How can managers encourage organizational citizenship?

7. *(communication question)* Suppose you are a manager in a customer service organization. Your group includes seven supervisors who report directly to you. Each supervisor manages a team of seven customer service representatives. One of your supervisors, Linda, has complained that Joe, one of her employees, has "an attitude problem." She has requested that Joe be transferred to another team. Write a memo to Linda explaining your position on this problem and what should be done.

8. *(communication question)* Select a company that you admire for its values. Use the resources of your university library to answer two questions. First, what are the company's values? Second, how do employees enact these values? Prepare an oral presentation to present in class.

9. *(communication question)* Think of a time when you have experienced cognitive dissonance. Analyze your experience in terms of the attitude and behavior involved. What did you do to resolve the cognitive dissonance? What other actions could you have taken? Write a brief description of your experience and your responses to the questions.

Ethical Dilemma

Sara, a manager in a large software development company, sits at her desk looking out the window. The challenge before her is to pick a project manager for a major new project just given to her department. She has narrowed down her choice to two employees. Sara's first option is Paula, who is probably the most qualified candidate for this project. No one knows this area of software development better than Paula. She also has extensive knowledge of the client. Paula has one other attribute, which can be a positive or a negative factor: attitude. She is the best at her job and she knows it. She also lets everyone else know it. Because of this, she always gets the top projects. The problem is that Paula cares only about Paula and little else. She is not a team player and does little to contribute to the department as a whole. She can be arrogant and extremely self-centered.

Sara's other option is Mark. Mark is also talented with all the markings of becoming a great project manager if given the chance. In addition to his technical skills, Mark is a great coworker. He is a team player that cares as much about the success of the department as he does about his own personal success. He is well-liked by everyone, especially Sara. As a manager, she always appreciates Mark's willingness to consider the department's needs and not just the work that would lead to personal success.

Sara's predicament needs to be resolved by the end of the day. She knows everyone expects her to again choose Paula to head this project. However, Sara really believes it is time to give Mark a chance. She realizes the fallout for not choosing Paula would be great, but she is really tired of doing what everyone, including Paula, expects her to do within her own department.

Questions

1. What is Sara's obligation to the client?

2. Does this obligation affect her decision?

3. Using rule, virtue, right, and justice theories, evaluate Sara's decision options.

Experiential Exercises

4.1 Chinese, Indian, and American Values

Purpose
To learn some differences among Chinese, Indian, and American value systems.

Group size
Any number of groups of five to eight people.

Time required
50+ minutes

Exercise Schedule

1. Complete rankings (preclass)
Students rank the fifteen values for either Chinese and American orientations or for Indian and American systems. If time permits, all three can be done.

	Unit time	Total time
2. Small groups (optional)	15 min.	15 min.

Groups of five to eight members try to achieve consensus on the ranking values for both Chinese and American cultures.

	Unit time	Total time
3. Group presentations (optional)	15 min.	30 min.

Each group presents its rankings and discusses reasons for making those decisions.

	Unit time	Total time
4. Discussion	20+ min.	50 min.

Instructor leads a discussion on the differences between Chinese and American value systems and presents the correct rankings.

Value Rankings
Rank each of the fifteen values below according to what you think they are in the Chinese, Indian (from India), and American cultures. Use "1" as the most important value for the culture and "15" as the least important value for that culture.

Value	American	Chinese	Indian
Achievement			
Deference			
Order			
Exhibition			
Autonomy			
Affiliation			
Intraception			
Succorance			
Dominance			
Abasement			
Nurturance			
Change			
Endurance			
Heterosexuality			
Aggression			

Some Definitions
Intraception: The tendency to be governed by subjective factors, such as feelings, fantasies, speculations, and aspirations; the other side of extraception, where one is governed by concrete, clearly observable physical conditions.
Succorance: Willingness to help another or to offer relief.
Abasement: To lower oneself in rank, prestige, or esteem.

Internal/External Locus of Control
Consider American and Chinese groups. Which would tend to have more internal locus of control (tend to feel in control of one's destiny, that rewards come as a result of hard work, perseverance, and responsibility)? Which would be more external (fate, luck or other outside forces control destiny)?

Machiavellianism
This concept was defined by Christie and Geis as the belief that one can manipulate and deceive people for personal gain. Do you think Americans or Chinese would score higher on the Machiavellian scale?

Discussion Questions

1. What are some main differences among the cultures? Did any pattern emerge?

2. Were you surprised by the results?

3. What behaviors could you expect in business dealings with Chinese (or Indians) based on their value system?

4. How do American values dictate Americans' behaviors in business situations?

SOURCE: "Chinese, Indian, and American Values" by Dorothy Marcic, copyright 1993. Adapted from Michael Harris Bond, ed., *The Psychology of the Chinese People,* Hong Kong: Oxford University Press, 200 Madison Ave., NY 10016, 1986. The selection used here is a portion of "Chinese Personality and Its Change," by Kuo-Shu Yang, pp. 106–170. Reprinted by permission.

4.2 Is This Behavior Ethical?

The purpose of this exercise is to explore your opinions about ethical issues faced in organizations. The class should be divided into twelve groups. Each group will randomly be assigned one of the following issues, which reflect the twelve ethical themes found in *The Wall Street Journal* study shown in Table 4.3.

1. Is it ethical to take office supplies from work for home use? Make personal long-distance calls from the office? Use company time for personal business? Or do these behaviors constitute stealing?

2. If you exaggerate your credentials in an interview, is it lying? Is lying in order to protect a coworker acceptable?

3. If you pretend to be more successful than you are in order to impress your boss, are you being deceitful?

4. How do you differentiate between a bribe and a gift?

5. If there are slight defects in a product you are selling, are you obligated to tell the buyer? If an advertised "sale" price is really the everyday price, should you divulge the information to the customer?

6. Suppose you have a friend who works at the ticket office for the convention center where Shania Twain will be appearing. Is it cheating if you ask the friend to get you tickets so that you won't have to fight the crowd to get them? Is buying merchandise for your family at your company's cost cheating?

7. Is it immoral to do less than your best in terms of work performance? Is it immoral to accept workers' compensation when you are fully capable of working?

8. What behaviors constitute emotional abuse at work? What would you consider an abuse of one's position of power?

9. Are high-stress jobs a breach of ethics? What about transfers that break up families?

10. Are all rule violations equally important? Do employees have an ethical obligation to follow company rules?

11. To what extent are you responsible for the ethical behavior of your coworkers? If you witness unethical behavior and don't report it, are you an accessory?

12. Is it ethical to help one work group at the expense of another group? For instance, suppose one group has excellent performance and you want to reward its members with an afternoon off. The other work group will have to pick up the slack and work harder if you do this. Is this ethical?

Once your group has been assigned its issue, you have two tasks:

1. First, formulate your group's answer to the ethical dilemmas.

2. After you have formulated your group's position, discuss the individual differences that may have contributed to your position. You will want to discuss the individual differences presented in this chapter as well as any others that you feel affected your position on the ethical dilemma.

Your instructor will lead the class in a discussion of how individual differences may have influenced your positions on these ethical dilemmas.

SOURCE: Kluwer Academic Publishers, by J. O. Cherrington and D. J. Cherrington, "A Menu of Moral Issues: One Week in the Life of *The Wall Street Journal*," *Journal of Business Ethics* 11 (1992): 255–265. Reprinted with kind permission of Springer Science and Business Media.

Biz Flix | The Emperor's Club

William Hundert (Kevin Kline), a professor at Saint Benedict's Academy for Boys, believes in teaching his students about living a principled life. He also wants them to learn his beloved classical literature. New student, Sedgewick Bell (Emile Hirsch), challenges Hundert's principled ways. Bell's behavior during the seventy-third annual Mr. Julius Caesar Contest causes Hundert to suspect that Bell leads a less than principled life, a suspicion reinforced years later during a repeat of the competition.

This scene appears at the end of the film. It is an edited portion of the Mr. Julius Caesar Contest reenactment at former student Sedgewick Bell's (Joel Gretsch) estate. Bell wins the competition, but Hundert notices Bell's earpiece. Earlier in the film, Hundert had suspected that young Bell also wore an earpiece during the original competition. Bell announced his candidacy for the U.S. Senate just before talking to Hundert in the bathroom. In his announcement, he described his commitment to specific values he would pursue if elected.

What to Watch for and Ask Yourself:

> Does William Hundert describe a specific type of life that one should lead? If so, what are its elements?

> Does Sedgewick Bell lead that type of life? Is he committed to any specific ethics view or theory?

> What consequences or effects do you predict for Sedgewick Bell because of the way he chooses to live his life?

Workplace Video | The Timberland Company: Ethics and Social Responsibility

Timberland is a global retailer that designs premium-quality footwear, apparel, and accessories for consumers who value the outdoors. Timberland's dedication to making quality products is matched by the company's commitment to "doing well and doing good"—forging powerful partnerships among employees, consumers, and service partners to carry out various social responsibility initiatives. In addition to making quality products, Timberland strongly believes that it has a responsibility to help effect positive change in local communities.

Timberland considers a broad range of stakeholders in its business dealings. The company first recognizes the responsibility to be profitable for investors. In addition to bottom-line considerations, Timberland seeks to serve its employee stakeholders—the company is committed to diversity in its workforce and employs a high percentage of non-Caucasian minorities and women. Timberland also believes in bettering communities through a variety of service projects. Employees for the apparel maker have contributed literally hundreds of thousands of hours to company-sponsored community service events. Finally, Timberland considers the impact that its activities may have on the environment. The company's Environmental Affairs department has a specific mission to minimize harmful effects on the ecosystem and to support environmental causes.

TAKE 2

While the true value of Timberland's social responsibility efforts is difficult to measure using traditional bottom-line metrics, the company believes its community efforts increase sales, build marketing relationships, and enhance research and development, resulting in increased value for all stakeholders.

Questions

1. *Identify one of the community service programs sponsored by Timberland, and explain why company leaders consider it important.*
2. *How do Timberland's social responsibility efforts and high ethical standards benefit the company?*
3. *List the constituencies to whom companies have traditionally been responsible. What has happened to that old model of corporate responsibility?*

Canine Companions for Independence: Values-Based Service for Disabled People

Founded in July 1975 in Santa Rosa, California, Canine Companions for Independence (CCI) is a not-for-profit organization that trains and provides dogs to assist people with physical or developmental disabilities. CCI operates nationwide with centers in Santa Rosa and Oceanside, California; Delaware, Ohio; Farmingdale, New York; and Orlando, Florida. CCI provides assistance dogs, called Canine Companions, to enhance the independence or quality of life of disabled people. Private donations cover all of the costs associated with breeding, raising, and training Canine Companions. The breed stock for Canine Companions consists of Golden Retrievers, Labrador Retrievers, or a crossbreed between the two. Users of the program, known as CCI graduates, pay only a $100 Team Training registration fee to cover the cost of materials for the two-week training program in which they must participate. The training program matches the human user with a Canine Companion and prepares them to work well with each other. CCI graduates are responsible for the proper care and housing of their Canine Companions.

People with physical or developmental disabilities who want an assistance dog must complete an application process, and if selected for the CCI program, they attend the Team Training course. Professionals who work for organizations that provide physical or mental health care to clients may also apply to the program. To be eligible, the professional must demonstrate that clients would benefit from having a Canine Companion in the facility where they care for disabled clients.

Types of CCI Assistance Teams

CCI trains four types of assistance teams: service teams, skilled companion teams, facility teams, and hearing teams. A service team consists of a child or adult with physical disabilities and a Canine Companion that performs physical tasks, such as picking up dropped items, turning light switches on or off, pulling a wheelchair, or opening doors, on behalf of the disabled person. The skilled companion team consists of an adolescent or adult with physical, emotional, or developmental disabilities as well as a human primary caretaker and a Canine Companion. The role of the Canine Companion on a skilled companion team is to help the disabled person with physical tasks and to provide companionship and affection. A facility team links a Canine Companion with a rehabilitation professional or caregiver to help improve the physical, mental, or emotional health of people the professional takes care of in a facility setting. A hearing team utilizes a Canine Companion to alert deaf or hard-of-hearing adults to everyday sounds like alarm clocks, smoke alarms, telephones, and doorbells.

Approximately 2,100 teams have been developed since CCI's founding in 1975. Approximately 81 percent of the Canine Companion placements were in service teams and skilled companion teams. About 12 percent of the placements were in facility teams, and the remaining 7 percent of placements were in hearing teams. In the summer of 2004, over 1,000 active teams were operating.

The Role of Volunteers in Training Canine Companions

Volunteers raise and train the puppies that are destined to be Canine Companions. The puppy raisers care for the CCI puppies, take them to puppy classes, and train them in appropriate behaviors and house manners. Upon reaching the required age, the CCI puppies enter a formal training program at one of the five regional CCI centers.

Famed professional basketball player Bill Walton and his wife, Lori, are puppy raiser volunteers. For fourteen months they raised, trained, and socialized a puppy named Loma. At fourteen months of age, Loma was placed in advanced training for nine months at one of CCI's regional training centers. During this time, the Waltons could not have any contact with Loma. Turning Loma over to the

Oceanside, California, regional training center was an emotional time for the Waltons, given the relationship they had established with the dog. Loma was destined to be the Canine Companion for David Grucca, a quadriplegic. Upon Loma's completion of the advanced training, the Waltons ceremonially presented Loma to David Grucca and began a friendship with him that is likely to be permanent. The Waltons are now raising another CCI puppy.

Two other volunteers, Amy Witherel and Karissa White, both employees of Perot Systems Corp., located in Plano, Texas, are also raising puppies to become Canine Companions. Witherel and White give their puppies, Hilani and Orenda, lots of love and affection while training them to be well-mannered and housebroken. To become effectively socialized, the puppies go everywhere with their raisers, including the grocery store, sporting events, restaurants, movies theaters, the beauty parlor, and even work. Neither Witherel nor White relish the thought of parting with their beloved puppies, but they recognize that ultimately they will help people who really need the Canine Companions.

Many other volunteers are involved in raising puppies for the Canine Companions program. Indeed, as of mid-2004, there were 860 active puppy raisers. Unfortunately, the demand for CCI assistance dogs exceeds the supply of volunteer puppy raisers—there is a four-year waiting list for getting a Canine Companion.

Discussion Questions

1. Using the five attributes of attitude-behavior correspondence that are discussed in the chapter, explain the linkage between the volunteer puppy raisers' attitudes and their behaviors.
2. What instrumental values and terminal values become evident through the activities of Canine Companions for Independence? For the CCI puppy raisers?
3. What impact might the instrumental and terminal values of CCI puppy raisers have on their propensity to behave ethically or unethically?

SOURCE: This case was written by Michael K. McCuddy, The Louis S. and Mary L. Morgal Chair of Christian Business Ethics and Professor of Management, College of Business Administration, Valparaiso University. This case was developed from material contained on the Canine Companions for Independence Web site at http://www.caninecompanions.org and in the following articles: L. S. Ball, "Pups Waggle into Texas Workplace as Future Helpers in Training," *The Dallas Morning News* (January 25, 2003): accessed from Newspaper Source; "Basketball Hall of Famer Bill Walton Raises and Trains Assistance Dog, Presents to Man With Quadriplegia," *Ascribe Health & Fitness News Services* (August 20, 2003): 3–4; "Canine Companions for Independence Exceeds Goals; 137 Assistance Dog Teams Placed in 2002 to Serve the Disabled," *Ascribe Health & Fitness News Services* (January 23, 2003): 8–9.

Motivation at Work

THINKING AHEAD: CANINE COMPANIONS FOR INDEPENDENCE (CCI)

Volunteers ... Motivated by Love

Jack Warnock is a retired Pacific Gas & Electric (PG&E) executive with multiple sclerosis who also suffered a stroke. These health problems have not stopped Warnock; he still makes about 50 speaking appearances each year in his wheelchair with his dog, Ellie, by his side. Ellie is a Canine Companion dog that has changed his life in a positive way. Ellie knew 49 basic commands when she first met Warnock. She can gently pull off his socks and slacks at bedtime and fetch things out of the refrigerator. Ellie even closes the refrigerator door when Warnock says "Ellie, were you raised in a barn?"[1] He recognizes that most people cannot imagine how Canine Companion dogs change a person's life nor how much work is involved for the puppy-raisers who prepare these dogs to serve.

Canine Companions for Independence (CCI) has provided highly trained assistance dogs and ongoing support to people with disabilities for more than 25 years. Nationally headquartered on the Schulz Campus in Santa Rosa, California, CCI has four other regional training centers where dogs and humans work together as a team. More than 2,000 assistance dog-and-human teams have gone through the training. Canine Companions may enter the program as puppies in training or as "mama" dogs. The cost of raising and training one assistance dog for Canine Companions is approximately $10,000. This cost includes medical care, food, and training by specialists. This cost does not include the important contributions of volunteers who raise the assistance dogs from pups. Emily Williams is one of these dedicated volunteers.

A Canine Companion volunteer for well over a decade, Emily Williams is motivated by love, not money. She receives no salary; all she does is love puppies. She knows the name of every dog she has cared for—a total of 180 special dogs entrusted to Emily over the years. She has served as canine midwife, helping to whelp 19 litters, and raised 10 assistance dogs in training. CCI cannot put a price tag on what Emily and its other volunteers do. Nor could CCI afford to pay them for everything they do in loving these puppies into mature dogs ready for assistance training. Emily is motivated and inspired by the difficult road chosen by disabled persons who sign up for a service dog. In recognition for her dedicated volunteer service, Emily was recognized with CCI's 2003 Jack Warnock Award for outstanding volunteer service.

At the end of CCI's silver anniversary year, 9/11 struck. The tragic events of that day would unfortunately increase the need for the indispensable services of Canine Companions.

This is the first of two chapters about motivation, behavior, and performance at work. A comprehensive approach to understanding motivation, behavior, and performance must consider three elements of the work situation—the individual, the job, and the work environment—and how these elements interact.[2] This chapter emphasizes internal and process theories of motivation. It begins with individual need theories of motivation, turns to the two-factor theory of motivation, and finishes by examining two individual–environment interaction or process theories of motivation. The next chapter (Chapter 6) emphasizes external theories of motivation and focuses on factors in the environment to help understand good or bad performance.

Motivation and Work Behavior

1. Define *motivation*.

motivation

The process of arousing and sustaining goal-directed behavior.

Motivation is the process of arousing and sustaining goal-directed behavior. Motivation is one of the more complex topics in organizational behavior. *Motivation* comes from the Latin root word *movere*, which means "to move." Motivation theories attempt to explain and predict observable behavior. The wide range and variety of motivation theories result from the great diversity of people and the complexity of their behavior in organizations. Motivation theories may be broadly classified into internal, process, and external theories of motivation. Internal theories of motivation give primary consideration to variables within the individual that give rise to motivation and behavior. The hierarchy of needs theory exemplifies the internal theories. Process theories of motivation emphasize the nature of the interaction between the individual and the environment. Expectancy theory exemplifies the process theories. External theories of motivation focus on the elements in the environment, including the consequences of behavior, as the basis for understanding and explaining people's behavior at work. Any single motivation theory explains only a small portion of the variance in human behavior. Therefore, alternative theories have developed over time in an effort to account for the unexplained portions of the variance in behavior.

Internal Needs

Philosophers and scholars have theorized for centuries about human needs and motives. During the past century, attention narrowed to understanding motivation in businesses and other organizations.[3] Max Weber, an early German organizational scholar, argued that the meaning of work lay not in the work itself but in its deeper potential for contributing to a person's ultimate salva-

Protestant Ethic

Rate the following statements from 1 (for *disagree completely*) to 6 (for *agree completely*).

____ 1. When the workday is finished, people should forget their jobs and enjoy themselves.

____ 2. Hard work makes us better people.

____ 3. The principal purpose of people's jobs is to provide them with the means for enjoying their free time.

____ 4. Wasting time is as bad as wasting money.

____ 5. Whenever possible, a person should relax and accept life as it is rather than always striving for unreachable goals.

____ 6. A good indication of a person's worth is how well he or she does his or her job.

____ 7. If all other things are equal, it is better to have a job with a lot of responsibility than one with little responsibility.

____ 8. People who "do things the easy way" are the smart ones.

____ Total your score for the pro-Protestant ethic items (2, 4, 6, and 7).

____ Total your score for the non-Protestant ethic items (1, 3, 5, and 8).

A pro-Protestant ethic score of 20 or over indicates you have a strong work ethic; 15–19 indicates a moderately strong work ethic; 9–14 indicates a moderately weak work ethic; 8 or less indicates a weak work ethic.

A non-Protestant ethic score of 20 or over indicates you have a strong non-work ethic; 15–19 indicates a moderately strong non-work ethic; 9–14 indicates a moderately weak non-work ethic; 8 or less indicates a weak non-work ethic.

SOURCE: M. R. Blood, "Work Values and Job Satisfaction," *Journal of Applied Psychology* 53 (1969): 456–459. Copyright © 1969 by the American Psychological Association. Reprinted with permission.

tion.[4] From this Calvinistic perspective, the Protestant ethic was the fuel for human industriousness. The Protestant ethic said people should work hard because those who prospered at work were more likely to find a place in heaven. You 5.1 gives you an opportunity to evaluate how strongly you have a pro-Protestant versus a non-Protestant ethic. Although Weber, and later Blood, both used the term *Protestant ethic*, many see the value elements of this work ethic in the broader Judeo-Christian tradition. We concur.

A more complex motivation theory was proposed by Sigmund Freud. For him, a person's organizational life was founded on the compulsion to work and the power of love.[5] He saw much of human motivation as unconscious by nature. *Psychoanalysis* was Freud's method for delving into the unconscious mind to better understand a person's motives and needs. Freud's psychodynamic theory offers explanations for irrational and self-destructive behavior, such as suicide or workplace violence. The motives underlying such traumatic work events may be understood by analyzing a person's unconscious needs and motives. The psychoanalytic approach also helps explain workplace deviant behavior, which can have a negative impact on business unit performance.[6] Freud's theorizing is important as the basis for subsequent need theories of motivation. Research suggests that people's deeper feelings may transcend culture, with most people caring deeply about the same few things.[7]

Internal needs and external incentives both play an important role in motivation. Although extrinsic motivation is important, so too is intrinsic motivation,

psychoanalysis

Sigmund Freud's method for delving into the unconscious mind to better understand a person's motives and needs.

which varies by the individual.[8] Therefore, it is important for managers to consider both internal needs and external incentives when attempting to motivate their employees. Further, managers who are more supportive and less controlling appear to elicit more intrinsic motivation from their employees.

External Incentives

Early organizational scholars made economic assumptions about human motivation and developed differential piece-rate systems of pay that emphasized external incentives. They assumed that people were motivated by self-interest and economic gain. The Hawthorne studies confirmed the positive effects of pay incentives on productivity and also found that social and interpersonal motives were important.[9]

Those who made economic assumptions about human motivation emphasized financial incentives for behavior. The Scottish political economist and moral philosopher Adam Smith argued that a person's *self-interest* was God's providence, not the government's.[10] More recently, executives have focused on "enlightened" self-interest. Self-interest is what is in the best interest and benefit to the individual; enlightened self-interest additionally recognizes the self-interest of other people. Adam Smith laid the cornerstone for the free enterprise system of economics when he formulated the "invisible hand" and the free market to explain the motivation for individual behavior. The "invisible hand" refers to the unseen forces of a free market system that shape the most efficient use of people, money, and resources for productive ends. Smith's basic assumption was that people are motivated by self-interest for economic gain to provide the necessities and conveniences of life. Thus, employees are most productive when motivated by self-interest.

Technology is an important concept in Smith's view, because he believed that a nation's wealth is determined primarily by the productivity of its labor force. Thus, the more efficient and effective the labor force, the greater the abundance of the nation. Technology is important as a force multiplier for the productivity of labor.[11]

Frederick Taylor, the founder of scientific management, was also concerned with labor efficiency and effectiveness.[12] His central concern was to change the relationship between management and labor from one of conflict to one of cooperation.[13] Taylor believed the basis of their conflict was the division of the profits. Instead of continuing this conflict over the division of profits, labor and management should form a cooperative relationship aimed at enlarging the total profits.

Employee Recognition and Ownership

Modern management practices, such as employee recognition programs, flexible benefit packages, and stock ownership plans, build on Smith's and Taylor's original theories. These modern practices emphasize external incentives, which may take either strictly economic form or more material form, such as "outstanding employee" plaques, gold watches, and other organizational symbols of distinction. One bridge approach to employee motivation that considers both psychological needs and external incentives is psychological ownership. An increasing number of scholars and managers emphasize the importance of "feelings of ownership" for the organization. One study of 800 managers and employees in three different organizations found that psychological ownership increased organizational citizenship behavior, a key contextual performance beyond the call of duty as discussed in Chapter 3.[14]

self-interest
What is in the best interest and benefit to an individual.

Maslow's Need Hierarchy

Abraham Maslow, a psychologist, proposed a need theory of motivation emphasizing psychological and interpersonal needs in addition to physical needs and economic necessity. His theory was based on a need hierarchy later applied through Theory X and Theory Y, two sets of assumptions about people at work. In addition, his need hierarchy was reformulated in an ERG theory of motivation using a revised classification scheme for basic human needs.

The Hierarchy of Needs

The core of Maslow's theory of human motivation is a hierarchy of five need categories.[15] Although he recognized that there were factors other than one's needs (for example, culture) that were determinants of behavior, he focused his theoretical attention on specifying people's internal needs. Maslow labeled the five hierarchical categories as physiological needs, safety and security needs, love (social) needs, esteem needs, and the need for self-actualization. Maslow's *need hierarchy* is depicted in Figure 5.1, which also shows how the needs relate to Douglas McGregor's assumptions about people, which will be discussed next.

Maslow conceptually derived the five need categories from the early thoughts of William James[16] and John Dewey,[17] coupled with the psychodynamic thinking of Sigmund Freud and Alfred Adler.[18] Maslow's need theory was later tested in research with working populations. For example, one study reported that middle managers and lower-level managers had different perceptions of their need deficiencies and the importance of their needs.[19] One distinguishing feature of Maslow's need hierarchy is the following progression hypothesis. Although some research has challenged the assumption, the theory says that only ungratified needs motivate behavior.[20] Further, it is the lowest level of ungratified needs in the hierarchy that motivates behavior. As one level of need is met, a person progresses to the next higher level of need as a source of motivation. Hence, people progress up the hierarchy as they successively gratify each level of need.

need hierarchy
The theory that behavior is determined by a progression of physical, social, and psychological needs by higher order needs.

FIGURE 5.1   Human Needs, Theory X, and Theory Y

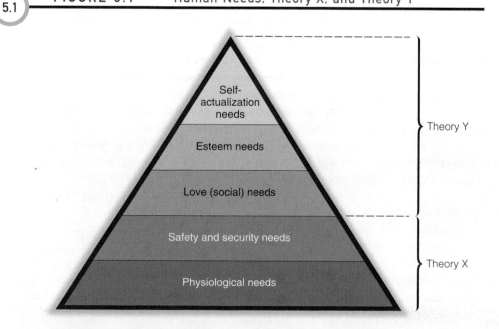

Theory X and Theory Y

2. Explain how Theory X and Theory Y relate to Maslow's hierarchy of needs.

Theory X

A set of assumptions of how to manage individuals who are motivated by lower order needs.

Theory Y

A set of assumptions of how to manage individuals who are motivated by higher order needs.

One important organizational implication of the need hierarchy concerns how to manage people at work (see Figure 5.1). Douglas McGregor understood people's motivation using Maslow's need theory. He grouped the physiological and safety needs as "lower order" needs and the social, esteem, and self-actualization needs as "upper order" needs, as shown in Figure 5.1. McGregor proposed two alternative sets of assumptions about people at work based on which set of needs were the motivators.[21] His *Theory X* and *Theory Y* assumptions are included in Table 5.1. McGregor saw the responsibility of management as the same under both sets of assumptions. Specifically, "management is responsible for organizing the elements of productive enterprise—money, materials, equipment, people—in the interest of economic ends."[22]

McGregor believed that Theory X assumptions are appropriate for employees motivated by lower order needs. Theory Y assumptions, in contrast, are appropriate for employees motivated by higher order needs. Employee participation programs are one consequence of McGregor's Theory Y assumptions. Therefore, *Fortune 1000* corporations use employee involvement as one motivation strategy for achieving high performance.[23] Whole Foods founder and CEO John Mackey relies on Maslow's hierarchy of needs in leading the company, as discussed in The Real World 5.1.

Gordon Forward, founding CEO of world-class Chaparral Steel Company, considered the assumptions made about people central to motivation and management.[24] He viewed employees as resources to be developed. Using Maslow's need hierarchy and Theory Y assumptions about people, he cultivated and developed a productive, loyal workforce in TXI's Chaparral Steel unit.

ERG Theory

Clayton Alderfer recognized Maslow's contribution to understanding motivation, yet believed that the original need hierarchy was not quite accurate in identifying and categorizing human needs.[25] As an evolutionary step, Alderfer

---

5.1   TABLE 5.1   McGregor's Assumptions About People

THEORY X	THEORY Y
■ People are by nature indolent. That is, they work as little as possible. ■ People lack ambition, dislike responsibility, and prefer to be led. ■ People are inherently self-centered and indifferent to organizational needs. ■ People are by nature resistant to change. ■ People are gullible and not very bright, the ready dupes of the charlatan and the demagogue.	■ People are not by nature passive or resistant to organizational needs. They have become so as a result of experience in organizations. ■ The motivation, the potential for development, the capacity for assuming responsibility, and the readiness to direct behavior toward organizational goals are all present in people. Management does not put them there. It is a responsibility of management to make it possible for people to recognize and develop these human characteristics for themselves. ■ The essential task of management is to arrange conditions and methods of operation so that people can achieve their own goals best by directing their own efforts toward organizational objectives.

Food ... Basic in Maslow's Hierarchy of Needs

Whole Foods CEO John Mackey subscribes to Maslow's hierarchy of needs in building and running his natural-food chain.

© David McNew/Staff/Getty Images

Whole Foods is the largest natural-food chain and the fastest-growing company in the competitive U.S. grocery business. Founded in 1980 with a single shop by unconventional CEO John Mackey, Whole Foods grew to 143 stores with 23,000 employees by 2003. Its stock soared 131 percent in three years, and its revenues doubled in five years to $2.8 billion in 2002. Whole Foods plans to grow to 260 stores and revenues of $10 billion by 2010.

Mackey shuns the spotlight and relies on Abraham Maslow's hierarchy of needs in building Whole Foods. He says that humans' needs begin with food and safety; then move to community and a sense of belonging; to the need for beauty; and next to education, esteem, and self-actualization. This is classic Maslow . . . and food is basic in his hierarchy of needs.

Mackey's formal education is not in business but in philosophy and religion. He supports employee empowerment and teamwork for self-actualization but thinks unions have their own self-interest motivations. In search of his own self-actualization, Mackey took five months off to hike the entire length of the 2,168-mile Appalachian Trail (his trail name was Strider) during 2002, when he was turning 50 and the economy was in one of its worst slumps in decades. John Mackey and Whole Foods are clearly a business success, if unconventionally so, and they reach back to Maslow's theory for their framework to understand human motivation.

SOURCE: J. Boorstin, "No Preservatives. No Unions. Lots of Dough," *Fortune* 148 (September 15, 2003): 127–129, http://www.fortune.com/fortune/ceo/articles/0,15114,480416,00.html.

proposed the ERG theory of motivation, which grouped human needs into only three basic categories: existence, relatedness, and growth.[26] Alderfer classified Maslow's physiological and physical safety needs in an existence need category; Maslow's interpersonal safety, love, and interpersonal esteem needs in a relatedness need category; and Maslow's self-actualization and self-esteem needs in a growth need category.

In addition to the differences in categorizing human needs, ERG theory added a regression hypothesis to go along with the progression hypothesis originally proposed by Maslow. Alderfer's regression hypothesis helped explain people's behavior when frustrated at meeting needs at the next higher level in the hierarchy. Specifically, the regression hypothesis states that people regress to the next lower category of needs and intensify their desire to gratify these needs. Hence, ERG theory explains both progressive need gratification and regression when people face frustration.

McClelland's Need Theory

A second major need theory of motivation focuses on personality and learned needs. Henry Murray developed a long list of motives and manifest needs in his early studies of personality.[27] David McClelland was inspired by Murray's early work.[28] McClelland identified three learned or acquired needs, called manifest needs. These manifest needs were the needs for achievement, for power,

3. Discuss the needs for achievement, power, and affiliation.

and for affiliation. Some individuals have a high need for achievement, whereas others have a moderate or low need for achievement. The same is true for the other two needs. Hence, it is important to emphasize that different needs are dominant in different people. For example, a manager may have a strong need for power, a moderate need for achievement, and a weak need for affiliation. Each need has quite different implications for people's behavior. The Murray Thematic Apperception Test (TAT) was used as an early measure of the achievement motive and was further developed by McClelland and his associates.[29] The TAT is a projective test, and projective tests were discussed in Chapter 3.

Need for Achievement

need for achievement

A manifest (easily perceived) need that concerns individuals' issues of excellence, competition, challenging goals, persistence, and overcoming difficulties.

The *need for achievement* concerns issues of excellence, competition, challenging goals, persistence, and overcoming difficulties.[30] A person with a high need for achievement seeks excellence in performance, enjoys difficult and challenging goals, and is persevering and competitive in work activities. Example questions that address the need for achievement are: Do you enjoy difficult, challenging work activities? Do you strive to exceed your performance objectives? Do you seek out new ways to overcome difficulties?

McClelland found that people with a high need for achievement perform better than those with a moderate or low need for achievement, and he has noted national differences in achievement motivation. Individuals with a high need for achievement have three unique characteristics. First, they set goals that are moderately difficult, yet achievable. Second, they like to receive feedback on their progress toward these goals. Third, they do not like having external events or other people interfere with their progress toward the goals.

High achievers often hope and plan for success. They may be quite content to work alone or with other people—whichever is more appropriate to their task. High achievers like being very good at what they do, and they develop expertise and competence in their chosen endeavors. Research shows that need for achievement generalizes well across countries with adults who are employed full-time.[31] In addition, international differences in the tendency for achievement have been found. Specifically, achievement tendencies are highest for the United States, an individualistic culture, and lowest for Japan and Hungary, collectivistic societies.[32]

Achievement tendencies vary internationally, ranging high for individualistic cultures, such as the United States, to lowest for collectivistic societies, such as Japan.

Need for Power

need for power

A manifest (easily perceived) need that concerns an individual's need to make an impact on others, influence others, change people or events, and make a difference in life.

The *need for power* is concerned with making an impact on others, the desire to influence others, the urge to change people or events, and the desire to make a difference in life. The need for power is interpersonal, because it involves influence with other people. People with a high need for power like to control people and events. McClelland makes an important distinction between socialized power, which is used for the benefit of many, and personalized power, which is used for individual gain. The former is a constructive force, whereas the latter may be a very disruptive, destructive force.

A high need for power was one distinguishing characteristic of managers rated the "best" in McClelland's research. Specifically, the best managers had a very high need for socialized power, as opposed to personalized power.[33] These managers are concerned for others; have an interest in organizational goals; and have a desire to be useful to the larger group, organization, and society.

While successful managers have the greatest upward velocity in an organization and rise to higher managerial levels more quickly than their contemporaries, they benefit their organizations most if they have a high socialized power need.[34] The need for power is discussed further in Chapter 11, on power and politics.

Need for Affiliation

The *need for affiliation* is concerned with establishing and maintaining warm, close, intimate relationships with other people.[35] People with a high need for affiliation are motivated to express their emotions and feelings to others while expecting other people to do the same in return. They find conflicts and complications in their relationships disturbing and are strongly motivated to work through any such barriers to closeness. The relationships they have with others are therefore close and personal, emphasizing friendship and companionship.

Over and above these three needs, Murray's manifest needs theory included the need for autonomy. This is the desire for independence and freedom from any constraints. People with a high need for autonomy like to work alone and to control the pace of their work. They dislike bureaucratic rules, regulations, and procedures. The need for relationships is important in each theory. The accompanying Science feature is based on a study that found that intrinsic motivation increased with supportive relationships on the job. Figure 5.2 summarizes Maslow's hierarchy of needs with its two extensions in the work of McGregor and Alderfer. The figure also summarizes McClelland's need theory of motivation. The figure shows the parallel structures of these four motivational theories.

need for affiliation
A manifest (easily perceived) need that concerns an individual's need to establish and maintain warm, close, intimate relationships with other people.

Herzberg's Two-Factor Theory

Frederick Herzberg departed from the need theories of motivation and examined the experiences that satisfied or dissatisfied people at work. This motivation theory became known as the two-factor theory.[36] Herzberg's original study included 200 engineers and accountants in western Pennsylvania during the

4. Describe the two-factor theory of motivation.

FIGURE 5.2   Need Theories of Motivation

5.2

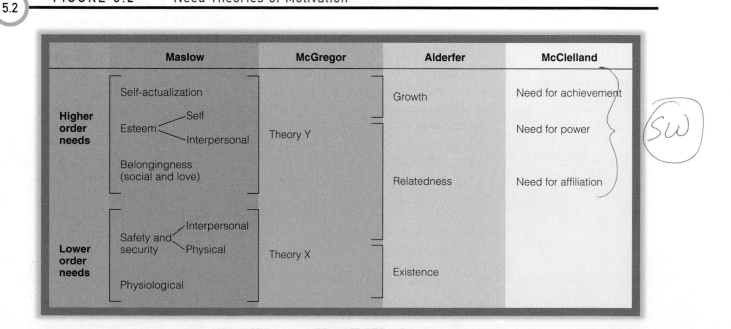

Intrinsic Motivation Increases with Instrumental Support on the Job

A recent study examined the effects of job demands, job control, and job social support on fatigue and intrinsic motivation among 555 nurses in specialized units for patients with different levels of mental deficiency. The investigators thought that intrinsic motivation among these nurses would increase when job demands and job control were high, and also when job social support was high. Further, they thought that fatigue among the nurses would be high when job demands were high and job control low, as well as when job social support was low.

The investigators did find that job control reduced fatigue in highly demanding jobs but found no evidence that support on the job made any difference in the nurses' level of fatigue. Further, they found that the availability of high levels of instrumental support on the job produced elevated levels of intrinsic motivation for the nurses. This latter finding concerning high levels of instrumental support and intrinsic motivation held true regardless of the level of job demands or job control.

The investigators suggest that increasing job social support is the most effective way to enhance intrinsic motivation for employees. Further, an important managerial implication of the study is that refining interpersonal skills associated with exchanging social support with others, such as asking for help from others on the job, may have very positive motivational effects for employees at work.

SOURCE: N. W. van Yperen and M. Hagedoorn, "Do High Job Demands Increase Intrinsic Motivation or Fatigue or Both? The Role of Job Control and Job Social Support," *Academy of Management Journal* 46 (2003): 339–348.

1950s. Herzberg asked these people to describe two important incidents at their jobs: one that was very satisfying and made them feel exceptionally good at work, and another that was very dissatisfying and made them feel exceptionally bad at work.

Herzberg and his colleagues believed that people had two sets of needs—one related to the avoidance of pain and one related to the desire for psychological growth. Conditions in the work environment would affect one or the other of these needs. Work conditions related to satisfaction of the need for psychological growth were labeled *motivation factors*. Work conditions related to dissatisfaction caused by discomfort or pain were labeled *hygiene factors*. Each set of factors related to one aspect of what Herzberg identified as the human being's dual nature regarding the work environment. Thus, motivation factors relate to job satisfaction, and hygiene factors relate to job dissatisfaction,[37] as shown in Figure 5.3.

motivation factor
A work condition related to satisfaction of the need for psychological growth.

hygiene factor
A work condition related to dissatisfaction caused by discomfort or pain.

Motivation Factors

Job satisfaction is produced by building motivation factors into a job, according to Herzberg. This process is known as job enrichment. In the original research, the motivation factors were identified as responsibility, achievement, recognition, advancement, and the work itself. When these factors are present, they lead to superior performance and effort on the part of job incumbents. Figure 5.3 also shows that salary is a motivational factor in some studies. Many organizational reward systems now include other financial benefits, such as stock options, as part of an employee's compensation package. A long-term study of young men in the United States and West Germany found job satisfaction positively linked to earnings and changes in earnings, as well as voluntary turnover.[38]

Motivation factors lead to positive mental health and challenge people to grow, contribute to the work environment, and invest themselves in the orga-

Hygiene: Job dissatisfaction	Motivators: Job satisfaction
	Achievement
	Recognition of achievement
	Work itself
	Responsibility
	Advancement
	Growth
Company policy and administration	
Supervision	
Interpersonal relations	
Working conditions	
Salary*	
Status	
Security	

*Because of its ubiquitous nature, salary commonly shows up as a motivator as well as hygiene. Although primarily a hygiene factor, it also often takes on some of the properties of a motivator, with dynamics similar to those of recognition for achievement.

SOURCE: Reprinted from Frederick Herzberg, *The Managerial Choice: To Be Efficient or to Be Human* (Salt Lake City: Olympus, 1982). Reprinted by permission.

nization. According to the theory and original research, the absence of these factors does not lead to dissatisfaction. Rather, it leads to the lack of satisfaction. The motivation factors are the more important of the two sets of factors, because they directly affect a person's motivational drive to do a good job. When they are absent, the person is demotivated to perform well and achieve excellence. The hygiene factors are a completely distinct set of factors unrelated to the motivation to achieve and do excellent work.

Hygiene Factors

Job dissatisfaction occurs when the hygiene factors are either not present or not sufficient. In the original research, the hygiene factors were company policy and administration, technical supervision, salary, interpersonal relations with one's supervisor, and working conditions, salary, and status. These factors relate to the context of the job and may be considered support factors. They do not directly affect a person's motivation to work but influence the extent of the person's discontent. They cannot stimulate psychological growth or human development but may be thought of as maintenance factors. Excellent hygiene factors result in employees' being *not dissatisfied* and contribute to the absence of complaints about these contextual considerations.

When these hygiene factors are poor or absent, the person complains about "poor supervision," "poor medical benefits," or whatever hygiene factor is poor. Employees experience a deficit and are dissatisfied when the hygiene factors are not present. Even in the absence of good hygiene factors, employees may still be very motivated to perform their jobs well if the motivation factors are present. Although this may appear to be a paradox, it is not, because the motivation and hygiene factors are independent of each other.

The combination of motivation and hygiene factors can result in one of four possible job conditions. First, a job high in both motivation and hygiene factors leads to high motivation and few complaints among employees. Second, a job low in both factors leads to low motivation and many complaints among employees. Third, a job high in motivation factors and low in hygiene factors leads to high employee motivation to perform coupled with complaints about aspects of the work environment. Fourth, a job low in motivation factors and high in hygiene factors leads to low employee motivation to excel but few complaints about the work environment.

Two conclusions can be drawn at this point. First, hygiene factors are of some importance up to a threshold level, but beyond the threshold there is little value in improving the hygiene factors. Second, the presence of motivation factors is essential to enhancing employee motivation to excel at work. You 5.2 asks you to rank a set of ten job reward factors in terms of their importance to the average employee, to supervisors, and to you.

Critique of the Two-Factor Theory

Herzberg's two-factor theory has been critiqued. One criticism concerns the classification of the two factors. Data have not shown a clear dichotomization of incidents into hygiene and motivator factors. For example, employees almost equally classify pay as a hygiene factor and as a motivation factor. A second criticism is the absence of individual differences in the theory. Specifically, individual differences such as age, sex, social status, education, or occupational level may influence the classification of factors. A third criticism is that intrinsic job factors, such as the work flow process, may be more important in determining satisfaction or dissatisfaction on the job. Finally, almost all of the supporting data for the theory come from Herzberg and his students using his peculiar critical-incident technique. These criticisms challenge and qualify, yet do not invalidate, the theory. Independent research found his theory valid in a government research and development environment.[39] Herzberg's two-factor theory has important implications for the design of work, as discussed in Chapter 14.

What's Important to Employees?

There are many possible job rewards that employees may receive. Listed below are ten possible job reward factors. Rank these factors three times. First, rank them as you think the average employee would rank them. Second, rank them as you think the average employee's supervisor would rank them for the employee. Finally, rank them according to what you consider important.

Your instructor has normative data for 1,000 employees and their supervisors that will help you interpret your results and place the results in the context of Maslow's need hierarchy and Herzberg's two-factor theory of motivation.

Employee	Supervisor	You	MGT	
		7		**1.** job security
		4		**2.** full appreciation of work done
		5		**3.** promotion and growth in the organization
		6		**4.** good wages
		1		**5.** interesting work
		2		**6.** good working conditions
		8		**7.** tactful discipline
		10		**8.** sympathetic help with personal problems
		3		**9.** personal loyalty to employees
		9		**10.** a feeling of being in on things

SOURCE: "Crossed Wires on Employee Motivation," *Training and Development* 49 (1995): 59–60. American Society for Training and Development. Reprinted with permission. All rights reserved.

Two New Ideas in Motivation

While executives like Whole Foods' CEO John Mackey value traditional motivation theories such as Maslow's, others like PepsiCo's CEO Steve Reinemund use new motivational ideas with their employees. Two new ideas in motivation have emerged in the past decade. One new idea centers on eustress, strength, and hope. This idea comes from the new discipline of positive organizational scholarship. A second new idea centers on positive energy and full engagement. This idea translates what was learned from high-performance athletes for *Fortune 500* executives and managers, such as those at PepsiCo. Both new ideas concern motivation, behavior, and performance at work.

5. Explain two new ideas in human motivation.

Which one is SW?

Eustress, Strength, and Hope

Our detailed discussion of stress and health at work will come in Chapter 7. The positive side of stress discussed in Chapter 7 concerns its value as a motivational force, as in eustress. *Eustress* is healthy, normal stress.[40] Aligned with eustress in the new discipline of positive organizational scholarship are investing in strengths, finding positive meaning in work, displaying courage and principled action, and drawing on positive emotions at work.[41] This new, positive perspective on organizational life encourages optimism, hope, and health for people at work. Rather than focusing on the individual's needs, or alternatively on the rewards or punishment metered out in the work environment, this new idea in motivation focuses on the individual's interpretation of events.

eustress

Healthy, normal stress.

Eustress is one manifestation of this broad, positive perspective. People are motivated by eustress when they see opportunities rather than obstacles, when they experience challenges rather than barriers, and when they feel energized rather than frustrated by the daily experiences of organizational life. Thus, eustress is a healthy and positive motivational force for individuals who harness its energy for productive work and organizational contributions.

Positive Energy and Full Engagement

The second new idea in motivation takes lessons learned from professional athletes and applies them in order to develop corporate athletes.[42] Jim Loehr's central tenets are the management of energy rather than time and the strategic use of disengagement to balance the power of full activity engagement.[43] This approach to motivation suggests that individuals do not need to be activated by unmet needs but are already activated by their own physical, emotional, mental, and spiritual energy. A manager's task is to help individuals learn to manage their energy so that they can experience periodic renewal and recovery and thus build positive energy and capacity for work.

A key to positive energy and full engagement is the concept that energy recovery is equally important to, if not more important than, energy expenditure. Individuals may be designed more as sprinters than long-distance runners, putting forth productive energy for short periods and then requiring time for recovery to reenergize. This approach to motivation and work is based on a balanced approach to the human body's potential to build or enhance its capacity, thus enabling the individual to sustain a high level of performance in the face of increasing work demands.

Social Exchange and Equity Theory

Equity theory is a social exchange process theory of motivation that focuses on the individual–environment interaction. In contrast to internal needs theories of motivation, equity theory is concerned with the social processes that influence motivation and behavior. Power and exchange are important considerations in understanding human behavior.[44] In the same vein, Amitai Etzioni developed three categories of exchange relationships that people have with organizations: committed, calculated, and alienated involvements.[45] The implications of these relationships for power are discussed in detail in Chapter 11. Etzioni characterized committed relations as moral ones of high positive intensity, calculated relationships as ones of low positive or low negative intensity, and alienated relationships as ones of high negative intensity. Committed relationships may characterize a person's involvement with a religious group, and alienated relationships may characterize a person's incarceration in a prison. Social exchange theory may be the best way to understand effort–reward relationships and the sense of fairness at work as seen in a Dutch study.[46] Moral principles in workplace fairness are important because failures in fairness, or unfairness, lead to such things as theft, sabotage, and even violence.[47]

Demands and Contributions

Calculated involvements are based on the notion of social exchange in which each party in the relationship demands certain things of the other and contributes accordingly to the exchange. Business partnerships and commercial deals are excellent examples of calculated involvements. When they work well and both parties to the exchange benefit, the relationship has a positive orientation. When losses occur or conflicts arise, the relationship has a negative orientation. A model for examining these calculated exchange relationships is set out in Figure 5.4. We use this model to examine the nature of the relationship between a person and his or her employing organization.[48] The same basic model can be used to examine the relationship between two individuals or two organizations.

DEMANDS Each party to the exchange makes demands upon the other. These demands express the expectations that each party has of the other in the relationship. The organization expresses its demands on the individual in the form of goal or mission statements, job expectations, performance objectives, and performance feedback. These are among the primary and formal mechanisms through which people learn about the organization's demands and expectations of them.

The organization is not alone in making demands of the relationship. The individual has needs to be satisfied as well, as we have previously discussed. These needs form the basis for the expectations or demands placed on the organization by the individual. Employee need fulfillment and the feeling of belonging are both important to a healthy exchange and to organizational membership.[49] These needs may be conceptualized from the perspective of Maslow, Alderfer, Herzberg, or McClelland. When employees are well taken care of by the company, then they take care of the business, as discussed in The Real World 5.2.

_SW_

CONTRIBUTIONS Just as each party to the exchange makes demands upon the other, each also has contributions to make to the relationship. These

FIGURE 5.4   The Individual–Organizational Exchange Relationship

5.4

	Organization	Individual
Demands	• Organizational goals • Departmental objectives • Job tasks	• Physiological needs • Security needs • Physical needs
Contributions	• Company status • Benefits • Income	• Developmental potential • Employee knowledge • Employee skills and abilities

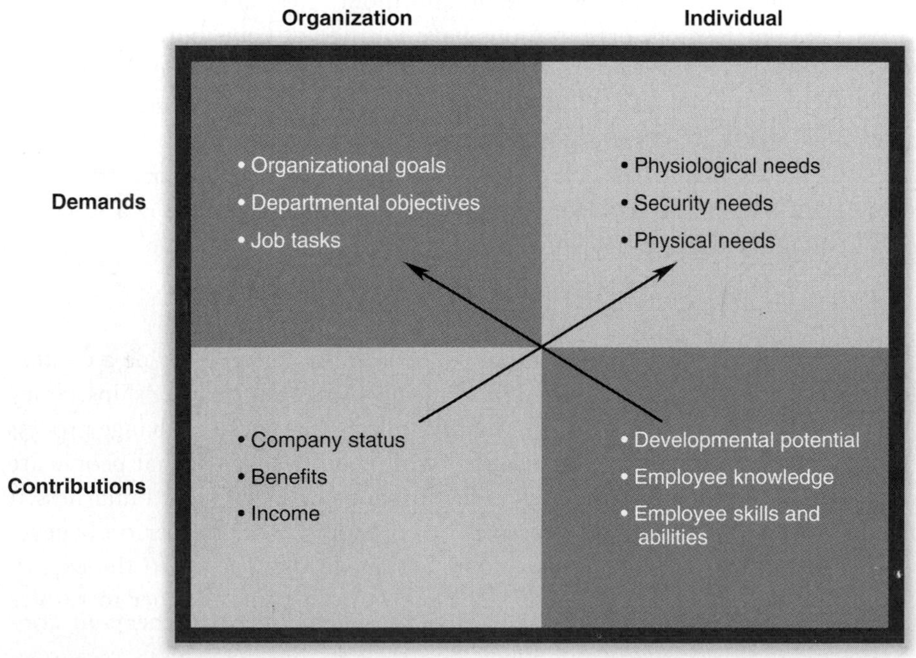

SOURCE: J. P. Campbell, M. D. Dunnette, E. E. Lawler, III, and K. E. Weick, Jr., _Managerial Behavior, Performance, and Effectiveness_ (New York: McGraw-Hill, Inc., 1970). Reproduced with permission from McGraw-Hill, Inc.

Take Care of People . . . They'll Take Care of Business

Can a modern steel company be worker friendly? Hamilton, Ontario-based Dofasco, Inc., is! While tiny by industry standards with just 8,500 employees and a market cap of $2.3 billion, this steel company has outperformed many of its big competitors. Dofasco's approach is to keep an eye on the "triple bottom line." The triple-bottom-line thinking refers to financial metrics, impact on society, and effect on the environment. The company's approach is to keep shareholders happy by having satisfied customers who, in turn, are satisfied by happy employees who, in turn, live in healthy, supportive communities. So, when Dofasco takes care of people, the people take care of business.

Dofasco treats employees fairly and equitably, in exchange for which the employees are highly motivated and highly productive. When the company does well, employees prosper, as in 1999 when employees split a record bonus pot of $36 million. In addition, when times are tough, few people . . . if any . . . are laid off. Turnover in Dofasco's primary facility in Hamilton is less than two percent.

While tracking financial metrics conforms to accepted industry practice, Dofasco measures its impact on society and effect on the environment. Four tips in this regard are (1) think long term and look to the environment; (2) shoot for zero adverse impact in the community; (3) put employee satisfaction numbers in historical and industry context; and (4) experiment with various measures because triple-bottom-line reporting is still in its infancy.

SOURCE: C. Dahle, "A Steelmaker's Heart of Gold," *Fast Company* 71 (June 2003): 46, http://www.fastcompany.com/magazine /71/smartcompany.html.

contributions are the basis for satisfying the demands expressed by the other party in the relationship. Employees are able to satisfy organizational demands through a range of contributions, including their skills, abilities, knowledge, energy, professional contacts, and native talents. As people grow and develop over time, they are able to increasingly satisfy the range of demands and expectations placed upon them by the organization.

In a similar fashion, organizations have a range of contributions available to the exchange relationship to meet individual needs. These contributions include salary, benefits, advancement opportunities, security, status, and social affiliation. Some organizations are richer in resources and better able to meet employee needs than other organizations. Thus, one of the concerns that individuals and organizations alike have is whether the relationship is a fair deal or an equitable arrangement for both members of the relationship.

Adams's Theory of Inequity

6. Describe how inequity influences motivation and can be resolved.

inequity
The situation in which a person perceives he or she is receiving less than he or she is giving, or is giving less than he or she is receiving.

Blau's and Etzioni's ideas about social process and exchange provide a context for understanding fairness, equity, and inequity in work relationships. Stacy Adams explicitly developed the idea that *inequity* in the social exchange process is an important motivator. Adams's theory of inequity suggests that people are motivated when they find themselves in situations of inequity or unfairness.[50] Inequity occurs when a person receives more, or less, than the person believes is deserved based on effort and/or contribution. Inequity leads to the experience of tension, and tension motivates a person to act in a manner to resolve the inequity.

When does a person know that the situation is inequitable or unfair? Adams suggests that people examine the contribution portion of the exchange relationship just discussed. Specifically, people consider their inputs (their own contributions to the relationship) and their outcomes (the organization's contributions to the relationship). People then calculate an input/outcome ratio, which they compare with that of a generalized or comparison other. Figure 5.5 shows one equity situation and two inequity situations, one negative and one positive. For example, inequity in (b) could occur if the comparison other earned a higher salary, and inequity in (c) could occur if the person had more vacation time, in both cases all else being equal. Although not illustrated in the example, nontangible inputs, like emotional investment, and nontangible outcomes, like job satisfaction, may well enter into a person's equity equation.

Pay inequity has been a particularly thorny issue for women in some professions and companies. Eastman Kodak and other companies have made real progress in addressing this inequity through pay equity.[51] As organizations become increasingly international, it may be difficult to determine pay and benefit equity/inequity across national borders.

equitable pay

Adams would consider the inequity in Figure 5.5(b) to be a first level of inequity. A more severe, second level of inequity would occur if the comparison other's inputs were lower than the person's. Inequalities in one (inputs or outcomes) coupled with equality in the other (inputs or outcomes) are experienced as a less severe inequity than inequalities in both inputs and outcomes. Adams's theory, however, does not provide a way of determining if some inputs (such as effort or experience) or some outcomes are more important or weighted more than others, such as a degree or certification.

The Resolution of Inequity

Once a person establishes the existence of an inequity, a number of strategies can be used to restore equity to the situation. Adams's theory provides seven basic strategies to restore equity for the person: (1) alter the person's outcomes, (2) alter the person's inputs, (3) alter the comparison other's outcomes, (4) alter the comparison other's inputs, (5) change who is used as a comparison other, (6) rationalize the inequity, and (7) leave the organizational situation.

Within each of the first four strategies, a wide variety of tactics can be employed. For example, if an employee has a strategy to increase his or her income by $11,000 per year to restore equity, the tactic might be a meeting between the employee and his or her manager concerning the issue of salary

FIGURE 5.5   Equity and Inequity at Work

5.5

	Person		Comparison other
(a) Equity	$\dfrac{\text{Outcomes}}{\text{Inputs}}$	$=$	$\dfrac{\text{Outcomes}}{\text{Inputs}}$
(b) Negative Inequity	$\dfrac{\text{Outcomes}}{\text{Inputs}}$	$<$	$\dfrac{\text{Outcomes}}{\text{Inputs}}$
(c) Positive Inequity	$\dfrac{\text{Outcomes}}{\text{Inputs}}$	$>$	$\dfrac{\text{Outcomes}}{\text{Inputs}}$

equity. The person would present relevant data on the issue. Another tactic would be for the person to work with the company's compensation specialists. A third tactic would be for the person to bring the matter before an equity committee in the company. A fourth tactic would be for the person to seek advice from the legal department.

The selection of a strategy and a set of tactics is a sensitive issue with possible long-term consequences. In this example, a strategy aimed at reducing the comparison other's outcomes may have the desired short-term effect of restoring equity while having adverse long-term consequences in terms of morale and productivity. Similarly, the choice of legal tactics may result in equity but have the long-term consequence of damaged relationships in the workplace. Therefore, as a person formulates the strategy and tactics to restore equity, the range of consequences of alternative actions must be taken into account. Hence, not all strategies or tactics are equally preferred. The equity theory does not include a hierarchy predicting which inequity reduction strategy a person will or should choose.

Field studies on equity theory suggest that it may help explain important organizational behaviors. For example, one study found that workers who perceived compensation decisions as equitable displayed greater job satisfaction and organizational commitment.[52] In addition, equity theory may play an important role in labor–management relationships with regard to union-negotiated benefits.

New Perspectives on Equity Theory

Since the original formulation of the theory of inequity, now usually referred to as equity theory, a number of revisions have been made in light of new theories and research. One important theoretical revision proposes three types of individuals based on preferences for equity.[53] *Equity sensitives* are those people who prefer equity based on the originally formed theory. Equity sensitivity contributes significantly to variation in free time spent working.[54] *Benevolents* are people who are comfortable with an equity ratio less than that of their comparison other, as exhibited in the Calvinistic heritage of the Dutch.[55] These people may be thought of as givers. *Entitleds* are people who are comfortable with an equity ratio greater than that of their comparison other, as exhibited by some offspring of the affluent who want and expect more.[56] These people may be thought of as takers. Females and minorities have not always been equitably treated in business and commerce.

Research on organizational justice has a long history.[57] One study suggests that a person's organizational position influences self-imposed performance expectations.[58] Specifically, a two-level move up in an organization with no additional pay creates a higher self-imposed performance expectation than a one-level move up with modest additional pay. Similarly, a two-level move down in an organization with no reduction in pay creates a lower self-imposed performance expectation than a one-level move down with a modest decrease in pay. This suggests that organizational position may be more important than pay in determining the level of a person's performance expectations.

One of the unintended consequences of inequity and organizational injustice is dysfunctional behavior. For example, workplace injustice can trigger aggressive reactions or other forms of violent and deviant behavior that do harm to both individuals and the organization. Fortunately, only a small number of individuals respond to such unfairness through dysfunctional behavior.[59]

Although most studies of equity theory take a short-term perspective, equity comparisons over the long term should be considered as well. Increasing, de-

equity sensitive

An individual who prefers an equity ratio equal to that of his or her comparison other.

benevolent

An individual who is comfortable with an equity ratio less than that of his or her comparison other.

entitled

An individual who is comfortable with an equity ratio greater than that of his or her comparison other.

creasing, or constant experiences of inequity over time may have very different consequences for people.[60] For example, do increasing experiences of inequity have a debilitating effect on people? In addition, equity theory may help companies implement two-tiered wage structures, such as the one used by American Airlines in the early 1990s. In a two-tiered system, one group of employees receives different pay and benefits than another group of employees. A study of 1,935 rank-and-file members in one retail chain using a two-tiered wage structure confirmed the predictions of equity theory.[61] The researchers suggest that unions and management may want to consider work location and employment status (part-time versus full-time) prior to the implementation of a two-tiered system.

Expectancy Theory of Motivation

Whereas equity theory focuses on a social exchange process, Vroom's expectancy theory of motivation focuses on personal perceptions of the performance process. His theory is founded on the basic notions that people desire certain outcomes of behavior and performance, which may be thought of as rewards or consequences of behavior, and that they believe there are relationships between the effort they put forth, the performance they achieve, and the outcomes they receive. Expectancy theory is a cognitive process theory of motivation.

The key constructs in the expectancy theory of motivation are the *valence* of an outcome, *expectancy*, and *instrumentality*.[62] Valence is the value or importance one places on a particular reward. Expectancy is the belief that effort leads to performance (for example, "If I try harder, I can do better"). Instrumentality is the belief that performance is related to rewards (for example, "If I perform better, I will get more pay"). A model for the expectancy theory notions of effort, performance, and rewards is depicted in Figure 5.6.

Valence, expectancy, and instrumentality are all important to a person's motivation. Expectancy and instrumentality concern a person's beliefs about how effort, performance, and rewards are related. For example, a person may firmly believe that an increase in effort has a direct, positive effect on performance and that a reduced amount of effort results in a commensurate reduction in performance. Another person may have a very different set of beliefs about the

7. Describe the expectancy theory of motivation.

$\varsigma\omega$

valence
The value or importance one places on a particular reward.

expectancy
The belief that effort leads to performance.

instrumentality
The belief that performance is related to rewards.

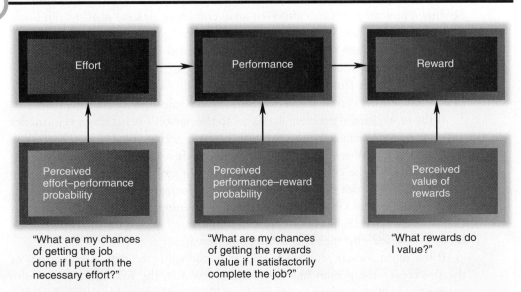

FIGURE 5.6   An Expectancy Model for Motivation

5.6

effort–performance link. The person might believe that regardless of the amount of additional effort put forth, no improvement in performance is possible. Therefore, the perceived relationship between effort and performance varies from person to person and from activity to activity.

In a similar fashion, people's beliefs about the performance–reward link vary. One person may believe that an improvement in performance has a direct, positive effect on the rewards received, whereas another person may believe that an improvement in performance has no effect on the rewards received. Again, the perceived relationship between performance and rewards varies from person to person and from situation to situation. From a motivation perspective, it is the person's belief about the relationships between these constructs that is important, not the actual nature of the relationship. During volatile times in business, the performance–reward linkage may be confusing.

Expectancy theory has been used by managers and companies to design motivation programs.[63] Sometimes called performance planning and evaluation systems, these motivation programs are designed to enhance a person's belief that effort would lead to better performance and that better performance would lead to merit pay increases and other rewards. Valence and expectancy are particularly important in establishing priorities for people pursuing multiple goals.[64]

A person's motivation increases along with his or her belief that effort leads to performance and that performance leads to rewards, assuming the person wants the rewards. This is the third key idea within the expectancy theory of motivation. It is the idea that the valence, or value, that people place on various rewards varies. One person prefers salary to benefits, whereas another person prefers just the reverse. All people do not place the same value on each reward. Expectancy theory has been used in a wide variety of contexts, including test-taking motivation among students.[65]

Motivational Problems

Within the expectancy theory framework, motivational problems stem from three basic causes. These causes are a disbelief in a relationship between effort and performance, a disbelief in a relationship between performance and rewards, and lack of desire for the rewards offered.

If the motivational problem is related to the person's belief that effort will not result in performance, the solution lies in altering this belief. The person can be shown how an increase in effort, or an alteration in the kind of effort put forth, can be converted into improved performance. For example, the textbook salesperson who does not believe more calls (effort) will result in greater sales (performance) might be shown how to distinguish departments with high-probability sales opportunities from those with low-probability sales opportunities. Hence, more calls (effort) can be converted into greater sales (performance).

If the motivational problem is related to the person's belief that performance will not result in rewards, the solution lies in altering this belief. The person can be shown how an increase in performance or a somewhat altered form of performance will be converted into rewards. For example, the textbook salesperson who does not believe greater sales (performance) will result in overall higher commissions (rewards) might be shown computationally or graphically that a direct relationship does exist. Hence, greater sales (performance) are directly converted into higher commissions (rewards).

If the motivational problem is related to the value the person places on, or the preference the person has for, certain rewards, the solution lies in influencing the value placed on the rewards or altering the rewards themselves. For example, the textbook salesperson may not particularly want higher commissions, given the small incremental gain he would receive at his tax level. In this case, the company might establish a mechanism for sheltering commissions from being taxed or alternative mechanisms for deferred compensation.

Research results on expectancy theory have been mixed.[66] The theory has been shown to predict job satisfaction accurately.[67] However, the theory's complexity makes it difficult to test the full model, and the measures of instrumentality, valence, and expectancy have only weak validity.[68] In addition, measuring the expectancy constructs is time consuming, and the values for each construct change over time for an individual. Finally, a theory assumes the individual is totally rational and acts as a minicomputer, calculating probabilities and values. In reality, the theory may be more complex than people as they typically function.

Motivation and Moral Maturity

Expectancy theory would predict that people work to maximize their personal outcomes. This is consistent with Adam Smith's ideas of working for one's own self-interest. Ultimately, Adam Smith and expectancy theories believe that people work to benefit themselves alone. Expectancy theory would not explain altruistic behavior for the benefit of others. Therefore, it may be necessary to consider an individual's *moral maturity* in order to better understand altruistic, fair, and equitable behavior. Moral maturity is the measure of a person's cognitive moral development, which was discussed in Chapter 4. Morally mature people act and behave based on universal ethical principles, whereas morally immature people act and behave based on egocentric motivations.[69]

moral maturity
The measure of a person's cognitive moral development.

Cultural Differences in Motivation

Most motivation theories in use today have been developed by Americans in the United States and are about Americans.[70] When researchers have examined the universality of these theories, they have found cultural differences, at least with regard to Maslow's, McClelland's, and Herzberg's theories. For example, while self-actualization may be the pinnacle need for Americans in Maslow's need hierarchy, security may be the most important need for people in cultures such as Greece and Japan who have a high need to avoid uncertainty.[71] Although achievement is an important need for Americans, research noted earlier in the chapter suggested that other cultures do not value achievement as much as Americans do.

The two-factor theory has been tested in other countries as well. Results in New Zealand did not replicate the results found in the United States; supervision and interpersonal relationships were important motivators in New Zealand rather than hygienic factors as in America.[72] Finally, expectancy theory may hold up very nicely in cultures that value individualism but break down in more collectivist cultures that value cooperative efforts. In collectivist cultures, rewards are more closely tied to group and team efforts, thus rendering unnecessary the utility of expectancy theory.

8. Describe the cultural differences in motivation.

Managerial Implications: Many Ways to Motivate People

Managers must realize that all motivation theories are not equally good or equally useful. The later motivation theories, such as the equity and expectancy theories, may be more scientifically sound than earlier theories, such as the two-factor theory. Nevertheless, the older theories of motivation have conceptual value, show us the importance of human needs, and provide a basis for the later theories. The individual, internal theories of motivation and the individual–environment interaction process theories uniquely contribute to our overall understanding of human behavior and motivation at work.

Managers cannot assume they understand employees' needs. They should recognize the variety of needs that motivate employee behavior and ask employees for input to better understand their needs. Individual employees differ in their needs, and managers should be sensitive to ethnic, national, gender, and age differences in this regard. Employees with high needs for power must be given opportunities to exercise influence, and employees with high needs for achievement must be allowed to excel at work.

Managers can increase employee motivation by training (increased perceptions of success because of increased ability), coaching (increased confidence), and task assignments (increased perceptions of success because of more experience). Managers should ensure that rewards are contingent on good performance and that valued rewards, such as time off or flexible work schedules, are available. Managers must understand what their employees want.

Finally, managers should be aware that morally mature employees are more likely to be sensitive to inequities at work. At the same time, these employees are less likely to be selfish or self-centered and more likely to be concerned about equity issues for all employees. Morally mature employees will act ethically for the common good of all employees and the organization.

LOOKING BACK: CANINE COMPANIONS FOR INDEPENDENCE

Canine Companions for Independence trains its dogs to not only physically help the disabled but also to comfort and uplift the spirits of those in need.

© Tom Nebbia/CORBIS

9/11 Brings out the Need for Emotional Support

Watching the events of September 11, 2001, unfold on television, hospital administrative director Dr. Tom Demaria realized that the children and families of those killed would need long-term emotional support. Dr. Demaria acted quickly and signed a lease for a 5,000-square-foot storefront in Rockville Centre to house a counseling center. This counseling facility became the World Trade Center Child and Family Counseling Program, sponsored by South Nassau Communities Hospital and financed largely from two memorial funds—Project Liberty and the September 11th Fund. Anyone who lost a relative on 9/11 receives the program's services for free. The events of 9/11 are the kind of tragedy that threatens our security and our sense of safety and triggers our need for emotional support and nurturance. Dr. Demaria created a safe place where parents could bring their children and be cared for themselves. The families made the rules in the counseling center, not the counseling program's 25 therapists, including psychologists, social workers, and art therapists from the South Nassau hospital staff

These therapists are not alone in providing emotional support for the grieving. CCI prepares its assistance dogs to help the disabled and also to be a source of support and comfort for the grieving. Tom Flynn drove Derek, his three-year-old Canine Companion golden retriever, every three weeks to Rockville Centre from his home in Pennsylvania. For Kiersten Haub, who lost her firefighter father Michael Haub in the 9/11 tragedy, Derek was a source of emotional support as he would lay on the carpet, letting Kiersten ruffle his fur. Derek was trained at CCI's regional center at the State University at Farmingdale.

The trauma of sudden, violent death as caused by 9/11 is abnormal, threatens people, and elicits deeper needs than usually experienced. These events take us all out of the realm of normal human motivation and into the realm of coping and recovery. The frustration, anger, and confusion experienced in these traumatic circumstances are often labeled by victims as abnormal, while in fact they are quite normal reactions to abnormal events. As people rebuild their self-confidence and lives in the face of such tragedy, the wise words of an experienced therapist can be helpful. So, too, can the gentle stroking of a Canine Companion by a traumatized child be therapeutic and aid that child in the process of healing and recovery. Coworkers, friends, family, and Canine Companions are all part of an emotional support network in a person's darkest hour before the dawn of a new day and renewed strength.[73]

Chapter Summary

1. Early economic theories of motivation emphasized extrinsic incentives as the basis for motivation and technology as a force multiplier.

2. Maslow's hierarchy of needs theory of motivation was the basis for McGregor's Theory X and Theory Y assumptions about people at work.

3. According to McClelland, the needs for achievement, power, and affiliation are learned needs that differ among diverse cultures.

4. The two-factor theory found that the presence of motivation factors led to job satisfaction, and the presence of hygiene factors prevented job dissatisfaction.

5. New ideas in motivation emphasize eustress, hope, positive energy, and full engagement.

6. Social exchange theory holds that people form calculated working relationships and expect fair, equitable, ethical treatment.

7. Expectancy theory says that effort is the basis for motivation and that people want their effort to lead to performance and rewards.

8. Theories of motivation are culturally bound, and differences occur among nations.

Key Terms

benevolent (p. 166)
entitled (p. 166)
equity sensitive (p. 166)
eustress (p. 161)
expectancy (p. 167)
hygiene factor (p. 158)
inequity (p. 164)

instrumentality (p. 167)
moral maturity (p. 169)
motivation (p. 150)
motivation factor (p. 158)
need for achievement (p. 156)
need for affiliation (p. 157)
need for power (p. 156)

need hierarchy (p. 153)
psychoanalysis (p. 151)
self-interest (p. 152)
Theory X (p. 154)
Theory Y (p. 154)
valence (p. 167)

Review Questions

1. How can knowledge of motivation theories help managers?

2. What are the five categories of motivational needs described by Maslow? Give an example of how each can be satisfied.

3. What are the Theory X and Theory Y assumptions about people at work? How do they relate to the hierarchy of needs?

4. What three manifest needs does McClelland identify?

5. How do hygiene and motivational factors differ? What are the implications of the two-factor theory for managers?

6. What are two new ideas in motivation that managers are using?

7. How is inequity determined by a person in an organization? How can inequity be resolved if it exists?

8. What are the key concepts in the expectancy theory of motivation?

Discussion and Communication Questions

1. What do you think are the most important motivational needs for the majority of people? Do you think your needs differ from those of most people?

2. At what level in Maslow's hierarchy of needs are you living? Are you basically satisfied at this level?

3. Assume you are leaving your current job to look for employment elsewhere. What will you look for that you do not have now? If you do not have a job, assume you will be looking for one soon. What are the most important factors that you will seek?

4. If you were being inequitably paid in your job, which strategy do you think would be the most helpful to you in resolving the inequity? What tactics would you consider using?

5. Do you believe you can do a better job of working or do a better job of studying than you are currently doing? Do you think you would get more pay and benefits or better grades if you did a better job? Do you care about the rewards (or grades) in your organization (or university)?

6. What important experiences have contributed to your moral and ethical development? Are you working to further your own moral maturity at this time?

7. *(communication question)* Prepare a memo describing the two employees you work with who most closely operate according to Theory X and Theory Y assumptions about human nature. Be as specific and detailed in your description as you can, using quotes and/or observational examples.

8. *(communication question)* Develop an oral presentation about the most current management practices in employee motivation. Find out what at least four different companies are doing in this area. Be prepared to compare these practices with the theory and research in the chapter.

9. *(communication question)* Interview a manager and prepare a memo summarizing the relative importance that manager places on the needs for achievement, power, and affiliation. Include (1) whether these needs have changed over time and (2) what job aspects satisfy these needs.

Ethical Dilemma

Mitch heard the alarm blaring. "It couldn't be 5:00 A.M. already," he thought. He sat on the edge of the bed wondering how he had gotten himself into this mess. Mitch graduated from a good school with a bachelor's degree in management and a good GPA. He had dreams of a great job and a wonderful life. Instead, he found himself working 60 or more hours per week and feeling constantly pressured to work more.

Mitch started working at Acme, an electronics retailer, right out of college. At the time, the company recruiter had painted a picture of great opportunity for the "right" people. Acme wanted employees who had a high need for achievement and a desire to attain positions of power and authority. It sounded perfect for Mitch. He knew he was executive material. The problem was that the company hired only people who were willing to go the extra mile.

Now, two years later, Mitch realized that the company was using his own personal needs against him. When he was hired by Acme, Mitch was told that the average workweek would be 50 hours. It was not the cushy job he had envisioned, but if it led to the advancement the company alluded to, it was well worth it. Although he was not required to go beyond the stated 50 hours, Mitch had never worked less than 60 hours and often approached 70. From day one, the company had pushed for full commitment. "The only way to advance is to prove yourself and your commitment to the company," was heard more than once. It was the mantra to every unit

manager in the organization. Mitch was beginning to believe that the whole process had been a game. Acme hired employees who were highly motivated to achieve and then used that internal motivation against them to get as much productivity from them as possible. The company caused managers to burn out and simply hired new ones when they left. Mitch had never before felt so deceived and used.

Questions

1. Did Acme mislead Mitch and the other managers?

2. Does Acme have an obligation to its shareholders to maximize productivity and profitability?

3. Using rule, virtue, right, and justice theories, evaluate Acme's hiring practices.

Experiential Exercises

5.1 What Do You Need from Work?

This exercise provides an opportunity to discuss your basic needs and those of other students in your class. Refer back to You 5.2, What's Important to Employees?, and look over your ranking of the ten possible job reward factors. Think about basic needs you may have that are possibly work related and yet would not be satisfied by one or another of these ten job reward factors.

Step 1. The class will form into groups of approximately six members each. Each group elects a spokesperson and answers the following questions. The group should spend at least five minutes on the first question and make sure each member of the group makes a contribution. The second question will probably take longer for your group to answer, up to fifteen minutes. The spokesperson should be ready to share the group's answers.

a. *What important basic needs do you have that are not addressed by one or another of these ten job reward factors?* Members should focus on the whole range of needs discussed in the different need theories of motivation covered in Chapter 5. Develop a list of the basic needs overlooked by these ten factors.

5.2 What to Do?

According to Stacy Adams, the experience of inequity or social injustice is a motivating force for human behavior. This exercise provides you and your

b. *What is important to members of your group?* Rank-order all job reward factors (the original ten and any new ones your group came up with in Step 1) in terms of their importance for your group. If group members disagree about the rankings, take time to discuss the differences among group members. Work for consensus and also note points of disagreement.

Step 2. Each group will share the results of its answers to the questions in Step 1. Cross-team questions and discussion follow.

Step 3. If your instructor has not already shared the normative data for 1,000 employees and their supervisors mentioned in You 5.2, the instructor may do that at this time.

Step 4 (Optional). Your instructor may ask you to discuss the similarities and differences in your group's rankings with the employee and supervisory normative rankings. If he or she does, spend some time addressing two questions.

a. *What underlying reasons do you think may account for the differences that exist?*

b. *How have the needs of employees and supervisors changed over the past twenty years? Are they likely to change in the future?*

group with a brief scenario of an inequity at work. Your task is to consider feasible actions for redress of this inequity.

John and Mary are full professors in the same medical school department of a large private university. As a private institution, neither the school nor the university makes the salaries and benefits of its faculty a matter of public record. Mary has pursued a long-term (fourteen years) career in the medical school, rising through the academic ranks while married to a successful businessman with whom she has raised three children. Her research and teaching contributions have been broad ranging and award winning. John joined the medical school within the last three years and was recruited for his leading-edge contribution to a novel line of research on a new procedure. Mary thought he was probably attracted with a comprehensive compensation package, yet she had no details until an administrative assistant gave her some information about salary and benefits a month ago. Mary learned that John's base contract salary is 16 percent higher than hers ($250,000 versus $215,000), that he was awarded an incentive pay component for the commercialization of his new procedure, and that he was given an annual discretionary travel budget of $35,000 and a membership in an exclusive private club. Mary is in a quandary about what to do. Given pressures from the board of trustees to hold down costs associated with public and private pressure to keep tuition increases low, Mary wonders how to begin to close this $70,000+ inequity gap.

Step 1. Working in groups of six, discuss the equity issues in this medical school department situation using the text material on social exchange and equity theory. Do the outcome differences here appear to be gender based, age based, performance based, or marital status based? Do you need more information? If so, what additional information do you need?

Step 2. Consider each of the seven strategies for the resolution of inequity as portrayed in this situation. Which ones are feasible to pursue based on what you know? Which ones are not feasible? Why? What are the likely consequences of each strategy or course of action? What would you advise Mary to do?

Step 3. Once your group has identified feasible resolution strategies, choose the best strategy. Next, develop a specific plan of action for Mary to follow in attempting to resolve the inequity so that she can achieve the experience and reality of fair treatment at work.

Step 4 (Optional). Your group may be asked to share its preferred strategy for this situation and your rationale for the strategy.

Biz Flix | For Love of the Game

Billy Chapel (Kevin Costner), a twenty-year veteran pitcher for the Detroit Tigers, learns just before the season's last game that the team's new owners want to trade him. He also learns that his partner, Jane Aubrey (Kelly Preston), intends to leave him. Faced with these daunting blows, Chapel wants to pitch a perfect final game. Director Raimi's love of baseball shines through in some striking visual effects.

The scene from *For Love of the Game* is a slightly edited version of the "Just Throw" sequence that begins the film's exciting closing scenes. In this scene, Tigers' catcher Gus Sinski (John C. Reilly) comes out to the pitching mound to talk to Chapel. It is the beginning of Chapel's last game.

What to Watch for and Ask Yourself:

> At what level are Billy Chapel's esteem needs at this point in the game?

> Do you expect Gus Sinski's talk to have any effect on Chapel? If it will, what effect do you expect it to have?

> What rewards potentially exist for Billy Chapel? Remember, this is the last baseball game of his career.

Workplace Video | Buffalo Zoo: Motivation in Organizations

When Donna Fernandes first arrived at the Buffalo Zoo in upstate New York, she encountered an organization plagued by flagging attendance, low employee morale, and a reputation for being poorly managed and operated. The autocratic leadership style and heavy-handed policies of former management had created an unpleasant work environment, and the well-trained and educated keepers and staff were not granted the freedom necessary to provide expert animal care.

Under the direction of Fernandes, the Buffalo Zoo has enjoyed a turnaround of mammoth proportions. Fernandes' participatory management style and natural enthusiasm for the job have made her mission to restore greatness to the Buffalo Zoo a dream shared by all.

How Donna Fernandes got everyone to transform a run-down, sparsely visited zoo in the space of just a few years is a testimony to her motivational abilities. By understanding the underlying needs of her employees, Fernandes was able to foster a motivated staff committed to the dream of making the Buffalo Zoo an educational and entertaining attraction for individuals and families throughout the region.

Questions

1. *Based on the personal testimonies given in the video, which needs in Maslow's hierarchy do you think are most important to the employees at the Buffalo Zoo? What actions has Donna Fernandes taken to help meet those needs?*
2. *How does Fernandes use positive reinforcement and the principle of instrumentality to motivate her employees? Give specific examples.*
3. *Why did Fernandes set up regular job rotation for the zoo's employees? Explain how job rotation works and what benefits it offers.*

Motivating Creativity at Pixar Animation Studios

Pixar Animation Studios, led by co-founder, chairman, and CEO Steven Jobs, "combines creative and technical artistry to create original films in the medium of computer animation." Pixar's notable animated films include *Toy Story*, *Toy Story 2*, and *Finding Nemo*, among others. Pixar's innovative proprietary technology reflects technical creativity as well as supporting animation creativity. The creative genius of Pixar's employees provides the solid foundation for the company's ongoing success.

Creative genius is evident in the collaborative efforts of Pixar's technical and creative teams in developing Marionette™, Ringmaster™, and Render-Man®. Each is a proprietary software system that supports different aspects of computerized animation. RenderMan®, for instance, is used to synthesize high-quality, photo-realistic images. Ed Catmull, Pixar's co-founder, president, and leader of the company's technology division, is overseeing development of a new animation software package called Luxo. Luxo allows fewer people to do more work, thus enhancing productivity. Luxo also promotes creativity by automatically making adjustments to the animation environment when changes are made, as in the appearance of animated characters.

Pixar's technological and creative genius has resulted in widespread acclaim and numerous film industry awards. The Academy of Motion Picture Arts and Sciences recognized the technical and creative advancements exemplified by RenderMan® by awarding an Oscar to Ed Catmull, Loren Carpenter (senior scientist), and Rob Cook (vice president of software engineering). The Producer's Guild of America honored Pixar for achievement in new media and technology with its first Vanguard Award in 2002. John Lasseter, co-founder of Pixar and executive vice president in charge of the creative division, has won two Oscars for his direction of animated films. Pixar employees have won a total of 16 Academy Awards® as well as numerous other awards.

Ed Catmull established Pixar University to provide educational opportunities for all employees and to encourage collaboration among them. Pixar University is a key element in attracting and retaining quality, artistically oriented employees. Pixar University aims to "raise the level of the best, cross-train, and develop mastery." Pixar University not only trains animators on the company's software but also offers classes in various artistic endeavors, including photography, screenwriting, acting, sculpting, painting, and drawing, among numerous others. All of the courses at Pixar University are geared toward fostering creativity, promoting collaboration, and preventing burnout.

The challenges at Pixar are enormous and the creative opportunities appear to be unlimited. Along with the challenges and creative opportunities, however, comes the risk of job stress and burnout. Pixar seeks to prevent burnout among its employees so they can have long, productive careers. As one means of preventing burnout, Pixar's animators are not allowed to work more than 50 hours per week without a manager's permission. Another approach is a weekly visit by a masseuse and a physician to Pixar's campus.

Pixar's campus-like environment also has a gym, a swimming pool, a soccer field, and volleyball courts. The large atrium area has games of ping-pong, table football, and billiards. There is a self-service canteen called Café Luxo. The animators area has a bar and stage. After work on Fridays employees can go there to play their music. Some employees have transformed their workspaces into a bachelor pad or a Hawaiian beach hut; others skateboard to meetings.

While key Pixar employees receive significant financial incentives, this does not seem to be the force that drives them. Rather, the driving force seems to be the creative freedom they are granted. Andrew Stanton, one of the co-writers and co-directors of *Finding Nemo*, is impressed with the creativity and quality of people at Pixar. He observes that people outside of Pixar "pale in comparison" to Pixar's employees.

John Lasseter guides the creative inspiration of Pixar. He maintains that good animated filmmaking is more about good storytelling than it is about innovative technology. Pixar makes films with stories that both make people laugh and grab their emotions. Technology helps to tell the story; it supports and enhances creativity. However, Lasseter maintains that animated film failures are never about bad technology but are always about bad storytelling. Under Lasseter's guidance, Pixar has assembled a "creative brain trust"—a group of individuals who contribute ideas and suggest improvements on every animation project.

Pixar has created a working environment and working conditions that help to attract, motivate, and retain quality employees. "The enviably progressive working environment nurtures and sustains creativity, and the dividend has been a box-office winning streak that stands in notable contrast to the hit-and-miss model of almost every other movie studio."

Discussion Questions

1. What needs does Pixar appeal to through its working environment and working conditions, its corporate university, and its commitment to creative innovation and excellence?

2. What is important to you in terms of your personal work motivation? How do the things that motivate you fit with Pixar's approach to motivating employees?

3. Using the model of the individual–organizational exchange relationship shown in Figure 5.4, explain the relationship that Pixar seeks to develop with its employees. How might this exchange relationship influence the employees' perceptions of equity?

SOURCE: This case was written by Michael K. McCuddy, The Louis S. and Mary L. Morgal Chair of Christian Business Ethics and Professor of Management, College of Business Administration, Valparaiso University. This case was developed from material contained on the Pixar Animation Studios Web site at http://www.pixar.com and in the following articles: P. Burrows, "Pixar's Unsung Hero," *Business Week* (June 30, 2003): 68–69; C. Gant, "Gone Fishin'—Pixar Studios and the Fish that Ate Disney," *The Australian* (December 20, 2003): accessed from newspaper source.

Chapter 6

Learning and Performance Management

LEARNING OBJECTIVES

After reading this chapter, you should be able to do the following:

1 Define *learning, reinforcement, punishment, extinction,* and *goal setting.*

2 Distinguish between classical and operant conditioning.

3 Explain the use of positive and negative consequences of behavior in strategies of reinforcement and punishment.

4 Identify the purposes of goal setting and five characteristics of effective goals.

5 Describe 360-degree feedback.

6 Compare individual and team-oriented reward systems.

7 Describe strategies for correcting poor performance.

THINKING AHEAD: VIRGIN GROUP, LTD.

People, Power, and Performance

Sir Richard Branson grew up in the 1960s, a product of the democratizing ideals of that period.[1] While leading Virgin Group more than twenty-five years later, he has not given up either his ideals that all people should be treated with respect or his great belief in people power. He has built his business on the premise that people—both customers and employees—come first. Actually, he likes to refer to Virgin employees as belonging to a large extended family. This may be a difficult posture to take in a publicly traded company, but it is quite feasible in a private company like Virgin Group. Everyone in the company continues to call Branson by his first name, and he still eschews the trappings of status and power, as he has from the very start. He may have been well ahead of his time when he focused on persons and not just behavior. As in many families, rewards are shared.

Two examples of Branson's personal approach are reflected in how a British Airways (BA) libel settlement was handled and how Virgin Atlantic responded during the recessionary period of the early 1990s brought on by Operations Desert Shield and Desert Storm. In the first case, Branson used a classic touch by sharing the £610,000 settlement from the libel suit against BA. The money was divided equally among all Virgin staff, each receiving £166. This was known as the "BA Bonus." The message was that they had all conquered BA together. In the second case, when the airline business was depressed by the Gulf War, the company managed not to lay off staff, and there was a common sharing of the pain with everyone suffering a little less.

While many companies are in the midst of flattening out, dismantling their hierarchies, and eliminating outward signs of executive privilege, Virgin has never gone to these places in building its successful business model.

Many companies also put into place formalized performance management systems that focus on observable and measurable behaviors, but Virgin is a counterpoint in its personal and familial ways of treating employees. Branson considers keeping faith with his employees to be extremely important. This does not mean that no one at Virgin loses his or her job or that no one is ever fired. Employees are fired occasionally, and the company is always interested in avoiding redundancies for its own benefit. However, the employee who believes that he or she was unjustly fired can appeal directly to the chairman. Branson has been known to intervene personally if he thinks the appeal is justified.

How does Virgin approach performance management within its legal team? Read the Looking Back at the end of this chapter.

This is the second of two chapters addressing motivation and behavior. Chapter 5 emphasized internal and process theories of motivation. This chapter focuses on external theories of motivation and factors in the work environment that influence good and bad performance. The first section addresses learning theory and the use of reinforcement, punishment, and extinction at work. It also touches on Bandura's social learning theory and Jung's personality approach to learning. The second section presents theory, research, and practice related to goal setting in organizations. The third section addresses the definition and measurement of performance. The fourth section is concerned with rewarding performance. The fifth and concluding section addresses how to correct poor performance.

Learning in Organizations

1. Define *learning, reinforcement, punishment, extinction,* and *goal setting.*

learning
A change in behavior acquired through experience.

Learning is a change in behavior acquired through experience. Learning may begin with the cognitive activity of developing knowledge about a subject, which then leads to a change in behavior. Alternatively, the behaviorist approach to learning assumes that observable behavior is a function of its consequences. According to the behaviorists, learning has its basis in classical and operant conditioning. Learning helps guide and direct motivated behavior.

Classical Conditioning

2. Distinguish between classical and operant conditioning.

classical conditioning
Modifying behavior so that a conditioned stimulus is paired with an unconditioned stimulus and elicits an unconditioned response.

Classical conditioning is the process of modifying behavior so that a conditioned stimulus is paired with an unconditioned stimulus and elicits an unconditioned response. It is largely the result of the research on animals (primarily dogs) by the Russian physiologist Ivan Pavlov.[2] Pavlov's professional exchanges with Walter B. Cannon and other American researchers during the early 1900s led to the application of his ideas in the United States.[3] Classical conditioning builds on the natural consequence of an unconditioned response to an unconditioned stimulus. In dogs, this might be the natural production of saliva (unconditioned response) in response to the presentation of meat (unconditioned stimulus). By presenting a conditioned stimulus (for example, a bell) simultaneously with the unconditioned stimulus (the meat), the researcher caused the dog to develop a conditioned response (salivation in response to the bell).

Classical conditioning may occur in a similar fashion in humans.[4] For example, a person working at a computer terminal may get lower back tension (unconditioned response) as a result of poor posture (unconditioned stimulus). If the person becomes aware of that tension only when the manager enters the work area (conditioned stimulus), then the person may develop a conditioned response (lower back tension) to the appearance of the manager.

Although this example is logical, classical conditioning has real limitations in its applicability to human behavior in organizations—for at least three reasons. First, humans are more complex than dogs and less amenable to simple cause-and-effect conditioning. Second, the behavioral environments in organizations are complex and not very amenable to single stimulus–response manipulations. Third, complex human decision making makes it possible to override simple conditioning.

Operant Conditioning

Operant conditioning is the process of modifying behavior through the use of positive or negative consequences following specific behaviors. It is based on the notion that behavior is a function of its consequences,[5] which may be either positive or negative. The consequences of behavior are used to influence, or shape, behavior through three strategies: reinforcement, punishment, and extinction.

Organizational behavior modification (O.B. Mod., commonly known as OBM) is a form of operant conditioning used successfully in a variety of organizations to shape behavior by Luthans and his colleagues.[6] The three types of consequences used in OBM to influence behavior are financial reinforcement, nonfinancial reinforcement, and social reinforcement. A major review of the research on the influence of OBM in organizations found that it had significant and positive influence on task performance in both manufacturing and service organizations, but that the effects were most powerful in manufacturing organizations.[7] Recent research showed that money-based (financial) reinforcement improved performance more than routine pay for performance, social recognition, and performance feedback.[8]

The Strategies of Reinforcement, Punishment, and Extinction

Reinforcement is used to enhance desirable behavior, and punishment and extinction are used to diminish undesirable behavior. The application of reinforcement theory is central to the design and administration of organizational reward systems. Well-designed reward systems help attract and retain the very best employees. Strategic rewards help motivate behavior, actions, and accomplishments, which advance the organization toward specific business goals.[9] Strategic rewards go beyond cash to include training and educational opportunities, stock options, and recognition awards such as travel. Strategic rewards are important positive consequences of people's work behavior.

Reinforcement and punishment are administered through the management of positive and negative consequences of behavior. *Positive consequences* are the results of a person's behavior that the person finds attractive or pleasurable. They might include a pay increase, a bonus, a promotion, a transfer to a more desirable geographic location, or praise from a supervisor. *Negative consequences* are the results of a person's behavior that the person finds unattractive or aversive. They might include disciplinary action, an undesirable transfer, a demotion, or harsh criticism from

© Reuters/Ruben Sprich/Landov

operant conditioning
Modifying behavior through the use of positive or negative consequences following specific behaviors.

3. Explain the use of positive and negative consequences of behavior in strategies of reinforcement and punishment.

positive consequences
Results of a behavior that a person finds attractive or pleasurable.

negative consequences
Results of a behavior that a person finds unattractive or aversive.

The awarding of medals to Olympic athletes is a tangible example of a positive consequence.

a supervisor. Positive and negative consequences must be defined for the person receiving them. Therefore, individual, gender, and cultural differences may be important in their classification.

The use of positive and negative consequences following a specific behavior either reinforces or punishes that behavior.[10] Thorndike's law of effect states that behaviors followed by positive consequences are more likely to recur and behaviors followed by negative consequences are less likely to recur.[11] Figure 6.1 shows how positive and negative consequences may be applied or withheld in the strategies of reinforcement and punishment.

reinforcement

The attempt to develop or strengthen desirable behavior by either bestowing positive consequences or withholding negative consequences.

REINFORCEMENT *Reinforcement* is the attempt to develop or strengthen desirable behavior by either bestowing positive consequences or withholding negative consequences. Positive reinforcement results from the application of a positive consequence following a desirable behavior. Bonuses paid at the end of successful business years are an example of positive reinforcement. Marriott International provides positive reinforcement by honoring ten to twenty employees each year with its J. Willard Marriott Award of Excellence. Each awardee receives a medallion engraved with the words that express the basic values of the company: dedication, achievement, character, ideals, effort, and perseverance.

Negative reinforcement results from withholding a negative consequence when a desirable behavior occurs. For example, a manager who reduces an employee's pay (negative consequence) if the employee comes to work late (undesirable behavior) and refrains from doing so when the employee is on time (desirable behavior) has negatively reinforced the employee's on-time behavior. The employee avoids the negative consequence (a reduction in pay) by exhibiting the desirable behavior (being on time to work).

Either continuous or intermittent schedules of reinforcement may be used. These reinforcement schedules are described in Table 6.1. When managers design organizational reward systems, they consider not only the type of reinforcement but also how often the reinforcement should be provided.

punishment

The attempt to eliminate or weaken undesirable behavior by either bestowing negative consequences or withholding positive consequences.

PUNISHMENT *Punishment* is the attempt to eliminate or weaken undesirable behavior. It is used in two ways. One way to punish a person is to ap-

FIGURE 6.1   Reinforcement and Punishment Strategies

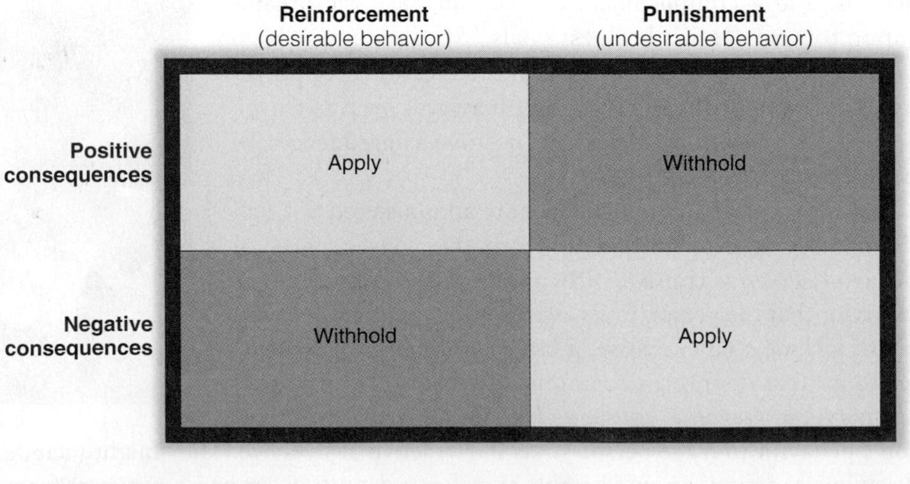

6.1

	Reinforcement (desirable behavior)	Punishment (undesirable behavior)
Positive consequences	Apply	Withhold
Negative consequences	Withhold	Apply

TABLE 6.1   Schedules of Reinforcement

SCHEDULE	DESCRIPTION	EFFECTS ON RESPONDING
Continuous	Reinforcer follows every response.	1. Steady high rate of performance as long as reinforcement follows every response 2. High frequency of reinforcement may lead to early satiation 3. Behavior weakens rapidly (undergoes extinction) when reinforcers are withheld 4. Appropriate for newly emitted, unstable, low-frequency responses
Intermittent	Reinforcer does not follow every response.	1. Capable of producing high frequencies of responding 2. Low frequency of reinforcement precludes early satiation 3. Appropriate for stable or high-frequency responses
Fixed Ratio	A fixed number of responses must be emitted before reinforcement occurs.	1. A fixed ratio of 1:1 (reinforcement occurs after every response) is the same as a continuous schedule 2. Tends to produce a high rate of response that is vigorous and steady
Variable Ratio	A varying or random number of responses must be emitted before reinforcement occurs.	Capable of producing a high rate of response that is vigorous, steady, and resistant to extinction
Fixed Interval	The first response after a specific period of time has elasped is reinforced.	Produces an uneven response pattern varying from a very slow, unenergetic response immediately following reinforcement to a very fast, vigorous response immediately preceding reinforcement
Variable Interval	The first response after varying or random periods of time have elapsed is reinforced.	Tends to produce a high rate of response that is vigorous, steady, and resistant to extinction

SOURCE: Table from *Organizational Behavior Modification* by Fred Luthans and Robert Kreitner. Copyright © 1985, p. 58, by Scott Foresman and Company and the authors. Reprinted by permission of the authors.

ply a negative consequence following an undesirable behavior. For example, a professional athlete who is excessively offensive to an official (undesirable behavior) may be ejected from a game (negative consequence). The other way to punish a person is to withhold a positive consequence following an undesirable behavior. For example, a salesperson who makes few visits to companies (undesirable behavior) and whose sales are well below the quota (undesirable behavior) is likely to receive a very small commission check (positive consequence) at the end of the month.

One problem with punishment is that it may have unintended results. Because punishment is discomforting to the individual being punished, the experience of punishment may result in negative psychological, emotional, performance, or behavioral consequences. For example, the person being punished may become angry, hostile, depressed, or despondent. From an organizational standpoint, this result becomes important when the punished person translates negative emotional and psychological responses into negative actions.

The power of Pos. relationships [have] has

THE REAL WORLD 6.1

The Fear Factor? . . . Not at Southwest Airlines

Fear can motivate people in the short run and get results. Fear may be evoked by outright intimidation, or more subtly fostered by Machiavellian strategies of divide and conquer. Fear can have its effects especially in the presence of the intimidator or the enforcer who carries the threat of punishment and coercion. However, fear backfires when people find hidden and surreptitious ways to retaliate against their managers and hide information for protection against punishment.

The fear factor is *not* used at Southwest Airlines to achieve the world class performance results sustained over the long run. Rather, the company builds sustained, consistently high levels of performance through the power of positive relationships. Positive relationships for sustained high performance are particularly important in the case of boundary spanning positions that require coordination across internal and external organizational boundaries. Southwest practices "relational coordination." The power of this approach is in the elements of shared goals, shared knowledge, mutual respect, frequent communication, and a problem-solving focus rather than finger pointing. The power of positive relationships and the absence of the fear factor in motivating Southwest employees results in few passenger complaints, excellent on-time performance and baggage handling, fast aircraft gate service, and high employee productivity. While the company's fun culture may be its hallmark, its highly disciplined approach to performance management systems and positive relationships is what gets great results.

SOURCE: M. Maccoby, J. Hoffer Gittell, and M. Ledeen, "Leadership and the Fear Factor," *Sloan Management Review* 148 (Winter 2004): 14–18.

Threat of punishment may also elicit fear, as noted in The Real World 6.1. Clearly, the fear factor is not used at Southwest Airlines as a management strategy for employee behavior.

extinction

The attempt to weaken a behavior by attaching no consequences to it.

EXTINCTION An alternative to punishing undesirable behavior is *extinction*—the attempt to weaken a behavior by attaching no consequences (either positive or negative) to it. It is equivalent to ignoring the behavior. The rationale for using extinction is that a behavior not followed by any consequence is weakened. Some patience and time may be needed for extinction to be effective, however.

Extinction may be practiced, for example, by not responding (no consequence) to the sarcasm (behavior) of a colleague. Extinction may be most effective when used in conjunction with the positive reinforcement of desirable behaviors. Therefore, in the example, the best approach might be to compliment the sarcastic colleague for constructive comments (reinforcing desirable behavior) while ignoring sarcastic comments (extinguishing undesirable behavior).

Extinction is not always the best strategy, however. In cases of dangerous behavior, punishment might be preferable to deliver a swift, clear lesson. It might also be preferable in cases of seriously undesirable behavior, such as employee embezzlement and other illegal or unethical behavior.

Bandura's Social Learning Theory

A social learning theory proposed by Albert Bandura is an alternative and complement to the behavioristic approaches of Pavlov and Skinner.[12] Bandura believes learning occurs through the observation of other people and the modeling of their behavior. Executives might teach their subordinates a wide range of behaviors, such as leader–follower interactions and stress management, by exhibiting these behaviors. Since employees look to their supervisors for acceptable norms of behavior, they are likely to pattern their own responses on the supervisor's.

Central to Bandura's social learning theory is the notion of *task-specific self-efficacy*, an individual's beliefs and expectancies about his or her ability to perform a specific task effectively. (Generalized self-efficacy was discussed in Chapter 3.) Individuals with high self-efficacy believe that they have the ability to get things done, that they are capable of putting forth the effort to accomplish the task, and that they can overcome any obstacles to their success. Self-efficacy is higher in a learning context than in a performance content, especially for individuals with a high learning orientation.[13] There are four sources of task-specific self-efficacy: prior experiences, behavior models (witnessing the success of others), persuasion from other people, and assessment of current physical and emotional capabilities.[14] Believing in one's own capability to get something done is an important facilitator of success. There is strong evidence that self-efficacy leads to high performance on a wide variety of physical and mental tasks.[15] High self-efficacy has also led to success in breaking addictions, increasing pain tolerance, and recovering from illnesses. Conversely, success can enhance one's self-efficacy. For example, women who trained in physical self-defense increased their self-efficacy, both for specific defense skills and for coping in new situations.[16]

Alexander Stajkovic and Fred Luthans draw on Bandura's ideas of self-efficacy and social learning in expanding their original work in behavioral management and OBM into a more comprehensive framework for performance management.[17] Bandura saw the power of social reinforcement, recognizing that financial and material rewards often occur following or in conjunction with the approval of others, whereas undesirable experiences often follow social disapproval. Thus, self-efficacy and social reinforcement can be powerful influences over behavior and performance at work. A comprehensive review of 114 studies found that self-efficacy is positively and strongly related to work performance, especially for tasks that are not too complex.[18] Stajkovic and Luthans suggest that managers and supervisors can be confident that employees with high self-efficacy are going to perform well. The challenge managers face is how to select and develop employees so that they achieve high self-efficacy.

Managers can help employees develop self-efficacy. The strongest way for an employee to develop self-efficacy is to succeed at a challenging task. Managers can help by providing job challenges, coaching and counseling for improved performance, and rewarding employees' achievements. Empowerment, or sharing power with employees, can be accomplished by interventions that help employees increase their self-esteem and self-efficacy. Given the increasing diversity of the workforce, managers may want to target their efforts toward women and minorities in particular. Research has indicated that women and minorities tend to have lower than average self-efficacy.[19]

Learning and Personality Differences

The cognitive approach to learning mentioned at the beginning of the chapter is based on the *Gestalt* school of thought and draws on Jung's theory of personality differences (discussed in Chapter 3). Two elements of Jung's theory have important implications for learning and subsequent behavior.

The first element is the distinction between introverted and extraverted people. Introverts need quiet time to study, concentrate, and reflect on what they are learning. They think best when they are alone. Extraverts need to interact with other people, learning through the process of expressing and exchanging ideas with others. They think best in groups and while they are talking.

task-specific self-efficacy

An individual's beliefs and expectancies about his or her ability to perform a specific task effectively.

TABLE 6.2 Personality Functions and Learning

PERSONALITY PREFERENCE	IMPLICATIONS FOR LEARNING BY INDIVIDUALS
Information Gathering	
Intuitors	Prefer theoretical frameworks.
	Look for the meaning in material.
	Attempt to understand the grand scheme.
	Look for possibilities and interrelations.
Sensors	Prefer specific, empirical data.
	Look for practical applications.
	Attempt to master details of a subject.
	Look for what is realistic and doable.
Decision Making	
Thinkers	Prefer analysis of data and information.
	Work to be fairminded and evenhanded.
	Seek logical, just conclusions.
	Do not like to be too personally involved.
Feelers	Prefer interpersonal involvement.
	Work to be tenderhearted and harmonious.
	Seek subjective, merciful results.
	Do not like objective, factual analysis.

SOURCE: O. Kroeger and J. M. Thuesen, *Type Talk: The 16 Personality Types That Determine How We Live, Love, and Work* (New York: Dell Publishing Co., 1989).

The second element is the personality functions of intuition, sensing, thinking, and feeling. These functions are listed in Table 6.2, along with their implications for learning by individuals. The functions of intuition and sensing determine the individual's preference for information gathering. The functions of thinking and feeling determine how the individual evaluates and makes decisions about newly acquired information.[20] Each person has a preferred mode of gathering information and a preferred mode of evaluating and making decisions about that information. For example, an intuitive thinker may want to skim research reports about implementing total quality programs and then, based on hunches, decide how to apply the research findings to the organization. A sensing feeler may prefer viewing videotaped interviews with people in companies that implemented total quality programs and then identify people in the organization most likely to be receptive to the approaches presented.

Goal Setting at Work

Goal setting is the process of establishing desired results that guide and direct behavior. Goal-setting theory is based on laboratory studies, field research experiments, and comparative investigations by Edwin Locke, Gary Latham, John M. Ivancevich, and others.[21] Goals help crystallize the sense of purpose and mission that is essential to success at work. Priorities, purpose, and goals are important sources of motivation for people at work, often leading to collective achievement, even in difficult times.

Characteristics of Effective Goals

Various organizations define the characteristics of effective goals differently. For the former Sanger-Harris, a retail organization, the acronym SMART com-

4. Identify the purposes of goal setting and five characteristics of effective goals.

goal setting
The process of establishing desired results that guide and direct behavior.

municated the approach to effective goals. SMART stands for *Specific*, *Measurable*, *Attainable*, *Realistic*, and *Time-bound*. Five commonly accepted characteristics of effective goals are specific, challenging, measurable, time-bound, and prioritized.

Specific and challenging goals serve to cue or focus the person's attention on exactly what is to be accomplished and to arouse the person to peak performance. In a wide range of occupations, people who set specific, challenging goals consistently outperform people who have easy or unspecified goals, as Figure 6.2 shows. How difficult and challenging are your work or school goals? You 6.1 gives you an opportunity to evaluate your goals for five dimensions.

Breaking records is a measurable goal, as epitomized here when Hank Aaron broke Babe Ruth's homerun record in baseball.

Measurable, quantitative goals are useful as a basis for feedback about goal progress. Qualitative goals are also valuable. The Western Company of North America (now part of BJ Services Company) allowed about 15 percent of a manager's goals to be of a qualitative nature.[22] A qualitative goal might be to improve relationships with customers. Further work might convert the qualitative goal into quantitative measures such as number of complaints or frequency of complimentary letters. In this case, however, the qualitative goal may well be sufficient and most meaningful.

Time-bound goals enhance measurability. The time limit may be implicit in the goal, or it may need to be made explicit. For example, without the six-month time limit, an insurance salesperson might think the sales goal is for the whole year rather than for six months. Many organizations work on standardized cycles, such as quarters or years, where very explicit time limits are assumed. If there is any uncertainty about the time period of the goal effort, the time limit should be explicitly stated.

The priority ordering of goals allows for effective decision making about resource allocation.[23] As time, energy, or other resources become available, a person can move down the list of goals in descending order. The key concern is with achieving the top-priority goals. Priority helps direct a person's efforts and behavior. Although these characteristics help increase motivation and performance,

6.2 **FIGURE 6.2**   **Goal Level and Task Performance**

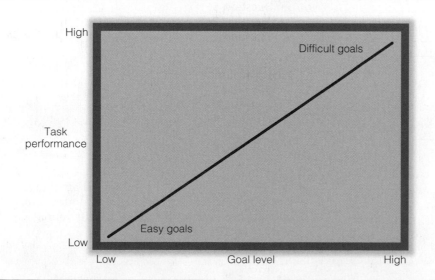

Task–Goal Attribute Questionnaire

Listed below is a set of statements that may or may not describe the job or school objectives toward which you are presently working. Please read each statement carefully and rate each on a scale from 1 (agree completely) to 7 (disagree completely) to describe your level of agreement or disagreement with the statement. *Please answer all questions.*

____ **1.** I am allowed a high degree of influence in the determination of my work/school objectives.
____ **2.** I should not have too much difficulty in reaching my work/school objectives; they appear to be fairly easy.
____ **3.** I receive a considerable amount of feedback concerning my quantity of output on the job/in school.
____ **4.** Most of my coworkers and peers try to outperform one another on their assigned work/school goals.
____ **5.** My work/school objectives are very clear and specific; I know exactly what my job/assignment is.
____ **6.** My work/school objectives will require a great deal of effort from me to complete them.
____ **7.** I really have little voice in the formulation of my work/school objectives.
____ **8.** I am provided with a great deal of feedback and guidance on the quality of my work.
____ **9.** I think my work/school objectives are ambiguous and unclear.
____ **10.** It will take a high degree of skill and know-how on my part to attain fully my work/school objectives.
____ **11.** The setting of my work/school goals is pretty much under my own control.
____ **12.** My boss/instructors seldom let(s) me know how well I am doing on my work toward my work/school objectives.
____ **13.** A very competitive atmosphere exists among my peers and me with regard to attaining our respective work/school goals; we all want to do better than anyone else in attaining our goals.
____ **14.** I understand fully which of my work/school objectives are more important than others; I have a clear sense of priorities on these goals.
____ **15.** My work/school objectives are quite difficult to attain.
____ **16.** My supervisor/instructors usually ask(s) for my opinions and thoughts when determining my work/school objectives.

Scoring:

Place your response (1 through 7) in the space provided. For questions 7, 12, 9, and 2, subtract your response from 8 to determine your adjusted score.

For each scale (e.g., participation in goal setting), add the responses and divide by the number of questions in the scale.

Participation in Goal Setting:
Question 1 ____
Question 7 (8 – ____) = ____
Question 11 ____
Question 16 ____
Total divided by 4 = ____

Feedback on Goal Effort:
Question 3 ____
Question 8 ____
Question 12 (8 – ____) = ____
Total divided by 3 = ____

Peer Competition:
Question 4 ____
Question 13 ____
Total divided by 2 = ____

Goal Specificity:
Question 5 ____
Question 9 (8 – ____) = ____
Question 14 ____
Total divided by 3 = ____

Goal Difficulty:
Question 2 (8 – ____) = ____
Question 6 ____
Question 10 ____
Question 15 ____
Total divided by 4 = ____

Interpreting your average scale scores:
6 or 7 are very high on this task–goal attribute.
4 is a moderate level on this task–goal attribute.
1 or 2 is very low on this task–goal attribute.

SOURCE: Adapted from R. M. Steers, "Factors Affecting Job Attitudes in a Goal-Setting Environment," *Academy of Management Journal* 19 (1976): 9. Permission conveyed through Copyright Clearance Center, Inc.

that is not the only function of goal setting in organizations. One new study of goal setting suggests that it may be a theory of ability as well as a theory of motivation, especially in a learning context versus a performance context.[24]

Goal setting serves one or more of three functions. First, it can increase work motivation and task performance.[25] Second, it can reduce the role stress that is associated with conflicting or confusing expectations.[26] Third, it can improve the accuracy and validity of performance evaluation.[27]

Increasing Work Motivation and Task Performance

Goals are often used to increase employee effort and motivation, which in turn improve task performance. The higher the goal, the better the performance; that is, people work harder to reach difficult goals. The positive relationship between goal difficulty and task performance is depicted in Figure 6.2.

Three important behavioral aspects of enhancing performance motivation through goal setting are employee participation, supervisory commitment, and useful performance feedback. Employee participation in goal setting leads to goal acceptance by employees. Goal acceptance is thought to lead to goal commitment and then to goal accomplishment. Special attention has been given to factors that influence commitment to difficult goals, such as participation in the process of setting the difficult goals.[28] Even in the case of assigned goals, goal acceptance and commitment are considered essential prerequisites to goal accomplishment.

Supervisory goal commitment is a reflection of the organization's commitment to goal setting. Organizational commitment is a prerequisite for successful goal-setting programs, such as management by objectives (MBO) programs.[29] The organization must be committed to the program, and the employee and supervisors must be committed to specific work goals as well as to the program. (MBO is discussed in more detail later in the chapter.)

The supervisor plays a second important role by providing employees with interim performance feedback on progress toward goals. Performance feedback is most useful when the goals are specific, and specific goals improve performance most when interim feedback is given.[30] When done correctly, negative performance feedback can lead to performance improvement.[31] For example, assume an insurance salesperson has a goal of selling $500,000 worth of insurance in six months but has sold only $200,000 after three months. During an interim performance feedback session, the supervisor may help the salesperson identify his problem—that he is not focusing his calls on the likeliest prospects. This useful feedback coupled with the specific goal helps the salesperson better focus his efforts to achieve the goal. Feedback is most helpful when it is useful (helping the salesperson identify high-probability prospects) and timely (halfway through the performance period).

Reducing Role Stress, Conflict, and Ambiguity

A second function of goal setting is to reduce the role stress associated with conflicting and confusing expectations. This is done by clarifying the task–role expectations communicated to employees. Supervisors, coworkers, and employees are all important sources of task-related information. A fourteen-month evaluation of goal setting in reducing role stress found that conflict, confusion, and absenteeism were all reduced through the use of goal setting.[32]

The improved role clarity resulting from goal setting may be attributable to improved communication between managers and employees. An early study of the MBO goal-setting program at Ford Motor Company found an initial 25 percent lack of agreement between managers and their bosses concerning the definition of the managers' jobs. Through effective goal-setting activities, this lack of agreement was reduced to about 5 percent.[33] At FedEx, managers are encouraged to include communication-related targets in their annual MBO goal-setting process.[34]

Improving Performance Evaluation

The third major function of goal setting is improving the accuracy and validity of performance evaluation. One of the best methods of doing so is to use *management by objectives (MBO)*—a goal-setting program based on interaction and negotiation between employees and managers. MBO programs have been pervasive in organizations for nearly thirty years.[35]

According to Peter Drucker, who originated the concept, the objectives-setting process begins with the employee writing an "employee's letter" to the manager. The letter explains the employee's general understanding of the scope of the manager's job, as well as the scope of the employee's own job, and lays out a set of specific objectives to be pursued over the next six months or year. After some discussion and negotiation, the manager and the employee finalize these items into a performance plan.

Drucker considers MBO a participative and interactive process. This does not mean that goal setting begins at the bottom of the organization. It means that goal setting is applicable to all employees, with lower level organizational members and professional staff having a clear influence over the goal-setting process.[36] (The performance aspect of goal setting is discussed in the next section of the chapter.)

Goal-setting programs have operated under a variety of names, including goals and controls at Purex (now part of Dial Corporation), work planning and review at Black & Decker and General Electric, and performance planning and evaluation at IBM. Most of these programs are designed to enhance performance,[37] especially when incentives are associated with goal achievement.

The two central ingredients in goal-setting programs are planning and evaluation. The planning component consists of organizational and individual goal setting. Organizational goal setting is an essential prerequisite to individual goal setting; the two must be closely linked for the success of both.[38] At FedEx, all individual objectives must be tied to the overall corporate objectives of people, service, and profit.

In planning, discretionary control is usually given to individuals and departments to develop operational and tactical plans to support the corporate objectives. The emphasis is on formulating a clear, consistent, measurable, and ordered set of goals to articulate *what* to do. It is also assumed that operational support planning helps determine *how* to do it. The concept of intention is used to encompass both the goal (*what*) and the set of pathways that lead to goal attainment (*how*), thus recognizing the importance of both what and how.[39]

The evaluation component consists of interim reviews of goal progress, conducted by managers and employees, and formal performance evaluation. The reviews are mid-term assessments designed to help employees take self-corrective action. They are not designed as final or formal performance evaluations. The formal performance evaluation occurs at the close of a reporting period, usually once a year. To be effective, performance reviews need to be tailored to

management by objectives (MBO)
A goal-setting program based on interaction and negotiation between employees and managers.

Predicting Job Performance

General mental ability has been found to be highly predictive of job knowledge in military jobs.

A recent study focuses on occupational attainment and job performance within one's chosen occupation. General mental ability (GMA), when measured early in life, predicts later life occupational attainment in longitudinal studies. While GMA was originally introduced about 100 years ago, more recent research on job performance has attempted to differentiate more specific aptitudes as predictors of job performance and occupational attainment. These more specific aptitudes include quantitative aptitude measures of math knowledge and arithmetic reasoning, verbal aptitudes of word knowledge and general science concepts, and technical aptitude tests of electronics information and mechanical comprehension. This more recent approach to job performance led to specific aptitude theory, which was dramatically refuted in an earlier large sample research study of U.S. Air Force, Marine, and Army personnel. Other earlier research did not find the predictive validity of job experience very compelling. In the present study, GMA was found to be quite important for job performance and, from an explanatory perspective, it was found that job knowledge is an important mediating link between GMA and job performance. Specifically, GMA was found to be highly predictive of job knowledge in both civilian and military jobs. Further, job performance is highly predicted by GMA directly and as mediated through job knowledge, again for both civilian and military jobs.

SOURCE: F. L. Schmidt and J. Hunter, "General Mental Ability in the World of Work: Occupational Attainment and Job Performance," *Journal of Personality and Social Psychology* 86 (2004): 162–173.

the business, capture what goes on in the business, and easily changed when the business changes.[40]

Because goal-setting programs are somewhat mechanical by nature, they are most easily implemented in stable, predictable industrial settings. Although most programs allow for some flexibility and change, they are less useful in organizations where high levels of unpredictability exist, as in basic research and development, or where the organization requires substantial adaptation or adjustment. Finally, individual, gender, and cultural differences do not appear to threaten the success of goal-setting programs.[41] Thus, goal-setting programs may be widely applied and effective in a diverse workforce.

Performance: A Key Construct

Goal setting is designed to improve work performance, an important organizational behavior directly related to the production of goods or the delivery of services. Performance is most often thought of as task accomplishment, the term *task* coming from Taylor's early notion of a worker's required activity.[42] Some early management research found performance standards and differential piece-rate pay to be key ingredients in achieving high levels of performance, while other early research found stress helpful in improving performance up to an optimum point.[43] Hence, outcomes and effort are both important for good performance. This section focuses on task-oriented performance.

Predicting job performance has been a concern for over 100 years. Early theories around the time of World War I focused on the importance of intelligence and general mental ability, the subject of the research in the Science feature. As important to predicting job performance is defining job performance.

performance management

A process of defining, measuring, appraising, providing feedback on, and improving performance.

Performance management is a process of defining, measuring, appraising, providing feedback on, and improving performance.[44] The skill of defining performance in behavioral terms is an essential first step in the performance management process. Once defined, performance can be measured and assessed. This information about performance can then be fed back to the individual and used as a basis for setting goals and establishing plans for improving performance. Positive performance behaviors should be rewarded, and poor performance behaviors should be corrected. This section of the chapter focuses on defining, measuring, appraising, and providing feedback on performance. The last two sections of the chapter focus on rewarding, correcting, and improving performance.

Defining Performance

Performance must be clearly defined and understood by the employees who are expected to perform well at work. Performance in most lines of work is multidimensional. For example, a sales executive's performance may require administrative and financial skills along with the interpersonal skills needed to motivate a sales force. Or a medical doctor's performance may demand the positive interpersonal skills of a bedside manner to complement the necessary technical diagnostic and treatment skills for enhancing the healing process. Each specific job in an organization requires the definition of skills and behaviors essential to excellent performance. Defining performance is a prerequisite to measuring and evaluating performance on the job.

Although different jobs require different skills and behaviors, organizational citizenship behavior (OCB) is one dimension of individual performance that spans many jobs. OCB was defined in Chapter 4 as behavior that is above and beyond the call of duty. OCB involves individual discretionary behavior that promotes the organization and is not explicitly rewarded; it includes helping behavior, sportsmanship, and civic virtue. According to supervisors, OCB is enhanced most through employee involvement programs aimed at engaging employees in the work organization rather than through employee involvement in employment decisions in nonunion operations.[45] OCB emphasizes collective performance in contrast to individual performance or achievement. OCB is just one of a number of performance dimensions to consider when defining performance for a specific job within an organization.

performance appraisal

The evaluation of a person's performance.

Performance appraisal is the evaluation of a person's performance once it is well defined. Accurate appraisals help supervisors fulfill their dual roles as evaluators and coaches. As a coach, a supervisor is responsible for encouraging employee growth and development. As an evaluator, a supervisor is responsible for making judgments that influence employees' roles in the organization. Although procedural justice is often thought of as a unidimensional construct, recent research shows that in the performance appraisal content it can be conceptualized as two dimensional.[46]

Cross-cultural research has found that North American, Asian, and Latin American managers' perceptions of their employees' motivation are different and that their perceptions affect their appraisals of employee performance.[47]

The major purposes of performance appraisals are to give employees feedback on performance, to identify the employees' developmental needs, to make promotion and reward decisions, to make demotion and termination decisions, and to develop information about the organization's selection and placement decisions. For example, a review of 57,775 performance appraisals found higher ratings on appraisals done for administrative reasons and lower ratings on appraisals done for research or for employee development.[48]

Measuring Performance

Ideally, actual performance and measured performance are the same. Practically, this is seldom the case. Measuring operational performance is easier than measuring managerial performance because of the availability of quantifiable data. Measuring production performance is easier than measuring research and development performance because of the reliability of the measures. Recent research has focused on measuring motivation for task performance and has found that wording and context may influence the validity of direct self-reports.[49]

Performance appraisal systems are intended to improve the accuracy of measured performance and increase its agreement with actual performance. The extent of agreement is called the true assessment, as Figure 6.3 shows. The figure also identifies the performance measurement problems that contribute to inaccuracy. These include deficiency, unreliability, and invalidity. Deficiency results from overlooking important aspects of a person's actual performance. Unreliability results from poor-quality performance measures. Invalidity results from inaccurate definition of the expected job performance.

Early performance appraisal systems were often quite biased. See, for example, Table 6.3, which is a sample of officer effectiveness reports from an infantry company in the early 1800s. Even contemporary executive appraisals have a dark side, arousing managers' and executives' defenses. Addressing emotions and defenses is important to making appraisal sessions developmental.[50] Some performance review systems lead to forced rankings of employees, which may be controversial.

Performance-monitoring systems using modern electronic technology are sometimes used to measure the performance of vehicle operators, computer

6.3 **FIGURE 6.3**   Actual and Measured Performance

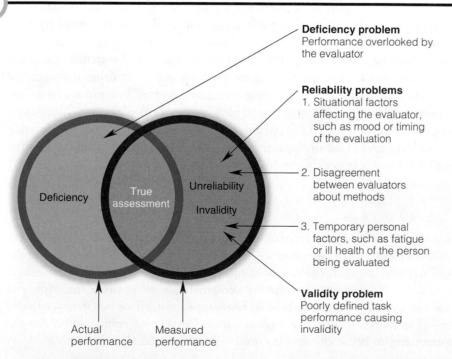

Deficiency problem
Performance overlooked by the evaluator

Reliability problems
1. Situational factors affecting the evaluator, such as mood or timing of the evaluation

2. Disagreement between evaluators about methods

3. Temporary personal factors, such as fatigue or ill health of the person being evaluated

Validity problem
Poorly defined task performance causing invalidity

Deficiency

True assessment

Unreliability

Invalidity

Actual performance

Measured performance

TABLE 6.3   Officer Effectiveness Reports, Circa 1813

Alexander Brown—Lt. Col., Comdg.—A good natured man.

Clark Crowell—first Major—A good man, but no officer.

Jess B. Wordsworth—2nd Major—An excellent officer.

Captain Shaw—A man of whom all unite in speaking ill. A knave despised by all.

Captain Thomas Lord—Indifferent, but promises well.

Captain Rockwell—An officer of capacity, but imprudent and a man of violent passions.

1st Lt. Jas. Kearns—Merely good, nothing promising.

1st Lt. Robert Cross—Willing enough—has much to learn—with small capacity.

2nd Lt. Stewart Berry—An ignorant unoffending fellow.

Ensign North—A good young man who does well.

SOURCE: Table from *The Air Officer's Guide*, 6th ed., Copyright © 1952 Stackpole Books. Used with permission.

technicians, and customer service representatives. For example, such systems might record the rate of keystrokes or the total number of keystrokes for a computer technician. The people subject to this type of monitoring are in some cases unaware that their performance is being measured. What is appropriate performance monitoring? What constitutes inappropriate electronic spying on the employee? Are people entitled to know when their performance is being measured? The ethics of monitoring performance may differ by culture. The United States and Sweden, for example, respect individual freedom more than Japan and China do. The overriding issue, however, is how far organizations should go in using modern technology to measure human performance.

Goal setting and MBO are results-oriented methods of performance appraisal that do not necessarily rely on modern technology. Like performance-monitoring systems, they shift the emphasis from subjective, judgmental performance dimensions to observable, verifiable results. Goals established in the planning phase of goal setting become the standard against which to measure subsequent performance. However, rigid adherence to a results-oriented approach may risk overlooking performance opportunities.

FedEx has incorporated a novel and challenging approach to evaluation in its blueprint for service quality. All managers at FedEx are evaluated by their employees through a survey-feedback-action system. Employees evaluate their managers using a five-point scale on twenty-nine standard statements and ten local option ones. Low ratings suggest problem areas requiring management attention. For example, the following statement received low ratings from employees in 1990: Upper management pays attention to ideas and suggestions from people at my level. CEO Fred Smith became directly involved in addressing this problem area. One of the actions he took to correct the problem was the development of a biweekly employee newsletter.

Performance Feedback: A Communication Challenge

Once clearly defined and accurate performance measures are developed, there is still the challenge of performance feedback. Feedback sessions are among the more stressful events for supervisors and employees. Early research at General Electric found employees responded constructively to positive feedback and were defensive over half the time in response to critical or negative feedback. Typical responses to negative feedback included shifting responsibility for the shortcoming or behavior, denying it outright, or providing a wide range of excuses for it.[51]

Both parties to a performance feedback session should try to make it a constructive learning experience, since positive and negative performance feedback has long-term implications for the employee's performance and for the working relationship. American Airlines follows three guidelines in providing evaluative feedback so that the experience is constructive for supervisor and employee alike.[52] First, refer to specific, verbatim statements and specific, observable behaviors displayed by the person receiving the feedback. This enhances the acceptance of the feedback while reducing the chances of denial. Second, focus on changeable behaviors, as opposed to intrinsic or personality-based attributes. People are often more defensive about who they are than about what they do. Third, plan and organize for the session ahead of time. Be sure to notify the person who will receive the feedback. Both the leader and the follower should be ready.

In addition to these ideas, many companies recommend beginning coaching and counseling sessions with something positive. The intent is to reduce defensiveness and enhance useful communication. There is almost always at least one positive element to emphasize. Once the session is under way and rapport is established, then the evaluator can introduce more difficult and negative material. Because people are not perfect, there is always an opportunity for them to learn and to grow through performance feedback sessions. Critical feedback is the basis for improvement and is essential to a performance feedback session. Specific feedback is beneficial for initial performance but discourages exploration and undermines the learning needed for later, more independent performance.[53]

360-Degree Feedback

Many organizations use *360-degree feedback* as a tactic to improve the accuracy of performance appraisals because it is based on multiple sources of information. When self-evaluations are included in this process, there is evidence that the evaluation interviews can be more satisfying, more constructive, and less defensive.[54] One of the criticisms of self-evaluations is their low level of agreement with supervisory evaluations.[55] However, high levels of agreement may not necessarily be desirable if the intent of the evaluation is to provide a full picture of the person's performance. This is a strength of the 360-degree feedback method, which provides a well-rounded view of performance from superiors, peers, followers, and customers.[56]

An example of a 360-degree feedback evaluation occurred in a large military organization for a midlevel civilian executive. The midlevel executive behaved very differently in dealing with superiors, peers, and followers. With superiors, he was positive, compliant, and deferential. With peers, he was largely indifferent, often ignoring them. With followers, he was tough and demanding, bordering on cruel and abusive. Without each of these perspectives, the executive's performance would not have been accurately assessed. When the executive received feedback, he was then able to see the inconsistency in his behavior.

Two recommendations have been made to improve the effectiveness of the 360-degree feedback method. The first one is to add a systematic coaching component to the 360-degree feedback.[57] By focusing on enhanced self-awareness and behavioral management, this feedback-coaching model can enhance performance as well as satisfaction and commitment, and reduce intent to turnover. The second one is that the performance feedback component of the 360-degree appraisal be separated from the management development component.[58] The feedback component should emphasize quantitative feedback and performance

5. Describe 360-degree feedback.

360-degree feedback
A process of self-evaluation and evaluations by a manager, peers, direct reports, and possibly customers.

measures, while the management development component should emphasize qualitative feedback and competencies for development.

Developing People and Enhancing Careers

A key function of a good performance appraisal system is to develop people and enhance careers. Developmentally, performance appraisals should emphasize individual growth needs and future performance. If the supervisor is to coach and develop employees effectively, there must be mutual trust. The supervisor must be vulnerable and open to challenge from the subordinate while maintaining a position of responsibility for what is in the subordinate's best interests.[59] The supervisor must also be a skilled, empathetic listener who encourages the employee to talk about hopes and aspirations.[60]

The employee must be able to take active responsibility for future development and growth. This might mean challenging the supervisor's ideas about future development as well as expressing individual preferences and goals. Passive, compliant employees are unable to accept responsibility for themselves or to achieve full emotional development. Individual responsibility is a key characteristic of the culture of the Chaparral Steel Company (part of TXI). The company joke is that the company manages by "adultry" (pun intended). Chaparral Steel treats people like adults and expects adult behavior from them.

Key Characteristics of an Effective Appraisal System

An effective performance appraisal system has five key characteristics: validity, reliability, responsiveness, flexibility, and equitability. Its validity comes from capturing multiple dimensions of a person's job performance. Its reliability comes from capturing evaluations from multiple sources and at different times over the course of the evaluation period. Its responsiveness allows the person being evaluated some input into the final outcome. Its flexibility leaves it open to modification based on new information, such as federal requirements. Its equitability results in fair evaluations against established performance criteria, regardless of individual differences.

Rewarding Performance

One function of a performance appraisal system is to provide input for reward decisions. If an organization wants good performance, then it must reward good performance. If it does not want bad performance, then it must not reward bad performance. If companies talk "teamwork," "values," and "customer focus," then they need to reward behaviors related to these ideas. Although this idea is conceptually simple, it can become very complicated in practice. Reward decisions are among the most difficult and complicated decisions made in organizations, and among the most important decisions. When leaders confront decisions about pay every day, they should know that it is a myth that people work for money.[61] While pay and rewards for performance have value, so too do trust, fun, and meaningful work.

A Key Organizational Decision Process

Reward and punishment decisions in organizations affect many people throughout the system, not just the persons being rewarded or punished. Reward allocation involves sequential decisions about which people to reward, how to reward them, and when to reward them. Taken together, these decisions shape the behavior of everyone in the organization, because of the vicarious learning that occurs as people watch what happens to others, especially when new programs or initiatives are implemented. People carefully watch what happens to peers who make mistakes or have problems with the new system; then they gauge their own behavior accordingly.

Individual versus Team Reward Systems

One of the distinguishing characteristics of Americans is the value they place on individualism. Systems that reward individuals are common in organizations in the United States. One of the strengths of these systems is that they foster autonomous and independent behavior that may lead to creativity, to novel solutions to old problems, and to distinctive contributions to the organization. Individual reward systems directly affect individual behavior and may encourage competitive striving within a work team. Although motivation and reward techniques in the United States are individually focused, they are often group focused outside the United States.[62]

6. Compare individual and team-oriented reward systems.

Too much competition within a work environment, however, may be dysfunctional. At the Western Company of North America (now part of BJ Services Company), individual success in the MBO program was tied too tightly to rewards, and individual managers became divisively competitive. For example, some managers took last-minute interdepartmental financial actions in a quarter to meet their objectives, but by doing so, they caused other managers to miss their objectives. These actions raise ethical questions about how far individual managers should go in serving their own self-interest at the expense of their peers.

Team reward systems solve the problems caused by individual competitive behavior. These systems emphasize cooperation, joint efforts, and the sharing of information, knowledge, and expertise. The Japanese and Chinese cultures, with their collectivist orientations, place greater emphasis than Americans on the individual as an element of the team, not a member apart from the team. Digital Equipment Corporation (now part of Hewlett-Packard) used a partnership approach to performance appraisals. Self-managed work group members participated in their own appraisal process. Such an approach emphasizes teamwork and responsibility.

Some organizations have experimented with individual and group alternative reward systems.[63] At the individual level, these include skill-based and pay-for-knowledge systems. Each emphasizes skills or knowledge possessed by an employee over and above the requirements for the basic job. At the group level, gain-sharing plans emphasize collective cost reduction and allow workers to share in the gains achieved by reducing production or other operating costs. In such plans, everyone shares equally in the collective gain. Avnet, Inc., found that collective profit sharing improved performance.

The Power of Earning

The purpose behind both individual and team reward systems is to shape productive behavior. Effective performance management can be the lever of change that boosts individual and team achievements in an organization. So, if one wants the rewards available in the organization, then one should work to earn them. Performance management and reward systems assume a demonstrable connection between performance and rewards. Organizations get the performance they reward, not the performance they say they want.[64] Further, when there is no apparent link between performance and rewards, people may begin to believe they are entitled to rewards regardless of how they perform. The concept of entitlement is very different from the concept of earning, which assumes a performance–reward link.

The notion of entitlement at work is counterproductive when taken to the extreme because it counteracts the power of earning.[65] People who believe they are entitled to rewards regardless of their behavior or performance are not motivated to behave constructively. Merit raises in some organizations, for example, have come to be viewed as entitlements, thus reducing their positive value in the organizational reward system. People believe they have a right to be taken care of by someone, whether that is the organization or a specific person. Entitlement engenders passive, irresponsible behavior, whereas earning engenders active, responsible, adult behavior. If rewards depend on performance, then people must perform responsibly to receive them. The power of earning rests on a direct link between performance and rewards.

Correcting Poor Performance

7. Describe strategies for correcting poor performance.

Often a complicated, difficult challenge for supervisors, correcting poor performance is a three-step process. First, the cause or primary responsibility for the poor performance must be identified. Second, if the primary responsibility is a person's, then the source of the personal problem must be determined. Third, a plan of action to correct the poor performance must be developed. You 6.2 gives you an opportunity to examine a poor performance you have experienced.

Poor performance may result from a variety of causes, the more important being poorly designed work systems, poor selection processes, inadequate training and skills development, lack of personal motivation, and personal problems intruding on the work environment. Not all poor performance is self-motivated; some is induced by the work system. Therefore, a good diagnosis should pre-

Loop Customer Management's Performance Management Framework

Loop Customer Management Ltd. is a UK-based organization originally formed to provide managed customer services to Yorkshire Water. The company now has other external clients for its services. Because Loop originated in a utility industry environment, it developed a performance management system that would work in that context. However, as the company moved into outsourced customer services, it needed to change many of its performance management practices.

Loop operated on five brand values: performance, partnership, people, innovation, and best value. The company wanted to puts its values into action and found it essential that employees be involved in creating the performance standards and measures that would be used. Loop had line managers and employees describe the behaviors of the best employees and the behaviors of poor employees. Through this process, the company built performance competencies for groups of its employees from front-line agents, to team leaders and specialists, and for business leaders. Competencies and behaviors were specified for each group of employees. For example, a team leader just learning the job should be able to identify development needs for team members, while an advanced team leader should be able to develop and coach other managers. Loop's new performance management framework has been a success and contributed to the company's inclusion in the 2004 *Financial Times* list of "50 Best Workplaces in the UK."

SOURCE: N. Wilson, "Rewarding Values at Loop Customer Management," *Strategic HR Review* 3 (January/February 2004): 12–13.

cede corrective action. For example, it may be that an employee is subject to a work design or selection system that does not allow the person to exhibit good performance. The Real World 6.2 describes how Loop Customer Management Ltd. involved employees to help change its performance management system to fit its new work design. Identifying the cause of the poor performance comes first and should be done in communication with the employee. If the problem is with the system and the supervisor can fix it, then everyone wins as a result.

If the poor performance is not attributable to work design or organizational process problems, then attention should be focused on the employee. At least three possible causes of poor performance can be attributed to the employee. The problem may lie in (1) some aspect of the person's relationship to the organization or supervisor, (2) some area of the employee's personal life, or (3) a training or developmental deficiency. In the latter two cases, poor performance may be treated as a symptom as opposed to a motivated consequence. In such cases, identifying financial problems, family difficulties, or health disorders may enable the supervisor to help the employee solve problems before they become too extensive. Employee assistance programs (EAPs) can be helpful to employees managing personal problems and are discussed in Chapter 7 in relation to managing stress.

Poor performance may also be motivated by an employee's displaced anger or conflict with the organization or supervisor. In such cases, the employee may or may not be aware of the internal reactions causing the problem. In either event, sabotage, work slowdowns, work stoppages, and similar forms of poor performance may result from such motivated behavior. The supervisor may attribute the cause of the problem to the employee, and the employee may attribute it to the supervisor or organization. To solve motivated performance problems requires treating the poor performance as a symptom with a deeper cause. Resolving the underlying anger or conflict results in the disappearance of the symptom (poor performance).

According to attribution theory, managers make attributions (inferences) concerning employees' behavior and performance.[66] The attributions may not always be accurate. For example, an executive with Capital Cities Corporation/ABC (now part of the Disney Company) who had a very positive relationship with his boss was not held responsible for profit problems in his district. The boss attributed the problem to the economy instead. Supervisors and employees who share perceptions and attitudes, as in the Capital Cities situation, tend to evaluate each other highly.[67] Supervisors and employees who do not share perceptions and attitudes are more likely to blame each other for performance problems.

Harold Kelley's attribution theory aims to help us explain the behavior of other people. He also extended attribution theory by trying to identify the antecedents of internal and external attributions. Kelley proposed that individuals make attributions based on information gathered in the form of three informational cues: consensus, distinctiveness, and consistency.[68, 69] We observe an individual's behavior and then seek out information in the form of these three cues. *Consensus* is the extent to which peers in the same situation behave the same way. *Distinctiveness* is the degree to which the person behaves the same way in other situations. *Consistency* refers to the frequency of a particular behavior over time.

We form attributions based on whether these cues are low or high. Figure 6.4 shows how the combination of these cues helps us form internal or external attributions. Suppose you have received several complaints from customers regarding one of your customer service representatives, John. You have not received complaints about your other service representatives (low consensus). Upon reviewing John's records, you note that he also received customer complaints during his previous job as a sales clerk (low distinctiveness). The complaints have been coming in steadily for about three months (high consistency). In this case, you would most likely make an internal attribution and conclude that the complaints must stem from John's behavior. The combination of low consensus, low distinctiveness, and high consistency leads to internal attributions.

Other combinations of these cues, however, produce external attributions. High consensus, high distinctiveness, and low consistency, for example, produce external attributions. Suppose one of your employees, Mary, is performing poorly on collecting overdue accounts. You find that the behavior is widespread within your work team (high consensus) and that Mary is performing poorly only on this aspect of the job (high distinctiveness), and that most of the time she handles this aspect of the job well (low consistency). You will probably decide that something about the work situation caused the poor performance—perhaps work overload or an unfair deadline.

Consensus, distinctiveness, and consistency are the cues used to determine whether the cause of behavior is internal or external. The process of determining the cause of a behavior may not be simple and clear-cut, however, because of some biases that occur in forming attributions.

Figure 6.5 presents an attribution model that specifically addresses how supervisors respond to poor performance. A supervisor who observes poor performance seeks cues about the employee's behavior in the three forms discussed above: consensus, consistency, and distinctiveness.

On the basis of this information, the supervisor makes either an internal (personal) attribution or an external (situational) attribution. Internal attributions might include low effort, lack of commitment, or lack of ability. External attributions are outside the employee's control and might include equipment

consensus
An informational cue indicating the extent to which peers in the same situation behave in a similar fashion.

distinctiveness
An informational cue indicating the degree to which an individual behaves the same way in other situations.

consistency
An informational cue indicating the frequency of behavior over time.

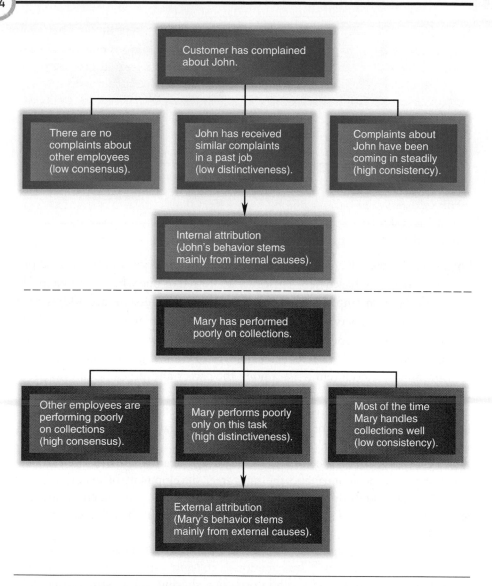

failure or unrealistic goals. The supervisor then determines the source of responsibility for the performance problem and tries to correct the problem.

Supervisors may choose from a wide range of responses. They can, for example, express personal concern, reprimand the employee, or provide training. Supervisors who attribute the cause of poor performance to a person (an internal cause) will respond more harshly than supervisors who attribute the cause to the work situation (an external cause). Supervisors should try not to make either of the two common attribution errors discussed in Chapter 3: the fundamental attribution error and the self-serving bias.

Coaching, Counseling, and Mentoring

Supervisors have important coaching, counseling, and mentoring responsibilities to their subordinates. Supervisors and coworkers have been found to be more effective in mentoring functions than assigned, formal mentors from higher up in the organizational hierarchy.[70] Success in the mentoring relationship also

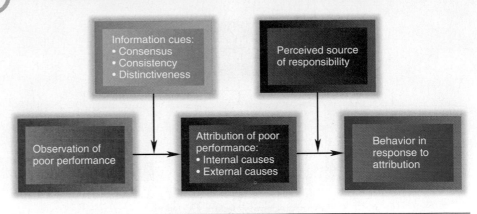

hinges on the presence of openness and trust.[71] This relationship may be one where performance-based deficiencies are addressed or one where personal problems that diminish employee performance, such as depression, are addressed.[72] In either case, the supervisors can play a helpful role in employee problem-solving activities without accepting responsibility for the employees' problems. One important form of help is to refer the employee to trained professionals.

Coaching and counseling are among the career and psychosocial functions of a mentoring relationship.[73] *Mentoring* is a work relationship that encourages development and career enhancement for people moving through the career cycle. Mentor relationships typically go through four phases: initiation, cultivation, separation, and redefinition. For protégés, mentoring offers a number of career benefits.[74] The relationship can significantly enhance the early development of a newcomer and the midcareer development of an experienced employee. One study found that good performance by newcomers resulted in leaders giving more delegation.[75] Career development can be enhanced through peer relationships as an alternative to traditional mentoring relationships.[76] Executive coaching is increasingly being used as a way of outsourcing the business mentoring functions.[77] Informational, collegial, and special peers aid the individual's development through information sharing, career strategizing, job-related feedback, emotional support, and friendship. Hence, mentors and peers may both play constructive roles in correcting an employee's poor performance and in enhancing overall career development.

mentoring

A work relationship that encourages development and career enhancement for people moving through the career cycle.

Managerial Implications: Performance Management Is a Key Task

People in organizations learn from the consequences of their actions. Therefore, managers must exercise care in applying positive and negative consequences to ensure that they are connected to the behaviors the managers intend to reward or punish. Managers should also be judicious in the use of punishment and should consider extinction coupled with positive reinforcement as an alternative to punishment for shaping employee behavior. The strategic use of training and educational opportunities, stock options, and recognition awards is instrumental to successful organizational reward systems. Managers can serve as positive role models for employees' vicarious learning about ethical behavior and high-quality performance.

Goal-setting activities may be valuable to managers in bringing out the best performance from employees. Managers can use challenging, specific goals for this purpose and must be prepared to provide employees with timely, useful feedback on goal progress so that employees will know how they are doing. Goal-setting activities that are misused may create dysfunctional competition in an organization and lead to lower performance.

Good performance management systems are a valuable tool for providing employees with clear feedback on their actions. Managers who rely on valid and reliable performance measures may use them in employee development and to correct poor performance. Managers who use high-technology performance monitoring systems must remember that employees are humans, not machines. Managers are responsible for creating a positive learning atmosphere in performance feedback sessions, and employees are responsible for learning from these sessions. 360-degree feedback is especially effective when combined with coaching.

Finally, managers can use rewards as one of the most powerful positive consequences for shaping employee behavior. If rewards are to improve performance, managers must make a clear connection between specific performance and the rewards. Employees should be expected to earn the rewards they receive; they should expect rewards to be related to performance quality and skill development.

LOOKING BACK: VIRGIN GROUP, LTD.

Performance through Collaboration, Not Dictation

Performance management emphasizes behaviors, gives careful attention to evaluation and feedback, and is concerned with performance improvement, often through goal setting. While this approach is successful and appropriate in a variety of work contexts, it is not universally used. As we saw in the opening Thinking Ahead, Sir Richard Branson's Virgin Group, Ltd. is a counterpoint organization that does not always follow the conventional wisdom, conventional approach, or traditional pathway to business success and achievement. This is true for Virgin's legal team, which is not a muscular, in-house one. Helena Samaha is Virgin's legal director who works in the group's London headquarters.[78] Rather than a large in-house legal staff, Samaha oversees Virgin's relationship with external lawyers who do about £10 million in legal work annually. In addition, she does Virgin's legal work on new ventures.

Across the entire company, there are only fourteen in-house lawyers, some housed in the group's companies such as Virgin Atlantic, Virgin Trains, its hot-air balloon company, or its myriad of other smaller companies. In her words, Samaha does not dictate behavior to the lawyers or executives in these groups. Rather, she uses and encourages a collaborative style of relationship that fits Virgin's entrepreneurial culture, not the combative, antagonistic style stereotypical of the legal profession and courtroom dramas. In this view, she does not evaluate the performance of Virgin's lawyers within the companies but rather leaves that to the executives who are actually managing the companies. This approach opens up a way of macro-managing Virgin's legal work rather than micro-managing the behavior of its lawyers.

Samaha's management style does not mean she's disengaged from performance evaluations and performance management. On the contrary, she conducts a full review of Virgin's external legal panel annually. Because it outsources 80 percent of its legal work to external lawyers, Virgin must keep these lawyers motivated and performing well for the company. Samaha achieves this by annual evaluations of the external legal panel. Annual reviews give her the flexibility to retain legal firms who perform well, such as Allen & Overy, while letting others, such as Hammonds, drop off retainer. In addition, she looks carefully at the possibility of renegotiating fees with the external lawyers. This activity is all aimed at enhancing both motivation and performance among the external lawyers because of the contingent rewards offered. While Virgin Group has kept its in-house legal team minimal, it has stayed on top of its legal work through a motivated panel of external lawyers who are managed well by the company and who give it flexibility in meeting its legal needs.

Chapter Summary

1. Learning is a change in behavior acquired through experience.

2. The operant conditioning approach to learning states that behavior is a function of positive and negative consequences.

3. Reinforcement is used to develop desirable behavior; punishment and extinction are used to decrease undesirable behavior.

4. Bandura's social learning theory suggests that task-specific self-efficacy is important to effective learning.

5. Goal setting improves work motivation and task performance, reduces role stress, and improves the accuracy and validity of performance appraisal.

6. Performance management and 360-degree feedback can lead to improved performance.

7. Making accurate attributions about the behavior of others is an essential prerequisite to correcting poor performance.

8. High-quality performance should be rewarded and poor performance should be corrected.

9. Mentoring is a relationship for encouraging development and career enhancement for people moving through the career cycle.

Key Terms

classical conditioning (p. 180)
consensus (p. 200)
consistency (p. 200)
distinctiveness (p. 200)
extinction (p. 184)
goal setting (p. 186)
learning (p. 180)

management by objectives (MBO) (p. 190)
mentoring (p. 202)
negative consequences (p. 181)
operant conditioning (p. 181)
performance appraisal (p. 192)

performance management (p. 192)
positive consequences (p. 181)
punishment (p. 182)
reinforcement (p. 182)
task-specific self-efficacy (p. 185)
360-degree feedback (p. 195)

Review Questions

1. Define the terms *learning, reinforcement, punishment*, and *extinction*.

2. What are positive and negative consequences in shaping behavior? How should they be managed? Explain the value of extinction as a strategy.

3. How can task-specific self-efficacy be enhanced? What are the differences in the way introverted and extroverted and intuitive and sensing people learn?

4. What are the five characteristics of well-developed goals? Why is feedback on goal progress important?

5. What are the purposes of conducting performance appraisals? What are the benefits of 360-degree feedback?

6. What are the two possible attributions of poor performance? What are the implications of each?

7. How can managers and supervisors best provide useful performance feedback?

8. How do mentors and peers help people develop and enhance their careers?

Discussion and Communication Questions

1. Which learning approach—the behavioral approach or Bandura's social learning theory—do you find more appropriate for people?

2. Given your personality type, how do you learn best? Do you miss learning some things because of how they are taught?

3. What goals do you set for yourself at work? In your personal life? Will you know if you achieve them?

4. If a conflict occurred between your self-evaluation and the evaluation given to you by your supervisor or instructor, how would you respond? What, specifically, would you do? What have you learned from your supervisor or instructor during the last reporting period?

5. What rewards are most important to you? How hard are you willing to work to receive them?

6. *(communication question)* Prepare a memo detailing the consequences of behavior in your work or university environment (e.g., grades, awards, suspensions, and scholarships). Include in your memo your classification of these consequences as positive or negative. Should your organization or university change the way it applies these consequences?

7. *(communication question)* Develop an oral presentation about the most current management practices in employee rewards and performance management. Find out what at least four different companies are doing in this area. Be prepared to discuss their fit with the text materials.

8. *(communication question)* Interview a manager or supervisor who is responsible for completing performance appraisals on people at work. Ask the manager which aspects of performance appraisal and the performance appraisal interview process are most difficult and how he or she manages these difficulties.

Ethical Dilemma

Donna Hermann shuffled the papers on her desk. She was very surprised by what she read. On her desk sat the annual evaluations of Julie Stringer, an employee in Donna's department. Both worked for Telecom Solutions, a large call center in the Midwest where it was the policy to do 360° annual evaluation on all employees. Each individual was evaluated by his or her supervisor, peers, and subordinates if the person was in a management position. As Julie's supervisor, Donna was looking at the evaluations completed by three of Julie's peers and three of her subordinates.

Julie's peers' opinion of her performance closely matched Donna's. Working at Telecom was intense and the managers had worked hard to create an environment where they supported each other. They felt that Julie was not supporting this environment. She never got in anyone's way but she never pitched in to help either. Julie came to Telecom everyday to work, nothing else. She never cared to make friends or to be a part of the team. Donna felt this was not good for the morale of her department and had hoped this annual evaluation would help her start the process of replacing Julie. However, the problem was Julie's employees loved her. Quite frankly, Donna had never seen such glowing reviews by anyone's subordinates. Obviously, Julie was not remote with her team. One of Julie's highest ratings from her team was her willingness to pitch in at any time for any reason. This was a very different perception from the management team.

Donna had no personal problem with Julie; she was concerned about her entire department. Since Julie joined the company, things had not been the same. However, was it more important for Julie's peers to be happy or her employees? Her group was always productive. Also, was it fair to punish someone for coming to the office to work? But, was it right to let Julie's behaviors to continue chipping away at the culture that Donna and the other managers had worked so hard to achieve?

Questions

1. What is Donna's primary responsibility?

2. Does Donna have a greater responsibility to her direct reports or to those one level down.

3. Using rule, virtue, right, and justice theories, evaluate Donna's decision regarding Julie.

Experiential Exercises

6.1 Positive and Negative Reinforcement

Purpose: To examine the effects of positive and negative reinforcement on behavior change.

1. Two or three volunteers are selected to receive reinforcement from the class while performing a particular task. The volunteers leave the room.

2. The instructor identifies an object for the student volunteers to locate when they return to the room. (The object should be unobtrusive but clearly visible to the class. Some that have worked well are a small triangular piece of paper that was left behind when a notice was torn off a classroom bulletin board, a smudge on the chalkboard, and a chip in the plaster of a classroom wall.)

3. The instructor specifies the reinforcement contingencies that will be in effect when the volunteers return to the room. For negative reinforcement, students should hiss, boo, and throw things (although you should not throw anything harmful) when the first volunteer is moving away from the object; cheer and applaud when the second volunteer is getting closer to the object; and if a third volunteer is used, use both negative and positive reinforcement.

4. The instructor should assign a student to keep a record of the time it takes each of the volunteers to locate the object.

5. Volunteer number 1 is brought back into the room and is instructed: "Your task is to locate and touch a particular object in the room, and the class has agreed to help you. You may begin."

6. Volunteer number 1 continues to look for the object until it is found while the class assists by giving negative reinforcement.

7. Volunteer number 2 is brought back into the room and is instructed: "Your task is to locate and touch a particular object in the room, and the class has agreed to help you. You may begin."

8. Volunteer number 2 continues to look for the object until it is found while the class assists by giving positive reinforcement.

9. Volunteer number 3 is brought back into the room and is instructed: "Your task is to locate and touch a particular object in the room, and the class has agreed to help you. You may begin."

10. Volunteer number 3 continues to look for the object until it is found while the class assists by giving both positive and negative reinforcement.

11. In a class discussion, answer the following questions:

   a. How did the behavior of the volunteers differ when different kinds of reinforcement (positive, negative, or both) were used?

   b. What were the emotional reactions of the volunteers to the different kinds of reinforcement?

   c. Which type of reinforcement—positive or negative—is most common in organizations? What effect do you think this has on motivation and productivity?

6.2 Correcting Poor Performance

This exercise provides an opportunity for you to engage in a performance diagnosis role-play as either the assistant director of the Academic Computing Service Center or as a member of a university committee appointed by the president of the university at the request of the center director. The instructor will form the class into groups of five or six students and either ask the group to select who is to be the assistant director or assign one group member to be the assistant director.

Performance diagnosis, especially where some poor performance exists, requires making attributions and determining causal factors as well as formulating a plan of action to correct any poor performance.

Step 1. (5 minutes) Once the class is formed into groups, the instructor provides the assistant director with a copy of the role description and each university committee member with a copy of the role context information. Group members are to read through the materials provided.

Step 2. (15 minutes) The university committee is to call in the assistant director of the Academic Computing Service Center for a performance diagnostic interview. This is an information-gathering interview, not an appraisal session. The purpose is to gather information for the center director.

Step 3. (15 minutes) The university committee is to agree on a statement that reflects their understanding of the assistant director's poor performance and to include a specification of the causes. Based on this problem statement, the committee is to formulate a plan of action to correct the poor performance. The assistant director is to do the same, again ending with a plan of action.

Step 4. (10–15 minutes, optional) The instructor may ask the groups to share the results of their work in Step 3 of the role-play exercise.

Biz Flix | Seabiscuit

Combine a jockey who is blind in one eye with an undersized, ill-tempered thoroughbred and an unusual trainer. The result: the Depression era champion race horse Seabiscuit. This engaging film shows the training and development of Seabiscuit by trainer "Silent" Tom Smith (Chris Cooper) and jockey Red Pollard (Tobey Maguire). The enduring commitment of owner Charles Howard (Jeff Bridges) ensures the ultimate success of Seabiscuit on the racing circuit. Based on *Seabiscuit: An American Legend*, the best selling book by Laura Hillenbrand, *Seabiscuit* received seven 2003 Academy Award nominations, including Best Picture.

The *Seabiscuit* scene is an edited composite from DVD Chapters 21 and 22 toward the end of the film. In earlier scenes, Red severely injured a leg and cannot ride Seabiscuit in the competition against War Admiral. Samuel Riddle (Eddie Jones), War Admiral's owner, described any new rider as immaterial to the race's result. The scene begins with Red giving George Wolff (Gary Stevens), Seabiscuit's new jockey, some tips about riding him. Red starts by saying to George, "He's got a strong left lead, Georgie. He banks like a frigg'n airplane." The film continues to its exciting and unexpected ending.

What to Watch for and Ask Yourself:

> Does Red set clear performance goals for George? If he does, what are they?

> Does Red help George reach those performance goals? How?

> Does Red give George any positive reinforcement while he tries to reach the performance goals?

Workplace Video | Fannie Mae: Human Resource Management

Fannie Mae is a financial services company that works with primary lenders such as banks, credit unions, mortgage companies, and government housing agencies to increase the availability and affordability of home ownership for low- and middle-income Americans. With more than 12 million active mortgages issued to its target clientele of women, minorities, and single parents, Fannie Mae is the nation's largest source of financing for homebuyers. The Washington D.C.-based firm is known for fostering rich diversity among its over 4,000 employees, and each individual at the company contributes to the corporate mission of helping families achieve the American dream of home ownership.

Fannie Mae's success can be attributed in part to its ability to attract and retain a motivated and highly skilled workforce. The firm's employment polices are designed to achieve core objectives such as treating employees with respect, creating opportunities for learning and growth, and helping employees find ways to balance work and family life. Fannie Mae's human resources personnel consider specific benefits such as job training, advanced education, mentoring, and flexible scheduling to be essential towards developing a productive workforce.

By ensuring that human resources programs have a positive impact on the lives of its employees, Fannie Mae is able to achieve its corporate objective to reduce barriers, lower costs, and present opportunities for home ownership to all Americans.

TAKE 2

1. *List three specific benefit programs Fannie Mae offers to its employees. How do such programs create a more productive workforce?*
2. *Why does Fannie Mae pay for employees to take college classes? How does the firm benefit from this continuing education program?*
3. *Describe Fannie Mae's mentorship program. What is the purpose of mentoring employees?*

Hewlett-Packard's Approach to Encouraging and Rewarding Employee Performance

Scott Cohen, an expert on performance management, says: "Performance management programs represent a lost opportunity for most companies. These systems, if designed and implemented properly, can have a strong positive impact on individual performance and financial results—our studies suggest a possible 20 percent improvement in shareholder value." Cohen goes on to observe that too many companies use performance management programs merely as "window dressing" rather than to add real value.

One key to having a successful pay-for-performance plan is to have an organizational culture that embraces pay for performance. Such a culture will emphasize goal setting, rating and/or ranking of performance, and performance dialogue between supervisors and subordinates. A performance-based culture places a premium on obtaining desired behaviors and results, recognizes that the organization's success depends on the employees' successful performance, lets strategic outcomes and goals drive the work of the organization, and rewards desired performance but not poor performance.

Hewlett-Packard's Performance-Based Culture

Hewlett-Packard, operating in 178 countries and doing business in more than ten languages, is a company with a performance-based culture. Employing more than 140,000 people, Hewlett-Packard is known as a great place to work. Hewlett-Packard values ideas and believes that ideas are best developed in a teamwork culture. "That is why everyone at every level in every function is encouraged to have original ideas to express them, and to share them." Each employee is valued for the unique skills, experiences, and perspectives that he or she brings to the job and organization.

Hewlett-Packard provides employees "every opportunity to learn, grow, and develop skills to drive the company toward achieving its business goals." It encourages employees "to develop their work and life skills in order to achieve personal as well as career goals." Hewlett-Packard encourages employees to plan individual development paths that are discussed with their respective managers. Employees and their managers reach mutual agreement upon the individual development paths. Learning within the context of these development plans is intended to be flexible, fast, and rewarding. Hewlett-Packard prides itself on having an "empowering culture that allows people to make the most of their skills, personality, and career."

Not only is goal setting an important part of employees' development plans, but it is also a crucial element in on-the-job performance management. Employees have three sets of goals: threshold, target, and aspirational. Threshold goals represent the minimum acceptable performance. Target goals represent the desired and expected level of performance. Aspirational goals exceed the desired and expected level of performance by a significant amount. Attainment of these goals is evaluated using appropriate criteria.

Hewlett-Packard's Total Rewards Program

Performance management at Hewlett-Packard relies, in part, on a *Total Rewards* program that encourages employees to contribute ideas and attain a high level of achievement. The *Total Rewards* program includes six major components: competitive base pay, performance-related pay, comprehensive benefits, stock ownership, work life navigation, and sports and social facilities.

While the *Total Rewards* program differs from nation to nation and by organizational level, all employees are paid market rates for their locations and have benefits packages that are designed to address needs of the location. For instance, differences occur in benefits plans from country to country because of the different laws and regulations that govern the distribution of benefits. In the United States, for example, the benefits package includes a variety of programs for managing work and life demands (e.g., flexible work hours, flexible work arrangements, and educational assistance, among others), staying healthy (e.g., medical, dental, and vision plans), and protecting employees (e.g., life insurance and disability insurance).

All employees also receive performance-related pay that is linked to their attainment of threshold, target, and aspirational goals. "When aspirational goals are met, employees may exceed their target pay potential. Conversely, when minimal thresholds are not met, no variable payment will be made." This provides employees the opportunity to share in HP's success.

Performance-related pay may be one of three types: a company performance bonus, pay for results, or sales incentives. *The company performance bonus* links individual rewards to HP's overall success. The *pay for results* variable incentive links compensation for executives and managers to individual, business organization, and company performance results. *Sales incentives* link the compensation of sales professionals to the attainment of individual, business organization, and company performance goals.

The ultimate effect of and justification for Hewlett-Packard *Total Rewards* program is perhaps best captured in its corporate rewards philosophy: "Our philosophy on rewards is simple: We believe that when excellent performance is acknowledged and rewarded, people are more motivated and work smarter."

Discussion Questions

1. Evaluate the performance management impact of performance-related pay in terms of goal setting and reinforcement.

2. Why should a performance management system be flexible yet embedded in a company's culture?

3. What are the primary characteristics of an organizational culture that strongly supports performance management?

4. How does Hewlett-Packard's organizational culture support its performance-management philosophy?

5. Why is it important to link an organization's performance management system to its reward system?

SOURCE: This case was written by Michael K. McCuddy, The Louis S. and Mary L. Morgal Chair of Christian Business Ethics and Professor of Management, College of Business Administration, Valparaiso University. This case was developed from material contained on the Hewlett-Packard Web site at http://www.jobs.hp.com and in the following articles: J. Graham, "Developing a Performance-Based Culture," *The Journal for Quality & Participation* (Spring 2004): 4–8; "Making Performance Management Work," *Executive Edge Newsletter* (July 1997): 15; A. Saunier and M. Mavis, "Fixing a Broken System," *HR Focus* (March 1998): 1–3; "Survey Reveals Successful PFP Plans Have a Profound Effect on Your Top Workers," *IOMA's Pay for Performance Report* (August 2004, Vol. 4, No. 8): 1 and 11–13; "The Benefits of Performance Management," *Worklife Report* (1998, Vol. 11, No. 2): 10–12; "U.S. Workers Give Performance Management Programs a Failing Grade," *PA Times* (May 2004): 13.

© AP/Wide World Photos

Stress and Well-Being at Work

After reading this chapter, you should be able to do the following:

1 Define *stress, distress,* and *strain.*

2 Compare four different approaches to stress.

3 Explain the psychophysiology of the stress response.

4 Identify work and nonwork causes of stress.

5 Describe the benefits of eustress and the costs of distress.

6 Discuss individual differences in the stress–strain relationship.

7 Distinguish the primary, secondary, and tertiary stages of preventive stress management.

8 Discuss organizational and individual methods of preventive stress management.

THINKING AHEAD: PIXAR ANIMATION STUDIOS

Stress, Academy Awards, and Creativity

Pixar's employees work really hard to produce its Academy Award-winning movies, and hard work is stressful. However, hard work does not have to be distressing, and Pixar's employees recognize the importance of letting off steam.[1] The Pixar Studios campus has a magical quality that appeals to the kid in most people and to the kid in Pixar's employees. While Hollywood and the film industry are stereotyped as a fantasy world of make believe, those who know the world also know that there is plenty of stress, pressure, and uncertainty there, too. Success and achievement are not guaranteed any more than are Academy Awards. Therefore, Pixar's Academy Awards are the product of good, hard, successful work with its associated stress, tension, and pressure. As we know, stress can be a positive, motivating force for people at work. This seems to be the case at Pixar. How does the firm do it?

One of the ways that Pixar turns stress into achievement is through creativity. Pixar more than allows its employees to express their creative sides; it encourages creativity. For example, activities like the company paper airplane contest provide a forum for employees to act out their creative ideas and designs. Imagination reigns in this competition, with designs that range from tiny darts to three-foot monsters, and all of a sudden work is turned into play. Employees from all over the company gather in the scenic atrium to watch their colleagues launch their airplanes from the upper-level suspended walkway. Once launched, these unique and imaginative designs come alive. While some fly better than others, it's all in good fun and an opportunity to let off some of the steam that builds up in a high-performance company.

Another way that Pixar's employees let off steam is by roaming the halls wearing bright Hawaiian shirts or backward baseball caps. These employees simply look wholesomely too-cool-for-school in their jolly get-ups. On a good day, some employees might zip around the halls on shiny razor scooters, passing those on foot. Some really fortunate visitors may be invited to tour the "Tiki Room," a private club built by a Pixar employee inside a ventilation cavity accessible only through a grate in the wall of his office. A visitor might even get to meet the office chimpanzee, who might be an intern for all anyone knows. All in all, Pixar is a pretty zany and peppy workplace with many of the same production pressures of other organizations, but one that uses innovative ways to reduce stress. Is it all fun and games at Pixar Studios?

Stress is an important topic in organizational behavior, in part due to the increase in competitive pressures that take a toll on workers and managers alike. Poor leadership, work–family conflicts, and sexual harassment are among the leading causes of work stress.[2] This chapter has five major sections, each addressing one aspect of stress. The first section examines the question "What is stress?" The discussion includes four approaches to the stress response. The second section reviews the demands and stressors that trigger the stress response at work. The third section examines the performance and health benefits of stress and the individual and organizational forms of distress. The fourth section considers individual difference factors, such as gender and personality hardiness, that help moderate the stress–distress relationship. The fifth section presents a framework for preventive stress management and reviews a wide range of individual and organizational stress management methods.

What Is Stress?

1. Define *stress*, *distress*, and *strain*.

stress
The unconscious preparation to fight or flee that a person experiences when faced with any demand.

stressor
The person or event that triggers the stress response.

distress
The adverse psychological, physical, behavioral, and organizational consequences that may arise as a result of stressful events.

strain
Distress.

Stress is one of the most creatively ambiguous words in the English language, with as many interpretations as there are people who use the word. In other languages, the term *stress* has a variety of meanings, and Spanish does not even have a direct translation of the word. Even the stress experts do not agree on its definition. Stress carries a negative connotation for some people, as though it were something to be avoided. This is unfortunate, because stress is a great asset in managing legitimate emergencies and achieving peak performance. *Stress*, or the stress response, is the unconscious preparation to fight or flee that a person experiences when faced with any demand.[3] A *stressor*, or demand, is the person or event that triggers the stress response. *Distress* or *strain* refers to the adverse psychological, physical, behavioral, and organizational consequences that *may* occur as a result of stressful events. You 7.1 gives you an opportunity to examine how overstressed and angry you may be.

Four Approaches to Stress

The stress response was discovered by Walter B. Cannon, a medical physiologist, early in the twentieth century.[4] Later researchers defined stress differently than Cannon. We will review four different approaches to defining stress: the

The Frazzle Factor

Then + Now

Read each of the following statements and rate yourself on a scale of 0 to 3, giving the answer that best describes how you generally feel (3 points for *always*, 2 points for *often*, 1 point for *sometimes*, and 0 points for *never*). Answer as honestly as you can, and do not spend too much time on any one statement.

Am I Overstressed?

_1._ 1. I have to make important snap judgments and decisions.

0 ~~2.~~ 2. I am not consulted about what happens ~~on my job or~~ in my classes.

0 3. I feel I am underpaid.

0 ~~4.~~ 4. I feel that no matter how hard I work, the system will mess it up.

0 5. I do not get along with some of my coworkers or fellow students.

0 6. I do not trust my superiors at work or my professors at school.

2 7. The paperwork burden on my job or at school is getting to me.

0 8. I feel people outside the job or the university do not respect what I do.

Am I Angry?

2 1. I feel that people around me make too many irritating mistakes.

1 2. I feel annoyed because I do good work or perform well in school, but no one appreciates it.

1 3. When people make me angry, I tell them off.

0 4. When I am angry, I say things I know will hurt people.

0 5. I lose my temper easily.

1 6. I feel like striking out at someone who angers me.

1 7. When a coworker or fellow student makes a mistake, I tell him or her about it.

3 8. I cannot stand being criticized in public.

12

SCORING

To find your level of anger and potential for aggressive behavior, add your scores from both quiz parts.

40–48: The red flag is waving, and you had better pay attention. You are in the danger zone. You need guidance from a counselor or mental health professional, and you should be getting it now.

30–39: The yellow flag is up. Your stress and anger levels are too high, and you are feeling increasingly hostile. You are still in control, but it would not take much to trigger a violent flare of temper.

10–29: Relax, you are in the broad normal range. Like most people, you get angry occasionally, but usually with some justification. Sometimes you take overt action, but you are not likely to be unreasonably or excessively aggressive.

0–9: Congratulations! You are in great shape. Your stress and anger are well under control, giving you a laid-back personality not prone to violence.

SOURCE: Questionnaire developed by C. D. Spielberger. Appeared in W. Barnhill, "Early Warning," *The Washington Post* (August 11, 1992): B5.

---

homeostatic/medical, cognitive appraisal, person–environment fit, and psychoanalytic approaches. These four approaches to stress will give you a more complete understanding of what stress really is.

THE HOMEOSTATIC/MEDICAL APPROACH When Walter B. Cannon originally discovered stress, he called it "the emergency response" or "the militaristic response," arguing that it was rooted in "the fighting emotions." His early writings provide the basis for calling the stress response the *fight-or-flight* response. According to Cannon, stress resulted when an external, environmental demand upset the person's natural steady-state balance.[5] He referred

2. Compare four different approaches to stress.

to this steady-state balance, or equilibrium, as *homeostasis*. Cannon believed the body was designed with natural defense mechanisms to keep it in homeostasis. He was especially interested in the role of the sympathetic nervous system in activating a person under stressful conditions.[6]

Perception and cognitive appraisal may carry more weight than the physiological aspects of a stressful situation.

THE COGNITIVE APPRAISAL APPROACH Richard Lazarus was more concerned with the psychology of stress. He de-emphasized the medical and physiological aspects, emphasizing instead the psychological and cognitive aspects of the response.[7] Like Cannon, Lazarus saw stress as a result of a person–environment interaction, and he emphasized the person's cognitive appraisal in classifying persons or events as stressful or not. Individuals differ in their appraisal of events and people. What is stressful for one person may not be stressful for another. Perception and cognitive appraisal are important processes in determining what is stressful, and a person's organizational position can shape such perception. For example, an employee would more likely be stressed by an upset supervisor than another supervisor would be. Lazarus also introduced problem-focused and emotion-focused coping. Problem-focused coping emphasizes managing the stressor, and emotion-focused coping emphasizes managing your response.

THE PERSON–ENVIRONMENT FIT APPROACH Robert Kahn was concerned with the social psychology of stress. His approach emphasized how confusing and conflicting expectations of a person in a social role create stress for the person.[8] He extended the approach to examine a person's fit in the environment. A good person–environment fit occurs when a person's skills and abilities match a clearly defined, consistent set of role expectations. This results in a lack of stress for the person. Stress occurs when the role expectations are confusing and/or conflicting or when a person's skills and abilities are not able to meet the demands of the social role. After a period of this stress, the person can expect to experience strain, such as strain in the form of depression.

THE PSYCHOANALYTIC APPROACH Harry Levinson defined stress based on Freudian psychoanalytic theory.[9] Levinson believes that two elements of the personality interact to cause stress. The first element is the *ego-ideal*— the embodiment of a person's perfect self. The second element is the *self-image*— how the person really sees himself or herself, both positively and negatively. Although not sharply defined, the ego-ideal encompasses admirable attributes of parental personalities, wished-for and/or imaginable qualities a person would like to possess, and the absence of any negative or distasteful qualities. Stress results from the discrepancy between the idealized self (ego-ideal) and the real self-image; the greater the discrepancy, the more stress a person experiences. More generally, psychoanalytic theory helps us understand the role of unconscious personality factors as causes of stress within a person.

The Stress Response

Whether activated by an ego-ideal/self-image discrepancy, a poorly defined social role, cognitive appraisal suggesting threat, or a lack of balance, the resulting stress response is characterized by a predictable sequence of mind and body events. The stress response begins with the release of chemical messengers, primarily adrenaline, into the bloodstream. These messengers activate the sympathetic nervous system and the endocrine (hormone) system. These two systems work together and trigger four mind–body changes to prepare the person for fight or flight:

3. Explain the psychophysiology of the stress response.

1. The redirection of the blood to the brain and large-muscle groups and away from the skin, internal organs, and extremities.

2. Increased alertness by way of improved vision, hearing, and other sensory processes through the activation of the brainstem (ancient brain).

3. The release of glucose (blood sugar) and fatty acids into the bloodstream to sustain the body during the stressful event.

4. Depression of the immune system, as well as restorative and emergent processes (such as digestion).

This set of four changes shifts the person from a neutral, or naturally defensive, posture to an offensive posture. The stress response can be very functional in preparing a person to deal with legitimate emergencies and to achieve peak performance. It is neither inherently bad nor necessarily destructive.

Sources of Work Stress

Work stress is caused both by factors in the work environment and by pressures from outside the workplace that have spillover effects into the workplace. An example of the latter would be when a working mother or father is called at work to come pick up a sick child from the day-care center so that the child does not expose other children to a health risk. Therefore, the two major categories of sources of work stress are the work demands and nonwork demands shown in Table 7.1. As the table suggests, one of the most complex causes of work stress is role conflict. An innovative study by Pam Perrewé and her colleagues examined the dysfunctional physical and psychological consequences of role conflict. The study is discussed in the accompanying Science feature. The researchers found political skill to be an antidote for role conflict, one of a range of preventive stress management strategies discussed later in the chapter.

4. Identify work and nonwork causes of stress.

Work Demands

Role ambiguity is the second major role demand identified in Table 7.1 that causes work stress. In addition, role demands, task demands, interpersonal demands, and physical demands are shown in the table. The table does not present an exhaustive list of work demands but rather aims to show major causes of work stress in each of the four major domains of the work environment.

TASK DEMANDS Globalization is creating dramatic changes at work, causing on-the-job pressure and stress.[10] Change leads to uncertainty, a lack of predictability in a person's daily tasks and activities, and may be caused by job

TABLE 7.1   Work and Nonwork Demands

WORK DEMANDS

Task Demands	**Role Demands**
Change	Role conflict:
Lack of control	Interrole
Career progress	Intrarole
New technologies	Person–role
Time pressure	Role ambiguity

Interpersonal Demands	**Physical Demands**
Emotional toxins	Extreme environments
Sexual harassment	Strenuous activities
Poor leadership	Hazardous substances
	Global travel

NONWORK DEMANDS

Home Demands	**Personal Demands**
Family expectations	Workaholism
Child-rearing/day-care arrangements	Civic and volunteer work
Parental care	Traumatic events

insecurity related to difficult economic times. Even as the U.S. economy recovered strongly in 2004, creating hundreds of thousands of jobs, nearly 80,000 U.S. workers continue to lose their jobs monthly. For those who do not lose their jobs, underemployment, monotony, and boredom may be problems. Technology and technological innovation create further change and uncertainty for many employees, requiring adjustments in training, education, and skill development. Intended to make life and work easier and more convenient, information technology may have a paradoxical effect and be a source of stress rather than a stress-reliever.

Lack of control is a second major source of stress, especially in work environments that are difficult and psychologically demanding. The lack of control may be caused by inability to influence the timing of tasks and activities, to select tools or methods for accomplishing the work, to make decisions that influence work outcomes, or to exercise direct action to affect the work outcomes. One study found that male workers in occupations with low job autonomy (lack of control) and high job demands (heavy workloads) experienced more heart attacks than other male workers.[11]

Concerns over career progress, new technologies, and time pressures (or work overload) are three additional task demands triggering stress for the person at work. Career stress is related to the career gridlock that has occurred in many organizations as the middle-manager ranks have been thinned due to mergers, acquisitions, and downsizing during the past two decades.[12] Thinning the organizational ranks also often leaves an abundance of work for those who are still employed. Time pressure is a leading stressor for people at work and in school. Time pressure is often associated with work overload and may result from poor time management skills. New technologies also create both career stress and "technostress" for people at work who wonder if they will be replaced by "smart" machines.[13] Although they enhance the organization's productive capacity, new technologies may be viewed as the enemy by workers who must ultimately learn to use them. This creates a real dilemma for management.

Political Skill as an Antidote for Role Conflict

Job stress is a major problem that costs organizations billions of dollars in employee disability claims, employee absenteeism, and lost productivity. One long-known cause of job stress is role conflict, which is linked to several measures of job strain. Role conflict is often a chronic problem because of the multiple roles (e.g., employee, wife, mother, and daughter) that an employee occupies. While the link between role conflict and job strain is well known, little is known about the potential benefits of political skill as an antidote for role conflict.

Recent research studied 230 full-time employees, many with supervisory responsibilities. In addition to a battery of psychological tests to measure the individual's political skills, experienced role conflict, and job strain as indicated by psychological anxiety and somatic complaints, the study included physiological measures. Specifically, heart rate was measured with a stethoscope, and blood pressure was measured with a sphygmomanometer. The blood pressure readings included both the systolic value (i.e., maximum pressure when the heart beats) and the diastolic value (i.e., minimum pressure between heartbeats). Hence, this study is unique because it includes four mind–body measures of job strain. The results showed that higher levels of political skill did in fact have a positive, moderating effect on all types of job strain, thus reducing the adverse effects of role conflict on both the mind and the body, specifically the cardiovascular system.

SOURCE: P. L. Perrewé, K. L. Zellars, G. R. Ferris, A. M. Rossi, C. J. Kacmar, and D. A. Ralston, "Neutralizing Job Stressors: Political Skill as an Antidote to the Dysfunctional Consequences of Role Conflict," *Academy of Management Journal* 47 (2004): 141–152.

ROLE DEMANDS The social–psychological demands of the work environment may be every bit as stressful as task demands at work. People encounter two major categories of role stress at work: role conflict and role ambiguity.[14] Role conflict results from inconsistent or incompatible expectations communicated to a person. The conflict may be an interrole, intrarole, or person–role conflict.

Interrole conflict is caused by conflicting expectations related to two separate roles, such as employee and parent. For example, the employee with a major sales presentation on Monday and a sick child at home Sunday night is likely to experience interrole conflict. Work–family conflicts like these can lead individuals to withdrawal behaviors.[15]

Intrarole conflict is caused by conflicting expectations related to a single role, such as employee. For example, the manager who presses employees for both very fast work *and* high-quality work may be viewed at some point as creating a conflict for employees.

Ethics violations are likely to cause person–role conflicts. Employees expected to behave in ways that violate personal values, beliefs, or principles experience conflict. The unethical acts of committed employees exemplify this problem. Organizations with high ethical standards, such as Johnson & Johnson, are less likely to create ethical conflicts for employees. Person–role conflicts and ethics violations create a sense of divided loyalty for an employee.

The second major cause of role stress is role ambiguity. Role ambiguity is the confusion a person experiences related to the expectations of others. Role ambiguity may be caused by not understanding what is expected, not knowing how to do it, or not knowing the result of failure to do it. For example, a new magazine employee asked to copyedit a manuscript for the next issue may experience confusion because of lack of familiarity with copyediting procedures and conventions for the specific magazine.

A twenty-one-nation study of middle managers examined their experiences of role conflict, role ambiguity, and role overload. The results indicated that role stress varies more by country than it does by demographic and organizational factors. For example, non-Western managers experience less role ambiguity and more role overload than do their Western counterparts.[16] A study of U.S. military personnel found that when role clarity was high in a supportive work group, then psychological strain was low.[17]

INTERPERSONAL DEMANDS Emotional toxins, sexual harassment, and poor leadership in the organization are interpersonal demands for people at work. Emotional toxins are often generated at work by abrasive personalities.[18] These emotional toxins can spread through a work environment and cause a range of disturbances. Even emotional dissonance can be a cause of work stress.[19] Organizations are increasingly less tolerant of sexual harassment, a gender-related interpersonal demand that creates a stressful working environment both for the person being harassed and for others. The vast majority of sexual harassment is directed at women in the workplace and is a chronic yet preventable workplace problem.[20] Poor leadership in organizations and excessive, demanding management styles are a leading cause of work stress for employees. Employees who feel secure with strong, directive leadership may be anxious with an open management style. Those comfortable with participative leaders may feel restrained by a directive style. Trust is an important characteristic of the leader–follower interpersonal relationship, and a threat to a worker's reputation with her or his supervisor may be especially stressful.[21] Functional diversity in project groups also causes difficulty in the establishment of trusting relationships, thus increasing job stress, which leads to lower cohesiveness within the group.[22]

PHYSICAL DEMANDS Extreme environments, strenuous activities, hazardous substances, and global travel create physical demands for people at work. Work environments that are very hot or very cold place differing physical demands on people and create unique risks. One cross-cultural study that examined the effects of national culture and ambient temperature on role stress concluded that ambient temperature does affect human well-being, leading to the term *sweat shop* for inhumane working conditions.[23] Dehydration is one problem of extremely hot climates, whereas frostbite is one problem of extremely cold climates. The strenuous job of a steelworker and the hazards associated with bomb disposal work are physically demanding in different ways. The unique physical demands of work are often occupation specific, such as the risk of gravitationally induced loss of consciousness for military pilots flying high-performance fighters[24] or jet lag and loss of sleep for globe-trotting CEOs like IBM's Samuel J. Palmisano and Xerox's Anne Mulcahy. The demands of business travel are increasingly recognized as sources of stress.[25] However, the positive aspects of business trips are also increasingly recognized.[26]

Office work has its physical hazards as well. Noisy, crowded offices, such as those of some stock brokerages, can prove stressful for work. Working with a computer terminal can also be stressful, especially if the ergonomic fit between the person and machine is not correct. Eyestrain, neck stiffness, and arm and wrist problems can occur. Office designs that use partitions (cubicles) rather than full walls can create stress. These systems offer little privacy for the occupant (for example, to conduct employee counseling or performance appraisal sessions) and little protection from interruptions.

Nonwork demands also create stress for people, which may carry over into the work environment, or vice versa.[27] Nonwork demands may broadly be identified as home demands from an individual's personal life environment and personal demands that are self-imposed.

HOME DEMANDS Not all workers are subject to family demands related to marriage, child rearing, and parental care. The wide range of home and family arrangements in contemporary American society has created great diversity in this arena. For those in traditional families, these demands may create role conflicts or overloads that are difficult to manage. For example, the loss of good day care for children may be especially stressful for dual-career and single-parent families.[28] The tension between work and family may lead to a real struggle to achieve balance in life. This struggle led Rocky Rhodes, cofounder of Silicon Graphics, to establish four priorities for his life: God, family, exercise, and work.[29] These priorities helped him reallocate his time to achieve better balance in his life. As a result of the maturing of the American population, an increasing number of people face the added demand of parental care. Even when a person works to achieve an integrative social identity, integrating many social roles into a "whole" identity for a more stress-free balance in work and nonwork identities, the process of integration is not an easy one.[30]

PERSONAL DEMANDS Self-imposed, personal demands are the second major category of nonwork demands identified in Table 7.1. While self-imposed and personal, they can and do contribute to work stress on the job. *Workaholism* may be the most notable of the self-imposed, personal demands that causes stress for people at work and has been identified as a form of addiction.[31] Some of the early warning signs of workaholism include overcommitment to work, inability to enjoy vacations and respites from work, preoccupation with work problems when away from the workplace, and constantly taking work home on the weekend. Another type of personal demand comes from civic activities, volunteer work, and nonwork organizational commitments, such as in churches, synagogues, and public service organizations. These demands become more or less stressful depending on their compatibility with the person's work and family life and their capacity to provide alternative satisfactions for the person. Finally, traumatic events, such as 9/11, and their aftermath are stressful for people who experience them.[32] Not all traumatic events are as catastrophic as 9/11, however. Job loss, examination failures, and termination of romantic attachments are all traumatic, though less catastrophic, and may lead to distress if not addressed and resolved.

workaholism
An imbalanced preoccupation with work at the expense of home and personal life satisfaction.

The Consequences of Stress

Stress can be good or bad. Some managers and executives thrive under pressure because they practice what world-class athletes already know.[33] That is, to bring mind, body, and spirit to peak condition requires recovering energy, which is just as important as expending energy. Hence, world-class athletes and managers who practice what they know get high marks on any "stress test" because they use stress-induced energy in positive, healthy, and productive ways. The consequences of healthy, normal stress (called *eustress*, for "euphoria + stress") include a number of performance and health benefits to be balanced against the more commonly known costs of individual and organizational

5. Describe the benefits of eustress and the costs of distress.

TABLE 7.2   Benefits of Eustress and Costs of Distress

BENEFITS OF EUSTRESS

Performance	**Health**
Increased arousal	Cardiovascular efficiency
Bursts of physical strength	Balance in the nervous system
Full engagement	Enhanced focus in an emergency

COSTS OF DISTRESS

Individual	**Organizational**
Psychological disorders	Participation problems
Medical illnesses	Performance decrements
Behavioral problems	Compensation awards

distress.[34] The benefits of eustress and the costs of distress are listed in Table 7.2. An organization striving for high-quality products and services needs a healthy workforce to support the effort. Eustress is a characteristic of healthy people; distress is not.

Performance and Health Benefits

The Yerkes-Dodson law, shown in Figure 7.1, indicates that stress leads to improved performance up to an optimum point.[35] Beyond the optimum point, further stress and arousal have a detrimental effect on performance. Therefore, healthy amounts of eustress are desirable to improve performance by arousing a person to action. It is in the midrange of the curve that the greatest performance benefits from stress are achieved. Joseph McGrath has suggested that performance declines beyond the midpoint in the Yerkes-Dodson curve because

FIGURE 7.1   Yerkes-Dodson Law

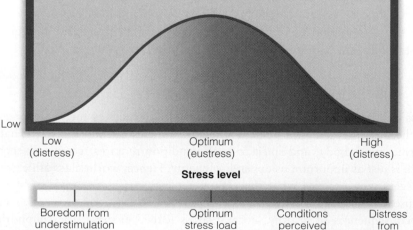

of the increasing difficulty of the task to be performed.[36] The stress response does provide momentary strength and physical force for brief periods of exertion, thus providing a basis for peak performance in athletic competition or other events. In addition, psychological well-being contributes positively to job performance.[37]

Specific stressful activities, including aerobic exercise, weight training, and flexibility training, improve health and enhance a person's ability to manage stressful demands or situations. Cannon argued that the stress response better prepares soldiers for combat.[38] In survival or combat situations, stress provides one with the necessary energy boost to manage the situation successfully.

The stress response is not inherently bad or destructive. The various individual and organizational forms of distress often associated with the word *stress* are the result of prolonged activation of the stress response, mismanagement of the energy induced by the response, or unique vulnerabilities in a person. We next examine the forms of individual distress and then the forms of organizational distress.

Individual Distress

An extreme preoccupation with work may result in acute individual distress, such as the unique Japanese phenomenon of *karoshi*, or death by overwork.[39] In general, individual distress usually takes one of the three basic forms shown in Table 7.2. Work-related psychological disorders are among the ten leading health disorders and diseases in the United States, according to the National Institute for Occupational Safety and Health.[40] The most common types of psychological distress are depression, burnout, and psychosomatic disorders. Depression and burnout can lead to emotional exhaustion with its associated negative consequences.[41] Emotional exhaustion may also be caused by the requirements for emotional expression on the job.[42] The Real World 7.1 discusses rust-out as another form of psychological distress. Psychosomatic disorders are physical disorders with a psychological origin. For example, the intense stress of public speaking may result in a speech disorder; that is, the person is under so much stress that the mind literally will not allow speech to occur.

A number of medical illnesses have a stress-related component.[43] The most significant medical illnesses of this form are heart disease and strokes, backaches, peptic ulcers, and headaches. Ford Motor Company found that cardiovascular diseases, the leading cause of death in the United States since 1910, constituted only 1.5 percent of the medical incidents among 800 salaried employees at its headquarters but accounted for 29 percent of the reported medical costs.[44] On the positive side, premature death and disability rates have dropped 24 to 36 percent since the mid-1970s. Backaches are a nonfatal medical problem to which stress contributes through the strong muscular contractions related to preparation for fight or flight. Headaches may be related to eyestrain or have a migraine component, but tension headaches are caused by the contraction of the head and neck muscles under stressful conditions. Finally, stress is a contributing factor to peptic ulcers. A popular comedian commented, "I don't get angry; I just grow a tumor!" There is no clear evidence that stress is a direct causal agent in the onset of cancer. However, stress may play an indirect role in the progression of the disease.[45]

Behavioral problems are the third form of individual distress. These problems include workplace aggression, substance abuse of various kinds, and accidents. Workplace agression may be triggered by perceptions of injustice in

Routing Rust-Out . . . at Sainsbury's and Elsewhere

Tom McPate is the occupational health manager at Sainsbury's, the British food retailer. While burnout was the disease of the dot.com era, rust-out may be the epidemic of this more sober decade. McPate discovered several years ago that the symptoms he was observing were alarmingly similar to burnout, such as depression and apathy which can lead to both physical ailments and psychological disorders, but the problem was not really burnout. *Rust-out* is a term used for over twenty years to describe workers who are wasting away, unchallenged and uninspired, at their desks. This is in contrast to workers who are burning out because they are over challenged and wholly consumed by the demands of their work.

Rust-out had previously been common among older workers and middle managers who had run out of gas. McPate found a new group suffering from rust-out: the young, overqualified workers stuck at first base in undemanding jobs. This lack of fit between educational achievement and job demands has created underemployment among some in the younger generation.

Here is one five-step approach that managers and employees can use to combat rust-out in their organizations.

1. *Spot it.* Performing regular stress audits can provide early warnings of rust-out.
2. *Prevent it.* A good fit between individual skills and job demands leads to engagement.
3. *Lead it.* Leaders can set the tone and be an example for healthy stress management.
4. *Confess it.* Always be willing to ask for help at the first signs of apathy or cynicism.
5. *Risk it.* Revisit your purpose at work and your definition of success.

SOURCE: I. Wylie, "Routing Rust-Out," © 2004 Gruner & Jahr USA Publishing. First published in *Fast Company* Magazine (January 2004): 40. Reprinted with permissions. http://www.fastcompany.com/magazinee/78/5things.html.

the workplace.[46] Interpersonal conflicts can be a form of nonphysical aggression. One study found that conflicts with workmates, neighbors, and other "nonintimates" account for about 80 percent of our bad moods.[47] Ethnic and cultural differences are too often a basis for interpersonal conflicts and may escalate into physical violence in the workplace. For example, some U.S. employees of Arab descent experienced ethnic slurs at work during the War on Terror with Iraq, a largely Arab nation.

Substance abuse ranges from legal behaviors such as alcohol abuse, excessive smoking, and the overuse of prescription drugs to illegal behaviors such as heroin addiction. Former surgeon general C. Everett Koop's war on smoking was warranted based on health risk information reported by the American Heart Association. However, the war on smoking also raises an ethical debate about the restriction of individual behavior. How far can the government or society go in restricting individual behavior that has adverse health consequences for many? This is even more problematic in light of recent research results showing the adverse health effects nonsmokers experience as a result of passive smoke.

Accidents, both on and off the job, are another behavioral form of distress that can sometimes be traced to work-related stressors. For example, an unresolved problem at work may continue to preoccupy or distract an employee driving home and result in the employee having an automobile accident.

These three forms of individual distress—psychological disorders, medical illnesses, and behavioral problems—cause a burden of personal suffering. They also cause a collective burden of suffering reflected in organizational distress.

The University of Michigan studies on organizational stress identified a variety of indirect costs of mismanaged stress for the organization, such as low morale, dissatisfaction, breakdowns in communication, and disruption of working relationships. Subsequent research at the Survey Research Center at Michigan established behavioral costing guidelines, which specify the direct costs of organizational distress.[48] New research suggests that even positive performance stereotypes can have an adverse effect on organizational health.[49]

Participation problems are the costs associated with absenteeism, tardiness, strikes and work stoppages, and turnover. In the case of absenteeism, the organization may compensate by hiring temporary personnel who take the place of the absentee, thus elevating personnel costs. When considering turnover, a distinction should be made between dysfunctional and functional turnover. Dysfunctional turnover occurs when an organization loses a valuable employee. It is costly for the organization. Replacement costs, including recruiting and retraining, for the valued employee range from five to seven months of the person's monthly salary. Functional turnover, in contrast, benefits the organization by creating opportunities for new members, new ideas, and fresh approaches. Functional turnover occurs when an organization loses an employee who has little or no value or is a problem. Functional turnover is good for the organization. The "up or out" promotion policy for members of some organizations is designed to create functional turnover.

Performance decrements are the costs resulting from poor quality or low quantity of production, grievances, and unscheduled machine downtime and repair. As in the case of medical illnesses, stress is not the only causal agent in these performance decrements. Stress does play a role, however, whether the poor quality or low quantity of production is motivated by distressed employees or by an unconscious response to stress on the job. In California, some employees have the option of taking a "stress leave" rather than filing a grievance against the boss.

Compensation awards are the organizational costs resulting from court awards for job distress.[50] One former insurance employee in Louisiana filed a federal suit against the company, alleging it created a high-strain job for him that resulted in an incapacitating depression.[51] A jury awarded him a $1.5 million judgment that was later overturned by the judge. Job stress-related claims have skyrocketed and threaten to bankrupt the workers' compensation system in some states, although claims and costs are down in other states.[52] However, employers need not panic because fair procedures go a long way toward avoiding legal liability, and legal rulings are setting realistic limits on employers' obligations.[53]

Individual Differences in the Stress–Strain Relationship

The same stressful events may lead to distress and strain for one person and to excitement and healthy results for another. Individual differences play a central role in the stress–strain relationship. The weak organ hypothesis in medicine, also known as the Achilles' heel phenomenon, suggests that a person breaks down at his or her weakest point. Some individual differences, such as gender and Type A behavior pattern, enhance vulnerability to strain under stressful conditions. Other individual differences, such as personality hardiness and self-reliance, reduce vulnerability to strain under stressful conditions.

participation problem
A cost associated with absenteeism, tardiness, strikes and work stoppages, and turnover.

performance decrement
A cost resulting from poor quality or low quantity of production, grievances, and unscheduled machine downtime and repair.

compensation award
An organizational cost resulting from court awards for job distress.

6. Discuss individual differences in the stress–strain relationship.

Reasearch has revealed that a woman's behavioral response to stress differs from a man's behavioral response.

Gender Effects

While prevailing stereotypes suggest that women are the weaker sex, the truth is that the life expectancy for American women is approximately seven years longer than for American men. This suggests that women may be stronger. The stereotype is challenged by research in public accounting, which finds that female public accountants have no higher turnover rates than males even though they report more stress, thus suggesting that women respond differently to stress.[54] This is further supported by research that finds women's behavioral responses to stress are in fact different from men's responses to stress.[55]

Some literature suggests that there are differences in the stressors to which the two sexes are subject.[56] For example, sexual harassment is a gender-related source of stress for many working women. There is also substantive evidence that the important differences in the sexes are in vulnerabilities.[57] For example, males are more vulnerable at an earlier age to fatal health problems, such as cardiovascular disorders, whereas women report more non-fatal, but long-term and disabling, health problems. Although we can conclude that gender indeed creates a differential vulnerability between the two sexes, it may actually be more important to examine the differences *among* women or *among* men.

Type A Behavior Pattern

Type A behavior pattern

A complex of personality and behavioral characteristics, including competitiveness, time urgency, social status insecurity, aggression, hostility, and a quest for achievements.

Type A behavior pattern is also labeled *coronary-prone behavior*.[58] *Type A behavior pattern* is a complex of personality and behavioral characteristics, including competitiveness, time urgency, social status insecurity, aggression, hostility, and a quest for achievements. Table 7.3 lists four primary components of the Type A behavior pattern.

There are two primary hypotheses concerning the lethal part of the Type A behavior pattern. One hypothesis suggests that the problem is time urgency, whereas the other hypothesis suggests that it is the hostility and aggression. The weight of evidence suggests that hostility and aggression, not time urgency, are the lethal agents.[59] Look back at your result in You 7.1. Are you too angry and overstressed?

The alternative to the Type A behavior pattern is the Type B behavior pattern. People with Type B personalities are relatively free of the Type A behaviors and characteristics identified in Table 7.3. Type B people are less coronary prone, but if they do have a heart attack, they do not appear to recover as well as those with Type A personalities. Organizations can also be characterized as Type A or Type B organizations.[60] Type A individuals in Type B organizations and Type B individuals in Type A organizations experience stress related to a misfit between their personality type and the pre-

7.3 TABLE 7.3   Type A Behavior Pattern Components

1. Sense of time urgency (a kind of "hurry sickness").
2. The quest for numbers (success is measured by the number of achievements).
3. Status insecurity (feeling unsure of oneself deep down inside).
4. Aggression and hostility expressed in response to frustration and conflict.

PART 2 INDIVIDUAL PROCESSES AND BEHAVIOR

dominant type of the organization. However, preliminary evidence suggests that Type A individuals in Type A organizations are most at risk of health disorders.

Type A behavior can be modified. The first step is recognizing that an individual is prone to the Type A pattern. Another possible step in modifying Type A behavior is to spend time with Type B individuals. Type B people often recognize Type A behavior and can help Type A individuals take hassles less seriously and see the humor in situations. Type A individuals can also pace themselves, manage their time well, and try not to do multiple things at once. Focusing only on the task at hand and its completion, rather than worrying about other tasks, can help Type A individuals cope more effectively.

Personality Hardiness

People who have personality hardiness resist strain reactions when subjected to stressful events more effectively than do people who are not hardy.[61] The components of *personality hardiness* are commitment (versus alienation), control (versus powerlessness), and challenge (versus threat). Commitment is a curiosity and engagement with one's environment that leads to the experience of activities as interesting and enjoyable. Control is an ability to influence the process and outcomes of events that leads to the experience of activities as personal choices. Challenge is the viewing of change as a stimulus to personal development, which leads to the experience of activities with openness.

The hardy personality appears to use these three components actively to engage in transformational coping when faced with stressful events.[62] *Transformational coping* is the act of actively changing an event into something less subjectively stressful by viewing it in a broader life perspective, by altering the course and outcome of the event through action, and/or by achieving greater understanding of the process. The alternative to transformational coping is regressive coping, a much less healthy form of coping with stressful events characterized by a passive avoidance of events by decreasing interaction with the environment. Regressive coping may lead to short-term stress reduction at the cost of long-term healthy life adjustment.

Self-Reliance

There is increasing evidence that social relationships have an important impact on health and life expectancy.[63] *Self-reliance* is a personality attribute related to how people form and maintain supportive attachments with others. Self-reliance was originally based in attachment theory, a theory about normal human development.[64] The theory identifies three distinct patterns of attachment, and research suggests that these patterns extend into behavioral strategies during adulthood, in professional as well as personal relationships.[65] Self-reliance results in a secure pattern of attachment and interdependent behavior. Interpersonal attachment is emotional and psychological connectedness to another person. The two insecure patterns of attachment are counterdependence and overdependence.

Self-reliance is a healthy, secure, *interdependent* pattern of behavior. It may appear paradoxical, because a person appears independent while maintaining a host of supportive attachments.[66] Self-reliant people respond to stressful, threatening situations by reaching out to others appropriately. Self-reliance is a flexible, responsive strategy of forming and maintaining multiple, diverse

personality hardiness
A personality resistant to distress and characterized by commitment, control, and challenge.

transformational coping
A way of managing stressful events by changing them into less subjectively stressful events.

self-reliance
A healthy, secure, *interdependent* pattern of behavior related to how people form and maintain supportive attachments with others.

counterdependence

An unhealthy, insecure pattern of behavior that leads to separation in relationships with other people.

overdependence

An unhealthy, insecure pattern of behavior that leads to preoccupied attempts to achieve security through relationships.

relationships. Self-reliant people are confident, enthusiastic, and persistent in facing challenges.

Counterdependence is an unhealthy, insecure pattern of behavior that leads to separation in relationships with other people. When faced with stressful and threatening situations, counterdependent people draw into themselves, attempting to exhibit strength and power. Counterdependence may be characterized as a rigid, dismissing denial of the need for other people in difficult and stressful times. Counterdependent people exhibit a fearless, aggressive, and actively powerful response to challenges.

Overdependence is also an unhealthy, insecure pattern of behavior. Overdependent people respond to stressful and threatening situations by clinging to other people in any way possible. Overdependence may be characterized as a desperate, preoccupied attempt to achieve a sense of security through relationships. Overdependent people exhibit an active but disorganized and anxious response to challenges. Overdependence prevents a person from being able to organize and maintain healthy relationships and thus creates much distress. It is interesting to note that both counterdependence and overdependence are exhibited by some military personnel who are experiencing adjustment difficulties during the first thirty days of basic training.[67] In particular, basic military trainees who have the most difficulty have overdependence problems and find it difficult to function on their own during the rigors of training.

You 7.2 gives you an opportunity to examine how self-reliant (interdependent), counterdependent, and/or overdependent you are.

Preventive Stress Management

7. Distinguish the primary, secondary, and tertiary stages of preventive stress management.

preventive stress management

An organizational philosophy that holds that people and organizations should take joint responsibility for promoting health and preventing distress and strain.

primary prevention

The stage in preventive stress management designed to reduce, modify, or eliminate the demand or stressor causing stress.

secondary prevention

The stage in preventive stress management designed to alter or modify the individual's or the organization's response to a demand or stressor.

tertiary prevention

The stage in preventive stress management designed to heal individual or organizational symptoms of distress and strain.

Stress is an inevitable feature of work and personal life. It is neither inherently bad nor destructive. Stress can be managed. The following is the central principle of *preventive stress management*: Individual and organizational distress are not inevitable. Preventive stress management is an organizational philosophy about people and organizations taking joint responsibility for promoting health and preventing distress and strain. Preventive stress management is rooted in the public health notions of prevention, which were first used in preventive medicine. The three stages of prevention are primary, secondary, and tertiary prevention. A framework for understanding preventive stress management is presented in Figure 7.2, which includes the three stages of prevention in a preventive medicine context, as well as an organizational context.

Primary prevention is intended to reduce, modify, or eliminate the demand or stressor causing stress. The idea behind primary prevention is to eliminate or ameliorate the source of a problem. True organizational stress prevention is largely primary in nature, because it changes and shapes the demands the organization places on people at work. *Secondary prevention* is intended to alter or modify the individual's or the organization's response to a demand or stressor. People must learn to manage the inevitable, inalterable work stressors and demands so as to avert distress and strain while promoting health and well-being. *Tertiary prevention* is intended to heal individual or organizational symptoms of distress and strain. The symptoms may range from early warning signs (such as headaches or absenteeism) to more severe forms of distress (such as hypertension, work stoppages, and strikes). One innovative approach that blends treatment and prevention with a full-time former grief counselor on staff is discussed in The Real World 7.2. We discuss these stages of prevention in the context of organizational prevention, individual prevention, and comprehensive health promotion.

Are You Self-Reliant?

Each of the following questions relates to how you form relationships with people at work, at home, and in other areas of your life. Read each statement carefully and rate each on a scale from 0 (strongly dis- agree) to 5 (strongly agree) to describe your degree of disagreement or agreement with the statement. *Answer all 15 questions.*

_4_ **1.** It is difficult for me to delegate work to others.
_3_ **2.** Developing close relationships at work will backfire on you.
_1_ **3.** I avoid depending on other people because I feel crowded by close relationships.
_1_ **4.** I am frequently suspicious of other people's motives and intentions.
_5_ **5.** Asking for help makes me feel needy, and I do not like that.
_4_ **6.** It is difficult for me to leave home or work to go to the other.
_5_ **7.** People will always be there when I need them.
_1_ **8.** I regularly and easily spend time with other people during the workday.
_5_ **9.** I trust at least two other people to have my best interests at heart.
_5_ **10.** I have a healthy, happy home life.
_0_ **11.** I need to have colleagues or subordinates close in order to feel secure about my work.
_5_ **12.** I become very concerned when I have conflict with family members at home.
_4_ **13.** I get very upset and disturbed if I have conflicts in relationship(s) at work.
_3_ **14.** I prefer very frequent feedback from my boss to know I am performing well.
_2_ **15.** I always consult others when I make decisions.

Scoring:

Follow the instructions to determine your score for each subscale of the Self-Reliance Inventory. *Note: Question 6 is used twice in scoring.*

Self-Reliance/Counterdependence

Step 1: Total your responses to Questions 1–6   _18_
Step 2: Total your responses to Questions 7–10   _16_
Step 3: Subtract your Step 2 total from 20 (20 − _16_) = _4_
Step 4: Add your results in Steps 1 and 3   _38_

Self-Reliance/Overdependence

Step 5: Total your responses to Questions 6 and 11–15   _4 + 14 = 18_

A score lower than 16 in Step 4 or Step 5 indicates self-reliance on that particular subscale. _NO_

A score higher than 20 in Step 4 suggests possible counterdependence and a score higher than 20 in Step 5 suggests possible overdependence. _NO_

SOURCE: Adapted from J. C. Quick, D. L. Nelson, and J. D. Quick, "The Self-Reliance Inventory," in J. W. Pfeiffer, ed., *The 1991 Annual: Developing Human Resources* (San Diego: Pfeiffer & Co., 1991), 149–161.

Organizational Stress Prevention

Some organizations are low-stress, healthy environments, whereas others are high-stress environments that may place their employees' health at risk. The experience of organizational justice and fairness is emerging as one contextual factor at work that leads to a positive low-stress work environment.[68] One comprehensive approach to organizational health and preventive stress management

8. Discuss organizational and individual methods of preventive stress management.

FIGURE 7.2   A Framework for Preventive Stress Management

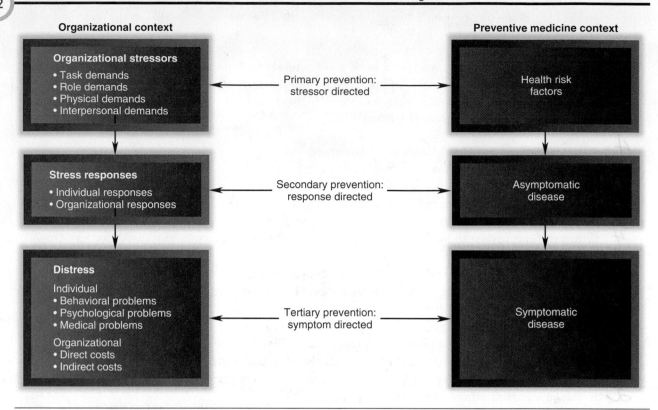

Organizational context

Organizational stressors
- Task demands
- Role demands
- Physical demands
- Interpersonal demands

Stress responses
- Individual responses
- Organizational responses

Distress

Individual
- Behavioral problems
- Psychological problems
- Medical problems

Organizational
- Direct costs
- Indirect costs

Preventive medicine context

Health risk factors

Asymptomatic disease

Symptomatic disease

Primary prevention: stressor directed

Secondary prevention: response directed

Tertiary prevention: symptom directed

SOURCE: J. D. Quick, R. S. Horn, and J. C. Quick, "Health Consequences of Stress," *Journal of Organizational Behavior Management* 8, No. 2, figure 1 (Fall 1986): 21. Reprinted with permission of Haworth Press, Inc., 10 Alice Street, Binghamton, NY 13904. Copyright 1986.

was pioneered in the U.S. Air Force by Colonel Joyce Adkins, who developed an Organizational Health Center (OHC) at the Sacramento Air Logistics Center.[69] The OHC's goal is to keep people happy, healthy, and on the job, while increasing efficiency and productivity to their highest levels by focusing on workplace stressors, organizational and individual forms of distress, and managerial and individual strategies for preventive stress management. This comprehensive, organizational health approach addresses primary, secondary, and tertiary prevention. Most organizational prevention, however, is primary prevention, including job redesign, goal setting, role negotiation, and career management. Two organizational stress prevention methods, team building and social support at work, are secondary prevention. Because team building is discussed extensively in Chapter 9, we do not discuss it separately here. Finally, companies such as Kraft Foods (a subsidiary of Altria Group, Inc.) and Hardee's Food Systems (part of CKE Restaurants, Inc.) have developed specific violence prevention programs to combat the rise in workplace violence. Violence in organizations is a category of dysfunctional behaviors that are often motivated by stressful events and whose negative consequences organizations want to prevent.[70]

JOB REDESIGN The job strain model presented in Figure 7.3 suggests that the combination of high job demands and restricted job decision latitude or worker control leads to a high-strain job. A major concern in job redesign should be to enhance worker control. Increasing worker control reduces distress and strain without necessarily reducing productivity in many cases.

Dead Hard Drive? . . . Oh, Good Grief!

DriveSavers was able to retrieve an episode of *The Simpsons* from a dead hard drive and alleviate a lot of headaches and rework.

One problem with personal computers is that the hard drive sometimes dies. This problem can be anywhere from a nuisance to a serious business problem. For example, the "Who Killed Mr. Burns?" episode of *The Simpsons* was lost to a hard-drive crash before it was finished and aired. DriveSavers got the call to recover the episode and save *The Simpsons*' bacon. The company was successful in doing so and is just one of two companies able to get data off dead hard drives. DriveSavers works on about 1,000 hard drives each month and has fixed a lot of celebrity drives, such as for *The Simpsons*. Companies and individuals pay anywhere from $1,000 to $25,000 for dead hard-drive service.

A dead hard drive, especially one in which the company loses all of its data, can cause big headaches and stress for DriveSavers' customers, which in turn can be transferred to DriveSavers' employees. So, the company has on staff a full-time grief counselor who used to do suicide prevention. Having a psychological expert for employees in time of need becomes a positive preventive resource for employees at DriveSavers in three possible ways. First, the company legitimizes stress, grief, and emotional toxins as potential problems, thus normalizing the human dilemma of dealing with difficult emotions. Second, the counselor is available for early intervention with employees before they are in crisis, helping them deal with their own emotions. Finally, the counselor can coach employees to relate positively to shocked, grief-stricken, distressed customers.

SOURCE: J. C. Dvorak, "Baffling," *PC Magazine* 3 (November 4, 2003): 61, http://www.pcmag.com/article2/0,4149,1369270,00.asp.

Job redesign to increase worker control is one strategy of preventive stress management. It can be accomplished in a number of ways, the most common being to increase job decision latitude. Increased job decision latitude might include greater decision authority over the sequencing of work activities, the timing of work schedules, the selection and sequencing of work tools, or the selection of work teams. A second objective of job redesign should be to reduce uncertainty and increase predictability in the workplace. Uncertainty is a major stressor.

GOAL SETTING Organizational preventive stress management can also be achieved through goal-setting activities. These activities are designed to increase task motivation, as discussed in Chapter 6, while reducing the degree of role conflict and ambiguity to which people at work are subject. Goal setting focuses a person's attention while directing energy into a productive channel. Implicit in much of the goal-setting literature is the assumption that people participate in, and accept, their work goals. Chapter 6 addressed goal setting in depth.

ROLE NEGOTIATION The organizational development technique of role negotiation has value as a stress management method because it allows people to modify their work roles.[71] Role negotiation begins with the

FIGURE 7.3 Job Strain Model

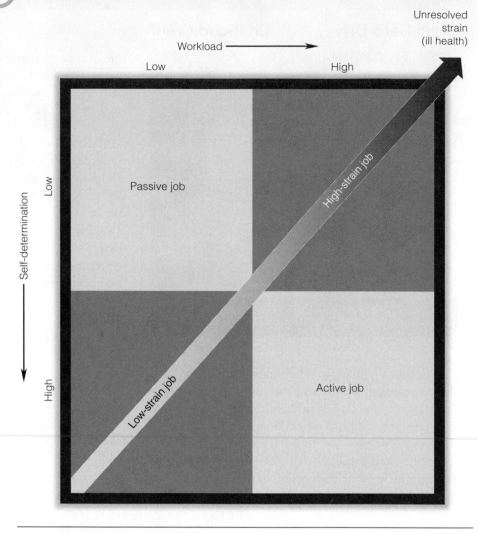

SOURCE: B. Gardell, "Efficiency and Health Hazards in Mechanized Work," in J. C. Quick, R. S. Bhagat, J. E. Dalton, and J. D. Quick, eds., *Work Stress: Health Care Systems in the Workplace.* Copyright © 1987. Reproduced with permission of Greenwood Publishing Group, Inc., Westport, CT.

definition of a specific role, called the focal role, within its organizational context. The person in the focal role then identifies the expectations understood for that role, and key organizational members specify their expectations of the person in the focal role. The actual negotiation follows from the comparison of the role incumbent's expectations and key members' expectations. The points of confusion and conflict are opportunities for clarification and resolution. The final result of the role negotiation process should be a clear, well-defined focal role with which the incumbent and organizational members are all comfortable.

SOCIAL SUPPORT SYSTEMS Team building, discussed in Chapter 9, is one way to develop supportive social relationships in the workplace. However, team building is primarily task oriented, not socioemotional, in nature. Although employees may receive much of their socioemotional support from personal relationships outside the workplace, some socioemotional support within the workplace is also necessary for psychological well-being.

Social support systems can be enhanced through the work environment in a number of ways. Interpersonal communication is the key to unlocking social support for preventive stress management.[72] Figure 7.4 identifies key elements in a person's work and nonwork social support system. These relations provide emotional caring, information, evaluative feedback, modeling, and instrumental support.

Individual Prevention

Clinical research shows that individuals may use a number of self-directed interventions to help prevent distress and enhance positive well-being.[73] Individual prevention can be of a primary, secondary, or tertiary nature. The primary prevention activities we discuss are learned optimism, time management, and leisure time activities. The secondary prevention activities we discuss are physical exercise, relaxation, and diet. The tertiary prevention activities we discuss are opening up and professional help. These eight methods and their benefits are summarized in Table 7.4.

POSITIVE THINKING The power of positive thinking is found as an optimistic, nonnegative thinking style used by people to explain the good and bad events in their lives to themselves.[74] A positive, optimistic explanatory style is a habit of thinking learned over time, though some people are predisposed to positive thinking. Pessimism is an alternative explanatory style leading to depression, physical health problems, and low levels of achievement. In contrast, positive thinking and optimism enhance physical health and achievement and avert susceptibility to depression.

Optimistic people avoid distress by viewing the bad events and difficult times in their lives as temporary, limited, and caused by something other than

FIGURE 7.4   Social Support at Work and Home

7.4

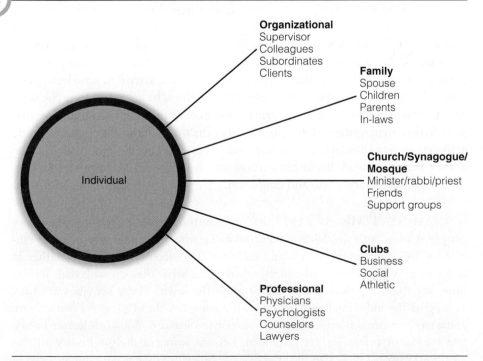

SOURCE: From J. C. Quick, J. D. Quick, D. L. Nelson, and J. J. Hurrell, Jr., in *Preventive Stress Management in Organizations*, 1997, p. 198. Copyright © 1997 by The American Psychological Association. Reprinted with permission.

Primary Prevention

Positive thinking:	Optimistic, nonnegative self-talk that reduces depression.
Time management:	Improves planning and prioritizes activities.
Leisure time activity:	Balances work and nonwork activities.

Secondary Prevention

Physical exercise:	Improves cardiovascular function and muscular flexibility.
Relaxation training:	Lowers all indicators of the stress response.
Diet:	Lowers the risk of cardiovascular disease and improves overall physical health.

Tertiary Prevention

Opening up:	Releases internalized traumas and emotional tensions.
Professional help:	Provides information, emotional support, and therapeutic guidance.

themselves. Optimistic people face difficult times and adversity with hope. Optimistic people take more credit for the good events in their lives; they see these good events as more pervasive and generalized. Learned optimism begins with identifying pessimistic thoughts and then distracting oneself from these thoughts or disputing them with evidence and alternative thoughts. Learned optimism is nonnegative thinking. This is one of the five dimensions of positive organizational behavior (POB), the other four dimensions being confidence/self-efficacy, hope, subjective well-being/happiness, and emotional intelligence.[75]

TIME MANAGEMENT Time pressure is one of the major sources of stress listed in Table 7.1 for people both at work and in school. The leading symptoms of poor time management include constant rushing, missed deadlines, work overload and the sense of being overwhelmed, insufficient rest time, and indecision. Good time managers are "macro" time managers who use a GP³ method of time management.[76] The GP³ method includes (1) setting *goals* that are challenging yet attainable; (2) *prioritizing* these goals in terms of their relative importance; (3) *planning* for goal attainment through specific tasks, activities, scheduling, and even delegation; and (4) *praising* oneself for specific achievements along the way. Setting concrete goals and prioritizing these goals are the most important first steps in time management skills, ensuring that the most important work and study activities receive enough time and attention. This system of time management enables a person to track his or her success over time and goes a long way toward reducing unnecessary stress and confusion.

LEISURE TIME ACTIVITIES Unremitted striving characterizes many people with a high need for achievement. Leisure time activities provide employees an opportunity for rest and recovery from strenuous activities either at home or at work. Many individuals, when asked what they do with their leisure time, say that they clean the house or mow the lawn. These activities are fine, as long as the individual gets the stress-reducing benefit of pleasure from them. Some say our work ethic is a cultural barrier to pleasure. We work longer hours, and two-income families are the norm. Leisure is increasingly a luxury among working people. The key to the effective use of leisure time is enjoyment. Leisure time can be used for spontaneity, joy, and connection with others in our lives.

While vacations can be a relief from job burnout, there can be fade-out effects.[77] Hence, leisure time and vacations must be periodic, recurring activities.

PHYSICAL EXERCISE Different types of physical exercise are important secondary stress prevention activities for individuals. Colleges and universities often implement physical exercise through physical education classes, while military organizations implement it through physical fitness standards. Aerobic exercise improves a person's responsiveness to stressful activities. Kenneth Cooper has long advocated aerobic exercise.[78] Research at the Aerobics Center in Dallas has found that aerobically fit people (1) have lower levels of adrenaline in their blood at rest; (2) have a slower, stronger heart functioning; and (3) recover from stressful events more quickly.

Flexibility training is an important type of exercise because of the muscular contractions associated with the stress response. One component of the stress response is the contraction of the flexor muscles, which prepares a person to fight or flee. Flexibility training enables a person to stretch and relax these muscles to prevent the accumulation of unnecessary muscular tension.[79] Flexibility exercises help maintain joint mobility, increase strength, and play an important role in the prevention of injury.

RELAXATION TRAINING Herbert Benson was one of the first people to identify the relaxation response as the natural counterresponse to the stress response.[80] In studying Western and Eastern peoples, Benson found that Judeo-Christian people have elicited this response through their time-honored tradition of prayer, whereas Eastern people have elicited it through meditation. The relaxation response does not require a theological or religious component. If you have a practice of regular prayer or meditation, you may already elicit the relaxation response regularly. Keep in mind that digestion may interfere with the elicitation of the response, so avoid practicing relaxation shortly after eating.

DIET Diet may play an indirect role in stress and stress management. High sugar content in the diet can stimulate the stress response, and foods high in cholesterol can adversely affect blood chemistry. Good dietary practices contribute to a person's overall health, making the person less vulnerable to distress. In his nonsurgical, nonpharmacological approach to reversing heart disease, Dean Ornish proposes a very stringent "reversal diet" for people with identifiable blockage of the arteries.[81] Ornish recommends a somewhat less stringent "prevention diet" as one of four elements for opening up the arteries. Another element in his program is being open in relationships with other people.

OPENING UP Everyone experiences a traumatic, stressful, or painful event in life at one time or another. One of the most therapeutic, curative responses to such an event is to confide in another person.[82] Discussing difficult experiences with another person is not always easy, yet health benefits, immune system improvement, and healing accrue through self-disclosure. In one study comparing those who wrote once a week about traumatic events with those who wrote about nontraumatic events, significant health benefits and reduced absenteeism were found in the first group.[83] Confession need not be through a personal relationship with friends. It may occur through a private diary. For example, a lawyer might write each evening about all of his or her most troubling thoughts, feelings, and emotions during the course of the day. The process of opening up and confessing appears to counter the detrimental effects of stress.

PROFESSIONAL HELP Confession and opening up may occur through professional helping relationships. People who need healing have psychological counseling, career counseling, physical therapy, medical treatment, surgical intervention, and other therapeutic techniques available. Employee assistance programs (EAPs) may be very helpful in referring employees to the appropriate caregivers. Even combat soldiers who experience battle stress reactions severe enough to take them out of action can heal and be ready for subsequent combat duty.[84] The early detection of distress and strain reactions, coupled with prompt professional treatment, can be instrumental in averting permanent physical and psychological damage.

Comprehensive Health Promotion

Whereas organizational stress prevention is aimed at eliminating health risks at work, comprehensive health promotion programs are aimed at establishing a "strong and resistent host" by building on individual prevention and lifestyle change.[85] Physical fitness and exercise programs characterize corporate health promotion programs in the United States and Canada.[86] A health promotion and wellness survey of accredited medical schools in the United States, Canada, and Puerto Rico found that these programs place the most emphasis on physical well-being and the least emphasis on spiritual well-being.[87] A new approach to comprehensive health promotion places the focus on the organization and organizational wellness.[88] Still, social and cognitive processes are key considerations in the successful implementation of stress prevention programs.[89]

Johnson & Johnson developed a comprehensive health promotion program with a significant number of educational modules for individuals and groups. These educational modules addressed a specific topic, such as Type A behavior, exercise, diet (through cooperative activities with the American Heart Association), stress, and risk assessment (through regular risk assessments and health profiles for participants). Johnson & Johnson found that the health status of employees who are not participating in health promotion programs in the workplace improves if the worksite does have a health promotion program.

Managerial Implications: Stress Without Distress

Stress is an inevitable result of work and personal life. Distress is not an inevitable consequence of stressful events, however; in fact, well-managed stress can improve health and performance. Managers must learn how to create healthy stress for employees to facilitate performance and well-being without distress. Managers can help employees by adjusting workloads, avoiding ethical dilemmas, being sensitive to diversity among individuals concerning what is stressful, and being sensitive to employees' personal life demands.

New technologies create demands and stress for employees. Managers can help employees adjust to new technologies by ensuring that their design and implementation are sensitive to employees and that employee involvement is strong.

Managers can be sensitive to early signs of distress at work, such as employee fatigue or changes in work habits, in order to avoid serious forms of distress. The serious forms of distress include violent behavior, psychological depression, and cardiovascular problems. Distress is important to the organization because of the costs associated with turnover and absenteeism, as well as poor-quality production.

Managers should be aware of gender, personality, and behavioral differences when analyzing stress in the workplace. Men and women have different vulnerabilities when it comes to distress. Men are at greater risk of fatal disorders, for example, and women are more vulnerable to nonfatal disorders, such as depression. Managers should be aware that even positive performance stereotypes may place undue stress on employees, leading to chronic disorders such as hypertension. Personality hardiness and self-reliance are helpful in managing stressful events.

Managers can use the principles and methods of preventive stress management to create healthier work environments. They can practice several forms of individual stress prevention to create healthier lifestyles for themselves, and they can encourage employees to do the same. Large organizations can create healthier workforces through the implementation of comprehensive health promotion programs. Setting an example is one of the best things a manager can do for employees when it comes to preventive stress management.

LOOKING BACK: PIXAR ANIMATION STUDIOS

Every Story Does Not Have a Happy Ending . . .

Contrary to the Hollywood myth, every story, every act, and every scene does not have a happy ending. The Thinking Ahead feature portrays the happy and magical quality of Pixar Studios. Of course, the story never ends until the final curtain, so work and life are an ongoing process of stress and challenge. Death is the only way to avoid stress and is not a good alternative when one has positive skills and tools for preventive stress management. However, speed bumps at work are an occurrence that managers and employees alike need to anticipate and recognize as inevitable. Pixar Studios hit one of these speed bumps when Pixar's Steve Jobs and Disney's Michael Eisner got into a high-stress conflict that led Pixar to walk away from Mickey Mouse & Company.

Steve Jobs is one of his generation's most creative and accomplished entrepreneurs who first made his mark by cofounding Apple in 1976. His defining characteristic is an unalloyed confidence that borders on arrogance: that his own judgment is correct. He combines this great confidence with extraordinary powers of persuasion. These two personality features are said to create a "reality distortion field" that surrounds him and enables him to convince anyone in his immediate vicinity that he is right. Wow! With this confidence and power of persuasion, Jobs entered the computer-animated film business when he bought Pixar for $10 million in 1986. Pixar's five films have brought in $2.5 billion in revenues, and Jobs became a billionaire himself when the company went public in 1995. All this had to be positive and exhilarating.

However, it's not over 'til it's over. The stress and tension in Steve Jobs and Michael Eisner's relationship built up when Jobs wanted to rewrite their agreement so that Pixar got more than half of the profits from *The Incredibles* and *Cars*, two Pixar films scheduled for release in 2004 and 2005 under the Disney agreement. Disney refused to rewrite the deal because it would have cost the company hundreds of millions of dollars. By walking away from Disney, Steve Jobs is costing Pixar some significant profits over the next two years, profits that would have accrued had Jobs succeeded in winning a better deal. However, hardly anyone at a senior level left Pixar Studios, and Steve Jobs' judgment has proved correct in some big-stakes situations. While the company has some challenges to meet as a result of the change, Steve Jobs' personal stress level is way down because he does not have to deal with Michael Eisner. Yes, some stories do have a happy ending.[90]

Chapter Summary

1. Stress is the unconscious preparation to fight or flee when faced with any demand. Distress is the adverse consequence of stress.

2. Four approaches to understanding stress are the homeostatic/medical approach, the cognitive appraisal approach, the person–environment fit approach, and the psychoanalytic approach.

3. The stress response is a natural mind–body response characterized by four basic mind–body changes.

4. Employees face task, role, interpersonal, and physical demands at work, along with nonwork demands. Globalization, international competition, and advanced technologies create new stresses at work.

5. Nonwork stressors, such as family problems and work–home conflicts, can affect an individual's work life and home life.

6. Stress has health benefits, including enhanced performance.

7. Distress is costly to both individuals and organizations.

8. Individual diversity requires attention to gender, Type A behavior, personality hardiness, and self-reliance in determining the links between stress and strain.

9. Preventive stress management aims to enhance health and reduce distress or strain. Primary prevention focuses on the stressor, secondary prevention focuses on the response to the stressor, and tertiary prevention focuses on symptoms of distress.

Key Terms

compensation award (p. 225)
counterdependence (p. 228)
distress (p. 214)
ego-ideal (p. 216)
homeostasis (p. 216)
overdependence (p. 228)
participation problem (p. 225)
performance decrement (p. 225)

personality hardiness (p. 227)
preventive stress management (p. 228)
primary prevention (p. 228)
secondary prevention (p. 228)
self-image (p. 216)
self-reliance (p. 227)
strain (p. 214)

stress (p. 214)
stressor (p. 214)
tertiary prevention (p. 228)
transformational coping (p. 227)
Type A behavior pattern (p. 226)
workaholism (p. 221)

Review Questions

1. Define *stress*, *distress*, and *strain*.

2. Describe four approaches to understanding stress. How does each add something new to our understanding of stress?

3. What are the four changes associated with the stress response?

4. List three demands of each type: task, role, interpersonal, and physical.

5. What is a nonwork demand? How does it affect an individual?

6. Describe the relationship between stress and performance.

7. What are the major medical consequences of distress? The behavioral consequences? The psychological consequences?

8. Why should organizations be concerned about stress at work? What are the costs of distress to organizations?

9. How do individual differences such as gender, Type A behavior, personality hardiness, and self-reliance moderate the relationship between stress and strain?

10. What is primary prevention? Secondary prevention? Tertiary prevention? Describe major organizational stress prevention methods.

11. Describe eight individual preventive stress management methods.

12. What is involved in comprehensive health promotion programs?

Discussion and Communication Questions

1. Why should organizations help individuals manage stress? Isn't stress basically the individual's responsibility?

2. Is there more stress today than in past generations? What evidence is available concerning this question?

3. Discuss the following statement: Employers should be expected to provide stress-free work environments.

4. If an individual claims to have job-related anxiety or depression, should the company be liable?

5. Do you use any stress prevention methods that are not discussed in the chapter? If so, what are they?

6. (*communication question*) Write a memo describing the most challenging demands and/or stressors at your workplace (or university). Be specific in describing the details of these demands and/or stressors. How might you go about changing these demands and/or stressors?

7. (*communication question*) Interview a medical doctor, a psychologist, or another health care professional about the most common forms of health problems and distress seen in their work. Summarize your interview and compare the results to the categories of distress discussed in the chapter.

8. (*communication question*) Do research on social support and diaries as ways to manage stressful and/or traumatic events. Develop an oral presentation for class that explains the benefits of each of these approaches for preventive stress management. Include guidelines on how to practice each.

Ethical Dilemma

Josh Newland is very excited about the proposal that sits on his desk. If this proposal is accepted, it could be the turning point in his career. Josh is an analyst for Barnes and Associates, a financial services company. Josh has been with the company for five years and is beginning to be noticed. He has put a lot of time and effort into this proposal in hopes of turning that attention into a promotion. He just wishes he felt better about turning it in.

Josh looked up from the proposal to the pictures on his desk. The eyes of his wife and two sons look back. They are the only drawbacks to this proposal being the success Josh is certain it will be. The promotion Josh wants so badly would allow even less time to spend with Mary and the kids. But he has worked very hard to get where he is. His parents had worked hard to send him to the best schools. It would be wrong to ignore everyone's efforts.

But Mary has worked hard too. She has career dreams as well. While she is happy to take time off while the children are small, she has definite plans to return to work. However, if Josh gets this promotion, there will be little time for him to support her career as she has supported his. He would not be able to watch the kids while Mary works late nights to get noticed. Nor would he be able to perform any other parental duties so that Mary would not have to ask for time off. Mary has so willingly put her ca-

reer on hold so that they could have a family. Is it fair not to give her a chance to regain what she has lost? Is it right to allow his sons to grow up with a dad who is rarely there? But is it wrong for him to take advantage of the best career opportunity he may ever have? He only wants to provide the best life possible for his family.

Questions

1. Does Josh have a responsibility to question submitting this proposal?

2. Evaluate Josh's alternatives using rule, virtue, rights, and justice theories.

Experiential Exercises

7.1 Gender Role Stressors

The major sources of stress are not necessarily the same for men and women. This exercise will help you identify the similarities and differences in the stressors and perceptions of men and women.

Step 1. Individually, list the major sources of stress for you because of your gender. Be as specific as possible, and within your list, prioritize your stressors.

Step 2. Individually, list what you think are the major sources of stress for those of the opposite gender. Again, be as specific as possible, and prioritize your list.

Step 3. In teams of five or six members of the same sex, share your two lists of stressors. Discuss these

stressors, and identify the top five sources of stress for your group because of your gender and the top five sources of stress for those of the opposite gender. Again, be as specific as possible, and prioritize your list.

Step 4. The class will then engage in a cross-team exchange of lists. Look for similarities and differences among the teams in your class as follows. Select one gender to be addressed first. If the females are first, for example, the male groups will post their predictions. This will be followed by the actual stressor lists from the female groups. Then do the same for the other gender.

7.2 Workplace Stress Diagnosis

The following exercise gives you an opportunity to work within a group to compare the work demands and job stressors found in different work settings. Intervention for preventive stress management should always be based on a good diagnosis. This exercise gives you a start in this direction.

Step 1. Rate the degree to which each of the following work demands is a source of stress for you and your coworkers at work. Use a 7-point rating scale for assigning the stressfulness of the work demand, with 7 = very high source of stress, 4 = moderate source of stress, and 1 = very little source of stress.

___ Uncertainty about various aspects of the work environment

___ Lack of control over people, events, or other aspects of work

___ Lack of career opportunities and progress

___ The implementation of new technologies

___ Work overload; that is, too much to do and not enough time

___ Conflicting expectations from one or more people at work

___ Confusing expectations from one or more people at work

___ Dangerous working conditions and/or hazardous substances

___ Sexual harassment by supervisors, coworkers, or others

___ Abrasive personalities and/or political conflicts

___ Rigid, insensitive, unresponsive supervisors or managers

Step 2. Write a brief description of the most stressful event that has occurred in your work environment during the past twelve-month period.

Step 3. The class will form into groups of approximately six members each. Each group elects a spokesperson and then compares the information developed by each person in Steps 1 and 2. In the process of this comparison, answer the following questions:

a. What are the similarities between work environments in terms of their most stressful work demands?

b. What are the differences among work environments in terms of their most stressful work demands?

c. Are there similarities in the descriptions of the most stressful events? If so, what are they?

Step 4. Each group will share the results of its answers to the questions in Step 3. Cross-team questions and discussion follow.

Step 5 (Optional). Your instructor may ask you to choose one or another of the work environments in which to develop some preventive stress management strategies. Complete parts a and b below in your group.

a. Identify one to three preventive stress management strategies that you think are the best to use in the work environment. Why have you chosen them?

b. How should the effectiveness of these strategies be evaluated?

Biz Flix | Meet the Parents

Greg Focker (Ben Stiller) hopes his weekend visit to his girlfriend Pam's (Teri Polo) home will leave a positive impression on her parents. Unfortunately, Jack (Robert De Niro), Pam's father, immediately dislikes him. Jack's fondness does not improve after Greg accidentally breaks the urn holding Jack's mother's ashes. Other factors do not help the developing relationship: Greg is Jewish, while Jack is a WASP ex-CIA psychological profiler. These factors blend well to cause the continuous development of stress and stress responses of all parties involved.

The scene from *Meet the Parents* comes from the "Bomb's the Word" segment in the last quarter of the film. Greg has boarded his flight to return home after his excruciating weekend visit with Pam's family. By this time, he has experienced an almost endless stream of stressors: meeting Pam's parents for the first time, taking a polygraph test administered by Jack, adjusting to Jinx the Himalayan cat's odd behavior, and . . . the film continues to a predictable happy ending.

What to Watch for and Ask Yourself:

> Does Greg experience the stress response during this scene? What evidence appears in the scene?

> Does he experience distress or eustress?

> Why does Greg respond so harshly to the simple request to check his bag?

Workplace Video | Fallon Worldwide: Corporate Culture

Fallon Worldwide is a growing advertising agency with billings of more than $800 million per year and a client list that reads like a Who's Who of corporate giants. The Minneapolis-based ad firm is known for its creative culture, and the people who work at Fallon rave about the company's cozy, quirky, sometimes outrageous spirit.

But when Paris-based Publicis Group SA announced its acquisition of the agency, worry was on everyone's mind. There was a lurking fear that the firm could lose the inspiring environment and creative freedom that helped make the company great. The agency's founders, however, firmly believed that keeping everyone calm and comfortable boiled down to one thing: culture. By focusing upon preserving Fallon's fun and laid back corporate culture, employees would be able to continue producing their very best creative in a pleasant, productive workplace.

There's no doubt that Fallon will face difficult challenges as it seeks to integrate with Publicis without losing its own identity or talented staff. But employees appear confident that by leaning on the company's unique culture, they will be able to handle change and continue to deliver top-notch creativity for clients.

Questions

1. *Describe some of the fun and unusual features of Fallon's unique work environment. How might Fallon's creative culture affect workers' stress and well-being?*
2. *Why are globalization and new technology sources of on-the-job pressure and stress?*
3. *What stress prevention measures can be implemented at both the organizational and individual levels to help Fallon's employees manage stress and stay productive?*

The American Red Cross: Providing Training to Protect Employees' Health and Safety

The American Red Cross (ARC), with well over a million volunteers, is the largest humanitarian organization in the world. The ARC also provides about half of the nation's blood supply and about one-quarter of the tissue used for transplantation. In addition, the Red Cross trains millions of people in vital life-saving skills, mobilizes relief to victims in thousands of disasters nationwide, provides direct health services to millions of people, assists international disaster and conflict victims in more than 50 countries, and transmits hundreds of thousands of emergency messages to the members of the Armed Forces and their families.

But these activities are not all that the American Red Cross does. To increase its workplace relevancy, the American Red Cross has introduced a variety of training programs that are designed to create a safer workplace and to protect employees' health and safety. Included in the program mix are courses in first aid, cardiopulmonary resuscitation (CPR), use of automated external defibrillator (AED) machines, dealing with workplace violence, reducing repetitive motion injuries and back injuries, preventing disease transmission from bloodborne pathogens, oxygen administration for breathing problems, and controlling risk factors for heart disease, among others.

Some of the more notable workplace training efforts of the American Red Cross include two different programs that provide first-aid training for employees. One program is an hour to an hour-and-one-half long and the other, much more comprehensive one is five-and-one-half hours long. Another ARC workplace initiative is a half-day program on adult CPR that is designed to prepare employees to deal with cardiac and breathing emergencies in adults. Another workplace program involves a series of one-hour injury control modules that focus on ergonomics; workplace violence awareness; slips, trips, and falls; managing stress; back injury prevention; and the benefits of a healthy heart. In the injury control modules, self-assessments are used to help employees identify risky habits they are pursuing and tips are offered for preventing the occurrence of injuries.

Employers can select from these courses to create a training package that meets their particular needs. Program costs depend on the number of employees taking part and the number of courses in the training package. Businesses can also have an employee trained as a trainer in order to have an in-house training resource.

Three American Red Cross training programs are especially relevant to the experience of stress in the workplace. These training programs focus on rapid response to workplace heart attacks, preparedness for workplace violence, and stress management/reduction.

Heart attacks are often stress-related events. A quick response is often essential to saving a person's life. Consequently, having employees who are trained in emergency resuscitation techniques can make the difference between life and death for someone having a heart attack in the workplace. To prepare businesses for handling situations like these, the American Red Cross offers a training program that combines basic first aid, cardiopulmonary resuscitation, and the use of automated external defibrillators. Through lectures, videos, live demonstrations, and hands-on activities, this training program teaches employees of a business "how to administer CPR, how to use an AED for an adult cardiac arrest, and how to recognize other injuries."

Another stress-related event is workplace violence. Indeed, workplace violence can be a response to stress that emanates from work and/or nonwork sources. Moreover, workplace violence can create additional stress for its victims. The American Red Cross is helping to address workplace violence through a training module that was introduced in early 2000. The focus of this training module is to help employees recognize the warning signs of workplace violence as well as to reduce their chances of becoming a victim of workplace violence. "As with any emergency preparedness training, the workplace violence training offers employees steps to take that could help them react quickly and calmly in a crisis."

The American Red Cross also provides a program for managing and reducing stress. This program is designed to help workers identify sources of stress and provides exposure to techniques for reducing stress.

Increased interest in the various workplace training programs provided by the ARC is a direct reflection of employers' increased concern with workplace safety. The concern with safety, in turn, is traceable to an aging workforce and terrorism. Another reason for the increased interest in ARC training programs is that "more and more businesses have begun to realize that their employees are their most valuable resource."

Discussion Questions

1. Why would an organization like the American Red Cross be interested in providing businesses with training programs that deal with stress-related issues?

2. What can the American Red Cross training programs accomplish in terms of equipping organizations to better deal with workplace stress or its consequences?

3. How could you personally benefit from the American Red Cross training programs that are related to the issue of workplace stress?

SOURCE: This case was written by Michael K. McCuddy, The Louis S. and Mary L. Morgal Chair of Christian Business Ethics and Professor of Management, College of Business Administration, Valparaiso University. This case was developed from material contained on the American Red Cross Web site at http://www.redcross.org and in the following articles: N. Glor, "Red Cross Training Helps Preserve Human Resources," *Health-Care Quarterly* (August 8, 2003): 4A–4B; A. Keen, "Red Cross Increasing Workplace Safety Training," *Fort Worth Business Press* (June 16, 2000): 16; E. Hlotyak, "Workers Learn to Provide Emergency Cardiac," *Westchester County Business Journal* (February 19, 2001): 18; K. Watt, "Red Cross Offers Workplace Training Courses," *Inside Tucson Business* (January 22, 2001): 9.

Google™ (B)

When Larry Page and Sergey Brin first met as doctoral students in computer science at Stanford University, they argued about everything they discussed. Both had strong opinions and differing viewpoints, but eventually they found "common ground in a unique approach to solving one of computing's biggest challenges: retrieving relevant information from a massive set of data."

Interestingly, Brin and Page had backgrounds that were both similar and dissimilar. Thirty-year-old Brin, originally from Moscow and the son of a mathematics professor, had trained on the trapeze with the intent of joining the circus. Prior to entering Stanford, he received a bachelor's degree with honors in mathematics and computer science from the University of Maryland. Thirty-one-year-old Page, from Lansing, Michigan, has had a love affair with computers for nearly his entire life. The son of a Michigan State University computer science professor, Page, who started using computers at six years of age, earned a bachelor's degree with honors in computer engineering from the University of Michigan.

As doctoral students at Stanford University, both Page and Brin were passionate about their collaborative research that focused on creating a unique Internet search engine. They broke away from the common practice of designing a search engine to focus on the frequency with which a given word appeared on a Web site. Instead of this commonly used approach, Brin and Page developed a search engine that reflected both the relevance of a Web site to a search query and the number of other Web pages that linked to that Web site. Creating the search engine was a time-consuming process that increasingly took over their lives. Even though Brin and Page committed long hours to their work, they made sure they had fun with it.

The Challenges of Growing Google

The potential of the search engine soon became apparent, and the rapid march toward commercial-ization soon took place. Brin and Page founded Google Inc., which grew rapidly in terms of search engine usage but struggled to generate an ongoing stream of substantial revenue. What little revenue the company generated was mostly from licensing the search service to other Internet sites. Brin and Page were geniuses at computer technology and sensing what search engine users wanted, but they were not as skilled at handling the organizational and operational issues of the business and at transforming the company into a profitable, revenue-generating enterprise. Realizing their limitations, and under pressure from the company's board of directors, Brin and Page sought out professional business management expertise.

Eric Schmidt, who has a bachelor's degree in electrical engineering from Princeton University as well as masters and doctoral degrees in computer science from the University of California-Berkley, was recruited to be chairman of the executive committee and chief executive officer of Google Inc. Previously, Schmidt had been chairman and CEO at Novell, where he led the company's strategic planning, management, and technology development. Schmidt's leadership of Novell capped "a 20-year record of achievement as an Internet strategist, entrepreneur, and developer of great technologies." Schmidt, in his late 40s and almost old enough to be Brin's or Page's father, became the professional business counterbalance to the youthful exuberance of Page and Brin. Schmidt, however, "wasn't interested in pushing them aside, or in replacing the culture they had created." Instead, Schmidt focused on transforming Google into a sustainable business enterprise.

Getting Other People to Be Dedicated and Passionate— and to Have Fun

Preserving the company's culture while transforming the company into a self-sustaining business required, among other things, the ongoing recruitment of employees who would be a "good fit" with Google's culture and keeping employees excited about working for the company. All employees are called *Googlers*—

a designation that conveys a profound belief in the employees' commitment to and excitement about the company and the opportunities that it provides.

Brin and Page are involved in all hiring decisions, and work experience counts far less than educational background. Brin, Page, and Schmidt agree that brainpower is often valued more than experience. Schmidt notes that the result has been a company where fewer people are needed to accomplish more. As of mid-2004, Google has grown to the point of having more than 1,900 employees, including "some of the most experienced technology and business professionals" in California's Silicon Valley. Jobs at Google are highly desirable—approximately 1,000 people apply every day.

Google identifies its top ten reasons for people desiring to work at the company. These reasons, which reveal much about the company's culture, management philosophy, leadership, and employees, are:

> *Lend a helping hand*—employees help to connect people with the information they need.

> *Life is beautiful*—being a part of making a meaningful difference is remarkably fulfilling.

> *Appreciation is the best motivation*—Google has a fun and inspiring workplace that shows employees the company truly cares about them.

> *Work and play are not mutually exclusive*—both can be accomplished within the workplace.

> *We love our employees, and we want them to know it*—Google provides a family-friendly environment and a range of benefits to appeal to employees.

> *Innovation is our bloodline*—Google provides endless opportunities for employees to develop technological innovations.

> *Good company everywhere you look*—the employees' diversity of backgrounds and talents makes for interesting co-workers.

> *Uniting the world, one user at a time*—as a global company, Google seeks to contribute to making the world a better place.

> *Boldly go where no man has gone before*—Google provides employees with numerous challenges and opportunities to be innovative and creative.

> *There is such a thing as a free lunch after all*—Google provides free lunches to employees.

According to Google insiders, "You won't find any bored engineers at Google. You will find friendly colleagues, fascinating projects, and the opportunity to make life better for tens of millions of people every day. We work on challenging, real-world problems. . . . We're constantly pushing the limits of what can be done with information. And while we work hard, we also have fun doing it."

What else would one expect from a company founded by two highly motivated, intellectually gifted, fun loving computer enthusiasts? Nowadays, Brin and Page are described as "calm, even confident, in the face of a rising tide of competitors, technology challenges and the tricky process of using the principles of disorganization to build a substantial company out of one unquestionably brilliant idea."

Discussion Questions

1. Using relevant concepts from Chapter 3 through 7 of the text, how would you characterize Sergey Brin and Larry Page?

2. From a motivational and perceptual perspective, what seems to explain Eric Schmidt's career success?

3. What do Google's hiring practices reveal about the potential attributions being made regarding prospective employees?

4. What do the "top ten reasons for working at Google" indicate about the nature of Google's employees?

SOURCE: This case was written by Michael K. McCuddy, The Louis S. and Mary L. Morgal Chair of Christian Business Ethics and Professor of Management, College of Business Administration, Valparaiso University. This case was developed from material contained on the Google Inc. Web site at http://www.google.com and in the following article: S. Levy, "Next Frontiers: All Eyes on Google," *Newsweek* (March 29, 2004): 48–50, 52, 54–56, 58.

PART 3

Interpersonal Processes and Behavior

© AP/Wide World Photos

Chapter 8

Communication

After reading this chapter, you should be able to do the following:

1 Understand the roles of the communicator, the receiver, perceptual screens, and the message in interpersonal communication.

2 Practice good reflective listening skills.

3 Describe the five communication skills of effective supervisors.

4 Explain five communication barriers and gateways through them.

5 Distinguish between defensive and nondefensive communication.

6 Explain positive, healthy communication.

7 Describe Information Communication Technology (ICT) used by managers.

THINKING AHEAD: CISCO SYSTEMS

Behind the Firewall

The very latest in information technology is a central aspect of the overall communications strategy within an organization. E-mails have become the quintessential paradox in many organizations as these electronic communications flood employees' mailboxes. Managers may well receive hundreds of e-mail communications each day, depending upon their industry and functional position within the company. The flood of e-mails comes both from within an organization and from external customers or other constituents. SPAM screening devices installed by many companies can be helpful in reviewing and sorting this communications flow, but there is always the risk that these SPAM screens may put important messages in the electronic recycle bin, erroneously. Thus, building an effective and functional firewall for internal organizational communications that does not kill important inbound messages from external customers is a real system design challenge.

Inside the corporate walls, however, Cisco Systems aims for a win–win strategy with its intranet such that the fun and business elements of using this electronic communications device are blended into a seamless package. That is, Cisco's intranet aims to be effective and fun at the same time. Cisco has worked to achieve this combined objective by positioning its intranet in the context of its overall communications strategy as an organization. A primary focus for Cisco was on ways to make the intranet helpful to employees in managing e-mails. One of the nice features within Cisco's intranet enables e-mails on related subjects to be presented in a Web interface with checkboxes to speed the replies. For example, one natural grouping of e-mails for a Cisco manager might be grouping e-mails from all employees requesting vacation time.

The Cisco intranet also supports a great deal of personalization of content access and delivery, and the company has found the benefits of this to be considerable. However, the ultimate focus of a successful intranet must be on the content, regardless of all the other features that may make it fun or entertaining. If employees cannot find the information they need in their e-mails and other electronic communications, or if they cannot trust the information to be both correct and current, then all the other entertaining and fun features serve to only highlight the deficiencies of the company's intranet. The fun features are the attention getters in the communications, but employees know that the message content must be sound, dependable, reliable, and substantive. That is where the real heart of any high-quality communication is, electronic or otherwise. So, Cisco's intranet does satisfy the company's internal customers. But how well does Cisco take care of communication with external customers in its supply chain?[1]

communication
The evoking of a shared or common meaning in another person.

interpersonal communication
Communication between two or more people in an organization.

Communication is the evoking of a shared or common meaning in another person. *Interpersonal communication* is communication that occurs between two or more people in an organization. Reading, listening, managing and interpreting information, and serving clients are among the interpersonal communication skills identified by the Department of Labor as being necessary for successful functioning in the workplace.[2] In Chapter 7, we noted that interpersonal communication is the key to social support for preventive stress management.[3] Interpersonal communication is central to health and well-being.

This chapter addresses the interpersonal and technological dimensions of communication in organizations. The first section presents an interpersonal communication model and a reflective listening technique intended to improve communication. The next section of the chapter addresses the five communication skills that characterize effective supervisors. The third section examines five barriers to effective communication and gives suggestions for overcoming them. The fourth section compares defensive and nondefensive communication. The fifth section discusses kinds of nonverbal communication. The final section gives an overview of the latest technologies for information management in organizations.

Interpersonal Communication

1. Understand the roles of the communicator, the receiver, perceptual screens, and the message in interpersonal communication.

Interpersonal communication is important in building and sustaining human relationships at work. Interpersonal communication cannot be replaced by the advances in information technology and data management that have taken place during the past several decades. The model in this section of the chapter provides a basis for understanding the key elements of interpersonal communication. These elements are the communicator, the receiver, the perceptual screens, and the message. Reflective listening is a valuable tool for improving interpersonal communication.

communicator
The person originating a message.

receiver
The person receiving a message.

perceptual screen
A window through which we interact with people that influences the quality, accuracy, and clarity of the communication.

An Interpersonal Communication Model

Figure 8.1 presents an interpersonal communication model as a basis for the discussion of communication. The model has four basic elements: the communicator, the receiver, perceptual screens, and the message. The *communicator* is the person originating the message. The *receiver* is the person receiving the message. The receiver must interpret and understand the message. *Perceptual screens* are the windows through which we interact with people in the world.

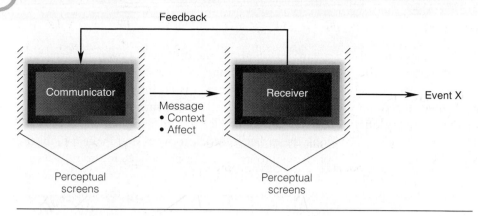

The communicator's and the receiver's perceptual screens influence the quality, accuracy, and clarity of the message. The screens influence whether the message sent and the message received are the same or whether distortion occurs in the message. Perceptual screens are composed of the personal factors each person brings to interpersonal communication, such as age, gender, values, beliefs, past experiences, cultural influences, and individual needs. The extent to which these screens are open or closed significantly influences both the sent and received messages.

The *message* contains the thoughts and feelings that the communicator intends to evoke in the receiver. The message has two primary components. The thought or conceptual component of the message (its content) is contained in the words, ideas, symbols, and concepts chosen to relay the message. The feeling or emotional component of the message (its affect) is contained in the intensity, force, demeanor, and sometimes the gestures of the communicator. This component of the message adds the emotional overtones, such as joy or anger, fear, or pain, to the conceptual component. This addition often enriches and clarifies the message. The feeling component gives the message its full meaning.

Feedback may or may not be activated in the model. Feedback occurs when the receiver provides the communicator with a response to the message. More broadly, feedback occurs when information is fed back that completes two-way communication. The Real World 8.1 describes how Intuit Corporation has established a direct feedback mechanism from its customers to its employees.

The *language* of the message is increasingly important because of the multinational nature of many organizations. Language is the words, their pronunciation, and the methods of combining them used by a community of people. Language will be addressed as a possible barrier to communication. For example, special language barriers arise for non-Japanese-speaking Americans who work with Japanese workers and for non-Spanish-speaking Canadians who work with Spanish-speaking workers.

Data are the uninterpreted, unanalyzed elements of a message. *Information* is data with meaning to some person who has interpreted or analyzed them. Messages are conveyed through a medium, such as a telephone or face-to-face discussion. Messages differ in *richness*, the ability of the medium to convey the meaning.[4] Table 8.1 compares different media with regard to data capacity and information richness. Attributes of communication media affect how influence-seeking behavior is generated and perceived in organizations.[5]

message
The thoughts and feelings that the communicator is attempting to elicit in the receiver.

feedback
Information fed back that completes two-way communication.

language
The words, their pronunciation, and the methods of combining them used and understood by a group of people.

data
Uninterpreted and unanalyzed facts.

information
Data that have been interpreted, analyzed, and have meaning to some user.

richness
The ability of a medium or channel to elicit or evoke meaning in the receiver.

Feedback at Intuit Corporation

Intuit Corporation has transformed business and financial management for small businesses, accounting professionals, and consumers for twenty years in the United States, Canada, and the United Kingdom. However, all did not go well for the company during the 2003 tax filing season. The company discovered that while many people do not like to call and complain about products or services, they are more than happy to complain on-line, and Intuit customers did. While everyone's blood boils at tax time, especially an accountant's, Intuit customers' Blood really boiled at tax time, and they flooded on-line forums with complaints about some product features they did not like, especially those having to do with antipiracy safeguards. A boycott of Intuit products was even threatened. The company's prompt response smoothed ruffled feathers, and the company learned a hard lesson about the Internet's power to tarnish a corporate reputation.

Since the 2003 tax season, Intuit monitors various Web sites to ensure that criticisms, or even falsehoods, are not going unaddressed. In addition, the company took the earlier feedback to heart and made a number of changes to its TurboTax products, including a feedback mechanism that allows customers to communicate confusion or displeasure directly to the employee responsible for the part of the program in question. Opening communication lines between its customers and its employees has paid dividends. While monitoring on-line sites and responding to feedback is time consuming, the time and effort are well worth it to the company.

SOURCE: CFO Staff, "Hold that Golden Spike," *CFO Magazine* 20 (Spring 2004): 9, http://www.cfo.com/article/1,5309,12606||M| 846,00.html.

Reflective Listening

2. Practice good reflective listening skills.

reflective listening
A skill intended to help the receiver and communicator clearly and fully understand the message sent.

Reflective listening is the skill of carefully listening to another person and repeating back to the speaker the heard message to correct any inaccuracies or misunderstandings. This kind of listening emphasizes the role of the receiver or audience in interpersonal communication. Managers use it to understand other people and help them solve problems at work.[6] Reflective listening enables the listener to understand the communicator's meaning, reduce perceptual distortions, and overcome interpersonal barriers that lead to communication failures. Reflective listening ensures that the meanings of the sent and received messages are the same. Reflecting back the message helps the communicator clarify and sharpen the intended meaning. It is especially

	Communication Media: Information Richness and Data Capacity	
TABLE 8.1		
MEDIUM	**INFORMATION RICHNESS**	**DATA CAPACITY**
Face-to-face discussion	Highest	Lowest
Telephone	High	Low
Electronic mail	Moderate	Moderate
Individualized letter	Moderate	Moderate
Personalized note or memo	Moderate	Moderate
Formal written report	Low	High
Flyer or bulletin	Low	High
Formal numeric report	Lowest	Highest

SOURCE: Created by E. A. Gerloff from "Information Richness: A New Approach to Managerial Behavior and Organizational Design" by Richard L. Daft and R. H. Lengel in *Research in Organizational Behavior* 6 (1984): 191–233. Reprinted by permission of JAI Press Inc.

Reflective Listening Affects Behaviors and Emotions

Reflective listening has been a cornerstone of nondirective counseling and applied in a wide range of other settings, including the corporate setting. Reflective listening is a communication skill that may be taught and learned. A series of three studies devised and evaluated a communication skills training program with managers and employees in an insurance company. These studies were conducted to determine the effects of the training, and student evaluators assisted in rating reflective listening skills in conversations with employees.

Study 1 compared a group of managers trained in reflective listening to a control group of managers in an experimental setting. The results suggested that the trained managers used more reflective listening responses than the control group managers, and the trained managers were evaluated more positively on their conversation skills than the control group managers. Study 2 tested whether the trained managers would generalize their reflective listening skills to an authentic customer setting. The results showed that the trained managers were able to generalize their reflective listening skills into a corporate setting. Study 3 used a larger sample of judges to confirm the results of Study 1, which suggested that trained managers received more positive evaluations of their conversation skills than control group managers. In this case, the results did not confirm the initial results of Study 1. The researchers concluded that reflective listening can be learned in a relatively short period of time and it does have a positive effect on both behaviors and emotions.

SOURCE: E. Rautalinko and H. O. Lisper, "Effects of Training Reflective Listening in a Corporate Setting," *Journal of Business and Psychology* 18 (2004): 281–299.

useful in problem solving. As we see in the accompanying Science feature, reflective listening can be learned in a short time with positive effects on behaviors and emotions in corporate settings.

Reflective listening can be characterized as personal, feeling oriented, and responsive.[7] First, reflective listening emphasizes the personal elements of the communication process, not the impersonal or abstract elements of the message. The reflective listener demonstrates empathy and concern for the communicator as a person, not an inanimate object. Second, reflective listening emphasizes the feelings communicated in the message. Thoughts and ideas are often the primary focus of a receiver's response, but that is not the case in reflective listening. The receiver should pay special attention to the feeling component of the message. Third, reflective listening emphasizes responding to the communicator, not leading the communicator. Receivers should distinguish their own feelings and thoughts from those of the speaker so as not to confuse the two. The focus must be on the speaker's feelings and thoughts in order to respond to them. A good reflective listener does not lead the speaker according to the listener's own thoughts and feelings.

Four levels of verbal response by the receiver are part of active reflective listening: affirming contact, paraphrasing expressed thoughts and feelings, clarifying implicit thoughts and feelings, and reflecting "core" feelings not fully expressed. Nonverbal behaviors also are useful in reflective listening. Specifically, silence and eye contact are responses that enhance reflective listening.

Each reflective response is illustrated through the case of a software engineer and her supervisor. The engineer has just discovered a major problem, which is not yet fully defined, in a large information system she is building for a very difficult customer.

AFFIRMING CONTACT The receiver affirms contact with the communicator by using simple statements such as "I see," "Uh-huh," and "Yes, I understand." The purpose of an affirmation response is to communicate attentiveness, not necessarily agreement. In the case of the software engineer, the supervisor might most appropriately use several affirming statements as the engineer begins to talk through the problem. Affirming contact is especially reassuring to a speaker in the early stages of expressing thoughts and feelings about a problem, especially when there may be some associated anxiety or discomfort. As the problem is more fully explored and expressed, it is increasingly useful for the receiver to use additional reflective responses.

PARAPHRASING THE EXPRESSED After an appropriate time, the receiver might paraphrase the expressed thoughts and feelings of the speaker. Paraphrasing is useful because it reflects back to the speaker the thoughts and feelings as the receiver heard them. This verbal response enables the receiver to build greater empathy, openness, and acceptance into the relationship while ensuring the accuracy of the communication process.

In the case of the software engineer, the supervisor may find paraphrasing the engineer's expressed thoughts and feelings particularly useful for both of them in developing a clearer understanding of the system problem. For example, the supervisor might say, "I hear you saying that you are very upset about this problem and that you are not yet clear about what is causing it." It is difficult to solve a problem until it is clearly understood.

CLARIFYING THE IMPLICIT People often communicate implicit thoughts and feelings about a problem in addition to their explicitly expressed thoughts and feelings. Implicit thoughts and feelings are not clearly or fully expressed. The receiver may or may not assume that the implicit thoughts and feelings are within the awareness of the speaker. For example, the software engineer may be anxious about how to talk with a difficult customer concerning the system problem. This may be implicit in her discussion with her supervisor because of the previous discussions about this customer. If her anxiety feelings are not expressed, the supervisor may want to clarify them. For example, the supervisor might say, "I hear that you are feeling very upset about the problem and may be worried about the customer's reaction when you inform him." This would help the engineer shift the focus of her attention from the main problem, which is in the software, to the important and related issue of discussing the matter with the customer.

REFLECTING "CORE" FEELINGS Next, the receiver should go beyond the explicit or implicit thoughts and feelings that the speaker is expressing. The receiver, in reflecting the core feelings that the speaker may be experiencing, is reaching beyond the immediate awareness level of the speaker. "Core" feelings are the deepest and most important ones from the speaker's perspective. For example, if the software engineer had not been aware of any anxiety in her relationship with the difficult customer, her supervisor's ability to sense the tension and bring it to the engineer's awareness would exemplify reflecting core feelings.

The receiver runs a risk of overreaching in reflecting core feelings if a secure, empathetic relationship with the speaker does not already exist or if strongly repressed feelings are reflected back. Even if the receiver is correct, the speaker may not want those feelings brought to awareness. Therefore, it is important to exercise caution and care in reflecting core feelings to a speaker.

SILENCE Long, extended periods of silence may cause discomfort and be a sign or source of embarrassment, but silence can help both speaker and listener in reflective listening. From the speaker's perspective, silence may be useful in moments of thought or confusion about how to express difficult ideas or feelings. The software engineer may need some patient, silent response as she thinks through what to say next. Listeners can use brief periods of silence to sort out their own thoughts and feelings from those of the speaker. Reflective listening focuses only on the latter. In the case of the software engineer's supervisor, any personal, angry feelings toward the difficult customer should not intrude on the engineer's immediate problem. Silence provides time to identify and isolate the listener's personal responses and exclude them from the dialogue.

EYE CONTACT Eye contact is a nonverbal behavior that may help open up a relationship and improve communication between two people. The absence of any direct eye contact during an exchange tends to close communication. Cultural and individual differences influence what constitutes appropriate eye contact. For example, some cultures, such as in India, place restrictions on direct eye contact initiated by women or children. Too much direct eye contact, regardless of the individual or culture, has an intimidating effect.

Moderate direct eye contact, therefore, communicates openness and affirmation without causing either speaker or listener to feel intimidated. Periodic aversion of the eyes allows for a sense of privacy and control, even in intense interpersonal communication.

ONE-WAY VERSUS TWO-WAY COMMUNICATION Reflective listening encourages two-way communication. *Two-way communication* is an interactive form of communication in which there is an exchange of thoughts, feelings, or both and through which shared meaning often occurs. Problem solving and decision making are often examples of two-way communication. *One-way communication* occurs when a person sends a message to another person and no feedback, questions, or interaction follow. Giving instructions or giving directions are examples of one-way communication. One-way communication occurs whenever a person sends a one-directional message to a receiver with no reflective listening or feedback in the communication.

One-way communication is faster, although how much faster depends on the amount and complexity of information communicated and the medium chosen. Even though it is faster, one-way communication is often less accurate than two-way communication. This is especially true for complex tasks where clarifications and iterations may be required for task completion. Where time and accuracy are both important to the successful completion of a task, such as in combat or emergency situations, extensive training prior to execution enhances accuracy and efficiency of execution without two-way communication.[8] Fire fighters and military combat personnel engage extensively in such training to minimize the need for communication during emergencies. These highly trained professionals rely on fast, abbreviated, one-way communication as a shorthand for more complex information. However, this communication only works within the range of situations for which the professionals are specifically trained.

It is difficult to draw general conclusions about people's satisfaction with one-way versus two-way communication. For example, communicators with a stronger need for feedback or who are not uncomfortable with conflicting or confusing questions may find two-way communication more satisfying. In contrast, receivers who believe that a message is very straightforward may be sat-

two-way communication
A form of communication in which the communicator and receiver interact.

one-way communication
Communication in which a person sends a message to another person and no feedback, questions, or interaction follow.

isfied with one-way communication and dissatisfied with two-way communication because of its lengthy, drawn-out nature.

Five Keys To Effective Supervisory Communication

3. Describe the five communication skills of effective supervisors.

Interpersonal communication, especially between managers and employees, is a critical foundation for effective performance in organizations, as well as for health and well-being as seen later in the chapter. Language and power are intertwined in the communication that occurs between managers and their employees.[9] One large study of managers in a variety of jobs and industries found that managers with the most effective work units engaged in routine communication within their units, whereas the managers with the highest promotion rates engaged in networking activities with superiors.[10] Another study of male and female banking managers suggested that higher performing managers are better and less apprehensive communicators than lower performing managers.[11] Oral communication (voice) and cooperative behaviors are important contextual performance skills that have positive effects on the psychosocial quality of the work environment.[12]

A review of the research on manager–employee communication identified five communication skills that distinguish "good" from "bad" supervisors.[13] These skills include being expressive speakers, empathetic listeners, persuasive leaders, sensitive people, and informative managers. Some supervisors are good and effective without possessing each of these skills, and some organizations value one or another skill over the others. Thus, dyadic relationships are at the core of much organization-based communication.[14]

Expressive Speakers

Better supervisors express their thoughts, ideas, and feelings and speak up in meetings. They are comfortable expressing themselves. They tend toward extroversion. Supervisors who are not talkative or who tend toward introversion may at times leave their employees wondering what their supervisors are thinking or how they feel about certain issues. Supervisors who speak out let the people they work with know where they stand, what they believe, and how they feel.

Empathetic Listeners

In addition to being expressive speakers, the better supervisors are willing, empathetic listeners. They use reflective listening skills; they are patient with, and responsive to, problems that employees, peers, and others bring to them about their work. They respond to and engage the concerns of other people. For example, the president of a health care company estimated that he spent 70 percent of his interpersonal time at work listening to others.[15] He listens empathetically to personal and work dilemmas without taking responsibility for others' problems. Empathetic listeners are able to hear the feelings and emotional dimensions of the messages people send them, as well as the content of the ideas and issues. Better supervisors are approachable and willing to listen to suggestions and complaints. You 8.1 gives you an opportunity to evaluate how active a listener you are. Active listening is one key communication skill that closes the feedback gap between managers and employees.[16]

Persuasive Leaders (and Some Exceptions)

Better supervisors are persuasive leaders rather than directive, autocratic ones. All supervisors and managers must exercise power and influence in organiza-

tions if they are to ensure performance and achieve results. These better supervisors are distinguished by their use of persuasive communication when influencing others. Specifically, they encourage others to achieve results instead of telling others what to do. They are not highly directive or manipulative in their influence attempts. Patience may be a virtue in this context because the sleeper effect, or delayed influence, may be active in some situations.[17]

The exceptions to this pattern of communication occur in emergency or high-risk situations, such as life-threatening traumas in medical emergency rooms or in oil rig firefighting. In these cases, the supervisor must be directive and assertive.

Dr. Martin Luther King, Jr., combined the traits of an expressive speaker with a persuasive leader.

Sensitive to Feelings

Better supervisors are also sensitive to the feelings, self-image, and psychological defenses of their employees. Although the supervisor is capable of giving criticism and negative feedback to employees, he or she does it confidentially and constructively. Care is taken to avoid giving critical feedback or reprimanding employees in public. Those settings are reserved for the praise of employees' accomplishments, honors, and achievements. In this manner, the better supervisors are sensitive to the self-esteem of others. They work to enhance that self-esteem as appropriate to the person's real talents, abilities, and achievements.

Informative Managers

Finally, better supervisors keep those who work for them well informed and are skilled at appropriately and selectively disseminating information. This role involves receiving large volumes of information, through a wide range of written and verbal communication media and then filtering through the information before distributing it appropriately. The failure to filter and disseminate information selectively to employees can lead to either information overload for the employees or a lack of sufficient information for performance and task accomplishment. Better supervisors favor giving advance notice of organizational changes and explaining the rationale for organizational policies.

A person may become a good supervisor even in the absence of one of these communication skills. For example, a person with special talents in planning and organizing or in decision making may compensate for a shortcoming in expressiveness or sensitivity. Further, when supervisors and employees engage in overt behaviors of communication and forward planning, they have a greater number of agreements about the employee's performance and behavior.[18] Overall, interpersonal communication is a key foundation for human relationships.

Barriers and Gateways to Communication

Barriers to communication are factors that block or significantly distort successful communication. About 20 percent of communication problems that cause organizational problems and drain profitability can be prevented or solved by communication policy guidelines.[19] *Gateways to communication* are pathways through these barriers and serve as antidotes to the problems caused by communication barriers. These barriers to communication in organizations may be temporary and can be overcome. Awareness and recognition are the first steps in formulating ways to overcome the barriers. Five communication barriers are physical separation, status differences, gender differences, cultural diversity, and language. The discussion of each concludes with one or two ways to overcome the barrier.

Physical Separation

The physical separation of people in the work environment poses a barrier to communication. Telephones and technology, such as electronic mail, often help bridge the physical gap. We address a variety of new technologies in the closing section of the chapter. Although telephones and technology can be helpful, they are not as information rich as face-to-face communication (see Table 8.1).

Periodic face-to-face interactions is one antidote to physical separation problems, because the communication is much richer, largely because of nonverbal cues. The richer the communication, the less the potential for confusion or misunderstandings. Another gateway through the barrier of physical separation is regularly scheduled meetings for people who are organizationally interrelated.

Status Differences

Status differences related to power and the organizational hierarchy pose another barrier to communication among people at work, especially within manager–employee pairs.[20] Because the employee is dependent on the manager as the primary link to the organization, the employee is more likely to distort upward communication than either horizontal or downward communication.

Effective supervisory skills, discussed at the beginning of the chapter, make the supervisor more approachable and are an antidote to the problems related to status differences. In addition, when employees feel secure, they are more likely to be straightforward in upward communication. The absence of status, power, and hierarchical differences, however, is not a cure-all. New information technologies provide another way to overcome status-difference barriers because they encourage the formation of nonhierarchical working relationships.[21]

Gender Differences

Communication barriers can be explained in part by differences in conversational styles.[22] Thus, when people of different ethnic or class backgrounds talk to one another, what the receiver understands may not be the same as what the speaker meant. In a similar way, men and women have different conversational styles, which may pose a communication barrier between those of opposite sexes. For example, women prefer to converse face to face, whereas men are comfortable sitting side by side and concentrating on some focal point in front of them. Hence, conversation style differences may result in a failure to communicate between men and women. Again, what is said by one may be understood to have an entirely different meaning by the other. Male–female conversation is really cross-cultural communication. In a work context, one study found that female employees sent less information to their supervisors and experienced less information overload than did male employees.[23]

An important gateway through the gender barrier to communication is developing an awareness of gender-specific differences in conversational style. These differences can enrich organizational communication and empower professional relationships.[24] A second gateway is to actively seek clarification of the person's meaning rather than freely interpreting meaning from one's own frame of reference.

Cultural Diversity

Cultural values and patterns of behavior can be very confusing barriers to communication. Important international differences in work-related values exist among people in the United States, Germany, the United Kingdom, Japan, and other nations.[25] These value differences have implications for motivation, leadership, and teamwork in work organizations.[26] Habitual patterns of interaction within a culture often substitute for communication. Outsiders working in a culture foreign to them often find these habitual patterns confusing and at times bizarre. For example, the German culture places greater value on authority and hierarchical differences. It is therefore more difficult for German workers to engage in direct, open communication with their supervisors than it is for U.S. workers.[27]

These types of cultural stereotypes can be confusing and misleading in cross-cultural communications. When people from one culture view those in another culture through the lens of stereotypes, they in effect are discounting the individual differences within the other culture. For example, an Asian stereotype of Americans may be that they are aggressive and arrogant and, thus, insensitive and unapproachable. Or, an American stereotype of Chinese and Japanese may be that they are meek and subservient, unable to be appropriately strong and assertive. Individuals who depend on the accuracy of these forms of cultural stereotypes may be badly misled in communicating with those in other cultures.

One gateway through cultural diversity as a communication barrier is increasing awareness and sensitivity. In addition, companies can provide seminars for expatriate managers as part of their training for overseas assignments.

Bernard Isautier, chairman, president, and CEO of PetroKazakstan, believes that understanding and communication are two keys to success with workplace diversity, which is an essential ingredient for success in international markets.[28] A second gateway is developing or acquiring a guide, map, or beacon for understanding and interacting with members of other cultures. One approach to doing this is to describe a nation in terms of a suitable and complex metaphor.[29] For example, Irish conversations, the Spanish bullfight, and American football are consensually derived metaphors that can enable those outside the culture to understand members within the culture.

Language

Language is a central element in communication. It may pose a barrier if its use obscures meaning and distorts intent. Although English is the international language of aviation, it is not the international language of business. Where the native languages of supervisors and employees differ, the risk of barriers to communication exists. However, increasing numbers of business men and women are bilingual or multilingual. For example, Honeywell former CEO Michael Bonsignore's ability to speak four languages helped him conduct business around the world more fluently. Less obvious are subtle distinctions in dialects within the same language, which may cause confusion and miscommunication. For example, the word *lift* means an elevator in Great Britain and a ride in the United States. In a different vein, language barriers are created across disciplines and professional boundaries by technical terminology. Acronyms may be very useful to those on the inside of a profession or discipline as means of shorthand communication. Technical terms can convey precise meaning between professionals. However, acronyms and technical terms may only serve to confuse, obscure, and derail any attempt at clear understanding for people unfamiliar with their meaning and usage. For example, while "probable" is a meaningful word for the forecaster, "likely" is a better term for the layperson to avoid miscommunication.[30] Use simple, direct, declarative language. Speak in brief sentences and use terms or words you have heard from your audience. As much as possible, speak in the language of the listener. Do not use jargon or technical language except with those who clearly understand it.

Defensive and Nondefensive Communication

5. Distinguish between defensive and nondefensive communication.

defensive communication
Communication that can be aggressive, attacking, and angry, or passive and withdrawing.

nondefensive communication
Communication that is assertive, direct, and powerful.

Defensive communication in organizations also can create barriers between people, whereas nondefensive communication helps open up relationships.[31] *Defensive communication* includes both aggressive, attacking, angry communication and passive, withdrawing communication. *Nondefensive communication* is an assertive, direct, powerful form of communication. It is an alternative to defensive communication. Although aggressiveness and passiveness are both forms of defensive communication, assertiveness is nondefensive communication. Organizations are increasingly engaged in courtroom battles and media exchanges, which are especially fertile settings for defensive communication. Catherine Crier had extensive experience as a trial lawyer and judge in dealing with defensive people. She carried this knowledge over into her position as a news anchor for CNN, ABC, Fox News, and currently on Court TV as the host of "Catherine Crier Live." Her four basic rules are (1) define the situation, (2) clarify the person's position, (3) acknowledge the person's feelings, and (4) bring the focus back to the facts.

Defensive communication in organizations leads to a wide range of problems, including injured feelings, communication breakdowns, alienation in working relationships, destructive and retaliatory behaviors, nonproductive efforts, and problem-solving failures. When such problems arise in organizations, everyone is prone to blame everyone else for what is not working.[32] The defensive responses of counterattack or sheepish withdrawal derail communication. Such responses tend to lend heat, not light, to the communication. An examination of eight defensive tactics follows the discussion of the two basic patterns of defensiveness in the next section.

Court TV host Catherine Crier channels defensive communication and turns it into nondefensive communication.

Nondefensive communication, in contrast, provides a basis for asserting and defending oneself when attacked, without being defensive. There are appropriate ways to defend oneself against aggression, attack, or abuse. An assertive, nondefensive style restores order, balance, and effectiveness in working relationships. A discussion of nondefensive communication follows the discussion of defensive communication.

Defensive Communication at Work

Defensive communication often elicits defensive communication in response. The two basic patterns of defensiveness are dominant defensiveness and subordinate defensiveness. One must be able to recognize various forms of defensive communication before learning to engage in constructive, nondefensive communication. You 8.2 helps you examine your defensive communication. Complete it before reading the following text material.

SUBORDINATE DEFENSIVENESS Subordinate defensiveness is characterized by passive, submissive, withdrawing behavior. The psychological attitude of the subordinately defensive person is "You are right, and I am wrong." People with low self-esteem may be prone to this form of defensive behavior, as well as people at lower organizational levels. When people at lower organizational levels fear sending bad news up the organization, information that is sensitive and critical to organizational performance may be lost.[33] People who are subordinately defensive do not adequately assert their thoughts and feelings in the workplace. Passive-aggressive behavior is a form of defensiveness that begins as subordinate defensiveness and ends up as dominant defensiveness. It is behavior that appears very passive but, in fact, masks underlying aggression and hostility.

DOMINANT DEFENSIVENESS Dominant defensiveness is characterized by active, aggressive, attacking behavior. It is offensive in nature: "The best defense is a good offense." The psychological attitude of the dominantly defensive person is "I am right, and you are wrong." People who compensate for low self-esteem may exhibit this pattern of behavior, as well as people who are in higher-level positions within the organizational hierarchy.

Junior officers in a regional banking organization described such behavior in the bank chairman, euphemistically called "The Finger." When giving orders or admonishing someone, he would point his index finger in a domineering, intimidating, emphatic manner that caused defensiveness on the part of the recipient.

What Kind of a Defender Are You?

Not all of our communication is defensive, but each of us has a tendency to engage in either subordinate or dominant defensiveness. The following table presents twelve sets of choices that will help you see whether you tend to be more subordinate or dominant when you communicate defensively.

Complete the questionnaire by allocating 10 points between the two alternatives in each of the twelve rows.

For example, if you never ask permission when it is not needed, but you do give or deny permission frequently, you may give yourself 0 and 10 points, respectively, in the third row. However, if you do each of these behaviors about equally, though at different times, you may want to give yourself 5 points for each alternative.

Add your total points for each column. Whichever number is larger identifies your defensive style.

Subordinate Defensiveness

____ Explain, prove, justify your actions, ideas, or feelings more than is required for results wanted.

____ Ask why things are done the way they are, when you really want to change them. *Why don't they . . . ?*

____ Ask permissions when not needed. *Is it okay with you if . . . ?*

____ Give away decisions, ideas, or power when it would be appropriate to claim them as your own. *Don't you think that . . . ?*

____ Apologize, feel inadequate, say *I'm sorry* when you're not.

____ Submit or withdraw when it's not in your best interest. *Whatever you say . . .*

____ Lose your cool, lash out, cry where it's inappropriate (turning your anger toward yourself).

____ Go blank, click off, be at a loss for words just when you want to have a ready response. *I should've said . . .* (afterwards)

____ Use coping humor, hostile jocularity, or put yourself down when "buying time" or honest feedback would get better results. *Why don't you lay off?*

____ Use self-deprecating adjectives and reactive verbs. *I'm just a . . . I'm just doing what I was told.*

____ Use the general *you* and *they* when *I* and personal names would state the situation more clearly. *They really hassle you here.*

____ Smile to cover up feelings or put yourself down since you don't know what else to do and it's *nice.*

____ TOTAL Subordinate Points

Dominant Defensiveness

____ Prove that you're right. *I told you so. Now see, that proves my point.*

____ Give patient explanations but few answers. *It's always been done this way. We tried that before, but . . .*

____ Give or deny permission. *Oh, I couldn't let you do that.*

____ Make decisions or take power as your natural right. *The best way to do it is . . . Don't argue, just do as I say.*

____ Prod people to get the job done. *Don't just stand there . . .*

____ Take over a situation or decision even when it's delegated; get arbitrary. *My mind is made up.*

____ Lose your cool, yell, pound the desk where it's inappropriate (turning your anger toward others).

____ Shift responsibility for something you should have taken care of yourself. *You've always done it before. What're you all of a sudden upset for now?*

____ Use coping humor, baiting, teasing, hostile jocularity, mimicry to keep other people off balance so you don't have to deal with them. *What's the matter, can't you take it?*

____ Impress others with how many important people you know. *The other night at Bigname's party when I was talking to . . .*

____ Don't listen: interpret. Catch the idea of what they're saying, then list rebuttals or redefine their point. *Now what you really mean is . . .*

____ Use verbal dominance, if necessary, to make your point. Don't let anyone interrupt what you have to say.

____ TOTAL Dominant Points

Unfortunately, defensive tactics are all too common in work organizations. Eight major defensive tactics are summarized in Table 8.2. They might be best understood in the context of a work situation: Joe is in the process of completing a critical report for his boss, and the report's deadline is drawing near. Mary, one of Joe's peers at work, is to provide him with some input for the report, and the department secretary is to prepare a final copy of the report. Each work example in the table is related to this situation.

Until defensiveness and defensive tactics are recognized for what they are, it is difficult either to change them or to respond to them in nondefensive ways. Defensive tactics are how defensive communication is acted out. In many cases, such tactics raise ethical dilemmas and issues for those involved. For example, is it ethical to raise doubts about another person's values, beliefs, or sexuality? At what point does simple defensiveness become unethical behavior?

Power plays are used by people to control and manipulate others through the use of choice definition (defining the choice another person is allowed to make), either/or conditions, and overt aggression. The underlying dynamic in power plays is that of domination and control.

A put-down is an effort by the speaker to gain the upper hand in the relationship. Intentionally ignoring another person or pointing out his or her mistakes in a meeting are kinds of put-downs.

Labeling is often used to portray another person as abnormal or deficient. Psychological labels are often used out of context for this purpose, such as calling a person "paranoid," a word that has a specific, clinical meaning.

Raising doubts about a person's abilities, values, preferential orientations, or other aspects of his or her life creates confusion and uncertainty. This tactic tends to lack the specificity and clarity present in labeling.

Giving misleading information is the selective presentation of information designed to leave a false and inaccurate impression in the listener's mind. It is

TABLE 8.2   Defensive Tactics

DEFENSIVE TACTIC	SPEAKER	WORK EXAMPLE
Power play	The boss	"Finish this report by month's end or lose your promotion."
Put-down	The boss	"A capable manager would already be done with this report."
Labeling	The boss	"You must be a slow learner. Your report is still not done?"
Raising doubts	The boss	"How can I trust you, Joe, if you can't finish an easy report?"
Misleading information	Joe	"Mary has not gone over with me the information I need from her for the report." (She left him a copy.)
Scapegoating	Joe	"Mary did not give me her input until just today."
Hostile jokes	Joe	"You can't be serious! The report isn't that important."
Deception	Joe	"I gave it to the secretary. Did she lose it?"

not the same as lying or misinforming. Giving misleading information is one form of deception.

Scapegoating and its companion, buck-passing, are methods of shifting responsibility to the wrong person. Blaming other people is another form of scapegoating or buck-passing.

Hostile jokes should not be confused with good humor, which is both therapeutic and nondefensive. Jokes created at the expense of others are destructive and hostile.

Deception may occur through a variety of means, such as lying or creating an impression or image that is at variance with the truth. Deception can be very useful in military operations, but it can be a destructive force in work organizations.

Nondefensive Communication

Nondefensive communication is a constructive, healthy alternative to defensive communication in working relationships. The person who communicates nondefensively may be characterized as centered, assertive, controlled, informative, realistic, and honest. Nondefensive communication is powerful, because the speaker is exhibiting self-control and self-possession without rejecting the listener. Converting defensive patterns of communication to nondefensive ones enhances relationship building at work. Relationship building behaviors and communication help reduce adverse responses, such as blame and anger, following negative events at work.[34]

The subordinately defensive person needs to learn to be more assertive. This can be done in many ways, of which two examples follow. First, instead of asking for permission to do something, report what you intend to do, and invite confirmation. Second, instead of using self-deprecating words, such as "I'm just following orders," drop the *just*, and convert the message into a self-assertive, declarative statement. Nondefensive communication should be self-affirming without being self-aggrandizing. Some people overcompensate for subordinate defensiveness and inadvertently become domineering.

The person prone to be domineering and dominantly defensive needs to learn to be less aggressive. This may be especially difficult because it requires overcoming the person's sense of "I am right." People who are working to overcome dominant defensiveness should be particularly sensitive to feedback from others about their behavior. There are many ways to change this pattern of behavior. Here are two examples. First, instead of giving and denying permission, give people free rein except in situations where permission is essential as a means of clearing approval or ensuring the security of the task. Second, instead of becoming inappropriately angry, provide information about the adverse consequences of a particular course of action.

Nonverbal Communication

Much defensive and nondefensive communication focuses on the language used. However, most of the meaning in a message (an estimated 65 to 90 percent) is conveyed through nonverbal communication.[35] *Nonverbal communication* includes all elements of communication, such as gestures and the use of space, that do not involve words or do not involve language.[36] The four basic kinds of nonverbal communication are proxemics, kinesics, facial and eye behavior, and paralanguage. They are important topics for managers attempting to understand the types and meanings of nonverbal signals from employees. Non-

nonverbal communication

All elements of communication that do not involve words.

verbal communication is influenced by both psychological and physiological processes.[37]

Some scholars consider this area of communication to be less scientifically rigorous than other areas of communication. In any case, the interpretation of nonverbal communication is specific to the context of the interaction and the actors. That is, nonverbal cues only give meaning in the context of the situation and the interaction of the actors. For example, some federal and state judges attempt to curb nonverbal communication in the courtroom. The judges' primary concern is that nonverbal behavior may unfairly influence jurors' decisions. It is also important to note that nonverbal behavior is culturally bound. Gestures, facial expressions, and body locations have different meanings in different cultures. The globalization of business means managers should be sensitive to the nonverbal customs of other cultures in which they do business.

Proxemics

The study of an individual's perception and use of space, including territorial space, is called *proxemics*.[38] *Territorial space* refers to bands of space extending outward from the body. These bands constitute comfort zones. In each comfort zone, different cultures prefer different types of interaction with others. Figure 8.2 presents four zones of territorial space based on U.S. culture.

The first zone, intimate space, extends outward from the body to about 1½ feet. In this zone, we interact with spouses, significant others, family members, and others with whom we have an intimate relationship. The next zone, the personal distance zone, extends from 1½ feet outward to 4 feet. Friends typically

---

8.2 FIGURE 8.2   Zones of Territorial Space in U.S. Culture

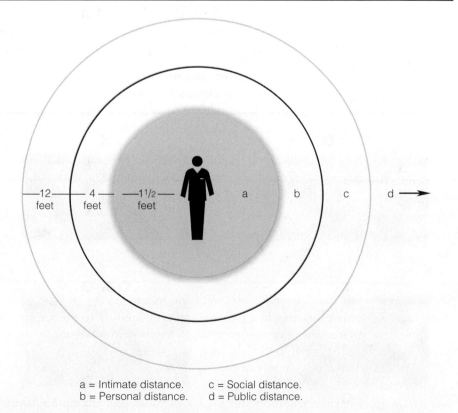

a = Intimate distance.   c = Social distance.
b = Personal distance.   d = Public distance.

interact within this distance. The third zone, the social distance zone, spans the distance from 4 to 12 feet. We prefer that business associates and acquaintances interact with us in this zone. The final zone is the public distance zone, extending 12 feet from the body outward. Most of us prefer that strangers stay at least 12 feet from us, and we become uncomfortable when they move closer.

Territorial space varies greatly across cultures. People often become uncomfortable when operating in territorial spaces different from those in which they are familiar. Edward Hall, a leading proxemics researcher, says Americans working in the Middle East tend to back away to a comfortable conversation distance when interacting with Arabs. Because Arabs' comfortable conversation distance is closer than that of Americans, Arabs perceive Americans as cold and aloof. One Arab wondered, "What's the matter? Does he find me somehow offensive?"[39] Personal space tends to be larger in cultures with cool climates, such as the United States, Great Britain, and northern Europe, and smaller in cultures with warm climates, such as southern Europe, the Caribbean, India, or South America.[40]

Our relationships shape our use of territorial space. For example, we hold hands with, or put an arm around, significant others to pull them into intimate space. Conversely, the use of territorial space can shape people's interactions. A 4-foot-wide business desk pushes business interactions into the social distance zone. An exception occurred for one SBC manager who met with her seven first-line supervisors around her desk. Being elbow to elbow placed the supervisors in one another's intimate and personal space. They appeared to act more like friends and frequently talked about their children, favorite television shows, and other personal concerns. When the manager moved the staff meeting to a larger room and the spaces around each supervisor were in the social distance zone, the personal exchanges ceased, and they acted more like business associates again.

Seating dynamics, another aspect of proxemics, is the art of seating people in certain positions according to the person's purpose in communication. Figure 8.3 depicts some common seating dynamics. To encourage cooperation, you should

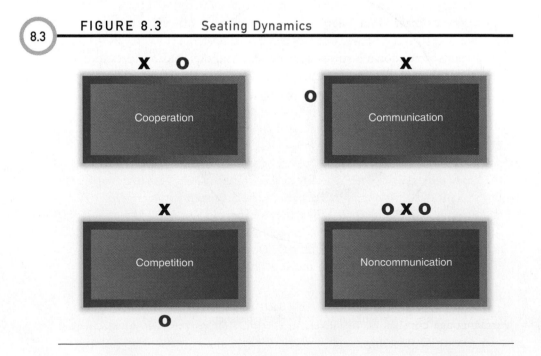

FIGURE 8.3   Seating Dynamics

seat the other party beside you, facing the same direction. To facilitate direct and open communication, seat the other party across a corner of your desk from you or in another place where you will be at right angles. This allows for more honest disclosure. To take a competitive stand with someone, position the person directly across from you. Suppose you hold a meeting around a conference table, and two of the attendees are disrupting your meeting. Where should you seat them? If you place one on each side of yourself, it should stifle the disruptions (unless one is so bold as to lean in front of you to keep chatting).

Kinesics

Kinesics is the study of body movements, including posture.[41] Like proxemics, kinesics is culturally bound; there is no single universal gesture. For example, the U.S. hand signal for "okay" is an insult in other countries. With this in mind, we can interpret some common U.S. gestures. Rubbing one's hands together or exhibiting a sharp intake of breath indicates anticipation. Stress is indicated by a closed hand position (that is, tight fists), hand wringing, or rubbing the temples. Nervousness may be exhibited through drumming fingers, pacing, or jingling coins in the pocket. Perhaps most fun to watch is preening behavior, seen most often in couples on a first date. Preening communicates "I want to look good for you" to the other party and consists of smoothing skirts, straightening the tie, or arranging the hair. No discussion of gestures would be complete without mention of insult gestures—some learned at an early age, much to the anxiety of parents. Sticking out one's tongue and waving fingers with one's thumbs in the ears is a childhood insult gesture.

Facial and Eye Behavior

The face is a rich source of nonverbal communication. Facial expression and eye behavior are used to add cues for the receiver. The face may give unintended clues to emotions the sender is trying to hide. Dynamic facial actions and expressions in a person's appearance are key clues of truthfulness, especially in deception situations.[42]

Although smiles have universal meaning, frowns, raised eyebrows, and wrinkled foreheads must all be interpreted in conjunction with the actors, the situation, and the culture. One study of Japanese and U.S. students illustrates the point. The students were shown a stress-inducing film, and their facial expressions were videotaped. When alone, the students had almost identical expressions. However, the Japanese students masked their facial expressions of unpleasant feelings much better than did the American students when another person was present.[43]

As mentioned earlier, eye contact can enhance reflective listening and, along with smiling, is one good way of displaying positive emotion.[44] However, eye contact must be understood in a cultural context. A direct gaze indicates honesty, truthfulness, and forthrightness in the United States. This may not be true in other cultures. For example, Barbara Walters was uncomfortable interviewing Muammar al-Qaddafi in Libya because he did not look directly at her. However, in Libya, it is a serious offense to look directly at a woman.[45] In Asian cultures it is considered good behavior to bow the head in deference to a superior rather than to look in the supervisor's eyes.

Paralanguage

Paralanguage consists of variations in speech, such as pitch, loudness, tempo, tone, duration, laughing, and crying.[46] People make attributions about the sender by deciphering paralanguage cues. A high-pitched, breathy voice in a female may contribute to the stereotype of the "dumb blonde." Rapid, loud speech may be taken as a sign of nervousness or anger. Interruptions such as "mmm" and "ah-hah" may be used to speed up the speaker so that the receiver can get in a few words. Clucking of the tongue or the "tsk-tsk" sound is used to shame someone. All these cues relate to how something is said.

How Accurately Do We Decode Nonverbal Cues?

Peoples' confidence in their ability to decode nonverbal communication is greater than their accuracy in doing so. Judges with several years' experience in interviewing were asked in one study to watch videotapes of job applicants and to rate the applicants' social skills and motivation levels.[47] The judges were fairly accurate about the social skills, but not about motivation. The judges relied on smiling, gesturing, and speaking as cues to motivation, yet none of these cues are motivation indicators. Thus, incorrectly interpreting nonverbal codes leads to inaccuracy.

Studies of deception emphasize how to use nonverbal cues to interpret whether someone is lying. In one simulation study, customers were asked to detect whether or not automobile salespeople were lying. The customers' ability to detect lies in this study was no better than chance. Does this suggest that salespeople are skilled deceivers who control nonverbal behaviors to prevent detection?[48]

Paul Ekman, a psychologist who has trained judges, Secret Service agents, and polygraphers to detect lies, says that the best way to detect lies is to look for inconsistencies in the nonverbal cues. Rapidly shifting facial expressions and discrepancies between the person's words and body, voice, or facial expressions are some clues.[49]

Nonverbal communication is important for managers because of its impact on the meaning of the message. However, a manager must consider the total message and all media of communication. A message can only be given meaning in context, and cues are easy to misinterpret. Table 8.3 presents common nonverbal behaviors exhibited by managers and how employees may interpret them. Nonverbal cues can give others the wrong signal.

Positive, Healthy Communication

6. Explain positive, healthy communication.

communicative disease
The absence of heartfelt communication in human relationships leading to loneliness and social isolation.

The absence of heartfelt communication in human relationships leads to loneliness and social isolation and has been labeled *communicative disease* by James Lynch.[50] Communicative disease has adverse effects on the heart and cardiovascular system and can ultimately lead to premature death. According to Lynch, heartfelt communication is a healing dialogue and central antidote for communicative disease. Positive, healthy communication is central to health and well-being. While communication may often be thought of as a cognitive activity of the head, Lynch suggests that the heart may be more important in the communications process.

Positive, healthy communication is one important aspect of working together when the term "working together" is taken for its intrapersonal meaning as well as its interpersonal meaning.[51] The balance between head and heart is achieved when a person displays positive emotional competence and is able to have a healthy internal conversation between his or her thoughts and feelings, ideas, and emotions. In addition, working together occurs when there are cooperative work behaviors between people based upon positive, healthy, and open communica-

NONVERBAL COMMUNICATION	SIGNAL RECEIVED	REACTION FROM RECEIVER
Manager looks away when talking to the employee.	Divided attention.	My supervisor is too busy to listen to my problem or simply does not care.
Manager fails to acknowledge greeting from fellow employee.	Unfriendliness.	This person is unapproachable.
Manager glares ominously (i.e., gives the evil eye).	Anger.	Reciprocal anger, fear, or avoidance, depending on who is sending the signal in the organization.
Manager rolls the eyes.	Not taking person seriously.	This person thinks he or she is smarter or better than I am.
Manager sighs deeply.	Disgust or displeasure.	My opinions do not count. I must be stupid or boring to this person.
Manager uses heavy breathing (sometimes accompanied by hand waving).	Anger or heavy stress.	Avoid this person at all costs.
Manager does not maintain eye contact when communicating.	Suspicion or uncertainty.	What does this person have to hide?
Manager crosses arms and leans away.	Apathy or closed-mindedness.	This person already has made up his or her mind; my opinions are not important.
Manager peers over glasses.	Skepticism or distrust.	He or she does not believe what I am saying.
Manager continues to read a report when employee is speaking.	Lack of interest.	My opinions are not important enough to get the supervisor's undivided attention.

SOURCE: From "Steps to Better Listening" by C. Hamilton and B. H. Kleiner. Copyright © February 1987. Reprinted with permission, *Personnel Journal,* all rights reserved.

tion that is based on trust and truthfulness. Honest competition within the workplace is not inconsistent with this notion of working together; forthright, well-managed, honest competition can bring out the best in all those involved.

Positive, healthy communication is at the core of personal integrity as displayed by healthy executives.[52] Former President Ronald Reagan was a great communicator who displayed strong ethical character, personal integrity, and simplicity in his communication. He exemplified communication from the heart in the sense that his messages came from his core values, beliefs, and aspirations for himself and others. His optimism shone through from the core of his person, displaying a continuing positive attitude that drew even his opponents to like him. Communication from core values and beliefs is communication anchored in personal integrity and ethical character.

Personal integrity in positive, healthy communication is achieved through emotional competence and the head-to-heart dialogue mentioned earlier. In addition to the public self, as is familiar in the case of Ronald Reagan, all executives have a private self. Karol Wasylyshyn has shown that one dimension of coaching star executives is to enhance their emotional competence

© 2004 AFP/Getty Images

Former President Ronald Reagan's core values and beliefs reverberated in his public speeches.

and capacity to talk through challenging issues, both personally and professionally.[53] Quick and Macik-Frey focus on the private-self aspect of positive, healthy communication in developing their model of executive coaching through deep interpersonal communication.[54] Their executive coaching model relies on what Lynch might call a healing dialogue between executive and coach. However, their model of deep interpersonal communication is one that can enhance positive, healthy communication in a wider range of human relationships.

Communicating through New Technologies

7. Describe Information Communication Technology (ICT) used by managers.

Nonverbal behaviors can be important in establishing trust in working relationships, but modern technologies may challenge our ability to maintain trust in relationships. New technologies are an essential feature of modern management. Many organizations around the world are now plugging into the Internet, an electronic and computer-based technology that allows for the easy transfer of information and data across continents. The Real World 8.2 describes two communication advances at FedEx that have been made possible by investments in information technology.

Managers in today's business world have access to more communication tools than ever before. All of these new technologies are, surprisingly, having relatively little impact on work culture. In addition, security concerns since 9/11 have complicated wireless access. An understanding of the use of these new technologies influences effective, successful communication. In addition, it is important to understand how these new technologies affect others' communication and behavior. Finally, information technology can encourage or discourage moral dialogue, and moral conversations are central to addressing ethical issues at work.[55]

Written Communication

Many organizations are working toward paperless offices and paperless interfaces with their customers. Some written communication is still required, however. Forms are one category of written communication. Manuals are another. Policy manuals are important in organizations because they set out guidelines for decision making and rules of actions for organizational members. Operations and procedures manuals explain how to perform various tasks and resolve problems that may occur at work. Reports are a third category of written communication; company annual reports are an example. Reports may summarize the results of a committee's or department's work or provide information on progress toward certain objectives.

Letters and memorandums are briefer, more frequently used categories of written communication in organizations. Letters are a formal means of communication—often with people outside the organization—and may vary substantially in length. Memorandums are another formal means of communication, often to constituencies within the organization. Memos are sometimes used to create a formal, historical record of a specific event or occurrence to which people in the organization may want to refer at some future date. Referring back to Table 8.1, we can conclude that written communication has the advantage of high to moderate data capacity and the possible disadvantage of moderate to low information richness.

Communication Technologies

Computer-mediated communication was once used only by technical specialists but now influences virtually all managers' behavior in the work environ-

Communication Advances at FedEx

Information technology (IT) investments can advance communication and save money at the same time. FedEx receives nearly 600,000 phone calls per day at its 800-GO-FEDEX line, of which about 100,000 result in a package tracking request. Each one of those tracking request phone calls costs $2.30 for a total daily cost of $230,000. By contrast, at FedEx.com, the company averages more than 2.4 million tracking queries per day, but each of those queries costs the company less than 5¢. In thinking of new ways to communicate with customers, FedEx has made two communication advances through IT investments that have resulted in saving about $25 million per month. One of these, called FedEx InSight, is a Web-based communication advance that lets customers check on the status of inbound shipments regardless of who sent them. Best of all, the customer does not even need a tracking number. Thus, customers can better manage their supply chain and do business with FedEx on the Internet, and FedEx saves money in the process by avoiding the high phone tracking costs. In addition to making it easier for customers, FedEx launched a second communication advance called PowerPad for 40,000 of its couriers. PowerPad allows couriers to send and receive near-real-time information and updates from any location via a wireless network. This ability enables couriers to communicate without returning to their vans to upload information or refer to a manual for shipping rates.

SOURCE: R. Carter, "Fast Talk: The New IT Agenda," *Fast Company* 69 (April 2003): 53, http://www.fastcompany.com/magazine/69/fasttalk.html.

ment. Informational databases are becoming more commonplace. These databases provide a tremendous amount of information with the push of a button. Another example of an informational database is the type of system used in many university libraries, in which books and journals are available through an electronic card catalog.

Electronic mail systems represent another technology; users can leave messages via the computer to be accessed at any time by the receiver. This eliminates the time delay of regular mail and allows for immediate reply. Research comparing e-mail versus face-to-face communication on choices individuals make found that the effects vary with the nature of the decisions and may depend on the complexity and content of what needs to be communicated.[56] Thus, e-mail has strengths and advantages in communication as well as limitations with which to exercise caution. Unfortunately, some people feel much less inhibited when using e-mail and end up sending caustic messages they would never consider saying in person. The MoodWatch software system helps guard against "flaming" e-mails by notifying users if their message contains hostile, abusive, or bullying content (flames). In addition and on a positive note, there are also devices that enable international e-mail users to have their messages translated to and from French, German, Spanish, Portuguese, and English.

Voice mail systems are another widely used communication mode, especially in sales jobs where people are away from the office. Voice behavior influences the quality of the work environment. This has implications for the quality of voice mail as well. Some voice mail systems allow the user to retrieve messages from remote locations. Timely retrieval of messages is important. One manager in the office furniture industry had a problem with her voice mail when first learning to use it. She would forget to check it until late in the day. Employees with problems early in the day felt frustrated with her slow response time. When using voice mail, it is important to remember that the receiver may not retrieve the messages in a timely manner. Urgent messages must be delivered directly.

Facsimile (fax) machine systems allow the immediate transmission of documents. This medium allows the sender to communicate facts, graphs, and illustrations very rapidly. Fax machines are used in cars, as well as offices and remote locations.

Cell phones are also commonplace, permitting communication while away from the office and on the commute to and from work. They are used extensively in sales jobs involving travel. Not all reactions to car phones are positive. For example, one oil producer did not want his thinking time while driving disturbed by a cell phone. Cell phones while driving are also risky, with some estimates suggesting that using a cell phone while driving is as risky as driving while under the influence of alcohol. For this reason, some states have outlawed the use of cell phones while driving a motor vehicle.

How Do Communication Technologies Affect Behavior?

Information Communication Technology (ICT)

The various new technologies, such as electronic mail, voice mail, teleconferencing, and wireless access, which are used for interpersonal communication.

Information Communication Technology (ICT) provides faster, more immediate access to information than was available in the past. It provides instant exchange of information in minutes or seconds across geographic boundaries and time zones. Schedules and office hours become irrelevant. The normal considerations of time and distance become less important in the exchange. Hence, these technologies have important influences on people's behavior.

One aspect of computer-mediated communication is its impersonal nature. The sender interacts with a machine, not a person. As mentioned earlier, studies show that using these technologies results in an increase in flaming, or making rude or obscene outbursts by computer.[57] Interpersonal skills like tact and graciousness diminish, and managers are more blunt when using electronic media. People who participate in discussions quietly and politely when face to face may become impolite, more intimate, and uninhibited when they communicate using computer conferencing or electronic mail.[58]

Another effect of the new technologies is that the nonverbal cues we rely on to decipher a message are absent. Gesturing, touching, facial expressions, and eye contact are not available, so the emotional element of the message is difficult to access. In addition, clues to power, such as organizational position and departmental membership, may not be available, so the social context of the exchange is altered.

Communication via technologies also changes group interaction. It tends to equalize participation, because group members participate more equally, and charismatic or higher status members may have less power.[59] Studies of groups that make decisions via computer interaction (computer-mediated groups) have shown that the computer-mediated groups took longer to reach consensus than face-to-face groups. In addition, they were more uninhibited, and there was less influence from any one dominant person. It appears that groups that communicate by computer experience a breakdown of social and organizational barriers.

The potential for overload is particularly great with the new communication technologies. Not only is information available more quickly, the sheer volume of information at the manager's fingertips also is staggering. An individual can easily become overwhelmed by information and must learn to be selective about the information accessed.

A paradox created by the new, modern communication technology lies in the danger it may pose for managers. The danger is that managers cannot get away from the office as much as in the past, because they are more accessible to coworkers, subordinates, and the boss via telecommunications. Interactions are no longer confined to the 8:00 to 5:00 work hours.

In addition, the use of new technologies encourages polyphasic activity (that is, doing more than one thing at a time). Managers can simultaneously make phone calls, send computer messages, and work on memos. Polyphasic activity has its advantages in terms of getting more done—but only up to a point. Paying attention to more than one task at a time splits a person's attention and may reduce effectiveness. Constantly focusing on multiple tasks can become a habit, making it psychologically difficult for a person to let go of work.

Finally, the new technologies may make people less patient with face-to-face communication. The speed advantage of the electronic media may translate into an expectation of greater speed in all forms of communication. However, individuals may miss the social interaction with others and may find their social needs unmet. Communicating via computer means an absence of small talk; people tend to get to the point right away.

With many of these technologies, the potential for immediate feedback is reduced, and the exchange can become one-way. Managers can use the new technologies more effectively by keeping the following hints in mind:

1. Strive for completeness in your message.

2. Build in opportunities for feedback.

3. Do not assume you will get an immediate response.

4. Ask yourself if the communication is really necessary.

5. "Disconnect" yourself from the technology at regular intervals.

6. Provide opportunities for social interaction at work.

Managerial Implications: Communicate with Strength and Clarity

Interpersonal communication is important for the quality of working relationships in organizations. Managers who are sensitive and responsive in communicating with employees encourage the development of trusting, loyal relationships. Managers and employees alike benefit from secure working relations. Managers who are directive, dictatorial, or overbearing with employees, in contrast, are likely to find such behavior counterproductive, especially in periods of change.

Encouraging feedback and practicing reflective listening skills at work can open up communication channels in the work environment. Open communication benefits decision-making processes, because managers are better informed and more likely to base decisions on complete information. Open communication encourages nondefensive relationships, as opposed to defensive relationships, among people at work. Defensive relationships create problems because of the use of tactics that create conflict and division among people.

Managers benefit from sensitivity to employees' nonverbal behavior and territorial space, recognizing that understanding individual and cultural diversity is important in interpreting a person's nonverbal behavior. Seeking verbal clarification on nonverbal cues improves the accuracy of the communication and helps build trusting relationships. In addition, managers benefit from an awareness of their own nonverbal behaviors. Seeking employee feedback about their own nonverbal behavior helps managers provide a message consistent with their intentions.

Managers may complement good interpersonal contact with the appropriate use of new information technology. New information technologies' high data capacity is an advantage in a global workplace. The high information richness of interpersonal contacts is an advantage in a culturally diverse workforce. Therefore, managers benefit from both interpersonal and technological media by treating them as complementary modes of communication, not as substitutes for each other.

LOOKING BACK: CISCO SYSTEMS

Cisco Came, It Surveyed, and It Improved

While Cisco System's intranet focuses on employees as internal communications customers, communication pathways to its external customers are important to Cisco as well. The company is well aware of the current mantra in a very competitive global market concerning delighting these customers to ensure that they *remain* customers. Customers! Customers! Customers! Yes, customers are important to both manufacturing and service companies. In addition, for manufacturing companies, the beginning of the supply chain can be just as important. For this reason, Cisco recognized the importance of starting well in its supply chain by having excellent interaction and communication with its strategic supplier partners. The company found that it needed honest information about whether it was causing "undue pain" for any of its suppliers because its goal was to have a virtual, closed-loop supply chain that worked and worked well.

This concern for suppliers was in the context of Cisco's larger operational framework of three-to-five year goals, an approach that was a huge cultural shift for the company. These goals are communicated as specific milestones and outcomes that allow the company to fulfill its larger mission and vision concept. We know the power of goal setting in transforming performance in a positive way. However, goals cannot transform performance if they are not communicated or not understood. Once goals are set and communicated, then strategies must be developed that support the goals and enable the fulfillment of the vision. That is where the supply chain comes in for a manufacturing company and where strategic supply partners become critical to achieving milestones and desired outcomes. At Cisco, the communication interaction may demand change.

In the case of suppliers, Cisco developed targeted surveys through which it could communicate with its supply partners and receive feedback on performance. In one situation, a survey returned from one supplier gave low scores in communication and spurred internal discussion about how to improve. The supplier's specific need was for executive representation and two-way communication during supplier performance reviews. Once Cisco understood what the need was, the company developed an action plan to get its executives more involved in quarterly supplier performance reviews. Going one step further, the company developed a new executive sponsorship program in which one contact is designated to facilitate communications with strategic suppliers. Thus, Cisco works a dynamic process of communicating with its suppliers to ensure that all goes well at the start of its virtual and essential supply chain.[60]

Chapter Summary

1. The perceptual screens of communicators and listeners either help clarify or distort a message that is sent and received. Age, gender, and culture influence the sent and received messages.

2. Reflective listening involves affirming contact, paraphrasing what is expressed, clarifying the implicit, reflecting "core" feelings, and using appropriate nonverbal behavior to enhance communication.

3. The best supervisors talk easily with diverse groups of people, listen empathetically, are generally persuasive and not directive, are sensitive to a person's self-esteem, and are communication minded.

4. Physical separation, status differences, gender differences, cultural diversity, and language are potential communication barriers that can be overcome.

5. Active or passive defensive communication destroys interpersonal relationships, whereas assertive, nondefensive communication leads to clarity.

6. Nonverbal communication includes the use of territorial space, seating arrangements, facial gestures, eye contact, and paralanguage. Nonverbal communication varies by nation and culture around the world.

7. Communicative disease is the absence of heartfelt communication in human relationship and can lead to loneliness and social isolation.

8. Information Communication Technology (ICT) includes electronic mail, voice mail, and cell phones. High-tech innovations require high-touch responses.

Key Terms

barriers to communication (p. 258)
communication (p. 250)
communicative disease (p. 268)
communicator (p. 250)
data (p. 251)
defensive communication (p. 260)
feedback (p. 251)
gateways to communication (p. 258)

information (p. 251)
Information Communication Technology (ICT) (p. 272)
interpersonal communication (p. 250)
language (p. 251)
message (p. 251)
nondefensive communication (p. 260)

nonverbal communication (p. 264)
one-way communication (p. 255)
perceptual screen (p. 250)
receiver (p. 250)
reflective listening (p. 252)
richness (p. 251)
two-way communication (p. 255)

Review Questions

1. What different components of a person's perceptual screens may distort communication?

2. What are the three defining features of reflective listening?

3. What are the four levels of verbal response in reflective listening?

4. Compare one-way communication and two-way communication.

5. What are the five communication skills of effective supervisors and managers?

6. Describe dominant and subordinate defensive communication. Describe nondefensive communication.

7. What four kinds of nonverbal communication are important in interpersonal relationships?

8. What are helpful nonverbal behaviors in the communication process? Unhelpful behaviors?

9. What is communicative disease?

10. Describe at least five new communication technologies in terms of data richness.

Discussion and Communication Questions

1. Who is the best communicator you know? Why do you consider that person to be so?

2. Who is the best listener you have ever known? Describe what that person does that makes him or her so good at listening.

3. What methods have you found most helpful in overcoming barriers to communication that are physical? That are status-based? That are cultural? That are linguistic?

4. Who makes you the most defensive when you talk with that person? What does the person do that makes you so defensive or uncomfortable?

5. With whom are you the most comfortable and nondefensive in conversation? What does the person do that makes you so comfortable or nondefensive?

6. What nonverbal behaviors do you find most helpful in others when you are attempting to talk with them? When you try to listen to them?

7. (communication question) Identify a person at work or at the university who is difficult to talk to and arrange an interview in which you practice good reflective listening skills. Ask the person questions about a topic in which you think he or she is interested. Pay particular attention to being patient, calm, and nonreactive. After the interview, summarize what you learned.

8. (communication question) Go to the library and read about communication problems and barriers. Write a memo categorizing the problems and barriers you find in the current literature (last five years). What changes do organizations or people need to make to solve these problems?

9. (communication question) Develop a role-playing activity for class that demonstrates defensive (dominant or subordinate) and nondefensive communication. Write brief role descriptions that classmates can act out.

10. (communication question) Read everything you can find in the library about a new communication technology. Write a two-page memo summarizing what you have learned and the conclusions you draw about the new technology's advantages and disadvantages.

Ethical Dilemma

Pat Williams sat at her desk listening to the conversation in the next cubical. She didn't want to listen, but it was impossible to miss. The discussion was between Jake Timmons, a coworker and their supervisor, Mark Andersen. They were in a heated discussion about one of the company's biggest clients, Patel Manufacturing.

An executive from Patel had contacted Mark to tell him that Jake had not been giving them the attention such a large client deserved. He claimed that Jake did not return phone calls and often missed appointments. Mark was furious about the situation and was demanding an explanation. Jake tried to explain that he was doing everything he could to effectively manage the account, but the breakdown was on the other end. John, his contact at Patel, was the problem. He rarely responded to any of Jake's calls or e-mail. Jake had thought about reporting him but didn't want to get him in trouble with his manager.

Mark seemed not to hear a word Jake was saying. He simply continued to accuse Jake of endangering their most important customer. As Pat listened to this conversation, she considered whether or not she should get involved. It was obvious that Mark was not listening to anything Jake said. She had overheard Jake on several occasions trying to reach John without success. She could testify to that. But, she had worked with John herself and had never experienced any problems. Also, she had only Jake's word for just how bad things were. She really didn't know Jake very well, and what if he was really slacking on his end and using John as an excuse? She didn't want to add to the disparaging comments about John if they weren't true. But she also didn't think it was fair that Mark was not giving any credit to what Jake was trying to explain. She didn't want to get Mark angry at her but felt she needed to support Jake in some way.

Experiential Exercises

8.1 Communicate, Listen, Understand

The following exercise gives you an opportunity to work within a three-person group to do a communication skill-building exercise. You can learn to apply some of the reflective listening and two-way communication materials from the early sections of the chapter, as well as some of the lessons managing difficult communication in a nondefensive manner.

Step 1. The class is formed into three-person groups and each group designates its members "A," "B," and "C." There will be three 5- to 7-minute conversations among the group members: first, between A and B; second, between B and C; third, between C and A. During each conversation, the nonparticipating group member is to observe and make notes about two communicating group members.

Step 2. Your instructor will give you a list of controversial topics and ask A to pick a topic. A is then asked to discuss her or his position on this topic, with the rationale for the position, with B. B is to practice reflective listening and engage in listening checks periodically by paraphrasing what he or she understands to be A's position. C should observe whether B is practicing good listening skills or be-

Questions

1. Does Pat have a duty to support Jake?

2. Does she have a responsibility to John?

3. Evaluate Pat's decision using rule, virtue, rights, and justice theory.

coming defensive. C should also observe whether A is becoming dominantly defensive in the communication. This should be a two-way communication.

Step 3. Repeat Step 2 with B as communicator, C as listener, and A as observer.

Step 4. Repeat Step 2 with C as communicator, A as listener, and B as observer.

Step 5. After your instructor has had all groups complete Steps 1 through 4, your three-person group should answer the following questions.

a. *Did either the listener or the communicator become visibly (or internally) angry or upset during the discussion?*

b. *What were the biggest challenges for the listeners in the controversial communication? For the communicator?*

c. *What are the most important skill improvements (e.g., better eye contact or more patience) the listener and communicator could have made to improve the quality of understanding achieved through the communication process?*

8.2 Preparing for an Employment-Selection Interview

The purpose of this exercise is to help you develop guidelines for an employment-selection interview. Employment-selection interviews are one of the more important settings in which supervisors and job candidates use applied communication skills. There is always the potential for defensiveness and confusion as well as lack of complete information exchange in this interview. This exercise allows you to think through ways to maximize the value of an employment-selection interview, whether you are the supervisor or the candidate, so that it is a productive experience based on effective applied communication.

Your instructor will form your class into groups of students. Each group should work through Steps 1 and 2 of the exercise.

Step 1. *Guidelines for the Supervisor*
Develop a set of guidelines for the supervisor in preparing for and then conducting an employment-selection interview. Consider the following questions in developing your guidelines.

a. What should the supervisor do before the interview?

b. How should the supervisor act and behave during the interview?

c. What should the supervisor do after the interview?

Step 2. *Guidelines for the Employee*
Develop another set of guidelines for the employee in preparing for and then being involved in an employment-selection interview. Consider the following questions in developing your guidelines.

a. What should the employee do before the interview?

b. How should the employee act and behave during the interview?

c. What should the employee do after the interview?

Once each group has developed the two sets of guidelines, the instructor will lead the class in a general discussion in which groups share and compare their guidelines. Consider the following questions during this discussion.

1. What similarities are there among the groups for each set of guidelines?

2. What unique or different guidelines have some of the groups developed?

3. What are essential guidelines for conducting an employment-selection interview?

Biz Flix | Patch Adams

Hunter "Patch" Adams (Robin Williams), a maverick medical student, believes that laughter is the best medicine. The rest of the medical community believes that medicine is the best medicine. Unlike traditional physicians who remain aloof, Patch Adams prefers closeness to his patients. Williams's wackiness comes through clearly in this film, which is based on a true story.

The scene from *Patch Adams* comes from an early sequence, "The Experiment," which takes place after the students' medical school orientation. Patch Adams and fellow medical student Truman Schiff (Daniel London) leave the University Diner. They begin Patch's experiment for changing the programmed responses of people they meet on the street. Along the way, they stumble upon a meat packer's convention where this scene occurs. The film continues with the convention and then returns to the medical school.

What to Watch for and Ask Yourself:

> What parts of the communication process appear in this scene? Note each part of the process that you see in the scene.

> What type of communication does this scene show? Small group, large audience, or persuasive?

> Is Patch Adams an effective communicator? Why or why not?

Workplace Video | Le Meridien Hotel: Communicating in Organizations

Le Meridien is a luxury hotel chain famous for offering a unique European experience with a French flair to its more than 100,000 visitors each year. The hotel group operates over 130 hotels in 56 countries around the globe.

For Assistant General Manager Bob van den Oord, communication plays a crucial role in managing Le Meridien. His job involves communicating with department heads, staff, guests, suppliers, and senior management, through both formal and informal channels. The assistant general manager is personable and has become known for his "management by walkabout" style—a daily routine of monitoring operations and staff by conducting a walk-through inspection of the entire hotel.

Van den Oord creates a variety of meetings where managers can discuss their duties and schedules while receiving important feedback. In between meetings, employees utilize various communications technologies to coordinate efforts and report back to the assistant general manager. Although van den Oord concedes that technology-based communications like e-mail and text messaging are convenient and have a place in hotel operations, he prefers the channel richness of face-to-face communication.

Questions

1. *What barriers to effective communication were discussed in the video?*
2. *How important is nonverbal communication at Le Meridien Hotel? On what types of nonverbal communication does Bob van den Oord rely?*
3. *How does van den Oord foster effective communication at Le Meridien Hotel?*

Implications of Communicating through New Technologies

Richard Smith, a human resources expert, observes: "Internet access is now commonplace in our workplaces and has become an essential part of the way we work. However, it offers a host of distractions, from Internet banking and buying the weekly groceries, to catching up on gossip or planning a holiday—not to mention the temptation of popular sites such as Hotmail, eBay and Amazon." Indeed, it is difficult to imagine how a modern workplace would function effectively and efficiently without Internet access.

The Internet and e-mail are technological innovations that have, in a relatively few years, transformed the way people communicate within the workplace. Gone are the days when communication was primarily in person, by telephone, or through what is now called "snail mail." In vogue are e-mail communication and instant messaging 24 hours a day, seven days a week around the globe; company and personal Web sites that invite communications from others; intranets to facilitate communication among employees; and extranets to support communication with customers and suppliers.

While information technology has transformed communications among people in the workplace, it has not been accomplished without an accompanying set of challenges and problems. Patrice Rapalus, director of the Computer Security Institute in San Francisco, California, says: "There is much more illegal and unauthorized activity . . . than corporations admit to their clients, stockholders and business partners, or report to law enforcement." Illegal and unauthorized activity appears to be quite widespread. For instance, a 2002 study by the Computer Security Institute found that 78 percent of the responding organizations had detected employee abuse of Internet access privileges and that 80 percent had significant financial losses due to computer breaches, including employee abuse of privileges. Financial losses attributable to all sources of computer breaches were $455 million for the 223 responding companies.

A very insidious form of unauthorized usage of company computer resources and Internet access occurs when employees create "extracurricular Web sites" to serve key customers and suppliers rather than use the company's official Web site. "A clever and ambitious employee has every incentive to use technology to make himself more indispensable to both his company and his client. The firm, of course, has every incentive to deploy technology that empowers employees and their customers—but not enough so that they become a threat to the business. That's a conflict."

In a presentation to the attendees of the 2002 annual conference of the Society for Human Resource Management, Rodney Glover, a partner with the law firm Wiley Rein and Fielding LLP, reported some revealing statistics regarding employees' Internet usage and companies' responses to that usage. Specifically, over 80 percent of major U.S. companies monitor employee use of the Internet; almost 70 percent have disciplined employees for Internet misuse; slightly more than 30 percent of these companies have fired people for Internet misuse; employees spend an average six work hours a week surfing the Internet for personal reasons; and legal claims concerning violations of employee privacy have increased by 3,000 percent since 1990. More recently, Websense, a computer security company, reported in its 2004 annual survey of computer users that "employees aren't shy about using their Internet connections at work for personal reasons, but most believe productivity doesn't suffer." Collectively, these data strongly indicate that significant organizational resources are being expended on monitoring employee communications via the Internet and e-mail.

Monitoring employee Internet and e-mail usage serves a variety of purposes for an organization. Among the various reasons for this sort of organizational surveillance are the following:

> Preventing decrements in employee productivity and the corresponding negative financial impact on the company.

> Effectively managing the company's liability for employee misuse of the technology it provides.

> Protecting the company's trade secrets.

> Preventing corporate defamation.

> Protecting the company against discovery in litigation.

By taking action to accomplish these objectives, organizations run the risk of unduly trampling on employee privacy. The key to resolving this conundrum, according to several experts, is to make employees aware in advance that they "shouldn't expect privacy when using corporate resources, including the Internet and e-mail." Moreover, permitting personal use of the Internet and e-mail could provide beneficial outcomes for both the employees and the company. Richard Smith, the previously mentioned human resources expert, suggests that providing employees with some work time to use the Internet for personal reasons might even boost morale and concentration, thereby contributing to enhanced productivity.

Discussion Questions

1. How are the Internet and e-mail transforming the way people communicate in the workplace?

2. Does the illegal and unauthorized use of company computer resources and Internet access constitute a major problem for businesses?

3. Why should an organization monitor its employees' use of the company's computer resources, e-mail, and Internet access?

4. What has been your experience with the use of an organization's computer resources and Internet access? How did the organization's computer usage policies influence what you did?

SOURCE: This case was written by Michael K. McCuddy, The Louis S. and Mary L. Morgal Chair of Christian Business Ethics and Professor of Management, College of Business Administration, Valparaiso University. This case was developed from material contained in the following articles: "Balancing Security & Privacy in the Internet Age," *HR Focus* (August 2002: Vol.79, No. 2): 1 4; R. Breeden, "Workers See Personal Use of Web as Aiding Jobs," *The Wall Street Journal* (July 13, 2004): accessed from *The Wall Street Journal* on-line at http://www.wsj.com; A. Conry-Murray, "The Pros and Cons of Employee Surveillance," *Network Magazine* (February 2001, Vol. 16, No. 2): 62–65; "Managing Internet Surfing," Management Services (July 2004, Vol. 48, No. 7): 8; E. Marcus, "Why Your Company Needs a Computer-Use Policy," *NH Business Review* (February 21–March 6, 2003): 5B; M. Schrage, "Internet: Internal Threat?" *Fortune* (July 9, 2001, Vol. 144, No. 1): 184.

© Photodisc Collection/Getty Images

Chapter 9

Work Teams and Groups

LEARNING OBJECTIVES

After reading this chapter, you should be able to do the following:

1 Define *group* and *work team.*

2 Explain four important aspects of group behavior.

3 Describe group formation, the four stages of a group's development, and the characteristics of a mature group.

4 Explain the task and maintenance functions in groups.

5 Identify the social benefits of group and team membership.

6 Discuss diversity and creativity in teams.

7 Discuss empowerment, teamwork, and self-managed teams.

8 Explain the importance of upper echelons and top management teams.

THINKING AHEAD: WHOLE FOODS MARKET

Team Member Excellence and Happiness

Whole Foods Market's motto "Whole Foods, Whole People, Whole Planet" emphasizes its dedication to its retail customers and employees. The company says that there is no place for the "us-versus-them" thinking that permeates some organizations. Employees at Whole Foods are referred to as *team members*, whether they are retail team members or "behind the scene" team members. The company strives to build positive and healthy relationships among all team members. Its goal is to achieve unity of vision and to build trust among team members in the organization while supporting a balanced life for each team member. The best way to achieve these aims, goals, and outcomes is to encourage participation and involvement at all levels of the business. Whole Foods does this by having a collective, team-oriented focus in much of its organizational life.

Whole Foods encourages teamwork in the organization along a number of dimensions. Self-directed teams meet regularly to discuss issues, solve problems, and appreciate each other's contributions to the business. Communication throughout the company is increased through team member forums and team member advisory groups. In addition, communication is enhanced through open-book, open-door, and open-people practices that build relationships and trust among team members. Team member incentive programs, such as labor gainsharing, emphasize team-oriented behaviors as opposed to individual effort and achievement. The company's stock options and stock purchase plan further highlight this collective emphasis. These policies and practices aim to help each team member reach his or her full potential.

Despite the best efforts at teamwork in some organizations, an us-versus-them mentality does materialize. Whole Foods is the nation's largest nonunion food retailer after Wal-Mart. Some unions would love to organize the large Whole Foods workforce, just as they would like to do in the case of Wal-Mart. Whole Foods' CEO John

Mackey knows that this can happen when management does not listen to employees. When employees are not heard, they have a tendency to turn to unions for the sympathetic ear not available within the organization. While some managers and executives may not pay enough attention to employees throughout their organizations, others truly do care about their employees' attitudes, concerns, and feelings. In either case, employees who feel neglected, unheard, unappreciated, or in the more extreme cases, mistreated are highly likely to turn to unions to have their needs met.[1] Will the spirit of teamwork be strong enough at Whole Foods to fend off efforts by some employees to unionize?

1. Define *group* and *work team*.

Northrop Grumman was able to achieve teamwork among employees, customers, and partners through knowledge sharing in integrated product teams.[2] Not all teams and groups work face to face. In today's information age, advanced computer and telecommunications technologies enable organizations to be more flexible through the use of virtual teams.[3] Virtual teams also address new workforce demographics, enabling companies to access expertise and the best employees who may be located anywhere in the world. Whether a traditional group or a virtual team, groups and teams continue to play a vital role in organizational behavior and performance at work.

A *group* is two or more people having common interests, objectives, and continuing interaction. Table 9.1 summarizes the characteristics of a well-functioning, effective group.[4] A *work team* is a group of people with complementary skills who are committed to a common mission, performance goals, and approach for which they hold themselves mutually accountable.[5] All work teams are groups, but not all groups are work teams. Groups emphasize individual leadership, individual accountability, and individual work products. Work teams emphasize shared leadership, mutual accountability, and collective work products.

The chapter begins with a traditional discussion of group behavior and group development in the first two sections. The third section discusses teams. The final two sections explore the contemporary team issues of empowerment, self-managed teams, and upper echelon teams.

group

Two or more people with common interests, objectives, and continuing interaction.

work team

A group of people with complementary skills who are committed to a common mission, performance goals, and approach for which they hold themselves mutually accountable.

TABLE 9.1   Characteristics of a Well-Functioning, Effective Group

(9.1)

- The atmosphere tends to be relaxed, comfortable, and informal.
- The group's task is well understood and accepted by the members.
- The members listen well to one another; most members participate in a good deal of task-relevant discussion.
- People express both their feelings and their ideas.
- Conflict and disagreement are present and centered around ideas or methods, not personalities or people.
- The group is aware and conscious of its own operation and function.
- Decisions are usually based on consensus, not majority vote.
- When actions are decided, clear assignments are made and accepted by members of the group.

Group Behavior

Group behavior has been a subject of interest in social psychology for a long time, and many different aspects of group behavior have been studied over the years. We now look at four topics relevant to groups functioning in organizations: norms of behavior, group cohesion, social loafing, and loss of individuality. Group behavior topics related to decision making, such as polarization and groupthink, are addressed in Chapter 10.

2. Explain four important aspects of group behavior.

① Norms of Behavior

The standards that a work group uses to evaluate the behavior of its members are its *norms of behavior*. These norms may be written or unwritten, verbalized or not verbalized, implicit or explicit. As long as individual members of the group understand the norms, the norms can be effective in influencing behavior. Norms may specify what members of a group should do (such as a specified dress code for men and for women), or they may specify what members of a group should not do (such as executives not behaving arrogantly with employees).

Norms may exist in any aspect of work group life. They may evolve informally or unconsciously within a group, or they may arise in response to challenges, such as the norm of disciplined behavior by firefighters in responding to a three-alarm fire to protect the group.[6] Performance norms are among the most important group norms from the organization's perspective. For example, cooperative standards within teams lead to members working for mutual benefit, which in turn facilitate team performance.[7] We discuss performance standards further in a later section of this chapter. Organizational culture and corporate codes of ethics, such as Johnson & Johnson's credo (see Chapter 2), reflect behavioral norms expected within work groups. Finally, norms that create awareness of emotions and help regulate emotions are critical to groups' effectiveness.[8]

norms of behavior
The standards that a work group uses to evaluate the behavior of its members.

② Group Cohesion

The "interpersonal glue" that makes the members of a group stick together is *group cohesion*. Group cohesion can enhance job satisfaction for members and improve organizational productivity.[9] Highly cohesive groups are able to control and manage their membership better than work groups low in cohesion. In one study of 381 banking teams in Hong Kong and the United States, increased job complexity and task autonomy led to increased group cohesiveness, which translated into better performance.[10] In addition to performance, highly cohesive groups are strongly motivated to maintain good, close relationships among the members. We examine group cohesion in further detail, along with factors leading to high levels of group cohesion, when discussing the common characteristics of well-developed groups.

group cohesion
The "interpersonal glue" that makes members of a group stick together.

③ Social Loafing

Social loafing occurs when one or more group members rely on the efforts of other group members and fail to contribute their own time, effort, thoughts, or other resources to a group.[11] This may create a real drag on the group's efforts and achievements. Some scholars argue that, from the individual's standpoint, social loafing, or free riding, is rational behavior in response to an experience of inequity or when individual efforts are hard to observe. However, it shortchanges the group, which loses potentially valuable resources possessed by individual members.[12]

social loafing
The failure of a group member to contribute personal time, effort, thoughts, or other resources to the group.

A number of methods for countering social loafing exist, such as having identifiable individual contributions to the group product and member self-evaluation systems. For example, if each group member is responsible for a specific input to the group, a member's failure to contribute will be noticed by everyone. If members must formally evaluate their contributions to the group, they are less likely to loaf.

Loss of Individuality

loss of individuality

A social process in which individual group members lose self-awareness and its accompanying sense of accountability, inhibition, and responsibility for individual behavior.

Social loafing may be detrimental to group achievement, but it does not have the potentially explosive effects of *loss of individuality*. Loss of individuality, or deindividuation, is a social process in which individual group members lose self-awareness and its accompanying sense of accountability, inhibition, and responsibility for individual behavior.[13]

When individuality is lost, people may engage in morally reprehensible acts and even violent behavior as committed members of their group or organization. For example, loss of individuality was one of several contributing factors in the violent and aggressive acts that led to the riot that destroyed sections of Los Angeles following the Rodney King verdict in the early 1990s. Loss of individuality is not always negative or destructive, however. The loosening of normal ego control mechanisms in the individual may lead to prosocial behavior and heroic acts in dangerous situations.[14] A group that successfully develops into a mature group may not encounter problems with loss of individuality.

Group Formation and Development

3. Describe group formation, the four stages of a group's development, and the characteristics of a mature group.

After its formation, a group goes through predictable stages of development. If successful, it emerges as a mature group. One logical group development model proposes four stages following the group's formation.[15] These stages are mutual acceptance, decision making, motivation and commitment, and control and sanctions. To become a mature group, each of the stages in development must be successfully negotiated.

According to this group development model, a group addresses three issues: interpersonal issues, task issues, and authority issues.[16] The interpersonal issues include matters of trust, personal comfort, and security. The task issues include the mission or purpose of the group, the methods the group employs, and the outcomes expected of the group. The authority issues include decisions about who is in charge, how power and influence are managed, and who has the right to tell whom to do what. This section addresses group formation, each stage of group development, and the characteristics of a mature group.

Group Formation

Formal and informal groups form in organizations for different reasons. The Real World 9.1 discusses the formation of a formal group at General Motors. Formal groups are sometimes called official or assigned groups, and informal groups may be called unofficial or emergent groups. Formal groups gather to perform various tasks and include an executive and staff, standing committees of the board of directors, project task forces, and temporary committees. An example of a formal group was the task force assembled by The University of Texas at Arlington (UTA), whose mission was to design the Goolsby Leadership Academy that bridges academics and practice. Chaired by the associate dean of business, the task force was composed of seven members with diverse

Breaking All the Rules at GM

GM's Mike DiGiovanni handpicked an unconventional team to build the highly successful H2.

© Reuters/CORBIS

When GM's all-powerful strategy board gave Mike DiGiovanni the go-ahead to snag the marketing rights to Hummer from its manufacturer AM General, his core idea was to take the military vehicle made famous during the Gulf War and create the "son of Hummer." Also known as H2, this would be a smaller, friendlier version of the original. GM's unanticipated success

with this idea over a four-year period came from the passion and personal commitment of an unlikely team of unorthodox veterans. DiGiovanni knew that the Hummer needed a good team, so he used a three-pronged strategy to put together the right team to build the H2. First, DiGiovanni picked people who had been slapped on the wrist for speaking their minds. His euphemism was that these people had been "sent to the rock pile." He wanted team members with somewhat irreverent attitudes who were willing to stand up for what they thought was right, even if it was not politically correct. Second, DiGiovanni threw out the hiring lists because he did not want people who were next in line for a job. Rather, he wanted people with passion who wanted to be on the team. Third, DiGiovanni did not go with the conventional wisdom of hiring newcomers because they were more innovative. Instead, he sought out networkers who had been around the system. In the end, Mike DiGiovanni won with a savvy team of GM veterans.

SOURCE: F. Warner, "GM Goes Off-Road," *Fast Company* 67 (February 2003): 40, http://www.fastcompany.com/magazine/67/smartcompany.html.

academic expertise and business experience. The task force envisioned a five-year developmental plan to create a national center of excellence in preparing Goolsby Fellows and Goolsby Associates for authentic leadership in the twenty-first century.

Diversity is an important consideration in the formation of groups. For example, Monsanto Agricultural Company, now simply Monsanto Company, created a task force titled Valuing Diversity to address subtle discrimination resulting from workforce diversity.[17] The original task force was titled Eliminating Subtle Discrimination (ESD) and was composed of fifteen women, minorities, and white males. Subtle discrimination might include the use of gender- or culture-specific language. Monsanto and the task force's intent was to build on individual differences—whether in terms of gender, race, or culture—in developing a dominant heterogeneous culture. Diversity can enhance group performance. One study of gender diversity among U.S. workers found that men and women in gender-balanced groups had higher job satisfaction than those in homogeneous groups.[18]

Ethnic diversity has characterized many industrial work groups in the United States since the 1800s. This was especially true during the early years of the 1900s, when waves of immigrant workers arrived from Germany, Yugoslavia, Italy, Poland, Scotland, the Scandinavian countries, and many other nations. Organizations were challenged to blend these culturally and linguistically diverse peoples into effective work groups.

In addition to ethnic, gender, and cultural diversity, there is interpersonal diversity. Chaparral Steel Company (part of Texas Industries) has a team of officers who achieved compatibility through interpersonal diversity. Successful interpersonal relationships are the basis of group effort, a key foundation for business success. In the case of the Chaparral Steel officers, they differed in their needs for inclusion in activities, control of people and events, and interpersonal affection from others. Though diverse in their interpersonal needs, the officers as a group found strength through balance and complementarity.

Informal groups evolve in the work setting to gratify a variety of member needs not met by formal groups. For example, organizational members' inclusion and affection needs might be satisfied through informal athletic or interest groups. Athletic teams representing a department, unit, or company may achieve semiofficial status, such as the AT&T National Running Team that uses the corporate logo on its race shirts.

Stages of Group Development

All groups, formal and informal, go through stages of development as noted on page 286, from forming interpersonal relationships among the members to becoming a mature and productive unit. Mature groups are able to work through the necessary interpersonal, task, and authority issues to achieve at high levels. Demographic diversity and group fault lines (i.e., potential breaking points in a group) are two potential predictors of the sense-making process, subgroup formation patterns, and nature of group conflict at various stages of group development.[19] Hence, group development through these stages may not always be smooth.

In addition to the Bennis and Shepard group development model, we want to look at two other group development models. These two well-known models are Tuckman's and Gersick's. Each of these models looks at the evolution of behavior in teams, and Tuckman's model also focuses on leadership.

THE FIVE-STAGE MODEL Bruce Tuckman's five-stage model of group development proposes that team behavior progresses through five stages: forming, storming, norming, performing, and adjourning.[20] These stages and the emphasis on relationships and leadership styles in each are shown in Figure 9.1.

Dependence on guidance and direction is the defining characteristic in the *forming* stage. Team members are unclear about individual roles and responsibilities and tend to rely heavily on the leader to answer questions about the team's purpose, objectives, and external relationships. Moving from this stage requires that team members feel they are part of the team.

FIGURE 9.1   Tuckman's Five-Stage Model of Group Development

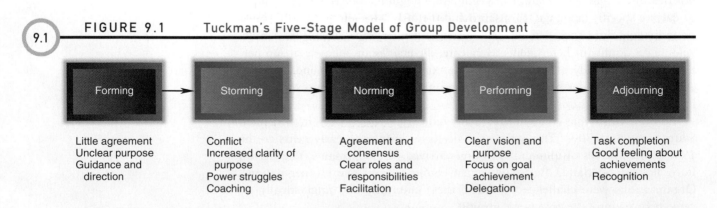

Forming	Storming	Norming	Performing	Adjourning
Little agreement Unclear purpose Guidance and direction	Conflict Increased clarity of purpose Power struggles Coaching	Agreement and consensus Clear roles and responsibilities Facilitation	Clear vision and purpose Focus on goal achievement Delegation	Task completion Good feeling about achievements Recognition

Team members compete for position in the *storming* stage. As the name suggests, this is a stage of considerable conflict as power struggles, cliques, and factions within the group begin to form. Clarity of purpose increases, but uncertainties still exist. This is also the stage when members assess one another with regard to trustworthiness, emotional comfort, and evaluative acceptance. For the Valuing Diversity task force at Monsanto, trust was one of the early issues to be worked through. A coaching style by the leader is key during this stage of group development as team members may challenge him or her.

Agreement and consensus are characteristic of team members in the *norming* stage. It is in this stage that roles and responsibilities become clear and accepted with big decisions being made by group agreement. The focus turns from interpersonal relations to decision-making activities related to the group's task accomplishment. Small decisions may be delegated to individuals or small teams within the group. The group addresses authority questions like these: Who is responsible for what aspects of the group's work? Does the group need one primary leader and spokesperson? Wallace Supply Company, an industrial distributor of pipes, valves, and fittings, has found employee teams particularly valuable in this aspect of work life.[21] Leadership is facilitative with some leadership responsibilities being shared by the team.

As a team moves into the *performing* stage, it becomes more strategically aware and clear about its mission and purpose. In this stage of development, the group has successfully worked through the necessary interpersonal, task, and authority issues and can stand on its own two feet with little interference from the leader. Primarily, the team makes decisions, and disagreements are resolved positively with necessary changes to structure and processes attended to by the team. A mature group is able to control its members through the judicious application of specific positive and negative sanctions based on the evaluation of specific member behaviors. Recent research shows that evaluation biases stemming from liking someone operate in face-to-face groups but not in electronic groups, such as virtual teams.[22] Members at this stage do not need to be instructed but may ask for assistance from the leader with personal or interpersonal development. The team requires a leader who delegates and oversees.

The final stage of group development is the *adjourning* stage. When the task is completed, everyone on the team can move on to new and different things. Team members have a sense of accomplishment and feel good knowing that their purpose is fulfilled. The leader's role is primarily one of recognition of the group's achievements. Unless the group is a task force or other informal team, most groups in organizations remain at the performing stage and do not disband as the adjourning stage suggests.

PUNCTUATED EQUILIBRIUM MODEL Though it is still highly cited in team and group research, Tuckman's "forming–norming–storming–performing–adjourning" model may be unrealistic from an organizational perspective. In fact, research has shown that many teams experience relational conflicts at different times and in different contexts. Connie Gersick proposes that groups do not necessarily progress linearly from one step to another in a predetermined sequence but alternate between periods of inertia with little visible progress toward goal achievement *punctuated* by bursts of energy as work groups develop. It is in these periods of energy where the majority of a group's work is accomplished.[23] For example, a task force given nine months to complete a task may use the first four months to choose its norms, explore contextual issues, and determine how it will communicate.

The description of a well-functioning, effective group in Table 9.1 characterizes a mature group. Such a group has four distinguishing characteristics: a clear purpose and mission, well-understood norms and standards of conduct, a high level of group cohesion, and a flexible status structure.

PURPOSE AND MISSION The purpose and mission may be assigned to a group (as in the previous example of the Goals by Leadership Academy task force of UTA) or emerge from within the group (as in the case of the AT&T National Running Team). Even in the case of an assigned mission, the group may reexamine, modify, revise, or question the mission. It may also embrace the mission as stated. The importance of mission is exemplified in IBM's Process Quality Management, which requires that a process team of not more than twelve people develop a clear understanding of mission as the first step in the process.[24] The IBM approach demands that all members agree to go in the same direction. The mission statement is converted into a specific agenda, clear goals, and a set of critical success factors. Stating the purpose and mission in the form of specific goals enhances productivity over and above any performance benefits achieved through individual goal setting.[25]

BEHAVIORAL NORMS Behavioral norms, which evolve over a period of time, are well-understood standards of behavior within a group.[26] They are benchmarks against which team members are evaluated and judged by other team members. Some behavioral norms become written rules, such as an attendance policy or an ethical code for a team. Other norms remain informal, although they are no less understood by team members. Dress codes and norms about after-hours socializing may fall into this category. Behavioral norms also evolve around performance and productivity.[27] Productivity norms even influence the performance of sports teams.[28] The group's productivity norm may or may not be consistent with, and supportive of, the organization's productivity standards. A high-performance team sets productivity standards above organizational expectations with the intent to excel. Average teams set productivity standards based on, and consistent with, organizational expectations. Noncompliant or counterproductive teams may set productivity standards below organizational expectations with the intent of damaging the organization or creating change.

GROUP COHESION Group cohesion was earlier described as the interpersonal attraction binding group members together. It enables a group to exercise effective control over its members in relation to its behavioral norms and standards. Goal conflict in a group, unpleasant experiences, and domination of a subgroup are among the threats to a group's cohesion. Groups with low levels of cohesion have greater difficulty exercising control over their members and enforcing their standards of behavior. A classic study of cohesiveness in 238 industrial work groups found cohesion to be an important factor influencing anxiety, tension, and productivity within the groups.[29] Specifically, work-related tension and anxiety were lower in teams high in cohesion, and they were higher in teams low in cohesion, as depicted in Figure 9.2. This suggests that cohesion has a calming effect on team members, at least concerning work-related tension and anxiety. In addition, actual productivity was found to vary significantly less in highly cohesive teams, making these teams much more predictable with regard to their productivity. The actual productivity lev-

FIGURE 9.2   Cohesiveness and Work-Related Tension*

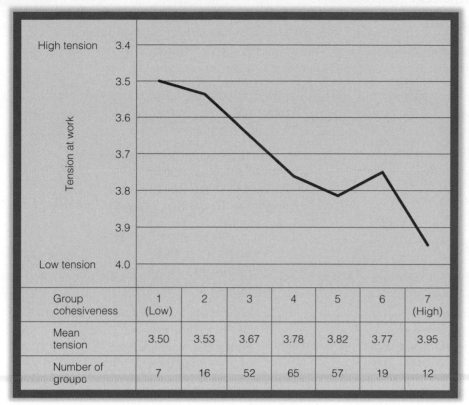

Group cohesiveness	1 (Low)	2	3	4	5	6	7 (High)
Mean tension	3.50	3.53	3.67	3.78	3.82	3.77	3.95
Number of groups	7	16	52	65	57	19	12

Note: Product–moment correlation is 0.28, and critical ratio is 4.20; the group cohesion–tension relationship is highly significant at the .001 level.

*The measure of tension at work is based on group mean response to the question "Does your work ever make you feel 'jumpy' or nervous?" A low numerical score represents relatively high tension.

SOURCE: From S. E. Seashore, *Group Cohesiveness in the Industrial Work Group*, 1954. Research conducted by Stanley E. Seashore at the Institute for Social Research, University of Michigan. Reprinted by permission.

els were primarily determined by the productivity norms within each work group. That is, highly cohesive groups with high production standards are very productive. Similarly, highly cohesive groups with low productivity standards are unproductive. Member satisfaction, commitment, and communication are better in highly cohesive groups. Groupthink may be a problem in highly cohesive groups and is discussed in Chapter 10. You 9.1 includes the three group cohesion questions from this research project. Complete You 9.1 to determine the level of cohesion in a group of which you are a member.

Group cohesion is influenced by a number of factors, most notably time, size, the prestige of the team, external pressure, and internal competition. Group cohesion evolves gradually over time through a group's normal development. Smaller groups—those of five or seven members, for example—are more cohesive than those of more than twenty-five, although cohesion does not decline much with size after forty or more members. Prestige or social status also influences a group's cohesion, with more prestigious groups, such as the U.S. Air Force Thunderbirds or the U.S. Navy Blue Angels, being highly cohesive. However, even groups of very low prestige may be highly cohesive in how they stick together. Finally, external pressure and internal competition influence group cohesion. Although the mechanics' union, pilots, and other internal constituencies at Eastern Airlines had various differences of opinion, they all pulled

How Cohesive Is Your Group?

Think about a group of which you are a member. Answer each of the following questions in relation to this group by circling the number next to the alternative that most reflects your feelings.

1. Do you feel that you are really a part of your group?
   5—Really a part of the group.
   4—Included in most ways.
   3—Included in some ways, but not in others.
   2—Do not feel I really belong.
   1—Do not work with any one group of people.

2. If you had a chance to do the same activities in another group, for the same pay if it is a work group, how would you feel about moving?
   1—Would want very much to move.
   2—Would rather move than stay where I am.
   3—Would make no difference to me.
   4—Would rather stay where I am than move.
   5—Would want very much to stay where I am.

3. How does your group compare with other groups that you are familiar with on each of the following points?

   • The way people get along together.
     5—Better than most.
     3—About the same as most.
     1—Not as good as most.

   • The way people stick together.
     5—Better than most.
     3—About the same as most.
     1—Not as good as most.

   • The way people help one another on the job.
     5—Better than most.
     3—About the same as most.
     1—Not as good as most.

Add up your circled responses. If you have a number of 20 or above, you view your group as highly cohesive. If you have a number between 10 and 19, you view your group's cohesion as average. If you have a number of 7 or less, you view your group as very low in cohesion.

SOURCE: From S. E. Seashore, *Group Cohesiveness in the Industrial Work Group*, University of Michigan, 1954. Reprinted by permission.

together in a cohesive fashion in resisting Frank Lorenzo when he came in to reshape the airline before its demise. Whereas external pressures tend to enhance cohesion, internal competition usually decreases cohesion within a team. One study found that company-imposed work pressure disrupted group cohesion by increasing internal competition and reducing cooperative interpersonal activity.[30]

status structure

The set of authority and task relations among a group's members.

(4) **STATUS STRUCTURE** *Status structure* is the set of authority and task relations among a group's members. The status structure may be hierarchical or egalitarian (i.e., democratic), depending on the group. Successful resolution of the authority issue within a team results in a well-understood status structure of leader–follower relationships. Where leadership problems arise, it is important to find solutions and build team leader effectiveness.[31] Whereas groups tend to have one leader, teams tend to share leadership. For example, one person may be the team's task master who sets the agenda, initiates much of the work activity, and ensures that the team meets its deadlines. Another team member may take a leadership role in maintaining effective interpersonal relationships in the group. Hence, shared leadership is very feasible in teams. An effective status structure results in role interrelatedness among group members.

Diversity in a group is healthy, and members may contribute to the collective effort through one of four basic styles.[32] These are the contributor, the collaborator, the communicator, and the challenger. The contributor is data driven, supplies necessary information, and adheres to high performance standards. The collaborator sees the big picture and is able to keep a constant focus on the mission and urge other members to join efforts for mission accomplishment. The communicator listens well, facilitates the group's process, and humanizes the collective effort. The challenger is the devil's advocate who questions everything from the group's mission, purpose, and methods to its ethics. Members may exhibit one or more of these four basic styles over a period of time. In addition, an effective group must have an integrator.[33] This can be especially important in cross-functional teams, where different perspectives carry the seeds of conflict. However, cross-functional teams are not necessarily a problem. Effectively managing cross-functional teams of artists, designers, printers, and financial experts enabled Hallmark Cards to cut its new-product development time in half.[34]

Emergent leadership in groups was studied among sixty-two men and sixty women.[35] Groups performed tasks not classified as either masculine or feminine, that is, "sex-neutral" tasks. Men and women both emerged as leaders, and neither gender had significantly more emergent leaders. However, group members who described themselves in masculine terms were significantly more likely to emerge as leaders than group members who described themselves in feminine, androgynous (both masculine and feminine), or undifferentiated (neither masculine nor feminine) terms. Hence, gender stereotypes may play a role in emergent leadership.

Task and Maintenance Functions

An effective group or team carries out various task functions to perform its work successfully and various maintenance functions to ensure member satisfaction and a sense of team spirit.[36] Teams that successfully fulfill these functions afford their members the potential for psychological intimacy and integrated involvement. Table 9.2 presents nine task and nine maintenance functions in teams or groups.

Task functions are those activities directly related to the effective completion of the team's work. For example, the task of initiating activity involves suggesting ideas, defining problems, and proposing approaches and/or solutions to problems. The task of seeking information involves asking for ideas, suggestions, information, or facts. Effective teams have members who fulfill various task functions as they are required.

4. Explain the task and maintenance functions in groups.

task function
An activity directly related to the effective completion of a team's work.

TABLE 9.2 **Task and Maintenance Functions in Teams or Groups**

TASK FUNCTIONS	MAINTENANCE FUNCTIONS
Initiating activities	Supporting others
Seeking information	Following others' leads
Giving information	Gatekeeping communication
Elaborating concepts	Setting standards
Coordinating activities	Expressing member feelings
Summarizing ideas	Testing group decisions
Testing ideas	Consensus testing
Evaluating effectiveness	Harmonizing conflict
Diagnosing problems	Reducing tension

Some task functions are more important at one time in the life of a group, and other functions are more important at other times. For example, during the engineering test periods for new technologies, the engineering team needs members who focus on testing the practical applications of suggestions and those who diagnose problems and suggest solutions.

The effective use of task functions leads to the success of the group, and the failure to use them may lead to disaster. For example, the successful initiation and coordination of an emergency room (ER) team's activities by the senior resident saved the life of a knife wound victim.[37] The victim was stabbed one-quarter inch below the heart, and the ER team acted quickly to stem the bleeding, begin intravenous fluids, and monitor the victim's vital signs.

Maintenance functions are those activities essential to the effective, satisfying interpersonal relationships within a group or team. For example, following another group member's lead may be as important as leading others. Communication gatekeepers within a group ensure balanced contributions from all members. Because task activities build tension into teams and groups working together, tension-reduction activities are important to drain off negative or destructive feelings. For example, in a study of twenty-five work groups over a five-year period, humor and joking behavior were found to enhance the social relationships in the groups.[38] The researchers concluded that performance improvements in the twenty-five groups indirectly resulted from improved relationships attributable to the humor and joking behaviors. Maintenance functions enhance togetherness, cooperation, and teamwork, enabling members to achieve psychological intimacy while furthering the success of the team. Jody Grant's supportive attitude and comfortable demeanor as chairman and CEO of Texas Capital Bancshares enabled him to build a vibrant bank in the aftermath of the great Texas banking crash. Grant was respected for his expertise *and* his ability to build relationships. Both task and maintenance functions are important for successful groups and teams.

Work Teams in Organizations

Work teams are task-oriented groups, though in some organizations the term *team* has a negative connotation for unions and union members. Work teams make important and valuable contributions to the organization and are important to the member need satisfaction. For example, an idea to implement a simple change in packaging from a work team at Glenair, a UK-based aerospace and defense contractor, saved the company twenty-five minutes of packaging time per unit. Additionally, a job that used to take one worker half an hour to complete was reduced to only five minutes, freeing the worker to perform other work in the factory.[39]

Several kinds of work teams exist. One classification scheme uses a sports analogy. Some teams work like baseball teams with set responsibilities, other teams work like football teams through coordinated action, and still other teams work like doubles tennis teams with primary yet flexible responsibilities. In addition, crews are a distinct type of work teams that can be studied using the concept of "crewness."[40] Although each type of team may have a useful role in the organization, the individual expert should not be overlooked.[41] That is, at the right time and in the right context, individual members must be allowed to shine.

Why Work Teams?

Teams are very useful in performing work that is complicated, complex, interrelated, and/or more voluminous than one person can handle. Harold Geneen,

---

maintenance function

An activity essential to effective, satisfying interpersonal relationships within a team or group.

while chairman of ITT, said, "If I had enough arms and legs and time, I'd do it all myself." Obviously, people working in organizations cannot do everything because of the limitations of arms, legs, time, expertise, knowledge, and other resources. Individual limitations are overcome and problems are solved through teamwork and collaboration. World-class U.S. corporations, such as Motorola Inc., are increasingly deploying work teams in their global affiliates to meet the competition and gain an advantage.[42] Motorola's "Be Cool" team in the Philippines has a family atmosphere and may even begin a meeting with a prayer, yet is committed to improving individual and team performance.

Teams make important contributions to organizations in work areas that lend themselves to teamwork. *Teamwork* is a core value at Hewlett-Packard. Complex, interdependent work tasks and activities that require collaboration particularly lend themselves to teamwork. Teams are appropriate where knowledge, talent, skills, and abilities are dispersed across organizational members and require integrated effort for task accomplishment. The recent emphasis on team-oriented work environments is based on empowerment with collaboration, not on power and competition. Larry Hirschhorn labels this "the new team environment" founded on a significantly more empowered workforce in the industrial sectors of the American economy. This new team environment is compared with the old work environment in Table 9.3. The spirit of teamwork can also improve worker satisfaction as described in The Real World 9.2.

That teams are necessary is a driving principle of total quality efforts in organizations. Total quality efforts often require the formation of teams—especially cross-functional teams composed of people from different functions, such as manufacturing and design, who are responsible for specific organizational processes. Former Eastman Kodak CEO George Fisher believed in the importance of participation and cooperation as foundations for teamwork and a total quality program. In a study of forty machine crews in a northeastern U.S. paper mill, organizational citizenship behaviors, specifically helping behavior and sportsmanship, contributed significantly to the quantity and quality of work group performance.[43]

teamwork
Joint action by a team of people in which individual interests are subordinated to team unity.

TABLE 9.3 | A Comparison of the New Team Environment versus the Old Work Environment

NEW TEAM ENVIRONMENT	OLD WORK ENVIRONMENT
Person comes up with initiatives.	Person follows orders.
Team has considerable authority to chart its own steps.	Team depends on the manager to chart its course.
Members form a team because people learn to collaborate in the face of their emerging right to think for themselves. People both rock the boat and work together.	Members were a team because people conformed to direction set by the manager. No one rocked the boat.
People cooperate by using their thoughts and feelings. They link up through direct talk.	People cooperated by suppressing their thoughts and feelings. They wanted to get along.

SOURCE: *Managing in the New Team Environment,* by Hirschhorn. © 1991. Reprinted by permission of Prentice-Hall, Inc., Upper Saddle River, N.J.

Teamwork for a Cause

The World Wildlife Fund has as its foundation a true team concept with a unified sense of purpose.

© Photolink/Photodisc/Getty Images

David Southern used to work at Citibank, but he wanted two things he did not have with the bank. He wanted more work/life balance, and he wanted to work for something he believed in—for a cause. So Southern became head of information technology (IT) at the World Wildlife Fund (WWF), which is headquartered in Switzerland and has offices in England, Northern Ireland, Scotland, and Wales. He has a small IT department but one that works in a highly professional environment. He and his staff are trusted within the WWF because they have service-level agreements with their users,

they measure their own performance, and they have clear processes in place. The IT team members are not there for big company salaries, because the WWF does not pay them. They are there because of the charity's work and because of the spirit of teamwork that pervades the fund.

While the IT team members in particular have bonded well, it is not because they have done specific team-building activities such as whitewater rafting. Rather, they have bonded well because of their unity and common sense of purpose in their work. In addition, the small IT staff size has led to high satisfaction due to a high level of responsibility, a lot of job variety, and the ability to nurture people's careers around their strengths and interests. A tribute to Southern's leadership and the teamwork in the department is the fact that only one person has left the IT staff in four years.

SOURCE: J. Vowler, "Teamwork Key to Charity's Success," *Computer Weekly* (February 25, 2004): 24, http://www.computerweekly.com/Article128526.htm.

Work Team Structure and Work Team Process

structure

Work team effectiveness in the new team environment requires attention by management to both work team structure and work team process.[44] The primary structural issues for work teams are goals and objectives, operating guidelines, performance measures, and the specification of roles. A work team's goals and objectives specify what must be achieved, while the operating guidelines set the organizational boundaries and decision-making limits within which the team must function. The goal-setting process was discussed in Chapter 6 and has applicability for work teams, too. In addition to these two structural elements, the work team needs to know what performance measures are being used to assess its task accomplishment. For example, a medical emergency team's performance measures might include the success rate in saving critically injured patients and the average number of hours a patient is in the emergency room before being transferred to a hospital bed. Finally, work team structure requires a clearly specified set of roles for the executives and managers who oversee the work of the team, for the work team leaders who exercise influence over team members, and for team members. These role specifications should include information about required role behaviors, such as decision making and task performance, as well as restrictions or limits on role behaviors, such as the limitations on managerial interventions in work team activities and decision making. Expectations as well as experience may be especially important for newcomer role performance in work teams.[45]

Process

Work team process is the second important dimension of effectiveness. Two of the important process issues in work teams are the managing of cooperative behaviors and the managing of competitive behaviors. Both sets of behaviors are helpful in task accomplishment, and they should be viewed as complementary sets of behaviors. Cooperative teamwork skills include open communication, trust, personal integrity, positive interdependence, and mutual support. On the other hand, positive competitive teamwork skills include the ability to enjoy competition, play fair, be a good winner or loser; to have access to information for monitoring where the team and members are in the competition; and not to overgeneralize or exaggerate the results of any specific competition. In a study of reward structures in 75 four-member teams, competitive rewards enhanced speed of performance, while cooperative rewards enhanced accuracy of performance.[46]

Work team process issues have become more complex in the global workplace with teams composed of members from many cultures and backgrounds. This is enhanced by the presence of virtual work teams operating on the global landscape. Our discussions of diversity earlier in the text have particular relevance to multicultural work teams. In addition to the process issues of cooperation, competition, and diversity, three other process issues are related to topics we discuss elsewhere in the text. These are empowerment, discussed in the next major section of this chapter; team decision making, which is discussed in Chapter 10; and conflict management and resolution, which are discussed in Chapter 13.

Quality Teams and Circles

Quality teams and quality circles are part of a total quality program. Decision making in *quality teams* is discussed in detail in Chapter 10. Quality teams are different from QCs in that they are more formal and are designed and assigned by upper-level management. Quality teams are not voluntary and have formal power, whereas quality circles have less formal power and decision authority. Although less commonly used than a decade ago, quality circle principles continue to have value.

Quality circles (QCs) are small groups of employees who work voluntarily on company time—typically one hour per week—to address work-related problems such as quality control, cost reduction, production planning and techniques, and even product design. Membership in a QC is typically voluntary and is fixed once a circle is formed, although some changes may occur as appropriate. QCs are trained in various problem-solving techniques and use them to address the work-related problems.

QCs were popularized as a Japanese management method when an American, W. Edwards Deming, exported his thinking about QCs to Japan following World War II.[47] QCs became popular in the United States in the 1980s, when companies such as Ford, Hewlett-Packard, and Eastman Kodak implemented them. The Camp Red Cloud Garrison in South Korea saved $2 million by implementing the Six Sigma quality program that involved all garrison supervisors and looked at efficiencies from the customer's perspective. Some of the money saved from technology improvements has gone back to employees in an effort to improve safety equipment, work facilities, and employee recreation.

Quality teams and quality circles must deal with substantive issues if they are to be effective; otherwise, employees begin to believe the quality effort is simply a management ploy. QCs do not necessarily require final decision authority

quality team
A team that is part of an organization's structure and is empowered to act on its decisions regarding product and service quality.

quality circle (QC)
A small group of employees who work voluntarily on company time, typically one hour per week, to address work-related problems such as quality control, cost reduction, production planning and techniques, and even product design.

to be effective if their recommendations are always considered seriously and implemented when appropriate. One study found that QCs are effective for a period of time, and then their contributions begin to diminish.[48] This may suggest that quality teams and QCs must be reinforced and periodically reenergized to maintain their effectiveness over long periods of time.

Social Benefits

5. Identify the social benefits of group and team membership.

Two sets of social benefits are available to team or group members. One set of social benefits accrues from achieving psychological intimacy. The other comes from achieving integrated involvement.[49]

psychological intimacy
Emotional and psychological closeness to other team or group members.

emotion-based

① *Psychological intimacy* is emotional and psychological closeness to other team or group members. It results in feelings of affection and warmth, unconditional positive regard, opportunity for emotional expression, openness, security and emotional support, and giving and receiving nurturance. Failure to achieve psychological intimacy results in feelings of emotional isolation and loneliness. This may be especially problematic for chief executives who experience loneliness at the top. Although psychological intimacy is valuable for emotional health and well-being, it need not necessarily be achieved in the work setting.

integrated involvement
Closeness achieved through tasks and activities.

② *Integrated involvement* is closeness achieved through tasks and activities. It results in enjoyable and involving activities, social identity and self-definition, being valued for one's skills and abilities, opportunity for power and influence, conditional positive regard, and support for one's beliefs and values. Failure to achieve integrated involvement results in social isolation. Whereas psychological intimacy is more emotion based, integrated involvement is more behavior and activity based. Integrated involvement contributes to social psychological health and well-being.

Psychological intimacy and integrated involvement each contribute to overall health. It is not necessary to achieve both in the same team or group. For example, while chief executive at Xerox Corporation, David Kearns was also a marathon runner; he found integrated involvement with his executive team and psychological intimacy with his athletic companions on long-distance runs.

Teams and groups have two sets of functions that operate to enable members to achieve psychological intimacy and integrated involvement. These are task and maintenance functions.

Diversity and Creativity in Teams

6. Discuss diversity and creativity in teams.

Diversity and creativity are important, emerging issues in the study of teams and teamwork. Recent research in diversity has focused on the issue of dissimilarity and its effect within the team itself. This is often studied based on social identity theory and self-categorization theory. Later in the chapter, we specifically address the issue of multicultural diversity in upper echelons, or top management teams, in the global workplace. Creativity concerns new and/or dissimilar ideas or ways of doing things within teams. Novelty and innovation are creativity's companions. While creativity is developed in some detail in Chapter 10, we treat it briefly here in the context of teams.

Dissimilarity

We defined diversity in Chapter 1 in terms of individual differences. Recent relational demography research finds that demographic dissimilarity influences employees' absenteeism, commitment, turnover intentions, beliefs, workgroup relationships, self-esteem, and organizational citizenship behavior (OCB).[50] Thus, dissimilarity may have positive or negative effects in teams and on team members. While value dissimilarity may be positively related to task and relationship conflict, it is negatively related to team involvement.[51] This highlights the importance of managing dissimilarity in teams, being open to diversity, and turning conflicts over ideas into positive outcomes.

Functional background is one way to look at dissimilarity in teams. One study of 262 professionals in thirty-seven cross-functional teams found that promoting functional background social identification helped individuals perform better as team members.[52] Another study of multifunctional management teams in a *Fortune* 100 company found that functional background predicted team involvement.[53] Finally, in a slightly different study of 129 members on twenty multidisciplinary project teams, informational dissimilarity had no adverse effects when there was member task and goal congruence.[54] Where there was incongruence, dissimilarity adversely affected team identification and OCBs.

Creativity

Creativity is often thought of in an individual context rather than a team context. However, there is such a thing as team creativity. In a study of fifty-four research and development teams, one study found that team creativity scores would be explained by aggregation processes across both people and time.[55] The investigators concluded that it is important to consider aggregation across time as well as aggregation across individuals when one is attempting to understand team creativity.

Some think that the deck is stacked against teams as agents of creativity. Leigh Thompson thinks differently and suggests that team creativity and divergent thinking can be enhanced through greater diversity in teams, brainwriting, training facilitators, membership change in teams, electronic brainstorming, and building a playground.[56] These practices can overcome social loafing, conformity, and downward norm setting in teams and organizations. Team members might exercise care in timing the insertion of their novel ideas into the team process so as to maximize the positive impact and benefits.[57]

Empowerment and Self-Managed Teams

Quality teams and quality circles, as we discussed earlier, are one way to implement teamwork in organizations. Self-managed teams are broad-based work teams that deal with issues beyond quality. Decision making in self-managed teams is also discussed in Chapter 10. On a dysfunctional note, employee resistance behavior can emerge in self-managed work teams. It is influenced by cultural values and can affect employee attitudes.[58] However, self-managed teams have an overall positive history and are increasingly used by U.S. multinational corporations in global operations.

Empowerment may be thought of as an attribute of a person or of an organization's culture.[59] As an organizational culture attribute, empowerment encourages participation, an essential ingredient for teamwork.[60] Quality action teams (QATs) at FedEx are the primary quality improvement process (QIP) technique used by the company to engage management and hourly employees in four- to-ten-member problem-solving teams.[61] The teams are empowered to act and solve problems as specific as charting the best route from the Phoenix airport to the local distribution center or as global as making major software enhancements to the on-line package-tracking system.

7. Discuss empowerment, teamwork, and self-managed teams.

Empowerment may give employees the power of a lightning strike, but empowered employees must be properly focused through careful planning and preparation before they strike.[62]

You 9.2 includes several items from FedEx's survey-feedback-action (SFA) survey related to employee empowerment. Complete You 9.2 to see if you are empowered.

Empowerment Skills

Empowerment through employee self-management is an alternative to empowerment through teamwork.[63] Whether through self-management or teamwork, empowerment requires the development of certain skills if it is to be enacted effectively. Competence skills are the first set of skills required for empowerment. Mastery and experience in one's chosen discipline and profession provide an essential foundation for empowerment. This means that new employees and trainees should experience only limited empowerment until they demonstrate the capacity to accept more responsibility, a key aspect of empowerment.

Empowerment also requires certain process skills. The most critical process skills for empowerment include negotiating skills, especially with allies, opponents, and adversaries.[64] Allies are the easiest people to negotiate with because they agree with you about the team's mission, and you can trust their actions and behavior. Opponents require a different negotiating strategy; although you can predict their actions and behavior, they do not agree with your concept of the team's mission. Adversaries are dangerous, difficult people to negotiate with because you cannot predict their actions or behaviors, and they do not agree with your concept of the team's mission.

A third set of empowerment skills involves the development of cooperative and helping behaviors.[65] Cooperative people are motivated to maximize the gains for everyone on the team; they engage in encouraging, helpful behavior to bring about that end. The alternatives to cooperation are competitive, individualistic, and egalitarian orientations. Competitive people are motivated to maximize their personal gains regardless of the expense to other people. This can be very counterproductive from the standpoint of the team. Individualistic people are motivated to act autonomously, though not necessarily to maximize their personal gains. They are less prone to contribute to the efforts of the team. Egalitarian people are motivated to equalize the outcomes for each team member, which may or may not be beneficial to the team's well-being.

Communication skills are a final set of essential empowerment skills.[66] These skills include self-expression skills and skills in reflective listening. Empowerment cannot occur in a team unless members are able to express themselves effectively, as well as listen carefully to one another.

Self-Managed Teams

self-managed team

A team that makes decisions that were once reserved for managers.

Self-managed teams are teams that make decisions that were once reserved for managers. They are also called *self-directed teams* or *autonomous work groups*. Self-managed teams are one way to implement empowerment in organizations. Even so, managers have an important role in providing leadership and influence as discussed in the accompanying Science feature. A one-year study of self-managed teams suggests that they have a positive impact on employee attitudes but not on absenteeism or turnover.[67] Evaluative research is helpful in achieving a better understanding of this relatively new way of approaching teamwork and the design of work. Research can help

Are You an Empowered Employee?*

Read each of the following statements carefully. Then, to the right, indicate which answer best expresses your level of agreement (5 = strongly agree, 4 = agree, 3 = sometimes agree/sometimes disagree, 2 = disagree, 1 = strongly disagree, and 0 = undecided/do not know). Mark only one answer for each item, and respond to all items.

		5	4	3	2	1	0
4	**1.** I feel free to tell my manager what I think.	5	4	3	2	1	0
0	**2.** My manager is willing to listen to my concerns.	5	4	3	2	1	0
3	**3.** My manager asks for my ideas about things affecting our work.	5	4	3	2	1	0
0	**4.** My manager treats me with respect and dignity.	5	4	3	2	1	0
0	**5.** My manager keeps me informed about things I need to know.	5	4	3	2	1	0
0	**6.** My manager lets me do my job without interfering.	5	4	3	2	1	0
0	**7.** My manager's boss gives us the support we need.	5	4	3	2	1	0
0	**8.** Upper management (directors and above) pays attention to ideas and suggestions from people at my level.	5	4	3	2	1	0

Scoring

To determine if you are an empowered employee, add your scores.

32–40: You are empowered! Managers listen when you speak, respect your ideas, and allow you to do your work.

24–31: You have *some* power! Your ideas are considered sometimes, and you have some freedom of action.

16–23: You must exercise caution. You cannot speak or act too boldly, and your managers appear to exercise close supervision.

8–15: Your wings are clipped! You work in a powerless, restrictive work environment.

*If you are not employed, discuss these questions with a friend who is employed. Is your friend an empowered employee?

SOURCE: *Survey-Feedback-Action (SFA)*, FedEx Corporation, Memphis, TN.

---

in establishing expectations for self-managed teams. For example, one study of antonomous work teams found that a key ingredient to enhancing organizational commitment and job satisfaction involves the perception that one has the required skills and abilities to perform well.[68] Further, there are risks, such as groupthink, in self-managing teams that must be prevented or managed if the team is to achieve full development and function.[69] Finally, one evaluation of empowerment, teams, and TQM programs found that companies associated with these popular management techniques did not have higher economic performance.[70]

Other evaluations of self-managed teams are more positive. Southwest Industries, a high-technology aerospace manufacturing firm, embarked on a major internal reorganization in the early 1990s that included the creation of self-managed teams to fit its high-technology production process. Southwest's team approach resulted in a 30 percent increase in shipments, a 30 percent decrease in lead time, a 40 percent decrease in total inventory, a decrease in machinery downtime, and almost a one-third decrease in production costs.[71] Self-managed teams were also the foundation for the miraculous resurrection

Self-Directed Work Teams

Heightened competitive pressures, elevated quality expectations, and calls for employee empowerment have led increasing numbers of companies to turn to self-directed work teams (SDWTs). The purpose of a recent study was to understand how influence and leadership can serve to enhance SDWT effectiveness. This study was conducted in one multilevel manufacturing organization in which multiple departments were adopting teams. The specific research site was a large unionized plant with over 800 employees. The investigators were interested in examining managers' behaviors and influence tactics over an eighteen-month implementation period for SDWTs. They were particularly interested in hard influence tactics, such as coalition, legitimating, and pressure versus soft tactics, such as rational persuasion, consultation, and inspirational appeals. In addition, they were interested in the managers' ability to self-monitor.

The results suggested that despite the transition to self-directed work teams, managers' use of influence tactics was focused at the individual level versus the group level. Managers did, however, increase their use of soft influence tactics and decrease their use of hard influence tactics during the transition. In addition, high self-monitoring managers were more prone to increase their use of soft influence tactics and to decrease their use of hard influence tactics over the course of the transition. Thus, influence and leadership clearly changed over time in a self-directed work team environment.

SOURCE: C. Douglas and W. L. Gardner, "Transition to Self-Directed Work Teams: Implications of Transition Time and Self-Monitoring for Managers' Use of Influence Tactics," *Journal of Organizational Behavior* 25 (2004): 47–65.

of the former Chrysler (now DaimlerChrysler) Corporation's oldest plant in New Castle, Indiana, as the United Auto Workers' union and company management forged a partnership for success.[72]

A game (Learning Teams) is available to help people create self-directed teams, learn cooperatively, and master factual information.[73] With no outside help, an engineering team in the Defense Systems and Electronics Group (DSEG), now part of Raytheon, developed themselves into a highly effective, productive, self-managed team. They then helped DSEG in its successful effort to win a Malcolm Baldrige National Quality Award.

Upper Echelons: Teams at the Top

8. Explain the importance of upper echelons and top management teams.

upper echelon

A top-level executive team in an organization.

Self-managed teams at the top of the organization—top-level executive teams—are referred to as *upper echelons*. Organizations are often a reflection of these upper echelons.[74] Upper echelon theory argues that the background characteristics of the top management team can predict organizational characteristics. Furthermore, upper echelons are one key to the strategic success of the organization.[75] Thus, the teams at the top are instrumental in defining the organization over time such that the values, competence, ethics, and unique characteristics of the top management team are eventually reflected throughout the organization. This ability to exert power and influence throughout the entire organization makes the top management team a key to the organization's success. This ability may be compromised if the top team sends mixed signals about teamwork and if executive pay systems foster competition, politics, and individualism.[76]

For example, when Lee Iacocca became CEO at the former Chrysler Corporation, his top management team was assembled to bring about strategic realignment within the corporation by building on Chrysler's historical engineering strength. The dramatic success of Chrysler during the early 1980s was followed by struggle and accommodation during the late 1980s. This raises the question of how long a CEO and the top management team can sustain organizational success.

Hambrick and Fukutomi address this question by examining the dynamic relationship between a CEO's tenure and the success of the organization.[77] They found five seasons in a CEO's tenure: (1) response to a mandate, (2) experimentation, (3) selection of an enduring theme, (4) convergence, and (5) dysfunction. A summary of each season is shown in Table 9.4. All else being equal, this seasons model has significant implications for organizational performance. Specifically, organizational performance increases during a CEO's tenure to a peak, after which performance declines. This relationship is depicted in Figure 9.3. The peak has been found to come at about seven years—somewhere in the middle of the executive's seasons. As indicated by the dotted lines in the figure, the peak may be extended, depending on several factors, such as diversity in the executive's support team.

Diversity at the Top

From an organizational health standpoint, diversity and depth in the top management team enhance the CEO's well-being.[78] From a performance standpoint, the CEO's top management team can influence the timing of the performance peak, the degree of dysfunction during the closing season of the CEO's tenure, and the rate of decline in organizational performance. Diversity and heterogeneity in the top management team help sustain high levels of organizational performance at the peak and help maintain the CEO's vitality. The presence of a "wild turkey" in the top management team can be a particularly positive force. The wild turkey is a devil's advocate who challenges the thinking of the CEO and other top executives and provides a counterpoint during debates. If

TABLE 9.4   The Five Seasons of a CEO's Tenure

CRITICAL CEO CHARACTERISTICS	1 RESPONSE TO MANDATE	2 EXPERIMENTATION	3 SELECTION OF AN ENDURING THEME	4 CONVERGENCE	5 DYSFUNCTION
Commitment to a Paradigm	Moderately strong	Could be strong or weak	Moderately strong	Strong; increasing	Very strong
Task Knowledge	Low but rapidly increasing	Moderate; somewhat increasing	High; slightly increasing	High; slightly increasing	High; slightly increasing
Information Diversity	Many sources; unfiltered	Many sources but increasingly filtered	Fewer sources; moderately filtered	Few sources; highly filtered	Very few sources; highly filtered
Task Interest	High	High	Moderately high	Moderately high but diminishing	Moderately low and diminishing
Power	Low; increasing	Moderate; increasing	Moderate; increasing	Strong; increasing	Very strong; increasing

SOURCE: D. Hambrick and G. D. S. Fukutomi, "The Seasons of a CEO's Tenure," *Academy of Management Review*, 1991, p. 729. Permission conveyed through Copyright Clearance Center, Inc.

FIGURE 9.3   Executive Tenure and Organizational Performance

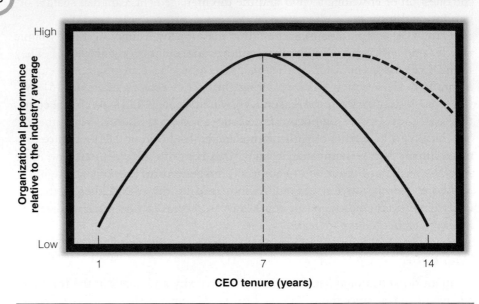

SOURCE: D. Hambrick, The Seasons of an Executive's Tenure, keynote address, the Sixth Annual Texas Conference on Organizations, Lago Vista, Texas, April 1991.

not shouted down or inhibited, the wild turkey helps the CEO and the team sustain peak performance and retard the CEO's dysfunction and decline. For example, President George W. Bush had his administration enhanced by the independent voice of Secretary of State Colin Powell. Often taking a more moderate position on policy issues than either the secretary of defense or the vice president, Powell brought variance and value to the voice of President Bush's administration.

No organization can succeed without a senior team that, collectively, captures a diversity of attributes: vision, task mastery, stewardship, and facilitation.[79] Leaders must evolve communication strategies to bring together a team that is functionally diverse, intellectually diverse, demographically diverse, temperamentally diverse, and so on, in order to complement each other. It is out of dissimilarity that strength is developed, and it is out of similarity that connections are built.

We can conclude that the leadership, composition, and dynamics of the top management team have an important influence on the organization's performance. In some cases, corporations have eliminated the single CEO. Current research has shown a dramatic increase in the number of co-CEO arrangements in both public and private corporations.[80] While more common in Europe than in the United States in the past, historical U.S. examples exist as well, such as when Walter Wriston created a three-member team when he was chairman at Citicorp (now part of Citigroup). At Southwest Airlines, the new top management team is emerging from the long shadow of legendary founder Herb Kelleher. This new top team led Southwest successfully through the terrorist crisis of September 2001.

Multicultural Top Teams

The backgrounds of group members may be quite different in the global workplace. Homogeneous groups in which all members share similar backgrounds are giving way to token groups in which all but one member come from the same background, bicultural groups in which two or more members represent each of two distinct cultures, and multicultural groups in which members represent three or more ethnic backgrounds.[81] Diversity within a group may increase the uncertainty, complexity, and inherent confusion in group processes, making it more difficult for the group to achieve its full, potential productivity.[82] On the positive side, Merck attributes its long-term success to its leadership model that promotes and develops the leadership skills of all Merck employees. Ray Gilmartin, chairman, president, and CEO, values diversity in Merck's top management team because he believes that diversity sparks innovation when employees with different perspectives work together to offer solutions. The design and function of top management teams in Great Britian, Denmark, and the Netherlands have been studied by international researchers.[83] The advantages of culturally diverse groups include the generation of more and better ideas while limiting the risk of groupthink, to be discussed in Chapter 10.

Some companies believe diversity in teams leads to creative problem solving by bringing differing perspectives to the table.

Managerial Implications: Teamwork for Productivity and Quality

Work groups and teams are important vehicles through which organizations achieve high-quality performance. The current emphasis on the new team environment, shown in Table 9.3, places unique demands on managers, teams, and individuals in leading, working, and managing. Managing these demands requires an understanding of individual diversity and the interrelationships of individuals, teams, and managers, as depicted in the triangle in Figure 9.4. Expectations associated with these three key organizational roles for people at work are different. The first role is as an individual, empowered employee. The second is as an active member of one or more teams. The third is the

FIGURE 9.4

9.4

The Triangle for Managing in the New Team Environment

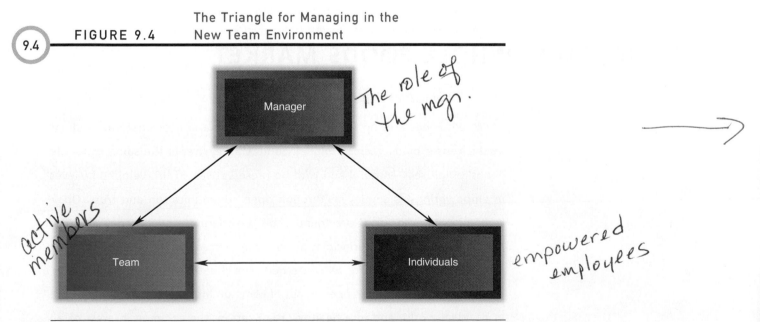

SOURCE: *Managing in the New Team Environment*, by Hirschhorn. © 1991. Reprinted by permission of Prentice-Hall, Inc., Upper Saddle River, N.J.

role of manager or formal supervisor. Earlier in the chapter, we discussed the foundations for teamwork, empowerment, az working in the new team environment. Individual empowerment must be balanced with collaborative teamwork.

The manager in the triangle is responsible for creating a receptive organizational environment for work groups and teams. This requires that the manager achieve a balance between setting limits (so that individuals and teams do not go too far afield) and removing barriers (so that empowered individuals and self-managed teams can accomplish their work). In addition, the manager should establish a flexible charter for each team. Once the charter is established, the manager continues to be available to the team as a coaching resource, as necessary. The manager establishes criteria for evaluating the performance effectiveness of the team, as well as the individuals, being supervised. In an optimum environment, this involves useful and timely performance feedback to teams that carries a sense of equity and fairness with it. The manager's responsibilities are different from the team leader's.

Effective team leaders may guide a work group or share leadership responsibility with their teams, especially self-managed teams. Team leaders are active team members with responsibility for nurturing the development and performance of the team.[84] They require skills different from those of the manager. Whereas the manager establishes the environment in which teams flourish, the team leader teaches, listens, solves problems, manages conflict, and enhances the dynamics of team functioning to ensure the team's success. It is the team leader's task to bring the team to maturity; help the team work through interpersonal, task, and authority issues; and be skilled in nurturing a cohesive, effective team. A team leader requires the hands-on skills of direct involvement and full membership in the team. Flexibility, delegation, and collaboration are characteristics of healthy teams and team leaders. Increasing globalization requires team leaders to be skilled at forging teamwork among diverse individuals, whereas managers must be skilled at forging collaboration among diverse groups.

LOOKING BACK: WHOLE FOODS MARKET

Empowerment, Trust, and Open Communication

Whole Foods uses no preservatives in its foods and keeps natural products at the center of its business model. John Mackey wants the same in Whole Foods' employees—natural and with no preservatives. In this vein, he believes in empowering his employees through open communication and trust. Open communication and trust are founded on the sharing and exchange of influence and power. These principles assume the existence of a common purpose and a common interest for all concerned. The greatest benefits of teamwork come when team members operate out of common interest and not self-interest. In an ideal world, and in a healthy organization, the common interest of all and the self-interest of the individual are joined as one. In a healthy, team-based organization, empowered employees act in the best interests of all concerned!

Whole Foods has no unions, and John Mackey is opposed to unionization because of the risks its poses for the spirit of teamwork in the company. Unions may have a place in some organizations, but the potential exists for union leadership to become a self-interested power center in conflict with the interests of management. Debbie Rasmussen was fired by Whole Foods for breaking the rules and store policy in the Madison, Wisconsin, store. Rasmussen claims she was fired for pro-union activism. Regardless of who is right and who is not in this conflict, teamwork is damaged. However, management cannot go too far either. Whole Foods has put a ceiling on executive pay such that no executive can earn cash pay more than 14 times what its average employee makes. Balancing employee and executive interests is important.

Companies often get the type of union that management deserves whenever the unionization process first occurs. In a healthy organization with open communication and trust, management is able to hear employee concerns and/or grievances in such a way that they become addressed for a win–win outcome. John Mackey clearly understood this and recognized that Whole Foods may have neglected its team members over a several-year period. He also recognized that the concern for team members could be put back in balance. One example of how the company did that was by allowing employees to vote on benefit plans to choose how much money individuals might allocate for everything from health care to tuition reimbursement. Organizations that give employees voice, such as this example at Whole Foods, are able to preclude the need for a union in the first place. When management addresses employee concerns and employees support management direction and plans, then the organization truly is operating within the spirit and the practice of teamwork.[85]

Chapter Summary

1. Groups are often composed of diverse people at work. Teams in organizations are a key to enhance quality and achieve success.

2. Important aspects of group behavior include norms of behavior, group cohesion, social loafing, and loss of individuality.

3. Once a group forms, it generally goes through five stages of development. If successful, the group can function independently, with little interference from its leader.

4. Quality circles, originally popularized in Japan, and quality teams contribute to solving technological and quality problems in the organization.

5. Teams provide social benefits for team members, as well as enhancing organizational performance.

6. Functional and value dissimilarity may have positive or negative effects on teams. Managing dissimilarity in teams and being open to diversity is highly important for promoting creativity.

7. Empowerment and teamwork require specific organizational design elements and individual psychological characteristics and skills.

8. Upper echelons and top management teams are key to the strategy and performance of an organization. Diversity and a devil's advocate in the top team enhance performance.

9. Managing in the new team environment places new demands on managers, teams, and individuals. Managers must create a supportive and flexible environment for collaborative teams and empowered individuals. Team leaders must nurture the team's development.

Key Terms

group (p. 284)

group cohesion (p. 285)

integrated involvement (p. 298)

loss of individuality (p. 286)

maintenance function (p. 294)

norms of behavior (p. 285)

psychological intimacy (p. 298)

quality circle (QC) (p. 297)

quality team (p. 297)

self-managed team (p. 300)

social loafing (p. 285)

status structure (p. 292)

task function (p. 293)

teamwork (p. 295)

upper echelon (p. 302)

work team (p. 284)

Review Questions

1. What is a group? A work team?

2. Explain four aspects of group behavior. How can each aspect help or hinder the group's functioning?

3. Describe what happens in each stage of a group's development according to Tuckman's Five-Stage Model. What are the leadership requirements in each stage?

4. Describe the four characteristics of mature groups.

5. Why are work teams important to organizations today? How and why are work teams formed?

6. Describe at least five task and five maintenance functions that effective work teams must perform.

7. Discuss diversity and creativity in teams.

8. Describe the necessary skills for empowerment and teamwork.

9. What are the benefits and potential drawbacks of self-managed teams?

10. What is the role of the manager in the new team environment? What is the role of the team leader?

Discussion and Communication Questions

1. Which was the most effective group (or team) of which you have been a member? What made that group (or team) so effective?

2. Have you ever experienced peer pressure to act more in accordance with the behavioral norms of a group? Have you ever engaged in a little social loafing? Have you ever lost your head and been caught up in a group's destructive actions?

3. Name a company that successfully uses teamwork and empowerment. What has that company done that makes it so successful at teamwork and empowerment? Has its team approach made a difference in its performance? How?

4. Name a person you think is a particularly good team member. What makes this person a good team member? Name a person who is a problem as a team member. What makes this person a problem?

5. Think about your current work environment. Does your work environment use quality circles or self-managed teams? What are the barriers to teamwork and empowerment in that environment? What elements of the environment en-

hance or encourage teamwork and empowerment? (If you do not work, discuss this question with a friend who does.)

6. (*communication question*) Prepare a memo describing your observations about work teams and groups in your workplace or your university. Where have you observed teams or groups to be most effective? Why? What changes might be made at work or in the university to make teams more effective?

7. (*communication question*) Develop an oral presentation about what the most important norms of behavior should be in an academic community and workplace. Be specific. Discuss how these norms should be established and reinforced.

8. (*communication question*) Interview an employee or manager about what he or she believes contributes to cohesiveness in work groups and teams. Ask the person what the conclusions are based on. Be prepared to discuss what you have learned in class.

9. Do you admire the upper echelons in your organization or university? Why or why not? Do they communicate effectively with groups and individuals throughout the organization?

Ethical Dilemma

Greg Towns and Michele Brown sat chatting. Michele had come to Greg's office to discuss the first meeting of the strategic planning team. Michele had found out only last week that she would be the team leader for this very important project. Recently, upper management had discovered that many of their employees didn't feel that their needs, desires, or capabilities were being considered in the formation of company goals. In response, the president had requested that a team of employees be formed to provide employee input for the new plan.

This would be Michele's first time in a leadership position. She was excited, especially since she had been handpicked by the president. She had come to Greg's office to ask for his support in the meetings. Michele did not have confidence in her leadership skills and wanted to know that she could count on someone to back her. Greg confidently assured Michele that she could count on him.

Everyone was excited as the meeting began. They were all happy to be working for a company that cared enough about its employees to create this committee. Michele began the meeting by reminding everyone why they were called together. She felt this was their time to shine for management. People began offering suggestions. Michele dismissed the first two as too broad. The third she called juvenile. The room fell silent. Michele was surprised by the silence and asked if everyone was out of suggestions. Allen Jamison finally spoke up. He told Michele that no one wanted to make suggestions if she was just going to shoot down every idea. Michele denied that she was discounting the others' ideas. She just wanted to be sure that they sent management their very best suggestions. Michele looked to Greg, waiting for the promised support.

Greg felt trapped. He agreed with Allen. Michele's behavior did not encourage input. She was acting like a dictator, not a team leader. He had promised to support her, but he never dreamt that she would act this way. Supporting her behavior went against his beliefs. But he had promised.

Questions

1. How would Greg's promise to support Michele still hold given Michele's behavior?

2. Evaluate Greg's decision using rule, virtue, rights, and justice theory.

Experiential Exercises

9.1 Tower Building: A Group Dynamics Activity
This exercise gives you an opportunity to study group dynamics in a task-oriented situation. Each group must bring materials to class for building a tower. All materials must fit in a box no greater than eight cubic feet (i.e., 2 ft. × 2 ft. × 2 ft. or 1 ft. × 2 ft. × 4 ft.).

Step 1. Each group is assigned a meeting place and a workplace. One or two observers should be assigned in each group. The instructor may assign a manager to each group.

Step 2. Each group plans for the building of the paper tower (no physical construction is allowed during this planning period). Towers will be judged on the basis of height, stability, beauty, and meaning. (Another option is to have the groups do the planning outside of class and come prepared to build the tower.)

Step 3. Each group constructs its tower.

Step 4. Groups inspect other towers, and all individuals rate towers other than their own. See the evaluation sheet at the right. Each group turns in its point totals (i.e., someone in the group adds up each person's total for all groups rated) to the instructor, and the instructor announces the winner.

Step 5. Group dynamics analysis. Observers report observations to their own groups, and each group analyzes the group dynamics that occurred during the planning and building of the tower.

Step 6. Groups report on major issues in group dynamics that arose during the tower planning and building. Complete the tower building aftermath

questionnaire as homework if requested by your instructor.

CRITERIA	GROUPS							
	1	2	3	4	5	6	7	8
Height								
Stability/Strength								
Beauty								
Meaning/ Significance								
TOTALS								

Rate each criterion on a scale of 1–10, with 1 being lowest or poorest, and 10 being highest or best.

SOURCE: From *Organizational Behavior and Performance*, 5/e by Szilagyi/Wallace. © 1997. Reprinted by permission of Prentice-Hall, Inc., Upper Saddle River, N.J.

9.2 Design a Team

The following exercise gives you an opportunity to design a team. Working in a six-person group, address the individual characteristics, team composition, and norms for an effective group whose task is to make recommendations on improving customer relations. The president of a small clothing manufacturer is concerned that his customers are not satisfied enough with the company's responsiveness, product quality, and returned-orders process. He has asked your group to put together a team to address these problems.

Step 1. The class will form into groups of approximately six members each. Each group elects a spokesperson and answers the following questions. The group should spend an equal amount of time on each question.

a. *What characteristics should the individual members of the task team possess?* Members may

consider professional competence, skills, department, and/or personality and behavioral characteristics in the group's discussion.

b. *What should the composition of the task team be?* Once your group has addressed individual characteristics, consider the overall composition of the task team. Have special and/or unique competencies, knowledge, skills, and abilities been considered in your deliberations?

c. *What norms of behavior do you think the task team should adopt?* A team's norms of behavior may evolve, or they may be consciously discussed and agreed upon. Take the latter approach.

Step 2. Each group will share the results of its answers to the questions in Step 1. Cross-team questions and discussion follow.

Biz Flix | Apollo 13

This superb film dramatically shows the NASA mission to the moon that had an in-space disaster. Innovative problem solving and decision making amid massive ambiguity saved the crew. *Apollo 13* has many examples of problem solving and decision making.

The scene from the film shows day 5 of the mission, about two-thirds of the way through *Apollo 13*. Earlier in the mission, Jack Swigert (Kevin Bacon) stirred the oxygen tanks at mission control's request. An explosion in the spacecraft happened shortly after this procedure, causing unknown damage to the command module. Before this scene takes place, the damage has forced the crew to move into the LEM (Lunar Exploration Module), which becomes their lifeboat for return to earth.

What to Watch for and Ask Yourself:

> What triggers the conflict in this scene?

> Is this intergroup conflict or intragroup conflict? What effects can such conflict have on the group dynamics on board *Apollo 13*?

> Does mission commander Jim Lovell (Tom Hanks) successfully manage the group dynamics to return the group to a normal state?

Workplace Video | Cannondale Corporation: Teamwork in Organizations

Cannondale is one of the world's leading manufacturers of high-performance bicycles, providing state-of-the-art racing bikes, technical expertise, and sponsorship support for the competitive riding market.

Manufacturing technologically advanced racing bikes that customers can afford requires teamwork, and Cannondale utilizes cross-functional teams both to ensure continuous improvement in quality and to capitalize on the collective strengths of its design and marketing professionals. In the video, the design team for Cannondale's popular Jekyll series works together to meet production objectives set by the entire company.

Cannondale's team members are selected based on particular areas of expertise. Once the right people are in place, the research and development group begins designing bicycles on advanced computer systems, developing prototypes of new-model bicycles that eventually gain approval for mass production. If product designs for new bicycles meet company specifications, raw materials are then sent to the factory for manufacturing purposes. Production managers oversee the process from start to finish, ensuring that costs are kept within budget.

Questions

1. *Why does Cannondale organize in teams instead of having individuals work alone?*
2. *At which stage of development was the Jekyll design team? Explain your answer.*
3. *What challenges do work teams face at Cannondale? What managerial competencies do Cannondale's managers need in order to deal with these challenges?*

The Eden Alternative: Implications for Empowerment and Teamwork

Long-term nursing care facilities for the sick and elderly can be sterile and even depressing places—particularly for the residents of the facilities. This typical nursing home environment disturbed Dr. William Thomas, the sole physician and medical director for Chase Memorial Nursing Home, an 80-bed facility in rural New York State. After taking the position at Chase Memorial, Dr. Thomas soon realized that nursing homes usually fostered loneliness, helplessness, and boredom—what he now refers to as "the three plagues of nursing homes."

Dr. Thomas decided that a different approach was needed, so he developed a holistic approach to long-term nursing care known as *The Eden Alternative*. The basic philosophy of The Eden Alternative is to create a "human habitat" where residents thrive, grow, and flourish rather than wither, decay, and die. Infusing Edenized facilities with life—in the form of animals, plants, and children—creates this human habitat. The emphasis is on incorporating plants, animals, and children into the daily lives of the residents. While there are therapeutic benefits, Edenization is not trying to turn plants, animals, and children into some dramatic form of therapy.

Edenization Requires Attitudinal and Organizational Transformation

Edenization is far more than simply bringing plants, animals, and children into a long-term care facility. The mission of The Eden Alternative is "to improve the well-being of elders and those who care for them by transforming the communities in which they live and work." Edenization requires an attitudinal transformation on the part of the facility's staff and a cultural transformation of the organization.

Staff members' reactions to Edenization at Chase Memorial Nursing Home illustrate the importance of attitudinal transformation. Initially, they reacted negatively. It was not uncommon to hear comments such as: "You're buying parakeets? Why not give us a raise instead?" "Do you really think I'm going to clean up after a dog? That's not my job." Dr. Thomas kept pushing the Edenization concept; resistance gradually diminished, and the staff began to embrace Edenization.

The reaction of the staff at Chase Memorial is symptomatic of a more profound issue with Edenization. While plants, animals, and children help turn a long-term nursing care facility into a "human habitat," those elements are only cosmetic in nature if not accompanied by more fundamental changes in how the nursing home staff works together. Empowering staff, particularly frontline caregivers, is at the heart of The Eden Alternative.

David Zimmerman, director of The Center for Health Systems Research and Analysis at the University of Wisconsin-Madison, says: "The Eden Alternative's primary benefit and greatest challenge is that it involves a truly fundamental change in the entire culture of the facility, the interaction between management and staff, staff and each resident." Dr. Thomas points out that Edenization "is replacing top-down bureaucratic management with decision-making authority in the hands of frontline staff."

A nursing home in North Carolina provides an excellent illustration of how the facility's staff must work together to realize the full benefits of Edenization. Central to the implementation of The Eden Alternative at this facility "is building and empowering staff for total commitment and participation in the project." Multidisciplinary teams have been created and given responsibility for ensuring that all the elements of Edenization are being implemented and nurtured. Led by staff members from different areas, these teams meet regularly to discuss residents' needs and capacities. The teams are responsible for addressing resident-centered issues and working on continually improving the residents' quality of life. Edenization is an ongoing process; it is always evolving, always changing. The teams look for problems and solutions. Empowered staff members examine resident needs and how best to meet them.

At another long-term care facility, located in northern Virginia, flexible staffing policies are used to support an emphasis on teamwork. Instead of having only specifically assigned responsibilities, many duties are shared among the registered and licensed nurses, nursing assistants, and activities staff members.

Moving Beyond Basic Edenization

Recently, The Eden Alternative has undertaken a new initiative known as The Green House Project. "The Green House is a group home for elders built to a residential scale that situates necessary clinical care within a habilitative, social model in which primacy is given to the elder's quality of life."

The Green House Project is a direct reflection of The Eden Alternative principles, one of which has special relevance to the transformation and management of elder-care facilities. As stated on The Eden Alternative Web site, "An elder-centered community honors its elders by de-emphasizing top-down bureaucratic authority, seeking instead to place the maximum possible decision-making authority in the hands of the elders or in the hands of those closest to them."

Green Houses operate very differently from traditional nursing homes. The traditional nursing home has a highly bureaucratic organization structure, the nurses are in control of all unit activity, and staff members make decisions. Green Houses, however, are characterized by flattened organization structures and empowerment of the direct care staff. Nurses visit the Green House to provide needed skilled services. House councils, composed of the facility's residents, make decisions about menus, activities, and house routines. This places decisions as close to the elders as possible, thereby giving them greater control over their lives.

The Green House Project represents another progressive alternative in the way long-term, elder-care facilities are operated. Adopting this alternative will provide continuing management and leadership challenges to staff members and house councils alike.

Discussion Questions

1. Using Table 9.1, discuss the extent to which the characteristics of well-functioning, effective groups accurately describe the Edenized facilities discussed in the case.
2. Explain why teamwork is important for the effective implementation of The Eden Alternative.
3. Using Table 9.2, explain how the task functions and maintenance functions might be used to facilitate effective implementation of teamwork in a facility undergoing Edenization.
4. Explain the relevance of empowerment and self-managed teams to the Green House Project.

SOURCE: This case was written by Michael K. McCuddy, The Louis S. and Mary L. Morgal Chair of Christian Business Ethics and Professor of Management, College of Business Administration, Valparaiso University. This case was developed from material contained on The Eden Alternative Web site at http://www.edenalt.com and in the following articles: L. Bruck, "Welcome to Eden," *Nursing Homes Long-Term Care Management* (January 1997): 28–33; "Cats, Dogs and Kids Add Cozy Touch . . . . At 'Eden Alternative' Nursing Homes," *CQ Researcher* (February 20, 1998): 150–151; D. Reese, " 'Alternative' Lifestyle: The Eden Alternative Is More than Just Life Gone to the Dogs!" *Contemporary Long-Term Care* (July 2000): 38–42; M. Stermer, "Notes From an Eden Alternative Pioneer," *Nursing Homes Long-Term Care Management* (Nov./Dec. 1998): 35–36.

© George Bulard

Chapter 10

Decision Making by Individuals and Groups

THINKING AHEAD: CANINE COMPANIONS FOR INDEPENDENCE

Making Tough Decisions

Hali (rhymes with "alley") is a loveable two-year-old yellow lab. In the next few hours, a group of strangers will make a crucial decision: where she will spend the rest of her life.

Canine Companions for Independence (CCI) is a not-for-profit organization that breeds and trains skilled assistance dogs to enhance the lives of people with disabilities. Founded in 1975 in Santa Clara, California, CCI has trained and placed more than 2,000 service dogs; the current wait to receive a dog is one to two years. While each dog's training costs more than $10,000, CCI is funded exclusively by donations, and each recipient pays only a $100 fee for training and supplies.

CCI dogs—mostly labs, golden retrievers, and crosses of these two breeds—are bred specifically for this role. At eight weeks of age, CCI puppies go to live with one of seven hundred "puppy raisers," whose job is to socialize the dogs, teach them basic obedience, and take them everywhere the puppy raiser goes.

At fourteen to sixteen months of age, the dogs relocate to CCI for six to nine months of advanced training, where they learn advanced skills in one of several specific roles that CCI dogs fill. This training is rigorous, and less than half the dogs graduate. Hali's job for the next eight years will be to assist a disabled child with such daily tasks as opening doors, turning on lights, and retrieving dropped objects.

Dog owners know that dogs, like people, have unique personalities, making the "match" of dog with owner one of the most important decisions CCI workers will face. A mismatched team will have trouble functioning efficiently; in the worst case, it might fail entirely. Needless to say, CCI takes the matching decision very seriously, and the two-week team training is among the most critical parts of the entire process.

Hali's class consists of six human clients and eight dogs, including Hali and classmates Lazer, Logan, Kenda, and Cajun. By the second day of classes, clients are beginning to work with various dogs in the class. As they practice, CCI employees watch closely, making extensive notes about the traits of both dogs and people, gathering as much information as possible for the coming decision.

Finally, the time for the matching meeting arrives, and armed with years of experience and stacks of notes, the staff gathers to prematch humans and dogs. These meetings can be as short as half an hour, but this particular session stretches from its 5 P.M. start well into the evening! At 10 P.M., the group decides to adjourn with no final decision reached. The decision is postponed until the following day. Hali's future remains undecided.[1]

The Decision-Making Process

programmed decision

A simple, routine matter for which a manager has an established decision rule.

nonprogrammed decision

A new, complex decision that requires a creative solution.

Decision making is a critical activity in the lives of managers. The decisions a manager faces can range from very simple, routine matters for which the manager has an established decision rule (*programmed decisions*) to new and complex decisions that require creative solutions (*nonprogrammed decisions*).[2] Scheduling lunch hours for one's work group is a programmed decision. The manager performs the decision activity on a daily basis, using an established procedure with the same clear goal in mind. In contrast, decisions like buying out another company are nonprogrammed. The decision to acquire a company is unique and unstructured and requires considerable judgment. Regardless of the type of decision made, it is helpful to understand as much as possible about how individuals and groups make decisions.

Decision making is a process involving a series of steps, as shown in Figure 10.1. The first step is recognition of the problem; that is, the manager realizes that a decision must be made. Identification of the real problem is important; otherwise, the manager may be reacting to symptoms and firefighting rather than dealing with the root cause of the problem. Next, a manager must identify the objective of the decision. In other words, the manager must determine what is to be accomplished by the decision.

The third step in the decision-making process is gathering information relevant to the problem. The manager must pull together sufficient information about why the problem occurred. This involves conducting a thorough diagnosis of the situation and going on a fact-finding mission.

The fourth step is listing and evaluating alternative courses of action. During this step, a thorough "what-if" analysis should also be conducted to de-

FIGURE 10.1   The Decision-Making Process

10.1

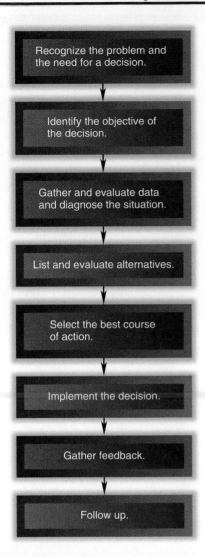

termine the various factors that could influence the outcome. It is important to generate a wide range of options and creative solutions in order to be able to move on to the fourth step.

Next, the manager selects the alternative that best meets the decision objective. If the problem has been diagnosed correctly and sufficient alternatives have been identified, this step is much easier.

Finally, the solution is implemented. The situation must then be monitored to see whether the decision met its objective. Consistent monitoring and periodic feedback are essential parts of the follow-up process.

Decision making can be stressful. Managers must make decisions with significant risk and uncertainty, and often without full information. They must trust and rely on others in arriving at their decisions, but they are ultimately responsible. Sometimes the decisions are painful and involve exiting businesses, firing people, and admitting wrong. Blue Man Group has a history of making effective decisions. They have grown wildly famous and successful by making sound business choices, as you can see in The Real World 10.1.

Blue Man Group—Staying True Blue

The Blue Man Group stays true to its artistic vision and founding principles.

© Blue Man Group

When you think of effective managers, you probably don't think of them wearing blue greasepaint and playing music on fifty-five-gallon drums; yet that's exactly how these successful decision makers can be described. Blue Man Group profits millions of dollars per year by keeping true to its artistic vision and by making sound business decisions in line with that vision.

The founding members—Chris Wink, Matt Goldman, and Phil Stanton—have made Blue Man Group an excellent case study on how to grow a company without losing focus. Although they have no formal training in music, acting, or business, they have permanent shows in New York, Boston, Chicago, Las Vegas, and Berlin. There are now forty-four Blue Man Group performers; one is actually a woman!

After a record of success, Blue Man Group has been offered product endorsements, a bigger Broadway theater, and a Disney movie deal and theme ride. The group turned down offers to sell credit cards, soft drinks, breath mints, and paint, all of course related to the color blue. With each new opportunity, the three founders use the same evaluation. "Okay, that's all good and well, that's a nice thought—but is it Blue Man?" They also have achieved what a lot of businesses want to do but never complete: a detailed one hundred thirty-two page operating manual. The founders make decisions by unanimous agreement, and despite their huge success, they still share a single office. The group's next opportunities are shows in London and Toronto.

SOURCE: R. Walker, "Brand Blue," *Fortune* (April 28, 2003): 118B–118H, http://www.fortune.com/fortune/smallbusiness/articles/0,15114,426909,00.html.

Models of Decision Making

effective decision

A timely decision that meets a desired objective and is acceptable to those individuals affected by it.

The success of any organization depends on managers' abilities to make *effective decisions*. An effective decision is timely, is acceptable to the individuals affected by it, and meets the desired objective.[3] This section describes three models of decision making: the rational model, the bounded rationality model, and the garbage can model.

Rational Model

rationality

A logical, step-by-step approach to decision making, with a thorough analysis of alternatives and their consequences.

Rationality refers to a logical, step-by-step approach to decision making, with a thorough analysis of alternatives and their consequences. The rational model of decision making comes from classic economic theory and contends that the decision maker is completely rational in his or her approach. The rational model has the following important assumptions:

1. The outcome will be completely rational.

2. The decision maker has a consistent system of preferences, which is used to choose the best alternative.

3. The decision maker is aware of all the possible alternatives.

4. The decision maker can calculate the probability of success for each alternative.[4]

In the rational model, the decision maker strives to optimize, that is, to select the best possible alternative.

Given the assumptions of the rational model, it is unrealistic. There are time constraints and limits to human knowledge and information-processing capabilities. In addition, a manager's preferences and needs change often. The rational model is thus an ideal that managers strive for in making decisions. It captures the way a decision should be made but does not reflect the reality of managerial decision making.[5]

Bounded Rationality Model

Recognizing the deficiencies of the rational model, Herbert Simon suggested that there are limits on how rational a decision maker can actually be. His decision theory, the bounded rationality model, earned a Nobel Prize in 1978.

Simon's model, also referred to as the "administrative man" theory, rests on the idea that there are constraints that force a decision maker to be less than completely rational. The bounded rationality model has four assumptions:

1. Managers select the first alternative that is satisfactory.

2. Managers recognize that their conception of the world is simple.

3. Managers are comfortable making decisions without determining all the alternatives.

4. Managers make decisions by rules of thumb or heuristics.

Bounded rationality assumes that managers *satisfice*; that is, they select the first alternative that is "good enough," because the costs of optimizing in terms of time and effort are too great.[6] Further, the theory assumes that managers develop shortcuts, called *heuristics*, to make decisions in order to save mental activity. Heuristics are rules of thumb that allow managers to make decisions based on what has worked in past experiences.

Does the bounded rationality model more realistically portray the managerial decision process? Research indicates that it does.[7] One of the reasons managers face limits to their rationality is that they must make decisions under risk and time pressure. The situation they find themselves in is highly uncertain, and the probability of success is not known.

Garbage Can Model

Sometimes the decision-making process in organizations appears to be haphazard and unpredictable. In the *garbage can model*, decisions are random and unsystematic.[8] Figure 10.2 depicts the garbage can model. In this model, the organization is a garbage can in which problems, solutions, participants, and choice opportunities are floating around randomly. If the four factors happen to connect, a decision is made.[9] The quality of the decision depends on timing. The right participants must find the right solution to the right problem at the right time.

The garbage can model illustrates the idea that not all organizational decisions are made in a step-by-step, systematic fashion. Especially under conditions of high uncertainty, the decision process may be chaotic. Some decisions appear to happen out of sheer luck.

On the high-speed playing field of today's businesses, managers must make critical decisions quickly, with incomplete information, and must also involve employees in the process.

1. Explain the assumptions of bounded rationality.

bounded rationality
A theory that suggests that there are limits to how rational a decision maker can actually be.

satisfice
To select the first alternative that is "good enough," because the costs in time and effort are too great to optimize.

heuristics
Shortcuts in decision making that save mental activity.

garbage can model
A theory that contends that decisions in organizations are random and unsystematic.

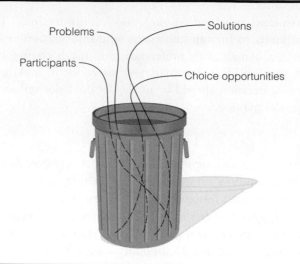

SOURCE: From M. D. Cohen, J. G. March, and J. P. Olsen in *Administrative Science Quarterly* 17 (March 1972): 1–25. Reprinted by permission of the *Administrative Science Quarterly.*

Decision Making and Risk

Many decisions involve some element of risk. For managers, hiring decisions, promotions, delegation, acquisitions and mergers, overseas expansions, new product development, and other decisions make risk a part of the job.

Risk and the Manager

risk aversion

The tendency to choose options that entail fewer risks and less uncertainty.

Individuals differ in terms of their willingness to take risks. Some people experience *risk aversion*. They choose options that entail fewer risks, preferring familiarity and certainty. Other individuals are risk takers; that is, they accept greater potential for loss in decisions, tolerate greater uncertainty, and in general are more likely to make risky decisions. Risk takers are also more likely to take the lead in group discussions.[10]

Research indicates that women are more averse to risk taking than men and that older, more experienced managers are more risk averse than younger managers. There is also some evidence that successful managers take more risks than unsuccessful managers.[11] However, the tendency to take risks or avoid them is only part of behavior toward risk. Risk taking is influenced not only by an individual's tendency but also by organizational factors. In commercial banks, loan decisions that require the assessment of risk are made every day.

Upper-level managers face a tough task in managing risk-taking behavior. By discouraging lower-level managers from taking risks, they may stifle creativity and innovation. If upper-level managers are going to encourage risk taking, however, they must allow employees to fail without fear of punishment. One way to accomplish this is to consider failure "enlightened trial and error."[12] The key is establishing a consistent attitude toward risk within the organization.

When individuals take risks, losses may occur. Suppose an oil producer thinks there is an opportunity to uncover oil by reentering an old drilling site. She gathers a group of investors and shows them the logs, and they chip in to finance the venture. The reentry is drilled to a certain depth, and nothing is found. Convinced they did not drill deep enough, the producer goes back to the investors and requests additional financial backing to continue drilling. The investors consent, and she drills deeper, only to find nothing. She approaches the investors, and after lengthy discussion, they agree to provide more money to drill deeper. Why do decision makers sometimes throw good money after bad? Why do they continue to provide resources to what looks like a losing venture?

Escalation of Commitment

Continuing to support a failing course of action is known as *escalation of commitment*.[13] In situations characterized by escalation of commitment, individuals who make decisions that turn out to be poor choices tend to hold fast to those choices, even when substantial costs are incurred.[14] An example of escalation is the price wars that often occur between airlines. The airlines reduce their prices in response to competitors until at a certain stage, both airlines are in a "no-win" situation. Yet they continue to compete despite the heavy losses they are incurring. The desire to win is a motivation to continue to escalate, and each airline continues to reduce prices (lose money) based on the belief that the other airline will pull out of the price war. Another example of escalation of commitment is NASA's enormous International Space Station. Originally estimated to cost $8 billion, the Space Station has been redesigned five times and remains unfinished. As of 2003, its estimated cost topped $30 billion, and some pundits speculate that the total bill may reach $100 billion for what physicist Robert Park describes as "the biggest technological blunder in history." Despite the station's drain on virtually every other NASA program, it remains a focal point of NASA's work and continues to consume vast resources.[15]

Why does escalation of commitment occur? One explanation is offered by cognitive dissonance theory, as we discussed in Chapter 4. This theory assumes that humans dislike inconsistency, and that when there is inconsistency among their attitudes or inconsistency between their attitudes and behavior, they strive to reduce the dissonance.[16]

Other reasons why people may hang on to a losing course of action are optimism and control. Some people are overly optimistic and overestimate the likelihood that positive things will happen to them. Other people operate under an illusion of control—that they have special skills to control the future that other people don't have.[17] In addition, sunk costs may encourage escalation. Individuals think, "Well, I've already invested this much . . . what's a few dollars more?" And the closer a project is to completion, the more likely escalation is to occur.[18]

Hanging on to a poor decision can be costly to organizations. While most U.S. airlines (including United, American, and TWA) originally placed orders for the prestigious Mach 2 Concorde airliner during the 1960s, all U.S. orders for the plane were eventually cancelled, leaving only British Airways and Air France as customers. While these two firms doggedly held onto their marginally profitable Concorde operations for almost three decades, a crash in 2000 led to closer scrutiny of the aging fleet, which was eventually retired in 2003.

escalation of commitment
The tendency to continue to support a failing course of action.

© Uli Deck/EPA/Landov

British Airways hung onto its Concorde operations for too long because of escalation of commitment.

Industry insiders estimate that every customer who took the Concorde rather than a 747 cost British Airways more than $1,200 in profits.[19] Organizations can deal with escalation of commitment in several ways. One is to split the responsibility for decisions about projects. One individual can make the initial decision, and another individual can make subsequent decisions on the project. Companies have also tried to eliminate escalation of commitment by closely monitoring decision makers.[20] Another suggestion is to provide individuals with a graceful exit from poor decisions so that their images are not threatened. One way of accomplishing this is to reward people who admit to poor decisions before escalating their commitment to them. A study also suggested that having groups, rather than individuals, make an initial investment decision would reduce escalation. Support has been found for this idea. Participants in group decision making may experience a diffusion of responsibility for the failed decision rather than feeling personally responsible; thus, they can pull out of a bad decision without threatening their image.[21]

We have seen that there are limits to how rational a manager can be in making decisions. Most managerial decisions involve considerable risk, and individuals react differently to risk situations.

Jung's Cognitive Styles

2. Describe Jung's cognitive styles and how they affect managerial decision making.

cognitive style
An individual's preference for gathering information and evaluating alternatives.

In Chapter 3 we introduced Jungian theory as a way of understanding and appreciating differences among individuals. This theory is especially useful in pointing out that individuals have different styles of making decisions. Carl Jung's original theory identified two styles of information gathering (sensing and intuiting) and two styles of making judgments (thinking and feeling). You already know what each individual preference means. Jung contended that individuals prefer one style of perceiving and one style of judging.[22] The combination of a perceiving style and a judging style is called a *cognitive style*. There are four cognitive styles: sensing/thinking (ST), sensing/feeling (SF), intuiting/thinking (NT), and intuiting/feeling (NF). Each of the cognitive styles affects managerial decision making.[23]

STs rely on facts. They conduct an impersonal analysis of the situation and then make an analytical, objective decision. The ST cognitive style is valuable in organizations because it produces a clear, simple solution. STs remember details and seldom make factual errors. Their weakness is that they may alienate others because of their tendency to ignore interpersonal aspects of decisions. In addition, they tend to avoid risks.

SFs also gather factual information, but they make judgments in terms of how they affect people. They place great importance on interpersonal relationships but also take a practical approach to gathering information for problem solving. The SFs' strength in decision making lies in their ability to handle interpersonal problems well and their ability to take calculated risks. SFs may have trouble accepting new ideas that break the rules in the organization.

NTs focus on the alternative possibilities in a situation and then evaluate the possibilities objectively and impersonally. NTs love to initiate ideas, and they like to focus on the long term. They are innovative and will take risks. This makes NTs good at things like new business development.[24] Weaknesses of NTs include their tendencies to ignore arguments based on facts and to ignore the feelings of others.

NFs also search out alternative possibilities, but they evaluate the possibilities in terms of how they will affect the people involved. They enjoy participative decision making and are committed to developing their employees.

However, NFs may be prone to making decisions based on personal preferences rather than on more objective data. They may also become too responsive to the needs of others.

Research supports the existence of these four cognitive styles and their influences on managerial decision making.[25] One study asked managers to describe their ideal organization, and the researchers found strong similarities in the descriptions of managers with the same cognitive style.[26] STs wanted an organization that relied on facts and details and that exercised impersonal methods of control. SFs focused on facts, too, but they did so in terms of the relationships within the organization. NTs emphasized broad issues and described impersonal, idealistic organizations. NFs described an organization that would serve humankind well and focused on general, humanistic values.

All four cognitive styles have much to contribute to organizational decision making.[27] Isabel Briggs Myers, creator of the MBTI, also developed the Z problem-solving model, which capitalizes on the strengths of the four separate preferences (sensing, intuiting, thinking, and feeling). By using the Z problem-solving model, managers can use both their preferences and nonpreferences to make decisions more effectively. The Z model is presented in Figure 10.3.

According to this model, good problem solving has four steps:

1. *Examine the facts and details.* Use sensing to gather information about the problem.

2. *Generate alternatives.* Use intuiting to develop possibilities.

FIGURE 10.3   The Z Problem-Solving Model

(10.3)

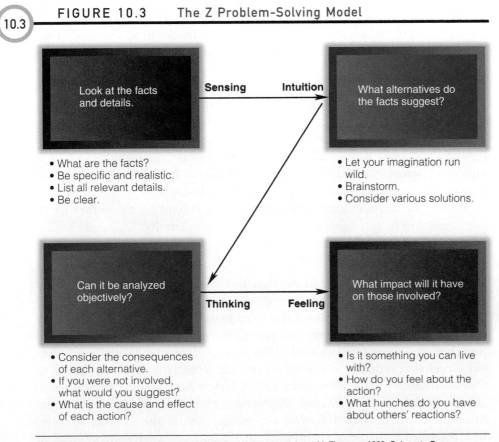

SOURCE: Excerpted from *Type Talk at Work* by Otto Kroeger and Janet M. Thuesen. 1992. Delacorte Press. Reprinted by permission of Otto Kroeger Associates.

3. *Analyze the alternatives objectively.* Use thinking to logically determine the effects of each alternative.

4. *Weigh the impact.* Use feeling to determine how the people involved will be affected.

Using the Z model can help an individual develop his or her nonpreferences. Another way to use the Z model is to rely on others to perform the nonpreferred activities. For example, an individual who is an NF might want to turn to a trusted NT for help in analyzing alternatives objectively.

Other Individual Influences on Decision Making

In addition to the cognitive styles just examined, many other individual differences affect a manager's decision making. Other personality characteristics, attitudes, and values, along with all of the individual differences variables that were discussed in Chapters 3 and 4, have implications for managerial decision making. Managers must use both their logic and their creativity to make effective decisions. Most of us are more comfortable using either logic or creativity, and we show that preference in everyday decision making. You 10.1 is an activity that will tell you which process, logic or creativity, is your preferred one. Take You 10.1 now, and then read on to interpret your score.

Brain hemispheric dominance is related to students' choices of college majors. Left-brained students gravitate toward business, engineering, and sciences, whereas right-brained students are attracted to education, nursing, communication, and literature.[28]

Our brains have two lateral halves (Figure 10.4). The right side is the center for creative functions, while the left side is the center for logic, detail, and planning. There are advantages to both kinds of thinking, so the ideal situation is to be "brain-lateralized" or to be able to use either logic or creativity or both, depending on the situation. There are ways to develop the side of the brain you are not accustomed to using. To develop your right side, or creative side, you can ask "what-if" questions, engage in play, and follow your intuition. To develop the left side, you can set goals for completing tasks and work to attain these goals. For managers, it is important to see the big picture, craft a vision, and plan strategically—all of which require right-brain skills. It is equally important to be able to understand day-to-day operations and flow chart work processes, which are left-hemisphere brain skills.

Two particular individual influences that can enhance decision-making effectiveness will be highlighted next: intuition and creativity.

The Role of Intuition

intuition

A fast, positive force in decision making that is utilized at a level below consciousness and involves learned patterns of information.

There is evidence that managers use their *intuition* to make decisions.[29] Henry Mintzberg, in his work on managerial roles, found that in many cases managers do not appear to use a systematic, step-by-step approach to decision making. Rather, Mintzberg argued, managers make judgments based on "hunches."[30] Daniel Isenberg studied the way senior managers make decisions and found that intuition was used extensively, especially as a mechanism to evaluate decisions made more rationally.[31] Robert Beck studied the way managers at BankAmerica (now Bank of America) made decisions about the future direction of the company following the deregulation of the banking industry. Beck described their use of intuition as an antidote to "analysis paralysis," or the tendency to analyze decisions rather than developing innovative solutions.[32]

Which Side of Your Brain Do You Favor?

There are no "right" or "wrong" answers to this questionnaire. It is more of a self-assessment than a test. Do not read the questions more than once. Don't overanalyze. Merely circle "A" or "B" to indicate which answer is more typical of you.

1. Typically, when I have a problem to solve,
   - (A) I make a list of possible solutions, prioritize them, and then select the best answer.
   - B I "let it sit" for a while or talk it over with someone before I attempt to reach a solution.

2. When I sit with my hands clasped in my lap (FOLD YOUR HANDS THAT WAY RIGHT NOW BEFORE GOING ON, THEN LOOK AT YOUR HANDS), the thumb that is on top is
   - (A) my right thumb.
   - B my left thumb.

3. I have hunches
   - A sometimes, but do not place much faith in them.
   - (B) frequently and I usually follow them.

4. If I am at a meeting or lecture, I tend to take extensive notes.
   - (A) True
   - (B) False

5. I am well-organized, have a system for doing things, have a place for everything and everything in its place, and can assimilate information quickly and logically.
   - (A) True
   - B False

6. I am good with numbers.
   - (A) True
   - B False

7. Finding words in a dictionary or looking up names in a telephone book is something I can do easily and quickly.
   - (A) True
   - B False

8. If I want to remember directions or other information,
   - A I make notes.
   - (B) I visualize the information.

9. I express myself well verbally.
   - (A) True
   - B False

10. To learn dance steps or athletic moves,
    - (A) I try to understand the sequence of the steps and repeat them mentally.
    - B I don't think about it; I just try to get the feel of the game or the music.

Interpretation:

> Four, five, or six "A" answers indicate lateralization—an ability to use either hemisphere easily and to solve problems according to their nature rather than according to a favored manner.

> One, two, or three "A" answers indicate right-hemisphere dominance; corresponding traits include inventiveness, creativity, innovation, risk taking, whimsy, and an ability to see the "big picture."

> Seven, eight, or nine "A" answers indicate a left-hemisphere dominance—a tendency toward attention to detail, the use of logic, and traits of thoroughness and accuracy.

SOURCE: "Which Side of the Brain Do You Favor?" from *Quality Driven Designs*. Copyright 1992 Pfeiffer/Jossey-Bass. Reprinted by permission of Jossey-Bass, Inc., a subsidiary of John Wiley & Sons, Inc.

Just what is intuition? In Jungian theory, intuiting (N) is one preference used to gather data. This is only one way that the concept of intuition has been applied to managerial decision making, and it is perhaps the most widely researched form of the concept of intuition. There are, however, many definitions of *intuition* in the managerial literature. Chester Barnard, one of the early influential management researchers, argued that intuition's main attributes were speed and the inability of the decision maker to determine how the decision was made.[33] Other researchers have contended that intuition occurs at an unconscious level and that this is why the decision maker cannot verbalize how the decision was made.[34]

FIGURE 10.4   Functions of the Left and Right Brain Hemispheres

10.4

Two Brains, Two Cognitive Styles

Left hemisphere   **Right hemisphere**

Verbal   Nonverbal, visuospatial
Sequential, temporal, digital Simultaneous, spatial,
                               analogical
Logical, analytic   Gestalt, synthetic
Rational   Intuitive
Western thought   Eastern thought

Comic strip:

Panel 1: AS YOUR CONSULTANT I'LL BE ABLE TO UNLEASH RIGHT-BRAIN POTENTIAL IN YOUR EMPLOYEES.

Panel 2: THEY'LL LEARN TO FIND CREATIVE ANSWERS, NOT JUST RELY ON LEFT-BRAIN QUANTITATIVE ANALYSIS.

Panel 3: WHICH PART OF THE BRAIN DO WE USE FOR MEETINGS?   THAT WOULD BE THE STEM.

SOURCES: Created based on ideas from *Left Brain, Right Brain* by Springer and Deutsch, p. 272. © 1993 by Sally P. Springer and Georg Deutsch (New York: W. H. Freeman and Company, 1993). DILBERT reprinted by permission of United Feature Syndicate, Inc.

Intuition has been variously described as follows:

> The ability to know or recognize quickly and readily the possibilities of a situation.[35]

> Smooth automatic performance of learned behavior sequences.[36]

> Simple analyses frozen into habit and into the capacity for rapid response through recognition.[37]

These definitions share some common assumptions. First, there seems to be a notion that intuition is fast. Second, intuition is utilized at a level below consciousness. Third, there seems to be agreement that intuition involves learned patterns of information. Fourth, intuition appears to be a positive force in decision making.

The use of intuition may lead to more ethical decisions. Intuition allows an individual to take on another's role with ease, and role taking is a fundamental part of developing moral reasoning. You may recall from Chapter 4 the role of cognitive moral development in ethical decision making. One study found a strong link between cognitive moral development and intuition. The development of new perspectives through intuition leads to higher moral growth, and thus to more ethical decisions.[38]

One question that arises is whether managers can be taught to use their intuition. Weston Agor, who has conducted workshops on developing intuitive skills in managers, has attained positive results in organizations such as the city of Phoenix and entertainment powerhouse Walt Disney Enterprises. After giving intuition tests to more than 10,000 executives, he has concluded that in most cases, higher management positions are held by individuals with higher levels of intuition. Just as the brain needs both hemispheres to work, Agor cautions that organizations need both analytical and intuitive minds to function at their peak. Consider Grant Tinker, former head of NBC. "Sometimes the boss has to go by his gut, hold his nose, and jump," Tinker writes in *Tinker in Television*. Lee Iaccoca, in his autobiography, spends pages extolling intuition: "To a certain extent, I've always operated by gut feeling."[39] Agor suggests relaxation techniques, using images to guide the mind, and taking creative pauses before making a decision.[40] A review of the research on intuition suggests that although intuition itself cannot be taught, managers can be trained to rely more fully on the promptings of their intuition.[41]

Intuition is an elusive concept, and one with many definitions. There is an interesting paradox regarding intuition. Some researchers view "rational" methods as preferable to intuition, yet satisfaction with a rational decision is usually determined by how the decision feels intuitively.[42] Intuition appears to have a positive effect on managerial decision making, but it is not without controversy. Some writers argue that intuition has its place and that instincts should be trusted, but not as a substitute for reason. With new technologies, managers can analyze a lot more information in a lot less time, making the rational method less time consuming than it once was.[43]

Creativity at Work

Creativity is a process influenced by individual and organizational factors that results in the production of novel and useful ideas, products, or both.[44] The social and technological changes that organizations face require creative decisions.[45] Managers of the future need to develop special competencies to deal with the turbulence of change, and one of these important competencies is the ability to promote creativity in organizations.[46]

creativity
A process influenced by individual and organizational factors that results in the production of novel and useful ideas, products, or both.

Creativity is a process that is at least in part unconscious. The four stages of the creative process are preparation, incubation, illumination, and verification.[47] Preparation means seeking out new experiences and opportunities to learn, because creativity grows from a base of knowledge. Travel and educational opportunities of all kinds open the individual's mind. Incubation is a process of reflective thought and is often conducted subconsciously. During incubation, the individual engages in other pursuits while the mind considers the problem and works on it. Illumination occurs when the individual senses an insight for solving the problem. Finally, verification is conducted to determine if the solution or idea is valid. This is accomplished by thinking through the implications of the decision, presenting the idea to another person, or trying out the decision. Sleep is an important contributor to creative problem solving,

For Creative Problem Solving, Sleep on It!

Have you ever worried about a problem, gone to sleep, and found that when you awoke in the morning you had the answer? An experiment showed that this is possible. Researchers taught subjects two simple rules for converting a string of numbers into a new order. A third rule that was kept secret from the subjects could only be discovered through insight. This hidden rule would dramatically improve the performance on the task. Subjects who worked on the problem in the evening and then slept for eight hours were twice as likely to discover the secret rule as those who stayed awake. Subjects who tried the problem in the morning and then worked a full day were just as bad at finding the secret rule as those who stayed awake all night.

The study is a good demonstration of what many of us have experienced. Sleep tends to facilitate creative problem solving. Employers who want creative employees may need to encourage restful sleep at night. Does this mean "power napping" at work will become acceptable?

SOURCE: U. Wagner, S. Gais, H. Haider, and J. Born, "Sleep Inspires Insight," *Nature* 427 (2004): 352–355.

as you can see in the Science feature. Momentary quieting of the brain through relaxation can also increase "coherence" or the ability of different parts of the brain to work together.[48, 49] Both individual and organizational influences affect the creative process.

INDIVIDUAL INFLUENCES Several individual variables are related to creativity. One group of factors involves the cognitive processes that creative individuals tend to use. One cognitive process is divergent thinking, meaning the individual's ability to generate several potential solutions to a problem.[50] In addition, associational abilities and the use of imagery are associated with creativity.[51] Unconscious processes such as dreams are also essential cognitive processes related to creative thinking.[52]

Personality factors have also been related to creativity in studies of individuals from several different occupations. These characteristics include intellectual and artistic values, breadth of interests, high energy, concern with achievement, independence of judgment, intuition, self-confidence, and a creative self-image.[53] Tolerance of ambiguity, intrinsic motivation, risk taking, and a desire for recognition are also associated with creativity.[54]

There is also evidence that people who are in a good mood are more creative. One study found that individuals who were in a good mood were more successful at creative problem solving than people whose mood was neutral.[55]

ORGANIZATIONAL INFLUENCES The organizational environment in which people work can either support creativity or impede creative efforts. Creativity killers include focusing on how work is going to be evaluated, being closely monitored while you are working, and competing with other people in win–lose situations. In contrast, creativity facilitators include feelings of autonomy, being part of a team with diverse skills, and having creative supervisors and coworkers.[56] High-quality, supportive relationships with supervisors are related to creativity.[57] Flexible organizational structures and participative decision making have also been associated with creativity. An organization can also present impediments to creativity. These barriers include internal political problems, harsh criticism of new ideas, destructive internal competition, and avoidance of risk.[58] The physical environment can also hamper creativity. Companies like Oticon, a Danish hearing-aid manufacturer, and Ethicon Endo-Surgery, a division of Johnson & Johnson, use open-plan offices that eliminate office walls and cubicles so that employees interact more frequently. When people mix, ideas mix as well.[59]

Studies of the role of organizational rewards in encouraging creativity have mixed results. Some studies have shown that monetary incentives improve creative performance, whereas others have found that material rewards do not influence innovative activity.[60] Still other studies have indicated that explicitly contracting to obtain a reward led to lower levels of creativity when compared with contracting for no reward, being presented with just the task, or being presented with the task and receiving the reward later.[61] Organizations can therefore enhance individuals' creative decision making by providing a supportive environment, participative decision making, and a flexible structure.

INDIVIDUAL/ORGANIZATION FIT Research has indicated that creative performance is highest when there is a match, or fit, between the individual and organizational influences on creativity. For example, when individuals who desire to be creative are matched with an organization that values creative ideas, the result is more creative performance.[62]

A common mistaken assumption regarding creativity is that either you have it or you do not. Research refutes this myth and has shown that individuals can be trained to be more creative.[63] The Disney Institute features a wide range of programs offered to companies, and one of their best-sellers is creativity training. You 10.2 allows you to determine whether you prefer creative or logical problem solving.

Part of creativity training involves learning to open up mental locks that keep us from generating creative alternatives to a decision or problem. The following are some mental locks that diminish creativity:

> Searching for the "right" answer.

> Trying to be logical.

> Following the rules.

> Avoiding ambiguity.

> Striving for practicality.

> Being afraid to look foolish.

> Avoiding problems outside our own expertise.

> Fearing failure.

> Believing we are not really creative.

> Not making play a part of work.[64]

Note that many of these mental locks stem from values within organizations. Organizations can facilitate creative decision making in many ways. Rewarding creativity, allowing employees to fail, making work more fun, and providing creativity training are a few suggestions. Also, companies can encourage creativity by exposing employees to new ideas. This can be done in several ways, including job rotation, which moves employees through different jobs and gives them exposure to different information, projects, and teams. Employees can also be assigned to work with groups outside the company, such as suppliers or consultants. Finally, managers can encourage employees to surround themselves with stimuli that they have found to enhance their creative

3. Understand the role of creativity in decision making and practice ways to increase your own creativity.

Creative or Logical Problem Solving: What Is Your Preference?

Try the following creative problem-solving challenge.

Each of the following problems is an equation that can be solved by substituting the appropriate words for the letters. Have fun with them!

Examples: 3F = 1Y (3 feet = 1 yard.)
4LC = GL (4 leaf clover = Good luck.)

1. M + M + NH + V + C + RI = NE.
2. "1B in the H = 2 in the B."
3. 8D – 24H = 1W.
4. 3P = 6.
5. HH & MH at 12 = N or M.
6. 4J + 4Q + 4K = All the FC.
7. S & M & T & W & T & F & S are D of W.
8. A + N + AF + MC + CG = AF.
9. T = LS State.
10. 23Y – 3Y = 2D.
11. E – 8 = Z.
12. Y + 2D = T.
13. C + 6D = NYE.
14. Y – S – S – A = W.
15. A & E were in the G of E.
16. My FL and South P are both MC.
17. "NN = GN."
18. N – P + SM = S of C.
19. 1 + 6Z = 1M.
20. "R = R = R."
21. AL & JG & WM & JK were all A.
22. N + V + P + A + A + C + P + I = P of S.
23. S + H of R = USC.

SOURCE: From *A Whack on the Side of the Head* by Roger Von Oech. Copyright © 1983, 1990, 1998 by Roger Von Oech. By permission of Warner Books.

Now try the following logical problem-solving exercise, entitled "Who Owns the Fish?", which is attributed to Albert Einstein.

There are five houses in a row and in five different colors. In each house lives a person from a different country. Each person drinks a certain drink, plays a certain game, and keeps a certain pet. No two people drink the same drink, play the same game, or keep the same pet.

> The Brit lives in a red house.
> The Swede keeps dogs.
> The Dane drinks tea.
> The green house is on the left of the white house.
> The green house owner drinks coffee.
> The person who plays tennis rears birds.
> The owner of the yellow house plays chess.
> The man living in the house right in the center drinks milk.

> The Norwegian lives in the first house.
> The man who plays poker lives next to the man who keeps cats.
> The man who keeps horses lives next to the one who plays chess.
> The man who plays billiards drinks beer.
> The German plays golf.
> The Norwegian lives next to the blue house.
> The man who plays poker has a neighbor who drinks water.

Question: Who owns the fish?

Answer: Your instructor can provide the solutions to this exercise.

SOURCE: By E. O. Welles, © 2004 Gruner + Jahr USA Publishing. "The Billionaire Next Door," first published in *Inc. Magazine*, 23(6) (May 2001): pp. 80–85. Reprinted with permission.

processes. These may be music, artwork, books, or anything else that encourages creative thinking.[65]

We have seen that both individual and organizational factors can produce creativity. Creativity can also mean finding problems as well as fixing them. Recently, four different types of creativity have been proposed, based on the source of the trigger (internal or external) and the source of the problem (presented versus discovered). Responsive creativity means responding to a problem that is presented to you by others because it is part of your job. Expected creativity is discovering problems because you are expected to by the organization. Contributory creativity is responding to problems presented to you because you want to be creative. Proactive creativity is discovering problems because you want to be creative.[66]

3M consistently ranks among the top ten in *Fortune*'s annual list of most admired corporations. It earned this reputation through innovation: More than one-quarter of 3M's sales are from products less than four years old. Post-It Notes, for example, were created by a worker who wanted little adhesive papers to mark hymns for church service. He thought of another worker who had perfected a light adhesive, and the two spent their "free time" developing Post-It Notes. 3M has continued its tradition of innovation with Post-It Flags, Pop-Up Tape Strips, and Nexcare Ease-Off Bandages.

Leaders can play key roles in modeling creative behavior. Sir Richard Branson, founder and chairman of U.K.-based Virgin Group, believes that if you do not use your employees' creative potential, you are doomed to failure. At Virgin Group, the culture encourages risk taking and rewards innovation. Rules and regulations are not its thing, nor is analyzing ideas to death. Branson says an employee can have an idea in the morning and implement it in the afternoon.[67]

Creativity is a global concern. Poland, for example, is undergoing a major shift from a centrally planned economy and monoparty rule to a market economy and Western-style democracy. One of the major concerns for Polish managers is creativity. Finding ingenious solutions and having the ability to think creatively can be a question of life or death for Polish organizations, which are making the transition to a faster pace of learning and change.[68]

Both intuition and creativity are important influences on managerial decision making. Both concepts require additional research so that managers can better understand how to use intuition and creativity, as well as how to encourage their employees to use them to make more effective decisions.

Participation in Decision Making

Effective management of people can improve a company's economic performance. Firms that capitalize on this fact share several common practices. Chief among them is participation of employees in decision making.[69] Many companies do this through highly empowered self-managed teams like the ones we discussed in Chapter 9. Even in situations where formal teams are not feasible, decision authority can be handed down to front-line employees who have the knowledge and skills to make a difference. At Hampton Inn hotels, for example, guest services personnel are empowered to do whatever is necessary to make guests happy—without consulting their superiors.

The Effects of Participation

Participative decision making occurs when individuals who are affected by decisions influence the making of those decisions. Participation buffers employees

participative decision making
Decision making in which individuals who are affected by decisions influence the making of those decisions.

from the negative experiences of organizational politics.[70] In addition, participative management has been found to increase employee creativity, job satisfaction, and productivity.[71]

GE Capital believes in participation. Each year it holds dreaming sessions, and employees from all levels of the company attend strategy and budget meetings to discuss where the company is heading. As a result, young employees came up with e-commerce ideas like http://www.financiallearning.com and http://www.gefn.com, which were highly successful.[72]

As our economy becomes increasingly based on knowledge work, and as new technologies make it easier for decentralized decision makers to connect, participative decision making will undoubtedly increase.[73] Consider the city and county of San Francisco, a combined city/county government organization. When the city and county of San Francisco needed to adopt a single messaging system to meet the needs of more than 20,000 users, it faced a huge challenge in getting all the users to provide input into the decision. Technology helped craft a system that balanced the needs of all the groups involved, and IT planners developed a twenty-eight-page spreadsheet to pull together the needs and desires of all sixty departments into a focused decision matrix. Within two years, 90 percent of the users had agreed on and moved to a single system, reducing costs and complexity.[74]

Foundations for Participation and Empowerment

Organizational and individual foundations underlie empowerment that enhances task motivation and performance. The organizational foundations for empowerment include a participative, supportive organizational culture and a team-oriented work design. A supportive work environment is essential because of the uncertainty that empowerment can cause within the organization. Empowerment requires that lower-level organizational members be able to make decisions and take action on those decisions. As operational employees become empowered to make decisions, real fear, anxiety, or even terror can be created among middle managers in the organization.[75] Senior leadership must create an organizational culture that is supportive and reassuring for these middle managers as the power dynamics of the system change. If not supported and reassured, the middle managers can become a restraining, disruptive force to participative decision-making efforts.

A second organizational foundation for empowerment concerns the design of work. The old factory system relied on work specialization and narrow tasks with the intent of achieving routinized efficiency.[76] This approach to the design of work had some economic advantages, but it also had some distressing disadvantages leading to monotony and fatigue. This approach to the design of work is inconsistent with participation, because the individual feels absolved of much responsibility for a whole piece of work. Team-oriented work designs are a key organizational foundation because they lead to broader tasks and a greater sense of responsibility. For example, Volvo builds cars using a team-oriented work design in which each person does many different tasks, and each person has direct responsibility for the finished product.[77] These work designs create a context for effective participation as long as the empowered individuals meet necessary individual prerequisites.

The three individual prerequisites for participation and empowerment are (1) the capability to become psychologically involved in participative activities, (2) the motivation to act autonomously, and (3) the capacity to see the relevance of participation for one's own well-being.[78] First, people must be psychologically equipped to become involved in participative activities if they are to be empowered and become effective team members. Not all people are so predisposed. For example, Germany has an authoritarian tradition that runs counter to participation and empowerment at the individual and group level. General Motors encountered significant difficulties implementing quality circles in its German plants, because workers expected to be directed by supervisors, not to engage in participative problem solving. The German initiatives to establish supervisory/worker boards in corporations are intended to change this authoritarian tradition.

A second individual prerequisite is the motivation to act autonomously. People with dependent personalities are predisposed to be told what to do and to rely on external motivation rather than internal, intrinsic motivation.[79] These dependent people are not effective contributors to decision making.

Finally, if participative decision making is to work, people must be able to see how it provides a personal benefit to them. The personal payoff for the individual need not be short term. It may be a long-term benefit that results in people receiving greater rewards through enhanced organizational profitability.

What Level of Participation?

Participative decision making is complex, and one of the things managers must understand is that employees can be involved in some, or all, of the stages of the decision-making process. For example, employees could be variously involved in identifying problems, generating alternatives, selecting solutions, planning implementations, or evaluating results. Research shows that greater involvement in all five of these stages has a cumulative effect. Employees who are involved in all five processes have higher satisfaction and performance levels. And, all decision processes are not created equal. If employees can't be provided with full participation in all stages, the highest payoffs seem to come with involvement in generating alternatives, planning implementations, and evaluating results.[80] Styles of participation in decision making may need to change as the company grows or as its culture changes.

The Group Decision-Making Process

Managers use groups to make decisions for several reasons. One is *synergy*, which occurs when group members stimulate new solutions to problems through the process of mutual influence and encouragement within the group. Another reason for using a group is to gain commitment to a decision. Groups also bring more knowledge and experience to the problem-solving situation.

Group decisions can sometimes be predicted by comparing the views of the initial group members with the final group decision. These simple relationships are known as *social decision schemes*. One social decision scheme is the majority-wins rule, in which the group supports whatever position is taken by the majority of its members. Another scheme, the truth-wins rule, predicts that the correct decision will emerge as an increasing number of members realize its appropriateness. The two-thirds-majority rule means that the decision favored by two-thirds or more of the members is supported. Finally, the first-shift rule states that members support a decision represented by the first shift in opinion shown by a member.

Research indicates that these social decision schemes can predict a group decision as much as 80 percent of the time.[81] Current research is aimed at

synergy
A positive force that occurs in groups when group members stimulate new solutions to problems through the process of mutual influence and encouragement within the group.

social decision schemes
Simple rules used to determine final group decisions.

discovering which rules are used in particular types of tasks. For example, studies indicate that the majority-wins rule is used most often in judgment tasks (that is, when the decision is a matter of preference or opinion), whereas the truth-wins rule predicts decisions best when the task is an intellectual one (that is, when the decision has a correct answer).[82]

Advantages and Disadvantages of Group Decision Making

4. Identify the advantages and disadvantages of group decision making.

Both advantages and disadvantages are associated with group decision making. The advantages include (1) more knowledge and information through the pooling of group member resources; (2) increased acceptance of, and commitment to, the decision, because the members had a voice in it; and (3) greater understanding of the decision, because members were involved in the various stages of the decision process. The disadvantages of group decision making include (1) pressure within the group to conform and fit in; (2) domination of the group by one forceful member or a dominant clique, who may ramrod the decision; and (3) the amount of time required, because a group makes decisions more slowly than an individual.[83]

Given these advantages and disadvantages, should an individual or a group make a decision? Substantial empirical research indicates that whether a group or an individual should be used depends on the type of task involved. For judgment tasks requiring an estimate or a prediction, groups are usually superior to individuals because of the breadth of experience that multiple individuals bring to the problem.[84] On tasks that have a correct solution, other studies have indicated that the most competent individual outperforms the group.[85] This finding has been called into question, however. Much of the previous research on groups was conducted in the laboratory, where group members interacted only for short periods of time. Researchers wanted to know how a longer experience in the group would affect decisions. Their study showed that groups who worked together for longer periods of time outperformed the most competent member 70 percent of the time. As groups gained experience, the best members became less important to the group's success.[86] This study demonstrated that experience in the group is an important variable to consider when evaluating the individual versus group decision-making question.

Given the emphasis on teams in the workplace, many managers believe that groups produce better decisions than do individuals, yet the evidence is mixed. It is evident that more research needs to be conducted in organizational settings to help answer this question.

Two potential liabilities are found in group decision making: groupthink and group polarization. These problems are discussed in the following sections.

Groupthink

5. Discuss the symptoms of groupthink and ways to prevent it.

groupthink
A deterioration of mental efficiency, reality testing, and moral judgment resulting from pressures within the group.

One liability of a cohesive group is its tendency to develop *groupthink*, a dysfunctional process. Irving Janis, the originator of the groupthink concept, describes groupthink as "a deterioration of mental efficiency, reality testing, and moral judgment" resulting from pressures within the group.[87]

Certain conditions favor the development of groupthink. One of the conditions is high cohesiveness. Cohesive groups tend to favor solidarity because members identify strongly with the group.[88] High-ranking teams that make decisions without outside help are especially prone to groupthink because they are likely to have shared mental models; that is, they are more likely to think alike.[89] And homogeneous groups (ones with little to no diversity among members) are more likely to suffer from groupthink.[90] Two other conditions that encourage groupthink are having to make a highly consequential decision and time constraints.[91] A highly consequential decision is one that will have a great impact on the group members and on outside parties. When group members feel that they have a limited time in which to make a decision, they may rush through the process. These antecedents cause members to prefer concurrence in decisions and to fail to evaluate one another's suggestions critically. A group suffering from groupthink shows recognizable symptoms. Table 10.1 presents these symptoms and makes suggestions on how to avoid groupthink.

An incident cited as a prime example of groupthink is the 1986 *Challenger* disaster, in which the shuttle exploded and killed all seven crew members. A presidential commission concluded that flawed decision making was the primary cause of the accident. Sadly, organizations often struggle to learn from

TABLE 10.1   Symptoms of Groupthink and How to Prevent It

SYMPTOMS OF GROUPTHINK

- *Illusions of invulnerability.* Group members feel that they are above criticism. This symptom leads to excessive optimism and risk taking.
- *Illusions of group morality.* Group members feel they are moral in their actions and therefore above reproach. This symptom leads the group to ignore the ethical implications of their decisions.
- *Illusions of unanimity.* Group members believe there is unanimous agreement on the decisions. Silence is misconstrued as consent.
- *Rationalization.* Group members concoct explanations for their decisions to make them appear rational and correct. The results are that other alternatives are not considered, and there is an unwillingness to reconsider the group's assumptions.
- *Stereotyping the enemy.* Competitors are stereotyped as evil or stupid. This leads the group to underestimate its opposition.
- *Self-censorship.* Members do not express their doubts or concerns about the course of action. This prevents critical analysis of the decisions.
- *Peer pressure.* Any members who express doubts or concerns are pressured by other group members who question their loyalty.
- *Mindguards.* Some members take it upon themselves to protect the group from negative feedback. Group members are thus shielded from information that might lead them to question their actions.

GUIDELINES FOR PREVENTING GROUPTHINK

- Ask each group member to assume the role of the critical evaluator who actively voices objections or doubts.
- Have the leader avoid stating his or her position on the issue prior to the group decision.
- Create several groups that work on the decision simultaneously.
- Bring in outside experts to evaluate the group process.
- Appoint a devil's advocate to question the group's course of action consistently.
- Evaluate the competition carefully, posing as many different motivations and intentions as possible.
- Once consensus is reached, encourage the group to rethink its position by reexamining the alternatives.

SOURCE: Janis, Irving L., *Groupthink: Psychological Studies of Policy Decisions and Fiascoes,* Second Edition. Copyright © 1982 by Houghton Mifflin Company. Used with permission.

their mistakes. In 2003, the shuttle *Columbia* exploded over Texas upon reentering the earth's atmosphere, killing all seven crew members. Within days of the *Columbia* disaster, questions began to surface about the decision-making process that led flight engineers to assume that damage caused to the shuttle upon take-off was minor and to continue the mission. The subsequent investigation of the disaster led observers to note that NASA's decision-making process appears just as flawed today as it was in 1986, exhibiting all the classic symptoms of groupthink. The final accident report blamed the NASA culture that downplayed risk and suppressed dissent for the decision.[92, 93]

Consequences of groupthink include an incomplete survey of alternatives, failure to evaluate the risks of the preferred course of action, biased information processing, and a failure to work out contingency plans. The overall result of groupthink is defective decision making. This was evident in the *Challenger* situation. The group considered only two alternatives: launch or no launch. They failed to consider the risks of their decision to launch the shuttle, and they did not develop any contingency plans.

Table 10.1 presents Janis's guidelines for avoiding groupthink. Many of these suggestions center around the notion of ensuring that decisions are evaluated completely, with opportunities for discussion from all group members. This strategy helps encourage members to evaluate one another's ideas critically.

Janis has used the groupthink framework to conduct historical analyses of several political and military fiascoes, including the Bay of Pigs invasion, the Vietnam War, and Watergate. One review of the decision situation in the *Challenger* incident proposed that two variables, time and leadership style, are important to include.[94] When a decision must be made quickly, there is more potential for groupthink. Leadership style can either promote groupthink (if the leader makes his or her opinion known up front) or avoid groupthink (if the leader encourages open and frank discussion).

There are few empirical studies of groupthink, and most of these involved students in a laboratory setting. More applied research may be seen in the future, however, as a questionnaire has been developed to measure the constructs associated with groupthink.[95] Janis's work on groupthink has led to several interdisciplinary efforts at understanding policy decisions.[96] The work underscores the need to examine multiple explanations for failed decisions.

Group Polarization

Another group phenomenon was discovered by a graduate student. His study showed that groups made riskier decisions; in fact, the group and each individual accepted greater levels of risk following a group discussion of the issue. Subsequent studies uncovered another shift—toward caution. Thus, group discussion produced shifts both toward more risky positions and toward more cautious positions.[97] Further research revealed that individual group member attitudes simply became more extreme following group discussion. Individuals who were initially against an issue became more radically opposed, and individuals who were in favor of the issue became more strongly supportive following discussion. These shifts came to be known as *group polarization*.[98]

The tendency toward polarization has important implications for group decision making. Groups whose initial views lean a certain way can be expected to adopt more extreme views following interaction.

Several ideas have been proposed to explain why group polarization occurs. One explanation is the social comparison approach. Prior to group discussion, individuals believe they hold better views than the other members. During group

group polarization

The tendency for group discussion to produce shifts toward more extreme attitudes among members.

discussion, they see that their views are not so far from average, so they shift to more extreme positions.[99] A second explanation is the persuasive arguments view. It contends that group discussion reinforces the initial views of the members, so they take a more extreme position.[100] Both explanations are supported by research. It may be that both processes, along with others, cause the group to develop more polarized attitudes.

Group polarization leads groups to adopt extreme attitudes. In some cases, this can be disastrous. For instance, if individuals are leaning toward a dangerous decision, they are likely to support it more strongly following discussion. Both groupthink and group polarization are potential liabilities of group decision making, but several techniques can be used to help prevent or control these two liabilities.

Techniques for Group Decision Making

Once a manager has determined that a group decision approach should be used, he or she can determine the technique that is best suited to the decision situation. Seven techniques will be briefly summarized: brainstorming, nominal group technique, Delphi technique, devil's advocacy, dialectical inquiry, quality circles and quality teams, and self-managed teams.

6. Evaluate the strengths and weaknesses of several group decision-making techniques.

Brainstorming

Brainstorming is a good technique for generating alternatives. The idea behind *brainstorming* is to generate as many ideas as possible, suspending evaluation until all of the ideas have been suggested. Participants are encouraged to build upon the suggestions of others, and imagination is emphasized. One company that benefits from brainstorming is Toyota. Despite its success with the baby-boomer generation, Toyota's executives realized that they were failing to connect with younger buyers who viewed the firm as stodgy. In response, Toyota assembled a group of younger employees to brainstorm new products for this market. The result was the Toyota Echo, as well as Scion, an entirely new line of boxy crossover vehicles aimed at the younger set.[101, 102, 103] Evidence suggests, however, that group brainstorming is less effective than a comparable number of individuals working alone. In groups, participants engage in discussions that can make them lose their focus.[104]

One recent trend is the use of electronic brainstorming instead of verbal brainstorming in groups. Electronic brainstorming overcomes two common problems that can produce group brainstorming failure: production blocking and evaluation apprehension. In verbal brainstorming, individuals are exposed to the inputs of others. While listening to others, individuals are distracted from their own ideas.[105] This is referred to as production blocking. When ideas are recorded electronically, participants are free from hearing the interruptions of others; thus, production blocking is reduced. Some individuals suffer from evaluation apprehension in brainstorming groups. They fear that others might respond negatively to their ideas. In electronic brainstorming, input is anonymous, so evaluation apprehension is reduced. Studies indicate that anonymous electronic brainstorming groups outperform face-to-face brainstorming groups in the number of ideas generated.[106]

brainstorming
A technique for generating as many ideas as possible on a given subject, while suspending evaluation until all the ideas have been suggested.

Nominal Group Technique

A structured approach to decision making that focuses on generating alternatives and choosing one is called *nominal group technique (NGT)*. NGT involves the following discrete steps:

nominal group technique (NGT)
A structured approach to group decision making that focuses on generating alternatives and choosing one.

1. Individuals silently list their ideas.

2. Ideas are written on a chart one at a time until all ideas are listed.

3. Discussion is permitted but only to clarify the ideas. No criticism is allowed.

4. A written vote is taken.

NGT is a good technique to use in a situation where group members fear criticism from others.[107]

Delphi Technique

Delphi technique
Gathering the judgments of experts for use in decision making.

The *Delphi technique*, which originated at the Rand Corporation, involves gathering the judgments of experts for use in decision making. Experts at remote locations respond to a questionnaire. A coordinator summarizes the responses to the questionnaire, and the summary is sent back to the experts. The experts then rate the various alternatives generated, and the coordinator tabulates the results. The Delphi technique is valuable in its ability to generate a number of independent judgments without the requirement of a face-to-face meeting.[108]

Devil's Advocacy

devil's advocacy
A technique for preventing groupthink in which a group or individual is given the role of critic during decision making.

In the *devil's advocacy* decision method, a group or individual is given the role of critic. This devil's advocate has the task of coming up with the potential problems of a proposed decision. This helps organizations avoid costly mistakes in decision making by identifying potential pitfalls in advance.[109] As we discussed in Chapter 9, a devil's advocate who challenges the CEO and top management team can help sustain the vitality and performance of the upper echelon.

Dialectical Inquiry

dialectical inquiry
A debate between two opposing sets of recommendations.

Dialectical inquiry is essentially a debate between two opposing sets of recommendations. Although it sets up a conflict, it is a constructive approach, because it brings out the benefits and limitations of both sets of ideas.[110] When using this technique, it is important to guard against a win–lose attitude and to concentrate on reaching the most effective solution for all concerned. Research has shown that the way a decision is framed (that is, win–win versus win–lose) is very important. A decision's outcome could be viewed as a gain or a loss, depending on the way the decision is framed.[111]

Quality Circles and Quality Teams

As you recall from Chapter 9, quality circles are small groups that voluntarily meet to provide input for solving quality or production problems. Quality circles are also a way of extending participative decision making into teams. Managers often listen to recommendations from quality circles and implement the suggestions. The rewards for the suggestions are intrinsic—involvement in the decision-making process is the primary reward.

Quality circles are often generated from the bottom up; that is, they provide advice to managers, who still retain decision-making authority. As such, quality circles are not empowered to implement their own recommendations. They operate in parallel fashion to the organization's structure, and they rely on voluntary participation.[112] In Japan, quality circles have been integrated into the organization instead of added on. This may be one reason for Japan's success with this technique. In contrast, the U.S. experience is not as positive. It has been estimated that 60 to 75 percent of the quality circles have failed. Reasons for the failures have included lack of top management support and lack of problem-solving skills among quality circle members.[113]

Quality teams, in contrast, are included in total quality management and other quality improvement efforts as part of a change in the organization's structure. Quality teams are generated from the top down and are empowered to act on their own recommendations. Whereas quality circles emphasize the generation of ideas, quality teams make data-based decisions about improving product and service quality. Various decision-making techniques are employed in quality teams. Brainstorming, flow charts, and cause-and-effect diagrams help pinpoint problems that affect quality.

Some organizations have moved toward quality teams, but Toyota has stuck with quality circles. The company has used them since 1963 and was the second company in the world to do so. Toyota's quality circles constitute a limited form of empowerment—and they like it that way. The members want to participate but don't have the desire to be self-directed. They would rather leave certain decisions to managers who are trusted to take good care of them. Toyota attributes its success with quality circles to the longevity of their use and to its view of them as true methods of participation.[114]

Quality circles and quality teams are methods for using groups in the decision-making process. Self-managed teams take the concept of participation one step further.

Self-Managed Teams

Another group decision-making method is the use of self-managed teams, which we also discussed in Chapter 9. The decision-making activities of self-managed teams are more broadly focused than those of quality circles and quality teams, which usually emphasize quality and production problems. Self-managed teams make many of the decisions that were once reserved for managers, such as work scheduling, job assignments, and staffing. Unlike quality circles, whose role is an advisory one, self-managed teams are delegated authority in the organization's decision-making process.

Many organizations have claimed success with self-managed teams. At Northern Telecom (now Nortel Networks), revenues rose 63 percent and sales increased 26 percent following the implementation of self-managed teams.[115] Research evidence shows that self-managed teams can lead to higher productivity, lower turnover among employees, and flatter organization structure.[116]

Self-managed teams, like any cohesive group, can fall victim to groupthink. The key to stimulating innovation and better problem solving in these groups is welcoming dissent among members. Dissent breaks down complacency and sets in motion a process that results in better decisions. Team members must know that dissent is permissible so that they won't fear embarrassment or ridicule.[117] Before choosing a group decision-making technique, the manager should carefully evaluate the group members and the decision situation. Then the best method for accomplishing the objectives of the group decision-making process can be selected. If the goal is generating a large number of alternatives, for example, brainstorming would be a good choice. If group members are reluctant to contribute ideas, the nominal group technique would be appropriate. The need for expert input would be best facilitated by the Delphi technique. To guard against groupthink, devil's advocacy or dialectical inquiry would be effective. Decisions that concern quality or production would benefit from the advice of quality circles or the empowered decisions of quality teams. Finally, a manager who wants to provide total empowerment to a group should consider self-managed teams.

Cultural Issues in Decision Making

Styles of decision making vary greatly among cultures. Many of the dimensions proposed by Hofstede that were presented in Chapter 2 affect decision making. Uncertainty avoidance, for example, can affect the way people view decisions. In the United States, a culture with low uncertainty avoidance, decisions are seen as opportunities for change. In contrast, cultures such as those of Indonesia and Malaysia attempt to accept situations as they are rather than to change them.[118] Power distance also affects decision making. In more hierarchical cultures, such as India, top-level managers make decisions. In countries with low power distance, lower-level employees make many decisions. The Swedish culture exemplifies this type.

The individualist/collectivist dimension has implications for decision making. Japan, with its collectivist emphasis, favors group decisions. The United States has a more difficult time with group decisions because it is an individualistic culture. Time orientation affects the frame of reference of the decision. In China, with its long-term view, decisions are made with the future in mind. In the United States, many decisions are made considering only the short term.

The masculine/feminine dimension can be compared to the Jungian thinking/feeling preferences for decision making. Masculine cultures, as in many Latin American countries, value quick, assertive decisions. Feminine cultures, as in many Scandinavian countries, value decisions that reflect concern for others.

Managers should learn as much as possible about the decision processes in other cultures. NAFTA, for example, has eliminated many barriers to trade with Mexico. In Mexican organizations, decision-making authority is centralized, autocratic, and retained in small groups of top managers. As a consequence, Mexican employees are reluctant to participate in decision making and often wait to be told what to do rather than take a risk. In addition, joint ventures with family-owned *grupos* (large groups of businesses) can be challenging. It may be difficult to identify the critical decision maker in the family and to determine how much decision-making authority is held by the grupo's family board.[119] Mexican managers may be more likely to engage in escalation of commitment or continue to invest in a losing venture. However, because lower-level managers in Mexico have control over smaller amounts of resources, they tend to invest in smaller increments than do U.S. managers.[120]

Technological Aids to Decision Making

7. Describe the effects that expert systems and group decision support systems have on decision making in organizations.

Many computerized decision tools are available to managers. These systems can be used to support the decision-making process in organizations.

Expert Systems

Artificial intelligence is used to develop an expert system, which is a programmed decision tool. The system is set up using decision rules, and the effectiveness of the expert system is highly dependent on its design. Because expert systems are sources of knowledge and experience and not just passive software, the organization must decide who is responsible for the decisions made by expert systems. Organizations must therefore be concerned about the liability for using the recommendations of expert systems.

TriPath Imaging has found a way to automate a critical but tedious process: screening Pap smears for signs of cancer. Programmers developing this software, called FocalPoint, met with numerous pathologists to learn which criteria they look for, such as the color of a cell's nucleus. They then allowed the software to learn by "practicing" on slides that had already been examined by experts. Today, FocalPoint software screens about 10 percent of all Pap smear slides in the United States.[121]

Expert systems hold great potential for affecting managerial decisions. Thus, managers must carefully scrutinize the expert system rather than simply accepting its decisions.

Decision Support Systems

Managers use decision support systems (DSS) as tools to enhance their ability to make complex decisions. DSS are computer and communication systems that process incoming data and synthesize pertinent information for managers to use. One example is the Fire Management Information System (FMIS) developed by a team of five partners from companies representing four European countries. Fire managers who are in charge of emergencies are bombarded with information and stress as situations change. The team sought to design a system that would help the fire managers in their decision-making tasks during forest fires. Although emergencies can take different forms, managers do not require radically different plans for dealing with them. This makes it possible to develop and store skeletal plans that can be accessed using the DSS instead of starting from scratch with each forest fire.

The team combined five decision support services in putting together the system:

> Weather monitoring synthesized information from remote meteorological stations.

> Fire risk rating assessed risk using an expert system.

> Fighting adviser proposed plans for preventing and fighting the fire.

> Fire detection used a network of imaging sensors for early detection of fires.

> Fire modeling simulated the fire's pattern and spread, taking into account vegetation, topography, and weather.

The fire manager uses the system in two modes. In standby mode, the system constantly updates databases and maps. In operational mode, the fire manager navigates through different functions when an emergency arises. In this way, the FMIS integrates all the decision support tools the manager needs to make the quick decisions needed to fight forest fires.[122]

Group Decision Support Systems

Another tool for decision making focuses on helping groups make decisions. A group decision support system (GDSS) uses computer support and communication facilities to support group decision-making processes in either face-to-face meetings or dispersed meetings. The GDSS has been shown to affect conflict management within a group by depersonalizing the issue and by forcing the group to discuss its conflict management process.[123] Team decisions often improve by using a GDSS because members share information more fully when they use a GDSS.[124]

Shell Oil realized several years ago that its engineers were wasting time and money finding answers to questions when other people in the firm already had the solutions. To help leverage its internal knowledge, Shell devised a massive but simple system based on the familiar model of Web discussion groups. Within these "communities," engineers can pose questions to experts in other segments of the business. But perhaps more important, Shell indexes and archives the discussions from these boards, creating a living, growing knowledge base that future generations of engineers will rely on even more heavily. To date, Shell estimates that it has saved $200 for every dollar invested in the project.[125]

Northrop Grumman, a major defense contractor, works with a dazzling array of advanced technologies. But what happens when an aircraft engineer faces a decision involving an area with which he is unfamiliar, even though he is fairly sure that one of Grumman's other 10,000 employees probably knows the answer? Today, he can use a piece of decision support software called ActiveNet. ActiveNet digs through mountains of data, including employee profiles and internal documents—from e-mail to PowerPoint slides—to identify individuals whose interests or backgrounds might match the need. In some cases, the key people may be just down the hall; in others, they might be on another continent. By bringing workers together with other experts, ActiveNet helps them broaden their decision-making abilities by tapping the resources already present around them.[126]

The success of GDSS as an aid to decision making depends on a number of factors. Organizations in which people are open to change and in which managers attach importance to flexible and creative decision processes are more likely to benefit. Evidence also shows that a GDSS that encourages full participation and promotes raising questions and expressing concerns is more likely to be successful. Further, managers should carefully consider the group's size and the type of task in planning for a GDSS. In the initial stages of decision making, such as generating alternatives, larger groups may work well with a GDSS. For more complex problem solving and choice making, however, small groups (fifteen members or fewer) are more effective.[127]

The effects of GDSS need further investigation. In a study that involved making investment decisions, minority opinion holders expressed their views most frequently using a GDSS. However, these minority views were more influential under face-to-face communication. This means that GDSS may facilitate the expression of minority viewpoints, but GDSS may also diminish their influence on group decisions.[128]

Decision Making in the Virtual Workplace

Managers today are working in flexible organizations—so flexible in fact that many workplaces are unconstrained by geography, time, and organizational boundaries. Virtual teams are emerging as a new form of working arrangement. Virtual teams are groups of geographically dispersed coworkers who work together using a combination of telecommunications and information technologies to accomplish a task. Virtual teams seldom meet face to face, and membership often shifts according to the project at hand.

How are decisions made in virtual teams? These teams require advanced technologies for communication and decision making. Three basic technologies aid virtual teams in decision making: desktop videoconferencing systems (DVCS); group decision support systems (GDSS), as described in the previous section; and Internet/intranet systems.[129]

Desktop videoconferencing systems are the major technologies that form the basis for other virtual team technologies. DVCS recreate the face-to-face interactions of teams and go one step beyond by supporting more complex levels of communication among virtual team members. Small cameras on top of computer monitors provide video feeds, and voice transmissions are made possible through earpieces and microphones. High-speed data connections are used for communication. All team members can be connected, and outside experts can even be added. A local group can connect with up to fifteen different individuals or groups. Users can simultaneously work on documents, analyze data, or map out ideas.

GDSS make real-time decision making possible in the virtual team. They are ideal systems for brainstorming, focus groups, and group decisions. By using support tools within the GDSS, users can turn off their individual identities and interact with anonymity, and can poll participants and assemble statistical information relevant to the decision being made. GDSS are thus the sophisticated software that makes collaboration possible in virtual teams.

Internal internets, or intranets, are adaptations of Internet technologies for use within a company. For virtual teams, the Internet and intranets can be rich communication and decision-making resources. These tools allow virtual teams to archive text, visual, audio, and data files for use in decision making. They permit virtual teams to inform other organization members about the team's progress and enable the team to monitor other projects within the organization.

By using DVCS, GDSS, and Internet/intranet technologies, virtual teams can capitalize on a rich communications environment for decision making. It is difficult, however, to duplicate the face-to-face environment. The effectiveness of a virtual team's decision making depends on its members' ability to use the tools that are available. Collaborative systems can enhance virtual teams' decision quality if they are used well.[130]

Ethical Issues in Decision Making

One criterion that should be applied to decision making is the ethical implications of the decision. Ethical decision making in organizations is influenced by many factors, including individual differences and organizational rewards and punishments.

8. Utilize an "ethics check" for examining managerial decisions.

Kenneth Blanchard and Norman Vincent Peale proposed an "ethics check" for decision makers in their book *The Power of Ethical Management*.[131] They contend that the decision maker should ponder three questions:

1. Is it legal? (Will I be violating the law or company policy?)

2. Is it balanced? (Is it fair to all concerned in the short term and long term? Does it promote win–win relationships?)

3. How will it make me feel about myself? (Will it make me proud of my actions? How will I feel when others become aware of the decision?)

As we mentioned in Chapter 2, there are many ethical issues surrounding drug testing in organizations. In The Real World 10.2, you can see this dilemma as faced by Caterpillar.

General Dynamics, a major defense contractor that builds weapons ranging from submarines to fighter jets, faced charges of defrauding the government out of more than $2 billion on the Los Angeles class submarine project. While the company ultimately admitted no guilt, the scandal cost Admiral Hyman Rickover his career. And audiotapes of the firm's CEO and CFO discussing their plans to "screw the Navy," combined with revelations that a company vice president billed the Navy for the cost of kenneling his dog while he was out of town, started a long downhill slide which ultimately cost the two executives their jobs and cost General Dynamics its reputation.[132, 133]

Drug Testing Dilemmas at Caterpillar, Inc.

When company needs and employee needs collide, who decides which will give? Caterpillar makes heavy construction equipment, and its need for factory safety led it to institute random employee drug tests at its Georgia plant in late 2002. Many companies use random drug tests for the same reasons; approximately 45 million drug tests are done each year. But while Caterpillar says it follows drug testing guidelines set by the U.S. Department of Transportation, one former employee says the policy is unfair. Tom Smith was fired when, after waiting three hours and drinking more than a quart of water, he was still unable to provide a urine specimen. Smith says he has always been embarrassed to "go" with other people around, and Dr. Michael Chancellor, a urology professor, notes that this condition (paruresis, also known as shy bladder syndrome) is actually fairly common. In North America, roughly 20 million people suffer from the disorder. But while Smith claims he was *unable* to provide the specimen, company rules state that after three hours of waiting, an employee is considered *unwilling* to comply and will be fired.

As drug testing has become more common, such conflicts have become more frequent, with some workers claiming that the condition is a disability and they are protected by law, and others accusing firms of discriminating against them because of their difficulty. Where do company rights end and employee rights begin? Is an employee's offer to provide blood samples or hair samples instead of urine a reasonable compromise, or simply a waste of time? And who will make the final decision?

SOURCE: J. Barbian, "Stand and Deliver," *Training* 39 (2002): 22, http://www.cbsnews.com/stories/2004/02/09/national/main598991.shtml.

In summary, all decisions, whether made by individuals or by groups, must be evaluated for their ethics. Organizations should reinforce ethical decision making among employees by encouraging and rewarding it. Socialization processes should convey to newcomers the ethical standards of behavior in the organization. Groups should use devil's advocates and dialectical methods to reduce the potential for groupthink and the unethical decisions that may result. Effective and ethical decisions are not mutually exclusive.

Managerial Implications: Decision Making Is a Critical Activity

Decision making is important at all levels of every organization. At times managers may have the luxury of optimizing (selecting the best alternative), but more often they are forced to satisfice (select the alternative that is good enough). And, at times, the decision process can even seem unpredictable and random.

Individuals differ in their preferences for risk, as well as in their styles of gathering information and making judgments. Understanding individual differences can help managers maximize strengths in employee decision styles and build teams that capitalize on strengths. Creativity is one such strength. It can be encouraged by providing employees with a supportive environment that nourishes innovative ideas. Creativity training has been used in some organizations with positive results.

Some decisions are best made by individuals and some by teams or groups. The task of the manager is to diagnose the situation and implement the appropriate level of participation. To do this effectively, managers should know the advantages and disadvantages of various group decision-making techniques and should minimize the potential for groupthink. Finally, decisions made by individuals or groups should be analyzed to see whether they are ethical.

LOOKING BACK: CANINE COMPANIONS FOR INDEPENDENCE

Good Decisions, Happy Endings

While the clients at team training are eager to learn which dog they have been prematched with, Hali couldn't care less; in fact, she is largely oblivious to the important decisions about her future being made nearby. Morning comes and the CCI staff once again creates various human/dog pairings, putting them through their paces as they search for that perfect match. The morning goes well, and a quick lunchtime conference confirms the pairings.

A canine companion undergoes testing and training to determine for whom it will be a good match.

That afternoon, Hali is paired with a seven-year-old boy from Oklahoma named Matthew. Matthew was born with O. I., commonly known as brittle bone disease. His bones fracture easily, often for no apparent reason, and he uses a wheelchair to get around. Hali, Matthew, and Matthew's mother spend the rest of the two-week training session learning to work together, and after a tearful graduation ceremony and words of thanks to Hali's puppy raiser, they board the plane for home.

Hali quickly settles into her new home, finding her way around the house and learning specific skills to help Matthew. Her days start with the words, "Hali, light," which tells her to pull the cord attached to Matthew's room light switch. During the day, they play ball and Hali works on such tasks as putting Matthew's clothes in the hamper and helping him fix her meals. Her days end with Matthew's favorite command, "Hali, snuggle," which is her signal to lie down and put her head on his bed so they can drift off to sleep together. A good match, to be sure.[134]

Chapter Summary

1. Bounded rationality assumes that there are limits to how rational managers can be.

2. The garbage can model shows that under high uncertainty, decision making in organizations can be an unsystematic process.

3. Jung's cognitive styles can be used to help explain individual differences in gathering information and evaluating alternatives.

4. Intuition and creativity are positive influences on decision making and should be encouraged in organizations.

5. Empowerment and teamwork require specific organizational design elements and individual characteristics and skills.

6. Techniques such as brainstorming, nominal group technique, Delphi technique, devil's advocacy, dialectical inquiry, quality circles and teams, and self-managed teams can help managers reap the benefits of group methods while limiting the possibilities of groupthink and group polarization.

7. Technology is providing assistance to managerial decision making, especially through expert systems

and group decision support systems. More research is needed to determine the effects of these technologies.

8. Managers should carefully weigh the ethical issues surrounding decisions and encourage ethical decision making throughout the organization.

Key Terms

bounded rationality (p. 319)
brainstorming (p. 337)
cognitive style (p. 322)
creativity (p. 327)
Delphi technique (p. 338)
devil's advocacy (p. 338)
dialectical inquiry (p. 338)
effective decision (p. 318)

escalation of commitment (p. 321)
garbage can model (p. 319)
group polarization (p. 336)
groupthink (p. 334)
heuristics (p. 319)
intuition (p. 324)
nominal group technique (NGT) (p. 337)

nonprogrammed decision (p. 316)
participative decision making (p. 331)
programmed decision (p. 316)
rationality (p. 318)
risk aversion (p. 320)
satisfice (p. 319)
social decision schemes (p. 333)
synergy (p. 333)

Review Questions

1. Compare the garbage can model with the bounded rationality model. Compare the usefulness of these models in today's organizations.

2. List and describe Jung's four cognitive styles. How does the Z problem-solving model capitalize on the strengths of the four preferences?

3. What are the individual and organizational influences on creativity?

4. What are the organizational foundations of empowerment and teamwork? The individual foundations?

5. Describe the advantages and disadvantages of group decision making.

6. Describe the symptoms of groupthink, and identify actions that can be taken to prevent it.

7. What techniques can be used to improve group decisions?

Discussion and Communication Questions

1. Why is identification of the real problem the first and most important step in the decision-making process? How does attribution theory explain mistakes that can be made as managers and employees work together to explain why the problem occurred?

2. How can organizations effectively manage both risk taking and escalation of commitment in the decision-making behavior of employees?

3. How will you most likely make decisions based on your cognitive style? What might you overlook using your preferred approach?

4. How can organizations encourage creative decision making?

5. What are some organizations that use expert systems? Group decision support systems? How will these two technologies affect managerial decision making?

6. How do the potential risks associated with participating in quality circles differ from those associated with participating in quality teams? If you were a member of a quality circle, how would management's decisions to reject your recommendations affect your motivation to participate?

7. (communication question) Form a team of four persons. Find two examples of recent decisions made in organizations: one that you consider a good decision, and one that you consider a bad decision. Two members should work on the good decision, and two on the bad decision. Each pair should write a brief description of the decision. Then write a summary of what went right, what went wrong, and what could be done to improve the decision process. Compare and contrast your two examples in a presentation to the class.

8. *(comunication question)* Reflect on your own experiences in groups with groupthink. Describe the situation in which you encountered groupthink, the symptoms that were present, and the outcome. What remedies for groupthink would you prescribe? Summarize your answers in a memo to your instructor.

Ethical Dilemma

Slowly the managers of Beckman Services began arriving. An unexpected meeting had been called for 8:30 this morning and not everyone anticipated the news they were about to hear. Beckman was a financial services company that sold their services to individuals and companies. Since the terrorists' attacks on 9/11, Beckman had been experiencing financial difficulties. In order to boost sales, an incentive plan had been rolled out last December which management hoped would solve the problem. The plan challenged the sales force to increase sales by 15%. A daunting task, but the generous incentives made the challenge well worth the endeavor.

The meeting began and CEO Frank May opened by welcoming everyone to "one of the most difficult meetings he has ever had to call." Frank explained that although the incentive plan seemed to be working very well, the company's cash reserves were not as strong as they had hoped and delivering the promised bonuses would be more difficult than they had anticipated. He realized this was not going to be a popular decision, but Frank felt sure the salespeople would understand.

Richard Johnson, VP of Human Recourses, sat quietly in the meeting. He could not believe what was happening. It was now early November and the salespeople had been working hard for the last 10 months. He knew many of the salespeople well, and they were counting on the promised bonuses. What message was the company sending if they cancel this program at the last minute? He also knew he should say something, but disagreeing with Frank was never a good idea, especially when everyone else seemed to agree with the plan. Richard looked up and realized that the meeting was coming to an end. To challenge Frank in front of the team could be the end of his career at Beckman. But it couldn't be possible that everyone really agreed with Frank, could they? "Any questions or concerns about proceeding?" Frank asked. Richard needed to make a decision and make it fast.

Questions

1. Who are the stakeholders in Beckman Services and what is Frank May's responsibility to them?

2. To whom does Richard Johnson have a responsibility?

3. Evaluate Richard Johnson's decision using rule, virtue, right, and justice theories.

Experiential Exercises

10.1 Making a Layoff Decision

Purpose
In this exercise, you will examine how to weigh a set of facts and make a difficult personnel decision about laying off valued employees during a time of financial hardship. You will also examine your own values and criteria used in the decision-making process.

The Problem
Walker Space Institute (WSI) is a medium-sized firm located in Connecticut. The firm essentially has been a subcontractor on many large space contracts that have been acquired by firms like Alliant Techsystems and others.

With the cutback in many of the National Aeronautics and Space Administration programs, Walker has an excess of employees. Stuart Tartaro, the head of one of the sections, has been told by his superior that he must reduce his section of engineers from nine to six. He is looking at the following summaries of their vitae and pondering how he will make this decision:

1. *Roger Allison*, age twenty-six, married, two children. Allison has been with WSI for a year and a half. He is a very good engineer, with a degree from Rensselaer Polytech. He has held two prior jobs and lost both of them because of cutbacks in the space program. He moved to Connecticut from California to take this job. Allison is well liked by his coworkers.

2. *Dave Jones*, age twenty-four, single. Jones is an African-American, and the company looked hard to get him because of affirmative action pressure.

He is not very popular with his coworkers. Because he has been employed less than a year, not too much is known about his work. On his one evaluation (which was average), Jones accused his supervisor of bias against African-Americans. He is a graduate of the Detroit Institute of Technology.

3. *William Foster*, age fifty-three, married, three children. Foster is a graduate of "the school of hard knocks." After serving in the Vietnam War, he started to go to school but dropped out because of high family expenses. Foster has worked at the company for twenty years. His ratings were excellent for fifteen years. The last five years they have been average. Foster feels his supervisor grades him down because he does not "have sheepskins covering his office walls."

4. *Donald Boyer*, age thirty-two, married, no children. Boyer is well liked by his coworkers. He has been at WSI five years, and he has a B.S. and M.S. in engineering from Purdue University. Boyer's ratings have been mixed. Some supervisors rated him high and some average. Boyer's wife is an M.D.

5. *Ann Shuster*, age twenty-nine, single. Shuster is a real worker, but a loner. She has a B.S. in engineering from the University of California. She is working on her M.S. at night, always trying to improve her technical skills. Her performance ratings have been above average for the three years she has been at WSI.

6. *Sherman Soltis*, age thirty-seven, divorced, two children. He has a B.S. in engineering from Ohio State University. Soltis is very active in community affairs: Scouts, Little League, and United Way. He is a friend of the vice president through church work. His ratings have been average, although some recent ones indicate that he is out of date. He is well liked and has been employed at WSI for fourteen years.

7. *Warren Fortuna*, age forty-four, married, five children. He has a B.S. in engineering from Georgia Tech. Fortuna headed this section at one time. He worked so hard that he had a heart attack. Under doctor's orders, he resigned from the supervisory position. Since then he has done good work, though because of his health, he is a bit slower than the others. Now and then he must spend extra time on a project because he did get out of date during the eight years he headed the section. His performance evaluations for the last two years have been above average. He has been employed at WSI for fourteen years.

8. *Robert Treharne*, age forty-seven, single. He began an engineering degree at MIT but had to drop out for financial reasons. He tries hard to stay current by regular reading of engineering journals and taking all the short courses the company and nearby colleges offer. His performance evaluations have varied, but they tend to be average to slightly above average. He is a loner, and Tartaro thinks this has negatively affected Treharne's performance evaluations. He has been employed at WSI sixteen years.

9. *Sandra Rosen*, age twenty-two, single. She has a B.S. in engineering technology from the Rochester Institute of Technology. Rosen has been employed less than a year. She is enthusiastic, a very good worker, and well liked by her coworkers. She is well regarded by Tartaro.

Tartaro does not quite know what to do. He sees the good points of each of his section members. Most have been good employees. They all can pretty much do one another's work. No one has special training.

He is fearful that the section will hear about the downsizing and morale will drop. Work would fall off. He does not even want to talk to his wife about it, in case she would let something slip. Tartaro has come to you, Edmund Graves, personnel manager at WSI, for some guidelines on this decision—legal, moral, and best personnel practice.

Assignment
You are Edmund Graves. Write a report with your recommendations for termination and a careful analysis of the criteria for the decision. You should also carefully explain to Tartaro how you would go about the terminations and what you would consider reasonable termination pay. You should also advise him about the pension implications of this decision. Generally, fifteen years' service entitles you to at least partial pension.

SOURCE: W. F. Glueck. *Cases and Exercises in Personnel* (Dallas: Business Publications, 1978), 24–26.

10.2 Dilemma at 29,000 Feet

Purpose

Making ethical decisions often requires taking decisive actions in ambiguous situations. Making these decisions entails not just weighing options and making rational choices but making choices between competing but equally important demands. Managers must not only take action, but they also must provide compelling reasons that make their choices rationally accountable to others. This exercise requires you to think through an ethical situation, take an action, and create a convincing justification for your action. The exercise is designed to encourage critical thinking about complex problems and to encourage thinking about how you might resolve a dilemma outside your area of expertise.

The Problem

Imagine you are the sole leader of a mountain-climbing expedition and have successfully led a group of three climbers to the mountain summit. However, on your descent, trouble sets in as a fierce storm engulfs the mountain and makes progression down nearly impossible. One climber collapses from exhaustion at 24,000 feet and cannot continue down the mountain. The two stronger climbers insist on continuing down without you because they know if they stay too long at high altitude death is certain. No one has ever survived overnight on the mountain. A rescue attempt is impossible because helicopters cannot reach you above 18,000 feet.

As the leader, you are faced with a difficult choice: abandon your teammate and descend alone or stay with your dying teammate and face almost certain death. On one hand, you might stay with your dying teammate in hopes that the storm might clear and a rescue party will be sent. However, you know that if you stay both of you will most likely die. On the other hand, you are still strong and may be able to make it down to safety, abandoning your teammate to die alone on the mountain.

Assignment

Your assignment is to make an argument for one of the actions: staying with your teammate or descending alone. The technical aspects of mountain climbing are not important, nor is it good enough to state that you would not get in this situation in the first place! What is important is that you provide a well-reasoned argument for your action. A good argument might address the following points:

1. A discussion of the pros and cons of each action: staying with your teammate or descending alone.

2. A discussion of the underlying values and assumptions of each action. For example, staying with the teammate implies that you have a particular obligation as the leader of a team; descending alone suggests that you may place a higher value on your own life.

3. A discussion of your own values and viewpoints on the topic. In other words, take a stand and justify your position. How, for example, might you justify to the family of the abandoned climber your decision to descend alone? How might you justify to your own family your decision to stay with the ailing climber?

4. What prior experience, knowledge, or beliefs lead you to your conclusion?

5. How might this situation be similar to or different from the dilemmas faced in more typical organizations? For example, do leaders need to take actions that require them to make similar difficult decisions? Have you experienced any similar dilemmas that had no easy answer in the workplace, and how did you resolve them?

Final Thoughts

Remember, there is no right or wrong answer to this case. The point is to consider and make clear your own ethical choices by evaluating all relevant information, evaluating the underlying assumptions of each, and creating a clear and convicing argument for action. A quote by philosopher Martha Craven Nussbaum might act as a starting point for your study. She writes,

"Both alternatives make a serious claim on your practical attention. You might sense that no matter how you choose, you will be left with some regret that you did not do the other thing. Sometimes you may be clear about which is the better choice and yet feel pain over the frustration of the other significant concerns. It is extremely important to realize that the problem is not just one difficult decision but that conflicts arise when the final decision itself is perfectly obvious."

Good luck in your decision!

SOURCE: D. C. Kayes, "Dilemma at 29,000 Feet: An Exercise in Ethical Decision Making Based on the 1996 Mt. Everest Climbing Disaster." *Journal of Management Education* 26 (2002): 307–321. Reprinted by permission of Sage Publications.

TAKE 2

Biz Flix | Dr. Seuss' How the Grinch Stole Christmas

Readers and lovers of the Dr. Seuss original tale may feel put off by Ron Howard's loose adaptation of the story. Whoville, a magical, mythical land, features the Whos who love Christmas and the Grinch (Jim Carrey) who hates it. Cindy Lou Who (Taylor Momsen) tries to bring the Grinch back to the Yuletide celebrations, an effort that backfires on all involved. Sparkling special effects will dazzle most viewers and likely distract them from the film's departures from the original story.

The selected scene is an edited version of the "Second Thoughts" sequence early in the film. Just before this scene, fearless Cindy Lou entered the Grinch's lair to invite him to be the Holiday Cheermeister at the Whobilation One-Thousand celebration. In typical Grinch fashion, he pulls the trap door on Cindy Lou, who unceremoniously slides out of his lair to land on a snowy Whoville street. The Grinch now must decide whether to accept the invitation. The film continues with the Cheermeister award ceremony.

What to Watch for and Ask Yourself:

> What are the Grinch's decision alternatives or options?

> What decision criteria does the Grinch use to choose from the alternatives?

> Describe the steps in the Grinch's decision-making process.

Workplace Video | Machado & Silvetti: Managerial Decision Making

Machado & Silvetti Associates specializes in creating housing and other building structures for colleges, universities, and cities, both in the U.S. and around the world. The Boston-based architecture and urban-design firm has received widespread acclaim for its unique architecture and boasts an impressive list of clients including the J. Paul Getty Trust, the Utah Museum of Fine Arts, Harvard University, and the City of Vienna.

Rodolfo Machado and Jorge Silvetti, seasoned professionals in the world of architecture, became partners in the 1970s and began building a business together based on hard work and successful collaboration with others. Like most architectural firms, Machado & Silvetti Associates is organized around its building projects, and employees at the company must coordinate with architects, project managers, and clients to make key decisions related to design and construction assignments. Regardless of how simple or complex the building project, important decisions have to be made concerning materials and dimensions, and great effort goes into reducing uncertainty and risk—especially with regard to budgets. Some decisions at Machado & Silvetti are routine and scripted; others are made on-the-spot by teams of experienced professionals.

Decision-making skills are critical to the success of any architectural firm. In a fast-changing world, decisions have to be made quickly and managers have to keep themselves open to creativity and innovation. Machado & Silvetti Associates demonstrates that a business can make timely, intelligent, cost effective choices and still remain true to its creative vision.

Questions

1. *List some of the important decisions that have to be made throughout the design and construction of Machado & Silvetti's building projects.*

2. *Which model of decision making do you think is most common to the teams working for Machado & Silvetti Associates: the rational model, bounded rationality model, or garbage can model? Explain.*

3. *What decision-making pitfalls must teams avoid as they try to make good decisions on architectural building projects?*

The Context of Decision Making at Whole Foods Market

As the world's largest retailer of natural and organic foods, Whole Foods Market had sales of $3.1 billion in the fiscal year ended September 2003. Started as one small store in Austin, Texas, in 1980, Whole Foods Market has grown to 158 stores in North America and the United Kingdom as of mid-2004. Much of the growth has occurred through targeted mergers and acquisitions that fit well with the company's mission and vision. The mergers and acquisitions include Wellspring Grocery, Fresh Fields, Bread of Life, Merchant of Vino, Allegro Coffee, Nature's Heartland, and Harry's Farmers Market, among others. Even with all this growth, Whole Foods Market has maintained its commitment to: (a) selling only the highest quality natural and organic food products; (b) satisfying and delighting its customers; (c) supporting the excellence and happiness of its employees (called "team members"); (d) promoting environmental stewardship; and (e) exercising financial stewardship.

The company's mission is succinctly captured in its "Whole Foods, Whole People, Whole Planet" logo. Whole Foods Market describes its mission as follows: "Our mission is to offer the highest quality, least processed, most flavorful and naturally preserved foods. We are dedicated to creating a respectful workplace where people are treated fairly and are highly motivated to succeed. And we believe companies, like individuals, must assume their share of responsibility as tenants of the earth."

The vision of Whole Foods Market is articulated through its "Declaration of Interdependence" which explicitly recognizes the close linkages that exist among the company's various stakeholders and the need to balance the interests, wants, and needs of these stakeholders. The company's vision focuses on a sustainable future that involves holistic thinking regarding all of the obligations and repercussions associated with the decisions and actions of being a food retailer. "Our motto—Whole Foods, Whole People, Whole Planet—emphasizes that our vision reaches far beyond just being a food retailer. Our success in fulfilling our vision is measured by customer satisfaction, team member excellence and happiness, return on capital investments, improvement in the state of the environment, and local and larger community support."

Key Elements of Decision Making at Whole Foods

Decision making at Whole Foods Market relies on decentralization within a regional organizational structure and the use of self-directed teams. The company's eight regions enable it to better serve its different communities and markets by focusing on what works well in each region. Even though merchandising and operational differences exist among regions, all of them adhere to the company's core values that are manifested in its mission and vision.

Within each region, self-directed teams make merchandising and operational decisions at the store level. Each store has up to eleven different teams, and each team is responsible for a different aspect of store operations or for a different product category. Team members are empowered to make decisions within their responsibility areas.

Two-way communication with customers is essential for effective decision making by both Whole Foods Market and its customers. Each store has a bulletin board where customers can post their ideas and comments about products and the store. Customers can also post requests on the store's bulletin board. Team members respond to these requests by telephone or by posting a reply on the bulletin board. Empowered decision making at the store level results in each store having products and services that reflect the unique wants and needs of its market.

Whole Foods Market provides customers with lots of information about the products and services it offers. Pamphlets on various aspects of Whole Foods' products and services are found throughout each store. Signs in each department also provide detailed information about products and services. These communications to customers help them to make more informed choices about the foods they buy.

Decision Making Regarding Product Sourcing

Supply chain choices at Whole Foods Market are targeted toward ensuring a steady supply of high quality, fresh organic products for the stores. Much of the produce sold in each store comes from local farms. Whole Foods views itself as being in partnership with local farmers. The company encourages and supports farmers who are changing from conventional to organic production methods. Whole Foods Market pays a fair price for locally grown produce, advertises it as locally grown, and even displays a miniature biography of the farmers in its in-store advertising. Locally grown produce ensures freshness. Whole Foods purchases only the highest quality produce.

Whole Foods also seeks the utmost in freshness and quality in its fish and seafood products. Purchasing the catches from day-trip and short-trip fishing boats ensures freshness and facilitates quality control. Whole Foods Market also pays a fair price for the catches.

The company goes around the world in search of the best coffee beans, for which it pays premium prices. The decision to pay premium prices helps the coffee farmers to stay in business, invest in their farms, and hire and retain the best employees.

Collectively, these decisions and actions by Whole Foods Market encourage, support, and help sustain their small business suppliers. In turn, this ensures that reliable sources of quality natural and organic products are available to satisfy customers' wants and needs.

Discussion Questions

1. How would you describe the merchandising and operational decisions made by Whole Foods Market in terms of the rational, bounded rationality, and garbage can models of decision making?
2. What role does participation play in the decision-making process at Whole Foods Market?
3. How does Whole Foods Market incorporate ethical considerations into its decision making?

SOURCE: This case was written by Michael K. McCuddy, The Louis S. and Mary L. Morgal Chair of Christian Business Ethics and Professor of Management, College of Business Administration, Valparaiso University. This case was developed from material contained on the Whole Foods Market Web site at http://www.wholefoods.com and in the following article: J. Tarnowski, "Doing What Comes Naturally," *Convenience Store News* (October 12, 2003): 174–181.

© Reuters/CORBIS

Chapter 11

Power and Political Behavior

THINKING AHEAD: CISCO SYSTEMS

The Highs and Lows of Power

John Chambers, CEO of Cisco, has known both the highs and the lows that often accompany power. From his humble roots in West Virginia, Chambers, though mildly dyslexic, graduated second in his high school class. Throughout most of the 1990s, Cisco was at the top of the world, and John Chambers was clearly at the top of Cisco. Sales tripled in his first three years at the helm. From a relatively small maker of switching equipment, Cisco grew to power the Internet bubble, at one time boasting that its equipment handled 75 percent of all Internet traffic. As the Internet grew, Cisco grew even faster, and at its amazing peak in March 2000, Cisco briefly became the most valuable company on the planet, worth more than half a trillion dollars. John Chambers was named *Chief Executive*'s 2000 CEO of the Year, and he and Cisco were truly powerful.

The peak of power was short-lived. Almost exactly one year later, the Internet bubble had burst, and Chambers sat with top managers finalizing plans to lay off almost 20 percent of the firm's employees. Along the way, more than 3,000 resellers and 800 suppliers were eliminated, and the firm wrote off more than $2 billion in inventory. Shortly after the layoffs, major customers including AT&T called a meeting to deliver a chilling message: Cisco's telecom software was too buggy, and unless the firm provided an immediate fix, they would take their business elsewhere.

The year 2001 ended with a net loss of $1 billion and Cisco's stock price languishing. Chambers, previously touted as a business icon in the same league as Bill Gates or Alfred P. Sloan, and who had once enjoyed serving ice cream to his employees on Fridays, found himself forced to hire bodyguards to travel with him in the face of threats from disgruntled former employees. From prince to pariah, John Chambers had experienced both the highs and the lows of corporate power. Only time would reveal the next chapter in his story.[1,2,3,4]

The Concept of Power

power
The ability to influence another person.

influence
The process of affecting the thoughts, behavior, and feelings of another person.

authority
The right to influence another person.

zone of indifference
The range in which attempts to influence a person will be perceived as legitimate and will be acted on without a great deal of thought.

Power is the ability to influence someone else. As an exchange relationship, it occurs in transactions between an agent and a target. The agent is the person using the power, and the target is the recipient of the attempt to use power.[5]

Because power is an ability, individuals can learn to use it effectively. *Influence* is the process of affecting the thoughts, behavior, and feelings of another person. *Authority* is the right to influence another person.[6] It is important to understand the subtle differences among these terms. For instance, a manager may have authority but no power. She may have the right, by virtue of her position as boss, to tell someone what to do. But she may not have the skill or ability to influence other people.

In a relationship between the agent and the target, there are many influence attempts that the target considers legitimate. Working forty hours per week, greeting customers, solving problems, and collecting bills are actions that, when requested by the manager, are considered legitimate by a customer service representative. Requests such as these fall within the employee's *zone of indifference*—the range in which attempts to influence the employee are perceived as legitimate and are acted on without a great deal of thought.[7] The employee accepts that the manager has the authority to request such behaviors and complies with the requests. Some requests, however, fall outside the zone of indifference, so the manager must work to enlarge the employee's zone of indifference. Enlarging the zone is accomplished with power (an ability) rather than with authority (a right).

Suppose the manager asks the employee to purchase a birthday gift for the manager's wife or to overcharge a customer for a service call. The employee may think that the manager has no right to ask these things. These requests fall outside the zone of indifference; they're viewed as extraordinary, and the manager has to operate from outside the authority base to induce the employee to fulfill them. In some cases, no power base is enough to induce the employee to comply, especially if the behaviors requested by the manager are considered unethical by the employee.

Failures to understand power and politics can be costly in terms of your career. The former CEO of American Airlines found this out the hard way, as shown in The Real World 11.1. Managers must learn as much as possible about power and politics to be able to use them effectively and to manage the inevitable political behavior in organizations.

Forms and Sources of Power in Organizations

Individuals have many forms of power to use in their work settings. Some of them are interpersonal—used in interactions with others. One of the earliest and most influential theories of power comes from French and Raven, who tried to determine the sources of power manager uses to influence other people.

Interpersonal Forms of Power

French and Raven identified five forms of interpersonal power that managers use. They are reward, coercive, legitimate, referent, and expert power.[8]

Reward power is power based on the agent's ability to control rewards that a target wants. For example, managers control the rewards of salary increases, bonuses, and promotions. Reward power can lead to better performance, but only as long as the employee sees a clear and strong link between performance

reward power
Power based on an agent's ability to control rewards that a target wants.

American Airlines—Power Blunder

When the world's largest airline was less than ten minutes from filing bankruptcy, CEO Donald Carty managed to pull it out of its nosedive. So why was he forced to resign just twenty-four days later?

In the wake of the attacks on September 11, 2001, Carty called for the layoffs of 20,000 American Airlines employees, citing the need for the cuts to ensure American's survival. "If at times I've been blunt, it's because the facts in front of us are stark, and I knew I would only be worthy of your trust if I were totally honest with you," Carty informed employees. After heated and prolonged negotiations, Carty managed to wrest over a billion dollars from unions in terms of concessions to keep American Airlines from having to file bankruptcy. That agreement was a milestone in the U.S. airline industry, which has always suffered from huge labor costs.

Unfortunately, on the same day the agreement was announced, more news was made. It was disclosed that special pension trust funding and huge retention bonuses were given to American Airlines executives, including Carty—despite the fact that union workers had agreed to the steep pay cuts.

Carty spent the next three-and-a-half weeks apologizing, even giving the money back, before falling on his sword. He may have lost his job because he lost the trust of his American Airlines employees.

SOURCES: Reuters Limited, "Canadian Carty Had Rough Ride at American Airlines," *USA Today* (April 25, 2003), http://www.usatoday.com/travel/news/2003/2003-04-25-aa-carty-profile.htm; S. Tully, "The Airlines' New Deal," *Fortune* (April 28, 2003): 79–80, http://www.fortune.com/fortune/articles/0,15114,443062,00.html.

---

and rewards. To use reward power effectively, then, the manager should be explicit about the behavior being rewarded and should make the connection clear between the behavior and the reward.

Coercive power is power that is based on the agent's ability to cause the target to have an unpleasant experience. To coerce someone into doing something means to force the person to do it, often with threats of punishment. Managers using coercive power may verbally abuse employees or withhold support from them.

coercive power
Power that is based on an agent's ability to cause an unpleasant experience for a target.

Legitimate power, which is similar to authority, is power that is based on position and mutual agreement. The agent and target agree that the agent has the right to influence the target. It doesn't matter that a manager thinks he has the right to influence his employees; for legitimate power to be effective, the employees must also believe the manager has the right to tell them what to do. In Native American societies, the chieftain has legitimate power; tribe members believe in his right to influence the decisions in their lives.

legitimate power
Power that is based on position and mutual agreement; agent and target agree that the agent has the right to influence the target.

Referent power is an elusive power that is based on interpersonal attraction. The agent has referent power over the target because the target identifies with or wants to be like the agent. Charismatic individuals are often thought to have referent power. Interestingly, the agent need not be superior to the target in any way. People who use referent power well are most often individualistic and respected by the target.

referent power
An elusive power that is based on interpersonal attraction.

Expert power is the power that exists when the agent has specialized knowledge or skills that the target needs. For expert power to work, three conditions must be in place. First, the target must trust that the expertise given is accurate. Second, the knowledge involved must be relevant and useful to the target. Third, the target's perception of the agent as an expert is crucial. Using easy-to-understand language signals the target that the expert has an appreciation for real-world concerns and increases the target's trust in the expert.[9]

expert power
The power that exists when an agent has specialized knowledge or skills that the target needs.

Which type of interpersonal power is most effective? Research has focused on this question since French and Raven introduced their five forms of power. Some of the results are surprising. Reward power and coercive power have similar effects.[10] Both lead to compliance. That is, employees will do what the manager asks them to, at least temporarily, if the manager offers a reward or threatens them with punishment. Reliance on these sources of power is dangerous, however, because it may require the manager to be physically present and watchful in order to apply rewards or punishment when the behavior occurs. Constant surveillance creates an uncomfortable situation for managers and employees and eventually results in a dependency relationship. Employees will not work unless the manager is present.

Legitimate power also leads to compliance. When told "Do this because I'm your boss," most employees will comply. However, the use of legitimate power has not been linked to organizational effectiveness or to employee satisfaction.[11] In organizations where managers rely heavily on legitimate power, organizational goals are not necessarily met.

Referent power is linked with organizational effectiveness. It is the most dangerous power, however, because it can be too extensive and intensive in altering the behavior of others. Charismatic leaders need an accompanying sense of responsibility for others. Christopher Reeve's referent power made him a powerful spokesperson for research on spinal injuries and stem cell research.

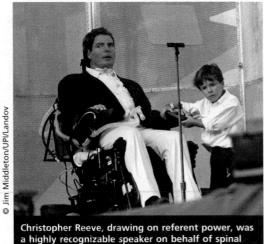

Christopher Reeve, drawing on referent power, was a highly recognizable speaker on behalf of spinal cord research.

Expert power has been called the power of the future.[12] Of the five forms of power, it has the strongest relationship with performance and satisfaction. It is through expert power that vital skills, abilities, and knowledge are passed on within the organization. Employees internalize what they observe and learn from managers they perceive to be experts.

The results on the effectiveness of these five forms of power pose a challenge in organizations. The least effective power bases—legitimate, reward, and coercive—are the ones most likely to be used by managers.[13] Managers inherit these power bases as part of the position when they take a supervisory job. In contrast, the most effective power bases—referent and expert—are ones that must be developed and strengthened through interpersonal relationships with employees.

Using Power Ethically

3. Understand the ethical use of power.

Managers can work at developing all five of these forms of power for future use. The key to using them well is using them ethically, as Table 11.1 shows. Coercive power, for example, requires careful administration if it is to be used in an ethical manner. Employees should be informed of the rules in advance, and any punishment should be used consistently, uniformly, and privately. The key to using all five types of interpersonal power ethically is to be sensitive to employees' concerns and to communicate well.

TABLE 11.1   Guidelines for the Ethical Use of Power

FORM OF POWER	GUIDELINES FOR USE
Reward power	Verify compliance.
	Make feasible, reasonable requests.
	Make only ethical requests.
	Offer rewards desired by subordinates.
	Offer only credible rewards.
Coercive power	Inform subordinates of rules and penalties.
	Warn before punishing.
	Administer punishment consistently and uniformly.
	Understand the situation before acting.
	Maintain credibility.
	Fit punishment to the infraction.
	Punish in private.
Legitimate power	Be cordial and polite.
	Be confident.
	Be clear and follow up to verify understanding.
	Make sure request is appropriate.
	Explain reasons for request.
	Follow proper channels.
	Exercise power consistently.
	Enforce compliance.
	Be sensitive to subordinates' concerns.
Referent power	Treat subordinates fairly.
	Defend subordinates' interests.
	Be sensitive to subordinates' needs and feelings.
	Select subordinates similar to oneself.
	Engage in role modeling.
Expert power	Maintain credibility.
	Act confident and decisive.
	Keep informed.
	Recognize employee concerns.
	Avoid threatening subordinates' self-esteem.

SOURCE: *Leadership in Organizations* by Gary A. Yukl. Copyright © 1981. Reprinted by permission of Prentice-Hall, Upper Saddle River, N.J.

To French and Raven's five power sources, we can add a source that is very important in today's organizations. *Information power* is access to and control over important information. Consider, for example, the CEO's administrative assistant. He or she has information about the CEO's schedule that people need if they are going to get in to see the CEO. Central to the idea of information power is the person's position in the communication networks in the organization, both formal and informal. Also important is the idea of framing, which is the "spin" that managers put on information. Managers not only pass information on to subordinates; they interpret this information and influence the subordinates' perceptions of it. Information power occurs not only in the downward direction; it may also flow upward from subordinates to managers. In manufacturing plants, database operators often control information about plant metrics and shipping performance that is vital to managerial decision making.

information power
Access to and control over important information.

Information power can also flow laterally. Salespersons convey information from the outside environment (their customers) that is essential for marketing efforts.

Determining whether a power-related behavior is ethical is complex. Another way to look at the ethics surrounding the use of power is to ask three questions that show the criteria for examining power-related behaviors:[14]

1. *Does the behavior produce a good outcome for people both inside and outside the organization?* This question represents the criterion of *utilitarian outcomes*. The behavior should result in the greatest good for the greatest number of people. If the power-related behavior serves only the individual's self-interest and fails to help the organization reach its goals, it is considered unethical. A salesperson might be tempted to discount a product deeply in order to make a sale that would win a contest. Doing so would be in her self-interest but would not benefit the organization.

2. *Does the behavior respect the rights of all parties?* This question emphasizes the criterion of *individual rights*. Free speech, privacy, and due process are individual rights that are to be respected, and power-related behaviors that violate these rights are considered unethical.

3. *Does the behavior treat all parties equitably and fairly?* This question represents the criterion of *distributive justice*. Power-related behavior that treats one party arbitrarily or benefits one party at the expense of another is unethical. Granting a day of vacation to one employee in a busy week in which coworkers must struggle to cover for him might be considered unethical.

To be considered ethical, power-related behavior must meet all three criteria. If the behavior fails to meet the criteria, then alternative actions should be considered. Unfortunately, most power-related behaviors are not easy to analyze. Conflicts may exist among the criteria; for example, a behavior may maximize the greatest good for the greatest number of people but may not treat all parties equitably. Individual rights may need to be sacrificed for the good of the organization. A CEO may need to be removed from power for the organization to be saved. Still, these criteria can be used on a case-by-case basis to sort through the complex ethical issues surrounding the use of power.

Two Faces of Power: One Positive, One Negative

We turn now to a theory of power that takes a strong stand on the "right" versus "wrong" kind of power to use in organizations. David McClelland has spent a great deal of his career studying the need for power and the ways managers use power. As was discussed in Chapter 5, he believes that there are two distinct faces of power, one negative and one positive.[15] The negative face of power is *personal power*—power used for personal gain. Managers who use personal power are commonly

Dennis Koslowski, former Tyco CEO, abused personal power to lead a lavish lifestyle to the detriment of his company and its stockholders.

personal power

Power used for personal gain.

There's Power in Family-Owned Businesses

There is a perception, even among financial analysts, that founding-family ownership and control of businesses is a less profitable way of operating. Family owners may sacrifice business success for private gain. Because the family controls the cash flow, they have the power to take actions that benefit themselves at the expense of firm performance. They may limit top management positions to only family members, who may not have the skills and talents to run the business efficiently. At the extreme, families could expropriate wealth from the firm through excessive compensation, transactions within the family, or special dividends to family members. In short, families may use personal power instead of social power.

Researchers set out to test the link between family ownership and firm performance, among others, in a study of the Standard & Poor's (S&P) 500 companies. Family companies are those in which the founders or their families are in senior management positions, are on the board of directors, or are significant shareholders.

Over one-third of the S&P 500 are family businesses. Contrary to popular belief, the family firms outperform the nonfamily firms! The Wrigley chewing gum business, Walgreens, and Clear Channel Communications are examples of family firms. So why do family firms perform well? It could be that with family leaders, decision making is faster, there is lower turnover among family members, and most importantly, family members are in it for the long haul. Unlike outside executives whose tenure may be short, families may be more likely to reinvest in the business.

SOURCE: R. C. Anderson and D. M. Reeb, "Founding-Family Ownership and Firm Performance: Evidence from the S&P 500," *Journal of Finance* 58 (2003): 1301–1328.

described as "power hungry." Dennis Koslowski's tenure as CEO of Tyco was marked by one of the most massive strings of acquisitions by any American firm, earning him the nickname "Deal-A-Month Dennis." But as questions began to mount about why Tyco continued to expand when many of its existing divisions were not profitable, Koslowski simply dismissed them. Only later would it come to light that not only had Koslowski mismanaged the firm, but he had also looted it for more than $240 million, which he spent on artwork, houses, yachts, and a $2 million birthday party for his wife.[16] People who approach relationships with an exchange orientation often use personal power to ensure that they get at least their fair share—and often more—in the relationship. They are most interested in their own needs and interests. Some people think, for example, that family-owned firms don't perform as well as others because the families are out for themselves—they're more interested in personal power. You'll be surprised to learn that this isn't the case, as shown in the Science feature.

Individuals who rely on personal power at its extreme might be considered Machiavellian—willing to do whatever it takes to get one's own way. Niccolo Machiavelli was an Italian statesman during the sixteenth century who wrote *The Prince*, a guide for acquiring and using power.[17] Among his methods for using power was manipulating others, believing that it was better to be feared than loved. Machiavellians (or high Machs) are willing to manipulate others for personal gain, and are unconcerned with others' opinions or welfare.

The positive face of power is *social power*—power used to create motivation or to accomplish group goals. McClelland clearly favors the use of social power by managers. People who approach relationships with a communal orientation focus on the needs and interests of others. They rely on social power.[18] McClelland has found that managers who use power successfully have four power-oriented characteristics:

social power

Power used to create motivation or to accomplish group goals.

1. *Belief in the authority system.* They believe that the institution is important and that its authority system is valid. They are comfortable influencing and being influenced. The source of their power is the authority system of which they are a part.

2. *Preference for work and discipline.* They like their work and are very orderly. They have a basic value preference for the Protestant work ethic, believing that work is good for a person over and beyond its income-producing value.

3. *Altruism.* They publicly put the company and its needs before their own needs. They are able to do this because they see their own well-being as integrally tied to the corporate well-being.

4. *Belief in justice.* They believe justice is to be sought above all else. People should receive that to which they are entitled and that which they earn.

McClelland takes a definite stand on the proper use of power by managers. When power is used for the good of the group, rather than for individual gain, it is positive.

Intergroup Sources of Power

Groups or teams within an organization can also use power from several sources. One source of intergroup power is control of *critical resources.*[19] When one group controls an important resource that another group desires, the first group holds power. Controlling resources needed by another group allows the power-holding group to influence the actions of the less powerful group. This process can continue in an upward spiral. Groups seen as powerful tend to be given more resources from top management.[20]

strategic contingencies
Activities that other groups depend on in order to complete their tasks.

Groups also have power to the extent that they control *strategic contingencies*—activities that other groups depend on in order to complete their tasks.[21] The dean's office, for example, may control the number of faculty positions to be filled in each department of a college. The departmental hiring plans are thus contingent on approval from the dean's office. In this case, the dean's office controls the strategic contingency of faculty hiring, and thus has power.

Three factors can give a group control over a strategic contingency.[22] One is the *ability to cope with uncertainty.* If a group can help another group deal with uncertainty, it has power. One organizational group that has gained power in recent years is the legal department. Faced with increasing government regulations and fears of litigation, many other departments seek guidance from the legal department.

Another factor that can give a group control power is a *high degree of centrality* within the organization. If a group's functioning is important to the organization's success, it has high centrality. The sales force in a computer firm, for example, has power because of its immediate effect on the firm's operations and because other groups (accounting and servicing groups, for example) depend on its activities.

The third factor that can give a group power is *nonsubstitutability*—the extent to which a group performs a function that is indispensable to an organization. A team of computer specialists may be powerful because of its expertise with a system. It may have specialized experience that another team cannot provide.

The strategic contingencies model thus shows that groups hold power over other groups when they can reduce uncertainty, when their functioning is central to the organization's success, and when the group's activities are difficult to replace.[23] The key to all three of these factors, as you can see, is dependency. When one group controls something that another group needs, it creates a dependent relationship—and gives one group power over the other.

Power Analysis: A Broader View

Amitai Etzioni takes a more sociological orientation to power. Etzioni has developed a theory of power analysis.[24] He says that there are three types of organizational power and three types of organizational involvement, or membership, that will lead to either congruent or incongruent uses of power. The three types of organizational power are the following:

4. Explain power analysis, an organizational-level theory of power.

1. *Coercive power*—influencing members by forcing them to do something under threat of punishment or through fear and intimidation.

2. *Utilitarian power*—influencing members by providing them with rewards and benefits.

3. *Normative power*—influencing members by using the knowledge that they want very much to belong to the organization and by letting them know that what they are expected to do is the "right" thing to do.

Along with these three types of organizational power, Etzioni proposes that we can classify organizations by the type of membership they have:

1. *Alienative membership.* The members have hostile, negative feelings about being in the organization. They don't want to be there. Prisons are a good example of alienative memberships.

2. *Calculative membership.* Members weigh the benefits and limitations of belonging to the organization. Businesses are good examples of organizations with calculative memberships.

3. *Moral membership.* Members have such positive feelings about organizational membership that they are willing to deny their own needs. Organizations with many volunteer workers, such as the American Heart Association, are examples of moral memberships. Religious groups are another example.

Etzioni argues that the type of organizational power should be matched to the type of membership in the organization in order to achieve congruence. Figure 11.1 shows the matches in his power analysis theory.

In an alienative membership, members have hostile feelings. In prisons, for example, Etzioni would contend that coercive power is the appropriate type to use.

A calculative membership is characterized by an analysis of the good and bad aspects of being in the organization. In a business partnership, for example, each partner weighs the benefits from the partnership against the costs entailed in the contractual arrangement. Utilitarian or reward-based power is the most appropriate type to use.

In a moral membership, the members have strong positive feelings about the particular cause or goal of the organization. Normative power is the most appropriate to use because it capitalizes on the members' desires to belong.

FIGURE 11.1 Etzioni's Power Analysis

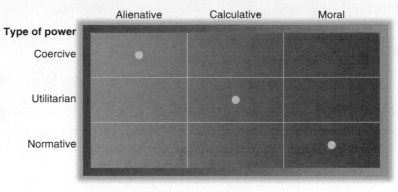

SOURCE: Adapted from Amitai Etzioni, *Modern Organizations* (Upper Saddle River, N.J.: Prentice-Hall, 1964), 59–61. Reprinted by permission of Pearson Education, Inc., Upper Saddle River, N.J.

Etzioni's power analysis is an organizational-level theory. It emphasizes that the characteristics of an organization play a role in determining the type of power appropriate for use in the organization. Etzioni's theory is controversial in its contention that a single type of power is appropriate in any organization.

Symbols of Power

5. Identify symbols of power and power-lessness in organizations.

Organization charts show who has authority, but they do not reveal much about who has power. We'll now look at two very different ideas about the symbols of power. The first one comes from Rosabeth Moss Kanter. It is a scholarly approach to determining who has power and who feels powerless. The second is a semiserious look at the tangible symbols of power by Michael Korda.

Kanter's Symbols of Power

Kanter provides several characteristics of powerful people in organizations:[25]

1. *Ability to intercede for someone in trouble.* An individual who can pull someone out of a jam has power.

2. *Ability to get placements for favored employees.* Getting a key promotion for an employee is a sign of power.

3. *Exceeding budget limitations.* A manager who can go above budget limits without being reprimanded has power.

4. *Procuring above-average raises for employees.* One faculty member reported that her department head distributed 10 percent raises to the most productive faculty members although the budget allowed for only 4 percent increases. "I don't know how he did it; he must have pull," she said.

5. *Getting items on the agenda at meetings.* If a manager can raise issues for action at meetings, it's a sign of power.

6. *Access to early information.* Having information before anyone else does is a signal that a manager is plugged into key sources.

7. *Having top managers seek out their opinion.* When top managers have a problem, they may ask for advice from lower-level managers. The managers they turn to have power.

A theme that runs through Kanter's list is doing things for others: for people in trouble, for employees, for bosses. There is an active, other-directed element in her symbols of power.

You can use Kanter's symbols of power to identify powerful people in organizations. They can be particularly useful in finding a mentor who can effectively use power.

Kanter's Symbols of Powerlessness

Kanter also wrote about symptoms of *powerlessness*—a lack of power—in managers at different levels of the organization. First-line supervisors, for example, often display three symptoms of powerlessness: overly close supervision, inflexible adherence to the rules, and a tendency to do the job themselves rather than training their employees to do it. Staff professionals such as accountants and lawyers display different symptoms of powerlessness. When they feel powerless, they tend to resist change and try to protect their turf. Top executives can also feel powerless. They show symptoms such as focusing on budget cutting, punishing others, and using dictatorial, top-down communication. Acting in certain ways can lead employees to believe that a manager is powerless. By making external attributions (blaming others or circumstances) for negative events, a manager looks as if he or she has no power.[26]

powerlessness
A lack of power.

What can you do when you recognize that employees are feeling powerless? The key to overcoming powerlessness is to share power and delegate decision-making authority to employees.

Korda's Symbols of Power

Michael Korda takes a different look at symbols of power in organizations.[27] He discusses three unusual symbols: office furnishings, time power, and standing by.

Furniture is not just physically useful; it also conveys a message about power. Locked file cabinets are signs that the manager has important and confidential information in the office. A rectangular (rather than round) conference table enables the most important person to sit at the head of the table. The size of one's desk may convey the amount of power. Most executives prefer large, expensive desks.

Time power means using clocks and watches as power symbols. Korda says that the biggest compliment a busy executive can pay a visitor is to remove his watch and place it face down on the desk, thereby communicating "my time is yours." He also notes that the less powerful the executive, the more intricate the watch; moreover, managers who are really secure in their power wear no watch at all, since they believe nothing important can happen without them. A full calendar is also proof of power. Personal planners are left open on the desk to display busy schedules.

Standing by is a game in which people are obliged to keep their cell phones, pagers, etc. with them at all times so executives can reach them. The idea is that the more you can impose your schedule on other people, the more power you have. In fact, Korda defines *power* as follows: There are more people who inconvenience themselves on your behalf than there are people on whose behalf you would inconvenience yourself. Closely tied to this is the ability to make others perform simple tasks for you, such as getting your coffee or fetching the mail.

While Kanter's symbols focus on the ability to help others, Korda's symbols focus on status—a person's relative standing in a group based on prestige and having other people defer to him or her.[28] By identifying powerful people and learning from their modeled behavior, you can learn the keys to power use in the organization.

Political Behavior in Organizations

6. Define organizational politics and understand the major influence tactics.

organizational politics
The use of power and influence in organizations.

political behavior
Actions not officially sanctioned by an organization that are taken to influence others in order to meet one's personal goals.

Like power, the term politics in organizations may conjure up a few negative images. However, *organizational politics* is not necessarily negative; it is the use of power and influence in organizations. Because organizations are arenas in which people have competing interests, effective managers must reconcile competing interests. Organizational politics are central to managing. As people try to acquire power and expand their power base, they use various tactics and strategies. Some are sanctioned (acceptable to the organization); others are not. *Political behavior* refers to actions not officially sanctioned by an organization that are taken to influence others in order to meet one's personal goals.[29] Sometimes personal goals are aligned with team or organizational goals, and they can be achieved in support of others' interests. But other times personal goals and the interests of others collide, and individuals pursue politics at the expense of others' interests.[30]

Politics is a controversial topic among managers. Some managers take a favorable view of political behavior; others see it as detrimental to the organization. Some workers who perceive their workplace as highly political actually find the use of political tactics more satisfying and report greater job satisfaction when they engage in political behavior. Some people may therefore thrive in political environments, while others may find office politics distasteful and stressful.[31]

Most people are also amazingly good at recognizing political behavior at all levels of the firm. Employees are not only keenly aware of political behavior at their level but can also spot political behavior at both their supervisor's level and the topmost levels of the organization.[32]

Many organizational conditions encourage political activity. Among them are unclear goals, autocratic decision making, ambiguous lines of authority, scarce resources, and uncertainty.[33] Even supposedly objective activities may involve politics. One such activity is the performance appraisal process. A study of sixty executives who had extensive experience in employee evaluation indicated that political considerations were nearly always part of the performance appraisal process.[34]

Individuals who use power in organizations are organizational politicians. You 11.1 shows the personal characteristics of effective organizational politicians and can help you assess your own political potential.

The effects of political behavior in organizations can be quite negative when the political behavior is strategically undertaken to maximize self-interest. If people within the organization are competitively pursuing selfish ends, they're unlikely to be attentive to the concerns of others. The workplace can seem less helpful, more threatening, and more unpredictable. People focus on their own concerns rather than on organizational goals. This represents the negative face of power described earlier by David McClelland as personal power. If employees view the organization's political climate as extreme, they experience more anxiety, tension, fatigue, and burnout. They are also dissatisfied with their jobs

Evaluate Your Political Potential

Examine the following table and answer the questions that follow it.

Personal Characteristics of Effective Political Actors

Personal Characteristic	Behavioral Example
Articulate	• Must be able to clearly communicate ideas.
Sensitive	• Must be sensitive to other individuals, situations, and opportunities.
Socially adept	• Must understand the social norms of the organization and behave so as to be perceived by influential others as "fitting in well."
Competent	• Must have the necessary skills and qualifications.
Popular	• Must be liked or admired by others in the organization.
Extraverted	• Must be interested in what happens outside of him or her.
Self-confident	• Must have confidence in his or her abilities.
Aggressive	• Must be self-assertive and forceful.
Ambitious	• Must be eager to attain success.
Devious	• Must be willing to use any tactic to get his or her way.
"Organization man or woman"	• Must emphasize the well-being of the organization.
Highly intelligent	• Must be able to use his or her knowledge to solve problems.
Logical	• Must be capable of reasoning.

1. Which characteristics do you possess? Which do you need to work on? Ask a friend what characteristics you possess.

2. On the basis of the table, are you an effective political actor? Explain.

3. Can we assume that all of these characteristics are worth having?

SOURCE: Table from "Organizational Politics: Tactics and Characteristics of Its Actors" by R. N. Allen, D. L. Madison, L. W. Porter, P. A. Renwick, and B. T. Mayes. Copyright © 1979 by The Regents of the University of California. Reprinted from the *California Management Review*, Vol. 22, No. 1, Fall 1979, 77–83. By permission of The Regents.

and are more likely to leave.[35] Not all political behavior is destructive. Constructive political behavior is selfless, rather than selfish, in nature. In this respect, it is similar to David McClelland's concept of social power. Constructive organizational politicians see the difference between ethical and unethical behavior, understand that relationships drive the political process, and use power with a sense of responsibility.[36]

Influence Tactics

Influence is the process of affecting the thoughts, behavior, or feelings of another person. That other person could be the boss (upward influence), an employee (downward influence), or a coworker (lateral influence). There are eight basic types of influence tactics. They are listed and described in Table 11.2.[37]

Research has shown that the four tactics used most frequently are consultation, rational persuasion, inspirational appeals, and ingratiation. Upward appeals and coalition tactics are used moderately. Exchange tactics are used least often.

Influence tactics are used for impression management, which was described in Chapter 3. In impression management, individuals use influence tactics to control others' impressions of them. One way in which people engage

TABLE 11.2   Influence Tactics Used in Organizations

TACTICS	DESCRIPTION	EXAMPLES
Pressure	The person uses demands, threats, or intimidation to convince you to comply with a request or to support a proposal.	If you don't do this, you're fired. You have until 5:00 to change your mind, or I'm going without you.
Upward appeals	The person seeks to persuade you that the request is approved by higher management or appeals to higher management for assistance in gaining your compliance with the request.	I'm reporting you to my boss. My boss supports this idea.
Exchange	The person makes an explicit or implicit promise that you will receive rewards or tangible benefits if you comply with a request or support a proposal or reminds you of a prior favor to be reciprocated.	You owe me a favor. I'll take you to lunch if you'll support me on this.
Coalition	The person seeks the aid of others to persuade you to do something or uses the support of others as an argument for you to agree also.	All the other supervisors agree with me. I'll ask you in front of the whole committee.
Ingratiation	The person seeks to get you in a good mood or to think favorably of him or her before asking you to do something.	Only you can do this job right. I can always count on you, so I have another request.
Rational persuasion	The person uses logical arguments and factual evidence to persuade you that a proposal or request is viable and likely to result in the attainment of task objectives.	This new procedure will save us $150,000 in overhead. It makes sense to hire John; he has the most experience.
Inspirational appeals	The person makes an emotional request or proposal that arouses enthusiasm by appealing to your values and ideals or by increasing your confidence that you can do it.	Being environmentally conscious is the right thing. Getting that account will be tough, but I know you can do it.
Consultation	The person seeks your participation in making a decision or planning how to implement a proposed policy, strategy, or change.	This new attendance plan is controversial. How can we make it more acceptable? What do you think we can do to make our workers less fearful of the new robots on the production line?

SOURCE: First two columns from G. Yukl and C. M. Falbe, "Influence Tactics and Objectives in Upward, Downward, and Lateral Influence Attempts," *Journal of Applied Psychology* 75 (1990): 132–140. Copyright © 1990 by the American Psychological Association. Reprinted with permission.

in impression management is through image building. Another way is to use impression management to get support for important initiatives or projects.

Ingratiation is an example of one tactic often used for impression management. Ingratiation can take many forms, including flattery, opinion conformity, and subservient behavior.[38] Exchange is another influence tactic that may be used for impression management. Offering to do favors for someone in an effort to create a favorable impression is an exchange tactic.

Which influence tactics are most effective? It depends on the target of the influence attempt and the objective. Individuals use different tactics for different purposes, and they use different tactics for different people. Influence attempts with subordinates, for example, usually involve assigning tasks or changing behavior. With peers, the objective is often to request help. With superiors, influence attempts are often made to request approval, resources, political support, or personal benefits. Rational persuasion and coalition tactics are used most often to get support from peers and superiors to change company policy. Consultation and inspirational appeals are particularly effective for gaining support and resources for a new project.[39] Overall, the most effective tactic in terms of achieving objectives is rational persuasion. Pressure is the least effective tactic.

Influence tactics are often used on bosses in order to get the boss to evaluate the employee more favorably or to give the employee a promotion. Two tactics—rational persuasion and ingratiation—appear to work effectively. Employees who use these tactics receive higher performance evaluations than other employees who don't use rational persuasion and ingratiation.[40] When supervisors believe an employee's motive for doing favors for the boss is simply to be a good citizen, they are likely to reward that employee. However, when the motive is seen as brownnosing (ingratiation), supervisors respond negatively.[41] And, as it becomes more obvious that the employee has something to gain by impressing the boss, the likelihood that ingratiation will succeed decreases.

Still, a well-disguised ingratiation is hard to resist. Attempts that are not obvious usually succeed in increasing the target's liking for the ingratiator.[42] Most people have trouble remaining neutral when someone flatters them or agrees with them. However, witnesses to the ingratiation are more likely to question the motive behind the flattery or agreement. Observers are more skeptical than the recipients of the ingratiation.

There is evidence that men and women view politics and influence attempts differently. Men tend to view political behavior more favorably than do women. When both men and women witness political behavior, they view it more positively if the agent is of their gender and the target is of the opposite gender.[43] Women executives often view politics with distaste and expect to be recognized and promoted only on the merit of their work. A lack of awareness of organizational politics is a barrier that holds women back in terms of moving into senior executive ranks.[44] Women may have fewer opportunities to develop political skills because of a lack of mentors and role models and because they are often excluded from informal networks.[45]

Different cultures prefer different influence tactics at work. One study found that American managers dealing with a tardy employee tended to rely on pressure tactics such as "If you don't start reporting on time for work, I will have no choice but to start docking your pay." In contrast, Japanese managers relied on influence tactics that either appealed to the employee's sense of duty ("It is your duty as a responsible employee of this company to begin work on time.") or emphasized a consultative approach ("Is there anything I can do to help you overcome the problems that are preventing you from coming to work on time?").[46]

It is important to note that influence tactics do have some positive effects. When investors form coalitions and put pressure on firms to increase their research and development efforts, it works.[47] However, some influence tactics, including pressure, coalition building, and exchange, can have strong ethical implications. There is a fine line between being an impression manager and being seen as a manipulator.

How can a manager use influence tactics well? First, a manager can develop and maintain open lines of communication in all directions: upward, downward, and lateral. Then, the manager can treat the targets of influence attempts—whether managers, employees, or peers—with basic respect. Finally, the manager can understand that influence relationships are reciprocal—they are two-way relationships. As long as the influence attempts are directed toward organizational goals, the process of influence can be advantageous to all involved.

Managing Political Behavior in Organizations

Politics cannot and should not be eliminated from organizations. Managers can, however, take a proactive stance and manage the political behavior that inevitably occurs.[48]

Open communication is one key to managing political behavior. Uncertainty tends to increase political behavior, and communication that reduces the uncertainty is important. One form of communication that will help is to clarify the sanctioned and nonsanctioned political behaviors in the organization. For example, you may want to encourage social power as opposed to personal power.[49]

Another key is to clarify expectations regarding performance. This can be accomplished through the use of clear, quantifiable goals and through the establishment of a clear connection between goal accomplishment and rewards.[50]

Participative management is yet another key. Often, people engage in political behavior when they feel excluded from decision-making processes in the organization. By including them, you will encourage positive input and eliminate behind-the-scenes maneuvering.

Encouraging cooperation among work groups is another strategy for managing political behavior. Managers can instill a unity of purpose among work teams by rewarding cooperative behavior and by implementing activities that emphasize the integration of team efforts toward common goals.[51]

Managing scarce resources well is also important. An obvious solution to the problem of scarce resources is to increase the resource pool, but few managers have this luxury. Clarifying the resource allocation process and making the connection between performance and resources explicit can help discourage dysfunctional political behavior.

Providing a supportive organizational climate is another way to manage political behavior effectively. A supportive climate allows employees to discuss controversial issues promptly and openly. This prevents the issue from festering and potentially causing friction among employees.[52]

Managing political behavior at work is important. The perception of dysfunctional political behavior can lead to dissatisfaction.[53] When employees perceive that there are dominant interest groups or cliques at work, they are less satisfied with pay and promotions. When they believe that the organization's reward practices are influenced by who you know rather than how well you perform, they are less satisfied.[54] In addition, when employees believe that their coworkers are exhibiting increased political behavior, they are less satisfied with their coworkers. Open communication, clear expectations about performance and rewards, participative decision-making practices, work group cooperation, effective management of scarce resources, and a supportive organizational climate can help managers prevent the negative consequences of political behavior.

Managing Up: Managing The Boss

7. Develop a plan for managing employee-boss relationships.

One of the least discussed aspects of power and politics is the relationship between you and your boss. This is a crucial relationship, because your boss is your most important link with the rest of the organization.[55] The employee–boss relationship is one of mutual dependence; you depend on your boss to give you performance feedback, provide resources, and supply critical information. She depends on you for performance, information, and support. Because it's a mutual relationship, you should take an active role in managing it. Too often, the management of this relationship is left to the boss; but if the relationship doesn't meet your needs, chances are you haven't taken the responsibility to manage it proactively.

Table 11.3 shows the basic steps to take in managing your relationship with your boss. The first step is to try to understand as much as you can about your boss. What are the person's goals and objectives? What kind of pressures does the person face in the job? Many individuals naively expect the boss to be perfect and are disappointed when they find that this is not the case. What are the boss's strengths, weaknesses, and blind spots? Because this is an emotionally charged relationship, it is difficult to be objective; but this is a critical step in forging an effective working relationship. What is the boss's preferred work style? Does the person prefer everything in writing or hate detail? Does the boss prefer that you make appointments or is dropping in at the boss's office acceptable? The point is to gather as much information about your boss as you can and to try to put yourself in that person's shoes.

The second step in managing this important relationship is to assess yourself and your own needs much in the same way you analyzed your boss's. What are your strengths, weaknesses, and blind spots? What is your work style? How do you normally relate to authority figures? Some of us have tendencies toward counterdependence; that is, we rebel against the boss as an authority and view the boss as a hindrance to our performance. Or, in contrast, we might take an overdependent stance, passively accepting the employee–boss relationship and treating the boss as an all-wise, protective parent. What is your tendency? Knowing how you react to authority figures can help you understand your interactions with your boss.

TABLE 11.3   Managing Your Relationship with Your Boss

Make Sure You Understand Your Boss and Her Context, Including:

Her goals and objectives.

The pressures on her.

Her strengths, weaknesses, and blind spots.

Her preferred work style.

Assess Yourself and Your Needs, Including:

Your own strengths and weaknesses.

Your personal style.

Your predisposition toward dependence on authority figures.

Develop and Maintain a Relationship that:

Fits both your needs and styles.

Is characterized by mutual expectations.

Keeps your boss informed.

Is based on dependability and honesty.

Selectively uses your boss's time and resources.

Once you have done a careful self-analysis and tried to understand your boss, the next step is to work to develop an effective relationship. Both parties' needs and styles must be accommodated. A fundraiser for a large volunteer organization related a story about a new boss, describing him as cold, aloof, unorganized, and inept. She made repeated attempts to meet with him and clarify expectations, and his usual reply was that he didn't have the time. Frustrated, she almost looked for a new job. "I just can't reach him!" was her refrain. Then she stepped back to consider her boss's and her own styles. Being an intuitive-feeling type of person, she prefers constant feedback and reinforcement from others. Her boss, an intuitive-thinker, works comfortably without feedback from others and has a tendency to fail to praise or reward others. She sat down with him and cautiously discussed the differences in their needs. This discussion became the basis for working out a comfortable relationship. "I still don't like him, but I understand him better," she said.

Another aspect of managing the relationship involves working out mutual expectations. One key activity is to develop a plan for work objectives and have the boss agree to it.[56] It is important to do things right, but it is also important to do the right things. Neither party to the relationship is a mind reader, and clarifying the goals is a crucial step.

Keeping the boss informed is also a priority. No one likes to be caught off guard, and there are several ways to keep the boss informed. Give the boss a weekly to-do list as a reminder of the progress towards goals. When you read something pertaining to your work, clip it out for the boss. Most busy executives appreciate being given materials they don't have time to find for themselves. Give the boss interim reports, and let the boss know if the work schedule is slipping. Don't wait until it's too late to take action.

The employee–boss relationship must be based on dependability and honesty. This means giving and receiving positive and negative feedback. Most of us are reluctant to give any feedback to the boss, but positive feedback is welcomed at the top. Negative feedback, while tougher to initiate, can clear the air. If given in a problem-solving format, it can even bring about a closer relationship.[57]

Finally, remember that the boss is on the same team you are. The golden rule is to make the boss look good, because you expect the boss to do the same for you.

Sharing Power: Empowerment

8. Discuss how managers can empower others.

empowerment
Sharing power within an organization.

Another positive strategy for managing political behavior is *empowerment*— sharing power within an organization. As modern organizations grow flatter, eliminating layers of management, empowerment becomes more and more important. Jay Conger defines *empowerment* as "creating conditions for heightened motivation through the development of a strong sense of personal self-efficacy."[58] This means sharing power in such a way that individuals learn to believe in their ability to do the job. The driving idea of empowerment is that the individuals closest to the work and to the customers should make the decisions and that this makes the best use of employees' skills and talents. You can empower yourself by developing your sense of self-efficacy. You 11.2 helps you assess your progress in terms of self-empowerment.

Four dimensions comprise the essence of empowerment: meaning, competence, self-determination, and impact.[59] *Meaning* is a fit between the work role and the employee's values and beliefs. It is the engine of empowerment through which employees become energized about their jobs. If employees' hearts are not in their work, they cannot feel empowered. *Competence* is the belief that

Are You Self-Empowered?

Check either a. or b. to indicate how you usually are in these situations:

1. If someone disagrees with me in a class or a meeting, I
   a. immediately back down
   b. explain my position further
2. When I have an idea for a project, I
   a. typically take a great deal of time to start it
   b. get going on it fairly quickly
3. If my boss or teacher tells me to do something that I think is wrong, I
   a. do it anyway, telling myself he or she is "the boss"
   b. ask for clarification and explain my position
4. When a complicated problem arises, I usually tell myself
   a. I can take care of it
   b. I will not be able to solve it
5. When I am around people of higher authority, I often
   a. feel intimidated and defer to them
   b. enjoy meeting important people
6. As I awake in the morning, I usually feel
   a. alert and ready to conquer almost anything
   b. tired and have a hard time getting myself motivated
7. During an argument I
   a. put a great deal of energy into "winning"
   b. try to listen to the other side and see if we have any points of agreement
8. When I meet new people, I
   a. always wonder what they are "really" up to
   b. try to learn what they are about and give them the benefit of the doubt until they prove otherwise
9. During the day I often
   a. criticize myself on what I am doing or thinking
   b. think positive thoughts about myself
10. When someone else does a great job, I
    a. find myself picking apart that person and looking for faults
    b. often give a sincere compliment
11. When I am working in a group, I try to
    a. do a better job than the others
    b. help the group function more effectively

12. If someone pays me a compliment, I typically
    a. try not to appear boastful and I downplay the compliment
    b. respond with a positive "thank you" or similar response
13. I like to be around people who
    a. challenge me and make me question what I do
    b. give me respect
14. In love relationships I prefer the other person to
    a. have his/her own selected interests
    b. do pretty much what I do
15. During a crisis I try to
    a. resolve the problem
    b. find someone to blame
16. After seeing a movie with friends, I
    a. wait to see what they say before I decide whether I liked it
    b. am ready to talk about my reactions right away
17. When work deadlines are approaching, I typically
    a. get flustered and worry about completion
    b. buckle down and work until the job is done
18. If a job comes up I am interested in, I
    a. go for it and apply
    b. tell myself I am not qualified enough
19. When someone treats me unkindly or unfairly, I
    a. try to rectify the situation
    b. tell other people about the injustice
20. If a difficult conflict situation or problem arises, I
    a. try not to think about it, hoping it will resolve itself
    b. look at various options and may ask others for advice before I figure out what to do

Scoring:

Score one point for each of the following circled: 1b, 2b, 3b, 4a, 5b, 6a, 7b, 8b, 9b, 10b, 11b, 12b, 13a, 14a, 15a, 16b, 17b, 18a, 19a, 20b.

Analysis of Scoring

16–20 You are a take-charge person and generally make the most of opportunities. When others tell you something cannot be done, you may take this as a challenge and do it anyway. You see the world as an oyster with many pearls to harvest.

(continued)

one has the ability to do the job well. Without competence, employees will feel inadequate and lack a sense of empowerment. _Self-determination_ is having control over the way one does his or her work. Employees who feel they're just following orders from the boss cannot feel empowered. _Impact_ is the belief that one's job makes a difference within the organization. Without a sense of contributing to a goal, employees cannot feel empowered.

Employees need to experience all four of the empowerment dimensions in order to feel truly empowered. Only then will organizations reap the hoped-for rewards from empowerment efforts. The rewards sought are increased effectiveness, higher job satisfaction, and less stress.

Empowerment is easy to advocate but difficult to put into practice. Conger offers some guidelines on how leaders can empower others.

First, managers should express confidence in employees and set high performance expectations. Positive expectations can go a long way toward enabling good performance, as the Pygmalion effect shows (Chapter 3).

Second, managers should create opportunities for employees to participate in decision making. This means participation in the forms of both voice and choice. Employees should not just be asked to contribute their opinions about any issue; they should also have a vote in the decision that is made. One method for increasing participation is using self-managed teams, as we discussed in Chapter 9.

Third, managers should remove bureaucratic constraints that stifle autonomy. Often, companies have antiquated rules and policies that prevent employees from managing themselves. An example is a collection agency where a manager's signature was once required to approve long-term payment arrangements for delinquent customers. Collectors, who spoke directly with customers, were the best judges of whether the payment arrangements were workable, and having to consult a manager made them feel closely supervised and powerless. The rule was dropped, and collections increased.

Fourth, managers should set inspirational or meaningful goals. When individuals feel they "own" a goal, they are more willing to take personal responsibility for it.

Empowerment is a matter of degree. Jobs can be thought of in two dimensions: job content and job context. Job content consists of the tasks and procedures necessary for doing a particular job. Job context is broader. It is the reason the organization needs the job and includes the way the job fits into the organization's mission, goals, and objectives. These two dimensions are depicted in Figure 11.2, the employee empowerment grid.

Both axes of the grid contain the major steps in the decision-making process. As shown on the horizontal axis, decision-making authority over job content increases in terms of greater involvement in the decision-making process. Sim-

FIGURE 11.2   Employee Empowerment Grid

11.2

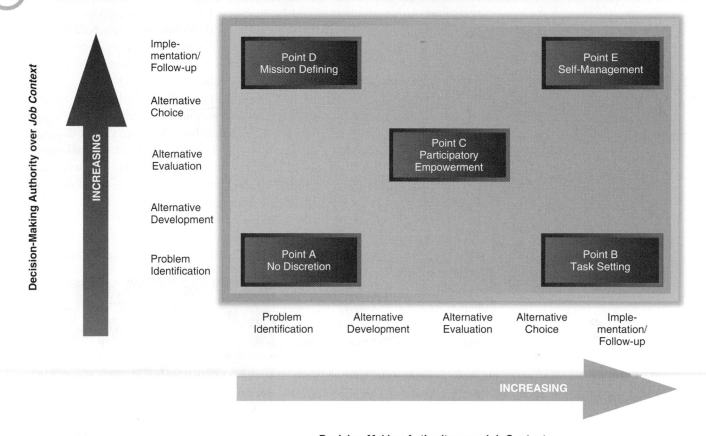

Decision-Making Authority over *Job Content*

ilarly, the vertical axis shows that authority over job context increases with greater involvement in that decision-making process. Combining job content and job context authority in this way produces five points that vary in terms of the degree of empowerment.[60]

No Discretion (point A) represents the traditional, assembly-line job: highly routine and repetitive, with no decision-making power. Recall from Chapter 7 that if these jobs have a demanding pace and if workers have no discretion, distress will result.

Task Setting (point B) is the essence of most empowerment programs in organizations today. In this case, the worker is empowered to make decisions about the best way to get the job done but has no decision responsibility for the job context.

Participatory Empowerment (point C) represents a situation that is typical of autonomous work groups that have some decision-making power over both job content and job context. Their involvement is in problem identification, developing alternatives, and evaluating alternatives, but the actual choice of alternatives is often beyond their power. Participatory empowerment can lead to job satisfaction and productivity.

Mission Defining (point D) is an unusual case of empowerment and is seldom seen. Here, employees have power over job context but not job content. An example would be a unionized team that is asked to decide whether their jobs could be better done by an outside vendor. Deciding to outsource would dramatically affect the mission of the company, but would not affect job content, which is specified in the union contract. Assuring these employees of continued employment regardless of their decision would be necessary for this case of empowerment.

Self-Management (point E) represents total decision-making control over both job content and job context. It is the ultimate expression of trust. One example is TXI Chaparral Steel (part of Texas Industries), where employees redesign their own jobs to add value to the organization.

Empowerment should begin with job content and proceed to job context. Because the workforce is so diverse, managers should recognize that some employees are more ready for empowerment than others. Managers must diagnose situations and determine the degree of empowerment to extend to employees.

When most firms talk about "empowerment," they mean allowing employees to play a bigger role in day-to-day activities; when David Zipper and Peter Murray of Empowered Painters discuss it, they mean that one day they plan to give the company to the workers entirely!

Zipper and Murray were economics students at Strathmore College when they hit on a plan to help revitalize rundown sections of Philadelphia. With countless hours of work and $40,000 in start-up funds, they began their project in 1999, hiring seven unemployed men as employees and renting a rundown house for $200 a month to serve as their home and office. While finding houses in need of paint was not hard, keeping the business going was, with long days and countless complications, including illiterate workers.[61]

The goal of the company Empowered Painters is to truly empower its workers to the point where they own and run the company.

The success of Empowered Painters has been recognized not just in Philadelphia, but elsewhere; Murray recently received the Eli Segal Entrepreneurship Award for his work,[62] while Zipper was awarded the prestigious Truman Scholarship.[63] In 2003, the organization received an $80,000 grant from the Pew Fund for Health and Human Services in Philadelphia Charitable Trust for its ongoing work.[64] The two young entrepreneurs believe their business model can work elsewhere and have plans to expand it to other cities. While many organizations talk about empowerment, Empowered Painters practices it.

The empowerment process also carries with it a risk of failure. When you delegate responsibility and authority, you must be prepared to allow employees to fail; and failure is not something most managers tolerate well. At Merck, some say the CEO empowered scientists too much and that their failures cost Merck its profitability and reputation as one of *Fortune*'s Most Admired Companies. The Real World 11.2 details this empowerment crisis at Merck.

Managerial Implications: Using Power Effectively

Sydney Finkelstein, a professor at Dartmouth University, spends his time studying why executives fail. Interestingly, most of these failures involve the misuse of power and organizational politics. Here are several reasons why executives fail:

> *They see themselves and their companies as dominating their environments.* While confidence is helpful, the perception that a company is without peer is a recipe for failure. On a more personal level, CEOs who come to see

Merck—Empowerment Backfires

Merck & Company, the pharmaceutical giant, is in trouble. Its five biggest selling drugs lost their patent protection, and the company has been unable to make any earth shattering discoveries of new drugs to replace them. CEO Ray Gilmartin has refused to play the merger game, and unlike other CEOs in the industry, has so far not pursued buying up smaller companies with good drugs in development. Instead, he has placed huge faith in Merck's scientists. But is that faith misplaced?

Merck has a reputation for having the best scientists in the industry, but some claim that Gilmartin has grown a culture of scientific arrogance that is harming the company. He refused to go after "me too" drugs—copies of drugs that other companies introduced. "We go for novel medicines that are true advances," Gilmartin stated. He gave his research scientists a great amount of power because he was not a scientist himself. One example of this empowerment involved a diabetes drug that early research showed caused tumors in mice. Scientists argued that despite early studies showing the drug wasn't viable, research should continue, and it did . . . until the drug was finally axed, costing the company considerably in terms of time and money. More than ten years of effort went into testing aprepitant, a revolutionary depression drug that set Merck apart from its competitors, who were concentrating on drugs that work on serotonin. Unfortunately, studies showed that the drug was no more effective than a placebo. Profits fell flat, and 3,200 employees were laid off. Will Gilmartin last two more years until his retirement? Will Merck change its culture of scientific arrogance in order to survive? Only time will tell.

SOURCE: J. Simons, "Merck's Man in the Hot Seat," *Fortune* (February 23, 2004): 111–114.

themselves as uniquely gifted in comparison to their competitors and coworkers are generally ripe for a fall.

> *They think they have all the answers.* While decisive leadership and vision often lead to the executive suite, an unwillingness to admit ignorance or seek others' input is a recipe for disaster. A reluctance to empower others leads to failure.

> *They ruthlessly eliminate anyone who isn't 100 percent behind them.* Business history is replete with leaders who culled the ranks of those who were willing to voice different opinions, only to find themselves blundering down the road to disaster without anyone to yell "Stop!"

> *They stubbornly rely on what worked for them in the past.* Like most of us, business leaders tend to fall back on what has worked before. Unfortunately, yesterday's solution is rarely an ideal fit for today's challenge, and successes of the past may well inhibit success in the future.

> *They have no clear boundaries between their personal interests and corporate interests.* As a top leader invests more time and effort in a firm, it's easy for him or her to become convinced that the firm is simply a reflection of his or her own enormous ego. Ironically, leaders who fail to make this distinction tend to be far less careful about spending corporate resources, leading to often embarrassing revelations of executive excess at employee and stockholder expense.[65]

While Finkelstein is quick to point out that corporate executives are, almost without exception, amazingly bright and talented individuals, they also tend to succumb to the same temptations as lesser mortals. Given the extreme power they wield, their failures tend to be much more visible, painful, and far reaching than most. Corporate executives need accountability to help them avoid these blunders.

In addition to learning from failure, there is research on how to use power successfully. John Kotter argues that managers therefore need to develop power strategies to operate effectively.[66] Kotter offers some guidelines for managing dependence on others and for using power successfully:

> *Use power in ethical ways.* People make certain assumptions about the use of power. One way of using the various forms of power ethically is by applying the criteria of utilitarian outcomes, individual rights, and distributive justice.

> *Understand and use all of the various types of power and influence.* Successful managers diagnose the situation, understand the people involved, and choose a compatible influence method.

> *Seek jobs that allow you to develop your power skills.* Recognize that managerial positions are dependent ones, and look for positions that allow you to focus on a critical issue or problem.

> *Use power tempered by maturity and self-control.* Power for its own sake should not be a goal, nor should power be used for self-aggrandizement.

> *Accept that influencing people is an important part of the management job.* Power means getting things accomplished; it is not a dirty word. Acquiring and using power well is a key to managerial success.

You can use these guidelines to enhance your own power skills. Mastering the power and politics within an organization takes respect and patience. When all people are empowered, the total amount of power within the organization will increase.

LOOKING BACK: **CISCO SYSTEMS**

Powering Up

Coworkers who endured the Cisco layoffs of 2001 recall how devastated John Chambers was by the difficult decision; as one put it, the normally optimistic Chambers was somber for a full year following the cuts. Others note that Cisco's dark years noticeably aged the CEO, putting a full decade of lines on his congenial face in only three years.

Amazingly, out of the rubble of the dot.com bust, a handful of firms have emerged stronger than ever; perhaps not surprisingly, John Chambers and Cisco appear to be among the survivors. Chambers' reputation was scorched in 2001 when he refused to lower his projections of Cisco's performance; even when he finally scaled back profit projections, he was still proven harshly wrong. And the firm's reputation for being obsessively customer focused was also called into question, as its clients began to pound the firm's products. Furthermore, many of its former suppliers were alienated, as two-thirds of them were eliminated and others were forced to offer discounts and longer warranty periods. And in perhaps his toughest sell to date, Chambers tried to tame the firm's freewheeling culture by requiring executives to provide regular reports on productivity and adding new procedures to bring some organization to the firm's chaotic ordering process. Perhaps most impressively, Chambers tied top executives' bonuses to teamwork, with 30 percent of their bonuses based on how well they collaborated with others in the firm. The result? Despite flat revenues, earnings for 2003 almost doubled those of 2002.

Chambers also took on the task of personally repairing customer relations, calling several telecom executives to apologize for his arrogance. The result? Orders rose 20 percent over the previous year. And in perhaps the most telling sign of his persistence, Chambers himself appears to have regained his optimism about the firm's future, albeit now tempered with a dose of hard-earned wisdom. In retrospect, Chambers was late to react, but he made the tough decisions, regardless of how they might be perceived. His appropriate use of power, along with his ability to learn from mistakes, are the reasons Cisco is still in business today when many of its former dot.com rivals no longer exist.

Chapter Summary

1. Power is the ability to influence others. Influence is the process of affecting the thoughts, behavior, and feelings of others. Authority is the right to influence others.

2. French and Raven's five forms of interpersonal power are reward, coercive, legitimate, referent, and expert power. Information power is another form of interpersonal power.

3. The key to using all of these types of power well is to use them ethically.

4. McClelland believes personal power is negative and social power is positive.

5. Intergroup power sources include control of critical resources and strategic contingencies.

6. According to Etzioni's power analysis, the characteristics of the organization are an im-

portant factor in deciding the type of power to use.

7. Recognizing symbols of both power and powerlessness is a key diagnostic skill for managers.

8. Organizational politics is an inevitable feature of work life. Political behavior consists of actions not officially sanctioned that are taken to influence others in order to meet personal goals. Managers should take a proactive role in managing politics.

9. The employee–boss relationship is an important political relationship. Employees can use their skills to develop more effective working relationships with their bosses.

10. Empowerment is a positive strategy for sharing power throughout the organization.

Key Terms

authority (p. 356)
coercive power (p. 357)
empowerment (p. 372)
expert power (p. 357)
influence (p. 356)
information power (p. 359)

legitimate power (p. 357)
organizational politics (p. 366)
personal power (p. 360)
political behavior (p. 366)
power (p. 356)
powerlessness (p. 365)

referent power (p. 357)
reward power (p. 356)
social power (p. 361)
strategic contingencies (p. 362)
zone of indifference (p. 356)

Review Questions

1. What are the five types of power according to French and Raven? What are the effects of these types of power? What is information power?

2. What are the intergroup sources of power?

3. Distinguish between personal and social power. What are the four power-oriented characteristics of the best managers?

4. According to Rosabeth Moss Kanter, what are the symbols of power? The symptoms of powerlessness?

5. How do organizations encourage political activity?

6. Which influence tactics are most effective?

7. What are some of the characteristics of an effective relationship between you and your boss?

8. What are some ways to empower people at work?

Discussion and Communication Questions

1. Who is the most powerful person you know personally? What is it that makes the person so powerful?

2. Why is it hard to determine if power has been used ethically?

3. What kinds of membership (alienative, calculative, moral) do you currently have? Is the power used in these relationships congruent?

4. As a student, do you experience yourself as powerful, powerless, or both? On what symbols or symptoms are you basing your perception?

5. How does attribution theory explain the reactions supervisors can have to influence tactics?

How can managers prevent the negative consequences of political behavior?

6. Are people in your work environment empowered? How could they become more empowered?

7. Chapter 2 discussed power distance as a dimension of cultural differences. How would empowerment efforts be different in a country with high power distance?

8. *(communication question)* Think of a person you admire. Write a newspaper feature analyzing the person's use of power in terms of the ideas presented in the chapter.

Ethical Dilemma

James Allen, a manager for a large retail department store, sat at his desk remembering how this whole thing began. He had called a meeting of his team in early June in which he had laid out his plan to increase productivity over the next six months. Between back to school and the holidays, July through December was always a busy time in retail, but this year needed to be exceptional. Just weeks before that meeting, James had been informed that the store manager was retiring and his successor would be appointed from within the organization. Specifically, the manager whose department was the most productive and efficient through the end of the year would be named the new general manager.

It was now October, and the evaluation period was half over. James felt confident that things were

going well in his department. His concern at the moment was Tom Sharp's department. One of Tom's employees had confided that Tom was promising favors to his employees who helped him gain this promotion. Once promoted, he would be in a position to give raises or even promote those who had helped him advance. To help Tom accomplish his goals, the department employees were willing to do just about anything, even work overtime off the clock to reduce labor costs.

James knew that these practices were wrong and against the company's mission and policies. His concern was how to handle it. He felt confident that his department would be the best, so Tom's unethical practices would not affect the outcome. And if he were the new general manager, he could handle the problem then. However, was it right to let these behaviors continue for another three months? Was James sending the wrong signal to his own employees by keeping quiet? Was it enough to say that fair and just practices win in the end? If he did blow the whistle, would the people he would soon supervise think badly of him for being a snitch? James really wanted to do the right thing, but he just was not sure what that was.

Experiential Exercises

11.1 Social Power Role Plays

1. Divide the class into five groups of equal size, each of which is assigned one of the French and Raven types of power.

2. Read the following paragraph and prepare an influence plan using the type of power that has been assigned to your group. When you have finished your planning, select one member to play the role of instructor. Then choose from your own or another group a "student" who is to be the recipient of the "instructor's" efforts.

You are an instructor in a college class and have become aware that a potentially good student has been repeatedly absent from class and sometimes is unprepared when he is there. He seems to be satisfied with the grade he is getting, but you would like to see him attend regularly, be better prepared, and thus do better in the class. You even feel that the student might get really turned on to pursuing a career in this field, which is an exciting one for you. You are respected and liked by your students, and it irritates you that this person treats your dedicated teaching

Questions

1. Who are the stakeholders that would be affected by James's decision?

2. Does James have a responsibility to come forward with this information?

3. Using rule, virtue, right, and justice theories, evaluate James's decision options.

with such a cavalier attitude. You want to influence the student to start attending regularly.

3. Role-playing.

   a. Each group role-plays its influence plan.
   b. During the role-playing, members in other groups should think of themselves as the student being influenced. Fill out the following "Reaction to Influence Questionnaire" for each role-playing episode, including your own.

4. Tabulate the results of the questionnaire within your group. For each role-playing effort, determine how many people thought the power used was reward, coercive, and so on; then add up each member's score for item 2, then for items 3, 4, and 5.

5. Group discussion.

   a. As a class, discuss which influence strategy is the most effective in compliance, long-lasting effect, acceptable attitude, and enhanced relationships.
   b. What are the likely side effects of each type of influence strategy?

Reaction to Influence Questionnaire

Role-Play #1

1. Type of power used (mark one):

   Reward—Ability to influence because of potential reward.

   Coercive—Ability to influence because of capacity to coerce or punish.

   Legitimate—Stems from formal position in organization.

   Referent—Comes from admiration and liking.

   Expert—Comes from superior knowledge or ability to get things done.

Role-Plays				
1	2	3	4	5

Think of yourself on the receiving end of the influence attempt just described and record your own reaction with an "X" in the appropriate box.

2. As a result of this influence attempt I will . . .

definitely not comply definitely comply

1 2 3 4 5

3. Any change that does come about will be . . .

temporary long-lasting

1 2 3 4 5

4. My own personal reaction is . . .

resistant accepting

1 2 3 4 5

5. As a result of this influence attempt, my relationship with the instructor will probably be . . .

worse better

1 2 3 4 5

Role-Plays

1	2	3	4	5

SOURCE: Gib Akin. *Exchange* 3. No. 4 (1978): 38–39. Reprinted by permission of Gib Akin. McIntire School of Commerce. University of Virginia.

11.2 Empowerment in the Classroom

1. Divide the class into groups of six people.

2. Each group is to brainstorm ways in which students might be more empowered in the classroom. The ideas do not have to be either feasible or reasonable. They can be as imaginative as possible.

3. Each group should now analyze each of the empowerment ideas for feasibility, paying attention to administrative or other constraints that may hamper implementation. This feasibility discussion might include ideas about how the college or university could be altered.

4. Each group should present its empowerment ideas along with its feasibility analysis. Questions of clarification for each group should follow each presentation.

5. Discuss the following questions as a class:

a. Who is threatened by the power changes caused by empowerment?

b. Are there unintended or adverse consequences of empowerment? Explain.

Biz Flix | Scarface

Cuban refugee Antonio "Tony" Montana (Al Pacino) comes to Miami to pursue the American dream. He quickly rises in power within the Miami drug world until life turns against him. This lengthy, punishing film will leave unforgettable images and thoughts on almost any viewer. It is a remake of the 1931 *Scarface*, a classic gangster film starring Paul Muni that set an early standard for films of this type.

The scene from *Scarface* comes from the "Shakedown" sequence that occurs about halfway through the film. The sequence takes place at a disco before Tony's confrontation with his sister Gina (Mary Elizabeth Mastrantonio) about the man she is dating.

Mel Bernstein (Harris Yulin), Chief Detective, Narcotics and Tony Montana discuss Mel's proposal to protect Tony's drug operation. After Mel says, "Thank you for the drink" and leaves, Tony goes to Elvira's (Michelle Pfeiffer) table. The film continues through more of Tony Montana's complex drug deals and to its well-known violent ending.

What to Watch for and Ask Yourself:

> What are Mel's sources or bases of power in this interaction with Tony Montana?

> What are Tony Montana's sources or bases of power?

> What type of power relationship forms between the two men?

Workplace Video | Buffalo Zoo: Leadership in Organizations

After years of overreaching leadership, flagging attendance, and sinking employee morale, the Buffalo Zoo struggled to update its vision and find its place in the world. Part of finding that place was the selection of Donna Fernandes as the zoo's new president.

At first, senior staff were cynical about the arrival of Ms. Fernandes. The Buffalo Zoo's former executives had been unable to follow through on creating and executing a master plan or working effectively with the board to raise money for the organization. The staff soon learned that Ms. Fernandes was a charismatic leader capable of using her power to set realistic goals and establish plans that were both actionable and empowering to employees.

Good leadership requires vision, charisma, and the ability to use power effectively, and Donna Fernandes possesses the right qualities to lead the Buffalo Zoo. Ms. Fernandes has been described as "energetic," "smart," and "willing to get in the trenches"—traits that endear her to her colleagues. Ms. Fernandes's ability to build relationships with her staff and the board has prepared the zoo for a bright and promising future.

Questions

1. *Which of French and Raven's five forms of interpersonal power does Donna Fernandes embody? How do employees at the zoo respond to her use of power?*
2. *What is "empowerment," and how does Ms. Fernandes seek to empower others?*
3. *In what ways does Ms. Fernandes utilize "expert knowledge" at the Buffalo Zoo, and how does such knowledge help her lead the organization?*

The American Heart Association: Exercising Influence through Public Advocacy

The American Heart Association (AHA) has the "goal of reducing heart disease and stroke by 25% by the year 2010." One major approach to achieving this goal is the AHA's public advocacy programs. These programs are geared toward influencing policy makers and legislators to make a difference in the fight against heart disease, stroke, and other cardiovascular diseases. Some of the policy issues in which the AHA is interested include funding for relevant research, access to quality health care, tobacco control, emergency cardiovascular care, overweight and obesity, and physical activity.

The American Heart Association encourages the public to get involved in its advocacy programs by becoming active in the Grassroots Network or through use of the Legislative Action Center. Through the Grassroots Network, the AHA asks members to write, call, or visit decision makers at the local, state, and federal levels to express their views on important AHA issues. The American Heart Association provides a variety of advocacy tools that members can use in their contacts with decision makers. The Legislative Action Center provides e-mail action alerts to members of the Grassroots Network. These action alerts enable Grassroots members to quickly and easily contact public officials on important issues. In addition to action alerts, the AHA Legislative Action Center provides Grassroots members with tips on communicating with elected officials, including tips on telephoning, writing, and e-mailing members of Congress. The American Heart Association also publishes the *Advocacy Pulse* on the Internet to keep AHA members and other interested parties informed about the latest legislative developments and other fast-breaking government news regarding issues of interest.

Advocacy Coalitions

The American Heart Association also seeks to influence policy and resource allocation decisions through its participation in *The National Coalition for Heart and Stroke Research*. This coalition, consisting of 18 organizations, seeks to achieve the following three goals: (1) increasing awareness within Congress regarding the importance of heart and stroke research; (2) increasing public awareness about the importance of heart and stroke research; and (3) increasing federal funding for heart and stroke research. "The coalition is a catalyst for the coordination of research advocacy efforts of its member organizations. This includes the coordination of strategy development, information sharing, participation in 'lobby day,' and developing coordinated grassroots efforts."

Another coalition that the AHA promotes is *The Congressional Heart and Stroke Coalition*. As of mid-2004, this coalition consisted of more than 200 members of Congress. It works to raise awareness of cardiovascular diseases, serves as a resource center on relevant issues, and seeks to advance public policy aimed at fighting cardiovascular diseases. The American Heart Association encourages its Web site visitors to e-mail their senators and representatives, asking them to join *The Congressional Heart and Stroke Coalition*.

On another front, Rose Marie Robertson, the AHA's president and chief science officer, has worked vigorously to establish a strategic alliance with four agencies of the federal government that will help the AHA achieve its goal of significantly improving cardiovascular health. This public/private partnership has four specific goals:

> To prevent the development of risk factors for cardiovascular disease.

> To detect and treat risk factors for cardiovascular disease and stroke.

> To achieve early identification and treatment of acute coronary disease and stroke.

> To prevent the recurrence and complications of cardiovascular disease and stroke.

Key AHA Advocacy Interests

Two high-profile current AHA advocacy interests are tobacco control and obesity prevention. "Tobacco is the only legal product sold in the United States that, when used exactly according to the manufacturer's instructions, causes death and disability (including one out of every five deaths from heart disease)." Tobacco products are regularly used daily by approximately 50 million Americans, one third of whom will eventually die as a result of tobacco use. The death rate escalates to 50 percent for lifetime tobacco users. This does not include the harm caused by exposure to secondary smoke. The American Heart Association strongly supports the bills introduced into the United States Senate and House of Representatives by a bipartisan group of Democrats and Republicans to grant regulatory authority over tobacco products to the Food and Drug Administration (FDA). The bill would authorize the FDA to regulate the manufacture, labeling, advertising, promotion, distribution, and sale of tobacco products.

Overweight and obesity are leading risk factors for heart disease. Approximately 61 percent of American adults are overweight or obese, and about 8.8 million children and adolescents ages 6 to 19 are overweight or obese. The incidence of these risk factors has risen dramatically for both adults and children during the last ten years. Legislation, sponsored by a bipartisan group of three senators and three representatives, has been introduced into Congress to help address the obesity problem. The legislation—known as the Improved Nutrition and Physical Activity Act (IMPACT bill)—would commit substantial federal resources to the diagnosis, treatment, and prevention of obesity. Through its advocacy efforts, the American Heart Association is working toward the passage of the IMPACT bill. The AHA, along with other advocacy groups, also supports efforts of restaurant chains to alter their menus to help fight obesity, particularly in children.

Advocacy Impact

Taken together, the various public advocacy programs of the American Heart Association provide the means for influencing policy makers and decision makers to establish appropriate policies and programs and to direct sufficient resources toward the fight against cardiovascular disease. Progress in winning this fight will be an indicator of the effectiveness of the American Heart Association's public advocacy programs.

Discussion Questions

1. The chapter defines influence as "the process of affecting the thoughts, behavior, or feelings of another person." Explain the American Heart Association's public advocacy programs in the context of this definition.

2. Using Table 11.2 as a point of departure, describe the influence tactics that the American Heart Association uses in its various approaches to public advocacy.

3. Suppose that you joined the Grassroots Network of the American Heart Association. Why would you join the Network and what would you do to try to exercise influence through the Network?

SOURCE: This case was written by Michael K. McCuddy, The Louis S. and Mary L. Morgal Chair of Christian Business Ethics and Professor of Management, College of Business Administration, Valparaiso University. This case was developed from material contained on the American Heart Association Web site at http://www.americanheart.org and in the following articles: S. Rector, "Demise of McDonald's Super-Size Fries May Be Just Small Potatoes," *Detroit Free Press* (March 4, 2004): accessed from newspaper source; P. Wenske, "On Kids' Menus, Fat Becomes a Burning Issue," *The Kansas City Star* (February 27, 2004): accessed from newspaper source.

Chapter 12

Leadership and Followership

After reading this chapter, you should be able to do the following:

1 Define *leadership* and *followership*.

2 Discuss the differences between leadership and management and between leaders and managers.

3 Compare autocratic, democratic, and laissez-faire leadership styles.

4 Explain initiating structure and consideration, leader behaviors, and the Leadership Grid.

5 Explain Fiedler's contingency theory of leadership.

6 Distinguish among the path–goal theory, the Vroom-Yetton-Jago theory, and the Situational Leadership® model.

7 Distinguish among transformational, transactional, and charismatic leaders.

8 Discuss the characteristics of effective and dynamic followers.

THINKING AHEAD: VIRGIN GROUP LTD.

Richard Branson—Not Your Average Leader

Sir Richard Branson, head of Virgin Group, is a lot like other corporate CEOs . . . and yet nothing like them at all. Like many corporate leaders, he starts his day early, often at 4:30 A.M. But unlike most of them, he typically begins it lying in a hammock in his swim trunks, thinking through the business of the day and jotting notes or writing letters in a small black book. Like many other CEOs, Branson is comfortable discussing technology, having been invited to speak at a recent Microsoft conference; unlike most of them, he never uses a computer, preferring to jot down e-mail messages, which he then dictates to his administrative assistant. For urgent reminders, he simply writes a note on the back of his hand.

Branson's eccentricities extend to other parts of his life. He sports a costly Breitling watch, a gift from its maker, which includes an emergency transmitter to summon a rescue helicopter; alas, the watch shows the incorrect time, since the pin to change the time is next to the pin for summoning help, and Branson can never remember which is which. More than once, he has been caught without cash for a cab fare or lunch, although his net worth is estimated to be more than $2 billion. His preferred briefcase is an athletic duffle bag.

Branson's unique personal style influences every aspect of his companies, which have succeeded in a diverse array of markets from bridal gowns to airlines. In each case, Richard Branson's peculiar perspective on life has helped shape the company's unique and creative business strategies and the way it competes against more traditional firms.[1]

1. Define *leadership* and *followership*.

leadership

The process of guiding and directing the behavior of people in the work environment.

formal leadership

Officially sanctioned leadership based on the authority of a formal position.

informal leadership

Unofficial leadership accorded to a person by other members of the organization.

followership

The process of being guided and directed by a leader in the work environment.

2. Discuss the differences between leadership and management and between leaders and managers.

leader

An advocate for change and new approaches to problems.

manager

An advocate for stability and the status quo.

Leadership in organizations is the process of guiding and directing the behavior of people in the work environment. The first section of the chapter distinguishes leadership from management. *Formal leadership* occurs when an organization officially bestows on a leader the authority to guide and direct others in the organization. *Informal leadership* occurs when a person is unofficially accorded power by others in the organization and uses influence to guide and direct their behavior. Leadership is among the most researched topics in organizational behavior and one of the least understood social processes in organizations.

Leadership has a long, rich history in organizational behavior. In this chapter, we explore many of the theories and ideas that have emerged along the way in that history. To begin, we examine the differences between leaders and managers. Next, we explore the earliest theories of leadership, the trait theories, which tried to identify a set of traits that leaders have in common. Following the trait theories, behavioral theories were developed, proposing that leader behaviors, not traits, are what counts. Contingency theories followed soon after. These theories argue that appropriate leader behavior depends on the situation and the followers. Next, we present some exciting contemporary theories of leadership, followed by the "hot" and exciting new issues that are arising in leadership. We end by discussing *followership* and providing you with some guidelines for using this leadership knowledge.

Leadership and Management

John Kotter suggests that leadership and management are two distinct, yet complementary systems of action in organizations.[2] Specifically, he believes that effective leadership produces useful change in organizations and that good management controls complexity in the organization and its environment. Fred Smith, who founded Federal Express (FedEx) in 1971, has been producing constant change since the company's start. FedEx began with primarily high-dollar medical and technology shipments. The company recently bought Kinko's to extend its reach from the back office to the front.[3] Bill Gates has successfully controlled complexity—Microsoft has grown exponentially from early times when his company's sole product was DOS. Healthy organizations need both effective leadership and good management.

For Kotter, the management process involves (1) planning and budgeting, (2) organizing and staffing, and (3) controlling and problem solving. The management process reduces uncertainty and stabilizes an organization. Alfred P. Sloan's integration and stabilization of General Motors after its early growth years are an example of good management.

In contrast, the leadership process involves (1) setting a direction for the organization; (2) aligning people with that direction through communication; and (3) motivating people to action, partly through empowerment and partly through basic need gratification. The leadership process creates uncertainty and change in an organization. Donald Peterson's championing of a quality revolution at Ford Motor Company is an example of effective leadership.

Abraham Zaleznik proposes that leaders have distinct personalities that stand in contrast to the personalities of a manager.[4] Zaleznik suggests that both leaders and managers make a valuable contribution to an organization and that each one's contribution is different. Whereas *leaders* agitate for change and new approaches, *managers* advocate stability and the status quo. There is a dynamic tension between leaders and managers that makes it difficult for each to understand the other. Leaders and managers differ along four separate dimensions of personality: attitudes toward goals, conceptions of work, relationships with other people, and sense of self. The differences between these two personality types are summarized in Table 12.1. Zaleznik's distinction between leaders and managers is similar to the distinction made between transactional and transformational leaders, or between leadership and supervision. Transactional leaders use formal rewards and punishment to engage in deal making and contractual obligations, which you will read about later in this chapter.

It has been proposed that some people are strategic leaders who embody both the stability of managers and the visionary abilities of leaders. Thus, strategic leaders combine the best of both worlds in a synergistic way. The unprecedented success of both Coca-Cola and Microsoft suggests that their leaders, the late Robert Goizueta (of Coke) and Bill Gates, were strategic leaders.[5]

Early Trait Theories

The first studies of leadership attempted to identify what physical attributes, personality characteristics, and abilities distinguished leaders from other members of a group.[6] The physical attributes considered have been height, weight, physique, energy, health, appearance, and even age. This line of research yielded some interesting findings. However, very few valid generalizations emerged from this line of inquiry. Therefore, there is insufficient evidence to conclude that leaders can be distinguished from followers on the basis of physical attributes.

Leader personality characteristics that have been examined include originality, adaptability, introversion–extroversion, dominance, self-confidence, integrity, conviction, mood optimism, and emotional control. There is some evidence that leaders may be more adaptable and self-confident than the average group member.

(12.1) TABLE 12.1   Leaders and Managers

PERSONALITY DIMENSION	MANAGER	LEADER
Attitudes toward goals	Has an impersonal, passive, functional attitude; believes goals arise out of necessity and reality	Has a personal and active attitude; believes goals arise from desire and imagination
Conceptions of work	Views work as an enabling process that combines people, ideas, and things; seeks moderate risk through coordination and balance	Looks for fresh approaches to old problems; seeks high-risk positions, especially with high payoffs
Relationships with others	Avoids solitary work activity, preferring to work with others; avoids close, intense relationships; avoids conflict	Is comfortable in solitary work activity; encourages close, intense working relationships; is not conflict averse
Sense of self	Is once born; makes a straightforward life adjustment; accepts life as it is	Is twice born; engages in a struggle for a sense of order in life; questions life

SOURCE: Reprinted by permission of *Harvard Business Review*. From "Managers and Leaders: Are They Different?" by A. Zaleznik (January 2004). Copyright © 2004 by the Harvard Business School Publishing Corporation; all rights reserved.

With regard to leader abilities, attention has been devoted to such constructs as social skills, intelligence, scholarship, speech fluency, cooperativeness, and insight. In this area, there is some evidence that leaders are more intelligent, verbal, and cooperative and have a higher level of scholarship than the average group member.

These conclusions suggest traits leaders possess, but the findings are neither strong nor uniform. For each attribute or trait claimed to distinguish leaders from followers, there were always at least one or two studies with contradictory findings. For some, the trait theories are invalid, though interesting and intuitively of some relevance. The trait theories have had very limited success in being able to identify the universal, distinguishing attributes of leaders.

Behavioral Theories

Behavioral theories emerged as a response to the deficiencies of the trait theories. Trait theories told us what leaders were like, but didn't address how leaders behaved. Three theories are the foundations of many modern leadership theories: the Lewin, Lippitt, and White studies; the Ohio State studies; and the Michigan studies.

Lewin Studies

The earliest research on leadership style, conducted by Kurt Lewin and his students, identified three basic styles: autocratic, democratic, and laissez-faire.[7] Each leader uses one of these three basic styles when approaching a group of followers in a leadership situation. The specific situation is not an important consideration, because the leader's style does not vary with the situation. The *autocratic style* is directive, strong, and controlling in relationships. Leaders with an autocratic style use rules and regulations to run the work environment. Followers have little discretionary influence over the nature of the work, its accomplishment, or other aspects of the work environment. The leader with a *democratic style* is collaborative, responsive, and interactive in relationships and emphasizes rules and regulations less than the autocratic leader. Followers have a high degree of discretionary influence, although the leader has ultimate authority and responsibility. The leader with a *laissez-faire style* leads through nonleadership. A laissez-faire leader abdicates the authority and responsibility of the position, and this style often results in chaos.

Ohio State Studies

The leadership research program at The Ohio State University also measured specific leader behaviors. The initial Ohio State research studied aircrews and pilots.[8] The aircrew members, as followers, were asked a wide range of questions about their lead pilots using the Leader Behavior Description Questionnaire (LBDQ). The results using the LBDQ suggested that there were two important underlying dimensions of leader behaviors.[9] These were labeled initiating structure and consideration.

Initiating structure is leader behavior aimed at defining and organizing work relationships and roles, as well as establishing clear patterns of organization, communication, and ways of getting things done. *Consideration* is leader behavior aimed at nurturing friendly, warm working relationships, as well as encouraging mutual trust and interpersonal respect within the work unit. These two leader behaviors are independent of each other. That is, a leader may be high on both, low on both, or high on one while low on the other. The Ohio

3. Compare autocratic, democratic, and laissez-faire leadership styles.

autocratic style
A style of leadership in which the leader uses strong, directive, controlling actions to enforce the rules, regulations, activities, and relationships in the work environment.

democratic style
A style of leadership in which the leader takes collaborative, responsive, interactive actions with followers concerning the work and work environment.

laissez-faire style
A style of leadership in which the leader fails to accept the responsibilities of the position.

4. Explain initiating structure and consideration, leader behaviors, and the Leadership Grid.

initiating structure
Leader behavior aimed at defining and organizing work relationships and roles, as well as establishing clear patterns of organization, communication, and ways of getting things done.

consideration
Leader behavior aimed at nurturing friendly, warm working relationships, as well as encouraging mutual trust and interpersonal respect within the work unit.

State studies were intended to describe leader behavior, not to evaluate or judge behavior.[10]

Michigan Studies

Another approach to the study of leadership, developed at the University of Michigan, suggests that the leader's style has very important implications for the emotional atmosphere of the work environment and, therefore, for the followers who work under that leader. Two styles of leadership were identified: employee oriented and production oriented.[11]

A production-oriented style leads to a work environment characterized by constant influence attempts on the part of the leader, either through direct, close supervision or through the use of many written and unwritten rules and regulations for behavior. The focus is clearly on getting work done.

In comparison, an employee-oriented leadership style leads to a work environment that focuses on relationships. The leader exhibits less direct or less close supervision and establishes fewer written or unwritten rules and regulations for behavior. Employee-oriented leaders display concern for people and their needs.

These three groups of studies (the Lewin, Lippitt, and White studies; Ohio State studies; and Michigan studies) taken together form the building blocks of many recent leadership theories. What the studies have in common is that two basic leadership styles were identified, with one focusing on tasks (autocratic, production oriented, initiating structure) and one focusing on people (democratic, employee oriented, consideration). Use You 12.1 to assess your supervisor's task- versus people-oriented styles.

The Leadership Grid: A Contemporary Extension

Robert Blake and Jane Mouton's *Leadership Grid*, originally called the Managerial Grid, was developed with a focus on attitudes.[12] The two underlying dimensions of the grid are labeled Concern for Results and Concern for People. These two attitudinal dimensions are independent of each other and in different combinations form various leadership styles. Blake and Mouton originally identified five distinct managerial styles, and further development of the grid has led to the seven distinct leadership styles shown in Figure 12.1.

The *organization man manager (5,5)* is a middle-of-the-road leader who has a medium concern for people and production. This leader attempts to balance a concern for both people and production without a commitment to either.

The *authority-compliance manager (9,1)* has great concern for production and little concern for people. This leader desires tight control in order to get tasks done efficiently and considers creativity and human relations unnecessary. Authority-compliance managers may become so focused on running an efficient organization that they actually use tactics such as bullying. Some authority-compliance managers may intimidate, verbally and mentally attack, and otherwise mistreat subordinates. This form of abuse is quite common, with one in six U.S. workers reporting that they have been bullied by a manager.[13] The *country club manager (1,9)* has great concern for people and little concern for production, attempts to avoid conflict, and seeks to be well liked. This leader's goal is to keep people happy through good interpersonal relations, which are more important to him or her than the task. (This style is not a sound human relations approach but rather a soft Theory X approach.)

The *team manager (9,9)* is considered ideal and has great concern for both people and production. This leader works to motivate employees to reach their

The authority-compliance manager might use aggressive body language to more forcefully get his or her point across.

Leadership Grid

An approach to understanding a leader's or manager's concern for results (production) and concern for people.

organization man manager (5,5)

A middle-of-the-road leader.

authority-compliance manager (9,1)

A leader who emphasizes efficient production.

country club manager (1,9)

A leader who creates a happy, comfortable work environment.

team manager (9,9)

A leader who builds a highly productive team of committed people.

How Does Your Supervisor Lead?

Answer the following sixteen questions concerning your supervisor's (or professor's) leadership behav- iors using the seven-point Likert scale. Then complete the summary to examine your supervisor's behaviors.

	Not at All					Very Much	
1. Is your superior strict about observing regulations?	1	2	3	4	5	6	7
2. To what extent does your superior give you instructions and orders?	1	2	3	4	5	6	7
3. Is your superior strict about the amount of work you do?	1	2	3	4	5	6	7
4. Does your superior urge you to complete your work by the time he or she has specified?	1	2	3	4	5	6	7
5. Does your superior try to make you work to your maximum capacity?	1	2	3	4	5	6	7
6. When you do an inadequate job, does your superior focus on the inadequate way the job was done instead of on your personality?	1	2	3	4	5	6	7
7. Does your superior ask you for reports about the progress of your work?	1	2	3	4	5	6	7
8. Does your superior work out precise plans for goal achievement each month?	1	2	3	4	5	6	7
9. Can you talk freely with your superior about your work?	1	2	3	4	5	6	7
10. Generally, does your superior support you?	1	2	3	4	5	6	7
11. Is your superior concerned about your personal problems?	1	2	3	4	5	6	7
12. Do you think your superior trusts you?	1	2	3	4	5	6	7
13. Does your superior give you recognition when you do your job well?	1	2	3	4	5	6	7
14. When a problem arises in your workplace, does your superior ask your opinion about how to solve it?	1	2	3	4	5	6	7
15. Is your superior concerned about your future benefits like promotions and pay raises?	1	2	3	4	5	6	7
16. Does your superior treat you fairly?	1	2	3	4	5	6	7

Add up your answers to Questions 1 through 8. This total indicates your supervisor's performance orientation:

Task orientation = _____

Add up your answers to Questions 9 through 16. This total indicates your supervisor's maintenance orientation:

People orientation = _____

A score above 40 is high, and a score below 20 is low.

SOURCE: Reprinted from "The Performance-Maintenance Theory of Leadership: Review of a Japanese Research Program" by J. Misumi and M. F. Peterson, published in *Administrative Science Quarterly* 30 (1985): 207. By permission of Administrative Science Quarterly © 1985.

impoverished manager (1.1)

A leader who exerts just enough effort to get by.

paternalistic "father knows best" manager (9+9)

A leader who promises reward and threatens punishment.

highest levels of accomplishment, is flexible, responsive to change, and understands the need for change. The *impoverished manager (1,1)* is often referred to as a laissez-faire leader. This leader has little concern for people or production, avoids taking sides, and stays out of conflicts; he or she does just enough to get by. Two new leadership styles have been added to these five original leadership styles within the grid. The *paternalistic "father knows best" manager (9+9)* promises reward for compliance and threatens punishment for noncompliance. The *opportunistic "what's in it for me" manager (Opp)* uses the style that he or she feels will return him or her the greatest self-benefits.

FIGURE 12.1   The Leadership Grid

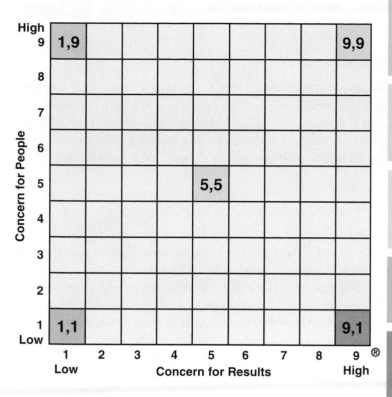

1,9 Country Club Management:
Thoughtful attention to the needs of the people for satisfying relationships leads to a comfortable, friendly organization atmosphere and work tempo.

9,9 Team Management:
Work accomplishment is from committed people; interdependence through a "common stake" in organization purpose leads to relationships of trust and respect.

5,5 Middle-of-the-Road Management:
Adequate organization performance is possible through balancing the necessity to get work out while maintaining morale of people at a satisfactory level.

1,1 Impoverished Management:
Exertion of minimum effort to get required work done is appropriate to sustain organization membership.

9,1 Authority-Compliance Management:
Efficiency in operations results from arranging conditions of work in such a way that human elements interfere to a minimum degree.

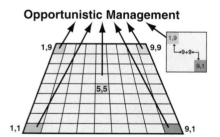

In Opportunisitic Management, people adapt and shift to any grid style needed to gain the maximum advantage. Performance occurs according to a system of selfish gain. Effort is given only for an advantage for personal gain.

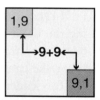

9+9: Paternalism/Maternalism Management:
Reward and approval are bestowed to people in return for loyalty and obedience; failure to comply leads to punishment.

SOURCE: "The Leadership Grid®" figure, Paternalism Figure and Opportunism from *Leadership Dilemmas—Grid Solutions*, by Robert R. Blake and Anne Adams McCanse (Formerly the Managerial Grid by Robert R. Blake and Jane S. Mouton). Houston: Gulf Publishing Company (Grid Figure: p. 29; Paternalism Figure: p. 30; Opportunism Figure: p. 31). Copyright 1991 by Blake and Mouton, and Scientific Methods, Inc. Reproduced by permission of the owners.

The Leadership Grid is distinguished from the original Ohio State research in two important ways. First, it has attitudinal overtones that are not present in the original research. Whereas the LBDQ aims to describe behavior, the grid addresses both the behavior and the attitude of the leader. Second, the Ohio State approach is fundamentally descriptive and nonevaluative, whereas the grid is normative and prescriptive. Specifically, the grid evaluates the team manager (9,9) as the very best style of managerial behavior. This is the basis on which the grid has been used for team building and leadership training in an organization's

opportunistic "what's in it for me" manager (Opp)
A leader whose style aims to maximize self-benefit.

development. As an organizational development method, the grid aims to transform the leader in the organization to lead in the "one best way," which according to the grid is the team approach. The team style is one that combines optimal concern for people with optimal concern for results.

Contingency Theories

Contingency theories involve the belief that leadership style must be appropriate for the particular situation. By their nature, contingency theories are "if–then" theories: If the situation is ____, then the appropriate leadership behavior is ____. We examine four such theories, including Fiedler's contingency theory, path–goal theory, normative decision theory, and situational leadership theory.

Fiedler's Contingency Theory

5. Explain Fiedler's contingency theory of leadership.

Fiedler's contingency theory of leadership proposes that the fit between the leader's need structure and the favorableness of the leader's situation determine the team's effectiveness in work accomplishment. This theory assumes that leaders are either task oriented or relationship oriented, depending upon how the leaders obtain their primary need gratification.[14] Task-oriented leaders are primarily gratified by accomplishing tasks and getting work done. Relationship-oriented leaders are primarily gratified by developing good, comfortable interpersonal relationships. Accordingly, the effectiveness of both types of leaders depends on the favorableness of their situation. The theory classifies the favorableness of the leader's situation according to the leader's position power, the structure of the team's task, and the quality of the leader–follower relationships.

THE LEAST PREFERRED COWORKER Fiedler classifies leaders using the Least Preferred Coworker (LPC) Scale.[15] The LPC Scale is a projective technique through which a leader is asked to think about the person with whom he or she can work least well (the *least preferred coworker*, or *LPC*).

least preferred coworker (LPC)

The person a leader has least preferred to work with over his or her career.

The leader is asked to describe this least preferred coworker using sixteen eight-point bipolar adjective sets. Two of these bipolar adjective sets follow (the leader marks the blank most descriptive of the least preferred coworker):

| Efficient | : | : | : | : | : | : | : | : | Inefficient |
| Cheerful | : | : | : | : | : | : | : | : | Gloomy |

Leaders who describe their least preferred coworker in positive terms (that is, pleasant, efficient, cheerful, and so on) are classified as high LPC, or relationship-oriented, leaders. Those who describe their least preferred coworker in negative terms (that is, unpleasant, inefficient, gloomy, and so on) are classified as low LPC, or task-oriented, leaders.

The LPC score is a controversial element in contingency theory.[16] The LPC score has been critiqued conceptually and methodologically because it is a projective technique with low measurement reliability.

task structure

The degree of clarity, or ambiguity, in the work activities assigned to the group.

position power

The authority associated with the leader's formal position in the organization.

SITUATIONAL FAVORABLENESS The leader's situation has three dimensions: task structure, position power, and leader–member relations. Based on these three dimensions, the situation is either favorable or unfavorable for the leader. *Task structure* refers to the number and clarity of rules, regulations, and procedures for getting the work done. *Position power* refers to the leader's legitimate authority to evaluate and reward performance, punish errors, and demote group members.

The quality of *leader–member relations* is measured by the Group-Atmosphere Scale, composed of nine eight-point bipolar adjective sets. Two of these bipolar adjective sets follow:

leader–member relations
The quality of interpersonal relationships among a leader and the group members.

Friendly : : : : : : : : : Unfriendly
Accepting : : : : : : : : : Rejecting

A favorable leadership situation is one with a structured task for the work group, strong position power for the leader, and good leader–member relations. In contrast, an unfavorable leadership situation is one with an unstructured task, weak position power for the leader, and moderately poor leader–member relations. Between these two extremes, the leadership situation has varying degrees of moderate favorableness for the leader.

LEADERSHIP EFFECTIVENESS The contingency theory suggests that low and high LPC leaders are each effective if placed in the right situation.[17] Specifically, low LPC (task-oriented) leaders are most effective in either very favorable or very unfavorable leadership situations. In contrast, high LPC (relationship-oriented) leaders are most effective in situations of intermediate favorableness. Figure 12.2 shows the nature of these relationships and suggests

FIGURE 12.2 Leadership Effectiveness in the Contingency Theory

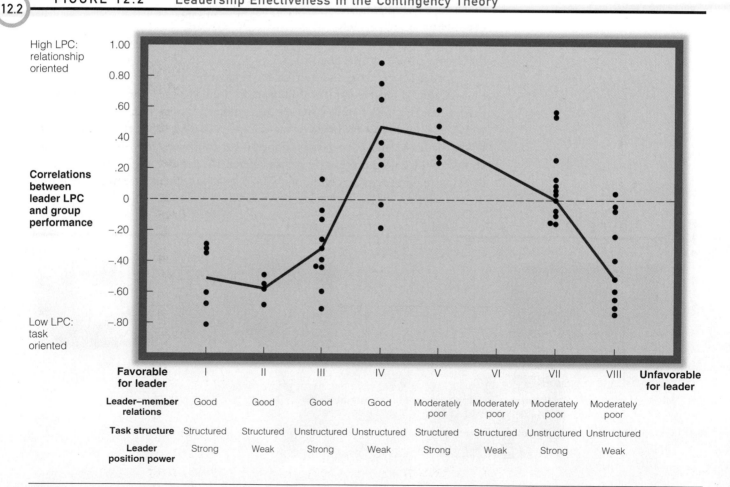

SOURCE: F. E. Fiedler. *A Theory of Leader Effectiveness* (New York: McGraw-Hill, 1964). Reprinted with permission of the author.

that leadership effectiveness is determined by the degree of fit between the leader and the situation. Recent research has shown that relationship-oriented leaders encourage team learning and innovativeness, which helps products get to market faster. This means that most relationship-oriented leaders perform well in leading new product development teams. In short, the right team leader can help get creative new products out the door faster, while a mismatch between the leader and the situation can have the opposite effect.[18]

What, then, is to be done if there is a misfit? That is, what happens when a low LPC leader is in a moderately favorable situation or when a high LPC leader is in a highly favorable or highly unfavorable situation? It is unlikely that the leader can be changed, according to the theory, because the leader's need structure is an enduring trait that is hard to change. Fiedler recommends that the leader's situation be changed to fit the leader's style.[19] A moderately favorable situation would be reengineered to be more favorable and therefore more suitable for the low LPC leader. A highly favorable or highly unfavorable situation would be changed to one that is moderately favorable and more suitable for the high LPC leader.

Fiedler's theory makes an important contribution in drawing our attention to the leader's situation.

Path–Goal Theory

6. Distinguish among the path–goal theory, the Vroom-Yetton-Jago theory, and the Situational Leadership® model.

Robert House developed a path–goal theory of leader effectiveness based on an expectancy theory of motivation.[20] From the perspective of path–goal theory, the basic role of the leader is to clear the follower's path to the goal. The leader uses the most appropriate of four leader behavior styles to help followers clarify the paths that lead them to work and personal goals. The key concepts in the theory are shown in Figure 12.3.

A leader selects from the four leader behavior styles, shown in Figure 12.3, the one that is most helpful to followers at a given time. The directive style is used when the leader must give specific guidance about work tasks, schedule work, and let followers know what is expected. The supportive style is used when the leader needs to express concern for followers' well-being and social status. The participative style is used when the leader must engage in joint decision-making activities with followers. The achievement-oriented style is used

FIGURE 12.3   The Path–Goal Theory of Leadership

12.3

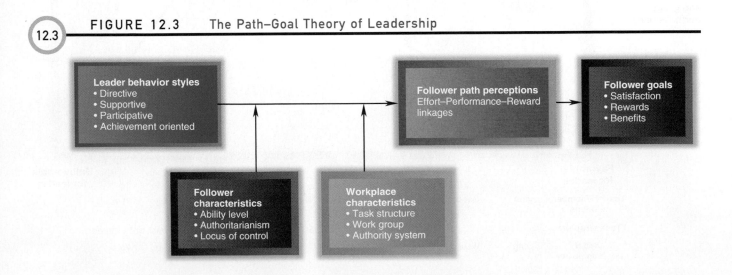

when the leader must set challenging goals for followers and show strong confidence in those followers.

In selecting the appropriate leader behavior style, the leader must consider both the followers and the work environment. A few characteristics are included in Figure 12.3. Let us look at two examples. In Example 1, the followers are inexperienced and working on an ambiguous, unstructured task. The leader in this situation might best use a directive style. In Example 2, the followers are highly trained professionals, and the task is a difficult, yet achievable one. The leader in this situation might best use an achievement-oriented style. The leader always chooses the leader behavior style that helps followers achieve their goals.

The path–goal theory assumes that leaders adapt their behavior and style to fit the characteristics of the followers and the environment in which they work. Actual tests of the path–goal theory and its propositions provide conflicting evidence.[21] The path–goal theory does have intuitive appeal and reinforces the idea that the appropriate leadership style depends on both the work situation and the followers. Research is focusing on which style works best in specific situations. For example, in small organizations, leaders who used visionary, transactional, and empowering behaviors, while avoiding autocratic behaviors, were most successful.[22]

Vroom-Yetton-Jago Normative Decision Model

The Vroom-Yetton-Jago normative decision model helps leaders and managers know when to have employees participate in the decision-making process. Victor Vroom, Phillip Yetton, and Arthur Jago developed and refined the normative decision model, which helps managers determine the appropriate decision-making strategy to use. The model recognizes the benefits of authoritative, democratic, and consultive styles of leader behavior.[23] Five forms of decision making are described in the model:

> *Decide.* The manager makes the decision alone and either announces it or "sells" it to the group.

> *Consult individually.* The manager presents the problem to the group members individually, gets their input, and then makes the decision.

> *Consult group.* The manager presents the problem to the group members in a meeting, gets their inputs, and then makes the decision.

> *Facilitate.* The manager presents the problem to the group in a meeting and acts as a facilitator, defining the problem and the boundaries that surround the decision. The manager's ideas are not given more weight than any other group member's ideas. The objective is to get concurrence.

> *Delegate.* The manager permits the group to make the decision within the prescribed limits, providing needed resources and encouragement.[24]

The key to the normative decision model is that a manager should use the decision method most appropriate for a given decision situation. The manager arrives at the proper method by working through matrices like the one in Figure 12.4. The factors across the top of the model (decision significance, commitment, leader expertise, etc.) are the situational factors in the normative decision model. This matrix is for decisions that must be made under time pressure, but other matrices are also available. For example, there is a different matrix managers can use when their objective is to develop subordinates' decision-making skills. Vroom

TIME-DRIVEN MODEL

Instructions: The matrix operates like a funnel. You start at the left with a specific decision problem in mind. The column headings denote situational factors which may or may not be present in that problem. You progress by selecting High or Low (H or L) for each relevant situational factor. Proceed down from the funnel, judging only those situational factors for which a judgment is called for, until you reach the recommended process.

Problem Statement	Decision Significance	Importance of Commitment	Leader Expertise	Likelihood of Commitment	Group Support	Group Expertise	Team Competence	Recommended Process
P R O B L E M S T A T E M E N T	H	H	H	H	–	–	–	Decide
				L	H	H	H	Delegate
							L	Consult (Group)
						L	–	Consult (Group)
					L	–	–	Consult (Group)
			L		H	H	H	Facilitate
							L	Consult (Individually)
						L	–	Consult (Individually)
					L	H	H	Facilitate
							L	Consult (Group)
						L	–	Consult (Group)
		L	H	–	–	–	–	Decide
			L	–	H	H	H	Facilitate
							L	Consult (Individually)
						L	–	Consult (Individually)
					L	–	–	Consult (Individually)
	L	H	–	H	–	–	–	Decide
				L	–	–	H	Delegate
							L	Facilitate
		L	–	–	–	–	–	Decide

SOURCE: Reprinted from *Organizational Dynamics*, 28, by V. H. Vroom, "Leadership and the Decision-Making Process," 82–94 (Spring 2000) with permission from Elsevier.

has also developed a Windows-based computer program called Expert System that can be used by managers to determine which style to use.

Although the model offers very explicit predictions as well as prescriptions for leaders, its utility is limited to the leader decision-making tasks.

One unique study applied the normative decision model of leadership to the battlefield behavior of ten commanding generals in six major battles of the American Civil War. When the commanders acted consistently with the prescriptions of the Vroom-Yetton-Jago model, they were more successful in accomplishing their military goals. The findings also suggested that a lack of information sharing and consensus building resulted in serious disadvantages.[25]

The Situational Leadership® Model

The Situational Leadership® model, developed by Paul Hersey and Kenneth Blanchard, suggests that the leader's behavior should be adjusted to the maturity level of the followers.[26] The model employs two dimensions of leader behavior as used in the Ohio State studies; one dimension is task oriented, and the other is relationship oriented. Follower maturity is categorized into four levels, as shown in Figure 12.5. Follower readiness is determined by the follower's ability and willingness to complete a specific task. Readiness can therefore be low or high depending on the particular task. In addition, readiness varies within a single person according to the task. One person may be willing and able to satisfy simple requests from customers (high readiness) but less able or willing to give highly technical advice to customers (low readiness). It is important that the leader be able to evaluate the readiness level of each follower for each task. The four styles of leader behavior associated with the four readiness levels are depicted in the figure as well.

According to the Situational Leadership® model, a leader should use a telling style (S1) when a follower is unable and unwilling to do a certain task. This style involves providing instructions and closely monitoring performance. As such, the telling style involves considerable task behavior and low relationship behavior. When a follower is unable but willing and confident to do a task, the leader can use the selling style (S2) in which there is high task behavior and high relationship behavior. In this case, the leader explains decisions and provides opportunities for the employee to seek clarification or help. Sometimes a follower will be able to complete a task but may seem unwilling or insecure about doing so. In these cases, a participating style (S3) is warranted, which involves high relationship but low task behavior. The leader in this case encourages the follower to participate in decision making. Finally, for tasks in which a follower is able and willing, the leader is able to use a delegating style (S4), characterized by low task behavior and low relationship behavior. In this case, follower readiness is high, and low levels of leader involvement (task or relationship) are needed.

One key limitation of the Situational Leadership® model is the absence of central hypotheses that could be tested, which would make it a more valid, reliable theory of leadership.[27] However, the theory has intuitive appeal and is widely used for training and development in corporations. In addition, the theory focuses attention on follower maturity as an important determinant of the leadership process.

Recent Developments in Leadership Theory

Leadership is an exciting area of organizational behavior, one in which new research is constantly emerging. Four new developments are important to understand. These are leader–member exchange, substitutes for leadership, transformational leadership, and charismatic leadership.

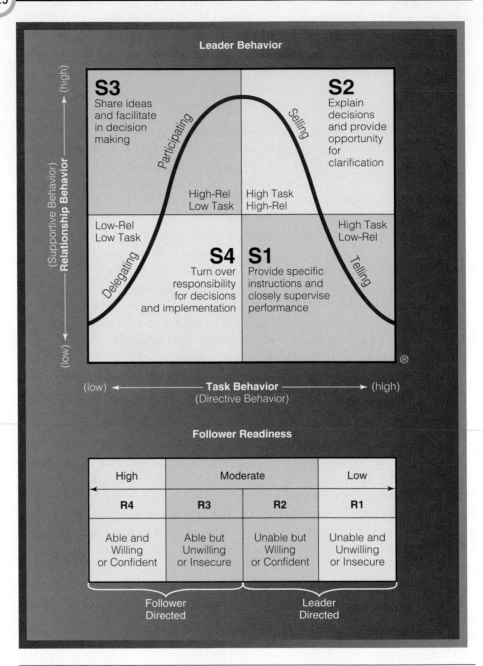

SOURCE: P. Hersey, K. H. Blanchard, and D. E. Johnson, *Management of Organizational Behavior: Leading Human Resources*, 8th ed. (Upper Saddle River, N.J.: Pearson Education, Inc., 2001), 182. Copyright © 2001, Center for Leadership Studies, Escondido, CA. Used with permission.

Leader–Member Exchange

Leader–member exchange theory, or LMX, recognizes that leaders may form different relationships with followers. The basic idea behind LMX is that leaders form two groups, in-groups and out-groups, of followers. In-group members tend to be similar to the leader and given greater responsibilities, more rewards, and more attention. They work within the leader's inner circle of communication. As a result, in-group members are more satisfied, have lower turnover, and have higher organizational commitment. In contrast, out-group members are outside the circle and receive less attention and fewer rewards. They are managed by formal rules and policies.[28]

Research on LMX is supportive. In-group members are more likely to engage in organizational citizenship behavior, while out-group members are more likely to retaliate against the organization.[29] And, the type of stress varies by the group to which a subordinate belongs. In-group members' stress comes from the additional responsibilities placed on them by the leader, whereas out-group members' stress comes from being left out of the communication network.[30] One surprising finding is that more frequent communication with the boss may either help or hurt a worker's performance ratings, depending on whether the worker is in the in-group or the out-group. Among the in-group, more frequent communication generally leads to higher performance ratings, while members of the out-group who communicate more often with the superior tend to receive lower performance ratings. Perhaps the out-group members get to talk to the boss only when something has gone wrong![31]

Employees who enjoy more frequent contact with the boss also have a better understanding of what the boss's expectations are. Such agreement tends to lead to better performance by the employee and fewer misunderstandings between employer and employee.[32]

In-group members are also more likely to support the values of the organization and to become models of appropriate behavior. If the leader, for example, wants to promote safety at work, in-group members model safe work practices, which leads to a climate of workplace safety.[33]

Substitutes for Leadership

Sometimes situations can neutralize or even replace leader behavior. This is the central idea behind the substitutes for leadership theory.[34] When a task is very satisfying and employees get feedback about performance, leader behavior is irrelevant, because the employee's satisfaction comes from the interesting work and the feedback. Other things that can substitute for leadership include high skill on the part of the employee, team cohesiveness, and formal controls on the part of the organization. Research on this idea is generally supportive, and other factors that act as substitutes are being identified.[35] Even a firm's customers can be a substitute for leadership. In service settings, employees with lots of customer contact actually receive significant leadership and direction from customer demands, allowing the firm to provide less formal supervision to these employees than to workers with little customer contact. This finding adds new weight to the old adage about the customer being boss.[36]

Transformational Leadership

Transformational leaders inspire and excite followers to high levels of performance.[37] They rely on their personal attributes instead of their official position to manage followers. In contrast, transactional leaders use rewards and punishments to make deals with subordinates. There is some evidence that transformational leadership can be learned.[38] As U.S. corporations increasingly operate in a global economy, there is a greater demand for leaders who can practice transformational leadership by converting their visions into reality[39] and by inspiring followers to perform "above and beyond the call of duty."[40] Howard Schultz, founder and chairman of Starbucks Coffee, is the transformational leader and visionary heart of Starbucks. He has grown his firm from a small specialty coffee bar into one of the best-known brands in the world.

7. Distinguish among transformational, transactional, and charismatic leaders.

With the firm hoping to continue its rapid growth pace of 25–30 percent per year, Schultz's ability to develop new leaders within the firm (which helped Starbucks get where it is today) will be sorely tested. But given the enormous market for coffee worldwide (Starbucks currently has less than 10 percent of the market), the potential for further growth exists if the company can develop the people to tap it.[41]

Leaders can be both transformational and transactional.[42] Transformational leadership adds to the effects of transactional leadership, but exceptional transactional leadership cannot substitute for transformational leadership.[43] One reason that transformational leadership is effective is that transformational leaders encourage followers to set goals congruent with the followers' own authentic interests and values. Because of this, followers see their work as important and their goals as aligned with who they are.[44]

There is some evidence that transformational leadership may work in military organizations. One study showed that military leaders who practiced transformational leadership produced both greater development and better performance among their subordinates than leaders who used other leadership styles.[45]

Charismatic Leadership

Steve Jobs, the pioneer behind the Macintosh computer and the growing music download market, has an uncanny ability to create a vision and convince others to become part of it. This was evidenced by Apple's continual overall success despite its major blunders in the desktop computer wars. Jobs' unique ability is so powerful that Apple employees coined a term in the 1980s for it, the *reality-distortion field*. This expression is used to describe the persuasive ability and peculiar charisma of managers like Steve Jobs. This reality-distortion field allows Jobs to convince even skeptics that his plans are worth supporting, no matter how unworkable they may appear. Those close to these managers become passionately committed to possibly insane projects, without regard to the practicality of their implementation or competitive forces in the marketplace.[46]

charismatic leadership

A leader's use of personal abilities and talents in order to have profound and extraordinary effects on followers.

Charismatic leadership results when a leader uses the force of personal abilities and talents to have profound and extraordinary effects on followers.[47] Some scholars see transformational leadership and charismatic leadership as very similar, but others believe they are different. *Charisma* is a Greek word meaning "gift"; the charismatic leader's unique and powerful gifts are the source of the leader's great influence with followers.[48] In fact, followers often view the charismatic leader as one who possesses superhuman, or even mystical, qualities.[49] Charismatic leaders rely heavily on referent power, discussed in Chapter 11, and charismatic leadership is especially effective in times of uncertainty.[50] Charismatic leadership falls to those who are chosen (are born with the "gift" of charisma) or who cultivate that gift. Some say charismatic leaders are born, and others say they are taught.

Some charismatic leaders rely on humor as a tool for communication. In the Science feature, research shows the positive effects of humor in the workplace.

Charismatic leadership carries with it not only great potential for high levels of achievement and performance on the part of followers but also shadowy risks of destructive courses of action that might harm followers or other people. Several researchers have attempted to demystify charismatic leadership and distinguish its two faces.[51] The ugly face of charisma is revealed in the personalized power motivations of Adolf Hitler in Nazi Germany and David Koresh of the Branch Davidian cult in Waco, Texas. Both men led their followers into

Does Clowning Around Pay Off? A Look at Leadership and Humor

The old adage "Laughter is the best medicine" applies in the workplace as it does elsewhere.

Do class clowns actually get the last laugh? Maybe so. A recent study compared the use of humor by several executives in a large food and beverage company. Executives who had previously been evaluated as "outstanding" performers used humor more than twice as often as executives who had been rated merely as "average" (17.8 times per hour versus only 7.5 times per hour). Whether laughter makes for better leadership or whether successful leadership makes one happier is unclear, but one thing is certain: laughter seems to be part of the formula for successful business leaders [including Sir Richard Branson, who includes "play" as one of the five principles that have helped him succeed (see the Looking Back feature of this chapter)]. Humor can reduce hostility at work, deflect criticism, relieve tension, and improve morale. When used skillfully, humor can be one of a leader's best tools.

SOURCE: F. Sala, "Laughing All the Way to the Bank," *Harvard Business Review* 81 (September 2003): 16–17.

struggle, conflict, and death. The brighter face of charisma is revealed in the socialized power motivations of U.S. President Franklin D. Roosevelt. Former presidents Bill Clinton and Ronald Reagan, while worlds apart in terms of their political beliefs, were actually quite similar in their use of personal charisma to inspire followers and motivate them to pursue the leader's vision. In each case, followers perceived the leader as imbued with a unique vision for America and unique abilities to lead the country there.

Despite the warm emotions charismatic leaders can evoke, some charismatic leaders are narcissists who listen only to those who agree with them and do not need advice from those who disagree.[52] Whereas charismatic leaders with socialized power motivation are concerned about the collective well-being of their followers, charismatic leaders with a personalized power motivation are driven by the need for personal gain and glorification.[53]

Charismatic leadership styles are associated with several positive outcomes. One study reported that firms headed by more charismatic leaders outperformed other firms, particularly in difficult economic times. Perhaps even more important, charismatic leaders were able to raise more outside financial support for their firms than noncharismatic leaders, meaning that charisma at the top may translate to greater funding at the bottom.[54]

Emerging Issues in Leadership

Along with the recent developments in theory, some exciting issues have emerged of which leaders must be aware. These include emotional intelligence, trust, women leaders, and servant leadership.

Emotional Intelligence

It has been suggested that effective leaders possess emotional intelligence, which is the ability to recognize and manage emotion in oneself and in others. In fact, some researchers argue that emotional intelligence is more important for effective leadership than either IQ or technical skills.[55] Emotional intelligence is made up of several competencies, including self-awareness, empathy, adaptability, and self-confidence. While most people gain emotional intelligence as they age, not everyone starts with an equal amount. Fortunately, emotional intelligence can be learned. With honest feedback from coworkers and ongoing guidance, almost any leader can improve emotional intelligence, and with it, the ability to lead in times of adversity.[56]

Emotional intelligence affects the way leaders make decisions. Under high stress, leaders with higher emotional intelligence tend to keep their cool and make better decisions, while leaders with low emotional intelligence make poor decisions and lose their effectivness.[57]

Joe Torre, manager of the New York Yankees, gets the most out of his team, makes his boss happy, and delivers wins. He is a model of emotional intelligence: compassionate, calm under stress, and a great motivator. He advocates "managing against the cycle," which means staying calm when situations are tough, but turning up the heat on players when things are going well.[58]

Trust

Trust is an essential element in leadership. Trust is the willingness to be vulnerable to the actions of another.[59] This means that followers believe that their leader will act with the followers' welfare in mind. Trustworthiness is also one of the competencies in emotional intelligence. Trust among top management team members facilitates strategy implementation; that means that if team members trust each other, they have a better chance of getting "buy-in" from employees on the direction of the company.[60] And if employees trust their leaders, they will buy in more readily.

How would you go about leading a team of people in different organizations, in different geographic locations around the world, who had never met? They would not have shared understandings of problems, norms, work distribution, roles, or responsibilities. This is a challenge that is becoming more common, and one that Boeing-Rocketdyne faced. What Boeing-Rocketdyne learned is that the leader of such teams needs to be the "spoke in the center of the wheel" in terms of coordination. The leader also needs to help the team create a common language and document results for the entire team.[61] Not surprisingly, Boeing's largest rival—Airbus Industries of Europe—has developed its own virtual teams. Called Elab, this network helps Airbus coordinate work by aerospace firms all over Europe, including British Aerospace, Rolls Royce, and Snecma. Using complex communications tools, including high-quality video, Elab allows these member firms to create complete working environments for groups of engineers scattered throughout the continent.[62] Leading virtual teams requires trust, because face-to-face interaction that is the hallmark of leadership is not possible. Leaders must not only come to trust their subordinates, but they must also express that trust. Research has shown that workers who believe their boss trusts them (called "felt trustworthiness") enjoy their work more, are more productive, and are more likely to "go the extra mile" at work and perform organizational citizenship behaviors.[63]

Effective leaders also understand both *who* to trust and *how* to trust. At one extreme, leaders often trust a close circle of advisors, listening only to them and gradually cutting themselves off from dissenting opinions. At the opposite extreme, lone-wolf leaders may trust nobody, leading to preventable mistakes. Wise leaders carefully evaluate both the competence and the position of those they trust, seeking out a variety of opinions and input.[64]

Women Leaders

An important, emergent leadership question is this: Do women and men lead differently? Historical stereotypes persist, and people characterize successful managers as having more male-oriented attributes than female-oriented attributes.[65] Although legitimate gender differences may exist, the same leadership traits may be interpreted differently in a man and a woman because of stereotypes. The real issue should be leader behaviors that are not bound by gender stereotypes.

Early evidence shows that women tend to use a more people-oriented style that is inclusive and empowering. Women managers excel in positions that demand strong interpersonal skills.[66] More and more women are assuming positions of leadership in organizations. Donna Dubinsky, founder and CEO of palmOne, cofounded Palm and Handspring, and is known as the mother of the handheld computer. She wants to change the world such that PDAs outsell PCs. Interestingly, much of what we know about leadership is based on studies that were conducted on men. We need to know more about the ways women lead.

Servant Leadership

Robert Greenleaf was director of management research at AT&T for many years. He believed that leaders should serve employees, customers, and the community, and his essays are the basis for today's view called servant leadership. His personal and professional philosophy was that leaders lead by serving others. Other tenets of servant leadership are that work exists for the person as much as the person exists for work, and that servant leaders try to find out the will of the group and lead based on that. Servant leaders are also stewards who consider leadership a trust and desire to leave the organization in better shape for future generations.[67] Although Greenleaf's writings were completed thirty years ago, many have now been published and are becoming more popular. Interestingly, one particular teacher who claims to be motivated by selfish reasons may end up benefiting many people who need help. Read his story in The Real World 12.1.

Followership

In contrast to leadership, the topic of followership has not been extensively researched. Much of the leadership literature suggests that leader and follower roles are highly differentiated. The traditional view casts followers as passive, whereas a more contemporary view casts the follower role as an active one with potential for leadership.[68] The follower role has alternatively been cast as one of self-leadership in which the follower assumes responsibility for influencing his or her own performance.[69] This approach emphasizes the follower's individual responsibility and self-control. Self-led followers perform naturally motivating tasks and do work that must be done but that is not naturally motivating. Self-leadership enables followers to be disciplined and effective, essential first steps if one is to become a leader. Organizational programs such as empowerment and self-managed work teams may be used to further activate the follower role.[70]

Types of Followers

Contemporary work environments are ones in which followers recognize their interdependence with leaders and learn to challenge them while at the same time respecting the leaders' authority.[71] Effective followers are active, responsible,

8. Discuss the characteristics of effective and dynamic followers.

A Selfish Leader Among the Selfless? The Boston Cure Project

When *Fortune* named its ten greatest CEOs of all time, two men stood out for their benevolent, selfless perspectives: David Packard (of Hewlett-Packard) and George Merck (of Merck pharmaceuticals). These two men, founders of the firms that still bear their names, stated clearly and repeatedly that business was about more than personal gain. Packard, early in his career, told a group of business leaders that companies have a responsibility to their employees, while Merck, appearing on the cover of *Time* magazine in 1952, declared that medicine existed to help people, not to earn profits. In both cases, these founding values guided their respective firms for decades, gaining these men both financial success and tremendous respect.

But today, not all entrepreneurs are guided by such selfless motives. Art Mellor, a successful entrepreneur who cofounded three companies, was told in 2000 that he had multiple sclerosis (MS), an incurable, degenerative diease. Today, he is the executive director of Boston Cure Project, a not-for-profit organization whose sole purpose is to find a cure for MS. And while some might applaud this humanitarian turn from a wealthy businessman, Mellor makes it clear that he is motivated solely by his own desire to be cured of MS. Ironically, he chose the nonprofit route to avoid accountability to any outside shareholder group. He has even suggested that if his company does find a cure for his disease, he might abandon the organization entirely. While positive results will undoubtedly emerge from Mellor's efforts, his motivation stands in stark contrast to Packard, Merck, and others who focused on more than their own interests. Interestingly, his seemingly selfish motives may end up helping countless individuals with MS.

SOURCES: J Collins, "The 10 Greatest CEOs of All Time," *Fortune* (July 21, 2003): 54–69, http://www.fortune.com/fortune/ceo/articles/0,15114,462692,00.html; D. Whitford, "The Nonprofit Motive," *Fortune* (October 13, 2003): 2143a–2143d, http://www.fortune.com/fortune/smallbusiness/articles/0,15114,489758,00.html.

and autonomous in their behavior and critical in their thinking without being insubordinate or disrespectful. Effective followers and four other types of followers are identified based on two dimensions: (1) activity versus passivity and (2) independent, critical thinking versus dependent, uncritical thinking.[72] Figure 12.6 shows these follower types.

Alienated followers think independently and critically, yet are very passive in their behavior. As a result, they become psychologically and emotionally distanced from their leaders. Alienated followers are potentially disruptive and a threat to the health of the organization. Sheep are followers who do not think independently or critically and are passive in their behavior. They simply do as they are told by their leaders. Yes people are followers who also do not think independently or critically, yet are very active in their behavior. They uncritically reinforce the thinking and ideas of their leaders with enthusiasm, never questioning or challenging the wisdom of the leaders' ideas and proposals. Yes people are the most dangerous to a leader because they are the most likely to give a false positive reaction and give no warning of potential pitfalls. Survivors are the least disruptive and the lowest risk followers in an organization. They perpetually sample the wind, and their motto is "better safe than sorry."

Effective followers are the most valuable to a leader and an organization because of their active contributions. Effective followers share four essential qualities. First, they practice self-management and self-responsibility. A leader can delegate to an effective follower without anxiety about the outcome. Second, they are committed to both the organization and a purpose, principle, or person outside themselves. Effective followers are not self-centered or self-aggrandizing. Third, effective followers invest in their own competence and pro-

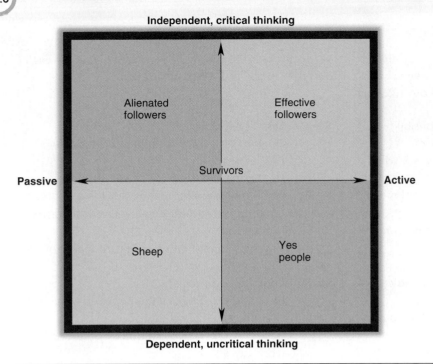

fessionalism and focus their energy for maximum impact. Effective followers look for challenges and ways in which to add to their talents or abilities. Fourth, they are courageous, honest, and credible. You 12.2 gives you an opportunity to consider your effectiveness as a follower.

Effective followers might be thought of as self-leaders who do not require close supervision.[73] The notion of self-leadership, or superleadership, blurs the distinction between leaders and followers. Caring leaders are able to develop dynamic followers.

The Dynamic Follower

The traditional stereotype of the follower or employee is of someone in a powerless, dependent role rather than in a potent, active, significant role. The latter, in which the follower is dynamic, is a more contemporary, healthy role.[74] The *dynamic follower* is a responsible steward of his or her job, is effective in managing the relationship with the boss, and practices responsible self-management.

The dynamic follower becomes a trusted adviser to the boss by keeping the supervisor well informed and building trust and dependability into the relationship. He or she is open to constructive criticism and solicits performance feedback. The dynamic follower shares needs and is responsible.

It takes time and patience to nurture a good relationship between a follower and a supervisor. Once this relationship has been developed, it is a valuable resource for both. In The Real World 12.2, you will see that Denny's has gone from diversity trouble to becoming one of the world's best companies for minorities. Ray Hood-Phillips, who is both an effective leader and a dynamic follower, gets credit for Denny's dramatic transformation.

dynamic follower

A follower who is a responsible steward of his or her job, is effective in managing the relationship with the boss, and practices self-management.

Are You an Effective Follower?

To determine whether you are an effective follower, read the text section on "Types of Followers," look back at your self-reliance results on You 7.2, and work through the following four steps. Answer each question in the four steps yes or no.

Step 1. Self-Management and Self-Responsibility

_____ Do you take the initiative at work?

_____ Do you challenge the system at work when appropriate?

_____ Do you ask questions when you need more information?

_____ Do you successfully bring your projects to completion?

Step 2. Commitment beyond Yourself

_____ Are you committed to your boss's and company's success?

_____ Is there a higher purpose in life that you value deeply?

_____ Is there a principle(s) that you will not compromise?

_____ Is there a person at work or elsewhere you admire greatly?

Step 3. Self-Development

_____ Do you attend a professional development class annually?

_____ Do you have a program of self-study or structured learning?

_____ Do you take at least one class each semester in the year?

_____ Have you identified new skills to learn for your job?

Step 4. Courage and Honesty

_____ Have you disagreed with your boss twice this year?

_____ Have you taken two unpopular positions at work this year?

_____ Have you given critical feedback to someone, kindly?

_____ Have you taken one risk at work to do a better job?

Scoring:

Count the number of "yes" answers in Steps 1 through 4: _____

If you have 10 to 16 "yes" answers, this would suggest that you are an effective follower. If you have 7 or fewer "yes" answers, this may suggest that you fall into one of the other four categories of followers.

People who are self-reliant may also be effective followers, and effective followers may also be self-reliant. If you are an effective follower, were you also self-reliant in You 7.2? If you were not self-reliant in You 7.2, did you fall into a category other than the effective follower category?

SOURCE: Reprinted by permission of *Harvard Business Review*. From "In Praise of Followers" by R. E. Kelley, (November–December 1988). Copyright © 1988 by Harvard Business School Publishing Corporation; all rights reserved.

Cultural Differences in Leadership

The situational approaches to leadership would lead to the conclusion that a leader must factor in culture as an important situational variable when exercising influence and authority. Thus, global leaders should expect to be flexible enough to alter their approaches when crossing national boundaries and working with people from foreign cultures.[75]

We are beginning to learn more about how perspectives on effective leadership vary across cultures. You might assume that most Europeans view leadership in the same way. Research tells us instead that there are many differences among European countries. In Nordic countries like Finland, leaders who are direct and close to subordinates are viewed positively, while in Turkey, Poland, and Russia this is not the case. And leaders who give subordinates autonomy are viewed more positively in Germany and Austria than in the Czech Repub-

THE REAL WORLD 12.2

Ray Hood-Phillips: A Leader and Dynamic Follower

© Advantica Restaurant Group

Ray Hood-Phillips, embracing diversity with open arms at Denny's.

Ten years ago, a lot of people were talking about Denny's and race, as Denny's name became almost synonymous with racial tension. Today, people are still talking about Denny's and race, but in a different way. *Fortune* recently named Denny's one of the Best Companies for Minorities. What brought about the change?

Somebody had to lead the change. Denny's CEO, Jim Adamson, believed that he had to find someone with a passion for diversity and the fire to make it happen. He knew that Ray Hood-Phillips had led Burger King toward an inclusive workplace, so he called her and asked for help. She agreed to consult for two or three days a week, getting up at 3:00 A.M. to commute from her home in Miami to Denny's headquarters in Spartanburg. After a few months of working eighteen-hour days, Hood-Phillips agreed to join Denny's.

Hood-Phillips's passion is diversity and inclusion. She led big changes at Denny's but was also a dynamic follower who didn't hesitate to challenge the boss (Adamson). Speaking to a group of executives, Adamson remarked, "You know, we need to be color-blind; we can't see color." Once they were out the door, Hood-Phillips pulled the CEO aside and took him to the woodshed. She told him that all humans have differences and that people from different racial and ethnic backgrounds also have different cultural and social references—people shouldn't be expected to think or act in the same ways. Adamson listened and credits Hood-Phillips with helping him see that Denny's could not pretend that everyone in the United States is the same. This distinction made all the difference.

Hood-Phillips has helped Denny's get diversity right. She monitors diversity progress in every area of Denny's operations, including purchasing contracts, management positions, training and education, philanthropy, performance evaluations, and trade partnerships with minority groups. She has led the diversity charge at Denny's and is not afraid to be a dynamic follower in terms of challenging authority.

SOURCES: Fortune Magazine, "50 Best Companies for Minorities 2003," *Fortune* (July 7, 2003): 103, http://www.fortune.com/fortune/diversity/subs/fulllist/2003/0,17538,,00.html; J. Adamson, *The Denny's Story: How a Company in Crisis Resurrected Its Good Name and Reputation* (John Wiley & Sons, Inc., 2000).

lic and Portugal.[76] There are even differences between the American view of transformational leadership and that found in the United Kingdom. The U.K. approach to transformational leadership is much closer to what we in the United States refer to as servant leadership. It involves more connectedness between leaders and followers and more vulnerability on the part of the leader.[77]

To be effective, leaders must understand other cultures. U.S. executives often perceive specific global regions as being made up of relatively homogenous individuals. For example, some U.S. leaders think that most of Latin America is populated with people of similar values and beliefs. But a recent study of more than 1,000 small business owners in the region demonstrated that despite similarities, these business leaders are quite diverse in terms of their individual goals. Mexican and Brazilian leaders had values that were very different from leaders in other countries in the region. This means that we cannot stereotype people from Latin America as being totally similar.[78]

Whereas most American workers follow traditional Protestant work values, workers from other countries base their work values on very different sets of beliefs, drawing in some cases from multiple philosophies. China, for instance, draws from not one but three perspectives, as Buddhism, Taoism, and Confucianism harmonize to create work values such as trust, hierarchy, loyalty, and networks.[79]

Guidelines for Leadership

Leadership is a key to influencing organizational behavior and achieving organizational effectiveness. When artifacts are eliminated, studies of leadership succession show a moderately strong leader influence on organizational performance.[80] With this said, it is important to recognize that other factors also influence organizational performance. These include environmental factors (such as general economic conditions) and technological factors (such as efficiency).

Corporate leaders play a central role in setting the ethical tone and moral values for their organizations. While many corporate leaders talk about ethics, many never have to actually risk the firm's fortune on an ethical decision. In 1976, when James Burke, head of Johnson & Johnson, challenged his management team to reaffirm the company's historic commitment to ethical behavior, he had no idea he would be asked to demonstrate that commitment in action. But six years later, when poisoned packages of Tylenol appeared on store shelves, Burke did not hesitate to act on what he had pledged. The company pulled the product from the shelves at a cost of $100 million. It also offered a reward and revamped the product's packaging. In the end, Tylenol recovered and is once again the leading pain medication in the United States. Jim Burke was recently recognized by *Fortune* as one of the ten greatest CEOs of all time, and Johnson & Johnson continues to be rated one of the best companies for which to work.[81]

Five useful guidelines appear to emerge from the extensive leadership research of the past sixty years:

> First, leaders and organizations should appreciate the unique attributes, predispositions, and talents of each leader. No two leaders are the same, and there is value in this diversity.

> Second, although there appears to be no single best style of leadership, there are organizational preferences in terms of style. Leaders should be chosen who challenge the organizational culture, when necessary, without destroying it.

> Third, participative, considerate leader behaviors that demonstrate a concern for people appear to enhance the health and well-being of followers in the work environment. This does not imply, however, that a leader must ignore the team's work tasks.

> Fourth, different leadership situations call for different leadership talents and behaviors. This may result in different individuals taking the leader role, depending on the specific situation in which the team finds itself.

> Fifth, good leaders are likely to be good followers. Although there are distinctions between their social roles, the attributes and behaviors of leaders and followers may not be as distinct as is sometimes thought.

LOOKING BACK: VIRGIN GROUP LTD.

Leadership Advice from Richard Branson

Even an unconventional leader like Sir Richard Branson is sometimes asked to break it all down to a few rules. Here are the basic principles he practices and preaches:

1. *Follow your passions*. Love to fly? Start an airline. Hire drop-dead-gorgeous flight attendants and an onboard masseuse. Enter a hot-air balloon race. It'll get you some ink, and it's fun.

2. *Keep it simple*. Running your life out of a black book and a gym bag means you know where everything is. It also means you stay focused on what's important.

3. *Get the best people to help you*. If you don't like math, hire some bean counters. If you're an optimist, hire some realists. Make sure you do enough outrageous stuff that their lives never get boring. Treat them to nice vacations.

4. *Recreate yourself*. Kids buying less music from your stores? Start a cell phone business. Variety wards off boredom—and it could save your hide.

5. *Play*. Play practical jokes on your CEOs. Play tennis with your kids. Wear your bathing suit all day long.[82]

Chapter Summary

1. Leadership is the process of guiding and directing the behavior of followers in organizations. Followership is the process of being guided and directed by a leader. Leaders and followers are companions in these processes.

2. A leader creates meaningful change in organizations, whereas a manager controls complexity. Charismatic leaders have a profound impact on their followers.

3. Autocratic leaders create high pressure for followers, whereas democratic leaders create healthier environments for followers.

4. The five styles in the Leadership Grid are manager, authority-obedience manager, country club manager, team manager, and impoverished manager.

5. According to Fiedler's contingency theory, task-oriented leaders are most effective in highly favorable or highly unfavorable leadership situations, and relationship-oriented leaders are most effective in moderately favorable leadership situations.

6. The path–goal theory, Vroom-Yetton-Jago theory, and Situational Leadership® model say that a leader should adjust his or her behavior to the situation and should appreciate diversity among followers.

7. There are many developments in leadership. Emerging issues include emotional intelligence, trust, women leaders, and servant leadership.

8. Effective, dynamic followers are competent and active in their work, assertive, independent thinkers, sensitive to their bosses' needs and demands, and responsible self-managers. Caring leadership and dynamic followership go together.

Key Terms

authority-compliance manager (9,1) (p. 391)

autocratic style (p. 390)

charismatic leadership (p. 402)

consideration (p. 390)

country club manager (1,9) (p. 391)

democratic style (p. 390)

dynamic follower (p. 407)

followership (p. 388)

formal leadership (p. 388)

impoverished manager (1,1) (p. 392)

informal leadership (p. 388)

initiating structure (p. 390)

laissez-faire style (p. 390)

leader (p. 388)

leader–member relations (p. 395)

leadership (p. 388)

Leadership Grid (p. 391)

least preferred coworker (LPC) (p. 394)

manager (p. 388)

opportunistic "what's in it for me" manager (Opp) (p. 393)

organization man manager (5,5) (p. 391)

paternalistic "father knows best" manager (9+9) (p. 392)

position power (p. 394)

task structure (p. 394)

team manager (9,9) (p. 391)

Review Questions

1. Define *leadership* and *followership*. Distinguish between formal leadership and informal leadership.

2. Discuss transformational and charismatic leadership. Would you expect these styles of leadership to exist in all cultures? Differ across cultures?

3. Describe the differences between autocratic and democratic work environments. How do they differ from a laissez-faire workplace?

4. Define *initiating structure* and *consideration* as leader behaviors.

5. Describe the middle-of-the-road manager, authority-compliance manager, country club manager, team manager, and impoverished manager.

6. How does the LPC scale measure leadership style? What are the three dimensions of the leader's situation?

7. Describe the alternative decision strategies used by a leader in the Vroom-Yetton-Jago normative decision theory.

8. Compare House's path–goal theory of leadership with the Situational Leadership® model.

9. Describe alienated followers, sheep, yes people, survivors, and effective followers.

Discussion and Communication Questions

1. Do you (or would you want to) work in an autocratic, democratic, or laissez-faire work environment? What might be the advantages of each work environment? The disadvantages?

2. Is your supervisor or professor someone who is high in concern for production? High in concern for people? What is his or her Leadership Grid style?

3. What decision strategies does your supervisor use to make decisions? Are they consistent or inconsistent with the Vroom-Yetton-Jago model?

4. Discuss the similarities and differences between effective leadership and dynamic followership. Are you dynamic?

5. Describe the relationship you have with your supervisor or professor. What is the best part of the relationship? The worst part? What could you do to make the relationship better?

6. *(communication question)* Who is the leader you admire the most? Write a description of this person's characteristics and attributes that you admire. Note any aspects of this leader's behavior that you find less than wholly admirable.

7. *(communication question)* Refresh yourself on the distinction between leaders (also called transformational leaders) and managers (also called transactional leaders) in the text. Then read about four contemporary business leaders. Prepare a brief summary of each and classify them as leaders or managers.

8. *(communication question)* Interview a supervisor or manager about the best follower the supervi-

sor or manager has worked with. Ask questions about the characteristics and behaviors that made this person such a good follower. Note in particular how this follower responds to change. Be prepared to present your interview results in class.

Ethical Dilemma

Sam Bennett has been president of Chateau Bank for the past 35 years. Next to his family, running the bank has been the focus of his life. When Sam took over as president, the bank was small and poorly run. Today, there are 50 branch offices across three counties, an accomplishment in which Sam takes great pride. Now Sam is almost 70 and is ready to retire. He has been preparing for this event for some time. Grooming his replacement is very important and something he has been working on for years.

For several years, Chris Hollister has been the heir apparent. Chris had caught Sam's eye when he first joined the bank. Sam has watched with great interest as Chris rose through the ranks. As Chris began moving into the upper echelons, Sam made it well known that Chris was his choice to succeed him as president. The problem Sam now faces is that Chateau is not the same bank. It has, and rightly so, become a bank of the 21st century. Computers run everything. But Chris is from the old school. He understands computers well enough, but to move this company into the future, it needs someone who understands that technology is the catalyst to do that.

Dana Heart might just be that person. Dana joined the company at the management level just 12 years ago, straight from graduate school. She grew up in the technology era and knows how to use technology to her and the bank's advantage. Dana is not only good at what she does, but she also has a vision for the future. Sam likes Dana, but how can he turn his back on Chris?

Should his loyalty be with the man he has been grooming for so long or with the growth needs of the organization? Sam is sure that Chris could get the job done, but Dana would move the company forward.

Questions

1. Does Sam have an obligation to appoint Chris as the next president?

2. Evaluate each of Sam's alternatives, choosing Chris or Dana, using rule, virtue, right, and justice theories.

Experiential Exercises

12.1 National Culture and Leadership

Effective leadership often varies by national culture, as Hofstede's research has shown. This exercise gives you the opportunity to examine your own and your group's leadership orientation compared to norms from ten countries, including the United States.

Exercise Schedule

1. Preparation (before class)
Complete the 29-item questionnaire.

2. Individual and Group Scoring
Your instructor will lead you through the scoring of the questionnaire, both individually and as a group.

3. Comparison of Effective Leadership Patterns by Nation
Your instructor leads a discussion on Hofstede's value system and presents the culture dimension scores for the ten countries.

In the questionnaire below, indicate the extent to which you agree or disagree with each statement. For example, if you strongly agree with a particular statement, circle the 5 next to the statement.

1 = strongly disagree
2 = disagree
3 = neither agree nor disagree
4 = agree
5 = strongly agree

QUESTIONNAIRE	STRONGLY DISAGREE				STRONGLY AGREE
1. It is important to have job instructions spelled out in detail so that employees always know what they are expected to do.	1	2	3	4	5
2. Managers expect employees to closely follow instructions and procedures.	1	2	3	4	5

(continued)

QUESTIONNAIRE	STRONGLY DISAGREE				STRONGLY AGREE
3. Rules and regulations are important because they inform employees what the organization expects of them.	1	2	3	4	5
4. Standard operating procedures are helpful to employees on the job.	1	2	3	4	5
5. Instructions for operations are important for employees on the job.	1	2	3	4	5
6. Group welfare is more important than individual rewards.	1	2	3	4	5
7. Group success is more important than individual success.	1	2	3	4	5
8. Being accepted by the members of your work group is very important.	1	2	3	4	5
9. Employees should pursue their own goals only after considering the welfare of the group.	1	2	3	4	5
10. Managers should encourage group loyalty even if individual goals suffer.	1	2	3	4	5
11. Individuals may be expected to give up their goals in order to benefit group success.	1	2	3	4	5
12. Managers should make most decisions without consulting subordinates.	1	2	3	4	5
13. Managers should frequently use authority and power when dealing with subordinates.	1	2	3	4	5
14. Managers should seldom ask for the opinions of employees.	1	2	3	4	5
15. Managers should avoid off-the-job social contacts with employees.	1	2	3	4	5
16. Employees should not disagree with management decisions.	1	2	3	4	5
17. Managers should not delegate important tasks to employees.	1	2	3	4	5
18. Managers should help employees with their family problems.	1	2	3	4	5
19. Managers should see to it that employees are adequately clothed and fed.	1	2	3	4	5
20. A manager should help employees solve their personal problems.	1	2	3	4	5
21. Management should see that all employees receive health care.	1	2	3	4	5
22. Management should see that children of employees have an adequate education.	1	2	3	4	5
23. Management should provide legal assistance for employees who get into trouble with the law.	1	2	3	4	5
24. Managers should take care of their employees as they would their children.	1	2	3	4	5
25. Meetings are usually run more effectively when they are chaired by a man.	1	2	3	4	5
26. It is more important for men to have a professional career than it is for women to have a professional career.	1	2	3	4	5
27. Men usually solve problems with logical analysis; women usually solve problems with intuition.	1	2	3	4	5
28. Solving organizational problems usually requires an active, forcible approach, which is typical of men.	1	2	3	4	5
29. It is preferable to have a man, rather than a woman, in a high-level position.	1	2	3	4	5

SOURCES: By Peter Dorfman. *Advances in International Comparative Management*, vol. 3, pages 127–150, 1988. Reprinted by permission of JAI Press Inc. D. Marcic and S. M. Puffer. "Dimensions of National Culture and Effective Leadership Patterns: Hofstede Revisited," *Management International* (Minneapolis/St. Paul: West Publishing, 1994), 10–15. All rights reserved. May not be reproduced without written permission of the publisher.

12.2 Leadership and Influence

To get a better idea of what your leadership style is and how productive it would be, fill out the following questionnaire. If you are currently a manager or have been a manager, answer the questions considering "members" to be your employees. If you have never been a manager, think of situations when you were a leader in an organization and consider "members" to be people working for you.

Response choices for each item:

A = always   B = often   C = occasionally
D = seldom   E = never

A B C D E

1. I would act as the spokesperson of the group.
2. I would allow the members complete freedom in their work.
3. I would encourage overtime work.
4. I would permit the members to use their own judgment in solving problems.
5. I would encourage the use of uniform procedures.
6. I would needle members for greater effort.
7. I would stress being ahead of competing groups.
8. I would let the members do their work the way they think best.
9. I would speak as the representative of the group.
10. I would be able to tolerate postponement and uncertainty.
11. I would try out my ideas in the group.
12. I would turn the members loose on a job, and let them go on it.
13. I would work hard for a promotion.
14. I would get swamped by details.
15. I would speak for the group when visitors are present.
16. I would be reluctant to allow the members any freedom of action.
17. I would keep the work moving at a rapid pace.

A B C D E

18. I would let some members have authority that I should keep.
19. I would settle conflicts when they occur in the group.
20. I would allow the group a high degree of initiative.
21. I would represent the group at outside meetings.
22. I would be willing to make changes.
23. I would decide what will be done and how it will be done.
24. I would trust the members to exercise good judgment.
25. I would push for increased production.
26. I would refuse to explain my actions.
27. Things usually turn out as I predict.
28. I would permit the group to set its own pace.
29. I would assign group members to particular tasks.
30. I would act without consulting the group.
31. I would ask the members of the group to work harder.
32. I would schedule the work to be done.
33. I would persuade others that my ideas are to their advantage.
34. I would urge the group to beat its previous record.
35. I would ask that group members follow standard rules and regulations.

Scoring

People oriented: Place a check mark by the number if you answered either A or B to any of these questions:

Question #   2 ____   10 ____   22 ____
               4 ____   12 ____   24 ____
               6 ____   18 ____   28 ____
               8 ____   20 ____

Place a check mark by the number if you answered either D or E to any of these questions:

       14 ____ 16 ____ 26 ____ 30 ____

Count your check marks to get your total people-oriented score. ____

Task oriented: Place a check mark by the number if you answered either A or B to any of these questions:

     3 ____   7 ____   11 ____   13 ____
   17 ____   25 ____   29 ____   31 ____
   34 ____

Place a check mark by the number if you answered C or D to any of these questions:

     1 ____   5 ____   9 ____   15 ____
   19 ____   21 ____   23 ____   27 ____
   32 ____   33 ____   35 ____

Count your check marks to get your total task-oriented score. ____

Range People	Range Task		
People 0–7;	Task 0–10	You are not involved enough in either the task or the people.	Uninvolved
People 0–7;	Task 10–20	You tend to be autocratic, a whip-snapper. You get the job done, but at a high emotional cost.	Task-oriented
People 8–15;	Task 0–10	People are happy in their work, but sometimes at the expense of productivity.	People-oriented
People 8–15;	Task 10–20	People enjoy working for you and are productive. They naturally expend energy because they get positive reinforcement for doing a good job.	Balanced

As a leader, most people tend to be more task-oriented or more people-oriented. Task-orientation is concerned with getting the job done, while people-orientation focuses on group interactions and the needs of individual workers.

Effective leaders, however, are able to use both styles, depending on the situation. There may be times when a rush job demands great attention placed on task completion. During a time of low morale, though, sensitivity to workers' problems would be more appropriate. The best managers are able to balance both task and people concerns. Therefore, a high score on both would show this balance. Ultimately, you will gain respect, admiration, and productivity from your workers.

Exercise Schedule

1. Preparation (before class)
Complete and score inventory.

2. Group discussion
The class should form four groups based on the scores on the Leadership Style Inventory. Each group will be given a separate task.

Uninvolved: Devise strategies for developing task-oriented and people-oriented styles.

Task-oriented: How can you develop a more people-oriented style? What problems might occur if you do not do so?

People-oriented: How can you develop a more task-oriented style? What problems might occur if you do not do so?

Balanced: Do you see any potential problems with your style? Are you a fully developed leader?

SOURCE: From Thomas Sergiovanni, Richard Metzcus, and Larry Burden, "Toward a Particularistic Approach to Leadership Style: Some Findings," *American Educational Research Journal*, vol. 6(1), January 1969. Copyright 1969 The American Educational Research Association. Reprinted with permission of AERA.

Biz Flix | U-571

This action-packed World War II thriller shows a U.S. submarine crew's efforts to retrieve an Enigma encryption device from a disabled German submarine. After the crew gets the device, a German vessel torpedoes and sinks their submarine. The survivors must now use the disabled German submarine to escape from the enemy with their prize.

The *U-571* scene is an edited composite of the "To Be a Captain" sequence early in the film and the "A Real Sea Captain" sequence in about the middle of the film. A "chalkboard" (title screen) that reads, "Mr. Tyler, permission to speak freely?" separates the two parts. You can pause and separately study each part of the scene.

The first part occurs before the crew boards the disabled German U-boat. The second part occurs after the crew of survivors board the U-boat and try to return to England. Andrew Tyler (Matthew McConaughey), formerly the executive officer, is now the submarine's commander following the drowning death of Mike Dahlgren (Bill Paxton), the original commander. Just before this part of the scene, Tyler overheard some crewmen questioning his decision about taking a dangerous route to England. They also question why Chief Petty Officer Henry Klough (Harvey Keitel) is not the commander. The film continues with a German reconnaissance airplane circling their submarine and a crewman challenging Tyler's authority.

What to Watch for and Ask Yourself:

> What aspects of leadership does Dahlgren describe as important for a submarine commander?

> Which leadership behaviors or traits does Klough emphasize?

> Are these traits or behaviors right for this situation? Why or why not?

Workplace Video | The Vermont Teddy Bear Company: Liz Robert —CEO

The Vermont Teddy Bear Company is a direct marketer in the gift delivery industry and the only major American manufacturer of premium teddy bears. Faced with increasing competition and the reality that its market was smaller than first believed, The Vermont Teddy Bear Company decided it needed new leadership that could inspire confidence, empower workers, and carry out a vision for future growth. After conducting an extensive search, the company promoted CFO Liz Robert to the position of president and CEO. Whereas the company's former CEOs relied heavily on intuition as a core leadership competency, Robert is known for taking a more scientific approach to understanding the company's market and customers, relying upon market research and other data to help make key decisions.

Questions

1. *According to the video, what is the difference between a manager and a leader?*
2. *What are Liz Robert's core leader competencies?*
3. *How might Liz Robert's leadership style influence the culture of The Vermont Teddy Bear Company?*

Norman Brinker and Brinker International

Among other labels and titles, Norman Brinker has been called entrepreneur, pioneer, visionary, and mentor. These titles and labels were acquired through the 40+ years of his legendary career in the restaurant industry.

Always looking for a challenge, Brinker started his restaurant career in the late 1950s as a partner in the Jack-in-the-Box restaurant chain. This initial experience forged a love for the restaurant business. In 1966, he developed Steak and Ale, the forerunner of what is now referred to as casual dining. In 1971, he sought out another challenge in the restaurant industry, developing the Bennigan's chain. In 1976, he sold the Steak and Ale and Bennigan's chains to the Pillsbury Corporation, becoming a vice president for Pillsbury. He quickly ascended to the presidency of Pillsbury, but he left in 1983 to buy a 40 percent interest in the Chili's restaurant chain. In 1984, Brinker International was formed, and Norman Brinker pursued an aggressive growth strategy for the company.

Since it was formed, Brinker International has developed into "the premier casual dining restaurant company in the world and has received numerous accolades through the years for its outstanding performance." As of the end of fiscal year 2003, Brinker International had 1,402 company-operated, jointly developed, and franchised units in 49 states and 22 nations. The Brinker International brands include Chili's Grill and Bar, Romano's Macaroni Grill, On the Border Mexican Grill and Cantina, Maggiano's Little Italy, Big Bowl Asian Kitchen, Corner Bakery Café, and Rockfish Seafood Grill. Brinker International had annual revenues of approximately $3.8 billion in fiscal year 2003. Each year from 2000 to 2003, Brinker International was listed among the "400 Best Companies in America" by *Forbes* magazine.

Norman Brinker has been recognized on numerous occasions for his leadership capabilities. He is "widely regarded as one of the most influential chain builders in food service history." Brinker's leadership philosophy is that "winners attract winners." Brinker clearly has confidence in himself, and justifiably so. He has successfully led several companies in a highly competitive industry in which many fail. Moreover, Brinker likes to surround himself with people who believe in themselves and are (or can be) successful. He says: "The people I've been able to attract over the years are terrific individuals. They want to do better. And the success is contagious."

Under his leadership, Brinker International developed a culture "driven by integrity, teamwork, passion, and an unwavering commitment to making sure each and every guest has an enjoyable dining experience." Through example and personal involvement, Norman Brinker promoted an ethical organizational culture where people respect one another and work collaboratively in seeking to provide excellent meals and excellent service.

Norman Brinker has ended his formal leadership within the restaurant industry, but his influential reach will continue. In retiring from Brinker International in 2000 but remaining as chairman emeritus, Norman Brinker formally turned over the leadership reins of the company to Ron McDougall, a protégé whom he had groomed since the two began working together in 1974 at Steak and Ale. In passing the leadership torch to McDougall, Brinker observed that his successor "is one of the strongest, most visionary individuals that I've ever been associated with. He is a born leader, an adept team-builder, and the best strategist in the business."

McDougall has served as Brinker's Chief Executive Officer since 1995 and as Chairman since Norman Brinker became chairman emeritus in 2000. According to *Brinker's 2003 Annual Report,* McDougall will hand over the CEO duties to Doug Brooks while remaining as chairman of the board. Brooks is a 25-year Brinker employee and president and chief operating officer since 1999. Todd Diener, a member of the Brinker management team since 1981, will succeed Brooks. The top management transitioning and continued success of Brinker International is due in no small part to the mentoring provided by Norman Brinker.

As chairman emeritus, Norman Brinker is not involved in the day-to-day operations of Brinker International. However, he will "travel and address franchisee groups, spreading his casual dining gospel of good management, great food and fun that was his hallmark throughout his career." He most assuredly will be listening to customers, trying to find out what they are thinking. "He even visits competitors' restaurants, walking around as if he runs the place, stopping to inquire about the food and service." As Richie Jackson, executive vice president of the Texas Restaurant Association, observes: "Norman will still be building leadership and mentoring in his capacity as chairman emeritus."

Discussion Questions

1. In what ways was Norman Brinker a manager? In what ways was he a leader?

2. Describe the nature of followership that Norman Brinker has sought to develop at Brinker International.

3. What skills would you personally need to develop to become a leader like Norman Brinker? What could you do to develop or refine those skills?

4. What do you think is the most important leadership lesson in this case? Explain your answer.

SOURCE: This case was written by Michael K. McCuddy, The Louis S. and Mary L. Morgal Chair of Christian Business Ethics and Professor of Management, College of Business Administration, Valparaiso University. This case was developed from material contained on the Brinker International Web site at http://www.brinker.com and in the following articles: P. LaHue, "Norman Brinker," *Restaurant Hospitality* (March 2001): 42; R. B. Tucker, "Value Added Services," *American Salesman* (June 2004): 28–30; C. Walkup, "Colleagues, Analysts Expect Brinker to Remain a Force in New Emeritus Role," *Nation's Restaurant News* (November 20, 2000): 76.

© 2004 Getty Images

Conflict and Negotiation

LEARNING OBJECTIVES

After reading this chapter, you should be able to do the following:

<u>1</u> Diagnose functional versus dysfunctional conflict.

<u>2</u> Identify the causes of conflict in organizations.

<u>3</u> Identify the different forms of conflict.

<u>4</u> Understand the defense mechanisms that individuals exhibit when they engage in interpersonal conflict.

<u>5</u> Describe effective and ineffective techniques for managing conflict.

<u>6</u> Understand five styles of conflict management, and diagnose your own preferred style.

THINKING AHEAD: WHOLE FOODS MARKET

Conflict within One of the "Best Companies"

Only a relative handful of companies ever make *Fortune's* list of "100 Best Companies to Work For." At Austin, Texas-based Whole Foods Market, making the esteemed list has become something of an annual tradition. In fact, the company's place on the 2004 list marked its seventh consecutive appearance there. Whole Foods is one of only twenty-four firms in the country to have made the list in every single year of its existence.

What makes Whole Foods such a great place to work? Employees cite perks like solid health care for both full- and part-time employees, generous stock options for nonexecutives, and a profit-sharing plan that boosts employee earnings when the firm prospers. John Mackey, the firm's president, says this has been his plan since day one: to empower his people as a means to achieve business success. When it comes to keeping employees happy, Whole Foods appears to have the recipe for success down.

Yet, Whole Foods is not immune to conflict. If Whole Foods is such a perfect place to work, why did workers at the Madison, Wisconsin, store vote in 2002 to organize a labor union? And if Whole Foods is committed to empowering its workers, why did the company quickly announce that it would not recognize its workers' legally organized union? And is it just coincidence that shortly after the organizing drive, two of the organizers were fired? Is Whole Foods really a great place to work or not?[1]

The Nature of Conflicts in Organizations

All of us have experienced conflict of various types, yet we probably fail to recognize the variety of conflicts that occur in organizations. *Conflict* is defined as any situation in which incompatible goals, attitudes, emotions, or behaviors lead to disagreement or opposition between two or more parties.[2]

conflict

Any situation in which incompatible goals, attitudes, emotions, or behaviors lead to disagreement or opposition between two or more parties.

Today's organizations may face greater potential for conflict than ever before in history. The marketplace, with its increasing competition and globalization, magnifies differences among people in terms of personality, values, attitudes, perceptions, languages, cultures, and national backgrounds.[3] With the increasing diversity of the workforce, furthermore, comes the potential for incompatibility and conflict.

Importance of Conflict Management Skills for the Manager

Estimates show that managers spend about 21 percent of their time dealing with conflict.[4] That is the equivalent of one day every week. And conflict management skills are a major predictor of managerial success.[5] Emotional intelligence (EI) relates to the ability to manage conflict. It is the power to control one's emotions and perceive emotions in others, adapt to change, and manage adversity. Conflict management skills may be more a reflection of EI than of IQ. People who lack emotional intelligence, especially empathy or the ability to see life from another person's perspective, are more likely to be causes of conflict than managers of conflict.[6] EI seems to be valid across cultures. It is common among successful people not only in North America, but also in Nigeria, India, Argentina, and France.

Functional versus Dysfunctional Conflict

1. Diagnose functional versus dysfunctional conflict.

Not all conflict is bad. In fact, some types of conflict encourage new solutions to problems and enhance creativity in the organization. In these cases, managers will want to encourage the conflicts. Thus, the key to conflict management is to stimulate functional conflict and prevent or resolve dysfunctional conflict. The difficulty, however, is distinguishing between dysfunctional and functional conflicts. The consequences of conflict can be positive or negative, as shown in Table 13.1.

functional conflict
A healthy, constructive disagreement between two or more people.

Functional conflict is a healthy, constructive disagreement between two or more people. Functional conflict can produce new ideas, learning, and growth among individuals. When individuals engage in constructive conflict, they develop a better awareness of themselves and others. In addition, functional conflict can improve working relationships; when two parties work through their disagreements, they feel they have accomplished something together. By releasing tensions and solving problems in working together, morale is improved.[7] Functional conflict can lead to innovation and positive change for the organization.[8] Because it tends to encourage creativity among individuals, this positive form of conflict can translate into increased productivity.[9] A key to

TABLE 13.1   Consequences of Conflict

POSITIVE CONSEQUENCES	NEGATIVE CONSEQUENCES
• Leads to new ideas	• Diverts energy from work
• Stimulates creativity	• Threatens psychological well-being
• Motivates change	• Wastes resources
• Promotes organizational vitality	• Creates a negative climate
• Helps individuals and groups establish identities	• Breaks down group cohesion
• Serves as a safety valve to indicate problems	• Can increase hostility and aggressive behaviors

recognizing functional conflict is that it is often cognitive in origin; that is, it arises from someone challenging old policies or thinking of new ways to approach problems.

Dysfunctional conflict is an unhealthy, destructive disagreement between two or more people. Its danger is that it takes the focus away from the work to be done and places the focus on the conflict itself and the parties involved. Excessive conflict drains energy that could be used more productively. A key to recognizing a dysfunctional conflict is that its origin is often emotional or behavioral. Disagreements that involve personalized anger and resentment directed at specific individuals rather than specific ideas are dysfunctional.[10] Individuals involved in dysfunctional conflict tend to act before thinking, and they often rely on threats, deception, and verbal abuse to communicate. In dysfunctional conflict, the losses to both parties may exceed any potential gain from the conflict. For an extremely dysfunctional conflict, take a look at The Real World 13.1.

dysfunctional conflict

An unhealthy, destructive disagreement between two or more people.

Diagnosing conflict as good or bad is not easy. The manager must look at the issue, the context of the conflict, and the parties involved. The following questions can be used to diagnose the nature of the conflict a manager faces:

> Are the parties approaching the conflict from a hostile standpoint?

> Is the outcome likely to be a negative one for the organization?

> Do the potential losses of the parties exceed any potential gains?

> Is energy being diverted from goal accomplishment?

If the majority of the answers to these questions are yes, then the conflict is probably dysfunctional. Once the manager has diagnosed the type of conflict, he or she can either work to resolve it (if it is dysfunctional) or to stimulate it (if it is functional).

It is easy to make mistakes in diagnosing conflicts. Sometimes task conflict, which is functional, can be misattributed as being personal, and dysfunctional conflict can follow. Developing trust within the work group can keep this misattribution from occurring.[11] A study of group effectiveness found that American decision-making groups made up of friends were able to more openly engage in disagreement than groups made up of strangers, allowing the friends' groups to make more effective decisions. When group members (friends) felt comfortable and trusting enough to express conflicting opinions, optimal performance resulted. But similar groups made up of Chinese friends and strangers exhibited both high levels of conflict *and* low levels of performance, suggesting that open disagreement in these groups was not helpful. This finding should serve as a cautionary tale for managers trying to apply one country's management style and techniques in another cultural setting.[12]

One occasion when managers should work to stimulate conflict is when they suspect their group is suffering from groupthink, discussed in Chapter 10.[13] When a group fails to consider alternative solutions and becomes stagnant in its thinking, it might benefit from healthy disagreements. Teams exhibiting symptoms of groupthink should be encouraged to consider creative problem solving and should appoint a devil's advocate to point out opposing perspectives. These actions can help stimulate constructive conflict in a group.

Causes of Conflict in Organizations

Conflict is pervasive in organizations. To manage it effectively, managers should understand the many sources of conflict. They can be classified into two broad

2. Identify the causes of conflict in organizations.

Do Lawyers Need Hazardous Duty Pay?

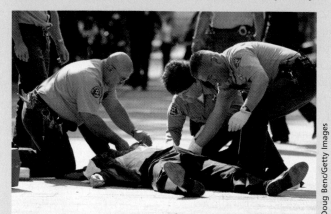

Attorney Jerry Curry falling victim to extreme dysfunctional conflict.

© Doug Benc/Getty Images

You've heard the tasteless lawyer jokes. Q: What do you call a thousand lawyers at the bottom of the ocean? A: A good start.

What happened to attorney Jerry Curry was no joke. You probably saw the footage of the incident on television. A man named William Striler tried to shoot him as Curry played "dodge the bullets" behind a tree. Although Striler fired five or six shots, none connected with any of the lawyer's vital organs. During the attack, Striler shouted, "You took my money, that's what you get." It seems that Striler was upset because Curry was being paid from his trust fund, which Curry was hired to manage. Curry staggered from behind the tree, bleeding from the face, and held up his hands before collapsing in the street.

Striler, the gunman, calmly walked past stunned reporters before an off-duty sheriff's reserve officer tackled him. Work-related violence is an extreme outcome of dysfunctional conflict.

SOURCE: Associated Press, "Lawyer Shot Outside L.A. Court," *MSNBC News* (October 31, 2003), http://www.msnbc.com/news /987626.asp.

categories: structural factors, which stem from the nature of the organization and the way in which work is organized, and personal factors, which arise from differences among individuals. Figure 13.1 summarizes the causes of conflict within each category.

Structural Factors

The causes of conflict related to the organization's structure include specialization, interdependence, common resources, goal differences, authority relationships, status inconsistencies, and jurisdictional ambiguities.

SPECIALIZATION When jobs are highly specialized, employees become experts at certain tasks. For example, one software company has one specialist for databases, one for statistical packages, and another for expert systems.

13.1

FIGURE 13.1   Causes of Conflict in Organizations

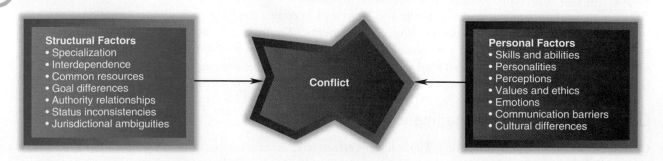

Structural Factors	Personal Factors
• Specialization	• Skills and abilities
• Interdependence	• Personalities
• Common resources	• Perceptions
• Goal differences	• Values and ethics
• Authority relationships	• Emotions
• Status inconsistencies	• Communication barriers
• Jurisdictional ambiguities	• Cultural differences

Conflict

Highly specialized jobs can lead to conflict, because people have little awareness of the tasks that others perform.

A classic conflict of specialization may occur between salespeople and engineers. Engineers are technical specialists responsible for product design and quality. Salespeople are marketing experts and liaisons with customers. Salespeople are often accused of making delivery promises to customers that engineers cannot keep because the sales force lacks the technical knowledge necessary to develop realistic delivery deadlines.

INTERDEPENDENCE Work that is interdependent requires groups or individuals to depend on one another to accomplish goals.[14] Depending on other people to get work done is fine when the process works smoothly. When there is a problem, however, it becomes very easy to blame the other party, and conflict escalates. In a garment manufacturing plant, for example, when the fabric cutters get behind in their work, the workers who sew the garments are delayed as well. Considerable frustration may result when the workers at the sewing machines feel their efforts are being blocked by the cutters' slow pace, and their pay is affected because they are paid piece-rate.

COMMON RESOURCES Any time multiple parties must share resources, there is potential for conflict.[15] This potential is enhanced when the shared resources become scarce. For example, managers often share secretarial support. Not uncommonly, one secretary supports ten or more managers, each of whom believes his or her work is most important. This puts pressure on the secretary and leads to potential conflicts in prioritizing and scheduling work.

GOAL DIFFERENCES When work groups have different goals, these goals may be incompatible. For example, in one cable television company, the salesperson's goal was to sell as many new installations as possible. This created problems for the service department, because its goal was timely installations. With increasing sales, the service department's workload became backed up, and orders were delayed. Often these types of conflicts occur because individuals do not have knowledge of another department's objectives.

AUTHORITY RELATIONSHIPS A traditional boss–employee relationship is hierarchical in nature with a boss who is superior to the employee. For many employees, such a relationship is not a comfortable one, because another individual has the right to tell them what to do. Some people resent authority more than others, and obviously this creates conflicts. In addition, some bosses are more autocratic than others; this compounds the potential for conflict in the relationship. As organizations move toward the team approach and empowerment, there should be less potential for conflict from authority relationships.

STATUS INCONSISTENCIES Some organizations have a strong status difference between management and nonmanagement workers. Managers may enjoy privileges—such as flexible schedules, reserved parking spaces, and longer lunch hours—that are not available to nonmanagement employees. This may result in resentment and conflict.

JURISDICTIONAL AMBIGUITIES Have you ever telephoned a company with a problem and had your call transferred through several different jurisdictional ambiguity

The presence of unclear lines of
responsibility within an organization.

people and departments? This situation illustrates *jurisdictional ambiguity*—that is, unclear lines of responsibility within an organization.[16] The classic situation here involves the hardware/software dilemma. You call the company that made your computer, and they inform you that the problem is caused by the software. You call the software division, and they tell you it's the hardware . . . you get the idea.

The factors just discussed are structural in that they arise from the ways in which work is organized. Other conflicts come from differences among individuals.

Personal Factors

The causes of conflict that arise from individual differences include skills and abilities, personalities, perceptions, values and ethics, emotions, communication barriers, and cultural differences.

SKILLS AND ABILITIES The workforce is composed of individuals with varying levels of skills and ability. Diversity in skills and abilities may be positive for the organization, but it also holds potential for conflict, especially when jobs are interdependent. Experienced, competent workers may find it difficult to work alongside new and unskilled recruits. Workers can become resentful when their new boss, fresh from college, knows a lot about managing people but is unfamiliar with the technology with which they are working.

PERSONALITIES Individuals do not leave their personalities at the doorstep when they enter the workplace. Personality conflicts are realities in organizations. To expect that you will like all of your coworkers may be a naive expectation, as would be the expectation that they will all like you.

One personality trait that many people find difficult to deal with is abrasiveness.[17] An abrasive person ignores the interpersonal aspects of work and the feelings of colleagues. Abrasive individuals are often achievement oriented and hardworking, but their perfectionist, critical style often leaves others feeling unimportant. This style creates stress and strain for those around the abrasive person.[18] Can Bill Gates be abrasive? Read about him in The Real World 13.2.

PERCEPTIONS Differences in perception can also lead to conflict. For example, managers and workers may not have a shared perception of what motivates people. In this case, the reward system can create conflicts if managers provide what they think employees want rather than what employees really want.

VALUES AND ETHICS Differences in values and ethics can be sources of disagreement. Older workers, for example, value company loyalty and probably would not take a sick day when they were not really ill. Younger workers, valuing mobility, like the concept of "mental health days," or calling in sick to get away from work. This may not be true for all workers, but it illustrates that differences in values can lead to conflict.

Most people have their own sets of values and ethics. The extent to which they apply these ethics in the workplace varies. Some people have strong desires for approval from others and will work to meet others' ethical standards. Some people are relatively unconcerned about approval from others and strongly apply their own ethical standards. Still others operate seemingly without regard to ethics or values.[19] When conflicts about values or ethics do arise, heated disagreement is common because of the personal nature of the differences.

"Bully" Gates?

In a small conference room on the Microsoft campus, Bill Gates is meeting with twenty young Microsoft employees, all looking fearful. Gates is peeved, to put it mildly. "You've studied it and studied it and decided that it's turning bits on and off! And it's a BRILLIANT INSIGHT! . . . And then there's this relationship with Hewlett-Packard that we KEEP SCREWING UP! . . . What about this [expletive] thing with no definition!"

The "sour smell of sweaty terror" permeates the room. One of the Microsofties gets exactly five words out of his mouth when Gates cuts him off with a string of obscenities. He sits down and one of his more composed teammates takes a turn. Someone timidly offers Gates a proposition. Gates screams at him. Someone else tries a rebuttal. Gates screams at him. This pattern continues for an hour.

A young, soft-spoken Chinese woman directs comments at Gates while he is in mid-tirade. Both times, no one but Gates seems to understand her—her voice is barely audible, and English appears to be her fourth language, after Chinese, C, and C++. Incredibly, her comments seem to calm Bill Gates down. "Okay," he says quietly, "this looks good. Go ahead"—and abruptly he leaves the meeting. His prisoners run away, afraid he might suddenly change his mind and begin berating them again. Is Bill Gates a bully? Or, does he just hate incompetence?

SOURCE: F. Moody, "Wonder Women in the Rude Boys' Paradise," *Fast Company* 3 (June/July 1996): 85, http://www.fastcompany.com/magazine/03/microsof.html.

EMOTIONS The emotions of others can be a source of conflict in the workplace. Problems at home often spill over into the work arena, and the related moods can be hard for others to deal with.

Conflict by its nature is an emotional interaction,[20] and the emotions of the parties involved in conflict play a pivotal role in how they perceive the negotiation and respond to one another. In fact, emotions are now considered critical elements of any negotiation that must be included in any examination of the process and how it unfolds.[21]

One important research finding has been that emotion can play a problematic role in negotiations. In particular, when negotiators begin to act based on emotions rather than on cognitions, they become much more likely to reach an impasse.[22]

COMMUNICATION BARRIERS Communication barriers such as physical separation and language can create distortions in messages, and these can lead to conflict. Another communication barrier is value judgment, in which a listener assigns a worth to a message before it is received. For example, suppose a team member is a chronic complainer. When this individual enters the manager's office, the manager is likely to devalue the message before it is even delivered. Conflict can then emerge.

CULTURAL DIFFERENCES Although cultural differences are assets in organizations, sometimes they can be seen as sources of conflict. Often, these conflicts stem from a lack of understanding of another culture. In one MBA class, for example, Indian students were horrified when American students challenged the professor. Meanwhile, the American students thought the students from India were too passive. Subsequent discussions revealed that professors in India expected to be treated deferentially and with great respect. While students might challenge an idea vigorously, they would rarely challenge the professor.

Diversity training that emphasizes education on cultural differences can make great strides in preventing misunderstandings.

Globalization and Conflict

Large transnational corporations employ many different ethnic and cultural groups. In these multiethnic corporations, the widely differing cultures represent vast differences among individuals, so the potential for conflict increases.[23] As indicated in Chapter 2, Hofstede has identified five dimensions along which cultural differences may emerge: individualism/collectivism, power distance, uncertainty avoidance, masculinity/femininity, and long-term/short-term orientation.[24] These cultural differences have many implications for conflict management in organizations.

Individualism means that people believe that their individual interests take priority over society's interests. Collectivism, in contrast, means that people put the good of the group first. For example, the United States is a highly individualistic culture, whereas Japan is a very collectivist culture. The individualism/collectivism dimension of cultural differences strongly influences conflict management behavior. People from collectivist cultures tend to display a more cooperative approach to managing conflict.[25]

Hofstede's second dimension of cultural differences is power distance. In cultures with high power distance, individuals accept that people in organizations have varying levels of power. In contrast, in cultures with low power distance, individuals do not automatically respect those in positions of authority. For example, the United States is a country of low power distance, whereas Brazil is a country with a high power distance. Differences in power distance can lead to conflict. Imagine a U.S. employee managed by a Brazilian supervisor who expects deferential behavior. The supervisor would expect automatic respect based on legitimate power. When this respect is not given, conflict would arise.

Uncertainty avoidance also varies by culture. In the United States, employees can tolerate high levels of uncertainty, whereas employees in Israel tend to prefer certainty in their work settings. A U.S.-based multinational firm might run into conflicts operating in Israel. Suppose such a firm is installing a new technology. Its expatriate workers from the United States would tolerate the uncertainty of the technological transition better than would their Israeli coworkers, and this might lead to conflicts among the employees.

Masculinity versus femininity illustrates the contrast between preferences for assertiveness and material goods versus preferences for human capital and quality of life. The United States is a masculine society, whereas Sweden is considered a feminine society. Adjustment to the assertive interpersonal style of U.S. workers may be difficult for Swedish coworkers.

Conflicts can also arise between cultures that vary in their time orientation of values. China, for example, has a long-term orientation; the Chinese prefer values that focus on the future, such as saving and persistence. The United States and Russia, in contrast, have short-term orientations. These cultures emphasize values in the past and present, such as respect for tradition and fulfillment of social obligations. Conflicts can arise when managers fail to understand the nature of differences in values.

An organization whose workforce consists of multiple ethnicities and cultures holds potential for many types of conflict because of the sheer volume of individual differences among workers. The key to managing conflict in a multicultural workforce is understanding cultural differences and appreciating their value.

Forms of Conflict in Organizations

Conflict can take on any of several different forms in an organization, including interorganizational, intergroup, intragroup, interpersonal, and intrapersonal conflicts. It is important to note that the prefix *inter* means "between," whereas the prefix *intra* means "within."

3. Identify the different forms of conflict.

Interorganizational Conflict

Conflict that occurs between two or more organizations is called *interorganizational conflict*. Competition can heighten interorganizational conflict. Corporate takeovers, mergers, and acquisitions can also produce interorganizational conflict. What about the interorganizational conflict between Major League Baseball's players' union and management, which is sometimes characterized as a battle between millionaires and multimillionaires (not sure which is which)? The players regularly go on strike to extract more of the profits from management, while management cries that it is not making a dime.

Conflicts among organizations abound. Some of these conflicts can be functional, as when firms improve the quality of their products and services in the spirit of healthy competition. Other interorganizational conflicts can have dysfunctional results. *that inevitably led to several resignations*

interorganizational conflict
Conflict that occurs between two or more organizations.

© REUTERS/Chip East/Landov

The heated Major League Baseball strike negotiations are examples of interorganizational conflict.

Intergroup Conflict

When conflict occurs between groups or teams, it is known as *intergroup conflict*. Conflict between groups can have positive effects within each group, such as increased group cohesiveness, increased focus on tasks, and increased loyalty to the group. There are, however, negative consequences as well. Groups in conflict tend to develop an "us against them" mentality whereby each sees the other team as the enemy, becomes more hostile, and decreases its communication with the other group. Groups are even more competitive and less cooperative than individuals. The inevitable outcome is that one group gains and the other group loses.[26]

Competition between groups must be managed carefully so that it does not escalate into dysfunctional conflict. Research has shown that when groups compete for a goal that only one group can achieve, negative consequences like territoriality, aggression, and prejudice toward the other group can result.[27] Managers should encourage and reward cooperative behaviors across groups. Some effective ways of doing this include modifying performance appraisals to include assessing intergroup behavior and using an external supervisor's evaluation of intergroup behavior. Group members will be more likely to help other groups when they know that the other group's supervisor will be evaluating their behavior, and that they will be rewarded for cooperation.[28] In addition, managers should encourage social interactions across groups so that trust can be developed. Trust allows individuals to exchange ideas and resources with members of other groups and results in innovation when members of different groups cooperate.[29] Conflict often results when older employees fear that younger new-hires may take over their jobs. Social interaction can help reduce these perceived threats, creating trust and reducing the intergroup conflict in the process.[30]

intergroup conflict
Conflict that occurs between groups or teams in an organization.

intragroup conflict
Conflict that occurs within groups or teams.

follow 13.1 (handwritten)

interpersonal conflict
Conflict that occurs between two or more individuals.

intrapersonal conflict
Conflict that occurs within an individual.

interrole conflict
A person's experience of conflict among the multiple roles in his or her life.

(2) state emp v advocate for (handwritten)
fam & infants (handwritten)
2 dir (handwritten)

intrarole conflict
Conflict that occurs within a single role, such as when a person receives conflicting messages from role senders about how to perform a certain role.

(3) emp → boss → owner (handwritten)
loyal save $ (handwritten)

person–role conflict
Conflict that occurs when an individual is expected to perform behaviors in a certain role that conflict with his or her personal values.

(4) (handwritten)
term. therapist (handwritten)

Intragroup Conflict

Conflict that occurs within groups or teams is called *intragroup conflict*. Some conflict within a group is functional. It can help the group avoid groupthink, as we discussed in Chapter 10.

Even the newest teams, virtual teams, are not immune to conflict. The nuances and subtleties of face-to-face communication are often lacking in these teams, and misunderstandings can result. To avoid dysfunctional conflicts, virtual teams should make sure their tasks fit their methods of interacting. Complex strategic decisions may require face-to-face meetings rather than e-mails or threaded discussions. Face-to-face and telephone interactions early on can eliminate later conflicts and allow virtual teams to move on to use electronic communication because trust has been developed.[31]

Teams can experience many types of conflict. Using You 13.1, you can assess the types of conflict in a team you belong to, as well as design ways to manage those conflicts.

Interpersonal Conflict

Conflict between two or more people is *interpersonal conflict*. Conflict between people can arise from many individual differences, including personalities, attitudes, values, perceptions, and the other differences we discussed in Chapters 3 and 4. Later in this chapter, we look at defense mechanisms that individuals exhibit in interpersonal conflict and at ways to cope with difficult people.

Intrapersonal Conflict

When conflict occurs within an individual, it is called *intrapersonal conflict*. There are several types of intrapersonal conflict, including interrole, intrarole, and person–role conflicts. A role is a set of expectations placed on an individual by others.[32] The person occupying the focal role is the role incumbent, and the individuals who place expectations on the person are role senders. Figure 13.2 depicts a set of role relationships.

Interrole conflict occurs when a person experiences conflict among the multiple roles in his or her life. One interrole conflict that many employees experience is work/home conflict, in which their role as worker clashes with their role as spouse or parent.[33] Work/home conflict has become even more common with the rise of work-at-home professionals and telecommuting because the home becomes the office, blurring the boundary between work and family life.[34]

Intrarole conflict is conflict within a single role. It often arises when a person receives conflicting messages from role senders about how to perform a certain role. Suppose a manager receives counsel from her department head that she needs to socialize less with the nonmanagement employees. She also is told by her project manager that she needs to be a better team member, and that she can accomplish this by socializing more with the other nonmanagement team members. This situation is one of intrarole conflict.

Person–role conflict occurs when an individual in a particular role is expected to perform behaviors that clash with his or her values.[35] Salespeople, for example, may be required to offer the most expensive item in the sales line first to the customer, even when it is apparent that the customer does not want or cannot afford the item. A computer salesman may be required to offer a large, elaborate system to a student he knows is on a tight budget. This may conflict with the salesman's values, and he may experience person–role conflict.

Assess Your Team's Conflict

Think of a team you're a member of or one you were part of in the past. Answer the following eight questions regarding that team.

1. How much emotional tension was there in your team?

    No tension   Lots of tension
      1   2   3   4   (5)

2. How much conflict of ideas was there in your team?

    No idea conflict   Lots of idea conflict
      1   2   3   4   (5)

3. How often did people get angry while working in your team?

    Never   Often
      1   2   3   4   (5)

4. How different were your views on the content of your project?

    Very similar views   Very different views
      1   2   3   4   (5)

5. How much were personality clashes evident in your team?

    No clashes   Personality clashes
    evident   very evident
      1   2   3   4   (5)

6. How much did you talk through disagreements about your team projects?

    Never talked   Always talked
    through   through
    disagreements   disagreements
      1   (2)   3   4   (5)

7. How much interpersonal friction was there in your team?

    No friction   Lots of friction
      1   2   3   4   (5)

8. How much disagreement was there about task procedure in your team?

    No disagreement   Lots of disagreement
    about procedure   about procedure
      1   2   3   4   (5)

Total for items 2, 4, 6, and 8 = ___17___ indicating task conflict.
Total for items 1, 3, 5, and 7 = ___20___ indicating relationship conflict.

*   Did your team experience higher relationship or task conflict?
*   What actions can you take to better manage task conflict? Relationship conflict?
*   Was there an absence of both, or either, types of conflict in your team? What does this indicate?

SOURCE: Adapted from K. Jehn, "A Multimethod Examination of the Benefits and Detriments of Intragroup Conflict," *Administrative Science Quarterly* 40 (1995): 256–282.

Intrapersonal conflicts can have positive consequences. Often, professional responsibilities clash with deeply held values. A budget shortfall may force you to lay off a loyal, hardworking employee. Your daughter may have a piano recital on the same day your largest client is scheduled to be in town visiting the office. In such conflicts, we often have to choose between right and right; that is, there's no correct response. These may be thought of as *defining moments* that challenge us to choose between two or more things in which we believe.[36] Character is formed in defining moments because they cause us to shape our identities. They help us crystallize our values and serve as opportunities for personal growth.

Intrapersonal Conflict

Intrapersonal conflict can be managed with careful self-analysis and diagnosis of the situation. Three actions in particular can help prevent or resolve intrapersonal conflicts.

FIGURE 13.2   An Organization Member's Role Set

13.2

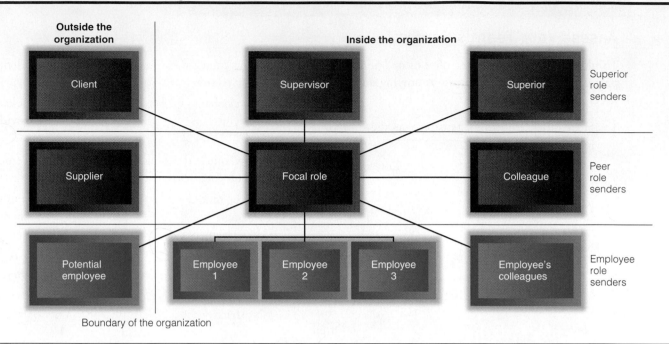

SOURCE: J. C. Quick, J. D. Quick, D. L. Nelson, and J. J. Hurrell, Jr., *Preventive Stress Management in Organizations*, 1997. Copyright © 1997 by the American Psychological Association. Reprinted with permission.

First, when seeking a new job, you should find out as much as possible about the values of the organization.[37] Many person–role conflicts center around differences between the organization's values and the individual's values. Research has shown that when there is a good fit between the values of the individual and the organization, the individual is more satisfied and committed and is less likely to leave the organization.[38]

Second, to manage intrarole or interrole conflicts, role analysis is a good tool.[39] In role analysis, the individual asks the various role senders what they expect of him or her. The outcomes are clearer work roles and the reduction of conflict and ambiguity.[40] Role analysis is a simple tool that clarifies the expectations of both parties in a relationship and reduces the potential for conflict within a role or between roles.

Third, political skills can help buffer the negative effects of stress that stem from role conflicts. Effective politicians, as we discussed in Chapter 11, can negotiate role expectations when conflicts occur. For more on how political skills can help you deal with conflict, see the accompanying Science feature.

All these forms of conflict can be managed. An understanding of the many forms is a first step. The next section focuses more extensively on interpersonal conflict because of its pervasiveness in organizations.

Interpersonal Conflict

When a conflict occurs between two or more people, it is known as interpersonal conflict. To manage interpersonal conflict, it is helpful to understand power networks in organizations, defense mechanisms exhibited by individuals, and ways to cope with difficult people.

A Positive Role for Political Skill

While personality traits like Type A behavior appear to play a major role in how we respond to stress, there are also skills that help us handle conflict and stress in ways that reduce their potentially damaging effects on health. In a recent study, researchers wondered whether political skills would help individuals deal with role conflict. Participants, who were all experiencing role conflict, were assessed for their level of political skill, as well as physiological measures of stress such as pulse and blood pressure. The study found that workers with stronger political skills suffered less severe physical impact from the role conflict. This finding suggests that while role conflict and other work stressors may be a fact of modern life, good political skills can reduce the damage they cause. Perhaps more importantly, because political skills can be taught, the potential exists for firms to "stress-proof" their employees, reducing both employee discomfort and future stress-related medical costs.

SOURCE: P. L. Perrewe, K. L. Zellars, G. R. Ferris, A. M. Rossi, C. J. Kacmar, and D. A. Ralston, "Neutralizing Job Stressors: Political Skill as an Antidote to the Dysfunctional Consequences of Role Conflict," *Academy of Management Journal* 47 (2004): 141–153.

Power Networks

According to Mastenbroek, individuals in organizations are organized in three basic types of power networks.[41] Based on these power relationships, certain kinds of conflict tend to emerge. Figure 13.3 illustrates three basic kinds of power relationships in organizations.

The first relationship is equal versus equal, in which there is a horizontal balance of power among the parties. An example of this type of relationship would be a conflict between individuals from two different project teams. The behavioral tendency is toward suboptimization; that is, the focus is on a win–lose approach to problems, and each party tries to maximize its power at the expense of the other party. Conflict within this type of network can lead to depression, low self-esteem, and other distress symptoms. Interventions like improving coordination between the parties and working toward common interests can help manage these conflicts.

The second power network is high versus low, or a powerful versus a less powerful relationship. Conflicts that emerge here take the basic form of the powerful individuals trying to control others, with the less powerful people trying to become more autonomous. Conflict in this network can lead to job dissatisfaction, low organizational commitment, and turnover.[42] Organizations typically respond to these conflicts by tightening the rules. However, the more successful ways of managing these conflicts are to try a different style of leadership, such as a coaching and counseling style, or to change the structure to a more decentralized one.

The third power network is high versus middle versus low. This power network illustrates the classic conflicts felt by middle managers. Two particular conflicts are evident for middle managers: role conflict, in which conflicting expectations are placed on the manager from bosses and employees, and role ambiguity, in which the expectations of the boss are unclear. Improved communication among all parties can reduce role conflict and ambiguity. In addition, middle managers can benefit from training in positive ways to influence others.

Knowing the typical kinds of conflicts that arise in various kinds of relationships can help a manager diagnose conflicts and devise appropriate ways to manage them.

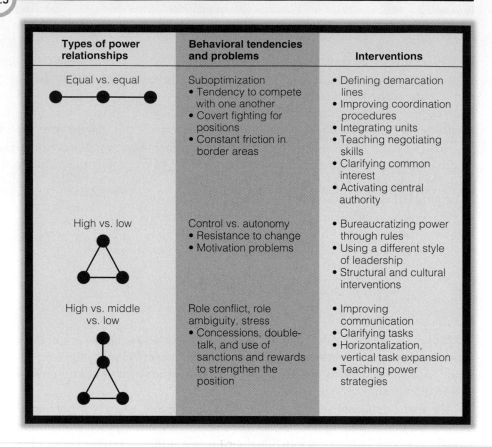

Types of power relationships	Behavioral tendencies and problems	Interventions
Equal vs. equal	Suboptimization • Tendency to compete with one another • Covert fighting for positions • Constant friction in border areas	• Defining demarcation lines • Improving coordination procedures • Integrating units • Teaching negotiating skills • Clarifying common interest • Activating central authority
High vs. low	Control vs. autonomy • Resistance to change • Motivation problems	• Bureaucratizing power through rules • Using a different style of leadership • Structural and cultural interventions
High vs. middle vs. low	Role conflict, role ambiguity, stress • Concessions, double-talk, and use of sanctions and rewards to strengthen the position	• Improving communication • Clarifying tasks • Horizontalization, vertical task expansion • Teaching power strategies

SOURCE: W. F. G. Mastenbroek, *Conflict Management and Organization Development,* 1987. Copyright John Wiley & Sons Limited. Reproduced with permission.

Defense Mechanisms

When individuals are involved in conflict with another human being, frustration often results.[43] Conflicts can often arise within the context of a performance appraisal session. Most people do not react well to negative feedback, as was illustrated in a classic study.[44] In this study, when employees were given criticism about their work, over 50 percent of their responses were defensive.

When individuals are frustrated, as they often are in interpersonal conflict, they respond by exhibiting defense mechanisms.[45] Defense mechanisms are common reactions to the frustration that accompanies conflict. Table 13.2 describes several defense mechanisms seen in organizations.

Aggressive mechanisms, such as fixation, displacement, and negativism, are aimed at attacking the source of the conflict. In *fixation*, an individual fixates on the conflict, or keeps up a dysfunctional behavior that obviously will not solve the conflict. An example of fixation occurred in a university, where a faculty member became embroiled in a battle with the dean because the faculty member felt he had not received a large enough salary increase. He persisted in writing angry letters to the dean, whose hands were tied because of a low budget allocation to the college. *Displacement* means directing anger toward someone who is not the source of the conflict. For example, a manager may respond harshly to an employee after a telephone confrontation with an angry customer. Another aggressive defense mechanism is *negativism*, which is active or passive resistance. Negativism is illustrated by a manager who, when ap-

---

4. Understand the defense mechanisms that individuals exhibit when they engage in interpersonal conflict.

fixation

An aggressive mechanism in which an individual keeps up a dysfunctional behavior that obviously will not solve the conflict.

displacement

An aggressive mechanism in which an individual directs his or her anger toward someone who is not the source of the conflict.

negativism

An aggressive mechanism in which a person responds with pessimism to any attempt at solving a problem.

TABLE 13.2   Common Defense Mechanisms

DEFENSE MECHANISM	PSYCHOLOGICAL PROCESS
AGGRESSIVE MECHANISMS	
• Fixation	Person maintains a persistent, nonadjustive reaction even though all the cues indicate the behavior will not cope with the problem.
• Displacement	Individual redirects pent-up emotions toward persons, ideas, or objects other than the primary source of the emotion.
• Negativism	Person uses active or passive resistance, operating unconsciously.
COMPROMISE MECHANISMS	
• Compensation	Individual devotes himself or herself to a pursuit with increased vigor to make up for some feeling of real or imagined inadequacy.
• Identification	Individual enhances own self-esteem by patterning behavior after another's, frequently also internalizing the values and beliefs of the other person; also vicariously shares the glories or suffering in the disappointments of other individuals or groups.
• Rationalization	Person justifies inconsistent or undesirable behavior, beliefs, statements, and motivations by providing acceptable explanations for them.
WITHDRAWAL MECHANISMS	
• Flight or withdrawal	Through either physical or psychological means, person leaves the field in which frustration, anxiety, or conflict is experienced.
• Conversion	Emotional conflicts are expressed in muscular, sensory, or bodily symptoms of disability, malfunctioning, or pain.
• Fantasy	Person daydreams or uses other forms of imaginative activity to obtain an escape from reality and obtain imagined satisfactions.

SOURCE: Timothy W. Costello and Sheldon S. Zalkind, adapted table from "Psychology in Administration: A Research Orientation" from *Journal of Conflict Resolution* III 1959, pp. 148–149. Reprinted by permission of Sage Publications, Inc.

pointed to a committee on which she did not want to serve, made negative comments throughout the meeting.

Compromise mechanisms, such as compensation, identification, and rationalization, are used by individuals to make the best of a conflict situation. *Compensation* occurs when an individual tries to make up for an inadequacy by putting increased energy into another activity. Compensation can be seen when a person makes up for a bad relationship at home by spending more time at the office. *Identification* occurs when one individual patterns his or her behavior after another's. One supervisor at a construction firm, not wanting to acknowledge consciously that she was not likely to be promoted, mimicked the behavior of her boss, even going so far as to buy a car just like the boss's. *Rationalization* is trying to justify one's behavior by constructing bogus reasons for it. Employees may rationalize unethical behavior like padding their expense accounts because "everyone else does it."

compensation

A compromise mechanism in which an individual attempts to make up for a negative situation by devoting himself or herself to another pursuit with increased vigor.

identification

A compromise mechanism whereby an individual patterns his or her behavior after another's.

rationalization

A compromise mechanism characterized by trying to justify one's behavior by constructing bogus reasons for it.

flight/withdrawal

A withdrawal mechanism that entails physically escaping a conflict (flight) or psychologically escaping (withdrawal).

conversion

A withdrawal mechanism in which emotional conflicts are expressed in physical symptoms.

fantasy

A withdrawal mechanism that provides an escape from a conflict through daydreaming.

Withdrawal mechanisms are exhibited when frustrated individuals try to flee from a conflict using either physical or psychological means. Flight, conversion, and fantasy are examples of withdrawal mechanisms. Physically escaping a conflict is *flight*. When an employee takes a day off after a blowup with the boss is an example. *Withdrawal* may take the form of emotionally leaving a conflict, such as exhibiting an "I don't care anymore" attitude. *Conversion* is a process whereby emotional conflicts become expressed in physical symptoms. Most of us have experienced the conversion reaction of a headache following an emotional exchange with another person. *Fantasy* is an escape by daydreaming. In the Internet age, fantasy as an escape mechanism has found new meaning. A study conducted by International Data Corporation (IDC) showed that 30 to 40 percent of all Internet surfing at work is nonwork-related and that more than 70 percent of companies have had sex sites accessed from their networks, suggesting that employees' minds aren't always focused on their jobs.[46]

When employees exhibit withdrawal mechanisms, they often fake it by pretending to agree with their bosses or coworkers in order to avoid facing an immediate conflict. Many employees fake it because the firm informally rewards agreement and punishes dissent. The long-term consequence of withdrawal and faking it is emotional distress for the employee.[47]

Knowledge of these defense mechanisms can be extremely beneficial to a manager. By understanding the ways in which people typically react to interpersonal conflict, managers can be prepared for employees' reactions and help them uncover their feelings about a conflict.

Conflict Management Strategies and Techniques

The overall approach (or strategy) you use in a conflict is important in determining whether the conflict will have a positive or negative outcome.

These overall strategies are competitive versus cooperative strategies. Table 13.3 depicts the two strategies and four different conflict scenarios. The competitive strategy is founded on assumptions of win–lose and entails dishonest communication, mistrust, and a rigid position from both parties.[48] The cooperative strategy is founded on different assumptions: the potential for win–win outcomes, honest communication, trust, openness to risk and vulnerability, and the notion that the whole may be greater than the sum of the parts.

To illustrate the importance of the overall strategy, consider the case of two groups competing for scarce resources. Suppose budget cuts have to be made at an insurance company. The claims manager argues that the sales training staff should be cut, because agents are fully trained. The sales training manager argues that claims personnel should be cut, because the company is processing fewer claims. This could turn into a dysfunctional brawl, with both sides refusing to give ground. This would constitute a win–lose, lose–win, or lose–lose scenario. Personnel cuts could be made in only one department, or in

TABLE 13.3   Win–Lose versus Win–Win Strategies

STRATEGY	DEPARTMENT A	DEPARTMENT B	ORGANIZATION
Competitive	Lose	Lose	Lose
	Lose	Win	Lose
	Win	Lose	Lose
Cooperative	Win–	Win–	Win

both departments. In all three cases, with the competitive approach the organization winds up in a losing position.

Even in such intense conflicts as those over scarce resources, a win–win strategy can lead to an overall win for the organization. In fact, conflicts over scarce resources can be productive if the parties have cooperative goals—a strategy that seeks a winning solution for both parties. To achieve a win–win outcome, the conflict must be approached with open-minded discussion of opposing views. Through open-minded discussion, both parties integrate views and create new solutions that facilitate productivity and strengthen their relationship; the result is feelings of unity rather than separation.[49]

In the example of the conflict between the claims manager and sales training manager, open-minded discussion might reveal that there are ways to achieve budget cuts without cutting personnel. Sales support might surrender part of its travel budget, and claims might cut out overtime. This represents a win–win situation for the company. The budget has been reduced, and relationships between the two departments have been preserved. Both parties have given up something (note the "win–" in Table 13.3), but the conflict has been resolved with a positive outcome.

You can see the importance of the broad strategy used to approach a conflict. We now move from broad strategies to more specific techniques.

Ineffective Techniques

There are many specific techniques for dealing with conflict. Before turning to techniques that work, it should be recognized that some actions commonly taken in organizations to deal with conflict are not effective.[50]

Nonaction is doing nothing in hopes that the conflict will disappear. Generally, this is not a good technique, because most conflicts do not go away, and the individuals involved in the conflict react with frustration.

Secrecy, or trying to keep a conflict out of view of most people, only creates suspicion. An example is an organizational policy of pay secrecy. In some organizations, discussion of salary is grounds for dismissal. When this is the case, employees suspect that the company has something to hide. Secrecy may result in secret political activity by employees who hope to uncover the secret![51]

Administrative orbiting is delaying action on a conflict by buying time, usually by telling the individuals involved that the problem is being worked on or that the boss is still thinking about the issue. Like nonaction, this technique leads to frustration and resentment.

Due process nonaction is a procedure set up to address conflicts that is so costly, time consuming, or personally risky that no one will use it. Some companies' sexual harassment policies are examples of this technique. To file a sexual harassment complaint, detailed paperwork is required, the accuser must go through appropriate channels, and the accuser risks being branded a troublemaker. Thus, the company has a procedure for handling complaints (due process), but no one uses it (nonaction).

Character assassination is an attempt to label or discredit an opponent. Character assassination can backfire and make the individual who uses it appear dishonest and cruel. It often leads to name-calling and accusations by both parties, and both parties end up losers in the eyes of those who witness the conflict.

Effective Techniques

Fortunately, there are effective conflict management techniques. These include appealing to superordinate goals, expanding resources, changing personnel, changing structure, and confronting and negotiating.

5. Describe effective and ineffective techniques for managing conflict.

nonaction
Doing nothing in hopes that a conflict will disappear.

secrecy
Attempting to hide a conflict or an issue that has the potential to create conflict.

administrative orbiting
Delaying action on a conflict by buying time.

due process nonaction
A procedure set up to address conflicts that is so costly, time consuming, or personally risky that no one will use it.

character assassination
An attempt to label or discredit an opponent.

superordinate goal

An organizational goal that is more important to both parties in a conflict than their individual or group goals.

SUPERORDINATE GOALS An organizational goal that is more important to both parties in a conflict than their individual or group goals is a *superordinate goal.*[52] Superordinate goals cannot be achieved by an individual or by one group alone. The achievement of these goals requires cooperation by both parties.

One effective technique for resolving conflict is to appeal to a superordinate goal—in effect, to focus the parties on a larger issue on which they both agree. This helps them realize their similarities rather than their differences.

In the conflict between service representatives and cable television installers that was discussed earlier, appealing to a superordinate goal would be an effective technique for resolving the conflict. Both departments can agree that superior customer service is a goal worthy of pursuit and that this goal cannot be achieved unless cables are installed properly and in a timely manner, and customer complaints are handled effectively. Quality service requires that both departments cooperate to achieve the goal.

EXPANDING RESOURCES One conflict resolution technique is so simple that it may be overlooked. If the conflict's source is common or scarce resources, providing more resources may be a solution. Of course, managers working with tight budgets may not have the luxury of obtaining additional resources. Nevertheless, it is a technique to be considered. In the example earlier in this chapter, one solution to the conflict among managers over secretarial support would be to hire more secretaries.

CHANGING PERSONNEL In some cases, long-running severe conflict may be traced to a specific individual. For example, managers with lower levels of emotional intelligence have been demonstrated to have more negative work attitudes, to exhibit less altruistic behavior, and to produce more negative work outcomes. A chronically disgruntled manager who exhibits low EI may not only frustrate his employees but also impede his department's performance. In such cases, transferring or firing an individual may be the best solution, but only after due process.[53]

CHANGING STRUCTURE Another way to resolve a conflict is to change the structure of the organization. One way of accomplishing this is to create an integrator role. An integrator is a liaison between groups with very different interests. In severe conflicts, it may be best that the integrator be a neutral third party.[54] Creating the integrator role is a way of opening dialogue between groups that have difficulty communicating.

Using cross-functional teams is another way of changing the organization's structure to manage conflict. In the old methods of designing new products in organizations, many departments had to contribute, and delays resulted from difficulties in coordinating the activities of the various departments. Using a cross-functional team made up of members from different departments improves coordination and reduces delays by allowing many activities to be performed at the same time rather than sequentially.[55] The team approach allows members from different departments to work together and reduces the potential for conflict. In teamwork, it is helpful to break up a big task so that it becomes a collection of smaller, less complex tasks, and to have smaller teams work on the smaller tasks. This helps to reduce conflict, and organizations can potentially improve the performance of the overall team by improving the outcomes in each subteam.[56]

CONFRONTING AND NEGOTIATING Some conflicts require confrontation and negotiation between the parties. Both these strategies require skill on the part of the negotiator and careful planning before engaging in negotiations. The process of negotiating involves an open discussion of problem solutions, and the outcome often is an exchange in which both parties work toward a mutually beneficial solution.

Negotiation is a joint process of finding a mutually acceptable solution to a complex conflict. Negotiating is a useful strategy under the following conditions:

> There are two or more parties. Negotiation is primarily an interpersonal or intergroup process.

> There is a conflict of interest between the parties such that what one party wants is not what the other party wants.

> The parties are willing to negotiate because each believes it can use its influence to obtain a better outcome than by simply taking the side of the other party.

> The parties prefer to work together rather than to fight openly, give in, break off contact, or take the dispute to a higher authority.

There are two major negotiating approaches: distributive bargaining and integrative negotiation.[57] *Distributive bargaining* is an approach in which the goals of one party are in direct conflict with the goals of the other party. Resources are limited, and each party wants to maximize its share of the resources (get its part of the pie). It is a competitive or win–lose approach to negotiations. Sometimes distributive bargaining causes negotiators to focus so much on their differences that they ignore their common ground. In these cases, distributive bargaining can become counterproductive. The reality is, however, that some situations are distributive in nature, particularly when the parties are interdependent. If a negotiator wants to maximize the value of a single deal and is not worried about maintaining a good relationship with the other party, distributive bargaining may be an option.

In contrast, *integrative negotiation* is an approach in which the parties' goals are not seen as mutually exclusive and in which the focus is on making it possible for both sides to achieve their objectives. Integrative negotiation focuses on the merits of the issues and is a win–win approach. (How can we make the pie bigger?) For integrative negotiation to be successful, certain preconditions must be present. These include having a common goal, faith in one's own problem-solving abilities, a belief in the validity of the other party's position, motivation to work together, mutual trust, and clear communication.[58]

Cultural differences in negotiation must be acknowledged. Japanese negotiators, for example, when working with American negotiators, tend to see their power as

distributive bargaining
A negotiation approach in which the goals of the parties are in conflict, and each party seeks to maximize its resources.

integrative negotiation
A negotiation approach that focuses on the merits of the issues and seeks a win–win solution.

To be effective negotiators in a multicultural setting, the negotiating parties should have a respectful understanding of their differing cultural influences.

coming from their role (buyer versus seller). Americans, in contrast, view their power as their ability to walk away from the negotiations.[59] Neither culture understands the other very well, and the negotiations can resemble a dance in which one person is waltzing and the other doing a samba. The collectivism–individualism dimension (discussed in Chapter 2) has a great bearing on negotiations. Americans, with their individualism, negotiate from a position of self-interest; Japanese focus on the good of the group. Cross-cultural negotiations can be more effective if you learn as much about other cultures as possible.

Gender may also play a role in negotiation. There appears to be no evidence that men are better negotiators that women or vice versa. The differences lie in how negotiators are treated. Women are blatantly discriminated against in terms of the offers made to them in negotiations.[60] Gender stereotypes also affect the negotiating process. Women may be seen as accommodating, conciliatory, and emotional (negatives in negotiations) and men may be seen as assertive, powerful, and convincing (positive for negotiations) in accordance with traditional stereotypes. Sometimes, when women feel they're being stereotyped, they exhibit stereotype reactance, which is a tendency to display behavior inconsistent with (or opposite of) the stereotype. This means they become more assertive and convincing. Alternatively, men may choke when they're expected to fulfill the stereotype, fearing that they might not be able to live up to the stereotype.

One way to help men and women avoid stereotyping each other is to promote shared, positive identities between the negotiators. This means recognizing similarities between the two parties; for example, recognizing each other as highly successful professionals. This results in more cooperation because of shared and equal status, as opposed to more competition because of gender stereotypes.[61]

Conflict Management Styles

6. Understand five styles of conflict management, and diagnose your own preferred style.

Managers have at their disposal a variety of conflict management styles: avoiding, accommodating, competing, compromising, and collaborating. One way of classifying styles of conflict management is to examine the styles' assertiveness (the extent to which you want your goals met) and cooperativeness (the extent to which you want to see the other party's concerns met).[62] Figure 13.4 graphs the five conflict management styles using these two dimensions. Table 13.4 lists appropriate situations for using each conflict management style.

Avoiding

Avoiding is a style low on both assertiveness and cooperativeness. Avoiding is a deliberate decision to take no action on a conflict or to stay out of a conflict situation. Some relationship conflicts, such as those involving political norms and personal tastes, may distract team members from their tasks and avoiding may be an appropriate strategy.[63] When the parties are angry and need time to cool down, it may be best to use avoidance. There is a potential danger in using an avoiding style too often, however. Research shows that overuse of this style results in negative evaluations from others in the workplace.[64]

Accommodating

A style in which you are concerned that the other party's goals be met but relatively unconcerned with getting your own way is called accommodating.

FIGURE 13.4 Conflict Management Styles

13.4

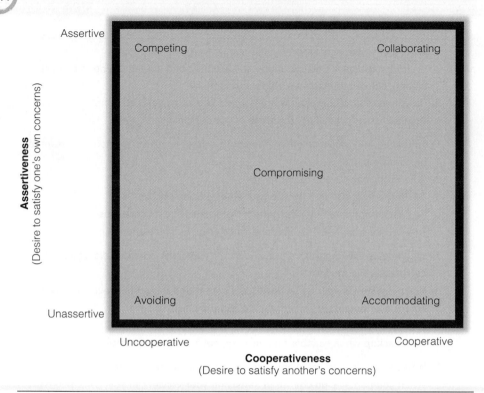

SOURCE: K. W. Thomas, "Conflict and Conflict Management," in M. D. Dunnette. *Handbook of Industrial and Organizational Psychology* (Chicago: Rand McNally, 1976), 900. Used with permission of M. D. Dunnette.

It is cooperative but unassertive. Appropriate situations for accommodating include times when you find you are wrong, when you want to let the other party have his or her way so that that individual will owe you similar treatment later, or when the relationship is important. Overreliance on accommodating has its dangers. Managers who constantly defer to others may find that others lose respect for them. In addition, accommodating managers may become frustrated because their own needs are never met, and they may lose self-esteem.[65]

Competing

Competing is a style that is very assertive and uncooperative. You want to satisfy your own interests and are willing to do so at the other party's expense. In an emergency or in situations where you know you are right, it may be appropriate to put your foot down. For example, environmentalists forced Shell Oil Company (part of Royal Dutch/Shell Group) to scrap its plans to build a refinery in Delaware after a bitter "To Hell with Shell" campaign.[66] Relying solely on competing strategies is dangerous, though. Managers who do so may become reluctant to admit when they are wrong and may find themselves surrounded by people who are afraid to disagree with them.

Compromising

The compromising style is intermediate in both assertiveness and cooperativeness, because each party must give up something to reach a solution to the conflict. Compromises are often made in the final hours of union–management

TABLE 13.4   Uses of Five Styles of Conflict Management

CONFLICT-HANDLING STYLE	APPROPRIATE SITUATION
Competing	1. When quick, decisive action is vital (e.g., emergencies). 2. On important issues where unpopular actions need implementing (e.g., cost cutting, enforcing unpopular rules, discipline). 3. On issues vital to company welfare when you know you are right. 4. Against people who take advantage of noncompetitive behavior.
Collaborating	1. To find an integrative solution when both sets of concerns are too important to be compromised. 2. When your objective is to learn. 3. To merge insights from people with different perspectives. 4. To gain commitment by incorporating concerns into a consensus. 5. To work through feelings that have interfered with a relationship.
Compromising	1. When goals are important but not worth the effort or potential disruption of more assertive modes. 2. When opponents with equal power are committed to mutually exclusive goals. 3. To achieve temporary settlements to complex issues. 4. To arrive at expedient solutions under time pressure. 5. As a backup when collaboration or competition is unsuccessful.
Avoiding	1. When an issue is trivial or more important issues are pressing. 2. When you perceive no chance of satisfying your concerns. 3. When potential disruption outweighs the benefits of resolution. 4. To let people cool down and regain perspective. 5. When gathering information supersedes immediate decision. 6. When others can resolve the conflict more effectively. 7. When issues seem tangential or symptomatic of other issues.
Accommodating	1. When you find you are wrong—to allow a better position to be heard, to learn, and to show your reasonableness. 2. When issues are more important to others than to yourself—to satisfy others and maintain cooperation. 3. To build social credits for later issues. 4. To minimize loss when you are outmatched and losing. 5. When harmony and stability are especially important. 6. To allow employees to develop by learning from mistakes.

SOURCE: K. W. Thomas, "Toward Multidimensional Values in Teaching: The Example of Conflict Behaviors," *Academy of Management Review* 2 (1977): 309–325.

negotiations, when time is of the essence. Compromise may be an effective backup style when efforts toward collaboration are not successful.[67]

It is important to recognize that compromises are not optimal solutions. Compromise means partially surrendering one's position for the sake of coming to terms. Often, when people compromise, they inflate their demands to begin with. The solutions reached may only be temporary, and often compromises do nothing to improve relationships between the parties in the conflict.

Collaborating

A win–win style that is high on both assertiveness and cooperativeness is known as collaborating. Working toward collaborating involves an open and thorough discussion of the conflict and arriving at a solution that is satisfactory to both parties. Situations where collaboration may be effective include times when both parties need to be committed to a final solution or when a combination of different perspectives can be formed into a solution. Collaborating requires open, trusting behavior and sharing information for the benefit of both parties. Long term, it leads to improved relationships and effective performance.[68]

Research on the five styles of conflict management indicates that although most managers favor a certain style, they have the capacity to change styles as the situation demands.[69] A study of project managers found that managers who used a combination of competing and avoiding styles were seen as ineffective by the engineers who worked on their project teams.[70] In another study of conflicts between R&D project managers and technical staff, competing and avoiding styles resulted in more frequent conflict and lower performance, whereas the collaborating style resulted in less frequent conflict and better performance.[71] Use You 13.2 to assess your dominant conflict management style.

Cultural differences also influence the use of different styles of conflict management. For example, one study compared Turkish and Jordanian managers with U.S. managers. All three groups preferred the collaborating style. Turkish managers also reported frequent use of the competing style, whereas Jordanian and U.S. managers reported that it was one of their least used styles.[72]

The human resources manager of one U.S. telecommunications company's office in Singapore engaged a consultant to investigate the conflict in the office.[73] Twenty-two expatriates from the United States and Canada and thirty-eight Singaporeans worked in the office. The consultant used the Thomas model (Figure 13.4) and distributed questionnaires to all managers to determine their conflict management styles. The results were not surprising: The expatriate managers preferred the competing, collaborating, and compromising styles, while the Asians preferred the avoiding and accommodating styles.

Workshops were conducted within the firm to develop an understanding of the differences and how they negatively affected the firm. The Asians interpreted the results as reflecting the tendency of Americans to "shout first and ask questions later." They felt that the Americans had an arrogant attitude and could not handle having their ideas rejected. The Asians attributed their own styles to their cultural background. The Americans attributed the results to the stereotypical view of Asians as unassertive and timid, and they viewed their own results as reflecting their desire to "get things out in the open."

The process opened a dialogue between the two groups, who began to work on the idea of harmony through conflict. They began to discard the traditional stereotypes in favor of shared meanings and mutual understanding.

It is important to remember that preventing and resolving dysfunctional conflict is only half the task of effective conflict management. Stimulating functional conflict is the other half.

Managerial Implications: Creating a Conflict-Positive Organization

Dean Tjosvold argues that well-managed conflict adds to an organization's innovation and productivity.[74] He discusses procedures for making conflict positive. Too many organizations take a win–lose, competitive approach to conflict or avoid conflict altogether. These two approaches view conflict as negative. A positive view of conflict, in contrast, leads to win–win solutions. Figure 13.5 illustrates these three approaches to conflict management.

What Is Your Conflict-Handling Style?

Instructions:

For each of the fifteen items, indicate how often you rely on that tactic by circling the appropriate number.

		Rarely Always
1.	I argue my case with my coworkers to show the merits of my position.	1—2—3—4—5
2.	I negotiate with my coworkers so that a compromise can be reached.	1—2—3—4—5
3.	I try to satisfy the expectations of my coworkers.	1—2—3—4—5
4.	I try to investigate an issue with my coworkers to find a solution acceptable to us.	1—2—3—4—5
5.	I am firm in pursuing my side of the issue.	1—2—3—4—5
6.	I attempt to avoid being "put on the spot" and try to keep my conflict with my coworkers to myself.	1—2—3—4—5
7.	I hold on to my solution to a problem.	1—2—3—4—5
8.	I use "give and take" so that a compromise can be made.	1—2—3—4—5
9.	I exchange accurate information with my coworkers to solve a problem together.	1—2—3—4—5
10.	I avoid open discussion of my differences with my coworkers.	1—2—3—4—5
11.	I accommodate the wishes of my coworkers.	1—2—3—4—5
12.	I try to bring all our concerns out in the open so that the issues can be resolved in the best possible way.	1—2—3—4—5
13.	I propose a middle ground for breaking deadlocks.	1—2—3—4—5
14.	I go along with the suggestions of my coworkers.	1—2—3—4—5
15.	I try to keep my disagreements with my coworkers to myself in order to avoid hard feelings.	1—2—3—4—5

Scoring Key:

Collaborating		Accommodating		Competing		Avoiding		Compromising	
Item	**Score**	**Item**	**Score**	**Item**	**Score**	**Item**	**Score**	**Item**	**Score**
4.	___	3.	___	1.	___	6.	___	2.	___
9.	___	11.	___	5.	___	10.	___	8.	___
12.	___	14.	___	7.	___	15.	___	13.	___
Total = ___		Total = ___		Total = ___		Total = ___		Total = ___	

Your primary conflict-handling style is: _____   Your backup conflict-handling style is: _____
(The category with the highest total.)   (The category with the second highest total.)

SOURCE: Reprinted with permission of Academy of Management, PO Box 3020, Briar Cliff Manor, NY 10510-8020. *A Measure of Styles of Handling Interpersonal Conflict* (Adaptation), M. A. Rahim, *Academy of Management Journal*, June 1983. Reproduced by permission of the publisher via Copyright Clearance Center, Inc.

Four interrelated steps are involved in creating a conflict-positive organization:

1. *Value diversity and confront differences.* Differences should be seen as opportunities for innovation, and diversity should be celebrated. Open and honest confrontations bring out differences, and they are essential for positive conflict.

2. *Seek mutual benefits and unite behind cooperative goals.* Conflicts have to be managed together. Through conflict, individuals learn how much

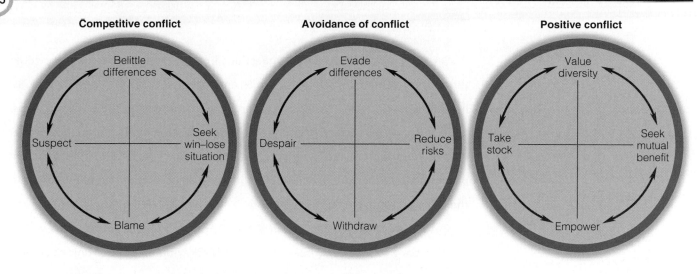

SOURCE: *The Conflict Positive Organization*, by Tjsovold. © 1991. Reprinted by permission of Prentice-Hall, Inc., Upper Saddle River, N.J.

they depend on one another. Even when employees share goals, they may differ on how to accomplish the goals. The important point is that they are moving toward the same objectives. Joint rewards should be given to the whole team for cooperative behavior.

3. *Empower employees to feel confident and skillful.* People must be made to feel that they control their conflicts and that they can deal with their differences productively. When they do so, they should be recognized.

4. *Take stock to reward success and learn from mistakes.* Employees should be encouraged to appreciate one another's strengths and weaknesses and to talk directly about them. They should celebrate their conflict management successes and work out plans for ways they can improve in the future.

Tjosvold believes that a conflict-positive organization has competitive advantages for the future.

A complimentary perspective comes from Peter J. Frost, who proposed that over time, organizational practices like poor conflict management can "poison" the organization as well as those who work within it. He describes how compassionate leaders can help reduce the effects of organizational toxins on their coworkers and how these toxin handlers should be rewarded for this crucial role in maintaining organizational health. Frost's position echoes Tjosvold's, as he calls for firms to become emotionally healthy workplaces for the good of their employees as well as for the good of their stockholders.[75]

Finally, don't overlook the importance of high emotional intelligence in the work of a good conflict manager. The ability to influence your own and others' emotions is not just a practical tool, but it can also serve as an important tactical asset, making you a better negotiator in a variety of situations and helping reduce conflict and increase productivity in your organization.[76]

LOOKING BACK: WHOLE FOODS MARKET

There Are No Easy Answers

Whole Foods, in response to suggestions from throughout the company, took the unprecedented step of allowing its employees to vote on benefits such as health care and purchase discounts at company stores. In what the company terms an example of democracy in action, Whole Foods' employees were allowed the type of input that is typically reserved for unionized employees. Further, the firm plans to repeat the vote in future years, making it, at least at first glance, one of the most responsive employers around.

But questions still remain about Whole Foods and the way it treats its workers. Company founder and libertarian John Mackey bundles labor unions (which he has compared to "herpes") with other outsiders, such as organized crime, who might try to interfere with his firm's operations. Some Web sites condemn his actions as union busting, while others call for Whole Foods' workers throughout the country to organize.[77, 78]

Is John Mackey's anti-union position consistent with Whole Foods' stated values of helping its people grow and prosper, or is it simply a way to keep wages low and profits up? Who holds the high ground in this long-running battle? Expect to see further encounters between Whole Foods and organized labor in the future. And, unless things change radically, expect to see Whole Foods back on *Fortune*'s list of "100 Best Companies to Work For" again next year, despite the conflict.

Chapter Summary

1. Conflict management skills are keys to management success. The manager's task is to stimulate functional conflict and prevent or resolve dysfunctional conflict.

2. Structural causes of conflict include specialization, interdependence, common resources, goal differences, authority relationships, status inconsistencies, and jurisdictional ambiguities.

3. Personal factors that lead to conflict include differences in skills and abilities, personalities, perceptions, or values and ethics; emotions; communication barriers; and cultural differences. The increasing diversity of the workforce and globalization of business have potential to increase conflict arising from these differences.

4. The levels of conflict include interorganizational, intergroup, interpersonal, and intrapersonal.

5. Individuals engaged in interpersonal conflict often display aggressive, compromise, or withdrawal defense mechanisms.

6. Ineffective techniques for managing conflict include nonaction, secrecy, administrative orbiting, due process nonaction, and character assassination.

7. Effective techniques for managing conflict include appealing to superordinate goals, expanding resources, changing personnel, changing structure, and confronting and negotiating.

8. In negotiating, managers can use a variety of conflict management styles, including avoiding, accommodating, competing, compromising, and collaborating.

9. Managers should strive to create a conflict-positive organization—one that values diversity, empowers employees, and seeks win–win solutions to conflicts.

Key Terms

administrative orbiting (p. 437)

character assassination (p. 437)

compensation (p. 435)

conflict (p. 421)

conversion (p. 436)

displacement (p. 434)

distributive bargaining (p. 439)

due process nonaction (p. 437)

dysfunctional conflict (p. 423)

fantasy (p. 436)

fixation (p. 434)

flight/withdrawal (p. 436)

functional conflict (p. 422)

identification (p. 435)

integrative negotiation (p. 439)

intergroup conflict (p. 429)

interorganizational conflict (p. 429)

interpersonal conflict (p. 430)

interrole conflict (p. 430)

intragroup conflict (p. 430)

intrapersonal conflict (p. 430)

intrarole conflict (p. 430)

jurisdictional ambiguity (p. 426)

negativism (p. 434)

nonaction (p. 437)

person–role conflict (p. 430)

rationalization (p. 435)

secrecy (p. 437)

superordinate goal (p. 438)

Review Questions

1. Discuss the differences between functional and dysfunctional conflict. Why should a manager understand conflict?

2. Identify the structural and personal factors that contribute to conflict.

3. Discuss the four major forms of conflict in organizations.

4. What defense mechanisms do people use in interpersonal conflict?

5. What are the most effective techniques for managing conflict at work? What are some ineffective techniques?

6. Identify and discuss five styles of conflict management.

Discussion and Communication Questions

1. What causes you the most conflict at work or school?

2. Identify the different intragroup, interrole, intrarole, and person–role conflicts that you experience.

3. Which defense mechanism do you see people exhibiting most frequently? Why do you think this is the case? How can you manage this type of reaction to a conflict?

4. Are you comfortable with your preferred conflict management style? Would you consider modifying it?

5. *(communication question)* Think of a person with whom you have had a recent conflict. Write a letter to this person, attempting to resolve the conflict. Use the concepts from the chapter to accomplish your objective. Be sure to address whether the conflict is functional or dysfunctional, what styles each party has used, effective strategies for resolving the conflict, and ineffective strategies that should be avoided.

Ethical Dilemma

Scott Davis sat at his desk anxiously waiting for the next few minutes to pass. It was almost time for the meeting he had scheduled between Debra Cronin and Ken Brown. Scott knew this meeting would be challenging for everyone. Debra and Ken had been at odds for quite some time. The prob-lems started soon after Ken joined the company. At first Scott thought the conflict was healthy and would bring some much needed change to the department. Scott soon learned that the disputes between Debra and Ken were more personal than professional.

Debra had been with the company for seven years. Scott had no complaints about her performance. She was a hard worker that got the job done. Unfortunately, Debra was also the source of a lot of conflict in the department. She always felt she knew the best way to do everything and freely shared that opinion with everyone, whether they wanted it or not. Scott has spent many hours listening to employees' complaints about Debra's insistence on showing them the "proper" way to do their jobs. Debra's interference had caused a fair amount of discontent in the department, but Scott never felt it was enough to consider termination. The meeting today may well change that opinion.

Ken Brown was new to the company. He had joined Scott's department just four months ago. He was young with a lot of fresh, new ideas. Scott liked everything about Ken and thought he would be great for the department and the company. But just like those before him, Ken found working with Debra difficult. She was set in her ways and was not going to change. Worse, she was undermining the other employees' interest in changing. Scott felt that he had done everything he could to resolve the conflict between the two, without success. He felt sure that today's meeting would end with one person leaving the company. His decision was which one: Debra, the longtime employee, or Ken, the newcomer, with the vision for the future?

Questions

1. Does Scott have a greater responsibility to Debra than to Ken?

2. To whom does Scott owe the greatest responsibility?

3. Evaluate Scott's decision alternatives using rule, virtue, rights, and justice theories.

Experiential Exercises

13.1 Conflicts over Unethical Behavior

Many conflicts in work organizations arise over differences in beliefs concerning what constitutes ethical versus unethical behavior. The following questionnaire provides a list of behaviors that you or your coworkers might engage in when working for a company. Go over each item, and circle the number that best indicates the frequency with which you personally would (or do, if you work now) engage in that behavior. Then put an X over the number you think represents how often your coworkers would (or do) engage in that behavior. Finally, put a check mark beside the item (in the "Needs Control" column) if you believe that management should control that behavior.

	At Every Opportunity	Often	About Half the Time	Seldom	Never	Needs Control
1. Passing blame for errors to an innocent coworker.	5	4	3	2	1	_____
2. Divulging confidential information.	5	4	3	2	1	_____
3. Falsifying time/quality/quantity reports.	5	4	3	2	1	_____
4. Claiming credit for someone else's work.	5	4	3	2	1	_____
5. Padding an expense account by over 10 percent.	5	4	3	2	1	_____
6. Pilfering company materials and supplies.	5	4	3	2	1	_____
7. Accepting gifts/favors in exchange for preferential treatment.	5	4	3	2	1	_____
8. Giving gifts/favors in exchange for preferential treatment.	5	4	3	2	1	_____
9. Padding an expense account by up to 10 percent.	5	4	3	2	1	_____
10. Authorizing a subordinate to violate company rules.	5	4	3	2	1	_____
11. Calling in sick to take a day off.	5	4	3	2	1	_____
12. Concealing one's errors.	5	4	3	2	1	_____
13. Taking longer than necessary to do a job.	5	4	3	2	1	_____
14. Using company services for personal use.	5	4	3	2	1	_____
15. Doing personal business on company time.	5	4	3	2	1	_____

	At Every Opportunity	Often	About Half the Time	Seldom	Never	Needs Control
16. Taking extra personal time (lunch hour, breaks, early departure, and so forth).	5	4	3	2	1	_____
17. Not reporting others' violations of company policies and rules.	5	4	3	2	1	_____
18. Overlooking a superior's violation of policy to prove loyalty to the boss.	5	4	3	2	1	_____

Discussion Questions

1. Would (do) your coworkers seem to engage in these behaviors more often than you would (do)? Why do you have this perception?

2. Which behaviors tend to be most frequent?

3. How are the most frequent behaviors different from the behaviors engaged in less frequently?

4. What are the most important items for managers to control? How should managers control these behaviors?

5. Select a particular behavior from the list. Have two people debate whether the behavior is ethical or not.

6. What types of conflicts could emerge if the behaviors in the list occurred frequently?

SOURCE: From Managerial Experience, 3e and 3rd Edition by Jauch L. © 1983. Reprinted with permission of South-Western, a division of Thomson Learning: www.thomsonlearning.com. Fax 800-730-2215.

13.2 The World Bank Game: An Intergroup Negotiation

The purposes of this exercise are to learn about conflict and trust between groups and to practice negotiation skills. In the course of the exercise, money will be won or lost. Your team's objective is to win as much money as it can. Your team will be paired with another team, and both teams will receive identical instructions. After reading these instructions, each team will have ten minutes to plan its strategy.

Each team is assumed to have contributed $50 million to the World Bank. Teams may have to pay more or may receive money from the World Bank, depending on the outcome.

Each team will receive twenty cards. These cards are the weapons. Each card has a marked side (X) and an unmarked side. The marked side signifies that the weapon is armed; the unmarked side signifies that the weapon is unarmed.

At the beginning, each team will place ten of its twenty weapons in their armed position (marked side up) and the remaining ten in their unarmed position (marked side down). The weapons will remain in the team's possession and out of sight of the other team at all times.

The game will consist of *rounds* and *moves*. Each round will be composed of seven moves by each team. There will be two or more rounds in the game, depending on the time available. Payoffs will be determined and recorded after each round. The rules are as follows:

1. A move consists of turning two, one, or none of the team's weapons from armed to unarmed status, or vice versa.

2. Each team has one and a half minutes for each move. There is a thirty-second period between each move. At the end of the one and a half minutes, the team must have turned two, one, or none of its weapons from armed to unarmed status or from unarmed to armed status. If the team fails to move in the allotted time, no change can be made in weapon status until the next move.

3. The two-minute length of the period between the beginning of one move and the beginning of the next is unalterable.

Finances:

The funds each team has contributed to the World Bank are to be allocated in the following manner: $30 million will be returned to each team to be used as the team's treasury during the course of the game, and $20 million will be retained for the operation of the World Bank.

Payoffs:

1. If there is an attack:

   a. Each team may announce an attack on the other team by notifying the banker during the thirty seconds following any minute-and-a-half period used to decide upon the move (including the seventh, or final, decision period in any round). The choice of each team during the decision period just ended counts as a move. An attack may not be made during negotiations.

b. If there is an attack by one or both teams, two things happen: (1) the round ends, and (2) the World Bank assesses a penalty of $2.5 million on each team.

c. The team with the greater number of armed weapons wins $1.5 million for each armed weapon it has over and above the number of armed weapons of the other team. These funds are paid directly from the treasury of the losing team to the treasury of the winning team. The banker will manage the transfer of funds.

2. If there is no attack:

At the end of each round (seven moves), each team's treasury will receive from the World Bank $1 million for each of its weapons that is at that point unarmed; and each team's treasury will pay to the World Bank $1 million for each of its weapons remaining armed.

Negotiations:

Between moves, each team will have the opportunity to communicate with the other team through its negotiations. Either team may call for negotiations by notifying the banker during any of the thirty-second periods between decisions. A team is free to accept or reject any invitation to negotiate.

Negotiators from both teams are required to meet after the third and sixth moves (after the thirty-second period following the move, if there is no attack).

Negotiations can last no longer than three minutes. When the two negotiators return to their teams, the minute-and-a-half decision period for the next move will begin once again.

Negotiators are bound only by (a) the three-minute time limit for negotiations and (b) their required appearance after the third and sixth moves. They are always free to say whatever is necessary to benefit themselves or their teams. The teams are not bound by agreements made by their negotiators, even when those agreements are made in good faith.

Special Roles:

Each team has ten minutes to organize itself and plan team strategy. During this period, before the first round begins, each team must choose persons to fill the following roles:

- A *negotiator*—activities stated above.
- A *representative*—to communicate the team's decisions to the banker.
- A *recorder*—to record the moves of the team and to keep a running balance of the team's treasury.
- A *treasurer*—to execute all financial transactions with the banker.

The instructor will serve as the banker for the World Bank and will signal the beginning of each of the rounds.

At the end of the game, each participant should complete the following questionnaire, which assesses reactions to the World Bank Game.

World Bank Questionnaire:

1. To what extent are you satisfied with your team's strategy?

    Highly   1 2 3 4 5 6 7   Highly
    dissatisfied   satisfied

2. To what extent do you believe the other team is trustworthy?

    Highly   1 2 3 4 5 6 7   Highly
    untrustworthy   trustworthy

3. To what extent are you satisfied with the performance of your negotiator?

    Highly   1 2 3 4 5 6 7   Highly
    dissatisfied   satisfied

4. To what extent was there a consensus on your team regarding its moves?

    Very little   1 2 3 4 5 6 7   A great deal

5. To what extent do you trust the other members of your team?

    Very little   1 2 3 4 5 6 7   A great deal

6. Select one word that describes how you feel about your team: _____.

7. Select one word that describes how you feel about the other team: _____.

Negotiators only:

    How did you see the other team's negotiator?

    Phony and   1 2 3 4 5 6 7   Authentic
    insincere   and sincere

At the end of the game, the class will reconvene and discuss team members' responses to the World Bank Questionnaire. In addition, the following questions are to be addressed:

1. What was each team's strategy for winning? What strategy was most effective?

2. Contrast the outcomes in terms of win–win solutions to conflict versus win–lose solutions.

SOURCE: Adapted by permission from N. H. Berkowitz and H. A. Hornstein, "World Bank: An Intergroup Negotiation," in J. W. Pfeiffer and J. E. Jones, eds., *The 1975 Handbook for Group Facilitators* (San Diego: Pfeiffer), 58–62. Copyright © 1975 Pfeiffer/Jossey-Bass. This material is used by permission of John Wiley & Sons, Inc.

WORLD BANK RECORD SHEET

		Round One		Round Two		Round Three		Round Four	
		Armed	Unarmed	Armed	Unarmed	Armed	Unarmed	Armed	Unarmed
Move		10	10	10	10	10	10	10	10
	1								
	2								
	3								
Required Negotiation	4								
	5								
	6								
Required Negotiation	7								

Funds in Team Treasury	$30 million				
Funds of Other Treasury	$30 million				
Funds in World Bank	$40 million				

Biz Flix | The Guru

"Deepak Chopra meets Dr. Ruth" is a possible alternate title or subtitle for this film. The film follows Ramu Gupta's (Jimi Mistry) journey from India to the United States where he wants to become a film star. Unlucky at keeping a job, Ramu is fired from a waiter's job and a pornographic film role. By closely following the advice of Sharrona (Heather Graham), his ex-pornographic co-star, Ramu becomes a highly acclaimed though mystical sex therapist.

The scene from *The Guru* appears in the final quarter of the film. It occurs after Ramu starts his performance at the Broadway Playhouse to a packed, enthusiastic audience. By this time in the film, he has become a renowned sex therapist who has moved from individual therapy to public performances. The film continues after this scene with self-appointed manager Vijay (Emil Marwa) bringing several beautiful women to Ramu's new apartment.

What to Watch for and Ask Yourself:

> What is the latent conflict (cause of conflict) that triggered this conflict event or episode?

> What conflict management style do Ramu and Sharrona use during this episode?

> Do they end the conflict with a clear conflict aftermath? Do you expect the conflict to continue? Why or why not?

Workplace Video | Fallon Worldwide: Managing in a Global Environment

Advertising agency Fallon Worldwide has grown from a Minneapolis-based American firm into an international business with billings of over $800 million and clients all over the globe. From the beginning, the agency's founders showed an interest in global markets, recruiting employees from Europe, South America, and Australia while creating a client base of multinational corporations such as BMW, United Airlines, and L'Oreal.

Fallon has gained many advantages through globalization. By going global, the ad agency reaches consumers well beyond the North American region. Expansion into emerging markets like Sao Paulo and Hong Kong allows the firm to develop campaigns that effectively advertise brands across geographic and cultural borders. Additionally, by becoming a global organization, Fallon has been able to benefit from the perspective and experience of marketers from around the world.

Despite its advantages, globalization can also be a source of conflict in organizations. Global expansion has created organizational and technological challenges for Fallon's employees, and many workers have expressed fears about the possibility of losing the creative freedom and inspiring corporate culture that helped make the company great. In addition, the global environment introduces language and cultural barriers that create many challenges for Fallon's managers.

The pressures associated with becoming an international agency are enormous. Yet even with all the difficulties, working globally can be fun. Alliances have to be forged, and managers have to think seriously about guiding a business through different cultures. In the end, it all comes down to planning, strategy, and taking a risk or two.

Questions

1. *What factors did Fallon consider when deciding to expand its business globally? How does the advertising firm manage the conflict between global and local objectives?*

2. *What common sources of conflict are associated with globalization?*

3. *What interpersonal hurdles do managers face when operating in a global setting?*

Vying for Control of Molson Inc.

Molson Inc., the Canadian brewing company, was founded in 1786 by John Molson and has remained family controlled for all but a few years since then. After an era of extensive diversification into such businesses as lumbering, furniture making, and pipe and furnace manufacturing, Molson sold control of its brewing operations to Australia's Foster's Group Ltd. in the mid-1990s. The sale was made in part in anticipation of "tough competition from U.S. beer makers as trade barriers fell." At about the same time a dispute began brewing between rival factions of the Molson family for control of the Molson business empire. Eric Molson and Ian Molson were pitted against one another in the struggle for control.

Family Relationships as a Backdrop for the Struggle

John Molson passed the ownership of the company to the family's eldest sons, whereas the top management positions at the company were given to outsiders or Molson relatives with business acumen. This long-established tradition eventually created a rift in the family—"the shareholders considered themselves 'real' or 'brewery' Molsons and viewed other family members as hired help."

Eric Molson's side of the family held the majority of shares and controlled the top operating positions throughout the latter half of the twentieth century. In 1988, Eric became the company's chairman and inherited his father's voting shares in the company. Eric is a shy man who is uncomfortable with public speaking. Eric's supporters say that he deserves more credit for his business competence than he has received.

Eric's younger cousin Ian eventually became an aspirant for the chairman's job. Ian's branch of the Molson family, which was not viewed as being "brewing line," fell into disfavor after it sold the Montreal Canadiens hockey team in 1971. Ian began working at the brewery during the summer when he was a teenager in the early 1970s and then went on to become a Harvard-educated international banker. In 1996, Ian joined the Molson board of directors. "Ian used his deal-making skills to sell non-core businesses and buy back control of Molson's beer operations." Ian also was primarily responsible for the acquisition of a Brazilian brewer, which turned out to be a poor investment decision. Further, Ian increased his holdings of Molson's voting stock.

The Evolving Conflict

Ian maintains that Eric endangered the company's future due to his lack of business acumen. Ian charged that Eric's refusal to work with him had destabilized the company. Eric's supporters, however, stress that Ian has destabilized the company through his impatience and aggressiveness.

Eric and Ian clashed at board meetings, with Ian often interrupting Eric. Their differences became increasingly intense and embittered. At a January 2003 board meeting, Eric announced a review of Molson's corporate governance. While a surprise to the board, the review was nonetheless conducted. The governance report recommended eliminating Ian's position as deputy chairman. Ian confronted Eric, but nothing was resolved. At the November board meeting, the recommendation to eliminate Ian's position was defeated. At the May 2004 meeting, three board members, including Ian, resigned in protest over Eric's leadership of the company. The remainder of the board chose to reaffirm Eric's status as chairman. At the company's annual meeting the following month, Ian and four other members of the family-controlled board refused to stand for reelection.

In an effort to wrest control of the company from Eric after the May board meeting, Ian began "lobbying family members to pool votes and blunt Eric's voting control." Some members of the Molson extended family were quietly questioning Eric's leadership of the company. At the company's annual meeting, Ian's brother William openly challenged Eric, pointing out that "Ian's involvement has been good for the company and the shareholders." Eric denied that the feud with Ian was having a negative effect on the board and the company. He insisted that the board was being pared down for governance reasons.

Meanwhile, Molson Inc. and Adolph Coors Co. initiated merger talks. The two companies had been working together since 1998 with each company distributing the other's products in its home territory. The major hurdle to the proposed merger was the feud between the two factions of the Molson family. Eric, who along with allied family members controlled more than half the voting shares, favored the merger. Ian, with approximately 10 percent of the voting shares, was against the merger. A shareholder agreement between Ian and Eric prevented either one from transferring or selling his voting shares without the consent of the other. Eric maintained that he had found a legal way to circumvent the agreement. Ian, on the other hand, was preparing to offer as much as $4 billion to acquire Molson Inc. in order to prevent the merger with Coors.

On July 22, 2004, the two companies jointly announced the merger of Molson and Coors. The merged company would be known as Molson Coors Brewing Company and would have established brands in Canada, the United States, the United Kingdom, and Brazil. The merger would make Molson Coors Brewing Company the world's fifth largest brewer and is expected to deliver substantial value to shareholders.

Discussion Questions

1. From your perspective, were the consequences of the conflict between Eric Molson and Ian Molson positive or negative?
2. What structural factors and personal factors were likely causes of the conflict between Eric Molson and Ian Molson?
3. What conflict management styles do Eric Molson and Ian Molson seem to be using?

SOURCE: This case was written by Michael K. McCuddy, The Louis S. and Mary L. Morgal Chair of Christian Business Ethics and Professor of Management, College of Business Administration, Valparaiso University. This case was developed from material contained on the Molson Web site at http://www.molson.com and in the following articles: E. Cheney and R. Frank, "Molson Chairman Resists Calls for Ouster Amid a Family Feud," *The Wall Street Journal* (June 23, 2004): B46; R. Frank and D. K. Berman, "Molson, Coors Talks Heat Up, But a Deal Faces Several Hurdles," *The Wall Street Journal* (July 19, 2004): B2; R. Frank and D. K. Berman, "Ian Molson May Thwart Coors Deal," *The Wall Street Journal* (July 22, 2004): A3; and R. Frank and E. Cheney, "Canadian Club: A Brewing Family Feud Poses Risks for Molson Beer Empire," *The Wall Street Journal* (June 29, 2004): A1.

Google™ (C)

In the span of five years, Google Inc. experienced phenomenal growth, going from a loss of $6.1 million on revenues of $220,000 in calendar year 1998 to a net income of $105.6 million on revenues of $961.9 million for calendar year 2003. Starting with one employee and themselves, Sergey Brin and Larry Page now help lead a company with approximately 2,000 employees. While such growth is impressive, it has not been problem free. Brin and Page, along with Eric Schmidt, whom they hired as chairman and chief executive officer in 2001, have tried to keep the company on the cutting edge of innovation both with respect to its products and services and its operational approach. Still, these innovation efforts, while being successful, have also led to some potential problematic consequences.

The innovation efforts with respect to products and services have not only placed Google in a favorable competitive position, but also have fostered the growth of competition. For instance, AOL, eBay, and Amazon, among others, are competing for some of Google's advertising revenues. On another competitive front, Yahoo!, a licensee of Google's search technology, has invested more than a $1 billion in a bid to compete directly with Google's search engine. A third challenge to Google's product and service innovations is Microsoft's efforts to develop a new operating system that contains a richer search engine than Google's current search engine.

Google's innovative operational approaches can be best captured through its culture of informality, equality, involvement, and empowerment; its aversion to bureaucracy; and its top leadership. Each represents an area in which Google has tried to operate in ways that are distinctly different from many other companies. Yet, in doing so, Google has encountered or is likely to encounter some rather interesting and challenging unintended consequences.

Google's Culture of Informality, Equality, Involvement, and Empowerment

Google tries to treat employees like family. Google provides employees with free lunch and dinner, pre-pared by the former chef of the rock band, Grateful Dead. Beanbag chairs and lava lamps are common decorations at the company's headquarters in Mountain View, California. Animals are welcome at the company's headquarters. The staff goes to Lake Tahoe for a weekend retreat once a year.

Google's family atmosphere seems to foster a spirit of inclusion. However, this effort at inclusion goes beyond the amenities and benefits. Every Friday, for instance, the entire staff meets to talk about the business—a practice that has endured since the company's founding. Business information is shared with the employees, and ideas are sought from them.

Still, the spirit of inclusiveness has not been as successful as Brin and Page might have desired. For example, an implied caste system at Google has resulted from hiring hundreds of contract workers who do not have the same benefits as the other full-time employees. Engineers, who reflect the image of Brin and Page, are at the top of this unwritten and unspoken caste system. Contract workers—some 30 percent of Google's workforce—are at the bottom of the caste system. They work alongside those at the top of the caste system but they do not have the "benefits, stock options, or access to the company intranet, not to mention meetings or social events" that those at the top have.

Google's Aversion to Bureaucracy

Google operates with very little bureaucracy in order to encourage engineers to rapidly develop good ideas. Indeed, Google has an aversion to bureaucracy. Brin, Page, and Schmidt strive to keep the structure as simple as possible and the reporting relationships direct. Given the competencies of the people they hire, they expect that clear and direct relationships will be beneficial in addressing the work and issues of the company. Employees are empowered to take meaningful actions within their areas of responsibility.

While Google's aversion to bureaucracy may be seen as positive, some observers wonder whether things might be out of control. Some of Google's business partners have reported difficulty in determining which Google employees are responsible for making certain decisions. "Google has hired so many people in its middle ranks and given so many the same title—project manager—that no one can figure out who's in charge or even what Google's licensing policy is." While acknowledging that Google is disorganized, Brin and Page maintain that it is a result of deliberate choices, not mismanagement, inattention, or arrogance. To support this contention, Brin and Page point out that employees must spend 20 percent of their working time interviewing outside job candidates and another 20 percent on self-directed projects. Consequently, such things as preparing for meetings with partners or clients—or even arriving on time—sometimes are not high priority activities.

Google's Top Leadership

With Sergey Brin as a Google cofounder and President, Technology, Larry Page as a cofounder and President, Products, and Eric Schmidt, as Chairman of the Executive Committee and Chief Executive Officer, some people wonder: "Who is really in charge at Google?" Employees and business partners are frequently confused about who is responsible for which activities. There is controversy concerning whether CEO Schmidt is actually in charge of the company or whether cofounders Brin and Page are in charge. Some people believe that Brin and Page are actually in charge and that Schmidt is just a figurehead. Other people believe that Google is performing too well for Schmidt to realistically attempt any major changes.

Schmidt indicates that he isn't interested in pushing Brin and Page aside or in changing Google's culture. Instead, he has focused on building the revenue side of the business, shepherding the development of Google AdWords and Google AdSense. Schmidt points out that whenever Brin, Page, and he disagree, they take a vote and whoever gets two votes wins. Schmidt says that as CEO there may be a rare occasion when he will override Brin and Page if the issue is sufficiently important and he disagrees with them.

In Google's April 29, 2004 filing with the Securities and Exchange Commission of the United States

for its initial public offering (IPO) of stock, the executive roles of Sergey Brin, Larry Page, and Eric Schmidt are described as a triumvirate. Brin and Page write: "Sergey and I have worked closely together for the last eight years, five at Google. Eric, our CEO, joined Google three years ago. The three of us run the company collaboratively with Sergey and me as presidents. The structure is unconventional, but we have worked successfully in this way." Brin's responsibilities focus on engineering and business deals. Page's responsibilities encompass engineering and product management. As CEO, Schmidt has the legal responsibilities associated with that position and coordinates the activities of the company's vice presidents and sales organization.

Brin, Page, and Schmidt meet on a daily basis to update one another and to collaboratively focus on important and immediate issues. Although decisions are often made by one of the three individually, the other two are always briefed later. This enables the triumvirate to manage the company on the basis of healthy debate accompanied by the absence of significant internal conflict.

Discussion Questions

1. What effect does Google's culture seem to have on work group dynamics and cohesiveness?
2. Why does Google have an aversion to bureaucracy, and what effects does it have on how employees interact with one another and approach their jobs?
3. How would you describe the top leadership at Google, and why is effective communication and decision making so essential to this form of leadership?

SOURCE: This case was written by Michael K. McCuddy, The Louis S. and Mary L. Morgal Chair of Christian Business Ethics and Professor of Management, College of Business Administration, Valparaiso University. This case was developed from material contained on the Google Inc. Web site at http://www.google.com and in the following articles: J. Boorstin, "STREET LIFE: Google's IPO Filing: Nearly Everything is Unorthodox," *Fortune* (April 29, 2004): accessed at http://www.fortune.com/fortune/streetlife/0,15704,631301,00.html; *Form S-1 Registration Statement Under The Securities Act of 1933: Google Inc.* (April 29,

2004): accessed at http://sec.gov/Archives/edgar/data/1288776/00011931250407339/ds1.htm; S. Levy, "Next Frontiers: All Eyes on Google," *Newsweek* (March 29, 2004): 48–50, 52, 54–56, 58; F. Vogelstein, "Can Google Grow Up? Google Is One of the Best Things to Happen to the Net. So Will Its IPO, Expected This Spring, Be a Must-Buy? A Look Inside Reveals a Talented Company Facing Trouble," *Fortune* (December 8, 2003): accessed at http://www.fortune.com/fortune/technology/articles/0,15114,548765,00.html; F. Vogelstein and A. Lashinsky, "At Google, Beware the IPO Aftermath. Welcome to the World of Employee Envy and Financial Disclosure," *Fortune* (May 17, 2004): accessed at http://www.fortune.com/fortune/technology/articles/0,15114,632052,00.html.

PART 4

Organizational Processes and Structure

Chapter 14

Jobs and the Design of Work

After reading this chapter, you should be able to do the following:

1 Define the term *job* and identify six patterns of defining *work*.

2 Discuss the four traditional approaches to job design.

3 Describe the Job Characteristics Model.

4 Compare the social information-processing (SIP) model with traditional job design approaches.

5 Explain ergonomics and the interdisciplinary framework for the design of work.

6 Compare Japanese, German, and Scandinavian approaches to work.

7 Explain how job control, uncertainty, and conflict can be managed for employee well-being.

8 Discuss five contemporary issues in the design of work.

THINKING AHEAD: PIXAR ANIMATION STUDIOS

Playing at Pixar

The work environment at Pixar has been described as "semicontrolled chaos," which is guided by the Pixar philosophy that good work and performance come from creative people bouncing ideas off each other. Common areas like the cafeteria, mailroom, and even the restrooms encourage people from different departments to meet and trade ideas. Hence, common functions facilitate the bouncing. The imagination of the artists, writers, animators, and programmers who work at Pixar is evident in their office décor. One row of offices is noted for its varied roofing materials. One is topped with a thatch tiki-room design, the next in Spanish tile, and a third in suburban shingles with a satellite dish. Hanging from the ceiling is the large Canadian flag that flew from a pole at Pixar's front entrance in honor of Glenn McQueen, an animator who died of cancer in 2002.

All this happens in the context of a two-story, 220,000-square-foot building of brick, steel beams, and filtered glass set on a 16-acre campus of rolling green that includes an outdoor amphitheater and half a soccer field. The studio resembles a community college rather than a business. This contextual design was not as intended. The original plan called for having a separate building for those who worked on the story lines, another one for those who worked on animation, a third for those whose work was technology, and so on. This is actually how a "regular" movie studio would have its work done. While this approach to work appears logical and rational and gets people to focus narrowly on their type of work (e.g., animation) that contributes to the whole, there is also a definite downside to the approach.

The downside is reflected in a story. Disney animators, Frank Thomas and Ollie Johnston, recollected what Walt Disney did for them after their success with *Snow White and the Seven Dwarfs*. Disney had a set built for them that was to be the utopian animation studio. Every person had an office, and each wing of the building was separated so that every office would have natural light. This design served to separate and isolate people so that no one knew what was going on. There was no real interaction. Based on this story, Pixar scrapped the multibuilding plan. Pixar's CEO Steve Jobs wanted to go even further than one building; he wanted one bathroom to create a "bathroom effect" where people would interact and be creative.[1] Will the creativity and imagination of Pixar's artists, writers, animators, and programmers be enough to take them "to infinity and beyond"?

job
A set of specified work and task activities that engage an individual in an organization.

A *job* is defined as an employee's specific work and task activities in an organization. A job is not the same as an organizational position or a career. *Organizational position* identifies a job in relation to other parts of the organization; career refers to a sequence of job experiences over time.

This chapter focuses on jobs and the design of work as elements of the organization's structure. Jobs help people define their work and become integrated into the organization. The first section in the chapter examines the meaning of work in organizations. The second major section addresses four traditional approaches to job design developed between the late 1800s and the 1970s. The third major section examines four alternative approaches to job design developed over the past couple of decades. The final section addresses emerging issues in job design.

Work in Organizations

work
Mental or physical activity that has productive results.

Work is effortful, productive activity resulting in a product or a service. Work is one important reason why organizations exist. A job is composed of a set of specific tasks, each of which is an assigned piece of work to be done in a specific time period. Work is an especially important human endeavor because it has a powerful effect in binding a person to reality. Through work, people become securely attached to reality and securely connected in human relationships. However, work may also overshadow one's personal life. This is an emerging concern in the United Kingdom, as discussed in The Real World 14.1.

Work has different meanings for different people. For all people, work is organized into jobs, and jobs fit into the larger structure of an organization. The structure of jobs is the concern of this chapter, and the structure of the organization is the concern of the next chapter. Both chapters emphasize organizations as sets of task and authority relationships through which people get work done.

The Meaning of Work

meaning of work
The way a person interprets and understands the value of work as part of life.

The *meaning of work* differs from person to person, and from culture to culture. In an increasingly global workplace, it is important to understand and appreciate differences among individuals and cultures with regard to the meaning of work. One study found six patterns people follow in defining *work*, and these help explain the cultural differences in people's motivation to work.[2]

Croner Consulting Looks at Work in the United Kingdom

In the early 1980s, the United Kingdom had the lowest divorce rate among European nations. Today, it has the highest divorce rate, and work/life balance is a hugely contentious issue in the United Kingdom because employees are torn between work and family commitments. Work has become a dominating issue at the expense of family life and balance.

In this context, Croner Consulting conducts surveys of work life. Croner is the United Kingdom's leading supplier of business information, advice, and support. Croner has concluded that the United Kingdom is the hardest working nation in Europe. Employees have a difficult time moving between jobs, and job security is at an all-time low in the country. Sixty-one percent of Britons are reluctant to take benefits, such as holiday time off, for fear that it will hinder their career prospects. The number of work-ing parents in the United Kingdom has also risen, along with the divorce rate and the length of commuting time.

Work is increasingly dominating the lives of Britons. Further, the work culture in the United Kingdom supports the belief that longer hours equal a more devoted, loyal, and productive worker. Croner Consulting points out that the system is not designed that way. In fact, both management and government believe employees should take advantage of benefits such as generous holiday entitlements and flexible working arrangements. Unfortunately, employee fear of job loss appears to be an overarching angst and dark specter shadowing the British working class.

SOURCE: F. Warner, "Employees Choosing Work over Perks," *Management Services* 48 (March 2004): 3.

Pattern A people define *work* as an activity in which value comes from performance and for which a person is accountable. It is generally self-directed and devoid of negative affect.

Pattern B people define *work* as an activity that provides a person with positive personal affect and identity. Work contributes to society and is not unpleasant.

Pattern C people define *work* as an activity from which profit accrues to others by its performance and that may be done in various settings other than a working place. Work is usually physically strenuous and somewhat compulsive.

Pattern D people define *work* as primarily a physical activity a person must do that is directed by others and generally performed in a working place. Work is usually devoid of positive affect and is unpleasantly connected to performance.

Pattern E people define *work* as a physically and mentally strenuous activity. It is generally unpleasant and devoid of positive affect.

Pattern F people define *work* as an activity constrained to specific time periods that does not bring positive affect through its performance.

These six patterns were studied in six different countries: Belgium, Germany, Israel, Japan, the Netherlands, and the United States. Table 14.1 summarizes the percentage of workers in each country who defined work according to each of the six patterns. An examination of the table shows that a small percentage of workers in all six countries used either Pattern E or Pattern F to define *work*. Furthermore, there are significant differences among countries in how *work* is defined. In the Netherlands, *work* is defined most positively and with the most balanced personal and collective reasons for doing it. *Work* is defined least positively and with the most collective reason for doing it in Germany and Japan.

TABLE 14.1   Work Definition Patterns by Nation

SAMPLE	PATTERN[a]					
	A	B	C	D	E	F
Total Sample (*N* × 4,950)	11%	28%	18%	22%	11%	12%
Nation						
Belgium	8%	40%	13%	19%	11%	9%
Germany	8%	26%	13%	28%	11%	14%
Israel	4%	22%	33%	23%	9%	9%
Japan	21%	11%	13%	29%	10%	17%
The Netherlands	15%	43%	12%	11%	9%	9%
United States	8%	30%	19%	19%	12%	11%

Note: $X^2 = 680.98$ (25 degrees of freedom). $P < .0001$ Significance level

[a]In Pattern A, work is valued for its performance. The person is accountable and generally self-directed. In Pattern B, work provides a person with positive affect and identity. It contributes to society. In Pattern C, work provides profit to others by its performance. It is physical and not confined to a working place. In Pattern D, work is a required physical activity directed by others and generally unpleasant. In Pattern E, work is physically and mentally strenuous. It is generally unpleasant. In Pattern F, work is constrained to specific time periods. It does not bring positive affect through performance.

SOURCE: From G. W. England and I. Harpaz, "How Working Is Defined: National Contexts and Demographic and Organizational Role Influences," from *Journal of Organizational Behavior*, 11, 1990. Copyright John Wiley & Sons, Limited. Reproduced with permission.

Belgium, Israel, and the United States represent a middle position between these two. Future international studies should include Middle Eastern countries, India, Central and South American countries, and other Asian countries to better represent the world's cultures.

In another international study, 5,550 people across ten occupational groups in twenty different countries completed the Work Value Scales (WVS).[3] The WVS is composed of thirteen items measuring various aspects of the work environment, such as responsibility and job security. The study found two common basic work dimensions across cultures. Work content is one dimension, measured by items such as "the amount of responsibility on the job." Job context is the other dimension, measured by items such as "the policies of my company." This finding suggests that people in many cultures distinguish between the nature of the work itself and elements of the context in which work is done. This supports Herzberg's two-factor theory of motivation (see Chapter 5) and his job enrichment method discussed later in this chapter. Although the meaning of *work* differs among countries, new theorizing about crafting a job also suggests that individual employees can alter work meaning and work identity by changing task and relationship configurations in their work.[4]

Jobs in Organizations

Task and authority relationships define an organization's structure. Jobs are the basic building blocks of this task–authority structure and are considered the micro-structural element to which employees most directly relate. Jobs are usually designed to complement and support other jobs in the organization. Isolated jobs are rare, although one was identified at Coastal Corporation during the early 1970s. Shortly after Oscar Wyatt moved the company from Corpus Christi, Texas, to Houston, Coastal developed organizational charts and job descriptions because the company had grown so large. In the process of charting the organization's structure, it was discovered that the beloved corporate economist reported to no one. Everyone assumed he worked for someone else. Such peculiarities are rare, however.

Jobs in organizations are interdependent and designed to make a contribution to the organization's overall mission and goals. For salespeople to be successful, the production people must be effective. For production people to be effective, the material department must be effective. These interdependencies require careful planning and design so that all of the "pieces of work" fit together into a whole. For example, an envelope salesperson who wants to take an order for one million envelopes from John Hancock Financial Services must coordinate with the production department to establish an achievable delivery date. The failure to incorporate this interdependence into his planning could create conflict and doom the company to failure in meeting John Hancock's expectations. The central concerns of this chapter are designing work and structuring jobs to prevent such problems and to ensure employee well-being. Inflexible jobs that are rigidly structured have an adverse effect and lead to stressed-out employees.

Chapter 15 addresses the larger issues in the design of organizations. In particular, it examines the competing processes of differentiation and integration in organizations. Differentiation is the process of subdividing and departmentalizing the work of an organization. Jobs result from differentiation, which is necessary because no one can do it all (contrary to the famous statement made by Harold Geneen, former chairman of ITT: "If I had enough arms and legs and time, I'd do it all myself"). Even small organizations must divide work so that each person is able to accomplish a manageable piece of the whole. At the same time the organization divides up the work, it must also integrate those pieces back into a whole. Integration is the process of connecting jobs and departments into a coordinated, cohesive whole. For example, if the envelope salesperson had coordinated with the production manager before finalizing the order with John Hancock, the company could have met the customer's expectations, and integration would have occurred.

Traditional Approaches to Job Design

Failure to differentiate, integrate, or both may result in badly designed jobs, which in turn cause a variety of performance problems in organizations. Good job design helps avoid these problems, improves productivity, and enhances employee well-being. Four approaches to job design that were developed during the twentieth century are scientific management, job enlargement/job rotation, job enrichment, and the job characteristics theory. Each approach offers unique benefits to the organization, the employee, or both, but each also has limitations and drawbacks. Furthermore, an unthinking reliance on a traditional approach can be a serious problem in any company. The later job design approaches were developed to overcome the limitations of traditional job design approaches. For example, job enlargement was intended to overcome the problem of boredom associated with scientific management's narrowly defined approach to jobs.

2. Discuss the four traditional approaches to job design.

Scientific Management

Scientific management, an approach to work design first advocated by Frederick Taylor, emphasized work simplification. *Work simplification* is the standardization and the narrow, explicit specification of task activities for workers.[5] Jobs designed through scientific management have a limited number of tasks,

work simplification
Standardization and the narrow, explicit specification of task activities for workers.

and each task is scientifically specified so that the worker is not required to think or deliberate. According to Taylor, the role of management and the industrial engineer is to calibrate and define each task carefully. The role of the worker is to execute the task. The elements of scientific management, such as time and motion studies, differential piece-rate systems of pay, and the scientific selection of workers, all focus on the efficient use of labor to the economic benefit of the corporation. Employees who are satisfied with various aspects of repetitive work may like scientifically designed jobs.

Two arguments supported the efficient and standardized job design approach of scientific management in the early days of the American Industrial Revolution. The first argument was that work simplification allowed workers of diverse ethnic and skill backgrounds to work together in a systematic way. This was important during the first great period of globalization in the late 1800s during which Germans, Scots, Hungarians, Poles, and other immigrants came to work in America.[6] Taylor's unique approach to work standardization allowed diverse individuals to be blended into a functional workforce.

The second argument for scientific management was that work simplification led to production efficiency in the organization and, therefore, to higher profits. This economic argument for work simplification tended to treat labor as a means of production and dehumanized it. This is a problem in some modern service jobs, such as flipping hamburgers.

A fundamental limitation of scientific management is that it undervalues the human capacity for thought and ingenuity. Jobs designed through scientific management use only a portion of a person's capabilities. This underutilization makes work boring, monotonous, and understimulating. The failure to fully utilize the workers' capacity in a constructive fashion may cause a variety of work problems. Contemporary approaches to enhancing motivation through pay and compensation work to overcome these problems through modern job designs that retain talent and reduce turnover.[7]

Job Enlargement/Job Rotation

job enlargement

A method of job design that increases the number of activities in a job to overcome the boredom of overspecialized work.

job rotation

A variation of job enlargement in which workers are exposed to a variety of specialized jobs over time.

Job enlargement is a traditional approach to overcome the limitations of overspecialized work, such as boredom.[8] *Job enlargement* is a method of job design that increases the number of tasks in a job. *Job rotation*, a variation of job enlargement, exposes a worker to a variety of specialized job tasks over time. The reasoning behind these approaches to the problems of overspecialization is as follows. First, the core problem with overspecialized work was believed to be lack of variety. That is, jobs designed by scientific management were too narrow and limited in the number of tasks and activities assigned to each worker. Second, a lack of variety led to understimulation and underutilization of the worker. Third, the worker would be more stimulated and better utilized by increasing the variety in the job. Variety could be increased by increasing the number of activities or by rotating the worker through different jobs. For example, job enlargement for a lathe operator in a steel plant might include selecting the steel pieces to be turned and performing all of the maintenance work on the lathe. As an example of job rotation, an employee at a small bank might take new accounts one day, serve as a cashier another day, and process loan applications on a third day.

One of the first studies of the problem of repetitive work was conducted at IBM after World War II. The company implemented a job enlargement program during the war and evaluated the effort after six years.[9] The two most important results were a significant increase in product quality and a reduction in idle time, both for people and for machines. Less obvious and measurable are the benefits of job enlargement to IBM through enhanced worker status and improved manager–worker communication. IBM concluded that job enlargement countered the problems of work specialization. A contemporary study in a Swedish electronics assembly plant used physiological measures of muscle tension.[10] Job enlargement had a positive effect on mechanical exposure variability.

A later study examined the effects of mass production jobs on assembly-line workers in the automotive industry.[11] Mass production jobs have six characteristics: mechanically controlled work pace, repetitiveness, minimum skill requirements, predetermined tools and techniques, minute division of the production process, and a requirement for surface mental attention, rather than thoughtful concentration. The researchers conducted 180 private interviews with assembly-line workers and found generally positive attitudes toward pay, security, and supervision. They concluded that job enlargement and job rotation would improve other job aspects, such as repetition and a mechanical work pace.

Job rotation and *cross-training* programs are variations of job enlargement. Pharmaceutical company Eli Lilly has found that job rotation can be a proactive means for enhancing work experiences for career development and can have tangible benefits for employees in the form of salary increases and promotions.[12] In cross-training, workers are trained in different specialized tasks or activities. All three kinds of programs horizontally enlarge jobs; that is, the number and variety of an employee's tasks and activities are increased. Graphic Controls Corporation (now a subsidiary of Tyco International) used cross-training to develop a flexible workforce that enabled the company to maintain high levels of production.[13]

Job Enrichment

Whereas job enlargement increases the number of job activities through horizontal loading, job enrichment increases the amount of job responsibility through vertical loading. Both approaches to job design are intended, in part, to increase job satisfaction for employees. A study to test whether job satisfaction results from characteristics of the job or of the person found that an interactionist approach is most accurate and that job redesign can contribute to increased job satisfaction for some employees. Another two-year study found that intrinsic job satisfaction and job perceptions are reciprocally related to each other.[14]

Job enrichment is a job design or redesign method aimed at increasing the motivational factors in a job. Job enrichment builds on Herzberg's two-factor theory of motivation, which distinguished between motivational and hygiene factors for people at work. Whereas job enlargement recommends increasing and varying the number of activities a person does, job enrichment recommends increasing the recognition, responsibility, and opportunity for achievement. For example, enlarging the lathe operator's job means adding maintenance activities, and enriching the job means having the operator meet with customers who buy the products.

Herzberg believes that only certain jobs should be enriched and that the first step is to select the jobs appropriate for job enrichment.[15] He recognizes that some people prefer simple jobs. Once jobs are selected for enrichment, management should brainstorm about possible changes, revise the list to include only specific changes related to motivational factors, and screen out generalities and suggestions that would simply increase activities or numbers of tasks. Those

cross-training
A variation of job enlargement in which workers are trained in different specialized tasks or activities.

job enrichment
Designing or redesigning jobs by incorporating motivational factors into them.

whose jobs are to be enriched should not participate in this process because of a conflict of interest. Two key problems can arise in the implementation of job enrichment. First, an initial drop in performance can be expected as workers accommodate to the change. Second, first-line supervisors may experience some anxiety or hostility as a result of employees' increased responsibility.

A seven-year implementation study of job enrichment at AT&T found the approach beneficial.[16] Job enrichment required a big change in management style, and AT&T found that it could not ignore hygiene factors in the work environment just because it was enriching existing jobs. Although the AT&T experience with job enrichment was positive, a critical review of job enrichment did not find that to be the case generally.[17] One problem with job enrichment as a strategy for work design is that it is based on an oversimplified motivational theory. Another problem is the lack of consideration for individual differences among employees. Job enrichment, like scientific management's work specialization and job enlargement/job rotation, is a universal approach to the design of work and thus does not differentiate among individuals.

Job Characteristics Theory

The job characteristics theory, which was initiated during the mid-1960s, is a traditional approach to the design of work that makes a significant departure from the three earlier approaches. It emphasizes the interaction between the individual and specific attributes of the job; therefore, it is a person–job fit model rather than a universal job design model. It originated in a research study of 470 workers in forty-seven different jobs across eleven industries.[18] The study measured and classified relevant task characteristics for these forty-seven jobs and found four core job characteristics: job variety, autonomy, responsibility, and interpersonal interaction. The study also found that core job characteristics did not affect all workers in the same way. A worker's values, religious beliefs, and ethnic background influenced how the worker responded to the job. Specifically, workers with rural values and strong religious beliefs preferred jobs high in core characteristics, and workers with urban values and weaker religious beliefs preferred jobs low in core characteristics.

Richard Hackman and his colleagues modified the original model by including three critical psychological states of the individual and refining the measurement of core job characteristics. The result is the *Job Characteristics Model* shown in Figure 14.1.[19] The *Job Diagnostic Survey (JDS)* was developed to diagnose jobs by measuring the five core job characteristics and three critical psychological states shown in the model. The core job characteristics stimulate the critical psychological states in the manner shown in Figure 14.1. This results in varying personal and work outcomes, as identified in the figure.

The five core job characteristics are defined as follows:

1. *Skill variety.* The degree to which a job includes different activities and involves the use of multiple skills and talents of the employee.

2. *Task identity.* The degree to which the job requires completion of a whole and identifiable piece of work—that is, doing a job from beginning to end with a tangible outcome.

3. *Task significance.* The degree to which the job has a substantial impact on the lives or work of other people, whether in the immediate organization or in the external environment.

3. Describe the Job Characteristics Model.

Job Characteristics Model

A framework for understanding person–job fit through the interaction of core job dimensions with critical psychological states within a person.

Job Diagnostic Survey (JDS)

The survey instrument designed to measure the elements in the Job Characteristics Model.

PART 4 [ORGANIZATIONAL PROCESSES AND STRUCTURE

FIGURE 14.1   The Job Characteristics Model

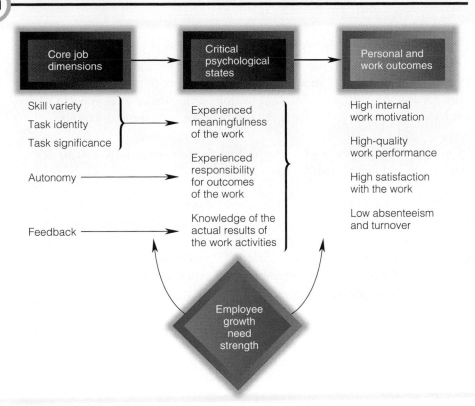

SOURCE: J. R. Hackman and G. R. Oldham, "The Relationship Among Core Job Dimensions, the Critical Psychological States, and On-the-Job Outcomes." *The Job Diagnostic Survey: An Instrument for the Diagnosis of Jobs and the Evaluation of Job Redesign Projects,* 1974. Reprinted by permission of Greg R. Oldham.

4. *Autonomy.* The degree to which the job provides the employee with substantial freedom, independence, and discretion in scheduling the work and in determining the procedures to be used in carrying it out.

5. *Feedback from the job itself.* The degree to which carrying out the work activities results in the employee's obtaining direct and clear information about the effectiveness of his or her performance.

Hackman and his colleagues say that the five core job characteristics interact to determine an overall Motivating Potential Score (MPS) for a specific job. The MPS indicates a job's potential for motivating incumbents. An individual's MPS is determined by the following equation:

$$MPS = \frac{\begin{bmatrix} \text{Skill} \\ \text{variety} \end{bmatrix} + \begin{bmatrix} \text{Task} \\ \text{identity} \end{bmatrix} + \begin{bmatrix} \text{Task} \\ \text{significance} \end{bmatrix}}{3} \times [\text{Autonomy}] \times [\text{Feedback}].$$

You 14.1 enables you to answer five questions from the JDS short form to get an idea about the motivating potential of your present job or any job you have held.

The Job Characteristics Model includes *growth need strength* (the desire to grow and fully develop one's abilities) as a moderator. People with a high growth need strength respond favorably to jobs with high MPSs, and individuals with

Diagnosing Your Job

This questionnaire challenges you to examine the motivating potential in your job. If you are not currently working, complete the questionnaire for any job you have ever held for which you want to examine the motivating potential. For each of the following five questions, circle the number of the most accurate description of the job. Be as objective as you can in describing the job by answering these questions.

1. How much *autonomy* is there in the job? That is, to what extent does the job permit a person to decide *on his or her own* how to go about doing the work?

1	2	3	4	5	6	7

Very little; the job gives a person almost no personal say about how and when the work is done.

Moderate autonomy; many things are standardized and not under the control of the person, but he or she can make some decisions about the work.

Very much; the job gives the person almost complete responsibility for deciding how and when the work is done.

2. To what extent does the job involve doing a *"whole"* and *identifiable piece of work*? That is, is the job a complete piece of work that has an obvious beginning and end? Or is it a small part of the overall piece of work, which is finished by other people or by automatic machines?

1	2	3	4	5	6	7

The job is only a tiny part in the overall piece of work; the results of the person's activities cannot be seen in the final product or service.

The job is a moderate-sized "chunk" of the overall piece of work; the person's own contribution can be seen in the final outcome.

The job involves doing the whole piece of work, from start to finish; the results of the person's activities are easily seen in the final product or service.

3. How much *variety* is there in the job? That is, to what extent does the job require a person to do many different things at work, using a variety of his or her skills and talents?

1	2	3	4	5	6	7

Very little; the job requires the person to do the same routine things over and over again.

Moderate variety.

Very much; the job requires the person to do many different things, using a number of different skills and talents.

4. In general, how *significant* or *important* is the job? That is, are the results of the person's work likely to affect significantly the lives or well-being of other people?

1	2	3	4	5	6	7

Not at all significant; the outcome of the work is *not* likely to affect anyone in any important way.

Moderately significant.

Highly significant; the outcome of the work can affect other people in very important ways.

(continued)

5. To what extent *does doing the job itself* provide the person with information about his or her work performance? That is, does the actual work itself provide clues about how well the person is doing—aside from any feedback coworkers or supervisors may provide?

1	2	3	4	5	6	7

Very little; the job itself is set up so a person could work forever without finding out how well he or she is doing.

Moderately; sometimes doing the job provides feedback to the person; sometimes it does not.

Very much; the job is set up so that a person gets almost constant feedback as he or she works about how well he or she is doing.

To score your questionnaire, place your responses to Questions 3, 2, 4, 1, and 5, respectively, in the blank spaces in the following equation:

$$\text{Motivating Potential Score (MPS)} = \frac{\overset{Q\#3}{[\quad]} + \overset{Q\#2}{[\quad]} + \overset{Q\#4}{[\quad]}}{3} \times \overset{Q\#1}{[\quad]} \times \overset{Q\#5}{[\quad]} = \underline{\quad}.$$

If the MPS for the job you rated is between

> 200 and 343, it is high in motivating potential.

> 120 and 199, it is moderate in motivating potential.

> 0 and 119, it is low in motivating potential.

SOURCE: J. R. Hackman and G. R. Oldham, "The Job Diagnostic Survey: An Instrument for the Diagnosis of Jobs and the Evaluation of Job Redesign Projects," *Technical Report No. 4*, 1974, 2–3 of the Short Form. Reprinted by permission of Greg R. Oldham.

low growth need strength respond less favorably to such jobs. The job characteristics theory further suggests that core job dimensions stimulate three critical psychological states according to the relationships specified in the model. These critical psychological states are defined as follows:

1. *Experienced meaningfulness of the work*, or the degree to which the employee experiences the job as one that is generally meaningful, valuable, and worthwhile.

2. *Experienced responsibility for work outcomes*, or the degree to which the employee feels personally accountable and responsible for the results of the work he or she does.

3. *Knowledge of results*, or the degree to which the employee knows and understands, on a continuous basis, how effectively he or she is performing the job.

In one early study, Hackman and Oldham administered the JDS to 658 employees working on sixty-two different jobs in seven business organizations.[20] The JDS was useful for job redesign efforts through one or more of five implementing concepts: (1) combining tasks into larger jobs, (2) forming natural work teams to increase task identity and task significance, (3) establishing relationships with customers, (4) loading jobs vertically with more responsibility, and/or (5) opening feedback channels for the job incumbent. For example, if an automotive mechanic received little feedback on the quality of repair work performed, one redesign strategy would be to solicit customer feedback one month after each repair.

A more recent sequence of two studies conducted in Egypt aimed to disaggregate work autonomy, one important component in job design theory.[21] Study 1 included 534 employees in two Egyptian organizations. Study 2 involved 120 managers in four organzations. The results indicated that separate work method, work schedule, and work criteria autonomy were three separate facets of work autonomy.

In another international study, the Job Characteristics Model was tested in a sample of fifty-seven jobs from thirty-seven organizations in Hong Kong.[22] Job incumbents and their supervisors both completed questionnaires about the incumbents' jobs.[23] The supervisory version asked the supervisor to rate the employee's job. The study supported the model in general. However, task significance was not a reliable core job dimension in Hong Kong, which suggests either national differences in the measurement of important job dimensions or cultural biases about work. This result also suggests that value differences may exist between American and Asian people with regard to jobs.

An alternative to the Job Characteristics Model is the Job Characteristics Inventory (JCI) developed by Henry Sims and Andrew Szilagyi.[24] The JCI primarily measures core job characteristics. It is not as comprehensive as the JDS because it does not incorporate critical psychological states, personal and work outcomes, or employee needs. The JCI does give some consideration to structural and individual variables that affect the relationship between core job characteristics and the individual.[25] One comparative analysis of the two models found similarities in the measures and in the models' predictions.[26] The comparative analysis also found two differences. First, the variety scales in the two models appear to have different effects on performance. Second, the autonomy scales in the two models appear to have different effects on employee satisfaction. Overall, the two models together support the usefulness of a person–job fit approach to the design of work over the earlier, universal theories.

Engagement

Psychological conditions related to job design features are a particular concern of the Job Characteristics Model.[27] One study of over 200 managers and employees in a midwestern insurance company found that meaningfulness, safety, and availability were three important psychological conditions that affected employees' *engagement* in their jobs and work roles. Engagement at work is important for its positive individual and organizational outcomes. Engagement is the harnessing of organizational members to their work roles. When engaged, people employ and express themselves physically, cognitively, and emotionally as they perform their jobs and their work roles. The Real World 14.2 discusses how Gallup's Q was used to improve engagement for a clinical nutrition group at St. Mary's/Duluth Clinic Health System.

Full engagement requires the strategic management of one's energy in response to the environment.[28] Being fully engaged in one's work role and job can be highly appropriate and yet demand energy, time, and effort. To achieve balance and afford opportunity for recovery, there is a commensurate need to strategically and appropriately disengage from one's job and work role on a periodic basis. The effective management of energy in response to one's job and work role leads to both high performance and personal renewal. Thus, while the design of work is important, the human spirit's response to job characteristics and work design features is equally important.

Cultural biases about work could account for why Hong Kong does not consider task significance a reliable core job dimension.

© D. Normark/Photolink/Getty Images

engagement

The expression of oneself as one performs in work or other roles.

Nourishing Engagement

When Mary Grassinger was hired as clinical nutrition manager for St. Mary's/Duluth Clinic Health System in Duluth, Minnesota, she did not know she would face insufficient staff and low morale. However, shortly after she took the job, her clinic participated in the Gallup Q employee survey that focused attention on the most important attributes of effective work groups. While her clinical nutrition group's overall engagement score was not bad, it was at best mediocre.

Armed with this feedback and feedback on her own positive core strengths, Grassinger initiated several changes in her immediate work environment. She began with an office redesign that added modular furniture to improve the physical setting. She then included regular team meetings and individualized review sessions with each of the clinical dieticians. Finally, she carefully analyzed the workload for her unit and its clinicians. Grassinger was able to show St. Mary's Position Review Committee, using the workload data she had developed, that the unit needed two additional positions for clinicians and one for a clerk.

These physical and personnel changes led to the unit turning a corner. One year later when her clinical nutrition unit took the Gallup Q, the results were a remarkable improvement. Rather than being mediocre at slightly below average (50 percentile), the unit scored at the 92 percentile level. Mary Grassinger had clearly turned the unit around, and its members were highly engaged, energized, and effective in their jobs.

SOURCE: R. Wagner, "Nourishing Employee Engagement," *Gallup Management Journal* (February 12, 2004): 1–7, http://gmj.gallup.com/content/default.asp?ci=10504.

Alternative Approaches to Job Design

Because each of the traditional job design approaches has limitations, several alternative approaches to job design have emerged over the past couple of decades. This section examines four of these alternatives that are in the process of being tried and tested. First, it examines the social information-processing model. Second, it reviews ergonomics and the interdisciplinary framework of Michael Campion and Paul Thayer. Their framework builds on the traditional job design approaches. Third, this section examines the international perspectives of the Japanese, Germans, and Scandinavians. Finally, it focuses on the health and well-being aspects of work design. Healthy work enables individuals to adapt, function well, and balance work with private life activities.[29] An emerging fifth approach to the design of work through teams and autonomous work groups was addressed in Chapter 9.

Social Information Processing

The traditional approaches to the design of work emphasize objective core job characteristics. In contrast, the *social information-processing (SIP) model* emphasizes the interpersonal aspects of work design. Specifically, the SIP model says that what others tell us about our jobs is important.[30] The SIP model has four basic premises about the work environment.[31] First, other people provide cues we use to understand the work environment. Second, other people help us judge what is important in our jobs. Third, other people tell us how they see our jobs. Fourth, other people's positive and negative feedback helps us understand our feelings about our jobs.

People's perceptions and reactions to their jobs are shaped by information from other people in the work environment.[32] In other words, what others believe about a person's job may be important to understanding the person's

4. Compare the social information-processing (SIP) model with traditional job design approaches.

social information-processing (SIP) model
A model that suggests that the important job factors depend in part on what others tell a person about the job.

perceptions of, and reactions to, the job. This does not mean that objective job characteristics are unimportant; rather, it means that others can modify the way these characteristics affect us. For example, one study of task complexity found that the objective complexity of a task must be distinguished from the subjective task complexity experienced by the employee.[33] While objective task complexity may be a motivator, the presence of others in the work environment, social interaction, or even daydreaming may be important additional sources of motivation. The SIP model makes an important contribution to the design of work by emphasizing the importance of other people and the social context of work. In some cases, these aspects of the work environment may be more important than objective core job characteristics. For example, the subjective feedback of other people about how difficult a particular task is may be more important to a person's motivation to perform than an objective probability estimate of the task's difficulty.

Ergonomics and Interdisciplinary Framework

5. Explain ergonomics and the interdisciplinary framework for the design of work.

ergonomics
The science of adapting work and working conditions to the employee or worker.

Michael Campion and Paul Thayer use *ergonomics* based on engineering, biology, and psychology to develop an interdisciplinary framework for the design of work. Actually, they say that four approaches—the mechanistic, motivational, biological, and perceptual/motor approaches—are necessary because no one approach can solve all performance problems caused by poorly designed jobs. Each approach has its benefits as well as its limitations. The ergonomics study discussed in the accompanying Science feature found lower levels of upper body pain along with other positive outcomes of the workstation redesign.

The interdisciplinary framework allows the job designer or manager to consider trade-offs and alternatives among the approaches based on desired outcomes. If a manager finds poor performance a problem, for example, the manager should analyze the job to ensure a design aimed at improving performance. The interdisciplinary framework is important because badly designed jobs cause far more performance problems than managers realize.[34]

Table 14.2 summarizes the positive and negative outcomes of each job design approach. The mechanistic and motivational approaches to job design are very similar to scientific management's work simplification and to the Job Characteristics Model, respectively. Because these were discussed earlier in the chapter, they are not further elaborated here.

The biological approach to job design emphasizes the person's interaction with physical aspects of the work environment and is concerned with the amount of physical exertion, such as lifting and muscular effort, required by the position. For example, an analysis of medical claims at TXI's Chaparral Steel Company identified lower back problems as the most common physical problem experienced by steel workers and managers alike. As a result, the company instituted an education and exercise program under expert guidance to improve care of the lower back. Program graduates received back cushions for their chairs with "Chaparral Steel Company" embossed on them. Herman Miller designed an office chair to support the lower back and other parts of the human body.[35] The chair was tested in several offices including that of the director of human resources for Valero Energy Corporation prior to large-scale production. Lower back problems associated with improper lifting may be costly, but they are not fatal. Campion describes the potentially catastrophic problem that occurred at Three Mile Island, when nuclear materials contami-

Ergonomic Office Design

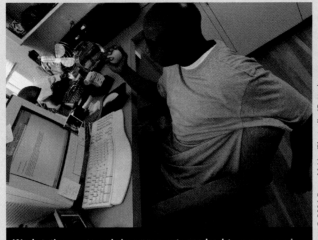

Workstation ergonomic improvements can lead to a more positive employee attitude.

© 2004 Ryan McVay/Photodisc/Getty images

Physical discomfort, pain symptoms, and eyestrain are among the negative employee responses to poor office designs. A recent study used a quasi-experimental design to examine the effects of ergonomic improvements in workstation design for eighty-seven administrative employees in the municipal offices of a large midwestern U.S. city. Four major types of workstation ergonomic interventions were undertaken. These were seating enhancements (e.g., new chairs, back supports, or chair cushions), keyboard-related improvements (e.g., wrist rests/pads or keyboard trays), computer relocations (e.g., workstation rearrangement), and computer screen modifications (e.g., computer glare guards or new computer screens). The employee responses that the researchers measured were persistent pain, eyestrain, and workstation satisfaction. The study included measures of employee age, job tenure, and positive affectivity. The results suggested that workstation improvements led to positive perceptions of the workstation's ergonomic qualities, lower levels of upper back pain, and greater workstation satisfaction. These positive responses increased more for younger employees than older employees. These results support the "impressionable years" framework in the psychology of aging. For human resource managers in particular, the results imply that systematic ergonomic job redesign efforts can have positive effects on employee health and attitudes in offices.

SOURCE: D. R. May, K. Reed, C. E. Schwoerer, and P. Potter, "Ergonomic Office Design and Aging: A Quasi-Experimental Field Study of Employee Reactions to an Ergonomics Intervention Program," *Journal of Occupational Health Psychology* 9 (2004): 123–135.

nated the surrounding area and threatened disaster. Campion concluded that poor design of the control room operator's job caused the problem.

The perceptual/motor approach to job design also emphasizes the person's interaction with physical aspects of the work environment and is based on engineering that considers human factors such as strength or coordination, ergonomics, and experimental psychology. It places an important emphasis on human interaction with computers, information, and other operational systems. This approach addresses how people mentally process information acquired from the physical work environment through perceptual and motor skills. The approach emphasizes perception and fine motor skills, as opposed to the gross motor skills and muscle strength emphasized in the mechanistic approach. The perceptual/motor approach is more likely to be relevant to operational and technical work, such as keyboard operations and data entry jobs, which may tax a person's concentration and attention, than to managerial, administrative, and custodial jobs, which are less likely to strain concentration and attention.

One study using the interdisciplinary framework to improve jobs evaluated 377 clerical, 80 managerial, and 90 analytical positions.[36] The jobs were improved by combining tasks and adding ancillary duties. The improved jobs provided greater motivation for the incumbents and were better from a perceptual/motor standpoint. The jobs were poorly designed from a mechanical

TABLE 14.2   Summary of Outcomes from Various Job Design Approaches

JOB DESIGN APPROACH (DISCIPLINE)	POSITIVE OUTCOMES	NEGATIVE OUTCOMES
Mechanistic Approach (mechanical engineering)	Decreased training time Higher personnel utilization levels Lower likelihood of error Less chance of mental overload Lower stress levels	Lower job satisfaction Lower motivation Higher absenteeism
Motivational Approach (industrial psychology)	Higher job satisfaction Higher motivation Greater job involvement Higher job performance Lower absenteeism	Increased training time Lower personnel utilization levels Greater chance of errors Greater chance of mental overload and stress
Biological Approach (biology)	Less physical effort Less physical fatigue Fewer health complaints Fewer medical incidents Lower absenteeism Higher job satisfaction	Higher financial costs because of changes in equipment or job environment
Perceptual Motor Approach (experimental psychology)	Lower likelihood of error Lower likelihood of accidents Less chance of mental stress Decreased training time Higher personnel utilization levels	Lower job satisfaction Lower motivation

SOURCE: Reprinted from *Organizational Dynamics*, Winter/1987 Copyright © 1987, with permission from Elsevier Science.

engineering standpoint, however, and they were unaffected from a biological standpoint. Again, the interdisciplinary framework considers trade-offs and alternatives when evaluating job redesign efforts.

International Perspectives on the Design of Work

6. Compare Japanese, German, and Scandinavian approaches to work.

Each nation or ethnic group has a unique way of understanding and designing work.[37] As organizations become more global and international, an appreciation of the perspectives of other nations is increasingly important. The Japanese, Germans, and Scandinavians in particular have distinctive perspectives on the design and organization of work.[38] Each country's perspective is forged within its unique cultural and economic system, and each is distinct from the approaches used in North America.

THE JAPANESE APPROACH The Japanese began harnessing their productive energies during the 1950s by drawing on the product quality ideas of W. Edwards Deming.[39] In addition, the central government became actively involved in the economic resurgence of Japan, and it encouraged companies to conquer industries rather than to maximize profits.[40] Such an industrial policy, which built on the Japanese cultural ethic of collectivism, has implications for how work is done. Whereas Frederick Taylor and his successors in the United States emphasized the job of an individual worker, the Japanese work system emphasizes the strategic level and encourages collective and cooperative working arrangements.[41] As Table 14.1 shows, the Japanese emphasize performance, accountability, and other- or self-directedness in defining work, whereas Americans emphasize the positive affect, personal identity, and social benefits of work.

The Japanese success with lean production has drawn the attention of managers. *Lean production* methods are similar to the production concept of *sociotechnical systems (STS)*, although there are some differences.[42] In particular, STS gives greater emphasis to teamwork and self-managed and autonomous work groups, to the ongoing nature of the design process, and to human values in the work process. The approaches are similar, however, in that both differ from Taylor's scientific management and both emphasize job variety, feedback to work groups and teams, support of human resources, and control of production variance close to the point of origin. One three-year evaluation of lean teams, assembly lines, and workflow formalization as lean production practices was conducted in Australia.[43] Employees in all lean production groups were negatively affected, and the assembly line employees the worst.

THE GERMAN APPROACH The German approach to work has been shaped by Germany's unique educational system, cultural values, and economic system. The Germans are a highly educated and well-organized people. For example, their educational system has a multitrack design with technical and university alternatives. The German economic system puts a strong emphasis on free enterprise, private property rights, and management–labor cooperation. A comparison of voluntary and mandated management–labor cooperation in Germany found that productivity was superior under voluntary cooperation.[44] The Germans value hierarchy and authority relationships and, as a result, are generally disciplined.[45] Germany's workers are highly unionized, and their discipline and efficiency have enabled Germany to be highly productive while its workers labor substantially fewer hours than do Americans.

The traditional German approach to work design was *technocentric*, an approach that placed technology and engineering at the center of job design decisions. Recently, German industrial engineers have moved to a more *anthropocentric* approach, which places human considerations at the center of job design decisions. The former approach uses a natural scientific process in the design of work, whereas the latter relies on a more humanistic process, as shown in Figure 14.2. In the anthropocentric approach, work is evaluated using the criteria of practicability and worker satisfaction at the individual level and the criteria of endurability and acceptability at the group level. Figure 14.2 also identifies problem areas and disciplines concerned with each aspect of the work design.

THE SCANDINAVIAN APPROACH The Scandinavian cultural values and economic system stand in contrast to the German system. The social democratic tradition in Scandinavia has emphasized social concern rather than industrial efficiency. The Scandinavians place great emphasis on a work design model that encourages a high degree of worker control and good social support systems for workers.[46] Lennart Levi believes that circumstantial and inferential scientific evidence provides a sufficiently strong basis for legislative and policy actions for redesigns aimed at enhancing worker well-being. An example of such an action for promoting good working environments and occupational health was Swedish Government Bill 1976/77:149, which stated, "Work should be safe both physically and mentally *but also* provide opportunities for involvement, job satisfaction, and personal development." In 1991,

lean production
Using committed employees with ever-expanding responsibilities to achieve zero waste, 100 percent good product, delivered on time, every time.

sociotechnical systems (STS)
Giving equal attention to technical and social considerations in job design.

technocentric
Placing technology and engineering at the center of job design decisions.

anthropocentric
Placing human considerations at the center of job design decisions.

Scientific approaches of labor sciences	Levels of evaluation of human work	Problem areas and assignment to disciplines
View from natural science	Practicability	Technical, anthropometric, and psychophysical problems (ergonomics)
	Endurability	Technical, physiological, and medical problems (ergonomics and occupational health)
Primarily oriented to individuals / Primarily oriented to groups	Acceptability	Economical and sociological problems (occupational psychology and sociology, personnel management)
View from cultural studies	Satisfaction	Sociopsychological and economic problems (occupational psychology and sociology, personnel management)

SOURCE: H. Luczak, "'Good Work' Design: An Ergonomic, Industrial Engineering Perspective," in J. C. Quick, L. R. Murphy, and J. J. Hurrell, eds., *Stress and Well-Being at Work* (Washington, D.C.). Copyright ©1997 by the American Psychological Association. Reprinted with permission.

the Swedish Parliament set up the Swedish Working Life Fund to fund research, intervention programs, and demonstration projects in work design. For example, a study of Stockholm police on shift schedules found that going from a daily, counterclockwise rotation to a clockwise rotation was more compatible with human biology and resulted in improved sleep, less fatigue, lower systolic blood pressure, and lower blood levels of triglycerides and glucose.[47] Hence, the work redesign improved the police officers' health.

Work Design and Well-Being

7. Explain how job control, uncertainty, and conflict can be managed for employee well-being.

An international group of scholars, including American social scientists, has been concerned about designing work and jobs that are both healthy and productive.[48] This issue was discussed briefly in Chapter 7. Economic and industry-specific upheavals in the United States during the 1990s led to job loss and unemployment, and the adverse health impact of these factors has received attention.[49] Attention has also been devoted to the effects of specific work design parameters on psychological health.[50] Frank Landy believes that organizations should redesign jobs to increase worker control and reduce worker uncertainty, while at the same time managing conflict and task/job demands. These objectives can be achieved in several ways.

Control in work organizations can be increased by (1) giving workers the opportunity to control several aspects of the work and the workplace; (2) designing machines and tasks with optimal response times and/or ranges; and (3) implementing performance-monitoring systems as a source of relevant feedback to workers. Uncertainty can be reduced by (1) providing employees with timely and complete information needed for their work; (2) making clear and unambiguous work assignments; (3) improving communication at shift change time;

and (4) increasing employee access to information sources. Conflict at work can be managed through (1) participative decision making to reduce conflict; (2) using supportive supervisory styles to resolve conflict; and (3) having sufficient resources available to meet work demands, thus preventing conflict. Task/job design can be improved by enhancing core job characteristics and not patterning service work after assembly-line work.

Task uncertainty was shown to have an adverse effect on morale in a study of 629 employment security work units in California and Wisconsin.[51] More important, the study showed that morale was better predicted by considering both the overall design of the work unit and the task uncertainty. This study suggests that if one work design parameter, such as task uncertainty, is a problem in a job, its adverse effects on people may be mitigated by other work design parameters. For example, higher pay may offset an employee's frustration with a difficult coworker, or a friendly, supportive working environment may offset frustration with low pay. You 14.2 provides you with an opportunity to evaluate how psychologically healthy your work environment is.

Contemporary Issues in the Design of Work

A number of contemporary issues related to specific aspects of the design of work have an effect on increasing numbers of employees. Rather than addressing job design or worker well-being in a comprehensive way, these issues address one or another aspects of a job. The issues include telecommuting, alternative work patterns, technostress, task revision, and skill development. Telecommuting and alternative work patterns such as job sharing can increase flexibility for employees. Companies use these and other approaches to the design of work as ways to manage a growing business while contributing to a better balance of work and family life for employees.

8. Discuss five contemporary issues in the design of work.

Telecommuting

Telecommuting, as noted in Chapter 2, is when employees work at home or in other locations geographically separate from their company's main location. Telecommuting may entail working in a combination of home, satellite office, and main office locations. This flexible arrangement is designed to achieve a better fit between the needs of the individual employee and the organization's task demands. Cisco Systems manager Christian Renaud moved from California and began telecommuting from Johnston, Iowa, when he and his wife began their family.

Telecommuting has been around since the 1970s but was slower to catch on than some expected.[52] This was due to the inherent paradoxes associated with telecommuting.[53] Actually, with a greater emphasis on managing the work rather than the worker, managers can enhance control, effectively decentralize, and even encourage teamwork through telecommuting. A number of companies, such as AT&T in Phoenix and Bell Atlantic (now part of Verizon Communications), have programs in telecommuting for a wide range of employees. These flexible arrangements help some companies respond to changing demographics and a shrinking labor pool. The Travelers Group (now part of Citigroup) was one of the first companies to try telecommuting and was considered an industry leader in telecommuting. Because of its confidence in its employees, Travelers reaped rewards from telecommuting, including higher productivity, reduced absenteeism, expanded opportunities for workers with disabilities, and an increased ability to attract and retain talent.[54]

Is Your Work Environment a Healthy One?

To determine whether your work environment is a healthy one, read the text section on "Work Design and Well-Being," then complete the following four steps. Answer each question in the five steps "yes" or "no."

Step 1. Control and Influence

_____ Do you have influence over the pace of your work?

_____ Are system response times neither too fast nor too slow?

_____ Do you have a say in your work assignments and goals?

_____ Is there an opportunity for you to comment on your performance appraisal?

Step 2. Information and Uncertainty

_____ Do you receive timely information to complete your work?

_____ Do you receive complete information for your work assignments?

_____ Is there adequate planning for changes that affect you at work?

_____ Do you have access to all the information you need at work?

Step 3. Conflict at Work

_____ Does the company apply policies clearly and consistently?

_____ Are job descriptions and task assignments clear and unambiguous?

_____ Are there adequate policies and procedures for the resolution of conflicts?

_____ Is your work environment an open, participative one?

Step 4. Job Scope and Task Design

_____ Is there adequate variety in your work activities and/or assignments?

_____ Do you receive timely, constructive feedback on your work?

_____ Is your work important to the overall mission of the company?

_____ Do you work on more than one small piece of a big project?

Scoring:

Count the number of "yes" answers in Steps 1 through 4: _____

If you have 10 to 16 "yes" answers, this suggests that your work environment is a psychologically healthy one.

If you have 7 or fewer "yes" answers, this may suggest that your work environment is not as psychologically healthy as it could be.

Pacific Bell (now part of SBC Communications) tried telecommuting on a large scale.[55] In 1990, Pacific Bell had 1,500 managers who telecommuted. For example, an employee might work at home four days a week as an information systems designer and spend one day a week at the main office location in meetings, work exchanges, and coordination with others. Of 3,000 Pacific Bell managers responding to a mail survey, 87 percent said telecommuting would reduce employee stress, 70 percent said it would increase job satisfaction while reducing absenteeism, and 64 percent said it would increase productivity.

Telecommuting is neither a cure-all nor a universally feasible alternative. Many telecommuters feel a sense of social isolation. Furthermore, not all forms of work are amenable to telecommuting. For example, firefighters and police officers must be at their duty stations to be successful in their work. Employees for whom telecommuting is not a viable option within a company may feel jealous of those able to telecommute. In addition, telecommuting may have the potential to create the sweatshops of the twenty-first century. Thus, telecommuting is a novel, emerging issue.

Alternative Work Patterns

Job sharing is an alternative work pattern in which more than one person occupies a single job. Job sharing may be an alternative to telecommuting for addressing demographic and labor pool concerns. Job sharing is found throughout a wide range of managerial and professional jobs, as well as in production and service jobs. It is not common among senior executives.

The *four-day workweek* is a second type of alternative work schedule. Information systems personnel at the United Services Automobile Association (USAA) in San Antonio, Texas, work four ten-hour days and enjoy a three-day weekend. This arrangement provides the benefit of more time for those who want to balance work and family life through weekend travel. However, the longer workdays may be a drawback for employees with many family or social activities on weekday evenings. Hence, the four-day workweek has both benefits and limitations.

Flextime is a third alternative work pattern. Flextime, in which employees can set their own daily work schedules, has been applied in numerous ways in work organizations and can lead to reduced absenteeism. Companies in highly concentrated urban areas, like Houston, Los Angeles, and New York City, may allow employees to set their own daily work schedules as long as they start their eight hours at any thirty-minute interval from 6:00 A.M. to 9:00 A.M. This arrangement is designed to ease traffic and commuting pressures. It also is somewhat responsive to individual biorhythms, allowing early risers to go to work early and nighthawks to work late. Typically, 9:00 A.M. to 3:00 P.M. is the required core working time for everyone in the company. Even in companies without formal flextime programs, flextime may be an individual option arranged between supervisor and subordinate. For example, a first-line supervisor who wants to complete a college degree may negotiate a work schedule accommodating both job requirements and course schedules at the university. Flextime options may be more likely for high performers who assure their bosses that work quality and productivity will not suffer.[56] On the cautionary side, one study found that a woman on a flexible work schedule was perceived to have less job–career dedication and less advancement motivation, though no less ability.[57]

Technology at Work

New technologies and electronic commerce are here to stay and are changing the face of work environments, dramatically in some cases. Many government jobs expect to change, and even disappear, with the advent of e-government using Internet technology. As forces for change, new technologies are a double-edged sword that can be used to improve job performance or to create stress. On the positive side, modern technologies are helping to revolutionize the way jobs are designed and the way work gets done. The *virtual office* is a mobile platform of computer, telecommunication, and information technology and services that allows mobile workforce members to conduct business virtually anywhere, anytime, globally. While virtual offices have benefits, they may also lead to a lack of social connection or to technostress.

Technostress is stress caused by new and advancing technologies in the workplace, most often information technologies.[58] For example, the widespread use of electronic bulletin boards as a forum for rumors of layoffs may cause feelings of uncertainty and anxiety (technostress). However, the same electronic bulletin boards can be an important source of information and thus reduce uncertainty for workers.

job sharing
An alternative work pattern in which more than one person occupies a single job.

flextime
An alternative work pattern that enables employees to set their own daily work schedules.

virtual office
A mobile platform of computer, telecommunication, and information technology and services.

technostress
The stress caused by new and advancing technologies in the workplace.

New information technologies enable organizations to monitor employee work performance, even when the employee is not aware of the monitoring.[59] These new technologies also allow organizations to tie pay to performance because performance is electronically monitored.[60] Three guidelines can help make electronic workplace monitoring, especially of performance, less distressful. First, workers should participate in the introduction of the monitoring system. Second, performance standards should be seen as fair. Third, performance records should be used to improve performance, not to punish the performer. In the extreme, new technologies that allow for virtual work in remote locations take employees beyond such monitoring.[61]

Task Revision

task revision

The modification of incorrectly specified roles or jobs.

A new concept in the design of work is *task revision*.[62] Task revision is an innovative way to modify an incorrectly specified role or job. Task revision assumes that organizational roles and job expectations may be correctly or incorrectly defined. Furthermore, a person's behavior in a work role has very different performance consequences depending on whether the role is correctly or incorrectly defined. Table 14.3 sets out the performance consequences of three categories of role behaviors based on the definition of the role or job. As indicated in the table, standard role behavior leads to good performance if the role is correctly defined, and it leads to poor performance if the role is incorrectly defined. These performances go to the extreme when incumbents exhibit extreme behavior in their jobs.[63] Going to extremes leads one to exceed expectations and display extraordinary behavior (extrarole behavior); this results in either excellent performance or very poor performance, depending on the accuracy of the defined role.

counter-role behavior

Deviant behavior in either a correctly or incorrectly defined job or role.

Counter-role behavior is when the incumbent acts contrary to the expectations of the role or exhibits deviant behavior. This is a problem if the role is correctly defined. For example, poor performance occurred on a hospital ward when the nursing supervisor failed to check the administration of all medications for the nurses she was supervising, resulting in one near fatality because a patient was not given required medication by a charge nurse. The nursing supervisor exhibited counter-role behavior in believing she could simply trust the nurses and did not have to double-check their actions. The omission was caught on the next shift. When a role or task is correctly defined (for example, double-checking medication administration), counter-role behavior leads to poor performance.

TABLE 14.3   Performance Consequences of Role Behaviors

ROLE CHARACTERISTICS	STANDARD ROLE BEHAVIOR (MEETS EXPECTATIONS)	EXTRA ROLE BEHAVIOR (GOES BEYOND EXPECTATIONS)	COUNTER-ROLE BEHAVIOR (DIFFERS FROM EXPECTED)
Correctly specified role	Ordinary good performance	Excellent performance (organizational citizenship and prosocial behavior)	Poor performance (deviance, dissent, and grievance)
Incorrectly specified role	Poor performance (bureaucratic behavior)	Very poor performance (bureaucratic zeal)	Excellent performance (task revision and redirection, role innovation)

SOURCE: Republished with permission of Academy of Management, PO Box 3020, Briar Cliff Manor, NY 10510-8020. "Task Revision: A Neglected Form of Work Performance," (Table), R. M. Staw & R. D. Boettger, *Academy of Management Journal*, 1990, Vol. 33. Reproduced by permission of the publisher via Copyright Clearance Center, Inc.

Task revision is counter-role behavior in an incorrectly specified role and is a useful way to correct the problem in the role specification (see Table 14.3). Task revision is a form of role innovation that modifies the job to achieve a better performance. Task revision is the basis for long-term adaptation when the current specifications of a job are no longer applicable.[64] For example, the traditional role for a surgeon is to complete surgical procedures in an accurate and efficient manner. Based on this definition, socio-emotional caregiving is counter-role behavior on the part of the surgeon. However, if the traditional role were to be labeled incorrect, the surgeon's task revision through socio-emotional caregiving would be viewed as leading to much better medical care for patients.

Skill Development

Problems in work system design are often seen as the source of frustration for those dealing with technostress.[65] However, system and technical problems are not the only sources of technostress in new information technologies. Some experts see a growing gap between the skills demanded by new technologies and the skills possessed by employees in jobs using these technologies.[66] Although technical skills are important and are emphasized in many training programs, the largest sector of the economy is actually service-oriented, and service jobs require interpersonal skills. Managers also need a wide range of nontechnical skills to be effective in their work.[67] Therefore, any discussion of jobs and the design of work must recognize the importance of incumbent skills and abilities to meet the demands of the work. Organizations must consider the talents and skills of their employees when they engage in job design efforts. The two issues of employee skill development and job design are interrelated. The knowledge and information requirements for jobs of the future are especially high.

Managerial Implications: The Changing Nature of Work

Work is an important aspect of a healthy life. The two central needs in human nature are to engage in productive work and to form healthy relationships with others. Work means different things to different ethnic and national groups. Therefore, job design efforts must be sensitive to cultural values and beliefs.

In crafting work tasks and assignments, managers should make an effort to fit the jobs to the people who are doing them. There are no universally accepted ways to design work, and early efforts to find them have been replaced by a number of alternatives. Early approaches to job design were valuable for manufacturing and administrative jobs of the mid-1900s. Now, however, the changing nature of work in the United States and the Americans with Disabilities Act (ADA) challenge managers to find new ways to define work and design jobs.

The distinguishing feature of job design in the foreseeable future is flexibility. Dramatic global, economic, and organizational changes dictate that managers be flexible in the design of work in their organizations. Jobs must be designed to fit the larger organizational structures discussed in Chapter 15. Organizations must ask, does the job support the organization's mission? Employees must ask, does the job meet my short- and long-term needs?

Technology is one of the distinguishing features of the modern workplace. Advances in information, mechanical, and computer technology are transforming work into a highly scientific endeavor demanding employees who are highly educated, knowledgeable workers. American workers can expect these technological advances to continue during their lifetimes and should expect to meet the challenge through continuous skill development and enhancement.

LOOKING BACK: PIXAR ANIMATION STUDIOS

John Lasseter, Executive Vice President of Pixar Studios.

Pixar—To Infinity and Beyond

When callers reach the main number at Pixar, they hear an enthusiastic phone message that is unlike the kind of "corporate-speak" that most U.S. businesses present to the public. The phone greeting reflects Pixar's philosophy of not taking itself too seriously. Take the "bathroom effect" mentioned in the opening Thinking Ahead. CEO Steve Jobs had an interesting idea of installing one bathroom for the whole building. However, 700 people is a lot of traffic. So, the studios placed eight restrooms on two floors in the central atrium. This concentration of four men's rooms and four women's rooms still serves the purpose of creating interactions between people from all over the building. This arrangement exemplifies the entire culture of not taking anything or anyone too seriously, except maybe for the work.

The studios' creative types are engaged in the time-consuming and expensive process of animation. When Pixar started in 1985, it took eight hours to render one frame of computer animation. That frame of computer animation played in 1/24th of a second—quicker than a heartbeat. Twenty years later, it still takes eight hours to create one frame of computer animation because the artwork in each frame is far more complex. Technology has been infused into the world of animation in a big way. The brain of Pixar's computers is a collection of some 300 machines, each with eight processors that collectively can perform 400 billion computations per second. There is a serious leveraging of human talent with advanced technology to produce leading-edge computer animations. While the computers are powerful, the animators are still in charge.

The animators and creative types at Pixar are excited about the possibilities of taking the technology even further, to the next level. However, an organization needs more than creativity and technology to stay afloat. With its split from Disney, Pixar faces some economic uncertainty as it works to craft a new business model that factors Disney out of, rather than into, the picture. The risk for Pixar is that the studios may become overly cautious, accountant driven, and bureaucratic. Reenter John Lasseter whose formal job is executive vice president and whose real position is the studios' longtime creative leader. Lasseter's humor and imagination keep the creative juices flowing. As he wanders around visiting Pixar's creative types, he may play with most of the toys in the office—and there are plenty of toys. He wants to know the story behind this toy or that toy. If he occasionally stays too long, that is OK. In the long run, Lasseter's job is to keep Pixar very much alive and vital and take it "to infinity and beyond"![68]

Chapter Summary

1. Different countries have different preferences for one or more of six distinct patterns of defining work.

2. Scientific management, job enlargement/job rotation, job enrichment, and the job characteristics theory are traditional American approaches to the design of work and the management of workforce diversity.

3. The social information-processing (SIP) model suggests that information from others and the social context are important in a job.

4. Ergonomics and the interdisciplinary framework draw on engineering, psychology, and biology in considering the advantages and disadvantages of job and work design efforts.

5. The cultural values and social organizations in Japan, Germany, and Scandinavia lead to unique approaches to the design of work.

6. Control, uncertainty, conflict, and job/task demands are important job design parameters to consider when designing work for the well-being of the workers.

7. Telecommuting, alternative work patterns, technostress, task revision, and skill development are emerging issues in the design of work and the use of information technology.

Key Terms

anthropocentric (p. 477)
counter-role behavior (p. 482)
cross-training (p. 467)
engagement (p. 472)
ergonomics (p. 474)
flextime (p. 481)
job (p. 462)
Job Characteristics Model (p. 468)
Job Diagnostic Survey (JDS) (p. 468)

job enlargement (p. 466)
job enrichment (p. 467)
job rotation (p. 466)
job sharing (p. 481)
lean production (p. 477)
meaning of work (p. 462)
social information-processing (SIP) model (p. 473)
sociotechnical systems (STS) (p. 477)

task revision (p. 482)
technocentric (p. 477)
technostress (p. 481)
virtual office (p. 481)
work (p. 462)
work simplification (p. 465)

Review Questions

1. Define a job in its organizational context.

2. Describe six patterns of working that have been studied in different countries.

3. Describe four traditional approaches to the design of work in America.

4. Identify and define the five core job dimensions and the three critical psychological states in the Job Characteristics Model.

5. What are the salient features of the social information-processing (SIP) model of job design?

6. List the positive and negative outcomes of the four job design approaches considered by the interdisciplinary framework.

7. How do the Japanese, German, and Scandinavian approaches to work differ from one another and from the American approach?

8. Describe the key job design parameters considered when examining the effccts of work design on health and well-being.

9. What are five emerging issues in jobs and the design of work?

Discussion and Communication Questions

1. Is there ever one best way to design a particular job?

2. What should managers learn from the traditional approaches to the design of work used in the United States?

3. It is possible for American companies to apply approaches to the design of work that were developed in other countries?

4. What is the most important emerging issue in the design of work?

5. *(communication question)* Read about new approaches to jobs, such as job sharing. Prepare a memo comparing what you have learned from your reading with one or more approaches to job design discussed in the chapter. What changes in approaches to jobs and job design do you notice from this comparison?

6. *(communication question)* Interview an employee in your organization or another organization and develop an oral presentation about how the job the employee is doing could be enriched. Make sure you ask questions about all aspects of the employee's work (e.g., what specific tasks are done and with whom the employee interacts on the job).

7. *(communication question)* Based on the materials in the chapter, prepare a memo detailing the advantages and disadvantages of flextime job arrangements. In a second part of the memo, identify the specific conditions and characteristics required for a successful flextime program. Would you like to work under a flextime arrangement?

Ethical Dilemma

Bill Rider is the manager for the medical records department of a large university-based hospital. He really loves his job, but there are times when it really stretches his tolerance. He has been dealing with one such challenge for the last several weeks. Bill is trying to hire someone for a key position in his department. The hospital is in a large city that usually offers a great applicant pool from which to fill openings. But this position has always been different. It is a very demanding job and one that is often extremely stressful. Bill has tried everything he knows to restructure the position, but it remains one of the most difficult jobs in his department.

The position has been open for two months now, and the pressure to hire someone is increasing. Bill has interviewed many people. Only one person stands out in Bill's mind: Elizabeth Murry. She is smart and has plenty of medical records experience. She would be perfect for the job except for Bill's concerns about putting her in such a stressful position.

During the interview process, Bill and Elizabeth had chatted about her life as a single mom. Bill had respected Elizabeth's honesty. He also recognized

how badly she needs this job. The position comes with a generous pay raise and a much shorter commute. Both things would allow Elizabeth to provide better for her children.

Bill's concern is that Elizabeth does not realize just how demanding this job could be. He also realizes that Elizabeth does not fully understand the dynamics of the job. Bill had not lied, but he had not been completely honest either. He is afraid she will not accept the position if she really understands what she is getting into. No job is perfect, but this one has some real flaws. Bill is unsure what to do. He could be honest and chance losing Elizabeth, or he could just be quiet and hope Elizabeth is willing to live with the negatives of the position.

Questions

1. Where does Bill's primary responsibility lie?

2. Will his responsibilities to his employer be met if he hires Elizabeth under these conditions?

3. Evaluate Bill's decision using rule, virtue, rights, and justice theories.

Experiential Exercises

14.1 Chaos and the Manager's Job

Managers' jobs are increasingly chaotic as a result of high rates of change, uncertainty, and turbulence. Some managers thrive on change and chaos, but others have a difficult time responding to high rates of change and uncertainty in a positive manner. This questionnaire gives you an opportunity to evaluate how you would react to a manager's job that is rather chaotic.

Exercise Schedule

1. Preparation (preclass)
   Complete the questionnaire.

2. Individual Scoring
   Give yourself 4 points for each A, 3 points for each B, 2 points for each C, 1 point for each D, and 0 points for each E. Compute the total, divide by 24, and round to one decimal place.

3. Group Discussion

Your instructor may have you discuss your scores in groups of six students. The higher your score, the more you respond positively to change and chaos; the lower your score, the more difficulty you would have responding to this manager's job in a positive manner. In addition, answer the following questions.

a. If you could redesign this manager's job, what are the two or three aspects of the job that you would change first?

b. What are the two or three aspects of the job that you would feel no need to change?

SOURCE: "Chaos and the Manager's Job" in D. Marcic, "Option B. Quality and the New Management Paradigm," *Organizational Behavior: Experiences and Cases*, 4th ed. (Minneapolis/St. Paul: West Publishing, 1995): 296–297. Reprinted by permission.

A Manager's Job[a]

Listed below are some statements a thirty-seven-year-old manager made about his job at a large and successful corporation. If your job had these characteristics, how would you react to them? After each statement are five letters, A–E. Circle the letter that best describes how you would react according to the following scale:

A. I would enjoy this very much; it's completely acceptable.

B. This would be enjoyable and acceptable most of the time.

C. I'd have no reaction one way or another, or it would be about equally enjoyable and unpleasant.

D. This feature would be somewhat unpleasant for me.

E. This feature would be very unpleasant for me.

1. I regularly spend 30–40 percent of my time in meetings.　　A B C D E
2. A year and a half ago, my job did not exist, and I have been essentially inventing it as I go along.　　A B C D E
3. The responsibilities I either assume or am assigned consistently exceed the authority I have for discharging them.　　A B C D E
4. At any given moment in my job, I average about a dozen phone calls to be returned.　　A B C D E
5. There seems to be very little relation in my job between the quality of my performance and my actual pay and fringe benefits.　　A B C D E
6. I need about two weeks of management training a year to stay current in my job.　　A B C D E
7. Because we have very effective equal employment opportunity in my company and because it is thoroughly multinational, my job consistently brings me into close contact at a professional level with people of many races, ethnic groups, and nationalities and of both sexes.　　A B C D E
8. There is no objective way to measure my effectiveness.　　A B C D E
9. I report to three different bosses for different aspects of my job, and each has an equal say in my performance appraisal.　　A B C D E
10. On average, about a third of my time is spent dealing with unexpected emergencies that force all scheduled work to be postponed.　　A B C D E
11. When I need to meet with the people who report to me, it takes my secretary most of a day to find a time when we are all available, and even then I have yet to have a meeting where everyone is present for the entire meeting.　　A B C D E
12. The college degree I earned in preparation for this type of work is now obsolete, and I probably should return for another degree.　　A B C D E
13. My job requires that I absorb about 100–200 pages a week of technical material.　　A B C D E
14. I am out of town overnight at least one night a week.　　A B C D E
15. My department is so interdependent with several other departments in the company that all distinctions about which department is responsible for which tasks are quite arbitrary.　　A B C D E
16. I will probably get a promotion in about a year to a job in another division that has most of these same characteristics.　　A B C D E
17. During the period of my employment here, either the entire company or the division I worked in has been reorganized every year or so.　　A B C D E
18. While I face several possible promotions, I have no real career path.　　A B C D E

19. While there are several possible promotions I can see ahead of me, I think I have no realistic chance of getting to the top levels of the company. A B C D E

20. While I have many ideas about how to make things work better, I have no direct influence on either the business policies or the personnel policies that govern my division. A B C D E

21. My company has recently put in an "assessment center" where I and other managers must go through an extensive battery of psychological tests to assess our potential. A B C D E

22. My company is a defendant in an antitrust suit, and if the case comes to trial, I will probably have to testify about some decisions that were made a few years ago. A B C D E

23. Advanced computer and other electronic office technology is continually being introduced into my division, necessitating constant learning on my part. A B C D E

24. The computer terminal and screen I have in my office can be monitored in my boss's office without my knowledge. A B C D E

a"A Manager's Job" by Peter B. Vaill in *Managing as a Performing Art: New Ideas for a World of Chaotic Change.* 1989. Reprinted by permission of Jossey-Bass Inc., Publishers.

14.2 A Job Redesign Effort

This activity will help you consider ways in which work can be redesigned to improve its impact on people and its benefit to the organization. Consider the following case:

Eddie is a quality control inspector for an automotive assembly line. His job is to inspect the body, interior, and engine of cars as they roll off the assembly line. Eddie's responsibility is to identify quality problems that either hinder the functioning of these parts of the car or noticeably mar the car's appearance. He is to report the problem so that it can be corrected. Sometimes late in the day, especially on Thursdays and Fridays, Eddie lets assembly problems slip past him. In addition, Eddie's back feels sore at the end of the day, and sometimes he is very stiff in the morning. There are times when he is not sure whether he is seeing a serious problem or just a glitch.

As a five-person team, your job is to evaluate two alternative approaches to redesigning Eddie's job using theories presented in the chapter. Answer the following questions as a team. Your team should be prepared to present its recommendations to the class as a whole.

Discussion Questions

Your instructor will lead a class discussion of each of the following questions:

1. For this particular job, which are the two best models to use in a redesign effort? Why?

2. Does your team need any additional information before it begins to redesign Eddie's job? If so, what information do you need?

3. Using the two models you chose in Question 1, what would your team specifically recommend to redesign Eddie's job?

Biz Flix | Reality Bites

Four Generation X'ers meet life's realities after their college graduation. Life's realities play cruel tricks on them as they continue developing together. Lelaina Pierce (Winona Ryder) records their reality interactions in an almost endless documentary video. Ben Stiller, in his directorial debut with this film, tries to make penetrating observations on this generation's growth, development, and shared life expectations.

This scene from *Reality Bites* is the "Wienerdude" segment that appears about one-third of the way through the film. Lelaina, her class's valedictorian, desperately seeks a job after her termination as a TV morning show production assistant. She has had three unsuccessful job interviews before the one shown in this scene at a local Wienerschnitzel. Just before this scene, Lelaina asked her mother (Susan Norfleet) for a loan. Lelaina's mother noted that times are hard, and Lelaina should perhaps find a job at a fast-food restaurant. The film continues with Lelaina trying to escape her depression by chain-smoking cigarettes, watching mindless television programs, and talking to a psychic telephone partner (voiced by Amy Stiller).

What to Watch for and Ask Yourself:

> Assess the proposed job using the core job characteristics of the Job Characteristics Model. Is each job characteristic high or low?

> Do you expect the job described by Wienderdude (David Spade, uncredited) to induce high levels of internal work motivation and work satisfaction? Why or why not?

> Would you expect the work context (working conditions, supervision, coworkers) to positively or negatively affect a person's motivation and satisfaction?

Workplace Video | Machado & Silvetti: Using Structural Design to Achieve Strategic Goals

Machado & Silvetti Associates specializes in creating housing and other building structures for colleges, universities, and cities, both in the U.S. and around the world. Machado & Silvetti has approximately 50 employees, and its core leadership structure consists of the founders, two vice presidents, and nine associates. The firm's horizontal, task-based approach to organization fosters innovation among the company's designers and architects, and its flexible team structure enables rapid response and clear focus on project tasks.

Questions

1. *Briefly describe the work environment at Machado & Silvetti.*
2. *Identify some of the different job roles at Machado & Silvetti and explain how they complement each other.*
3. *Do you think there is a downside to the way jobs and teams are defined at Machado & Silvetti? Why or why not?*

Creating Jobs for Improved Performance: The Coca-Cola Way

The Coca-Cola Company, headquartered in Atlanta, Georgia, produces approximately 400 beverage brands in over 200 nations around the world. Over 70 percent of the company's revenue comes from outside the United States. In 2003, revenue was just over $21 billion, up 8 percent from the preceding year, and net income was $4.3 billion, an increase of 43 percent from 2002.

The Coca-Cola Company describes itself as "a local employer, with responsibility to enable our people to tap into their full potential, working at their innovative best and representing the diversity of the world we serve." Encouraging performance excellence by creating meaningful and involving jobs seems to be one hallmark of Coca-Cola's approach to employee motivation throughout its global operations. The Coca-Cola Company "strives to focus its resources on enabling and empowering employees to be and do their best, every day." Moreover, "it is the policy of The Coca-Cola Company to provide associates with opportunities to develop the knowledge and skills that lead to effective job performance."

The Coca-Cola Company gives employees a significant voice in the operation of the company. It seeks to create a workplace that values all employees' ideas and contributions. Listening to employees' ideas and encouraging them to share their insights helps to create new opportunities for the company. Giving employees a significant voice also helps in making decisions that benefit the company's multiple stakeholders. Productive dialogue between employees and leaders is fostered through a variety of mechanisms, including but not limited to: weekly open discussions between senior leaders and employees, "no-agenda" brown bag lunches involving senior leaders and small groups of employees at the company's headquarters, the biennial employee insights survey, and employee forums that focus on a variety of organizational initiatives.

Continuous learning is a high priority for The Coca-Cola Company; it is a key to the company's ongoing pursuit of continuous improvement and organizational success. Coca-Cola's emphasis on continuous learning reflects its philosophy of holding each employee "accountable for continually expanding and growing the business." To facilitate continuous learning, Coca-Cola offers its employees a variety of programs to aid in their personal career planning and development. Career planning includes company assistance to employees in developing realistic personal career goals. By using a series of guided personal assessments and self-reflections as well as external information, employees are able to define goals, better understand how to be effective in their current jobs, identify appropriate career paths, and add value to the organization. Career development activities help employees to enhance their competencies for their current jobs as well as imparting those skills that are needed for making progress on their career plans. The company provides just-in-time learning through more than 1,200 on-line courses that are relevant to employees' present job skills and anticipated future needs.

Performance feedback is an essential element of Coca-Cola's human resource practices. The company states: "We believe that the success of our employees depends on their clear understanding of how their work aligns with organizational objectives and a strong process of ongoing guidance, feedback, and coaching." Consequently, the company uses performance management to ensure that every employee knows the requirements and expectations of his or her job, how the job connects with the objectives of the operating unit or functional area, and the steps that are essential for achieving higher levels of performance. Although formal performance reviews occur at least twice a year, there is ongoing communication between managers and employees where they discuss progress, exchange ideas, solve performance problems, remove performance barriers, and identify strengths and future developmental needs.

The content of jobs and the emphasis on performance management are not the only ways in which The Coca-Cola Company attempts to foster high employee motivation and superior achievement. The company also provides a variety of mechanisms and programs to support employees' efforts to achieve work/life balance. Flexible working schedules are available to accommodate employees' personal needs while simultaneously fulfilling work responsibilities. In addition, job sharing is available in those positions for which it is appropriate. The underlying managerial philosophy for these types of programs is to support employees' work needs and lifestyle preferences, thereby enhancing their work experiences and performance results.

Taken together, these programs reflect The Coca-Cola Company's commitment to providing employees with meaningful and satisfying work opportunities.

Discussion Questions

1. Using the Job Characteristics Model, analyze and discuss the work design implications of The Coca-Cola Company's approach to creating jobs for improved performance.

2. How can the social information-processing model be applied to understanding The Coca-Cola Company's approach to creating jobs for improved performance?

3. What alternative work patterns does The Coca-Cola Company offer its employees, and why does it use them?

SOURCE: This case was written by Michael K. McCuddy, The Louis S. and Mary L. Morgal Chair of Christian Business Ethics and Professor of Management, College of Business Administration, Valparaiso University. This case was developed from material contained on The Coca-Cola Company Web site at http://www.coca-cola.com and in the following reports: *The Coca-Cola Company: 2003 Summary Annual Report, 2003 Report*, http://www2.coca-cola.com/investors/annualandotherreports/2003/intro.shtml; and *The Coca-Cola Company: Our Workplace in the United States, 2003 Report*, http://www.workplacereport.coca-cola.com.

Chapter 15

© John Dominis/Time Life Pictures/Getty Images

Organizational Design and Structure

THINKING AHEAD: THE COCA-COLA COMPANY

Coca-Cola . . . Strengthening the Brand for Battle

Coca-Cola is a brand name product, no question about it. The creation and maintenance of powerful, positive brand names requires consistency. Customers need to know what they are getting every time, again and again. Consistency is the most important brand issue for any company with a brand name. When the lion's share of a company's messages is electronic, then unifying the means of communication and correspondence is a critical brand issue. Marketing campaigns, point-of-sale data, and customer service all benefit when the company's information technology (IT) infrastructure and interdepartmental coordination are integrated. Coke is looking to IT initiatives to help it reorganize and advance its brand name. Using IT initiatives to drive restructuring activities can lead to efficiencies for the company.

At the beginning of 2003, Coca-Cola's chairman and CEO described in a memo to employees his goal to seek these efficiencies and eliminate redundancies among functionally similar business units through the use of IT initiatives. He did this by combining three North American business units into a single integrated operating model. The three business units were Coca-Cola North America, Minute Maid, and Fountain. The company created one integrated team to execute a clear strategy with common processes and procedures. This restructuring of the organization unified functionally similar business units, including IT departments, to strip out redundancies that hindered efficiencies. Coke may be on the leading edge of using IT to drive its restructuring and reorganization, but it is not alone. PepsiCo is another consumer packaged-goods company involved in the huge trend to use IT to improve business processes and reduce costs.

The "cola wars" have been raging for years, with Coke and Pepsi as the two heavyweight combatants. Market share and profitability are two of the leading indicators in these wars. The first way to win in profitability is to grow the bottom-line, revenue side of the business. This initiative overlaps with increasing market share. This can be tough to do in a highly competitive industry. The second way to win in profitability is to reduce the expense side of the equation; in other words, reduce the cost structure. This goal is the aim of the IT initiatives and corporate restructuring activities going on within Coke. As in any war, however, there is an ebb and flow on the battlefield, and clear-cut victors are rarely found because it is an ongoing competitive landscape.[1] So, will the latest reorganization of Coca-Cola's businesses give it a competitive advantage in the cola wars?

---

organizational design

The process of constructing and adjusting an organization's structure to achieve its goals.

organizational structure

The linking of departments and jobs within an organization.

Organizational design is the process of constructing and adjusting an organization's structure to achieve its goals. The design process begins with the organization's goals. These goals are broken into tasks as the basis for jobs, as discussed in Chapter 14. Jobs are grouped into departments, and departments are linked to form the *organizational structure*. Chapter 15 builds on Chapter 14 by examining the macro structure of the organization in a parallel fashion to how Chapter 14 examines the micro structure of the organization. One of the most elegantly designed organizations of the last century was General Motors. GM's muscular organization structure has given way to a very different organization, as discussed in The Real World 15.1.

The first section of the chapter examines the design processes of differentiation and integration. The second section addresses the six basic design dimensions of an organization's structure. The organization's structure gives it the form to fulfill its function in the environment. As Louis Sullivan, the father of the skyscraper, said, "Form ever follows function." The third section of the chapter presents five structural configurations for organizations. Based on its mission and purpose, an organization determines the best structural configuration for its unique situation. The fourth section examines size, technology, environment, and strategy and goals as *contextual variables* influencing organizational design. When the organization's contextual variables change, the organization must redesign itself to meet new demands and functions. The fifth section examines five forces shaping organizations today. The final section notes several areas where managers should be cautious with regard to structural weaknesses and dysfunctional structural constellations.

contextual variables

A set of characteristics that influence the organization's design processes.

Key Organizational Design Processes

1. Define *differentiation* and *integration* as organizational design processes.

Differentiation is the design process of breaking the organizational goals into tasks. Integration is the design process of linking the tasks together to form a structure that supports goal accomplishment. These two processes are the keys to successful organizational design. The organizational structure is designed to prevent chaos through an orderly set of reporting relationships and communication channels. Understanding the key design processes and organizational structure helps a person understand the larger working environment and may prevent confusion in the organization.

GM—The Way It Was . . . The Way It Is

When Alfred P. Sloan built the GM juggernaut organization in the 1920s, it was truly amazing. General Motors came to dominate American industry for years. The company's power rested over the middle decades of the last century on its operating divisions—Chevrolet, Pontiac, Oldsmobile, Buick, Cadillac—that were almost autonomous enterprises and were multibillion-dollar companies. The money was controlled at headquarters, as were key design and engineering decisions. Centralized control and decentralized operation made General Motors the largest company in the world with 60 percent of the American car market. But after the 1960s, the reorganizations began and continued . . . and continued. The operating divisions had become large and clumsy and had begun competing with each other in dysfunctional ways. Restructuring was desperately needed.

GM continues to be a huge automotive organization. Yet, the organization is nothing like the elegant powerhouse that Alfred Sloan built. The divisions are now largely marketing organizations that work on sales and advertising rather than dynamic operating companies. This dramatic change in organization and structure has left GM with two not easily answered questions. How do the divisions build historical memory? What is the career upward mobility route for the car people? In the beginning, the car guys ran General Motors; that's the way *it was*. Today, a GM manager may parachute in from the snack food industry, or somewhere like that; that's the way *it is*.

SOURCE: J. Flint, "When Car Guys Ran GM," *Forbes* 173 (April 19, 2004): 77, http://www.forbes.com/columnists/business/forbes/2004/0419/077.html.

The organization chart is the most visible representation of the organization's structure and underlying components. Figure 15.1 is the organizational chart for the World Trade Organization. Most organizations have a series of organization charts showing reporting relationships throughout the system. The underlying components are (1) formal lines of authority and responsibility (the organizational structure designates reporting relationships by the way jobs and departments are grouped) and (2) formal systems of communication, coordination, and integration (the organizational structure designates the expected patterns of formal interaction among employees).[2]

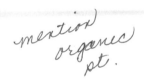

Differentiation

Differentiation is the process of deciding how to divide the work in an organization.[3] Differentiation ensures that all essential organizational tasks are assigned to one or more jobs and that the tasks receive the attention they need. Many dimensions of differentiation have been considered in organizations. Lawrence and Lorsch found four dimensions of differentiation in one study: (1) manager's goal orientation, (2) time orientation, (3) interpersonal orientation, and (4) formality of structure.[4] Table 15.1 shows some typical differences

differentiation

The process of deciding how to divide the work in an organization.

TABLE 15.1   Differentiation between Marketing and Engineering

BASIS FOR DIFFERENCE	MARKETING	ENGINEERING
Goal orientation	Sales volume	Design
Time orientation	Long run	Medium run
Interpersonal orientation	People oriented	Task oriented
Structure	Less formal	More formal

FIGURE 15.1 Organizational Chart for the World Trade Organization

15.1

WTO structure

All WTO members may participate in all councils, committees, etc., except Appellate Body, Dispute Settlement panels, Textiles Monitoring Body, and plurilateral committees.

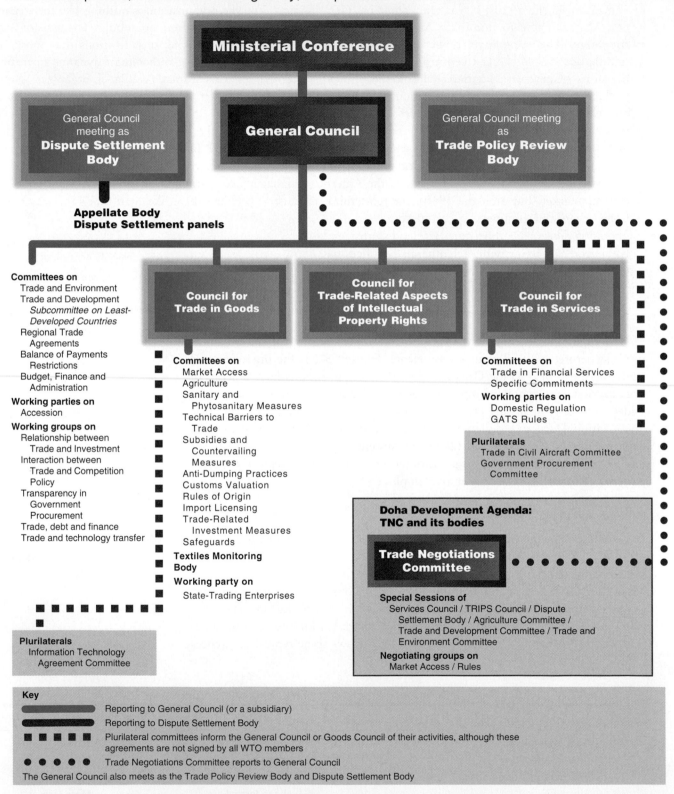

Ministerial Conference

General Council meeting as **Dispute Settlement Body**

General Council

General Council meeting as **Trade Policy Review Body**

Appellate Body
Dispute Settlement panels

Committees on
Trade and Environment
Trade and Development
Subcommittee on Least-Developed Countries
Regional Trade
  Agreements
Balance of Payments
  Restrictions
Budget, Finance and
  Administration
Working parties on
Accession
Working groups on
Relationship between
  Trade and Investment
Interaction between
  Trade and Competition
  Policy
Transparency in
  Government
  Procurement
Trade, debt and finance
Trade and technology transfer

Plurilaterals
Information Technology
  Agreement Committee

Council for Trade in Goods

Committees on
Market Access
Agriculture
Sanitary and
  Phytosanitary Measures
Technical Barriers to
  Trade
Subsidies and
  Countervailing
  Measures
Anti-Dumping Practices
Customs Valuation
Rules of Origin
Import Licensing
Trade-Related
  Investment Measures
Safeguards
Textiles Monitoring Body
Working party on
State-Trading Enterprises

Council for Trade-Related Aspects of Intellectual Property Rights

Council for Trade in Services

Committees on
Trade in Financial Services
Specific Commitments
Working parties on
Domestic Regulation
GATS Rules

Plurilaterals
Trade in Civil Aircraft Committee
Government Procurement
Committee

Doha Development Agenda:
TNC and its bodies

Trade Negotiations Committee

Special Sessions of
Services Council / TRIPS Council / Dispute
  Settlement Body / Agriculture Committee /
  Trade and Development Committee / Trade and
  Environment Committee
Negotiating groups on
Market Access / Rules

Key
———— Reporting to General Council (or a subsidiary)
———— Reporting to Dispute Settlement Body
■ ■ ■ ■ ■ Plurilateral committees inform the General Council or Goods Council of their activities, although these agreements are not signed by all WTO members
● ● ● ● ● Trade Negotiations Committee reports to General Council
The General Council also meets as the Trade Policy Review Body and Dispute Settlement Body

SOURCE: WTO Organization Chart http://www.wto.org/english/thewto_e/whatis_e/tif_e/org2_e.htm

in orientation for various functional areas of an organization. Three different forms of differentiation are horizontal, vertical, and spatial.

Horizontal differentiation is the degree of differentiation between organizational subunits and is based on employees' specialized knowledge, education, or training. For example, two university professors who teach specialized subjects in different academic departments are subject to horizontal differentiation. Horizontal differentiation increases with specialization and departmentation.

Specialization refers to the particular grouping of activities performed by an individual.[5] The degree of specialization or the division of labor in the organization gives an indication of how much training is needed, what the scope of a job is, and what individual characteristics are needed for job holders. Specialization can also lead to the development of a specialized vocabulary, as well as other behavioral norms. As the two college professors specialize in their subjects, abbreviations or acronyms take on unique meanings. For example, OB means "organizational behavior" to a professor of management but "obstetrics" to a professor of medicine.

Usually, the more specialized the jobs within an organization, the more departments are differentiated within that organization (the greater the departmentation). Departmentation can be by function, product, service, client, geography, process, or some combination of these. A large organization may departmentalize its structure using all or most of these methods at different levels of the organization.

Vertical differentiation is the difference in authority and responsibility in the organizational hierarchy. Vertical differentiation occurs, for example, between a chief executive and a maintenance supervisor. Tall, narrow organizations have greater vertical differentiation, and flat, wide organizations have less vertical differentiation. The height of the organization is also influenced by level of horizontal differentiation and span of control. The span of control refers to and defines the number of subordinates a manager can and should supervise.[6]

Tall structures—those with narrow spans of control—tend to be characterized by closer supervision and tighter controls. In addition, the communication becomes more burdensome, since directives and information must be passed through more layers. The banking industry has often had tall structures. Flat structures—those with wider spans of control—have simpler communication chains and reduced promotion opportunities due to fewer levels of management. Sears is an example of an organization that has gone to a flat structure. With the loss of more than a million middle management positions in organizations, many organizations are now flatter. The degree of vertical differentiation affects organizational effectiveness, but there is no consistent finding that flatter or taller organizations are better.[7] Organizational size, type of jobs, skills and personal characteristics of employees, and degree of freedom must all be considered in determining organizational effectiveness.[8]

Spatial differentiation is the geographic dispersion of an organization's offices, plants, and personnel. A salesperson in New York and one in Portland experience spatial differentiation. An increase in the number of locations increases the complexity of organizational design but may be necessary for organizational goal achievement or organizational protection. For example, if an organization wants to expand into a different country, it may be best to form a separate subsidiary that is partially owned and managed by citizens of that country. Few U.S. citizens think of Shell Oil Company as being a subsidiary of Royal Dutch/Shell Group, a company whose international headquarters is in the Netherlands.

Spatial differentiation may give an organization political and legal advantages in a country because it is identified as a local company. Distance is as important as political and legal issues in making spatial differentiation decisions. For example, a salesperson in Lubbock, Texas, would have a hard time servicing accounts in Beaumont, Texas (over 500 miles away), whereas a salesperson in Delaware might be able to cover all of that state, as well as parts of one or two others.

Horizontal, vertical, and spatial differentiation indicate the amount of width, height, and breadth an organizational structure needs. Just because an organization is highly differentiated along one of these dimensions does not mean it must be highly differentiated along the others. The university environment, for example, is generally characterized by great horizontal differentiation but relatively little vertical and spatial differentiation. A company such as Coca-Cola is characterized by a great deal of all three types of differentiation. The more structurally differentiated an organization is, the more complex it is.[9]

Complexity refers to the number of activities, subunits, or subsystems within the organization. Lawrence and Lorsch suggest that an organization's complexity should mirror the complexity of its environment. As the complexity of an organization increases, its need for mechanisms to link and coordinate the differentiated parts also increases. If these links do not exist, the departments or differentiated parts of the organization can lose sight of the organization's larger mission, and the organization runs the risk of chaos. Designing and building linkage and coordination mechanisms is known as *integration*.

Integration

integration

The process of coordinating the different parts of an organization.

Integration is the process of coordinating the different parts of an organization. Integration mechanisms are designed to achieve unity among individuals and groups in various jobs, departments, and divisions in the accomplishment of organizational goals and tasks.[10] Integration helps keep the organization in a state of dynamic equilibrium, a condition in which all the parts of the organization are interrelated and balanced.

Vertical linkages are used to integrate activities up and down the organizational chain of command. A variety of structural devices can be used to achieve vertical linkage. These include hierarchical referral, rules and procedures, plans and schedules, positions added to the structure of the organization, and management information systems.[11]

The vertical lines on an organization chart indicate the lines of hierarchical referral up and down the organization. When employees do not know how to solve a problem, they can refer it up the organization for consideration and resolution. Work that needs to be assigned is usually delegated down the chain of command as indicated by the vertical lines.

Rules and procedures, as well as plans and schedules, provide standing information for employees without direct communication. These vertical integrators, such as an employee handbook, communicate to employees standard information or information that they can understand on their own. These integrators allow managers to have wider spans of control, because the managers do not have to inform each employee of what is expected and when it is expected. Vertical integrators encourage managers to use management by exception—to make decisions when employees bring problems up the hierarchy. Military organizations depend heavily on vertical linkages. The army, for example, has a well-defined chain of command. Certain duties are expected to be carried out, and proper paperwork is to be in place. In times of crisis, however, much more information is processed, and the proper paperwork becomes secondary to "getting the job done." Vertical linkages help individuals understand their roles in the organization, especially in times of crisis.

Adding positions to the hierarchy is used as a vertical integrator when a manager becomes overloaded by hierarchical referral or problems arise in the chain of command. Positions such as "assistant to" may be added or another level may be added. Adding levels to the hierarchy often reflects growth and increasing complexity. This action tends to reduce the span of control, thus allowing more communication and closer supervision.

Management information systems that are designed to process information up and down the organization also serve as a vertical linkage mechanism. With the advent of computers and network technology, it has become easier for managers and employees to communicate through written reports that are entered into a network and then electronically compiled for managers in the hierarchy. Electronic mail systems allow managers and employees greater access to one another without having to be in the same place at the same time or even attached by telephone. These types of systems make information processing up and down the organization more efficient.

Generally, the taller the organization, the more vertical integration mechanisms are needed. This is because the chains of command and communication are longer. Additional length requires more linkages to minimize the potential for misunderstandings and miscommunications.

Horizontal integration mechanisms provide the communication and coordination that are necessary for links across jobs and departments in the organization. The need for horizontal integration mechanisms increases as the complexity of the organization increases. The horizontal linkages are built into the design of the organization by including liaison roles, task forces, integrator positions, and teams.

A liaison role is created when a person in one department or area of the organization has the responsibility for coordinating with another department (for example, a liaison between the engineering and production departments). Task forces are temporary committees composed of representatives from multiple departments who assemble to address a specific problem affecting these departments.[12]

A stronger device for integration is to develop a person or department designed to be an integrator. In most organizations, the integrator has a good deal of responsibility but not much authority. Such an individual must have the ability to get people together to resolve differences within the perspective of organizational goals.[13]

The strongest method of horizontal integration is through teams. Horizontal teams cut across existing lines of organizational structure to create new entities that make organizational decisions. An example of this may occur in product development with the formation of a team that includes marketing, research, design, and production personnel. Ford used such a cross-functional team to develop the Taurus automobile, which was designed to regain market share in the United States. The information exchanged by such a product development team should lead to a product that is acceptable to a wider range of organizational groups, as well as to customers.[14]

The use of these linkage mechanisms varies from organization to organization, as well as within areas of the same organization. In general, the flatter the organization, the more necessary are horizontal integration mechanisms.

Basic Design Dimensions

2. Discuss six basic design dimensions of an organization.

Differentiation, then, is the process of dividing work in the organization, and integration is the process of coordinating work in the organization. From a structural perspective, every manager and organization look for the best combination of differentiation and integration for accomplishing the goals of the organization. There are many ways to approach this process. One way is to establish a desired level of each structural dimension on a high to low continuum and then develop a structure that meets the desired configuration. These structural dimensions include the following:[15]

formalization
The degree to which the organization has official rules, regulations, and procedures.

centralization
The degree to which decisions are made at the top of the organization.

specialization
The degree to which jobs are narrowly defined and depend on unique expertise.

standardization
The degree to which work activities are accomplished in a routine fashion.

complexity
The degree to which many different types of activities occur in the organization.

hierarchy of authority
The degree of vertical differentiation across levels of management.

1. *Formalization:* The degree to which an employee's role is defined by formal documentation (procedures, job descriptions, manuals, and regulations).

2. *Centralization:* The extent to which decision-making authority has been delegated to lower levels of an organization. An organization is centralized if the decisions are made at the top of the organization and decentralized if decision making is pushed down to lower levels in the organization.

3. *Specialization:* The degree to which organizational tasks are subdivided into separate jobs. The division of labor and the degree to which formal job descriptions spell out job requirements indicate the level of specialization in the organization.

4. *Standardization:* The extent to which work activities are described and performed routinely in the same way. Highly standardized organizations have little variation in the defining of jobs.

5. *Complexity:* The number of activities within the organization and the amount of differentiation needed within the organization.

6. *Hierarchy of authority:* The degree of vertical differentiation through reporting relationships and the span of control within the structure of the organization.

An organization that is high on formalization, centralization, specialization, standardization, and complexity and has a tall hierarchy of authority is said to be highly bureaucratic. Bureaucracies are not in and of themselves bad; however, they are often tainted by abuse and red tape. The Real World 15.2 describes how The Royal Bank of Canada has redesigned its mortgage process to be more decentralized.

An organization that is on the opposite end of each of these continua is very flexible and loose. Control is very hard to implement and maintain in such an organization, but at certain times such an organization is appropriate. The research and development departments in many organizations are often more flexible than other departments in order to stimulate creativity. An important organizational variable, which is not included in the structural dimensions, is trust.

Another approach to the process of accomplishing organizational goals is to describe what is and is not important to the success of the organization rather than worry about specific characteristics. Henry Mintzberg feels that the following questions can guide managers in designing formal structures that fit each organization's unique set of circumstances:[16]

The Royal Bank of Canada Decentralizes

© Norm Betts/Bloomberg News/Landov

RBC attempts to avoid bottle-necks in mortgage processing by decentralizing.

Proponents of centralization in banking services, including mortgages, argue that centralized processing is faster and cheaper. In addition, by centralizing mortgage processing, loan officers have more freedom to focus on sales. While many home lenders are centralizing or even outsourcing more of their processing, The Royal Bank of Canada (RBC) Mortgage Company maintains that a lender needs to be "local" to sign up the best loan officers. In 2004, RBC fired 200 of its loan officers for underperformance.

At the same time, it planned to hire about 400 to 500 loan officers in line with a major retooling of its business model for mortgages. RBC's plan is to have most of the mortgage loan-processing work, from taking an application to funding a loan, performed at the branch level. By decentralizing mortgages, RBC anticipates avoiding bottlenecks that occur in central processing handoffs. Even those who argue for centralization agree that it frustrates loan officers because they lose a sense of control while waiting for work done elsewhere to come back to them. While branch bank units may be self-sufficient in many functions that support loan officers, underwriting can be an exception. Loan approvals can usually be secured through automated underwriting, leaving the branch to call on outside underwriters only for unusual cases.

SOURCE: J. Shenn, "RBC Idea for Processing Mortgages: Decentralize," *American Banker* 169 (April 12, 2004): 1.

1. How many tasks should a given position in the organization contain, and how specialized should each task be?

2. How standardized should the work content of each position be?

3. What skills, abilities, knowledge, and training should be required for each position?

4. What should be the basis for the grouping of positions within the organization into units, departments, divisions, and so on?

5. How large should each unit be, and what should the span of control be (that is, how many individuals should report to each manager)?

6. How much standardization should be required in the output of each position?

7. What mechanisms should be established to help individuals in different positions and units to adjust to the needs of other individuals?

8. How centralized or decentralized should decision-making power be in the chain of authority? Should most of the decisions be made at the top of the organization (centralized) or be made down in the chain of authority (decentralized)?

The manager who can answer these questions has a good understanding of how the organization should implement the basic structural dimensions. These basic design dimensions act in combination with one another and are not entirely independent characteristics of an organization. You 15.1 gives you (or a friend) an opportunity to consider how decentralized your company is.

Five Structural Configurations

3. Briefly describe five structural configurations for organizations.

Differentiation, integration, and the basic design dimensions combine to yield various structural configurations. Very early organization structures were often either based on product or function. The matrix organization structure crossed these two ways of organizing.[17] Mintzberg moved beyond these early approaches and proposed five structural configurations: the simple structure, the machine bureaucracy, the professional bureaucracy, the divisionalized form, and the adhocracy.[18] Table 15.2 summarizes the prime coordinating mechanism, the key part of the organization, and the type of decentralization for each of these structural configurations. The five basic parts of the organization, for Mintzberg, are the upper echelon or strategic apex; the middle level; the operating core, where work is accomplished; the technical staff; and the support staff. Figure 15.2 depicts these five basic parts with a small strategic apex, connected by a flaring middle line to a large, flat operating core. Each configuration affects people in the organization somewhat differently.

Simple Structure

simple structure

A centralized form of organization that emphasizes the upper echelon and direct supervision.

The *simple structure* is an organization with little technical and support staff, strong centralization of decision making in the upper echelon, and a minimal middle level. This structure has a minimum of vertical differentiation of authority and minimal formalization. It achieves coordination through direct supervision, often by the chief executive in the upper echelon. An example of a simple structure is a small, independent landscape practice in which one or two landscape architects supervise the vast majority of work with no middle-level managers. Even an organization with as few as thirty people can become dysfunctional as a simple structure after an extended period.

Machine Bureaucracy

machine bureaucracy

A moderately decentralized form of organization that emphasizes the technical staff and standardization of work processes.

The *machine bureaucracy* is an organization with a well-defined technical and support staff differentiated from the line operations of the organization, limited horizontal decentralization of decision making, and a well-defined hierarchy of authority. The technical staff is powerful in a machine bureaucracy. There is strong formalization through policies, procedures, rules, and regulations. Coordination is achieved through the standardization of work processes.

TABLE 15.2   Five Structural Configurations of Organizations

STRUCTURAL CONFIGURATION	PRIME COORDINATING MECHANISM	KEY PART OF ORGANIZATION	TYPE OF DECENTRALIZATION
Simple structure	Direct supervision	Upper echelon	Centralization
Machine bureaucracy	Standardization of work processes	Technical staff	Limited horizontal decentralization
Professional bureaucracy	Standardization of skills	Operating level	Vertical and horizontal decentralization
Divisionalized form	Standardization of outputs	Middle level	Limited vertical decentralization
Adhocracy	Mutual adjustment	Support staff	Selective decentralization

SOURCE: H. Mintzberg, *The Structuring of Organizations.* © 1979, 301. Reprinted by permission of Prentice-Hall, Inc., Upper Saddle River, N.J.

How Decentralized Is Your Company?

Decentralization is one of the key design dimensions in an organization. It is closely related to several behavioral dimensions of an organization, such as leadership style, degree of participative decision making, and the nature of power and politics within the organization.

The following questionnaire allows you to get an idea about how decentralized your organization is. (If you do not have a job, have a friend who does work complete the questionnaire to see how decentralized his or her organization is.) Which level in your organization has the authority to make each of the following eleven decisions? Answer the questionnaire by circling one of the following:

0 = The board of directors makes the decision.
1 = The CEO makes the decision.
2 = The division/functional manager makes the decision.
3 = A subdepartment head makes the decision.
4 = The first-level supervisor makes the decision.
5 = Operators on the shop floor make the decision.

Decision Concerning:	**Circle Appropriate Level**					
a. The number of workers required.	0	1	2	3	4	5
b. Whether to employ a worker.	0	1	2	3	4	5
c. Internal labor disputes.	0	1	2	3	4	5
d. Overtime worked at shop level.	0	1	2	3	4	5
e. Delivery dates and order priority.	0	1	2	3	4	5
f. Production planning.	0	1	2	3	4	5
g. Dismissal of a worker.	0	1	2	3	4	5
h. Methods of personnel selection.	0	1	2	3	4	5
i. Method of work to be used.	0	1	2	3	4	5
j. Machinery or equipment to be used.	0	1	2	3	4	5
k. Allocation of work among workers.	0	1	2	3	4	5

Scoring

Add up all your circled numbers.
Total = _____.
The higher your number (for example, 45 or more), the more decentralized your organization. The lower your number (for example, 25 or less), the more centralized your organization.

SOURCE: From D. Miller and C. Droge, "Psychological and Traditional Determinants of Structure," *Administrative Science Quarterly* 31 (1986): 558. Reprinted by permission of the Administrative Science Quarterly.

An example of a machine bureaucracy is an automobile assembly plant with routinized operating tasks. The strength of the machine bureaucracy is efficiency of operation in stable, unchanging environments. The weakness of the machine bureaucracy is its slow responsiveness to external changes and to individual employee preferences and ideas.

Professional Bureaucracy

The *professional bureaucracy* emphasizes the expertise of the professionals in the operating core of the organization. The technical and support staffs serve the professionals. There is both vertical and horizontal differentiation in the professional bureaucracy. Coordination is achieved through the standardization of

professional bureaucracy
A decentralized form of organization that emphasizes the operating core and standardization of skills.

FIGURE 15.2   Mintzberg's Five Basic Parts of an Organization

15.2

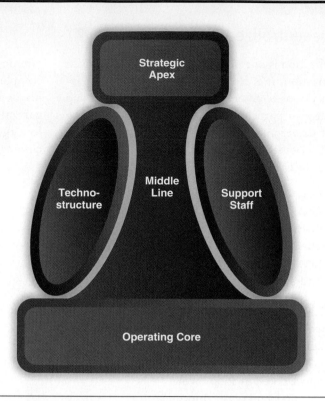

SOURCE: From H. Mintzberg, *The Structuring of Organizations*, © 1979, 20. Reprinted by permission of Pearson Education, Inc., Upper Saddle River, N.J.

the professionals' skills. Examples of professional bureaucracies are hospitals and universities. The doctors, nurses, and professors are given wide latitude to pursue their work based on professional training and indoctrination through professional training programs. Large accounting firms may fall into the category of professional bureaucracies.

Divisionalized Form

divisionalized form

A moderately decentralized form of organization that emphasizes the middle level and standardization of outputs.

The *divisionalized form* is a loosely coupled, composite structural configuration.[19] It is a configuration composed of divisions, each of which may have its own structural configuration. Each division is designed to respond to the market in which it operates. There is vertical decentralization from the upper echelon to the middle of the organization, and the middle level of management is the key part of the organization. This form of organization may have one division that is a machine bureaucracy, one that is an adhocracy, and one that is a simple structure. An example of this form of organization is Valero Energy Corporation, headquartered in San Antonio, Texas, with oil refining operations throughout the country. The divisionalized organization uses standardization of outputs as its coordinating mechanism.

Adhocracy

adhocracy

A selectively decentralized form of organization that emphasizes the support staff and mutual adjustment among people.

The *adhocracy* is a highly open and decentralized, rather than highly structured, configuration with minimal formalization and order. It is designed to fuse interdisciplinary experts into smoothly functioning ad hoc project teams. Liaison devices are the primary mechanism for integrating the project teams through a process of mutual adjustment. There is a high degree of horizontal specialization based on formal training and expertise. Selective decentralization of the project teams occurs within the adhocracy. An example of this form of organization is the National Aeronautics and Space Administration (NASA), which is composed of many talented experts who work in small teams on a wide range of projects related to America's space agenda. New high-technology businesses also often select an adhocracy design. Paradoxically, though, some new high-tech ventures choose bureaucratic design strategies as antidotes for the uncertainty, anxiety, and stress of their typically turbulent operating environments.

Contextual Variables

The basic design dimensions and the resulting structural configurations play out in the context of the organization's internal and external environments. Four contextual variables influence the success of an organization's design: size, technology, environment, and strategy and goals. These variables provide a manager with key considerations for the right organizational design, although they do not determine the structure. The amount of change in the contextual variables throughout the life of the organization influences the amount of change needed in the basic dimensions of the organization's structure.[20] For example, competitive pressures in many industries have led to outsourcing, labeled one of the greatest shifts in organization structure in a century.[21]

> 4. Describe four contextual variables for an organization.

Size

The total number of employees is the appropriate definition of size when discussing the design of organizational structure. This is logical, because people and their interactions are the building blocks of structure. Other measures, such as net assets, production rates, and total sales, are usually highly correlated with the total number of employees but may not reflect the actual number of interpersonal relationships that are necessary to effectively structure an organization.

Electronic Data Systems (EDS) began as an entrepreneurial venture of H. Ross Perot and had grown into an internationally prominent provider of information technology services when it was bought by General Motors Corporation (GM) in the early 1980s. Nearly half of EDS's revenues came from GM at the time of the buyout. The early culture of EDS placed a premium on technical competence, high achievement drive, an entrepreneurial attitude, and a maverick spirit. EDS has continued to grow and to change. In 1996, it was spun off by GM and became an autonomous company once again.[22] However, following the spin-off, the company has struggled to find a clear focus and identity and has lost two chairmen (Les Aberthal and Dick Brown) in the process.

Although there is some argument over the degree of influence that size has on organizational structure, there is no argument that it does influence design options. In one study, Meyer found size of the organization to be the most important of all variables considered in influencing the organization's structure and design, whereas other researchers argue that the decision to expand the organization's business causes an increase in size as the structure is adjusted to accommodate the planned growth.[23] Downsizing is a planned strategy to reduce the size of an organization, and is often accompanied by related restructuring and revitalization activities.[24]

How much influence size exerts on the organization's structure is not as important as the relationship between size and the design dimensions of structure. In other words, when exploring structural alternatives, what should the manager know about designing structures for large and small organizations?

Table 15.3 illustrates the relationships among each of the design dimensions and organizational size. Formalization, specialization, and standardization all tend to be greater in larger organizations because they are necessary to control activities within the organization. For example, larger organizations are more likely to use documentation, rules, written policies and procedures, and detailed job descriptions than to rely on personal observation by the manager. The more relationships that have to be managed by the structure, the more formalized and standardized the processes need to be. McDonald's has several volumes that describe how to make all its products, how to greet customers, how to maintain the facilities, and so on. This level of

McDonald's relies on formalization, specialization, and standardization to ensure consistency of its products across the chains.

standardization, formalization, and specialization helps McDonald's maintain the same quality of product no matter where a restaurant is located. In contrast, at a small, locally owned café, your hamburger and french fries may taste a little different every time you visit. This is evidence of a lack of standardization.

Formalization and specialization also help a large organization decentralize decision making. Because of the complexity and number of decisions in a large organization, formalization and specialization are used to set parameters for decision making at lower levels. Can you imagine the chaos if the President of the United States, commander-in-chief of all U.S. military forces, had to make operational-level decisions in the war on terrorism? By decentralizing decision making, the larger organization adds horizontal and vertical complexity, but not necessarily spatial complexity. However, it is more common for a large organization to have more geographic dispersion.

TABLE 15.3	Relationship between Organizational Size and Basic Design Dimensions	
BASIC DESIGN DIMENSIONS	SMALL ORGANIZATIONS	LARGE ORGANIZATIONS
Formalization	Less	More
Centralization	High	Low
Specialization	Low	High
Standardization	Low	High
Complexity	Low	High
Hierarchy of authority	Flat	Tall

Another dimension of design, hierarchy of authority, is related to complexity. As size increases, complexity increases; thus, more levels are added to the hierarchy of authority. This keeps the span of control from getting too large. However, there is a balancing force, because formalization and specialization are added. The more formalized, standardized, and specialized the roles within the organization, the wider the span of control can be.

Although some have argued that the future belongs to small, agile organizations, others argue that size continues to be an advantage. To take advantage of size, organizations must become centerless corporations with a global core.[25] These concepts are pioneered by Booz Allen Hamilton based on its worldwide technology and management consulting. The global core provides strategic leadership, helps distribute and provide access to the company's capabilities and knowledge, creates the corporate identity, ensures access to low cost capital, and exerts control over the enterprise as a whole.

Technology

An organization's technology is an important contextual variable in determining the organization's structure, as noted in Chapter 2.[26] Technology is defined as the tools, techniques, and actions used by an organization to transform inputs into outputs.[27] The inputs of the organization include human resources, machines, materials, information, and money. The outputs are the products and services that the organization offers to the external environment. Determining the relationship between technology and structure is complicated, because different departments may employ very different technologies. As organizations become larger, there is greater variation in technologies across units in the organization. Joan Woodward, Charles Perrow, and James Thompson have developed ways to understand traditional organizational technologies. More work is needed to better understand the contemporary engineering, research and development, and knowledge-based technologies of the information age.

Woodward introduced one of the best-known classification schemes for technology, identifying three types: unit, mass, or process production. Unit technology is small-batch manufacturing technology and, sometimes, made-to-order production. Examples include Smith & Wesson's arms manufacture and the manufacture of fine furniture. Mass technology is large-batch manufacturing technology. Examples include American automotive assembly lines and latex glove production. Process production is continuous-production processes. Examples include oil refining and beer making. Woodward classified unit technology as the least complex, mass technology as more complex, and process technology as the most complex. The more complex the organization's technology, the more complex the administrative component or structure of the organization needs to be.

Perrow proposed an alternative to Woodward's scheme based on two variables: task variability and problem analyzability. Task variability considers the number of exceptions encountered in doing the tasks within a job. Problem analyzability examines the types of search procedures followed to find ways to respond to task exceptions. For example, for some exceptions encountered while doing a task, the appropriate response is easy to find. If you are driving down a street and see a sign that says, "Detour—Bridge Out," it is very easy to respond to the task variability. When Thomas Edison was designing the first electric light bulb, however, the problem analyzability was very high for his task.

Perrow went on further to identify the four key aspects of structure that could be modified to the technology. These structural elements are (1) the amount of discretion that an individual can exercise to complete a task, (2) the power of groups to control the unit's goals and strategies, (3) the level of interdependence among groups, and (4) the extent to which organizational units coordinate work using either feedback or planning. Figure 15.3 summarizes Perrow's findings about types of technology and basic design dimensions.[28]

Thompson offered yet another view of technology and its relationship to organizational design. This view is based on the concept of *technological interdependence* (i.e., the degree of interrelatedness of the organization's various technological elements) and the pattern of an organization's work flows. Thompson's research suggests that greater technological interdependence leads to greater organizational complexity and that the problems of this greater complexity may be offset by decentralized decision making.[29]

The research of these three early scholars on the influence of technology on organizational design can be combined into one integrating concept—routineness in the process of changing inputs into outputs in an organization. This routineness has a very strong relationship with organizational structure. The more routine and repetitive the tasks of the organization, the higher the degree of formalization that is possible; the more centralized, specialized, and standardized the organization can be; and the more hierarchical levels with wider spans of control that are possible.

Since the work of Woodward, Perrow, and Thompson, however, an important caveat to the discussion of technology has emerged: the advance of in-

technological interdependence

The degree of interrelatedness of the organization's various technological elements.

FIGURE 15.3 15.3

Summary of Perrow's Findings about the Relationship between Technology and Basic Design Dimensions

	Task Variability	
	Few Exceptions	**Many Exceptions**
Ill-defined and Unanalyzable	Craft 1. Moderate 2. Moderate 3. Moderate 4. Low-moderate 5. High 6. Low	Nonroutine 1. Low 2. Low 3. Low 4. Low 5. High 6. Low
Well-defined and Analyzable	Routine 1. High 2. High 3. Moderate 4. High 5. Low 6. High	Engineering 1. Moderate 2. Moderate 3. High 4. Moderate 5. Moderate 6. Moderate

Problem Analyzability (vertical axis label)

Key:
1. Formalization   4. Standardization
2. Centralization   5. Complexity
3. Specialization   6. Hierarchy of authority

SOURCE: Built from C. Perrow, "A Framework for the Comparative Analysis of Organizations," *American Sociological Review* (April 1967): 194–208.

formation technology has influenced how organizations transform inputs into outputs. The introduction of computer-integrated networks, CAD/CAM systems, and computer-integrated manufacturing has broadened the span of control, flattened the organizational hierarchy, decentralized decision making, and lowered the amount of specialization and standardization.[30] Advances in information technology have allowed for other advances in manufacturing, such as mass customization. Hewlett-Packard has found a key to mass customization in postponing the task of differentiating a product for a specific customer until the latest possible time.[31]

Further, the emergence of new digital technologies along with the globalization of the economy are major forces for change. These two forces affect all organizations throughout the economy, ushering in a new economy that has four characteristics. Stanley M. Davis describes these as (1) *any time*—customers can get their goods and services 24/7; (2) *any place*—customers can order from anywhere if they have Internet access; (3) *no matter*—intangibles are adding value to products, such as through digital photography; and (4) *mass customization*—technology and information allow for rapid, responsive customization of products.[32] Thus, digital technology and economic change have resulted in downsizing and restructuring activities in the private sector.

Environment

The third contextual variable for organizational design is *environment*. The environment of an organization is most easily defined as anything outside the boundaries of that organization. Different aspects of the environment have varying degrees of influence on the organization's structure. In one study of 318 CEOs between 1996 and 2000, strategic decision speed was found to moderate the relationship between the environment and the organization structure and performance.[33] For example, in response to the 9/11 terrorist attack on The World Trade Centers, President George W. Bush acted swiftly to restructure the U.S. federal government and create the Department of Homeland Security. The general environment includes all conditions that may have an impact on the organization. These conditions could include economic factors, political considerations, ecological changes, sociocultural demands, and governmental regulation.

environment
Anything outside the boundaries of an organization.

TASK ENVIRONMENT When aspects of the general environment become more focused in areas of direct interest to the organization, those aspects become part of the *task environment*, or specific environment. The task environment is that part of the environment that is directly relevant to the organization. Typically, this level of environment includes stakeholders such as unions, customers, suppliers, competitors, government regulatory agencies, and trade associations.

The domain of the organization refers to the area the organization claims for itself with respect to how it fits into its relevant environments. The domain is particularly important because it is defined by the organization, and it influences how the organization perceives and acts within its environments.[34] For example, Wal-Mart and Neiman Marcus both sell clothing apparel, but their domains are very different.

The organization's perceptions of its environment and the actual environment may not be the same. The environment that the manager perceives is the environment that the organization responds to and organizes for.[35] Therefore, two organizations may be in relatively the same environment from an objective standpoint, but if the managers perceive differences, the organizations may enact very different structures to deal with this same environment.

task environment
The elements of an organization's environment that are related to its goal attainment.

environmental uncertainty

The amount and rate of change in the organization's environment.

mechanistic structure

An organizational design that emphasizes structured activities, specialized tasks, and centralized decision making.

organic structure

An organizational design that emphasizes teamwork, open communication, and decentralized decision making.

ENVIRONMENTAL UNCERTAINTY The perception of *environmental uncertainty* or the perception of the lack of environmental uncertainty is how the contextual variable of environment most influences organizational design. Some organizations have relatively static environments with little uncertainty, whereas others are so dynamic that no one is sure what tomorrow may bring. Binney & Smith, for example, has made relatively the same product for more than fifty years with very few changes in the product design or packaging. The environment for its Crayola products is relatively static. In fact, customers rebelled when the company tried to get rid of some old colors and add new ones. In contrast, in the last two decades, competitors in the airline industry have encountered deregulation, mergers, bankruptcies, safety changes, changes in cost and price structures, changes in customer and employee demographics, and changes in global competition. The uncertainty of the environment of the major airlines has been relatively high during this period.

The amount of uncertainty in the environment influences the structural dimensions. Burns and Stalker labeled two structural extremes that are appropriate for the extremes of environmental uncertainty—*mechanistic structure* and *organic structure*.[36] Table 15.4 compares the structural dimensions of these two extremes. The mechanistic and organic structures are opposite ends of a continuum of organizational design possibilities. The accompanying Science feature discusses a study of sixty-eight organizations that found mechanistic versus organic structures moderated organizational justice processes and perceptions. Although the general premise of environmental uncertainty and structural dimensions has been upheld by research, the organization must make adjustments for the realities of its perceived environment when designing its structure.[37]

The question for those trying to design organizational structures is how to determine environmental uncertainty. Dess and Beard defined three dimensions of environment that should be measured in assessing the degree of uncertainty: capacity, volatility, and complexity.[38] The capacity of the environment reflects the abundance or scarcity of resources. If resources abound, the environment supports expansion, mistakes, or both. In contrast, in times of scarcity, the environment demands survival of the fittest. Volatility is the degree of instability. The airline industry is in a volatile environment. This makes it difficult for managers to know what needs to be done. The complexity of the environment refers to the differences and variability among environmental elements.

If the organization's environment is uncertain, dynamic, and complex and resources are scarce, the manager needs an organic structure that is better able to adapt to its environment. Such a structure allows the manager to monitor the environment from a number of internal perspectives, thus helping the organization maintain flexibility in responding to environmental changes.[39]

TABLE 15.4 Mechanistic and Organic Organizational Forms

BASIC DESIGN DIMENSIONS	MECHANISTIC	ORGANIC
Formalization	High	Low
Centralization	High	Low
Specialization	High	Low
Standardization	High	Low
Complexity	Low	High
Hierarchy of authority	Strong, tall	Weak, flat

Organization Structure as a Moderator

Organizational justice researchers recognize the importance of organization context in individuals' perceptions of justice, yet few studies systematically examine the organizational context for these perceptions. A recent research study suggests that organization structure moderates the relationship between interactional justice and supervisory social exchange, as evidenced by supervisory trust. Further, the study suggests that organization structure moderates the relationship between procedural justice and organizational social exchange, as evidenced by perceived organizational support.

The researchers included sixty-eight organizations and 102 departments in their study in the Southeastern United States. They were able to distinguish between mechanistic organizations and or-

ganic organizations on a continuum. The results did support the study's two hypotheses. Specifically, they found that the relationship between interactional justice and supervisory trust was stronger in organic organization structures than in mechanistic ones. Further, they found that the relationship between procedural justice and perceived organizational support was stronger in mechanistic organization structures than in organic ones. Therefore, the organization structure and context are important in shaping individuals' perceptions and experience of justice and fairness at work.

SOURCE: M. L. Ambrose and M. Schminke, "Organization Structure as a Moderator of the Relationship between Procedural Justice, Interactional Justice, Perceived Organizational Support, and Supervisory Trust," *Journal of Applied Psychology* 88 (2003): 293–303.

Strategy and Goals

The fourth contextual variable that influences how the design dimensions of structure should be enacted is the strategies and goals of the organization. Strategies and goals provide legitimacy to the organization, as well as employee direction, decision guidelines, and criteria for performance.[40] In addition, strategies and goals help the organization fit into its environment.

As more understanding of the contextual influence of strategies and goals has developed, several strategic dimensions that influence structure have been defined. One of these definitions was put forth by Danny Miller.[41] His framework for these strategic dimensions and their implications for organizational structure is shown in Table 15.5.

TABLE 15.5 Miller's Integrative Framework of Structural and Strategic Dimensions

STRATEGIC DIMENSION	PREDICTED STRUCTURAL CHARACTERISTICS
Innovation—to understand and manage new processes and technologies	Low formalization Decentralization Flat hierarchy
Market differentiation—to specialize in customer preferences	Moderate to high complexity Moderate to high formalization Moderate centralization
Cost control—to produce standardized products efficiently	High formalization High centralization High standardization Low complexity

SOURCE: D. Miller, "The Structural and Environmental Correlates of Business Strategy," *Strategic Management Journal* 8 (1987): 55–76. Copyright © John Wiley & Sons Limited. Reproduced with permission.

For example, when Apple Computer introduced personal computers to the market, its strategies were very innovative. The structure of the organization was relatively flat and very informal. Apple had Friday afternoon beer and popcorn discussion sessions, and eccentric behavior was easily accepted. As the personal computer market became more competitive, however, the structure of Apple changed to help it differentiate its products and to help control costs. The innovative strategies and structures devised by Steve Jobs, one of Apple's founders, were no longer appropriate. The board of directors recruited John Scully, a marketing expert from PepsiCo, to help Apple better compete in the market it had created. In 1996 and 1997, Apple reinvented itself again and brought back Jobs to try to restore its innovative edge. Since his return, Apple has become a major player in the digital music market with its introduction of the iPod, selling over 200,000 units in one quarter.

Limitations exist, however, on how much strategies and goals influence structure. Because the structure of the organization includes the formal information-processing channels in the organization, it stands to reason that the need to change strategies may not be communicated throughout the organization. In such a case, the organization's structure influences its strategic choice.

The inefficiency of the structure to perceive environmental changes may even lead to organizational failure. In the airline industry, several carriers failed to adjust quickly enough to deregulation and the highly competitive marketplace. Only those airlines that were generally viewed as lean structures with good information-processing systems have flourished in the turbulent years since deregulation. Examples of how different design dimensions can affect the strategic decision process are listed in Table 15.6.

The four contextual variables—size, technology, environment, and strategy and goals—combine to influence the design process. However, the existing structure of the organization influences how the organization interprets and reacts

TABLE 15.6   Examples of How Structure Affects the Strategic Decision Process

FORMALIZATION

As the level of formalization increases, so does the probability of the following:
1. The strategic decision process will become reactive to crisis rather than proactive through opportunities.
2. Strategic moves will be incremental and precise.
3. Differentiation in the organization will not be balanced with integrative mechanisms.
4. Only environmental crises that are in areas monitored by the formal organizational systems will be acted upon.

CENTRALIZATION

As the level of centralization increases, so does the probability of the following:
1. The strategic decision process will be initiated by only a few dominant individuals.
2. The decision process will be goal-oriented and rational.
3. The strategic process will be constrained by the limitations of top managers.

COMPLEXITY

As the level of complexity increases, so does the probability of the following:
1. The strategic decision process will become more politicized.
2. The organization will find it more difficult to recognize environmental opportunities and threats.
3. The constraints on good decision processes will be multiplied by the limitations of each individual within the organization.

SOURCE: Republished with permission of Academy of Management, PO Box 3020, Briar Cliff Manor, NY 10510-8020. "The Strategic Decision Process and Organizational Structure" (Table), J. Fredrickson, *Academy of Management Review* (1986): 284. Reproduced by permission of the publisher via Copyright Clearance Center, Inc.

to information about each of the variables. Each of the contextual variables has management researchers who claim that it is the most important variable in determining the best structural design. Because of the difficulty in studying the interactions of the four contextual dimensions and the complexity of organizational structures, the argument about which variable is most important continues.

What is apparent is that there must be some level of fit between the structure and the contextual dimensions of the organization. The better the fit, the more likely the organization will achieve its short-run goals. In addition, the better the fit, the more likely the organization will process information and design appropriate organizational roles for long-term prosperity, as indicated in Figure 15.4.

FIGURE 15.4   The Relationship among Key Organizational Design Elements

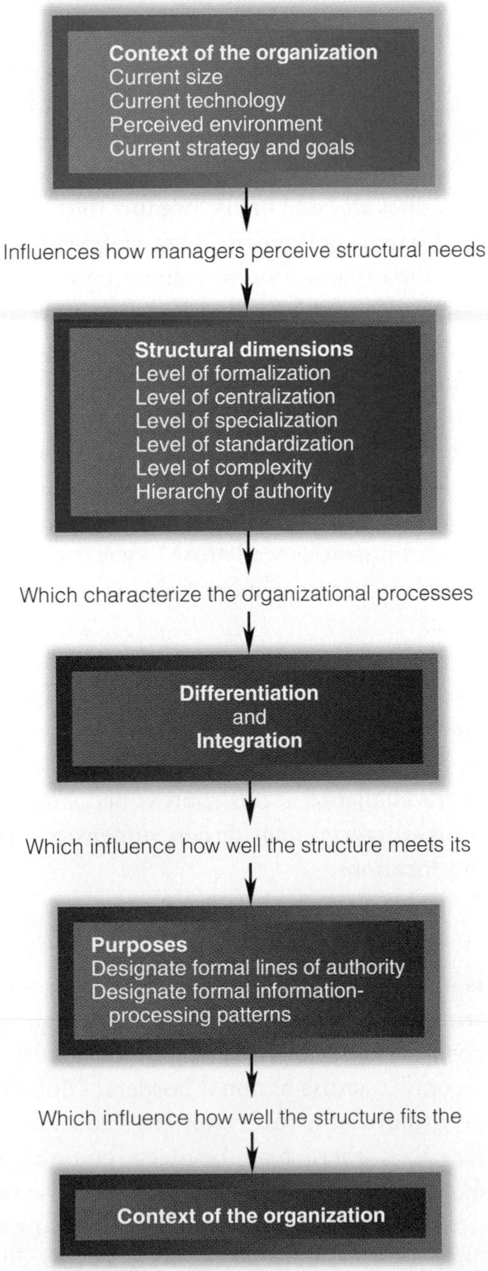

Context of the organization
Current size
Current technology
Perceived environment
Current strategy and goals

Influences how managers perceive structural needs

Structural dimensions
Level of formalization
Level of centralization
Level of specialization
Level of standardization
Level of complexity
Hierarchy of authority

Which characterize the organizational processes

Differentiation
and
Integration

Which influence how well the structure meets its

Purposes
Designate formal lines of authority
Designate formal information-
     processing patterns

Which influence how well the structure fits the

Context of the organization

Forces Reshaping Organizations

5. Explain the four forces reshaping organizations.

Managers and researchers traditionally examine organizational design and structure within the framework of basic design dimensions and contextual variables. Several forces reshaping organizations are causing managers to go beyond the traditional frameworks and to examine ways to make organizations more responsive to customer needs. Some of these forces include shorter life cycles within the organization, globalization, and rapid changes in information technology. These forces together increase the demands on process capabilities within the organization and emerging organizational structures. To successfully retain their health and vitality, organizations must function as open systems, as discussed in Chapter 1, that are responsive to their task environment.[42]

Life Cycles in Organizations

organizational life cycle

The differing stages of an organization's life from birth to death.

Organizations are dynamic entities. As such, they ebb and flow through different stages. Usually, researchers think of these stages as *organizational life cycles*. The total organization has a life cycle that begins at birth, moves through growth and maturity to decline, and possibly experiences revival.[43]

Organizational subunits may have very similar life cycles. Because of changes in technology and product design, many organizational subunits, especially those that are product based, are experiencing shorter life cycles. Hence, the subunits that compose the organization are changing more rapidly than in the past. These shorter life cycles enable the organization to respond quickly to external demands and changes.

When a new organization or subunit is born, the structure is organic and informal. If the organization or subunit is successful, it grows and matures. This usually leads to formalization, specialization, standardization, complexity, and a more mechanistic structure. If the environment changes, however, the organization must be able to respond. A mechanistic structure is not able to respond to a dynamic environment as well as an organic one. If the organization or subunit does respond, it becomes more organic and revives; if not, it declines and possibly dies.

Shorter life cycles put more pressure on the organization to be both flexible and efficient at the same time. Further, as flexible organizations use design to their competitive advantage, discrete organizational life cycles may give way to a kaleidoscope of continuously emerging, efficiency-seeking organizational designs.[44] The manager's challenge in this context becomes one of creating congruency among various organizational design dimensions to fit continuously changing markets and locations.

Globalization

Another force that is reshaping organizations is the process of globalization. In other words, organizations operate worldwide rather than in just one country or region. Global corporations can become pitted against sovereign nations when rules and laws conflict across national borders. Globalization makes spatial differentiation even more of a reality for organizations. Besides the obvious geographic differences, there may be deep cultural and value system differences. This adds another type of complexity to the structural design process and necessitates the creation of integrating mechanisms so that people are able to understand and interpret one another, as well as coordinate with one another.

© Kim Jae-Hwan/AFP/Getty Images

Global corporations, such as Nestlé, must take into account the cultural and values differences in day-to-day operations.

The choice of structure for managing an international business is generally based on choices concerning the following three factors:

1. *The level of vertical differentiation.* A hierarchy of authority must be created that clarifies the responsibilities of both domestic and foreign managers.

2. *The level of horizontal differentiation.* Foreign and domestic operations should be grouped in such a way that the company effectively serves the needs of all customers.

3. *The degree of formalization, specialization, standardization, and centralization.* The global structure must allow decisions to be made in the most appropriate area of the organization. However, controls must be in place that reflect the strategies and goals of the parent firm.[45]

Changes in Information-Processing Technologies

Many of the changes in information-processing technologies have allowed organizations to move into new product and market areas more quickly. However, just as shorter life cycles and globalization have caused new concerns for designing organizational structures, so has the increased availability of advanced information-processing technologies.

Organizational structures are already feeling the impact of advanced information-processing technologies. More integration and coordination are evident, because managers worldwide can be connected through computerized networks. The basic design dimensions have also been affected as follows:

1. The hierarchy of authority has been flattened.

2. The basis of centralization has been changed. Now managers can use technology to acquire more information and make more decisions, or they can use technology to push information and decision making lower in the hierarchy and thus decrease centralization.

3. Less specialization and standardization are needed, because people using advanced information-processing technologies have more sophisticated jobs that require a broader understanding of how the organization gets work done.[46]

Advances in information processing are leading to knowledge-based organizations, the outlines of which are now only seen dimly. Some of the hallmarks of these new organizational forms are virtual enterprising, dynamic teaming, and knowledge networking.[47] This fifth generation of management thought and practice leads to cocreation of products and services. Future organizations may well be defined by networks of overlapping teams.

Demands on Organizational Processes

Because of the forces reshaping organizations, managers find themselves trying to meet what seem to be conflicting goals: an efficiency orientation that results in on-time delivery *and* a quality orientation that results in customized, high-quality goods or services.[48] Traditionally, managers have seen efficiency and customization as conflicting demands.

To meet these conflicting demands, organizations need to become "dynamically stable."[49] To do so, an organization must have managers who see their roles as architects who clearly understand the "how" of the organizing process. Managers must combine long-term thinking with flexible and quick responses that help improve process and know-how. The organizational structure must help define, at least to some degree, roles for managers who hope to successfully address the conflicting demands of dynamic stability. The differences between the structural roles of managers today and managers of the future are illustrated in Table 15.7. You 15.2 allows you to examine the ways managers in your organization currently operate on the job.

Emerging Organizational Structures

6. Discuss emerging organizational structures.

The demands on managers and on process capabilities place demands on structures. The emphasis in organizations is shifting to organizing around processes. This process orientation emerges from the combination of three streams of applied organizational design: high-performance, self-managed teams; managing processes rather than functions; and the evolution of information technology. Information technology and advanced communication systems have led to internetworking. In a study of 469 firms, deeply internetworked firms were found to be more focused and specialized, less hierarchical, and more engaged in external partnering.[50] Three emerging organizational structures associated with these changes are network organizations, virtual organizations, and the circle organization.

Network organizations are weblike structures that contract some or all of their operating functions to other organizations and then coordinate their activities through managers and other employees at their headquarters. Information technology is the basis for building the weblike structure of the network organization and business unit managers that are essential to the success of

TABLE 15.7   Structural Roles of Managers Today versus Managers of the Future

ROLES OF MANAGERS TODAY

1. Strictly adhering to boss–employee relationships.
2. Getting things done by giving orders.
3. Carrying messages up and down the hierarchy.
4. Performing a prescribed set of tasks according to a job description.
5. Having a narrow functional focus.
6. Going through channels, one by one by one.
7. Controlling subordinates.

ROLES OF FUTURE MANAGERS

1. Having hierarchical relationships subordinated to functional and peer relationships.
2. Getting things done by negotiating.
3. Solving problems and making decisions.
4. Creating the job by developing entrepreneurial projects.
5. Having broad cross-functional collaboration.
6. Emphasizing speed and flexibility.
7. Coaching their workers.

SOURCE: Reprinted by permission of the publisher, from *Management Review*, January 1991 © 1991. Thomas R. Horton. American Management Association, New York. All rights reserved.

Managers of Today and the Future

Are the roles for managers in your organization more oriented toward today or toward the future? (If you do not work, think of an organization where you have worked or talk with a friend about managerial roles in his or her organization.)

Step 1. Reread Table 15.7 and check which orientation (today or future) predominates in your organization for each of the following seven characteristics:

	Today	Future
1. Boss–employee relationships.	_____	_____
2. Getting work accomplished.	_____	_____
3. Messenger versus problem solver.	_____	_____
4. Basis for task accomplishment.	_____	_____
5. Narrow versus broad functional focus.	_____	_____
6. Adherence to channels of authority.	_____	_____
7. Controlling versus coaching subordinates.	_____	_____

Step 2. Examine the degree of consistency across all seven characteristics. Could the organization make one or two structural changes to achieve a better alignment of the manager's role with today or with the future?

Step 3. Identify one manager in your organization who fits very well into the organization's ideal manager's role. What does this manager do that creates a good person–role fit?

Step 4. Identify one manager in your organization who does not fit very well into the organization's ideal manager's role. What does this manager do that creates a poor person–role fit?

these systems. This type of organization has arisen in the age of electronic commerce and brought into practice transaction cost economics, interorganizational collaborations, and strategic alliances. Network organizations can be global in scope.[51]

Virtual organizations are temporary network organizations consisting of independent enterprises. Many dot-coms were virtual organizations designed to come together swiftly to exploit an apparent market opportunity. They may function much like a theatrical troupe that comes together for a "performance."[52] Trust can be a challenge for virtual organizations because it is a complex phenomenon involving ethics, morals, emotions, values, and natural attitudes. However, trust and trustworthiness are important connective issues in virtual environments. Three key ingredients for the development of trust in virtual organizations are technology that can communicate emotion; a sharing of values, vision, and organizational identity; and a high standard of ethics.[53]

The circle organization is a third emerging structure crafted by Harley-Davidson in its drive to achieve teamwork without teams.[54] The company evolved the circle form of organization shown in Figure 15.5. The three organizational parts are those that (1) create demand, (2) produce product, and (3) provide support. As the figure indicates, these three parts are linked by the leadership and strategy council (LSC). The circle organization is a more open system and an organic structure for customer responsiveness. One innovation in this organizational scheme is the "circle coach," who possesses acute communication, listening, and influencing skills so as to be highly respected by circle members and the company's president.

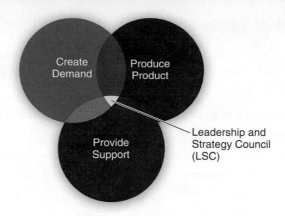

Cautionary Notes about Structure

7. Identify two cautions about the effect of organizational structures on people.

This chapter has identified the purposes of structure, the processes of organizational design, and the dimensions and contexts that must be considered in structure. In addition, it has looked at forces and trends in organizational design. Two cautionary notes are important for the student of organizational behavior. First, an organizational structure may be weak or deficient. In general, if the structure is out of alignment with its contextual variables, one or more of the following four symptoms appears. First, decision making is delayed because the hierarchy is overloaded and too much information is being funneled through one or two channels. Second, decision making lacks quality because information linkages are not providing the correct information to the right person in the right format. Third, the organization does not respond innovatively to a changing environment, especially when coordinated effort is lacking across departments. Fourth, a great deal of conflict is evident when departments are working against one another rather than working for the strategies and goals of the organization as a whole; the structure is often at fault.

The second caution is that the personality of the chief executive may adversely affect the structure of the organization.[55] Managers' personal, cognitive biases and political ideologies affect their good judgment and decision making.[56] Five dysfunctional combinations of personality and organization have been identified: the paranoid, the depressive, the dramatic, the compulsive, and the schizoid.[57] Each of these personality–organization constellations can create problems for the people who work in the organization. For example, in a paranoid constellation, people are suspicious of each other, and distrust in working relationships may interfere with effective communication and task accomplishment. For another example, in a depressive constellation, people feel depressed and inhibited in their work activities, which can lead to low levels of productivity and task accomplishment.

Managerial Implications: Fitting People and Structures Together

Organizations are complex social systems composed of numerous interrelated components. They can be complicated to understand. Managers who design, develop, and improve organizations must have a mastery of the basic concepts related to the anatomy and processes of organizational functioning. It is essential for executives at the top to have a clear concept of how the organization can be differentiated and then integrated into a cohesive whole.

People can work better in organizations if they understand how their jobs and departments relate to other jobs and teams in the organization. An understanding of the whole organization enables people to better relate their contribution to the overall mission of the organization and to compensate for structural deficiencies that may exist in the organization.

Different structural configurations place unique demands on the people who work within them. The diversity of people in work organizations suggests that some people are better suited for a simple structure, others are better suited to a professional bureaucracy, and still others are most productive in an adhocracy. Organizational structures are not independent of the people who work within them. This is especially true for organizations operating in a global work environment.

Managers must pay attention to the technology of the organization's work, the amount of change occurring in the organization's environment, and the regulatory pressures created by governmental agencies as the managers design effective organizations and subunits to meet emerging international demands and a diverse, multicultural workforce.

LOOKING BACK: THE COCA-COLA COMPANY

Coca-Cola Refreshes Its Supply Chain

The corporate warfare analogy brought forth in the press by reference to the "cola wars" brings attention to logistics and the supply chain of the force. Coke and other cola companies must focus attention on their supply chains and on procurement strategies if they are going to succeed in taking costs out of the system to boost their profitability and competitive advantage. Because the soft drink business is a low-margin business, careful management of costs as well as revenue is critical. However, this is not a simple accounting or bookkeeping matter. The structure of the organization can be a central dimension of competitive advantage and cost efficiency as we saw in the Thinking Ahead feature. Coca-Cola has partnered with software development giant SAP to facilitate the supply chain and close the gap between sales and delivery.

In such a low-growth business, Coca-Cola expects that putting new capabilities into its account managers, delivery drivers, and in-store merchants will speed products through the supply chain and improve its financial and competitive position. In the past, Coke has lacked direct store delivery functionality. The new SAP applications enable Coke to cost effectively replenish stock to retailers, accommodate more kinds of products, and maximize delivery truck space. Coca-Cola Enterprises' CIO is the executive in charge of driving this restructuring and reorganization, or companywide business transformation, under the banner of Project Pinnacle.

Profitability is a key success indicator for Coke and its competitors in the cola wars. Some of the initial returns on IT investments have been heartening for the company. For example, for the fiscal year ending in 2004, Coca-Cola Enterprises reported a net income of $676 million, or a 37 percent increase over the previous year. This is on revenue of $17.3 billion. However, the company predicted volume to grow only 1.5 percent in North America during 2004. In such a low-growth business, increasing profits requires further efficiencies in the system. An example of how to do that is the new supply chain management company in Japan created by The Coca-Cola Company and its bottling partners. Coke expects to reap $100 million in procurement, product, and logistics cost savings from this company in one year.[58] The cola wars are very competitive, and especially so given the low growth in the soft drink business. However, winning one battle at a time in the war of competition is possible with the right organization structures and processes in place.

Chapter Summary

1. Three basic types of differentiation occur in organizations: horizontal, vertical, and spatial.

2. The greater the complexity of an organization because of its degree of differentiation, the greater the need for integration.

3. Formalization, centralization, specialization, standardization, complexity, and hierarchy of authority are the six basic design dimensions in an organization.

4. Simple structure, machine bureaucracy, professional bureaucracy, divisionalized form, and adhocracy are five structural configurations of an organization.

5. The contextual variables important to organizational design are size, technology, environment, and strategy and goals.

6. Life cycles, globalization, changes in information-processing technologies, and demands on process capabilities are forces reshaping organizations today.

7. Network organizations, virtual organizations, and the circle organization are emerging organizational structures.

8. Organizational structures may be inherently weak, or chief executives may create personality–organization constellations that adversely affect employees.

Key Terms

adhocracy (p. 504)
centralization (p. 500)
complexity (p. 500)
contextual variables (p. 494)
differentiation (p. 495)
divisionalized form (p. 504)
environment (p. 509)
environmental uncertainty (p. 510)

formalization (p. 500)
hierarchy of authority (p. 500)
integration (p. 498)
machine bureaucracy (p. 502)
mechanistic structure (p. 510)
organic structure (p. 510)
organizational design (p. 494)
organizational life cycle (p. 514)

organizational structure (p. 494)
professional bureaucracy (p. 503)
simple structure (p. 502)
specialization (p. 500)
standardization (p. 500)
task environment (p. 509)
technological interdependence (p. 508)

Review Questions

1. Define the processes of differentiation and integration.

2. Describe the six basic dimensions of organizational design.

3. Discuss five structural configurations from the chapter.

4. Discuss the effects of the four contextual variables on the basic design dimensions.

5. Identify four forces that are reshaping organizations today.

6. Discuss the nature of emerging organizational structures.

7. List four symptoms of structural weakness and five unhealthy personality–organization combinations.

Discussion and Communication Questions

1. How would you describe the organization you work for (or your college) on each of the basic design dimensions? For example, is it a very formal organization or an informal organization?

2. Do the size, technology, and mission of your organization directly affect you? How?

3. Who are your organization's competitors? What changes do you see in information technology where you work?

4. Does your company show any one or more of the four symptoms of structural deficiency discussed at the end of the chapter?

5. *(communication question)* Write a memo classifying and describing the structural configuration of your university based on the five choices in Table 15.2. Do you need more information than you have to be comfortable with your classification and description? Where could you get the information?

6. *(communication question)* Interview an administrator in your college or university about possible changes in size (Will the college or university get bigger? Smaller?) and technology (Is the college or university making a significant investment in information technology?). What effects does the administrator anticipate from these changes? Be prepared to present your results orally to the class.

Ethical Dilemma

Kate Brown was a human resource manager for Summit Maintenance, a national commercial janitorial service company. She worked hard to represent the employees' best interest to management. Kate worked at one of Summit's regional headquarters. She had four regional human resource representatives that worked in the field to cover her region. Like many large, older companies, Summit was very bureaucratic with several levels of managers. Kate directly reported to the regional human resources vice president, but she also reported to the general manager for her regional office.

At the moment, Kate was feeling the burden of reporting to two different people. She had just left a meeting with Terry Beck, the general manager. Terry had explained that he wanted to make some small changes in the way they interpreted some of the company policies. Terry understood that these policies had been created for a lot of good reasons but

were not really appropriate for the more rural area their region covered. He went on to explain that he wasn't asking Kate to break the rules, just enforce them differently and more effectively for their employees.

After listening to Terry, Kate had to agree that his ideas would work much better in their area. The policies Terry was most concerned with were some of the safety policies that were developed for people working in large high-rise buildings or in high crime areas. Their employees worked in neither. They mostly worked in small, rural family businesses. The need to follow policies regarding terrorist attacks or escaping a high-rise fire seemed extremely remote. Yet day after day, employees were forced to carry extra equipment or go through extra procedures to ensure their safety against these dangers. Money, time, and space were wasted following policies that would probably never affect them.

Kate's only concern was her primary supervisor, Vernon Miller, the regional vice president. He would never go for this idea. He was a stickler for rules whether they made sense or not. Kate knew her first duty was to the HR executive, but she saw the value in easing the safety policies for their employees.

Experiential Exercises

15.1 Words-in-Sentences Company

Purpose: To design an organization for a particular task and carry through to production; to compare design elements with effectiveness.

Group Size: Any number of groups of six to fourteen persons.

Time Required: Fifty to ninety minutes.

Related Topics: Dynamics within groups and work motivation.

Background

You are a small company that manufactures words and then packages them in meaningful English-language sentences. Market research has established that sentences of at least three words but not more than six words are in demand. Therefore, packaging, distribution, and sales should be set up for three- to six-word sentences.

The "words-in-sentences" (WIS) industry is highly competitive; several new firms have recently entered what appears to be an expanding market. Since raw materials, technology, and pricing are all standard for the industry, your ability to compete depends on two factors: (1) volume and (2) quality.

Your Task

Your group must design and participate in running a WIS company. You should design your organization to be as efficient as possible during each ten-minute production run. After the first production run, you will have an opportunity to reorganize your company if you want.

Raw Materials

For each production you will be given a "raw material word or phrase." The letters found in the word or phrase serve as raw materials available to produce new words in sentences. For example, if the raw material word is "organization," you could produce the words and sentence: "Nat ran to a zoo."

Production Standards

Several rules must be followed in producing "words-in-sentences." If these rules are not followed, your

Questions

1. Does Kate have the right to interpret the policies they way she believes to be best?

2. Evaluate Kate's decision using rule, virtue, rights, and justice theories.

output will not meet production specifications and will not pass quality-control inspection.

1. The same letter may appear only as often in a manufactured word as it appears in the raw material word or phrase; for example, "organization" has two o's. Thus, "zoo" is legitimate, but not "zoonosis." It has too many o's and s's.

2. Raw material letters can be used again in different manufactured words.

3. A manufactured word may be used only once in a sentence and in only one sentence during a production run; if a word—for example, "a"—is used once in a sentence, it is out of stock.

4. A new word may not be made by adding "s" to form the plural of an already manufactured word.

5. A word is defined by its spelling, not its meaning.

6. Nonsense words or nonsense sentences are unacceptable.

7. All words must be in the English language.

8. Names and places are acceptable.

9. Slang is not acceptable.

Measuring Performance

The output of your WIS company is measured by the total number of acceptable words that are packaged in sentences. The sentences must be legible, listed on no more than two sheets of paper, and handed to the Quality Control Review Board at the completion of each production run.

Delivery

Delivery must be made to the Quality Control Review Board thirty seconds after the end of each production run, or else all points are lost.

Quality Control

If any word in a sentence does not meet the standards set forth above, all the words in the sentence will be rejected. The Quality Control Review Board (composed of one member from each company) is the final arbiter of acceptability. In the event of a tie on the Review Board, a coin toss will determine the outcome.

Exercise Schedule

	Unit Time	Total Time
1. Form groups, organizations, and assign workplaces Groups should have between six and fourteen members (if there are more than eleven or twelve persons in a group, assign one or two observers). Each group is a company.	2–5 min.	2–5 min.
2. Read "Background" Ask the instructor about any points that need clarification.	5 min.	10 min.
3. Design organizations Design your organizations using as many members as you see fit to produce your "words-in-sentences." You may want to consider the following.	7–15 min.	14–25 min.

a. What is your objective?

b. What technology would work here?

c. What type of division of labor is effective?

Assign one member of your group to serve on the Quality Review Board. This person may also take part in production runs.

	Unit Time	Total Time
4. Production Run #1 The instructor will hand each WIS company a sheet with a raw material word or phrase. When the instructor announces "Begin production," you are to manufacture as many words as possible and package them in sentences for delivery to the Quality Control Review Board. You will have ten minutes. When the instructor announces "Stop production," you will have thirty seconds to deliver your output to the Quality Control Review Board. Output received after thirty seconds does not meet the delivery schedule and will not be counted.	7–10 min.	21–35 min.
5. Quality Review Board meets, evaluates output While that is going on, groups discuss what happened during the previous production run.	5–10 min.	26–45 min.
6. Companies evaluate performance and type of organization Groups may choose to restructure and reorganize for the next production run.	5–10 min.	31–55 min.
7. Production Run #2 (same as Production Run #1)	7–10 min.	38–65 min.
8. Quality Review Board meets Quality Review Board evaluates output while groups draw their organization charts (for Runs #1 and #2) on the board.	5–10 min.	43–75 min.
9. Class discussion Instructor leads discussion of exercise as a whole. Discuss the following questions:	7–15 min.	50–90 min.

a. What were the companies' scores for Runs #1 and #2?

b. What type of structure did the "winning" company have? Did it reorganize for Run #2?

c. What type of task was there? Technology? Environment?

d.   What would Joan Woodward, Henry Mintzberg, Frederick Taylor, Lawrence and Lorsch, or Burns and Stalker say about WIS Company organization?

SOURCE: "Words-in-Sentences Company" in Dorothy Marcic, *Organizational Behavior: Experiences and Cases*, 4th ed. (St. Paul: West, 1995), 303–305. Reprinted by permission.

15.2 Design and Build a Castle

This exercise is intended to give your group an opportunity to design an organization and produce a product.

Your group is one of three product-development teams working within the research and development division of the GTM (General Turret and Moat) Corporation. GTM has decided to enter new markets by expanding the product line to include fully designed and produced castles, rather than selling components to other companies, as it has in the past.

Each of the three teams has been asked to design a castle for the company to produce and sell. Given its limited resources, the company cannot put more than one design on the market. Therefore, the company will have to decide which of the three designs it will use and will discard the other two designs.

Your task is to develop and design a castle. You will have forty-five minutes to produce a finished product. At the end of this period, several typical consumers, picked by scientific sampling techniques, will judge which is the best design. Before the consumers make their choice, each group will have one to two minutes to make a sales presentation.

Step 1. Each group is designated either 1, 2, or 3. The instructor will provide group members a memo-

randum appropriate for their group. One (or two for larger groups) observer is selected for each group. Observers read their materials.

Step 2. Groups design their organization in order to complete their goal.

Step 3. Each group designs its own castle and draws it on newsprint.

Step 4. "Typical consumers" (may be observers) tour building locations and hear sales pitches. Judges caucus to determine winner.

Step 5. Groups meet again and write up their central goal statement. They also write the organization chart on newsprint with the goal written beneath. These are posted around the room.

Step 6. Instructor leads a class discussion on how the different memos affected organization design. Which design seemed most effective for this task?

NOTE: Your instructor may allow more time and actually have you *build* the castles.

SOURCE: "Design and Build a Castle" from Dorothy Marcic and Richard C. Housley, *Organizational Behavior: Experiences and Cases* (St. Paul: West, 1989), 221–225. Reprinted by permission.

Biz Flix | Casino

Martin Scorcese's lengthy, complex, and beautifully photographed study of 1970s' Las Vegas gambling casinos and their organized crime connections completes his trilogy that includes *Mean Streets* (1973) and the 1990 *Goodfellas*. Ambition, greed, drugs, and sex destroy the mob's gambling empire. The film includes strong performances by Robert De Niro, Joe Pesci, and Sharon Stone. The violence and expletive-filled dialogue give *Casino* its R rating.

The *Casino* scene is part of "The Truth about Las Vegas" sequence early in the film. It follows the scenes of deceiving the Japanese gambler. It starts with a close-up of Sam "Ace" Rothstein (Robert De Niro) standing between his two casino executives (Richard Amalfitano, Richard F. Strafella). His voice-over says, "In Vegas, everybody's gotta watch everybody else." The scene ends after Sam Rothstein describes the excheaters who monitor the gambling floor with binoculars. The film continues with the introduction of Ginger (Sharon Stone).

What to Watch for and Ask Yourself:

> Which type or form of organizational design does this scene show?

> Does this scene show the results of the differentiation and integration organizational design processes?

> Does this scene show any behavioral demands of organizational design? What are they?

Workplace Video | Student Advantage: Fundamentals of Organizing

Student Advantage, Inc. is a leading integrated media and commerce company that works with hundreds of colleges, universities, and merchant locations to develop services that enable students to make purchases less expensively and more conveniently around campus. The primary aim at Student Advantage is to help college students make it through the lean years, providing discounts on merchandise and services from businesses such as Amtrak, Timberland, and Office Depot.

Ray Sozzi, the president and CEO of Student Advantage, believes in maintaining a flat organization where employees have authority to make and execute important plans with clients and partners. Sozzi is responsible for overseeing a broad vision that gets carried out by the firm's chief operating officer, department heads, and staff, but the employees take ownership for their specific duties and tasks. Delegation is important in the daily operations of the company, and Sozzi keeps employees directly responsible for the results of their plans.

Questions

1. *What does Student Advantage Founder Ray Sozzi mean when he says that management at small companies could be best summarized as "organized chaos," and what happens to that organized chaos when a company grows to a larger size?*
2. *Describe how the role of CEO and COO are differentiated at Student Advantage.*
3. *Briefly describe Student Advantage's organizational structure.*

Solectron Corporation—Integrated Supply Chain Solutions for Network Organizations

Solectron Corp., founded in 1977, is a leading provider of electronics manufacturing services. Solectron offers "a full range of integrated supply chain solutions" for the world's leading original equipment manufacturing companies in industries that rely on high-tech electronics. Headquartered in Milpitas, California, with operations on five continents and in more than 20 countries each in Asia, Europe, and the Americas, Solectron has major customer bases in computers, computer peripherals, telecommunications, semiconductors, computer networking, automotive controls and navigation systems, test and measurement instrumentation, home appliance electronic controls, medical electronics, avionics, and global positioning systems, among other markets.

Contract electronics manufacturers, like Solectron, are facilitating the development of "network organizations" that often do little besides designing and/or marketing a product. If a client both designs and markets a product, Solectron can handle the manufacturing and/or distribution of the product. If a client's core competency is product design, Solectron can manufacture, market, and distribute it. If a client's strength is marketing products, Solectron can perform all the other supply chain activities. Solectron aims "to minimize boundaries in the supply chain . . . in an effort to help its customers attain the fastest time-to-market with the lowest total costs, while helping them ensure the most efficient allocation of their scarce resources."

Solectron's Services

As a contract electronics manufacturer with a wide range of customers, Solectron needs to be flexible, and this is accomplished through Solectron's product design and launch support services, lean manufacturing and fulfillment services, and post-manufacturing services.

Solectron's collaborative approach to product design and launch support services "emphasizes value-adding activities that customers need." Chief among these activities are the collaborative design of products for both cost and production considerations, the design of products for manufacturability and Six Sigma quality, prototyping services and new product introduction processes, the management of mature product lines to extend the product life cycle, and ongoing design reviews for cost reduction opportunities as well as technological and functional product enhancements. "When customers partner with Solectron in design, they get to market faster, at lower cost, and with higher quality levels than they can consistently achieve on their own."

Solectron's "Lean Six Sigma manufacturing" emphasizes both exceptional quality and the use of lean operating principles to eliminate activities that do not add value to customers' businesses. Lean Six Sigma manufacturing enables Solectron to maximize its production flexibility, yield, and quality, while simultaneously eliminating factors that contribute to waste. Solectron accomplishes this by using common assembly systems and processes at all its factories around the world. Consequently, production can be easily and quickly transferred whenever and wherever Solectron's customers and the customers' markets require it.

Lean Six Sigma manufacturing seeks to eliminate waste and variability. It is driven by commitments to creating value for customers, identifying and strengthening those process steps that add value and eliminating those steps that produce waste, producing only what customers want when they want it, ensuring a continuous flow of goods through the supply chain, and embracing continuous improvement.

A critical element of Lean Six Sigma manufacturing is the development and maintenance of a responsive supplier network. Relying heavily on information technology, Solectron's global materials teams build partnerships with key suppliers to ensure an adequate supply of materials on a timely basis at the right price. The global materials teams also coordinate the movement of supplies within the company, and they work closely with the design and manufacturing operations.

The postmanufacturing services "range from product repair and remanufacturing to asset recovery and recycling," and are geared toward supporting "products from the time they are put into service until they are removed from the market." Solectron provides repair services for both components and complete electronic systems for a wide range of electronic products. Solectron's asset recovery operation significantly reduces waste resulting from repair work and helps address environmental concerns over the disposal of electronic products in the United States, Japan, and Europe.

The Need for Quality

Quality is essential in all aspects of Solectron's operations. Quality is crucial in securing, developing, and maintaining effective "partnering relationships" with Solectron's customers. Also, Solectron operates on thinner profit margins than its customers do. Consequently, the margin for error is small; anything less than superior quality can have a disastrous impact on the company's bottom line.

Every week the company asks its customers to grade it on quality, responsiveness, communication, service, and technical support. A grade of 'B−' or lower initiates a quality-improvement process; a grade of 'C' or lower triggers a formal customer complaint resolution process.

Solectron's concern with quality has generated very positive reactions among its customers. Solectron has received over 450 quality and service awards from its customers. In addition, Solectron is an Industry Week Best-Managed Company Award winner and the first two-time winner of the Malcolm Baldrige National Quality Award for Manufacturing.

Financial Success and the Future

In order to decrease costs, companies like IBM Corp., Nortel Networks Corp., and Cisco Systems Inc. are increasingly outsourcing work to Solectron and other contract electronic manufacturers. However, when declining sales hit the original equipment manufacturers, the contract electronic manufacturers are affected negatively—at least in the short term. For example, in fiscal year 2000 Solectron had sales of $14.1 billion with a profit $497 million, but then things turned sour in subsequent years. In fiscal 2001, sales peaked at $18.6 billion, but there was a loss of $123.5 million. Sales declined to around $11 billion in both fiscal 2002 and 2003 with losses exceeding $3 billion.

Over the long term, however, outsourcing of work to contract electronic manufacturers like Solectron most likely will continue, as customers seek to shave costs even more and to focus more intensely on their core competencies.

Discussion Questions

1. What is a network organization, and how does it differ from more traditional organization structures?
2. Why have network organizations come into existence? How has Solectron contributed to the rise of these types of organizations?
3. What are the key factors in Solectron's success in facilitating the rise of network organizations?
4. What advantages and disadvantages do you think arise from a network organization relationship?

SOURCE: This case was written by Michael K. McCuddy, The Louis S. and Mary L. Morgal Chair of Christian Business Ethics and Professor of Management, College of Business Administration, Valparaiso University. This case was developed from material contained on the Solectron Corp. Web site at http://www.solectron.com and in the following materials: R. Rothacker, "Milpitas, Calif., Electronics Maker Expects Strong Future in Tech Outsourcing," *The Charlotte Observer* (March 29, 2001); "Sierra Wireless Partners with Solectron Corporation to Manufacture Wireless Data Products," *Canadian Corporate News* (October 11, 2001); *Solectron 2003 Annual Report;* "Solectron Corporation and Nortel Networks Announce Industry's Largest-Ever Electronic Manufacturing Services Contract . . .," *PR Newswire* (April 4, 2000); and S. Thurm, "Behind the Scenes: Some Manufacturers Prosper by Facilitating Rise of 'Virtual' Firm," *The Wall Street Journal* (August 18, 1998): A1 & A6.

Chapter 16

Organizational Culture

LEARNING OBJECTIVES

After reading this chapter, you should be able to do the following:

1 Define *organizational culture* and explain its three levels.

2 Identify the four functions of culture within an organization.

3 Explain the relationship between organizational culture and performance.

4 Contrast the characteristics of adaptive and nonadaptive cultures.

5 Describe five ways leaders reinforce organizational culture.

6 Describe the three stages of organizational socialization and the ways culture is communicated in each step.

7 Identify ways of assessing organizational culture.

8 Explain actions managers can take to change organizational culture.

THINKING AHEAD: CANINE COMPANIONS FOR INDEPENDENCE

A Culture of Shared Values

The term "nonprofit corporation" is something of an oxymoron. To most Americans, business success is measured in terms of dollars earned, promotions received, and dividends paid. So why would any American choose to work each day at an organization that has no interest in profits, a place that by definition exists to give money and services away at little or no cost? What drives America's huge not-for-profit sector? And what is it like to work in these "noncompany" companies?

At Canine Companions for Independence (CCI), it's all about the dogs. "The dogs and what they bring to the people are the heart and soul of the program," says Judi Pierson, director of the Southwest Regional Center in Oceanside, California. "When they finish their training, the teams become part of the greater community. There's a lot of camaraderie, a lot of learning and training that goes on here to build solid, long lasting relationships."[1]

CCI has never earned a profit, at least not in the traditional sense. While its "income" in a typical year tops $10 million, none of this money goes to shareholders or owners, and less than 4 percent is spent on administration and salaries, which means that nobody at CCI is getting rich working there. Every employee and volunteer at CCI works there because of a strong belief in the organization's mission: enhancing the lives of people with disabilities by providing highly trained assistance dogs.[2] This shared mission says a lot about CCI's culture. In other words, CCI is without "profit" in the business sense, but hardly without purpose or benefit.

The Key Role of Organizational Culture

The concept of organizational culture has its roots in cultural anthropology. Just as there are cultures in larger human society, there seem to be cultures within organizations. These cultures are similar to societal cultures. They are shared, communicated through symbols, and passed down from generation to generation of employees.

The concept of cultures in organizations was alluded to as early as the Hawthorne studies, which described work group culture. The topic came into its own during the early 1970s, when managers and researchers alike began to search for keys to survival for organizations in a competitive and turbulent environment. Then, in the early 1980s, several books on corporate culture were published, including Deal and Kennedy's *Corporate Cultures*,[3] Ouchi's *Theory Z*,[4] and Peters and Waterman's *In Search of Excellence*.[5] These books found wide audiences, and research began in earnest on the elusive topic of organizational cultures. Executives indicated that these cultures were real and could be managed.[6]

Culture and Its Levels

1. Define *organizational culture* and explain its three levels.

organizational (corporate) culture
A pattern of basic assumptions that are considered valid and that are taught to new members as the way to perceive, think, and feel in the organization.

Many definitions of *organizational culture* have been proposed. Most of them agree that there are several levels of culture and that these levels differ in terms of their visibility and their ability to be changed. The definition adopted in this chapter is that *organizational (corporate) culture* is a pattern of basic assumptions that are considered valid and that are taught to new members as the way to perceive, think, and feel in the organization.[7]

Edgar Schein, in his comprehensive book on organizational culture and leadership, suggests that organizational culture has three levels. His view of culture is presented in Figure 16.1. The levels range from visible artifacts and creations to testable values to invisible and even preconscious basic assumptions. To achieve a complete understanding of an organization's culture, all three levels must be studied.

Artifacts

artifacts
Symbols of culture in the physical and social work environment.

Symbols of culture in the physical and social work environment are called *artifacts*. They are the most visible and accessible level of culture. The key to understanding culture through artifacts lies in figuring out what they mean. Artifacts are also the most frequently studied manifestation of organizational culture, perhaps because of their accessibility. Among the artifacts of culture are personal enactment, ceremonies and rites, stories, rituals, and symbols.[8]

PERSONAL ENACTMENT Culture can be understood, in part, through an examination of the behavior of organization members. Personal enactment is behavior that reflects the organization's values. In particular, personal enactment by the top managers provides insight into these values. Steve Irby is the founder and CEO of Stillwater Designs, the company that created Kicker audio speakers. He values good relationships and believes that people are the most important part of his company. Irby builds trust with his employees by sharing the financial results of the business each month. The employees know that if monthly sales are higher than the sales in the same month of the previous year, Irby will hold a cookout for the employees on the following Friday. Irby and the general manager always do the cooking. Eskimo Joe's, a Stillwater, Oklahoma, restaurant chain and one of the largest t-shirt sellers in the United States, could probably have become a national franchise years ago. But

PART 4 [ORGANIZATIONAL PROCESSES AND STRUCTURE

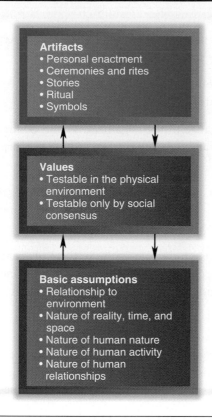

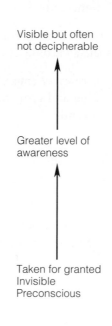

SOURCE: From Edgar H. Schein, *Organizational Culture and Leadership: A Dynamic View.* Copyright © 1985 Jossey-Bass Inc. Reprinted by permission of Jossey-Bass, Inc., a subsidiary of John Wiley & Sons, Inc.

founder Stan Clark, who began as co-owner of the once tiny bar, says his intent is to become better, not bigger. Clark still meets personally with new hires for the restaurant's serving staff, ensuring that they receive a firm grounding in his philosophy of food and fun.[9]

Modeled behavior is a powerful learning tool for employees, as Bandura's social learning theory demonstrated.[10] As we saw in Chapter 5, individuals learn vicariously by observing others' behavior and patterning their own behavior similarly. Culture can be an important leadership tool. Managerial behavior can clarify what is important and coordinate the work of employees, in effect negating the need for close supervision.[11]

Eskimo Joe's founder, Stan Clark, exhibits personal enactment by meeting personally with new employees and conveying to them his philosophy of mixing food with fun.

CEREMONIES AND RITES Relatively elaborate sets of activities that are enacted time and again on important occasions are known as organizational ceremonies and rites.[12] These occasions provide opportunities to reward and recognize employees whose behavior is congruent with the values of the company. Ceremonies and rites send a message that individuals who both espouse and exhibit corporate values are heroes to be admired.

The ceremonies also bond organization members together. Southwestern Bell (now part of SBC Communications) emphasized the importance of management training to the company. Training classes were kicked off by a high-ranking executive (a rite of renewal), and completion of the classes was signaled by a graduation ceremony (a rite of passage). Six kinds of rites in organizations have been identified:[13]

1. *Rites of passage* show that an individual's status has changed. Retirement dinners are an example.

2. *Rites of enhancement* reinforce the achievement of individuals. An example is the awarding of certificates to sales contest winners.

3. *Rites of renewal* emphasize change in the organization and commitment to learning and growth. An example is the opening of a new corporate training center.

4. *Rites of integration* unite diverse groups or teams within the organization and renew commitment to the larger organization. Company functions such as annual picnics fall into this category.

5. *Rites of conflict reduction* focus on dealing with conflicts or disagreements that arise naturally in organizations. Examples are grievance hearings and the negotiation of union contracts.

6. *Rites of degradation* are used by some organizations to visibly punish persons who fail to adhere to values and norms of behavior. Some CEOs, for example, are replaced quite publicly for unethical conduct or for failure to achieve organizational goals. In some Japanese organizations, employees who perform poorly are given ribbons of shame as punishment.

Wal-Mart's annual meeting is an important cultural ceremony. Almost 20,000 shareholders, associates (the company's preferred term for employees), and analysts attend the Wal-Mart annual meeting. Celebrities such as Nolan Ryan, Trisha Yearwood, and Amy Grant are featured. Although the meeting doesn't begin until 10 A.M., people start arriving at 7 A.M. for the extravaganza held for the benefit of the associates. Because it is the primary vehicle for perpetuating Wal-Mart's culture, videos of the meeting are played in Wal-Mart stores to motivate associates who are unable to attend.

The annual meeting is like a big family reunion. Patriotism is a common theme. The associates hear stories and watch videos about Wal-Mart's "Buy American" program, which has rescued jobs in small towns and created new ones. Associates who go the "extra mile" for customers are recognized and rewarded. One associate delivered a Sega Genesis on his own time on Christmas Eve, and another group of employees replaced presents for a family whose home was burglarized. Each example points to the generosity and compassion of Wal-Mart associates.[14]

STORIES Some researchers have argued that the most effective way to reinforce organizational values is through stories.[15] As they are told and retold, stories give meaning and identity to organizations and are especially helpful in orienting new employees. Part of the strength of organizational stories is that the listeners are left to draw their own conclusions—a powerful communication tool.[16]

Some corporate stories even transcend cultural and political boundaries. Visit the Web site of Wal-Mart China, and you will read the true story of Jeff, a pharmacist in Harrison, Arkansas, a small town deep in the Ozarks. When

Jeff received an early morning weekend call telling him that a diabetic patient needed insulin, he quickly opened his pharmacy and filled the prescription.[17] While Arkansas and Beijing are worlds apart, stories such as this one help transfer Wal-Mart's corporate "personality" to its new Asian associates.

Research by Joanne Martin and her colleagues has indicated that certain themes appear in stories across different types of organizations:[18]

1. *Stories about the boss.* These stories may reflect whether the boss is "human" or how the boss reacts to mistakes.

2. *Stories about getting fired.* Events leading to employee firings are recounted.

3. *Stories about how the company deals with employees who have to relocate.* These stories relate to the company's actions toward employees who have to move—whether the company is helpful and takes family and other personal concerns into account.

4. *Stories about whether lower-level employees can rise to the top.* Often, these stories describe a person who started out at the bottom and eventually became the CEO.

5. *Stories about how the company deals with crisis situations.* The example of the client crisis at IBM shows how the company overcomes obstacles.

6. *Stories about how status considerations work when rules are broken.* When Tom Watson, Sr., was CEO of IBM, he was once confronted by a security guard because he was not wearing an ID badge.

These are the themes that can emerge when stories are passed down. The information from these stories serves to guide the behavior of organization members.

To be effective cultural tools, stories must be credible. You can't tell a story about your flat corporate hierarchy and then have reserved parking spaces for managers. Stories that aren't backed by reality can lead to cynicism and mistrust.

Effective stories, however, can reinforce culture and create renewed energy. Lucasfilm is the home of director and producer George Lucas and the birthplace of such blockbusters as *Star Wars* and *Forrest Gump*. Stories of the company's legendary accomplishments are used to reinforce the creative culture and to rally the troops. When Gail Currey, former head of the company's digital division, found her 300 designers were grumbling, she reminded them of how they did *Gump* when everyone else said it was impossible and what a hit the film was. The geniuses would then head back to their computers to add to the company's success.[19]

RITUALS Everyday organizational practices that are repeated over and over are rituals. They are usually unwritten, but they send a clear message about "the way we do things around here." While some companies insist that people address each other by their titles (Mr., Mrs., Ms., Miss) and surnames to reinforce a professional image, others prefer that employees operate on a first-name basis—from the top manager on down. Hewlett-Packard values open communication, so its employees address one another by first names only.

In the fast-paced world of automotive manufacturing, the endless grind of the assembly line makes it tough for workers at most factories to imagine the person who will actually drive the car they are building. But at Saturn's Tennessee assembly plant, each car travels down the assembly line with the customer's name attached to it. And upon delivery, the customer is handed the keys and photographed by the dealer in a small ceremony commemorating the event. Not surprisingly, Saturn owners are among the most loyal in the industry.[20]

As everyday practices, rituals reinforce the organizational culture. Insiders who commonly practice the rituals may be unaware of their subtle influence, but outsiders recognize it easily.

SYMBOLS Symbols communicate organizational culture by unspoken messages. Southwest Airlines has used symbols in several ways. During its early years, the airline emphasized its customer service value by using the heart symbol (the "love" airline) and love bites (peanuts). More recently, the airline has taken on the theme of fun. Flight attendants wear casual sports clothes in corporate colors. Low fares are "fun fares," and weekend getaways are "fun packs." Some aircraft are painted to resemble Shamu the whale, underscoring the fun image. At Krispy Kreme, customers look for the famous "HOT DOUGHNUTS NOW" sign. Read about its origins in The Real World 16.1.

Symbols are representative of organizational identity and membership to employees. Nike's trademark "swoosh" is proudly tattooed above the ankles of some Nike employees. Apple Computer employees readily identify themselves as "Apple People." Symbols are used to build solidarity in the organizational culture.[21]

Personal enactment, rites and ceremonies, stories, rituals, and symbols serve to reinforce the values that are the next level of culture.

Values

Values are the second, and deeper, level of culture. They reflect a person's underlying beliefs of what should be or should not be. Values are often consciously articulated, both in conversation and in a company's mission statement or annual report. However, there may be a difference between a company's *espoused values* (what the members say they value) and its *enacted values* (values reflected in the way the members actually behave).[22] Values also may be reflected in the behavior of individuals, which is an artifact of culture.

A firm's values and how it promotes and publicizes those values can also affect how workers feel about their jobs and themselves. A study of 180 managers looked at their employers' effectiveness in communicating concern for employees' welfare. Managers in organizations that consistently communicated concern for workers' well-being and that focused on treating employees fairly reported feeling better about themselves and their role in the organization.[23] The lesson? *Treat* employees like valuable team members, and they are more likely to *feel* like valuable team members.

Values underlie the adaptable and innovative culture at Levi Strauss. As guides for behavior, they are reinforced in the aspirations statement and in the reward system of

espoused values

What members of an organization say they value.

enacted values

Values reflected in the way individuals actually behave.

"Get used to it. The first ten minutes of each meeting is devoted to ancestor worship."

Doughnut Culture in a Diet-Conscious World

Krispy Kreme's sign "Hot Doughnuts Now" symbolizes the company's commitment to providing the "fresh from the oven" doughnuts its customers have come to know and love.

What do Hank Aaron, Jimmy Buffett, and Dick Clark have in common? They all own Krispy Kreme store franchises. Krispy Kreme is a sixty-six-year-old firm that for years was regional and relatively unknown. Now, customers line up around the block in the middle of the night, wearing pajamas and waiting hours before a new store opens. Amazingly, the company spends nothing on national advertising. Before entering a new city, Krispy Kreme floods TV and radio stations with free doughnuts, finding this a cheaper and more effective way to "advertise."

The famous "HOT DOUGHNUTS NOW" sign originated in 1980. The folks at corporate headquarters noticed that the Chattanooga store's sales were outstanding, so they decided to investigate. Bob Glidden, the store manager, had posted a simple printed sign that read "HOT DOUGHNUTS NOW," but customers complained that the sign was posted even when the doughnuts weren't hot. Glidden bought a window shade and covered the sign until the doughnuts were hot; when the sign was posted, customers streamed in. Now the famous sign draws customers to Krispy Kreme stores around the country.

Krispy Kreme is a model of sweet success—but will that success continue in spite of the low-carbohydrate diet movement? Krispy Kreme plans to offer a new low-sugar/low-carb doughnut by the end of 2004, so only time will tell.

SOURCE: A. Serwer, "The Hole Story," *Fortune* (July 7, 2003): 51–62, http://www.fortune.com/fortune/subs/article/0,15114,460119,00.html.

the organization. Workforce diversity is valued at Levi Strauss. A former strong supporter of the Boy Scouts of America, the company discontinued its funding after the Scouts were shown to discriminate on the basis of sexual orientation. Mary Gross, a Levi Strauss spokesperson, expressed the company's position on valuing diversity: "One of the family values of this company is treating people who are different from you the same as you'd like to be treated. Tolerance is a pretty important family value."[24]

Some organizational cultures are characterized by values that support healthy lifestyle behaviors. When the workplace culture values worker health and psychological needs, there is enhanced potential for high performance and improved well-being.[25] Clif Bar, the energy bar maker, even has a twenty-two-foot rock climbing wall in its corporate office.

When Harley-Davidson hires new customer service employees, they had better be ready to do more than just answer telephones. Working at Harley-Davidson is not just a job, it's about an entire subculture that revolves around Harleys. New employees are immersed in this culture, typically through working at a Harley owners' rally and taking demonstration rides. Over time, most employees become Harley riders or owners, which helps them provide better service to other Harley lovers.[26]

Charles S. Schwab Corporation, a financial services firm, is a model of a values-driven business. Its core organizational values are as follows:

> Be fair, empathetic, and responsive in serving our clients.

> Respect and reinforce our fellow employees and the power of teamwork.

> Strive relentlessly to innovate what we do and how we do it.

> Always earn and be worthy of our clients' trust.[27]

Assumptions

Assumptions are the deeply held beliefs that guide behavior and tell members of an organization how to perceive and think about things. As the deepest and most fundamental level of an organization's culture, according to Edgar Schein, they are the essence of culture. They are so strongly held that a member behaving in any fashion that would violate them would be unthinkable. Another characteristic of assumptions is that they are often unconscious. Organization members may not be aware of their assumptions and may be reluctant or unable to discuss them or change them.

While unconscious assumptions often guide a firm's actions and decisions, some companies are quite explicit in their assumptions about employees. Earthlink, an Internet service provider, includes several of these assumptions on its Web site. The firm assumes that people who are treated with respect will respond by giving their best. It also assumes that because life is about more than work, that its employees will have fun. And the firm sees competition as a normal, even healthy part of work, due in part to its assumption that competition helps individuals, teams, and firms raise their level of performance. Earthlink is so confident of these assumptions, it encourages visitors who believe it is not living up to these values to "call us on it."[28]

Now that you understand Schein's three levels of culture, you can use You 16.1 to assess a culture you'd like to learn more about.

Functions and Effects of Organizational Culture

2. Identify the four functions of culture within an organization.

In an organization, culture serves four basic functions. First, culture provides a sense of identity to members and increases their commitment to the organization.[29] When employees internalize the values of the company, they find their work intrinsically rewarding and identify with their fellow workers. Motivation is enhanced, and employees are more committed.[30]

Second, culture is a sense-making device for organization members. It provides a way for employees to interpret the meaning of organizational events.[31]

Third, culture reinforces the values in the organization. The culture at SSM Health Care emphasizes patient care and continuous improvement. The St. Louis-based company, which owns and manages twenty-one acute care hospitals in four states, values compassionate, holistic, high-quality care. SSM was the first health care organization ever to win the Baldrige Quality Award.

Finally, culture serves as a control mechanism for shaping behavior. Norms that guide behavior are part of culture. If the norm the company wants to promote is teamwork, then its culture must reinforce that norm. The company's culture must be characterized by open communication, cooperation between teams, and integration of teams.[32]

The effects of organizational culture are hotly debated by organizational behaviorists and researchers. It seems that managers attest strongly to the positive effects of culture in organizations, but it is difficult to quantify these effects. John Kotter and James Heskett have reviewed three theories about the relationship between organizational culture and performance and the evidence that either supports or refutes these theories.[33] The three are the strong culture perspective, the fit perspective, and the adaptation perspective.

Analyzing the Three Levels of Culture

Select an organization you respect. Analyze its culture using the following dimensions.

The artifacts of _____'s culture are as follows:

Personal enactment:

Rites and ceremonies:

Stories:

Rituals:

Symbols:

The values embedded in _____'s culture are as follows:

The assumptions of _____'s culture are as follows:

1. On what information did you base your analysis?
2. How complete is your view of this organization's culture?

The Strong Culture Perspective

The strong culture perspective states that organizations with "strong" cultures perform better than other organizations.[34] A *strong culture* is an organizational culture with a consensus on the values that drive the company and with an intensity that is recognizable even to outsiders. Thus, a strong culture is deeply held and widely shared. It also is highly resistant to change. One example of a strong culture is IBM's. Its culture is one we are all familiar with: conservative, with a loyal workforce and an emphasis on customer service.

Strong cultures are thought to facilitate performance for three reasons. First, these cultures are characterized by goal alignment; that is, all employees share common goals. Second, strong cultures create a high level of motivation because of the values shared by the members. Third, strong cultures provide control without the oppressive effects of a bureaucracy.

To test the strong culture hypothesis, Kotter and Heskett selected 207 firms from a wide variety of industries. They used a questionnaire to calculate a culture strength index for each firm, and they correlated that index with the firm's economic performance over a twelve-year period. They concluded that strong cultures were associated with positive long-term economic performance, but only modestly.

There are also two perplexing questions about the strong culture perspectives. First, what can be said about evidence showing that strong economic performance can create strong cultures, rather than the reverse? Second, what if the strong culture leads the firm down the wrong path? Sears, for example, is an organization with a strong culture, but in the 1980s, it focused inward, ignoring competition and consumer preferences and damaging its performance. Changing Sears' strong but stodgy culture has been a tough task, with financial performance only recently showing an upward trend.[35]

strong culture
An organizational culture with a consensus on the values that drive the company and with an intensity that is recognizable even to outsiders.

3. Explain the relationship between organizational culture and performance.

The Fit Perspective

The "fit" perspective argues that a culture is good only if it fits the industry or the firm's strategy. For example, a culture that values a traditional hierarchical structure and stability would not work well in the computer manufacturing industry, which demands fast response and a lean, flat organization. Three particular characteristics of an industry may affect culture: the competitive environment, customer requirements, and societal expectations.[36] In the computer industry, firms face a highly competitive environment, customers who require highly reliable products, and a society that expects state-of-the-art technology and high-quality service.

A study of twelve large U.S. firms indicated that cultures consistent with industry conditions help managers make better decisions. It also indicated that cultures need not change as long as the industry doesn't change. If the industry does change, however, many cultures change too slowly to avoid negative effects on firms' performance.[37]

The fit perspective is useful in explaining short-term performance but not long-term performance. It also indicates that it is difficult to change culture quickly, especially if the culture is widely shared and deeply held. But it doesn't explain how firms can adapt to environmental change.

The Adaptation Perspective

The third theory about culture and performance is the adaptation perspective. Its theme is that only cultures that help organizations adapt to environmental change are associated with excellent performance. An *adaptive culture* is a culture that encourages confidence and risk taking among employees,[38] has leadership that produces change,[39] and focuses on the changing needs of customers.[40] 3M is a company with an adaptive culture in that it encourages new product ideas from all levels within the company.

To test the adaptation perspective, Kotter and Heskett interviewed industry analysts about the cultures of twenty-two firms. The contrast between adaptive cultures and nonadaptive cultures was striking. The results of the study are summarized in Table 16.1.

Adaptive cultures facilitate change to meet the needs of three groups of constituents: stockholders, customers, and employees. Nonadaptive cultures are characterized by cautious management that tries to protect its own interests. Adaptive firms showed significantly better long-term economic performance in Kotter and Heskett's study. One contrast that can be made is between Hewlett-Packard (HP), a high performer, and Xerox, a lower performer. The industry analysts viewed HP as valuing excellent leadership more than Xerox did and as valuing all three key constituencies more than Xerox did. Economic performance from 1977 through 1988 supported this difference: HP's index of annual net income growth was 40.2, as compared to Xerox's 13.1. Kotter and Heskett concluded that the cultures that promote long-term performance are those that are most adaptive. In the Science feature, you can discover why adaptive cultures are essential for companies that do business globally.

Given that high-performing cultures are adaptive ones, it is important to know how managers can develop adaptive cultures. In the next section, we will examine the leader's role in managing organizational culture.

The Leader's Role in Shaping and Reinforcing Culture

According to Edgar Schein, leaders play crucial roles in shaping and reinforcing culture.[41] The five most important elements in managing culture are (1)

---

adaptive culture
An organizational culture that encourages confidence and risk taking among employees, has leadership that produces change, and focuses on the changing needs of customers.

4. Contrast the characteristics of adaptive and nonadaptive cultures.

5. Describe five ways leaders reinforce organizational culture.

TABLE 16.1   Adaptive versus Nonadaptive Organizational Cultures

	ADAPTIVE ORGANIZATIONAL CULTURES	NONADAPTIVE ORGANIZATIONAL CULTURES
Core values	Most managers care deeply about customers, stockholders, and employees. They also strongly value people and processes that can create useful change (e.g., leadership up and down the management hierarchy).	Most managers care mainly about themselves, their immediate work group, or some product (or technology) associated with that work group. They value the orderly and risk-reducing management process much more highly than leadership initiatives.
Common behavior	Managers pay close attention to all their constituencies, especially customers, and initiate change when needed to serve their legitimate interests, even if that entails taking some risks.	Managers tend to behave somewhat insularly, politically, and bureaucratically. As a result, they do not change their strategies quickly to adjust to or take advantage of changes in their business environments.

SOURCE: Reprinted with the permission of The Free Press, a Division of Simon & Schuster, Inc. from *Corporate Culture and Performance* by John P. Kotter and James L. Heskett. Copyright © 1992 by Kotter Associates, Inc. and James L. Heskett.

what leaders pay attention to; (2) how leaders react to crises; (3) how leaders behave; (4) how leaders allocate rewards; and (5) how leaders hire and fire individuals.

The Enron Corporation fiasco illustrates each of these roles. "Enron ethics" is the term applied to the gap between words and deeds, and it illustrates that leader behavior deeply affects organizational culture.[42] Enron created deceptive partnerships and used questionable accounting practices to maintain its investment-grade rating. Employees recorded earnings before they were realized; they thought this was merely recording them early, not wrongly. Enron's culture was shaping the ethical boundaries of its employees, and Enron executives bent the rules for personal gain.

What Leaders Pay Attention To

Leaders in an organization communicate their priorities, values, and beliefs through the themes that consistently emerge from what they focus on. These themes are reflected in what they notice, comment on, measure, and control. If leaders are consistent in what they pay attention to, measure, and control, employees receive clear signals about what is important in the organization. If, however, leaders are inconsistent, employees spend a lot of time trying to decipher and find meaning in the inconsistent signals.

Enron leader Jeffrey Skilling paid attention to money and profit at all costs. Employees could take as much vacation as they wanted as long as they were delivering results; they could deliberately break company rules as long as they were making money.

How Leaders React to Crises

The way leaders deal with crises communicates a powerful message about culture. Emotions are heightened during a crisis, and learning is intense.

Difficult economic times present crises for many companies and illustrate their different values. Some organizations do everything possible to prevent

SCIENCE

Adaptive Cultures Are Important in Russia

Kotter and Heskett's research indicated that adaptive, flexible cultures are important to a firm's long-term success. Recent research indicates that in today's global economy, adapative cultures may be more important than ever before.

Researchers examined the link between organizational culture and firm effectiveness among foreign-owned firms that had operations in Russia. Russia's transitioning economy, its many subcultures, and the legacy of communism make Russia a unique environment for business. All of these characteristics make teamwork and coordination challenging.

To conduct the study, researchers compared 179 foreign-owned firms operating in Russia with firms operating in the United States. Their finding was that effectiveness in Russia depends even more on adaptable, flexible organizational cultures than it does in the United States. Firms that are adaptable can weather the storms of change and ultimately succeed in Russia's dynamic and unpredictable environment.

SOURCE: C. F. Fey and D. R. Denison, "Organizational Culture and Effectiveness: Can American Theory Be Applied in Russia?" *Organization Science* 14 (2003): 686–706.

laying off workers. Others may claim that employees are important but quickly institute major layoffs at the first signal of an economic downturn. Employees may perceive that the company shows its true colors in a crisis and thus may pay careful attention to the reactions of their leaders.

When the Enron crisis became public, managers quickly shifted blame and pointed fingers. Before bankruptcy was declared, managers began systematically firing any employee they could lay blame on, while denying that there was a problem with accounting irregularities. During the crisis, managers responded with anonymous whistle-blowing, hiding behind the Fifth Amendment and shredding documents.

How Leaders Behave

Through role modeling, teaching, and coaching, leaders reinforce the values that support the organizational culture. Employees often emulate leaders' behavior and look to the leaders for cues to appropriate behavior. Many companies are encouraging employees to be more entrepreneurial—to take more initiative and be more innovative in their jobs. A study showed that if managers want employees to be more entrepreneurial, they must demonstrate such behaviors themselves.[43] This is the case with any cultural value. Employees observe the behavior of leaders to find out what the organization values.

The behavior of Enron's managers spoke volumes; they broke the law as they created fake partnerships. They ignored and then denied that problems existed. While employees were unable to dump their Enron stocks, managers were hastily getting rid of their shares, all the while telling employees that the company would be fine.

How Leaders Allocate Rewards

To ensure that values are accepted, leaders should reward behavior that is consistent with the values. Some companies, for example, may claim that they use a pay-for-performance system that distributes rewards on the basis of performance. When the time comes for raises, however, the increases are awarded according to length of service with the company. Imagine the feelings of a high-performing newcomer who has heard leaders espouse the value of rewarding individual performance and then receives only a tiny raise.

Some companies may value teamwork. They form cross-functional teams and empower these teams to make important decisions. However, when performance is appraised, the criteria for rating employees focus on individual performance. This sends a confusing signal to employees about the company's culture: Is individual performance valued, or is teamwork the key?

At Enron, employees were rewarded only if they produced consistent results, with little regard for ethics. Managers were given extremely rich bonuses to keep the stock price up at any cost. Performance reviews were done in public, and poor performers were ridiculed.

How Leaders Hire and Fire Individuals

A powerful way that leaders reinforce culture is through the selection of newcomers to the organization. Leaders often unconsciously look for individuals who are similar to current organizational members in terms of values and assumptions. Some companies hire individuals on the recommendation of a current employee; this tends to perpetuate the culture because the new employees typically hold similar values. Promotion-from-within policies also serve to reinforce organizational culture.

The way a company fires an employee and the rationale behind the firing also communicate the culture. Some companies deal with poor performers by trying to find a place within the organization where they can perform better and make a contribution. Other companies seem to operate under the philosophy that those who cannot perform are out quickly.

The reasons for terminations may not be directly communicated to other employees, but curiosity leads to speculation. An employee who displays unethical behavior and is caught may simply be reprimanded even though such behavior is clearly against the organization's values. Other employees may view this as a failure to reinforce the values within the organization.

Enron hired employees who had aggressiveness, greed, a desire to win at all costs, and a willingness to break rules. It fired nonproductive employees, using a "rank and yank" system whereby the bottom 15–20 percent of employees were let go each year. Peers were required to rank each other, which led to cutthroat competition and extreme distrust among employees.

In summary, leaders play a critical role in shaping and reinforcing organizational culture. The Enron case provides an illustration of how powerful, and potentially damaging, that influence can be. The lesson for future managers is to create a positive culture through what they pay attention to, how they react to crises, how they behave, the way they allocate rewards, and how they hire and fire employees.

Organizational Socialization

We have seen that leaders play key roles in shaping an organization's culture. Another process that perpetuates culture is the way it is handed down from generation to generation of employees. Newcomers learn the culture through *organizational socialization*—the process by which newcomers are transformed from outsiders to participating, effective members of the organization.[44] The process is also a vehicle for bringing newcomers into the organizational culture. As we saw earlier, cultural socialization begins with the careful selection of newcomers who are likely to reinforce the organizational culture.[45] Once selected, newcomers pass through the socialization process.

6. Describe the three stages of organizational socialization and the ways culture is communicated in each step.

organizational socialization
The process by which newcomers are transformed from outsiders to participating, effective members of the organization.

The organizational socialization process is generally described as having three stages: anticipatory socialization, encounter, and change and acquisition. Figure 16.2 presents a model of the process and the key concerns at each stage of it.[46] It also describes the outcomes of the process, which will be discussed in the next section of the chapter.

anticipatory socialization

The first socialization stage, which encompasses all of the learning that takes place prior to the newcomer's first day on the job.

ANTICIPATORY SOCIALIZATION *Anticipatory socialization*, the first stage, encompasses all of the learning that takes place prior to the newcomer's first day on the job. It includes the newcomer's expectations. The two key concerns at this stage are realism and congruence.

Realism is the degree to which a newcomer holds realistic expectations about the job and about the organization. One thing newcomers should receive information about during entry into the organization is the culture. Information about values at this stage can help newcomers begin to construct a scheme for interpreting their organizational experiences. A deeper understanding of the organization's culture will be possible through time and experience in the organization.

There are two types of *congruence* between an individual and an organization: congruence between the individual's abilities and the demands of the job, and the fit between the organization's values and the individual's values. Organizations disseminate information about their values through their Web pages, annual reports, and recruitment brochures.[47] Value congruence is particularly important for organizational culture. It is also important in terms of newcomer adjustment. Newcomers whose values match the company's values are more satisfied with their new jobs, adjust more quickly, and say they intend to remain with the firm longer.[48]

FIGURE 16.2

The Organizational Socialization Process: Stages and Outcomes

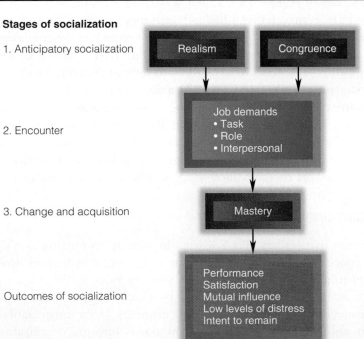

SOURCE: Reprinted from *Organizational Dynamics*, Autumn 1989, "An Ethical Weather Report: Assessing the Organization's Ethical Climate" by John B. Cullen, et al. Copyright © 1989, with permission from Elsevier Science.

ENCOUNTER The second stage of socialization, *encounter*, is when newcomers learn the tasks associated with the job, clarify their roles, and establish new relationships at work. This stage commences on the first day at work and is thought to encompass the first six to nine months on the new job. Newcomers face task demands, role demands, and interpersonal demands during this period.

Task demands involve the actual work performed. Learning to perform tasks is related to the organization's culture. In some organizations, newcomers are given considerable latitude to experiment with new ways to do the job, and creativity is valued. In others, newcomers are expected to learn the established procedures for their tasks. Early experiences with trying to master task demands can affect employees' entire careers. Auditors, for example, are often forced to choose between being thorough, on one hand, and being fast in completing their work, on the other. By pressuring auditors in this way, firms often set themselves up for problems later, when these pressures may lead auditors to make less-than-ethical decisions.

Role demands involve the expectations placed on newcomers. Newcomers may not know exactly what is expected of them (role ambiguity) or may receive conflicting expectations from other individuals (role conflict). The way newcomers approach these demands depends in part on the culture of the organization. Are newcomers expected to operate with considerable uncertainty, or is the manager expected to clarify the newcomers' roles? Some cultures even put newcomers through considerable stress in the socialization process, including humility-inducing experiences, so newcomers will be more open to accepting the firm's values and norms. Long hours, tiring travel schedules, and an overload of work are part of some socialization practices.

Interpersonal demands arise from relationships at work. Politics, leadership style, and group pressure are interpersonal demands. All of them reflect the values and assumptions that operate within the organization. Most organizations have basic assumptions about the nature of human relationships. The Korean chaebol LG Group strongly values harmony in relationships and in society, and its decision-making policy emphasizes unanimity.

In the encounter stage, the expectations formed in anticipatory socialization may clash with the realities of the job. It is a time of facing the task, role, and interpersonal demands of the new job.

CHANGE AND ACQUISITION In the third and final stage of socialization, *change and acquisition*, newcomers begin to master the demands of the job. They become proficient at managing their tasks, clarifying and negotiating their roles, and engaging in relationships at work. The time when the socialization process is completed varies widely, depending on the individual, the job, and the organization. The end of the process is signaled by newcomers being considered by themselves and others as organizational insiders.

Outcomes of Socialization

Newcomers who are successfully socialized should exhibit good performance, high job satisfaction, and the intention to stay with the organization. In addition, they should exhibit low levels of distress symptoms.[49] High levels of organizational commitment are also marks of successful socialization.[50] This commitment is facilitated throughout the socialization process by the communication of values that newcomers can buy into. Successful socialization is also signaled by mutual influence; that is, the newcomers have made adjustments in

encounter
The second socialization stage in which the newcomer learns the tasks associated with the job, clarifies roles, and establishes new relationships at work.

change and acquisition
The third socialization stage, in which the newcomer begins to master the demands of the job.

the job and organization to accommodate their knowledge and personalities. Newcomers are expected to leave their mark on the organization and not be completely conforming.

When socialization is effective, newcomers understand and adopt the organization's values and norms. This ensures that the company's culture, including its central values, survives. It also provides employees a context for interpreting and responding to things that happen at work, and it ensures a shared framework of understanding among employees.[51]

Newcomers adopt the company's norms and values more quickly when they receive positive support from organizational insiders. Sometimes this is accomplished through informal social gatherings.[52]

Socialization as Cultural Communication

Socialization is a powerful cultural communication tool. While the transmission of information about cultural artifacts is relatively easy, the transmission of values is more difficult. The communication of organizational assumptions is almost impossible, since organization members themselves may not be consciously aware of them.

The primary purpose of socialization is the transmission of core values to new organization members.[53] Newcomers are exposed to these values through the role models they interact with, the training they receive, and the behavior they observe being rewarded and punished. Newcomers are vigilant observers, seeking clues to the organization's culture and consistency in the cultural messages they receive. If they are expected to adopt these values, it is essential that the message reflect the underlying values of the organization.

One company known for its culture is The Walt Disney Company. Disney transmits its culture to employees though careful selection, socialization, and training. The Disney culture is built around customer service, and its image serves as a filtering process for applicants. Peer interviews are used to learn how applicants interact with each other. Disney tries to secure a good fit between employee values and the organization's culture. To remind employees of the image they are trying to project, employees are referred to as "cast members" and they occupy a "role." They work either "on stage" or "backstage" and wear "costumes," rather than uniforms. Disney operates its own "universities," which are attended by all new employees. Once trained at a Disney university, cast members are paired with role models to continue their learning on-site.

Companies such as Disney use the socialization process to communicate messages about organizational culture. Both individuals and organizations can take certain actions to ensure the success of the socialization process.

Assessing Organizational Culture

7. Identify ways of assessing organizational culture.

Although some organizational scientists argue for assessing organizational culture with quantitative methods, others say that organizational culture must be assessed with qualitative methods.[54] Quantitative methods, such as questionnaires, are valuable because of their precision, comparability, and objectivity. Qualitative methods, such as interviews and observations, are valuable because of their detail, descriptiveness, and uniqueness.

Two widely used quantitative assessment instruments are the Organizational Culture Inventory (OCI) and the Kilmann-Saxton Culture-Gap Survey. Both assess the behavioral norms of organizational cultures, as opposed to the artifacts, values, or assumptions of the organization.

The OCI focuses on behaviors that help employees fit into the organization and meet the expectations of coworkers. Using Maslow's motivational need hierarchy as its basis, it measures twelve cultural styles. The two underlying dimensions of the OCI are task/people and security/satisfaction. There are four satisfaction cultural styles and eight security cultural styles.

A self-report instrument, the OCI contains 120 questions. It provides an individual assessment of culture and may be aggregated to the work group and to the organizational level.[55] It has been used in firms throughout North America, Western Europe, New Zealand, and Thailand, as well as in U.S. military units, the Federal Aviation Administration, and nonprofit organizations.

Kilmann-Saxton Culture-Gap Survey

The Kilmann-Saxton Culture-Gap Survey focuses on what actually happens and on the expectations of others in the organization.[56] Its two underlying dimensions are technical/human and time (the short term versus the long term). With these two dimensions, the actual operating norms and the ideal norms in four areas are assessed. The areas are task support (short-term technical norms), task innovation (long-term technical norms), social relationships (short-term human orientation norms), and personal freedom (long-term human orientation norms). Significant gaps in any of the four areas are used as a point of departure for cultural change to improve performance, job satisfaction, and morale.

A self-report instrument, the Gap Survey provides an individual assessment of culture and may be aggregated to the work group. It has been used in firms throughout the United States and in not-for-profit organizations.

Triangulation

A study of a rehabilitation center in a 400-bed hospital incorporated *triangulation* (the use of multiple methods to measure organizational culture) to improve inclusiveness and accuracy in measuring the organizational culture.[57] Triangulation has been used by anthropologists, sociologists, and other behavioral scientists to study organizational culture. Its name comes from the navigational technique of using multiple reference points to locate an object. In the rehabilitation center study, the three methods used to triangulate on the culture were (1) obtrusive observations by eight trained observers, which provided an outsider perspective; (2) self-administered questionnaires, which provided quantitative insider information; and (3) personal interviews with the center's staff, which provided qualitative contextual information.

The study showed that each of the three methods made unique contributions toward the discovery of the rehabilitation center's culture. The complete picture could not have been drawn with just a single technique. Triangulation can lead to a better understanding of the phenomenon of culture and is the best approach to assessing organizational culture.

triangulation

The use of multiple methods to measure organizational culture.

Changing Organizational Culture

Changing situations may require changes in the existing culture of an organization. With rapid environmental changes such as globalization, workforce diversity, and technological innovation, the fundamental assumptions and basic values that drive the organization may need to be altered. One particular situation that may require cultural change is a merger or acquisition. The blending of two distinct organizational cultures may prove difficult.

Despite good-faith efforts, combining cultures is difficult. When dignified, established media giant Time Warner merged with free-wheeling Internet up-start America Online in 2001, few could imagine the fireworks that would result when these two "oil and water" firms tried to mix. Typical of the conflicts that followed was a client dinner in which AOL executive Neil Davis horrified Time Warner executives by describing how AOL preferred to handle weakened competitors. Taking a steak knife from the table, Davis raised his arm and drove the knife into the table top, explaining that, "What we like to do to a competitor that is damaged is drive the knife in their heart." The shocked client ultimately declined to buy ads on AOL, and the entire merger was eventually deemed a multibillion-dollar failure due, at least in part, to the culture clash between the two partners.[58]

Prior to the Daimler-Chrysler merger, both automotive giants enjoyed good performance. After the merger, however, it was a different story. The Chrysler division started losing money and instituted major, unanticipated layoffs. Differences in culture were cited as responsible for this failure. Daimler-Benz had a culture that was formal, with a very structured management style. Chrysler, in contrast, had a relaxed management style that accounted for its premerger success. The two divisions had vastly different views on pay scales and travel expenses. Chrysler executives and engineers began leaving in great numbers, and Chrysler employees believed that Daimler was trying to control the company and impose its culture on Chrysler. The stock price after the merger fell to half of its previous value following the initial postmerger high.[59, 60]

Alterations in culture may also be required when an organization employs people from different countries. Research indicates that some organizational cultures actually enhance differences in national cultures.[61] One study compared foreign employees working in a multinational organization with employees working in different organizations within their own countries. The assumption was that the employees from various countries working for the same multinational organization would be more similar than employees working in diverse organizations in their native countries. The results were surprising, in that there were significantly greater differences among the employees of the multinational than among managers working for different companies within their native countries. In the multinational, Swedes became more Swedish, Americans became more American, and so forth. It appears that employees enhance their national culture traditions even when working within a single organizational culture.[62] This is more likely to occur when diversity is moderate. When diversity is very high, employees are more likely to develop a shared identity in the organization's culture instead of relying on their own national culture.[63]

8. Explain actions managers can take to change organizational culture.

Changing an organization's culture is feasible but difficult.[64] One reason for the difficulty is that assumptions—the deepest level of culture—are often unconscious. As such, they are often nonconfrontable and nondebatable. Another reason for the difficulty is that culture is deeply ingrained and behavioral norms and rewards are well learned.[65] In a sense, employees must unlearn the old norms before they can learn new ones. Managers who want to change the culture should look first to the ways culture is maintained.

A model for cultural change that summarizes the interventions managers can use is presented in Figure 16.3. In this model, the numbers represent the actions managers can take. There are two basic approaches to changing the existing culture: (1) helping current members buy into a new set of values (actions 1, 2, and 3); or (2) adding newcomers and socializing them into the organization and removing current members as appropriate (actions 4 and 5).[66]

FIGURE 16.3   Interventions for Changing Organizational Culture

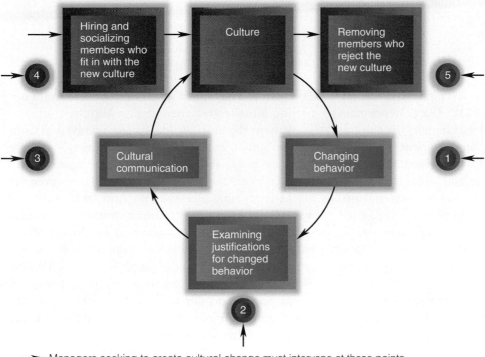

Managers seeking to create cultural change must intervene at these points.

SOURCE: From Vijay Sathe "How to Decipher and Change Corporate Culture," Chap. 13 in *Gaining Control of the Corporate Culture* (R. H. Kilmann et al., eds.) Fig. 1, p. 245. Copyright © 1985 Jossey-Bass, Inc. Reprinted by permission of Jossey-Bass, Inc., a subsidiary of John Wiley & Sons, Inc.

The first action is to change behavior in the organization. Even if behavior does change, however, this change is not sufficient for cultural change to occur. Behavior is an artifact (level 1) of culture. Individuals may change their behavior but not the values that drive it. They may rationalize, "I'm only doing this because my manager wants me to."

Therefore, managers must use action 2, which is to examine the justifications for the changed behavior. Are employees buying into the new set of values, or are they just complying?

The third action, cultural communication, is extremely important. All of the artifacts (personal enactment, stories, rites and ceremonies, rituals, and symbols) must send a consistent message about the new values and beliefs. It is crucial that the communication be credible; that is, managers must live the new values and not just talk about them. In The Real World 16.2, read about how the leaders at Continental Airlines managed artifacts to successfully change Continental's culture.

The two remaining actions (4 and 5) involve shaping the workforce to fit the intended culture. First, the organization can revise its selection strategies to more accurately reflect the new culture. Second, the organization can identify individuals who resist the cultural change or who are no longer comfortable with the values in the organization. Reshaping the workforce should not involve a ruthless pursuit of nonconforming employees; it should be a gradual and subtle change that takes considerable time. Changing personnel in the organization is a lengthy process; it cannot be done effectively in a short period of time without considerable problems.

Continental Airlines: Changing Corporate Culture by Changing Artifacts

One of the most successful corporate turnarounds in history was that of Continental Airlines, which was changed from a money loser to a profit maker by CEO Gordon Bethune and COO Greg Brenneman. Part of its success story involved changing its cultural artifacts to reinforce a new, service-oriented culture. Prior to the change, the norm at Continental was low productivity. Leaders Bethune and Brenneman instituted a bonus system whereby a check was given to every employee whose performance met or exceeded expectations—and the check came separately from the paycheck, with no tax deductions. The check and delivery system were symbols of the new emphasis on performance.

Bethune and Brenneman also communicated face to face with employees. They literally "walked the talk," personally explaining the value of customer service. Stories were passed among Continental employees about the new leaders who told jokes to employees, answered questions truthfully, and were good people to work for. The plan to save Continental was the "Go Forward Plan," also symbolic of the change. Brenneman created an airplane metaphor saying, "Did you know there are no rearview mirrors on an airplane? The runway behind is irrelevant." This plan and metaphor symbolized Continental's optimistic future rather than its dismal past.

Perhaps the most visible artifact involved in Continental's culture change was the company's massive 800-page policy manual, which had been universally despised by employees. It contained rules for even the most trivial things. To make it clear that bureaucracy was a relic of the past, human resource managers gathered hundreds of Continental employees in the parking lot and burned the manual, much to the employees' delight. A team of employees created a new manual, eighty pages long, that empowered employees to make good decisions without having to consult a manual for advice. Stories about the policy manual burning still abound.

By changing Continental's cultural artifacts, the leaders instituted a new, service-oriented, employee-empowering culture.

SOURCE: J. M. Higgins and C. McAllaster, "If You Want Strategic Change, Don't Forget to Change Your Cultural Artifacts," *Journal of Change Management* 4 (2004): 63–74.

Evaluating the success of cultural change may be best done by looking at behavior. Cultural change can be assumed to be successful if the behavior is intrinsically motivated—on "automatic pilot." If the new behavior would persist even if rewards were not present, and if the employees have internalized the new value system, then the behavior is probably intrinsically motivated. If employees automatically respond to a crisis in ways consistent with the corporate culture, then the cultural change effort can be deemed successful.

One organization that has changed its culture is AT&T. In 1984, the courts ordered the breakup of AT&T. Prior to the breakup, the company operated in a stable environment with low levels of uncertainty. The organization was a highly structured bureaucracy. The culture emphasized lifetime employment, promotion from within, and loyalty. AT&T faced minimal competition, and it offered individual security. When the courts ordered AT&T to divest its Bell operating companies, the old culture was no longer effective. The company had to move toward a culture that holds individuals accountable for their performance. Change at AT&T was painful and slow, but it was necessary for the company to be able to operate in the new competitive environment.[67] Changing environments may bring about changes in organizational culture.

Given the current business environment, managers may want to focus on three particular cultural modifications: (1) support for a global view of business, (2) reinforcement of ethical behavior, and (3) empowerment of employees to excel in product and service quality.

The values that drive the organizational culture should support a global view of the company and its efforts. To do so, the values should be clear to everyone involved so that everyone understands them. The values should also be strongly supported at the top. Management should embody the shared values and reward employees who support the global view. Finally, the values should be consistent over time. Consistent values give an organization a unifying theme that competitors may be unable to emulate.[68]

Global corporations suffer from the conflicting pressures of centralization and decentralization. An overarching corporate culture that integrates the decentralized subsidiaries in locations around the world can be an asset in the increasingly competitive global marketplace.

Following are six specific guidelines for managers who want to create a global culture[69]:

1. Create a clear and simple mission statement. A shared mission can unite individuals from diverse cultural backgrounds.

2. Create systems that ensure an effective flow of information. Coordination councils and global task forces can be used to ensure that information flows throughout the geographically dispersed organization are consistent.

3. Create "matrix minds" among managers; that is, broaden managers' minds to allow them to think globally. IBM does this through temporary overseas assignments. Managers with international experience share that experience when they return to the home organization.

4. Develop global career paths. This means ensuring not only that home country executives go overseas but also that executives from other countries rotate into service in the home office.

5. Use cultural differences as a major asset. The former Digital Equipment Corporation (now part of Hewlett-Packard), for example, transferred its research and development functions to Italy to take advantage of the free-flowing Italian management style that encouraged creativity. Its manufacturing operations went to Germany, which offered a more systematic management style.

6. Implement worldwide management education and team development programs. Unified training efforts that emphasize corporate values can help establish a shared identity among employees.

These guidelines are specifically aimed at multinational organizations that want to create a global corporate culture, but other organizations can also benefit from them. Companies that want to broaden employees' views or to use the diversity of their workforce as a resource will find several of these recommendations advantageous.

Developing an Ethical Organizational Culture

While a majority of U.S. firms have rushed to create and publicize codes of ethics in an effort to help their employees discern right from wrong, the impact of these codes is not always as positive as might be expected. While the implementation of formal ethics guidelines might be expected to improve ethical behavior, some studies have shown the exact opposite, with institution of formal ethics codes actually leading to less ethical behavior among employees. While the reasons for this are not clear, it appears that in some cases employees see the code of ethics as simply a management showpiece, leading to cynicism and resentment. In other cases, a heavy reliance on a strict set of rules may reduce the perceived need for employees to think about and be involved in ethical decision making, leading to inferior choices in the long run.[70]

The organizational culture, however, can have profound effects on the ethical behavior of organization members.[71] When a company's culture promotes ethical norms, individuals behave accordingly. Managers can encourage ethical behavior by being good role models for employees. They can institute the philosophy that ethical behavior makes good business sense and puts the company in congruence with the larger values of society.[72] Managers can also communicate that rationalizations for unethical behavior are not tolerated. For example, some salespersons justify padding their expense accounts because everyone else does it. Declaring these justifications illegitimate sends a clear message about the lack of tolerance for such behavior.

Trust is another key to effectively managing ethical behavior, especially in cultures that encourage whistle-blowing (as we saw in Chapter 2). Employees must trust that whistle-blowers will be protected, that procedures used to investigate ethical problems will be fair, and that management will take action to solve problems that are uncovered.

At John Deere & Company, a simple idea guides the firm's ethics and decision making: "No smoke, no mirrors, no tricks: just right down the middle of the field," as Robert Lane, chairman and CEO, puts it. John Deere's decision to donate a multimillion-dollar parcel of land to a university, rather than selling it to a developer, demonstrates its values and is one of the reasons the firm made the top ten in *Business Ethics* magazine's list of the "100 Best Corporate Citizens for 2004."[73]

The reasons most often cited for unethical corporate conduct are interesting.[74] They include the belief that a behavior is not really unethical, that it is in the organization's best interest, that it will not be discovered, and that the organization will support it because it offers a good outcome for the organization. An ethical corporate culture can eliminate the viability of these excuses by clearly communicating the boundaries of ethical conduct, selecting employees who support the ethical culture, rewarding organization members who exhibit ethical behavior, and conspicuously punishing members who engage in unethical behavior.

Organizations that seek to encourage ethical behavior can do so by using their organizational culture. By completing You 16.2, you can assess the ethical culture of an organization you're familiar with.

Developing a Culture of Empowerment and Quality

Throughout this book, we have seen that successful organizations promote a culture that empowers employees and excels in product and service quality. Empowerment serves to unleash employees' creativity and productivity. It requires eliminating traditional hierarchical notions of power. Cultures that emphasize empowerment and quality are preferred by employees. Companies that value empowerment and continuous improvement have cultures that promote high product and service quality.[75]

Organizational Culture and Ethics

Think about the organization you currently work for or one you know something about and complete the following Ethical Climate Questionnaire.

Use the scale below and write the number that best represents your answer in the space next to each item.

To what extent are the following statements true about your company?

Completely false	Mostly false	Somewhat false	Somewhat true	Mostly true	Completely true
0	1	2	3	4	5

____ **1.** In this company, people are expected to follow their own personal and moral beliefs.

____ **2.** People are expected to do anything to further the company's interests.

____ **3.** In this company, people look out for each other's good.

____ **4.** It is very important here to follow the company's rules and procedures strictly.

____ **5.** In this company, people protect their own interests above other considerations.

____ **6.** The first consideration is whether a decision violates any law.

____ **7.** Everyone is expected to stick by company rules and procedures.

____ **8.** The most efficient way is always the right way in this company.

____ **9.** Our major consideration is what is best for everyone in the company.

____ **10.** In this company, the law or ethical code of the profession is the major consideration.

____ **11.** It is expected at this company that employees will always do what is right for the customer and the public.

To score the questionnaire, first add up your responses to questions 1, 3, 6, 9, 10, and 11. This is subtotal number 1. Next, reverse the scores on questions 2, 4, 5, 7, and 8 (5 = 0, 4 = 1, 3 = 2, 2 = 3, 1 = 4, 0 = 5). Add the reverse scores to form subtotal number 2. Add subtotal number 1 to subtotal number 2 for an overall score.

Subtotal 1 _____ + Subtotal 2 _____ = Overall Score _____.

Overall scores can range from 0 to 55. The higher the score, the more the organization's culture encourages ethical behavior.

SOURCE: Reprinted from *Organizational Dynamics*, Autumn 1989, " An Ethical Weather Report: Assessing the Organization's Ethical Climate" by John B. Cullen et al. Copyright © 1989, with permission from Elsevier Science.

Corporate culture can also support values that help firms compete. New Balance Athletic Shoe competes with low-wage suppliers in Asia (where the average wage is less than $2 per hour), even though one-fourth of its products are produced in the United States. Part of the firm's success comes from its willingness to empower its employees by sharing information with them. For instance, the firm often shares cost data with employees, pointing out that a competitor's shoe can be made overseas for $15 and challenging them to meet that cost point. Today, New Balance workers in the United States receive twenty-two hours of training when they are hired and continual training on the factory floor. The result is that New Balance's U.S. workers can produce a pair of shoes in twenty-four minutes, compared to almost three hours in Asia.[76, 77]

Harley-Davidson might well be the ultimate old-line manufacturing firm trying to develop a culture of quality. From 1985, with the firm literally minutes from bankruptcy, to today, with demand for its high-quality cycles at an all-time high, Harley-Davidson has gone from the valley to the mountaintop.

Like many other old manufacturing firms, Harley tried to compete in the 1970s with techniques developed in the 1950s. Huge forklifts wandered the shop floor, shuffling millions of dollars worth of components among work stations; quality was poor; and in short, Harley was fat and inefficient. Over the last two decades, Harley has been reborn. Manufacturing has been streamlined to reflect more modern thinking on efficiency. Product quality has improved immensely, and the firm's workforce continues to improve, with close to half the company's employees taking training courses in any given year.

Harley's high level of quality is not merely an artifact of better shop practices. The company's management has worked to foster a unique congenial relationship with its unions, ensuring that continuous improvement is an organizational priority rather than simply the latest management fad. Today's Harley "hog" costs less to produce and is more reliable than any before it, due in large part to the firm's incessant drive to produce a better product.[78]

Medrad, Inc., won the 2003 Malcolm Baldrige Award for quality in manufacturing. Medrad makes devices that allow doctors to see through you; using diagnostic imaging technology, doctors get an inside view of the human body. It sells these products to hospitals and imaging centers around the world. CEO John Friel is committed to continuous improvement and quality, as well as employee empowerment. He spends at least one day a month in company shop floor operations—including customer service, tech support, and even sweeping the floor in maintenance. Friel's employees are committed to him, to Medrad, and to quality.[79]

Managers can learn from the experiences of New Balance, Harley-Davidson, and Medrad that employee empowerment is a key to achieving quality. Involving employees in decision making, removing obstacles to their performance, and communicating the value of product and service quality reinforce the values of empowerment and quality in the organizational culture.

Managerial Implications: The Organizational Culture Challenge

Managing organizational culture is a key challenge for leaders in today's organizations. With the trend toward downsizing and restructuring, maintaining an organizational culture in the face of change is difficult. In addition, such challenges as globalization, workforce diversity, technology, and managing ethical behavior often require that an organization change its culture. Adaptive cultures that can respond to changes in the environment can lead the way in terms of organizational performance.

Managers have at their disposal many techniques for managing organizational culture. These techniques range from manipulating the artifacts of culture, such as ceremonies and symbols, to communicating the values that guide the organization. The socialization process is a powerful cultural communication process. Managers are models who communicate the organizational culture to employees through personal enactment. Their modeled behavior sets the norms for the other employees to follow. Their leadership is essential for developing a culture that values diversity, supports empowerment, fosters innovations in product and service quality, and promotes ethical behavior.

LOOKING BACK: CANINE COMPANIONS FOR INDEPENDENCE

Starting Young and Learning Values

As a nationwide organization, CCI's culture has a wide-ranging impact, not just on its employees and volunteers, but often on others as well. Bridgit Sandford lives in Smithtown, New York, where she and her husband Robert have raised three CCI puppies. And beyond the impact of simply having the puppies in their house, the puppies' purpose has impacted their two-year-old son Rob, who has been known to approach strangers in wheelchairs and tell them, "I'm raising a puppy for you." As one of the organization's countless ambassadors, Rob is eager to tell disabled people about the potential of a CCI dog and how it can impact their lives. By playing a small part in CCI's work, Rob is learning about helping others, which is at the core of CCI's culture.[80]

Chapter Summary

1. Organizational (corporate) culture is a pattern of basic assumptions that are considered valid and that are taught to new members as the way to perceive, think, and feel in the organization.

2. The most visible and accessible level of culture is artifacts, which include personal enactment, ceremonies and rites, stories, rituals, and symbols.

3. Organizational culture has four functions: giving members a sense of identity and increasing their commitment, serving as a sense-making device for members, reinforcing organizational values, and serving as a control mechanism for shaping behavior.

4. Three theories about the relationship between culture and performance are the strong culture perspective, the fit perspective, and the adaptation perspective.

5. Leaders shape and reinforce culture by what they pay attention to, how they react to crises, how they behave, how they allocate rewards, and how they hire and fire individuals.

6. Organizational socialization is the process by which newcomers become participating, effective members of the organization. Its three stages are anticipatory socialization, encounter, and change and acquisition. Each stage plays a unique role in communicating organizational culture.

7. The Organizational Culture Inventory and Kilmann-Saxton Culture-Gap Survey are two quantitative instruments for assessing organizational culture. Triangulation, using multiple methods for assessing culture, is an effective measurement strategy.

8. It is difficult but not impossible to change organizational culture. Managers can do so by helping current members buy into a new set of values, by adding newcomers and socializing them into the organization, and by removing current members as appropriate.

Key Terms

adaptive culture (p. 538)
anticipatory socialization (p. 542)
artifacts (p. 530)
assumptions (p. 536)
change and acquisition (p. 543)

enacted values (p. 534)
encounter (p. 543)
espoused values (p. 534)
organizational (corporate) culture (p. 530)

organizational socialization (p. 541)
strong culture (p. 537)
triangulation (p. 545)

Review Questions

1. Explain the three levels of organizational culture. How can each level of culture be measured?

2. Describe five artifacts of culture and give an example of each.

3. Explain three theories about the relationship between organizational culture and performance. What does the research evidence say about each one?

4. Contrast adaptive and nonadaptive cultures.

5. How can leaders shape organizational culture?

6. Describe the three stages of organizational socialization. How is culture communicated in each stage?

7. How can managers assess the organizational culture? What actions can they take to change the organizational culture?

8. How does a manager know that cultural change has been successful?

9. What can managers do to develop a global organizational culture?

Discussion and Communication Questions

1. Name a company with a visible organizational culture. What do you think are the company's values? Has the culture contributed to the organization's performance? Explain.

2. Name a leader you think manages organizational culture well. How does the leader do this? Use Schein's description of how leaders reinforce culture to analyze the leader's behavior.

3. Suppose you want to change your organization's culture. What sort of resistance would you expect from employees? How would you deal with this resistance?

4. Given Schein's three levels, can we ever truly understand an organization's culture? Explain.

5. To what extent is culture manageable? Changeable?

6. *(communication question)* Select an organization that you might like to work for. Learn as much as you can about that company's culture, using library resources, on-line sources, contacts within the company, and as many creative means as you can. Prepare a brief presentation to the class summarizing the culture.

Ethical Dilemma

Jean Miller is the managing director of housekeeping at a large, upscale hotel. She feels good about working for an organization that cares a lot about its employees. The hotel respects its employees and does everything possible to create a culture of loyalty and commitment. Throughout Jean's 20 years, the hotel's strong commitment is among the most positive aspects of her job. Lately, Jean feels this loyalty is going too far, especially when it comes to Mary, one of the housekeeping supervisors.

Housekeeping is a very physical job that Mary excelled at for many years. Now Mary is ready to retire, but she is not in a financial position to do so. This greatly affects Mary's attitude, and unrest is beginning to spread among the people who work for her. There are three openings in Mary's department already and more are expected. The biggest obstacle,

from Jean's perspective, is that she feels any new hires sent to Mary would end up quitting. Jean has recently hired a very promising new person, Pat. Jean had even warned her about Mary's department. Within the first few weeks, Pat had been socialized into the negativity of the department. Jean tried to relocate Pat to a different department when she saw what was happening, but it was too late. Even in the new environment, Pat has retained the mindset she had already developed.

The most pressing challenge is what to do about the open positions. Jean is sure that any new person would react as Pat had to Mary, but it isn't fair to those who have to carry a great number of rooms everyday until the positions are filled. Jean has tried to move people from other departments but everyone has threatened to quit if they are transferred. Jean could also go to management and ask that Mary's retirement be enforced, but she doesn't want to do that either, given Mary's financial situation. Jean is unsure how to proceed but knows that she has to do something.

Questions

1. Is it Jean's responsibility to resolve this conflict?

2. Evaluate Jean's decision using rule, virtue, right, and justice theories.

Experiential Exercises

16.1 Identifying Behavioral Norms

This exercise asks you to identify campus norms at your university. Every organization or group has a set of norms that help determine individuals' behavior. A norm is an unwritten rule for behavior in a group. When a norm is not followed, negative feedback is given. It may include negative comments, stares, harassment, and exclusion.

1. As a group, brainstorm all the norms you can think of in the following areas:
   Dress
   Classroom behavior
   Studying
   Weekend activities
   Living arrangements
   Campus activities
   Dating (who asks whom)
   Relationships with faculty
   Eating on campus versus off campus
   Transportation

2. How did you initially get this information?

3. What happens to students who don't follow these norms?

4. What values can be inferred from these norms?

SOURCE: "Identifying Behavioral Norms" by Dorothy Marcic, *Organizational Behavior: Experiences and Cases* (St. Paul, Minn.: West Publishing, 1989). Reprinted by permission.

16.2 Contrasting Organizational Cultures

To complete this exercise, groups of four or five students should be formed. Each group should select one of the following pairs of organizations:

   American Airlines and Northwest Airlines
   Anheuser-Busch and Coors
   Hewlett-Packard and Xerox
   Albertsons and Winn-Dixie
   Dayton-Hudson (Target) and
      J. C. Penney

Use your university library's resources to gather information about the companies' cultures.

Contrast the cultures of the two organizations using the following dimensions:

   > Strength of the culture.
   > Fit of the culture with the industry's environment.
   > Adaptiveness of the culture.

Which of the two is the better performer? On what did you base your conclusion? How does the performance of each relate to its organizational culture?

SOURCE: Adapted with the permission of The Free Press, a Division of Simon & Schuster, Inc., from *Corporate Culture and Performance* by John P. Kotter and James L. Heskett. Copyright © 1992 by Kotter Associates, Inc., and James L. Heskett.

Biz Flix | Backdraft

Two brothers follow their late father, a legendary Chicago firefighter, and join the department. Stephen "Bull" McCaffrey (Kurt Russell) joins first and rises to the rank of lieutenant. Younger brother Brian (William Baldwin) joins later and becomes a member of Bull's Company 17. Sibling rivalry tarnishes their work relationships, but they continue to successfully fight Chicago fires. Add a plot element about a mysterious arsonist, and you have the basis for an extraordinary film. The intense, unprecedented special effects give the viewer an unparalleled experience of what it is like to fight a fire.

The scene appears early in the *Backdraft* as part of "The First Day" sequence. Brian McCaffrey has graduated from the fire academy, and the fire department has assigned him to his brother's company. This scene shows Company 17 preparing to fight a garment factory fire. The film continues with Brian receiving some harsh first-day lessons as Company 17 successfully fights the fire.

What to Watch for and Ask Yourself:

> What parts of the Chicago fire department culture does this scene show? Does the scene show any cultural artifacts or symbols? If it does, what are they?

> Does the scene show any values or norms that guide the firefighters' behavior? If it does, what are they?

> What does Brian McCaffrey learn on his first workday?

Workplace Video | Fannie Mae: Diversity and Corporate Culture

Fannie Mae is a financial services company that works with primary lenders such as banks, credit unions, mortgage companies, and government housing agencies to increase the availability of home ownership for low- and middle-income Americans. With more than 12 million active mortgages issued to its target clientele of women, minorities, and single parents, Fannie Mae is the nation's largest source of financing for homebuyers. The Washington D.C.-based firm is known for fostering rich diversity among its over 4,000 employees and each individual at the company contributes to the corporate mission of helping families achieve the American dream of home ownership.

Many companies seek to recruit and develop a truly diverse workforce, but at Fannie Mae diversity is a way of life. More than 47 percent of the company's management group, including officers and directors, are minorities, and nearly 54 percent of the company's workforce are women. In addition, the company is pledged to equal opportunity for workers with disabilities, older employees, and gay or lesbian workers. Fannie Mae aims to provide equal opportunity for all employees, and its corporate culture communicates the value of diversity throughout the whole company.

For Fannie Mae, diversity simply makes good business sense. By ensuring the fair treatment of all employees in everything from recruitment and hiring to developing internal talent, managers are able to promote accountability and improve relationships with all stakeholders. As the company has demonstrated, organizations that move beyond rules and regulations to embrace diversity as a core value can expect to reap rewards in employee satisfaction and performance.

Questions

1. *What is diversity, and why is it important to Fannie Mae?*
2. *How can a strong organizational culture help Fannie Mae achieve its objectives?*
3. *Do you think Fannie Mae's culture and emphasis on diversity would be equally effective for companies in other industries? Why or why not?*

Patagonia's Culture

Patagonia designs and manufactures clothing for use in a variety of sporting activities. Founded in the 1960s to make gear for mountain climbing, Patagonia has grown into a company that focuses on producing clothing for alpine climbing, skiing/snowboarding, rock climbing, surfing, fishing, paddling, mountain biking, and trail running. Patagonia tailors its clothing towards enabling its users "to move more freely through the natural world." Patagonia markets its products via the Internet, through catalogs, and in stores located in the United States, Europe, Asia/Oceana, and South America.

Patagonia views its clothing products as tools—tools that are used by various sports enthusiasts to enable them to fully engage in their activities while minimizing intrusiveness on the natural environment. Respect for the natural environment is a key element of Patagonia's core values. The company's commitment to environmental and social responsibility also influences the customers. Approximately 20 percent of Patagonia's customers indicate they buy the company's products because of its reputation and commitment to environmental and social responsibility.

In designing its products, Patagonia seeks to develop the "best tool" for the specific activity. Patagonia defines the "best tool" as the one that is "most functional, with the least material, with the smoothest lines, with strength and lasting qualities."

The company describes itself as "environmentally conscious makers of quality outdoor clothing." In developing and manufacturing the "best tools" in selected lines of sports clothing, Patagonia is very environmentally conscious. The company works vigorously to lessen the negative environmental impact of the materials and processes used in producing its products. This environmental consciousness and activism pervades the company's culture.

Another important value that permeates Patagonia's culture is the expectation for and appreciation of people. Patagonia places a high value on its employees, expecting significant contributions from them while encouraging them to follow their individual passions. Patagonia says, "We prefer the human scale to the corporate, vagabonding to tourism, the quirky and lively to the toned down and flattened out." Clearly, Patagonia places a high value on people and their interests and passions. In describing the types of employees it wants, Patagonia's Web site says, "We're especially interested in people who share our love of the outdoors, our passion for quality and our desire to make a difference." Moreover, Patgonia's employees can leave their jobs for up to two months to work full-time for a not-for-profit organization as long as the activity is in some way tied to social and environmental responsibility.

Patagoniacs

Members of the Patagonia "organizational family" are known as *Patagoniacs*. According to the company's self-description: "Patagoniacs are an eclectic bunch. Some would say we're quirky. Others, less understanding, might say wacky. But we make it work. Combining our different interests and lifestyles enhances our life experience and makes work more fun!"

Ron Hunter, for example, is a Patagoniac who works in the company's Environmental Programs Department. His job involves encouraging environmental activism among colleagues in the retail stores and in the Reno Service Center. He works to raise awareness and promote activism on a variety of environmental issues that are important to Patagonia. Ron uses climbing, skiing, hiking, and paddling to go to the outdoor places he loves. He understands the importance of "getting to know and love a place, while working for its protection."

Another Patagoniac is Chipper Bro Bell, formerly an itinerant freestyle Frisbee world champion. Initially employed as a switchboard operator even though he had no experience, Chipper started Patagonia's organic cotton T-shirt division in 1998. He disliked the paperwork associated with leading this division, however, and subsequently returned to the front desk. In this position "he has elevated the role of gatekeeper to high art, providing the same level of care and attention to the teenage job applicant as he does the visiting dignitary." Chipper also teaches surfing to Patagonia employees and continues his winning ways with a Frisbee, having won the World Beach Frisbee Championship a total of 11 times.

Still another Patagoniac is Kim Stroud, who manages the sample room. She invests a great deal of time and personal resources in caring for sick and injured birds. Kim runs an aviary at Patagonia that houses mostly owls and hawks. A few years ago Kim left the sample room to manage Patagonia's fledgling product development operation. Later she returned to the sample room to manage a team of 16 members, all of whom she treats like family.

Each Patagoniac is different, but all share some common characteristics. Being a Patagoniac means loving the outdoors; being passionately committed to quality, to people, and to the environment; and desiring to make a difference.

Discussion Questions

1. Explain Patagonia's culture using the levels of organizational culture model that is presented in Figure 16.1.
2. Using the concept of a strong culture, explain the nature of Patagonia's culture.
3. Can Patagonia's culture be described as an ethical organizational culture? Explain your answer.

SOURCE: This case was written by Michael K. McCuddy, The Louis S. and Mary L. Morgal Chair of Christian Business Ethics and Professor of Management, College of Business Administration, Valparaiso University. This case was developed from material contained on the Patagonia Web site at http://www.patagonia.com and from the following book: C. Laszlo, *The Sustainable Company: How to Create Last Value Through Social and Environmental Performance*, Washington, DC: Island Press (2002), 57–63.

© Tim Ockenden/EPA/Landov

Career Management

After reading this chapter, you should be able to do the following:

1 Define *career* and *career management*.

2 Explain occupational and organizational choice decisions.

3 Describe the four stages of the career model.

4 Explain the psychological contract.

5 Describe how mentors help organizational newcomers.

6 Describe ways to manage conflicts between work and home.

7 Explain how career anchors help form a career identity.

THINKING AHEAD: VIRGIN GROUP LTD.

A Career in the Airline Industry

By the age of fifteen, John Riordan knew there was something a little strange about the airline business. Even as a teenager, he remembers looking around a plane, counting the passengers, and thinking, "I paid a hundred bucks for this . . . they can't be making any money." Before long, however, John learned the truth about airline pricing: many of the people on the plane paid far more for their seats than he had. And this odd pricing model intrigued John.

John never intended to work for an airline, but his first job happened to be with USAir (now US Airways) in the early 1990s. At USAir, he was exposed to all kinds of marketing challenges, including the arrival of low fares from Southwest Airlines on the East Coast. While at USAir, John also ran the frequent-flier program. He even worked briefly (eight weeks) for a dot-com firm before a friend at USAir recommended him for a position at Virgin. John jumped at the chance to get back into the airline industry, especially with Virgin, which he refers to as "one of the best gigs in the airline business." He took the job of vice president of Marketing and Telephone Sales for North America in 1999.

Working at Virgin is different from working anywhere else, John says. Among the unique marketing ideas he's come up with were a giveaway of Handspring PDAs with the Virgin logo on them and the use of "wild postings" around Manhattan to encourage travel to London. Virgin recently announced a new transatlantic business class in which each seat pivots and folds down flat to make a bed. If discounter Southwest Airlines is the Sam Walton of the industry, Virgin is poised to become the P.T. Barnum of the field through constantly finding new ways to make dull airline flights more entertaining.[1]

Careers as Joint Responsibilities

1. Define *career* and *career management*.

Career management is an integral activity in our lives. There are three reasons why it is important to understand careers. First, if we know what to look forward to over the course of our careers, we can take a proactive approach to planning and managing them. Second, as managers, we need to understand the experiences of our employees and colleagues as they pass through the various stages of careers over their life spans. Third, career management is good business. It makes good financial sense to have highly trained employees keep up with their fields so that organizations can protect valuable investments in human resources.

A *career* is a pattern of work-related experiences that span the course of a person's life.[2] The two elements in a career are the objective element and the subjective element.[3] The objective element of the career is the observable, concrete environment. For example, you can manage a career by getting training to improve your skills. In contrast, the subjective element involves your perception of the situation. Rather than getting training (an objective element), you might change your aspirations (a subjective element). Thus, both objective events and the individual's perception of those events are important in defining a career.

Career management is a lifelong process of learning about self, jobs, and organizations; setting personal career goals; developing strategies for achieving the goals; and revising the goals based on work and life experiences.[4] Whose responsibility is career management? It is tempting to place the responsibility on individuals, and it is appropriate. However, it is also the organization's duty to form partnerships with individuals in managing their careers. Careers are made up of exchanges between individuals and organizations. Inherent in these exchanges is the idea of reciprocity, or give and take.

The balance between individuals and organizations in terms of managing careers has shifted in recent times. With restructuring and reengineering has come a new perspective of careers and career management.

career

The pattern of work-related experiences that span the course of a person's life.

career management

A lifelong process of learning about self, jobs, and organizations; setting personal career goals; developing strategies for achieving the goals, and revising the goals based on work and life experiences.

The New Career

The time of the fast track to the top of the hierarchical organization is past. Also gone is the idea of lifetime employment in a single organization. Today's environment demands leaner organizations. The paternalistic attitude that organizations take care of employees no longer exists. Individuals now take on more responsibility for managing their own careers. The concept of the career is undergoing a paradigm shift, as shown in Table 17.1. The old career is giving way to a new career characterized by discrete exchange, occupational excellence, organizational empowerment, and project allegiance.[5]

Discrete exchange occurs when an organization gains productivity while a person gains work experience. It is a short-term arrangement that recognizes that job skills change in value and that renegotiation of the relationship must occur as conditions change. This contrasts sharply with the mutual loyalty contract of the old career paradigm in which employee loyalty was exchanged for job security.

Occupational excellence means continually honing skills that can be marketed across organizations. The individual identifies more with the occupation (I am an engineer) than the organization (I am an IBMer). In contrast, the old one-employer focus meant that training was company specific rather than preparing the person for future job opportunities.

TABLE 17.1   The New versus Old Career Paradigms

NEW CAREER PARADIGM	OLD CAREER PARADIGM
Discrete exchange means:	**The mutual loyalty contract meant:**
• explicit exchange of specified rewards in return for task performance	• implicit trading of employee compliance in return for job security
• basing job rewards on the current market value of the work being performed	• allowing job rewards to be routinely deferred into the future
• engaging in disclosure and renegotiation on both sides as the employment relationship unfolds	• leaving the mutual loyalty assumptions as a political barrier to renegotiation
• exercising flexibility as each party's interests and market circumstances change	• assuming employment and career opportunities are standardized and prescribed by the firm
Occupational excellence means:	**The one-employer focus meant:**
• performance of current jobs in return for developing new occupational expertise	• relying on the firm to specify jobs and their associated occupational skill base
• employees identifying with and focusing on what is happening in their adopted occupation	• employees identifying with and focusing on what is happening in their particular firm
• emphasizing occupational skill development over the local demands of any particular firm	• forgoing technical or functional development in favor of firm-specific learning
• getting training in anticipation of future job opportunities; having training lead jobs	• doing the job first to be entitled to new training; making training follow jobs
Organizational empowerment means:	**The top-down firm meant:**
• strategic positioning is dispersed to separate business units	• strategic direction is subordinated to "corporate headquarters"
• everyone is responsible for adding value and improving competitiveness	• competitiveness and added value are the responsibility of corporate experts
• business units are free to cultivate their own markets	• business unit marketing depends on the corporate agenda
• new enterprise, spinoffs, and alliance building are broadly encouraged	• independent enterprise is discouraged, and likely to be viewed as disloyalty
Project allegiance means:	**Corporate allegiance meant:**
• shared employer and employee commitment to the overarching goal of the project	• project goals are subordinated to corporate policy and organizational constraints
• a successful outcome of the project is more important than holding the project team together	• being loyal to the work group can be more important than the project itself
• financial and reputational rewards stem directly from project outcomes	• financial and reputational rewards stem from being a "good soldier" regardless of results
• upon project completion, organization and reporting arrangements are broken up	• social relationships within corporate boundaries are actively encouraged

Organizational empowerment means that power flows down to business units and in turn to employees. Employees are expected to add value and help the organization remain competitive by being innovative and creative. The old top-down approach meant that control and strategizing were only done by the top managers, and individual initiative might be viewed as disloyalty or disrespect.

Project allegiance means that both individuals and organizations are committed to the successful completion of a project. The firm's gain is the project outcome; the individual's gain is experience and shared success. On project completion, the project team breaks up as individuals move on to new projects. Under the old paradigm, corporate allegiance was paramount. The needs of projects were overshadowed by corporate policies and procedures. Work groups were long term, and keeping the group together was often a more important goal than project completion.

While spending an entire career in one company was the old career model, times have changed, and job hopping and company hopping are becoming more the norm. You can expect to change jobs many times in your career. College graduates typically change jobs four times in their first ten years of work, a number that is projected to increase. At that rate, you could easily hold twenty different jobs in a typical career. In fact, the stigma associated with frequent job changes has largely disappeared. Some recruiters now view a résumé littered with different companies and locations as a sign of a smart self-promoter. The key is to know "why" you are making each job move, including both what it will cost and gain for you. By presenting your job-hopping career path as a growth process, rather than a series of impulsive changes, you may set yourself apart in the minds of recruiters.[6] Individuals must prepare for the new career and manage their careers with change in mind.

Becoming Your Own Career Coach

The best way to stay employed is to see yourself as being in business for yourself, even if you work for someone else. Know what skills you can package for other employers and what you can do to ensure that your skills are state of the art. Organizations need employees who have acquired multiple skills and are adept at more than one job. Employers want employees who have demonstrated competence in dealing with change.[7] To be successful, think of organizational change not as a disruption to your work but instead as the central focus of your work. You will also need to develop self-reliance, as we discussed in Chapter 7, to deal effectively with the stress of change. Self-reliant individuals take an interdependent approach to relationships and are comfortable both giving and receiving support from others.

The people who will be most successful in the new career paradigm are individuals who are flexible, team oriented (rather than hierarchical), energized by change, and tolerant of ambiguity. Those who will become frustrated in the new career are individuals who are rigid in their thinking and learning styles and who have high needs for control. A commitment to continuous, lifelong learning will prevent you from becoming a professional dinosaur.[8] An intentional and purposeful commitment to taking charge of your professional life will be necessary in managing the new career.

Emotional Intelligence and Career Success

Almost 40 percent of new managers fail within the first eighteen months on the job. What are the reasons for the failure? Newly hired managers flame out because they fail to build good relationships with peers and subordinates (82 percent of failures), are confused or uncertain about what their bosses expect (58 percent of failures), lack internal political skills (50 percent of failures), and are unable to achieve the two or three most important objectives of the new job (47 percent of failures).[9] You'll note that these failures are all due to a lack of human skills.

In Chapter 13, we introduced the concept of emotional intelligence (EI) as an important determinant of conflict management skills. Daniel Goleman argues that emotional intelligence is a constellation of the qualities that mark a star performer at work. These attributes include self-awareness, self-control, trustworthiness, confidence, and empathy, among others. Goleman's belief is that emotional competencies are twice as important to people's success today as raw intelligence or technical know-how. He also argues that the further up the corporate ranks you go, the more important emotional intelligence becomes.[10, 11] Employers, either consciously or unconsciously, look for emotional intelligence during the hiring process. In addition to traditionally recognized competencies such as communication and social skills, interns with higher levels of emotional intelligence are rated as more hireable by their host firms than those with lower levels of EI.[12] Neither gender seems to have cornered the market on EI. Both men and women who can demonstrate high levels of EI are seen as particularly gifted and may be promoted more rapidly.[13]

Emotional intelligence is important to career success in many cultures. A recent study in Australia found that high levels of emotional intelligence are associated with job success. EI improves one's ability to work with other team members and to provide high-quality customer service, and workers with high EI are more likely to take steps to develop their skills. This confirms U.S. studies that portray high emotional intelligence as an important attribute for the upwardly mobile worker.[14] You can assess your own emotional intelligence using You 17.1.

L'Oreal has found emotional intelligence to be a profitable selection tool. Salespeople selected on the basis of emotional competence outsold those selected using the old method by an average of $91,370 per year. As an added bonus for the firm, these salespeople also had 63 percent less turnover during the first year than those selected in the traditional way.[15]

The good news is that emotional intelligence can be developed and does tend to improve throughout life. Some companies are providing training in emotional intelligence competencies. American Express began sending managers through an emotional competence training program. It found that trained managers outperformed those who lacked this training. In the year after completing the course, managers trained in emotional competence grew their businesses by an average of 18.1 percent compared to 16.2 percent for those businesses whose managers were untrained.[16] In The Real World 17.1, see how The Trump Organization used EI in its television series *The Apprentice* and how Johnson & Johnson uses EI in the real world.

Before turning to the stages of an individual's career, we will examine the process of preparation for the world of work. Prior to beginning a career, individuals must make several important decisions.

Preparing for the World of Work

When viewed from one perspective, you might say that we spend our youth preparing for the world of work. Educational experiences and personal life experiences help an individual develop the skills and maturity needed to enter a career. Preparation for work is a developmental process that gradually unfolds over time.[17] As the time approaches for beginning a career, individuals face two difficult decisions: the choice of occupation and the choice of organization.

2. Explain occupational and organizational choice decisions.

Occupational Choice

In choosing an occupation, individuals assess their needs, values, abilities, and preferences and attempt to match them with an occupation that provides a fit.

What's Your EI at Work?

Answering the following 25 questions will allow you to rate your social skills and self-awareness.

EI, the social equivalent of IQ, is complex in no small part because it depends on some pretty slippery variables—including your innate compatibility, or lack thereof, with the people who happen to be your coworkers. But if you want to get a rough idea of how your EI stacks up, this quiz will help.

As honestly as you can, estimate how you rate in the eyes of peers, bosses, and subordinates on each of the following traits, on a scale of one to four, with four representing strong agreement, and one, strong disagreement.

_____ 1. I usually stay composed, positive, and unflappable even in trying moments.

_____ 2. I can think clearly and stay focused on the task at hand under pressure.

_____ 3. I am able to admit my own mistakes.

_____ 4. I usually or always meet commitments and keep promises.

_____ 5. I hold myself accountable for meeting my goals.

_____ 6. I'm organized and careful in my work.

_____ 7. I regulary seek out fresh ideas from a wide variety of sources.

_____ 8. I'm good at generating new ideas.

_____ 9. I can smoothly handle multiple demands and changing priorities.

_____ 10. I'm results-oriented, with a strong drive to meet my objectives.

_____ 11. I like to set challenging goals and take calculated risks to reach them.

_____ 12. I'm always trying to learn how to improve my performance, including asking advice from people younger than I am.

_____ 13. I readily make sacrifices to meet an important organizational goal.

_____ 14. The company's mission is something I understand and can identify with.

_____ 15. The values of my team—or of our division or department, or the company—influence my decisions and clarify the choices I make.

_____ 16. I actively seek out opportunities to further the overall goals of the organization and enlist others to help me.

_____ 17. I pursue goals beyond what's required or expected of me in my current job.

_____ 18. Obstacles and setbacks may delay me a little, but they don't stop me.

_____ 19. Cutting through red tape and bending outdated rules are sometimes necessary.

_____ 20. I seek fresh perspectives, even if that means trying something totally new.

_____ 21. My impulses or distressing emotions don't often get the best of me at work.

_____ 22. I can change tactics quickly when circumstances change.

_____ 23. Pursuing new information is my best bet for cutting down on uncertainty and findings ways to do things better.

_____ 24. I usually don't attribute setbacks to a personal flaw (mine or someone else's).

_____ 25. I operate from an expectation of success rather than a fear of failure.

A score below 70 indicates a problem. If your total is somewhere in the basement, don't despair: EI is not unimprovable. "Emotional intelligence can be learned, and in fact we are each building it, in varying degrees, throughout life. It's sometimes called maturity," says Daniel Goleman. "EI is nothing more or less than a collection of tools that we can sharpen to help ensure our own survival."

Personality plays a role in the selection of occupation. John Holland's theory of occupational choice contends that there are six types of personalities and that each personality is characterized by a set of interests and values.[18] Holland's six types are as follows:

The Trump Organization and Johnson & Johnson: Emotional Intelligence Can Make or Break Your Career

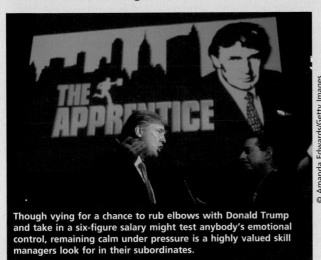

Though vying for a chance to rub elbows with Donald Trump and take in a six-figure salary might test anybody's emotional control, remaining calm under pressure is a highly valued skill managers look for in their subordinates.

You may have seen the hit show *The Apprentice* in which candidates compete for a position working directly for Donald Trump. Winners of each season's competition are granted the career of a lifetime with The Trump Organization and a massive six-figure salary. Candidates for the dream job are eliminated by Trump with his characteristic chopping hand motion and the now famous line, "You're fired!" Ereka Vetrini was one recipient of Trump's nonverbal and verbal firing. Trump said that Ereka, as a team leader, appeared frazzled and overwhelmed by her team's inability to sell enough Trump-brand bottled water, her team's challenge. Her teammates contended that she came unglued under stress and that her frazzled behavior affected the team's performance. In short, she was fired because of her inability to manage her emotions. But *The Apprentice* is only a TV show. What about the real world?

Peter Benton, former vice president at Johnson & Johnson, knows the value of emotional intelligence. He honed his emotional competencies by doing a 360-degree assessment of his EI, getting feedback from his boss, peers, and employees. Among the skills he developed as a result of the feedback were more effective leadership behaviors and the ability to remain calm under pressure. He knew his efforts to develop his EI were paying off when an employee noted that Benton was acting differently and that the employee felt more like they were a team.

Emotional intelligence doesn't mean holding in emotions; it means managing them for the benefit of yourself and others.

SOURCES: NBC, "The Apprentice—Weekly Recaps," http://www.nbc.com/nbc/The_Apprentice/weekly_recap/week08c.shtml; K. Maher, "Emotional Intelligence Is a Factor in Promotions," *The Wall Street Journal* (March 16, 2004): B8, http://www.collegejournal.com/columnists/thejungle/20040322-maher.html.

1. *Realistic:* stable, persistent, and materialistic.

2. *Artistic:* imaginative, emotional, and impulsive.

3. *Investigative:* curious, analytical, and independent.

4. *Enterprising:* ambitious, energetic, and adventurous.

5. *Social:* generous, cooperative, and sociable.

6. *Conventional:* efficient, practical, and obedient.

Holland also states that occupations can be classified using this typology. For example, realistic occupations include mechanic, restaurant server, and mechanical engineer. Artistic occupations include architect, voice coach, and interior designer. Investigative occupations include physicist, surgeon, and economist. Real estate agent, human resource manager, and lawyer are enterprising occupations. The social occupations include counselor, social worker, and member of the clergy. Conventional occupations include word processor, accountant, and data entry operator.

Holland's typology has been used to predict career choices with a variety of international participants, including Mexicans, Australians, Indians, New Zealanders, Taiwanese, Pakistanis, South Africans, and Germans.[19]

An assumption that drives Holland's theory is that people choose occupations that match their own personalities. People who fit Holland's social types are those who prefer jobs that are highly interpersonal in nature. They may see careers in physical and math sciences, for example, as not affording the opportunity for interpersonal relationships.[20] To fulfill the desire for interpersonal work, they may instead gravitate toward jobs in customer service or counseling in order to better match their personalities.

Although personality is a major influence on occupational choice, it is not the only influence. There are a host of other influences, including social class, parents' occupations, economic conditions, and geography.[21] Once a choice of occupation has been made, another major decision individuals face is the choice of organizations.

Organizational Choice and Entry

Several theories of how individuals choose organizations exist, ranging from theories that postulate very logical and rational choice processes to those that offer seemingly irrational processes. Expectancy theory, which we discussed in Chapter 5, can be applied to organizational choice.[22] According to the expectancy theory view, individuals choose organizations that maximize positive outcomes and avoid negative outcomes. Job candidates calculate the probability that an organization will provide a certain outcome and then compare the probabilities across organizations.

Other theories propose that people select organizations in a much less rational fashion. Job candidates may satisfice, that is, select the first organization that meets one or two important criteria and then justify their choice by distorting their perceptions.[23]

The method of selecting an organization varies greatly among individuals and may reflect a combination of the expectancy theory and theories that postulate less rational approaches. Entry into an organization is further complicated by the conflicts that occur between individuals and organizations during the process. Figure 17.1 illustrates these potential conflicts. The arrows in the figure illustrate four types of conflicts that can occur as individuals choose organizations and organizations choose individuals. The first two conflicts (1 and 2) occur between individuals and organizations. The first is a conflict between the organization's effort to attract candidates and the individual's choice of an organization. The individual needs complete and accurate information to make a good choice, but the organization may not provide it. The organization is trying to attract a large number of qualified candidates, so it presents itself in an overly attractive way.

The second conflict is between the individual's attempt to attract several organizations and the organization's need to select the best candidate. Individuals want good offers, so they do not disclose their faults. They describe their preferred job in terms of the organization's opening instead of describing a job they would really prefer.

Conflicts 3 and 4 are conflicts internal to the two parties. The third is a conflict between the organization's desire to recruit a large pool of qualified applicants and the organization's need to select and retain the best candidate. In recruiting, organizations tend to give only positive information, and this results in mismatches between the individual and the organization. The fourth

FIGURE 17.1   Conflicts during Organizational Entry

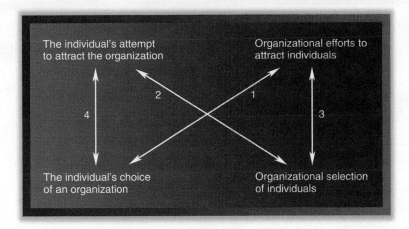

The individual's attempt to attract the organization

Organizational efforts to attract individuals

2

1

4

3

The individual's choice of an organization

Organizational selection of individuals

SOURCE: Figure in L. W. Porter, E. E. Lawler III, and J. R. Hackman, *Behavior in Organizations*, New York: McGraw-Hill, Inc., 1975, page 134. Reproduced with permission of The McGraw-Hill Companies.

conflict is internal to the individual; it is between the individual's desire for several job offers and the need to make a good choice. When individuals present themselves as overly attractive, they risk being offered positions that are poor fits in terms of their skills and career goals.[24]

The organizational choice and entry process is very complex due to the nature of these conflicts. Partial responsibility for preventing these conflicts rests with the individual. Individuals should conduct thorough research of the organization through published reports and industry analyses. Individuals also should conduct a careful self-analysis and be as honest as possible with organizations to ensure a good match. The job interview process can be stressful, but also fun. In The Real World 17.2, you can see the unusual questions that Microsoft uses when interviewing job applicants.

Partial responsibility for good matches also rests with the organization. One way of avoiding the conflicts and mismatches is to utilize a realistic job preview.

Realistic Job Previews

The conflicts just discussed may result in unrealistic expectations on the part of the candidate. People entering the world of work may expect, for example, that they will receive explicit directions from their boss, only to find that they are left with ambiguity about how to do the job. They may expect that promotions will be based on performance and find that promotions are based mainly on political considerations. Some new hires expect to be given managerial responsibilities right away; however, this is not often the case.

Giving potential employees a realistic picture of the job they are applying for is known as a *realistic job preview (RJP)*. When candidates are given both positive and negative information, they can make more effective job choices. Traditional recruiting practices produce unrealistically high expectations, which produce low job satisfaction when these unrealistic expectations hit the reality of the job situation. RJPs tend to create expectations that are much closer to reality, and they increase the numbers of candidates who withdraw from further

© Robert McNath/Idaho State Police

Though television shows may dramatize and even glamorize the jobs of state troopers, one must keep in mind that the job also entails mundane tasks and paperwork.

realistic job preview (RJP)

Both positive and negative information given to potential employees about the job they are applying for, thereby giving them a realistic picture of the job.

Microsoft: Crazy Interview Questions

Which question are you more likely to hear in a job interview?

How much work experience do you have?

or

If you are on a boat and toss a suitcase overboard, will the water level rise or fall?

As you prepare for job interviews, you probably consider possible answers to questions dealing with your qualifications, experience, and skills. But if you are interviewing with Microsoft or any of several other *Fortune 500* firms, you might just get questions like these (answers are at the end):

Why are manhole covers round rather than square?

How much does all the ice in a hockey rink weigh?

Mike and Todd have $21 between them. Mike has $20 more than Todd. How much does each one have? You cannot use fractions in your answer.

Microsoft receives about 12,000 résumés per month, or enough applicants to replace its entire workforce every four months! And because Microsoft so highly values creativity and problem-solving skills, it's hardly surprising that in the course of sifting through this mountain of applicants it frequently resorts to unusual questions.

Some researchers wonder just how effective these questions are. Given the questionable validity of interviews in general, concerns have been raised that questions like these don't really relate to on-the-job success. But at Microsoft and elsewhere, a firm belief exists that the problem-solving skills required to answer these odd questions are the very same skills needed to compete in the ever-changing marketplace of information technology.

So as you prepare for that next interview, be prepared for *any* question, and be ready to think on your feet. After all, some of the best companies use some of the oddest questions.

Answers:

a. Tossing the suitcase over the side will not raise or lower the water level, as long as the suitcase floats.

b. Manhole covers are round because a round cover can't fall in the hole, will fit no matter which direction it is facing, and can be rolled from place to place. A possible alternative answer is "because the holes are round."

c. The ice on a regulation hockey rink weighs about 60,000 pounds.

d. Mike has $20.50 and Todd has $0.50; this answer is mathematically correct and is in fact the only correct answer to this question. This question not only tests the candidate's math skills but also whether or not she will stand her ground when told she is wrong.

For more Microsoft-style interview questions, just type "Microsoft interview questions" into your search engine.

SOURCE: W. Poundstone, *How Would You Move Mount Fiji: Microsoft's Cult of the Puzzle* (Boston, MA: Little, Brown and Company, 2003).

consideration.[25] This occurs because candidates with unrealistic expectations tend to look for employment elsewhere. The Idaho State Police Department's on-line employment site provides an RJP, which begins with these words: " . . . you should put aside the images you have seen on television or in the movies and read carefully about the tasks an Idaho State Police Trooper performs."[26] It then goes on to provide an exhaustive list of tasks ranging from the exciting (manhunts and serving warrants) to the mundane (inspecting heavy trucks), as well as noting that troopers currently work rotating ten-hour shifts. While the site concludes with a summary of the rewards that accompany the job, it clearly notes that the work is at times tedious and far less glamorous than might be expected.

RJPs can also be thought of as inoculation against disappointment. If new recruits know what to expect in the new job, they can prepare for the experience. Newcomers who are not given RJPs may find that their jobs don't measure up to their expectations. They may then believe that their employer was deceitful in the hiring process, become unhappy and mishandle job demands, and ultimately leave the organization.[27]

Job candidates who receive RJPs view the organization as honest and also have a greater ability to cope with the demands of the job.[28] RJPs perform another important function: uncertainty reduction.[29] Knowing what to expect, both good and bad, gives a newcomer a sense of control that is important to job satisfaction and performance.

With today's emphasis on ethics, organizations need to do all they can to be seen as operating consistently and honestly. Realistic job previews are one way in which companies can provide ethically required information to newcomers. Ultimately, RJPs result in more effective matches, lower turnover, and higher organizational commitment and job satisfaction.[30] There is much to gain, and little to risk, in providing realistic job information.[31]

In summary, the needs and goals of individuals and organizations can clash during entry into the organization. To avoid potential mismatches, individuals should conduct a careful self-analysis and provide accurate information about themselves to potential employers. Organizations should present realistic job previews to show candidates both the positive and negative aspects of the job, along with the potential career paths available to the employee.

After entry into the organization, individuals embark on their careers. A person's work life can be traced through successive stages, as we see in the career stage model.

The Career Stage Model

A common way of understanding careers is viewing them as a series of stages through which individuals pass during their working lives.[32] Figure 17.2 presents the career stage model, which will form the basis for our discussion in the remainder of this chapter.[33] The career stage model shows that individuals pass through four stages in their careers: establishment, advancement, maintenance, and withdrawal. It is important to note that the age ranges shown are approximations; that is, the timing of the career transitions varies greatly among individuals.

Establishment is the first stage of a person's career. The activities that occur in this stage center around learning the job and fitting into the organization and occupation. *Advancement* is a high achievement-oriented stage in which people focus on increasing their competence. The *maintenance* stage finds the individual trying to maintain productivity while evaluating progress toward career goals. The *withdrawal* stage involves contemplation of retirement or possible career change.

Along the horizontal axis in Figure 17.2 are the corresponding life stages for each career stage. These life stages are based on the pioneering research on adult development conducted by Levinson and his colleagues. Levinson conducted extensive biographical interviews to trace the life stages of men and women. He interpreted his research in two books, *The Seasons of a Man's Life* and *The Seasons of a Woman's Life*.[34] Levinson's life stages are characterized by an alternating pattern of stability and transition.[35] Throughout the discussion of career stages that follows, we weave in the transitions of Levinson's life

3. Describe the four stages of the career model.

establishment
The first stage of a person's career in which the person learns the job and begins to fit into the organization and occupation.

advancement
The second, high achievement-oriented career stage in which people focus on increasing their competence.

maintenance
The third stage in an individual's career in which the individual tries to maintain productivity while evaluating progress toward career goals.

withdrawal
The final stage in an individual's career in which the individual contemplates retirement or possible career changes.

FIGURE 17.2   The Career Stage Model

17.2

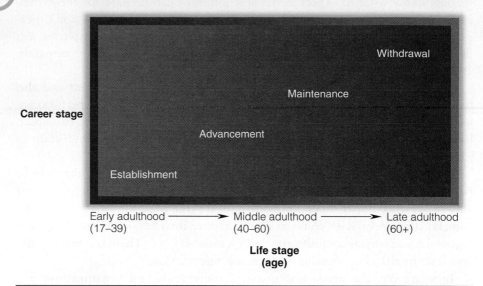

Career stage

Withdrawal

Maintenance

Advancement

Establishment

Early adulthood ——————➤ Middle adulthood ——————➤ Late adulthood
(17–39)   (40–60)   (60+)

**Life stage
(age)**

stages. Work and personal life are inseparable, and to understand a person's career experiences, we must also examine the unfolding of the person's personal experiences.

You can see that adult development provides unique challenges for the individual and that there may be considerable overlap between the stages. Now let us examine each career stage in detail.

The Establishment Stage

During the establishment stage, the individual begins a career as a newcomer to the organization. This is a period of great dependence on others, as the individual is learning about the job and the organization. The establishment stage usually occurs during the beginning of the early adulthood years (ages eighteen to twenty-five). During this time, Levinson notes, an important personal life transition into adulthood occurs: the individual begins to separate from his or her parents and becomes less emotionally and financially dependent. Following this period is a fairly stable time of exploring the adult role and settling down.

The transition from school to work is a part of the establishment stage. Many graduates find the transition to be a memorable experience. The following description was provided by a newly graduated individual who went to work at a large public utility:

We all tried to one-up each other about jobs we had just accepted . . . bragging that we had the highest salary, the best management training program, the most desirable coworkers, the most upward mobility . . . and believed we were destined to become future corporate leaders. . . . Every Friday after work we met for happy hour to visit and relate the events of the week. It is interesting to look at how the mood of those happy hours changed over the first few months . . . at first, we jockeyed for position in terms of telling stories about how great these new jobs were, or how weird our bosses were. . . . Gradually, things quieted down at happy hour. The mood went from "Wow, isn't this great" to

"What in the world have we gotten ourselves into?" There began to be general agreement that business wasn't all it was cracked up to be.[36]

Establishment is thus a time of big transitions in both personal and work life. At work, three major tasks face the newcomer: negotiating effective psychological contracts, managing the stress of socialization, and making a transition from organizational outsider to organizational insider.

Psychological Contracts

A *psychological contract* is an implicit agreement between the individual and the organization that specifies what each is expected to give and receive in the relationship.[37] Individuals expect to receive salary, status, advancement opportunities, and challenging work to meet their needs. Organizations expect to receive time, energy, talents, and loyalty in order to meet their goals. Working out the psychological contract with the organization begins with entry, but the contract is modified as the individual proceeds through the career.

Psychological contracts form and exist between individuals.[38] During the establishment stage, newcomers form attachment relationships with many people in the organization. Working out effective psychological contracts within each relationship is important. Newcomers need social support in many forms and from many sources. Table 17.2 shows the type of psychological contracts, in the form of social support, that newcomers may work out with key insiders in the organization.

One common newcomer concern, for example, is whose behavior to watch for cues to appropriate behavior. Senior colleagues can provide modeling support

4. Explain the psychological contract.

psychological contract
An implicit agreement between an individual and an organization that specifies what each is expected to give and receive in the relationship.

	TABLE 17.2	Newcomer–Insider Psychological Contracts for Social Support	
TYPE OF SUPPORT	**FUNCTION OF SUPPORTIVE ATTACHMENTS**	**NEWCOMER CONCERN**	**EXAMPLES OF INSIDER RESPONSE/ ACTION**
Protection from stressors	Direct assistance in terms of resources, time, labor, or environmental modification	What are the major risks/ threats in this environment?	*Supervisor* cues newcomer to risks/threats.
Informational	Provision of information necessary for managing demands	What do I need to know to get things done?	*Mentor* provides advice on informal political climate in organization.
Evaluative	Feedback on both personal and professional role performances	How am I doing?	*Supervisor* provides day-to-day performance feedback during first week on new job.
Modeling	Evidence of behavioral standards provided through modeled behavior	Whom do I follow?	Newcomer is apprenticed to *senior colleague*.
Emotional	Empathy, esteem, caring, or love	Do I matter? Who cares if I'm here or not?	*Other newcomers* empathize with and encourage individual when reality shock sets in.

SOURCE: Table from D. L. Nelson, J. C. Quick, and J. R. Joplin, "Psychological Contracting and Newcomer Socialization: An Attachment Theory Foundation," from *Journal of Social Behavior and Personality* 6 (1991): 65. Reprinted with permission.

by displaying behavior that the newcomer can emulate. This is only one of many types of support that newcomers need. Newcomers should contract with others to receive each of the needed types of support so that they can adjust to the new job. Organizations should help newcomers form relationships early and should encourage the psychological contracting process between newcomers and insiders. The influence of a broken psychological contract is often felt even after an employee leaves a job. Laid-off employees who feel that a psychological contract breach has occurred are not only unhappy with their former firms but may also be both more cynical and less trusting of their new employers.[39]

The Stress of Socialization

In Chapter 16 on organizational culture and socialization, we discussed three phases that newcomers go through in adjusting to a new organization: anticipatory socialization, encounter, and change and acquisition. (You may want to refer to Figure 16.2 for review.) Another way to look at these three phases is to examine the kinds of stress newcomers experience during each stage.[40]

In anticipatory socialization, the newcomer is gathering information from various sources about the job and organization. The likely stressor in this stage is ambiguity, so the provision of accurate information is important. During this stage, the psychological contract is formed. It is essential that both parties go into it with good intentions of keeping up their end of the agreement.

In the encounter phase, the demands of the job in terms of the role, task, interpersonal relationships, and physical setting become apparent to the newcomer. The expectations formed in anticipatory socialization may clash with the realities of organizational life, and reality shock can occur.[41] This very predictble "surprise" reaction may find the new employee thinking, "What have I gotten myself into?"[42] The degree of reality shock depends on the expectations formed in the anticipatory socialization stage. If these expectations are unrealistic or unmet, reality shock may be a problem.

While most organizations allow some time for newcomers to adapt, as little as two to three months may be allotted for new hires to reach some level of independence. This unwritten rule will mean that new hires who cannot quickly get up to speed on the organization's and their workgroup's norms and procedures will quickly find themselves experiencing negative feedback from coworkers.[43]

In the change and acquisition phase, the newcomer begins to master the demands of the job. Newcomers need to feel that they have some means of control over job demands.

Easing the Transition from Outsider to Insider

Being a newcomer in an organization is stressful. The process of becoming a functioning member of the organization takes time, and the newcomer needs support in making the transition. A successful transition from outsider to insider can be ensured if both the newcomer and the organization work together to smooth the way.

INDIVIDUAL ACTIONS Newcomers should ask about the negative side of the job if they were not given a realistic job preview. In particular, newcomers should ask about the stressful aspects of the job. Other employees are good sources of this information. Research has shown that newcomers who underestimate the stressfulness of job demands do not adjust well.[44] In addition, newcomers should present honest and accurate information about their own weaknesses. Both actions can promote good matches.

During the encounter phase, newcomers must prepare for reality shock. Realizing that slight depression is natural when adjusting to a new job can help alleviate the distress. Newcomers can also plan ways to cope with job stress ahead of time. If, for example, long assignments away from home are typical, newcomers can plan for these trips in advance. Part of the plan for dealing with reality shock should include ways to seek support from others. Networking with other newcomers who empathize can help individuals cope with the stress of the new job.

In the change and acquisition stage of adjusting to a new organization, newcomers should set realistic goals and take credit for the successes that occur as they master the job. Newcomers must seek feedback on job performance from their supervisors and coworkers. Organizations also can assist newcomers in their transition from outsiders to insiders.

ORGANIZATIONAL ACTIONS Realistic job previews start the relationship between the newcomer and the organization with integrity and honesty. Careful recruitment and selection of new employees can help ensure good matches.

During the encounter phase, organizations should provide early job assignments that present opportunities for the new recruit to succeed. Newcomers who experience success in training gain increased self-efficacy and adjust to the new job more effectively.[45] Newcomers who face early job challenges successfully tend to be higher performers later in their careers.[46] Providing encouragement and feedback to the newcomer during this stage is crucial. The immediate supervisor, peers, other newcomers, and support staff are important sources of support during encounter.[47] Otis Elevator has experimented with a program in which new hires, regardless of their specific job function (sales, manufacturing, finance, etc.), all complete a six-week training course covering all aspects of the elevator industry. During this program, they not only visit Otis's manufacturing and headquarters sites, they also visit construction sites to experience the gritty world of elevator installation.[48]

In contrast, some firms do little to help newcomers adjust. A recent survey of information technology firms found that only 38 percent have formal company policies regarding training for new employees. The remaining 62 percent answered that when it comes to new-hire training, they simply "wing it."[49]

During the change and acquisition phase, rewards are important. Organizations should tie the newcomers' rewards as explicitly as possible to performance.[50] Feedback is also crucial. Newcomers should receive daily, consistent feedback. This communicates that the organization is concerned about their progress and wants to help them learn the ropes along the way.

The establishment stage marks the beginning of an individual's career. Its noteworthy transitions include the transition from school to work, from dependence on parents to dependence on self, from organizational outsider to organizational insider. Individuals who successfully complete the establishment stage go through many positive changes, including increased self-confidence, interpersonal skills, and self-knowledge.[51] Once they have met their need to fit in, individuals move on to the advancement stage of their careers.

The Advancement Stage

The advancement stage is a period when many individuals strive for achievement. They seek greater responsibility and authority and strive for upward mobility. Usually around age thirty, an important life transition occurs.[52] Individuals reassess their goals and feel the need to make changes in their career dreams. The transition at age thirty is followed by a period of stability during which the individual tries to find a role in adult society and wants to succeed in the career. During this stage, several issues are important: exploring career paths, finding a mentor, working out dual-career partnerships, and managing conflicts between work and personal life.

Career Paths and Career Ladders

career path

A sequence of job experiences that an employee moves along during his or her career.

Career paths are sequences of job experiences along which employees move during their careers.[53] At the advancement stage, individuals examine their career dreams and the paths they must follow to achieve those dreams. For example, suppose a person's dream is to become a top executive in the pharmaceutical industry. She majors in chemistry in undergraduate school and takes a job with a nationally recognized firm. After she has adjusted to her job as a quality control chemist, she reevaluates her plan and decides that further education is necessary. She plans to pursue an MBA degree part-time, hoping to gain expertise in management. From there, she hopes to be promoted to a supervisory position within her current firm. If this does not occur within five years, she will consider moving to a different pharmaceutical company. An alternate route would be to try to transfer to a sales positon, from which she might advance into management.

The career paths of many women have moved from working in large organizations to starting their own businesses. Currently, there are 10.6 million women-owned firms in the United States, comprising almost half of all privately held firms in the country. What is the motivation for this exodus to entrepreneurship? The main reasons are to seek additional challenge and self-fulfillment and to have more self-determination and freedom.[54]

career ladder

A structured series of job positions through which an individual progresses in an organization.

A *career ladder* is a structured series of job positions through which an individual progresses in an organization. For example, at Southwestern Bell, it is customary to move through a series of alternating line and staff supervisory assignments to advance toward upper management. Supervisors in customer service might be assigned next to the training staff and then rotate back as line supervisors in network services to gain experience in different departments.

Some companies use the traditional concept of career ladders to help employees advance in their careers. Other organizations take a more contemporary approach to career advancement. Sony encourages creativity from its engineers by using nontraditional career paths. At Sony, individuals have the freedom to move on to interesting and challenging job assignments without notifying their supervisors. If they join a new project team, their current boss is expected to let them move on. This self-promotion philosophy at Sony is seen as a key to high levels of innovation and creative new product designs.

Another approach used by some companies to develop skills is the idea of a "career lattice"—an approach to building competencies by moving laterally through different departments in the organization or by moving through different projects. Top management support for the career lattice is essential, because in traditional terms an employee who has made several lateral moves might not be viewed with favor. However, the career lattice approach is an effective way to develop an array of skills to ensure one's employability.[55]

PART 4 [ORGANIZATIONAL PROCESSES AND STRUCTURE

Exploring career paths is one important activity in advancement. Another crucial activity during advancement is finding a mentor.

Finding a Mentor

A *mentor* is an individual who provides guidance, coaching, counseling, and friendship to a protégé. Mentors are important to career success because they perform both career and psychosocial functions.[56]

The career functions provided by a mentor include sponsorship, facilitating exposure and visibility, coaching, and protection. Sponsorship means actively helping the individual get job experiences and promotions. Facilitating exposure and visibility means providing opportunities for the protégé to develop relationships with key figures in the organization in order to advance. Coaching involves providing advice in both career and job performance. Protection is provided by shielding the protégé from potentially damaging experiences. Career functions are particularly important to the protégé's future success. One study found that the amount of career coaching received by protégés was related to more promotions and higher salaries four years later.[57]

The mentor also performs psychosocial functions. Role modeling occurs when the mentor displays behavior for the protégé to emulate. This facilitates social learning. Acceptance and confirmation is important to both the mentor and protégé. When the protégé feels accepted by the mentor, it fosters a sense of pride. Likewise, positive regard and appreciation from the junior colleague provide a sense of satisfaction for the mentor. Counseling by a mentor helps the protégé explore personal issues that arise and require assistance. Friendship is another psychosocial function that benefits both mentor and protégé alike.

There are characteristics that define good mentoring relationships. In effective mentoring relationships, there is regular contact between mentor and protégé that has clearly specified purposes. Mentoring should be consistent with the corporate culture and the organization's goals. Both mentors and protégés alike should be trained in ways to manage the relationship. Mentors should be held accountable and rewarded for their role. Mentors should be perceived (accurately) by protégés as having considerable influence within the organization.[58] While it may be tempting to go after the "top dog" as your mentor, personality compatibility is also an important factor in the success or failure of a mentoring relationship. Mentors who are similar to their protégés in terms of personality traits like extraversion, and whose expectations are largely met by the relationship, are more likely to show interest in continuing the arrangement.[59] Cigna Financial Advisors takes a proactive approach to integrating new employees. As part of the company's Partnership Program, all new hires work for up to twenty-seven months under the oversight of an experienced, successful mentor. This relationship provides the new hires with hands-on instruction in how to sell more effectively, as well as increasing sales levels for the mentors themselves. Cigna demonstrates its commitment to this approach by hiring no more new producers than it can assign to individual mentors.[60]

Mentoring programs are also effective ways of addressing the challenge of workforce diversity. The mentoring process, however, presents unique problems, including the availability of mentors, issues of language and acculturation, and cultural sensitivity, for minority groups such as Hispanic-Americans. Negative stereotypes can limit minority members' access to mentoring relationships and the benefits associated with mentoring.[61] To address this problem, companies can facilitate access to mentors in organizations. Informal

5. Describe how mentors help organizational newcomers.

mentor
An individual who provides guidance, coaching, counseling, and friendship to a protégé.

mentoring programs identify pools of mentors and protégés, provide training in the development of effective mentoring and diversity issues, and then provide informal opportunities for the development of mentoring relationships. Network groups are another avenue for mentoring. Network groups help members identify with those few others who are like them within an organization, build relationships with them, and build social support. Network groups enhance the chance that minorities will find mentors.[62] Lucent Technologies, for example, has several Employee Business Partner groups that serve networking functions. Some of these groups are HISPA, for Hispanic-Americans; 4A, which is for Asian-Americans; ABLE, for African-Americans; LUNA, for Native Americans; and Equal!, for gay, lesbian, and bisexual individuals. These groups serve as links to their respective communities within Lucent. Networks also increase the likelihood that individuals have more than one mentor. Individuals with multiple mentors, such as those gained from mentoring networks, have even greater career success than those with only one mentor.[63]

Some companies have formal mentoring programs. PricewaterhouseCoopers (PWC) also uses the mentoring model to help its interns. Each intern is assigned both a peer mentor to help with day-to-day questions and an experienced mentor to help with larger issues such as career path development. As an international firm, PWC also employs similar methods overseas. In PWC's Czech Republic operations, a team of two mentors—one of whom is called a "counselor"—fills the same guidance role as the two mentors generally fill for U.S. employees.[64]

Mentoring has had a strong impact in shaping the identities of the Big Four accounting firms. In one study, every partner who was interviewed reported having at least one mentor who played a critical role in his/her attainment of the partnership and beyond. Protégés' identities are shaped through mentoring, and their work goals, language, and even lifestyles reflect the imperatives of the Big Four firm.[65] Protégés are schooled on partners' "hot buttons" (what not to talk about), what to wear, to "tuck in the tie," and not to cut the grass without wearing a shirt.

Although some companies have formal mentoring programs, junior employees more often are left to negotiate their own mentoring relationships. The barriers to finding a mentor include lack of access to mentors, fear of initiating a mentoring relationship, and fear that supervisors or coworkers might not approve of the mentoring relationship. Individuals may also be afraid to initiate a mentoring relationship because it might be misconstrued as a sexual advance by the potential mentor or others. This is a fear of potential mentors as well. Some are unwilling to develop a relationship because of their own or because of the protégé's gender. Women report more of these barriers than men, and individuals who lack previous experience report more barriers to finding a mentor.[66]

Organizations can encourage junior workers to approach mentors by providing opportunities for them to interact with senior colleagues. The immediate supervisor is not always the best mentor for an individual, so exposure to other senior workers is important. Seminars, multilevel teams, and social events can serve as vehicles for bringing together potential mentors and protégés.

Mentoring relationships go through a series of phases: initiation, cultivation, separation, and redefinition. There is no fixed time length for each phase, because each relationship is unique. In the initiation phase, the mentoring relationship begins to take on significance for both the mentor and the protégé. In the cultivation phase, the relationship becomes more meaningful, and the protégé shows rapid progress because of the career and psychosocial support provided by the mentor. Protégés influence mentors as well.

In the separation phase, the protégé feels the need to assert independence and work more autonomously. Separation can be voluntary, or it can result from an involuntary change (the protégé or mentor may be promoted or transferred). The separation phase can be difficult if it is resisted, either by the mentor (who is reluctant to let go of the relationship) or by the protégé (who resents the mentor's withdrawal of support). Separation can proceed smoothly and naturally or can result from a conflict that disrupts the mentoring relationship.

The redefinition phase occurs if separation has been successful. In this phase, the relationship takes on a new identity as both parties consider themselves colleagues or friends. The mentor feels pride in the protégé, and the protégé develops a deeper appreciation for the support from the mentor.

Why are mentors so important? Aside from the support they provide, the research shows that mentors are important to the protégé's future success. For example, studies have demonstrated that individuals with mentors have higher promotion rates and higher incomes than individuals who do not have mentors.[67] Professionals who have mentors earn between $5,600 and $22,000 more per year than those who do not.[68] Individuals with mentors also are better decision makers.[69] And it is not just the presence of the mentor that yields these benefits. The quality of the relationship is most important.[70]

During the advancement stage, many individuals face another transition: They settle into a relationship with a life partner. This lifestyle transition requires adjustment in many respects: learning to live with another person, being concerned with someone besides yourself, dealing with an extended family, and many other demands. The partnership can be particularly stressful if both members are career oriented.

Dual-Career Partnerships

The two-career lifestyle has increased in recent years due in part to the need for two incomes to maintain a preferred standard of living. *Dual-career partnerships* are relationships in which both people have important career roles. This type of partnership can be mutually beneficial, but it can also be stressful. Often these stresses center around stereotypes that providing income is a man's responsibility and taking care of the home is the woman's domain. Among married couples, working women's satisfaction with the marriage is affected by how much the husband helps with child care. Men who adhere to traditional gender beliefs may be threatened when the wife's income exceeds their own. Beliefs about who should do what in the partnership complicate the dual-career issue.[71]

One stressor in a dual-career partnership is time pressure. When both partners work outside the home, there may be a time crunch in fitting in work, family, and leisure time. Another potential problem is jealousy. When one partner's career blooms before the other's, the partner may feel threatened.[72] Another issue to work out is whose career takes precedence. For example, what happens if one partner is transferred to another city? Must the other partner make a move that might threaten his or her own career in order to be with the individual who was transferred? Who, if anyone, will stay home and take care of a new baby?

Working out a dual-career partnership takes careful planning and consistent communication between the partners. Each partner must serve as a source of social support for the other. Couples can also turn to other family members, friends, and professionals for support if the need arises.

dual-career partnership
A relationship in which both people have important career roles.

6. Describe ways to manage conflicts between work and home.

An issue related to dual-career partnerships that is faced throughout the career cycle, but often first encountered in the advancement phase, is the conflicts that occur between work and personal life. Experiencing a great deal of work—home conflict negatively affects an individual's overall quality of life. Work—home conflicts can lead to emotional exhaustion. Dealing with customer complaints all day, failed sales calls, and missed deadlines can magnify negative events at home, and vice versa.[73] Responsibilities at home can clash with responsibilities at work, and these conflicts must be planned for. For example, suppose a child gets sick at school. Who will pick up the child and stay home with him or her? Couples must work together to resolve these conflicts. Even at Eli Lilly and Co., only 36 percent of workers said it is possible to get ahead in their careers and still devote sufficient time to family. This is surprising, because Lilly has a reputation as one of the world's most family-friendly workplaces.[74]

Work—home conflicts are particular problems for working women.[75] Women have been quicker to share the provider role than men have been to share responsibilities at home.[76] When working women experience work—home conflict, their performance declines, and they suffer more strain. Work—home conflict is a broad topic. It can be narrowed further into work—family conflict, in which work interferes with family, versus family—work conflict, in which family or home life interferes with work.[77] Cultural differences arise in these types of conflicts. One study showed that while Americans experience more family—work conflict, Chinese experience more work—family conflict.[78]

flexible work schedule

A work schedule that allows employees discretion in order to accommodate personal concerns.

To help individuals deal with work—home conflict, companies can offer *flexible work schedules*.[79] These programs, such as flextime, which we discussed in Chapter 14, give employees freedom to take care of personal concerns while still getting their work done.

Company-sponsored child care is another way to help. Companies with on-site day-care centers include Johnson & Johnson, Perdue Farms, and Campbell Soup. Mitchell Gold, an award-winning furniture maker, believes that treating people right must come first. Its 2,700-square-foot on-site day-care center is education based rather than activity based and operates at break-even rates to make it more accessible. The day-care facility was named the county's "Provider of the Year" in 2003.[80]

To help handle work—home conflict, some corporations, such as Mitchell Gold, offer an on-site day-care center.

Whereas large companies may offer corporate day care, small companies can also assist their workers by providing referral services for locating the type of child care the workers need. For smaller organizations, this is a cost-effective alternative.[81] At the very least, companies can be sensitive to work—home conflicts and handle them on a case-by-case basis with flexibility and concern.

eldercare

Assistance in caring for elderly parents and/or other elderly relatives.

A program of increasing interest that organizations can provide is *eldercare*. Often workers find themselves part of the sandwich generation: They are expected to care for both their children and their elderly parents. This extremely stressful role is reported more often by women than men.[82] The impact of caring for an aging loved one is often underestimated. But 17 percent of those who provide care eventually quit their jobs due to time constraints, and another 15 percent cut back their work hours for the same reason.[83] Caring for an elderly dependent at home can create severe work–home conflicts for employees and also takes a toll on the employee's own well-being and performance at work. This is especially the case if the organization is not one that provides a supportive climate for discussion of eldercare issues.[84] Harvard University has taken steps to help its faculty and staff deal with eldercare issues by contracting with Parents In A Pinch, a firm that specializes in nanny services and now also offers eldercare.[85]

John Beatrice is one of a handful of men making work fit their family, rather than trying to fit family around career. John remembers his father working most of the night so he could be at John's athletic events during the day, and John wants the same for his family. So while job sharing, flexible scheduling, and telecommuting have traditionally been viewed as meeting the needs of working mothers, John and other men are increasingly taking advantage of such opportunities. In John's case, flexible work hours at Ernst & Young allow him to spend part of his mornings and afternoons coaching a high school hockey team. In John's assessment, flexible work hours actually lead him to work more hours than he would otherwise, and he's happier about doing it. Not surprisingly, John's employer also benefits from the arrangement; after nineteen years, John is more loyal than ever and still loves what he does.[86]

Alternative work arrangements such as flextime, compressed workweeks, work-at-home arrangements, part-time hours, job sharing, and leave options can help employees manage work–home conflicts. Managers must not let their biases get in the way of these benefits. Top managers may be less willing to grant alternative work arrangements to men than to women, to supervisors than to subordinates, and to employees caring for elderly parents rather than children. It is important that family-friendly policies be applied fairly.[87]

The advancement stage is filled with the challenges of finding a mentor, balancing dual-career partnerships, and dealing with work–home conflicts. In the Science feature, you can read about the keys to success in advancing your career.

Developmental changes that occur in either the late advancement stage or the early maintenance stage can prove stressful, too. The midlife transition, which takes place approximately between ages forty and forty-five, is often a time of crisis. Levinson points out three major changes that contribute to the midlife transition. First, people realize that their lives are half over and that they are mortal. Second, age forty is considered by people in their twenties and thirties to be "over the hill" and not part of the youthful culture. Finally, people reassess their dreams and evaluate how close they have come to achieving those dreams. All of these factors make up the midlife transition.

The Maintenance Stage

Maintenance may be a misnomer for this career stage, because some people continue to grow in their careers, although the growth is usually not at the rate it was earlier. A career crisis at midlife may accompany the midlife transition. A senior product manager at Borden found himself in such a crisis and described it this way: "When I was in college, I had thought in terms of being president of a company. . . . But at Borden I felt used and cornered. Most of the guys in the next two rungs above me had either an MBA or fifteen to twenty years of experience in the food business. My long-term plans stalled."[88]

Some individuals who reach a career crisis are burned out, and a month's vacation will help, according to Carolyn Smith Paschal, who owns an executive

How to Succeed in the Boundaryless Career

Today, people change jobs and organizations frequently. This is known as the "boundaryless career." What makes people successful in this dynamic career environment? Researchers proposed three groups of factors that might be related to success: *knowing why* (knowing yourself and being adaptable), *knowing whom* (career-related networks and contacts), and *knowing how* (career skills and job-related knowledge). They measured career success using three indicators: perceived career satisfaction, perceived internal marketability, and perceived external marketability.

Using data from 458 alumni from a large southeastern university, the researchers found that knowing why, knowing whom, and knowing how each predicted career success. Specifically, individuals who were self-starters and knew their own strengths and weaknesses (knowing why) were more successful. Individuals who had extensive networks both within and outside of their organizations were more successful (knowing whom). And finally, individuals who built and diversified their skills and engaged in continuous learning were more successful (knowing how). These findings provide specific things that you can work on to ensure your career success in the constantly changing world of work.

SOURCE: L. T. Eby, M. Butts, and A. Lockwood, "Predictors of Success in the Era of the Boundaryless Career," *Journal of Organizational Behavior* 24 (2003): 689–708.

search firm. She recommends that companies give employees in this stage sabbaticals instead of bonuses. This would help rejuvenate them.

Some individuals reach the maintenance stage with a sense of achievement and contentment, feeling no need to strive for further upward mobility. Whether the maintenance stage is a time of crisis or contentment, however, there are two issues to grapple with: sustaining performance and becoming a mentor.

Sustaining Performance

career plateau

A point in an individual's career in which the probability of moving further up the hierarchy is low.

Remaining productive is a key concern for individuals in the maintenance stage. This becomes challenging when one reaches a *career plateau*, a point where the probability of moving further up the hierarchy is low. Some people handle career plateauing fairly well, but others may become frustrated, bored, and dissatisfied with their jobs.

To keep employees productive, organizations can provide challenges and opportunities for learning. Lateral moves are one option. Another option is to involve the employee in project teams that provide new tasks and skill development. The key is keeping the work stimulating and involving. Individuals at this stage also need continued affirmation of their value to the organization. They need to know that their contributions are significant and appreciated.[89]

Becoming a Mentor

During maintenance, individuals can make a contribution by sharing their wealth of knowledge and experience with others. Opportunities to be mentors to new employees can keep senior workers motivated and involved in the organization. It is important for organizations to reward mentors for the time and energy they expend. Some employees adapt naturally to the mentor role, but others may need training on how to coach and counsel junior workers.

Kathy Kram notes that there are four keys to the success of a formal mentoring program. First, participation should be voluntary. No one should be forced to enter a mentoring relationship, and careful matching of mentors and protégés is important. Second, support from top executives is needed to convey the intent of the program and its role in career development. Third, training should be provided to mentors so they understand the functions of the relationship. Finally, a graceful exit should be provided for mismatches or for people in mentoring relationships that have fulfilled their purpose.[90]

Maintenance is a time of transition, like all career stages. It can be managed by individuals who know what to expect and plan to remain productive, as well as by organizations that focus on maximizing employee involvement in work. According to Levinson, during the latter part of the maintenance stage, another life transition occurs. The age fifty transition is another time of reevaluating the dream and working further on the issues raised in the midlife transition. Following the age fifty transition is a fairly stable period. During this time, individuals begin to plan seriously for withdrawing from their careers.

The Withdrawal Stage

The withdrawal stage usually occurs later in life and signals that a long period of continuous employment will soon come to a close. Older workers may face discrimination and stereotyping. They may be viewed by others as less productive, more resistant to change, and less motivated. However, older workers are one of the most undervalued groups in the workforce. They can provide continuity in the midst of change and can serve as mentors and role models to younger generations of employees.

Discrimination against older workers is prohibited under the Age Discrimination in Employment Act.[91] Organizations must create a culture that values older workers' contributions. With their level of experience, strong work ethic, and loyalty, these workers have much to contribute. In fact, older workers have lower rates of tardiness and absenteeism, are more safety conscious, and are more satisfied with their jobs than are younger workers.[92]

Planning for Change

The decision to retire is an individual one, but the need for planning is universal. A retired sales executive from Boise Cascade said that the best advice is to "plan no unplanned retirement."[93] This means carefully planning not only the transition but also the activities you will be involved in once the transition is made. All options should be open for consideration. One recent trend is the need for temporary top-level executives. Some companies are hiring senior managers from the outside on a temporary basis. The qualities of a good temporary executive include substantial high-level management experience, financial security that allows the executive to choose only assignments that really interest him or her, and a willingness to relocate.[94] Some individuals at the withdrawal stage find this an attractive option.

Planning for retirement should include not only financial planning but also a plan for psychologically withdrawing from work. The pursuit of hobbies and travel, volunteer work, or more time with extended family can all be part of the plan. The key is to plan early and carefully, as well as to anticipate the transition with a positive attitude and a full slate of desirable activities.

Retirement

There are several retirement trends right now, ranging from early retirement to phased retirement to never retiring. Some adults are choosing a combination of these options, leaving their first career for some time off before reentering the workforce either part time or full time doing something they enjoy. For more and more Americans, the idea of a retirement spent sitting beside the swimming pool sounds, for lack of a better word, boring. Factors that influence the decision of when to retire include company policy, financial considerations, family support or pressure, health, and opportunities for other productive activities.[95]

During the withdrawal stage, the individual faces a major life transition that Levinson refers to as the late adulthood transition (ages sixty to sixty-five). One's own mortality becomes a major concern and the loss of one's family members and friends becomes more frequent. The person works to achieve a sense of integrity in life—that is, the person works to find the encompassing meaning and value in life.

Some retirement-agers may go through a second midlife crisis. People are living longer and staying more active. Vickie Ianucelli, for example, bought a condo on a Mexican beach, celebrated a birthday in Paris, bought herself a 9.5-karat ring, and got plastic surgery. And, it's her second midlife crisis. She's a psychologist who is also a 60-plus grandmother of two.[96]

phased retirement

An arrangement that allows employees to reduce their hours and/or responsibilities in order to ease into retirement.

Retirement need not be a complete cessation of work. Many alternative work arrangements can be considered, and many companies offer flexibility in these options. *Phased retirement* is a popular option for retirement-age workers who want to gradually reduce their hours and/or responsibilities. There are many forms of phased retirement, including reduced workdays or workweeks, job sharing, and consulting and mentoring arrangements. Many organizations cannot afford the loss of large numbers of experienced employees at once. In fact, although 50 percent of all U.S. workers are officially retired by age sixty, only 11 percent fully withdraw from work. This means there is an increase in *bridge employment*, which is employment that takes place after a person retires from a full-time position but before the person's permanent withdrawal from the workforce. Bridge employment is related to retirement satisfaction and overall life satisfaction.[97]

bridge employment

Employment that takes place after a person retires from a full-time position but before the person's permanent withdrawal from the workforce.

Some companies are helping employees transition to retirement in innovative ways. Retired individuals can continue their affiliation with the organization by serving as mentors to employees who are embarking on retirement planning or other career transitions. This helps diminish the fear of loss some people have about retirement, because the retiree has an option to serve as a mentor or consultant to the organization.

Lawrence Livermore National Labs (LLNL) employs some of the best research minds in the world. And when these great minds retire from full-time work, they have numerous opportunities to continue contributing. LLNL's retiree program Web site lists a wide variety of requests, ranging from guiding tours and making phone calls to providing guidance on current research and helping researchers make contact with other researchers.[98] Programs like this one help LLNL avoid the typical knowledge drain that takes place when seasoned veteran employees retire.

Now that you understand the career stage model, you can begin to conduct your own career planning. It is never too early to start.

7. Explain how career anchors help form a career identity.

career anchors

A network of self-perceived talents, motives, and values that guide an individual's career decisions.

Career Anchors

Much of an individual's self-concept rests upon a career. Over the course of the career, career anchors are developed. *Career anchors* are self-perceived talents, motives, and values that guide an individual's career decisions.[99] Edgar Schein developed the concept of career anchors based on a twelve-year study of MBA graduates from the Massachusetts Institute of Technology (MIT).

Schein found great diversity in the graduates' career histories but great similarities in the way they explained the career decisions they had made.[100] From extensive interviews with the graduates, Schein developed five career anchors:

1. *Technical/functional competence.* Individuals who hold this career anchor want to specialize in a given functional area (for example, finance or marketing) and become competent. The idea of general management does not interest them.

2. *Managerial competence.* Adapting this career anchor means individuals want general management responsibility. They want to see their efforts have an impact on organizational effectiveness.

3. *Autonomy and independence.* Freedom is the key to this career anchor, and often these individuals are uncomfortable working in large organizations. Autonomous careers such as writer, professor, or consultant attract these individuals.

4. *Creativity.* Individuals holding this career anchor feel a strong need to create something. They are often entrepreneurs.

5. *Security/stability.* Long-term career stability, whether in a single organization or in a single geographic area, fits people with this career anchor. Some government jobs provide this type of security.

Career anchors emerge over time and may be modified by work or life experiences.[101] The importance of knowing your career anchor is that it can help you find a match between yourself and an organization. For example, individuals with creativity as an anchor may find themselves stifled in bureaucratic organizations. Textbook sales may not be the place for an individual with a security anchor because of the frequent travel and seasonal nature of the business.

Managerial Implications: Managing Your Career

The challenges of globalization, diversity, technology, and ethics have provided unique opportunities and threats for career management. The ongoing restructuring of American organizations with its accompanying downsizing has resulted in a reduction of 25 percent of the jobs held in the *Fortune 500* companies.[102] The flattening of the organizational hierarchy has resulted in fewer opportunities for promotion. Forty-year careers with one organization, a phenomenon baby boomers saw their parents experience, are becoming less and less the norm. Negotiating the turbulent waters of the U.S. employment market will be a challenge in the foreseeable future.

Many industries are experiencing sinking employment, but there are some bright spots. According to Labor Department projections, the U.S. economy will add approximately 21.3 million jobs by the year 2012, with most of them in service industries. Figure 17.3 shows where the new jobs will be found. Of all the occupations expected to have faster than average employment growth, above average earnings, and below average unemployment, the ones shown in this chart have the largest number of projected openings. These occupations will account for 5 million new jobs, or 27 percent of all job growth. Most of these jobs require at least a bachelor's degree.

Andy Grove, chairman of Intel Corporation, suggests that as a general rule, you must accept that no matter where you work, you are not an employee.

FIGURE 17.3 High-Paying Occupations with Many Openings, Projected 2002–12

Over the 2002–12 decade, career choices abound for those seeking high earnings and lots of opportunities. High-paying occupations that are projected to have many openings are varied. This diverse group includes teachers, managers, and construction trades workers.

The job openings shown in the chart represent the total that are expected each year for workers who are entering these occupations for the first time. The job openings result from each occupation's growth and from the need to replace workers who retire or leave the occupation permanently for some other reason. Not included among these openings are ones that are created when workers move from job to job within an occupation.

Median earnings, such as those listed below, indicate that half of the workers in an occupation made more than that amount, and half made less. The occupations in the chart ranked in the highest or second-highest earnings quartiles for 2002 median earnings. This means that median earnings for workers in these occupations were higher than the earnings for at least 50 percent of all occupations in 2002.

Most of these occupations had another thing going for them in 2002: low or very low unemployment. Workers in occupations that had higher levels of unemployment—truck drivers, carpenters, and electricians—were more dependent on a strong economy or seasonal employment.

Occupation	Annual average job openings due to growth and net replacement needs, projected 2002–12	Median annual earnings, 2002
Registered nurses	110,119	$48,090
Postsecondary teachers	95,980	49,090
General and operations managers	76,245	68,210
Sales representatives, wholesale and manufacturing, except technical and scientific products	66,239	42,730
Truck drivers, heavy and tractor-trailer	62,517	33,210
Elementary school teachers, except special education	54,701	41,780
First-line supervisors or managers of retail sales workers	48,645	29,700
Secondary school teachers, except special and vocational education	45,761	43,950
General maintenance and repair workers	44,978	29,370
Executive secretaries and administrative assistants	42,444	33,410
First-line supervisors or managers of office and administrative support workers	40,909	38,820
Accountants and auditors	40,465	47,000
Carpenters	31,917	34,190
Automotive service technicians and mechanics	31,887	30,590
Police and sheriff's patrol officers	31,290	42,270
Licensed practical and licensed vocational nurses	29,480	31,440
Electricians	28,485	41,390
Management analysts	25,470	60,340
Computer systems analysts	23,735	62,890
Special education teachers	23,297	43,450

SOURCE: Bureau of Labor Statistics, "High-Paying Occupations with Many Openings, Projected 2002–12." *Occupational Outlook Quarterly* 48 (Spring 2004). http://www.bls.gov/opub/ooq/2004/spring/oochart.pdf.

Instead, you are in a business with one employee: yourself. You face tremendous competition with millions of other businesses. You own your career as a sole proprietor. Grove poses three key questions that are central to managing your career:

1. Continually ask: *Am I adding real value?* You add real value by continually looking for ways to make things truly better in your organization. In principle, every hour of your workday should be spent increasing the value of the output of the people for whom you're responsible.

2. Continually ask: *Am I plugged into what's happening around me?* Inside the company? The industry? Are you a node in a network of plugged-in people, or are you floating around by yourself?

3. Continually ask: *Am I trying new ideas, new techniques, and new technologies?* Try them personally—don't just read about them.[103]

The key to survival is to add more value every day and to be flexible. You can use You 17.2 to assess the current state of your flexibility skills.

YOU 17.2

Assess Your Flexibility Skills

Use the following scale to rate the frequency with which you perform the behaviors described in each question. Place the corresponding number (1–7) in the blank preceding the statement.

Rarely	Irregularly	Occasionally	Usually	Frequently	Almost Always	Consistently
1	2	3	4	5	6	7

_____ **1.** I manage a variety of assignments with varying demands and complexities.

_____ **2.** I adjust work plans to account for new circumstances.

_____ **3.** I modify rules and procedures in order to meet operational needs and goals.

_____ **4.** I work with ambiguous assignments when necessary and use these when possible to further my goals and objectives.

_____ **5.** I rearrange work or personal schedules to meet deadlines.

_____ **6.** In emergencies, I respond to the most pressing needs first.

_____ **7.** I change my priorities to accommodate unexpected events.

_____ **8.** I manage my personal work overload by seeking assistance or by delegating responsibility to others.

_____ **9.** I vary the way I deal with others according to their needs and personalities.

_____ **10.** I help others improve their job performance, or I assign tasks that will further their development.

_____ **11.** I accept the authority of my manager but continue to demonstrate my initiative and assertiveness.

_____ **12.** I work well with all types of personalities.

_____ **13.** I measure my performance on the job against the feedback I receive.

_____ **14.** I correct performance deficits that have been brought to my attention.

_____ **15.** When I disagree with my manager's appraisal of my work, I discuss our differences.

_____ **16.** I seek training and assignments that can help me improve my job-related skills.

_____ **17.** In disagreements concerning work-related issues, I look at matters impersonally and concentrate on the facts.

_____ **18.** I make compromises to get problems moving toward resolution.

_____ **19.** I look for new and better ways to accomplish my duties and responsibilities.

_____ **20.** I offer to negotiate all areas of disagreement.

(continued)

Skill Area	Items	Score
Working with new, changing, and ambiguous situations	1, 2, 3, 4	
Working under pressure	5, 6, 7, 8	
Dealing with different personal styles	9, 10, 11, 12	
Handling feedback	13, 14, 15, 16	
Resolving conflicts	17, 18, 19, 20	
TOTAL SCORE		

FIGURE B
Flexible Behaviors Questionnaire (FBQ) Evaluation

Total Score

Lowest score _____ Highest score

20   50   80   110   140

Category Scores

Working with new, changing, and ambiguous situations
_____
4   10   16   22   28

Working under pressure
_____
4   10   16   22   28

Dealing with different personality styles
_____
4   10   16   22   28

Handling feedback
_____
4   10   16   22   28

Resolving conflicts
_____
4   10   16   22   28

FBQ Scoring

The scoring sheet in Figure A summarizes your responses for the FBQ. It will help you identify your existing strengths and pinpoint areas that need improvement.

FBQ Evaluation

Figure B shows score lines for your total score and for each category measured on the FBQ. Each line shows a continuum from the lowest score to the highest.

The score lines in Figure B show graphically where you stand with regard to the five flexible behaviors. If you have been honest with yourself, you now have a better idea of your relative strengths and weaknesses in the categories that make up the skills of flexibility.

SOURCE: "Assess Your Flexibility Skills" by Fandt, from *Management Skills, Learning Through Practice and Experience, 1e*. pp. 431–433. © 1994. Reprinted with permission of Custom Publishing, a division of Thomson Learning: www.thomsonrights.com. Fax 800-730-2215.

LOOKING BACK: VIRGIN GROUP LTD.

A Good Career Fit

Virgin, like many other founder-led firms, is strongly reflective of its founder's values. And while it might be easy to dismiss Sir Richard Branson as a juvenile trickster, he is also a savvy businessman. In leading his growing firm, Branson makes sure that John Riordan and every other employee is well versed in five key values. Not surprisingly, at a company like Virgin, "fun" and "innovation" make the list. "Value" is there as well. Perhaps less expected are the final two: "honesty" and "caring."

In applying these values to daily work, Riordan makes several observations. He notes that if you have good, motivated people, focused on a brand they believe in, fun is never lacking. He also subscribes to an inverted business model, in which shareholder value is delivered as a *result* of creating employee value, rather than as a *goal* in itself. In this model, employees who are treated well respond by treating customers well, producing the profits that reward shareholders. In this analogy, as in so many other things, Virgin's employees just seem to see the world a little differently than most folks. Perhaps that is Virgin's biggest secret of all.[104]

Chapter Summary

1. Career management is a joint responsibility of individuals and organizations.

2. Good matches between individuals and organizations can be promoted with a realistic job preview (RJP).

3. The four stages in an individual's career are establishment, advancement, maintenance, and withdrawal. Each stage has unique challenges.

4. Psychological contracts are implicit agreements between individuals and organizations.

5. Mentoring is crucial to both the career success of young workers and the needs of older workers.

6. Child care, eldercare, and flexible work schedules can help employees manage work–home conflicts.

7. Career anchors help an individual form a career identity and formulate an effective career plan.

Key Terms

advancement (p. 571)
bridge employment (p. 584)
career (p. 562)
career anchors (p. 584)
career ladder (p. 576)
career management (p. 562)

career path (p. 576)
career plateau (p. 582)
dual-career partnership (p. 579)
eldercare (p. 580)
establishment (p. 571)
flexible work schedule (p. 580)

maintenance (p. 571)
mentor (p. 577)
phased retirement (p. 584)
psychological contract (p. 573)
realistic job preview (RJP) (p. 569)
withdrawal (p. 571)

Review Questions

1. What is career management?

2. What is the new career, and how does it differ from older notions about careers?

3. What are the sources of potential conflict during organizational entry? How can they be avoided?

4. What is a realistic job preview, and why is it important?

5. What are psychological contracts?

6. What stressors are associated with socialization?

7. What are the career functions provided by a mentor?

8. What are some of the most likely causes of home–work conflicts?

9. What are the two key issues to deal with during the maintenance career stage?

10. What is the key to career survival?

Discussion and Communication Questions

1. What are the realities of the new career? How can developing your emotional intelligence help you turn these realities into opportunities to improve your career?

2. What do you think will be the most stressful career stage? What type of stressors led you to make this choice?

3. Does the career stage model have exceptions? In other words, can it be applied to all careers? If not, what are the exceptions?

4. Do men and women have different expectations of a dual-career partnership? How do these expectations differ?

5. Given the downsizing and restructuring in many organizations, how can organizations help employees with career management if there are fewer opportunities for promotion?

6. How has each of the four challenges (globalization, diversity, technology, and ethics) affected career management in recent years?

7. *(communication question)* Contact the human resources manager of a local business. Ask if he or she would take a few minutes to discuss some is-sues about résumés with you. Structure your discussion around the following questions:

a. How often do you encounter "padded" résumés? What is the most common "padding," and how do you react to it?

b. Do you verify the information on résumés? How do you do this? How long does it take for you to be sure that an applicant has been honest about his/her qualifications?

c. What would you do if you found that a productive, loyal employee had lied on a résumé when he or she applied for a job? Is "résumé fraud" an offense that warrants firing?

Summarize the findings from your interview in a memo to your instructor.

8. *(communication question)* Select an individual in the field you want to work in or in a company you might want to work for. Contact the individual and ask if you might take a minute of his/her time for some career advice. Ask the following two questions, along with others you design yourself. First, how has the idea of a "career" changed over the past few years? Second, what advice would the person give to college students just beginning a new career? Be prepared to present your interview results in class.

Ethical Dilemma

Allen Jamison is manager of the information technology department of a small manufacturing firm. Allen's job is to ensure that everyone's computer systems work well. Allen is also responsible for the well-being of his employees. He knows only too well the challenges of being an IT employee. Everyone depends on their computers to do their jobs, and when a computer is down, no one wants to hear excuses. His employees are often on the receiving end of the frustration many people feel in these situations. Because of this, Allen feels it is his responsibility to create an environment of support in his department. He always makes it clear to everyone in the department what he expects from them. Allen frequently assures his employees that they can count on his support. "Do your best in every situation and I will always watch your back," he regularly states.

The problem now is that the organization has just experienced a serious network malfunction that has resulted in a 24-hour shutdown. Allen feels sure that his department has played a role in creating this situation, but this certainly is not the only cause. Allen is willing for his department to accept part of the blame, but he has just left a meeting in which he has been asked to take more of the responsibility than he feels his people deserve. The president described how critical it is that the organization gains buy-in for the new software platform by everyone. The president readily admitted that the new platform is in large part the reason for the shutdown. His concern is that this early failure will bias the employees against the equipment. He asked Allen if he would be willing to accept a larger part of the responsibility for the problem to keep dissatisfaction for the new system as low as possible.

Allen feels certain that his employees can handle the added criticism, but why should they? They have dealt with enough customer service problems already.

But Allen also knows how critical acceptance of the software platform is to its success.

Questions

1. Does Allen have a responsibility to do what the president is asking him to do?

2. Using rule, virtue, right, and justice theories, evaluate Allen's decision.

Experiential Exercises

17.1 The Individual–Organizational Dialogue

The purpose of this exercise is to help you gain experience in working out a psychological contract from both perspectives—the individual's and the organization's.

Students should form groups of six to eight members. Within each group, half of the students will be job candidates, and half will represent organization members (insiders).

Step 1. Each half should make two lists as follows:

List 1, candidate version. What information should you, as a job candidate, provide the organization to start an effective psychological contract?

List 2, candidate version. What information should you, as a job candidate, seek from the organization?

List 1, insider version. What information should you, as an organization insider, seek from potential employees?

List 2, insider version. What information should you, as an organization insider, provide to potential employees to start an effective psychological contract?

Step 2. Within each group, compare lists by matching the two versions of List 1. What were the similarities and differences in your lists? Then compare

List 2 from each half of the group. What were the similarities and differences in these lists?

Step 3. Review the lists, and select the most difficult information to obtain from the candidate and the organization. Select one person to play the candidate and one to play the insider. First, have the candidate role-play an interaction with the insider in which the candidate tries to get the difficult information from the organization. Then have the insider try to obtain the difficult information from the candidate.

Step 4. Reconvene as a class, and discuss the following questions:

1. What did you find to be the most difficult questions asked by candidates?

2. What did you find to be the most difficult questions asked by insiders?

3. What information is necessary for an effective psychological contract?

4. What keeps each party from fully disclosing the information needed for a good psychological contract?

5. What can organizations do to facilitate the process of forming good psychological contracts?

6. What can individuals do to facilitate the process?

17.2 The Ethics of Résumés and Recommendations

The purpose of this exercise is to explore ethical issues concerning résumés and recommendations. First, read the following brief introductory scenario.

Jason Eckerle returned to his desk from lunch with a single mission in mind: to select the half-dozen best candidates for a regional customer service manager's position. As he hung up his suit jacket, Eckerle sized up the stack of résumés and recommen-

dations he'd been dealing with all morning—more than 100 of them.

The work had been slow but steady, gradually forming into three distinct piles: one contained absolute rejects (not enough work experience, wrong academic credentials, or poor recommendations from former employers), the second contained a few definite candidates for personal interviews, while the third held the applications of those about whom he still had questions or reservations.

His task for the afternoon—selecting three more applicants to bring to the company headquarters for interviews—was complicated by the résumés and recommendation letters themselves. Some questions were obvious: "This guy lists five years' full time sales and marketing experience, yet he's only twenty-two years old. How can he go to school full time and have that kind of experience?" Here's another: "This young lady says she went to school at the Sorbonne in Paris for two years; yet on the application form, under the heading 'Foreign Languages' she's checked 'none.'" Here's one more: "This fella says he has a degree from the University of Texas, yet nowhere on his résumé does he say he lived or spent time there. Did he get that diploma by correspondence?"

Other issues are even more mysterious: "This young lady's résumé lists education and work experience, but there's a three-year gap from 1989 to 1992. What's that all about? Is she trying to conceal something, or just absent minded?" As Eckerle thumbed through another résumé, he noticed the application form declaring "fluency in Japanese, French, and Spanish." "How do you get to be *fluent* in a language unless you've lived where it's spoken?" he wondered. The résumé didn't list any of those languages as native, nor did the application mention living abroad.

"Some of this stuff is outright fraud," he observed. As he sifted through the "reject" pile, Eckerle pulled out one application with an education block that lists a degree the applicant didn't have. "When we checked," he said, "they told us he was close to finishing a master's degree, but he hadn't yet finished his thesis. The applicant said he had the degree in hand." Another listed work experience no one could verify. "This guy's résumé says he was a client service representative for Litiplex, Inc., of Boston, but the phone book doesn't list any firm by that name, no one in our business has ever heard of it, and we can't check out his claims. I asked the applicant about the company, and he says, 'Maybe they went out of business.'"

Résumés weren't Eckerle's only problem. Recommendations were almost as bad. "Letters of recommendation aren't particularly useful," he said. "In the first place, almost no one is dumb enough to ask for a recommendation from someone who'll give them a bad one. Second, most recommenders write in broad, general, vague terms that don't tell me much about an applicant's work history, aptitude, or potential. They use glowing, nonspecific words that tell me the applicant's a marvelous human being but don't say whether the guy's had any comparable work experience that I could use to help make a decision."

Eckerle mentioned one other recommendation problem. "Most of the people who write letters in support of a job applicant are fairly close friends of the applicant. They'll often say things that are laudatory, but just aren't true. By the time you're done reading the letter, you'd think the young man in question could walk on water. When he comes for an interview, he can't get his own name straight." Excessive praise in letters of recommendation, Eckerle noted, can be expensive for a firm when the recommendation just doesn't reflect the applicant's true potential. "It costs us nearly $1,000 to bring in an entry-level management candidate for interviews," he said, "and it's my job to make sure we don't bring in someone who's just not competitive." Inflated recommendations, he thought, can make that job much more difficult.

Next, the class should be divided into ten groups. Each group will be assigned one ethical issue. The group should formulate an answer to the dilemma and be ready to present the group's solution to the class.

1. Is a job applicant obligated to list *all employment* or *every work experience* on a résumé? What about jobs in which an applicant has had a bad relationship with a supervisor? Is it fair to "load up" a résumé only with positive work experience?

2. What if an applicant has been fired? Is a résumé *required* to reveal the exact circumstances under which he or she left the job?

3. Is it ethical to list educational institutions or degree programs that an applicant has attended but not completed? How much detail is necessary? Should an applicant explain *why* he or she left a degree program or school without finishing?

4. Is a job applicant *obliged* to list offenses against the law on a résumé? What about convictions or incarceration—say, 90 days' jail time for DWI?

5. Under such résumé categories as "Foreign Languages," how does an applicant determine whether he or she is "fluent," "conversant," or merely "familiar with" a language? Do the same general rules apply to listing technical skills, such

as computer languages and software applications?

6. In a letter of recommendation, is it ethical to lavish praise on a young man or woman, just because you know the person is in need of a job? Conversely, does faint praise mean that a job applicant will likely be refused?

7. Is it better to turn away a student for asking for a letter of recommendation, or should you do what's *honest* and tell a graduate school (or potential employer) exactly what you think of the person?

8. Is a résumé something like a *certificate of authenticity*, listing specifics and details with absolute adherence to honesty and accuracy, or is it more like a *sales brochure*, offering the best possible picture of a person in search of employment?

9. How well do you have to know someone before you can write an authentic, honest letter of recommendation? Is there a minimum time requirement before you can do so in good conscience?

10. Is the author of a letter of recommendation required to reveal *everything relevant* that he or she knows about an applicant? What about character or integrity flaws that may stand in the way of a job applicant's success? To whom is the author of such letters obligated? To the potential employer or to the applicant?

SOURCE: J. S. O'Rourke, "The Ethics of Résumés and Recommendations: When Do Filler and Fluff Become Deceptions and Lies?" *Business Communication Quarterly* 58 (1995): 54–56. Reprinted with permission by the author.

Biz Flix | The Secret of My Success

College graduate Brantley Foster (Michael J. Fox) leaves his Kansas home and goes to New York to look for a job. He is continually frustrated in his quest but eventually lands a mailroom job. An entertaining look at corporate life, this film features power, negotiation, and sexual shenanigans.

The scene from *The Secret of My Success* appears early in the film following Brantley's layoff from a job he never started. He looks up at a building while saying, "O.K., New York. If that's the way you want it, O.K." The scene ends after Ms. Miller (Judith Malina) says to Brantley, "Can you be a minority woman?" The film continues with Brantley talking to his mother on a public telephone.

What to Watch for and Ask Yourself:

> What do these scenes suggest about the job seeking process?

> Does Brantley behave ethically during his job interviews?

> What do these scenes suggest about career management?

Workplace Video | LaBelle Management: Career Management

In 1948, Norman LaBelle opened his first restaurant in Mt. Pleasant, Michigan. Since then, his two sons, Bart and Doug LaBelle, have grown their father's business into a very successful company known as LaBelle Management. Today, LaBelle Management is a leader in managing properties for businesses, hotels, and restaurants, operating a variety of business concepts with over 30 locations throughout the Midwest.

LaBelle's owners attribute the company's success to the dedicated managers and employees that operate the business on a day-to-day basis. In today's competitive job market where workers change jobs and professions routinely, it can be a challenge to find and retain qualified people. The loyalty and dedication that LaBelle receives from its workers is a result of the firm's focus on career management and development. LaBelle's career management program has two main objectives: to retain qualified employees and enable workers to achieve personal goals. Executives at LaBelle believe that employees need to be able to see a future at the organization and recognize a clear path for upward mobility if they are to stay. Furthermore, workers must get the message that the company will invest in them and help them achieve their personal goals through training, development, and new opportunities. LaBelle's career management program enables the company to achieve its recruitment and retention objectives, creating a strong foundation for future growth.

The days of working for a single employer are long gone. In today's business world, individuals may change jobs and professions many times in the course of a lifetime. Therefore, it is all the more important that managers find ways to keep workers satisfied and create incentives for them to stay with the company. LaBelle's career management program has proven effective in recruiting and maintaining quality workers, providing for the needs of both the company and its employees.

T A K E

2

Questions

1. *How might LaBelle Management's organizational needs be met through career management?*
2. *How does LaBelle motivate its managers to identify and train future leaders?*
3. *How might LaBelle meet the career needs of its employees?*

Oprah Winfrey's Career Impact

In late 1998, *Fortune* magazine published its first-ever list of the "50 Most Powerful Women in American Business." Oprah Winfrey was second on the list. In describing her as the second most powerful woman in American business, *Fortune* indicated that she "has redefined how American women think and what they read." In the ensuing years, Winfrey has received numerous honors, culminating in 2004 with *Time Magazine* recognizing her as one of the "100 Most Influential People in the World."

She produces and hosts *The Oprah Winfrey Show,* an enormously successful talk show; is chairman of HARPO Entertainment Group, which includes HARPO Productions, Inc., HARPO Films, and HARPO Video, Inc.; has had several notable acting successes where she has portrayed determined women dealing with their struggles and triumphs; is the publisher of *O: The Oprah Magazine;* is a noted philanthropist; and has taught at the Northwestern University Business School. Winfrey's "contributions can be felt beyond the world of television and into kareas such as publishing, music, film, philanthropy, education, health and fitness, and social awareness."

The Oprah Winfrey Show, seen by an estimated 30 million viewers a week in the United States and broadcast internationally in 109 countries, has been the number one talk show for 18 consecutive seasons. As a talk show host, Winfrey "helped usher in an age of confessional, ultrapersonal TV." In this context, *The Oprah Winfrey Show* has been characterized as "television that cared, that wanted to know, that wanted you to spill your feelings and guts." Just as guests are asked to "spill their guts," so has Oprah "spilled her own guts." She has been very self-disclosing about her life and her problems. Winfrey grew up "dirt-poor" in Mississippi. Although she felt powerless as a youngster, she was ambitious nonetheless. Winfrey has even revealed that she was raped at age nine and that she had used cocaine in her twenties. Such revelations are consistent with and reinforce her expectations for her guests and viewers. She "demands as much honesty from herself as she does from her guests and viewers."

Winfrey now recognizes that she is a person who commands a great deal of power—in her words, "the ability to have an impact with a purpose." She uses her show, her magazine, her various business ventures, her acting, her philanthropic activities, and her teaching to have an "impact with a purpose."

She uses *The Oprah Winfrey Show* "to enlighten, entertain and empower her viewers." In the mid-1990s, Winfrey expressed a desire to make her show more meaningful. She launched an on-air book club that has become enormously influential—vaulting books onto and to the top of the best seller lists. Later she added a regular feature to the show called *Remembering Your Spirit.* This segment "focuses on the rather lofty goal of soothing viewers' souls." She also launched *Oprah's Angel Network* in 1997. Initially, this was a year-long campaign to encourage people to help those in need. As one of its beginning projects, *Oprah's Angel Network* helped raise money to send 50 students—one from each state—to college. "To date, *Oprah's Angel Network* has raised nearly $20 million, with 100 percent of audience donations going to not-for-profit organizations across the globe. Oprah's Angel Network has helped establish scholarships and schools, support women's shelters and build youth centers and homes—changing the future for people all over the world."

Winfrey also uses her various business ventures to "have an impact with a purpose." For instance, nearly all the television and movie projects developed by Winfrey's production company, HARPO Films, "have been based on books that have had a personal impact on her." Included among these are projects about a youngster who is physically abused by her alcoholic mother, a woman trapped in a loveless marriage, and two teens who are in a mental institution. According to one of the company's executives, HARPO Films is interested in developing "projects that show individuals being responsible for themselves. It's all about seeing human beings as active creators of their lives rather than as passive victims."

Winfrey has acted in several big-screen films and made-for-television movies. Through this medium she has delivered powerful messages about the challenges faced by humanity and people's triumphs over human frailties. For example, in the film *Before Women Had Wings*, Oprah portrayed a wise and sorrowful woman who provided a refuge for a young girl struggling to cope with the alcoholism and abuse that was unleashed by her father's suicide.

As a philanthropist, Oprah "established The Oprah Winfrey Foundation to support the education and empowerment of women, children, and families in the United States and around the world." Through this foundation, Winfrey has awarded hundreds of grants to organizations that work to carry out the foundation's vision of education and empowerment. Committed to the belief that education is the door to freedom, Winfrey "has donated millions of dollars toward providing a better education for students who have merit but no means." She is particularly committed to awarding "scholarships to students determined to use their education to give back to their communities in the United States and abroad." In December 2002, The Oprah Winfrey Foundation expanded its global humanitarian efforts in announcing a partnership with South Africa's Ministry of Education to build "The Oprah Winfrey Leadership Academy for Girls" in South Africa. The Academy is scheduled to open in 2007.

"Winfrey is constantly working to get her message out. That's why she took the teaching job at Northwestern . . . the class was a way for her to groom a new crop of business leaders committed to developing purposeful and fulfilling careers."

Discussion Questions

1. Using the facts of the case, along with the career stage model shown in Figure 17.2, describe Oprah Winfrey's current stage of career development.

2. Andy Grove, Chairman of Intel Corporation, identifies three key questions that are central to the management of a person's career. These questions are: Am I adding real value? Am I plugged into what's happening around me? Am I trying new ideas, new techniques, and new technologies? How would you analyze Winfrey's career in light of these three questions?

3. In your judgment, what are the key factors in Oprah Winfrey's success?

4. What advice do you think Oprah Winfrey would give to someone just embarking on her/his career?

SOURCE: This case was written by Michael K. McCuddy, The Louis S. and Mary L. Morgal Chair of Christian Business Ethics and Professor of Management, College of Business Administration, Valparaiso University. This case was developed from material contained on Oprah Winfrey's Web site at http://www.oprah.com and in the following articles: L. Clemetson, J. Raymond, B. Begun, A. Figueroa, and J. Halpert, "Oprah on Oprah," *Newsweek* (January 8, 2001): 38–47; C. J. Farley, "Queen of All Media," *Time* (October 22, 1998) 82–84; P. Sellers, "The 50 Most Powerful Women in American Business," *Fortune* (October 12, 1998): 76–98.

© Ken Straiton/CORBIS

Chapter 18

Managing Change

LEARNING OBJECTIVES

After reading this chapter, you should be able to do the following:

1 Identify the major external and internal forces for change in organizations.

2 Define the terms *incremental change*, *strategic change*, *transformational change*, and *change agent*.

3 Describe the major reasons individuals resist change, and discuss methods organizations can use to manage resistance.

4 Apply force field analysis to a problem.

5 Explain Lewin's organizational change model.

6 Describe the use of organizational diagnosis and needs analysis as a first step in organizational development.

7 Discuss the major organization development interventions.

8 Identify the ethical issues that must be considered in organization development efforts.

THINKING AHEAD: THE COCA-COLA COMPANY

Has Coke Lost Its Fizz?

Coca-Cola is the most valuable brand name in the entire world. According to *Business Week*, the Coke name and logo are worth more than $70 million, topping other global giants such as Microsoft, Toyota, and Disney. It is more than six times as valuable as Pepsi-Cola.[1] Who says bubbly sugar water doesn't sell?

Lately, quite a few folks have noticed that it doesn't sell as well as it once did. Once a sure winner, the firm's stock has become a laggard. What is troubling this global marketing giant? In a word . . . change. The U.S. soda market, Coke's home turf, is growing less than 1 percent per year. And in the hottest drink markets, Coke is running a distant second to Pepsi brands, including Gatorade (with an 81 percent share of the hot sports drink market) and Aquafina, which leads the red-hot bottled water market. Even some of Coke's recent successes, such as Vanilla Coke, have been short-lived, with an initial sales punch quickly followed by declining sales. With 20 percent of its profits coming from Japan, the firm appears to be vulnerable to an aging population base, which is more likely to pick up low-margin bottles in the supermarket than high-margin cans in vending machines.[2]

In the 1980s, Coke's core business of producing soft drink concentrate was described as a "license to print money." Has Coke's money license run out? Has the global giant lost its fizz?

Forces for Change in Organizations

Change has become the norm in most organizations. Plant closings, business failures, mergers and acquisitions, and downsizing have become experiences common to American companies. **Adaptiveness, flexibility, and**

responsiveness are characteristics of the organizations that will succeed in meeting the competitive challenges that businesses face.[3] In the past, organizations could succeed by claiming excellence in one area—quality, reliability, or cost, for example—but this is not the case today. The current environment demands excellence in all areas and vigilant leaders. A recent survey of CEOs who were facing crises found that 50 percent of them said they believed the problems arrived "suddenly" and that they had not prepared adequately for them. More than 10 percent said they were, in fact, the last to know about the problems.[4]

As we saw in Chapter 1, change is what's on managers' minds. The pursuit of organizational effectiveness through downsizing, restructuring, reengineering, productivity management, cycle-time reduction, and other efforts is paramount. Organizations are in a state of tremendous turmoil and transition, and all members are affected. Continued downsizings may have left firms leaner but not necessarily richer. Though downsizing can increase shareholder value by better aligning costs with revenues, firms may suffer from public criticism for their actions. Laying off employees may be accompanied by increases in CEO pay and stock options, linking the misery of employees with the financial success of owners and management.[5]

Organizations must also deal with ethical, environmental, and other social issues. Competition is fierce, and companies can no longer afford to rest on their laurels. American Airlines has developed a series of programs to constantly reevaluate and change its operating methods to prevent the company from stagnating. General Electric holds off-site WorkOut sessions with groups of managers and employees whose goal is to make GE a faster, less complex organization that can respond effectively to change. In the WorkOut sessions, employees recommend specific changes, explain why they are needed, and propose ways the changes can be implemented. Top management must make an immediate response: an approval, a disapproval (with an explanation), or a request for more information. The GE WorkOut sessions eliminate the barriers that keep employees from contributing to change.

There are two basic forms of change in organizations. *Planned change* is change resulting from a deliberate decision to alter the organization. Companies that wish to move from a traditional hierarchical structure to one that facilitates self-managed teams must use a proactive, carefully orchestrated approach. Not all change is planned, however. *Unplanned change* is imposed on the organization and is often unforeseen. Changes in government regulations and changes in the economy, for example, are often unplanned. Responsiveness to unplanned change requires tremendous flexibility and adaptability on the part of organizations. Managers must be prepared to handle both planned and unplanned forms of change in organizations.

Forces for change can come from many sources. Some of these are external, arising from outside the company, whereas others are internal, arising from sources within the organization.

External Forces

The four major managerial challenges we have described throughout the book are major external forces for change. Globalization, workforce diversity, technological change, and managing ethical behavior are challenges that precipitate change in organizations.

GLOBALIZATION The power players in the global market are the multinational and transnational organizations. Conoco, for example, formed a joint

---

planned change

Change resulting from a deliberate decision to alter the organization.

unplanned change

Change that is imposed on the organization and is often unforeseen.

1. Identify the major external and internal forces for change in organizations.

venture with Arkhangelskgeoldobycha, a Russian firm, to develop a new oil field in Russia. This partnership, named Polar Lights, was the first Russian-American joint venture to develop an oil field in Russia. The project has been successful, and the production from Polar Lights has now passed the 75 million bbl production milestone.

NAFTA's impact has been felt across numerous industries. American agriculture has been a tremendous beneficiary, with annual U.S. exports of fruits and vegetables to Mexico climbing by more than $1 billion since 1993. This expanded market has been a tremendous windfall for U.S. producers, but trouble may be looming. Mexican farm leaders have accused the United States of unfairly dumping fruits and vegetables into the Mexican market.[6] They also claim that small Mexican farms cannot compete with large industrialized U.S. operations, and they have asked the Mexican government to renegotiate NAFTA to give them greater protection.[7] Because global business implicitly involves multiple governments and legal systems, it carries unique risks not found by firms competing within a single nation.

The United States is but one nation in the drive to open new markets. Japan and Germany are responding to global competition in powerful ways, and the emergence of the European Union as a powerful trading group will have a profound impact on world markets. By joining with their European neighbors, companies in smaller countries will begin to make major progress in world markets, thus increasing the fierce competition that already exists.

Kellogg's has long been a global company, and MTV is moving rapidly into global markets. In The Real World 18.1, read how the head of MTV India is learning from Kellogg's experience. Coca-Cola, this chapter's focus firm, faced a crisis when it introduced its Dasani bottled water in Great Britain. Coke had chosen a particularly compelling theme for its advertising, touting Dasani as even more pure than other bottled waters. After Coke had invested more than seven million pounds in this project, government regulators found that the water contained illegally high levels of bromate, a potentially cancer-causing chemical. To make matters worse, Coke was forced to admit that the contamination was introduced by its own production process. Coke's response was swift: it quickly pulled half a million bottles of Dasani from London shelves and postponed plans for product launches in France and Germany. Coke is still contemplating how best to respond to this debacle, which some British writers rank among the worst marketing disasters in Britain's history.[8]

All of these changes, along with others, have led companies to rethink the borders of their markets and to encourage their employees to think globally. Jack Welch, former CEO of GE, was among the first to call for a boundaryless company, in which there are no mental distinctions between domestic and foreign operations or between managers and employees.[9] The thought that drives the boundaryless company is that barriers that get in the way of people's working together should be removed. Globalizing an organization means rethinking the most efficient ways to use resources, disseminate and gather information, and develop people. It requires not only structural changes but also changes in the minds of employees.

WORKFORCE DIVERSITY Related to globalization is the challenge of workforce diversity. As we have seen throughout this book, workforce diversity is a powerful force for change in organizations. Let us recap the demographic trends contributing to workforce diversity that we discussed at length in Chapter 2. First, the workforce will see increased participation from females,

Kellogg's and MTV: Soggy Corn Flakes in India

Kellogg's anticipated warm embrace of its Corn Flakes cereal in India turned out instead to be a cold, soggy response. Kellogg's failed to consider India's breakfast preferences.

© Ravi Tahilramani/iStockphoto

Alex Kuruvilla is MTV's top man in Mumbai, and he faces tremendous challenges in bringing MTV into unfamiliar territory. He has experience, though, at this sort of thing. Kuruvilla was an account executive in Mumbai when Kellogg's decided to introduce Corn Flakes and other products into India. Kellogg's entered India with great enthusiasm, figuring that every Indian household would soon be enjoying Corn Flakes for breakfast.

What Kellogg's failed to recognize was that traditional Indian breakfasts are hot, fresh, and often spicy. Dalia, for instance, is a soup made of lentils, rice, peas, wheat, and onions, seasoned liberally with chili powder. The concept of "cold and crispy" at breakfast was odd to Indians. When Indian women were encouraged to at least try the Corn Flakes, they used hot milk, because traditionally, fresh milk is boiled to be pasteurized. The combination of Corn Flakes and hot milk was an unappetizing mess.

Kellogg's learned from this experience and ultimately introduced hot cereals in flavors that matched Indian taste preferences. And Alex Kuruvilla learned from observing Kellogg's experience. He praised Kellogg's for adapting quickly, noting that in India, as in any global endeavor, you have to adapt and reflect the local culture—which is what he intends to do with MTV India. He is probably on the right track in recognizing that *The Osbournes* is not a big hit among Indian teenagers, nor is rap music. MTV India will have to reflect the local culture.

SOURCE: M. Gunther, "MTV's Passage to India," *Fortune* (August 9, 2004): 117–125, http://www.fortune.com/fortune/subs/article/0,15114,672286,00.html.

because the majority of new workers will be female.[10] Second, the workforce will be more culturally diverse than ever. Part of this is attributable to globalization, but in addition, U.S. demographics are changing. The participation of African Americans and Hispanic Americans is increasing in record numbers. Third, the workforce is aging. There will be fewer young workers and more middle-aged Americans working.[11]

A few years ago, Denny's, the restaurant chain, was a name synonymous with racism. In 1994, the company paid $54.4 million to settle two lawsuits brought by black customers who claimed some restaurants refused to seat or serve them. Denny's undertook radical changes led by a blunt-talking CEO and a determined diversity officer in 1995. Because Denny's responded quickly, decisively, and sincerely, it weathered the crisis. Performance appraisals are now based on valuing diversity. A top manager who doesn't do so can have up to 25 percent of his or her bonus withheld. The company's response to a recent incident demonstrates that it takes this issue seriously: a cook and a waiter accused of racist behavior toward an African American customer in Florida were fired within twenty-four hours of the complaint. Almost half of Denny's 1,011 franchises are owned by minorities, 255 of them by Asian Indians, while one-third of restaurant managers and one-fifth of executives are also minorities. Denny's ranks fifth on *Fortune*'s list of the "50 Best Companies for Minorities."[12]

TECHNOLOGICAL CHANGE Rapid technological innovation is another force for change in organizations, and those that fail to keep pace can quickly fall behind. *Smart tags,* for example, are replacing bar codes for tracking and scanning products. Bar codes are passive identification markers whose stripes are unchangeable, and items must be lined up individually for scanning (like in a grocery store checkout line). Manufacturers are starting to use radio-frequency identification (RFID) tags that are as small as two matches laid side by side, and hold digital memory chips the size of a pinhead. RFIDs are also used in show dogs and cats. The tags are injected under a pet's skin with a syringe.

RFIDs contain a lot more information than bar codes, and users can alter the information on them. As many as fifty tags per second can be read—forty times faster than bar-code scanners. Ford uses RFIDs to track parts. Data such as a unique ID, part type, plant location, and time/date stamps are included on the tag. Because RFIDs are reusable, the long-term costs are about the same as bar codes.[13]

Technological innovations bring about profound change because they are not just changes in the way work is performed. Instead, the innovation process promotes associated changes in work relationships and organizational structures.[14] The team approach adopted by many organizations leads to flatter structures, decentralized decision making, and more open communication between leaders and team members.

MANAGING ETHICAL BEHAVIOR Recent ethical scandals have brought ethical behavior in organizations to the forefront of public consciousness. Ethical issues, however, are not always public and monumental. Employees face ethical dilemmas in their daily work lives. The need to manage ethical behavior has brought about several changes in organizations. Most center around the idea that an organization must create a culture that encourages ethical behavior.

All public companies issue annual financial reports. Gap Inc. has gone a step further by issuing an annual ethical report. The clothing industry is almost synonymous with the use of sweatshops, or low-paying overseas factories in which third-world workers (including children) labor for fifty to sixty hours each week for a few dollars in pay; in this sense, Gap is hardly alone in facing these issues. What sets Gap apart is its candor, beginning with its open admission that none of its 3,000 suppliers fully complies with the firm's ethical code of conduct. But rather than run from these problems, Gap has chosen to work with its suppliers to improve conditions overseas. The firm has more than ninety full-time employees charged with monitoring supplier operations around the world.[15]

The annual report includes extensive descriptions of these workers' activities, including which factories were monitored, what violations were found, and which factories are no longer used by Gap because of violations. It also addresses media reports critical of Gap and its operations.

Gap tries to improve worker conditions by providing training and encouraging suppliers to develop their own conduct codes. For example, in China it has encouraged lunchtime sessions in which workers are advised of their rights. While most facilities respond positively to these efforts, some don't, and Gap pulled its business from 136 factories it concluded were not going to improve. It also terminated contracts with two factories that had verifiable use of child labor. Gap's approach to overseas labor offers a model for other garment firms.[16]

Society expects organizations to maintain ethical behavior both internally and in relationships with other organizations. Ethical behavior is expected in relationships with customers, the environment, and society. These expectations may be informal, or they may come in the form of increased legal requirements.

These four challenges are forces that place pressures to change on organizations. There are other forces as well. Legal developments, changing stakeholder expectations, and shifting consumer demands can also lead to change.[17] And some companies change simply because others are changing.[18] Other powerful forces for change originate from within the organization.

Internal Forces

Pressures for change that originate inside the organization are generally recognizable in the form of signals indicating that something needs to be altered. A declining effectiveness is a pressure to change. A company that experiences its third quarterly loss within a fiscal year is undoubtedly motivated to do something about it. Some companies react by instituting layoffs and massive cost-cutting programs, whereas others look at the bigger picture, view the loss as symptomatic of an underlying problem, and seek the cause of the problem.

A crisis may also stimulate change in an organization. Strikes or walkouts may lead management to change the wage structure. The resignation of a key decision maker may cause the company to rethink the composition of its management team and its role in the organization. A much-publicized crisis that led to change at Exxon (now ExxonMobil) was the oil spill caused by the *Exxon Valdez* oil tanker. The accident brought about many changes in Exxon's environmental policies.

Changes in employee expectations can also trigger change in organizations. A company that hires a group of young newcomers may find that their expectations are very different from those expressed by older workers. The workforce is more educated than ever before. Although this has its advantages, workers with more education demand more of employers. Today's workers are also concerned with career and family balance issues, such as dependent care. The many sources of workforce diversity hold potential for a host of differing expectations among employees.

Changes in the work climate at an organization can also stimulate change. A workforce that seems lethargic, unmotivated, and dissatisfied is a symptom that must be addressed. This symptom is common in organizations that have experienced layoffs. Workers who have escaped a layoff may grieve for those who have lost their jobs and may find it hard to continue to be productive. They may fear that they will be laid off as well, and many feel insecure in their jobs.

Change Is Inevitable

We have seen that organizations face substantial pressures to change from both external and internal sources. Change in organizations is inevitable, but change is a process that can be managed. The scope of change can vary from small to quantum.

The Scope of Change

Change can be of a relatively small scope, such as a modification in a work procedure (an *incremental change*). Such changes, in essence, are a fine-tuning of the organization, or the making of small improvements. Intel and other chip producers must continually upgrade their manufacturing equipment just to stay competitive. Intel's 2004 plan to convert an Arizona "fab" or chip-making plant from older to newer technology is expected to cost $2 billion.[19] While radical

2. Define the terms *incremental change, strategic change, transformational change,* and *change agent.*

incremental change

Change of a relatively small scope, such as making small improvements.

change is more exciting and interesting to discuss, most research on change has focused on evolutionary (incremental) rather than revolutionary change.[20] Change can also be of a larger scale, such as the restructuring of an organization (a *strategic change*).[21] In strategic change, the organization moves from an old state to a known new state during a controlled period of time. Strategic change usually involves a series of transition steps. AT&T, the granddaddy of long distance companies, made a strategic decision in 2004 to get out of the residential long distance market entirely. Rather than simply cutting off its existing customers, the firm has stopped advertising to consumers and raised residential rates sharply.[22]

The most massive scope of change is *transformational change*, in which the organization moves to a radically different, and sometimes unknown, future state.[23] In transformational change, the organization's mission, culture, goals, structure, and leadership may all change dramatically.[24] Just over a century ago, two successful bicycle makers decided to leave the safety of the bike business to devote their time to building and selling an amazing new invention— the airplane—which transformed travel, warfare, communications, and the entire world. The Wright brothers transformed not only their bike business but the whole world! Of all the tasks a leader undertakes, many say that changing the form and nature of the organization itself may be the most difficult, an observation supported by research.[25]

One of the toughest decisions faced by leaders is the proper "pace" of change. Some scholars argue that rapid change is more likely to succeed, since it creates momentum,[26] while others argue that these short, sharp changes are actually rare and not experienced by most firms.[27] Still others observe that change in a large organization may occur incrementally in parts of the firm and quickly in others.[28] In summary, researchers agree that the pace of change is important, but they can't quite agree on which pace of change is most beneficial.

Very little long-term research has looked at change over a significant time period. One twelve-year study looked at change in the structure of Canadian National Sports Organizations (NSOs). It found that within NSOs, radical transition did not always require a fast pace of change. It also found that successful transitions often involve changing the high-impact elements of an organization (in this case, their decision-making structures) early in the process.[29]

The Change Agent's Role

The individual or group that undertakes the task of introducing and managing a change in an organization is known as a *change agent*. Change agents can be internal, such as managers or employees who are appointed to oversee the change process. In her book *The Change Masters*, Rosabeth Moss Kanter notes that at companies like Hewlett-Packard and Polaroid, managers and employees alike are developing the needed skills to produce change and innovation in the organization.[30] Change agents can also be external, such as outside consultants.

Internal change agents have certain advantages in managing the change process. They know the organization's past history, its political system, and its culture. Because they must live with the results of their change efforts, internal change agents are likely to be very careful about managing change. There are disadvantages, however, to using internal change agents. They may be associated with certain factions within the organization and may easily be accused of favoritism. Furthermore, internal change agents may be too close to the situation to have an objective view of what needs to be done.

strategic change
Change of a larger scale, such as organizational restructuring.

transformational change
Change in which the organization moves to a radically different, and sometimes unknown, future state.

change agent
The individual or group that undertakes the task of introducing and managing a change in an organization.

Change leaders within organizations tend to be young, in the twenty-five to forty age range. They are more flexible than ordinary general managers and much more people oriented. A high number of change leaders are women. The change leaders have a balance of technical and interpersonal skills. They are tough decision makers who focus on performance results. They also know how to energize people and get them aligned in the same direction. They get more out of people than ordinary managers can. In addition, they have the ability to operate in more than one leadership style and can shift from a team mode to command and control, depending on the situation. They are also comfortable with uncertainty.[31]

If change is large scale or strategic in nature, it may take a team of leaders to make change happen. A team assembling leaders with a variety of skills, expertise, and influence that can work together harmoniously may be needed to accomplish change of large scope.[32] In the Science feature, you can learn about the factors that lead to success for change management teams.

External change agents bring an outsider's objective view to the organization. They may be preferred by employees because of their impartiality. External change agents face certain problems, however; not only is their knowledge of the organization's history limited, but they may also be viewed with suspicion by organization members. External change agents have more power in directing changes if employees perceive the change agents as being trustworthy, possessing important expertise, having a track record that establishes credibility, and being similar to them.[33]

Different change agent competencies are required at different stages of the change process. Leadership, communication, training, and participation have varying levels of impact as the change proceeds, meaning change agents must be flexible in how they work through the different phases of the process.[34] Effective change leaders build strong relationships within their leadership team, between the team and organizational members, and between the team and key environmental players. Maintaining all three relationships simultaneously is quite difficult, so successful leaders are continually "coupling" and "uncoupling" with the different groups as the change process proceeds. Adaptability is a key skill for both internal and external change leaders.[35]

The Process of Change in Organizations

Organizations tend to respond to change by continuing to do what they are good at. After all, these strategies have been successful in the past. After periods of success, organizations can lose the ability to recognize when it is necessary to give up past strategies and try something new. Once an organization has made the decision to change, careful planning and analysis must take place. Change processes such as business process reengineering cannot ensure the success of the change. The people aspects of change are the most critically important for successful transformations.[36] Even Michael Hammer, who launched the reengineering movement, admits that he forgot about the "human aspects" of change. "I was reflecting on my engineering background and was insufficiently appreciative of the human dimension. I've learned that it's critical."[37] If people are not taken into account, a change process will be negatively affected or may even fail. Like organizations, people tend to cling to what has worked in the past, especially if they have been successful and they see no need for change.[38]

The challenge of managing the change process involves harnessing the energy of diverse individuals who hold a variety of views of change. It is impor-

Taking Care of Business with Team Citizenship Behaviors

Imagine you have been chosen to lead a team that has been asked to recommend and implement big changes within your company. You know it's going to be tough, and you have no clue how to begin. What things should you keep in mind in terms of helping the team work together effectively? A recent study asked this question. It examined multiple change management teams to find out what factors encouraged team members to help each other (behaviors called team citizenship behaviors, or TCBs). Several things were found to be important. First, the leader's use of encouragement was a major factor. Teams whose leaders encouraged teamwork demonstrated more of it. Also, team members who were more committed to the team at the beginning contributed more to it, suggesting that attention should be paid to member commitment in the initial stage of team formation. Third, high levels of support from the organization's management were associated with higher levels of TCB. So, from this study, you can conclude that encouraging members to demonstrate teamwork, building team members' commitment, and providing support will help your team succeed in its change management task.

SOURCE: C. L. Pearce and P. A. Herbik, "Citizenship Behavior at the Team Level of Analysis," *The Journal of Social Psychology* 144 (June 2004): 293–310.

tant to recognize that most changes will be met with varying degrees of resistance and to understand the basis of resistance to change.

Resistance to Change

People often resist change in a rational response based on self-interest. However, there are countless other reasons people resist change. Many of these center around the notion of reactance—that is, a negative reaction that occurs when individuals feel that their personal freedom is threatened.[39] Some of the major reasons for resisting change follow.

3. Describe the major reasons individuals resist change and discuss methods organizations can use to manage resistance.

FEAR OF THE UNKNOWN Change often brings with it substantial uncertainty. Employees facing a technological change, such as the introduction of a new computer system, may resist the change simply because it introduces ambiguity into what was once a comfortable situation for them. This is especially a problem when there has been little communication about the change.

FEAR OF LOSS When a change is impending, some employees may fear losing their jobs; this fear is particularly acute when an advanced technology like robotics is introduced. Employees may also fear losing their status because of a change.[40] Computer systems experts, for example, may feel threatened when they feel their expertise is eroded by the installation of a more user-friendly networked information system. Another common fear is that changes may diminish the positive qualities the individual enjoys in the job. Computerizing the customer service positions at Southwestern Bell (now part of SBC Communications), for example, threatened the autonomy that representatives previously enjoyed.

FEAR OF FAILURE Some employees fear changes because they fear their own failure. Employees may fear that changes will result in increased workloads or increased task difficulty, and they may question their own competencies for handling these. They may also fear that performance expectations will be elevated following the change, and that they may not measure up.[41] Resistance can also stem from a fear that the change itself will not really take place. In one large library that was undergoing a major automation effort, employees were doubtful that the vendor could really deliver the state-of-the-art system that was promised. In this case, the implementation never became a reality—the employees' fears were well founded.[42]

DISRUPTION OF INTERPERSONAL RELATIONSHIPS Employees may resist change that threatens to limit meaningful interpersonal relationships on the job. Librarians facing the automation effort described previously feared that once the computerized system was implemented, they would not be able to interact as they did when they had to go to another floor of the library to get help finding a resource. In the new system, with the touch of a few buttons on the computer, they would get their information without consulting another librarian.

PERSONALITY CONFLICTS When the change agent's personality engenders negative reactions, employees may resist the change. A change agent who appears insensitive to employee concerns and feelings may meet considerable resistance, because employees perceive that their needs are not being taken into account.

POLITICS Organizational change may also shift the existing balance of power in the organization. Individuals or groups who hold power under the current arrangement may be threatened with losing these political advantages in the advent of change.

CULTURAL ASSUMPTIONS AND VALUES Sometimes cultural assumptions and values can be impediments to change, particularly if the assumptions underlying the change are alien to employees. This form of resistance can be very difficult to overcome, because some cultural assumptions are unconscious. As we discussed in Chapter 2, some cultures tend to avoid uncertainty. In Mexican and Greek cultures, for example, change that creates a great deal of uncertainty may be met with great resistance.

Some individuals are more tolerant of ambiguity than others. You can assess your own attitude toward ambiguity in You 18.1.

We have described several sources of resistance to change. The reasons for resistance are as diverse as the workforce itself and vary with different individuals and organizations. The challenge for managers is introducing change in a positive manner and managing employee resistance.

Managing Resistance to Change

The traditional view of resistance to change treated it as something to be overcome, and many organizational attempts to reduce the resistance have only served to intensify it. The contemporary view holds that resistance is simply a form of feedback and that this feedback can be used very productively to manage the change process.[43] One key to managing resistance is to plan for it and to be ready with a variety of strategies for using the resistance as feedback and helping employees negotiate the transition. Three key strategies for managing resistance to change are communication, participation, and empathy and support.[44]

Communication about impending change is essential if employees are to adjust effectively.[45] The details of the change should be provided, but equally

Tolerance for Ambiguity

Tolerance for Ambiguity Survey Form

Read each of the following statements carefully. Then rate each of them in terms of the extent to which you either agree or disagree with the statement using the following scale:

Completely Disagree			**Neither Agree nor Disagree**			**Completely Agree**
1	**2**	**3**	**4**	**5**	**6**	**7**

Place the number that best describes your degree of agreement or disagreement in the blank to the left of each statement.

____ **1.** An expert who doesn't come up with a definite answer probably doesn't know much.

____ **2.** I would like to live in a foreign country for a while.

____ **3.** The sooner we all acquire similar values and ideals, the better.

____ **4.** A good teacher is one who makes you wonder about your way of looking at things.

____ **5.** I like parties where I know most of the people more than ones where all or most of the people are complete strangers.

____ **6.** Teachers or supervisors who hand out vague assignments give a chance for one to show initiative and originality.

____ **7.** A person who leads an even, regular life in which few surprises or unexpected happenings arise really has a lot to be grateful for.

____ **8.** Many of our most important decisions are based upon insufficient information.

____ **9.** There is really no such thing as a problem that can't be solved.

____ **10.** People who fit their lives to a schedule probably miss most of the joy of living.

____ **11.** A good job is one where what is to be done and how it is to be done are always clear.

____ **12.** It is more fun to tackle a complicated problem than to solve a simple one.

____ **13.** In the long run, it is possible to get more done by tackling small, simple problems rather than large and complicated ones.

____ **14.** Often the most interesting and stimulating people are those who don't mind being different and original.

____ **15.** What we are used to is always preferable to what is unfamiliar.

Scoring: For even-numbered questions, add the total points.
For odd-numbered questions, use reverse scoring and add the total points.
Your score is the total of the even- and odd-numbered questions.

Norms Using the Tolerance for Ambiguity Scale

Source: The Tolerance for Ambiguity Scale

Basis: The survey asks 15 questions about personal and work-oriented situations with ambiguity. You were asked to rate each situation on a scale from one (tolerant) to seven (intolerant). (Alternating questions have the response scale reversed.) The index scores the items. A perfectly tolerant person would score 15 and a perfectly intolerant person 105. Scores between 20 and 80 are reported, with means of 45. The responses to the even-numbered questions with 7 minus the score are added to the response for the odd-numbered questions.

(continued)

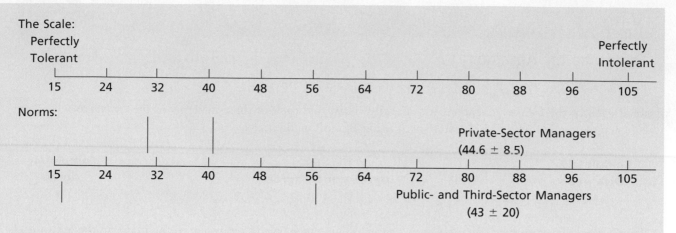

The Scale: Perfectly Tolerant												Perfectly Intolerant
15	24	32	40	48	56	64	72	80	88	96	105	

Norms:

Private-Sector Managers
(44.6 ± 8.5)

15	24	32	40	48	56	64	72	80	88	96	105

Public- and Third-Sector Managers
(43 ± 20)

SOURCE: "Tolerance for Ambiguity" from D. Marcic, *Organizational Behavior: Experiences and Cases* (St. Paul, Minn.: West Publishing, 1992), 339–340. Adapted from Paul Nutt. Used with permission.

important is the rationale behind the change. Employees want to know why change is needed. If there is no good reason for it, why should they favor the change? Providing accurate and timely information about the change can help prevent unfounded fears and potentially damaging rumors from developing. Delaying the announcement of a change and handling information in a secretive fashion can serve to fuel the rumor mill. Open communication in a culture of trust is a key ingredient for successful change.[46] It is also beneficial to inform people about the potential consequences of the change. Educating employees on new work procedures is often helpful. Studies on the introduction of computers in the workplace indicate that providing employees with opportunities for hands-on practice helps alleviate fears about the new technology. Employees who have experience with computers display more positive attitudes and greater efficacy—a sense that they can master their new tasks.[47]

There is substantial research support underscoring the importance of participation in the change process. Employees must be engaged and involved in order for change to work—as supported by the notion "That which we create, we support." Participation helps employees become involved in the change and establish a feeling of ownership in the process. When employees are allowed to participate, they are more committed to the change. Designer retailer Prada, famous for its extravagant clothing, decided to create an equally amazing retail location. In December 2001, the company opened per-

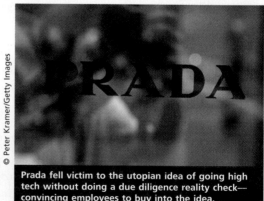

Prada fell victim to the utopian idea of going high tech without doing a due diligence reality check—convincing employees to buy into the idea.

© Peter Kramer/Getty Images

haps the world's most advanced boutique in New York City, spending one-fourth of the company's IT budget on the experiment. Wireless networks linked each item in inventory to a single database, allowing staff to walk the floor armed with wireless PDAs to check inventory. Automated dressing rooms with touch-screens offered additional information to customers. But by 2004, most of the technology sat abandoned, some of it malfunctioning, some of it simply too difficult to use. Like many other firms before it, Prada appears to have fallen in love with the "idea" of going high tech, without bothering to get the actual users (its employees) onboard. The company is currently reevaluating its strategy.[48]

Another strategy for managing resistance is providing empathy and support to employees who have trouble dealing with the change. Active listening is an excellent tool for identifying the reasons behind resistance and for uncovering fears. An expression of concerns about the change can provide important feedback that managers can use to improve the change process. Emotional support and encouragement can help an employee deal with the anxiety that is a natural response to change. Employees who experience severe reactions to change can benefit from talking with a counselor. Some companies provide counseling through their employee assistance plans.

Open communication, participation, and emotional support can go a long way toward managing resistance to change. Managers must realize that some resistance is inevitable, however, and should plan ways to deal with resistance early in the change process.

The Hartford Financial Services Group encountered some resistance to change in going global. When the company attempted to enter the lucrative British and Dutch insurance markets by acquiring British and Dutch companies, the overseas staff resisted changes suggested by Hartford, such as using laptops and introducing new financial products. The introduction of such U.S. business practices is often referred to as "economic imperialism" by employees who feel they are being forced to substitute corporate values for personal or national values.

Hartford needed its European staff to understand that they were part of a transnational company. Its solution was to offer a stock ownership plan that tied the personal fortunes of the staff to the company. This gave employees a considerable interest in Hartford's success and helped them identify with the company.[49]

Behavioral Reactions to Change

In spite of attempts to minimize the resistance to change in an organization, some reactions to change are inevitable. Negative reactions may be manifested in overt behavior or through more passive resistance to change. People show four basic, identifiable reactions to change: disengagement, disidentification, disenchantment, and disorientation.[50] Managers can use interventions to deal with these reactions, as shown in Table 18.1.

Disengagement is psychological withdrawal from change. The employee may appear to lose initiative and interest in the job. Employees who disengage may fear the change but approach it by doing nothing and simply hoping for the best. Disengaged employees are physically present but mentally absent. They lack drive and commitment, and they simply comply without real psychological

disengagement
Psychological withdrawal from change.

TABLE 18.1 Reactions to Change and Managerial Interventions

REACTION	EXPRESSION	MANAGERIAL INTERVENTION
Disengagement	Withdrawal	Confront, identify
Disidentification	Sadness, worry	Explore, transfer
Disenchantment	Anger	Neutralize, acknowledge
Disorientation	Confusion	Explain, plan

SOURCE: Table adapted from H. Woodward and S. Buchholz, *Aftershock: Helping People through Corporate Change*, p. 15. Copyright © 1987 John Wiley & Sons, Inc. Reprinted by permission of John Wiley & Sons, Inc.

investment in their work. Disengagement can be recognized by behaviors such as being hard to find or doing only the basics to get the job done. Typical disengagement statements include "No problem" or "This won't affect me."

One oil and gas company that started ventures in Russia found that the very idea of change was alien to Russian managers. They felt that the manager's task was to establish procedures and ensure continuity. When Western managers tried to institute change, the Russian managers disengaged, believing that their job was to secure stability rather than change.[51]

The basic managerial strategy for dealing with disengaged individuals is to confront them with their reaction and draw them out so that they can identify the concerns that need to be addressed. Disengaged employees may not be aware of the change in their behavior, and they need to be assured of your intentions. Drawing them out and helping them air their feelings can lead to productive discussions. Disengaged people seldom become cheerleaders for the change, but they can be brought closer to accepting and working with a change by open communication with an empathetic manager who is willing to listen.

Another reaction to change is *disidentification*. Individuals reacting in this way feel that their identity has been threatened by the change, and they feel very vulnerable. Many times they cling to a past procedure because they had a sense of mastery over it, and it gave them a sense of security. "My job is completely changed" and "I used to . . ." are verbal indications of disidentification. Disidentified employees often display sadness and worry. They may appear to be sulking and dwelling on the past by reminiscing about the old ways of doing things.

Because disidentified employees are so vulnerable, they often feel like victims in the change process. Managers can help them through the transition by encouraging them to explore their feelings and helping them transfer their positive feelings into the new situation. One way to do this is to help them identify what they liked in the old situation and then show them how it is possible to have the same positive experience in the new situation. Disidentified employees need to see that work itself and emotion are separable—that is, that they can let go of old ways and experience positive reactions to new ways of performing their jobs.

Disenchantment is also a common reaction to change. It is usually expressed as negativity or anger. Disenchanted employees realize that the past is gone, and they are mad about it. They may try to enlist the support of other employees by forming coalitions. Destructive behaviors like sabotage and backstabbing may result. Typical verbal signs of disenchantment are "This will never work" and "I'm getting out of this company as soon as I can." The anger of a disenchanted person may be directly expressed in organizational cultures where it is permissible to do so. This behavior tends to get the issues out in the open. More often, however, cultures view the expression of emotion at work as improper and unbusinesslike. In these cultures, the anger is suppressed and emerges in more passive-aggressive ways, such as badmouthing and starting rumors. One of the particular dangers of disenchantment is that it is quite contagious in the workplace.

It is often difficult to reason with disenchanted employees. Thus, the first step in managing this reaction is to bring these employees from their highly negative, emotionally charged state to a more neutral state. To neutralize the reaction does not mean to dismiss it; rather, it means to allow the individuals to let off the necessary steam so that they can come to terms with their anger. The second part of the strategy for dealing with disenchanted employees is to acknowledge that their anger is normal and that you do not hold it against them. Sometimes disenchantment is a mask for one of the other three reactions, and it must be worked

disidentification

Feeling that one's identity is being threatened by a change.

disenchantment

Feeling negativity or anger toward a change.

through to get to the core of the employee's reaction. Employees may also become cynical about change and lose faith in the leaders of change.

A final reaction to change is *disorientation*. Disoriented employees are lost and confused, and often they are unsure of their feelings. They waste energy trying to figure out what to do instead of how to do things. Disoriented individuals ask a lot of questions and become very detail oriented. They may appear to need a good deal of guidance and may leave their work undone until all of their questions have been answered. "Analysis paralysis" is characteristic of disoriented employees. They feel that they have lost touch with the priorities of the company, and they may want to analyze the change to death before acting on it. Disoriented employees may ask questions like "Now what do I do?" or "What do I do first?"

disorientation

Feelings of loss and confusion due to a change.

Disorientation is a common reaction among people who are used to clear goals and unambiguous directions. When change is introduced, it creates uncertainty and a lack of clarity. The managerial strategy for dealing with this reaction is to explain the change in a way that minimizes the ambiguity that is present. The information about the change needs to be put into a framework or an overall vision so that the disoriented individual can see where he or she fits into the grand scheme of things. Once the disoriented employee sees the broader context of the change, you can plan a series of steps to help this employee adjust. The employee needs a sense of priorities to work on.

Managers need to be able to diagnose these four reactions to change. Because each reaction brings with it significant and different concerns, no single universal strategy can help all employees adjust. By recognizing each reaction and applying the appropriate strategy, it is possible to help even strong resisters work through a transition successfully.

Lewin's Change Model

Kurt Lewin developed a model of the change process that has stood the test of time and continues to influence the way organizations manage planned change. Lewin's model is based on the idea of force field analysis.[52] Figure 18.1 shows a force field analysis of a decision to engage in exercise behavior.

4. Apply force field analysis to a problem.

FIGURE 18.1   Force Field Analysis of a Decision to Engage in Exercise

18.1

Forces for change	Forces for status quo
Weight gain	Lack of time
Minimally passing treadmill test	No exercise facility at work
Feeling lethargic; having no energy	Spouse/partner hates to exercise
Family history of cardiovascular disease	No interest in physical activity or sports
New, physically demanding job	Made a grade of D in a physical education class

Equilibrium

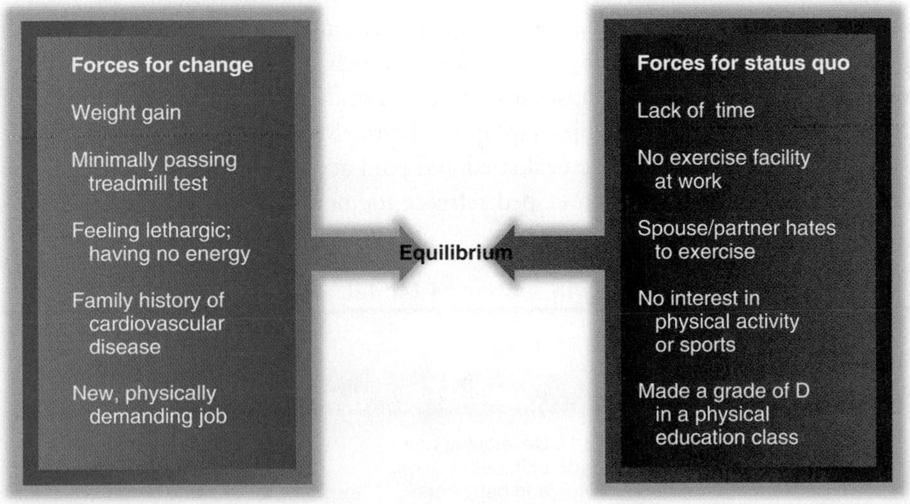

This model contends that a person's behavior is the product of two opposing forces; one force pushes toward preserving the status quo, and the other force pushes for change. When the two opposing forces are approximately equal, current behavior is maintained. For behavioral change to occur, the forces maintaining the status quo must be overcome. This can be accomplished by increasing the forces for change, by weakening the forces for the status quo, or by a combination of these actions. You 18.2 asks you to apply force field analysis to a problem in your life.

Lewin's change model is a three-step process, as shown in Figure 18.2. The process begins with *unfreezing*, which is a crucial first hurdle in the change process. Unfreezing involves encouraging individuals to discard old behaviors by shaking up the equilibrium state that maintains the status quo. Organizations often accomplish unfreezing by eliminating the rewards for current behavior and showing that current behavior is not valued. By unfreezing, individuals accept that change needs to occur. In essence, individuals surrender by allowing the boundaries of their status quo to be opened in preparation for change.[53]

The second step in the change process is *moving*. In the moving stage, new attitudes, values, and behaviors are substituted for old ones. Organizations accomplish moving by initiating new options and explaining the rationale for the change, as well as by providing training to help employees develop the new skills they need. Employees should be given the overarching vision for the change so that they can establish their roles within the new organizational structure and processes.[54]

Refreezing is the final step in the change process. In this step, new attitudes, values, and behaviors are established as the new status quo. The new ways of operating are cemented in and reinforced. Managers should ensure that the organizational culture and formal reward systems encourage the new behaviors and avoid rewarding the old ways of operating. Changes in the reward structure may be needed to ensure that the organization is not rewarding the old behaviors and merely hoping for the new behaviors. A study by Exxon Research and Engineering showed that framing and displaying a mission statement in managers' offices may eventually change the behavior of 2 percent of the managers. In contrast, changing managers' evaluation and reward systems will change the behavior of 55 percent of the managers almost overnight.[55]

The approach used by Monsanto to increase opportunities for women within the company is an illustration of how to use Lewin's model effectively. First, Monsanto emphasized unfreezing by helping employees debunk negative stereotypes about women in business. This also helped overcome resistance to change. Second, Monsanto moved employees' attitudes and behaviors by diversity training in which differences were emphasized as positive, and supervisors learned ways of training and developing female employees. Third, Monsanto changed its reward system so that managers were evaluated and paid according to how they coached and promoted women, which helped refreeze the new attitudes and behaviors.

5. Explain Lewin's organizational change model.

unfreezing
The first step in Lewin's change model, in which individuals are encouraged to discard old behaviors by shaking up the equilibrium state that maintains the status quo.

moving
The second step in Lewin's change model, in which new attitudes, values, and behaviors are substituted for old ones.

refreezing
The final step in Lewin's change model, in which new attitudes, values, and behaviors are established as the new status quo.

FIGURE 18.2 Lewin's Change Model

Unfreezing	Moving	Refreezing
Reducing forces for status quo	Developing new attitudes, values, and behaviors	Reinforcing new attitudes, values, and behaviors

Applying Force Field Analysis

Think of a problem you are currently facing. An example would be trying to increase the amount of study time you devote to a particular class.

1. Describe the problem, as specifically as possible.
2. List the forces driving change on the arrows at the left side of the diagram.
3. List the forces restraining change on the arrows at the right side of the diagram.
4. What can you do, specifically, to remove the obstacles to change?
5. What can you do to increase the forces driving change?
6. What benefits can be derived from breaking a problem down into forces driving change and forces restraining change?

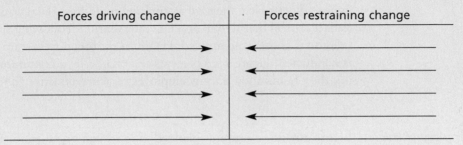

Forces driving change	Forces restraining change

One frequently overlooked issue is whether or not the change is consistent with the company's deeply held core values. Value consistency is critical to making a change "stick." Organizations whose members perceive the changes to be consistent with the firm's values adopt the changes much more easily and fully. Conversely, organizations whose members' values conflict with the changes may display "superficial conformity," in which members pay lip service to the changes, but ultimately revert to their old behaviors.[56]

Organizations that wish to change can select from a variety of methods to make a change become reality. Organization development is a method that consists of various programs for making organizations more effective.

Organization Development Interventions

Organization development (OD) is a systematic approach to organizational improvement that applies behavioral science theory and research in order to increase individual and organizational well-being and effectiveness.[57] This definition implies certain characteristics. First, OD is a systematic approach to planned change. It is a structured cycle of diagnosing organizational problems and opportunities and then applying expertise to them. Second, OD is grounded in solid research and theory. It involves the application of our knowledge of behavioral science to the challenges that organizations face. Third, OD recognizes the reciprocal relationship between individuals and organizations. It acknowledges that for organizations to change, individuals must change. Finally, OD is goal oriented. It is a process that seeks to improve both individual and organizational well-being and effectiveness.

Organization development has a rich history. Some of the early work in OD was conducted by Kurt Lewin and his associates during the 1940s. This work was continued by Rensis Likert, who pioneered the use of attitude surveys in

organization development (OD)

A systematic approach to organizational improvement that applies behavioral science theory and research in order to increase individual and organizational well-being and effectiveness.

OD. During the 1950s, Eric Trist and his colleagues at the Tavistock Institute in London focused on the technical and social aspects of organizations and how they affect the quality of work life. These programs on the quality of work life migrated to the United States during the 1960s. During this time, a 200-member OD network was established, and it has grown to more than 4,100 members worldwide. As the number of practitioners has increased, so has the number of different OD methods. One compendium of organizational change methods estimates that more than 300 different methods have been used.[58]

Organization development is also being used internationally. OD has been applied in Canada, Sweden, Norway, Germany, Japan, Australia, Israel, and Mexico, among others. Some OD methods are difficult to implement in other cultures. As OD becomes more internationally widespread, we will increase our knowledge of how culture affects the success of different OD approaches.

Prior to deciding on a method of intervention, managers must carefully diagnose the problem they are attempting to address. Diagnosis and needs analysis is a critical first step in any OD intervention. Following this, an intervention method is chosen and applied. Finally, a thorough follow-up of the OD process is conducted. Figure 18.3 presents the OD cycle, a continuous process of moving the organization and its employees toward effective functioning.

Diagnosis and Needs Analysis

6. Describe the use of organizational diagnosis and needs analysis as a first step in organizational development.

Before any intervention is planned, a thorough organizational diagnosis should be conducted. Diagnosis is an essential first step for any organization development intervention.[59] The term *diagnosis* comes from *dia* (through) and *gnosis* (knowledge of). Thus, the diagnosis should pinpoint specific problems and areas in need of improvement. Problems can arise in any part of the organization. Six areas to examine carefully are the organization's purpose, structure, reward system, support systems, relationships, and leadership.[60]

Harry Levinson's diagnostic approach asserts that the process should begin by identifying where the pain (the problem) in the organization is, what it is like, how long it has been happening, and what has already been done about it.[61] Then a four-part, comprehensive diagnosis can begin. The first part of the diagnosis involves achieving an understanding of the organization's history. In the second part, the organization as a whole is analyzed to obtain data about its structure and processes. In the third part, interpretive data about attitudes, relationships, and current organizational functioning are gathered. In the fourth part of the diagnosis, the data are analyzed and conclusions are reached. In each stage of the diagnosis, the data can be gathered

FIGURE 18.3   The Organization Development Cycle

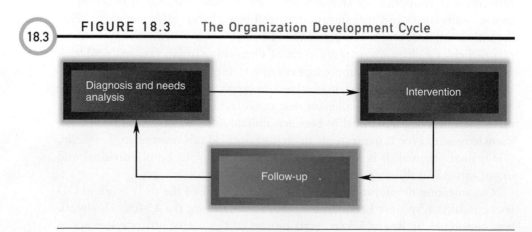

PART 4 [ORGANIZATIONAL PROCESSES AND STRUCTURE

using a variety of methods, including observation, interviews, questionnaires, and archival records.

The diagnostic process may yield the conclusion that change is necessary. As part of the diagnosis, it is important to address the following issues:

> What are the forces for change?

> What are the forces preserving the status quo?

> What are the most likely sources of resistance to change?

> What are the goals to be accomplished by the change?

This information constitutes a force field analysis, as discussed earlier in the chapter.

A needs analysis is another crucial step in managing change. This is an analysis of the skills and competencies that employees must have to achieve the goals of the change. A needs analysis is essential because interventions such as training programs must target these skills and competencies.

Hundreds of alternative OD intervention methods exist. One way of classifying these methods is by the target of change. The target of change may be the organization, groups within the organization, or individuals.

Organization- and Group-Focused Techniques

Some OD intervention methods emphasize changing the organization itself or changing the work groups within the organization. Intervention methods in this category include survey feedback, management by objectives, product and service quality programs, team building, and process consultation.

7. Discuss the major organization development interventions.

SURVEY FEEDBACK *Survey feedback* is a widely used intervention method whereby employee attitudes are solicited using a questionnaire. Once the data are collected, they are analyzed and fed back to the employees to diagnose problems and plan other interventions. Survey feedback is often used as an exploratory tool and then is combined with some other intervention. The effectiveness of survey feedback in actually improving outcomes (absenteeism or productivity, for example) increases substantially when this method is combined with other interventions.[62]

For survey feedback to be an effective method, certain guidelines should be used. Employees must be assured that their responses to the questionnaire will be confidential and anonymous. Unless this assurance is given, the responses may not be honest. Feedback should be reported in a group format; that is, no individual responses should be identified. Employees must be able to trust that there will be no negative repercussions from their responses. Employees should be informed of the purpose of the survey. Failing to do this can set up unrealistic expectations about the changes that might come from the surveys.

In addition, management must be prepared to follow up on the survey results. If some things cannot be changed, the rationale (for example, prohibitive cost) must be explained to the employees. Without appropriate follow-through, employees will not take the survey process seriously the next time.

survey feedback
A widely used method of intervention whereby employee attitudes are solicited using a questionnaire.

MANAGEMENT BY OBJECTIVES As an organization-wide technique, *management by objectives (MBO)* involves joint goal setting between employees and managers. The MBO process includes the setting of initial objectives, periodic progress reviews, and problem solving to remove any obstacles to

management by objectives (MBO)
An organization-wide intervention technique that involves joint goal setting between employees and managers.

goal achievement.[63] All these steps are joint efforts between managers and employees.

MBO is a valuable intervention because it meets three needs. First, it clarifies what is expected of employees. This reduces role conflict and ambiguity. Second, MBO provides knowledge of results, an essential ingredient in effective job performance. Finally, MBO provides an opportunity for coaching and counseling by the manager. The problem-solving approach encourages open communication and discussion of obstacles to goal achievement.[64]

Companies that have used MBO successfully include the former Tenneco, Mobil (now part of ExxonMobil), and General Electric. The success of MBO in effecting organizational results hinges on the linking of individual goals to the goals of the organization.[65] MBO programs should be used with caution, however. An excessive emphasis on goal achievement can result in cutthroat competition among employees, falsification of results, and striving for results at any cost.

quality program

A program that embeds product and service quality excellence in the organizational culture.

PRODUCT AND SERVICE QUALITY PROGRAMS *Quality programs*—programs that embed product and service quality excellence in the organizational culture—are assuming key roles in the organization development efforts of many companies. For example, the success or failure of a service company may depend on the quality of customer service it provides.[66]

The Ritz-Carlton Hotel Company (now part of Marriott International) integrated its comprehensive service quality program into marketing and business objectives. The Atlanta-based company, which managed twenty-eight luxury hotels, won the Malcolm Baldrige Award for service quality. Key elements of Ritz-Carlton's quality program included participatory executive leadership, thorough information gathering, coordinated execution, and employees who were empowered to "move heaven and earth" to satisfy customers.[67]

At Ritz-Carlton, the company president and thirteen senior executives made up the senior quality management team, which met weekly to focus on service quality. Quality goals were established at all levels of the company. The crucial product and service requirements of travel consumers were translated into Ritz-Carlton Gold Standards, which included a credo, a motto, three steps of service, and twenty Ritz-Carlton Basics. These standards guided service quality throughout the organization.

Employees were required to act on a customer complaint at once and were empowered to provide "instant pacification," no matter what it took. Quality teams set action plans at all levels of the company. Each hotel had a quality leader, who served as a resource to the quality teams. Daily quality production reports provided an early warning system for identifying areas that needed quality improvement.

After celebrating an award as the best hotel in the world, Ritz-Carlton did not stop its quality improvement process. At one hotel, the chief complaint was that room service was always late. A quality team was put together, including a cook, a waiter, and a room service order taker. They studied how the process flowed. When they discovered that the service elevator was slow, they added an engineer and a representative from the elevator company to the team. They found that the elevators worked well. Next, they posted a team member in the elevator twenty-four hours a day for a week. Every time the door opened, the team member had to find out why. Finally, a team member noticed that housemen who helped the maids got on the elevator a lot. It turned out that the housemen were stealing towels from other floors because their maids needed more. The problem with room service was that the hotel didn't own enough towels. Ritz-Carlton bought more towels, and room service complaints fell 50 percent.[68]

TEAM BUILDING *Team building* programs can improve the effectiveness of work groups. Team building usually begins with a diagnostic process through which team members identify problems, and it continues with the team's planning actions to take in order to resolve those problems. The OD practitioner in team building serves as a facilitator, and the work itself is completed by team members.[69]

Team building is a very popular OD method. A survey of *Fortune 500* companies indicated that human resource managers considered team building the most successful OD technique.[70] Managers are particularly interested in building teams that can learn. To build learning teams, members must be encouraged to seek feedback, discuss errors, reflect on successes and failures, and experiment with new ways of performing. Mistakes should be analyzed for ways to improve, and a climate of mutual support should be developed. Leaders of learning teams are good coaches who promote a climate of psychological safety so that team members feel comfortable discussing problems.[71]

One popular technique for team building is the use of outdoor challenges. Participants go through a series of outdoor activities, such as climbing a fourteen-foot wall. Similar physical challenges require the participants to work as a team and focus on trust, communication, decision making, and leadership. GE and Weyerhaeuser use outdoor challenges at the beginning of their team-building courses, and later in the training, team members apply what they have learned to actual business situations.[72] Now that adventure courses, paintball, and even high-powered go-karting have become common corporate training exercises, what's the next big thing? David Estes is betting he knows. At his new training center outside Sherman, Texas, uptight executives cut loose in real army tanks. At Tactical Tanks, team members develop their strategy and wear communication helmets and GPS locators. With a safety officer close by, they climb inside working, 50-ton military tanks to rumble around 265 acres of ground and afterwards meet to discuss what they learned. While the weapons aren't real, the experience certainly is, and participants rave about this newest form of team training.[73, 74] Preliminary studies indicate that team building can improve group processes.[75]

PROCESS CONSULTATION Pioneered by Edgar Schein, *process consultation* is an OD method that helps managers and employees improve the processes that are used in organizations.[76] The processes most often targeted are communication, conflict resolution, decision making, group interaction, and leadership.

One of the distinguishing features of the process consultation approach is that an outside consultant is used. The role of the consultant is to help employees help themselves. In this way, the ownership of a successful outcome rests with the employees.[77] The consultant guides the organization members in examining the processes in the organization and in refining them. The steps in process consultation are entering the organization, defining the relationship, choosing an approach, gathering data and diagnosing problems, intervening, and gradually leaving the organization.

team building
An intervention designed to improve the effectiveness of a work group.

© Bob Swain

A widely popular technique to enhance and foster team building is the use of outdoor challenges, like the conference bike shown here.

process consultation
An OD method that helps managers and employees improve the processes that are used in organizations.

Process consultation is an interactive technique between employees and an outside consultant, so it is seldom used as a sole OD method. Most often, it is used in combination with other OD interventions.

All the preceding OD methods focus on changing the organization or the work group. Other OD methods are aimed at facilitating change within individuals.

Individual-Focused Techniques

Organization development efforts that are targeted toward individuals include skills training, leadership training and development, executive coaching, role negotiation, job redesign, health promotion programs, and career planning.

skills training
Increasing the job knowledge, skills, and abilities that are necessary to do a job effectively.

SKILLS TRAINING The key question addressed by *skills training* is "What knowledge, skills, and abilities are necessary to do this job effectively?" Skills training is accomplished either in formal classroom settings or on the job. The challenge of integrating skills training into organization development is the rapid change that most organizations face. The job knowledge in most positions requires continual updates to keep pace with rapid change.

FedEx depends on more than 218,000 full- and part-time employees in 215 countries to deliver 100 percent customer satisfaction. The company is constantly changing its products and services, sometimes at the rate of 1,700 changes per year. FedEx decided to accomplish its mission using Web-based training and job skills testing. Employees find the training easy to use, convenient, and individualized. FedEx has found it to be economical as well because it eliminates travel expenses and the need for instructors. In job skills testing, every customer service employee takes a test every six months via computer. The test generates a unique prescription that informs employees what they do well and how they need to improve. It also directs employees to the interactive video lesson they need to practice to improve their skills.[78]

leadership training and development
A variety of techniques that are designed to enhance individuals' leadership skills.

LEADERSHIP TRAINING AND DEVELOPMENT Companies invest millions of dollars in *leadership training and development*, a term that encompasses a variety of techniques that are designed to enhance individuals' leadership skills. One popular technique is sending future leaders to off-site training classes. Research shows that this type of education experience can have some impact, but participants' enthusiastic return to work may be short-lived due to the challenges and realities of work life. Classroom learning alone thus has a limited effect on leadership skills.

The best leadership training and development programs combine classroom learning with on-the-job experiences. One way of accomplishing development is through the use of action learning, a technique that was pioneered in Europe.[79] In action learning, leaders take on unfamiliar problems or familiar problems in unfamiliar settings. The leaders work on the problems and meet weekly in small groups made up of individuals from different organizations. The outcome of action learning is that leaders learn about themselves through the challenges of their comrades. Other techniques that provide active learning for participants are simulation, business games, role-playing, and case studies.[80]

Eli Lilly has an action learning program that pulls together eighteen future company leaders and gives them a strategic business issue to resolve. For six weeks, the trainees meet with experts, best-practices organizations, and customers and then present their recommendations to top brass. One action learning team was charged with coming up with an e-business strategy; their plan was so good that executives immediately implemented it. At Eli Lilly and other firms, action learning programs provide developmental experiences for leaders and result in useful initiatives for the company.[81]

Leadership training and development is an ongoing process that takes considerable time and effort. There are no quick fixes. At IBM, managers are strongly held accountable for leadership development. In fact, IBM's managers will not be considered for promotion into senior executive positions unless they have a record of developing leaders. Top management must be committed to the process of leadership training and development if they want to create a pipeline of high-potential employees to fill leadership positions.[82]

EXECUTIVE COACHING *Executive coaching* is a technique in which managers or executives are paired with a coach in a partnership to help the executive perform more effectively at work and, sometimes, even in personal life. Although coaching is usually done in a one-on-one manner, it is sometimes attempted in groups. The popularity of executive coaching has increased dramatically in recent years. The International Coach Federation, a group that trains and accredits executive coaches, in just two years of existence doubled its membership, which is now at 7,000 members in thirty-five countries.

Coaching is typically a special investment in top-level managers. Coaches provide another set of eyes and ears and help executives see beyond their own blinders. They elicit solutions and ideas from the client rather than making suggestions; thus, they enhance the talents and capabilities within the client, in addition to developing new ones. Many coaching arrangements focus on developing the emotional intelligence of the client executive and may use a 360-degree assessment in which the executive, his or her boss, peers, subordinates, and even family members rate the executive's emotional competencies.[83, 84] This information is then fed back to the executive, and along with the coach, a development plan is put in place. Wachovia is one firm that leverages executive coaching, as you can see in The Real World 18.2.

Good coaches form strong connections with clients, exhibit professionalism, and deliver forthright, candid feedback. The top reasons executives seek out coaches are to make personal behavior changes, enhance their effectiveness, and foster stronger relationships. Does executive coaching pay off? Evidence suggests that successful coaching can result in sustained changes in executives' behavior, increased self-awareness and understanding, and more effective leadership competencies.[85] In one study, for example, executives who worked with executive coaches were more likely to set specific goals, ask for feedback from their supervisors, and were rated as better performers by their supervisors and subordinates when compared to executives who simply received feedback from surveys.[86] Effective coaching relationships depend on a professional, experienced coach, an executive who is motivated to learn and change, and a good fit between the two.

ROLE NEGOTIATION Individuals who work together sometimes have differing expectations of one another within the working relationship. *Role negotiation* is a simple technique whereby individuals meet and clarify their psychological contract. In doing this, the expectations of each party are clarified and negotiated. The outcome of role negotiation is a better understanding between the two parties of what each can be expected to give and receive in the

executive coaching
A technique in which managers or executives are paired with a coach in a partnership to help the executive perform more efficiently.

role negotiation
A technique whereby individuals meet and clarify their psychological contract.

Wachovia: Extensive Executive Coaching

Wachovia is a financial services provider based in Charlotte, North Carolina, that has a unique and comprehensive approach to executive coaching. It uses both internal and external coaches. Participants in Wachovia's executive learning program are given a 360-degree assessment as feedback to use with their internal coaches, who are always from different divisions within the company. Together, managers and coaches review the feedback and put together an action plan. Because internal coaches understand Wachovia's culture, they're extremely valuable; because they need to develop coaching skills, Wachovia puts them through extensive training on how to be a good coach.

Top executives who face challenges like moving into a new position at Wachovia are paired with external coaches. This is a special perk for high-potential leaders who are marked for success at the top three or four levels in the company. Wachovia uses strict criteria for hiring its external coaches, who use not only 360-degree assessments but also interviews and other psychological assessments to assist the executives. Objectivity is the main asset for Wachovia's external coaches, who work both one on one and in depth with executives over a long period of time.

Ultimately, Wachovia's internal and external executive coaches have the same objectives—engaging in a learning relationship that is personally valuable to each executive and tailored to his or her needs. Because of this, executives feel safe in seeking and receiving feedback, find a new view of themselves, and feel compelled to take purposeful action to improve.

SOURCE: H. Johnson, "The Ins and Outs of Executive Coaching," *Training* 41 (2004): 36–42.

---

reciprocal relationship. When both parties have a mutual agreement on expectations, there is less ambiguity in the process of working together.

job redesign

An OD intervention method that alters jobs to improve the fit between individual skills and the demands of the job.

JOB REDESIGN As an OD intervention method, *job redesign* emphasizes the fit between individual skills and the demands of the job. Chapter 14 outlined several approaches to job design. Many of these methods are used as OD techniques for realigning task demands and individual capabilities or for redesigning jobs to fit new techniques or organizational structures better.

Ford Motor Company has redesigned virtually all of its manufacturing jobs, shifting workers from individual to team-based roles in which they have greater control of their work and can take the initiative to improve products and production techniques. Ford began trying this technique more than a decade ago and found that it not only improved employee job satisfaction but also productivity and product quality.

Another form of job redesign is telecommuting, in which employees perform some or all of their work from home. Companies including American Express, AT&T, and Merrill Lynch have significant numbers of employees who work this way. When AT&T surveyed its managers to assess the impact of telecommuting, 76 percent were happier with their jobs, and 79 percent were happier with their careers in general since they began telecommuting.[87]

HEALTH PROMOTION PROGRAMS As organizations have become increasingly concerned with the costs of distress in the workplace, health promotion programs have become a part of larger organization development efforts. In Chapter 7, we examined stress and strain at work. Companies that have successfully integrated health promotion programs into their organizations include AT&T, Caterpillar, Kimberly-Clark, and Johnson & Johnson.

The American Psychological Association recently began recognizing companies for innovative programs that support psychologically healthy work environments. Winners included Small Dog Electronics, Inc., of Vermont and ARUP Laboratories, located in Utah. Small Dog Electronics, Inc., works hard to create a relaxing work environment. Employee work areas are painted in brilliant colors, while employees choose the music played in the office. Breaks are encouraged, pets are allowed in the office, and pet insurance is offered as an employee benefit. ARUP Laboratories offers comprehensive medical care by providing an on-site health clinic that employees may utilize free of charge. In addition to improving physical health, the clinic has improved employee morale.[88]

Although companies have long recognized the importance of maintenance on their machinery, many are only recently learning that their human assets need maintenance as well, in the form of employee wellness and health promotion activities. The components of these programs can include education about stress and coping, relaxation training, company-sponsored exercise, and employee assistance programs. All are focused on helping employees manage their stress and health in a preventive manner.

CAREER PLANNING Matching an individual's career aspirations with the opportunities in the organization is career planning. This proactive approach to career management is often part of an organization's development efforts. Career planning is a joint responsibility of organizations and individuals. Companies like IBM, Travelers Life & Annuity (part of Citigroup), and 3M have implemented career-planning programs.

Career-planning activities benefit the organization, as well as its individuals. Through counseling sessions, employees identify their skills and skill deficiencies. The organization then can plan its training and development efforts based on this information. In addition, the process can be used to identify and nurture talented employees for potential promotion.

Managers can choose from a host of organization development techniques to facilitate organizational change. Some of these techniques are aimed toward organizations or groups, and others focus on individuals. Large-scale changes in organizations require the use of multiple techniques. For example, implementing a new technology like robotics may require simultaneous changes in the structure of the organization, the configuration of work groups, and individual attitudes.

We should recognize at this point that the organization development methods just described are means to an end. Programs do not drive change; business needs do. The OD methods are merely vehicles for moving the organization and its employees in a more effective direction.

Ethical Considerations in Organization Development

Organization development is a process of helping organizations improve. It may involve resistance to change, shifts in power, losses of control, and redefinition of tasks.[89] These are all sensitive issues. Further, the change agent, whether a manager from within the organization or a consultant from outside, is in a position of directing the change. Such a position carries the potential for misuse of power. The ethical concerns surrounding the use of organization development center around four issues.[90]

The first issue is the selection of the OD method to be used. Every change agent has inherent biases about particular methods, but these biases must not enter into the decision process. The OD method used must be carefully chosen in accordance with the problem as diagnosed, the organization's culture, and the employees concerned. All alternatives should be given fair consideration in

8. Identify the ethical issues that must be considered in organization development efforts.

the choice of a method. In addition, the OD practitioner should never use a method he or she is not skilled in delivering. Using a method you are not an expert in is unethical, because the client assumes you are.

The second ethical issue is voluntary participation. No employee should be forced to participate in any OD intervention.[91] To make an informed decision about participation, employees should be given information about the nature of the intervention and what will be expected of them. They should also be afforded the option to discontinue their participation at any time they so choose.

The third issue of ethical concern is confidentiality. Change agents gather a wealth of information during organizational diagnoses and interventions. Successful change agents develop a trusting relationship with employees. They may receive privileged information, sometimes unknowingly. It is unethical for a change agent to reveal information in order to give some group or individual political advantage or to enhance the change agent's own standing. Consultants should not reveal information about an organization to its competitors. The use of information gathered from OD efforts is a sensitive issue and presents ethical dilemmas.

A final ethical concern in OD is the potential for manipulation by the change agent. Because any change process involves influence, some individuals may feel manipulated. The key to alleviating the potential for manipulation is open communication. Participants should be given complete knowledge of the rationale for change, what they can expect of the change process, and what the intervention will entail. No actions should be taken that limit the participants' freedom of choice.[92]

Are Organization Development Efforts Effective?

Because organization development is designed to help organizations manage change, it is important to evaluate the effectiveness of these efforts. The success of any OD intervention depends on a host of factors, including the technique used, the competence of the change agent, the organization's readiness for change, and top management commitment. No single method of OD is effective in every instance. Instead, multiple-method OD approaches are recommended because they allow organizations to capitalize on the benefits of several approaches.[93]

Efforts to evaluate OD efforts have focused on outcomes such as productivity. One review of more than 200 interventions indicated that worker productivity improved in 87 percent of the cases.[94] A separate analysis of 98 of these interventions revealed impressive productivity increases.[95] We can conclude that when properly applied and managed, organization development programs have positive effects on performance.[96]

Managerial Implications: Managing Change

Several guidelines can be used to facilitate the success of management change efforts.[97] First, managers should recognize the forces for change. These forces can come from a combination of sources both internal and external to the organization.

A shared vision of the change should be developed that includes participation by all employees in the planning process. Top management must be committed to the change and should visibly demonstrate support, because employees look to these leaders to model appropriate behavior. A comprehensive diagnosis and needs analysis should be conducted. The company then must ensure that there are adequate resources for carrying out the change.

Resistance to change should be planned for and managed. Communication, participation, and empathetic support are ways of helping employees adjust. The reward system within the organization must be carefully evaluated to ensure that new behaviors, rather than old ones, are being reinforced. Participation in the change process should also be recognized and rewarded.

The organization development technique used should be carefully selected to meet the goals of the change. Finally, organization development efforts should be managed in an ethical manner and should preserve employees' privacy and freedom of choice. Employees must be treated fairly, and management's explanations for change must be congruent with their actions. The congruence between talk and actions, or "walking the talk," is critical in managing organizational change.[98] By using these guidelines, managers can meet the challenges of managing change while enhancing productivity in their organizations.

LOOKING BACK: THE COCA-COLA COMPANY

Navigating Rough Waters

As Coke faced rapidly changing markets and declining profits in 2003, then CEO Douglas Daft stood at the helm of an enormous but listing ship. A few short months later, the board of directors decided that the ship needed a major change: a new captain. With the announcement of Daft's early retirement, the hunt was on once again for someone to lead Coke.[99] Ironically, Coke's finances appeared to be improving under Daft's oversight: net income in the first quarter of 2004 was up 35 percent on over $5 billion in sales.[100] But a slew of other problems had arisen at Coke.

An internal audit revealed that Coke had cheated partner Burger King by rigging a test of frozen Coke to make sales seem higher than they really were.[101] Coke's botched response to a whistle-blower's claims led to investigations by both the SEC and the U.S. Attorney's office in Atlanta. And protestors led by Jesse Jackson picketed the firm's annual meeting, accusing it of racism; Coke settled racial discrimination charges in 2000 for $192.5 million.[102]

To top it all off, Coke's inner workings appear convoluted and political, with a noticeable revolving door of top executives: as of mid-2004, only one of Coke's thirteen senior executives had been with the firm for five years, and he left soon thereafter.[103]

Coke named a new CEO, E. Neville Isdell, a former Coke executive who was drafted out of retirement.[104] Coke's stock was back in a nosedive, headed to its 52-week low after almost two weeks of consecutive declines.[105] U.S. soda sales remained flat, and the most valuable brand in the world faced the same challenges it did the year before: keeping the great ship afloat in a changing world.

Chapter Summary

1. Organizations face many pressures to change. Some forces are external, including globalization, workforce diversity, technological innovation, and ethics. Other forces are internal, such as declining effectiveness, crises, changing employee expectations, and a changing work climate.

2. Organizations face both planned and unplanned change. Change can be of an incremental, strategic, or transformational nature. The individual who directs the change, known as a change agent, can be internal or external to the organization.

3. Individuals resist change for many reasons, and many of these reasons are rooted in fear. Organizations can help manage resistance by educating workers and openly communicating the change, encouraging worker participation in the change efforts, and providing empathy and support to those who have difficulty dealing with change.

4. Reactions to change may be manifested in behaviors reflecting disengagement, disidentification, disenchantment, and disorientation. Managers can use separate interventions targeted toward each reaction.

5. Force field analysis states that when the forces for change are balanced by the forces restraining change, an equilibrium state exists. For change to occur, the forces for change must increase, or the restraining forces must decrease.

6. Lewin's change model proposes three stages of change: unfreezing, moving, and refreezing.

7. A thorough diagnosis and needs analysis is a critical first step in any organization development (OD) intervention.

8. OD interventions targeted toward organizations and groups include survey feedback, management by objectives, product and service quality programs, team building, and process consultation.

9. OD interventions that focus on individuals include skills training, leadership training and development, executive coaching, role negotiation, job redesign, health promotion programs, and career planning.

10. OD efforts should be managed ethically and should preserve individual freedom of choice and privacy.

11. When properly conducted, organization development can have positive effects on performance.

Key Terms

change agent (p. 605)
disenchantment (p. 612)
disengagement (p. 611)
disidentification (p. 612)
disorientation (p. 613)
executive coaching (p. 621)
incremental change (p. 604)
job redesign (p. 622)
leadership training and development (p. 620)

management by objectives (MBO) (p. 617)
moving (p. 614)
organization development (OD) (p. 615)
planned change (p. 600)
process consultation (p. 619)
quality program (p. 618)
refreezing (p. 614)
role negotiation (p. 621)

skills training (p. 620)
strategic change (p. 605)
survey feedback (p. 617)
team building (p. 619)
transformational change (p. 605)
unfreezing (p. 614)
unplanned change (p. 600)

Review Questions

1. What are the major external and internal forces for change in organizations?

2. Contrast incremental, strategic, and transformational change.

3. What is a change agent? Who plays this role?

4. What are the major reasons individuals resist change? How can organizations deal with resistance?

5. Name the four behavioral reactions to change. Describe the behavioral signs of each reaction,

and identify an organizational strategy for dealing with each reaction.

6. Describe force field analysis and its relationship to Lewin's change model.

7. What is organization development? Why is it undertaken by organizations?

8. Name six areas to be critically examined in any comprehensive organizational diagnosis.

9. What are the major organization-focused and group-focused OD intervention methods? The major individual-focused methods?

10. Which OD intervention is most effective?

Discussion and Communication Questions

1. What are the major external forces for change in today's organizations?

2. What are the advantages of using an external change agent? An internal change agent?

3. Review You 18.1. What can you learn from this challenge about how individuals' tolerance for ambiguity can lead to resistance?

4. Can organizations prevent resistance to change? If so, how?

5. What organization development techniques are the easiest to implement? What techniques are the most difficult to implement? Why?

6. Suppose your organization experiences a dramatic increase in turnover. How would you diagnose the underlying problem?

7. Downsizing has played a major role in changing U.S. organizations. Analyze the internal and external forces for change regarding downsizing an organization.

8. If you were in charge of designing the ideal management development program, what topics would you include? Why?

9. *(communication question)* Find an article that describes an organization that has gone through change and managed it well. Develop a Real World feature of your own about the example you find using the format in this book. Prepare a brief oral presentation of your Real World feature for your class.

10. *(communication question)* Think of a change you would like to make in your life. Using Figure 18.1 as a guide, prepare your own force field analysis for that change. How will you overcome the forces for the status quo? How will you make sure to "refreeze" following the change? Summarize your analysis in an action plan.

Ethical Dilemma

Tom Wood cannot contain his feelings of sadness. He is sitting at his desk considering the dismissal of his best department supervisor: Liz Williams. Liz has always been one of his best employees. She ran an efficient department and was always well within budget. Best of all, her employees were the happiest and most productive in the company. Tom had spent many days wishing that he had several more supervisors like Liz Williams working for him.

But that was the old Liz. Since the merger, Liz has become a very different employee. She has resented some of the changes that have taken place since the company has merged with a large multinational corporation. Tom has spoken with Liz on several occasions about the changes that have taken place. He knows Liz is struggling with the new management philosophy, and he does not want to lose her. Liz liked the way the previous company operated and is not making the necessary adjustments to become part of the new organization. She disagrees with the new company's procedures and she is not afraid to let people know it. On more than one occasion in the last six months, Tom has had to defend his decision to keep Liz as part of the team.

Recently, Tom believed things were getting better for Liz. She seemed to be settling down and adjusting to the new culture. At least that is what he thought until yesterday when Liz had a major dispute with her counterpart at the home office in Germany. It had been the last straw for upper management. Tom had gotten the phone message this morning that Liz needs to go. Tom needs to decide if he is pushing his luck too far by going to bat for Liz one more time. He isn't sure how much more his superiors are willing to listen to him defend Liz. Even he agrees that she is beginning to be a real problem. But she is also a good friend and under normal circumstances a very good worker. Does she deserve another chance?

Questions

1. How long does Tom need to defend Liz's behaviors?

2. What is Liz's responsibility to Tom?

3. Using rule, virtue, right, and justice theories, evaluate Tom's decision.

Experiential Exercises

18.1 Organizational Diagnosis of the University

The purpose of this exercise is to give you experience in organizational diagnosis. Assume that your team has been hired to conduct a diagnosis of problem areas in your university and to make preliminary recommendations for organization development interventions.

Each team member should complete the following University Profile. Then, as a team, evaluate the strengths and weaknesses within each area (acade-

mics, teaching, social, cultural, and administrative) using the accompanying University Diagnosis form. Finally, make recommendations concerning organization development interventions for each area. Be as specific as possible in both your diagnosis and your recommendations. Each team should then present its diagnosis to the class.

University Profile

Not True 1 2 3 4 5 **Very True**

I. Academics

1 2 3 4 5 1. There is a wide range of courses to choose from.
1 2 3 4 5 2. Classroom standards are too easy.
1 2 3 4 5 3. The library is adequate.
1 2 3 4 5 4. Textbooks are helpful.

II. Teachers

1 2 3 4 5 1. Teachers here are committed to quality instruction.
1 2 3 4 5 2. We have a high-quality faculty.

III. Social

1 2 3 4 5 1. Students are friendly to one another.
1 2 3 4 5 2. It is difficult to make friends.
1 2 3 4 5 3. Faculty get involved in student activities.
1 2 3 4 5 4. Too much energy goes into drinking and goofing off.

IV. Cultural Events

1 2 3 4 5 1. There are ample activities on campus.
1 2 3 4 5 2. Student activities are boring.
1 2 3 4 5 3. The administration places a high value on student activities.
1 2 3 4 5 4. Too much emphasis is placed on sports.
1 2 3 4 5 5. We need more "cultural" activities.

V. Organizational/Management

1 2 3 4 5 1. Decision making is shared at all levels of the organization.
1 2 3 4 5 2. There is unity and cohesiveness among departments and units.
1 2 3 4 5 3. Too many departmental clashes hamper the organization's effectiveness.
1 2 3 4 5 4. Students have a say in many decisions.
1 2 3 4 5 5. The budgeting process seems fair.
1 2 3 4 5 6. Recruiting and staffing are handled thoughtfully with student needs in mind.

University Diagnosis

	STRENGTH	WEAKNESS	INTERVENTION
1. Academic			
2. Teaching			
3. Social			
4. Cultural			
5. Administrative			

SOURCE: "Organizational Diagnosis of the University" by D. Marcic, *Organizational Behavior: Experiences and Cases* (St. Paul, Minn.: West Publishing Company, 1989), 326–329. Reprinted by permission.

18.2 Team Building for Team Effectiveness

This exercise will allow you and your team to engage in an organization development activity for team building. The two parts of the exercise are diagnosis and intervention.

Part 1. Diagnosis

Working as a team, complete the following four steps:

1. Describe how you have worked together this semester as a team.

2. What has your team done especially well? What has enabled this?

3. What problems or conflicts have you had as a team? (Be specific.) What was the cause of the problems your team experienced? Have the conflicts been over ideas, methods, or people?

4. Would you assess the overall effectiveness of your team as excellent, good, fair, poor, or a disaster? Explain your effectiveness rating.

Part 2. Intervention

A diagnosis provides the basis for intervention and action in organization development. Team building is a way to improve the relationships and effectiveness of teams at work. It is concerned with the results of work activities and the relationships among the members of the team. Complete the following three steps as a team.

Step 1. Answer the following questions with regard to the relationships within the team:

a. How could conflicts have been handled better?

b. How could specific relationships have been improved?

c. How could the interpersonal atmosphere of the team have been improved?

Step 2. Answer the following questions with regard to the results of the team's work:

a. How could the team have been more effective?

b. Are there any team process changes that would have improved the team's effectiveness?

c. Are there any team structure changes that would have improved the team's effectiveness?

Step 3. Answer the following questions with regard to the work environment in your place of employment:

a. What have you learned about team building that you can apply there?

b. What have you learned about team building that would not be applicable there?

TAKE 2

Biz Flix | Field of Dreams

Ray Kinsella (Kevin Costner) hears a voice while working in his Iowa cornfield that says, "If you build it, he will come." Ray concludes that "he" is legendary "Shoeless Joe" Jackson (Ray Liotta), a 1919 Chicago White Sox player suspended for rigging the 1919 World Series. With the support of his wife Annie (Amy Madigan), Ray jeopardizes his farm by replacing some corn fields with a modern baseball diamond. "Shoeless Joe" soon arrives, followed by the rest of the suspended players. This charming fantasy film, based on W. P. Kinsellas's novel *Shoeless Joe*, shows the rewards of pursuing a dream.

The scene is part of the "People Will Come" sequence toward the end of *Field of Dreams*. By this time in the story, Ray has met Terrence Mann (James Earl Jones). They have traveled together from Boston to Minnesota to find A. W. "Moonlight" Graham (Burt Lancaster). At this point, the three are at Ray's Iowa farm.

This scene follows Mark's (Timothy Busfield) arrival to discuss the foreclosure of Ray and Annie's mortgage. Mark, who is Annie's brother, cannot see the players on the field. Ray and Annie's daughter Karin (Gaby Hoffman) has proposed that people will come to Iowa City and buy tickets to watch a baseball game. Mark does not understand her proposal. The film continues to its end.

What to Watch for and Ask Yourself:

> Who is the target of change in this scene?

> What are the forces for change? Are the forces for change internal or external to the change target?

> Does the scene show the role of leadership in organizational change? If it does, who is the leader? What does this person do to get desired change?

Workplace Video | Peter Pan Bus Lines: Change and Development

Peter Pan Bus Lines Inc. has been in business since 1933, delivering a wide array of travel-related services including bus lines, charters, garages, and specialty vehicles. The Springfield, Massachusetts-based company boasts 1,500 employees, 4 million passengers, 400 coaches, and routes ranging from Concord, New Hampshire, to Washington, D.C.

Many changes have taken place at Peter Pan Bus Lines since it was first founded, but none have been quite as drastic as those made in recent years. Terrorist attacks in the United States and around the world have created many problems for the travel industry, and catastrophic events like 9/11 have forced Peter Pan and other companies to reexamine the safety of their businesses from top to bottom. While Peter Pan Bus Lines already had a reputation for safety, the attack on the World Trade Center in 2001 led company management to implement broad new changes that addressed the increasing threat of terrorism. From new technology upgrades and personnel changes to the redesign of corporate culture, recent improvements at Peter Pan have created a heightened alertness to safety issues.

TAKE 2

Change can be hard on companies, and it can take months for changes to settle into place. During the implementation of new changes, managers need to retrain employees and motivate them on a daily basis to see that fresh initiatives become standard operating procedures. When change begins at the top, it is very likely to succeed. Due to significant changes implemented at Peter Pan, safety is no mere buzzword—it's company policy.

Questions

1. *Describe the causes and scope of the change that took place at Peter Pan Bus Lines.*
2. *What specific changes were made at Peter Pan Bus Lines, and what was the purpose of such changes?*
3. *Explain why employees resisted some of the new safety procedures, and describe how the company addressed employee resistance.*

Forces for Innovation at Cisco Systems

Cisco Systems was founded in December 1984 by Len Bosack and Sandy Lerner, two computer scientists from Stanford University. It employed two technologists, Greg Satz and Kirk Lougheed and was geared toward enabling disparate computer networks to communicate with each other and share information. Cisco has grown into the worldwide sales leader of "networking equipment and software technology for routing, switching, and fiber- and Internet Protocol (IP)-based solutions" with "more than 35,000 employees in five theaters worldwide." In mid-2004 Cisco's rate of revenue generation was $18.9 billion per annum. Cisco has been recognized by *Fortune* magazine as one of the "Top 100 Best Companies to Work For" and as number 10 on the list of "Most Admired Companies." Additionally, *Mother's Magazine* has recognized Cisco as one of the "100 Best Companies for Working Mothers."

John Chambers, president and chief executive officer of Cisco Systems, observes: "There are a lot of market transitions going on in the industry, and it is the key to prioritize where we are going to go. It's now about the future. The company that brought you the routers to make the Internet work 20 years ago is now innovating and allowing people to enable the power of the Internet by a factor of 100, opening up new ideas that were previously unimaginable. This is truly the end of the beginning." Cisco has helped enable "the Internet to change the way the world works, lives, plays, and learns." After two decades of growth and success, Cisco Systems is seeking to continue its "tradition of innovation, business best practices, and social responsibility."

Start-up companies in the networking industry have been able to compete with Cisco, at least temporarily, because they introduced their products when Cisco was between product generations. However, over time Cisco has been able to catch up with them because of a constant pace of innovation being injected into its platforms. Cisco's constant pace of product innovation not only enables it to meet competitive threats but also contributes to its efforts to help shape the future of the networking industry.

According to one Cisco executive, networking products "must be able to transport many different types of information, such as voice, video, and data. The network must be able to extend across a great distance. It needs to support all types of users, including large enterprises, remote branches, and small businesses."

While the technology of computer networking and the Internet foster productivity increases for individuals, organizations, and nations, such technology is nonetheless disruptive. "It's disruptive because it has the potential for being less expensive and more productive while offering more functionality than any of the respective existing networks." John Chambers, Cisco's CEO, expresses the belief that the companies, countries, and governments that benefited from technology in the twentieth century have a responsibility to ensure that no one gets left behind in the twenty-first century. "When productivity of a country increases at 1% per year, the standard of living doubles every 70 years; at 3% the standard of living doubles every generation; and at 5% the standard of living doubles every 14 years. Technology can help bridge the gap between the world's developed and least-developed countries and raise the standard of living."

An ongoing study conducted by the Brookings Institution and economists at the University of California, Berkley, reports that Internet business solutions will provide European companies with about one-third of their expected future productivity increases and American companies with about one-half of their anticipated productivity increases. Productivity is obtained from the Internet in four progressive stages. First, the Internet is used for conveying *information*. Second, e-commerce and e-service are used to *interact* with customers. Third, Internet technologies are used to link people together on-line to foster *collaboration*. Fourth, the Internet *transforms* and becomes integral to all business activities.

"Cisco focuses its technology on where the market is going, not where it has been." John Chambers maintains that, "the Internet and education are the two great equalizers in life, leveling the playing field for people, companies, and countries worldwide. By providing greater access to educational opportunities through the Internet, students are able to learn more. Workers have greater access to e-learning opportunities to enhance and increase their skills. And companies and schools can decrease costs by utilizing technology for greater productivity."

Discussion Questions

1. Describe the *external* forces for change that seem to be affecting Cisco Systems.
2. Describe the *internal* forces for change that seem to be affecting Cisco Systems.
3. Explain the development of Cisco Systems from the perspectives of incremental change, strategic change, and transformational change.

SOURCE: This case was written by Michael K. McCuddy, The Louis S. and Mary L. Morgal Chair of Christian Business Ethics and Professor of Management, College of Business Administration, Valparaiso University. This case was developed from material contained on the Cisco Systems Web site at http://www.newsroom.cisco.com/, including the following articles written by Cisco executives: H.S. Charney, "A Positive Future for the Internet;" M. Mazzola, "Mario Mazzola Shares His Views on the Networking Challenges and Opportunities that Lie Ahead;" and M. Volpi, "Evolution of the Networking Industry."

Google™ (D)

Sergey Brin and Larry Page, Google's co-founders, along with Eric Schmidt, whom they recruited to be Google's Chairman and Chief Executive Officer, have led Google to enormous success by developing opportunities not identified by conventional wisdom or experience. In anticipation of the company's Initial Public Offering (IPO) of stock, one observer noted: "Soon, though, whatever they do will have to be done with shareholders in mind—a prospect that makes seat-of-the-pants governance impossible."

As pointed out in Google™ (C), the company is quite different from other businesses with respect to its culture of informality, equality, involvement, and empowerment; its aversion to bureaucracy; and its top leadership. Google's culture creates a family atmosphere that fosters a spirit of inclusion—but not everyone, particularly temporary contract workers, happen to be included. Google operates with very little bureaucracy in order to encourage engineers to rapidly develop good ideas; yet its aversion to bureaucracy causes some observers to wonder whether things might be out-of-control. Likewise, some people are wondering: "Who, among Sergey Brin, Larry Page, and Eric Schmidt, is really in charge at Google?"

Google's uniqueness with regard to culture, structure, and leadership reflects an underlying corporate philosophy that is based on the following ten principles:

> "Focus on the user and all else will follow."

> "It's best to do one thing really, really well."

> "Fast is better than slow."

> "Democracy on the Web works."

> "You don't need to be at your desk to need an answer."

> "You can make money without doing evil."

> "There's always more information out there."

> "The need for information crosses all borders."

> "You can be serious without a suit."

> "Great just isn't good enough."

While these principles provide guidance to regarding culture, structure, and leadership, they also create opportunities for challenges to arise.

Future Leadership Challenges

In taking the company public, Brin and Page intend to continue operating Google as a nonconventional company that emphasizes creativity and challenge. They "designed a corporate structure that will protect Google's ability to innovate and retain its most distinctive characteristics." This corporate structure basically leaves Brin and Page in control even after the initial public offering (IPO) of stock.

Google has set up a dual-class voting structure for public ownership of the company that will give Brin and Page "virtually unchallengeable authority as shareholders." After the IPO, each share held by Brin and Page will get ten votes, whereas each share held by the investing public will get one vote. Consequently, Brin and Page will remain in unquestionable control of Google. "Page and Brin get to have their billions without yet facing the day that a board controlled by outside investors can show them the door."

Google's IPO, which took place on August 19, 2004, "immediately vaulted hundreds of Google staff to millionaire status." While the company has not disclosed how many shares and stock options the employees other than top management hold, it is estimated that around 45 percent of Google staffers have options and shares worth $1 million or more. This newly created wealth presents some significant future challenges for Google. "The chief issues involve retaining newly rich staff, keeping workers focused and productive, and handling disaffection among employees and contractors whose own IPO paydays were small or nonexistent." Among the disaffected are the significant number of temporary workers employed by Google—workers who often are not eligible for stock options and similar benefits.

Anticipating and Embracing Change

Safia Rashtchy, an analyst from Piper Jaffray, estimates that Google had about one-fourth of the search industry's $4 billion annual revenue in 2003. With annual industry revenue being expected to increase to $12 billion by 2008, Google's maintenance of its market position would mean a revenue expansion to $3 billion over this time period.

Google's executives, however, are unlikely to be satisfied with simple maintenance of market position. Google is committed to innovation, improvement, and change—all of which suggest an aggressive growth approach. Larry Page, for instance, has a vision of developing the perfect search engine. Page believes the perfect search engine would do two things: (1) understand exactly what the user means, and (2) give the user exactly what he/she wants. Realizing this vision requires persistent innovation in developing "technology to provide a fast, accurate and easy-to-use search service that can be accessed from anywhere."

While these ambitions are admirable, they will not be realized without encountering considerable competitive challenges. Google has numerous powerful competitors. Amazon, AOL, and eBay are trying to capitalize on Google's lack of customer lock-in. Google says that instead of locking in customers, it will focus on creating and providing services that will keep customers coming back voluntarily. Microsoft is investing billions of dollars in developing its own search engine, which will be an essential component of its new operating system that is under development as well as part of its MSN on-line service. If Microsoft fully realizes its development goals, "it can offer people a richer version of search than Google can deliver—even before they bother to type their queries into a search field." Microsoft is developing "technology that enables users to employ a single search to locate information, data and files stored on their personal computers and the Internet." As some analysts observe, "Microsoft will try to use its PC-software expertise to try to overtake Google."

In the days preceding Google's IPO, the company settled two lawsuits brought by Yahoo! Google gave Yahoo! 2.7 million shares of its stock in exchange for "a perpetual license to Yahoo's patented technology for matching on-line advertisements to Web search results." The ad-matching technology issue arose from Yahoo's acquisition of Overture Services, a well-respected search engine company. Yahoo! elected to continue the suit that Overture Services had initiated against Google.

These competitive threats appear to have had little effect of the outlooks of Sergey Brin and Larry Page. Brin is unfazed by the competition. He observes that companies often self-destruct when they are obsessed with their competition. "If I had one magic bullet," says Brin, "I wouldn't spend it on a competitor. I'd spend it to make sure we're executing as well as we possibly can." Brin and Page are described as "calm, even confident, in the face of a rising tide of competitors, technology challenges, and the tricky process of using the principles of disorganization to build a substantial company out of one unquestionably brilliant idea."

Since the major breakthroughs in the search engine field are still in the future, the winners will be companies that are the best innovators. Google aims to be a major innovator in the search technology areas of deep content, multimedia, personalization, localization, and artificial intelligence. However, Google faces stiff competition in each of these areas as it works on shaping and developing its own future.

Discussion Questions

1. What insights about organization design can you derive by juxtaposing Google's aversion to bureaucracy with the stock ownership structure that will exist subsequent to the IPO?
2. Will Google's culture of informality, equality, involvement, and empowerment be able to deal effectively with the potential impact of the "haves" and "have nots" subsequent to the IPO?
3. What future competitive challenges await Google?
4. Do you think Google will be able to meet its competitive challenges?
5. What changes might need to take place in order for Google to retain its position as the "premier search engine" company?

SOURCE: This case was written by Michael K. McCuddy, The Louis S. and Mary L. Morgal Chair of Christian Business Ethics and Professor of Management, College of Business Administration, Valparaiso University. This case was developed from material contained on the Google Inc. Web site at http://www.google .com and in the following materials: K. J. Delaney, "Google, Yahoo! Settle Dispute Over Ad Patents, Service Deal," *The Wall Street Journal Online* (August 9, 2004): accessed at http://interactive .wsj.com; K. J. Delaney and J. S. Lubin, "Google's IPO: They're All Rich—Now the Problems Start," *The Wall Street Journal Online* (August 20, 2004): accessed at http://interactive.wsj.com;

Form S-1 Registration Statement Under The Securities Act of 1933: Google Inc. (April 29, 2004): accessed at http://sec.gov /Archives/edgar/data/1288776/00011931250407339/ds1.htm; S. Levy, "Next Frontiers: All Eyes on Google," *Newsweek* (March 29, 2004): 48–50, 52, 54–56, 58; "Microsoft Gives Glimpse of Plan to Battle Search Leader Google," *The Wall Street Journal Online* (July 30, 2004): accessed at http://interactive.wsj.com; F. Vogelstein, "Can Google Grow Up?," *Fortune* (December 8, 2003): accessed at http://www.fortune.com/technology/articles /0,15114,548765,00.html.

Appendix A

A Brief Historical Perspective

Organizational behavior may be traced back thousands of years, as noted in Sterba's analysis of the ancient Mesopotamian temple corporations. However, we will focus on the modern history of organizational behavior, which dates to the late 1800s. One of the more important series of studies conducted during this period was the Hawthorne studies. As these and other studies have unfolded, the six disciplines discussed in Chapter 1 of the text have contributed to the advancement of organizational behavior. An overview of the progress during the past century is presented in Table A.1 and the accompanying text. This is followed by a discussion of the Hawthorne studies.

One Hundred Years of Progress

Progress in any discipline, practice, or field of study is measured by significant events, discoveries, and contributions over time. The history of organizational

TABLE A.1	One Hundred Years of Progress in Organizational Behavior
1890s	• Frederick Taylor's development of scientific management
1900s	• Max Weber's concept of bureaucracy and the Protestant ethic
1910s	• Walter Cannon's discovery of the "emergency (stress) response"
1920s	• Elton Mayo's illumination studies in the textile industry
	• The Hawthorne studies at Western Electric Company
1930s	• Kurt Lewin's, Ronald Lippitt's, and Ralph White's early leadership studies
1940s	• Abraham Maslow's need hierarchy motivation theory
	• B. F. Skinner's formulation of the behavioral approach
	• Charles Walker's and Robert Guest's studies of routine work
1950s	• Ralph Stogdill's Ohio State leadership studies
	• Douglas McGregor's examination of the human side of enterprise
	• Frederick Herzberg's two-factor theory of motivation and job enrichment
1960s	• Arthur Turner's and Paul Lawrence's studies of diverse industrial jobs
	• Robert Blake's and Jane Mouton's Leadership Grid
	• Patricia Cain Smith's studies of satisfaction in work and retirement
	• Fred Fiedler's contingency theory of leadership
1970s	• J. Richard Hackman's and Greg Oldham's job characteristics theory
	• Edward Lawler's approach to pay and organizational effectiveness
	• Robert House's path–goal and charismatic theories of leadership
1980s	• Peter Block's political skills for empowered managers
	• Charles Manz's approach to self-managed work teams
	• Edgar Schein's approach to leadership and organizational culture
1990s	• Robert Solomon's personal integrity, character, and virtue ethics
	• Martin Seligman's positive psychology of hope and strength
2000s	• Fred Luthan's new framework of positive organzational behavior (POB)
	• Bruce Avolio's approach to authentic leadership

behavior begins, as noted in Table A.1, with the work of Frederick Taylor in scientific management at Midvale Steel Company, Bethlehem Steel Company, and elsewhere.[1] Taylor applied engineering principles to the study of people and their behavior at work. He pioneered the use of performance standards for workers, set up differential piece-rate systems of pay, and argued for the scientific selection of employees. He hoped to ultimately improve labor–management relationships in American industry. Taylor's lasting contributions include organizational goal-setting programs, incentive pay systems, and modern employee selection techniques.

The late 1800s also saw the United States make the transition from an agricultural society to an industrial one, and Taylor was part of this transformation process. About the same time Taylor was developing a uniquely American approach to the design of work, Max Weber was undertaking a classic work on religion and capitalism in Germany.[2] Weber's lasting legacies to management and organizational behavior are found in his notions of bureaucracies and the Protestant ethic, the latter an important feature of Chapter 5 in the text. Another major event of this era, as noted in Table A.1, was Walter Cannon's discovery of the stress response in about 1915. This discovery laid a foundation for psychosomatic medicine, industrial hygiene, and an understanding of the emotional components of health at work and play.[3] Finally, the first quarter of the twentieth century saw the initiation of the Hawthorne studies, a major research advancement in understanding people at work.[4] The Hawthorne studies are discussed in some depth in the second half of this brief history.

From the end of the 1930s through the 1950s, major contributions were made to the understanding of leadership, motivation, and behavior in organizations, as noted in Table A.1.[5] Lewin, Lippitt, and White's early examination of autocratic, democratic, and laissez-faire leadership styles was followed over a decade later by Ralph Stogdill's extensive studies at The Ohio State University focusing on leader behaviors. This marked a point of departure from earlier leadership studies, which had focused on the traits of the leader. Abraham Maslow proposed a need hierarchy of human motivation during the early 1940s, which served as a foundation for Douglas McGregor's theorizing in the 1950s about assumptions concerning the human side of a business enterprise. The 1950s was the decade in which Frederick Herzberg developed a new theory of motivation, which he later translated into an approach to job design, called *job enrichment*. This is quite different from the approach to designing work that Charles Walker and Robert Guest formulated a decade earlier in response to the problems they found with routine work. Attention was also given to group dynamics during this era in an effort to explain small group behavior.[6]

The 1960s and 1970s saw continued attention to theories of motivation, leadership, the design of work, and job satisfaction.[7] For example, Arthur Turner and Paul Lawrence's studies of diverse industrial jobs in various industries was a forerunner for the research program of Richard Hackman and Greg Oldham, which led to their job characteristics theory a decade later. Robert Blake and Jane Mouton's Leadership Grid was a variation on the Ohio State leadership studies of a decade earlier, while Fred Fiedler's contingency theory of leadership was an entirely new approach to leadership that emerged during the 1960s. Robert House proposed path–goal and charismatic theories of leadership during this era, and Edward Lawler drew attention to the importance of pay in performance and organizational effectiveness.

The 1980s saw attention shift to organizational culture, teamwork, and political skills in organizations. Peter Block drew our attention to the political skills required to empower managers in increasingly challenging work environments, while Charles Manz directed attention to teamwork and self-managed teams. Leadership continued to be an important topic, and Edgar Schein formulated a framework for understanding how leaders created, embedded, and maintained an organizational culture. Throughout the changing and unfolding story of the study of organizational behavior during the twentieth century there has been a common theme: How do we understand people, their psychology, and their behavior in the workplace?[8]

The 1990s saw an emerging concern for personal integrity, character, and virtue ethics as well as the new domain of positive psychology. The political scandals and impeachment hearings during the Clinton administration led to discussions in corporate boardrooms and college campuses about personal integrity and character. Robert Solomon framed an approach to personal virtues using an Aristotelian approach to business ethics.[9] Solomon extends his philosophy of personal integrity and character by articulating how they can lead to corporate success.[10] A second important development during the 1990s was the emergence of positive psychology, which Martin Seligman suggested was an underdeveloped aspect of the science of human behavior. The focus of positive psychology is building upon human strength and encouraging hope and optimism.[11] One early dissertation study in the management field linked positive psychology with eustress at work.[12] Since the year 2000, Fred Luthans has extended positive psychology with his emphasis on positive organizational behavior (POB), which emphasizes confidence, hope, optimism, and other positive attributes at work[13] Bruce Avolio draws upon POB research in his approach to authentic leadership.[14]

The intention of this brief historical review and time line in Table A.1 is to give you a sense of perspective on the drama of unfolding research programs, topics, and investigators who have brought us to the present state of knowledge and practice in organizational behavior. Although the text addresses the field in a topical manner by chapter, we think it is important that students of organizational behavior have a sense of historical perspective of the whole field. We now turn to the Hawthorne studies, one of the seminal research programs from the early part of the twentieth century.

The Hawthorne Studies

Initiated in 1925 with a grant from Western Electric, the Hawthorne studies were among the most significant advances in the understanding of organizational behavior during the past century. They were preceded by a series of studies of illumination conducted by Elton Mayo in the textile industry of Philadelphia. The research at the Hawthorne Works (an industrial manufacturing facility in Cicero, Illinois) was directed by Fritz Roethlisberger and consisted of four separate studies throughout a seven-year period.[15] These studies included (1) experiments in illumination, (2) the relay assembly test room study, (3) experiments in interviewing workers, and (4) the bank wiring room study. We will briefly examine this research program.

Experiments in Illumination

The experiments in illumination were a direct follow-up to Mayo's earlier work in the textile industry. At Hawthorne, the experiments in illumination consisted of a series of studies of test groups, in which the researchers varied illumination levels, and control groups, in which conditions were held constant. The purpose was to examine the relation of the quality and quantity of illumination to the efficiency of industrial workers. The experiments began in 1925 and extended over several years.

The researchers were surprised to discover that productivity increased to roughly the same rate in both test and control groups. It was only in the final experiment, where they decreased illumination levels to 0.06 footcandle (roughly moonlight intensity), that an appreciable decline in output occurred. The anticipated finding of a positive, linear relationship between illumination and industrial efficiency was simply not found. The researchers concluded that the results were "screwy" in the absence of this simple, direct cause-and-effect relationship.

It is from these first experiments that the term *Hawthorne Effect* was coined, referring originally to the fact that people's knowledge that they are being studied leads them to modify their behavior. A closer consideration of the Hawthorne Effect reveals that it is poorly understood and has taken on different meanings with the passage of time.[16] Hence, it has become somewhat an imprecise concept.

Relay Assembly Test Room Study

The researchers next set out to study workers segregated according to a range of working condition variables, such as workroom temperature and humidity, work schedule, rest breaks, and food consumption. The researchers chose five women in the relay assembly test room and kept careful records of the predictor variables, as well as output (measuring the time it took each woman to assemble a telephone relay of approximately forty parts).

Again, there was little the researchers were able to conclude from the actual data in this study in terms of a relationship between the predictor variables and industrial efficiency. However, they began to suspect that employee attitudes and sentiments were critically important variables not previously taken into account. Therefore, the researchers underwent a radical change of thought.

Experiments in Interviewing Workers

In 1928, a number of the researchers began a program of going into the workforce, without their normal tools and equipment, for the purpose of getting the workers to talk about what was important to them. Nearly 20,000 workers were interviewed over a period of two years, and in this interviewing process a major breakthrough occurred. The interview study was a form of research in which the investigators did not have a set of preconceptions concerning what they would find, as was the case in the two earlier phases of research. Rather, they set out to sympathetically and skillfully listen to what each worker was saying. As the interviewing progressed, the researchers discovered that the workers would open up and talk freely about what were the most important, and at times problematic, issues on their minds. The researchers discovered a rich and intriguing world previously unexamined within the Hawthorne Works.

Ultimately, Roethlisberger and his colleagues formulated guidelines for the conduct of interviews, and these guidelines became the basis for contemporary interviewing and active listening skills.[17] The discovery of the informal organization and its relationship to the formal organization began during the interview study. This led to a richer understanding of the social, interpersonal dynamics of people at work.

The concluding study at Hawthorne was significant because it confirmed the importance of one aspect of the informal organization on worker productivity. Specifically, the researchers studied workers in the bank wiring room and found that the behavioral norms set by the work group had a powerful influence over the productivity of the group. The higher the norms, the greater the productivity. The lower the norms, the lower the productivity. The power of the peer group and the importance of group influence on individual behavior and productivity were confirmed in the bank wiring room.

The Hawthorne studies laid a foundation for understanding people's social and psychological behavior in the workplace. Some of the methods used at Hawthorne, such as the experimental design methods and the interviewing technique, are used today for research in organizations. However, the discipline of organizational behavior is more than the psychology of people at work and more than the sociology of their behavior in organizations. Organizational behavior emerges from a wide range of interdisciplinary influences.

Appendix B

How Do We Know What We Know about Organizational Behavior?

By Uma Sekaran

This book has examined the skills and knowledge that managers need to be successful in their jobs. But how do you know how much faith to put in all the information you acquire from textbooks and management journals? Are some theories and statements more applicable than others? Even when applicable, will they apply at all times and under all circumstances? You can find answers to these important questions once you know the foundation on which theories and assertions rest. This appendix provides that foundation. It first examines why managers need to know about research and then discusses the basis for knowledge in this field. It then looks at the research process and research design and ends with a discussion of how research knowledge affects you.

Why Managers Should Know about Research

Why is it necessary for you to know about research? First, this knowledge helps you determine how much of what is offered in textbooks is of practical use to you as a manager. Second, a basic understanding of how good empirical research is done can make you an effective manager by helping you to make intelligent decisions about research proposals and reports that reach your desk. Third, it enables you to become an informed and discriminating consumer of research articles published in the management journals that you need to read to keep up with new ideas and technology. For your convenience, a list of the current academic and practitioner-oriented journals that frequently publish articles on organizational behavior is provided in Table B.1.

Understanding scientific research methods enables you to differentiate between good and appropriate research, which you can apply in your setting, and flawed or inappropriate research, which you cannot use. Moreover, knowledge of techniques such as sampling design enables you to decide whether the results of a study using a particular type of sample in certain types of organizations is applicable to your setting.

Managers need to understand, predict, and control the research-oriented problems in their environment. Some of these problems may be relatively simple and can be solved through simple data gathering and analysis. Others may be relatively complex, needing the assistance of researchers or consultants. In either case, without some basic knowledge of scientific research, managers will be unable to solve the problems themselves or to work effectively with consultants.

Managers need to discuss their problems with consultants in a useful way. This includes informing the problem solvers right at the start of the consulting process of any constraints (such as company records that are off limits to outsiders) or of types of recommendations that will not be considered (such as

APPENDIX B [HOW DO WE KNOW WHAT WE KNOW ABOUT ORGANIZATIONAL BEHAVIOR?

B-1

TABLE B.1   Journals with Organizational Behavior Articles

ACADEMIC JOURNALS	PRACTITIONER-ORIENTED JOURNALS
Academy of Management Journal	Academy of Management Executive
Academy of Management Review	Business Horizons
Administrative Science Quarterly	California Management Review
Advances in International	Columbia Journal of World Business
Comparative Management	Harvard Business Review
Group and Organization Studies	Human Resource Development
Human Relations	Quarterly
Human Resource Management	Industrial Relations
Human Resource Management	Industry Week
Review	Organizational Dynamics
Human Resource Planning	Personnel Journal
Industrial and Labor Relations	SAM Advanced Management
Review	Journal
International Journal of Human	Sloan Management Review
Resource Management	Supervision
International Journal of	Training
Management	Training and Development Journal
Journal of Applied Behavioral	
Science	
Journal of Applied Business	
Research	
Journal of Applied Psychology	
Journal of Business	
Journal of Business Ethics	
Journal of Business Research	
Journal of International Business	
Studies	
Journal of Management	
Journal of Management Studies	
Journal of Occupational Psychology	
Journal of Organizational Behavior	
Journal of Organizational Behavior	
Management	
Journal of Vocational Behavior	
Organizational Behavior and Human	
Decision Processes	
Personnel Administrator	
Sex Roles	
Women in Business	

laying off or hiring more people). Such discussions not only save time but also help the managers and researchers start off on the right foot. Managers who don't understand the important aspects of research will not be equipped to anticipate and forestall the inevitable hurdles in manager–researcher interactions. Also, paying a consultant handsomely for a research report will not help the company unless the manager is capable of determining how much scientific

B-2

APPENDIX B [HOW DO WE KNOW WHAT WE KNOW ABOUT ORGANIZATIONAL BEHAVIOR?

value can be placed on the findings. For these and other reasons, a working knowledge of the scientific research process and research design is necessary.

Our Basis for Knowledge

Observation and scientific data gathering have led to some of our knowledge about management. For instance, very early on, Frederick Winslow Taylor observed, studied, experimented, and demonstrated how coal-mining operations could be managed more efficiently by changing the way men shoveled coal— changing how the shovel was handled, how the body movements were made, and so on. The era of scientific management that Taylor's work ushered in provided much knowledge about how management could improve efficiency. This type of knowledge is not easy to come by, however, when we are examining employees' feelings, attitudes, and behaviors. Our knowledge of organizational behavior stems instead from armchair theories, case studies, and scientific research.

Armchair Theories

In trying to understand organizational behavior, management experts and scholars initially resorted to *armchair theorizing*—theorizing based on the observation of various phenomena and behaviors in the workplace. For instance, Douglas McGregor, through observation and experience, theorized that managers have two different world views of employees. Some managers (Theory X) assume that employees are, by nature, lazy and not very bright, that they dislike responsibility and prefer to be led rather than to lead, and that they resist change. Other managers (Theory Y) assume that employees have the opposite characteristics. McGregor's concept of Theory X and Theory Y managers has become a classic armchair theory.

Few people either totally accept or totally dispute this theory because of the lack of hard data to either substantiate or negate this interesting notion. Armchair theories are based on natural observation with no systematic experimentation and hence are not very useful for application in organizations.

Case Studies

Case studies—studies that examine the environment and background in which events occur in specific organizations in a particular period of time—help us to understand behavior in those organizations at that time. For example, we could study a particular organization in depth to determine the contributing factors that led to its fast recovery after a prolonged recession. We might find several factors, including price reductions, the offering of good incentives to a highly motivated workforce, and the taking of big risks. However, the findings from this one-time study of an organization offer only limited knowledge about fast recovery from recessions, because the findings may not hold true for other organizations or for even the same organization at another time. The replication of case studies is almost impossible, since environmental and background factors are rarely the same from organization to organization. Most of the companies whose problems you have been asked to solve are from real cases written by management scholars who studied the companies. The solutions they found may not work for other organizations experiencing similar problems, since differences in size, technology, environment, labor force, clientele, and other internal and external factors may exist. However, through case studies, we do gather information and gain insights and knowledge that might help us to develop theories and test them later.

APPENDIX B [HOW DO WE KNOW WHAT WE KNOW ABOUT ORGANIZATIONAL BEHAVIOR?

B-3

Empirical or data-based *scientific research* identifies a problem and solves it after a systematic gathering and analysis of the relevant data. This type of research offers in-depth understanding, confidence in the findings, and the capability of applying the knowledge gained to similar organizations. Scientific research is the main focus of this appendix.

Scientific Inquiry

Scientific inquiry involves a well-planned and well-organized systematic effort to identify and solve a problem. It encompasses a series of well-thought-out and carefully executed activities that help to solve the problem—as opposed to the symptoms—that is identified.

Purposes of Scientific Research: Applied and Basic Research

Scientific inquiry can be undertaken for two different purposes: (1) to solve an existing problem that a particular organization faces or (2) to examine problems that organizations generally encounter and to generate solutions, thereby expanding the knowledge base. Research undertaken to solve an existing problem in a specific setting is *applied research*. In this type of research, the findings are immediately applied to solve the problem. Many professors acting as consultants to organizations do applied research.

Research undertaken to add information to our existing base of knowledge is *basic research*. A large number of issues are of common interest to many organizations—for example, how to increase the productivity of a diverse workforce or how to eradicate sexual harassment in the workplace. The knowledge gained from research on such general issues can become useful later for application in organizational settings, but that is not the primary goal of basic research. The goal is to generate knowledge with which to build better theories that can be tested later. Basic research is often published in academic journals.

The Two Faces of Science: Theory and Empirical Research

Theory and empirical research are the two faces of science. Organizations benefit when good theories are developed and then substantiated through scientific research, because the results can then be confidently used for problem solving.

THEORY A *theory* is a postulated network of associations among various factors that a researcher is interested in investigating. For example, given what has been published thus far, you might theorize that self-confident employees perceive their work environment positively, which fosters their productivity, which in turn generates more profits for the company. In constructing this theory, you have postulated a positive relationship among (1) the self-confidence of employees and their positive attitude toward their work environment, (2) their attitude toward the work environment and their productivity, and (3) their productivity and the company's profits.

No doubt, this theory appeals to common sense. But in order to establish whether or not it holds true, we need to actually test it in organizations. Thus, theories offer the basis for doing scientific, data-based research; the theories and research together add to our knowledge. Conducting empirical

B-4

APPENDIX B [HOW DO WE KNOW WHAT WE KNOW ABOUT ORGANIZATIONAL BEHAVIOR?

research without the basis of sound theories does not steer us in the right direction, and building theories without empirically testing them limits their value.

The usefulness of good theories cannot be overstated. A good theory is formulated only after a careful examination of all the previous research and writings on the topic of interest, so that no factor already established as important is inadvertently omitted. Theory building offers unique opportunities to look at phenomena from different perspectives or to add new dimensions to existing ways of examining a phenomenon. New insights and creative ideas for theory building can come through personal observation, intuition, or even informal discussions with employees.

Testable theories are theories whose hypothesized relationships among measurable variables can be empirically tested and verified. When tested and substantiated repeatedly, such theories become the foundation on which subsequent theory building progresses. The next issue of interest is how theories are affirmed through empirical research.

EMPIRICAL RESEARCH As we have just seen, theories are of no practical use unless we have confidence that they work and can be applied to problem solving in organizational settings. Empirical research allows us to test the value of theories.

Empirical research is research that involves identifying the factors to be studied, gathering the relevant data, analyzing them, and drawing conclusions from the results of data analysis. It could involve simple qualitative analysis of the data, or it could be more complex, using a hypothetico-deductive approach. In *qualitative analysis*, responses to open-ended questions are obtained and meaningfully classified, and certain conclusions are drawn. In the *hypothetico-deductive approach*, a problem is identified, defined, and studied in depth. Then, a theory is formulated. From that theory, testable hypotheses are generated. Next, a research design is developed, relevant data are gathered and analyzed, results are interpreted, and conclusions (or deductions) are drawn from the results. Figure B.1 illustrates this approach.

To be called "scientific," research should conform to certain basic principles. It should be conducted objectively (without subjective biases). It should have a good and rigorous design (which we will examine shortly). It should be testable; that is, the conjectured relationships among factors in a setting should be capable of being tested. It should be replicable; that is, the results must be similar each time similar research is conducted. Finally, the findings should be generalizable (applicable to similar settings). It goes without saying, then, that scientific research offers precision (a good degree of exactitude) and a high degree of confidence in the results of the research (e.g. the researcher can say that 95 percent of the time, the results generated by the research will hold true, with only a 5 percent chance of its not being so).

The Research Process

The research process starts with a definition of the problem. To help define the problem, the researcher may interview people and study published materials in the area of interest in order to better understand what is happening in the environment. After defining the problem in clear and precise terms, the researcher develops a theoretical framework, generates hypotheses, creates the research design, collects data, analyzes data, interprets results, and draws conclusions.

APPENDIX B [HOW DO WE KNOW WHAT WE KNOW ABOUT ORGANIZATIONAL BEHAVIOR?

B-5

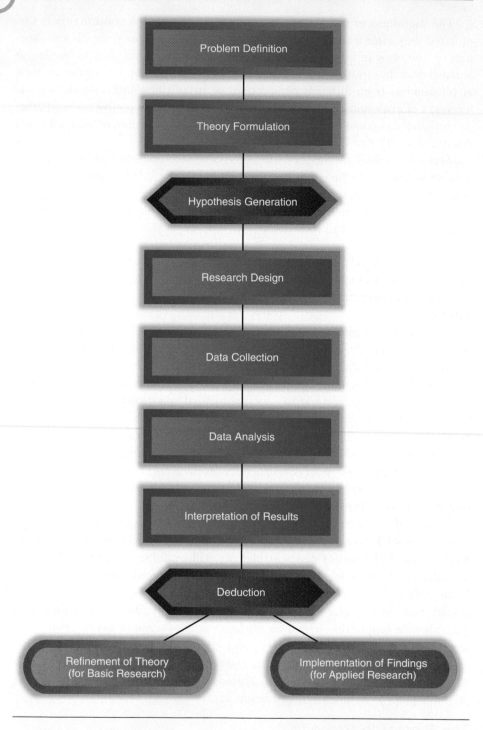

Problem Definition

The first job for the researcher is to define the problem. It is often difficult to state precisely the specific research question to be investigated. The researcher might simply know the broad area of interest—for instance, discrimination—without being clear about which aspect of discrimination to study. In order to focus on the issue to be investigated, the researcher might need to collect some preliminary information that will help to narrow down the issue.

B-6

APPENDIX B [HOW DO WE KNOW WHAT WE KNOW ABOUT ORGANIZATIONAL BEHAVIOR?

Such information can be obtained by interviewing people in organizations and by doing a literature survey. For example, employees of different gender, race, age, physical ability, and the like may be interviewed to determine the specific aspect of discrimination on which to focus. These interviews also provide insight into what the employees (rather than the researchers) consider important. The literature survey ensures that no pertinent variable is inadvertently omitted and that there is a credible and defensible basis for the research to be done. The researcher conducts an exhaustive search of all the published work in the area of interest to determine what research has been done thus far in the particular area and with what results. The search consumes a lot of time, as one must wade through several psychological, sociological, anthropological, and other relevant journals.

With all this information in hand, the researcher is now ready to define the problem. A well-defined, precise problem statement is a must for any study. The problem definition for the broad topic of discrimination could be this: *What are the important factors that contribute to employees' beliefs that they are being discriminated against by their immediate supervisor in cross-gender or cross-racial supervisor–employee relationships?*

Theoretical Framework

The next step is to develop a theoretical framework for the study. It involves focusing on the pertinent variables for the study and discussing the anticipated or theorized network of connections among the variables. For the discrimination problem, the framework might identify three factors related to employees' beliefs that they were discriminated against by the supervisor: (1) the level of mutual trust that is perceived by the employee to exist between the supervisor and employee (high to low), (2) the manner in which the supervisor offers performance feedback to the employee (in a forthright and helpful manner rather than in a derogatory and hurtful way), and (3) the extent to which the supervisor plays the role of mentor to the employee (training the subordinate and promoting the person's interests in career advancement to being indifferent toward the employee's career progress).

A network of logical connections among these four variables of interest to the study—discrimination (the dependent variable) and trust, performance feedback, and mentoring (the three independent variables)—can then be formulated. These connections with the anticipated nature and direction of the relationships among the variables are postulated in the theoretical framework.

Hypotheses

On the basis of the theoretical framework, the researcher next generates hypotheses. A *hypothesis* is a testable statement of the conjectured relationship between two or more variables. It is derived from the connections postulated in the theoretical framework. An example of a hypothesis is this: The more the employee perceives the supervisor as performing the mentoring role, the less the employee will feel discriminated against by the supervisor. The statement can be tested through data gathering and correlational analysis to see if it is supported.

Research Design

The next step in the research process is research design. Because this step is complex, it is covered in a separate section of the appendix, after the research process.

APPENDIX B [HOW DO WE KNOW WHAT WE KNOW ABOUT ORGANIZATIONAL BEHAVIOR?

B-7

Data Collection

After creating the research design, the researcher must gather the relevant data. In our example of the discrimination problem, we would collect data on the four variables of interest from employees in one or more organizations, obtain information about their race and gender and that of their supervisors, and seek such demographic data as age, educational level, and position in the organization. This information helps us describe the sample and enables us to see later if demographic characteristics make a difference in the results. For example, we might discover during data analysis that older employees sense less discrimination than their younger counterparts. Such information could even provide a basis for further theory development.

Data Analysis

Having collected the data, the researcher must next analyze it, using statistical procedures to test whether the hypotheses have been substantiated. In the case of the discrimination hypothesis, if a correlational analysis between the variables of mentoring and discrimination indicates a significant negative correlation, the hypothesis will have been supported. In other words, we have been correct in conjecturing that the more the supervisor is perceived as a mentor, the less the employee feels discriminated against. Each of the hypotheses formulated from the theoretical framework is tested, and the results are examined.

Interpreting Results and Drawing Conclusions

The final step is to interpret the results of the data analysis and draw conclusions about them. In our example, if a significant negative relationship is indeed found between mentoring and discrimination, then one of our conclusions might be that mentoring helps fight feelings of discrimination. We might therefore recommend that if the organization wants to create a climate where employees do not feel discriminated against, supervisors should actively engage in mentoring. If the organization accepts this recommendation, it might conduct training programs to make supervisors better mentors. By testing and substantiating each of the hypotheses, we might find a multitude of solutions to overcome the perception of discrimination by employees.

Summary

We can see that every step in the research process is important. Unless the problem is well defined, the research endeavor will be fruitless. If a thorough literature survey is not done, a defensible theoretical framework cannot be developed and useful hypotheses cannot be generated—which compromises effective problem solving. Using the correct methods in data gathering and analysis and drawing relevant conclusions are all indispensable methodological steps for conducting empirical research. We next examine some of the research design issues that are integral to conducting good research.

Research Design

Issues regarding research design relate particularly to how the variables are measured, how the data are collected, what sampling design is used, and how the data are analyzed. Before decisions in these areas are made, some details about the nature and purpose of the study have to be determined so there is a good match be-

B-8

APPENDIX B [HOW DO WE KNOW WHAT WE KNOW ABOUT ORGANIZATIONAL BEHAVIOR?

tween the purpose of the study and the design choices. If the research design does not mesh with the research goals, the right solutions will not be found.

Important Concepts in Research Design

Five important concepts in research design must be understood before an adequate design can be created: nature of study, study setting, types of study, researcher interference, and time horizon. The *nature of study* is the purpose of the study—whether it is to establish correlations among variables or causation. The *study setting* could be either the environment in which the phenomena studied normally and naturally occur—the *field*—or it could be in a contrived, artificial setting, such as a laboratory. The *type of study* is either experimental (to establish causal connections) or correlational (to establish correlations). An experiment could be conducted in an artificial setting—a *lab experiment*, or it could be conducted in the organization itself where events naturally occur—*field experiment*. *Researcher interference* is the extent to which the researcher manipulates the independent variable and controls other contaminating factors in the study setting that are likely to affect the cause–effect relationship. The *time horizon* is the number of data collection points in the study; the study could be either one-shot (various types of data are collected only once during the investigation) or longitudinal (same or similar data are collected more than once from the same system during the course of the study).

Purpose of Study and Design Choices

One of the primary issues to consider before making any research design decision is the purpose of the study. Is the research to establish a causal relationship (that variable X causes variable Y), or is it to detect any correlations that might exist between two or more variables? A study to establish a cause–effect relationship differs in many areas (for example, the setting, type of study, extent of researcher interference with the ongoing processes, and time frame of the study) from a study to examine correlations among factors. Figure B.2 depicts the fit between the goal of the study and the characteristics of the study.

Causal Studies

Studies conducted to detect causal relationships call for an experimental design, considerable researcher interference, and a longitudinal time span. The design could consist of laboratory experiments, field experiments, or simulations.

LABORATORY EXPERIMENTS A rigorous causal study may call for a *laboratory experiment*, where participants are exposed to an artificial environment and an artificial stimulus in order to establish a cause–effect relationship. The experiment is set up with maximum researcher interference; both manipulation and controls (described later) are used, and data are collected from the subjects more than once during the experiment (longitudinally). Following is an example of how a lab experiment is conducted.

Suppose a manager wants to know which of two incentives—offering stock options or giving a bonus—would better improve employee productivity. To determine this, the manager has to experiment with each of the two types of incentives to see which offers better results. Not knowing how to proceed, the manager might hire a researcher who is likely to recommend conducting a lab experiment first and then a field experiment. The lab experiment firmly establishes the causal relationship, and the field experiment confirms whether or not

APPENDIX B [HOW DO WE KNOW WHAT WE KNOW ABOUT ORGANIZATIONAL BEHAVIOR?

B-9

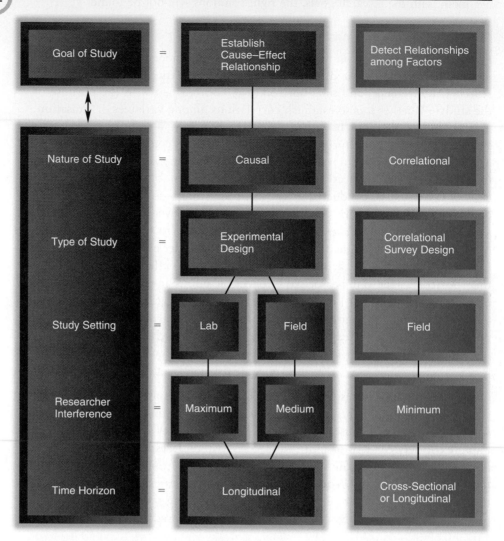

the causal relationship established during the lab experiment holds good in the organizational setting.

To set up a lab experiment in which thirty subjects participate, the following is done:

1. An artificial setting is created. It will consist of three conference rooms in which the experiment is conducted after regular work hours.

2. A simple task—assembling cardboard houses—is given to the subjects, who take part in the experiment for two hours.

3. The subjects receive an imaginary bonus in the form of cardboard chips and stock options in the form of fake certificates.

4. Each subject is randomly assigned to one of three conference rooms, thus forming three ten-member groups.

For the first hour, all three groups will be assigned the task of assembling the cardboard houses. Thereafter, the researcher manipulates the incentives—

giving one group stock options, another a bonus, and a third, called the control group, no incentives at all. The researcher has already exercised tight control to ensure that all three groups have more or less the same types of members in terms of ability, experience, and the like by randomly assigning members to each of the groups. In random assignment, every member has an equal chance of being assigned to any of the groups. This control helps avoid contamination of the cause–effect relationship, since all factors that might affect the causal relationship (age, ability, and so on) are randomly distributed among the groups.

The data are collected at two different times in the following manner. At the end of the first hour, when all three groups have worked without any incentives, the number of cardboard houses built by each group will be recorded by the researcher. The numbers are again counted and recorded at the end of the second hour, after the introduction of the incentives. Determining the difference between the number of houses assembled during the second hour and the number assembled during the first hour for the three groups clarifies the following two issues:

> Do the incentives make any difference at all to performance? Obviously, if the performance has increased during the second hour for either or both of the two groups provided with incentives, while there is no difference for the control group, then it is safe to surmise that either or both of the incentives have caused performance to rise. If there is no difference in the production between the second and first hour for all three groups, then, of course, the incentives have not caused an increase in performance.

> If the incentives do make a difference, which of the two incentives has worked better? By examining which group—the group that received the stock options or the group that received the bonus—performed better during the second hour, we know which of the two incentives worked better. The incentive that increases performance more will obviously be preferred by the company.

Because all possible contaminating factors have been controlled by the random assignment of members to the three groups, the cause–effect relationships found can be accepted with a high degree of confidence.

FIELD EXPERIMENTS What occurred in the tightly controlled artificial lab setting may or may not happen in an organizational setting, where many of the factors (such as employees' ages and experience) cannot be controlled and the jobs to be done might be quite complex. But having established a strong causal relationship in the lab setting, the researcher is eager to see if that relationship is generalizable to the organization, or field setting.

For the field experiment, three experimental cells (three branches or departments of the company, or whatever other units are appropriate for the organization) can be chosen. Real bonus and stock options can be offered to two groups, while the third group is treated as a control group and given no incentives. Work performance data can be collected for the three cells before the incentives are introduced and again six months after the incentives are introduced.

While it is possible to manipulate the incentive in a field experiment, it is not possible to control the contaminating factors (ability, experience, and so on). Because employees are already placed, members cannot be randomly assigned to the three units. Under these circumstances, researcher interference can be only partial, since the independent variable can be manipulated but other factors cannot be controlled. Even manipulating the independent variable is not easy, because people in organizations get suspicious and anxious as the word spreads that some strange changes are being made at some sites. Not only does this cause apprehension among employees, but it may also produce invalid results. Because of these difficulties, very few field experiments are conducted in organizational behavior research. However, if the manipulation is successful and the results of the field experiment are similar to those of the lab experiment, the manager can confidently introduce the changes needed to obtain the desired results.

If you read journal articles describing experimental designs, you will want to see how well the manipulations were done and how tightly the contaminating variables were controlled. Were the independent variables successfully manipulated, or did the subjects see through the manipulations? If the subjects in the various groups differed in some characteristics that are relevant to the cause–effect relationship, then it cannot be said with confidence that only the manipulated independent variable caused the dependent variable. Other factors in the setting might also have influenced the dependent variable, and they might be impossible to trace.[1]

SIMULATIONS Somewhere between lab and field experiments are *simulations*—experiments that are conducted in settings that closely resemble field settings. The specially created settings look much like actual environments in which events normally occur—for example, offices with desks, computers, and phones. Members of the experimental group are randomly selected and exposed to real-world experiences over a period of time, during which their behavior is studied. A free simulation for studying leadership styles, called "Looking Glass," has been used in management classes. This simulation enables students to study different kinds of behavior as the researcher manipulates some of the stimuli while allowing the flow of events to be governed by the reactions of the participants.[2]

Correlational Studies

Researchers and managers may not be interested in establishing causal connections. Instead, they may want to understand, describe, or predict occurrences in the workplace. In general, they want to know which factors are related to desirable outcomes (such as employee loyalty to the organization) and which to undesirable outcomes (such as high turnover rates). *Correlational studies* are studies that are not specifically geared toward establishing cause–effect relationships. Such studies may be *exploratory*—trying to understand certain relationships; *descriptive*—trying to describe certain phenomena at the workplace; or *analytical*—focusing on testing hypotheses. Correlational studies are always conducted in the field setting with minimum researcher interference, and they can be either one-shot or longitudinal. The vast majority of the research articles published in organizational behavior journals are field studies examining correlations among factors.

To conduct a scientific study, whether causal or correlational, certain research design decisions must be made. As Figure B.3 shows, these decisions involve measurement, issues, data collection methods, sampling design, and data analysis procedures.

Measurement Issues

We saw earlier that it is difficult to measure attitudes, feelings, and other abstract concepts. Since the measurement of variables in the organizational sci-

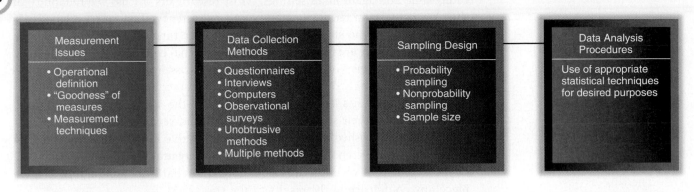

Measurement Issues	Data Collection Methods	Sampling Design	Data Analysis Procedures
• Operational definition • "Goodness" of measures • Measurement techniques	• Questionnaires • Interviews • Computers • Observational surveys • Unobtrusive methods • Multiple methods	• Probability sampling • Nonprobability sampling • Sample size	Use of appropriate statistical techniques for desired purposes

ences is not as exact as in the physical sciences, management research cannot be completely scientific. It is possible, however, to minimize biases in measurement by carefully developing valid and reliable measures for even abstract concepts. The primary aspects in measurement are operational definition, the "goodness" of measures, and the measurement techniques to be used.

OPERATIONAL DEFINITION Attitudes such as job satisfaction and organizational commitment do not easily lend themselves to measurement. To measure them, we first need to translate them into observable behaviors. *Operational definition* is the reduction of the level of abstraction of concepts so as to identify the observable behaviors and measure them.

For example, how can we measure the motivational level of individuals? We know that highly motivated people engage in the following types of behaviors, among others. They are driven by work, and they keep persevering even if they initially fail to accomplish what they want. We can measure the abstract concept of motivation by developing an instrument that asks subjects to respond to several suitably worded questions tapping these behaviors.[3] Most of the abstract concepts that are important to the study of organizational behavior have been operationally defined by scholars, who have developed "good" instruments for measuring them.[4]

"GOODNESS" OF MEASURES "Good" measurement instruments offer researchers the confidence that they do indeed measure what is desired to be measured and do so in a thorough and accurate manner. The goodness of instruments is established through their validity and reliability.

Validity is our confidence that the instrument used does indeed measure the concept it is supposed to measure. For instance, if a twenty-item instrument is developed to measure job satisfaction, we need to know that it does indeed measure job satisfaction, not employees' general happiness.

Researchers usually establish various types of validity for the measures they use. Among them are content validity, criterion-related validity, predictive validity, construct validity, and convergent and discriminant validity. Journal articles often explain the types of validity established for the instrument used, especially if it is newly developed. In general, only such measures as are both valid and reliable are frequently used by researchers.[5]

Reliability is the ability of an instrument to accurately and stably measure a concept over time and across situations. For example, it is not enough for an instrument to measure job satisfaction; it must do so consistently and accurately time and again in all settings. Most researchers discuss the reliability of their instruments in terms of stability and consistency. Test–retest reliability is one indicator of the stability of a measure over time. Cronbach's alpha and split-half reliability are two indicators of the internal consistency of instruments. These are the terms you are likely to come across in published empirical research.

Authors of studies usually provide details of the measures they use and, at a minimum, cite their source. Journal editors and reviewers try to ensure that studies to be published have used valid and reliable measures. Discriminating readers of journals reporting empirical studies pay attention to the "goodness" of the measures. If variables are not validly and reliably measured, how can we place any confidence in the results of the study?

MEASUREMENT TECHNIQUES Concepts are not measured solely through questionnaires or interviews. Sometimes, in order to tap certain ideas, feelings, and thoughts that are not easily verbalized, researchers use *projective tests*—word association, sentence completion, thematic apperception tests, and ink-blot tests are some familiar projective tests. In word association (e.g., work could be associated with excitement or drudgery) and sentence completion ("I like") tests, it is expected that the respondent will draw on deeply embedded feelings, attitudes, and orientations when answering. Marketing researchers use these techniques to assess consumer preferences. Thematic apperception tests and ink-blot tests ask the subject to offer a story or interpret an ink blot. They can be interpreted only by trained psychologists.

Data Collection Methods

Data can be collected through questionnaires, interviews, computers, observation, unobtrusive methods, or a combination of these. The most frequently used method in organizational behavior research is questionnaires.

QUESTIONNAIRES A *questionnaire* is a written set of questions to which respondents record their answers, usually within a close range of alternatives given to them. Questionnaires can be mailed to respondents or administered personally.

Mail questionnaires are commonly used because of the large number of people who can be reached economically even when they are geographically dispersed. As a rule, however, they do not elicit a good response rate, even when stamped, self-addressed envelopes are enclosed for their return. (Researchers sometimes even include, as a small token of their appreciation, a one-dollar bill.) A 30 percent response rate for mail questionnaires is considered good. Mail responses generally fall far short of even this low percentage. Because of the low response rate, certain types of nonresponse biases can creep into research. For example, we cannot know if those who responded to the survey differ from those who did not. Thus, we cannot be sure that the data are representative of the population we are trying to study.

Personally administered questionnaires are questionnaires given to groups of subjects by the researcher, who collects the responses immediately after completion. This method ensures practically a 100 percent response rate. However, many organizations are reluctant to spare company time for the research effort unless the study is of vital importance to them.

INTERVIEWS *Interviews* have the potential to elicit a good deal of information. In *structured interviews*, specific questions are asked of all respondents, and the responses are noted by the interviewer. In *unstructured interviews*, there is no predetermined format; questions are framed according to responses given to the previous question. Structured interviews are conducted when the interviewer knows precisely what sort of information is needed. They are efficient in terms of the amount of time involved in both obtaining the required information and categorizing the data obtained. Unstructured interviews are conducted when the researcher wants to explore a problem or become more knowledgeable about particular situations.

Face-to-face interviews offer the researcher the advantage of being able to observe the interviewees as they respond to questions. Nonverbal messages transmitted by the interviewees can be observed and explored further. *Telephone interviews*, on the other hand, help the researcher reach a vast number of geographically dispersed individuals. In both face-to-face and telephone interviews, certain types of biases can enter. The way a question is worded and asked, the inflection of a voice, the frame of mind of the interviewee at the time the interview is conducted, and other factors can all contribute to biases in the data.

COMPUTERS *Computer-assisted interviewing* and *computer-aided surveys* will become more popular in the future as more and more people become comfortable using their computers at home and responding to questions contained on diskettes or displayed on Web sites. Interview and questionnaire methods of data collection are greatly facilitated through computers. However, computer literacy of respondents is a prerequisite for using computer-assisted data collection techniques effectively.

OBSERVATIONAL SURVEYS *Observational surveys* are another data collection method whereby information is obtained without asking questions of subjects. In this method, the researcher observes firsthand what is going on and how people are behaving in the work setting. The data are collected by either nonparticipant observers (researchers who observe behavior as outsiders) or participant observers (integral members of the work team). An example of a nonparticipant study is one done by Henry Mintzberg, who observed the nature of managerial work over a period of time.

Like interviews, observational surveys can be either structured or unstructured. In a structured observational survey, the observer identifies the factors that are to be observed. For example, the observer might want to note the number of times a manager gives instructions to staff members and how much time this takes. In an unstructured observational survey, the observer might simply want to know how the manager spends the day at the workplace and might jot down all the activities the manager engages in and the time periods and frequencies involved.

Observational studies help prevent respondent bias, since information is not given by the subjects directly. Any bias that might creep in through the self-consciousness of subjects usually lasts only a few days. Then, subjects begin to function and behave normally, oblivious to the presence of the observer.

However, observer fatigue and observer bias cannot be totally avoided in observational studies. Moreover, when several observers are involved in a large research project, interobserver reliability could become an issue for concern; different observers might interpret and categorize the same behavior differently.

This problem can be minimized by training the observers before the start of the project.

UNOBTRUSIVE METHODS Data collection by *unobtrusive methods* offers valid and reliable information; bias is minimized because the source of the data is tangible elements rather than people. For example, the usage of library books can be determined by the wear and tear on them, a source of information more reliable than surveys of users of the library. The number of empty cans or bottles of pop in the recycling bins outside houses on garbage collection days would offer a good idea of the beverage consumption patterns in households. The personnel records of a company would indicate the absenteeism patterns of employees. Unobtrusive methods thus have the potential to offer the most reliable and unbiased data. They are, however, time consuming and labor intensive; also, the researcher must obtain the company's permission to gain access to such data.

MULTIPLE METHODS Each data collection method has advantages and disadvantages. The best approach is using multiple methods of collecting data, since it offers researchers a chance to cross-check the information obtained through the various methods. This approach, however, is expensive and thus is used infrequently in organizational behavior research.

When you read journal articles, you should assess the data collection methods used by the researchers to determine if they are adequate. Authors of published studies often discuss the limitations of their research and the biases they have attempted to minimize. The biases could relate to the types of measures used, the data collection methods adopted, the sampling design, and other research process and design issues. Sophisticated managers pay attention to all research design details in order to evaluate the quality of the research.

Sampling Design

Sampling is the process of drawing a limited number of subjects from a larger population or universe. Since researchers cannot possibly survey the entire universe of people they are interested in studying, they usually draw a sample of subjects from the population for investigation. The sampling design used makes a difference in the generalizability of the findings and determines the usefulness and scientific nature of the study. Sample size is another important issue. There are two broad categories of sampling—probability sampling and nonprobability sampling.

PROBABILITY SAMPLING *Probability sampling* is sampling that ensures that the elements in the population have some known chance, or probability, of being selected for the sample. Because of this, probability sampling designs offer more generalizability than nonprobability designs. There are many probability designs. The *simple random sampling* design, wherein every element in the population has a known and equal chance of being chosen, lends itself to the greatest generalizability. However, other probability designs can be more efficient and offer good generalizability as well. Among them are systematic sampling, stratified random sampling, cluster sampling, and area sampling.

In *systematic sampling*, every *n*th element in the population is chosen as a subject. In *stratified random sampling*, the population is first divided into meaningful strata (for example, blue-collar and white-collar employees); a sample is then drawn from each stratum using either simple random sampling or systematic sampling. *Cluster sampling* is the random selection of chunks (clusters or groups) of elements from the population; every chunk has an equal chance of being selected, and all the members in each chosen chunk participate in the research. For example, in an attitude survey, three departments in an organization can be randomly chosen; all the members of the three departments are the subjects. *Area sampling* is cluster sampling confined to particular geographical areas, such as counties or city blocks. Marketing researchers use cluster and area sampling extensively for surveys.

NONPROBABILITY SAMPLING For some research projects, probability sampling may be impossible or inappropriate. In such cases, *nonprobability sampling* may be used, even if generalizability is impaired or lost. In nonprobability sampling, the subjects do not have a known probability of being chosen for the study. For instance, the sample of subjects in a study of sexual harassment must come from those who have experienced such harassment; there is nothing to be gained by researching all the employees of the organization. When the choice of subjects for a study involves a limited number of people who are in a position to provide the required information, a probability sampling design is infeasible. The results of such a study are not generalizable; nevertheless, this type of sampling is the best way to learn about certain problems, such as sexual harassment.

Nonprobability sampling includes convenience sampling, judgment sampling, and quota sampling. In *convenience sampling*, information is collected from whoever is conveniently available. In *judgment sampling*, subjects who are in the best position to provide the required information are chosen. In *quota sampling*, people from different groups—some of which are underrepresented—are sampled for comparison purposes. One example might be a study of middle-class African-Americans and whites.

As noted earlier, nonprobability sampling does not lend itself to generalizability. In reading research articles, you should determine the type of sampling design being used and how much generalizability the author claims for the research.

SAMPLE SIZE Another critical issue in sampling is *sample size*. Too small or too large a sample could distort the results of the research. Tables providing ideal sample sizes for desired levels of precision and confidence are available to researchers. In examining any business report or journal article, you should note the sampling design and the sample size used by the researcher to assess the generalizability of the findings.

Data Analysis Procedures

Beyond good measures, appropriate data collection methods, and an acceptable sampling design, a good research project should also have suitable *data analysis procedures*. Some data cannot be subjected to sophisticated statistical tests. One example is data collected on a *nominal scale*, which divides subjects into mutually exclusive groups, such as men and women or the poor and the rich. Another example is data collected on an *ordinal scale*, which rank-orders the subjects and indicates a preference (X is better than Y). Various simple ways are available to analyze such data that are qualitative or nonparametric in nature. For instance, if we have categorized under distinct headings the verbal responses of organizational members to an open-ended question on how they perceive their work environment, a frequency count of the responses in each

APPENDIX B [HOW DO WE KNOW WHAT WE KNOW ABOUT ORGANIZATIONAL BEHAVIOR?

B-17

category would be adequate to describe how the work environment is perceived. Likewise, to detect if the gender of the worker (male versus female) is independent of members' commitment to the organization (less committed versus more committed), a simple x2 (chi-square) test would suffice.

Sophisticated statistical tests are possible when data have been gathered on interval or ratio scales. Data collected on interval scales—through individuals' responses to questions on equal-appearing multipoint scales—allow for the computation of the arithmetic mean and standard deviation. Data collected on ratio scales also allow us to compute proportions and ratios. For example, an individual who weighs 250 pounds is twice as heavy as one who weighs 125 pounds. Pearson correlations can be calculated, and multiple regression and many multivariate analyses can be made with data obtained on interval and ratio scales. These sorts of analyses cannot be made with data obtained on nominal and ratio scales. Illustrations of the four scales appear in Figure B.4.

One decision that needs to be made before collecting the data is what kinds of analyses are needed to find answers to the research question. This decision will determine which scales should be used in data collection. Sometimes researchers are tempted to apply more sophisticated statistical analyses to data that do not lend themselves to such analyses (this includes sample sizes below thirty). Using inappropriate methods can negatively affect the interpretation of the results and can compromise the problem solution.

B.4

FIGURE B.4   Illustrations of Four Data Analysis Scales

1. Nominal scale: Used for differentiating groups or categories

San Francisco 49ers   Dallas Cowboys   Buffalo Bills

2. Ordinal scale: Used for rank-ordering

Ranking in terms of sweetness:

Sweetest   Sweet   Not so sweet

3. Interval scale: Indicates the magnitude of differences

The extent to which a job is liked:

1	2	3	4	5
Very Much Disliked	Somewhat Disliked	Neither Liked nor Disliked	Somewhat Liked	Very Much Liked

4. Ratio scale: Indicates proportion of differences

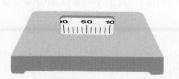

B-18

APPENDIX B [HOW DO WE KNOW WHAT WE KNOW ABOUT ORGANIZATIONAL BEHAVIOR?

Thus far, we have examined the biases that would result from poor research process and design decisions. Another source of bias is in the interpretation of results. Objectivity plays a large part in the validity of interpretations from the results of data analysis. Objectivity may be difficult, however, if the results of the study do not substantiate the theories painstakingly developed by the researcher.

When data analysis does not substantiate one or more of the hypotheses generated, the researcher may be tempted to downplay the results or try to explain them away. For example, a researcher may say that the results were actually in the expected direction even though they were not statistically significant. If a hypothesis has not passed the appropriate statistical test, the hypothesis is just not substantiated, regardless of whether the results were in the theorized direction. When authors try to explain their results, you have to decide for yourself whether the explanations offered are valid.

Organizational Behavior Research and You

It is seldom possible to do completely scientific research in the field of organizational behavior. First, adherence to good research design principles may not always be possible, since certain choices (such as obtaining the most representative sample for better generalizability or utilizing the best data collection methods) may be beyond the researcher's control. Second, attitudes and feelings cannot be measured accurately. Hence, there are likely to be several types of biases in research in this field. However, by paying careful attention to the research process and rigorously making good research design choices, we are able to minimize the biases and enhance the objectivity, testability, replicability, precision and confidence, and generalizability of our research.

Bias can enter at every stage of the process, from problem definition to problem solution. Errors can creep into experimental designs by way of poor or inadequate manipulations and controls. They can enter into measurement, data collection, sampling, data analysis, interpretation of results, and the drawing of conclusions therefrom.

Unless managers are knowledgeable about some of the methodological flaws that can adversely affect research results, they may inappropriately apply the conclusions drawn in published research to their own settings. Having been exposed to the rudiments of scientific research, *you* can critically examine and evaluate all published works before you assess their usefulness for your organization. For instance, you would not consider applying the results of good research done in a service organization to a manufacturing firm. Good research results in the hands of knowledgeable managers are highly useful tools. That is where research knowledge becomes invaluable. By grasping the essentials of good research, you will become a discriminating consumer of business reports and published articles and can become an effective manager. Research knowledge can often make the difference between managerial excellence and mediocrity.

References

Chapter 1

1. O. Malik, "The New Phone Company," *Business 2.0* 4 (November 2003): 82–89, http://www.business2.com/b2/subscribers/articles/0,17863,541290-1,00.html.
2. H. Schwartz, "The Clockwork or the Snakepit: An Essay on the Meaning of Teaching Organizational Behavior," *Organizational Behavior Teaching Review* 11, No. 2 (1987): 19–26.
3. M. Matcho, "Idea Fest," *Fast Company* 66 (January 2003): 95–105, http://www.fastcompany.com/online/66/ideafest.html.
4. H. G. Barkem, J. A. C. Baum, and E. A. Mannix, "Management Challenges in a New Time," *Academy of Management Journal* 45 (2002): 916–930.
5. K. Lewin, "Field Theory in Social Science," selected theoretical papers (edited by Dorin Cartwright) (New York: Harper, 1951).
6. N. Schmitt, ed., Industrial/Organizational Section in *Encyclopedia of Psychology* (Washington, D.C.: American Psychological Association, and New York: Oxford University Press, 2000).
7. R. M. Yerkes, "The Relation of Psychology to Military Activities," *Mental Hygiene* 1 (1917): 371–376.
8. N. Gross, W. Mason, and A. McEachen, *Explorations in Role Analysis: Studies of the School Superintendency Role* (New York: Wiley, 1958).
9. J. S. Adams, A. Tashchian, and T. H. Stone. "Codes of Ethics as Signals for Ethical Behavior," *Journal of Business Ethics* 29 (2001): 199–211.
10. F. W. Taylor, *The Principles of Scientific Management* (New York: Norton, 1911).
11. E. A. Locke and G. P. Latham, *A Theory of Goal Setting and Task Performance* (Englewood Cliffs, N.J.: Prentice-Hall, 1990).
12. A. L. Wilkins and W. G. Ouchi, "Efficient Cultures: Exploring the Relationship between Culture and Organizational Performance," *Administrative Science Quarterly* 28 (1983): 468–481.
13. M. F. R. Kets de Vries and D. Miller, "Personality, Culture, and Organization," *Academy of Management Review* 11 (1986): 266–279.
14. H. Schwartz, *Narcissistic Process and Corporate Decay: The Theory of the Organizational Ideal* (New York: NYU Press, 1990).
15. J. G. March and H. A. Simon, *Organizations* (New York: Wiley, 1958).
16. H. B. Elkind, *Preventive Management: Mental Hygiene in Industry* (New York: B. C. Forbes, 1931).
17. J. C. Quick, "Occupational Health Psychology: Historical Roots and Future Directions," *Health Psychology* 18 (1999).
18. K. R. Pelletier, *Mind as Healer, Mind as Slayer: A Holistic Approach to Preventing Stress Disorders* (New York: Delacorte, 1977).
19. D. R. Ilgen, "Health Issues at Work," *American Psychologist* 45 (1990): 273–283.
20. B. M. Staw, L. E. Sandelands, and J. E. Dutton, "Threat-Rigidity Effects in Organizational Behavior: A Multilevel Analysis," *Administrative Science Quarterly* 26 (1981): 501–524.
21. E. V. Brown, President of Proline International, Inc., "Commencement Address—College of Business Administration, the University of Texas at Arlington" (December 2003).
22. R. L. A. Sterba, "The Organization and Management of the Temple Corporations in Ancient Mesopotamia," *Academy of Management Review* 1 (1976): 16–26; S. P. Dorsey, *Early English Churches in America* (New York: Oxford University Press, 1952).
23. Sir I. Moncreiffe of That Ilk, *The Highland Clans: The Dynastic Origins, Chiefs, and Background of the Clans and of Some Other Families Connected to Highland History*, rev. ed. (New York: C. N. Potter, 1982).
24. D. Shambaugh, "The Soldier and the State in China: The Political Work System in the People's Liberation Army," *Chinese Quarterly* 127 (1991): 527–568.
25. L. L'Abate, ed., *Handbook of Developmental Family Psychology and Psychopathology* (New York: Wiley, 1993).
26. J. A. Hostetler, *Communitarian Societies* (New York: Holt, Rinehart & Winston, 1974).
27. J. M. Lewis, "The Family System and Physical Illness," in *No Single Thread: Psychological Health in Family Systems* (New York: Brunner/Mazel, 1976).
28. D. Katz and R. L. Kahn, *The Social Psychology of Organizations*, 2nd ed. (New York: John Wiley & Sons, 1978; H. J. Leavitt, "Applied Organizational Change in Industry: Structural, Technological, and Humanistic Approaches," in J. G. March, ed., *Handbook of Organizations* (Chicago: Rand McNally, 1965), 1144–1170.
29. J. D. Thompson, *Organizations in Action* (New York: McGraw-Hill, 1967).
30. F. J. Roethlisberger and W. J. Dickson, *Management and the Worker* (Cambridge, Mass.: Harvard University Press, 1939).
31. W. L. French and C. H. Bell, *Organization Development*, 4th ed. (Englewood Cliffs, N.J.: Prentice-Hall, 1990).
32. J. P. Kotter, "Managing External Dependence," *Academy of Management Review* 4 (1979): 87–92.
33. H. K. Steensma and D. G. Corley, "Organizational Context as a Moderator of Theories on Firm Boundaries for Technology Sourcing," *Academy of Management Journal* 44 (2001): 271–291.
34. Cisco Systems, Inc., "Annual Report—This Is the Power of Network" (November 2003).
35. Datamonitor.com, "The Coca-Cola Company—Company Profile," http://www.datamonitor.com/; Hoover's Online, "The Coca-Cola Company—Fact Sheet," http://www.hoovers.com.
36. Pixar, "Investor Relations Corporate Profile," http://corporate.pixar.com.
37. Hoover's Online, "Virgin Group Ltd.—Fact Sheet," http://www.hoovers.com/; B. Morris, "Richard Branson: What a Life," *Fortune* 7 (October 6, 2003), http://www.fortune.com/fortune/personalfortune/articles/0,15114,488581,00.html.
38. Hoover's Online, "Whole Foods Market, Inc.—Fact Sheet," http://www.hoovers.com/.
39. Charity Navigator, "Charity Summary—Canine Companions for Independence," http://www.charitynavigator.org/index.cfm/bay/search.summary/orgid/3418.htm, http://www.give.org/reports.
40. T. B. Lawrence and V. Corwin, "Being There: The Acceptance and Marginalization of Part-Time Professional Employees," *Journal of Organizational Behavior* 24 (2003): 923–943.
41. M. K. Gowing, J. D. Kraft, and J. C. Quick, *The New Organizational Reality: Downsizing, Restructuring and Revitalization* (Washington, D.C.: American Psychological Association, 1998); T. Tang and R. M. Fuller, "Corporate Downsizing: What Managers Can Do to Lessen the Negative Effects of Layoffs," *SAM Advanced Management Journal* 60 (1995): 12–15, 31.
42. L. R. Offermann and M. K. Gowing, "Organizations of the Future," *American Psychologist* 45 (1990): 95–108.
43. J. Chatman, J. Polzer, S. Barsade, and M. Neale, "Being Different Yet Feeling Similar: The Influence of Demographic Composition and Organizational Culture on Work Processes and Outcomes," *Administrative Science Quarterly* 43 (1998): 749–780.
44. L. E. Thurow, *Head to Head: The Coming Economic Battle among Japan, Europe, and America* (New York: William Morrow, 1992).
45. J. E. Patterson, *Acquiring the Future: America's Survival and Success in the Global Economy* (Homewood, Ill.: Dow Jones-Irwin, 1990); H. B. Stewart, *Recollecting the Future: A View of Business, Technology, and Innovation in the Next 30 Years* (Homewood, Ill.: Dow Jones-Irwin, 1989).
46. D. Ciampa, *Total Quality* (Reading, Mass.: Addison-Wesley, 1992).
47. T. J. Douglas and W. Q. Judge, Jr., "Total Quality Management Implementation and Competitive Advantage: The Role of Structural Control and Exploration," *Academy of Management Journal* 44 (2001): 158–169.

48. American Management Association, *Blueprints for Service Quality: The Federal Express Approach* (New York: American Management Association, 1991); P. R. Thomas, L. J. Gallace, and K. R. Martin, *Quality Alone Is Not Enough* (New York: American Management Association, 1992).

49. J. de Mast, "A Methodological Comparison of Three Strategies for Quality Improvement," *International Journal of Quality & Reliability Management* 21 (2004): 198–213.

50. M. Barney, "Motorola's Second Generation," *Six Sigma Forum Magazine* 1 (3) (May 2002): 13.

51. J. A. Edosomwan, "Six Commandments to Empower Employees for Quality Improvement," *Industrial Engineering* 24 (1992): 14–15.

52. See also the five articles in the Special Research Forum on Teaching Effectiveness in the Organizational Sciences, *The Academy of Management Journal* 40 (1997): 1265–1398.

53. R. M. Steers, L. W. Porter, and G. A. Bigley, *Motivation and Leadership at Work* (New York: McGraw-Hill, 1996).

54. H. Levinson, *Executive Stress* (New York: New American Library, 1975).

55. D. L. Whetzel, "The Department of Labor Identifies Workplace Skills," *Industrial/Organizational Psychologist* 29 (1991): 89–90.

56. D. A. Whetton and K. S. Cameron, *Developing Management Skills*, 3rd ed. (New York: HarperCollins, 1995).

57. C. Argyris and D. A. Schon, *Organizational Learning: A Theory of Action Perspective* (Reading, Mass.: Addison-Wesley, 1978).

58. D. Kirkpatrick, "Where the Action Is," *Fortune* 147 (May 12, 2003): 78, http://www.fortune.com/fortune/subs/article/0,15114,447123,00.html.

Chapter 2

1. J. Larsen, "The New Disney?" *The American Enterprise* 14 (July/August 2003): 50.

2. M. A. Hitt, R. E. Hoskisson, and J. S. Harrison, "Strategic Competitiveness in the 1990s: Challenges and Opportunities for U.S. Executives," *Academy of Management Executive* 5 (1991): 7–22.

3. H. G. Barkem, J. A. C. Baum, and E. A. Mannix, "Management Challenges in a New Time," *Academy of Management Journal* 45 (2002): 916–930.

4. S. C. Harper, "The Challenges Facing CEOs: Past, Present, and Future," *Academy of Management Executive* 6 (1992): 7–25.

5. T. R. Mitchell and W. G. Scott, "America's Problems and Needed Reforms: Confronting the Ethic of Personal Advantage," *Academy of Management Executive* 4 (1990): 23–25.

6. B. Spindle, "Sinking in Sync—The Global Slowdown Surprises Economists and Many Companies," *The Wall Street Journal* (December 21, 2000): A1–A10.

7. D. A. Harrison, J. H. Gavin, and A. T. Florey, "Time, Teams, and Task Performance: Changing Effects of Surface- and Deep-Level Diversity on Group Functioning," *Academy of Management Journal* 45 (2003): 1029–1045.

8. J. H. Gavin, J. C. Quick, C. L. Cooper, and J. D. Quick, "A Spirit of Personal Integrity: The Role of Character in Executive Health," *Organizational Dynamics* 32 (2003): 165–179.

9. K. Sera, "Corporate Globalization: A New Trend," *Academy of Management Executive* 6 (1992): 89–96.

10. K. Ohmae, *Borderless World: Power and Strategies in the Interlinked Economy* (New York: Harper & Row, 1990).

11. C. A. Bartlett and S. Ghoshal, *Managing across Borders: The Transnational Solution* (Boston: Harvard Business School Press, 1989).

12. K. R. Xin and J. L. Pearce, "Guanxi: Connections as Substitutes for Formal Institutional Support," *Academy of Management Journal* 39 (1996): 1641–1658.

13. P. S. Chan, "Franchise Management in East Asia," *Academy of Management Executive* 4 (1990): 75–85.

14. H. Weihrich, "Europe 1992: What the Future May Hold," *Academy of Management Executive* 4 (1990): 7–18.

15. E. H. Schein, "Coming to a New Awareness of Organizational Culture," *MIT Sloan Management Review* 25 (1984): 3–16.

16. S. S. Sarwano and R. M. Armstrong, "Microcultural Differences and Perceived Ethical Problems: An International Business Perspective," *Journal of Business Ethics* 30 (2001): 41–56.

17. R. Sharpe, "Hi-Tech Taboos," *The Wall Street Journal* (October 31, 1995): A1.

18. G. Hofstede, *Culture's Consequences: International Differences in Work-Related Values* (Beverly Hills, Calif.: Sage Publications, 1980).

19. G. Hofstede, "Motivation, Leadership, and Organization: Do American Theories Apply Abroad?" *Organizational Dynamics* (Summer 1980): 42–63.

20. R. Buda and S. M. Elsayed-Elkhouly, "Cultural Differences between Arabs and Americans," *Journal of Cross-Cultural Psychology* 29 (1998): 487–492.

21. G. Hofstede, "Gender Stereotypes and Partner Preferences of Asian Women in Masculine and Feminine Countries," *Journal of Cross Cultural Psychology* 27 (1996): 533–546.

22. G. Hofstede, "Cultural Constraints in Management Theories," *Academy of Management Executive* 7 (1993): 81–94.

23. G. M. Spreitzer, M. W. McCall, Jr., and J. D. Mahoney, "Early Identification of International Executive Potential," *Journal of Applied Psychology* 82 (1997): 6–29.

24. A. J. Michel, "Goodbyes Can Cost Plenty in Europe," *Fortune* (April 6, 1992): 16.

25. M. Adams, "Building a Rainbow One Stripe at a Time," *HR Magazine* 9 (August 1999): 72–79. Intel, "Diversity at Intel: Our Commitment," 2003, http://www.intel.com/jobs/Diversity/commitment.htm.

26. E. Brandt, "Global HR," *Personnel Journal* 70 (1991): 38–44.

27. J. C. Quick, J. H. Gavin, C. L. Cooper, and J. D. Quick, "Working Together: Balancing Head and Heart," in R. H. Rozensky, N. G. Johnson, C. D. Goodheart, and W. R. Hammond, eds., *Psychology Builds a Healthy World: Opportunities for Research and Practice* (Washington, D.C.: American Psychological Association, 2004) 219–232.

28. J. A. Gilbert and J. M. Ivancevich, "Valuing Diversity: A Tale of Two Organizations," *Academy of Management Executive* 4 (2000): 93–105.

29. R. W. Judy and C. D'Amico, *Workforce 2020* (Indianapolis, Ind.: Hudson Institute, 1997). U.S. Department of Labor, "Usual Weekly Earnings Summary," *Labor Force Statistics from the Current Population Survey* (Washington D.C.: U.S. Government, 2002).

30. S. Caudron, "Task Force Report Reveals Coke's Progress on Diversity," *Workforce* 82 (2003): 40, http://www.workforceonline.com/section/03/feature/23/42/44/234246.html.

31. L. S. Gottfredson, "Dilemmas in Developing Diversity Programs," in S. E. Jackson, ed., *Diversity in the Workplace: Human Resources Initiatives* (New York: Guilford Press, 1992), 279–305.

32. U.S. Department of Labor, "Employment Status of the Civilian Population by Sex and Age," (July 2004). Accessed on-line at http://stats.bls.gov/news.release/empsit.t01.htm.

33. Catalyst, *Catalyst Census of Women Corporate Officers and Top Earners*, 2001.

34. "2003: Year of the Women Among the 'Fortune' 500?," *USA Today* (December 30, 2003): 01b.

35. U.S. Department of Labor, "Highlights of Women's Earnings in 2002," *Report 972*, (September 2003).

36. A. M. Morrison, R. P. White, E. Van Velsor, and the Center for Creative Leadership, *Breaking the Glass Ceiling: Can Women Reach the Top of America's Largest Corporations?* (Reading, Mass.: Addison-Wesley, 1987).

37. D. E. Arfken, S. L. Bellar, and M. M. Helms, "The Ultimate Glass Ceiling Revisited: The Presence of Women on Corporate Boards," *Journal of Business Ethics* 50 (March 2004): 177–186.

38. N. J. Adler, "Global Leadership: Women Leaders," *Management International Review* 37 (1997): 171–196.

39. A. Eyring and B. A. Stead, "Shattering the Glass Ceiling: Some Successful Corporate Practices," *Journal of Business Ethics* 17 (1998): 245–251.

40. Catalyst, *Advancing Women in Business: The Catalyst Guide* (San Francisco: Jossey-Bass, 1998).

41. D. L. Nelson and M. A. Hitt, "Employed Women and Stress: Implications for Enhancing Women's Mental Health in the Work-

place," in J. C. Quick, L. R. Murphy, and J. J. Hurrell, Jr., eds., *Stress and Well-Being at Work* (Washington, D.C.: American Psychological Association, 1992), 164–177.

42. L. E. Atwater and D. D. Van Fleet, "Another Ceiling: Can Males Compete for Traditionally Female Jobs?" *Journal of Management* 23 (1997): 603–626.

43. U.S. Department of Health and Human Services, *Profile of Older Americans* (Washington, D.C.: U.S. Government, 1997).

44. W. B. Johnston, "Global Workforce 2000: The New World Labor Market," *Harvard Business Review* 69 (1991): 115–127.

45. S. E. Jackson and E. B. Alvarez, "Working through Diversity as a Strategic Imperative," in S. E. Jackson, ed., *Diversity in the Workplace: Human Resources Initiatives* (New York: Guilford Press, 1992), 13–36.

46. "Managing Generational Diversity," *HR Magazine* 36 (1991): 91–92.

47. C. M. Solomon, "Managing the Baby Busters," *Personnel Journal* (March 1992): 52–59.

48. S. R. Rhodes, "Age-Related Differences in Work Attitudes and Behavior: A Review and Conceptual Analysis," *Psychological Bulletin* 93 (1983): 338–367.

49. B. L. Hassell and P. L. Perrewe, "An Examination of Beliefs about Older Workers: Do Stereotypes Still Exist?" *Journal of Organizational Behavior* 16 (1995): 457–468.

50. U.S. Bureau of the Census, *Population Profile of the United States, 1997* (Washington, D.C.: U.S. Government Printing Office, 1997).

51. W. J. Rothwell, "HRD and the Americans with Disabilities Act," *Training and Development Journal* (August 1991): 45–47.

52. J. Waldrop, "The Cost of Hiring the Disabled," *American Demographics* (March 1991): 12.

53. J. J. Laabs, "The Golden Arches Provide Golden Opportunities," *Personnel Journal* (July 1991): 52–57.

54. L. Winfield and S. Spielman, "Making Sexual Orientation Part of Diversity," *Training and Development* (April 1995): 50–51.

55. N. E. Day and P. Schoenrade, "Staying in the Closet versus Coming Out: Relationships between Communication about Sexual Orientation and Work Attitudes," *Personnel Psychology* 50 (1997): 147–163.

56. J. Landau, "The Relationship of Race and Gender to Managers' Ratings of Promotion Potential," *Journal of Organizational Behavior* 16 (1995): 391–400.

57. P. Barnum, "Double Jeopardy for Women and Minorities: Pay Differences with Age," *Academy of Management Journal* 38 (1995): 863–880.

58. J. E. Rigdon, "PepsiCo's KFC Scouts for Blacks and Women for Its Top Echelons," *The Wall Street Journal* (November 13, 1991): A1.

59. P. A. Galagan, "Tapping the Power of a Diverse Workforce," *Training and Development Journal* 26 (1991): 38–44.

60. C. L. Holladay, J. L. Knight, D. L. Paige, and M. A. Quinones, "The Influence of Framing on Attitudes Toward Diversity Training," *Human Resource Development Quarterly* 14 (2003): 245–263.

61. R. Thomas, "From Affirmative Action to Affirming Diversity," *Harvard Business Review* 68 (1990): 107–117.

62. T. H. Cox, Jr., *Cultural Diversity in Organizations: Theory, Research and Practice* (San Francisco: Berrett-Koehler, 1994).

63. J. Gordon, "Different from What?" *Training* (May 1995): 25–33.

64. M. R. Fusilier, C. D. Aby, Jr., J. K. Worley, and S. Elliott, "Perceived Seriousness of Business Ethics Issues," *Business and Professional Ethics Journal* 15 (1996): 67–78.

65. J. S. Mill, *Utilitarianism, Liberty, and Representative Government* (London: Dent, 1910).

66. K. H. Blanchard and N. V. Peale, *The Power of Ethical Management* (New York: Morrow, 1988).

67. C. Fried, *Right and Wrong* (Cambridge, Mass.: Harvard University Press, 1978).

68. I. Kant, *Groundwork of the Metaphysics of Morals*, trans. H. J. Paton (New York: Harper & Row, 1964).

69. A. Smith, *An Inquiry into the Nature and Causes of the Wealth of Nations*, vol. 10 of The Harvard Classics, ed. C. J. Bullock (New York: P. F. Collier & Son, 1909).

70. R. C. Solomon, "Corporate Roles, Personal Virtues: Aristotelean Approach to Business Ethics," *Business Ethics Quarterly* 2 (1992): 317–339; R. C. Solomon, *A Better Way to Think about Business: How Personal Integrity Leads to Corporate Success* (New York: Oxford University Press, 1999).

71. D. Kemp, "Employers and AIDS: Dealing with the Psychological and Emotional Issues of AIDS in the Workplace," *American Review of Public Administration* 25 (1995): 263–278.

72. J. J. Koch, "Wells Fargo's and IBM's HIV Policies Help Protect Employees' Rights," *Personnel Journal* (April 1990): 40–48.

73. A. Arkin, "Positive HIV and AIDS Policies at Work," *Personnel Management* (December 1994): 34–37.

74. U.S. EEOC. 1980. Discrimination because of Sex under Title VII of the 1964 Civil Rights Act as amended: Adoption of interim guidelines—sexual harassment. *Federal Register* 45: 25024–25025; S. J. Adler, "Lawyers Advise Concerns to Provide Precise Written Policy to Employees," *The Wall Street Journal* (October 9, 1991): B1.

75. L. F. Fitzgerald, F. Drasgow, C. L. Hulin, M. J. Gelfand, and V. J. Magley, "Antecedents and Consequences of Sexual Harassment in Organizations: A Test of an Integrated Model," *Journal of Applied Psychology* 82 (1997): 578–589.

76. E. Felsenthal, "Rulings Open Way for Sex-Harass Cases," *The Wall Street Journal* (June 29, 1998): A10.

77. K. T. Schneider, S. Swan, and L. F. Fitzgerald, "Job-Related and Psychological Effects of Sexual Harassment in the Workplace: Empirical Evidence from Two Organizations," *Journal of Applied Psychology* 82 (1997): 401–415.

78. A. M. O'Leary-Kelly, R. L. Paetzold, and R. W. Griffin, "Sexual Harassment as Aggressive Behavior: An Actor-Based Perspective," *Academy of Management Review* 25 (2000): 372–388.

79. L. M. Goldenhar, N. G. Swanson, J. J. Hurrell, Jr., A. Ruder, and J. Deddens, "Stressors and Adverse Outcomes for Female Construction Workers," *Journal of Occupational Health Psychology* 3 (1998): 19–32; C. S. Piotrkowski, "Gender Harassment, Job Satisfaction and Distress Among Employed White and Minority Women," *Journal of Occupational Health Psychology* 3 (1998): 33–42.

80. G. N. Powell and S. Foley, "Something to Talk About: Romantic Relationships in Organizational Settings," *Journal of Management* 24 (1998): 421–448.

81. D. Fields, M. Pang, and C. Chio, "Distributive and Procedural Justice as Predictors of Employee Outcomes in Hong Kong," *Journal of Organizational Behavior* 21 (2000): 547–562.

82. H. L. Laframboise, "Vile Wretches and Public Heroes: The Ethics of Whistleblowing in Government," *Canadian Public Administration* (Spring 1991): 73–78.

83. A. Nyberg, "Whistle-Blower Woes," *CFO Magazine* 19 (October 2003): 50, http://www.cfo.com/article/1,5309,10790,00.html.

84. D. B. Turban and D. W. Greening, "Corporate Social Performance and Organizational Attractiveness to Prospective Employees," *Academy of Management Journal* 40 (1996): 658–672.

85. Task Force on Management of Innovation, *Technology and Employment: Innovation and Growth in the U.S. Economy* (Washington, D.C.: U.S. Government Research Council, 1987).

86. C. H. Ferguson, "Computers and the Coming of the U.S. Keiretsu," *Harvard Business Review* 68 (1990): 55–70.

87. J. Collins, *Good to Great: Why Some Companies Make the Leap . . . and Others Don't* (New York: HarperCollins, 2001).

88. C. Arnst, "The Networked Corporation," *Business Week* (June 26, 1995): 86–89.

89. J. A. Senn, *Information Systems in Management*, 4th ed. (Belmont, Calif.: Wadsworth, 1990).

90. D. K. Sorenson, O. Bouhaddou, and H. R. Warner, *Knowledge Engineering in Health Informatics* (New York: Springer, 1999).

91. M. T. Damore, "A Presentation and Examination of the Integration of Unlawful Discrimination Practices in the Private Business Sector with Artificial Intelligence" (Thesis, Oklahoma State University, 1992).

92. A. Tanzer and R. Simon, "Why Japan Loves Robots and We Don't," *Forbes* (April 16, 1990): 148–153.

93. E. Fingleton, "Jobs for Life: Why Japan Won't Give Them Up," *Fortune* (March 20, 1995): 119–125.

94. M. Iansitu, "How the Incumbent Can Win: Managing Technological Transitions in the Semiconductor Industry," *Management Science* 46 (2000): 169–185.

95. M. B. W. Fritz, S. Narasimhan, and H. Rhee, "Communication and Coordination in the Virtual Office," *Journal of Management Information Systems* 14 (1998): 7–28.

96. M. Apgar, IV, "The Alternative Workplace: Changing Where and How People Work," *Harvard Business Review* (May–June 1998): 121–136.

97. D. L. Nelson, "Individual Adjustment to Information-Driven Technologies: A Critical Review," *MIS Quarterly* 14 (1990): 79–98.

98. M. Allen, "Legislation Could Restrict Bosses from Snooping on Their Workers," *The Wall Street Journal* (September 24, 1991): B1–B8.

99. K. D. Hill and S. Kerr, "The Impact of Computer-Integrated Manufacturing Systems on the First Line Supervisor," *Journal of Organizational Behavior Management* 6 (1984): 81–87.

100. M. Reitzig, "Strategic Management of Intellectual Property," *MIT Sloan Management Review* 45 (Spring 2004): 35–40.

101. J. Anderson, "How Technology Brings Blind People into the Workplace," *Harvard Business Review* 67 (1989): 36–39.

102. D. L. Nelson and M. G. Kletke, "Individual Adjustment during Technological Innovation: A Research Framework," *Behaviour and Information Technology* 9 (1990): 257–271.

103. D. Mankin, T. Bikson, B. Gutek, and C. Stasz, "Managing Technological Change: The Process Is the Key," *Datamation* 34 (1988): 69–80.

104. J. Martin, "Inside the Pixar Dream Factory," *Fortune Small Business* 13 (2003): 45, http://www.fortune.com/fortune/smallbusiness/articles/0,15114,411065,00.html.

Chapter 3

1. Hoovers company information; http://www.hoovers.com.

2. K. Lewin, "Formalization and Progress in Psychology," in D. Cartwright, ed., *Field Theory in Social Science* (New York: Harper, 1951).

3. N. S. Endler and D. Magnusson, "Toward an Interactional Psychology of Personality," *Psychological Bulletin* 83 (1976): 956–974.

4. J. R. Terborg, "Interactional Psychology and Research on Human Behavior in Organizations," *Academy of Management Review* 6 (1981): 561–576.

5. T. J. Bouchard, Jr., "Twins Reared Together and Apart: What They Tell Us about Human Diversity," in S. W. Fox, ed., *Individuality and Determinism* (New York: Plenum Press, 1984).

6. R. D. Arvey, T. J. Bouchard, Jr., N. L. Segal, and L. M. Abraham, "Job Satisfaction: Environmental and Genetic Components," *Journal of Applied Psychology* 74 (1989): 235–248.

7. G. Allport, *Pattern and Growth in Personality* (New York: Holt, 1961).

8. R. B. Cattell, *Personality and Mood by Questionnaire* (San Francisco: Jossey-Bass, 1973).

9. J. M. Digman, "Personality Structure: Emergence of a Five-Factor Model," *Annual Review of Psychology* 41 (1990): 417–440.

10. T. A. Judge, J. J. Martocchio, and C. J. Thoresen, "Five-Factor Model of Personality and Employee Absence," *Journal of Applied Psychology* 82 (1997): 745–755.

11. H. J. Bernardin, D. K. Cooke, and P. Villanova, "Conscientiousness and Agreeableness as Predictors of Rating Leniency," *Journal of Applied Psychology* 85 (2000): 232–234.

12. S. E. Seibert and M. L. Kraimer, "The Five-Factor Model of Personality and Career Success," *Journal of Vocational Behavior* 58 (2001): 1–21.

13. T. A. Judge and R. Ilies, "Relationships of Personality to Performance Motivation: A Meta-Analytic Review," *Journal of Applied Psychology* 87 (2002): 797–807.

14. G. M. Hurtz and J. J. Donovan, "Personality and Job Performance: The Big Five Revisited," *Journal of Applied Psychology* 85 (2000): 869–879.

15. J. F. Salgado, S. Moscoso, and M. Lado, "Evidence of Cross-Cultural Invariance of the Big Five Personality Dimensions in Work Settings," *European Journal of Personality* 17 (2003): S67–S76; C. Rodriguez and T. H. Church, "The Structure and Personality Correlates of Affect in Mexico: Evidence of Cross-Cultural Comparability Using the Spanish Language," *Journal of Cross-Cultural Psychology* 34 (2003): 211–230.

16. H. C. Triandis, "Cultural Influences on Personality," *Annual Review of Psychology* 53 (2002): 133–160.

17. M. R. Barrick and M. K. Mount, "The Big Five Personality Dimensions and Job Performance: A Meta-Analysis," *Personnel Psychology* 44 (1991): 1–26.

18. S. Freud, *An Outline of Psychoanalysis* (New York: Norton, 1949).

19. C. Rogers, *On Becoming a Person: A Therapist's View of Psychotherapy*, 2nd ed. (Boston: Houghton Mifflin, 1970).

20. D. D. Clark and R. Hoyle, "A Theoretical Solution to the Problem of Personality-Situational Interaction," *Personality and Individual Differences* 9 (1988): 133–138.

21. D. Byrne and L. J. Schulte, "Personality Dimensions as Predictors of Sexual Behavior," in J. Bancroft, ed., *Annual Review of Sexual Research*, vol. 1 (Philadelphia: Society for the Scientific Study of Sex, 1990).

22. J. B. Rotter, "Generalized Expectancies for Internal vs. External Control of Reinforcement," *Psychological Monographs* 80, whole No. 609 (1966).

23. T. A. Judge and J. E. Bono, "Relationship of Core Self-Evaluations Traits—Self-Esteem, Generalized Self-Efficacy, Locus of Control, and Emotional Stability—with Job Satisfaction and Job Performance: A Meta-Analysis," *Journal of Applied Psychology* 86 (2001): 80–92.

24. S. S. K. Lam and J. Shaubroeck, "The Role of Locus of Control in Reactions to Being Promoted and to Being Passed Over: A Quasi Experiment," *Academy of Management Journal* 43 (2000): 66–78.

25. G. Chen, S. M. Gully, J. Whiteman, and R. N. Kilcullen, "Examination of Relationships Among Trait-Like Individual Differences, State-Like Individual Differences, and Learning Performance," *Journal of Applied Psychology* 85 (2000): 835–847; G. Chen, S. M. Gully, and D. Eden, "Validation of a New General Self-Efficacy Scale," *Organizational Research Methods* 4 (2001): 62–83.

26. A. Bandura, *Self-Efficacy: The Exercise of Control* (San Francisco: Freeman, 1997).

27. D. R. Avery, "Personality as a Predictor of the Value of Voice," *The Journal of Psychology* 137 (2003): 435–447.

28. B. W. Pelham and W. B. Swann, Jr., "From Self-Conceptions to Self-Worth: On the Sources and Structure of Global Self-Esteem," *Journal of Personality and Social Psychology* 57 (1989): 672–680.

29. A. H. Baumgardner, C. M. Kaufman, and P. E. Levy, "Regulating Affect Interpersonally: When Low Esteem Leads to Greater Enhancement," *Journal of Personality and Social Psychology* 56 (1989): 907–921.

30. J. Schimel, T. Pyszczynski, J. Arndt, and J. Greenberg, "Being Accepted for Who We Are: Evidence that Social Validation of the Intrinsic Self Reduces General Defensiveness," *Journal of Personality and Social Psychology* 80 (2001): 35–52.

31. P. Tharenou and P. Harker, "Moderating Influences of Self-Esteem on Relationships between Job Complexity, Performance, and Satisfaction," *Journal of Applied Psychology* 69 (1984): 623–632.

32. R. A. Ellis and M. S. Taylor, "Role of Self-Esteem within the Job Search Process," *Journal of Applied Psychology* 68 (1983): 632–640.

33. J. Brockner and T. Hess, "Self-Esteem and Task Performance in Quality Circles," *Academy of Management Journal* 29 (1986): 617–623.

34. B. R. Schlenker, M. F. Weingold, and J. R. Hallam, "Self-Serving Attributions in Social Context: Effects of Self-Esteem and Social Pressure," *Journal of Personality and Social Psychology* 57 (1990): 855–863.

35. M. K. Duffy, J. D. Shaw, and E. M. Stark, "Performance and Satisfaction in Conflicted Interdependent Groups: When and How Does Self-Esteem Make a Difference?" *Academy of Management Journal* 43 (2000): 772–782.

36. T. Mussweiler, S. Gabriel, and G. V. Bodenhausen, "Shifting Social Identities as a Strategy for Deflecting Threatening Social Comparisons," *Journal of Personality and Social Psychology* 79 (2000): 398–409.

37. M. Snyder and S. Gangestad, "On the Nature of Self-Monitoring: Matters of Assessment, Matters of Validity," *Journal of Personality and Social Psychology* 51 (1986): 123–139.

38. A. Mehra, M. Kilduff, and D. J. Brass, "The Social Networks of High and Low Self-Monitors: Implications for Workplace Performance," *Administrative Science Quarterly* 46 (2001): 121–146.

39. W. H. Turnley and M. C. Bolino, "Achieving Desired Images While Avoiding Undesired Images: Exploring the Role of Self-Monitoring in Impression Management," *Journal of Applied Psychology* 86 (2001): 351–360.

40. M. Kilduff and D. V. Day, "Do Chameleons Get Ahead? The Effects of Self-Monitoring on Managerial Careers," *Academy of Management Journal* 37 (1994): 1047–1060.

41. A. H. Church, "Managerial Self-Awareness in High-Performing Individuals in Organizations," *Journal of Applied Psychology* 82 (1997): 281–292.

42. C. Douglas and W. L. Gardner, "Transition to Self-Directed Work Teams: Implications of Transition Time and Self-Monitoring for Managers' Use of Influence Tactics," *Journal of Organizational Behavior* 25 (2004): 45–67.

43. A. M. Isen and R. A. Baron, "Positive Affect and Organizational Behavior," in B. M. Staw and L. L. Cummings, eds., *Research in Organizational Behavior*, vol. 12 (Greenwich, Conn.: JAI Press, 1990).

44. D. Watson and L. A. Clark, "Negative Affectivity: The Disposition to Experience Aversive Emotional States," *Psychological Bulletin* 96 (1984): 465–490.

45. R. Ilies and T. Judge, "On the Heritability of Job Satisfaction: The Mediating Role of Personality," *Journal of Applied Psychology* 88 (2003): 750–759.

46. J. M. George, "Mood and Absence," *Journal of Applied Psychology* 74 (1989): 287–324.

47. M. J. Burke, A. P. Brief, and J. M. George, "The Role of Negative Affectivity in Understanding Relations between Self-Reports of Stressors and Strains: A Comment on the Applied Psychology Literature," *Journal of Applied Psychology* 78 (1993): 402–412.

48. S. Barsade, A. Ward, J. Turner, and J. Sonnenfeld, "To Your Heart's Content: A Model of Affective Diversity in Top Management Teams," *Administrative Science Quarterly* 45 (2000): 802–836.

49. W. Mischel, "The Interaction of Person and Situation," in D. Magnusson and N. S. Endler, eds., *Personality at the Crossroads: Current Issues in Interactional Psychology* (Hillsdale, N.J.: Erlbaum, 1977).

50. H. Rorschach, *Psychodiagnostics* (Bern: Hans Huber, 1921).

51. C. G. Jung, *Psychological Types* (New York: Harcourt & Brace, 1923).

52. Consulting Psychologists Press.

53. R. Benfari and J. Knox, *Understanding Your Management Style* (Lexington, Mass.: Lexington Books, 1991).

54. O. Kroeger and J. M. Thuesen, *Type Talk* (New York: Delacorte Press, 1988).

55. S. Hirsch and J. Kummerow, *Life Types* (New York: Warner Books, 1989).

56. I. B. Myers and M. H. McCaulley, *Manual: A Guide to the Development and Use of the Myers-Briggs Type Indicator* (Palo Alto, Calif.: Consulting Psychologists Press, 1990).

57. G. P. Macdaid, M. H. McCaulley, and R. I. Kainz, *Myers-Briggs Type Indicator: Atlas of Type Tables* (Gainesville, Fla.: Center for Application of Psychological Type, 1987).

58. J. B. Murray, "Review of Research on the Myers-Briggs Type Indicator," *Perceptual and Motor Skills* 70 (1990): 1187–1202.

59. J. G. Carlson, "Recent Assessment of the Myers-Briggs Type Indicator," *Journal of Personality Assessment* 49 (1985): 356–365.

60. A. Thomas, M. Benne, M. Marr, F. Thomas, and R. Hume, "The Evidence Remains Stable: The MBTI Predicts Attraction and Attrition in an Engineering Program," *Journal of Psychological Type* 55 (2000): 35–42.

61. C. Walck, "Training for Participative Management: Implications for Psychological Type," *Journal of Psychological Type* 21 (1991): 3–12.

62. J. Michael, "Using the Myers-Briggs Indicator as a Tool for Leadership Development: Apply with Caution," *Journal of Leadership & Organizational Studies* 10 (2003): 68–78.

63. E. C. Webster, *The Employment Interview: A Social Judgment Process* (Schomberg, Canada: SIP, 1982).

64. N. Adler, *International Dimensions of Organizational Behavior*, 2nd ed. (Boston: PWS-Kent, 1991).

65. L. R. Offerman and M. K. Gowing, "Personnel Selection in the Future: The Impact of Changing Demographics and the Nature of Work," in Schmitt, Borman & Associates, eds., *Personnel Selection in Organizations* (San Francisco: Jossey-Bass, 1993).

66. J. Park and M. R. Banaji, "Mood and Heuristics: The Influence of Happy and Sad States on Sensitivity and Bias in Stereotyping," *Journal of Personality and Social Psychology* 78 (2000): 1005–1023.

67. M. W. Levine and J. M. Shefner, *Fundamentals of Sensation and Perception* (Reading, Mass.: Addison-Wesley, 1981).

68. R. L. Dipboye, H. L. Fromkin, and K. Willback, "Relative Importance of Applicant Sex, Attractiveness, and Scholastic Standing in Evaluations of Job Applicant Resumes," *Journal of Applied Psychology* 60 (1975): 39–43.

69. I. H. Frieze, J. E. Olson, and J. Russell, "Attractiveness and Income for Men and Women in Management," *Journal of Applied Social Psychology* 21 (1991): 1039–1057.

70. P. Ekman and W. Friesen, *Unmasking the Face* (Englewood Cliffs, N.J.: Prentice-Hall, 1975).

71. J. E. Rehfeld, "What Working for a Japanese Company Taught Me," *Harvard Business Review*, (November–December 1990): 167–176.

72. M. W. Morris and R. P. Larrick, "When One Cause Casts Doubt on Another: A Normative Analysis of Discounting in Causal Attribution," *Psychological Review* 102 (1995): 331–355.

73. G. B. Sechrist and C. Stangor, "Perceived Consensus Influences Intergroup Behavior and Stereotype Accessibility," *Journal of Personality and Psychology* 80 (2001): 645–654; A. Lyons and Y. Kashima, "How Are Stereotypes Maintained Through Communication? The Influence of Stereotype Sharedness," *Journal of Personality and Social Psychology* 85 (2003): 989–1005.

74. L. Copeland, "Learning to Manage a Multicultural Workforce," *Training* (May 1988): 48–56.

75. S. Ferrari, "Human Behavior in International Groups," *Management International Review* 7 (1972): 31–35.

76. A. Feingold, "Gender Differences in Effects of Physical Attractiveness on Romantic Attraction: A Comparison across Five Research Paradigms," *Journal of Personality and Social Psychology* 59 (1990): 981–993.

77. M. Snyder, "When Belief Creates Reality," *Advances in Experimental Social Psychology* 18 (1984): 247–305.

78. M. Biernat, "Toward a Broader View of Social Stereotyping," *American Psychologist* 58 (2003): 1019–1027.

79. E. Burnstein and Y. Schul, "The Informational Basis of Social Judgments: Operations in Forming an Impression of Another Person," *Journal of Experimental Social Psychology* 18 (1982): 217–234.

80. T. DeGroot and S. Motowidlo, "Why Visual and Vocal Cues Can Affect Interviewers' Judgments and Predict Job Performance," *Journal of Applied Psychology* 84 (1999): 986–993; M. C. L. Greene and L. Mathieson, *The Voice and Its Disorders* (London: Whurr, 1989).

81. R. L. Gross and S. E. Brodt, "How Assumptions of Consensus Undermine Decision Making," *MIT Sloan Management Review* 42 (Winter 2001): 86–94.

82. R. Rosenthal and L. Jacobson, *Pygmalion in the Classroom: Teacher Expectations and Pupils' Intellectual Development* (New York: Holt, Rinehart & Winston, 1968).

83. D. Eden and Y. Zuk, "Seasickness as a Self-Fulfilling Prophecy: Raising Self-Efficacy to Boost Performance at Sea," *Journal of Applied Psychology* 80 (1995): 628–635.

84. N. M. Kierein and M. A. Gold, "Pygmalion in Work Organizations: A Meta-Analysis," *Journal of Organizational Behavior* 21 (2000): 913–928.

85. D. Eden, "Pygmalion without Interpersonal Contrast Effects: Whole Groups Gain from Raising Manager Expectations," *Journal of Applied Psychology* 75 (1990): 394–398.

86. R. A. Giacolone and P. Rosenfeld, eds., *Impression Management in Organizations* (Hillsdale, N.J.: Erlbaum, 1990); J. Tedeschi and V. Melburg, "Impression Management and Influence in the Organization," in S. Bacharach and E. Lawler, eds., *Research in the Sociology of Organizations* (Greenwich, Conn.: JAI Press, 1984), 31–58.

87. A. Colella and A. Varma, "The Impact of Subordinate Disability on Leader–Member Exchange Relationships," *Academy of Management Journal* 44 (2001): 304–315.

88. D. C. Gilmore and G. R. Ferris, "The Effects of Applicant Impression Management Tactics on Interviewer Judgments," *Journal of Management* (December 1989): 557–564.

89. C. K. Stevens and A. L. Kristof, "Making the Right Impression: A Field Study of Applicant Impressions Management during Job Interviews," *Journal of Applied Psychology* 80 (1995): 587–606.

90. S. J. Wayne and R. C. Liden, "Effects of Impression Management on Performance Ratings: A Longitudinal Study," *Academy of Management Journal* 38 (1995): 232–260.

91. R. A. Baron, "Impression Management by Applicants during Employment Interviews: The 'Too Much of a Good Thing' Effect," in R. W. Eder and G. R. Ferris, eds., *The Employment Interview: Theory, Research, and Practice* (Newbury Park, Calif.: Sage Publications, 1989).

92. F. Heider, *The Psychology of Interpersonal Relations* (New York: Wiley, 1958).

93. B. Weiner, "An Attributional Theory of Achievement Motivation and Emotion," *Psychological Review* (October 1985): 548–573.

94. P. D. Sweeney, K. Anderson, and S. Bailey, "Attributional Style in Depression: A Meta-Analytic Review," *Journal of Personality and Social Psychology* 51 (1986): 974–991.

95. P. Rosenthal, D. Guest, and R. Peccei, "Gender Differences in Managers' Causal Explanations for Their Work Performance," *Journal of Occupational and Organizational Psychology* 69 (1996): 145–151.

96. J. Silvester, "Spoken Attributions and Candidate Success in Graduate Recruitment Interviews," *Journal of Occupational and Organizational Psychology* 70 (1997): 61–71.

97. L. Ross, "The Intuitive Psychologist and His Shortcomings: Distortions in the Attribution Process," in L. Berkowitz, ed., *Advances in Experimental Social Psychology* (New York: Academic Press, 1977); M. O'Sullivan, "The Fundamental Attribution Error in Detecting Deception: The Boy-Who-Cried Wolf Effect," *Personality & Social Psychology Bulletin* 29 (2003): 1316–1327.

98. D. T. Miller and M. Ross, "Self-Serving Biases in the Attribution of Causality: Fact or Fiction?" *Psychological Bulletin* 82 (1975): 313–325.

99. J. R. Schermerhorn, Jr., "Team Development for High-Performance Management," *Training and Development Journal* 40 (1986): 38–41.

100. J. G. Miller, "Culture and the Development of Everyday Causal Explanation," *Journal of Personality and Social Psychology* 46 (1984): 961–978.

101. G. Si, S. Rethorst, and K. Willimczik, "Causal Attribution Perception in Sports Achievement: A Cross-Cultural Study on Attributional Concepts in Germany and China," *Journal of Cross-Cultural Psychology* 26 (1995): 537–553.

102. http://www2.coca-cola.com.

Chapter 4

1. R. Levering and M. Moskowitz, "The 100 Best Companies to Work For," *Fortune* (January 12, 2004): 68.

2. J. Tarnowski, "Doing What Comes Naturally: A Far-Reaching Philosophy of Interdependence Has Made Whole Foods a Lifestyle Brand for Upscale Shoppers," *Progressive Grocer* (September 1, 2003): 22.

3. A. H. Eagly and S. Chaiken, *The Psychology of Attitudes* (Orlando, Fla.: Harcourt Brace Jovanovich, 1993).

4. M. J. Rosenberg, C. I. Hovland, W. J. McGuire, R. P. Abelson, and J. H. Brehm, *Attitude Organization and Change* (New Haven, Conn.: Yale University Press, 1960).

5. L. Festinger, *A Theory of Cognitive Dissonance* (Evanston, Ill.: Row, Peterson, 1957).

6. R. H. Fazio and M. P. Zanna, "On the Predictive Validity of Attitudes: The Roles of Direct Experience and Confidence," *Journal of Personality* 46 (1978): 228–243.

7. A. Tversky and D. Kahneman, "Judgment under Uncertainty: Heuristics and Biases," in D. Kahneman, P. Slovic, and A. Tversky, eds., *Judgment under Uncertainty* (New York: Cambridge University Press, 1982), 3–20.

8. D. Rajecki, *Attitudes*, 2nd ed. (Sunderland, Mass.: Sinauer Associates, 1989).

9. I. Ajzen and M. Fishbein, "Attitude–Behavior Relations: A Theoretical Analysis and Review of Empirical Research," *Psychological Bulletin* 84 (1977): 888–918.

10. B. T. Johnson and A. H. Eagly, "Effects of Involvement on Persuasion: A Meta-Analysis," *Psychological Bulletin* 106 (1989): 290–314.

11. K. G. DeBono and M. Snyder, "Acting on One's Attitudes: The Role of History of Choosing Situations," *Personality and Social Psychology Bulletin* 21 (1995): 629–636.

12. I. Ajzen and M. Fishbein, *Understanding Attitudes and Predicting Social Behavior* (Englewood Cliffs, N.J.: Prentice-Hall, 1980).

13. I. Ajzen, "From Intentions to Action: A Theory of Planned Behavior," in J. Kuhl and J. Beckmann, eds., *Action-Control: From Cognition to Behavior* (Heidelberg: Springer, 1985).

14. I. Ajzen, "The Theory of Planned Behavior," *Organizational Behavior and Human Decision Processes* 50 (1991): 1–33.

15. A. Sagie and M. Krausz, "What Aspects of the Job Have Most Effect on Nurses?" *Human Resource Management Journal* 13 (2003): 46–62.

16. C. P. Parker, B. B. Baltes, S. A. Young, J. W. Huff, R. A. Altman, H. A. LaCost, and J. E. Roberts, "Relationships between Psychological Climate Perceptions and Work Outcomes: A Meta-Analytic Review," *Journal of Organizational Behavior* 24 (2003): 389–416.

17. J. Lemmick and J. Mattsson, "Employee Behavior, Feelings of Warmth and Customer Perception in Service Encounters," *International Journal of Retail & Distribution Management* 30 (2002): 18–44.

18. E. A. Locke, "The Nature and Causes of Job Satisfaction," in M. Dunnette, ed., *Handbook of Industrial and Organizational Psychology* (Chicago: Rand McNally, 1976).

19. P. C. Smith, L. M. Kendall, and C. L. Hulin, *The Measurement of Satisfaction in Work and Retirement* (Skokie, Ill.: Rand McNally, 1969).

20. R. Ilies and T. A. Judge, "On the Heritability of Job Satisfaction: The Mediating Role of Personality," *Journal of Applied Psychology* 88 (2003): 750–759.

21. D. J. Weiss, R. V. Davis, G. W. England, and L. H. Lofquist, *Manual for the Minnesota Satisfaction Questionnaire* (Minneapolis: Industrial Relations Center, University of Minnesota, 1967).

22. C. D. Fisher, "Why Do Lay People Believe that Satisfaction and Performance Are Correlated? Possible Sources of a Commonsense Theory," *Journal of Organizational Behavior* 24 (2003): 753–777.

23. M. T. Iaffaldano and P. M. Muchinsky, "Job Satisfaction and Job Performance: A Meta-Analysis," *Psychological Bulletin* 97 (1985): 251–273.

24. L. A. Bettencourt, K. P. Gwinner, and M. L. Meuter, "A Comparison of Attitude, Personality, and Knowledge Predictors of Service-Oriented Organizational Citizenship Behaviors," *Journal of Applied Psychology* 86 (2001): 29–41.

25. Aplus.Net, "Aplus.Net Is Put to the Test with Firestorm 2003 and Passes with Flying Colors," http://www.aplus.net/comp_info_20031105.html, November 6, 2003.

26. D. W. Organ, *Organizational Citizenship Behavior: The Good Soldier Syndrome* (Lexington, Mass.: Lexington Books, 1988).

27. P. M. Podsakoff, S. B. Mackenzie, and C. Hui, "Organizational Citizenship Behaviors and Managerial Evaluations of Employee Performance: A Review and Suggestions for Future Research," G. Ferris, ed., in *Research in Personnel and Human Resources Management* (Greenwich, Conn.: JAI Press, 1993), 1–40.

28. O. Christ, R. Van Dick, and U. Wagner, "When Teachers Go the Extra Mile: Foci of Organizational Identification as Determinants of Different Forms of Organizational Citizenship Behavior Among Schoolteachers," *British Journal of Educational Psychology* 73 (2003): 329–341.

29. G. L. Blakely, M. C. Andrews, and J. Fuller, "Are Chameleons Good Citizens: A Longitudinal Study of the Relationship between Self-Monitoring and Organizational Citizenship Behavior," *Journal of Business & Psychology* 18 (2003): 131–144.

30. W. H. Bommer, E. W. Miles, and S. L. Grover, "Does One Good Turn Deserve Another? Coworker Influences on Employee Citizenship," *Journal of Organizational Behavior* 24 (2003): 181–196.

31. C. Ostroff, "The Relationship between Satisfaction, Attitudes and Performance: An Organizational Level Analysis," *Journal of Applied Psychology* 77 (1992): 963–974.

32. R. Griffin and T. Bateman, "Job Satisfaction and Organizational Commitment," in C. Cooper and I. Robertson, eds., *International Review of Industrial and Organizational Psychology* (New York: Wiley, 1986).

33. H. Y. Choi and H. Choi, "An Exploratory Study and Design of Cross-Cultural Impact of Information Systems Managers' Performance, Job Satisfaction, and Managerial Values," *Journal of Global Information Management* 11 (2003): 1–30.

34. X. Huang and E. Van De Vliert, "Where Intrinsic Job Satisfaction Fails to Work: National Moderators of Intrinsic Motivation," *Journal of Organizational Behavior* 24 (2003): 133–250.

35. R. T. Mowday, L. W. Porter, and R. M. Steers, *Employee-Organization Linkages: The Psychology of Commitment* (New York: Academic Press, 1982).

36. H. S. Becker, "Notes on the Concept of Commitment," *American Journal of Sociology* 66 (1960): 32–40.

37. J. P. Meyer, N. J. Allen, and C. A. Smith, "Commitment to Organizations and Occupations: Extension and Test of a Three-Component Model," *Journal of Applied Psychology* 78 (1993): 538–551.

38. J. P. Curry, D. S. Wakefield, J. L. Price, and C. W. Mueller, "On the Causal Ordering of Job Satisfaction and Organizational Commitment," *Academy of Management Journal* 29 (1986): 847–858.

39. B. Benkhoff, "Ignoring Commitment Is Costly: New Approaches Establish the Missing Link between Commitment and Performance," *Human Relations* 50 (1997): 701–726; N. J. Allen and J. P. Meyer, "Affective, Continuance, and Normative Commitment to the Organization: An Examination of Construct Validity," *Journal of Vocational Behavior* 49 (1996): 252–276.

40. M. J. Somers, "Organizational Commitment, Turnover, and Absenteeism: An Examination of Direct and Interaction Effects," *Journal of Organizational Behavior* 16 (1995): 49–58; L. Lum, J. Kervin, K. Clark, F. Reid, and W. Sirola, "Explaining Nursing Turnover Intent: Job Satisfaction, Pay Satisfaction, or Organizational Commitment?" *Journal of Organizational Behavior* 19 (1998): 305–320.

41. F. Stinglhamber and C. Vandenberghe, "Organizations and Supervisors as Sources of Support and Targets of Commitment," *Journal of Organizational Behavior* 24 (2003): 251–270.

42. R. Eisenberger *et al.*, "Reciprocation of Perceived Organizational Support," *Journal of Applied Psychology* 86 (2001): 42–51; J. E. Finegan, "The Impact of Person and Organizational Values on Organizational Commitment," *Journal of Occupational and Organizational Psychology* 73 (2000): 149–169.

43. E. Snape and T. Redman, "Too Old or Too Young? The Impact of Perceived Age Discrimination," *Human Resource Management Journal* 13 (2003): 78–89.

44. F. Luthans, H. S. McCaul, and N. C. Dodd, "Organizational Commitment: A Comparison of American, Japanese, and Korean Employees," *Academy of Management Journal* 28 (1985): 213–219.

45. C. Wong and I. Wong, "The Role of Perceived Quality of Social Relationships within Organizations in Chinese Societies," *International Journal of Management* 20 (2003): 216–223.

46. D. J. Koys, "The Effects of Employee Satisfaction, Organizational Citizenship Behavior, and Turnover on Organizational Effectiveness: A Unit-Level, Longitudinal Study," *Personnel Psychology* 54 (2001): 101–114.

47. J. A. Conger, "The Necessary Art of Persuasion," *Harvard Business Review* 76 (1998): 84–96.

48. J. Cooper and R. T. Croyle, "Attitudes and Attitude Change," *Annual Review of Psychology* 35 (1984): 395–426.

49. P. Sellers, "The Trials of John Mack," *Fortune* (August 11, 2003): 98–102.

50. D. M. Mackie and L. T. Worth, "Processing Deficits and the Mediation of Positive Affect in Persuasion," *Journal of Personality and Social Psychology* 57 (1989): 27–40.

51. J. W. Brehm, *Responses to Loss of Freedom: A Theory of Psychological Reactance* (New York: General Learning Press, 1972).

52. D. DeSteno, R. E. Petty, and D. D. Rucker, "Discrete Emotions and Persuasion: The Role of Emotion-Induced Expectancies," *Journal of Personality & Social Psychology* 86 (2004): 43–56.

53. R. Petty, D. T. Wegener, and L. R. Fabrigar, "Attitudes and Attitude Change," *Annual Review of Psychology* 48 (1997): 609–647.

54. P. Brinol and R. E. Petty, "Overt Head Movements and Persuasion: A Self-Validation Analysis," *Journal of Personality & Social Psychology* 84 (2003): 1123–1139.

55. W. Wood, "Attitude Change: Persuasion and Social Influence," *Annual Review of Psychology* 51 (2000): 539–570.

56. M. Rokeach, *The Nature of Human Values* (New York: Free Press, 1973).

57. M. Rokeach and S. J. Ball-Rokeach, "Stability and Change in American Value Priorities, 1968–1981," *American Psychologist* 44 (1989): 775–784.

58. G. W. England, "Organizational Goals and Expected Behavior of American Managers," *Academy of Management Journal* 10 (1967): 107–117.

59. E. C. Ravlin and B. M. Meglino, "Effects of Values on Perception and Decision Making: A Study of Alternative Work Values Measures," *Journal of Applied Psychology* 72 (1987): 666–673.

60. E. C. Ravlin and B. M. Meglino, "The Transitivity of Work Values: Hierarchical Preference Ordering of Socially Desirable Stimuli," *Organizational Behavior and Human Decision Processes* 44 (1989): 494–508.

61. B. M. Meglino, E. C. Ravlin, and C. L. Adkins, "A Work Values Approach to Corporate Culture: A Field Test of the Value Congruence Process and Its Relationship to Individual Outcomes," *Journal of Applied Psychology* 74 (1989): 424–432.

62. T. A. Judge and R. D. Bretz, Jr., "Effects of Work Values on Job Choice Decisions," *Journal of Applied Psychology* 77 (1992): 261–271.

63. Tony Jones, "Survey Finds Big Business Lacking in Social Responsibility," Australian Broadcasting Corporation (October 13, 2003), http://www.abc.net.au/lateline/content/2003/s966137.htm; RepuTex, http://www.reputex.com.au.

64. R. H. Doktor, "Asian and American CEOs: A Comparative Study," *Organizational Dynamics* 18 (1990): 46–56.

65. R. L. Tung, "Handshakes across the Sea: Cross-Cultural Negotiating for Business Success," *Organizational Dynamics* (Winter 1991): 30–40.

66. C. Gomez, B. L. Kirkman, and D. L. Shapiro, "The Impact of Collectivism and In-Group/Out-Group Membership on the Evaluation Generosity of Team Members," *Academy of Management Journal* 43 (2000): 1097–1106; J. Zhou and J. J. Martocchio, "Chinese and American Managers' Compensation Award Decisions: A Comparative Policy-Capturing Study," *Personnel Psychology* 54 (2001): 115–145.

67. A. J. Ali and M. Amirshahi, "The Iranian Manager: Work Values and Orientations," *Journal of Business Ethics* 40 (2002): 133–143.

68. R. Neale and R. Mindel, "Rigging Up Multicultural Teamworking," *Personnel Management* (January 1992): 27–30.

69. K. Hodgson, "Adapting Ethical Decisions to a Global Marketplace," *Management Review* 81 (1992): 53–57.

70. United States Department of Justice, "Foreign Corrupt Practices Act Antibribery Provisions," http://www.usdoj.gov/criminal/fraud/fcpa/dojdocb.htm, March 15, 2002.

71. F. Navran, "Your Role in Shaping Ethics," *Executive Excellence* 9 (1992): 11–12.

72. K. Labich, "The New Crisis in Business Ethics," *Fortune* (April 20, 1992): 167–176.

73. L. S. Paine, *Value Shift: Why Companies Must Merge Social and Financial Imperatives to Achieve Superior Performance* (New York: McGraw-Hill, 2003).

74. D. B. Turban and D. M. Cable, "Firm Reputation and Applicant Pool Characteristics," *Journal of Organizational Behavior* 24 (2003): 733–751.

75. E. A. Lind, J. Greenberg, K. S. Scott, and T. D. Welchans, "The Winding Road from Employee to Complainant: Situational and Psychological Determinants of Wrongful-Termination Claims," *Administrative Science Quarterly* 45 (2000): 557–590.

76. Miriam Schulman, "LittleBrother Is Watching You," http://www.scu.edu/ethics/publications/iie/v9n2/brother.html.

77. G. Flynn, "Make Employee Ethics Your Business," *Personnel Journal* (June 1995): 30–40.

78. M. S. Baucus and D. A. Baucus, "Paying the Piper: An Empirical Examination of Longer-Term Financial Consequences of Illegal Corporate Behavior," *Academy of Management Journal* 40 (1997): 129–151.

79. J. O. Cherrington and D. J. Cherrington, "A Menu of Moral Issues: One Week in the Life of The Wall Street Journal," *Journal of Business Ethics* 11 (1992): 255–265.

80. B. L. Flannery and D. R. May, "Environmental Ethical Decision Making in the U.S. Metal-Finishing Industry," *Academy of Management Journal* 43 (2000): 642–662.

81. K. R. Andrews, "Ethics in Practice," *Harvard Business Review* (September–October 1989): 99–104.

82. A. Bhide and H. H. Stevens, "Why Be Honest if Honesty Doesn't Pay?" *Harvard Business Review* (September–October 1990): 121–129.

83. Eli Lilly and Company, "Employee Volunteerism Policy," http://www.lilly.com/about/social/employee_giving/volunteerism _policy.html.

84. J. B. Rotter, "Generalized Expectancies for Internal versus External Control of Reinforcement," *Psychological Monographs* 80 (1966): 1–28.

85. L. K. Trevino and S. A. Youngblood, "Bad Apples in Bad Barrels: A Causal Analysis of Ethical Decision-Making Behavior," *Journal of Applied Psychology* 75 (1990): 378–385.

86. H. M. Lefcourt, *Locus of Control: Current Trends in Theory and Research*, 2nd ed. (Hillsdale, N.J.: Erlbaum, 1982).

87. N. Machiavelli, *The Prince*, trans. George Bull (Middlesex, England: Penguin Books, 1961).

88. R. Christie and F. L. Geis, *Studies in Machiavellianism* (New York: Academic Press, 1970).

89. R. A. Giacalone and S. B. Knouse, "Justifying Wrongful Employee Behavior: The Role of Personality in Organizational Sabotage," *Journal of Business Ethics* 9 (1990): 55–61.

90. S. B. Knouse and R. A. Giacalone, "Ethical Decision Making in Business: Behavioral Issues and Concerns," *Journal of Business Ethics* 11 (1992): 369–377.

91. L. Kohlberg, "Stage and Sequence: The Cognitive Developmental Approach to Socialization," in D. A. Goslin, ed., *Handbook of Socialization Theory and Research* (Chicago: Rand McNally, 1969), 347–480.

92. C. I. Malinowski and C. P. Smith, "Moral Reasoning and Moral Conduct: An Investigation Prompted by Kohlberg's Theory," *Journal of Personality and Social Psychology* 49 (1985): 1016–1027.

93. M. Brabeck, "Ethical Characteristics of Whistleblowers," *Journal of Research in Personality* 18 (1984): 41–53.

94. W. Y. Penn and B. D. Collier, "Current Research in Moral Development as a Decision Support System," *Journal of Business Ethics* 4 (1985): 131–136.

95. Trevino and Youngblood, "Bad Apples in Bad Barrels."

96. C. Gilligan, *In a Different Voice: Psychological Theory and Women's Development* (Cambridge, Mass.: Harvard University Press, 1982).

97. S. Jaffee and J. S. Hyde, "Gender Differences in Moral Orientation: A Meta-Analysis," *Psychological Bulletin* 126 (2000): 703–726.

98. G. R. Franke, D. F. Crown, and D. F. Spake, "Gender Differences in Ethical Perceptions of Business Practices: A Social Role Theory Perspective," *Journal of Applied Psychology* 82 (1997): 920–934.

99. S. A. Goldman and J. Arbuthnot, "Teaching Medical Ethics: The Cognitive-Developmental Approach," *Journal of Medical Ethics* 5 (1979): 171–181.

100. B. Horovitz, "Whole Foods Pledges to Be More Humane," *USA Today* (October 21, 2003): B1.

101. J. N. Frank, "VivaUSA Push Forces Whole Foods Change," *PR Week* (November 3, 2003): 4.

Chapter 5

1. R. Wolfe, "A Passion for Puppies: Volunteers for Canine Companions Raise and Train Dogs for Human Assistance," *The Press Democrat* 14 (August 31, 2003): B5.

2. L. W. Porter, G. Bigley, and R. M. Steers, *Motivation and Leadership at Work*, 7th ed. (New York: McGraw-Hill, 2002).

3. J. P. Campbell and R. D. Pritchard, "Motivation Theory in Industrial and Organizational Psychology," in M. D. Dunnette, ed., *Handbook of Industrial and Organizational Psychology* (Chicago: Rand McNally, 1976), 63–130.

4. M. Weber, *The Protestant Ethic and the Spirit of Capitalism* (London: Talcott Parson, tr., 1930).

5. S. Freud, *Civilization and Its Discontents*, trans. and ed. J. Strachey (New York: Norton, 1961).

6. P. D. Dunlop and K. Lee, "Workplace Deviance, Organizational Citizenship Behavior, and Business Unit Performance: The Bad Apples Do Spoil the Whole Barrel," *Journal of Organizational Behavior* 25 (2004): 67–80.

7. K. J. Sweetman, "Employee Loyalty around the Globe," *Sloan Management Review* 42 (2001): 16.

8. B. S. Frey, *Not Just for the Money: An Economic Theory of Personal Motivation* (Brookfield, Vt.: Edgar Elger, 1997).

9. F. J. Roethlisberger, *Management and Morale* (Cambridge, Mass.: Harvard University Press, 1941).

10. A. Smith, *An Inquiry into the Nature and Causes of the Wealth of Nations*, Vol. 10 of *The Harvard Classics*, C. J. Bullock, ed. (New York: Collier, 1909).

11. J. Jennings, *Less Is More: How Great Companies Use Productivity as a Competitive Tool in Business* (New York: Portfolio, 2002).

12. F. W. Taylor, *The Principles of Scientific Management* (New York: Norton, 1911).

13. Hearings before Special Committee of the House of Representatives to Investigate the Taylor and Other Systems of Shop Management under Authority of House Resolution 90, Vol. 3, 1377–1508 contains Taylor's testimony before the committee from Thursday, January 25, through Tuesday, January 30, 1912.

14. L. Van Dyne and J. L. Pierce, "Psychological Ownership and Feelings of Possession: Three Field Studies Predicting Employee Attitudes and Organizational Citizenship Behavior," *Journal of Organizational Behavior* 25 (2004): 439–459.

15. A. H. Maslow, "A Theory of Human Motivation," *Psychological Review* 50 (1943): 370–396.

16. W. James, *The Principles of Psychology* (New York: H. Holt & Co., 1890; Cambridge, Mass.: Harvard University Press, 1983).

17. J. Dewey, *Human Nature and Conduct: An Introduction to Social Psychology* (New York: Holt, 1922).

18. S. Freud, *A General Introduction to Psycho-Analysis: A Course of Twenty-Eight Lectures Delivered at the University of Vienna* (New York: Liveright, 1963); A. Adler, *Understanding Human Nature* (Greenwich, Conn.: Fawcett, 1927).

19. L. W. Porter, "A Study of Perceived Need Satisfactions in Bottom and Middle Management Jobs," *Journal of Applied Psychology* 45 (1961): 1–10.

20. E. E. Lawler, III and J. L. Suttle, "A Causal Correlational Test of the Need Hierarchy Concept," *Organizational Behavior and Human Performance* 7 (1973): 265–287.

21. D. M. McGregor, *The Human Side of Enterprise* (New York: McGraw-Hill, 1960).

22. D. M. McGregor, "The Human Side of Enterprise," *Management Review* (November 1957): 22–28, 88–92.

23. E. E. Lawler, G. E. Lawford, S. A. Mohrman, and G. E. Ledford, Jr., *Strategies for High Performance Organizations—The CEO Report: Employee Involvement, TQM, and Reengineering Programs in Fortune 1000 Corporations* (San Francisco: Jossey-Bass, Inc., 1998).

24. G. E. Forward, D. E. Beach, D. A. Gray, and J. C. Quick, "Mentofacturing: A Vision for American Industrial Excellence," *Academy of Management Executive* 5 (1991): 32–44.

25. C. P. Alderfer, *Human Needs in Organizational Settings* (New York: Free Press, 1972).

26. B. Schneider and C. P. Alderfer, "Three Studies of Need Satisfactions in Organizations," *Administrative Science Quarterly* 18 (1973): 489–505.

27. H. A. Murray, *Explorations in Personality: A Clinical and Experimental Study of Fifty Men of College Age* (New York: Oxford University Press, 1938).

28. D. C. McClelland, *Motivational Trends in Society* (Morristown, N.J.: General Learning Press, 1971).

29. J. P. Chaplin and T. S. Krawiec, *Systems and Theories of Psychology* (New York: Holt, Rinehart & Winston, 1960).

30. D. C. McClelland, "Achievement Motivation Can Be Learned," *Harvard Business Review* 43 (1965): 6–24.

31. E. A. Ward, "Multidimensionality of Achievement Motivation among Employed Adults," *Journal of Social Psychology* 134 (1997): 542–544.

32. A. Sagie, D. Elizur, and H. Yamauchi, "The Structure and Strength of Achievement Motivation: A Cross-Cultural Comparison," *Journal of Organizational Behavior* 17 (1996): 431–444.

33. D. C. McClelland and D. Burnham, "Power Is the Great Motivator," *Harvard Business Review* 54 (1976): 100–111; J. Hall and J. Hawker, *Power Management Inventory* (The Woodlands, Tex.: Teleometrics International, 1988).

34. F. Luthans, "Successful versus Effective Real Managers," *Academy of Management Executive* 2 (1988): 127–131.

35. S. Schachter, *The Psychology of Affiliation* (Stanford, Calif.: Stanford University Press, 1959).

36. F. Herzberg, B. Mausner, and B. Snyderman, *The Motivation to Work* (New York: Wiley, 1959).

37. F. Herzberg, *Work and the Nature of Man* (Cleveland: World, 1966).

38. D. S. Hamermesh, "The Changing Distribution of Job Satisfaction," *Journal of Human Resources* 36 (2001): 1–30.

39. F. J. Leach and J. D. Westbrook, "Motivation and Job Satisfaction in One Government Research and Development Environment," *Engineering Management Journal* 12 (2000): 3–8.

40. D. L. Nelson and B. L. Simmons, "Health Psychology and Work Stress: A More Positive Approach," in J. C. Quick and L. E. Tetrick, eds., *Handbook of Occupational Health Psychology* (Washington D. C.: American Psychological Association, 2003), 97–119.

41. K. S. Cameron, J. E. Dutton, and R. E. Quinn, eds., *Positive Organizational Scholarship: Foundations of a New Discipline* (San Francisco: Berrett-Keohler, 2003).

42. J. Loehr and T. Schwartz, "The Making of a Corporate Athlete," *Harvard Business Review* 79 (2001): 120–129.

43. J. Loehr and T. Schwartz, *The Power of Full Engagement: Managing Energy, Not Time, Is the Key to High Performance and Personal Renewal* (New York: Free Press, 2003).

44. P. M. Blau, *Exchange and Power in Social Life* (New York: Wiley, 1964).

45. A. Etzioni, "A Basis for Comparative Analysis of Complex Organizations," in A. Etzioni, ed., *A Sociological Reader on Complex Organizations*, 2nd ed., (New York: Holt, Rinehart & Winston, 1969), 59–76.

46. O. Janssen, "Job Demands, Perceptions of Effort–Reward Fairness and Innovative Work Behavior," *Journal of Occupational & Organizational Psychology* 73 (2000): 287–302.

47. R. Cropanzano, B. Goldman, and R. Folger, "Deontic Justice: The Role of Moral Principles in Workplace Fairness," *Journal of Organizational Behavior* 24 (2003): 1019–1024.

48. J. P. Campbell, M. D. Dunnette, E. E. Lawler, III, and K. E. Weick, Jr., *Managerial Behavior, Performance and Effectiveness* (New York: McGraw-Hill, 1970).

49. S. S. Masterson and C. L. Stamper, "Perceived Organizational Membership: An Aggregate Framework Representing the Employee–Organization Relationship," *Journal of Organizational Behavior* 24 (2003): 473–490.

50. J. S. Adams, "Inequity in Social Exchange," in L. Berkowitz, ed., *Advances in Experimental Social Psychology*, Vol. 2 (New York: Academic Press, 1965), 267–299; J. S. Adams, "Toward an Understanding of Inequity," *Journal of Abnormal and Social Psychology* 67 (1963): 422–436.

51. J. Nelson-Horchler, "The Best Man for the Job Is a Man," *Industry Week* (January 7, 1991): 50–52.

52. P. D. Sweeney, D. B. McFarlin, and E. J. Inderrieden, "Using Relative Deprivation Theory to Explain Satisfaction with Income and Pay Level: A Multistudy Examination," *Academy of Management Journal* 33 (1990): 423–436.

53. R. C. Huseman, J. D. Hatfield, and E. A. Miles, "A New Perspective on Equity Theory: The Equity Sensitivity Construct," *Academy of Management Review* 12 (1987): 222–234.

54. D. McLoughlin and S. C. Carr, "Equity and Sensitivity and Double Demotivation," *Journal of Social Psychology* 137 (1997): 668–670.

55. K. E. Weick, M. G. Bougon, and G. Maruyama, "The Equity Context," *Organizational Behavior and Human Performance* 15 (1976): 32–65.

56. R. Coles, *Privileged Ones* (Boston: Little, Brown, 1977).

57. J. A. Colquitt and J. Greenberg, "Organizational Justice: A Fair Assessment of the State of the Literature," in J. Greenberg, ed., *Organizational Behavior: The State of the Science*, 2nd ed. (Mahwah, N.J.: Erlbaum Associates, 2003).

58. J. Greenberg, "Equity and Workplace Status: A Field Experiment," *Journal of Applied Psychology* 73 (1988): 606–613.

59. J. Greenberg and B. Alge, "Aggressive Reactions to Workplace Injustice," in R. W. Griffin, A. O'Leary-Kelly, and J. Collins, eds., *Dysfunctional Behavior in Organizations, Vol. 1: Violent Behaviors in Organizations* (Greenwich, CT: JAI, 1998), 119–145.

60. R. A. Cosier and D. R. Dalton, "Equity Theory and Time: A Reformulation," *Academy of Management Review* 8 (1983): 311–319.

61. J. E. Martin and M. W. Peterson, "Two-Tier Wage Structures: Implications for Equity Theory," *Academy of Management Journal* 30 (1987): 297–315.

62. V. H. Vroom, *Work and Motivation* (New York: Wiley, 1964/1970).

63. U. R. Larson, "Supervisor's Performance Feedback to Subordinates: The Effect of Performance Valence and Outcome Dependence," *Organizational Behavior and Human Decision Processes* 37 (1986): 391–409.

64. M. C. Kernan and R. G. Lord, "Effects of Valence, Expectancies, and Goal-Performance Discrepancies in Single and Multiple Goal Environments," *Journal of Applied Psychology* 75 (1990): 194–203.

65. R. J. Sanchez, D. M. Truxillo, and T. N. Bauer, "Development and Examination of an Expectancy-Based Measure of Test-Taking Motivation," *Journal of Applied Psychology* 85 (2000): 739–750.

66. W. VanEerde and H. Thierry, "Vroom's Expectancy Models and Work-Related Criteria: A Meta-Analysis," *Journal of Applied Psychology* 81 (1996): 575–586.

67. E. D. Pulakos and N. Schmitt, "A Longitudinal Study of a Valence Model Approach for the Prediction of Job Satisfaction of New Employees," *Journal of Applied Psychology* 68 (1983): 307–312.

68. F. J. Landy and W. S. Becker, "Motivation Theory Reconsidered," in L. L. Cummings and B. M. Staw, eds., *Research in Organizational Behavior 9* (Greenwich, Conn.: JAI Press, 1987), 1–38.

69. L. Kohlberg, "The Cognitive-Developmental Approach to Socialization," in D. A. Goslin, ed., *Handbook of Socialization Theory and Research* (Chicago: Rand McNally, 1969).

70. N. J. Adler, *International Dimensions of Organizational Behavior*, 4th ed. (Mason, OH: South-Western, 2001).

71. G. Hofstede, "Motivation, Leadership, and Organization: Do American Theories Apply Abroad?" *Organizational Dynamics* 9 (1980): 42–63.

72. G. H. Hines, "Cross-Cultural Differences in Two-Factor Theory," *Journal of Applied Psychology* 58 (1981): 313–317.

73. L. Nadel, "For 9/11 Families, Shoulders to Cry On," *The New York Times* (March 31, 2002): 14LI.3.

Chapter 6

1. D. Dearlove, "Do the Hippy, Hippy Shake," in *Business the Richard Branson Way: 10 Secrets of the World's Greatest Brand Builder* (Oxford, UK: Capstone Publishing Ltd., 2002): 44–47.

2. I. P. Pavlov, *Conditioned Reflexes* (New York: Oxford University Press, 1927).

3. B. Cannon, "Walter B. Cannon: Reflections on the Man and His Contributions," *Centennial Session*, American Psychological Association Centennial Convention, Washington, D.C., 1992.

4. B. F. Skinner, *The Behavior of Organisms: An Experimental Analysis* (New York: Appleton-Century-Crofts, 1938).

5. B. F. Skinner, *Science and Human Behavior* (New York: Free Press, 1953).

6. F. Luthans and R. Kreitner, *Organizational Behavior Modification and Beyond* (Glenview, Ill.: Scott, Foresman, 1985).

7. A. D. Stajkovic and F. Luthans, "A Meta-Analysis of the Effects of Organizational Behavior Modification on Task Performance, 1975–95," *Academy of Management Journal* 40 (1997): 1122–1149.

8. A. D. Stajkovic and F. Luthans, "Differential Effects of Incentive Motivators on Work," *Academy of Management Journal* 44 (2001): 580–591.

9. J. Hale, "Strategic Rewards: Keeping Your Best Talent from Walking Out the Door," *Compensation & Benefits Management* 14 (1998): 39–50.

10. B. F. Skinner, *Contingencies of Reinforcement: A Theoretical Analysis* (New York: Appleton-Century-Crofts, 1969).

11. J. P. Chaplin and T. S. Krawiec, *Systems and Theories of Psychology* (New York: Holt, Rinehart & Winston, 1960).

12. A. Bandura, *Social Learning Theory* (Englewood Cliffs, N.J.: Prentice-Hall, 1977); A. Bandura, "Self-Efficacy: Toward a Unifying Theory of Behavioral Change," *Psychological Review* 84 (1977): 191–215.

13. J. J. Martocchio and E. J. Hertenstein, "Learning Orientation and Goal Orientation Context: Relationships with Cognitive and Affective Learning Outcomes," *Human Resource Development Quarterly* 14 (2003): 413–434.

14. A. Bandura, "Regulation of Cognitive Processes through Perceived Self-Efficacy," *Developmental Psychology* (September 1989): 729–735.

15. J. M. Phillips and S. M. Gully, "Role of Goal Orientation, Ability, Need for Achievement, and Locus of Control in the Self-Efficacy and Goal-Setting Process," *Journal of Applied Psychology* 82 (1997): 792–802.

16. J. C. Weitlauf, R. E. Smith, and D. Cervone, "Generalization Effects of Coping-Skills Training: Influence of Self-Defense Training on Women's Efficacy Beliefs, Assertiveness, and Aggression," *Journal of Applied Psychology* 85 (2000): 625–633.

17. A. D. Stajkovic and F. Luthans, "Social Cognitive Theory and Self-Efficacy: Going Beyond Traditional Motivational and Behavioral Approaches," *Organizational Dynamics* (Spring 1998): 62–74.

18. A. D. Stajkovic and F. Luthans, "Self-Efficacy and Work-Related Performance: A Meta-Analysis," *Psychological Bulletin* 124 (1998): 240–261.

19. V. Gecas, "The Social Psychology of Self-Efficacy," *Annual Review of Sociology* 15 (1989): 291–316.

20. O. Isachsen and L. V. Berens, *Working Together: A Personality Centered Approach to Management* (Coronado, Calif.: Neworld Management Press, 1988); O. Krueger and J. M. Thuesen, *Type Talk* (New York: Tilden Press, 1988).

21. E. A. Locke and G. P. Latham, *A Theory of Goal Setting and Task Performance* (Englewood Cliffs, N.J.: Prentice-Hall, 1990).

22. T. O. Murray, *Management by Objectives: A Systems Approach to Management* (Fort Worth, Tex.: Western Company, n.d.).

23. W. T. Brooks and T. W. Mullins, *High Impact Time Management* (Englewood Cliffs, N.J.: Prentice-Hall, 1989).

24. G. H. Seijts, G. P. Latham, K. Tasa, and B. W. Latham, "Goal Setting and Goal Orientation: An Integration of Two Different Yet Related Literatures," *Academy of Management Journal* 47 (2004): 227–239.

25. E. A. Locke, "Toward a Theory of Task Motivation and Incentives," *Organizational Behavior and Human Performance* 3 (1968): 157–189.

26. J. C. Quick, "Dyadic Goal Setting within Organizations: Role Making and Motivational Considerations," *Academy of Management Review* 4 (1979): 369–380.

27. D. McGregor, "An Uneasy Look at Performance Appraisal," *Harvard Business Review* 35 (1957): 89–94.

28. J. R. Hollenbeck, C. R. Williams, and H. J. Klein, "An Empirical Examination of the Antecedents of Commitment to Difficult Goals," *Journal of Applied Psychology* 74 (1989): 18–23.

29. R. C. Rodgers and J. E. Hunter, "The Impact of Management by Objectives on Organizational Productivity," unpublished paper (Lexington: University of Kentucky, 1989).

30. E. A. Locke, K. N. Shaw, L. M. Saari, and G. P. Latham, "Goal Setting and Task Performance: 1969–1980," *Psychological Bulletin* 90 (1981): 125–152.

31. D. B. Fedora, W. D. Davis, J. M. Maslync, and K. Mathiesond, "Performance Improvement Efforts in Response to Negative Feedback: The Roles of Source Power and Recipient Self-Esteem," *Journal of Management* 27 (2001): 79–98.

32. J. C. Quick, "Dyadic Goal Setting and Role Stress," *Academy of Management Journal* 22 (1979): 241–252.

33. G. S. Odiorne, *Management by Objectives: A System of Managerial Leadership* (New York: Pitman, 1965).

34. American Management Association, *Blueprints for Service Quality: The Federal Express Approach* (New York: American Management Association, 1991).

35. G. P. Latham and G. A. Yukl, "A Review of Research on the Application of Goal Setting in Organizations," *Academy of Management Journal* 18 (1975): 824–845.

36. P. F. Drucker, *The Practice of Management* (New York: Harper & Bros., 1954).

37. R. D. Prichard, P. L. Roth, S. D. Jones, P. J. Galgay, and M. D. Watson, "Designing a Goal-Setting System to Enhance Performance: A Practical Guide," *Organizational Dynamics* 17 (1988): 69–78.

38. C. L. Hughes, *Goal Setting: Key to Individual and Organizational Effectiveness* (New York: American Management Association, 1965).

39. M. E. Tubbs and S. E. Ekeberg, "The Role of Intentions in Work Motivation: Implications for Goal-Setting Theory and Research," *Academy of Management Review* 16 (1991): 180–199.

40. S. Vatave, "Managing Risk," *Supervision* 65 (2004): 6-9.

41. J. R. Hollenbeck and A. P. Brief, "The Effects of Individual Differences and Goal Origin on Goal Setting and Performance," *Organizational Behavior and Human Decision Processes* 40 (1987): 392–414.

42. R. A. Katzell and D. E. Thompson, "Work Motivation: Theory and Practice," *American Psychologist* 45 (1990): 144–153; M. W. McPherson, "Is Psychology the Science of Behavior?" *American Psychologist* 47 (1992): 329–335.

43. E. A. Locke, "The Ideas of Frederick W. Taylor: An Evaluation," *Academy of Management Review* 7 (1982): 15–16; R. M. Yerkes and J. D. Dodson, "The Relation of Strength of Stimulus to Rapidity of Habit-Formation," *Journal of Comparative Neurology and Psychology* 18 (1908): 459–482.

44. R. L. Cardy, *Performance Management: Concepts, Skills, and Exercises* (Armonk, New York and London, England: M.E. Sharpe, 2004).

45. P. Cappelli and N. Rogovsky, "Employee Involvement and Organizational Citizenship: Implications for Labor Law Reform and 'Lean Production,'" *Industrial & Labor Relations Review* 51 (1998): 633–653.

46. B. Erdogan, M. L. Kraimer, and R. C. Liden, "Procedural Justice as a Two-Dimensional Construct: An Examination in the Performance Appraisal Account," *Journal of Applied Behavioral Science* 37 (2001): 205–222.

47. S. E. DeVoe and S. S. Iyengar, "Managers' Theories of Subordinates: A Cross-Cultural Examination of Manager Perceptions of Motivation and Appraisal of Performance," *Organizational Behavior and Human Decision Processes* 93 (2004): 47–61.

48. I. M. Jawahar and C. R. Williams, "Where All the Children Are Above Average: The Performance Appraisal Purpose Effect," *Personnel Psychology* 50 (1997): 905–925.

49. M. E. Tubbs and M. L. Trusty, "Direct Reports of Motivation for Task Performance Levels: Some Construct-Related Evidence," *Journal of Psychology* 135 (2001): 185–205.

50. R. R. Kilburg, *Executive Coaching: Developing Managerial Wisdom in a World of Chaos* (Washington, D.C.: American Psychological Association, 2000).

51. H. H. Meyer, E. Kay, and J. R. P. French, "Split Roles in Performance Appraisal," *Harvard Business Review* 43 (1965): 123–129.

52. W. A. Fisher, J. C. Quick, L. L. Schkade, and G. W. Ayers, "Developing Administrative Personnel through the Assessment Center Technique," *Personnel Administrator* 25 (1980): 44–46, 62.

53. J. S. Goodman, R. E. Wood, and M. Hendrickx, "Feedback Specificity, Exploration, and Learning," *Journal of Applied Psychology* 89 (2004): 248–262.

54. M. B. DeGregorio and C. D. Fisher, "Providing Performance Feedback: Reactions to Alternative Methods," *Journal of Management* 14 (1988): 605–616.

55. G. C. Thornton, "The Relationship between Supervisory and Self-Appraisals of Executive Performance," *Personnel Psychology* 21 (1968): 441–455.

56. A. S. DeNisi and A. N. Kluger, "Feedback Effectiveness: Can 360-Degree Appraisals Be Improved?" *Academy of Management Executive* 14 (2000): 129–140.

57. F. Luthans and S. J. Peterson, "360-Degree Feedback with Systematic Coaching: Empirical Analysis Suggests a Winning Combination," *Human Resource Management* 42 (2003): 243–256.

58. G. Toegel and J. A. Conger, "360-Degree Assessment: Time for Reinvention," *Academy of Management Learning and Education* 2 (2003): 297–311.

59. L. Hirschhorn, "Leaders and Followers in a Postindustrial Age: A Psychodynamic View," *Journal of Applied Behavioral Science* 26 (1990): 529–542.

60. F. M Jablin, "Superior-Subordinate Communication: The State of the Art," *Psychological Bulletin* 86 (1979): 1201–1222.

61. J. Pfeffer, "Six Dangerous Myths about Pay," *Harvard Business Review* 76 (1998): 108–119.

62. M. Erez, "Work Motivation from a Cross-Cultural Perspective," in A. M. Bouvy, F. J. R. Van de Vijver, P. Boski, and P. G. Schmitz, eds., *Journeys into Cross-Cultural Psychology* (Amsterdam, Netherlands: Swets & Zeitlinger, 1994), 386–403.

63. George T. Milkovich and Jerry M. Newman, *Compensation*, 4th ed. (Homewood, Ill.: Irwin, 1993).

64. S. Kerr, "On the Folly of Rewarding A, While Hoping for B," *Academy of Management Journal* 18 (1975): 769–783.

65. J. M. Bardwick, *Danger in the Comfort Zone* (New York: American Management Association, 1991).

66. M. J. Martinko and W. L. Gardner, "The Leader/Member Attributional Process," *Academy of Management Review* 12 (1987): 235–249.

67. K. N. Wexley, R. A. Alexander, J. P. Greenawalt, and M. A. Couch, "Attitudinal Congruence and Similarity as Related to Interpersonal Evaluations in Manager-Subordinate Dyads," *Academy of Management Journal* 23 (1980): 320–330.

68. H. H. Kelley, *Attribution in Social Interaction* (New York: General Learning Press, 1971).

69. H. H. Kelley, "The Processes of Causal Attribution," *American Psychologist* 28 (1973): 107–128.

70. B. Raabe and T. A. Beehr, "Formal Mentoring versus Supervisor and Coworker Relationships: Differences in Perceptions and Impact," *Journal of Organizational Behavior* 24 (2003): 271–293.

71. A. M. Young and P. L. Perrewe, "What Did You Expect? An Examination of Career-Related Support and Social Support among Mentors and Protégés," *Journal of Management* 26 (2000): 611–633.

72. K. Doherty, "The Good News about Depression," *Business and Health* 3 (1989): 1–4.

73. K. E. Kram, "Phases of the Mentor Relationship," *Academy of Management Journal* 26 (1983): 608–625.

74. T. D. Allen, L. T. Eby, M. L. Poteet, E. Lentz, and L. Lima, "Career Benefits Associated with Mentoring for Protégés: A Meta-Analysis," *Journal of Applied Psychology* 89 (2004): 127–136.

75. T. N. Bauer and S. G. Green, "Development of Leader–Member Exchange: A Longitudinal Test," *Academy of Management Journal* 39 (1996): 1538–1567.

76. K. E. Kram and L. A. Isabella, "Mentoring Alternatives: The Role of Peer Relationships in Career Development," *Academy of Management Journal* 28 (1985): 110–132.

77. J. Greco, "Hey, Coach!" *Journal of Business Strategy* 22 (2001): 28–32.

78. H. Begum, "Branson's Force," *The Lawyer* (October 20, 2003): 15, http://www.thelawyer.com/cgi-bin/item.cgi?id=107286&d=11h=24&f=46.

Chapter 7

1. "Humans Only," *Monsters, Inc.* DVD (Walt Disney Home Video, released September 17, 2002).

2. J. Barling, E. K. Kelloway, and M. R. Frone, eds., *Handbook of Work Stress* (Thousand Oaks, CA: Sage Publications, 2005).

3. J. C. Quick, J. D. Quick, D. L. Nelson, and J. J. Hurrell, Jr., *Preventive Stress Management in Organizations* (Washington, D.C.: American Psychological Association, 1997).

4. S. Benison, A. C. Barger, and E. L. Wolfe, *Walter B. Cannon: The Life and Times of a Young Scientist* (Cambridge, Mass.: Harvard University Press, 1987).

5. W. B. Cannon, "Stresses and Strains of Homeostasis," *American Journal of the Medical Sciences* 189 (1935): 1–14.

6. W. B. Cannon, *The Wisdom of the Body* (New York: Norton, 1932).

7. R. S. Lazarus, *Psychological Stress and the Coping Process* (New York: McGraw-Hill, 1966).

8. D. Katz and R. L. Kahn, *The Social Psychology of Organizations*, 2nd ed. (New York: Wiley, 1978), 185–221.

9. H. Levinson, "A Psychoanalytic View of Occupational Stress," *Occupational Mental Health* 3 (1978): 2–13.

10. T. L. Friedman, *The Lexus and the Olive Tree* (New York: Vintage Anchor, 2000).

11. T. Theorell and R. A. Karasek, "Current Issues Relating to Psychosocial Job Strain and Cardiovascular Disease," *Journal of Occupational Health Psychology* 1 (1996): 9–26.

12. D. T. Hall and J. Richter, "Career Gridlock: Baby Boomers Hit the Wall," *Academy of Management Executive* 4 (1990): 7–22.

13. S. Zuboff, *In the Age of the Smart Machine: The Future of Work and Power* (New York: Basic Books, 1988).

14. R. L. Kahn, D. M. Wolfe, R. P. Quinn, J. D. Snoek, and R. A. Rosenthal, *Organizational Stress: Studies in Role Conflict and Ambiguity* (New York: Wiley, 1964).

15. L. B. Hammer, T. N. Bauer, and A. A. Grandey, "Work-Family Conflict and Work-Related Withdrawal Behaviors," *Journal of Business and Psychology* 17 (2003): 419–436.

16. M. F. Peterson, et al., "Role Conflict, Ambiguity, and Overload: A 21-Nation Study," *Academy of Management Journal* 38 (1995): 429–452.

17. P. D. Bliese and C. A. Castro, "Role Clarity, Work Overload and Organizational Support: Multilevel Evidence of the Importance of Support," *Work & Stress* 14 (2000): 65–74.

18. P. J. Frost, *Toxic Emotions at Work: How Compassionate Managers Handle Pain and Conflict* (Boston, MA: Harvard Business School Press, 2003).

19. S. Grebner, N. K. Semmer, L. L. Faso, S. Gut, W. Kalin, and A. Elfering, "Working Conditions, Well-Being, and Job-Related Attitudes Among Call Centre Agents," *European Journal of Work and Organizational Psychology* 12 (2003): 341–365.

20. M. P. Bell, J. C. Quick, and C. Cycota, "Assessment and Prevention of Sexual Harassment: An Applied Guide to Creating Healthy Organizations," *International Journal of Selection and Assessment* 10 (2002): 160–167.

21. L. T. Hosmer, "Trust: The Connecting Link between Organizational Theory and Philosophical Ethics," *Academy of Management Review* 20 (1995): 379–403; V. J. Doby and R. D. Caplan, "Organizational Stress as Threat to Reputation: Effects on Anxiety at Work and at Home," *Academy of Management Journal* 38 (1995): 1105–1123.

22. R. T. Keller, "Cross-Functional Project Groups in Research and New Product Development: Diversity, Communications, Job Stress, and Outcomes," *Academy of Management Journal* 33 (2001): 547–555.

23. M. F. Peterson and P. B. Smith, "Does National Culture or Ambient Temperature Explain Cross-National Differences in Role Stress? No Sweat!" *Academy of Management Journal* 40 (1997): 930–946.

24. K. K. Gillingham, "High-G Stress and Orientational Stress: Physiologic Effects of Aerial Maneuvering," *Aviation, Space, and Environmental Medicine* 59 (1988): A10–A20.

25. R. S. DeFrank, "Executive Travel Stress: Perils of the Road Warrior," *Academy of Management Executive* 14 (2000): 58–72.

26. M. Westman, "Strategies for Coping with Business Trips: A Qualitative Exploratory Study," *International Journal of Stress Management* 11 (2004): 167–176.

27. R. S. Bhagat, S. J. McQuaid, S. Lindholm, and J. Segovis, "Total Life Stress: A Multimethod Validation of the Construct and Its Effect on Organizationally Valued Outcomes and Withdrawal Behaviors," *Journal of Applied Psychology* 70 (1985): 202–214.

28. J. C. Quick, J. R. Joplin, D. A. Gray, and E. C. Cooley, "The Occupational Life Cycle and the Family," in L. L'Abate, ed., *Handbook of Developmental Family Psychology and Psychopathology* (New York: John Wiley, 1993).

29. S. Shellenbarger, "Work & Family," *The Wall Street Journal* (January 31, 1996): B1.

30. S. A. Lobel, "Allocation of Investment in Work and Family Roles: Alternative Theories and Implications for Research," *Academy of Management Review* 16 (1991): 507–521.

31. G. Porter, "Organizational Impact of Workaholism: Suggestions for Researching the Negative Outcomes of Excessive Work," *Journal of Occupational Health Psychology* 1 (1996): 70–84.

32. J. W. Pennebaker, C. F. Hughes, and R. C. O'Heeron, "The Psychophysiology of Confession: Linking Inhibitory and Psychosomatic Processes," *Journal of Personality and Social Psychology* 52 (1987): 781–793.

33. J. Loehr and T. Schwartz, "The Making of a Corporate Athlete," *Harvard Business Review* 79 (2001): 120–129.

34. J. D. Quick, R. S. Horn, and J. C. Quick, "Health Consequences of Stress," *Journal of Organizational Behavior Management* 8 (1986): 19–36.

35. R. M. Yerkes and J. D. Dodson, "The Relation of Strength of Stimulus to Rapidity of Habit-Formation," *Journal of Comparative Neurology and Psychology* 18 (1908): 459–482.

36. J. E. McGrath, "Stress and Behavior in Organizations," in M. D. Dunnette, ed., *Handbook of Industrial and Organizational Psychology* (Chicago: Rand McNally, 1976), 1351–1395.

37. T. A. Wright, R. Cropanzano, and D. G. Meyer, "State and Trait Correlates of Job Performance: A Tale of Two Perspectives," *Journal of Business and Psychology* 18 (2004): 365–383.

38. W. B. Cannon, *Bodily Changes in Pain, Hunger, Fear, and Rage* (New York: Appleton, 1915).

39. P. A. Herbig and F. A. Palumbo, "Karoshi: Salaryman Sudden Death Syndrome," *Journal of Managerial Psychology* 9 (1994): 11–16.

40. S. Sauter, L. R. Murphy, and J. J. Hurrell, Jr., "Prevention of Work-Related Psychological Distress: A National Strategy Proposed by the National Institute for Occupational Safety and Health," *American Psychologist* 45 (1990): 1146–1158.

41. R. Cropanzano, D. E. Rupp, and Z. S. Byrne, "The Relationship of Emotional Exhaustion to Work Attitudes, Job Performance, and Organizational Citizenship Behaviors," *Journal of Applied Psychology* 88 (2003): 160–169.

42. A. A. Grandey, "When 'The Show Must Go On': Surface Acting and Deep Acting as Determinants of Emotional Exhaustion and Peer-Rated Service Delivery," *Academy of Management Journal* 46 (2003): 86–96.

43. H. Selye, *Stress in Health and Disease* (Boston: Butterworth, 1976).

44. B. G. Ware and D. L. Block, "Cardiovascular Risk Intervention at a Work Site: The Ford Motor Company Program," *International Journal of Mental Health* 11 (1982): 68–75.

45. B. S. Siegel, *Love, Medicine, and Miracles* (New York: Harper & Row, 1986).

46. D. B. Kennedy, R. J. Homant, and M. R. Homant, "Perceptions of Injustice as a Predictor of Support for Workplace Aggression," *Journal of Business and Psychology* 18 (2004): 323–336.

47. N. Bolger, A. DeLongis, R. C. Kessler, and E. A. Schilling, "Effects of Daily Stress on Negative Mood," *Journal of Personality and Social Psychology* 57 (1989): 808–818.

48. B. A. Macy and P. H. Mirvis, "A Methodology for Assessment of Quality of Work Life and Organizational Effectiveness in Behavioral-Economic Terms," *Administrative Science Quarterly* 21 (1976): 212–226.

49. F. K. Cocchiara and J. C. Quick, "The Negative Effects of Positive Stereotypes: Ethnicity-Related Stressors and Implications on Organizational Health," *Journal of Organizational Behavior,* 25 (2004): 781–785.

50. J. M. Ivancevich, M. T. Matteson, and E. Richards, "Who's Liable for Stress on the Job?" *Harvard Business Review* 64 (1985): 60–72.

51. Frank S. Deus v. Allstate Insurance Company, civil action no. 88-2099, U.S. District Court, Western District of Louisiana.

52. R. S. DeFrank and J. M. Ivancevich, "Stress on the Job: An Executive Update," *Academy of Management Executive* 12 (1998): 55–66.

53. P. Wilson and M. Bronstein, "Employers: Don't Panic about Workplace Stress," *Personnel Today* (November 4, 2003): 10.

54. C. S. Troutman, K. G. Burke, and J. D. Beeler, "The Effects of Self-Efficacy, Assertiveness, Stress, and Gender on Intention," *Journal of Applied Business Research* 16 (2000): 63–75.

55. S. E. Taylor, L. C. Klein, G. P. Lewis, T. L. Gruenewald, R. A. R. Burung, and J. A. Updegraff, "Biobehavioral Responses to Stress in Females: Tend-and-Befriend, Not Fight-or-Flight," *Psychological Review* 107 (2000): 411–429.

56. D. L. Nelson and J. C. Quick, "Professional Women: Are Distress and Disease Inevitable?" *Academy of Management Review* 10 (1985): 206–218; T. D. Jick and L. F. Mitz, "Sex Differences in Work Stress," *Academy of Management Review* 10 (1985): 408–420.

57. L. Verbrugge, "Recent, Present, and Future Health of American Adults," *Annual Review of Public Health* 10 (1989): 333–361.

58. M. D. Friedman and R. H. Rosenman, *Type A Behavior and Your Heart* (New York: Knopf, 1974).

59. L. Wright, "The Type A Behavior Pattern and Coronary Artery Disease," *American Psychologist* 43 (1988): 2–14.

60. J. M. Ivancevich and M. T. Matteson, "A Type A–B Person–Work Environment Interaction Model for Examining Occupational Stress and Consequences," *Human Relations* 37 (1984): 491–513.

61. S. O. C. Kobasa, "Conceptualization and Measurement of Personality in Job Stress Research," in J. J. Hurrell, Jr., L. R. Murphy, S. L. Sauter, and C. L. Cooper, eds., *Occupational Stress: Issues and Developments in Research* (New York: Taylor & Francis, 1988), 100–109.

62. J. Borysenko, "Personality Hardiness," *Lectures in Behavioral Medicine* (Boston: Harvard Medical School, 1985).

63. J. S. House, K. R. Landis, and D. Umberson, "Social Relationships and Health," *Science* 241 (1988): 540–545.

64. J. Bowlby, *A Secure Base* (New York: Basic Books, 1988).

65. C. Hazan and P. Shaver, "Love and Work: An Attachment-Theoretical Perspective," *Journal of Personality and Social Psychology* 59 (1990): 270–280.

66. J. C. Quick, D. L. Nelson, and J. D. Quick, *Stress and Challenge at the Top: The Paradox of the Successful Executive* (Chichester, England: Wiley, 1990).

67. J. C. Quick, J. R. Joplin, D. L. Nelson, and J. D. Quick, "Self-Reliance for Stress and Combat" (*Proceedings of the 8th Combat Stress Conference*, U.S. Army Health Services Command, Fort Sam Houston, Texas, September 23–27, 1991): 1–5.

68. O. Janssen, "How Fairness Perceptions Make Innovative Behavior More or Less Stressful," *Journal of Organizational Behavior* 25 (2004): 201–215; T. A. Judge and J. A. Colquitt, "Organizational Justice and Stress: The Mediating Role of Work–Family Conflict," *Journal of Applied Psychology* 89 (2004): 395–404.

69. K. Hickox, "Content and Competitive," *Airman* (January 1994): 31–33.

70. R. W. Griffin, A. O'Leary-Kelly, and J. M. Collins, eds., *Dysfunctional Behavior in Organizations: Violent and Deviant Behavior* (Stamford, Conn.: JAI Press, 1998).

71. W. L. French and C. H. Bell, Jr., *Organizational Development: Behavioral Science Interventions for Organization Improvement,* 4th ed. (Englewood Cliffs, N.J.: Prentice-Hall, 1990).

72. M. Macik-Frey, J. C. Quick, and J. D. Quick, "Interpersonal Communication: The Key to Unlocking Social Support for Preventive Stress Management," in C. L. Cooper, ed., *Handbook of Stress, Medicine, and Health, Revised Edition* (Boca Raton, FL: CRC Press): in press.

73. J. C. Quick and C. L. Cooper, *FAST FACTS: Stress and Strain, Second Edition* (Oxford, England: Health Press, 2003).

74. M. E. P. Seligman, *Learned Optimism* (New York: Knopf, 1990).

75. F. Luthans, "Positive Organizational Behavior: Developing and Managing Psychological Strengths for Performance Improvement," *Academy of Management Executive* 16 (2002): 57–75.

76. W. T. Brooks and T. W. Mullins, *High-Impact Time Management* (Englewood Cliffs, N.J.: Prentice-Hall, 1989).

77. M. Westman and D. Eden, "Effects of a Respite from Work on Burnout: Vacation Relief and Fade-Out," *Journal of Applied Psychology* 82 (1997): 516–527.

78. C. P. Neck and K. H. Cooper, "The Fit Executive: Exercise and Diet Guidelines for Enhancing Performance," *Academy of Management Executive* 14 (2000): 72–84.

79. M. Davis, E. R. Eshelman, and M. McKay, *The Relaxation and Stress Reduction Workbook,* 3rd ed. (Oakland, Calif.: New Harbinger, 1988).

80. H. Benson, "Your Innate Asset for Combating Stress," *Harvard Business Review* 52 (1974): 49–60.

81. D. Ornish, *Dr. Dean Ornish's Program for Reversing Cardiovascular Disease* (New York: Random House, 1995).

82. J. W. Pennebaker, *Opening Up: The Healing Power of Expressing Emotions* (New York: Guilford, 1997).

83. M. E. Francis and J. W. Pennebaker, "Putting Stress into Words: The Impact of Writing on Physiological, Absentee, and Self-Reported Emotional Well-Being Measures," *American Journal of Health Promotion* 6 (1992): 280–287.

84. Z. Solomon, B. Oppenheimer, and S. Noy, "Subsequent Military Adjustment of Combat Stress Reaction Casualties: A Nine-Year Follow-Up Study," in N. A. Milgram, ed., *Stress and Coping in Time of War: Generalizations from the Israeli Experience* (New York: Brunner/Mazel, 1986), 84–90.

85. D. Wegman and L. Fine, "Occupational Health in the 1990s," *Annual Review of Public Health* 11 (1990): 89–103; J. C. Quick, "Occupational Health Psychology: Historical Roots and Future Directions," *Health Psychology* 17 (1999): 82–88.

86. D. Gebhardt and C. Crump, "Employee Fitness and Wellness Programs in the Workplace," *American Psychologist* 45 (1990): 262–272.

87. T. Wolf, H. Randall, and J. Faucett, "A Survey of Health Promotion Programs in U.S. and Canadian Medical Schools," *American Journal of Health Promotion* 3 (1988): 33–36.

88. S. Weiss, J. Fielding, and A. Baum, *Health at Work* (Hillsdale, N.J.: Erlbaum, 1990).

89. J. B. Bennett, R. F. Cook, and K. R. Pelletier, "Toward an Integrated Framework for Comprehensive Organizational Wellness: Concepts, Practices, and Research in Workplace Health Promotion," in J. C. Quick and L. E. Tetrick, eds., *Handbook of Occupational Health Psychology:* (Washington, D.C.: American Psychological Association, 2003): 69–95.

90. Finding Another Nemo," *The Economist* 370 (February 5, 2004), http://www.economist.com/people/displayStory.cfm?story_id=2404 681.

Chapter 8

1. M. White, "Does Your Intranet Have a Win–Win Strategy?" *EContent Magazine* 3 (March 2004): 41, http://www.ecmag.net/Articles/ArticleReader.aspx?ArticleID=6193&CategoryID=12.

2. D. L. Whetzel, "The Department of Labor Identifies Workplace Skills," *The Industrial/Organizational Psychologist* (July 1991): 89–90.

3. M. Macik-Frey, J. C. Quick, and J. D. Quick, "Interpersonal Communication: The Key to Unlocking Social Support for Preventive Stress Management," in C. L. Cooper, ed., *Handbook of Stress, Medicine, and Health, Revised Edition* (Boca Raton, FL: CRC Press), in press.

4. *Richness* is a term originally coined by W. D. Bodensteiner, "Information Channel Utilization under Varying Research and Development Project Conditions" (Ph.D. diss., University of Texas at Austin, 1970).

5. B. Barry and I. S. Fulmer, "The Medium and the Message: The Adaptive Use of Communication Media in Dyadic Influence," *Academy of Management Review* 29 (2004): 272–292.

6. T. Reik, *Listen with the Third Ear* (New York: Pyramid, 1972).

7. A. G. Athos and J. J. Gabarro, *Interpersonal Behavior: Communication and Understanding in Relationships* (Englewood Cliffs, N.J.: Prentice-Hall, 1978).

8. A. D. Mangelsdorff, "Lessons Learned from the Military: Implications for Management" (Distinguished Visiting Lecture, University of Texas at Arlington, 29 January 1993).

9. D. A. Morand, "Language and Power: An Empirical Analysis of Linguistic Strategies Used in Superior–Subordinate Communication," *Journal of Organizational Behavior* 21 (2000): 235–249.

10. F. Luthans, "Successful versus Effective Real Managers," *Academy of Management Executive* 2 (1988): 127–132.

11. L. E. Penley, E. R. Alexander, I. E. Jernigan, and C. I. Henwood, "Communication Abilities of Managers: The Relationship of Performance," *Journal of Management* 17 (1991): 57–76.

12. J. A. LePine and L. Van Dyne, "Voice and Cooperative Behavior as Contrasting Forms of Contextual Performance: Evidence of Differential Relationships with Big Five Personality Characteristics and Cognitive Ability," *Journal of Applied Psychology* 86 (2001): 326–336.

13. F. M. Jablin, "Superior-Subordinate Communication: The State of the Art," *Psychological Bulletin* 86 (1979): 1201–1222; W. C. Reddin, *Communication within the Organization: An Interpretive Review of Theory and Research* (New York: Industrial Communication Council, 1972).

14. B. Barry and J. M. Crant, "Dyadic Communication Relationships in Organizations: An Attribution Expectancy Approach," *Organization Science* 11 (2000): 648–665.

15. J. C. Quick, D. L. Nelson, and J. D. Quick, *Stress and Challenge at the Top: The Paradox of the Successful Executive* (Chichester, England: Wiley, 1990).

16. S. E. Moss and J. I. Sanchez, "Are Your Employees Avoiding You? Managerial Strategies for Closing the Feedback Gap," *Academy of Management Executive* 18 (2004): 32–44.

17. G. T. Kumkale and D. Albarracin, "The Sleeper Effect in Persuasion: A Meta-Analytic Review," *Psychological Bulletin* 130 (2004): 143–172.

18. A. Furhham and P. Stringfield, "Congruence in Job-Performance Ratings: A Study of 360 Degree Feedback Examining Self, Manager, Peers, and Consultant Ratings," *Human Relations* 51 (1998): 517–530.

19. J. W. Gilsdorf, "Organizational Rules on Communicating: How Employees Are—and Are Not—Learning the Ropes," *Journal of Business Communication* 35 (1998): 173–201.

20. E. A. Gerloff and J. C. Quick, "Task Role Ambiguity and Conflict in Supervision–Subordinate Relationships," *Journal of Applied Communication Research* 12 (1984): 90–102.

21. E. H. Schein, "Reassessing the 'Divine Rights' of Managers," *Sloan Management Review* 30 (1989): 63–68.

22. D. Tannen, *That's Not What I Mean! How Conversational Style Makes or Breaks Your Relations with Others* (New York: Morrow, 1986); D. Tannen, *You Just Don't Understand* (New York: Ballentine, 1990).

23. D. G. Allen and R. W. Griffeth, "A Vertical and Lateral Information Processing: The Effects of Gender, Employee Classification Level, and Media Richness on Communication and Work Outcomes," *Human Relations* 50 (1997): 1239–1260.

24. K. L. Ashcraft, "Empowering 'Professional' Relationships," *Management Communication Quarterly* 13 (2000): 347–393.

25. G. Hofstede, *Culture's Consequences: International Differences in Work-Related Values* (Beverly Hills, Calif.: Sage Publications, 1980).

26. G. Hofstede, "Motivation, Leadership, and Organization: Do American Theories Apply Abroad?" *Organizational Dynamics* 9 (1980): 42–63.

27. H. Levinson, *Executive* (Cambridge, Mass.: Harvard University Press, 1981).

28. P. Benimadhu, "Adding Value through Diversity: An Interview with Bernard F. Isautier," *Canadian Business Review* 22 (1995): 6–11.

29. M. J. Gannon and Associates, *Understanding Global Cultures: Metaphorical Journeys through 17 Countries* (Thousand Oaks, Calif.: Sage Publications, 1994).

30. T. M. Karelitz and D. V. Budescu, "You Say 'Probable' and I Say 'Likely': Improving Interpersonal Communication with Verbal Probability Phrases," *Journal of Experimental Psychology: Applied* 10 (2004): 25–41.

31. T. Wells, *Keeping Your Cool under Fire: Communicating Nondefensively* (New York: McGraw-Hill, 1980).

32. R. D. Laing, *The Politics of the Family and Other Essays* (New York: Pantheon, 1971).

33. H. S. Schwartz, *Narcissistic Process and Corporate Decay: The Theory of the Organizational Ideal* (New York: New York University Press, 1990).

34. W. R. Forrester and M. F. Maute, "The Impact of Relationship Satisfaction on Attribution, Emotions, and Behaviors Following Service Failure," *Journal of Applied Business Research* (2000): 1–45.

35. M. L. Knapp, *Nonverbal Communication in Human Interaction* (New York: Holt, Rinehart & Winston, 1978); J. McCroskey and L. Wheeless, *Introduction to Human Communication* (New York: Allyn & Bacon, 1976).

36. A. M. Katz and V. T. Katz, eds., *Foundations of Nonverbal Communication* (Carbondale, Ill.: Southern Illinois University Press, 1983).

37. M. D. Lieberman, "Intuition: A Social Cognitive Neuroscience Approach," *Psychological Bulletin* (2000): 109–138.

38. E. T. Hall, *The Hidden Dimension* (Garden City, N.Y.: Doubleday Anchor, 1966).

39. E. T. Hall, "Proxemics," in A. M. Katz and V. T. Katz, eds., *Foundations of Nonverbal Communication* (Carbondale, Ill.: Southern Illinois University Press, 1983).

40. R. T. Barker and C. G. Pearce, "The Importance of Proxemics at Work," *Supervisory Management* 35 (1990): 10–11.

41. R. L. Birdwhistell, *Kinesics and Context* (Philadelphia: University of Pennsylvania Press, 1970).

42. M. G. Frank and P. Ekman, "Appearing Truthful Generalizes Across Different Deception Situations," *Journal of Personality and Social Psychology* 86 (2004): 486–495.

43. P. Ekman and W. V. Friesen, "Research on Facial Expressions of Emotion," in A. M. Katz and V. T. Katz, eds., *Foundations of Nonverbal Communication* (Carbondale, Ill.: Southern Illinois University Press, 1983).

44. H. H. Tan, M. D. Foo, C. L. Chong, and R. Ng, "Situational and Dispositional Predictors of Displays of Positive Emotions," *Journal of Organizational Behavior* 24 (2003): 961–978.

45. C. Barnum and N. Wolniansky, "Taking Cues from Body Language," *Management Review* 78 (1989): 59.

46. Katz and Katz, *Foundations of Nonverbal Communication,* 181.

47. R. Gifford, C. F. Ng, and M. Wilkinson, "Nonverbal Cues in the Employment Interview: Links between Applicant Qualities and Interviewer Judgments," *Journal of Applied Psychology* 70 (1985): 729–736.

48. P. J. DePaulo and B. M. DePaulo, "Can Deception by Salespersons and Customers Be Detected through Nonverbal Behavioral Cues?" *Journal of Applied Social Psychology* 19 (1989): 1552–1577.

49. P. Ekman, *Telling Lies* (New York: Norton, 1985); D. Goleman, "Nonverbal Cues Are Easy to Misinterpret," *New York Times* (September 17, 1991): B5.

50. J. J. Lynch, *A Cry Unheard: New Insights into the Medical Consequences of Loneliness* (Baltimore, MD: Bancroft Press, 2000).

51. J. C. Quick, J. H. Gavin, C. L. Cooper, and J. D. Quick, "Working Together: Balancing Head and Heart," in N. G. Johnson, R. H. Rozensky, C. D. Goodheart, and R. Hammond, eds., *Psychology Builds a Healthy World*: (Washington, D.C.: American Psychological Association, 2004), 219–232.

52. J. C. Quick, C. L. Cooper, J. D. Quick, and J. H. Gavin, *The Financial Times Guide to Executive Health* (London, UK: Financial Times–Prentice Hall, 2003).

53. K. M. Wasylyshyn, "Coaching the Superkeepers," in L. A. Berger and D. R. Berger, eds., *The Talent Management Handbook: Creating Organizational Excellence by Identifying, Developing, and Positioning Your Best People*: (New York, NY: McGraw-Hill, 2003), 320–336.

54. J. C. Quick and M. Macik-Frey, "Behind the Mask: Coaching through Deep Interpersonal Communication," *Consulting Psychology Journal: Practice and Research* 56 (2004): 67–74.

55. B. Drake and K. Yuthas, "It's Only Words—Impacts of Information Technology on Moral Dialogue," *Journal of Business Ethics* 23 (2000): 41–60.

56. N. Frohlich and J. Oppenheimer, "Some Consequences of E-Mail vs. Face-to-Face Communication in Experiment," *Journal of Economic Behavior & Organization* 35 (1998): 389–403.

57. C. Brod, *Technostress: The Human Cost of the Computer Revolution* (Reading, Mass.: Addison-Wesley, 1984).

58. S. Kiesler, "Technology and the Development of Creative Environments," in Y. Ijiri and R. L. Kuhn, eds., *New Directions in Creative and Innovative Management* (Cambridge, Mass.: Ballinger Press, 1988).

59. S. Kiesler, J. Siegel, and T. W. McGuire, "Social Psychological Aspects of Computer-Mediated Communication," *American Psychologist* 39 (1984): 1123–1134.

60. L. H. Bastin, "All's Well that Starts Well," *Circuits Assembly* 15 (February 2004): 7.

Chapter 9

1. Whole Foods Market Press Release, "Declaration of Independence," (May 14, 2004), http://www.wholefoodmarket.com/company /declaration.html.

2. G. Garcia, "Measuring Performance at Northrop Grumman," *Knowledge Management Review* 3 (2001): 22–25.

3. A. M. Towsend, S. M. DeMarie, and A. R. Hendrickson, "Virtual Teams: Technology and the Workplace of the Future," *Academy of Management Executive* 12 (1998): 17–29.

4. D. M. McGregor, *The Human Side of Enterprise* (New York: McGraw-Hill, 1960).

5. J. R. Katzenbach and D. K. Smith, "The Discipline of Teams," *Harvard Business Review* 71 (1993): 111–120.

6. K. L. Bettenhausen and J. K. Murnighan, "The Development and Stability of Norms in Groups Facing Interpersonal and Structural Challenge," *Administrative Science Quarterly* 36 (1991): 20–35.

7. D. Tjosvold and Z. Yu, "Goal Interdependence and Applying Abilities for Team In-Role and Extra-Role Performance in China," *Group Dynamics: Theory, Research, and Practice* 8 (2004): 98–111.

8. V. U. Druskat and S. B. Wolff, "Building the Emotional Intelligence of Groups," *Harvard Business Review* 79 (2001): 80–90.

9. I. Summers, T. Coffelt, and R. E. Horton, "Work-Group Cohesion," *Psychological Reports* 63 (1988): 627–636.

10. D. C. Man and S. S. K. Lam, "The Effects of Job Complexity and Autonomy on Cohesiveness in Collectivistic and Individualistic Work Groups: A Cross-Cultural Analysis," *Journal of Organizational Behavior* 24 (2003): 979–1001.

11. K. H. Price, "Working Hard to Get People to Loaf," *Basic and Applied Social Psychology* 14 (1993): 329–344.

12. R. Albanese and D. D. Van Fleet, "Rational Behavior in Groups: The Free-Riding Tendency," *Academy of Management Review* 10 (1985): 244–255.

13. E. Diener, "Deindividuation, Self-Awareness, and Disinhibition," *Journal of Personality and Social Psychology* 37 (1979): 1160–1171.

14. S. Prentice-Dunn and R. W. Rogers, "Deindividuation and the Self-Regulation of Behavior," in P. Paulus, ed., *Psychology of Group Influence* (Hillsdale, N.J.: Erlbaum, 1989), 87–109.

15. B. M. Bass and E. C. Ryterband, *Organizational Psychology*, 2nd ed. (Boston: Allyn & Bacon, 1979).

16. W. G. Bennis and H. A. Shepard, "A Theory of Group Development," *Human Relations* 9 (1956): 415–438.

17. S. Caudron, "Monsanto Responds to Diversity," *Personnel Journal* (November 1990): 72–80.

18. D. L. Fields and T. C. Bloom, "Employee Satisfaction in Work Groups with Different Gender Composition," *Journal of Organizational Behavior* 18 (1997): 181–196.

19. D. C. Lau and J. K. Murnighan, "Demographic Diversity and Faultlines: The Compositional Dynamics of Organizational Groups," *Academy of Management Review* 23 (1998): 325–340.

20. B. Tuckman, "Developmental Sequence in Small Groups," *Psychological Bulletin* 63 (1965): 384–399; B. Tuckman and M. Jensen, "Stages of Small-Group Development," *Group and Organizational Studies* 2 (1977): 419–427.

21. D. Nichols, "Quality Program Sparked Company Turnaround," *Personnel* (October 1991): 24. For a commentary on Wallace's hard times and subsequent emergence from Chapter 11 bankruptcy, see R. C. Hill, "When the Going Gets Tough: A Baldrige Award Winner on the Line," *Academy of Management Executive* 7 (1993): 75–79.

22. S. Weisband and L. Atwater, "Evaluating Self and Others in Electronic and Face-to-Face Groups," *Journal of Applied Psychology* 84 (1999): 632–639.

23. C. J. G. Gersick, "Time and Transition in Work Teams: Toward a New Model of Group Development," *The Academy of Management Journal* 31 (1988): 9–41.

24. M. Hardaker and B. K. Ward, "How to Make a Team Work," *Harvard Business Review* 65 (1987): 112–120.

25. C. R. Gowen, "Managing Work Group Performance by Individual Goals and Group Goals for an Interdependent Group Task," *Journal of Organizational Behavior Management* 7 (1986): 5–27.

26. K. L. Bettenhausen and J. K. Murnighan, "The Emergence of Norms in Competitive Decision-Making Groups," *Administrative Science Quarterly* 30 (1985): 350–372; K. L. Bettenhausen, "Five Years of Groups Research: What We Have Learned and What Needs to Be Addressed," *Journal of Management* 17 (1991): 345–381.

27. J. E. McGrath, *Groups: Interaction and Performance* (Englewood Cliffs, N.J.: Prentice-Hall, 1984).

28. K. L. Gammage, A. V. Carron, and P. A. Estabrooks, "Team Cohesion and Individual Productivity," *Small Group Research* 32 (2001): 3–18.

29. S. E. Seashore, *Group Cohesiveness in the Industrial Work Group* (Ann Arbor, Mich.: University of Michigan, 1954).

30. S. M. Klein, "A Longitudinal Study of the Impact of Work Pressure on Group Cohesive Behaviors," *International Journal of Management* 12 (1996): 68–75.

31. N. Steckler and N. Fondas, "Building Team Leader Effectiveness: A Diagnostic Tool," *Organizational Dynamics* 23 (1995): 20–35.

32. G. Parker, *Team Players and Teamwork* (San Francisco: Jossey-Bass, 1990).

33. N. R. F. Maier, "Assets and Liabilities in Group Problem Solving: The Need for an Integrative Function," *Psychological Review* 74 (1967): 239–249.

34. T. A. Stewart, "The Search for the Organization of Tomorrow," *Fortune* (May 18, 1992): 92–98.

35. J. R. Goktepe and C. E. Schneier, "Role of Sex, Gender Roles, and Attraction in Predicting Emergent Leaders," *Journal of Applied Psychology* 74 (1989): 165–167.

36. W. R. Lassey, "Dimensions of Leadership," in W. R. Lassey and R. R. Fernandez, eds., *Leadership and Social Change* (La Jolla, Calif.: University Associates, 1976), 10–15.

37. J. D. Quick, G. Moorhead, J. C. Quick, E. A. Gerloff, K. L. Mattox, and C. Mullins, "Decision Making among Emergency Room Residents: Preliminary Observations and a Decision Model," *Journal of Medical Education* 58 (1983): 117–125.

38. W. J. Duncan and J. P. Feisal, "No Laughing Matter: Patterns of Humor in the Workplace," *Organizational Dynamics* 17 (1989): 18–30.

39. A. Hunter, "Best Practice Club," *Personnel Today* (April 15, 2003): 8.

40. S. S. Webber and R. J. Klimoski, "Crews: A Distinct Type of Work Team," *Journal of Business and Psychology* 18 (2004): 261–279.

41. P. F. Drucker, "There's More than One Kind of Team," *The Wall Street Journal* (February 11, 1992): A16.

42. B. L. Kirkman, C. B. Gibson, and D. L. Shapiro, "'Exporting' Teams: Enhancing the Implementation and Effectiveness of Work Teams in Global Affiliates," *Organizational Dynamics* 30 (2001): 12–29.

43. P. M. Podsakoff, M. Ahearne, and S. B. MacKenzie, "Organizational Citizenship Behavior and the Quantity and Quality of Work Group Performance," *Journal of Applied Psychology* 82 (1997): 262–270.

44. L. Hirschhorn, *Managing in the New Team Environment*, (Upper Saddle River, N.J.: Prentice-Hall), 521A.

45. G. Chen and R. J. Klimoski, "The Impact of Expectations on Newcomer Performance in Teams as Mediated by Work Characteristics, Social Exchanges, and Empowerment," *Academy of Management Journal* 46 (2003): 591–607.

46. B. Beersma, J. R. Hollenbeck, S. E. Humphrey, H. Moon, D. E. Conlon, and D. R. Ilgen, "Cooperation, Competition, and Team Performance: Toward a Contingency Approach," *Academy of Management Journal* 46 (2003): 572–590.

47. W. L. Mohr and H. Mohr, *Quality Circles: Changing Images of People at Work* (Reading, Mass.: Addison-Wesley, 1983).

48. R. W. Griffin, "A Longitudinal Assessment of the Consequences of Quality Circles in an Industrial Setting," *Academy of Management Journal* 31 (1988): 338–358.

49. P. Shaver and D. Buhrmester, "Loneliness, Sex-Role Orientation, and Group Life: A Social Needs Perspective," in P. Paulus, ed., *Basic Group Processes* (New York: Springer-Verlag, 1985), 259–288.

50. P. Chattopadhyay, M. Tluchowska, and E. George, "Identifying the Ingroup: A Closer Look at the Influence of Demographic Dissimilarity on Employee Social Identity," *Academy of Management Review* 29 (2004): 180–202.

51. E. V. Hobman, P. Bordia, and C. Gallois, "Consequences of Feeling Dissimilar from Others in a Work Team," *Journal of Business and Psychology* 17 (2003): 301–325.

52. A. E. Randel and K. S. Jaussi, "Functional Background Identity, Diversity, and Individual Performance in Cross-Functional Teams," *Academy of Management Journal* 46 (2003): 763–774.

53. J. S. Bunderson, "Team Member Functional Background and Involvement in Management Teams: Direct Effects and the Moderating Role of Power Centralization," *Academy of Management Journal* 46 (2003): 458–474.

54. G. S. Van Der Vegt, E. Van De Vliert, and A. Oosterhof, "Informational Dissimilarity and Organizational Citizenship Behavior: The Role of Intrateam Interdependence and Team Identification," *Academy of Management Journal* 46 (2003): 715–727.

55. A. Pirola-Merlo and L. Mann, "The Relationship between Individual Creativity and Team Creativity: Aggregating Across People and Time," *Journal of Organizational Behavior* 25 (2004): 235–257.

56. L. Thompson, "Improving the Creativity of Organizational Work Groups," *Academy of Management Executive* 17 (2003): 96–111.

57. C. Ford and D. M. Sullivan, "A Time for Everything: How the Timing of Novel Contributions Influences Project Team Outcomes," *Journal of Organizational Behavior* 25 (2004): 279–292.

58. B. L. Kirman and D. L. Shapiro, "The Impact of Cultural Values on Job Satisfaction and Organizational Commitment in Self-Managing Work Teams: The Mediating Role of Employee Resistance," *Academy of Management Journal* 44 (2001): 557–569.

59. K. W. Thomas and B. A. Velthouse, "Cognitive Elements of Empowerment: An 'Interpretive' Model of Intrinsic Task Motivation," *Academy of Management Review* 15 (1990): 666–681.

60. R. R. Blake, J. S. Mouton, and R. L. Allen, *Spectacular Teamwork: How to Develop the Leadership Skills for Team Success* (New York: Wiley, 1987).

61. American Management Association, *Blueprints for Service Quality: The Federal Express Approach*, AMA Management Briefing (New York: AMA, 1991).

62. W. C. Byham, *ZAPP! The Human Lightning of Empowerment* (Pittsburgh, Pa.: Developmental Dimensions, 1989).

63. F. Shipper and C. C. Manz, "Employee Self-Management without Formally Designated Teams: An Alternative Road to Empowerment," *Organizational Dynamics* (Winter 1992): 48–62.

64. P. Block, *The Empowered Manager: Positive Political Skills at Work* (San Francisco: Jossey-Bass, 1987).

65. V. J. Derlega and J. Grzelak, eds., *Cooperation and Helping Behavior: Theories and Research* (New York: Academic Press, 1982).

66. A. G. Athos and J. J. Gabarro, *Interpersonal Behavior: Communication and Understanding in Relationships* (Englewood Cliffs, N.J.: Prentice-Hall, 1978).

67. J. L. Cordery, W. S. Mueller, and L. M. Smith, "Attitudinal and Behavioral Effects of Autonomous Group Working: A Longitudinal Field Study," *Academy of Management Journal* 34 (1991): 464–476.

68. M. Workman and W. Bommer, "Redesigning Computer Call Center Work: A Longitudinal Field Experiment," *Journal of Organizational Behavior* 25 (2004): 317–337.

69. G. Moorhead, C. P. Neck, and M. S. West, "The Tendency Toward Defective Decision Making within Self-Managing Teams: The Relevance of Groupthink for the 21st Century," *Organizational Behavior & Human Decision Processes* 73 (1998): 327–351.

70. B. M. Staw and L. D. Epstein, "What Bandwagons Bring: Effects of Popular Management Techniques on Corporate Performance, Reputation, and CEO Pay," *Administrative Science Quarterly* 45 (2000): 523–556.

71. R. M. Robinson, S. L. Oswald, K. S. Swinehart, and J. Thomas, "Southwest Industries: Creating High-Performance Teams for High-Technology Production," *Planning Review* 19, published by the Planning Forum (November–December 1991): 10–47.

72. A. Lienert, "Forging a New Partnership," *Management Review* 83 (1994): 39–43.

73. S. Thiagaraian, "A Game for Cooperative Learning," *Training and Development* (May 1992): 35–41.

74. D. C. Hambrick and P. Mason, "Upper Echelons: The Organization as a Reflection of Its Top Managers," *Academy of Management Review* 9 (1984): 193–206.

75. D. C. Hambrick, "The Top Management Team: Key to Strategic Success," *California Management Review* 30 (1987): 88–108.

76. A. D. Henderson and J. W. Fredrickson, "Top Management Team Coordination Needs and the CEO Pay Gap: A Competitive Test of Economic and Behavioral Views," *Academy of Management Journal* 44 (2001): 96–117.

77. D. C. Hambrick and G. D. S. Fukutomi, "The Seasons of a CEO's Tenure," *Academy of Management Review* 16 (1991): 719–742.

78. J. C. Quick, D. L. Nelson, and J. D. Quick, "Successful Executives: How Independent?" *Academy of Management Executive* 1 (1987): 139–145.

79. I. Adizes, "Communication Strategies for Leading Teams," *Leader to Leader* (Winter 2004): 10–15.

80. L. G. Love, "The Evolving Pinnacle of the Corporation: An Explanatory Study of the Antecedents, Processes, and Consequences of Co-CEOs," 2003 (The University of Texas at Arlington).

81. N. J. Adler, *International Dimensions of Organizational Behavior* (Mason, Ohio: South-Western, 2001).

82. I. D. Steiner, *Group Process and Productivity* (New York: Academic Press, 1972).

83. U. Glunk, M. G. Heijltjes, and R. Olie, "Design Characteristics and Functioning of Top Management Teams in Europe," *European Management Journal* 19 (2001): 291–300.

84. J. W. Pfeiffer and C. Nolde, eds., *The Encyclopedia of Team-Development Activities* (San Diego: University Associates, 1991).

85. J. Boorstin, "No Preservatives. No Unions. Lots of Dough," *Fortune* 148 (September 15, 2003), http://www.fortune.com/fortune/subs/article/0,15114,480416,00.html; A. Blackman, "Putting a Ceiling on Pay: No Whole Foods Executive Can Earn Cash Pay of More Than 14 Times What Its Average Worker Makes; Will Other Companies Follow?" *The Wall Street Journal* (April 12, 2004): R11.

Chapter 10

1. Canine Companions for Independence—Exceptional Dogs for Exceptional People. Dogsatwork, http://www.Dogpark.com.
2. H. A. Simon, *The New Science of Management Decision* (New York: Harper & Row, 1960).
3. G. Huber, *Managerial Decision Making* (Glenview, Ill.: Scott, Foresman, 1980).
4. H. A. Simon, *Administrative Behavior* (New York: Macmillan, 1957).
5. E. F. Harrison, *The Managerial Decision-Making Process* (Boston: Houghton Mifflin, 1981).
6. R. L. Ackoff, "The Art and Science of Mess Management," *Interfaces* (February 1981): 20–26.
7. R. M. Cyert and J. G. March, eds., *A Behavioral Theory of the Firm* (Englewood Cliffs, N.J.: Prentice-Hall, 1963).
8. M. D. Cohen, J. G. March, and J. P. Olsen, "A Garbage Can Model of Organizational Choice," *Administrative Science Quarterly* 17 (1972): 1–25.
9. J. G. March and J. P. Olsen, "Garbage Can Models of Decision Making in Organizations," in J. G. March and R. Weissinger-Baylon, eds., *Ambiguity and Command* (Marshfield, Mass.: Pitman, 1986), 11–53.
10. D. van Knippenberg, B. van Knippenberg, and E. van Dijk, "Who Takes the Lead in Risky Decision Making? Effects of Group Members' Risk Preferences and Prototypicality," *Organizational Behavior and Human Decision Processes* 83 (2000): 213–234.
11. K. R. MacCrimmon and D. Wehrung, *Taking Risks* (New York: Free Press, 1986).
12. T. S. Perry, "How Small Firms Innovate: Designing a Culture for Creativity," *Research Technology Management* 28 (1995): 14–17.
13. B. M. Staw, "Knee-Deep in the Big Muddy: A Study of Escalating Commitment to a Chosen Course of Action," *Organizational Behavior and Human Performance* 16 (1976): 27–44; B. M. Staw, "The Escalation of Commitment to a Course of Action," *Academy of Management Review* 6 (1981): 577–587.
14. B. M. Staw and J. Ross, "Understanding Behavior in Escalation Situations," *Science* 246 (1989): 216–220.
15. T. Freemantle and M. Tolson, "Space Station Had Political Ties in Tow," *Houston Chronicle* (August 4, 2003), http://www.chron.com/cs/CDA/ssistory.mpl/space/2004947.
16. L. Festinger, *A Theory of Cognitive Dissonance* (Evanston, Ill.: Row, Peterson, 1957).
17. B. M. Staw, "The Escalation of Commitment: An Update and Appraisal," in Z. Shapira, ed., *Organizational Decision Making* (Cambridge, England: Cambridge University Press, 1997).
18. D. M. Boehne and P. W. Paese, "Deciding Whether to Complete or Terminate an Unfinished Project: A Strong Test of the Project Completion Hypothesis," *Organizational Behavior and Human Decision Processes* 81 (2000): 178–194; H. Moon, "Looking Forward and Looking Back: Integrating Completion and Sunk Cost Effects within an Escalation-of-Commitment Progress Decision," *Journal of Applied Psychology* 86 (2000): 104–113.
19. D. M. Rowell, "Concorde: An Untimely and Unnecessary Demise," (April 11, 2003), http://www.thetravelinsider.info/2003/0411.htm.
20. G. McNamara, H. Moon, and P. Bromiley, "Banking on Commitment: Intended and Unintended Consequences of an Organization's Attempt to Attenuate Escalation of Commitment," *Academy of Management Journal* 45 (2002): 443–452.
21. G. Whyte, "Diffusion of Responsibility: Effects on the Escalation Tendency," *Journal of Applied Psychology* 76 (1991): 408–415.
22. C. G. Jung, *Psychological Types* (London: Routledge & Kegan Paul, 1923).
23. W. Taggart and D. Robey, "Minds and Managers: On the Dual Nature of Human Information Processing and Management," *Academy of Management Review* 6 (1981): 187–195; D. Hellriegel and J. W. Slocum, Jr., "Managerial Problem-Solving Styles," *Business Horizons* 18 (1975): 29–37.
24. G. A. Stevens and J. Burley, "Piloting the Rocket of Radical Innovation," *Research Technology Management* 46 (2003): 16–26.
25. J. C. White, P. R. Varadarajan, and P. A. Dacin, "Market Situation Interpretation and Response: The Role of Cognitive Style, Organizational Culture, and Information Use," *Journal of Marketing* 67 (2003): 63–73.
26. I. I. Mitroff and R. H. Kilmann, "On Organization Stories: An Approach to the Design and Analysis of Organization through Myths and Stories," in R. H. Killman, L. R. Pondy, and D. P. Slevin, eds., *The Management of Organization Design* (New York: Elsevier–North Holland, 1976).
27. I. B. Myers, *Gifts Differing* (Palo Alto, Calif.: Consulting Psychologists Press, 1980).
28. A. Saleh, "Brain Hemisphericity and Academic Majors: A Correlation Study," *College Student Journal* 35 (2001): 193–200.
29. N. Khatri, "The Role of Intuition in Strategic Decision Making," *Human Relations* 53 (2000): 57–86.
30. H. Mintzberg, "Planning on the Left Side and Managing on the Right," *Harvard Business Review* 54 (1976): 51–63.
31. D. J. Isenberg, "How Senior Managers Think," *Harvard Business Review* 62 (1984): 81–90.
32. R. N. Beck, "Visions, Values, and Strategies: Changing Attitudes and Culture," *Academy of Managment Executive* 1 (1987): 33–41.
33. C. I. Barnard, *The Functions of the Executive* (Cambridge, Mass.: Harvard University Press, 1938).
34. R. Rowan, *The Intuitive Manager* (New York: Little, Brown, 1986).
35. W. H. Agor, *Intuition in Organizations* (Newbury Park, Calif.: Sage, 1989).
36. Isenberg, "How Senior Managers Think," 81–90.
37. H. A. Simon, "Making Management Decisions: The Role of Intuition and Emotion," *Academy of Management Executive* 1 (1987): 57–64.
38. J. L. Redford, R. H. McPhierson, R. G. Frankiewicz, and J. Gaa, "Intuition and Moral Development," *Journal of Psychology* 129 (1994): 91–101.
39. R. Wild, "Naked Hunch; Gut Instinct Is Vital to Your Business," *Success* (June 1998), http://www.findarticles.com/cf_dls/m3514/n6_v45/20746158/p1/article.jhtml.
40. W. H. Agor, "How Top Executives Use Their Intuition to Make Important Decisions," *Business Horizons* 29 (1986): 49–53.
41. O. Behling and N. L. Eckel, "Making Sense Out of Intuition," *Academy of Management Executive* 5 (1991): 46–54.
42. L. R. Beach, *Image Theory: Decision Making in Personal and Organizational Contexts* (Chichester, England: Wiley, 1990).
43. E. Bonabeau, "Don't Trust Your Gut," *Harvard Business Review* 81 (2003): 116–126.
44. L. Livingstone, "Person-Environment Fit on the Dimension of Creativity: Relationships with Strain, Job Satisfaction, and Performance" (Ph.D. diss., Oklahoma State University, 1992).
45. M. A. West and J. L. Farr, "Innovation at Work," in M. A. West and J. L. Farr, eds., *Innovation and Creativity at Work: Psychological and Organizational Strategies* (New York: Wiley, 1990), 3–13.
46. G. Morgan, *Riding the Waves of Change* (San Francisco: Jossey-Bass, 1988).
47. G. Wallas, *The Art of Thought* (New York: Harcourt Brace, 1926).
48. H. Benson and W. Proctor, *The Break-Out Principle* (Scribner: New York, 2003).
49. G. L. Fricchione, B. T. Slingsby, and H. Benson, "The Placebo Effect and the Relaxation Response: Neural Processes and Their Coupling to Constitutive Nitric Oxide," *Brain Research Reviews* 35 (2001): 1–19.
50. M. D. Mumford and S. B. Gustafson, "Creativity Syndrome: Integration, Application, and Innovation," *Psychological Bulletin* 103 (1988): 27–43.
51. T. Poze, "Analogical Connections—The Essence of Creativity," *Journal of Creative Behavior* 17 (1983): 240–241.
52. I. Sladeczek and G. Domino, "Creativity, Sleep, and Primary Process Thinking in Dreams," *Journal of Creative Behavior* 19 (1985): 38–46.

53. F. Barron and D. M. Harrington, "Creativity, Intelligence, and Personality," *Annual Review of Psychology* 32 (1981): 439–476.

54. R. J. Sternberg, "A Three-Faced Model of Creativity," in R. J. Sternberg, ed., *The Nature of Creativity* (Cambridge, England: Cambridge University Press, 1988), 125–147.

55. A. M. Isen, "Positive Affect and Decision Making," in W. M. Goldstein and R. M. Hogarth, eds., *Research on Judgment and Decision Making* (Cambridge, England: Cambridge University Press, 1997).

56. J. Zhou, "When the Presence of Creative Coworkers Is Related to Creativity: Role of Supervisor Close Monitoring, Developmental Feedback, and Creative Personality," *Journal of Applied Psychology* 88 (2003): 413–422.

57. C. Axtell, D. Holman, K. Unsworth, T. Wall, and P. Waterson, "Shopfloor Innovation: Facilitating the Suggestion and Implementation of Ideas," *Journal of Occupational Psychology* 73 (2000): 265–285.

58. T. M. Amabile, R. Conti, H. Coon, J. Lazenby, and M. Herron, "Assessing the Work Environment for Creativity," *Academy of Management Journal* 39 (1996): 1154–1184.

59. T. Tetenbaum and H. Tetenbaum, "Office 2000: Tear Down the Wall," *Training* (February 2000): 58–64.

60. D. M. Harrington, "Creativity, Analogical Thinking, and Muscular Metaphors," *Journal of Mental Imagery* 6 (1981): 121–126; R. M. Kanter, *The Change Masters* (New York: Simon & Schuster, 1983).

61. T. M. Amabile, B. A. Hennessey, and B. S. Grossman, "Social Influences on Creativity: The Effects of Contracted-for Reward," *Journal of Personality and Social Psychology* 50 (1986): 14–23.

62. Livingstone, "Person-Environment Fit."

63. R. L. Firestein, "Effects of Creative Problem-Solving Training on Communication Behaviors in Small Groups," *Small Group Research* (November 1989): 507–521.

64. R. Von Oech, *A Whack on the Side of the Head* (New York: Warner, 1983).

65. A. G. Robinson and S. Stern, *How Innovation and Improvement Actually Happen* (San Francisco: Berrett Koehler, 1997).

66. K. Unsworth, "Unpacking Creativity," *Academy of Management Review* 26 (2001): 289–297.

67. M. F. R. Kets de Vries, R. Branson, and P. Barnevik, "Charisma in Action: The Transformational Abilities of Virgin's Richard Branson and ABBS's Percy Barnevik," *Organizational Dynamics* 26 (1998): 7–21.

68. M. Kostera, M. Proppe, and M. Szatkowski, "Staging the New Romantic Hero in the Old Cynical Theatre: On Managers, Roles, and Change in Poland," *Journal of Organizational Behavior* 16 (1995): 631–646.

69. J. Pfeffer, "Seven Practices of Successful Organizations," *California Management Review* 40 (1998): 96–124.

70. L. A. Witt, M. C. Andrews, and K. M. Kacmar, "The Role of Participation in Decision Making in the Organizational Politics—Job Satisfaction Relationship," *Human Relations* 53 (2000): 341–358.

71. C. R. Leana, E. A. Locke, and D. M. Schweiger, "Fact and Fiction in Analyzing Research on Participative Decision Making: A Critique of Cotton, Vollrath, Froggatt, Lengnick-Hall, and Jennings," *Academy of Management Review* 15 (1990): 137–146; J. L. Cotton, D. A. Vollrath, M. L. Lengnick-Hall, and K. L. Froggatt, "Fact: The Form of Participation Does Matter—A Rebuttal to Leana, Locke, and Schweiger," *Academy of Management Review* 15 (1990): 147–153.

72. G. Hamel, "Reinvent Your Company," *Fortune* 141 (June 12, 2000): 98–118.

73. T. W. Malone, "Is Empowerment Just a Fad? Control, Decision Making, and Information Technology," *Sloan Management Review* 38 (1997): 23–35.

74. IBM Customer Success Stories, "City and County of San Francisco Lower Total Cost of Ownership and Build on Demand Foundation" (February 3, 2004), http://www-306.ibm.com/software/success/cssdb.nsf/cs/LWRT-5VTLM2?OpenDocument&Site=lotusmandc.

75. T. L. Brown, "Fearful of 'Empowerment': Should Managers Be Terrified?" *Industry Week* (June 18, 1990): 12.

76. L. Hirschhorn, "Stresses and Patterns of Adjustment in the Postindustrial Factory," in G. M. Green and F. Baker, eds., *Work, Health, and Productivity* (New York: Oxford University Press, 1991), 115–126.

77. P. G. Gyllenhammar, *People at Work* (Reading, Mass.: Addison-Wesley, 1977).

78. R. Tannenbaum and F. Massarik, "Participation by Subordinates in the Managerial Decision-Making Process," *Canadian Journal of Economics and Political Science* 16 (1950): 408–418.

79. H. Levinson, *Executive* (Cambridge, Mass.: Harvard University Press, 1981).

80. J. S. Black and H. B. Gregersen, "Participative Decision Making: An Integration of Multiple Dimensions," *Human Relations* 50 (1997): 859–878.

81. G. Stasser, L. A. Taylor, and C. Hanna, "Information Sampling in Structured and Unstructured Discussion of Three- and Six-Person Groups," *Journal of Personality and Social Psychology* 57 (1989): 67–78.

82. E. Kirchler and J. H. Davis, "The Influence of Member Status Differences and Task Type on Group Consensus and Member Position Change," *Journal of Personality and Social Psychology* 51 (1986): 83–91.

83. R. F. Maier, "Assets and Liabilities in Group Problem Solving," *Psychological Review* 74 (1967): 239–249.

84. M. E. Shaw, *Group Dynamics: The Psychology of Small Group Behavior*, 3rd ed. (New York: McGraw-Hill, 1981).

85. P. W. Yetton and P. C. Bottger, "Individual versus Group Problem Solving: An Empirical Test of a Best Member Strategy," *Organizational Behavior and Human Performance* 29 (1982): 307–321.

86. W. Watson, L. Michaelson, and W. Sharp, "Member Competence, Group Interaction, and Group Decision Making: A Longitudinal Study," *Journal of Applied Psychology* 76 (1991): 803–809.

87. I. Janis, *Victims of Groupthink* (Boston: Houghton Mifflin, 1972).

88. M. A. Hogg and S. C. Hains, "Friendship and Group Identification: A New Look at the Role of Cohesiveness in Groupthink," *European Journal of Social Psychology* 28 (1998): 323–341.

89. P. E. Jones and H. M. P. Roelofsma, "The Potential for Social Contextual and Group Biases in Team Decision Making: Biases, Conditions, and Psychological Mechanisms," *Ergonomics* 43 (2000): 1129–1152; J. M. Levine, E. T. Higgins, and H. Choi, "Development of Strategic Norms in Groups," *Organizational Behavior and Human Decision Processes* 82 (2000): 88–101.

90. A. L. Brownstein, "Biased Predecision Processing," *Psychological Bulletin* 129 (2003): 545–568.

91. C. P. Neck and G. Moorhead, "Groupthink Remodeled: The Importance of Leadership, Time Pressure, and Methodical Decision-Making Procedures," *Human Relations* 48 (1995): 537–557.

92. J. Schwartz and M. L. Ward, "Final Shuttle Report Cites 'Broken Safety Culture' at NASA," *New York Times* (August 26, 2003), http://www.nytimes.com/2003/08/26/national/26CND-SHUT.html?ex=1077253200&en=882575f2c17ed8ff&ei=5070.

93. C. Ferraris and R. Carveth, "NASA and the Columbia Disaster: Decision Making by Groupthink?" in Proceedings of the 2003 Convention of the Association for Business Communication Annual Convention, http://www.businesscommunication.org/conventions/Proceedings/2003/PDF/03ABC03.pdf.

94. G. Moorhead, R. Ference, and C. P. Neck, "Group Decision Fiascoes Continue: Space Shuttle *Challenger* and a Revised Groupthink Framework," *Human Relations* 44 (1991): 539–550.

95. J. R. Montanari and G. Moorhead, "Development of the Groupthink Assessment Inventory," *Educational and Psychological Measurement* 49 (1989): 209–219.

96. P. t'Hart, "Irving L. Janis' Victims of Groupthink," *Political Psychology* 12 (1991): 247–278.

97. J. A. F. Stoner, "Risky and Cautious Shifts in Group Decisions: The Influence of Widely Held Values," *Journal of Experimental Social Psychology* 4 (1968): 442–459.

98. S. Moscovici and M. Zavalloni, "The Group as a Polarizer of Attitudes," *Journal of Personality and Social Psychology* 12 (1969): 125–135.

99. G. R. Goethals and M. P. Zanna, "The Role of Social Comparison in Choice of Shifts," *Journal of Personality and Social Psychology* 37 (1979): 1469–1476.

100. A. Vinokur and E. Burnstein, "Effects of Partially Shared Persuasive Arguments on Group-Induced Shifts: A Problem-Solving Approach," *Journal of Personality and Social Psychology* 29 (1974): 305–315.

101. L. Armstrong, "Toyota's Scion: A Siren to Young Buyers?" *Business Week* (March 4, 2002), http://www.businessweek.com/bwdaily/dnflash/mar2002/nf2002034_8826.htm.

102. Edmunds.com, Inc., "Toyota Courts NetGen Youth with Echo Subcompact" (January 1, 1999), http://www.edmunds.com/news/autoshows/articles/44460/page020.html.

103. B. Young, "Mixing It Up: Crossover Vehicles Borrow Best of Cars, SUVs, Trucks," *Los Angeles Times*, http://www.latimes.com/extras/autoleasing/mixing.html.

104. K. Dugosh, P. Paulus, E. Roland, and H. Yang, "Cognitive Stimulation in Brainstorming," *Journal of Personality and Social Psychology* 79 (2000): 722–735.

105. B. A. Nijstad, W. Stroebe, and H. F. M. Lodewijkx, "Production Blocking and Idea Generation: Does Blocking Interfere with Cognitive Processes?" *Journal of Experimental Social Psychology* 39 (2003): 531–549.

106. W. H. Cooper, R. B. Gallupe, S. Pollard, and J. Cadsby, "Some Liberating Effects of Anonymous Electronic Brainstorming," *Small Group Research* 29 (1998): 147–178.

107. A. Van de Ven and A. Delbecq, "The Effectiveness of Nominal, Delphi and Interacting Group Decision-Making Processes," *Academy of Management Journal* 17 (1974): 605–621.

108. A. L. Delbecq, A. H. Van de Ven, and D. H. Gustafson, *Group Techniques for Program Planning: A Guide to Nominal, Group, and Delphi Processes* (Glenview, Ill.: Scott, Foresman, 1975).

109. R. A. Cosier and C. R. Schwenk, "Agreement and Thinking Alike: Ingredients for Poor Decisions," *Academy of Management Executive* 4 (1990): 69–74.

110. D. M. Schweiger, W. R. Sandburg, and J. W. Ragan, "Group Approaches for Improving Strategic Decision Making: A Comparative Analysis of Dialectical Inquiry, Devil's Advocacy, and Consensus," *Academy of Management Journal* 29 (1986): 149–159.

111. G. Whyte, "Decision Failures: Why They Occur and How to Prevent Them," *Academy of Management Executive* 5 (1991): 23–31.

112. E. E. Lawler III and S. A. Mohrman, "Quality Circles: After the Honeymoon," *Organizational Dynamics* (Spring 1987): 42–54.

113. T. L. Tang and E. A. Butler, "Attributions of Quality Circles' Problem-Solving Failure: Differences among Management, Supporting Staff, and Quality Circle Members," *Public Personnel Management* 26 (1997): 203–225.

114. S. R. Olberding, "Toyota on Competition and Quality Circles," *The Journal for Quality and Participation* 21 (1998): 52–54.

115. J. Schilder, "Work Teams Boost Productivity," *Personnel Journal* 71 (1992): 67–72.

116. L. I. Glassop, "The Organizational Benefits of Teams," *Human Relations* 55 (2002): 225–249.

117. C. J. Nemeth, "Managing Innovation: When Less Is More," *California Management Review* 40 (1997): 59–68.

118. N. Adler, *International Dimensions of Organizational Behavior*, 3rd ed. (Cincinnati, Ohio: South-Western, 1997).

119. G. K. Stephens and C. R. Greer, "Doing Business in Mexico: Understanding Cultural Differences," *Organization Dynamics* 24 (1995): 39–55.

120. C. R. Greer and G. K. Stephens, "Escalation of Commitment: A Comparison of Differences between Mexican and U. S. Decision Makers," *Journal of Management* 27 (2001): 51–78.

121. J. Khan, "It's Alive!" *Wired Magazine* 10.03 (March 2002), http://www.wired.com/wired/archive/10.03/everywhere_pr.html.

122. J. Wybo, "FMIS: A Decision Support System for Forest Fire Prevention and Fighting," *IEEE Transactions on Engineering Management* 45 (1998): 127–131.

123. M. S. Poole, M. Holmes, and G. DeSanctis, "Conflict Management in a Computer-Supported Meeting Environment," *Management Science* 37 (1991): 926–953.

124. S. S. K. Lam and J. Schaubroeck, "Improving Group Decisions by Better Pooling Information: A Comparative Advantage of Groups Decision Support Systems," *Journal of Applied Psychology* 85 (2000): 565–573.

125. O. Thomas, "At Shell, Everyone's the Answer Man," *Business 2.0* (February 2004): 55, http://www.business2.com/b2/web/articles/0,17863,582181,00.html.

126. P. Kaihla, "The Matchmaker in the Machine," *Business 2.0* (February 2004): 52, http://www.business2.com/b2/web/articles/0,17863,582487,00.html.

127. A. T. McCartt and J. Rohrbaugh, "Managerial Openness to Change and the Introduction of GDSS: Explaining Initial Success and Failure in Decision Conferencing," *Organization Science* 6 (1995): 569–584.

128. P. L. McLeod, R. S. Baron, M. W. Marti, and K. Yoon, "The Eyes Have It: Minority Influence in Face-to-Face and Computer-Mediated Group Discussion," *Journal of Applied Psychology* 82 (1997): 706–718.

129. A. M. Townsend, S. M. DeMarie, and A. R. Hendrickson, "Virtual Teams: Technology and the Workplace of the Future," *Academy of Management Executive* 12 (1998): 17–29.

130. L. M. Jessup and J. F. George, "Theoretical and Methodological Issues in Group Support Systems," *Small Group Research* 28 (1997): 394–413.

131. K. Blanchard and N. V. Peale, *The Power of Ethical Management* (New York: Fawcett Crest, 1988).

132. C. Schneider, "War Dance: Will SEC Go Light on DOD Contractors?" *CFO Magazine* April 7, 2003, http://www.cfo.com/article/1,5309,9121,00.html?f=related.

133. M. McGraw, "Another Whistleblower Down the Tubes," *Bulletin of the Atomic Scientists* 46 (June 1990), http://www.thebulletin.org/issues/1990/j90/j90mcgraw.html.

134. Personal conversation with Laura Phillips, Feb. 2004, "The matching process at CCI."

Chapter 11

1. G. Baum, "Cisco's CEO: John Chambers," *Forbes* (February 23, 1998): 52, http://www.forbes.com/asap/1998/0223/052.html.

2. J. P. Donlon, "Why John Chambers Is The CEO of the FUTURE," *Chief Executive* (June 2000), http://www.chiefexecutive.net/mag/157/cover1a.htm.

3. P. Burrows, "Cisco's Comeback," *Business Week* (November 24, 2003): 116, http://www.businessweek.com/magazine/content/03_47/b3859008.htm.

4. O. Malik, "The New Phone Company," *Business 2.0* (November 2003), http://www.business2.com/b2/web/articles/0,17863,541290,00.html.

5. G. C. Homans, "Social Behavior as Exchange," *American Journal of Sociology* 63 (1958): 597–606.

6. R. D. Middlemist and M. A. Hitt, *Organizational Behavior: Managerial Strategies for Performance* (St. Paul, Minn.: West Publishing, 1988).

7. C. Barnard, *The Functions of the Executive* (Cambridge, Mass.: Harvard University Press, 1938).

8. J. R. P. French and B. Raven, "The Bases of Social Power," in D. Cartwright, ed., *Group Dynamics: Research and Theory* (Evanston, Ill.: Row, Peterson, 1962); T. R. Hinkin and C. A. Schriesheim, "Development and Application of New Scales to Measure the French and Raven (1959) Bases of Social Power," *Journal of Applied Psychology* 74 (1989): 561–567.

9. K. D. Elsbach and G. Elofson, "How the Packaging of Decision Explanations Affects Perceptions of Trustworthiness," *Academy of Management Journal* 43, No. 1 (2000): 80–89.

10. P. M. Podsakoff and C. A. Schriesheim, "Field Studies of French and Raven's Bases of Power: Critique, Reanalysis, and Suggestions for Future Research," *Psychological Bulletin* 97 (1985): 387–411.

11. M. A. Rahim, "Relationships of Leader Power to Compliance and Satisfaction with Supervision: Evidence from a National Sample of Managers," *Journal of Management* 15 (1989): 545–556.

12. C. Argyris, "Management Information Systems: The Challenge to Rationality and Emotionality," *Management Science* 17 (1971): 275–292; J. Naisbitt and P. Aburdene, *Megatrends 2000* (New York: Morrow, 1990).

13. P. P. Carson, K. D. Carson, E. L. Knight, and C. W. Roe, "Power in Organizations: A Look through the TQM Lens," *Quality Progress* (November 1995): 73–78.

14. M. Velasquez, D. J. Moberg, and G. F. Cavanaugh, "Organizational Statesmanship and Dirty Politics: Ethical Guidelines for the Organizational Politician," *Organizational Dynamics* 11 (1982): 65–79.

15. D. E. McClelland, *Power: The Inner Experience* (New York: Irvington, 1975).

16. S. Finkelstein, *Why Smart Executives Fail: And What You Can Learn from Their Mistakes* (New York: Portfolio, 2003).

17. N. Machiavelli, *The Prince*, trans. by G. Bull (Middlesex, England: Penguin Books, 1961).

18. S. Chen, A. Y. Lee-Chai, and J. A. Bargh, "Relationship Orientation as a Moderator of the Effects of Social Power," *Journal of Personality and Social Psychology* 80, No. 2 (2001): 173–187.

19. J. Pfeffer and G. Salancik, *The External Control of Organizations* (New York: Harper & Row, 1978).

20. T. M. Welbourne and C. O. Trevor, "The Roles of Departmental and Position Power in Job Evaluation," *Academy of Management Journal* 43, No. 4 (2000): 761–771.

21. R. H. Miles, *Macro Organizational Behavior* (Glenview, Ill.: Scott, Foresman, 1980).

22. D. Hickson, C. Hinings, C. Lee, R. E. Schneck, and J. M. Pennings, "A Strategic Contingencies Theory of Intraorganizational Power," *Administrative Science Quarterly* 14 (1971): 219–220.

23. C. R. Hinings, D. J. Hickson, J. M. Pennings, and R. E. Schneck, "Structural Conditions of Intraorganizational Power," *Administrative Science Quarterly* 19 (1974): 22–44.

24. A. Etzioni, *Modern Organizations* (Upper Saddle River, N.J.: Prentice-Hall, 1964).

25. R. Kanter, "Power Failure in Management Circuits," *Harvard Business Review* (July–August 1979): 31–54.

26. F. Lee and L. Z. Tiedens, "Who's Being Served? 'Self-Serving' Attributions in Social Hierarchies," *Organizational Behavior and Human Decision Processes* 84, No. 2 (March 2001): 254–287.

27. M. Korda, *Power: How to Get It, How to Use It* (New York: Random House, 1975).

28. S. R. Thye, "A Status Value Theory of Power in Exchange Relations," *American Sociological Review* (2000): 407–432.

29. B. T. Mayes and R. T. Allen, "Toward a Definition of Organizational Politics," *Academy of Management Review* 2 (1977): 672–678.

30. M. Valle and P. L. Perrewe, "Do Politics Perceptions Relate to Political Behaviors? Tests of an Implicit Assumption and Expanded Model," *Human Relations* 53 (2000): 359–386.

31. W. A. Hochwarter, "The Interactive Effects of Pro-Political Behavior and Politics Perceptions on Job Satisfaction and Affective Commitment," *Journal of Applied Social Psychology* 33 (2003): 1360–1378.

32. W. A. Hochwarter, K. M. Kacmar, D. C. Treadway, and T. S. Watson, "It's All Relative: The Distinction and Prediction of Political Perceptions Across Levels," *Journal of Applied Social Psychology* 33 (2003): 1955–2016.

33. D. A. Ralston, "Employee Ingratiation: The Role of Management," *Academy of Management Review* 10 (1985): 477–487; D. R. Beeman and T. W. Sharkey, "The Use and Abuse of Corporate Politics," *Business Horizons* (March–April 1987): 25–35.

34. C. O. Longnecker, H. P. Sims, and D. A. Gioia, "Behind the Mask: The Politics of Employee Appraisal," *Academy of Management Executive* 1 (1987): 183–193.

35. M. Valle and P. L. Perrewe, "Do Politics Perceptions Relate to Political Behaviors? Tests of an Implicit Assumption and Expanded Model," *Human Relations* 53, No. 3 (2000): 359–386.

36. D. Butcher and M. Clarke, "Organizational Politics: The Cornerstone for Organizational Democracy," *Organizational Dynamics* 31 (2002): 35–46.

37. D. Kipnis, S. M. Schmidt, and I. Wilkinson, "Intraorganizational Influence Tactics: Explorations in Getting One's Way," *Journal of Applied Psychology* 65 (1980): 440–452; D. Kipnis, S. Schmidt, C. Swaffin-Smith, and I. Wilkinson, "Patterns of Managerial Influence: Shotgun Managers, Tacticians, and Bystanders," *Organizational Dynamics* (Winter 1984): 60–67; G. Yukl and C. M. Falbe, "Influence Tactics and Objectives in Upward, Downward, and Lateral Influence Attempts," *Journal of Applied Psychology* 75 (1990): 132–140.

38. G. R. Ferris and T. A. Judge, "Personnel/Human Resources Management: A Political Influence Perspective," *Journal of Management* 17 (1991): 447–488.

39. G. Yukl, P. J. Guinan, and D. Sottolano, "Influence Tactics Used for Different Objectives with Subordinates, Peers, and Superiors," *Groups & Organization Management* 20 (1995): 272–296.

40. C. A. Higgins, T. A. Judge, and G. R. Ferris, "Influence Tactics and Work Outcomes: A Meta-Analysis," *Journal of Organizational Behavior* 24 (2003): 89–106.

41. K. K. Eastman, "In the Eyes of the Beholder: An Attributional Approach to Ingratiation and Organizational Citizenship Behavior," *Academy of Management Journal* 37 (1994): 1379–1391.

42. R. A. Gordon, "Impact of Ingratiation on Judgments and Evaluations: A Meta-Analytic Investigation," *Journal of Personality and Social Psychology* 71 (1996): 54–70.

43. A. Drory and D. Beaty, "Gender Differences in the Perception of Organizational Influence Tactics," *Journal of Organizational Behavior* 12 (1991): 249–258.

44. S. Wellington, M. B. Kropf, and P. R. Gerkovich, "What's Holding Women Back?" *Harvard Business Review* (June 2003): 2–4.

45. P. Perrewe and D. Nelson, "Gender and Career Success: The Facilitative Role of Political Skill," *Organizational Dynamics*, in press.

46. R. Y. Hirokawa and A. Miyahara, "A Comparison of Influence Strategies Utilized by Managers in American and Japanese Organizations," *Communication Quarterly* 34 (1986): 250–265.

47. P. David, M. A. Hitt, and J. Gimeno, "The Influence of Activism by Institutional Investors on R&D," *Academy of Management Journal* 44, No. 1 (2001): 144–157.

48. K. Kumar and M. S. Thibodeaux, "Organizational Politics and Planned Organizational Change," *Group and Organization Studies* 15 (1990): 354–365.

49. McClelland, *Power*.

50. Beeman and Sharkey, "Use and Abuse of Corporate Politics," 37.

51. C. P. Parker, R. L. Dipboye, and S. L. Jackson, "Perceptions of Organizational Politics: An Investigation of Antecedents and Consequences," *Journal of Management* 21 (1995): 891–912.

52. S. J. Ashford, N. P. Rothbard, S. K. Piderit, and J. E. Dutton, "Out on a Limb: The Role of Context and Impression Management in Selling Gender-Equity Issues," *Administrative Science Quarterly* 43 (1998): 23–57.

53. J. Zhou and G. R. Ferris, "The Dimensions and Consequences of Organizational Politics Perceptions: A Confirmatory Analysis," *Journal of Applied Social Psychology* 25 (1995): 1747–1764.

54. M. L. Seidal, J. T. Polzer, and K. J. Stewart, "Friends in High Places: The Effects of Social Networks on Discrimination in Salary Negotiations," *Administrative Science Quarterly* 45 (2000): 1–24.

55. J. J. Gabarro and J. P. Kotter, "Managing Your Boss," *Harvard Business Review* (January–February 1980): 92–100.

56. P. Newman, "How to Manage Your Boss," Peat, Marwick, Mitchell & Company's *Management Focus* (May–June 1980): 36–37.

57. F. Bertolome, "When You Think the Boss Is Wrong," *Personnel Journal* 69 (1990): 66–73.

58. J. Conger and R. Kanungo, *Charismatic Leadership: The Elusive Factor in Organizational Effectiveness* (New York: Jossey-Bass, 1988).

59. G. M. Spreitzer, M. A. Kizilos, and S. W. Nason, "A Dimensional Analysis of the Relationship between Psychological Empowerment and Effectiveness, Satisfaction, and Strain," *Journal of Management* 23 (1997): 679–704.

60. R. C. Ford and M. D. Fottler, "Empowerment: A Matter of Degree," *Academy of Management Executive* 9 (1995): 21–31.

61. N. Furuichi, "Empowered Painters," *The Phoenix* (March 16, 2000), http://www.sccs.swarthmore.edu/org/phoenix/2000/2000-03-16/indepth/emppainters.html.

62. Corporation for National and Community Service, "Eli Segal Entrepreneurship Award: Americorps Alum Honored," *National Service News* 160 (June 10, 2002), http://www.nationalservice.org/news/nsn/160.html.

63. B. Karch, "Zipper '00 Awarded Truman Scholarship," *The Phoenix* (April 1, 1999), http://www.sccs.swarthmore.edu/org/phoenix/1999/1999-04-01/news/truman.html.

64. OMG Center for Collaborative Learning, "The Pew Fund for Health and Human Services in Philadelphia: 2003–2004 Grants to Agencies Serving Vulnerable Adults," http://www.omgcenter.org/pew/granteelist2003.html.

65. S. Finkelstein, *Why Smart Executives Fail: And What You Can Learn from Their Mistakes* (New York: Portfolio, 2003).

66. J. P. Kotter, "Power, Dependence, and Effective Management," *Harvard Business Review* 55 (1977): 125–136; J. P. Kotter, *Power and Influence* (New York: Free Press, 1985).

1. M. Broad, "The Greatest Briton in Management and Leadership," *Personnel Today* (February 18, 2003): 20–21.

2. J. P. Kotter, "What Leaders Really Do," *Harvard Business Review* 68 (1990): 103–111.

3. E. Florian, "2004 America's Most Admired Companies: Fred Smith of FedEx," *Fortune* (March 8, 2004): 88a, http://www.fortune.com/fortune/subs/article/0,15114,592448,00.html.

4. A. Zaleznik, "HBR Classic—Managers and Leaders: Are They Different?" *Harvard Business Review* 70 (1992): 126–135.

5. W. G. Rowe, "Creating Wealth in Organizations: The Role of Strategic Leadership," *Academy of Management Executive* 15 (2001): 81–94.

6. R. M. Stogdill, "Personal Factors Associated with Leadership: A Survey of the Literature," *Journal of Psychology* 25 (1948): 35–71.

7. K. Lewin, R. Lippitt, and R. K. White, "Patterns of Aggressive Behavior in Experimentally Created 'Social Climates,'" *Journal of Social Psychology* 10 (1939): 271–299.

8. R. M. Stogdill and A. E. Coons, eds., *Leader Behavior: Its Description and Measurement*, research monograph no. 88 (Columbus, Ohio: Bureau of Business Research, The Ohio State University, 1957).

9. A. W. Halpin and J. Winer, "A Factorial Study of the Leader Behavior Description Questionnaire," in R. M. Stogdill and A. E. Coons, eds., *Leader Behavior: Its Description and Measurement*, research monograph no. 88 (Columbus, Ohio: Bureau of Business Research, The Ohio State University, 1957), 39–51.

10. E. A. Fleishman, "Leadership Climate, Human Relations Training, and Supervisory Behavior," *Personnel Psychology* 6 (1953): 205–222.

11. R. Kahn and D. Katz, "Leadership Practices in Relation to Productivity and Morale," in D. Cartwright and A. Zander, eds., *Group Dynamics, Research and Theory* (Elmsford, NY: Row, Paterson, 1960).

12. R. R. Blake and J. S. Mouton, *The Managerial Grid III: The Key to Leadership Excellence* (Houston: Gulf, 1985).

13. W. Vandekerckhove and R. Commers, "Downward Workplace Mobbing: A Sign of the Times?" *Journal of Business Ethics* 45 (2003): 41–50.

14. F. E. Fiedler, *A Theory of Leader Effectiveness* (New York: McGraw-Hill, 1964).

15. F. E. Fiedler, *Personality, Motivational Systems, and Behavior of High and Low LPC Persons*, tech. rep. no. 70-12 (Seattle: University of Washington, 1970).

16. J. T. McMahon, "The Contingency Theory: Logic and Method Revisited," *Personnel Psychology* 25 (1972): 697–710; L. H. Peters, D. D. Hartke, and J. T. Pohlman, "Fiedler's Contingency Theory of Leadership: An Application of the Meta-Analysis Procedures of Schmidt and Hunter," *Psychological Bulletin* 97 (1985): 224–285.

17. F. E. Fiedler, "The Contingency Model and the Dynamics of the Leadership Process," in L. Berkowitz, ed., *Advances in Experimental and Social Psychology*, vol. 11 (New York: Academic Press, 1978).

18. S. Arin and C. McDermott, "The Effect of Team Leader Characteristics on Learning, Knowledge Application, and Performance of Cross-Functional New Product Development Teams," *Decision Sciences* 34 (2003): 707–739.

19. F. E. Fiedler, "Engineering the Job to Fit the Manager," *Harvard Business Review* 43 (1965): 115–122.

20. R. J. House, "A Path–Goal Theory of Leader Effectiveness," *Administrative Science Quarterly* 16 (1971): 321–338; R. J. House and T. R. Mitchell, "Path–Goal Theory of Leadership," *Journal of Contemporary Business* 3 (1974): 81–97.

21. C. A. Schriescheim and V. M. Von Glinow, "The Path–Goal Theory of Leadership: A Theoretical and Empirical Analysis," *Academy of Management Journal* 20 (1977): 398–405; E. Valenzi and G. Dessler, "Relationships of Leader Behavior, Subordinate Role Ambiguity, and Subordinate Job Satisfaction," *Academy of Management Journal* 21 (1978): 671–678; N. R. F. Maier, *Leadership Methods and Skills* (New York: McGraw-Hill, 1963).

22. J. P. Grinnell, "An Empirical Investigation of CEO Leadership in Two Types of Small Firms," *S.A.M. Advanced Management Journal* 68 (2003): 36–41.

23. V. H. Vroom and P. W. Yetton, *Leadership and Decision Making* (Pittsburgh: University of Pittsburgh, 1973).

24. V. H. Vroom, "Leadership and the Decision-Making Process," *Organizational Dynamics* 28 (2000): 82–94.

25. W. J. Duncan, K. G. LaFrance, and P. M. Ginter, "Leadership and Decision Making: A Retrospective Application and Assessment," *Journal of Leadership & Organizational Studies* 9 (2003): 1–20.

26. P. Hersey and K. H. Blanchard, "Life Cycle Theory of Leadership," *Training and Development* 23 (1969): 26–34; P. Hersey, K. H. Blanchard, and D. E. Johnson, *Management of Organizational Behavior: Leading Human Resources*, 8th ed. (Upper Saddle River, N.J.: Prentice-Hall, 2001).

27. B. M. Bass, *Bass and Stogdill's Handbook of Leadership: Theory, Research, and Managerial Applications*, 3rd ed. (New York: Free Press, 1990).

28. G. B. Graen and M. Uhl-Bien, "Relationship-Based Approach to Leadership: Development of Leader–Member Exchange (LMX) Theory of Leadership over 25 Years," *Leadership Quarterly* 6 (1995): 219–247; C. R. Gerstner and D. V. Day, "Meta-Analytic Review of Leader–Member Exchange Theory: Correlates and Construct Issues," *Journal of Applied Psychology* 82 (1997): 827–844; R. C. Liden, S. J. Wayne, and R. T. Sparrowe, "An Examination of the Mediating Role of Psychological Empowerment on the Relations between the Job, Interpersonal Relationships, and Work Outcomes," *Journal of Applied Psychology* 85 (2001): 407–416.

29. J. Townsend, J. S. Phillips, and T. J. Elkins, "Employee Retaliation: The Neglected Consequence of Poor Leader–Member Exchange Relations," *Journal of Occupational Health Psychology* 5 (2000): 457–463.

30. D. Nelson, R. Basu, and R. Purdie, "An Examination of Exchange Quality and Work Stressors in Leader–Follower Dyads," *International Journal of Stress Management* 5 (1998): 103–112.

31. K. M. Kacmar, L. A. Witt, S. Zivnuska, and S. M. Gully, "The Interactive Effect of Leader–Member Exchange and Communication Frequency on Performance Ratings," *Journal of Applied Psychology* 88 (2003): 764–772.

32. A. G. Tekleab and M. S. Taylor, "Aren't There Two Parties in an Employment Relationship? Antecedents and Consequences of Organization–Employee Agreement on Contract Obligations and Violations," *Journal of Organizational Behavior* 24 (2003): 585–608.

33. D. A. Hoffman, S. J. Gerras, and F. P. Morgeson, "Climate as a Moderator of the Relationship Between Leader–Member Exchange and Content Specific Citizenship: Safety Climate as an Exemplar," *Journal of Applied Psychology* 88 (2003): 170–178.

34. S. Kerr and J. M. Jermier, "Substitutes for Leadership: Their Meaning and Measurement," *Organizational Behavior and Human Performance* 22 (1978): 375–403.

35. P. M. Podsakoff, S. B. MacKenzie, and W. H. Bommer, "Meta-Analysis of the Relationships between Kerr and Jermier's Substitutes for Leadership and Employee Job Attitudes, Role Perceptions, and Performance," *Journal of Applied Psychology* 81 (1996): 380–399.

36. B. C. Skaggs and M. Youndt, "Strategic Positioning, Human Capital, and Performance in Service Organizations: A Customer Interaction Approach," *Strategic Management Journal* 25 (2004): 85–99.

37. J. M. Burns, *Leadership* (New York: Harper & Row, 1978); T. O. Jacobs, *Leadership and Exchange in Formal Organizations* (Alexandria, Va.: Human Resources Research Organization, 1971).

38. B. M. Bass, "From Transactional to Transformational Leadership: Learning to Share the Vision," *Organizational Dynamics* 19 (1990): 19–31; B. M. Bass, *Leadership and Performance beyond Expectations* (New York: Free Press, 1985).

39. W. Bennis, "Managing the Dream: Leadership in the 21st Century," *Training* 27 (1990): 43–48.

40. P. M. Podsakoff, S. B. MacKenzie, R. H. Moorman, and R. Fetter, "Transformational Leader Behaviors and Their Effects on Followers' Trust in Leader, Satisfaction, and Organizational Citizenship Behaviors," *Leadership Quarterly* 1 (1990): 107–142.

41. MyPrimeTime, Inc., "Great Entrepreneurs—Biography: Howard Schultz, Starbucks," http://www.myprimetime.com/work/ge/schultzbio/index.shtml.

42. C. P. Egri and S. Herman, "Leadership in the North American Environmental Sector: Values, Leadership Styles, and Contexts of En-

vironmental Leaders and Their Organizations," *Academy of Management Journal* 43 (2000): 571–604.

43. T. A. Judge and J. E. Bono, "Five-Factor Model of Personality and Transformational Leadership," *Journal of Applied Psychology* 85 (2001): 751–765.

44. J. E. Bono and T. A. Judge, "Self-Concordance at Work: Toward Understanding the Motivational Effects of Transformational Leaders," *Academy of Management Journal* 46 (2003): 554–571.

45. T. Dvir, D. Eden, B. J. Avolio, and B. Shamir, "Impact of Transformational Leadership on Follower Development and Performance: A Field Experiment," *Academy of Management Journal* 45 (2002): 735–744.

46. The Jargon Dictionary, "The **R** Terms: Reality-Distortion Field," http://info.astrian.net/jargon/terms/r/reality-distortion_field.html.

47. R. J. House and M. L. Baetz, "Leadership: Some Empirical Generalizations and New Research Directions," in B. M. Staw, ed., *Research in Organizational Behavior*, vol. 1 (Greenwood, Conn.: JAI Press, 1979), 399–401.

48. J. A. Conger and R. N. Kanungo, "Toward a Behavioral Theory of Charismatic Leadership in Organizational Settings," *Academy of Management Review* 12 (1987): 637–647.

49. A. R. Willner, *The Spellbinders: Charismatic Political Leadership* (New Haven, Conn.: Yale University Press, 1984).

50. D. Waldman, G. G. Ramirez, R. J. House, and P. Puranam, "Does Leadership Matter? CEO Leadership Attributes and Profitability under Conditions of Perceived Environmental Uncertainty," *Academy of Management Journal* 44 (2001): 134–143.

51. J. M. Howell, "Two Faces of Charisma: Socialized and Personalized Leadership in Organizations," in J. A. Conger, ed., *Charismatic Leadership: Behind the Mystique of Exceptional Leadership* (San Francisco: Jossey-Bass, 1988).

52. M. Maccoby, "Narcissistic Leaders: The Incredible Pros, the Inevitable Cons," *Harvard Business Review* 78 (2000): 68–77.

53. D. Sankowsky, "The Charismatic Leader as Narcissist: Understanding the Abuse of Power," *Organizational Dynamics* 23 (1995): 57–71.

54. F. J. Flynn and B. M. Staw, "Lend Me Your Wallets: The Effect of Charismatic Leadership on External Support for an Organization," *Strategic Management Journal* 25 (2004): 309–330.

55. D. Goleman, "What Makes a Leader?" *Harvard Business Review* 82 (2004): 82–91.

56. D. Goleman, "Never Stop Learning," *Harvard Business Review* 82 (2004): 28–30.

57. C. L. Gohm, "Mood Regulation and Emotional Intelligence: Individual Differences," *Journal of Personality and Social Psychology* 84 (2003): 594–607.

58. J. Useem, "A Manager for All Seasons," *Fortune* (April 30, 2001): 66–72.

59. R. C. Mayer, J. H. Davis, and F. D. Schoorman, "An Integrative Model of Organizational Trust," *Academy of Management Review* 20 (1995): 709–734.

60. R. S. Dooley and G. E. Fryxell, "Attaining Decision Quality and Commitment from Dissent: The Moderating Effects of Loyalty and Competence in Strategic Decision-Making Teams," *Academy of Management Journal* 42 (1999): 389–402.

61. A. Malhotra, A. Majchrzak, R. Carman, and V. Lott, "Radical Innovation without Collocation: A Case Study at Boeing-Rocketdyne," *MIS Quarterly* 25 (2001): 229–249.

62. P. Dixon, "Virtual Teams—Global Leadership," *Financial Times* 17 (February 2003), http://www.globalchange.com/vteams.htm.

63. S. W. Lester and H. H. Brower, "In the Eyes of the Beholder: The Relationship between Subordinates' Felt Trustworthiness and Their Work Attitudes and Behaviors," *Journal of Leadership & Organizational Studies* 10 (2003): 17–33.

64. Saj-nicole A. Joni, "The Geography of Trust," *Harvard Business Review* 82 (2003): 82–88.

65. M. E. Heilman, C. J. Block, R. F. Martell, and M. C. Simon, "Has Anything Changed? Current Characteristics of Men, Women, and Managers," *Journal of Applied Psychology* 74 (1989): 935–942.

66. A. H. Eagly, S. J. Darau, and M. Makhijani, "Gender and the Effectiveness of Leaders: A Meta-Analysis," *Psychological Bulletin* 117 (1995): 125–145.

67. R. K. Greenleaf, L. C. Spears, and D. T. Frick, eds., *On Becoming a Servant-Leader* (San Francisco: Jossey-Bass, 1996).

68. E. P. Hollander and L. R. Offerman, "Power and Leadership in Organizations: Relationships in Transition," *American Psychologist* 45 (1990): 179–189.

69. H. P. Sims, Jr., and C. C. Manz, *Company of Heros: Unleashing the Power of Self-Leadership* (New York: John Wiley & Sons, 1996).

70. C. C. Manz and H. P. Sims, "Leading Workers to Lead Themselves: The External Leadership of Self-Managing Work Teams," *Administrative Science Quarterly* 32 (1987): 106–128.

71. L. Hirschhorn, "Leaders and Followers in a Postindustrial Age: A Psychodynamic View," *Journal of Applied Behavioral Science* 26 (1990): 529–542.

72. R. E. Kelley, "In Praise of Followers," *Harvard Business Review* 66 (1988): 142–148.

73. C. C. Manz and H. P. Sims, "SuperLeadership: Beyond the Myth of Heroic Leadership," *Organizational Dynamics* 20 (1991): 18–35.

74. W. J. Crockett, "Dynamic Subordinancy," *Training and Development Journal* (May 1981): 155–164.

75. N. J. Adler, *International Dimensions in Organizational Behavior* (Boston: PWS-Kent, 1991).

76. F. C. Brodback *et al.*, "Cultural Variation of Leadership Prototypes across 22 European Countries," *Journal of Occupational and Organizational Psychology* 73 (2000): 1–29.

77. B. Alimo-Metcalfe and R. J. Alban-Metcalfe, "The Development of a New Transformational Leadership Questionnaire," *Journal of Occupational and Organizational Psychology* 74 (2001): 1–27.

78. T. Lenartowicz and J. P. Johnson, "A Cross-National Assessment of the Values of Latin American Managers: Contrasting Hues or Shades of Gray?" *Journal of International Business Studies* 34 (2003): 266–281.

79. Y. Hui-Chun and P. Miller, "The Generation Gap and Cultural Influence: A Taiwan Empirical Investigation," *Cross Cultural Management* 10 (2003): 23–42.

80. G. A. Yukl, *Leadership in Organizations*, 2nd ed. (Upper Saddle River, N.J.: Prentice-Hall, 1989).

81. Harvard Business School, "James E. Burke," *Working Knowledge* (October 27, 2003), http://hbswk.hbs.edu/pubitem.jhtml?id=3755&t =leadership.

82. B. Morris and P. Neering, "Sir Richard's Rules," *Fortune* 148 (October 6, 2003): 50+, http://www.fortune.com/fortune/subs/article /0,15114,488601,00.html.

Chapter 13

1. R. Levering and M. Moscovitz, "100 Best Companies to Work For," *Fortune* (January 12, 2004): 56–58.

2. Definition adapted from D. Hellriegel, J. W. Slocum, Jr., and R. W. Woodman, *Organizational Behavior* (St. Paul: West, 1992) and from R. D. Middlemist and M. A. Hitt, *Organizational Behavior* (St. Paul: West, 1988).

3. D. Tjosvold, *The Conflict-Positive Organization* (Reading, Mass.: Addison-Wesley, 1991).

4. K. Thomas and W. Schmidt, "A Survey of Managerial Interests with Respect to Conflict," *Academy of Management Journal* 19 (1976): 315–318; G. L. Lippitt, "Managing Conflict in Today's Organizations," *Training and Development Journal* 36 (1982): 66–74.

5. M. Rajim, "A Measure of Styles of Handling Interpersonal Conflict," *Academy of Management Journal* 26 (1983): 368–376.

6. D. Goleman, *Emotional Intelligence* (New York: Bantam Books, 1995); J. Stuller, "Unconventional Smarts," *Across the Board* 35 (1998): 22–23.

7. Tjosvold, *The Conflict-Positive Organization*, 4.

8. R. A. Cosier and D. R. Dalton, "Positive Effects of Conflict: A Field Experiment," *International Journal of Conflict Management* 1 (1990): 81–92.

9. D. Tjosvold, "Making Conflict Productive," *Personnel Administrator* 29 (1984): 121–130.

10. A. C. Amason, W. A. Hochwarter, K. R. Thompson, and A. W. Harrison, "Conflict: An Important Dimension in Successful Management Teams," *Organizational Dynamics* 24 (1995): 25–35.

11. T. L. Simons and R. S. Peterson, "Task Conflict and Relationship Conflict in Top Management Teams: The Pivotal Role of Intergroup Trust," *Journal of Applied Psychology* 85 (2000): 102–111.

12. R. Nibler and K. L. Harris, "The Effects of Culture and Cohesiveness on Intragroup Conflict and Effectiveness," *The Journal of Social Psychology* 143 (2003): 613–631.

13. I. Janis, *Groupthink*, 2nd ed. (Boston: Houghton Mifflin, 1982).

14. J. D. Thompson, *Organizations in Action* (New York: McGraw-Hill, 1967).

15. G. Walker and L. Poppo, "Profit Centers, Single-Source Suppliers, and Transaction Costs," *Administrative Science Quarterly* 36 (1991): 66–87.

16. R. Miles, *Macro Organizational Behavior* (Glenview, Ill.: Scott, Foresman, 1980).

17. H. Levinson, "The Abrasive Personality," *Harvard Business Review* 56 (1978): 86–94.

18. J. C. Quick and J. D. Quick, *Organizational Stress and Preventive Management* (New York: McGraw-Hill, 1984).

19. F. N. Brady, "Aesthetic Components of Management Ethics," *Academy of Management Review* 11 (1986): 337–344.

20. J. R. Ogilvie and M. L. Carsky, "Building Emotional Intelligence in Negotiations," *The International Journal of Conflict Management* 13 (2002): 381–400.

21. A. M. Bodtker and R. L. Oliver, "Emotion in Conflict Formation and Its Transformation: Application to Organizational Conflict Management," *International Journal of Conflict Management* 12 (2001): 259–275.

22. D. E. Conlon and S. H. Hunt, "Dealing with Feeling: The Influence of Outcome Representations on Negotiation," *International Journal of Conflict Management* 13 (2002): 35–58.

23. V. K. Raizada, "Multi-Ethnic Corporations and Inter-Ethnic Conflict," *Human Resource Management* 20 (1981): 24–27; T. Cox, Jr., "The Multicultural Organization," *Academy of Management Executive* 5 (1991): 34–47.

24. G. Hofstede, *Culture's Consequences: International Differences in Work-related Values* (Beverly Hills, Calif.: Sage, 1980); G. Hofstede and M. H. Bond, "The Confucius Connection: From Cultural Roots to Economic Growth," *Organizational Dynamics* (Spring 1988): 4–21; G. Hofstede, "Cultural Constraints in Management Theories," *Academy of Management Executive* 7 (1993): 81–94.

25. T. H. Cox, S. A. Lobel, and P. L. McLead, "Effects of Ethnic Group Cultural Differences on Cooperative and Competitive Behavior in a Group Task," *Academy of Management Journal* 34 (1991): 827–847.

26. J. Schopler, C. A. Insko, J. Wieselquist, *et al.*, "When Groups Are More Competitive than Individuals: The Domain of the Discontinuity Effect," *Journal of Personality and Social Psychology* 80 (2001): 632–644.

27. M. Sherif and C. W. Sherif, *Social Psychology* (New York: Harper & Row, 1969).

28. C. Song, S. M. Sommer, and A. E. Hartman, "The Impact of Adding an External Rater on Interdepartmental Cooperative Behaviors of Workers," *International Journal of Conflict Management* 9 (1998): 117–138.

29. W. Tsai and S. Ghoshal, "Social Capital and Value Creation: The Role of Intrafirm Networks," *Academy of Management Journal* 41 (1998): 464–476.

30. M. A. Zarate, B. Garcia, A. A. Garza, and R. T. Hitlan, "Cultural Threat and Perceived Realistic Group Conflict as Dual Predictors of Prejudice," *Journal of Experimental Social Psychology* 40 (2004): 99–105.

31. M. L. Maznevski and K. M. Chudoba, "Bridging Space over Time: Global Virtual-Team Dynamics and Effectiveness," *Organization Science* 11 (2000): 473–492.

32. D. Katz and R. Kahn, *The Social Psychology of Organizations*, 2nd ed. (New York: Wiley, 1978).

33. D. L. Nelson and J. C. Quick, "Professional Women: Are Distress and Disease Inevitable?" *Academy of Management Review* 10 (1985): 206–218; D. L. Nelson and M. A. Hitt, "Employed Women and Stress: Implications for Enhancing Women's Mental Health in the Workplace," in J. C. Quick, J. Hurrell, and L. A. Murphy, eds., *Stress and Well-Being at Work: Assessments and Interventions for Occupational Mental Health* (Washington, D.C.: American Psychological Association, 1992).

34. M. G. Pratt and J. A. Rosa, "Transforming Work-Family Conflict into Commitment in Network Marketing Organizations," *Academy of Management Journal* 46 (2003): 395–418.

35. R. L. Kahn, et al., *Organizational Stress: Studies in Role Conflict and Ambiguity* (New York: Wiley, 1964).

36. J. L. Badaracco, Jr., "The Discipline of Building Character," *Harvard Business Review* (March–April 1998): 115–124.

37. B. Schneider, "The People Make the Place," *Personnel Psychology* 40 (1987): 437–453.

38. C. A. O'Reilly, J. Chatman, and D. F. Caldwell, "People and Organizational Culture: A Profile Comparison Approach to Assessing Person-Organization Fit," *Academy of Management Journal* 34 (1991): 487–516.

39. I. Dayal and J. M. Thomas, "Operation KPE: Developing a New Organization," *Journal of Applied Behavioral Science* 4 (1968): 473–506.

40. R. H. Miles, "Role Requirements as Sources of Organizational Stress," *Journal of Applied Psychology* 61 (1976): 172–179.

41. W. F. G. Mastenbroek, *Conflict Management and Organization Development* (Chichester, England: Wiley, 1987).

42. M. R. Frone, "Interpersonal Conflict at Work and Psychological Outcomes: Testing a Model among Young Workers," *Journal of Occupational Health Psychology* 5 (2000): 246–255.

43. K. Thomas, "Conflict and Conflict Management," in M. D. Dunnette, ed., *Handbook of Industrial and Organizational Psychology* (New York: Wiley, 1976).

44. H. H. Meyer, E. Kay, and J. R. P. French, "Split Roles in Performance Appraisal," *Harvard Business Review* 43 (1965): 123–129.

45. T. W. Costello and S. S. Zalkind, *Psychology in Administration: A Research Orientation* (Englewood Cliffs, N.J.: Prentice-Hall, 1963).

46. Snapshot Spy, "Employee Computer & Internet Abuse Statistics," http://www.snapshotspy.com/employee-computer-abuse-statistics.htm; Data sources include U.S. Department of Commerce—Economics and Statistics Administration and the National Telecommunications and Information Administration—Greenfield and Rivet, "Employee Computer Abuse Statistics."

47. P. F. Hewlin, "And the Award for Best Actor Goes to . . . : Facades of Conformity in Organizational Settings," *Academy of Management Review* 28 (2003): 633–642.

48. C. A. Insko, J. Scholper, L. Gaertner, *et al.*, "Interindividual–Intergroup Discontinuity Reduction through the Anticipation of Future Interaction," *Journal of Personality and Social Psychology* 80 (2001): 95–111.

49. D. Tjosvold and M. Poon, "Dealing with Scarce Resources: Open-Minded Interaction for Resolving Budget Conflicts," *Group and Organization Management* 23 (1998): 237–255.

50. Miles, *Macro Organizational Behavior; R. Steers, Introduction to Organizational Behavior*, 4th ed. (Glenview, Ill.: Harper-Collins, 1991).

51. C. Morrill, M. N. Zold, and H. Rao, "Covert Political Conflict in Organizations: Challenges from Below," *Annual Review of Sociology* 29 (2003): 391–415.

52. A. Tyerman and C. Spencer, "A Critical Text of the Sherrif's Robber's Cave Experiments: Intergroup Competition and Cooperation between Groups of Well-Acquainted Individuals," *Small Group Behavior* 14 (1983): 515–531; R. M. Kramer, "Intergroup Relations and Organizational Dilemmas: The Role of Categorization Processes," in B. Staw and L. Cummings, eds., *Research in Organizational Behavior* 13 (Greenwich, Conn.: JAI Press, 1991), 191–228.

53. A. Carmeli, "The Relationship between Emotional Intelligence and Work Attitudes, Behavior and Outcomes: An Examination among Senior Managers," *Journal of Managerial Psychology* 18 (2003): 788–813.

54. R. Blake and J. Mouton, "Overcoming Group Warfare," *Harvard Business Review* 64 (1984): 98–108.

55. D. G. Ancona and D. Caldwell, "Improving the Performance of New Product Teams," *Research Technology Management* 33 (1990): 25–29.

56. C. K. W. DeDreu and L. R. Weingart, "Task versus Relationship Conflict, Team Performance, and Team Member Satisfaction: A Meta-Analysis," *Journal of Applied Psychology* 88 (2003): 741–749.

57. R. J. Lewicki, J. A. Litterer, J. W. Minton, and D. M. Saunders, *Negotiation*, 2nd ed. (Burr Ridge, Ill.: Irwin, 1994).

58. C. K. W. De Dreu, S. L. Koole, and W. Steinel, "Unfixing the Fixed Pie: A Motivated Information-Processing Approach to Integrative Negotiation," *Journal of Personality and Social Psychology* 79 (2000): 975–987.

59. M. H. Bazerman, J. R. Curhan, D. A. Moore, and K. L. Valley, "Negotiation," *Annual Review of Psychology* 51 (2000): 279–314.

60. I. Ayers and P. Siegelman, "Race and Gender Discrimination in Bargaining for a New Car," *American Economic Review* 85 (1995): 304–321.

61. L. J. Kray, L. Thompson, and A. Galinsky, "Battle of the Sexes: Gender Stereotype Confirmation and Reactance in Organizations," *Journal of Personality and Social Psychology* 80 (2001): 942–958.

62. K. W. Thomas, "Conflict and Conflict Management," in M. D. Dunnette, ed., *Handbook of Industrial and Organizational Psychology* (Chicago: Rand McNally, 1976), 900.

63. C. K. W. De Dreu and A. E. M. Van Vianen, "Managing Relationship Conflict and the Effectiveness of Organizational Teams," *Journal of Organizational Behavior* 22 (2001): 309–328.

64. R. A. Baron, S. P. Fortin, R. L. Frei, L. A. Hauver, and M. L. Shack, "Reducing Organizational Conflict: The Role of Socially Induced Positive Affect," *International Journal of Conflict Management* 1 (1990): 133–152.

65. S. L. Phillips and R. L. Elledge, *The Team Building Source Book* (San Diego: University Associates, 1989).

66. Gladwin and Walter, "How Multinationals Can Manage," 228.

67. K. W. Thomas, "Toward Multidimensional Values in Teaching: The Example of Conflict Behaviors," *Academy of Management Review* 2 (1977): 484–490.

68. S. Alper, D. Tjosvold, and K. S. Law, "Conflict Management, Efficacy, and Performance in Organizational Teams," *Personnel Psychology* 53 (2000): 625–642.

69. W. King and E. Miles, "What We Know and Don't Know about Measuring Conflict," *Management Communication Quarterly* 4 (1990): 222–243.

70. J. Barker, D. Tjosvold, and I. R. Andrews, "Conflict Approaches of Effective and Ineffective Project Managers: A Field Study in a Matrix Organization," *Journal of Management Studies* 25 (1988): 167–178.

71. M. Chan, "Intergroup Conflict and Conflict Management in the R&D Divisions of Four Aerospace Companies," *IEEE Transactions on Engineering Management* 36 (1989): 95–104.

72. M. K. Kozan, "Cultural Influences on Styles of Handling Interpersonal Conflicts: Comparisons among Jordanian, Turkish, and U.S. Managers," *Human Relations* 42 (1989): 787–799.

73. S. McKenna, "The Business Impact of Management Attitudes towards Dealing with Conflict: A Cross-Cultural Assessment," *Journal of Managerial Psychology* 10 (1995): 22–27.

74. Tjosvold, *The Conflict-Positive Organization.*

75. P. J. Frost, *Toxic Emotions at Work: How Compassionate Managers Handle Pain and Conflict* (Harvard Business School Press, 2003).

76. J. R. Ogilvie and M. L. Carsky, "Building Emotional Intelligence in Negotiations," *The International Journal of Conflict Management* 13 (2002): 381–400.

77. M. Rothschild, "Whole Foods Unionized," *The Progressive* (July 9, 2002), http://www.progressive.org/webex/wx071602.html.

78. A. Nathans, "Whole Foods Firings Stir Flap," *The Capital Times* (November 22, 2002), http://www.madison.com/captimes/news/stories/37339.php.

Chapter 14

1. S. P. Means, "Playing at Pixar," *The Salt Lake Tribune* (May 30, 2003), http://166.70.44.66/2003/May/05302003/friday/friday.asp.

2. G. W. England and I. Harpaz, "How Working Is Defined: National Contexts and Demographic and Organizational Role Influences," *Journal of Organizational Behavior* 11 (1990): 253–266.

3. L. R. Gomez-Mejia, "The Cross-Cultural Structure of Task-Related and Contextual Constructs," *Journal of Psychology* 120 (1986): 5–19.

4. A. Wrzesniewski and J. E. Dutton, "Crafting a Job: Revisioning Employees as Active Crafters of Their Work," *Academy of Management Review* 26 (2001): 179–201.

5. F. W. Taylor, *The Principles of Scientific Management* (New York: Norton, 1911).

6. T. Bell, *Out of This Furnace* (Pittsburgh: University of Pittsburgh Press, 1941).

7. P. Cappelli, "A Market-Driven Approach to Retaining Talent," *Harvard Business Review* 78 (2000): 103–111.

8. N. D. Warren, "Job Simplification versus Job Enlargement," *Journal of Industrial Engineering* 9 (1958): 435–439.

9. C. R. Walker, "The Problem of the Repetitive Job," *Harvard Business Review* 28 (1950): 54–58.

10. T. Moller, S. E. Mathiassen, H. Franzon, and S. Kihlberg, "Job Enlargement and Mechanical Exposure Variability in Cyclic Assembly Work," *Ergonomics* 47 (2004): 19–40.

11. C. R. Walker and R. H. Guest, *The Man on the Assembly Line* (Cambridge, Mass.: Harvard University Press, 1952).

12. M. A. Campion, L. Cheraskin, and M. J. Stevens, "Career-Related Antecedents and Outcomes of Job Rotation," *Academy of Management Journal* 37 (1994): 1518–1542.

13. E. Santora, "Keep Up Production Through Cross-Training," *Personnel Journal* (June 1992): 162–166.

14. R. P. Steel and J. R. Rentsch, "The Dispositional Model of Job Attitudes Revisited: Findings of a 10-Year Study," *Journal of Applied Psychology* 82 (1997): 873–879; C.-S. Wong, C. Hui, and K. S. Law, "A Longitudinal Study of the Job Perception–Job Satisfaction Relationship: A Text of the Three Alternative Specifications," *Journal of Occupational & Organizational Psychology* 71 (Part 2, 1998): 127–146.

15. F. Herzberg, "One More Time: How Do You Motivate Employees?" *Harvard Business Review* 46 (1968): 53–62.

16. R. N. Ford, "Job Enrichment Lessons from AT&T," *Harvard Business Review* 51 (1973): 96–106.

17. R. J. House and L. A. Wigdor, "Herzberg's Dual-Factor Theory of Job Satisfaction and Motivation: A Review of the Evidence and a Criticism," *Personnel Psychology* 20 (1967): 369–389.

18. A. N. Turner and P. R. Lawrence, *Industrial Jobs and the Worker* (Cambridge, Mass.: Harvard University Press, 1965).

19. J. R. Hackman and G. R. Oldham, "The Job Diagnostic Survey: An Instrument for the Diagnosis of Jobs and the Evaluation of Job Redesign Projects," *Technical Report No. 4* (New Haven, Conn.: Department of Administrative Sciences, Yale University, 1974).

20. J. R. Hackman and G. R. Oldham, "Development of the Job Diagnostic Survey," *Journal of Applied Psychology* 60 (1975): 159–170.

21. E. Sadler-Smith, G. El-Kot, and M. Leat, "Differentiating Work Autonomy Facets in a Non-Western Context," *Journal of Organizational Behavior* 24 (2003): 709–731.

22. P. H. Birnbaum, J. L. Farh, and G. Y. Y. Wong, "The Job Characteristics Model in Hong Kong," *Journal of Applied Psychology* 71 (1986): 598–605.

23. J. R. Hackman and G. R. Oldham, *Work Design* (Reading, Mass.: Addison-Wesley, 1980).

24. H. P. Sims, A. D. Szilagyi, and R. T. Keller, "The Measurement of Job Characteristics," *Academy of Management Journal* 19 (1976): 195–212.

25. H. P. Sims and A. D. Szilagyi, "Job Characteristic Relationships: Individual and Structural Moderators," *Organizational Behavior and Human Performance* 17 (1976): 211–230.

26. Y. Fried, "Meta-Analytic Comparison of the Job Diagnostic Survey and Job Characteristic Inventory as Correlates of Work Satisfaction and Performance," *Journal of Applied Psychology* 76 (1991): 690–698.

27. D. R. May, R. L. Gilson, and L. M. Harter, "The Psychological Conditions of Meaningfulness, Safety, and Availability and the Engagement of the Human Spirit at Work," *Journal of Occupational and Organizational Psychology* 77 (2004): 11–37.

28. J. Loehr and T. Schwartz, *The Power of Full Engagement: Managing Energy, Not Time, Is the Key to High Performance and Personal Renewal* (New York: Free Press, 2003).

29. M. F. R. Kets de Vries, "Creating Authentizotic Organizations: Well-Functioning Individuals in Vibrant Companies," *Human Relations* 54 (2001): 101–111.

30. G. R. Salancik and J. Pfeffer, "A Social Information Processing Approach to Job Attitudes and Task Design," *Administrative Science Quarterly* 23 (1978): 224–253.

31. J. Pfeffer, "Management as Symbolic Action: The Creation and Maintenance of Organizational Paradigms," in L. L. Cummings and B. M. Staw, eds., *Research in Organizational Behavior*, vol. 3 (Greenwich, Conn.: JAI Press, 1981), 1–52.

32. J. Thomas and R. Griffin, "The Social Information Processing Model of Task Design: A Review of the Literature," *Academy of Management Review* 8 (1983): 672–682.

33. D. J. Campbell, "Task Complexity: A Review and Analysis," *Academy of Management Review* 13 (1988): 40–52.

34. M. A. Campion and P. W. Thayer, "Job Design: Approaches, Outcomes, and Trade-Offs," *Organizational Dynamics* 16 (1987): 66–79.

35. J. Teresko, "Emerging Technologies," *Industry Week* (February 27, 1995): 1–2.

36. M. A. Campion and C. L. McClelland, "Interdisciplinary Examination of the Costs and Benefits of Enlarged Jobs: A Job Design Quasi-Experiment," *Journal of Applied Psychology* 76 (1991): 186–199.

37. B. Kohut, *Country Competitiveness: Organizing of Work* (New York: Oxford University Press, 1993).

38. J. C. Quick and L. E. Tetrick, eds., *Handbook of Occupational Health Psychology* (Washington, D.C.: American Psychological Association, 2002).

39. W. E. Deming, *Out of the Crisis* (Cambridge, Mass.: MIT Press, 1986).

40. L. Thurow, *Head to Head: The Coming Economic Battle among Japan, Europe, and America* (New York: Morrow, 1992).

41. M. A. Fruin, *The Japanese Enterprise System—Competitive Strategies and Cooperative Structures* (New York: Oxford University Press, 1992).

42. W. Niepce and E. Molleman, "Work Design Issue in Lean Production from a Sociotechnical System Perspective: Neo-Taylorism or the Next Step in Sociotechnical Design?" *Human Relations* 51 (1998): 259–287.

43. S. K. Parker, "Longitudinal Effects of Lean Production on Employee Outcomes and the Mediating Role of Work Characteristics," *Journal of Applied Psychology* 88 (2003): 620–634.

44. E. Furubotn, "Codetermination and the Modern Theory of the Firm: A Property-Rights Analysis," *Journal of Business* 61 (1988): 165–181.

45. H. Levinson, *Executive: The Guide to Responsive Management* (Cambridge, Mass.: Harvard University Press, 1981).

46. B. Gardell, "Scandinavian Research on Stress in Working Life" (Paper presented at the IRRA Symposium on Stress in Working Life, Denver, September 1980).

47. L. Levi, "Psychosocial, Occupational, Environmental, and Health Concepts; Research Results and Applications," in G. P. Keita and S. L. Sauter, eds., *Work and Well-Being: An Agenda for the 1990s* (Washington, D.C.: American Psychological Association, 1992), 199–211.

48. L. R. Murphy and C. L. Cooper, eds., *Healthy and Productive Work: An International Perspective* (London and New York: Taylor & Francis, 2000).

49. R. L. Kahn, *Work and Health* (New York: Wiley, 1981); M. Gowing, J. Kraft, and J. C. Quick, *The New Organizational Reality: Downsizing, Restructuring, and Revitalization* (Washington, D.C.: American Psychological Association, 1998).

50. F. J. Landy, "Work Design and Stress," in G. P. Keita and S. L. Sauter, eds., *Work and Well-Being: An Agenda for the 1990s* (Washington, D.C.: American Psychological Association, 1992), 119–158.

51. C. Gresov, R. Drazin, and A. H. Van de Ven, "Work-Unit Task Uncertainty, Design, and Morale," *Organizational Studies* 10 (1989): 45–62.

52. Y. Baruch, "The Status of Research on Teleworking and an Agenda for Future Research," *International Journal of Management Review* 3 (2000): 113–129.

53. K. E. Pearlson and C. S. Saunders, "There's No Place Like Home: Managing Telecommuting Paradoxes," *Academy of Management Executive* 15 (2001): 117–128.

54. S. Caudron, "Working at Home Pays Off," *Personnel Journal* (November 1992): 40–47.

55. D. S. Bailey and J. Foley, "Pacific Bell Works Long Distance," *HRMagazine* (August 1990): 50–52.

56. S. M. Pollan and M. Levine, "Asking for Flextime," *Working Women* (February 1994): 48.

57. S. A. Rogier and M. Y. Padgett, "The Impact of Utilizing a Flexible Work Schedule on the Perceived Career Advancement Potential of Women," *Human Resource Development Quarterly* 15 (2004): 89–106.

58. S. Zuboff, *In the Age of the Smart Machine: The Future of Work and Power* (New York: Basic Books, 1988).

59. B. A. Gutek and S. J. Winter, "Computer Use, Control over Computers, and Job Satisfaction," in S. Oskamp and S. Spacapan, eds., *People's Reactions to Technology in Factories, Offices, and Aerospace: The Claremont Symposium on Applied Social Psychology* (Newbury Park, Calif.: Sage, 1990), 121–144.

60. L. M. Schleifer and B. C. Amick III, "System Response Time and Method of Pay: Stress Effects in Computer-Based Tasks," *International Journal of Human-Computer Interaction* 1 (1989): 23–39.

61. K. Voight, "Virtual Work: Some Telecommuters Take Remote Work to the Extreme," *The Wall Street Journal Europe* (February 1, 2001): 1.

62. B. M. Staw and R. D. Boettger, "Task Revision: A Neglected Form of Work Performance," *Academy of Management Journal* 33 (1990): 534–559.

63. H. S. Schwartz, "Job Involvement as Obsession Compulsion," *Academy of Management Review* 7 (1982): 429–432.

64. C. J. Nemeth and B. M. Staw, "The Tradeoffs of Social Control and Innovation in Groups and Organizations," in L. Berkowitz, ed., *Advances in Experimental Social Psychology*, vol. 22 (New York: Academic Press, 1989), 175–210.

65. G. Salvendy, *Handbook of Industrial Engineering: Technology and Operations Management* (New York: John Wiley & Sons, 2001).

66. D. M. Herold, "Using Technology to Improve Our Management of Labor Market Trends," in M. Greller, ed., "Managing Careers with a Changing Workforce," *Journal of Organizational Change Management* 3 (1990): 44–57.

67. D. A. Whetten and K. S. Cameron, *Developing Management Skills*, 6th Edition (Upper Saddle River, N.J.: Prentice Hall, 2004).

68. M. Lasswell, "Pixar—To Infinity and Beyond," *Management Today* (May 1, 2004): 64–67.

Chapter 15

1. J. Foley, "Beverage Makers Seek Efficiencies," *InformationWeek* (February 17, 2003): 30, http://www.informationweek.com/story/IWK2003021450013.

2. J. Child, *Organization* (New York: Harper & Row, 1984).

3. P. Lawrence and J. Lorsch, "Differentiation and Integration in Complex Organizations," *Administrative Science Quarterly* 12 (1967): 1–47.

4. P. Lawrence and J. Lorsch, *Organization and Environment: Managing Differentiation and Integration*, rev. ed. (Cambridge, Mass.: Harvard University Press, 1986).

5. J. Hage, "An Axiomatic Theory of Organizations," *Administrative Science Quarterly* 10 (1965): 289–320.

6. W. Ouchi and J. Dowling, "Defining the Span of Control," *Administrative Science Quarterly* 19 (1974): 357–365.

7. L. Porter and E. Lawler, III, "Properties of Organization Structure in Relation to Job Attitudes and Job Behavior," *Psychological Bulletin* 65 (1965): 23–51.

8. J. Ivancevich and J. Donnelly, Jr., "Relation of Organization and Structure to Job Satisfaction, Anxiety-Stress, and Performance," *Administrative Science Quarterly* 20 (1975): 272–280.

9. R. Dewar and J. Hage, "Size, Technology, Complexity, and Structural Differentiation: Toward a Theoretical Synthesis," *Administrative Science Quarterly* 23 (1978): 111–136.

10. Lawrence and Lorsch, "Differentiation and Integration," 1–47.

11. J. R. R. Galbraith, *Designing Complex Organizations* (Reading, Mass.: Addison-Wesley-Longman, 1973).

12. W. Altier, "Task Forces: An Effective Management Tool," *Management Review* 76 (1987): 26–32.

13. P. Lawrence and J. Lorsch, "New Managerial Job: The Integrator," *Harvard Business Review* 45 (1967): 142–151.

14. J. Lorsch and P. Lawrence, "Organizing for Product Innovation," *Harvard Business Review* 43 (1965): 110–111.

15. D. Pugh, D. Hickson, C. Hinnings, and C. Turner, "Dimensions of Organization Structure," *Administrative Science Quarterly* 13 (1968): 65–91; B. Reimann, "Dimensions of Structure in Effective Organizations: Some Empirical Evidence," *Academy of Management Journal* 17 (1974): 693–708; S. Robbins, *Organization Theory: The Structure and Design of Organizations*, 3rd ed. (Englewood Cliffs, N.J.: Prentice-Hall, 1990).

16. H. Mintzberg, *The Structuring of Organizations* (Englewood Cliffs, N.J.: Prentice-Hall, 1979).
17. J. A. Kuprenas, "Implementation and Performance of a Matrix Organization Structure," *International Journal of Project Management* 21 (2003): 51–62.
18. Mintzberg, *Structuring of Organizations*.
19. K. Weick, "Educational Institutions as Loosely Coupled Systems," *Administrative Science Quarterly* (1976): 1–19.
20. D. Miller and C. Droge, "Psychological and Traditional Determinants of Structure," *Administrative Science Quarterly* 31 (1986): 540; H. Tosi, Jr., and J. Slocum, Jr., "Contingency Theory: Some Suggested Directions," *Journal of Management* 10 (1984): 9–26.
21. C. B. Clott, "Perspectives on Global Outsourcing and the Changing Nature of Work," *Business and Society Review* 109 (2004): 153–170.
22. D. Mack and J. C. Quick, "EDS: An Inside View of a Corporate Life Cycle Transition," *Organizational Dynamics* 30 (2002): 282–293.
23. M. Meyer, "Size and the Structure of Organizations: A Causal Analysis," *American Sociological Review* 37 (1972): 434–441; J. Beyer and H. Trice, "A Reexamination of the Relations between Size and Various Components of Organizational Complexity," *Administrative Science Quarterly* 24 (1979): 48–64; B. Mayhew, R. Levinger, J. McPherson, and T. James, "Systems Size and Structural Differentiation in Formal Organizations: A Baseline Generator for Two Major Theoretical Propositions," *American Sociological Review* 37 (1972): 26–43.
24. M. Gowing, J. Kraft, and J. C. Quick, *The New Organizational Reality: Downsizing, Restructuring, and Revitalization* (Washington, D.C.: American Psychological Association, 1998).
25. B. A. Pasternack and A. J. Viscio, *The Centerless Corporation: A New Model for Transforming Your Organization for Growth and Prosperity* (New York: Simon & Schuster, 1999).
26. J. Woodward, *Industrial Organization: Theory and Practices* (London: Oxford University Press, 1965).
27. C. Perrow, "A Framework for the Comparative Analysis of Organizations," *American Sociological Review* 32 (1967): 194–208; D. Rosseau, "Assessment of Technology in Organizations: Closed versus Open Systems Approaches," *Academy of Management Review* 4 (1979): 531–542.
28. Perrow, "A Framework for the Comparative Analysis of Organizations," 194–208.
29. J. D. Thompson, *Organizations in Action* (New York: McGraw-Hill, 1967).
30. P. Nemetz and L. Fry, "Flexible Manufacturing Organizations: Implication for Strategy Formulation and Organization Design," *Academy of Management Review* 13 (1988): 627–638; G. Huber, "The Nature and Design of Post-Industrial Organizations," *Management Science* 30 (1984): 934.
31. E. Feitzinger and H. L. Lee, "Mass Customization at Hewlett-Packard: The Power of Postponement," *Harvard Business Review* 75 (1997): 116–121.
32. S. M. Davis, *Future Perfect* (Reading, Mass.: Addison-Wesley, 1987).
33. J. R. Baum and S. Wally, "Strategic Decision Speed and Firm Performance," *Strategic Management Journal* 24 (2003): 1107–1129.
34. Thompson, *Organizations in Action*.
35. H. Downey, D. Hellriegel, and J. Slocum, Jr., "Environmental Uncertainty: The Construct and Its Application," *Administrative Science Quarterly* 20 (1975): 613–629.
36. T. Burns and G. Stalker, *The Management of Innovation* (London: Tavistock, 1961); Mintzberg, *Structuring of Organizations*.
37. M. Chandler and L. Sayles, *Managing Large Systems* (New York: Harper & Row, 1971).
38. G. Dess and D. Beard, "Dimensions of Organizational Task Environments," *Administrative Science Quarterly* 29 (1984): 52–73.
39. J. Courtright, G. Fairhurst, and L. Rogers, "Interaction Patterns in Organic and Mechanistic Systems," *Academy of Management Journal* 32 (1989): 773–802.
40. R. Daft, *Organization Theory and Design*, 7th ed. (Mason, OH: South-Western/Thomson Learning, 2000).
41. D. Miller, "The Structural and Environmental Correlates of Business Strategy," *Strategic Management Journal* 8 (1987): 55–76.
42. W. R. Scott, *Organizations: Rational, Natural, and Open Systems*, 4th ed. (Upper Saddle River, N.J.: Prentice-Hall, 1997).
43. D. Miller and P. Friesen, "A Longitudinal Study of the Corporate Life Cycle," *Management Science* 30 (1984): 1161–1183.
44. M. H. Overholt, "Flexible Organizations: Using Organizational Design as a Competitive Advantage," *Human Resource Planning* 20 (1997): 22–32; P. W. Roberts and R. Greenwood, "Integrating Transaction Cost and Institutional Theories: Toward a Constrained-Efficiency Framework for Understanding Organizational Design Adoption," *Academy of Management Review* 22 (1997): 346–373.
45. C. W. L. Hill and G. R. Jones, *Strategic Management Theory*, 5th ed. (Boston: Houghton Mifflin, 2000).
46. Daft, *Organization Theory and Design*.
47. C. M. Savage, *5th Generation Management, Revised Edition: Co-creating through Virtual Enterprising, Dynamic Teaming, and Knowledge Networking* (Boston: Butterworth-Heinemann, 1996).
48. S. M. Davis, *Future Perfect* (Perseus Publishing, 1997).
49. A. Boynton and B. Victor, "Beyond Flexibility: Building and Managing a Dynamically Stable Organization," *California Management Review* 8 (Fall 1991): 53–66.
50. P. J. Brews and C. L. Tucci, "Exploring the Structural Effects of Internetworking," *Strategic Management Journal* 25 (2004): 429–451.
51. J. Fulk, "Global Network Organizations: Emergence and Future Prospects," *Human Relations* 54 (2001): 91–100.
52. The use of the theatrical troupe as an analogy for virtual organizations was first used by David Mack, circa 1995.
53. E. C. Kasper-Fuehrer and N. M. Ashkanasy, "Communicating Trustworthiness and Building Trust in Interorganizational Virtual Organizations," *Journal of Management* 27 (2001): 235–254.
54. R. Teerlink and L. Ozley, *More than a Motorcycle: The Leadership Journey at Harley-Davidson* (Boston: Harvard Business School Press, 2000).
55. W. A. Cohen and N. Cohen, *The Paranoid Organization and 8 Other Ways Your Company Can Be Crazy: Advice from an Organizational Shrink* (New York: American Management Association, 1993).
56. P. E. Tetlock, "Cognitive Biases and Organizational Correctives: Do Both Disease and Cure Depend on the Politics of the Beholder?" *Administrative Science Quarterly* 45 (2000): 293–326.
57. M. F. R. Kets de Vries and D. Miller, "Personality, Culture, and Organization," *Academy of Management Review* 11 (1986): 266–279.
58. J. Foley, "Coca-Cola Plans to Refresh Supply Chain," *InformationWeek* (February 16, 2004): 22, http://www.informationweek.com/story/showArticle.jhtml?articleID=17700199&fb=20040323_software.

Chapter 16

1. D. H. Thomas, "Hot Diggity Dawg, A Dog's Life Ain't So Bad," *Accent on Living* 42 (Winter 1997): 62–68.
2. "Canine Companions for Independence—Charity Summary," http://www.charitynavigator.com/index.cfm/bay/search.summary/orgid/3418.htm.
3. T. E. Deal and A. A. Kennedy, *Corporate Cultures* (Reading, Mass.: Addison-Wesley, 1982).
4. W. Ouchi, *Theory Z* (Reading, Mass.: Addison-Wesley, 1981).
5. T. J. Peters and R. H. Waterman, *In Search of Excellence* (New York: Harper & Row, 1982).
6. M. Gardner, "Creating a Corporate Culture for the Eighties," *Business Horizons* (January–February 1985): 59–63.
7. Definition adapted from E. H. Schein, *Organizational Culture and Leadership* (San Francisco: Jossey-Bass, 1985), 9.
8. C. D. Sutton and D. L. Nelson, "Elements of the Cultural Network: The Communicators of Corporate Values," *Leadership and Organization Development* 11 (1990): 3–10.
9. J. Pagel, "Eskimo Joe's Getting Older, But Still Fun at 21," *Amarillo Business Journal* (November 20, 1996), http://www.businessjournal.net/entrepreneur1196.html.
10. A. Bandura, *Social Learning Theory* (Englewood Cliffs, N.J.: Prentice-Hall, 1977).
11. J. A. Chatman, "Leading by Leveraging Culture," *California Management Review* 45 (2003): 20–34.

12. J. M. Beyer and H. M. Trice, "How an Organization's Rites Reveal Its Culture," *Organizational Dynamics* 16 (1987): 5–24.

13. H. M. Trice and J. M. Beyer, "Studying Organizational Cultures through Rites and Ceremonials," *Academy of Management Review* 9 (1984): 653–669.

14. M. J. Schneider, "The Wal-Mart Annual Meeting: From Small-Town America to a Global Corporate Culture," *Human Organization* 57 (1998): 292–299.

15. H. Levinson and S. Rosenthal, *CEO: Corporate Leadership in Action* (New York: Basic Books, 1984).

16. V. Sathe, "Implications of Corporate Culture: A Manager's Guide to Action," *Organizational Dynamics* 12 (1987): 5–23.

17. "Wal-Mart Culture Stories—The Sundown Rule," http://www.wal-martchina.com/english/walmart/rule/sun.htm.

18. J. Martin, M. S. Feldman, M. J. Hatch, and S. B. Sitkin, "The Uniqueness Paradox in Organizational Stories," *Administrative Science Quarterly* 28 (1983): 438–453.

19. B. Durrance, "Stories at Work," *Training and Development* (February 1997): 25–29.

20. B. Siuru, "2003 Saturn L Series," http://www.autowire.net/2002-40.html.

21. R. Goffee and G. Jones, "What Holds the Modern Company Together?" *Harvard Business Review* (November–December 1996): 133–143.

22. C. Argyris and D. A. Schon, *Organizational Learning* (Reading, Mass.: Addison-Wesley, 1978).

23. D. J. McAllister and G. A. Bigley, "Work Context and the Definition of Self: How Organizational Care Influences Organization-Based Self-Esteem," *Academy of Management Journal* 45 (2002): 894–905.

24. "Sounds Like a New Woman," *New Woman* (February 1993): 144.

25. M. Peterson, "Work, Corporate Culture, and Stress: Implications for Worksite Health Promotion," *American Journal of Health Behavior* 21 (1997): 243–252.

26. R. Targos, "Big Bad Hog—Harley-Davidson Customer Service," *Child Care Business*, http://www.childcarebusiness.com/articles/161cover.html.

27. J. Rosenthal and M. A. Masarech, "High-Performance Cultures: How Values Can Drive Business Results," *Journal of Organizational Excellence* (Spring 2003): 3–18.

28. "Earthlink—Core Values and Beliefs," http://www.earthlink.net/about/cvb.

29. L. Smircich, "Concepts of Culture and Organizational Analysis," *Administrative Science Quarterly* (1983): 339–358.

30. Y. Weiner and Y. Vardi, "Relationships between Organizational Culture and Individual Motivation: A Conceptual Integration," *Psychological Reports* 67 (1990): 295–306.

31. M. R. Louis, "Surprise and Sense Making: What Newcomers Experience in Entering Unfamiliar Organizational Settings," *Administrative Science Quarterly* 25 (1980): 209–264.

32. T. L. Doolen, M. E. Hacker, and E. M. van Aken, "The Impact of Organizational Context on Work Team Effectiveness: A Study of Production Teams," *IEEE Transactions on Engineering Management* 50 (2003): 285–296.

33. J. P. Kotter and J. L. Heskett, *Corporate Culture and Performance* (New York: Free Press, 1992).

34. Deal and Kennedy, *Corporate Cultures.*

35. D. R. Katz, *The Big Store* (New York: Viking, 1987).

36. G. G. Gordon, "Industry Determinants of Organizational Culture," *Academy of Management Review* 16 (1991): 396–415.

37. G. Donaldson and J. Lorsch, *Decision Making at the Top* (New York: Basic Books, 1983).

38. R. H. Kilman, M. J. Saxton, and R. Serpa, eds., *Gaining Control of the Corporate Culture* (San Francisco: Jossey-Bass, 1986).

39. J. P. Kotter, *A Force for Change: How Leadership Differs from Management* (New York: Free Press, 1990); R. M. Kanter, *The Change Masters* (New York: Simon & Schuster, 1983).

40. T. Peters and N. Austin, *A Passion for Excellence: The Leadership Difference* (New York: Random House, 1985).

41. Schein, *Organizational Culture and Leadership.*

42. R. R. Sims and J. Brinkmann, "Enron Ethics (or Culture Matters More than Codes)," *Journal of Business Ethics* 45 (2003): 243–256.

43. J. A. Pearce II, T. R. Kramer, and D. K. Robbins, "Effects of Managers' Entrepreneurial Behavior on Subordinates," *Journal of Business Venturing* 12 (1997): 147–160.

44. D. C. Feldman, "The Multiple Socialization of Organization Members," *Academy of Management Review* 6 (1981): 309–318.

45. R. Pascale, "The Paradox of Corporate Culture: Reconciling Ourselves to Socialization," *California Management Review* 27 (1985): 26–41.

46. D. L. Nelson, "Organizational Socialization: A Stress Perspective," *Journal of Occupational Behavior* 8 (1987): 311–324.

47. D. M. Cable, L. Aiman-Smith, P. W. Mulvey, and J. R. Edwards, "The Sources and Accuracy of Job Applicants' Beliefs about Organizational Culture," *Academy of Management Journal* 43 (2000): 1076–1085.

48. J. Chatman, "Matching People and Organizations: Selection and Socialization in Public Accounting Firms," *Administrative Science Quarterly* 36 (1991): 459–484.

49. D. L. Nelson, J. C. Quick, and M. E. Eakin, "A Longitudinal Study of Newcomer Role Adjustment in U.S. Organizations," *Work and Stress* 2 (1988): 239–253.

50. N. J. Allen and J. P. Meyer, "Organizational Socialization Tactics: A Longitudinal Analysis of Links to Newcomers' Commitment and Role Orientation," *Academy of Management Journal* 33 (1990): 847–858.

51. T. N. Bauer, E. W. Morrison, and R. R. Callister, "Organizational Socialization: A Review and Directions for Future Research," *Research in Personnel and Human Resources Management* 16 (1998): 149–214.

52. D. M. Cable and C. K. Parsons, "Socialization Tactics and Person–Organization Fit," *Personnel Psychology* 54 (2001): 1–23.

53. M. R. Louis, "Acculturation in the Workplace: Newcomers as Lay Ethnographers," in B. Schneider, ed., *Organizational Climate and Culture* (San Francisco: Jossey-Bass, 1990), 85–129.

54. D. M. Rousseau, "Assessing Organizational Culture: The Case for Multiple Methods," in B. Schneider, ed., *Organizational Climate and Culture* (San Francisco: Jossey-Bass, 1990).

55. R. A. Cooke and D. M. Rousseau, "Behavioral Norms and Expectations: A Quantitative Approach to the Assessment of Organizational Culture," *Group and Organizational Studies* 12 (1988): 245–273.

56. R. H. Kilmann and M. J. Saxton, *Kilmann-Saxton Culture-Gap Survey* (Pittsburgh: Organizational Design Consultants, 1983).

57. W. J. Duncan, "Organizational Culture: 'Getting a Fix' on an Elusive Concept," *Academy of Management Executive* 3 (1989): 229–236.

58. C. Yang, "Merger of Titans, Clash of Cultures," *BusinessWeek Online* (July 14, 2003), http://www.businessweek.com/magazine/content/03_8/b3841042_mz005.htm.

59. R. A. Weber and C. F. Camerer, "Cultural Conflict and Merger Failure: An Experimental Approach," *Management Science* 49 (2003): 400–415.

60. S. Buchheit, W. R. Pasewark, and J. R. Strawser, "No Need to Compromise: Evidence of Public Accounting's Changing Culture Regarding Budgetary Performance," *Journal of Business Ethics* 42 (2003): 151–163.

61. N. J. Adler, *International Dimensions of Organizational Behavior*, 2nd ed. (Boston: PWS Kent, 1991).

62. A. Laurent, "The Cultural Diversity of Western Conceptions of Management," *International Studies of Management and Organization* 13 (1983): 75–96.

63. P. C. Earley and E. Mosakowski, "Creating Hybrid Team Cultures: An Empirical Test of Transnational Team Functioning," *Academy of Management Journal* 43 (2000): 26–49.

64. P. Bate, "Using the Culture Concept in an Organization Development Setting," *Journal of Applied Behavior Science* 26 (1990): 83–106.

65. K. R. Thompson and F. Luthans, "Organizational Culture: A Behavioral Perspective," in B. Schneider, ed., *Organizational Climate and Culture* (San Francisco: Jossey-Bass, 1990).

66. V. Sathe, "How to Decipher and Change Corporate Culture," in R. H. Kilman et al., *Managing Corporate Cultures* (San Francisco: Jossey-Bass, 1985).

67. J. B. Shaw, C. D. Fisher, and W. A. Randolph, "From Maternalism to Accountability: The Changing Cultures of Ma Bell and Mother Russia," *Academy of Management Executive* 5 (1991): 7–20.

68. D. Lei, J. W. Slocum, Jr., and R. W. Slater, "Global Strategy and Reward Systems: The Key Roles of Management Development and Corporate Culture," *Organizational Dynamics* 19 (1990): 27–41.

69. S. H. Rhinesmith, "Going Global from the Inside Out," *Training and Development Journal* 45 (1991): 42–47.

70. A. Pater and A. van Gils, "Stimulating Ethical Decision Making in a Business Context: Ethics of Ethical and Professional Codes," *European Management Journal* 21 (December 2003): 762–772.

71. L. K. Trevino and K. A. Nelson, *Managing Business Ethics: Straight Talk about How to Do It Right* (New York: John Wiley & Sons, 1995).

72. A. Bhide and H. H. Stevenson, "Why Be Honest if Honesty Doesn't Pay?" *Harvard Business Review* (September–October 1990): 121–129.

73. "Business Ethics Names 100 Best Corporate Citizens," *Business Ethics* (Spring 2004), http://www.business-ethics.com/100best.htm.

74. S. W. Gellerman, "Why Good Managers Make Bad Ethical Choices," *Harvard Business Review* 64 (1986): 85–90.

75. J. R. Detert, R. G. Schroeder, and J. J. Mauriel, "A Framework for Linking Culture and Improvement Initiatives in Organizations," *Academy of Management Review* 25 (2000): 850–863.

76. P. Panchak, "Executive Word—Manufacturing in the U.S. Pays Off," *Industry Week* (December 1, 2002), http://www.industryweek.com/CurrentArticles/Asp/articles.asp?ArticleId=1365.

77. A. Bernstein, "Low-Skilled Jobs: Do They Have to Move?" *Business Week* (February 26, 2001): 92.

78. R. Bruce, "A Case Study of Harley-Davidson's Business Practices," http://stroked.virtualave.net/casestudy.shtml.

79. T. A. Williams, "Do You Believe in Baldrige?" *Quality Magazine* 43 (2004): 6.

80. D. H. Thomas, "Hot Diggity Dawg, A Dog's Life Ain't So Bad," *Accent on Living* 42 (Winter 1997): 62–68.

Chapter 17

1. "Like Airplanes, Like Rugby," *Reveries Magazine* (November 2002), http://www.reveries.com/reverb/travel/riordan/.

2. J. H. Greenhaus, *Career Management* (Hinsdale, Ill.: CBS College Press, 1987).

3. D. T. Hall, *Careers in Organizations* (Pacific Palisades, Calif.: Goodyear, 1976).

4. Greenhaus, *Career Management;* T. G. Gutteridge and F. L. Otte, "Organizational Career Development: What's Going On Out There?" *Training and Development Journal* 37 (1983): 22–26.

5. M. B. Arthur, P. H. Claman, and R. J. DeFillippi, "Intelligent Enterprise, Intelligent Careers," *Academy of Management Executive* (November 1995): 7–22.

6. T. Lee, "Should You Stay Energized by Changing Jobs Frequently?" *CareerJournal* (January 11, 1998), http://www.careerjournal.com/jobhunting/strategies/19980111-reisberg.html.

7. P. Buhler, "Managing in the '90s," *Supervision* (July 1995): 24–26.

8. D. T. Hall and J. E. Moss, "The New Protean Career Contract: Helping Organizations and Employees Adapt," *Organizational Dynamics* (Winter 1998): 22–37.

9. A. Fisher, "Don't Blow Your New Job," *Fortune* (June 22, 1998): 159–162.

10. D. Goleman, *Working with Emotional Intelligence* (New York: Bantam, 1998).

11. A. Fisher, "Success Secret: A High Emotional IQ," *Fortune* (October 26, 1998): 293–298.

12. M. L. Maynard, "Emotional Intelligence and Perceived Employability for Internship Curriculum," *Psychological Reports* 93 (December 2003): 791–792.

13. K. V. Petrides, A. Furnham, and G. N. Martin, "Estimates of Emotional and Psychometric Intelligence," *Journal of Social Psychology* 144 (April 2004): 149–162.

14. C. Stough and D. de Guara, "Examining the Relationship between Emotional Intelligence and Job Performance," *Australian Journal of Psychology* 55 (2003): 145.

15. C. Chermiss, "The Business Case for Emotional Intelligence," *The Consortium for Research on Emotional Intelligence in Organizations* (2003), http://www.eiconsortium.org/research/business_case_for_ei.htm; L. M. Spencer, Jr. and S. Spencer, *Competence at Work: Models for Superior Performance* (New York: John Wiley & Sons, 1993); L. M. Spencer, Jr., D. C. McClelland, and S. Kelner, *Competency Assessment Methods: History and State of the Art* (Boston, MA: Hay/McBer, 1997).

16. Chermiss, "The Business Case for Emotional Intelligence."

17. D. E. Super, *The Psychology of Careers* (New York: Harper & Row, 1957); D. E. Super and M. J. Bohn, Jr., *Occupational Psychology* (Belmont, Calif.: Wadsworth, 1970).

18. J. L. Holland, *The Psychology of Vocational Choice* (Waltham, Mass.: Blaisdell, 1966); J. L. Holland, *Making Vocational Choices: A Theory of Careers* (Englewood Cliffs, N.J.: Prentice-Hall, 1973).

19. F. T. L. Leong and J. T. Austin, "An Evaluation of the Cross-Cultural Validity of Holland's Theory: Career Choices by Workers in India," *Journal of Vocational Behavior* 52 (1998): 441–455.

20. C. Morgan, J. D. Isaac, and C. Sansone, "The Role of Interest in Understanding the Career Choices of Female and Male College Students," *Sex Roles* 44 (2001): 295–320.

21. S. H. Osipow, *Theories of Career Development* (Englewood Cliffs, N.J.: Prentice-Hall, 1973).

22. J. P. Wanous, T. L. Keon, and J. C. Latack, "Expectancy Theory and Occupational/Organizational Choices: A Review and Test," *Organizational Behavior and Human Performance* 32 (1983): 66–86.

23. P. O. Soelberg, "Unprogrammed Decision Making," *Industrial Management Review* 8 (1967): 19–29.

24. J. P. Wanous, *Organizational Entry: Recruitment, Selection, and Socialization of Newcomers* (Reading, Mass.: Addison-Wesley, 1980).

25. S. L. Premack and J. P. Wanous, "A Meta-Analysis of Realistic Job Preview Experiments," *Journal of Applied Psychology* 70 (1985): 706–719.

26. Idaho State Police, "Realistic Job Preview," http://www.isp.state.id.us/hr/trooper_info/realistic_job.html.

27. P. W. Hom, R. W. Griffeth, L. E. Palich, and J. S. Bracker, "An Exploratory Investigation into Theoretical Mechanisms Underlying Realistic Job Previews," *Personnel Psychology* 41 (1998): 421–451.

28. J. A. Breaugh, "Realistic Job Previews: A Critical Appraisal and Future Research Directions," *Academy of Management Review* 8 (1983): 612–619.

29. G. R. Jones, "Socialization Tactics, Self-Efficacy, and Newcomers' Adjustment to Organizations," *Academy of Management Journal* 29 (1986): 262–279.

30. M. R. Buckley, D. B. Fedor, J. G. Veres, D. S. Wiese, and S. M. Carraher, "Investigating Newcomer Expectations and Job-Related Outcomes," *Journal of Applied Psychology* 83 (1998): 452–461.

31. M. R. Buckley, D. B. Fedor, S. M. Carraher, D. D. Frink, and D. Marvin, "The Ethical Imperative to Provide Recruits Realistic Job Previews," *Journal of Managerial Issues* 9 (1997): 468–484.

32. J. O. Crites, "A Comprehensive Model of Career Adjustment in Early Adulthood," *Journal of Vocational Behavior* 9 (1976): 105–118; S. Cytrynbaum and J. O. Crites, "The Utility of Adult Development in Understanding Career Adjustment Process," in M. B. Arthur, D. T. Hall, and B. S. Lawrence, eds., *Handbook of Career Theory* (Cambridge: Cambridge University Press, 1989), 66–88.

33. D. E. Super, "A Life-Span, Life-Space Approach to Career Development," *Journal of Vocational Behavior* 16 (1980): 282–298; L. Baird and K. Kram, "Career Dynamics: Managing the Superior/Subordinate Relationship," *Organizational Dynamics* 11 (1983): 46–64.

34. D. J. Levinson, *The Seasons of a Man's Life* (New York: Knopf, 1978); D. J. Levinson, *The Seasons of a Woman's Life*, 1997.

35. D. J. Levinson, "A Conception of Adult Development," *American Psychologist* 41 (1986): 3–13.

36. D. L. Nelson, "Adjusting to a New Organization: Easing the Transition from Outsider to Insider," in J. C. Quick, R. E. Hess, J. Hermalin, and J. D. Quick, eds., *Career Stress in Changing Times* (New York: Haworth Press, 1990), 61–86.

37. J. P. Kotter, "The Psychological Contract: Managing the Joining Up Process," *California Management Review* 15 (1973): 91–99.

38. D. M. Rousseau, "New Hire Perceptions of Their Own and Their Employers' Obligations: A Study of Psychological Contracts,"

Journal of Organizational Behavior 11 (1990): 389–400; D. L. Nelson, J. C. Quick, and J. R. Joplin, "Psychological Contracting and Newcomer Socialization: An Attachment Theory Foundation," *Journal of Social Behavior and Personality* 6 (1991): 55–72.

39. S. D. Pugh, D. P. Skarlicki, and B. S. Passell, "After the Fall: Lay-off Victims' Trust and Cynicism in Reemployment," *Journal of Occupational and Organizational Psychology* 76 (June 2003): 201–212.

40. D. L. Nelson, "Organizational Socialization: A Stress Perspective," *Journal of Occupational Behavior* 8 (1987): 311–324.

41. R. A. Dean, K. R. Ferris, and C. Konstans, "Reality Shock: Reducing the Organizational Commitment of Professionals," *Personnel Administrator* 30 (1985): 139–148.

42. Nelson, "Adjusting to a New Organization," 61–86.

43. G. Chen and R. J. Kilmoski, "The Impact of Expectations on Newcomer Performance in Teams as Mediated by Work Characteristics, Social Exchanges, and Empowerment," *Academy of Management Journal* 46 (October 2003): 591–607.

44. D. L. Nelson and C. D. Sutton, "The Relationship between Newcomer Expectations of Job Stressors and Adjustment to the New Job," *Work and Stress* 5 (1991): 241–254.

45. A. M. Saks, "Longitudinal Field Investigation of the Moderating and Mediating Effects of Self-Efficacy on the Relationship between Training and Newcomer Adjustment," *Journal of Applied Psychology* 80 (1995): 211–225.

46. G. F. Dreher and R. D. Bretz, Jr., "Cognitive Ability and Career Attainment: Moderating Effects of Early Career Success," *Journal of Applied Psychology* 76 (1991): 392–397.

47. D. L. Nelson and J. C. Quick, "Social Support and Newcomer Adjustment in Organizations: Attachment Theory at Work?" *Journal of Organizational Behavior* 12 (1991): 543–554.

48. Author conversation with Mark Phillips, Assistant Professor of Management, Abilene Christian University (July 2004).

49. TechRepublic Staff, "Most Organizations Wing It with New Employees," *TechRepublic* (April 5, 2002), http://techrepublic.com.com/5100-6317_11-1051414.html.

50. R. Pascale, "The Paradox of Corporate Culture: Reconciling Ourselves to Socialization," *California Management Review* 27 (1985): 27–41.

51. K. M. Davey and J. Arnold, "A Multi-Method Study of Accounts of Personal Change by Graduates Starting Work: Self-Ratings, Categories, and Women's Discourses," *Journal of Occupational and Organizational Psychology* 73 (2000): 461–486.

52. Levinson, "A Conception of Adult Development," 3–13.

53. J. W. Walker, "Let's Get Realistic about Career Paths," *Human Resource Management* 15 (1976): 2–7.

54. E. H. Buttner and D. P. Moore, "Women's Organizational Exodus to Entrepreneurship: Self-Reported Motivations and Correlates," *Journal of Small Business Management* 35 (1997): 34–46; Center for Women's Business Research Press Release, "Privately Held, 50% or More Women-Owned Businesses in the United States," 2004, http://www.nfwbo.org/pressreleases/nationalstatetrends/total.htm.

55. B. Filipczak, "You're on Your Own," *Training* (January 1995): 29–36.

56. K. E. Kram, *Mentoring at Work: Developmental Relationships in Organizational Life* (Glenview, Ill.: Scott, Foresman, 1985).

57. C. Orpen, "The Effects of Monitoring on Employees' Career Success," *Journal of Social Psychology* 135 (1995): 667–668.

58. J. Arnold and K. Johnson, "Mentoring in Early Career," *Human Resource Management Journal* 7 (1997): 61–70.

59. B. P. Madia and C. J. Lutz, "Perceived Similarity, Expectation-Reality Discrepancies, and Mentors' Expressed Intention to Remain in the Big Brothers/Big Sisters Programs," *Journal of Applied Social Psychology* 34 (March 2004): 598–622.

60. "A Guide to the Mentor Program Listings," *Mentors Peer Resources*, http://www.mentors.ca/mentorprograms.html.

61. B. R. Ragins, "Diversified Mentoring Relationships in Organizations: A Power Perspective," *Academy of Management Review* 22 (1997): 482–521.

62. R. Friedman, M. Kan, and D. B. Cornfield, "Social Support and Career Optimism: Examining the Effectiveness of Network Groups Among Black Managers," *Human Relations* 51 (1998): 1155–1177.

63. S. E. Seibert, M. L. Kraimer, and R. C. Liden, "A Social Capital Theory of Career Success," *Academy of Management Journal* 44 (2001): 219–237.

64. PricewaterhouseCoopers Czech Republic, "Graduate Recruitment—FAQs," http://www.pwcglobal.com/cz/eng/car-inexp/main/faq.html.

65. M. A. Covaleski, M. W. Dirsmuth, J. B. Heian, and S. Samuel, "The Calculated and the Avowed: Techniques of Discipline and Struggles over Identity in Big Six Public Accounting Firms," *Administrative Science Quarterly* 43 (1998): 293–327.

66. B. R. Ragins and J. L. Cotton, "Easier Said than Done: Gender Differences in Perceived Barriers to Gaining a Mentor," Academy of Management Journal 34 (1991): 939–951; S. D. Phillips and A. R. Imhoff, "Women and Career Development: A Decade of Research," *Annual Review of Psychology* 48 (1997): 31–43.

67. W. Whiteley, T. W. Dougherty, and G. F. Dreher, "Relationship of Career Mentoring and Socioeconomic Origin to Managers' and Professionals' Early Career Progress," *Academy of Management Journal* 34 (1991): 331–351; G. F. Dreher and R. A. Ash, "A Comparative Study of Mentoring among Men and Women in Managerial, Professional, and Technical Positions," *Journal of Applied Psychology* 75 (1990): 539–546; T. A. Scandura, "Mentorship and Career Mobility: An Empirical Investigation," *Journal of Organizational Behavior* 13 (1992): 169–174.

68. G. F. Dreher and T. H. Cox, Jr., "Race, Gender and Opportunity: A Study of Compensation Attainment and Establishment of Mentoring Relationships," *Journal of Applied Psychology* 81 (1996): 297–309.

69. D. D. Horgan and R. J. Simeon, "Mentoring and Participation: An Application of the Vroom-Yetton Model," *Journal of Business and Psychology* 5 (1990): 63–84.

70. B. R. Ragins, J. L. Cotton, and J. S. Miller, "Marginal Mentoring: The Effects of Type of Mentor, Quality of Relationship, and Program Design on Work and Career Attitudes," *Academy of Management Journal* 43 (2000): 1177–1194.

71. R. T. Brennan, R. C. Barnett, and K. C. Gareis, "When She Earns More than He Does: A Longitudinal Study of Dual-Earner Couples," *Journal of Marriage and Family* 63 (2001): 168–182.

72. F. S. Hall and D. T. Hall, *The Two-Career Couple* (Reading, Mass.: Addison-Wesley, 1979).

73. J. S. Boles, M. W. Johnston, and J. F. Hair, Jr., "Role Stress, Work–Family Conflict and Emotional Exhaustion: Inter-Relationships and Effects on Some Work-Related Consequences" *Journal of Personal Selling and Sales Management* 17 (1998): 17–28.

74. B. Morris, "Is Your Family Wrecking Your Career? (And Vice Versa)," *Fortune* (March 17, 1997): 70–80.

75. D. L. Nelson, J. C. Quick, M. A. Hitt, and D. Moesel, "Politics, Lack of Career Progress, and Work/Home Conflict: Stress and Strain for Working Women," *Sex Roles* 23 (1990): 169–185.

76. L. E. Duxbury and C. A. Higgins, "Gender Differences in Work–Family Conflict," *Journal of Applied Psychology* 76 (1991): 60–74.

77. R. G. Netemeyer, J. S. Boles, and R. McMurrian, "Development and Validation of Work–Family Conflict and Family–Work Conflict Scales," *Journal of Applied Psychology* 81 (1996): 400–410.

78. N. Yang, C. C. Chen, J. Choi, and Y. Zou, "Sources of Work–Family Conflict: A Sino–U.S. Comparison of the Effects of Work and Family Demands," *Academy of Management Journal* 43 (2000): 113–123.

79. D. L. Nelson and M. A. Hitt, "Employed Women and Stress: Implications for Enhancing Women's Mental Health in the Workplace," in J. C. Quick, L. R. Murphy, and J. J. Hurrell, eds., *Stress and Well-Being at Work: Assessments and Interventions for Occupational Mental Health* (Washington, D.C.: American Psychological Association, 1992), 164–177.

80. Mitchell Gold Co., "Day Care," http://www.mitchellgold.com/daycare.asp.

81. D. Machan, "The Mommy and Daddy Track," *Forbes* (April 6, 1990): 162.

82. E. M. Brody, M. H. Kleban, P. T. Johnsen, C. Hoffman, and C. B. Schoonover, "Work Status and Parental Care: A Comparison of Four Groups of Women," *Gerontological Society of America* 27 (1987): 201–208; J. W. Anastas, J. L. Gibson, and P. J. Larson, "Working Families and Eldercare: A National Perspective in an Aging America," *Social Work* 35 (1990): 405–411.

83. Cincinnati Area Senior Services, "Corporate Elder Care Program," http://www.senserv.org/elder.htm.

84. E. E. Kossek, J. A. Colquitt, and R. A. Noe, "Caregiving, Well-Being, and Performance: The Effects of Place and Provider as a Function

of Dependent Type and Work–Family Climates," *Academy of Management Journal* 44 (2001): 29–44.

85. Harvard University Office of Human Resources, "Work/Life Support Services—Elder Care Resources," http://atwork.harvard.edu/worklife/eldercare/.

86. M. Richards, "'Daddy Track' Is Road Taken More Often," *The Morning Call* (July 28, 2004), http://www.mcall.com/business/local/all-daddyjul28,0,1869593.story?coll=all-businesslocal-hed.

87. L. J. Barham, "Variables Affecting Managers' Willingness to Grant Alternative Work Arrangements," *Journal of Social Psychology* 138 (1998): 291–302.

88. J. Kaplan, "Hitting the Wall at Forty," *Business Month* 136 (1990): 52–58.

89. M. B. Arthur and K. E. Kram, "Reciprocity at Work: The Separate Yet Inseparable Possibilities for Individual and Organizational Development," in M. B. Arthur, D. T. Hall, and B. S. Lawrence, eds., *Handbook of Career Theory* (Cambridge: Cambridge University Press, 1989).

90. K. E. Kram, "Phases of the Mentoring Relationship," *Academy of Management Review* 26 (1983): 608–625.

91. B. Rosen and T. Jerdee, *Older Employees: New Roles for Valued Resources* (Homewood, Ill.: Irwin, 1985).

92. J. W. Gilsdorf, "The New Generation: Older Workers," *Training and Development Journal* (March 1992): 77–79.

93. J. F. Quick, "Time to Move On?" in J. C. Quick, R. E. Hess, J. Hermalin, and J. D. Quick, eds., *Career Stress in Changing Times* (New York: Haworth Press, 1990), 239–250.

94. D. Machan, "Rent-an-Exec," *Forbes* (January 22, 1990): 132–133.

95. E. McGoldrick and C. L. Cooper, "Why Retire Early?" in J. C. Quick, R. E. Hess, J. Hermalin, and J. D. Quick, eds., *Career Stress in Changing Times* (New York: Haworth Press, 1990), 219–238.

96. E. Daspin, "The Second Midlife Crisis," *The Baltimore Sun* (originally published in *The Wall Street Journal*) (May 10, 2004), http://www.baltimoresun.com/business/bal-crisis051004,0,614944.story?coll=bal-business-headlines.

97. S. Kim and D. C. Feldman, "Working in Retirement: The Antecedents of Bridge Employment and Its Consequences for Quality of Life in Retirement," *Academy of Management Journal* 43 (2000): 1195–1210.

98. Lawrence Livermore Retiree Program, "Tasks Requested by Lab Programs," http://www.llnl.gov/aadp/retiree/tasks.html.

99. E. Schein, *Career Anchors* (San Diego: University Associates, 1985).

100. G. W. Dalton, "Developmental Views of Careers in Organizations," in M. B. Arthur, D. T. Hall, and B. S. Lawrence, eds., *Handbook of Career Theory* (Cambridge: Cambridge University Press, 1989), 89–109.

101. D. C. Feldman, "Careers in Organizations: Recent Trends and Future Directions," *Journal of Management* 15 (1989): 135–156.

102. B. O'Reilly, "The Job Drought," *Fortune* (August 24, 1992): 62–74.

103. A. S. Grove, "A High-Tech CEO Updates His Views on Managing and Careers," *Fortune* (September 18, 1995): 229–230.

104. "Like Airplanes, Like Rugby," *Reveries Magazine* (November 2002), http://www.reveries.com/reverb/travel/riordan/.

Chapter 18

1. "2003 Global Brands Scorecard," *BusinessWeek Online* (August 4, 2003), http://bwnt.businessweek.com/brand/2003/index.asp.

2. J. Creswell and J. Schlosser, "Has Coke Lost Its Fizz?" *Fortune* 148 (November 10, 2003): 215, http://www.fortune.com/fortune/subs/article/0,15114,526363,00.html.

3. M. A. Verespej, "When Change Becomes the Norm," *Industry Week* (March 16, 1992): 35–38.

4. P. Mornell, "Nothing Endures But Change," *Inc. Magazine* 22 (July 2000): 131–132, http://www.inc.com/magazine/20000701/19555.html.

5. H. J. Van Buren III, "The Bindingness of Social and Psychological Contracts: Toward a Theory of Social Responsibility in Downsizing," *Journal of Business Ethics* 25 (2000): 205–219.

6. United States Embassy in Mexico Press Release, "Response to Criticism of U.S. Agricultural Policy and NAFTA" (December 5, 2002), http://www.usembassy-mexico.gov/releases/ep021205realitiesNAFTA.htm.

7. M. Stevenson, "Mexican Farmers Renew NAFTA Protests," *Yahoo! News* (January 20, 2003).

8. M. McCarthy, "PR Disaster as Coke Withdraws 'Purest' Bottled Water in Britain," *The New Zealand Herald* (March 20, 2004), http://www.nzherald.co.nz/business/businessstorydisplay.cfm?storyID=3555911&thesection=business&thesubsection=world&thesecondsubsection=europe.

9. L. Hirschhorn and T. Gilmore, "The New Boundaries of the 'Boundaryless' Company," *Harvard Business Review* (May–June 1992): 104–115.

10. L. R. Offerman and M. Gowing, "Organizations of the Future: Changes and Challenges," *American Psychologist* (February 1990): 95–108.

11. W. B. Johnston, "Global Work Force 2000: The New World Labor Market," *Harvard Business Review*, (March–April 1991): 115–127.

12. "50 Best Companies for Minorities: Full List," *Fortune* (June 28, 2004), http://www.fortune.com/fortune/diversity/subs/fulllist/0,20548,,00.html.

13. G. Bylinsky, "Hot New Technologies for American Factories," *Fortune* (June 26, 2000): 288A–288K.

14. R. M. Kanter, "Improving the Development, Acceptance, and Use of New Technology: Organizational and Interorganizational Challenges," in *People and Technology in the Workplace* (Washington, D.C.: National Academy Press, 1991), 15–56.

15. Gap Inc. Press Release, "Gap Inc. Joins the Ethical Trading Initiative," *CSRwire* (April 28, 2004), http://www.csrwire.com/article.cgi/2683.html.

16. "Gap Inc. 2003 Social Responsibility Report," *Gap Inc.* (September 17, 2004), http://ccbn.mobular.net/ccbn/7/645/696/index.html.

17. S. A. Mohrman and A. M. Mohrman, Jr., "The Environment as an Agent of Change," in A. M. Mohrman, Jr., et al., eds., *Large-Scale Organizational Change* (San Francisco: Jossey-Bass, 1989), 35–47.

18. T. D'Aunno, M. Succi, and J. A. Alexander, "The Role of Institutional and Market Forces in Divergent Organizational Change," *Administrative Science Quarterly* 45 (2000): 679–703.

19. Intel press release, Santa Clara, CA, April 21, 2004, http://www.intel.com/pressroom.

20. Q. N. Huy, "Emotional Balancing of Organizational Continuity and Radical Change: The Contribution of Middle Managers," *Administrative Science Quarterly* 47 (March 1, 2002): 31–69.

21. D. Nadler, "Organizational Frame-Bending: Types of Change in the Complex Organization," in R. Kilmann and T. Covin, eds., *Corporate Transformation* (San Francisco: Jossey-Bass, 1988), 66–83.

22. K. Belson, "AT&T Plans to Raise Its Rates for Residential Calling Plans," *The New York Times* (August 4, 2004), http://www.nytimes.com/2004/08/04/business/04phone.html.

23. L. Ackerman, "Development, Transition, or Transformation: The Question of Change in Organizations," *OD Practitioner* (December 1986): 1–8.

24. T. D. Jick, *Managing Change* (Homewood, Ill.: Irwin, 1993), 3.

25. J. M. Bloodgood and J. L. Morrow, "Strategic Organizational Change: Exploring the Roles of Environmental Structure, Internal Conscious Awareness, and Knowledge," *Journal of Management Studies* 40 (2003): 1761–1782.

26. D. Miller and M. J. Chen, "Sources and Consequences of Competitive Inertia. A Study of the U.S. Airline Industry," *Administrative Science Quarterly* 39 (1994): 1–23.

27. S. L. Brown and K. M. Eisenhardt, "The Art of Continuous Change: Linking Complexity Theory and Time-Paced Evolution in Relentlessly Shifting Organizations," *Administrative Science Quarterly* 42 (1997): 1–34.

28. J. Child and C. Smith, "The Context and Process of Organizational Transformation: Cadbury Ltd. In Its Sector," *Journal of Management Studies* 12 (1987): 12–27.

29. J. Amis, T. Slack, and C. R. Hinings, "The Pace, Sequence, and Linearity of Radical Change," *Academy of Management Journal* 47 (2004): 15–39.

30. R. M. Kanter, *The Change Masters* (New York: Simon & Schuster, 1983).

31. J. R. Katzenbach, *Real Change Leaders* (New York: Times Business, 1995).

32. J. L. Denis, L. Lamothe, and A. Langley, "The Dynamics of Collective Leadership and Strategic Change in Pluralistic Organizations," *Academy of Management Journal* 44 (2001): 809–837.

33. M. Beer, *Organization Change and Development: A Systems View* (Santa Monica, Calif.: Goodyear, 1980), 78.

34. K. Whalen-Berry and C. R. Hinings, "The Relative Effect of Change Drivers in Large-Scale Organizational Change: An Empirical Study," in W. Passmore and R. Goodman, eds., *Research in Organizational Change and Development* 14 (New York: JAI Press, 2003): 99–146.

35. J. L. Denis, L. Lamothe, and A. Langley, "The Dynamics of Collective Leadership and Strategic Change in Pluralistic Organizations," *Academy of Management Journal* 44 (2001): 809–837.

36. F. Cheyunski and J. Millard, "Accelerated Business Transformation and the Role of the Organizational Architect," *Journal of Applied Behavioral Science* 34 (1998): 268–285.

37. N. A. M. Worren, K. Ruddle, and K. Moore, "From Organizational Development to Change Management: The Emergence of a New Profession," *Journal of Applied Behavioral Science* 35 (1999): 273–286.

38. P. G. Audia, E. A. Locke, and K. G. Smith, "The Paradox of Success: An Archival and a Laboratory Study of Strategic Persistence Following Radical Environmental Change," *Academy of Management Journal* 43 (2000): 837–853.

39. J. W. Brehm, *A Theory of Psychological Reactance* (New York: Academic Press, 1966).

40. J. A. Klein, "Why Supervisors Resist Employee Involvement," *Harvard Business Review* 62 (1984): 87–95.

41. B. L. Kirkman, R. G. Jones, and D. L. Shapiro, "Why Do Employees Resist Teams? Examining the 'Resistance Barrier' to Work Team Effectiveness," *International Journal of Conflict Management* 11 (2000): 74–92.

42. D. L. Nelson and M. A. White, "Management of Technological Innovation: Individual Attitudes, Stress, and Work Group Attributes," *Journal of High Technology Management Research* 1 (1990): 137–148.

43. D. Klein, "Some Notes on the Dynamics of Resistance to Change: The Defender Role," in W. G. Bennis, K. D. Benne, R. Chin, and K. E. Corey, eds., *The Planning of Change*, 3rd ed. (New York: Holt, Rinehart & Winston, 1969), 117–124.

44. T. G. Cummings and E. F. Huse, *Organizational Development and Change* (St. Paul, Minn.: West, 1989).

45. N. L. Jimmieson, D. J. Terry, and V. J. Callan, "A Longitudinal Study of Employee Adaptation to Organizational Change: The Role of Change-Related Information and Change-Related Self Efficacy," *Journal of Occupational Health Psychology* 9 (2004): 11–27.

46. N. DiFonzo and P. Bordia, "A Tale of Two Corporations: Managing Uncertainty during Organizational Change," *Human Resource Management* 37 (1998): 295–303.

47. L. P. Livingstone, M. A. White, D. L. Nelson, and F. Tabak, "Delays in Technological Innovation Implementations: Some Preliminary Results on a Common but Understudied Occurrence," working paper, Oklahoma State University.

48. G. Lindsay, "Prada's High-Tech Misstep," *Business 2.0* (February 25, 2004): 72–75, http://www.business2.com/b2/web/articles/0,17863,594365,00.html.

49. M. Hickins, "Reconcilable Differences," *Management Review* 87 (1998): 54–58.

50. J. P. Kotter and L. A. Schlesinger, "Choosing Strategies for Change," *Harvard Business Review* 57 (1979): 109–112; W. Bridges, *Transitions: Making Sense of Life's Changes* (Reading, Mass.: Addison-Wesley, 1980); H. Woodward and S. Buchholz, *Aftershock: Helping People through Corporate Change* (New York: Wiley, 1987).

51. S. Michailova, "Contrasts in Culture: Russian and Western Perspectives on Organizational Change," *Academy of Management Executive* 14 (2000): 99–112.

52. K. Lewin, "Frontiers in Group Dynamics," *Human Relations* 1 (1947): 5–41.

53. W. McWhinney, "Meta-Praxis: A Framework for Making Complex Changes," in A. M. Mohrman, Jr., et al., eds., *Large-Scale Organizational Change* (San Francisco: Jossey-Bass, 1989), 154–199.

54. M. Beer and E. Walton, "Developing the Competitive Organization: Interventions and Strategies," *American Psychologist* 45 (1990): 154–161.

55. B. Bertsch and R. Williams, "How Multinational CEOs Make Change Programs Stick," *Long Range Planning* 27 (1994): 12–24.

56. J. Amis, T. Slack, and C. R. Hinings, "Values and Organizational Change," *Journal of Applied Behavioral Science* 38 (2002): 356–385.

57. W. L. French and C. H. Bell, *Organization Development: Behavioral Science Interventions for Organization Improvement*, 4th ed. (Englewood Cliffs, N.J.: Prentice-Hall, 1990); W. W. Burke, *Organization Development: A Normative View* (Reading, Mass.: Addison-Wesley, 1987).

58. A. Huczynski, *Encyclopedia of Organizational Change Methods* (Brookfield, Vt.: Gower, 1987).

59. A. O. Manzini, *Organizational Diagnosis* (New York: AMACOM, 1988).

60. M. R. Weisbord, "Organizational Diagnosis: Six Places to Look for Trouble with or without a Theory," *Group and Organization Studies* (December 1976): 430–444.

61. H. Levinson, *Organizational Diagnosis* (Cambridge, Mass.: Harvard University Press, 1972).

62. J. Nicholas, "The Comparative Impact of Organization Development Interventions," *Academy of Management Review* 7 (1982): 531–542.

63. G. Odiorne, *Management by Objectives* (Marshfield, Mass.: Pitman, 1965).

64. E. Huse, "Putting in a Management Development Program that Works," *California Management Review* 9 (1966): 73–80.

65. J. P. Muczyk and B. C. Reimann, "MBO as a Complement to Effective Leadership," *Academy of Management Executive* (May 1989): 131–138.

66. L. L. Berry and A. Parasuraman, "Prescriptions for a Service Quality Revolution in America," *Organizational Dynamics* 20 (1992): 5–15.

67. "Five Companies Win 1992 Baldridge Quality Awards," *Business America* (November 2, 1992): 7–16.

68. D. M. Anderson, "Hidden Forces," *Success* (April 1995): 12.

69. W. G. Dyer, *Team Building: Issues and Alternatives*, 2nd ed. (Reading, Mass.: Addison-Wesley, 1987).

70. E. Stephan, G. Mills, R. W. Pace, and L. Ralphs, "HRD in the Fortune 500: A Survey," *Training and Development Journal* (January 1988): 26–32.

71. A. Edmondson, "Psychological Safety and Learning Behavior in Work Teams," *Administrative Science Quarterly* 44 (1999): 350–383.

72. M. Whitmire and P. R. Nienstedt, "Lead Leaders into the '90s," *Personnel Journal* (May 1991): 80–85.

73. "Tactical Tanks: Sherman, Texas," *Life Adventures Online Magazine* (June 3, 2004), http://www.lifeadventures.com/tactical_tanks.htm.

74. Tactical Tanks (June 3, 2004), http://www.tacticaltanks.com.

75. E. Salas, T. L. Dickinson, S. I. Tannenbaum, and S. A. Converse, *A Meta-Analysis of Team Performance and Training, Naval Training System Center Technical Reports* (Orlando, Fla.: U.S. Government, 1991).

76. E. Schein, *Its Role in Organization Development*, vol. 1 of Process Consultation (Reading, Mass.: Addison-Wesley, 1988).

77. H. Hornstein, "Organizational Development and Change Management: Don't Throw the Baby Out with the Bath Water," *Journal of Applied Behavioral Science* 37 (2001): 223–226.

78. D. Filipowski, "How Federal Express Makes Your Package Its Most Important," *Personnel Journal* (February 1992): 40–46; P. Galagan, "Training Delivers Results to Federal Express," *Training and Development* (December 1991): 27–33.

79. R. W. Revans, *Action Learning* (London: Blonde & Briggs, 1980).

80. I. L. Goldstein, *Training in Organizations*, 3rd ed. (Pacific Grove, Calif.: Brooks/Cole, 1993).

81. J. A. Conger and R. M. Fulmer, "Developing Your Leadership Pipeline," *Harvard Business Review* 81 (2003): 76–84.

82. D. A. Ready and J. A. Conger, "Why Leadership Development Efforts Fail," *MIT Sloan Management Review* 44 (2003): 83–89.

83. M. Jay, "Understanding How to Leverage Executive Coaching," *Organization Development Journal* 21 (2003): 6–13.

84. D. Goleman, R. Boyaysis, and A. McKee, *Primal Leadership: Learning to Lead with Emotional Intelligence* (Harvard Business School Press, 2004).

85. K. M. Wasylyshyn, "Executive Coaching: An Outcome Study," *Consulting Psychology Journal* 55 (2003): 94–106.

86. J. W. Smither, M. London, R. Flautt, Y. Vargas, and I. Kucine, "Can Working with an Executive Coach Improve Multisource Feedback Ratings Over Time? A Quasi-Experimental Field Study," *Personnel Psychology* 56 (2003): 23–44.

87. "Occupational Stress and Employee Stress," *American Psychological Association* (June 6, 2004), http://www.psychologymatters.org/karasek.html.

88. J. D. Holloway, "Keeping Employees Healthy and Happy," *Monitor on Psychology* 34 (December 2003): 32–33, http://www.apapractice.org/apo/psychologically_healthy/keeping_employees.html.

89. D. A. Nadler, "Concepts for the Management of Organizational Change," in J. R. Hackman, E. E. Lawler III, and L. W. Porter, eds., *Perspectives on Organizational Behavior* (New York: McGraw-Hill, 1983).

90. Cummings and Huse, *Organizational Development*; P. E. Connor and L. K. Lake, *Managing Organizational Change* (New York: Praeger, 1988).

91. R. L. Lowman, "Ethical Human Resource Practice in Organizational Settings," in D. W. Bray, ed., *Working with Organizations* (New York: Guilford Press, 1991).

92. H. Kelman, "Manipulation of Human Behavior: An Ethical Dilemma for the Social Scientist," in W. Bennis, K. Benne, and R. Chin, eds., *The Planning of Change* (New York: Holt, Rinehart, & Winston, 1969).

93. A. M. Pettigrew, R. W. Woodman, and K. S. Cameron, "Studying Organizational Change and Development: Challenges for Future Research," *Academy of Management Journal* 44 (2001): 697–713.

94. R. A. Katzell and R. A. Guzzo, "Psychological Approaches to Worker Productivity," *American Psychologist* 38 (1983): 468–472.

95. R. A. Guzzo, R. D. Jette, and R. A. Katzell, "The Effects of Psychologically Based Intervention Programs on Worker Productivity," *Personnel Psychology* 38 (1985): 275–291.

96. Goldstein, *Training in Organizations*.

97. T. Covin and R. H. Kilmann, "Participant Perceptions of Positive and Negative Influences on Large-Scale Change," *Group and Organization Studies* 15 (1990): 233–248.

98. C. M. Brotheridge, "The Role of Fairness in Mediating the Effects of Voice and Justification on Stress and Other Outcomes in a Climate of Organizational Change," *International Journal of Stress Management* 10 (2003): 253–268.

99. P. Sellers, "Inside the CEO Change at Coke," *Fortune* 149 (March 8, 2004): 40, http://www.fortune.com/fortune/subs/article/0,15114,593448,00.html.

100. "KO'd: Coca-Cola Shares Fall 11 Straight Trading Rounds," *E*TRADE FINANCIAL Corp.* (July 29, 2004), http://us.etrade.com/e/t/invest/story?/ID=STORYID%3Detrade_2004_07_29_.

101. E. B. Smith, "Coke Exec Quits Over Frozen Coke Scandal," *USA Today* (August 25, 2003), http://www.usatoday.com/money/industries/food/2003-08-25-coke-resign_x.htm.

102. B. Morris, "Coca-Cola: The Real Story," *Fortune* (May 31, 2004): 84–98, http://www.fortune.com/fortune/subs/article/0,15114,638361,00.html.

103. Ibid.

104. Ibid.

105. "KO'd: Coca-Cola Shares Fall 11 Straight Trading Rounds," *E*TRADE FINANCIAL Corp.* (July 29, 2004), http://us.etrade.com/e/t/invest/story?/ID=STORYID%3Detrade_2004_07_29_.

Appendix A

1. F. W. Taylor, *The Principles of Scientific Management* (New York: Norton, 1911).

2. M. Weber, *The Protestant Ethic and the Spirit of Capitalism* (London: Talcott Parson, tr., 1930).

3. W. B. Cannon, *Bodily Changes in Pain, Hunger, Fear, and Rage* (New York: Appleton, 1915).

4. F. J. Roethlisberger and W. J. Dickson, *Management and the Worker* (Cambridge, Mass.: Harvard University Press, 1939).

5. K. Lewin, R. Lippitt, and R. K. White, "Patterns of Aggressive Behavior in Experimentally Created 'Social Climates,'" *Journal of Social Psychology* 10 (1939): 271–299; A. H. Maslow, *Motivation and Personality* (New York: Harper & Row, 1954); F. Herzberg, B. Mausner, and B. Snyderman, *The Motivation to Work*, 2nd ed. (New York: Wiley, 1959); E. A. Locke, "Toward a Theory of Task Motivation and Incentives," *Organizational Behavior and Human Performance* 3 (1968): 157–189; R. M. Stogdill, *Handbook of Leadership: A Survey of Theory and Research* (New York: Free Press, 1974); G. A. Yukl, *Leadership in Organizations*, 3rd ed. (Englewood Cliffs, N.J.: Prentice-Hall, 1995).

6. G. C. Homans, *The Human Group* (New York: Harcourt Brace Jovanovich, 1950).

7. J. R. Hackman and G. Oldham, *Work Redesign* (Reading, Mass.: Addison-Wesley, 1980); P. C. Smith, L. M. Kendall, and C. L. Hulin, *The Measurement of Satisfaction in Work and Retirement* (Chicago: Rand McNally, 1969).

8. N. R. F. Maier, *Psychology in Industry: A Psychological Approach to Industrial Problems*, 2nd ed. (Boston: Houghton Mifflin, 1955).

9. R. C. Solomon, "Corporate Roles, Personal Virtues: An Aristotelian Approach to Business Ethics," *Business Ethics Quarterly*, 2 (1992): 317–339.

10. R. C. Solomon, *A Better Way to Think about Business: How Personal Integrity Leads to Corporate Success* (New York: Oxford University Press, 1999).

11. M. E. P. Seligman, *Learned Optimism* (New York: Knopf, 1990) and M. E. P. Seligman and M. Csikszentmihalyi, "Positive Psychology," *American Psychologist*, 55 (2000): 5–14.

12. B. L. Simmons, *Eustress at Work: Accentuating the Positive* (unpublished doctoral dissertation, Oklahoma State University, 2000).

13. F. Luthans, "Positive Organizational Behavior: Developing and Managing Psychological Strengths," *Academy of Management Executive*, 16 (2002): 57–72; "The Need for and Meaning of Positive Organizational Behaviors," *Journal of Organizational Behavior*, 23 (2002): 695–706.

14. B. J. Avolio, *Full Leadership Development: Building the Vital Forces in Organizations* (Thousand Oaks, CA: Sage Publications, 1999).

15. F. J. Roethlisberger, *Management and Morale* (Cambridge, Mass: Harvard University Press, 1941).

16. J. G. Adair, "The Hawthorne Effect: A Reconsideration of Methodological Artifact," *Journal of Applied Psychology* 69 (1984): 334–345.

17. F. J. Roethlisberger, W. J. Dickson, and H. A. Wright, *Management and the Worker: An Account of a Research Program Conducted by the Western Electric Company, Hawthorne Works, Chicago* (Cambridge, Mass.: Harvard University Press, 1950); A. G. Athos and J. J. Gabarro, *Interpersonal Behavior: Communication and Understanding in Relationships* (Englewood Cliffs, N.J.: Prentice-Hall, 1978).

Appendix B

1. Two sources for further reference on experimental design are D. T. Campbell and J. C. Stanley, *Experimental and Quasi-Experimental Designs for Research* (Chicago: Rand McNally, 1966); and T. D. Cook and D. T. Campbell, *Quasi-Experimentation: Design and Analysis Issues for Field Settings* (Boston: Houghton Mifflin, 1979).

2. M. L. Lombardo, M. McCall, and D. L. DeVries, *Looking Glass* (Glenview, Ill.: Scott, Foresman, 1983).

3. Elaboration of how such measures are developed is beyond the scope of this appendix but can be found in U. Sekaran, *Research Methods for Business: A Skill Building Approach*, 2nd ed. (New York: Wiley, 1992).

4. Several measures are available in *Psychological Measurement Yearbooks*; J. L. Price, *Handbook of Organizational Measurement* (Lexington, Mass.: D. C. Heath, 1972); and *Michigan Organizational Assessment Packages* (Ann Arbor, Mich.: Institute of Survey Research).

5. One such instrument is the Job Descriptive Index, which is used to measure job satisfaction. It was developed by P. C. Smith, L. Kendall, and C. Hulin. See their book *The Measurement of Satisfaction in Work and Retirement* (Chicago: Rand McNally, 1969), pp. 79–84.

Glossary

A

adaptive culture An organizational culture that encourages confidence and risk taking among employees, has leadership that produces change, and focuses on the changing needs of customers.

adhocracy A selectively decentralized form of organization that emphasizes the support staff and mutual adjustment among people.

administrative orbiting Delaying action on a conflict by buying time.

advancement The second, highly achievement-oriented career stage in which people focus on increasing their competence.

affect The emotional component of an attitude.

affective commitment The type of organizational commitment that is based on an individual's desire to remain in an organization.

anthropocentric Placing human considerations at the center of job design decisions.

anthropology The science of the learned behavior of human beings.

anticipatory socialization The first socialization stage, which encompasses all of the learning that takes place prior to the newcomer's first day on the job.

artifacts Symbols of culture in the physical and social work environment.

assumptions Deeply held beliefs that guide behavior and tell members of an organization how to perceive and think about things.

attitude A psychological tendency expressed by evaluating an entity with some degree of favor or disfavor.

attribution theory A theory that explains how individuals pinpoint the causes of their own behavior and that of others.

authority The right to influence another person.

authority-compliance manager (9,1) A leader who emphasizes efficient production.

autocratic style A style of leadership in which the leader uses strong, directive, controlling actions to enforce the rules, regulations, activities, and relationships in the work environment.

B

barriers to communication Aspects of the communication content and context that can impair effective communication in a workplace.

behavioral measures Personality assessments that involve observing an individual's behavior in a controlled situation.

benevolent An individual who is comfortable with an equity ratio less than that of his or her comparison other.

bounded rationality A theory that suggests that there are limits to how rational a decision maker can actually be.

brainstorming A technique for generating as many ideas as possible on a given subject, while suspending evaluation until all the ideas have been suggested.

bridge employment Employment that takes place after a person retires from a full-time position but before the person's permanent withdrawal from the workforce.

C

career The pattern of work-related experiences that span the course of a person's life.

career anchors A network of self-perceived talents, motives, and values that guide an individual's career decisions.

career ladder A structured series of job positions through which an individual progresses in an organization.

career management A lifelong process of learning about self, jobs, and organizations; setting personal career goals; developing strategies for achieving the goals; and revising the goals based on work and life experiences.

career path A sequence of job experiences that an employee moves along during his or her career.

career plateau A point in an individual's career in which the probability of moving further up the hierarchy is low.

centralization The degree to which decisions are made at the top of the organization.

challenge The call to competition, contest, or battle.

change The transportation or modification of an organization and/or its stakeholders.

change agent The individual or group that undertakes the task of introducing and managing a change in an organization.

change and acquisition The third socialization stage, in which the newcomer begins to master the demands of the job.

character assassination An attempt to label or discredit an opponent.

character theory An ethical theory that emphasizes the character, personal virtues, and integrity of the individual.

charismatic leadership A leader's use of personal abilities and talents in order to have profound and extraordinary effects on followers.

classical conditioning Modifying behavior so that a conditioned stimulus is paired with an unconditioned stimulus and elicits an unconditioned response.

coercive power Power that is based on an agent's ability to cause an unpleasant experience for a target.

cognitive dissonance A state of tension that is produced when an individual experiences conflict between attitudes and behavior.

cognitive moral development The process of moving through stages of maturity in terms of making ethical decisions.

cognitive style An individual's preference for gathering information and evaluating alternatives.

collectivism A cultural orientation in which individuals belong to tightly knit social frameworks, and they depend strongly on large extended families or clans.

communication The evoking of a shared or common meaning in another person.

communicative disease The absence of heartfelt communication in human relationships leading to loneliness and social isolation.

communicator The person originating a message.

compensation A compromise mechanism in which an individual attempts to make up for a negative situation by devoting himself or herself to another pursuit with increased vigor.

compensation award An organizational cost resulting from court awards for job distress.

complexity The degree to which many different types of activities occur in the organization.

conflict Any situation in which incompatible goals, attitudes, emotions, or behaviors lead to disagreement or opposition between two or more parties.

consensus An informational cue indicating the extent to which peers in the same situation behave in a similar fashion.

consequential theory An ethical theory that emphasizes the consequences or results of behavior.

consideration Leader behavior aimed at nurturing friendly, warm working relationships, as well as encouraging mutual trust and interpersonal respect within the work unit.

consistency An informational cue indicating the frequency of behavior over time.

contextual variables A set of characteristics that influence the organization's design processes.

continuance commitment The type of organizational commitment that is based on the fact that an individual cannot afford to leave.

conversion A withdrawal mechanism in which emotional conflicts are expressed in physical symptoms.

counterdependence An unhealthy, insecure pattern of behavior that leads to separation in relationships with other people.

counter-role behavior Deviant behavior in either a correctly or incorrectly defined job or role.

country club manager (1,9) A leader who creates a happy, comfortable work environment.

creativity A process influenced by individual and organizational factors that results in the production of novel and useful ideas, products, or both.

cross-training A variation of job enlargement in which workers are trained in different specialized tasks or activities.

D

data Uninterpreted and unanalyzed facts.

defensive communication Communication that can be aggressive, attacking and angry, or passive and withdrawing.

Delphi technique Gathering the judgments of experts for use in decision making.

democratic style A style of leadership in which the leader takes collaborative, responsive, interactive actions with followers concerning the work and work environment.

devil's advocacy A technique for preventing groupthink in which a group or individual is given the role of critic during decision making.

dialectical inquiry A debate between two opposing sets of recommendations.

differentiation The process of deciding how to divide the work in an organization.

discounting principle The assumption that an individual's behavior is accounted for by the situation.

disenchantment Feeling negativity or anger toward a change.

disengagement Psychological withdrawal from change.

disidentification Feeling that one's identity is being threatened by a change.

disorientation Feelings of loss and confusion due to a change.

displacement An aggressive mechanism in which an individual directs his or her anger toward someone who is not the source of the conflict.

distinctiveness An informational cue indicating the degree to which an individual behaves the same way in other situations.

distress The adverse psychological, physical, behavioral, and organizational consequences that may arise as a result of stressful events.

distributive bargaining A negotiation approach in which the goals of the parties are in conflict, and each party seeks to maximize its resources.

distributive justice The fairness of the outcomes that individuals receive in an organization.

diversity All forms of individual differences, including culture, gender, age, ability, religion, personality, social status, and sexual orientation.

divisionalized form A moderately decentralized form of organization that emphasizes the middle level and standardization of outputs.

dual-career partnership A relationship in which both people have important career roles.

due process nonaction A procedure set up to address conflicts that is so costly, time consuming, or personally risky that no one will use it.

dynamic follower A follower who is a responsible steward of his or her job, is effective in managing the relationship with the boss, and practices self-management.

dysfunctional conflict An unhealthy, destructive disagreement between two or more people.

E

effective decision A timely decision that meets a desired objective and is acceptable to those individuals affected by it.

ego-ideal The embodiment of a person's perfect self.

eldercare Assistance in caring for elderly parents and/or other elderly relatives.

empowerment Sharing power within an organization.

enacted values Values reflected in the way individuals actually behave.

encounter The second socialization stage in which the newcomer learns the tasks associated with the job, clarifies roles, and establishes new relationships at work.

engagement The expression of oneself as one performs in work or other roles.

engineering The applied science of energy and matter.

entitled An individual who is comfortable with an equity ratio greater than that of his or her comparison other.

environment Anything outside the boundaries of an organization.

environmental uncertainty The amount and rate of change in the organization's environment.

equity sensitive An individual who prefers an equity ratio equal to that of his or her comparison other.

ergonomics The science of adapting work and working conditions to the employee or worker.

escalation of commitment The tendency to continue to support a failing course of action.

espoused values What members of an organization say they value.

establishment The first stage of a person's career, in which the person learns the job and begins to fit into the organization and occupation.

ethical behavior Acting in ways consistent with one's personal values and the commonly held values of the organization and society.

eustress Healthy, normal stress.

executive coaching A technique in which managers or executives are paired with a coach in a partnership to help the executive perform more efficiently.

expatriate manager A manager who works in a country other than his or her home country.

expectancy The belief that effort leads to performance.

expert power The power that exists when an agent has specialized knowledge or skills that the target needs.

expert system A computer-based application that uses a representation of human expertise in a specialized field of knowledge to solve problems.

extinction The attempt to weaken a behavior by attaching no consequences to it.

extraversion A preference indicating that an individual is energized by interaction with other people.

F

fantasy A withdrawal mechanism that provides an escape from a conflict through daydreaming.

feedback Information fed back that completes two-way communication.

feeling Making decisions in a personal, value-oriented way.

femininity The cultural orientation in which relationships and concern for others are valued.

first-impression error The tendency to form lasting opinions about an individual based on initial perceptions.

fixation An aggressive mechanism in which an individual keeps up a dysfunctional behavior that obviously will not solve the conflict.

flexible work schedule A work schedule that allows employees discretion in order to accommodate personal concerns.

flextime An alternative work pattern that enables employees to set their own daily work schedules.

flight/withdrawal A withdrawal mechanism that entails physically escaping a conflict (flight) or psychologically escaping (withdrawal).

followership The process of being guided and directed by a leader in the work environment.

formal leadership Officially sanctioned leadership based on the authority of a formal position.

formal organization The official, legitimate, and most visible part of the system.

formalization The degree to which the organization has official rules, regulations, and procedures.

functional conflict A healthy, constructive disagreement between two or more people.

fundamental attribution error The tendency to make attributions to internal causes when focusing on someone else's behavior.

G

garbage can model A theory that contends that decisions in organizations are random and unsystematic.

gateways to communication Pathways through barriers to communication and antidotes to communication problems.

general self-efficacy An individual's general belief that he or she is capable of meeting job demands in a wide variety of situations.

glass ceiling A transparent barrier that keeps women from rising above a certain level in organizations.

goal setting The process of establishing desired results that guide and direct behavior.

group Two or more people with common interests, objectives, and continuing interaction.

group cohesion The "interpersonal glue" that makes members of a group stick together.

group polarization The tendency for group discussion to produce shifts toward more extreme attitudes among members.

groupthink A deterioration of mental efficiency, reality testing, and moral judgment resulting from pressures within the group.

guanxi The Chinese practice of building networks for social exchange.

H

Hawthorne studies Studies conducted during the 1920s and 1930s that discovered the existence of the informal organization.

heuristics Shortcuts in decision making that save mental activity.

hierarchy of authority The degree of vertical differentiation across levels of management.

homeostasis A steady state of bodily functioning and equilibrium.

humanistic theory The personality theory that emphasizes individual growth and improvement.

hygiene factor A work condition related to dissatisfaction caused by discomfort or pain.

I

identification A compromise mechanism whereby an individual patterns his or her behavior after another's.

impoverished manager (1,1) A leader who exerts just enough effort to get by.

impression management The process by which individuals try to control the impression others have of them.

incremental change Change of a relatively small scope, such as making small improvements.

individual differences The way in which factors such as skills, abilities, personalities, perceptions, attitudes, values, and ethics differ from one individual to another.

individualism A cultural orientation in which people belong to loose social frameworks, and their primary concern is for themselves and their families.

inequity The situation in which a person perceives he or she is receiving less than he or she is giving, or is giving less than he or she is receiving.

influence The process of affecting the thoughts, behavior, and feelings of another person.

informal leadership Unofficial leadership accorded to a person by other members of the organization.

informal organization The unofficial and less visible part of the system.

information Data that have been interpreted, analyzed, and have meaning to some user.

Information Communication Technology (ICT) The various new technologies, such as electronic mail, voice mail, teleconferencing, and wireless access, which are used for interpersonal communication.

information power Access to and control over important information.

initiating structure Leader behavior aimed at defining and organizing work relationships and roles, as well as establishing clear patterns of organization, communication, and ways of getting things done.

instrumental values Values that represent the acceptable behaviors to be used in achieving some end state.

instrumentality The belief that performance is related to rewards.

integrated involvement Closeness achieved through tasks and activities.

integration The process of coordinating the different parts of an organization.

integrative approach The broad theory that describes personality as a composite of an individual's psychological processes.

integrative negotiation A negotiation approach that focuses on the merits of the issues and seeks a win–win solution.

interactional psychology The psychological approach that emphasizes that in order to understand human behavior, we must know something about the person and about the situation.

intergroup conflict Conflict that occurs between groups or teams in an organization.

interorganizational conflict Conflict that occurs between two or more organizations.

interpersonal communication Communication between two or more people in an organization.

interpersonal conflict Conflict that occurs between two or more individuals.

interrole conflict A person's experience of conflict among the multiple roles in his or her life.

intragroup conflict Conflict that occurs within groups or teams.

intrapersonal conflict Conflict that occurs within an individual.

intrarole conflict Conflict that occurs within a single role, such as when a person receives conflicting messages from role senders about how to perform a certain role.

introversion A preference indicating that an individual is energized by time alone.

intuiting Gathering information through "sixth sense" and focusing on what could be rather than what actually exists.

intuition A fast, positive force in decision making that is utilized at a level below consciousness that involves learned patterns of information.

J

job A set of specified work and task activities that engage an individual in an organization.

Job Characteristics Model A framework for understanding person–job fit through the interaction of core job dimensions with critical psychological states within a person.

Job Diagnostic Survey (JDS) The survey instrument designed to measure the elements in the Job Characteristics Model.

job enlargement A method of job design that increases the number of activities in a job to overcome the boredom of overspecialized work.

job enrichment Designing or redesigning jobs by incorporating motivational factors into them.

job redesign An OD intervention method that alters jobs to improve the fit between individual skills and the demands of the job.

job rotation A variation of job enlargement in which workers are exposed to a variety of specialized jobs over time.

job satisfaction A pleasurable or positive emotional state resulting from the appraisal of one's job or job experiences.

job sharing An alternative work pattern in which more than one person occupies a single job.

Judging Preference Preferring closure and completion in making decisions.

jurisdictional ambiguity The presence of unclear lines of responsibility within an organization.

L

laissez-faire style A style of leadership in which the leader fails to accept the responsibilities of the position.

language The words, their pronunciation, and the methods of combining them used and understood by a group of people.

leader An advocate for change and new approaches to problems.

leader–member relations The quality of interpersonal relationships among a leader and the group members.

leadership The process of guiding and directing the behavior of people in the work environment.

Leadership Grid An approach to understanding a leader's or manager's concern for results (production) and concern for people.

leadership training and development A variety of techniques that are designed to enhance individuals' leadership skills.

lean production Using committed employees with ever-expanding responsibilities to achieve zero waste, 100 percent good product, delivered on time, every time.

learning A change in behavior acquired through experience.

least preferred coworker (LPC) The person a leader has least preferred to work with over his or her career.

legitimate power Power that is based on position and mutual agreement; agent and target agree that the agent has the right to influence the target.

locus of control An individual's generalized belief about internal control (self-control) versus external control (control by the situation or by others).

loss of individuality A social process in which individual group members lose self-awareness and its accompanying sense of accountability, inhibition, and responsibility for individual behavior.

M

Machiavellianism A personality characteristic indicating one's willingness to do whatever it takes to get one's own way.

machine bureaucracy A moderately decentralized form of organization that emphasizes the technical staff and standardization of work processes.

maintenance The third stage in an individual's career in which the individual tries to maintain productivity while evaluating progress toward career goals.

maintenance function An activity essential to effective, satisfying interpersonal relationships within a team or group.

management The study of overseeing activities and supervising people in organizations.

management by objectives (MBO) A goal-setting program based on interaction and negotiation between employees and managers.

manager An advocate for stability and the status quo.

masculinity The cultural orientation in which assertiveness and materialism are valued.

meaning of work The way a person interprets and understands the value of work as part of life.

mechanistic structure An organizational design that emphasizes structured activities, specialized tasks, and centralized decision making.

medicine The applied science of healing or treatment of diseases to enhance an individual's health and well-being.

mentor An individual who provides guidance, coaching, counseling, and friendship to a protégé.

mentoring A work relationship that encourages development and career enhancement for people moving through the career cycle.

message The thoughts and feelings that the communicator is attempting to elicit in the receiver.

moral maturity The measure of a person's cognitive moral development.

motivation The process of arousing and sustaining goal-directed behavior.

motivation factor A work condition related to satisfaction of the need for psychological growth.

moving The second step in Lewin's change model, in which new attitudes, values, and behaviors are substituted for old ones.

Myers-Briggs Type Indicator (MBTI) An instrument developed to measure Carl Jung's theory of individual differences.

N

need for achievement A manifest (easily perceived) need that concerns individuals' issues of excellence, competition, challenging goals, persistence, and overcoming difficulties.

need for affiliation A manifest (easily perceived) need that concerns an individual's need to establish and maintain warm, close, intimate relationships with other people.

need for power A manifest (easily perceived) need that concerns an individual's need to make an impact on others, influence others, change people or events, and make a difference in life.

need hierarchy The theory that behavior is determined by a progression of physical, social, and psychological needs by higher order needs.

negative affect An individual's tendency to accentuate the negative aspects of himself or herself, other people, and the world in general.

negative consequences Results of a behavior that a person finds unattractive or aversive.

negativism An aggressive mechanism in which a person responds with pessimism to any attempt at solving a problem.

nominal group technique (NGT) A structured approach to group decision making that focuses on generating alternatives and choosing one.

nonaction Doing nothing in hopes that a conflict will disappear.

nondefensive communication Communication that is assertive, direct, and powerful.

nonprogrammed decision A new, complex decision that requires a creative solution.

nonverbal communication All elements of communication that do not involve words.

normative commitment The type of organizational commitment that is based on an individual's perceived obligation to remain with an organization.

norms of behavior The standards that a work group uses to evaluate the behavior of its members.

O

objective knowledge Knowledge that results from research and scholarly activities.

one-way communication Communication in which a person sends a message to another person and no questions, feedback, or interaction follow.

operant conditioning Modifying behavior through the use of positive or negative consequences following specific behaviors.

opportunistic "what's in it for me" manager (Opp) A leader whose style aims to maximize self-benefit.

opportunities Favorable times or chances for progress and advancement.

organic structure An organizational design that emphasizes teamwork, open communication, and decentralized decision making.

organization development (OD) A systematic approach to organizational improvement that applies behavioral science theory and research in order to increase individual and organizational well-being and effectiveness.

organization man manager (5,5) A middle-of-the-road leader.

organizational behavior The study of individual behavior and group dynamics in organizations.

organizational citizenship behavior Behavior that is above and beyond the call of duty.

organizational commitment The strength of an individual's identification with an organization.

organizational (corporate) culture A pattern of basic assumptions that are considered valid and that are taught to new members as the way to perceive, think, and feel in the organization.

organizational design The process of constructing and adjusting an organization's structure to achieve its goals.

organizational life cycle The differing stages of an organization's life from birth to death.

organizational politics The use of power and influence in organizations.

organizational socialization The process by which newcomers are transformed from outsiders to participating, effective members of the organization.

organizational structure The linking of departments and jobs within an organization.

overdependence An unhealthy, insecure pattern of behavior that leads to preoccupied attempts to achieve security through relationships.

P

participation problem A cost associated with absenteeism, tardiness, strikes and work stoppages, and turnover.

participative decision making Decision making in which individuals who are affected by decisions influence the making of those decisions.

paternalistic "father knows best" manager (9+9) A leader who promises reward and threatens punishment.

people The human resources of the organization.

Perceiving Preference Preferring to explore many alternatives and flexibility.

perceptual screen A window through which we interact with people that influences the quality, accuracy, and clarity of the communication.

performance appraisal The evaluation of a person's performance.

performance decrement A cost resulting from poor quality or low quantity of production, grievances, and unscheduled machine downtime and repair.

performance management A process of defining, measuring, appraising, providing feedback on, and improving performance.

person–role conflict Conflict that occurs when an individual is expected to perform behaviors in a certain role that conflict with his or her personal values.

personal power Power used for personal gain.

personality A relatively stable set of characteristics that influences an individual's behavior.

personality hardiness A personality resistant to distress and characterized by challenge, commitment, and control.

phased retirement An arrangement that allows employees to reduce their hours and/or responsibilities in order to ease into retirement.

planned change Change resulting from a deliberate decision to alter the organization.

political behavior Actions not officially sanctioned by an organization that are taken to influence others in order to meet one's personal goals.

position power The authority associated with the leader's formal position in the organization.

positive affect An individual's tendency to accentuate the positive aspects of himself or herself, other people, and the world in general.

positive consequences Results of a behavior that a person finds attractive or pleasurable.

power The ability to influence another person.

power distance The degree to which a culture accepts unequal distribution of power.

powerlessness A lack of power.

preventive stress management An organizational philosophy that holds that people and organizations should take joint responsibility for promoting health and preventing distress and strain.

primary prevention The stage in preventive stress management designed to reduce, modify, or eliminate the demand or stressor causing stress.

procedural justice The fairness of the process by which outcomes are allocated in an organization.

process consultation An OD method that helps managers and employers improve the processes that are used in organizations.

professional bureaucracy A decentralized form of organization that emphasizes the operating core and standardization of skills.

programmed decision A simple, routine matter for which a manager has an established decision rule.

projection Overestimating the number of people who share our own beliefs, values, and behaviors.

projective test A personality test that elicits an individual's response to abstract stimuli.

psychoanalysis Sigmund Freud's method for delving into the unconscious mind to better understand a person's motives and needs.

psychodynamic theory The personality theory that emphasizes the unconscious determinants of behavior.

psychological contract An implicit agreement between an individual and an organization that specifies what each is expected to give and receive in the relationship.

psychological intimacy Emotional and psychological closeness to other team or group members.

psychology The science of human behavior.

punishment The attempt to eliminate or weaken undesirable behavior by either bestowing negative consequences or withholding positive consequences.

Q

quality circle (QC) A small group of employees who work voluntarily on company time, typically one hour per week, to address work-related problems such as quality control, cost reduction, production planning and techniques, and even product design.

quality program A program that embeds product and service quality excellence into the organizational culture.

quality team A team that is part of an organization's structure and is empowered to act on its decisions regarding product and service quality.

R

rationality A logical, step-by-step approach to decision making, with a thorough analysis of alternatives and their consequences.

rationalization A compromise mechanism characterized by trying to justify one's behavior by constructing bogus reasons for it.

realistic job preview (RJP) Both positive and negative information given to potential employees about the job they are applying for, thereby giving them a realistic picture of the job.

receiver The person receiving a message.

referent power An elusive power that is based on interpersonal attraction.

reflective listening A skill intended to help the receiver and communicator clearly and fully understand the message sent.

refreezing The final step in Lewin's change model, in which new attitudes, values, and behaviors are established as the new status quo.

reinforcement The attempt to develop or strengthen desirable behavior by either bestowing positive consequences or withholding negative consequences.

reinvention The creative application of new technology.

reward power Power based on an agent's ability to control rewards that a target wants.

richness The ability of a medium or channel to elicit or evoke meaning in the receiver.

risk aversion The tendency to choose options that entail fewer risks and less uncertainty.

robotics The use of robots in organizations.

role negotiation A technique whereby individuals meet and clarify their psychological contract.

rule-based theory An ethical theory that emphasizes the character of the act itself rather than its effects.

S

satisfice To select the first alternative that is "good enough," because the costs in time and effort are too great to optimize.

secondary prevention The stage in preventive stress management designed to alter or modify the individual's or the organization's response to a demand or stressor.

secrecy Attempting to hide a conflict or an issue that has the potential to create conflict.

selective perception The process of selecting information that supports our individual viewpoints while discounting information that threatens our viewpoints.

self-esteem An individual's general feeling of self-worth.

self-fulfilling prophecy The situation in which our expectations about people affect our interaction with them in such a way that our expectations are fulfilled.

self-image How a person sees himself or herself, both positively and negatively.

self-interest What is in the best interest and benefit to an individual.

self-managed team A team that makes decisions that were once reserved for managers.

self-monitoring The extent to which people base their behavior on cues from other people and situations.

self-reliance A healthy, secure, interdependent pattern of behavior related to how people form and maintain supportive attachments with others.

self-report questionnaire A common personality assessment that involves an individual's responses to a series of questions.

self-serving bias The tendency to attribute one's own successes to internal causes and one's failures to external causes.

sensing Gathering information through the five senses.

simple structure A centralized form of organization that emphasizes the upper echelon and direct supervision.

Six Sigma A high-performance system to execute business strategy that is customer-driven, emphasizes quantitative decision making, and places a priority on saving money.

skill development The mastery of abilities essential to successful functioning in organizations.

skills training Increasing the job knowledge, skills, and abilities that are necessary to do a job effectively.

social decision schemes Simple rules used to determine final group decisions.

social information-processing (SIP) model A model that suggests that the important job factors depend in part on what others tell a person about the job.

social learning The process of deriving attitudes from family, peer groups, religious organizations, and culture.

social loafing The failure of a group member to contribute personal time, effort, thoughts, or other resources to the group.

social perception The process of interpreting information about another person.

social power Power used to create motivation or to accomplish group goals.

social responsibility The obligation of an organization to behave in ethical ways.

sociology The science of society.

sociotechnical systems (STS) Giving equal attention to technical and social considerations in job design.

specialization The degree to which jobs are narrowly defined and depend on unique expertise.

standardization The degree to which work activities are accomplished in a routine fashion.

status structure The set of authority and task relations among a group's members.

stereotype A generalization about a group of people.

strain Distress.

strategic change Change of a larger scale, such as organizational restructuring.

strategic contingencies Activities that other groups depend on in order to complete their tasks.

stress The unconscious preparation to fight or flee that a person experiences when faced with any demand.

stressor The person or event that triggers the stress response.

strong culture An organizational culture with a consensus on the values that drive the company and with an intensity that is recognizable even to outsiders.

strong situation A situation that overwhelms the effects of individual personalities by providing strong cues for appropriate behavior.

structure The manner in which an organization's work is designed at the micro level, as well as how departments, divisions, and the overall organization are designed at the macro level.

superordinate goal An organizational goal that is more important to both parties in a conflict than their individual or group goals.

survey feedback A widely used method of intervention whereby employee attitudes are solicited using a questionnaire.

synergy A positive force in groups that occurs when group members stimulate new solutions to problems through the process of mutual influence and encouragement in the group.

T

task An organization's mission, purpose, or goal for existing.

task environment The elements of an organization's environment that are related to its goal attainment.

task function An activity directly related to the effective completion of a team's work.

task revision The modification of incorrectly specified roles or jobs.

task structure The degree of clarity, or ambiguity, in the work activities assigned to the group.

task-specific self-efficacy An individual's beliefs and expectancies about his or her ability to perform a specific task effectively.

team building An intervention designed to improve the effectiveness of a work group.

team manager (9,9) A leader who builds a highly productive team of committed people.

teamwork Joint action by a team of people in which individual interests are subordinated to team unity.

technocentric Placing technology and engineering at the center of job design decisions.

technological interdependence The degree of interrelatedness of the organization's various technological elements.

technology The intellectual and mechanical processes used by an organization to transform inputs into products or services that meet organizational goals.

technostress The stress caused by new and advancing technologies in the workplace.

telecommuting Transmitting work from a home computer to the office using a modem.

terminal values Values that represent the goals to be achieved or the end states of existence.

tertiary prevention The stage in preventive stress management designed to heal individual or organizational symptoms of distress and strain.

Theory X A set of assumptions of how to manage individuals who are motivated by lower order needs.

Theory Y A set of assumptions of how to manage individuals who are motivated by higher order needs.

thinking Making decisions in a logical, objective fashion.

360-degree feedback A process of self-evaluation and evaluations by a manager, peers, direct reports, and possibly customers.

time orientation Whether a culture's values are oriented toward the future (long-term orientation) or toward the past and present (short-term orientation).

trait theory The personality theory that states that in order to understand individuals, we must break down behavior patterns into a series of observable traits.

transformational change Change in which the organization moves to a radically different, and sometimes unknown, future state.

transformational coping A way of managing stressful events by changing them into subjectively less stressful events.

transnational organization An organization in which the global viewpoint supersedes national issues.

triangulation The use of multiple methods to measure organizational culture.

two-way communication A form of communication in which the communicator and receiver interact.

Type A behavior pattern A complex of personality and behavioral characteristics, including competitiveness, time urgency, social status insecurity, aggression, hostility, and a quest for achievements.

U

uncertainty avoidance The degree to which a culture tolerates ambiguity and uncertainty.

unfreezing The first step in Lewin's change model, in which individuals are encouraged to discard old behaviors by shaking up the equilibrium state that maintains the status quo.

unplanned change Change that is imposed on the organization and is often unforeseen.

upper echelon A top-level executive team in an organization.

V

valence The value or importance one places on a particular reward.

values Enduring beliefs that a specific mode of conduct or end state of existence is personally or socially preferable to an opposite or converse mode of conduct or end state of existence.

virtual office A mobile platform of computer, telecommunication, and information technology and services.

W

whistle-blower An employee who informs authorities of the wrongdoings of his or her company or coworkers.

withdrawal The final stage in an individual's career in which the individual contemplates retirement or possible career changes.

work Mental or physical activity that has productive results.

work simplification Standardization and the narrow, explicit specification of task activities for workers.

work team A group of people with complementary skills who are committed to a common mission, performance goals, and approach for which they hold themselves mutually accountable.

workaholism An imbalanced preoccupation with work at the expense of home and personal life satisfaction.

Z

zone of indifference The range in which attempts to influence a person will be perceived as legitimate and will be acted on without a great deal of thought.

Company Index

I

Iacocca, Lee, 302, 327
Ianucelli, Vickie, 584
Irby, Steve, 530
Isautier, Bernard, 260
Isdell, E. Neville, 625
Isenberg, Daniel, 324
Ivancevich, John M., 186

J

Jackson, Richie, 419
Jago, Arthur, 397
James, William, 5, 153
Janis, Irving, 334, 335, 336
Jauch, Lawrence R., 446
Jehn, K., 431
Jensen, E., 21
Jewler, A. J., 21
Jobs, Steve, 13, 65, 176,
    237–238, 402, 462, 484, 512
Johnson, D. E., 400
Johnson, H., 622
Johnson, James, 32
Johnson, Mead, 32
Johnson, Robert Wood, 32
Johnson, Robert Wood, II, 32
Johnston, Ollie, 461
Jones, Eddie, 208
Jones, J. E., 451
Jones, James Earl, 630
Joplin, J. R. 573
Jung, Carl, 90–91, 92, 180, 185,
    322

K

Kacmar, C. J., 219, 433
Kahn, Robert, 8, 216
Kant, Immanuel, 53
Kanter, Rosabeth Moss,
    364–366, 605
Katz, D., 8
Kayes, D. C., 349
Kearns, David, 298
Keen, A., 244
Keitel, Harvey, 417
Kelleher, Herb, 305
Kelley, Harold, 200
Kelley, R. E., 407, 408
Kennedy, A. A., 530
Kilmann, R. H., 547

King, Dr. Martin Luther, Jr., 257
King, Rodney, 286
Kinni, T., 33
Kinsellas, W. P., 630
Kirkpatrick, D., 7
Kleiner, B. H., 257, 269
Kline, Kevin, 144
Kohlberg, Lawrence, 137–138
Koop, C. Everett, 224
Korda, Michael, 364–366
Koresh, David, 402
Koslowski, Dennis, 133, 360–361
Kotter, J. P., 371, 378, 388,
    536–540, 555
Kram, Kathy, 582
Kreitner, Robert, 183
Kroeger, Otto, 186, 323
Kuruvilla, Alex, 602

L

LaBelle, Bart, 594
LaBelle, Doug, 594
LaBelle, Norman, 594
LaHue, P., 419
Lancaster, Burt, 630
Landy, Frank, 478
Lane, Robert, 550
Larsen, Ralph, 33
Lashinsky, A., 459
Lasseter, John, 13, 176–177, 484
Laszlo, C., 558
Latham, Gary, 186
Lavelle, M., 75
Lawler, Edward, A-1–A-2
Lawler, E. E., III, 163, 569
Lawrence, Paul, 495, 498, A-1–A-2
Lax, David A., 71
Lay, Kenneth, 133
Lazarus, Richard, 216
Leavitt, Harold, 8, 9
Ledeen, M., 184
Lengel, R. H., 252
Lerner, Sandy, 632
Levi, Lennart, 477
Levinson, Harry, 216, 571–572,
    581, 583–584, 616
Levy, S., 78, 246, 459, 636
Lewin, Kurt, 5, 83, 390,
    613–615, A-1–A-2
Likert, Rensis, 615
Lilly, Eli, 136

Liotta, Ray, 630
Lippitt, Ronald, A-1–A-2
Lisper, H. O., 253
Locke, Edwin, 186
Lockwood, A., 582
Loehr, Jim, 162
Lofquist, L. H., 122
London, Daniel, 279
Lorenzo, Frank, 292
Lorsch, J., 495, 498
Lougheed, Kirk, 632
Lubin, J. S., 636
Lucas, George, 65, 533
Luczak, H., 478
Luthans, Fred, 183, 185, A-1, A-3
Lynch, James, 268, 270
Lynch, L. J., 133

M

Maccoby, M., 184
Machado, Rodolfo, 350
Machiavelli, Niccolò, 137, 361
Macik-Frey, M., 270
Mack, John, 125–126
Mackey, John, 14, 139–140, 154,
    155, 161, 283–284, 306–307,
    421, 446
Mackie, Anthony, 30
Madigan, Amy, 630
Madison, D. L., 367
Maguire, Tobey, 208
Malina, Judith, 594
Manz, Charles, A-1, A-3
March, J. G., 6, 9, 320
Marcic, Dorothy, 29, 70, 110,
    142, 374, 414, 487, 555, 610,
    628
Marcus, E., 281
Marois, R., 99
Marriott, J. Willard, 182
Martin, Joanne, 533
Marwa, Emil, 452
Maslow, Abraham, 153, 155,
    157, 163, 169, A-1–A-2
Mastenbroek, W. F. G., 433–434
Mastrantonio, Mary Elizabeth, 383
Mavis, M., 211
May, D. R., 475
Mayes, B. T., 367
Mayo, Elton, A-1, A-3
Mazzola, M., 633
McAllaster, C., 548